Law of Contract

Thirteenth Edition

Law of Contract

PAUL RICHARDS

Formerly Head of the School of Law, University of Huddersfield

 Pearson

Harlow, England • London • New York • Boston • San Francisco • Toronto • Sydney • Dubai • Singapore • Hong Kong
Tokyo • Seoul • Taipei • New Delhi • Cape Town • São Paulo • Mexico City • Madrid • Amsterdam • Munich • Paris • Milan

PEARSON EDUCATION LIMITED
Edinburgh Gate
Harlow CM20 2JE
United Kingdom
Tel: +44 (0)1279 623623
Web: www.pearson.com/uk

First published 1992 (print)
Second edition published 1995 (print)
Third edition published 1997 (print)
Fourth edition published 1999 (print)
Fifth edition published 2002 (print)
Sixth edition published 2004 (print)
Seventh edition published 2006 (print)
Eighth edition published 2007 (print)
Ninth edition published 2009 (print)
Tenth edition published 2011 (print)
Eleventh edition published 2013 (print and electronic)
Twelfth edition published 2015 (print and electronic)
Thirteenth edition published 2017 (print and electronic)

© Longman Group UK Limited 1992 (print)
© Pearson Professional Limited 1995 (print)
© Financial Times Professional Limited 1997 (print)
© Pearson Education Limited 1999, 2002, 2004, 2006, 2007, 2009, 2011 (print)
© Pearson Education Limited 2013, 2015, 2017 (print and electronic)

ISBN: 978-1-292-17610-9 (print)
      978-1-292-17611-6 (PDF)
      978-1-292-17612-3 (ePub)

British Library Cataloguing-in-Publication Data
A catalogue record for the print edition is available from the British Library

Library of Congress Cataloging-in-Publication Data
Names: Richards, Paul, 1951- author.
Title: Law of contract / Paul Richards, Formerly Head of the School of Law,
    University of Huddersfield.
Description: Thirteenth edition. | New York : Pearson, 2017.
Identifiers: LCCN 2016056451| ISBN 9781292176109 (print) | ISBN 9781292176116
    (pdf) | ISBN 9781292176123 (epub)
Subjects: LCSH: Contracts—England.
Classification: LCC KD1554 .R53 2017 | DDC 346.4202—dc23
LC record available at https://lccn.loc.gov/2016056451

10 9 8 7 6 5 4 3 2 1
21 20 19 18 17

Print edition typeset in 9/12 Stone Serif ITC Pro by SPi Global
Printed in Slovakia by Neografia

NOTE THAT ANY PAGE CROSS REFERENCES REFER TO THE PRINT EDITION

For my partner Maggie, my sons Phillip and William and my brother Anthony

Brief contents

Contents

Part 1 The formation of a contract

Part 3 Factors that vitiate a contract

Part 4 Discharge of contracts

Part 5 Remedies for breach of contract

Part 6 The rights and liabilities of third parties to the contract

Preface

At the time of writing the 12th edition of this book, the Consumer Rights Bill 2014 had just been introduced into Parliament and began what appeared to be a painfully slow path towards enactment. Like many legal authors this one found himself on the horns of a dilemma – to deal with the Bill or, take something of a gamble and treat the Bill as if it had been enacted. The safer route was adopted – one can never be sure of Parliamentarians! In this edition, therefore, with the Bill having progressed through to the Royal Assent, becoming law on 1 October 2015, it has been possible to deal with this important legislation in more definitive terms. On the face of things the Act seems to make the law in this area more complex, in that there is now a sharp divergence between implied terms and exemption clauses in consumer contracts from those in business contracts. Certainly this seemed to be the impression when the Act was in its embryonic stage as a Bill. Whilst working on this manuscript I came to the conclusion that whilst there is more law, it is nevertheless more accessible and clearer with regards to consumer rights. Gone are the Unfair Terms in Consumer Contract Regulations 1999, which at best were an unhealthy stop-gap process for the introduction of the European Directives in this area which caused great hand-wringing in the courts as they struggled to implement concepts that were largely alien to the law of contract as practised in the United Kingdom. The Act therefore implements the European dimension in a rather more measured and logical fashion in terms that are rather more readily recognisable. The Act is Certainly the biggest shake-up of consumer law for at least a generation and undoubtedly achieves its objective in providing a more transparent code for consumer rights. One other dimension to the Act is that Parts 1 to 3 largely extend to the whole of the UK. There are some exceptions where Part 3 does not apply to Scotland or Northern Ireland because of the differences in the law. For example, in Part 3 there are changes to the Sunday Trading Act 1994 which does not extend to Scotland or Northern Ireland. Similarly the provisions regarding the complaints handling scheme in higher education only apply to England and Wales on the basis that the original legislation only extended to these countries.

The law of contract has, as many lawyers and law students have no doubt lamented, been subject to the influence of European Directives and Regulations for some 40-odd years now. As Lord Denning famously observed in **Bulmer** v **Bollinger** regarding the incoming tide of EU law, 'it flows into the estuaries and up the rivers. It cannot be held back, Parliament has decreed that the Treaty is henceforward to be part of our law. It is equal in force to any statute'. It would seem that following the 'Brexit' vote in the referendum on the membership of the United Kingdom in the European Union, that tide may well begin to ebb. Whether that will be for the better or worse in terms of the law of contract in the United Kingdom is for the future; however, my own opinion is that our law will still and continue to be robust and indeed the choice of law in the vast majority of commercial transactions around the world. In any event, it can be seen already that the Supreme Court is increasingly taking on board decisions in Canadian, Australian, New Zealand and Singaporean courts where the jurisdictions have a great deal more affinity with our own common law system.

In this edition, I have considered a large number of cases but pre-eminent among these are *Marks and Spencer plc v BNP Baribas Securities Services Trust Co (Jersey) Ltd* [2015] UKSC 72 on implied terms; *Parkingeye Ltd v Beavis* [2015] UKSC 67 on unfair terms; *Hayward v Zurich Insurance Co plc* [2016] UKSC 48; *Versloot Dredging BV v HI Gerling Industrie Versicherung* AG [2016] UKSC 45 on misrepresentation; *Salt v Stratstone Specialist Ltd (t/a Stratstone Cadillac Newcastle)* [2015] EWCA Civ 745 on recission; *Hounga v Allen* [2014] UKSC 47 public policy considerations in illegality; *Bilta (UK) Ltd v Nazir (No 2)* [2015] UKSC 23; *Patel v Mirza* [2016] UKSC 42 on the illegality defence; *Bunge SA v Nidera BV* [2015] UKSC 43 the compensation rule in damages; *Wellesley Partners LLP v Withers LLP* [2015] EWCA Civ 1146 the reasonable foreseeability test in damages; *Fulton Shipping Inc. of Panama v Globalia Business travel (formerly Travelplan SAU) of Spain, The New Flamenco* [2015] EWCA Civ 1299 mitigation in damages; the conjoined appeals of *Cavendish Square Holding BV v Talal El Makdessi* and *ParkingEye Ltd v Beavis* [2015] UKSC 67 penalty clauses. Apart from the inclusion of these important cases I have endeavoured to rewrite some quite large areas of text, particularly with regard to Chapter 7 on terms and Chapter 8 on exemption clauses where the onset of the Consumer Rights Act 2015 has been more fully integrated into the text. Considerable chunks of new material have also been added to Chapter 9 on misrepresentation and Chapter 12 on illegality.

As in previous years, I have continued to refrain from making widespread use of unreported cases in order to maintain the original ethos of the book, in that it should so far as possible stand alone, and that if a student needs to look further, they should be able to obtain the information they want from a readily available source. Of course the objectives behind the writing of this book remain the same – that of presenting the law in a readable and accessible form by setting out the general principles of the subject with reference to the leading and most recent cases. I have attempted to avoid including new cases just because they are new. The courts hear many decisions and I have attempted to be conservative in choosing cases that have a real impact on the law wherever possible, as I see little point in cluttering up the text with minor decisions since these will only distract the student, create confusion and get in the way of developing a proper understanding of the law. The fact remains, however, that some of the judgements that are coming out of the courts, particularly the Supreme Court, are now of a very complex nature and reducing these to an easily understandable set of principles is now a challenging exercise in its own right. I hope I have done justice to these decisions for the reader.

Problem areas and other contentious aspects are also considered but as a means of leading the student into more specific reading. For this reason, there is a further reading section at the end of each chapter providing a selection of authoritative texts and articles in a variety of legal journals. Hopefully, these will also save students time when having to research particular topics. I have also attempted to continue to present the text in a user-friendly and structured form that eliminates footnotes that so often are a distraction and an intimidating presence which tend to obscure rather than clarify the principles behind the subject.

Whilst this book can be used as a stand-alone text, it is written not with this intention but to encourage students to undertake further reading so that they have a full understanding of the wider issues that surround this increasingly complex subject. The book has been written with the intention of providing a halfway house between a student's lecture notes, more substantive works and articles in legal journals and to encourage this learning process. In order to prompt student's into becoming more autonomous in their reading and learning I have included in this edition a number of 'Debates' and I hope that these will engage students in thought provoking exercises on the various topics contained within the 'Debates'.

All too often new students coming into higher education for the first time have not developed the learning skills to manage their own learning. Many academics have their own views on why this is the case but whatever those reasons, it is vital that the student of this subject spends time in the lawyers' laboratory, the library, reading around their subjects. It is also for this reason that the additional reading section is included.

Not that many years ago, the law of contract was regarded as one of the easier undergraduate law courses. I do not believe this to be true any longer (if, indeed, it ever was) and certainly some areas which in my days as a student were relatively straightforward are no longer the case, and the whole subject is now becoming quite a challenging one. The reception and comments received with respect to the last edition were extremely encouraging although, as ever, I welcome any suggestions that may improve it. In time-honoured tradition, all errors and omissions are entirely my responsibility.

It is a tradition and always a pleasure in the preface of a book to thank those who have given their help and assistance in the writing and production of it. I would like to give my thanks to Cheryl Cheasley and all the staff at Pearson or their continued support of this book and the Foundation Studies in Law Series in general. Their efforts, ideas and enthusiasm have contributed immensely to the success of both. The quality of the production of the book and the series is a tribute to their dedicated hard work. I thank them also for their patience when I overrun my date for submission of the manuscript.

There are many others who have given me support and help in terms of advising me about content or design and I thank them all for their input, particularly the students who have been so supportive of the this textbook. In particular, I have to thank Gerald Swaby at the University of Huddersfield for his telephone calls informing of new Supreme Court decisions and our discussions about those judgements. It has been a great privilege to act as Gerald's supervisor for his PhD and I am sure he will be very succesful in his viva later this year. I wish him and his lovely wife Hillary well for the future.

As in previous years I thank my sons Phillip and William for their love, support and companionship as they move on in life through difficult and what can be hard and challenging times. I thought that I had got rid of them but this seems to be a generation that keeps returning to the family nest! Phillip at least has his own place now and no doubt in the fullness of time William will find his place. The truth of course is that I love them both dearly and the home is never quite the same when they are not there. Such are the times we live in but at the end of the day it is their happiness that is of paramount importance to me.

I also thank my partner, Maggie, for her love, support, patience and for quite simply being there despite my long absences when I have been working on various manuscripts. I also thank my brother Antony Richards MBE for his unswerving support. We work together as a mutual support partnership and in between seeing some atrocious movies during our weekly dinner engagements as well as trying to hit a golf ball straight.

Paul Richards

August 2016

Acknowledgements

We are grateful to the following for permission to reproduce copyright material:

Text

Extract on page 10 from *Storer v Manchester City Council* [1974] 1 WLR 1403; Extract on page 10 from *The Leonidas D* [1985] 1 WLR 925; Extract on page 10 from *Attorney-General of Belize v Belize Telecom Ltd* [2009] 1 WLR 1988; Extract on page 10 from *Rainy Sky SA and others v Kookmin Bank* [2011] 1 WLR 2900; Extract on page 12 from *H.P. Bulmer Ltd and Another v J. Bollinger S.A.* [1974] Ch. 401; Extracts on page 17, page 82, page 84 from *New Zealand Shipping Co. Ltd v A M Satterthwaite and Co. Ltd, The Eurymedon* [1975] AC 154; Extracts on page 18, page 20 from *Carlill v Carbolic Smoke Ball Co.* [1893] 1 QB 256; Extract on page 21 from *Fisher v Bell* [1961] 1 QB 394; Extract on page 47 from *Brinkibon Ltd v Stahag Stahl und Stahlwarenhandelsgesellschaft GmbH* [1983] 2 AC 34; Extract on page 53 from *Errington v Errington and Woods* [1952] 1 KB 290; Extract on page 75 from *Chappell & Co. Ltd v Nestlé Co. Ltd* [1960] AC 87; Extract on page 86 from *Foakes v Beer* (1884) 9 App Cas 605; Extract on page 88 from *Hughes v Metropolitan Railway Co. Ltd* (1877) 2 App Cas 439; Extract on page 88 from *Combe v Combe* [1951] 2 KB 215; Extract on page 89 from *Central London Property Trust Ltd v High Trees House Ltd* [1947] KB 130; Extract on page 92 from *D & C Builders Ltd v Rees* [1966] 2 QB 617; Extract on page 98 from *Balfour v Balfour* [1919] 2 KB 571; Extract on page 100 from *Pettit v Pettit* [1970] AC 777; Extract on page 134 from *Moschi v Lep Air Services Ltd* [1973] AC 331; Extract on page 144 from *Jacobs v Batavia and General Plantations Trust* [1924] 1 Ch 287; Extract on page 145 from *Gillespie Bros & Co. v Cheney, Eggar and Co.* [1896] 2 QB 59; Extract on page 147 from *Heilbut, Symons & Co. v Buckleton* [1913] AC 30; Extracts on page 150, page 156, page 157 from *Prenn v Simmonds* [1971] 1 WLR 1381; Extract on pages 150–1 from *Reardon Smith Line Ltd v Yngvar Hansen-Tangen* [1976] 1 WLR 989; Extracts on pages 151–2, page 198 from *Investors Compensation Scheme Ltd v West Bromwich Building Society* [1998] 1 WLR 896; Extract on page 153 from *George Mitchell (Chesterhall) Ltd v Finney Lock Seeds* [1983] QB 284; Extracts on pages 153–4, pages 232–3, page 242 from *Photo Production Ltd v Securicor Transport Ltd* [1980] AC 827; Extract on page 160 *Antalos Compania Navlera SA v Salen Rederierna AB* [1985] AC 191, 201; Extract on page 163 from *Republic of India v India Steamship Co* [1998] AC 878; Extract on page 166 from *Geys v Société Générale* [2013] 1 AC 523; Extract on page 167 from *Shirlaw v Southern Foundries (1926) Ltd* [1939] 2 KB 206; Extract on page 190 from *Harlingdon & Leinster Enterprises Ltd v Christopher Hull Fine Art Ltd* [1992] 1 QB 564; Extract on page 197 from *Interfoto Picture Library Ltd v Stiletto Visual Programmes Ltd* [1989] QB 433; Extract on page 207 from *Hong Kong Fir Shipping Co. Ltd v Kawasaki Kisen Kaisha Ltd* [1962] 2 QB 26; Extract on page 220 from *Thornton v Shoe Lane Parking Ltd* [1971] QB 163; Extract on page 228 *Hollier v Rambler Motors* (A.M.C.) Ltd [1972] 2 QB 71; Extracts on page 230, pages 455–6 from *Vaswani v Italian Motor Cars Ltd* [1996] 1 WLR 270 (PC); Extracts on page 249, page 252 from *George Mitchell (Chesterhall) Ltd v Finney Lock Seeds* [1983] 2 AC 803; Extracts on page 263, pages 263–4, pages 264–5 from *Director General of Fair Trading v First National Bank* [2001] 3 WLR 1297 (HL); Extract on page 293 from *Edgington v Fitzmaurice* (1885) 29 ChD 459; Extract on pages 295–6 from *With v O'Flanagan* [1936] Ch 575; Extract on page 300 from *Downs v Chappell* [1997] 1 WLR 426; Extract on page 302 from *Standard Chartered Bank Ltd v Pakistan National Shipping Corporation Ltd (Nos 2 and 4)* [2003] 1 AC 959; Extract on page 305 from *BP Exploration Operating Co Ltd v Chevron Shipping Co.* [2003] 1 AC 197; Extract on page 308 from *Angus v Clifford* [1891] 2 Ch 449; Extract on page 309 from *Smith New Court Securities Ltd v Citibank NA* [1997] AC 254; Extracts on page 310, page 345 from *Manifest Shipping Co. Ltd v Uni-Polaris Shipping Co. Ltd (The "Star Sea")* [2001] 2 WLR 170; Extracts on page 326, page 384 from *William Sindall plc v Cambridgeshire County Council* [1994] 1 WLR 1016 (CA); Extract on page 329 from *Doyle v Olby (Ironmongers)*

Ltd [1969] 2 QB 158; Extracts on page 357, page 359 from *Bell* v *Lever Bros* [1932] AC 161; Extract on page 368 from *Smith* v *Hughes* (1871) LR 6 QB 597; Extract on page 369 from *Scriven Bros & Co.* v *Hindley & Co.* [1913] 3 KB 564; Extracts on page 379, page 384 from *Solle* v *Butcher* [1950] 1 KB 671; Extracts on page 382, page 385 from *Cooper* v *Phibbs* (1867) LR 2 HL 149; Extract on page 383 from *Huddersfield Banking Co. Ltd* v *Henry Lister & Son Ltd* [1895] 2 Ch 273; Extract on page 390 from *Frederick E Rose (London) Ltd* v *William H Pim Jnr & Co Ltd* [1953] 2 QB 450; Extract on pages 390–1 from *Thomas Bates Ltd* v *Wyndham's (Lingerie) Ltd* [1981] 1 WLR 505; Extract on page 400 from *Barton* v *Armstrong* [1976] AC 104; Extract on page 402 from *Universe Tankships Inc. of Monrovia* v *International Transport Workers' Federation (The Universe Sentinel)* [1983] 1 AC 366; Extract on page 402 from *Thorne v. Motor Trade Association* [1937] AC 797 806; Extract on page 414 from *Allcard* v *Skinner* (1887) 36 ChD 145; Extract on page 415 from *Goldsworthy* v *Brickell* [1987] Ch 378; Extract on page 427 from *Newbiggin* v *Adam* (1886) 34 ChD 582; Extract on page 428 from *Lloyds Bank Ltd* v *Bundy* [1975] QB 326; Extracts on page 435, pages 461–2 from *Vita Food Products Inc* v *Unus Shipping Co* [1939] AC 277; Extracts on page 439, page 440, page 449 from *St John Shipping Corporation* v *Joseph Rank Ltd* [1957] 1 QB 267; Extract on page 441 from *Enderby Town FC Ltd* v *The Football Association Ltd* [1971] Ch 591; Extract on page 443 from *Trendtex Trading Corporation* v *Crédit Suisse* [1982] AC 679 (HL); Extracts on page 450, page 451 from *Tinsley* v *Milligan* [1993] 3 WLR 126; Extract on page 465 from *Attorney General* v *Guardian Newspapers Ltd (No. 2)* [1990] 1 AC 109, 286; Extract on page 468 from *Nordenfelt* v *Maxim Nordenfelt Guns and Ammunition Co.* [1894] AC 535; Extract on page 469 from *Esso Petroleum Co. Ltd* v *Harper's Garage (Stourport) Ltd* [1968] AC 269; Extract on page 471 from *Littlewoods Organisation Ltd* v *Harris* [1977] 1 WLR 1472; Extracts on page 479, pages 481–2 from *Schroeder Music Publishing Co. Ltd* v *Macaulay* [1974] 1 WLR 1308; Extract on page 492 from *Arcos Ltd* v *E.A. Ronaasen & Son* [1933] AC 470; Extract on page 506 from *Maple Flock Co. Ltd* v *Universal Furniture Producers (Wembley) Ltd* [1934] 1 KB 148; Extracts on pages 508–9, page 512 from *White and Carter (Councils) Ltd* v *McGregor* [1962] AC 413; Extract on pages 514–5 from *Hounslow Borough Council* v *Twickenham Garden Developments Ltd* [1971] Ch 233; Extract on page 526 from *British Russian Gazette Ltd* v *Associated Newspapers Ltd* [1933] 2 KB 616; Extracts on page 533, pages 536–7, page 538 from *National Carriers Ltd* v *Panalpina (Northern) Ltd* [1981] AC 675; Extracts on page 557, page 558, page 561 from *Attorney-General* v *Blake* [2001] 1 AC 268; Extract on page 565 from *Darlington Borough Council* v *Wiltshier Northern Ltd* [1995] 1 WLR 68; Extracts on pages 573–4 from *Ageas (UK) Ltd* v *Kwik-Fit (GB) Ltd* [2014] QB 2178; Extract on page 575 from *Maredelanto Compania Naviera SA* v *Bergbau-Handel GmbH (The Mihalis Angelos)* [1971] 1 QB 164; Extract on page 582 from *Victoria Laundry (Windsor) Ltd* v *Newman Industries Ltd* [1949] 2 KB 528; Extracts on page 583, page 590 from *Koufos* v *Czarnikow Ltd, The Heron II* [1969] 1 AC 350; Extract on page 590 from *Transfield Shipping Inc.* v *Mercator Shipping Inc. (The Achilleas)* [2008] 3 WLR 345; Extract on pages 596–7 from *British Westinghouse Electric and Manufacturing Co. Ltd* v *Underground Electric Railways Co. of London Ltd* [1912] AC 673; Extract on page 600 from *Redgrave* v *Hurd* (1881) 20 ChD 1; Extract on pages 603–4 from *Dunlop Pneumatic Tyre Co. Ltd* v *New Garage and Motor Co. Ltd* [1915] AC 79; Extracts on page 604, page 605 from *Lordsvale Finance plc* v *Bank of Zambia* [1996] QB 752; Extract on page 609 from *Campbell Discount Ltd* v *Bridge* [1962] AC 600; Extract on page 610 from *Dies* v *British and International Mining and Finance Corporation* [1939] 1 KB 724; Extract on page 614 from *Jarvis* v *Swans Tours Ltd* [1973] 1 QB 233; Extract on page 628 from *Price* v *Strange* [1978] Ch 337; Extracts on page 636, page 637 from *Fibrosa Spolka Akcyjna* v *Fairbairn Lawson Combe Barbour Ltd* [1943] AC 32; Extracts on page 368, page 642 from *Rowland* v *Divall* [1923] 2 KB 500; Extract on page 644 from *Craven-Ellis* v *Cannons Ltd* [1936] 2 KB 403; Extract on page 651 from *Dunlop Pneumatic Tyre Co. Ltd* v *Selfridge & Co. Ltd* [1915] AC 847; Extract on page 660 from *Re Schebsman, Official Receiver* v *Cargo Superintendents (London) Ltd and Schebsman* [1944] Ch 83; Extract on page 668 from *Lord Strathcona Steamship Co.* v *Dominion Coal Co. Ltd* [1926] AC 108; Extract on page 691 from *William Brandt's Sons & Co.* v *Dunlop Rubber Co.* [1905] AC 454.

Contains public sector information licensed under the Open Government Licence v3.0.

Table of cases

Table of statutes

Part 1

The formation of a contract

1

1

The evolution and definition of the modern contract

Objectives

After reading this chapter you should be able to:

1. Understand how the law of contract evolved historically.
2. Understand how the law of contract has evolved in modern times and explain the nature of contracts of adhesion.
3. Define a contract.
4. Recognise when a contract arises in legal terms.

Evolution

The early development

Objective
1

The law of contract in England has a long history which dates back to the thirteenth and fourteenth centuries. Its early development was connected closely with the growth and expansion of the jurisdiction of the common law courts over the myriad courts that evolved before and after the Norman Conquest. Some local courts in the Middle Ages exercised a limited jurisdiction based on custom that was very similar to that of the law of contract. This jurisdiction was termed the 'law merchant' and was often administered at local fairs, markets and ports. It was, however, the common law courts that evolved a more generalised jurisdiction.

The evolution of contract began initially with forms of action based on covenant and debt, roughly equivalent to what we know today as contracts under seal and simple contracts. Under 'covenant' some agreements were regarded as so important that they were formalised in writing. In addition to this, and no doubt because of widespread illiteracy, the parties were required to acknowledge the written document by sealing it. Initially, the action was based on the need to enforce a specific promise to do something, such as ploughing a field, but it evolved into an action for damages for a sum of money, awarded by a jury for breach of the 'covenant' or agreement.

The informal contract evolved in a very different way since the action based on covenant could not be used in a parol (oral) contract. Here the action began on the basis of debt and detinue, whereby specific sums of money lent or otherwise owed (debt) or chattels sold or lent (detinue) could be recovered. These forms of action revolved around a fiction that the claimant was recovering their own money or property. The main deficiencies with these actions were that they could not be used to enforce a positive obligation, the only remedy being the recovery of the debt in all property. Further, the trial procedures were based on compurgation or wager of law, whereby a defendant could evade liability by producing a number of oath-swearers (usually 12) to swear their innocence in respect to the money or property alleged to be held by them. An action could be lost merely by the incorrect enunciation of the oath by one of the oath-swearers. Other rules made these actions inappropriate and often unjust, and it was at this time that the jurisdiction of the courts of chancery began to intervene to correct the inadequacies of the common law and evolve their own particular remedies applicable to agreements.

While the actions of debt and detinue were the earliest recognition of the enforcement of agreements, the modern law of contract in relation to informal agreements does not originate from these actions. As already stated, at this time there were a large number of different courts all vying to expand their own jurisdictions. The common law courts developed a jurisdiction over wrongs in which the king had a special interest. These were known as pleas of the Crown and involved actions relating to breaches of the king's peace. Such actions were founded on actions in **trespass** (i.e. actions in tort) which were particularly useful, in that the form of the writ was flexible and allowed the writ to be developed and used in many different situations. It is for this reason that Maitland called trespass 'the mother of all torts'. These types of writ were called 'actions on the case' and were tried by a jury which itself awarded damages as a remedy. Eventually the bringing of these actions ceased to be the sole prerogative of the Crown and could be used to remedy purely civil wrongs. Those torts that did not evolve in this way went on to form the basis of the criminal law. Among the torts that evolved at this time was an action in which the claimant alleged that the defendant had entered an informal agreement with them and then by a defective performance caused the claimant some damage. One particular anomaly in this early trespass on the case, known as 'assumpsit', was that it lay only for a **misfeasance**, that is performing one's obligations badly, rather than a **nonfeasance**, that is not performing one's obligations at all, though this restriction was removed after *Thoroughgood's case* (1584) 2 Co Rep 9a. The lifting of this anomaly was significant in the development of a law of contract since it meant that any breach of promise could be actionable, even though the agreement was merely informal.

The only remaining blot on the development of assumpsit was the relation of this action to debt. Again the significant factor was the competition for jurisdiction between the courts. With assumpsit, the Court of the King's Bench was prepared to allow the action to be used instead of the action on debt. The Court of Common Pleas regarded this use of assumpsit as improper, with the result that it would not allow a claimant to recover a specific sum of money by way of an action in assumpsit. It required such a claim to be brought in debt with all its incumbent defects. The dispute between the two courts was resolved in *Slade's case* (1602) 4 Co Rep 92a when the views of the Court of the King's Bench were upheld. The result of the case was to produce a single form of action for the enforcement of informal agreements and potentially produce an action that held no bounds in the enforcement of promises.

The open-ended scope of assumpsit needed to be controlled. The controlling element as to what types of promise fell within the general scope of assumpsit emerged also in the sixteenth and early seventeenth centuries when the doctrine of **consideration** evolved. How this doctrine arose in English law is unclear, but what is clear is that by the seventeenth century a principle had emerged that it was necessary not only to show a promise, but also some motivating reason for the existence of the promise. Put another way, a promise may be regarded as a statement of will but for that statement to have legal effect, it had to be supported by a motive for the exercise of that will or consideration. The establishment of the need to show consideration produced a broad form on which the modern law is now based and one which was not to be subject to radical reformulation until the nineteenth century.

The nineteenth century

The nineteenth century is regarded as the golden age of contract since it was at this time that the law of contract evolved into the structure that we have today. Perhaps just as important was the fact that the significance of contract changed within the legal psyche of lawyers since it emerged as a subject in its own right.

The emergence of the law of contract at this time has often been put down to the Industrial Revolution, though this development owes more to coincidence than to a substantive causative link. As Smith and Atiyah (2006) point out in *Atiyah's Introduction to the Law of Contract*, the emergence of the law of contract is really the result of the adoption of the theories of natural law, which propounded the idea of an inalienable right of people to own and deal with property, and that the state via the law should interfere as little as possible with the affairs of individuals. The effect of these two approaches was to elevate the law of contract to a higher plane and produce the notion of the sanctity of the contract, the function of the law being to uphold the contract and only to become involved when things went wrong, not concerning itself with the fairness or social justice of the situation.

This latter comment is of course too simplistic and creates an imbalance when the reality of the situation is assessed since the Courts of Chancery did attempt to protect individuals who found themselves bound by an onerous contract. Nevertheless, the protection offered by the Court of Chancery was limited and probably even reduced during this period, which was a time of great corruption within the court, as is graphically illustrated by Charles Dickens in *Bleak House*.

The result of the above changes produced, by the early part of the nineteenth century, a new concept of individualism, whereby the person in the street was regarded as self-sufficient and imbued with a new notion of self-reliance, in being able to control their own destiny. Given this development one then had to consider at what point the courts should become involved to settle any dispute that might arise from a contract, though central to this question was whether a contract had been entered into in the first place.

The answer here lies in the perhaps obvious statement that a contract materialises where there is an agreement between the parties. Again the statement is far too simplistic, since the stereotypical response where any breach of the contract is alleged is: 'I did not agree to that'. The problem is one of measuring the existence of the agreement. Further, in many situations, a party may not have expressly 'agreed' to anything. Thus, the act of buying a ticket and getting on a train shows no agreement on the face of things, the same being true of any standard form of contract, in that one has no option but to sign and accept; there is no question of 'agreement' here.

It is at this point that the notion of freedom of contract shows its frailty since the law imposes an objective test to find for the existence or not of an agreement, the court representing the so-called reasonable man. At the end of the day, then, the idea of individualism fails and the courts have to find for the existence of a contract based on the intention of the parties. That intention is found by reference to a legal rule rather than the intention of the individuals themselves, despite the fact that some judges at this time considered that *consensus ad idem* (total agreement) was an essential feature of the existence of an enforceable contract.

A further misconception of the notion of freedom of contract is the idea that it provides the parties with freedom of choice as to the terms on which the agreement is entered into. Such an idea holds good where there is equality of bargaining power but is plainly false where this is not the case. Indeed, it is the fact of the powerful imposing terms on the weak that led to the notions of collectivisation, the growth of the trade union movement, the intervention of government and the weakening of the notion of freedom of contract, with its laissez-faire basis, as the underlying principle on which the modern law of contract is based.

The classical theory of contract, as we have seen, played an important part in the early economic and social development of the country, when modern economic theory and power were still in their infancy and true freedom of choice existed. Once large, powerful industrial units developed, as in the railways, for instance, where there was no competition or freedom of choice, then the chinks in the armour of the classical theory began to open up, allowing interventionism and a new dawn of state paternalism to develop.

The modern era

Objective
2

The nineteenth century saw great social, economic and political change in Britain which heralded a swing away from the classic theory of freedom of contract. Britain became firmly established as an industrial leader and this brought with it large industrial concerns, mass production with a wide selection of goods readily available and the dawn of a new consumerism. While previously an individual was free to negotiate an agreement, now they were faced with **standard-form contracts**, large companies carrying great financial power and products which required a scientific knowledge beyond that of the person in the street. Political and social changes were also occurring, taking the form of a widening of the franchise and a movement towards a more socialist society, the result of which was a change from, as Smith and Atiyah put it, 'a corrective form of justice to one which was distributive'.

The modern era then became one of protectionism and a subsequent decline in the freedom of contract caused by the fettering of negotiating discretion. This decline was only partial and in many aspects of business freedom still persisted, particularly in the manufacturing industry. The new protectionism evolved in three ways, all of which often interacted with each other.

Social protectionism

The Industrial Revolution, culminating in the 1880s, the 'golden age' of Britain's economic and industrial transformation, produced a society dependent on earning a living since the population now became centred on major areas of industrial activity. The movement from the country to the towns presented massive social and infrastructure problems. The worker was treated by his employer as a commodity that without careful financial control could be a considerable liability. The effect of this was to produce slum dwellings, jerry-built with little or no sanitation, and working conditions that had the appearance of the devil's cauldron, with unsafe working practices and widespread pollution. These conditions could be seen to be the result of the need to further the profit motive, to produce housing and a workforce that allowed for the greatest maximisation of profit, this objective in turn being achieved by the negotiation of the contract between the manufacturer and the distributors of their goods. Freedom of contract in the classical theory could be seen as being at the centre of the exploitation of the most vulnerable members of society. It was to curtail these excesses that Parliament and the law were called in, and this they did, imposing planning controls, prohibiting certain types of contract and imposing terms into contracts.

So far we have seen how protectionism began but this process also continued right through the twentieth century and into the twenty-first. Thus there has developed a whole network of institutions designed to act as a safety net for the individual, to protect them from the extremes of commercial and industrial life, such as a system of national insurance, a national health service, statutory recognition of trade unions, a compensation scheme for those made redundant and a whole battery of legislation to protect tenants from the excesses of their landlords. There has also been a recognition of the dangers of the concentration of economic power with the development of restrictions on the growth of monopoly power.

Consumer protection

As already stated, the Industrial Revolution brought with it mass production, a great deal more freedom of choice and the development of goods of a complexity never before available. Britain had also become a consumer society, one where an individual generally had to work to earn a living to buy not only essentials such as food and clothing, but also those items which had hitherto been luxuries and beyond the aspirations of the ordinary person to acquire and which were available because of mass production techniques.

With this development the common law and Parliament imposed conditions on the parties to contracts, particularly sellers of goods, to comply with certain basic standards. Such legislation generally protected the individual against the vagaries of the commercial enterprise, though more limited protection was also imposed on contracts made between commercial enterprises. In contracts between private individuals the idea of freedom of contract encapsulated in the maxim *caveat emptor* (let the buyer beware) still persisted – as it does today.

Consumer protection legislation not only imposed civil liability, which left it to the individual to enforce the terms imposed by way of statute in an action for breach of contract, but also imposed criminal liability in some areas. Thus, the Trade Descriptions Act 1968 made it a criminal offence falsely to describe goods offered for sale.

Contracts of adhesion

Contracts of adhesion, generally known today as standard-form contracts, have now become part and parcel of the commercial life of the country. They derive from the time of the development of the passenger-carrying train when, for the first time, large numbers of contracts were entered into on any one day and it would clearly have been nonsensical to have to negotiate every single contract. The railway companies thus produced a standard contract which applied to everyone, the terms of which were not open to negotiation.

It might be thought, therefore, that such contracts are of recent origin, but they are not, and their history goes back to the very beginnings of mercantile enterprise. Initially, they could be found in trade usage, and eventually they were transformed into documents such as charter parties, insurance policies and bills of lading. Their purpose here was to save time and expense since clearly in complex matters such as those indicated, it would be commercially wasteful to have to sit down and negotiate each contract separately. A further purpose was to indicate where particular risks lay in carrying out the contract, so enabling a party to insure or guard against the risk becoming a loss. In contracts for export sales, for example, a strict **free on board** (or FOB) **contract** requires the seller to place the goods, at their own expense, on a ship nominated by the buyer. The price quoted on such a contract does not include the price of the freight or insurance, both of which must be provided for by the buyer.

Such contracts are quite legitimate when entered into between people of business at arm's length. Indeed, this might also be the case where a contract negotiated with a private individual can assume that the individual themselves would normally insure against a particular risk – for example, the cancellation of a holiday. Such contracts become illegitimate where the standard-form contract seeks to impose harsh and onerous terms on an individual who has no option but to accept them. Very often the weaker party will be unable either to renegotiate the contract or, very often, to go elsewhere since such contracts may be common to all operators within a particular industrial activity. A further criticism of such contracts is that they are often drafted in such a way as to be virtually incomprehensible to the ordinary person and often impose wide-ranging exemption clauses which preclude the stronger party from being liable for breach of the contract in almost any circumstances.

In the twentieth century such contracts became all-pervasive, and while the courts attempted to curtail the operation of such contracts – and in particular the effect of the exemption clause – by means of various rules regarding the construction of such clauses, a more radical step was required. This reform developed in a piecemeal fashion in various statutes until the passing of the Unfair Contract Terms Act in 1977.

The present day

Sir George Jessel in 1875 in *Printing and Numerical Registering Co.* v *Sampson* (1875) LR 19 Eq 462 stated:

> if there is one thing more than another which public policy requires, it is that men of full age and competent understanding shall have the utmost liberty in contracting, and that their contracts, when entered freely and voluntarily, shall be held sacred and shall be enforced by the Courts of Justice.

Such a view is clearly not one which sums up the evolution of the law of contract in the last quarter of the nineteenth century or in the twentieth century. The notion of freedom of contract lives on, but the reality is that it persists only in very limited areas of commercial life. The courts and Parliament have made substantial inroads into limiting the powers of those who exercise economic dominance.

In the 1980s, however, the notion of freedom of contract was given a new lease of life in the form of so-called Thatcherism, the idea that the controls that had evolved over the past 100 years had now become so restrictive and so protectionist that they had dulled the cutting edge of competitiveness which Britain required to succeed in the modern commercial world. The result of this dramatic policy change has been to privatise the once publicly-owned utilities which had become dilatory, safe in the knowledge that they were state-owned and protected monopolies which governments had to support no matter how inefficient. On a more individualistic level the government argued that the population was now better educated and more sophisticated, and that individuals were more able to look after their own interests.

The result of this change of policy has been to reduce the levels of protection offered and to allow the individual to have greater freedom of choice, thereby inducing a new competitive order to the economy. Thus the previously state-owned industries now had to become more efficient in order to make profits and to keep their customers. Failure to do so meant not only loss of business but also the asking of questions at the annual general meeting of the newly privatised company in question, since now their privatised customers, or at least some of them, were shareholders to whom the board was answerable.

Such changes occurred not only in relation to the old state-owned utilities, but also in relation to some of the benefits previously enjoyed and protected by the state. Thus individuals now became free to choose how to organise their pensions rather than being dependent on the state. Further, in the private sector, tenants had their rights to security of tenure reduced since it was recognised that the wide-ranging protection previously afforded had the effect of reducing investment in the rented housing market with a consequent reduction in the stock of rented accommodation throughout the country.

This new era of freedom of contract is not a complete one; some level of protection will always be required to protect those less able to look after themselves. It is of course not desirable to revert to the slums and deprivations that existed prior to the protectionist era and therefore some level of protection will be maintained. What that level should be is a matter of political debate, though it seems unlikely that, whatever the political colour of future governments, there will be a reversion to the protectionism prevalent prior to the 1980s. All political parties recognise that the competition prevalent in the notion of freedom of contract is essential to a sound national economy.

Definition

Objective 3

Treitel in *The Law of Contract* defines a contract as:

> an agreement giving rise to obligations which are enforced or recognised by law. The factor which distinguishes contractual from other legal obligations is that they are based on the agreement of the contracting parties.

Beatson in *Anson's Law of Contract*, takes his definition a little further than this, defining it as:

> A legally binding agreement made between two or more persons, by which rights are acquired by one or more to acts or forbearances on the part of the other or others.

Objectivity

Objective 4

The notion of agreement is central to both definitions and the question has to arise as to the point at which an agreement actually materialises. The problem of measuring the existence of the agreement has already been looked at in our discussions on the concept of freedom of contract. Nevertheless, it is worth restating the fact that the law requires more than some subjective indication of agreement between the parties. There is a clear need for some degree of evidence of the fact of agreement, otherwise there would be great uncertainty when one attempts to reconcile the theoretical basis of the law of contract with the actual intentions of the parties. An individual could escape their obligations merely by stating that they had no intention of being bound by any agreement. The courts thus require some outward objective evidence of the existence of an agreement. Any subjective element is subordinate to the objective one and is, to a large degree, of no consequence except where it corresponds with the intentions of the parties as ascertained by objective means. The point was emphasised by Lord Denning in **Storer v Manchester City Council** [1974] 1 WLR 1403 when he stated:

> In contracts you do not look into the actual intent in a man's mind. You look at what he said and did. A contract is formed when there is, to all outward appearances, a contract. A man cannot get out of a contract by saying, 'I did not intend to contract', if by his word he has done so.

In the case of **The Leonidas D** [1985] 1 WLR 925, Goff LJ, in analysing the discussions on the objective test that took place in **The Hannah Blumenthal** [1983] 1 AC 854, preferred the assertion of Lord Brightman in defining the objective test, stating:

> In his speech Lord Brightman was, as we understand it, asserting that if one party (O) so acts that his conduct, objectively considered, constitutes an offer, and the other party (A), believing that the conduct of O represents his actual intention, accepts O's offer, then a contract will come into existence, and on those facts it will make no difference if O did not in fact intend to make an offer, or if he misunderstood A's acceptance, so that O's state of mind is, in such circumstances, irrelevant.

The concept of objectivity in this context has, however, to be given some balance, since it is clearly not desirable for the law to impose an agreement where none existed simply because some hypothetical reasonable person says that there is such an agreement!

In the case of **The Golden Bear** [1987] 1 Lloyd's Rep 330 at 341, it was stated that the objective test would not apply, for instance, where X knows that Y's actual state of mind was not in accordance with the objective appearance created by Y's conduct. Moreover, the objective test will not apply when the result would be to cause hardship to the other party where, for instance, the apparent acceptance of one party is based on a mistake which has been induced by the negligent acts of the other.

For the most part this apparent conflict between finding for an agreement in objective or subjective terms will not materialise since in the vast majority of contracts there will be *consensus ad idem* between the parties, i.e. subjective agreement *and* an agreement as seen objectively. In such circumstances there is unlikely to be a dispute as to the existence of an agreement per se. The principle, however, remains that the test for a contract is based objectively on a reasonable man test but in asking this question one has to look at the circumstances surrounding the parties. This approach is replicated in other parts of the law of contract. Thus, in relation to the means by which the courts imply terms as a matter of fact, Lord Hoffmann stated in **Attorney-General of Belize v Belize Telecom Ltd** [2009] 1 WLR 1988:

> in every case in which it is said that some provision ought to be implied in an instrument, the question for the court is whether such a provision would spell out in express words what the instrument, read against the relevant background, would reasonably be understood to mean.

Similarly, the interaction between an objective test in a subjective context can be seen in **Rainy Sky SA and others v Kookmin Bank** [2011] 1 WLR 2900 where Lord Clarke stated:

> the exercise of construction is essentially one unitary exercise in which the court must consider the language used and ascertain what a reasonable person, that is a person who has all the background knowledge which would reasonably have been available to the parties in the situation in which they were at the time of the contract, would have understood the parties to have meant.

A similar approach is taken with regard to the finding for the existence of a contract and, while this is usually expressed in terms of offer and acceptance, the courts in appropriate cases can look at the whole of the transaction and determine for the existence or non-existence of a contract by assessing what the reasonable man would take to be the reality of the situation.

The notion of a bargain and legal relations

So far we have been discussing the need to establish an agreement before a contract becomes established, and certainly evidence must be submitted to prove this fact. English law of contract requires that there be not only an agreement but also the presence of a bargain since otherwise any promise could give rise to a binding obligation. Thus for the purposes of English law, a promise is not binding unless it is either made under seal or supported by 'consideration'.

See Chapter 3 for the doctrine of consideration.

While the doctrine of consideration will be examined in more depth later, one has to consider it briefly here as an essential element in finding for the mere existence of a contract. This requirement can be seen in Beatson's definition, where he indicates that there must be a degree of quid pro quo to establish the contract, or – to put it simply – the parties are each required to 'buy' the promise of the other party, as, for example, 'I promise to give you £500 if you promise to give me your car.'

In simple contracts, therefore, one must establish the existence of a bargain, and a bare promise, such as 'I promise to give you £500', is not enforceable, being simply a bare promise or *nudum pactum*. The only way such a promise is binding is if it is made in writing under seal as in a deed. However, here we are in the territory of speciality contracts and for the most part this book is about simple contracts.

A further factor in determining what sort of agreements are binding is the requirement of an intention to create a legal relationship. Even if evidence of an agreement is proved, together with consideration, not every such bargain will give rise to a legally enforceable contract.

Example

If *X* says to a neighbour, 'If you give me a lift to work, I will cut your lawns' and the neighbour agrees to this, there is prima facie no binding contract despite the clear existence of a bargain. The reason for this is that such a social arrangement is not one which a reasonable person would consider as giving rise to legally enforceable obligations. The law thus draws a line between agreements of a commercial nature and those of a social or domestic nature.

Debate

The international sphere of contract law

English law of contract does not exist in an isolated 'bubble', and indeed in the vast majority of business transactions around the world, English law of contract is law of choice and this is not just in relation to Commonwealth countries. The reason for this phenomenon is that it is stable, predictable and certain and is undoubtedly flexible, in that it is responsive to the needs and changing nature of commercial life. For many years, the decisions of the English courts stood aloof from decisions in former

Commonwealth countries but this is clearly no longer the case and indeed has not been for some time. The way the English courts have referred to decisions of other jurisdictions has meant that English law has continued to evolve and maintain its relevance internationally. This relevance has been maintained despite other codes being available to parties such as United Nations Convention on Contracts for the International Sale of Goods (the 'Vienna Convention'), the UNIDROIT Principles of International Commercial Contracts and the Principles of European Contract Law. It is an interesting fact that as of May 2016, while the Vienna Convention has been ratified by 85 states, the United Kingdom, recognised as a leading jurisdiction for the choice of law in international commercial contracts, is not a signatory. Apparently the grounds on which the United Kingdom has resiled from becoming a signatory is that, according to the UN, 'the government not viewing its ratification as a legislative priority, a lack of interest from business in supporting ratification, opposition from a number of large and influential organisations, a lack of public service resources, and a danger that London would lose its edge in international arbitration and litigation'.

Of course the greatest international influence on English law of contract is the European Union. This influence has been maintained since the UK acceded to the European Community Treaty by way of the European Communities Act 1972. It is well to remember the well-known retort of Lord Denning to this influence in the case of **H. P. Bulmer Ltd. and Another v J. Bollinger S.A.** [1974] Ch. 401 when he stated:

> The first and fundamental point is that the Treaty concerns only those matters which have a European element, that is to say, matters which affect people or property in the nine countries of the common market besides ourselves. The Treaty does not touch any of the matters which concern solely England and the people in it. These are still governed by English law. They are not affected by the Treaty. But when we come to matters with a European element, the Treaty is like an incoming tide. It flows into the estuaries and up the rivers. It cannot be held back, Parliament has decreed that the Treaty is henceforward to be part of our law. It is equal in force to any statute.

Of course things have moved on a great deal since Lord Denning first uttered these words and English law has now been subject to a huge influence in this field by way of a myriad of Directives and Regulations, much of it concerned with consumer protection. Much of this is to be welcomed, however, there is no getting away from the fact that English law is conceptually very different from many of the codes and legislative regimes that exist within the 27 member states of the EU. In some areas, concepts have been introduced that do not sit well within the UK, for instance, the notion of good faith as originally framed within the Consumer Rights Directive (CRD) 2011/83/EU and which, via the Unfair Contract Terms in Consumer Contract Regulations 1994 and 1999, is now embodied within the Consumer Rights Act 2015. This concept and its place in English law were considered at length by Leggatt J in **Yam Seng Pte Ltd v International Trade Corp Ltd**. In that case, he accepted that the existence of a contractual duty of good faith and fair dealing had been recognised in the United States and Australia and was cautiously gaining ground in Canada, though not in New Zealand. Leggatt J did not consider, however, that a duty of good faith had reached the point in English law that such a duty could be implied as a matter of law into contracts, though it does arise in some specific areas, such as insurance and the law of trusts.

The question arises then as to whether European law could eventually completely reform how English law operates. There is undoubtedly a powerful view that the law of contract should be subject to a harmonisation process across the European Union so that the principles will end up in a codified form. In one respect this would be useful, in that it would operate across all national boundaries and thereby facilitate commercial and business transactions. The wider question is whether this is necessary since parties negotiate a choice of law clauses within their contracts in any event and, as we have seen already, on a worldwide standing, English law of contract is by far the law of choice in commercial transactions. Such a move within the European Union should therefore be resisted and in any event it seems likely that with the Brexit referendum and the UK's withdrawal from the European Union, this threat to English law of contract will diminish.

Questions

1. Do you think that there should be a European law of contract?
2. Should English law of contract remain aloof from such an initiative?
3. What continued influences do think the European Union will have on the English law of contract post Brexit? Will it be reduced to simply being part of the wider notion of private international law?

Summary

This chapter deals with the evolution of the law of contract and its definition.

Evolution

- Early development from the thirteenth and fourteenth centuries encompassing the 'law merchant' and the early forms of action based on covenant, debt and assumpsit.
- Nineteenth-century 'golden age' of contract, the development of the notion of freedom of contract and the conflict with the objective test imposed to find for the existence of a contract.
- 'Classical theory' of contract and the development of interventionism as the notion of freedom of contract began to break down in the face of large-scale commercialism.
- Modern era – protectionism and the decline in the freedom of contract caused by the fettering of negotiating discretion. The new protectionism evolved in three ways: social protectionism, consumer protection, contracts of adhesion/standard-form contracts.
- Present day – rebirth of freedom of contract by the stripping away of state protectionism and the drive for a new competitive order.

Definition

Treitel:

An agreement giving rise to obligations which are enforced or recognised by law. The factor which distinguishes contractual from other legal obligations is that they are based on the agreement of the contracting parties.

Beatson:

> A legally binding agreement made between two or more persons, by which rights are acquired by one or more to acts or forbearances on the part of the other or others.

- The notion of agreement is central to both Treitel's and Beatson's definitions. The problem of measuring the existence of the agreement – the law requires more than some subjective indication of agreement between the parties.
- Need for some degree of evidence of the fact of agreement and the court's requirement for some outward objective evidence of the existence of an agreement.
- Subjective element is subordinate to the objective one and is, to a large degree, of no consequence except where it corresponds with the intentions of the parties as ascertained by objective means.

Further reading

Atiyah, *The Rise and Fall of the Freedom of Contract* (Oxford University Press, 1979)

Atiyah, 'The Hannah Blumenthal and Classical Contract Law' (1986) 102 *Law Quarterly Review* 363

Beatson, Burrows and Cartwright, *Anson's Law of Contract*, 30th edn (Oxford University Press, 2016)

Furmston, *Cheshire, Fifoot and Furmston's Law of Contract*, 16th edn (Oxford University Press, 2012)

Howarth, 'The Meaning of Objectivity in Contract' (1984) *100 Law Quarterly Review* 265

McKendrick, 'English Contract Law: A Rich Past, an Uncertain Future?' in Freeman and Lewis (eds) *Current Legal Problems 1997, Volume 50* (Oxford University Press, 1997)

Smith and Atiyah, *Atiyah's Introduction to the Law of Contract*, 6th edn (Oxford University Press, 2006)

Steyn, 'Contract Law: Fulfilling the Reasonable Expectations of Honest Men' (1997) 113 *Law Quarterly Review* 433

Peel, Treitel *Law of Contract*, 14th edn (Sweet and Maxwell, 2015)

Vorster, 'A Comment on the Meaning of Objectivity in Contract' (1987) 103 *Law Quarterly Review* 274

2

The fact of agreement

Objectives

After reading this chapter you should be able to:

1. Define an offer and compare it with other types of transactions, particularly invitations to treat.

2. Define an acceptance of an offer.

3. Understand the difference between an acceptance and a counter-offer.

4. Recognise the various means by which acceptances are communicated.

5. Explain when offers are terminated.

6. Appreciate the need for certainty in the formation of a contract.

Introduction

It has already been stated that there must be an intention to enter into a binding agreement, and that this intention is usually established by some outward objective indication of the existence of an agreement, rather than a subjective assessment of the actual intentions of the parties. On a practical level, however, the question arises as to what evidence of objective intention the law requires in deciding whether or not an agreement has been entered into.

Two very different approaches have been used to assess the presence of an agreement. The first is a liberal laissez-faire approach under which virtually anything at all could potentially be used in assessing the presence of an agreement. Such an approach almost invariably results in a subjective assessment of the parties' actions taking place and has the disadvantage of rendering the law uncertain and unpredictable. This approach found favour with Lord Denning who, in *Butler Machine Tool Co. Ltd* v *Ex-Cell-O Corporation (England) Ltd* [1979] 1 All ER 965, stated:

> In many cases our traditional analysis of offer, counter-offer, rejection, acceptance and so forth is out of date . . . The better way is to look at all the documents passing between the parties and glean from them or from the conduct of the parties, whether they have reached agreement on all material points.

Similarly, in *Gibson* v *Manchester City Council* [1979] 1 All ER 972, he also stated that one ought to:

> look at the correspondence as a whole and at the conduct of the parties and see therefrom whether the parties have come to an agreement on everything that was material.

In both these cases Lord Denning's approach was rejected in favour of the second, more traditional, approach which is to find the objective intention of the parties to enter into an agreement by reducing the agreement in terms of offers, counter-offers, acceptances, revocations and rejections. This method of finding whether an agreement has come into existence or not provides a more predictable, certain and objective means of assessment, though one that is artificial. One should always bear in mind that this process of breaking an agreement down into smaller, more manageable units is simply an evidential device and in difficult cases where this process of analysis is not possible, the courts may well adopt Lord Denning's approach. Lord Diplock in the *Gibson* case certainly considered it was a legitimate method of analysing a set of circumstances 'which do not fit easily into the normal analysis of offer and acceptance'. This legitimacy of Lord Denning's approach has since been affirmed in the following case.

G Percy Trentham Ltd v *Archital Luxfer* [1993] 1 Lloyd's Rep 25

The facts of the case were that the plaintiffs (Trentham) were engaged by Municipal Mutual Insurance as main contractors to design and build industrial units in two phases. Trentham employed Archital to design, supply and install the doors and window frames for the development. This work was eventually completed and, indeed, paid for by Trentham. The subcontracts were thus fully executed. Subsequently claims were made against Trentham by Municipal Mutual under the main contract for alleged delays and defects in carrying out the work. In order to obtain an indemnity against the damages that it had to pay out, Trentham began proceedings against several subcontractors, including Archital, alleging defects in the window works in both of the phases. In their defence Archital denied that any binding contracts had come into existence between themselves and Trentham. It was common ground in the dispute that no integrated written subcontracts had come into existence; instead there had been a series of exchanges of letters and telephone conversations but no corresponding offer and acceptance. The picture presented, then, was of two parties jockeying for position in a scenario very similar to a 'battle of forms' type of situation (see later in the chapter) where the parties both attempt to impose their own terms and conditions on a contract by the use of offers and counter-offers. The case is unusual, in that the issue is not one concerning whose standard terms and conditions predominate, but whether any contract at all has come into existence out of the exchange of correspondence. At first instance the judge held that a contract had been formed when the defendant carried out the work, basing his decision on *Brogden* v *Metropolitan Railway Co.* (1877) 2 App Cas 666 (see below). In other words, the plaintiff had made an offer which the defendants had accepted by conduct in carrying out the work. Archital appealed from this decision.

In the Court of Appeal, the only judgment was given by Steyn LJ, the two other members concurring. Steyn LJ agreed with the judge at first instance that there was a contract in existence. In arriving at this decision Steyn LJ considered that there were four matters which were of importance to the case. First, English law generally adopts an objective test to the issue of contract formation. As we have already seen, the law generally ignores a subjective assessment of the 'expectations and unexpressed mental reservations of the parties'. He stated that the governing criterion was 'the reasonable expectations of honest men', which he translated in the present case as the 'reasonable expectations of sensible businessmen'. Second, while in the vast majority of cases the presence of offer and acceptance will be the means of deciding the matter of contract formation, 'it is not necessarily so in the case of a contract alleged to have come into existence during and as a result of performance', citing **Brogden v Metropolitan Railway Co.**; **New Zealand Shipping Co. Ltd v A M Satterthwaite & Co. Ltd** [1974] 1 Lloyd's Rep 534 at 539; [1975] AC 154 at 167; **Gibson v Manchester City Council**, as supporting this proposition. Third, he stated that the fact that the contract in the case was executed (i.e. performance of the contract was completed) rather than executory was important since the fact that the transaction has been performed by both parties will make it very difficult for an argument to be sustained that there was no intention to create legal relations or that the contract is void for uncertainty. Indeed, on the specific matter of uncertainty Steyn LJ considered that the fact that the contract was executed 'makes it easier to imply a term resolving any uncertainty, or, alternatively, it may make it possible to treat a matter not finalised in negotiations as inessential'. Fourth, Steyn LJ stated that 'if a contract only comes into existence during and as a result of performance of the transaction it will frequently be possible to hold that the contract impliedly and retrospectively covers pre-contractual performance' as indicated in **Trollope and Colls Ltd v Atomic Power Constructions Ltd** [1962] 3 All ER 1035.

On the basis of these points, Steyn LJ concurred with the decision at first instance that there was sufficient evidence to conclude that there was a binding contract; the parties had clearly intended to create a legal relationship between each other. In arriving at this position Steyn LJ stated that 'one must not lose sight of the commercial nature of the transaction', that is one party carrying out work for which he expected to be paid, and this is what had occurred. There was no suggestion that there was a continuing stipulation that a contract would only be created if a written agreement was concluded. Thus Steyn LJ adopted an approach that was very similar to Lord Denning's in that he looked at the overall effect of what had been said and done by the parties, although he did not refer to Lord Denning's approach. He stated:

> The contemporary exchanges, and the carrying out of what was agreed in those exchanges, support the view that there was a course of dealing which on Trentham's side created a right to performance of the work by Archital, and on Archital's side it created a right to be paid on an agreed basis . . . The Judge (at first instance) analysed the matter in terms of offer and acceptance. I agree with his conclusion. But I am, in any event, satisfied that in this fully executed transaction a contract came into existence during performance even if it cannot be precisely analysed in terms of offer and acceptance.

Does this decision suggest an abandonment of offer and acceptance as central pillars in the formation of contracts? The answer to the question is clearly in the negative, since Steyn himself states that 'the coincidence of offer and acceptance will, in the vast majority of cases, represent the mechanism of contract formation'. What the decision does is to broaden the opportunity to find for a contract by examining the 'commercial reality' of the situation coupled with evidence of the parties' intentions and to this extent a level of uncertainty may have been created as to when a contract has actually been formed.

Despite the decision of Steyn, it should be borne in mind that the judge at first instance was able to find for a contract on the basis of offer and acceptance, that is by adopting the classical approach. More often than not, therefore, the courts will continue to go to great lengths to analyse the facts in terms of the classical approach.

As Lord Wilberforce stated in **New Zealand Shipping Co. Ltd v A M Satterthwaite and Co. Ltd** [1975] AC 154:

> English law, having committed itself to a rather technical and schematic doctrine of contract, in application takes a practical approach, often at the cost of forcing the facts to fit uneasily into the marked slots of offer, acceptance and consideration.

While one must always bear in mind Lord Denning's approach, the classical analysis is far more important and has to be considered in a great deal more depth. The basic proposition of the classical analysis may be summed up as:

offer + acceptance = agreement

Offer

The nature of an offer

Objective 1

An offer is an expression of a willingness to contract on certain terms made with the intention that a binding agreement will exist once the offer is accepted.

The task of a claimant seeking to enforce a contract is to prove the existence of an offer. An offer may be made either orally or in writing, or implied by the conduct of the person making the offer, namely, the offeror. Furthermore, the offer may be made to a specific person or group of persons or to the world at large. In the now famous case of ***Carlill v Carbolic Smoke Ball Co.***, it was argued that it was not possible to make an offer to the world at large.

Carlill v *Carbolic Smoke Ball Co.* [1893] 1 QB 256

In this case, the plaintiff bought a medical preparation called 'The Carbolic Smoke Ball' on the basis that the defendants advertised that they would pay £100 to any person who contracted influenza after using the smoke ball in the prescribed manner and for a specified period. Further, the defendants stated that 'to show their sincerity' they had deposited £1,000 with the Alliance Bank. The plaintiff bought one of the smoke balls and used it in the manner prescribed and promptly caught influenza! She sued for the £100. The defendants contended that there was no agreement between them and used considerable ingenuity in promoting this contention. One of the defences used was that it was not possible to make an offer to the whole world since this would enable the whole world to accept the offer, which was clearly beyond the realms of commercial reality. The Court of Appeal had no difficulty in rejecting this defence. Bowen LJ stated the position very clearly as follows:

> It was also said that the contract is made with the whole world – that is, with everybody and that you cannot contract with everybody. It is not a contract made with all the world. There is the fallacy of the argument. It is an offer made to all the world; and why should not an offer be made to all the world which is to ripen into a contract with anybody who comes forward and performs the condition? . . . Although the offer is made to the world, the contract is made with that limited portion of the public who come forward and perform the condition on the faith of the advertisement.

The defendants also contended that the plaintiff had not accepted their offer and therefore there was no consensus ad idem and thus no agreement. This defence, which was rejected, exposes the fact that offers may arise in two forms, either bilateral or unilateral. A bilateral offer arises where one party promises to do something in return for a promise made by the offeree. Both parties are agreeing to do something in return for some reciprocal promise from the other. An example of such an offer would be if A promises to sell their car in return for B promising to pay £5,000. The vast majority of offers are of this type.

A unilateral offer occurs where one party, the offeror, promises to pay for the act of another, that is, a conditional promise. The acceptance of the offer takes place when the offeree performs the act in question. The offer here is said to be unilateral because only one party is making a promise. The facts of the *Carlill* case provide an obvious example of such an offer but a modern example of the principle can be seen in the case of *O'Brien v MGN Ltd* [2001] EWCA Civ 1279. The facts of the case were that the claimant purchased a Sunday newspaper that contained a 'scratchcard' game that related to a competition being held during the following week in the *Daily Mirror*. The claimant's card revealed two 'windows' displaying £50,000 in each. The next week the claimant bought a copy of the *Daily Mirror* and in accordance with the 'rules' rang the 'hotline' and was told that the prize for that day was £50,000, and the claimant then believed he had won that amount. The court considered that the advertisement in the *Daily Mirror* constituted an offer which was accepted when those with a winning scratchcard rang up to claim their prize.

For more analysis of the *O'Brien v MGN Ltd* case refer to Chapter 8.

Two further features of offers to be noted are that the terms of an offer must be clear and that the offer is made with the intention that it should be binding. In connection with the latter requirement, a further defence propounded in the *Carlill* case was that the advertisement was a 'mere puff' and not intended to form the basis of a binding agreement. Such 'puffs' are very much part of commercial life today, particularly in the advertising industry. Clearly statements that allude to certain soap powders 'washing whiter than white' or certain types of beers working untold miracles are not intended to be taken seriously but to 'puff up' the propensities of the product to induce the all-suffering public to buy. In the *Carlill* case the allegation that the offer was a 'mere puff' was rejected on the basis that the advertisement also stated that the defendants had deposited £1,000 with the Alliance Bank 'to show their sincerity'. It was clear in this case that this fact indicated that they intended the promise to form the basis of a legal relationship.

So far everything presented is fairly straightforward, but unfortunately the situation is not so simple. There are many types of statement which, on the face of things, appear to be offers but in fact do not so comprise.

Offers compared with other types of transaction

Offers distinguished from invitations to treat

It has been seen that, according to one definition, an offer is an expression of a willingness to be bound by the terms of the offer should the offer be accepted. Clearly the implication here is that the statement of offer is the final statement of an individual who wishes to be bound by those terms; it is a person's final declaration of their readiness to be bound. It follows that if an individual is not willing to implement the terms of their promise but is merely seeking to initiate negotiations, then this cannot amount to an offer, such statements being termed 'invitations to treat'.

The distinction between an offer and an invitation to treat is not an easy one to make since it very often revolves around that elusive concept of intention. It may be that a statement amounts to an invitation to treat even though the statement is said to make an 'offer' and vice versa. The easiest way of making the distinction is by analysing how the law deals with the problem within certain stereotypical transactions, bearing in mind that the courts will look at the surrounding circumstances and the intention of the parties and will not necessarily have regard to the actual wording of the statement.

1. Advertisements and other notices

It has already been seen that the advertisement in the *Carlill* case amounted to an offer, though a unilateral one. In the words of Bowen LJ:

> It is not like cases in which you offer to negotiate or you issue advertisements that you have got a stock of books to sell, or houses to let, in which case there is no offer to be bound by any contract. Such advertisements are offers to negotiate – offers to receive offers – offers to chaffer.

The decision in the *Carlill* and *O'Brien* cases that the advertisement was an offer is peculiar to a situation where the statement is a conditional promise, a unilateral offer. A similar situation would result if an individual placed an advertisement offering a reward to the finder of a lost wallet. In such a case there is clearly a conditional promise and the advertisement would amount to an offer.

Most advertisements do not fall into this category and hence they are held not to be offers but statements inviting further negotiations or invitations to treat. An example of such a situation can be seen in the case of *Partridge* v *Crittenden* [1968] 2 All ER 421, where the appellants placed an advertisement in a periodical for bird fanciers stating, 'Bramblefinch cocks and hens 25s'. They were charged under the Protection of Birds Act 1954, s 6(1), in that they were unlawfully 'offering for sale' a certain live bird, a brambling, contrary to the provisions of the Act. At first instance the appellants were convicted but on appeal the conviction was quashed by the Divisional Court.

This decision affirms the much earlier decision of *Harris* v *Nickerson* (1873) LR 8 QB 286, where an auctioneer advertised that certain goods would be sold at a certain location on a certain date. The plaintiff went to the sale but all the lots he was interested in had been withdrawn. He sued the auctioneer for his loss of time and expenses. It was held that the claim must fail as the advertisement of the auction was merely a declaration of intent to hold a sale and did not amount to an offer capable of being accepted and thus forming the basis of a binding contract, that is, that the advertisement merely amounted to an invitation to treat.

The same conclusion was also reached in the case of a price list circulated by a wine merchant (*Grainger and Son* v *Gough* [1896] AC 325), though a notice declaring that deckchairs were for hire was held in *Chapelton* v *Barry UDC* [1940] 1 KB 532 as amounting to an offer. The moral of the story is clear that in this type of case, while one can draw on certain generalisations, as in advertisements, one must treat each case on its own merits, assessing the intentions of the parties.

2. Displays of goods for sale

By far the most common example of the occurrence of invitations to treat is in the case of goods displayed either in shop windows or within a shop itself. The issue that arises here is that if the display of the goods in question amounts to an offer, then a customer may enter the shop and purport to accept that offer, thus creating a binding obligation on the shopkeeper to sell the goods at the stated price. If, however, the display of goods only amounts to an invitation to treat, then it is the customer who makes the offer to the shopkeeper, who is free to accept or reject that offer as they wish. Almost invariably it is the latter approach that is adopted by the courts, though the reasoning behind the general rule is somewhat obscure and lost in the mists of time – some think the rule is a throwback to the time of the marketplace when bargaining and haggling were commonplace, a notion that is not particularly appropriate today. The rule could nevertheless produce some startling effects.

Example

A shopkeeper could refuse to sell the goods to a customer even if they offered certain goods for sale and wrote the words 'Special Offer' across the windows. The words 'Special Offer' import no specific legal meaning here and do not necessarily mean an offer at law. Such a conclusion may be somewhat unfair, however, if those words had induced a person to wait outside the shop all night, only to be told the next morning that their offer to buy had been rejected. Nevertheless, even if the goods subject to the 'Special Offer' were regarded as an offer at law, an offeror in any event is free to withdraw that offer at any time up to acceptance.

The general rule as regards goods displayed in shop windows is well illustrated in the case of *Fisher* v *Bell* [1961] 1 QB 394, where a price-marked flick-knife was displayed for sale in a shop window. The seller was prosecuted under the now repealed Restriction of Offensive Weapons Act 1961, which made it an offence to offer to sell such items, and was acquitted. Lord Parker stated:

> It is clear according to the ordinary law of contract that the display of an article with a price on it in a shop window is merely an invitation to treat. It is in no sense an offer for sale, the acceptance of which constitutes a contract.

A more problematical situation occurred in the following case.

Pharmaceutical Society of Great Britain v *Boots Cash Chemists (Southern) Ltd* [1952] 2 All ER 456; [1953] 1 All ER 482

The status of goods on the shelves of a self-service shop was called into question. The facts of the case were that the defendants were being prosecuted under the Pharmacy and Poisons Act 1933, s 17, in that they had allowed the sale of a listed poison to be effected without the supervision of a registered pharmacist. The arrangement in the shop was that a customer on entering was given a basket and he was then free to walk around the shop selecting items from the shelves. When he had selected such items as he required, they were taken to the cash desk, where the customer was required to pay for them. Near to the cash desk was a registered pharmacist who was authorised to prevent a customer removing any drug from the shop. The Pharmaceutical Society alleged that the goods on the shelves were offers to sell, which the customer accepted by placing the goods in the basket and that, thus, the sale took place at that point and not at the cash desk under the supervision of the registered pharmacist. In such a situation, it was alleged, Boots were clearly in breach of the provision and had committed a criminal offence. The court, however, decided that the goods on the shelves were only invitations to treat and that it was the customer who made an offer to buy when he presented the goods for payment at the cash desk. At this point the person at the cash desk or the registered pharmacist could accept or reject that offer. The effect of this reasoning was that the sale did take place under the supervision of the registered pharmacist and no criminal offence had been committed.

Some authorities, particularly American ones, dispute such a conclusion as regards the status of goods on display in a self-service shop. In *Lasky* v *Economy Grocery Stores*, 65 NE 305 (1946), it was stated that the goods displayed constituted offers but that the acceptance took place not on the placing of the goods in the basket, but on the customer presenting them at the cash desk for payment. Alternatively, in *Sheeskin* v *Giant Food Inc.*, 318 A 2d 894 (1974), it was stated that acceptance took place before the goods were presented at the cash desk, though the customer could cancel his acceptance before payment if he wished. Contradiction also exists in English law though, since in **R v Morris** [1984] AC 320 it was held that the taking of goods from a shelf and changing the price tags amounted to an 'appropriation' within the Theft Act 1968.

3. Auction sales

The status of the call for bids by an auctioneer was considered in the case of **Payne v Cave** (1789) 3 Term Rep 148. In this case, it was decided that a call for bids amounts to an invitation to treat, the bids themselves amounting to offers which the auctioneer is free to accept or reject as they wish. This situation is given implied authority in the Sale of Goods Act 1979, s 57(2), which provides that a sale in an auction is completed by the fall of the hammer and each party is allowed to withdraw up to this time.

Auction sales can take two forms, in that goods may be sold with or without a reserve price. Where the goods are put up for sale with a reserve price, it has been held (in **McManus v Fortescue** [1907] 2 KB 1) that no contract results if the auctioneer purports to accept a bid that is lower than the reserve price. Where the auction is held without reserve no contract of sale materialises between the owner of the property and the highest bidder if the auctioneer either refuses or otherwise fails to accept the highest bid. In **Warlow v Harrison** (1859) 1 E& E 309 it was stated, *obiter dicta*, that in such a case there is a collateral contract between the auctioneer and the highest bidder, whereby the auctioneer in calling for bids is offering to accept the highest bid and that this offer is accepted by bidding. Thus if the auctioneer refuses to sell to the highest bidder, the auctioneer may be sued for breach of contract. This position was affirmed in **Barry v Heathcote Ball & Co. (Commercial Auctions) Ltd** (2000) *The Times*, 31 August (CA). In this case, the defendant was auctioning two new machines on behalf of the Customs and Excise. The machines were valued at £14,251 each. The defendant was instructed to auction these machines without reserve. At the auction the claimant, who had been told that the sale was without reserve, bid £200 for each machine. When the defendant could not get a higher bid he withdrew the machines from the sale and sold them for £750 a few days later by way of a magazine advertisement. The claimant argued that on the highest bidder rule, the auctioneer was legally bound to accept his bid, since in an auction held without reserve the auctioneer was offering to accept the highest bid.

The Court of Appeal, affirming **Warlow v Harrison**, confirmed there was no contract between the vendors, the Customs and Excise, and the claimant. There was, however, a collateral contract between the auctioneer and the claimant. The measure of damages where a seller refused goods to the buyer was the difference between the contract price and the market price as set out in the Sale of Goods Act 1979, s 51(3). The Court of Appeal held that despite the fact that there was no contract between the vendor and the claimant, the same measure of damages would apply. Since the pledge considered that the machines were valued at £14,000 each, he awarded damages of £27,600.

4. Tenders

It was held in **Spencer v Harding** (1870) LR 5 CP 561 that a statement that goods are to be sold by tender is not normally an offer, and that thus no obligation is created to sell to the person making the highest tender. Similarly, an invitation for tenders for the supply of goods or services is not generally an offer but an invitation for offers to be submitted which can be accepted or rejected as the case may be.

In some circumstances, however, an invitation to tender may be held to be an offer.

Blackpool and Fylde Aero Club Ltd v Blackpool Borough Council [1990] 3 All ER 25

In this case, the Council owned and managed an airport, raising money by granting a concession to an operator to run pleasure flights from the airport. Shortly before the concession was about to expire in 1983 the Council invited tenders for the right to run the concession, invitations being sent to the plaintiffs and six other interested parties. The terms of submission of bids were that they were to be submitted in an envelope provided, which was to bear no mark which could identify the sender. Furthermore, the tender had to be submitted no later than 12 noon on 17 March 1983. The plaintiffs' tender was put in the Town Hall letter-box at 11 am on 17 March. However, although the box should have been cleared at noon, this did not occur. The plaintiffs' tender was subsequently marked down as being submitted late and was therefore not considered. The plaintiffs sued the Council for breach of contract on the basis that it had warranted that had a tender been submitted by the deadline it would be considered and that the Council had acted in breach of that warranty. It was held, on appeal, that in certain circumstances an invitation to tender could give rise to binding obligations. This was such an instance since tenders had been sought from a number of parties, all of them known to the Council, which had also imposed strict rules of compliance on them. It was thus implied that a person submitting a tender in compliance with those rules had the right to have their tender opened and considered along with the others.

Tenders may take two possible forms. They may be specific tenders or standing-offer tenders. The former comprises a tender for a definite quantity of goods to be delivered or sold at a specified time. Here the person requiring or selling the goods makes an invitation to tender, the person wishing to deliver or buy them making the offer, which will be converted into a trading contract when accepted by the first party.

The second type of tender arises when a person invites tenders for the supply of goods or services which *may* be required within a specified time at some future date. An example of such a tender may be where a company invites tenders for the supply of stationery as and when, or if and when, required. Here acceptance of the tender (i.e. the offer) does not create a binding contract. The supplier whose bid is successful is in fact making a standing offer which is accepted every time an order is placed for stationery. At this point the supplier is obliged to meet the order or be in breach of contract, though the supplier is free to revoke the standing offer at any time prior to an order being placed, though they are bound to fulfil orders already received.

The problem of standing offers was considered in the case of the **Great Northern Railway Co. v Witham** (1873) LR 9 CP 16 where the plaintiffs invited tenders for the supply of goods, including iron, for a period of 12 months. The defendant submitted a tender to supply the goods over the period at a fixed price in such quantities as may be ordered from time to time. The tender was accepted, but before the expiry of 12 months the defendant refused to supply any more goods and was sued for breach of contract. It was held that just as the plaintiffs were not bound to order goods, the defendant was only bound to supply goods actually ordered and that he could revoke his standing offer at any time provided that revocation was communicated to the other party.

The revocation thus only operated to free him from future obligations, not those which had actually accrued by virtue of the placing of an order. The case thus affirmed the earlier decision of **Offord v Davies** (1862) 12 CBNS 748.

In recent years, a new development has occurred in the area of tenders, namely, the referential bid. A referential bid occurs in a competitive tender situation where one party attempts to win the order by reference to a bid submitted by another party.

> **Example**
>
> X offers to pay £100,000 for a concession or £10,000 more than any other offer. The latter part of this bid is a referential bid.

The status of referential bids was considered in the following case.

Harvela Investments Ltd v *Royal Trust Co. of Canada (CI) Ltd* [1986] AC 207

> An invitation was made to two persons to submit 'offers' for the purchase of a quantity of shares. The first defendants, who were disposing of the shares, also agreed to accept the highest offer received provided it met with other stipulated conditions. The plaintiffs bid $2,175,000 while the second defendant bid $2,100,000 or '$10,000 in excess of any other offer which you may receive which is expressed as a fixed monetary amount whichever is higher'. The first defendants accepted the second defendant's offer. The House of Lords held that the referential bid was ineffective and that the fixed bid of the plaintiffs should have been accepted. The reasoning for this decision was that the House of Lords considered that the idea behind a competitive tender was that the bids were to be confidential and that no bidder would know the amount bid by the other person. The effect of a referential bid would be to defeat the notion of a confidential competitive tender.

5. Ticket cases

One problem that has recurred time and time again concerns the giving of a ticket during the course of entering into the contract. The problem revolves around whether the ticket is a contractual document, thereby rendering the parties subject to the terms and conditions printed or referred to on the ticket, or not. Two factors can influence the role of tickets in contracts: first, whether it was intended that the ticket should amount to a contractual document; and, second, the mode and timing of the issue of the ticket.

Chapelton v *Barry UDC* [1940] 1 KB 532

> In this case, the Court of Appeal considered that a sign by some deckchairs for hire constituted an offer, which the plaintiff accepted when he took two of the chairs. The tickets amounted to no more than mere receipts with the result that the terms and conditions on them formed no part of the contract since they were handed out after the contract was concluded.

With regard to timetables and passenger tickets, however, the law is not at all certain. Tickets have been held to be contractual documents on the basis that the proffering of the ticket by a bus conductor or ticket office clerk is an offer which is accepted by the taking of the ticket, as suggested in *Cockerton* v *Naviera Aznar SA* [1960] 2 Lloyd's Rep 450. Another view is that a timetable amounts to an offer which is accepted by a passenger either by applying for a ticket or by boarding the bus. The latter problem was discussed in the case of *Wilkie* v *London Passenger Transport Board* [1947] 1 All ER 258. In the *Wilkie* case, Lord Greene considered that on a bus a contract is made when the intending passenger 'puts himself either on the platform or inside the bus'. The implication here is that the company makes an offer of carriage by running the bus which the passenger accepts by boarding.

The fact that a contract arises here despite the fact that no fare has been paid, or ticket issued, renders the statement open to doubt. A better solution would surely be that the company makes an invitation to treat by virtue of its advertisement or sign on the front, the passenger making an offer when they get on the bus, which is accepted by the conductor's taking the fare and issuing the ticket. The question then arises as to whether the ticket issued is a contractual document or a mere receipt, but no doubt this is one for the court to answer in the circumstances of a particular case.

The question of the status of tickets also arose in the following case.

Thornton v *Shoe Lane Parking Ltd* [1971] 1 All ER 686

This case concerned the issue of a ticket by an automatic issuing machine in a car park. It will be discussed more fully when exemption clauses are analysed later, but in relation to offer and acceptance, the case also has a contribution to make. Broadly speaking, the facts are that the plaintiff went to park his car in the defendant's car park. At the entrance there was a sign which set out the charges and which stated: 'all cars parked at customer's risk'. As customers drove in, a light changed from red to green and a ticket was ejected from the machine. Lord Denning discussed the transaction as follows:

> The customer pays his money and gets a ticket. He cannot refuse it. He cannot get his money back. He may protest to the machine, even swear at it; but it will remain unmoved. He is committed beyond recall. He was committed at the very moment when he put his money in the machine; the contract was concluded at that time. It can be translated into offer and acceptance in this way. The offer is made when the proprietor of the machine holds out as being ready to receive the money. The acceptance takes place when the customer puts money in the slot. The terms of the offer are contained in the notice placed on or near the machine, stating what is offered for the money. He (the customer) is not bound by the terms printed on the ticket because the ticket comes too late. The contract had already been made.

The decision in the case is certainly a better solution to the status of tickets than Lord Greene's statement in the *Wilkie* case which would appear to be wrong.

6. E-commerce

Most people have heard of the possibility of buying goods via the Internet, even if they have not actually had experience of this commercial phenomenon. But what is the status of a supplier's website – does it represent an offer or an invitation to treat? Many of the electronic or virtual shopping sites are set out to resemble real stores, so that the potential purchaser browses through the products for sale in much the same way as one would do in a shop or supermarket. As the purchaser finds a product they want to buy, they place the item into a virtual shopping basket. When the purchaser has completed their 'shopping trip', the purchaser then submits details of the selected products, their identity (if they have shopped there before, otherwise they will have to register) and their credit/debit card details to the seller. The transaction is thus analogous to the situation seen in ***Pharmaceutical Society of Great Britain* v *Boots Cash Chemists (Southern) Ltd***. The goods on the website will constitute an invitation to treat, as in *Fisher* v *Bell*, the offer arising when the buyer submits their details to the seller.

The analysis above is of course dependent on the contents of the website. In appropriate cases it may be possible to argue that the site in fact constitutes an offer, possibly even a unilateral offer of the type seen in ***Carlill* v *Carbolic Smoke Ball Co.***, where the purchaser accepts the offer simply by pressing a button. Clearly website developers have to exercise great care in designing their websites to avoid such a situation from arising.

The sort of difficulties that can arise here can be seen in the recent case involving Argos Stores, where the company inadvertently offered television sets worth £300 for £3. Many customers purported to accept this offer but of course Argos would have argued that the website constituted an invitation to treat and that the purchasers were making an offer to buy. In such a situation, Argos was in a position to reject the offers made in response to the wrongly priced invitation to treat. No doubt this is a correct analysis but Argos might have found themselves in substantial difficulties if their website could have been considered to be a unilateral offer and the response by the purchasers clicking a button on the site to be an acceptance. Such a transaction would clearly not be in the interests of Argos in these particular circumstances. Of course, this would have required the customers to argue that the website constituted an offer. In the Argos scenario some customers had actually had their orders accepted and confirmed by Argos before the mistake was discovered. Presumably, therefore, they were entitled to insist on receiving a television set for £3. Sadly this is not the case since in **Hartog v Colin and Shields** [1939] 3 All ER 566 it was held that no contract arises where one party makes an offer to another and he is aware that the other party is acting under a fundamental mistake as to the terms of the offer.

For more on unilateral mistakes as to the terms of an offer refer to Chapter 10.

In spite of the fact that there have been a number of European Directives regulating various aspects of the law relating to electronic contracting, none purport to define the status of a website as either an invitation to treat or an offer. Thus reg 12 of the Electronic Commerce (EC Directive) Regulations 2002 states that an 'order may be but need not be a contractual offer', presumably implying that websites would normally constitute invitations to treat.

Offers distinguished from requests for information

Very often, particularly in commercial transactions, substantial negotiations may take place before the terms of the contract are agreed by the parties concerned and the contract itself is entered into. During the period of negotiation one of the parties may simply require further information before they can place themselves in the position of being able to enter the contract. Such a situation is very common where negotiations for the sale of land take place since there may be many questions of detail to be investigated before a formal contract can be entered into.

Harvey v Facey [1893] AC 552

The appellants sent a telegram to the respondent which read, 'Will you sell us Bumper Hall Pen? Telegraph lowest cash price'; the respondent replied, 'Lowest price for Bumper Hall Pen, £900.' The appellants then telegraphed, 'We agree to buy Bumper Hall Pen for £900 asked by you. Please send us your title deeds in order that we may get early possession.' The appellants received no reply and thereupon brought an action for specific performance. It was held that the action must fail since the respondent's reply was not an offer to sell but simply a statement as to the minimum price required should he decide to sell; his reply was a mere response to a request for information. The appellants' final telegram amounted to the offer to buy, which was not accepted by the respondent.

A similar case is that of **Clifton v Palumbo** [1944] 2 All ER 497, where the defendant was negotiating the purchase of a large estate owned by the plaintiff who wrote, 'I am prepared to offer you . . . my . . . estate for £600,000 . . . I also agree that a reasonable and sufficient time shall be granted to you for the examination and consideration of all the data and details necessary for the preparation of the Schedule of Completion.' It was held that, in the circumstances, this letter did not amount to an offer to sell but a mere preliminary statement as to price to enable negotiations to proceed.

So far the distinction between offers and requests for information is fairly straight-forward, though one wonders if some of the earlier decisions can be considered correct. Would the decision in *Harvey* v *Facey*, for instance, be the same today?

> ### Example
>
> If A walks up to B and says, 'How much do you want for your car?' and B replies, '£3,500', is this not a contract? Surely the situation is likely to be that if B does not wish to sell he will reply, '£3,500, but it is not for sale' or simply, 'The car is not for sale.'

The surrounding circumstances of the case will be important in this type of situation but on the face of things there would appear to be a binding contract today. The courts in any event are not consistent or predictable in this type of case.

Bigg v *Boyd Gibbons Ltd* [1971] 2 All ER 183

> In this case, negotiations were taking place for the sale of some freehold property belonging to the plaintiffs. The plaintiffs wrote to the defendants, stating: 'As you are aware that I paid £25,000 for this property, your offer of £20,000 would appear to be at least a little optimistic. For a quick sale I would accept £26,000.' The defendants replied: 'I accept your offer' and asked the plaintiffs to contact the defendants' solicitors. In their final letter the plaintiffs said: 'I am putting the matter in the hands of my solicitors . . . my wife and I are both pleased you are purchasing the property.' The plaintiffs alleged that this exchange of correspondence constituted an agreement for the sale of the property and sought specific performance. The Court of Appeal stated that an agreement on price did not necessarily mean an agreement for sale and purchase, nor did the use of the word 'offer' always amount to an offer in law; however, on the facts it was clear from the correspondence that the plaintiffs' first letter constituted an offer, the acceptance of which by the defendants constituted a binding contract. In this case the parties had gone so far down the road of negotiations that a binding agreement had resulted.

Quite clearly the background circumstances play an important part in determining the nature of a statement as to whether it is indeed an offer or simply a request for further information. The question is whether the offeror's words or conduct are such as to induce a reasonable person to believe that they intend to be bound, even though they have no such intention. In *Crest Nicholson (Londinium) Ltd* v *Akaria Investments Ltd* [2010] EWCA Civ 1331, Sir John Chadwick stated that the correct approach for determining whether there was an offer in a proposal that was capable of being accepted was to ask 'whether a person in the position of B (the offeree) (having the knowledge of the relevant circumstances which B had), acting reasonably, would understand that A (the offeror) was making a proposal to which he intended to be bound in the event of an unequivocal acceptance'.

Communication of offers

Clearly an offer cannot take effect until it has been received by the offeree, since they cannot accept something of which they are not aware. The principle can be seen in the case of *Taylor* v *Laird* (1856) 1 H& N 266; 25 LJ Ex 329, where the plaintiff, the captain of a ship, was employed to command a steamer 'for an exploring and trading voyage up the river Niger . . . at a rate of £50 per month'. The plaintiff took this ship as far as Dagbo, but refused to go further and resigned his command. He later helped to work the ship home and he claimed his wages for this work. It was held that the owners of the vessel were entitled to refuse payment as the plaintiff's offer to help to bring the ship back to its home port was not communicated to them. In other words, they were given no opportunity to either accept or reject his offer.

The timing of the communication of the offer can be of importance when determining the time within which it can be accepted by the offeree. From the above case it is clear that acceptance can only take place when the offer has been received; however, if the offer specifies some date by which the offer must be accepted and that date has passed when the offer is received, then the offeree is not able to accept the offer. Similarly, it may be that there has been a very long delay in the transmission of the offer to the offeree, and in these circumstances it may well be the case, depending on the subject matter of the offer, that the offer has in fact lapsed, rendering it incapable of acceptance.

One problem that arises in the latter context is what happens where the delay in the transmission of the offer is the fault of the offeror themselves. In *Adams* v *Lindsell* (1818) 1 B& Ald 681, the defendants offered to sell wool to the plaintiffs. Their letter of offer was wrongly addressed so that it reached the plaintiffs two days later than the defendants could, in normal circumstances, have expected it to arrive. The plaintiffs, on receiving the letter, immediately accepted the offer and it was held that they were entitled to do so, creating a binding contract, despite the fact that the defendants had considered that the offer had lapsed by the delay and sold the wool to a third party. It would seem from the case that the significant factor was the negligence of the defendants in addressing the letter and that if the delay had been caused by some other factor, then it is possible that the decision could have been the reverse.

Acceptance

The definition of acceptance

Objective 2

Treitel defines **acceptance** as 'a final unqualified expression of assent to all the terms of an offer'. The objective test, which was examined above in regard to offers, applies in the same manner to acceptance. In other words, evidence must be produced from which the courts can adduce an intention by the offeree to accept the offer communicated to them. Two principles evolve from the definition of acceptance and the requirement of its objective existence. First, the expression of intention to assent to the offer must, as seen in *Taylor* v *Laird* above, be in response to the offer and match the terms of the offer precisely. The acceptance, therefore, must be unequivocal and unconditional. Second, mere acknowledgement of the offer is insufficient: there must be a communication of the acceptance to the offeror.

These two factors can, however, lead to peculiar results in certain types of case, in particular where cross-offers materialise. The problem here occurs when two identical offers cross in the post.

> ### Example
> X offers to buy Y's car from him for £5,000, while at the same time Y offers to sell his car to X for £5,000. This is an example of a cross-offer.

In such an instance, no contract will be found to exist since, although the parties may undoubtedly be in subjective agreement, there must be an objective outward indication of the agreement, even if one could say there has been adequate communication of acceptance. In *Tinn v Hoffman and Co.* (1873) 29 LT 271, Blackburn J stated:

> When a contract is made between two parties, there is a promise by one in consideration of the promise made by the other; there are two assenting minds, the parties agreeing in opinion and one having promised in consideration of the promise made by the other – there is an exchange of promises. But I do not think exchanging offers would, upon principle, be at all the same thing . . . The promise or offer made on each side in ignorance of the promise or offer made on the other side, neither of them can be construed as an acceptance of the other.

The American case of *Fitch v Snedaker*, 38 NY 248 (1868), allegedly supports the judgment of Blackburn J. Indeed in that case Woodruff J asked, 'How can there be consent or assent to that of which the party has never heard?' Further support is also alleged in *R v Clarke* (1927) 40 CLR 227, where a reward of £1,000 was offered 'for such information as shall lead to the arrest and conviction of' the murderers of two police officers. The offer also added that if the information was given by an accomplice, he, not being one of the murderers, should receive a free pardon. Clarke saw the offer and later gave the necessary information and claimed the reward. In attempting to enforce his claim he admitted that at the time he gave the information he acted to save himself and that the reward was not at the forefront of his mind. The High Court of Australia held that his claim must fail. Isaacs CJ stated that Clarke was in the same position as if he had never heard of the reward:

> An offer of £100 to any person who should swim a hundred yards in the harbour on the first day of the year would not in my opinion be satisfied by a person who was accidentally or maliciously thrown overboard on that date and swam the distance simply to save his life, without any thought of the offer.

Similarly Higgins J stated:

> Clarke had seen the offer, indeed, but it was not present to his mind – he had forgotten it and gave no consideration to it in his intense excitement as to his own danger. There cannot be assent without knowledge of the offer, and ignorance of the offer is the same thing, whether it is due to never hearing of it or to forgetting it after the hearing.

Although these cases seem to support the decision of *Tinn v Hoffman*, *Cheshire, Fifoot and Furmston* believes that there are significant differences between the cases, pointing out that while the actions of the parties in *Tinn v Hoffman* are not 'in direct relation to that of the other and that the strict requirements of offer and acceptance are unsatisfied . . . each party does, in truth, contemplate legal relations upon an identical basis, and each is prepared to offer his own promise as consideration for the promise of the other'. *Cheshire, Fifoot and Furmston* also refers to the need for a coincidence of acts and a unanimity of mind in the case; the problem, however, is that while there is communication in the form of the transmission of the offer there is, in truth, no communication that conveys the idea of unanimity between the parties, the result being an absence of agreement in both subjective and objective terms.

The requirements of the transmission of unanimity might seem unduly harsh on the facts of *Tinn v Hoffman*, though it should be borne in mind that no more than a small act of performance by one of the parties would have been enough to bring about acceptance by conduct. It should also be borne in mind that without such a requirement a large element of uncertainty and confusion would be introduced into the case. Thus in *Henkel v Pape* (1870) LR 6 Ex 7, the defendant had previously intimated that he would have liked to buy as many as 50 rifles from the plaintiff. He sent a telegram to place an order for three but the telegraph clerk made a mistake and the telegram read, 'Send . . . the rifles', whereupon the plaintiff sent 50. It was held that the plaintiff could not recover the price of the extra 47. The acceptance was valid in the form as sent, not in the form as received. Without the requirement of the transmission of unanimity, who is to say what this contract is for, 50 or three rifles? There is no contract in this case since the manifestations of each party's willingness to enter a contract are not conjoined. The same is also true in *Tinn v Hoffman*, even though the parties' intentions are similar.

The fact of acceptance

The mode of acceptance

Acceptance of the offer may be communicated either orally or in writing, or inferred from conduct. Generally speaking, the first two methods of accepting an offer present little difficulty; however, where one attempts to infer acceptance by conduct, difficulties arise as to the nature and precise moment of the inferred conduct. It has been held in *Weatherby v Banham* (1832) 5 C& P 228 that where an offeror offered to supply goods to the offeree by sending the goods to him, acceptance of the offer arose when the offeree began using the goods. Such a set of circumstances must, however, be treated guardedly today. First, under the Unsolicited Goods and Services Act 1971, if an offeror sends unsolicited goods to an individual in certain circumstances, as stipulated by the Act, that individual may treat those goods as a gift and is able to treat the goods as his own, without incurring contractual liability. Second, it was stated in *Taylor v Allon* [1966] 1 QB 304, in true objective principle terms, that acceptance inferred from conduct can only have this effect if the offeree performed the act in question with the intention of accepting the offer. In that case it was held that an offeree did not accept an offer by an insurance company to provide car insurance merely by taking the vehicle out on the road where there was evidence that the offeree intended to take out insurance with another company. In *Pickfords Ltd v Celestica Ltd* [2003] EWCA Civ 1741, however, performance of the contract by the offeror following a counter-offer by the offeree was held to be deemed acceptance of the counter-offer.

The main difficulty concerning inferring acceptance from conduct usually arises where there have been protracted negotiations between the parties or where the negotiations have been so tentative that it is difficult to find when or if an agreement has been reached between the parties. Such a situation arose in the following case.

Brogden v Metropolitan Railway Co. (1877) 2 App Cas 666

Brogden had supplied the respondent railway company with coal for a number of years and then suggested that a formal contract should be entered into. A draft contract was submitted to Brogden who completed certain details on it, introduced a new term on it by adding the name of an arbitrator and then signed it, writing 'approved' at the end of the contract before returning it to the respondents. The company's agent put the contract in a drawer and nothing else was done to execute the contract. For some time afterwards coal was supplied and paid for on the basis of the draft agreement. Eventually, a dispute arose and Brogden denied that any binding long-term contract on the basis of the written contract had come into existence. The difficulty facing the court was to determine when, if ever, any mutual assent could be found. Because Brogden had introduced a new term into the contract his signature and return of the agreement could not amount to acceptance since, as we shall see later, qualified acceptance is no acceptance. The return of the contract could, however, amount to an offer on Brogden's part to supply coal, but where was the acceptance of this offer? Clearly the putting of the document into a drawer could not amount to acceptance by conduct, so where did the contract arise? In fact a court has considerable power to resolve uncertainties and in this case the court decided to exercise this discretion. To find that there was no contract would clearly be wrong since the parties had contracted on the basis of the agreement for a number of years and it was this conduct, which was explicable only on the basis of a mutual acceptance of the terms of the approved contract, that the court relied on. Subsequently, the House of Lords held that a contract came into existence either when the company ordered its first load of coal upon the terms of the approved contract or at least when Brogden first supplied the coal on those terms.

One final point must be made in relation to acceptance by conduct and that is that it is found most commonly in **unilateral contracts**. It has already been seen in *Carlill* v *Carbolic Smoke Ball Co.* that Mrs Carlill accepted the company's offer merely by using the smoke balls in the prescribed manner and subsequently catching influenza. Usually there will be some sort of communication of the fact that acceptance has been performed in order, as in Mrs Carlill's case, to claim the reward, but this is only notification of the fact that acceptance has taken place. It does not amount to acceptance itself. The act of acceptance must be completely performed for it to be valid. For instance, in Mrs Carlill's case the mere using of the smoke balls would not be enough – she had to use them in the prescribed manner and catch influenza. This requirement of complete performance was emphasised in *Daulia* v *Four Millbank Nominees Ltd* [1978] 2 All ER 557 by Goff LJ, who stated:

> I think the true view of a unilateral contract must in general be that the offeror is entitled to require full performance of the condition he has imposed and short of that he is not bound.

A related point is that very often an offer may prescribe a particular mode of acceptance; in such a case conduct cannot amount to acceptance until the mode stipulated is complied with, as stated in *Western Electric Ltd* v *Welsh Development Agency* [1983] 2 All ER 629, unless the offeror acquiesces in allowing the conduct to amount to acceptance.

Counter-offers

Objective 3

It has already been stated when defining acceptance that there must be an unqualified expression of assent. It follows that any attempt to introduce a new term amounts not to an acceptance of an offer, but in fact itself becomes a counter-offer. Such a result is manifestly fair since otherwise the offeror would be bound by a new term which they would not have had the opportunity to peruse and consider. The effect of a counter-offer is to destroy the original offer, that is, it operates as a rejection of the original offer.

Hyde v *Wrench* (1840) 3 Beav 334

The defendant offered to sell his farm for £1,000. The plaintiff at first made a counter-offer of £950, but two days later agreed to pay £1,000 and attempted to accept the original offer. The defendant refused to complete the sale and the plaintiff brought an action against him for a decree of specific performance. It was held that no contract existed since by his letter offering £950 the plaintiff had made a counter-offer, the effect of which was to reject and destroy the original offer, so that the latter was therefore not available for him to accept two days later.

Some care needs to be taken when discussing this whole area of counter-offers since the fact that acceptance needs to be unqualified does not by the same token mean that it needs to be precise. Very often communications take place which present themselves as counter-offers in that there appears to be a qualified acceptance when in fact there is nothing of the sort. Examples of such communications are as follows.

Conditional acceptances

On the face of things this may seem to be an exercise in pedantry but in fact the law makes a distinction between a conditional acceptance and a qualified acceptance. A conditional acceptance is neither a full acceptance of the original offer nor a counter-offer. Very often before an individual enters into a contract, they might wish to consult a third party for advice as to the nature of the contract or the wisdom of entering into a particular contract. Further, in some contracts there are many other ancillary matters to be arranged before an individual feels able to comply with the requirements of the contract. Such a situation commonly occurs in the purchase of a house, which is essentially a contract to purchase land. In this type of contract there are many factors to be considered by a purchaser before they can commit themselves to a formal contract, such as obtaining a surveyor's report on the property, obtaining a mortgage, making land registry or land charges searches, and so on. The result of these circumstances is that any agreement is usually arrived at 'subject to contract'.

The term 'subject to contract' now has a precise legal significance in that it raises a presumption that the parties do not intend to enter a legally binding contract. It is an expression of future intention to enter into a contract provided the offeree is satisfied as to any factors that may be of concern. It renders the entering of a formal contract, usually written, a condition precedent to a legally binding agreement. The words, however, do not invariably have this effect and in ***Alpenstow Ltd v Regalian Properties plc*** [1985] 2 All ER 545 the courts found for a legally binding contract despite the use of the expression, though it should be stated that this was an exceptional case.

From time to time attempts are made to adopt other language to indicate that any agreement is merely tentative and not meant to be final. The task facing the court here is to attempt to interpret the intention of the parties from their negotiations, correspondence and other surrounding circumstances of the case. It may be that the court will find that there is no condition precedent intended and that any further document is merely needed to formalise an already legally binding contract.

Branca v *Cobarro* [1947] KB 854

A vendor agreed to sell the lease and goodwill of his mushroom farm. The parties signed a document which contained the terms of their agreement. The document concluded, 'This is a provisional agreement until a fully legalised agreement drawn up by a solicitor and embodying all the conditions herewith stated is signed.' The purchaser sued for the return of his deposit and the vendor contended that their agreement was a binding contract despite the use of the expression 'provisional'. The court held that there was an immediately binding contract 'until' the document was replaced by one couched in more precise and formal language. The court commented that the decision would probably have been different if the parties had used the expression 'tentative' rather than 'provisional', though each case had to be decided on its own facts.

This latter point can be seen in the earlier case of ***Chillingworth v Esche*** [1924] 1 Ch 97, where the plaintiffs agreed to purchase the defendant's nursery for £4,800 'subject to a proper contract to be prepared by the vendor's solicitors'. The purchasers then refused to sign a contract prepared by the solicitors and executed by the vendor and failed to complete the transaction. It was held in this case that consent was conditional upon a 'proper contract' being signed and the plaintiffs could therefore recover their deposit.

In commercial contracts, the instinct of a judge is to find that the document indicates an intention to be bound, especially where trade usage forms the background to the transaction.

Hillas & Co. Ltd v *Arcos Ltd* (1932) 38 Com Cas 23

In this case, there was an agreement in writing for the supply of wood during 1930, together with an option to buy more wood the following year. The option clause did not specify the kind or size of timber required, nor the ports to which it had to be shipped or indeed the manner of shipment. The suppliers argued that the option clause was not binding and the fact of the absent factors was evidence that it was only to provide a basis for future negotiation and agreement. It was held that as the 1930 agreement had been expressed in a similar way and had been complied with, the option thus showed a sufficient intention to be bound and could create a binding obligation. With regard to the omissions the court held that these could be resolved by reference to the previous dealings between the parties and the trade usage of the timber trade.

The courts will not find for a binding contract if the agreement between the parties is too speculative, usually requiring some sort of previous course of dealings between the parties or some common business practice or usage before exercising discretion. Since the first instinct of the court is to exercise this discretion in commercial transactions, it follows that the courts will often allow retrospective acceptance to legitimise past informal arrangements between the parties as illustrated in *Trollope and Colls Ltd* v *Atomic Power Constructions Ltd* and restated by Steyn LJ in *G Percy Trentham Ltd* v *Archital Luxfer*. The approach of the courts is summed up by Lord Tomlin in *Hillas* v *Arcos* where he stated:

> The problem for a court of construction must always be so to balance matters that without the violation of essential principle, the dealings of men may as far as possible be treated as effective, and that the law may not incur the reproach of being the destroyer of bargains.

In *Tekdata Interconnections Ltd* v *Amphenol Ltd* [2009] EWCA Civ 1209 the Court of Appeal, while it considered it appropriate to look at the dealings between the parties, the longevity of their relationship and their conduct as giving rise to displacing the traditional approach, such an approach would usually be unnecessary.

Clarifying the terms of the offer

Just as the courts have difficulty in construing a particular contract, business people in lengthy or complex contracts often have similar problems when attempting to arrive at a finite and settled agreement. For this reason there may be many communications between the parties which are intended not to operate as counter-offers but merely as attempts to clarify the extent and terms of the offer, or to ascertain whether the offeror would consider changing certain aspects of the offer. The courts view such correspondence as mere requests for information which do not operate as counter-offers to destroy the original one. A typical such case is that of *Stevenson, Jacques & Co.* v *McLean*.

Stevenson, Jacques & Co. v *McLean* (1880) 5 QBD 346

In this case, the defendant offered to sell iron to the plaintiffs at 40s per ton. The plaintiffs sent a telegram to the defendant, 'Please wire whether you would accept 40 for delivery over two months, or if not, the longest limit you could give.' Later that day a further telegram was sent to the defendant by which the plaintiffs accepted the original offer. The defendant maintained, in the action brought by the plaintiffs for breach of contract, that the first telegram amounted to a counter-offer which destroyed the original offer so that it subsequently became incapable of acceptance. It was held that the first telegram was a mere request for information, not a counter-offer. There was no attempt here to introduce new terms into the contract as in *Hyde* v *Wrench*, but a genuine enquiry by the plaintiffs to see if the defendant would be willing to modify his terms.

A further refinement of this problem can occur where a person in accepting the offer makes reference to some other term. Ostensibly this would amount to a counter-offer. However, if this term would be implied into the contract in any event by operation of law, there would be a valid acceptance of the offer. Similarly Treitel indicates that where the acceptance 'adds new provision by way of indulgence to the offeror', then the acceptance will still be valid. In other words, the acceptance should still be valid provided any new term introduced is by way of benefit or concession to the offeror. He further indicates that should the offeree attempt to introduce a new term, which is not by way of concession to the offeror in their acceptance, that acceptance would still be valid if the offeree makes it clear that they will accept the offer even if the new term is rejected. This proposal was rejected in *Global Tankers Inc.* v *Amercoat Europa NV* [1975] 1 Lloyd's Rep 666, and indeed it is difficult to envisage the courts enabling the offeree to accept an offer once a counter-offer had been made. Clearly on a classical analysis the introduction of the new term must invariably destroy the original offer. In *Global Tankers*, it was suggested that the test as to whether an offeree is replying with a counter-offer or not is whether a reasonable person would regard the 'acceptance' as 'introducing a new term into the bargain and not as a clear acceptance of the offer'. The question is then reduced to one of the chicken or the egg – which comes first, the counter-offer or the acceptance?

The 'battle of the forms'

It has already been stated that one of the hallmarks of the modern environment of the law of contract is the use made of the standard form of contract. Most companies adopt such forms since it is clearly more efficient and convenient than to have to discuss and negotiate each contract with a customer on an individual basis, quite apart from the administrative nightmare created by having hundreds, possibly thousands, of individual contracts to supervise. It is not surprising, therefore, that in the offer, acceptance and counter-offer situation conflicts are likely to result when companies attempt to impose on the other party their own standard conditions of contract.

Example

Company X offers to, say, sell certain goods to company Y on company X's standard terms and conditions. Company Y replies, accepting company X's offer, but on company Y's terms and conditions – which could be materially different from company X's. The conflict now arises as to whose terms and conditions the contract is based on.

If the conflict is to be resolved by reference to the classical theory, then it is clear, as Megaw J stated in *Trollope and Colls Ltd v Atomic Power Constructions Ltd*, that 'the counter offer kills the original offer'. This being the case, the person who wins the 'battle of the forms' is the person who last submits the counter-offer which is accepted by the other party. This principle is sometimes referred to as the 'last shot' principle. The following case summary is the classic modern case illustrating this conflict.

Butler Machine Tool Co. Ltd v Ex-Cell-O Corporation (England) Ltd [1979] 1 All ER 965

The facts of the case were that on 23 May 1969, in response to an enquiry by the buyers, the sellers made a quotation offering to sell a machine tool to the buyers for £75,535, delivery to be made in ten months' time. The terms and conditions given in the quotation contained a price variation clause. The terms and conditions were also stated to 'prevail over any terms and conditions in the buyers' order'. On 27 May, the buyers replied by placing an order for the machine. This order was subject to terms and conditions that were materially different from those of the sellers, and in particular there was no price variation clause. At the end of the buyers' order there was a tear-off acknowledgement of the receipt of the order stating, 'We accept your order on the terms and conditions stated thereon'. On 5 June, the sellers completed and signed the acknowledgement and returned it to the buyers with a letter stating that the buyers' order was entered into in accordance with the sellers' quotation of 23 May. On delivering the machine, the sellers claimed the price had increased by £2,892. The buyers refused to pay and the sellers brought an action for the increase based on the price variation clause. It was held that the buyers' communication of 27 May was a counter-offer which was accepted by the sellers' returning the tear-off acknowledgement slip. The contract being thus made on the buyers' terms and conditions meant that the buyers were not subject to the price variation clause and were consequently not liable to pay the extra £2,892. The letter accompanying the acknowledgement slip, though the 'last shot' in the series, did not prevail because the reference in it to the sellers' original offer was not made with the intention of reiterating the terms and conditions contained in the original quotation/offer, but to identify the subject matter of the contract only.

The decision is clearly correct when analysed on the lines of the classical approach, given the interpretation of the letter accompanying the acknowledgement slip returned by the sellers. At first instance, though, the judge thought the additional moneys were recoverable because of the emphatic statement in the quotation of 23 May that the sellers' terms and conditions were to prevail. In the Court of Appeal the majority of the judges decided the case on classical lines though Lord Denning expressed sympathy for the views of the judge at first instance. He considered the classic view of offer, counter-offer, rejection and acceptance and so on to be out of date in the high-pressure commercial life of the twentieth century, reiterating Lord Wilberforce's view in *New Zealand Shipping Co. Ltd v AM Satterthwaite*, which we have already considered. Lord Denning thought the better approach was to examine all the documents passing between the parties and glean from them and the conduct of the parties whether agreement exists on the material terms. He thought that very often the end result may be no different, the man who fires the last shot being the winner. He puts forward his terms and conditions which are not objected to by the other, who is thus regarded as having agreed to those terms and conditions. Lord Denning went further, however, and considered that in appropriate cases different approaches may be justified. He stated:

> In some cases, however, the battle is won by the man who gets the blow in first. If he offers to sell at a named price on the terms and conditions stated on the back and the buyer orders the

goods purporting to accept the offer on an order form with his own different terms and conditions on the back, then, if the difference is so material that it would affect the price, the buyer ought not to be allowed to take advantage of the difference unless he draws it specifically to the attention of the seller. There are yet other cases where the battle depends on the shots fired on both sides. There is a concluded contract but the forms vary. The terms and conditions of both parties are to be construed together. If they can be reconciled so as to give a harmonious result, all well and good. If differences are irreconcilable, so that they are mutually contradictory, then the conflicting terms may have to be scrapped and replaced by a reasonable implication.

Lord Denning's approach can clearly be seen to be a subjective one which attempts to find for a consensus between the parties. We have already seen that such a view is not adopted today, the law preferring an objective approach. For this reason, the other judges in the Court of Appeal, Lawton and Bridge LJJ, decided the case on classical objective lines. Where does the above situation leave the modern business person? Clearly, in order to avoid losing the 'battle of the forms', it is essential that if they are to take part in a contract based on their own conditions they must ensure that they are the one who fires the last shot. Even here they cannot ensure that they will be the winner because of the possibility of a counter-offer coming from the other party. The only real certainty that can be achieved is a stalemate, and this is not a satisfactory state of affairs since it might be the case that the court will find that there is no contract at all in such a situation! For this reason, this approach was rejected in both *Johnson Matthey Bankers Ltd* v *State Trading Corporation of India* [1984] 1 Lloyd's Rep 427 and *Interfoto Picture Library Ltd* v *Stiletto Visual Programmes Ltd* [1988] 1 All ER 348. Whilst such a solution may be possible where the contract is purely executory with no or only a limited performance having taken place, it is neither desirable nor convenient in executed contracts where, as in the *Butler* case, an expensive custom-made machine has been produced and delivered. The idea of restitution here, that is a handing back of what has been received by both sides, is clearly nonsensical. In such a case a contract will be found to exist and the courts would then attempt to impose terms and conditions on the parties. This may not be a particularly elegant way for the courts to resolve the problem, but it fulfils an exigency. Such an approach was adopted in the case of *British Steel Corporation* v *Cleveland Bridge and Engineering Co. Ltd* [1984] 1 All ER 504. One should also take into account the approach taken by Steyn LJ in *G Percy Trentham Ltd* v *Archital Luxfer*, as examined earlier, and Dyson LJ in *Pickfords Ltd* v *Celestica Ltd* (see above).

It must be noted that Steyn LJ in *G Percy Trentham Ltd* v *Archital Luxfer* was clear that whilst the traditional analysis will normally apply in most cases, by way of an examination of the correspondence between the parties, this is not necessarily the case. It is equally possible for a contract to be objectively discerned by reference to the conduct of the parties. Some care needs to be exercised here since if a contract is discerned from the documentation, then any conduct subsequent to that will not usually be admissible in determining whether or not the documents have actually given rise to a contract. Thus in *Air Studios (Lyndhurst) Limited T/A Air Entertainment Group* v *Lombard North Central PLC* [2012] EWHC 3162 (QB), Males J stated:

> In deciding whether the parties have reached agreement, the whole course of the parties' negotiations must be considered and an objective test must be applied . . . Once the parties have to all outward appearances agreed in the same terms on the same subject matter, usually by a process of offer and acceptance, a contract will have been formed. The subjective

reservations of one party do not prevent the formation of a binding contract. Further, it is perfectly possible for the parties to conclude a binding contract, even though it is understood between them that a formal document recording or even adding to the terms agreed will need to be executed subsequently. Whether they do intend to be bound in such circumstances, or only as and when the formal document is executed, depends on an objective appraisal of their words and conduct.

A modern application of the above principles can be seen in the case of ***Sterling Hydraulics Ltd* v *Dichtomatik Ltd*** [2007] 1 Lloyd's Rep 8 where the judge accepted that the key to 'battle of the forms' scenarios is to make an analysis of the exchanges between the parties in terms of offer and acceptance. In reaching any conclusion it is necessary to decide the meaning and effect of the rival terms in order to discover if the response of one party is an offer and the response of the other party an acceptance of the offer or a counter-offer, which, as indicated in ***Trollope and Colls Ltd* v *Atomic Power Construction Ltd***, will 'kill the original offer'. In order to do this, however, one has to show that the acknowledgement of the offer was in conflict with the terms of the offer itself. Thus where the terms of the acknowledgement were substantially the same as the offer in terms of the date of payment there is no counter-offer but an acceptance of the terms set out in the order. The acknowledgement omitted to contain the defendant's own terms and conditions and therefore there was no indication that the acknowledgement attempted to introduce fresh terms or to modify or contradict the terms of the order sent by the claimant. As the judge stated, 'This was not one of those cases where victory goes to the party who fired the last shot. The first shot is the only one that counted. The "battle of the forms" was barely a skirmish!'

A similar stance was also taken in ***Balmoral Group Ltd* v *Borealis (UK) Ltd*** [2006] 2 Lloyd's Rep 629 where a purchaser had placed an order on its own terms though the purchaser had not supplied a copy of those terms to the supplier. A reference in poor typescript at the bottom of the purchase order was not considered to be a clear reference that the purchaser intended to contract on those terms. On the other hand, the supplier had provided a clear statement of its terms on the back of its invoices and these had been acknowledged by the purchasers by the managing director initialling the invoice. No objection was raised regarding the terms at this time. The court held that the purchasing company had accepted the supplier's terms.

In ***RTS Flexible Systems Ltd* v *Molkerei Alois Muller Gmbh & Co KG (UK Production)*** [2010] UKSC 14, the Supreme Court also wrestled with the issue as to whether a contract had come into existence and if so on what terms. The facts of the case were that RTS Flexible Systems Ltd (the 'claimant/respondent') specialised in the supply of automated machines for packaging and product handling in the food industry. The defendant/appellant was a leading supplier of dairy products. The respondent provided a number of quotations for the provision of work and equipment to the appellant and was awarded the contract, and then provided a further quotation. On 21 February 2005, a letter of intent was sent from the appellant to the respondent which confirmed that it wanted to proceed with the project 'as set out in the offer', subject to certain specified terms, which included that the full contractual terms would be based on the appellant's amended form of 'MF/1' conditions, which would be agreed and signed within four weeks, and that, prior to the full contract being agreed, only the appellant had the right to terminate the contract. By a letter of 1 March 2005 (the letter of intent contract) ('LOI'), the respondent confirmed that it had started work subject to two variations being made to the letter of intent, both of which were agreed by the appellant. Detailed negotiations as to the terms of the contract commenced, and, in mid-March, a first draft contract was produced by the appellant. Clauses 8 to 48 of that draft reflected the MF/1 terms, although significant amendments were made as negotiations continued. Clause 48 of the MF/1 conditions provided that a contract would only come into existence if a written agreement was entered into and signed by the parties – the so-called subject to contract clause. The LOI contract expired on 22 March 2005, but the parties agreed to extend it from time to time until 27 May 2005 to allow for execution of the full contract. By 26 May, the contract was substantially agreed and the respondent, who had begun work on the project, continued to work after expiry of the LOI contract. The contract was agreed as at 5 July, but was never signed. The parties agreed variations to the arrangements in August and subsequently the respondent issued invoices in relation to the work that it had done, and those invoices were paid for by the appellant. A dispute between the parties arose as to the delivery by the respondent of certain equipment to the appellant. The respondent brought proceedings in the High Court. The judge held that the parties had concluded a contract but that the contract did not incorporate the MF/1 terms.

The respondent appealed to the Court of Appeal. The Court of Appeal made a declaration that no contract came into existence after the termination of the letter of intent. The appellant then appealed to the Supreme Court. There were two issues to be considered as part of the appeal. First, had the parties made a contract after the expiry of the LOI contract? Second, was the contract subject to some or all of the MF/1 terms as amended?

The Supreme Court, with Lord Clarke giving the leading judgment, held that the appeal should be allowed. On the first point, the court held that whether there was a binding contract between parties depended upon what they had agreed on and not their subjective state of mind – a clear rejection of Denning's approach. The court decided that a contract had to be found on what had been communicated between the parties by words or conduct and whether that led to an objective conclusion that they had intended to create legal relations and the parties had agreed all the terms they regarded, or the law required as essential, for the formation of legally binding relations. Lord Clarke stated [at 45]:

> The general principles are not in doubt. Whether there was a binding contract between the parties and if so, upon what terms depends upon what they have agreed. It depends not upon their subjective state of mind, but upon a consideration of what was communicated between them by words or conduct, and whether that leads objectively to a conclusion that they intended to create legal relations and had agreed upon all the terms which they regarded or the law requires as essential for the formation of legally binding relations. Even if certain terms of economic or other significance have not been finalised, an objective appraisal of their words and conduct may lead to the conclusion that they did not intend agreement of such terms to be a precondition to a concluded and legally binding agreement.

Their Lordships decided that in cases where the contract was negotiated 'subject to contract' and work commenced before the formal contract was executed, it could not be said that there would always, or even usually, be a contract on the terms that were agreed 'subject to contract'. A court should not impose contracts on parties which they had not agreed to but should look at all the circumstances of the case. In assessing whether a contract had been concluded in correspondence as well as by oral communications and conduct 'subject to contract', the question to be asked was whether the parties had nevertheless agreed to enter into contractual relations on particular terms notwithstanding any earlier understanding or agreement. The court considered that it was possible for an agreement that was 'subject to contract' to become legally binding where the parties later agreed to waive that condition, with the consequence that a firm contract would come into existence on the terms of the earlier agreement.

The court also held that, since the parties had reached a final draft of the contractual terms and conditions which contained the general MF/1 terms as amended in their written correspondence between the parties, the terms had been agreed as at 5 July subject to the August variations. While the parties had not proceeded on the basis of all of the agreed conditions, that failure did not prevent the contract from having binding effect.

There are many examples of the 'battle of the forms' type of situation and a typical example of a modern case can be seen in the case of *Gulf International Ltd v Groupe Chimique Tunisien* [2009] EWHC 1684 (Comm). Similarly, the case of *Tekdata Interconnections Ltd v Amphenol Ltd* is another example where the Court of Appeal again reinforced the view that the traditional approach should be adopted rather than Lord Denning's subjective approach. Dyson LJ stated that the traditional approach 'has the great merit of providing a degree of certainty which is both desirable and necessary in order to promote effective commercial relationships'. Longmore LJ also emphasised the point by stating:

> I think it will always be difficult to displace the traditional analysis in a battle of the forms case, unless it can be said there was a clear course of dealing between the parties.

Similarly in *Trebor Bassett Holdings Ltd v ADT Fire and Security plc* [2011] EWHC 1936, the court reiterated the principle that in a 'battle of the forms' case the traditional analysis based on offer and acceptance had to be adopted, unless the parties' conduct and the documents passing between them showed that their common intention was that some other terms were to prevail and that it was difficult to displace the traditional approach unless there was a clear course of dealing between the parties: *Tekdata Interconnections Ltd v Amphenol Ltd* [2009] EWCA Civ 1209 followed. In *Trebor*, Coulson J considered that the 'last shot' principle was one to be applied with care and the mere existence of the principle was not one to be applied mechanically and that a court has to consider all the relevant circumstances. The effect is that the traditional analysis is applied unless there appears to be a course of dealing that demonstrates a common intention by the parties that other terms will apply.

The above principles were affirmed in *Transformers and Rectifiers Ltd v Need Ltd* [2015] EWHC 269 (TCC). In this case, a purchaser alleged that gaskets supplied by the defendant were not suitable for the purpose for which they were sold. The claimant alleged that the contract was entered into on their terms and conditions, which were printed on the back of the purchase order. There was no reference to the terms and conditions of the face of the order form. On the other hand, the defendant alleged that in fact its terms and conditions applied since they were referred to when they acknowledged the order. The defendants therefore alleged that their liability for breach of contract was limited or excluded according to those terms and conditions. The parties in fact had had a long relationship going back over 20 years on almost a weekly basis, whether by post, fax or by email attachments.

In his decision Edwards-Stuart J set out the principles which apply to cases of this nature, stating that where A makes an offer on its conditions and B accepts that offer on its conditions and performance follows, then the correct analysis is that the last shot principle applies, so that there is a contract on B's terms and conditions, provided each party's conditions have been reasonably drawn to the attention of the other, following *Tekdata Interconnections Ltd v Amphenol Ltd*.

Another method that can be used to attempt to avoid the 'battle of the forms' scenario is for a party to a contract steadfastly to maintain their bargaining proposals come what may.

The effect of this can be seen in the case of *Nissan UK Ltd v Nissan Motor Manufacturing (UK) Ltd* (1994) *Independent*, 26 October, where the Court of Appeal stated that if one of two contracting parties toing and froing with offers and counter-offers has maintained a proposal to the last, and has received no comeback from the other party, it could naturally be inferred that any subsequent conduct by that other party that was referable to the existence of some contract between the parties denoted the acceptance of the proposal.

No doubt, unless a person has a very clear perception of the different stages of a transaction, the 'battle of the forms' scenario can provide a trap for the commercially unwary. The result of this is that some suppliers have attempted to provide 'prevail clauses' among their terms and conditions. The aim of such clauses is of course to make sure that their terms and conditions prevail over the other party's. A typical 'prevail clause' may be as follows:

> These conditions form part of this contract entered into to the exclusion of all other terms and conditions, including those terms and conditions which the purchaser purports to apply in any purchase order, letter of confirmation or any other communication with this supplier.

Such clauses invariably have no legal effect, since to be effective, the purchaser would have to accept the clause. This is highly unlikely since the whole point of the battle of the forms is that the purchaser is attempting to impose their own terms and conditions, which would not include the 'prevail clause' set out by the supplier. Indeed, in such circumstances it is highly likely that the purchaser will include their own 'prevail clause'!

One final word regarding the battle of the forms is that it is not always necessary for a party's terms and conditions to be included or referred to in the documents forming the contract; it may be sufficient if they are clearly contained in or referred to in invoices sent subsequently. By contrast, an invoice following a concluded contract effected by a clear offer on standard terms which are accepted, even if only by delivery, will or may be too late: *Balmoral Group Ltd v Borealis (UK) Ltd* [2006] 2 Lloyd's Rep 629. Christopher Clarke J referring to *Albright & Wilson UK Ltd v Biachem Ltd* [2001] EWCA Civ 301 and the Scottish case of *Continental Tyre & Rubber Co Ltd v Trunk Trailer Ltd* [1987] S.L.T. 58 stated:

> These cases show two things. Firstly, at any rate where parties have dealt with each other more than once or twice, it may not be critical to the incorporation of standard terms that those terms be set out in a contractual document, i.e. one that itself constitutes an offer or its acceptance, or even in a purported record of the contract, nor that the document containing the terms relied on has preceded the making of every contract. Secondly, the sequence of events is important. An invoice following a concluded contract effected by a clear offer on standard terms which are accepted, even if only by delivery, will or may be too late. But, if there has been no reference to rival terms, the appearance of terms on the back of every invoice and the acceptance of delivery of goods without objection may indicate acceptance of the terms.

The communication of acceptance

The general rule

Objective 4

A further aspect of our analysis of the definition of acceptance is concerned with the communication of acceptance. The general rule here, as restated in *Holwell Securities Ltd v Hughes* [1974] 1 WLR 155, is that some objective or external manifestation of acceptance must be communicated to the offeror. The principle is also well illustrated in the case of *Powell v Lee* (1908) 99 LT 284, where the defendant decided to appoint the plaintiff as headmaster of a school. The terms of the appointment were never communicated to the plaintiff. It was held that there was no contract since the defendant's acceptance of the plaintiff's offer of service had not been communicated to him.

The need for communication of acceptance has raised several problems in this area of the law, to the extent that one really wonders why English law insists on such a requirement. One does not have to go very far to find compelling reasons for its need. First, substantial hardship would result for the offeror if they were to be held to be bound by the terms of their offer without first knowing that their offer had been accepted. It should be noted that communication of acceptance to the offeror's agent would be sufficient, provided that the agent has the authority to receive the acceptance, even though the offeror was unaware of that communication. On the other hand, communication, whether to the offeror directly or to their authorised agent, will not be effective if it was made by an agent of the offeree who had no authority to communicate such acceptance, this being expressed in the case of *Powell* v *Lee*, above. Second, as a simple matter of practical expediency, some outward sign of acceptance has to be present in order for it to be possible to decide whether a contract exists or not. Since this outward sign, of necessity, has to be measured in objective terms, it is easier to prove such existence by requiring the assent of the offeree to be communicated to the offeror.

It should be noted that acceptance has to be not only communicated to but also received by the offeror. In *Entores* v *Miles Far East Corporation* [1955] 2 QB 327, Lord Denning illustrated this principle by describing a situation where *A* shouts an offer to *B* across a river and *A* does not hear the reply because of the noise of an aircraft flying overhead. In such a situation there is no contract. A similar state of affairs could also exist if a person's reply was so indistinct that the offeror could not hear or understand what was being stated. This position does have to be qualified, however, since, if the acceptance would have been communicated and received by the offeror but this has not occurred because of the conduct of the offeror, they will be precluded from denying that they received the acceptance. In the *Entores* case, which will be examined in more detail later, Lord Denning explained the rule by stating that an offeror cannot deny receipt of the acceptance if 'it is his own fault that he did not get it', for example, 'if the listener on the telephone does not catch the words of acceptance but nevertheless does not . . . ask for them to be repeated'. Presumably the same principle applies if a message of acceptance is sent by telex but this is unread by the offeror, although Cairns LJ in *The Brimnes* [1975] QB 929 denied this. So far the general rule is fairly straightforward, but unfortunately such rules are rarely so simple and this aspect of acceptance is no exception to that principle.

For facts of this case, see below under '3. Instantaneous forms of communication'.

The exceptions to the general rule

1. The effect of silence

Is it possible to impose contractual liability on an individual, within the terms of the offer, by not requiring them to communicate their acceptance before becoming a party to the contract? On the basis of the general rule the answer to this question must be in the negative. Such a conclusion can be seen in the following case.

Felthouse v *Bindley* (1862) 11 CBNS 869

The case is rather unusual since it was based not on an action in contract but on an action in tort. The facts of the case were that the defendant was an auctioneer who had been instructed to sell the farming stock of John Felthouse. John's uncle was interested in one of the horses that was being sold and some negotiation took place between the parties. During the course of the negotiations a misunderstanding arose as to the price of the horse, namely whether it was for sale for £30 or 30 guineas. The uncle then wrote to John offering to split the difference and concluded: 'If I hear no more about him, I consider the horse mine at £30 15s'. John did not reply but instructed the defendant to withdraw the horse from the auction. By mistake the horse was put up for sale and sold. The uncle began an action against the defendant for the tort of conversion and failed. The court held that the uncle had no property in the horse as the silence of his nephew could not amount to acceptance of the uncle's offer. As *Cheshire, Fifoot and Furmston* states:

> Silence is usually equivocal as to consent and the uncle's letter did not render the nephew's failure to reply unequivocal since failure to reply to letters is a common human weakness.

Such a view found later support in *Allied Marine Transport Ltd* v *Vale Do Rio Doce Navegação SA, The Leonidas D* [1985] 2 All ER 796 where, in the Court of Appeal, Goff LJ stated:

> In the absence of special circumstances, silence and inaction by a party to a reference [to arbitration] are, objectively considered, just as consistent with his having inadvertently forgotten about the matter; or with his simply hoping that the matter will die a natural death . . . If so, there should, on ordinary principles, be no basis for the inference of an offer. Exactly the same comment can be made of silence and inaction of the other party, for the same reasons, there appears to be no basis for drawing the inference of an acceptance in response to the supposed offer, still less of the communication of that acceptance of the offeror . . . it is difficult to imagine how silence and inaction can be anything but equivocal.

It is an over-simplification to say that silence can never amount to acceptance since, as Goff LJ indicates, there may well be 'special circumstances' that will render silence as constituting acceptance of the offer. Treitel also discusses certain exceptions to the rule, arguing that:

> if an offer has been solicited by the offeree, the argument that he should not be put to the trouble of rejecting it loses much of its force, especially if the offer is made on a form provided by the offeree and that form stipulates that silence may amount to acceptance.

Further, he states that a previous course of dealing between the offeror and offeree might also give rise to acceptance by way of silence. An example of the operation of such a course of dealing may be seen in the American case of *Ammons* v *Wilson*, 176 Miss 645 (1936) where the offeror regularly ordered certain goods from the offeree. His order was usually given to the offeree's representative who would transmit the order to his head office, at the same time giving the offeror a booking. A dispute arose when the offeror was given a booking but not told until some 12 months later that the offeree had not accepted his order. The court held that a contract had been created since, given the previous course of dealing, it was reasonable that the offeree should notify the offeror if he did not intend to accept.

While English courts might be willing to adopt such a stance, it would be essential for there to be a previous course of dealing present since any attempt to render an offeror liable for a contract for goods or services which are not requested by the offeror amounts to a criminal offence under the Unsolicited Goods and Services Act 1971, and indeed, such goods or services can be enjoyed as an outright gift provided the provisions of the Act are complied with.

Although an offeror cannot impose liability on an offeree by not requiring them to communicate acceptance, subject to the exceptions discussed, it is possible for the offeror to waive the need for acceptance so that they run the risk of having contractual liability thrust upon themselves. This waiver of the need to communicate acceptance may be express or implied from the circumstances of the case. Such a situation occurs in the case of unilateral contracts. Thus in *Carlill* v *Carbolic Smoke Ball Co.*, there was no need for Mrs Carlill actively to communicate her acceptance of the company's offer. The company assumed such liability by Mrs Carlill's purchasing the smoke balls, using them in the prescribed manner and subsequently catching influenza. The company had impliedly waived the need for communication of acceptance. In this regard, Bowen LJ stated: '. . . as notification of acceptance is required for the benefit of the person who makes the offer, the person who makes the offer may dispense with notice to himself'. Thus the mode of acceptance was held by implication to be actually performing the conditions attached to the offer. Bowen LJ provided an example concerning a lost dog. If one offers £100 to anyone who finds a certain lost dog, everyone who reads the advertisement does not have to write to the owner and accept the offer. The owner has impliedly waived the need for such communication and anyone who finds and returns the dog is regarded as having accepted the offer, imposing a contractual obligation on the owner, whether or not acceptance has been communicated.

Such a situation also arose in the case of **Dresdner Kleinwort Ltd v Atrill** [2013] EWCA Civ 394. On 17 March 2008, the Chairman of Dresdner Bank AG ('DBAG') announced the intention to separate DBAG's commercial banking division from its investment banking division. This was a prelude to DBAG leaving investment banking, either by selling Dresdner Kleinwort ('DKIB'), its investment banking arm, or by drastically cutting back its operations, or winding it down. Notwithstanding that announcement, staff were told that the possibility of a sale was mere speculation; there was, nonetheless, a general belief that this might occur and it led to widespread uncertainty about the future of staff. There was a serious risk of a mass exodus of staff. In order to allay these fears and to retain staff the employer bank, Dresdner Kleinwort made an announcement to the employees of a company promising to pay a guaranteed employment bonus to the employees. The idea behind this bonus was to retain staff within a bank's investment arm which was being sold off. This was necessary since the Financial Services Authority had placed the company on a 'Firm Watch List' because of the risks posed by the proposed re-structuring. The FSA referred in particular to: '. . . the continuing uncertainty among management and staff [which] could lead to a significant number of key individuals leaving or becoming disaffected . . . '. Subsequently DBAG attempted to resile from its obligations under the bonus scheme claiming *inter alia*, that well-established contract theory requires acceptance and there was none provided by the employees. Elias LJ, following the dicta of Bowen LJ in *Carlill*, considered that it was plain that DBAG had dispensed with the need for any response to the offer at all. This was a promise without any disadvantage, actual or potential, of any kind to the employees. Nobody hearing the promise made in the announcement would for one moment expect that an employee would only be able to benefit from it if he or she positively accepted the offer. It would be a wholly formal and unnecessary exercise; the only sensible implication is that all employees who might potentially benefit from the promise would be deemed to have accepted it. Secondly, Elias LJ considered that the nature of the promise was inconsistent with the notion of individual acceptance. It would mean that if, say, a minority of the relevant staff accepted the offer, the employers would be bound to pay the whole of the bonus pool, if only to the minority. It was wholly unrealistic to think that the Bank would be willing to pay its bonuses from the fund by reference to whether the particular employee had formally accepted the offer or not. Indeed, if acceptance was needed, the minority who accepted the offer would arguably have a contractual claim against the Bank if it sought to diminish the fund by applying it for the benefit of those staff who had not accepted the offer and therefore had no claim on the fund, which would be a bizarre result.

2. The postal rule

The rule that acceptance must be communicated to the offeror is overturned when acceptance is sent via the post since here the rule is that acceptance takes place as soon as the letter is validly posted.

Adams v Lindsell (1818) 1 B & Ald 681

In this case, the defendants wrote to the plaintiffs on 2 September offering to sell them some wool on certain terms and requested a reply 'in course of post'. The letter containing the offer was wrongly addressed and only received on 5 September. As a result the letter of acceptance was received on 9 September, two days later than it should have been reasonably expected by the defendants. On the day before the letter of acceptance was received the defendants sold the wool to a third person, no reply having been received from the plaintiffs. The question which arose was whether a contract of sale had been entered into before 8 September when the wool was sold to the third party. Clearly if the acceptance was effective only when it arrived at the address or, at the latest, when it was brought to the attention of the defendant, then no contract would have been entered into, revocation of the offer being effected at that time by the later sale to the third party. The court held, however, that the offer had been accepted as soon as the letter of acceptance had been posted. The contract was thus in existence before the sale of the wool to the third party even though the letter of acceptance had not been received by the defendant, who was thus liable for breach of contract.

Adams v *Lindsell* was one of the earliest cases in this area of the law but any doubts as to its correctness or not were dispelled in *Household Fire and Carriage Accident Insurance Co.* v *Grant* (1879) 4 Ex D 216 where the defendant applied for shares in the plaintiff's company. The shares were allotted to him but the letter of allotment was never received. The company then went into liquidation and the liquidator claimed the balance of the purchase moneys from him. The defendant disputed the fact that he was a shareholder on the basis that he had not received an acceptance, in the form of the letter of allotment, to his offer to purchase the shares. It was held that the contract had been entered when the letter of allotment had been posted to him despite the fact that it had never arrived.

Today it has become firmly established in *Brinkibon Ltd* v *Stahag Stahl und Stahlwar-enhandelsgesellschaft GmbH* [1983] 2 AC 34 that acceptance is effective when it is placed in the control of the Post Office, that is, put into a postbox or handed to an officer of the post authorised to receive or collect letters. A postman delivering letters is not so authorised and the handing of a letter of acceptance to such an individual would take effect only when actually communicated to the offeror, as stated in *Re London and Northern Bank* [1900] 1 Ch 220. One conclusion that may be drawn from the above is that the letter must go into the postbox to be effective and if one arrives at the postbox just as it is being emptied it would not be a valid posting to place the letter directly into the postman's bag – they are not authorised to receive mail in this way. The letter must go into the box to be valid, even if this means that the postman simply has the door open and catches it as it falls in and places it in the bag! It also seems that the rules as regards letters apply equally to a telegram, the acceptance being valid as soon as its wording is communicated to a person authorised to receive it for transmission to the offeror. Treitel also suggests that the same rules apply to telemessages since there is nothing to doubt why these should be treated any differently.

Both Treitel (2011) and *Cheshire, Fifoot and Furmston* (2012) put forward theories to justify the existence of the rule but do not fully and conclusively provide an answer. One theory is that the rule prevents an offeree from accepting by post and then nullifying acceptance by communicating rejection of the offer by a quicker means of communication, such as telex, thereby preventing the letter of acceptance from being effective on receipt by the offeror. Another theory is that without the rule an offeree would not be able to know for certain whether they had actually entered into a contract or not. The truth of the matter is that the rule is one of expedience since whatever approach is adopted, one of the parties is bound to suffer hardship. The law, by taking a particular stance, is merely providing for certainty, though in *Holwell Securities Ltd v Hughes* it was stated that the rule would have no application if this would result in 'manifest inconvenience and absurdity'.

One theory often promoted as a reason for the existence of the postal rule is that if the offeror, either expressly or impliedly, indicates that postal acceptance is sufficient, then they should bear the consequences of the postal rule. This proposition leads us on to a discussion of whether it is possible for the offeror to circumvent the operation of the rule.

In *Henthorn v Fraser* [1892] 2 Ch 27, it was stated that the postal rule applied only where it was reasonable for the offeree to use the post as a means of communication. Indeed, in the case of *Quenerduaine v Cole* (1883) 32 WR 185, the view was taken that an offer by way of telegram was an indication that an equally expedient mode of acceptance was required, so that acceptance by post was held not to be valid. In these cases, the required mode of acceptance was inferred from the prevailing circumstances of the offer, but in the earlier case of *Household Fire and Carriage Accident Insurance Co.* v *Grant*, Bramwell LJ considered that the postal rule could be avoided by the prudent offeror saying, 'Your answer by post is only to bind if it reaches me'. The position has been supported in modern times by *Holwell Securities Ltd v Hughes* where there was an option said to be exercisable only by 'notice in writing'. It was held that these words were sufficient to negate the effects of the postal rule, so that a letter of acceptance posted but not received by the offeror was insufficient to form a contract.

From the latter cases it is clear that the offeror may also prevent the operation of the postal rule by expressly prescribing a particular mode of communication. The leading case in this area is *Manchester Diocesan Council for Education v Commercial and General Investments Ltd* [1969] 3 All ER 159, where Buckley J stated:

> An offeror may by the terms of his offer indicate that it may be accepted in a particular manner . . . an offeror, who by the terms of his offer insists on acceptance in a particular way is entitled to insist that he is not bound unless acceptance is effected or communicated in that precise way, although it seems probable that, even so, if the other party communicates his acceptance in some other way, the offeror may, by conduct or otherwise, waive his right to insist on the prescribed method of acceptance. Where, however, the offeror has prescribed a particular method of acceptance, but not in terms insisting that only acceptance in that mode shall be binding, I am of opinion that acceptance communicated to the offeror by any other mode which is no less advantageous to him will conclude the contract . . . If an offeror intends that he shall be bound only if his offer is accepted in some particular manner, it must be for him to make this clear.

The position, then, is that if the offeror requires acceptance by a particular mode and stipulates that only that mode will be sufficient, the offeree must comply with that stipulation, though the offeror can waive this requirement if they so wish. Where, however, the offeror merely asks for acceptance by a particular mode, an acceptance by the offeree will be sufficient even if it is by a different mode, provided that mode is more expeditious than (or equally as expeditious as) the method requested by the offeror. The latter position occurred in *Tinn* v *Hoffman and Co.* where the offeree was asked '*to reply by return of post*' and the court held that an equally expeditious method would suffice.

3. Instantaneous forms of communication

The postal rule as an exception to the general principle requiring communication is confined to communications through the post, telegrams and probably also telemessages. Modern technology, however, provides other methods of communication which are instantaneous in their operation to the extent that the parties are, as it were, in each other's presence. Such was the reasoning in *Entores v Miles Far East Corporation*.

Entores v *Miles Far East Corporation* [1955] 2 QB 327

The plaintiffs were a company based in London who were dealing with the defendants, an American company, with agents in Amsterdam. Both parties possessed telex equipment. The plaintiffs offered to buy goods from the defendants' agents using the equipment. The agents accepted the offer also by telex. Subsequently, a dispute arose between the parties and the plaintiffs wished to serve a writ on the defendants alleging breach of contract. This was only possible if the contract had in fact been made in England and it was this question that arose before the court. The Court of Appeal held that the parties were in the same position as they would have been if they had been in each other's presence. The consequence of this was that the contract was entered into when the acceptance by the agents was received in London by the plaintiffs, not when the telex was sent in Amsterdam, which would have meant that the contract would be subject to Dutch law. Lord Denning confirmed, obiter, that the same principles also apply to acceptances by telephone.

The decision in the **Entores** case was confirmed in **Brinkibon Ltd v Stahag Stahl GmbH** where the facts were very similar, except that the offer was made by telex in Vienna and accepted by telex sent in London. It was held that the contract was made in Vienna. In the two cases, both the telex messages were sent during ordinary office hours but what would happen if the acceptance had been sent out of office hours? Would the acceptance take place when received at the offeror's office or when it was read the next morning or the next time the office was open? Similarly, if the acceptance had been sent by telephone and recorded on an answering machine, would the acceptance take place when received or when the recording was next played back? What would happen if the recording was accidentally erased?

In **The Brimnes**, the Court of Appeal held that a notice of withdrawal that had been sent during office hours, but not seen by the office staff until the next Monday, was effective when received. One factor that may have influenced the decision here was a possibility of negligence on the part of the office staff. Such a solution may be appropriate where the erasing of a message on the telephone-answering machine could be regarded as a negligent act of the offeror or the offeror's agents/servants.

The decision in **The Brimnes** has been reinforced in **Mondial Shipping and Chartering BV v Astarte Shipping Ltd** [1995] CLC 1011. The case revolved around the issue as to when a telex notice of an intention to withdraw a ship from a charter for non-payment of the hire, sent by the shipowners to the charterers, was effective. The telex was sent at 23.41 hours on Friday 2 December 1994, and received instantaneously. Was it effective at that time or from the commencement of business the next working day, Monday 5 December? This was crucial since the charterers were entitled to tender payment at any time before midnight on Friday 2 December. If this notice took effect immediately at 23.41, it would have been invalid since the charterers were not in default of the terms of the charterparty at that time. If, however, the notice did not take effect until the start of business on Monday 5 December, it would have been valid and the shipowners would have been entitled to withdraw the ship from the charter. It was held that this notice was effectively communicated on the next working day and the owners were thus entitled to withdraw the ship. Gatehouse J stated:

> What matters is not when the notice is given/sent/despatched/issued by the owners but when its content reaches the mind of the charterers. If the telex is sent in ordinary business hours, the time of receipt is the same as the time of despatch because it is not open to the charterers to contend that it did not in fact then come to their attention.

This statement gives further clarification where a communication is sent outside normal business hours; however, it is no panacea to the problems associated with modern-day communication systems. These problems were discussed by Lord Wilberforce in the **Brinkibon** case, where he stated:

> Since 1955 the use of telex communications has been greatly expanded, and there are many variants on it. The senders and recipients may not be the principals to the contemplated contract. They may be servants or agents with limited authority. The message may not reach, or be intended to reach, the designated recipient immediately: messages may be sent out of office hours, or at night, with the intention, or on the assumption, that they will be read at a later time. There may be some error or fault at the recipient's end which prevents receipt at the time contemplated and believed in by the sender. The message may have been sent and/or received through machines operated by third persons. And many other variations may occur. No universal rule can cover all such cases; they must be resolved by reference to the intentions of the parties, by sound business practice and in some cases by a judgement where the risks should lie.

In this electronic age of instantaneous communications, whether one talks of telephones, telexes, electronic mailing systems or facsimile and telephone-answering machines, it is regrettable that Lord Wilberforce did not address more precisely the problem of when acceptance is effective. The result is that at the present time the law in this area is in a state of uncertainty.

Emails

Whilst there is some uncertainty in this area, there have been some tenuous developments that may offer some solution to this debate, though emails present particular problems with regard to communication. The starting point of course is that very often the parties, whilst starting off their negotiations electronically may actually stipulate that a signed letter of acceptance is required. In such a situation, the postal rule would apply, although, as we have seen, the offeror may even here stipulate that they must actually receive the letter of acceptance. In **Pretty Pictures v Quixote Films Ltd** [2003] EWHC 311 (QB), it was held that where the parties still had to negotiate some important terms and it was their common intention that for a binding contract to arise each had to sign a written agreement, then an exchange of emails would not give rise to a binding contract.

In terms of communicating acceptance, however, some difficult questions arise. Should an email amount to an electronic form of acceptance so that it is only communicated when received or read by the offeror or would simple 'delivery' to the offeror's server be sufficient? On the other hand, it could equally be argued that the postal rule should apply so that an acceptance in this mode takes effect as soon as it is sent. In this age of internet shopping when transactions can take place across national boundaries, if such a rule were adopted, then this might mean that the contract arises in a different jurisdiction. Thus, if the offeror, the customer, in England, makes an offer to buy an item from a supplier in Germany, for instance, then the fact that acceptance takes place according to the postal rule means that the acceptance takes place in Germany and is subject to the rules of that jurisdiction. On the other hand, if the normal rules of electronic communication apply, then the acceptance is only effective when received and the contract will be subject to English law, as per **Entores v Miles Far East Corporation**. This latter position was that opined by Blair J in **Thomas v BPE Solicitors** [2010] EWHC 306 (Ch) where an analogy with telexes was drawn, again, as per **Entores v Miles Far East Corporation** so that acceptance only takes place when received. Such an approach was also taken in the Singapore case of **Chwee Kin Keong v Digilandmall. com Pte Ltd** [2004] SLR (R) 594. The reasoning behind this decision lies in the fact communication by email is of a very different nature from communication via the post. It was also considered that the rule re instantaneous communication, the receipt rule, is considered globally as having greater acceptance. Similarly in **Greenclose v National Westminster Bank plc** [2014] EWHC (Ch) 1156 Andrews J stated: 'An email is not subject to the postal acceptance rule. It is a form of near-instantaneous communication . . . If the sender had to prove the <u>actual receipt</u> of a fax by someone with authority to act on behalf of the recipient, that suggests that the parties were concerned that there should be proof that the notice actually came to the attention of [the offeror] . . . If that is true for a fax message, the same reasoning should apply to an email.' Thus an email would only be effective once it is actually received. From **Greenclose** which rule operates largely depends on the terms of the offer. In that case it was clear that the acceptance had to be received but this position could be altered according to the express terms of the offer. Of course the other issue that arises here is what is actually meant by 'received' – received on the server or appears in the recipient's email box, in which case, does it have to be read?

4. E-commerce

The imprecision that can be seen in certain types of electronic means of instantaneous communication is not repeated when considering the nature of contracts made via the Internet. The way offers arise in this medium was examined earlier in this chapter (under 'Offers distinguished from invitations to treat'), where it was stated that the website would usually amount to an invitation to treat, as in **Fisher v Bell**. Once the purchaser has placed the required items in a virtual shopping basket, they click on a button or icon and proceed to the 'checkout'. Just as seen in the **Boots Cash Chemists** case, the purchaser can decide to change their mind at this point and not proceed with the purchase. However, if they do proceed with it, they will normally be asked to confirm their identity, or, if this is a first purchase from the website, they may be asked to register with the seller. The purchaser will then be asked to provide credit/debit card details or at least asked to confirm that the purchase will be made with a card that has previously been used. Assuming everything is in order, at this stage the seller will provide the purchaser with the details of the order and they will then be asked to confirm those details and that they wish to continue with the transaction. At this point the offer is transmitted to the seller, who may or may not accept the offer; for instance, the seller may consider that the credit card details are inaccurate or not acceptable. If everything is in order, then the seller will normally display another screen confirming the receipt and acceptance of the order. Usually this is followed up by an email to the purchaser.

There are two issues at this point. First, the confirmation/acceptance of the order by the seller is often generated electronically and thus the seller has to ensure that the information supplied on the website is correct. In the example of Argos Stores referred to above, if the purchasers had submitted their offers based on the television sets being sold for £3 instead of £300, then, prima facie, a contract would have arisen once the confirmation/acceptance of the order had been sent by the seller notwithstanding the further complication of a unilateral mistake as to the terms of the offer. Second, the problems already highlighted in **Brinkibon** as to determining the time at which the confirmation/acceptance is received also apply here. For example, can the purchaser revoke the offer prior to the confirmation/acceptance screen being communicated to them? Does the acceptance still take place if the confirmation screen is not seen or the confirming email ignored? No doubt such issues would have to be dealt with on the facts, as indicated by Lord Wilberforce in **Brinkibon**, as discussed above. These problems do not arise, however, where the seller's website constitutes an offer or where the confirmation screen itself is considered to be an offer that requires the purchaser to click on an icon to accept the offer. Just as the Electronic Commerce (EC Directive) Regulations 2002 do not help in deciding the status of the website as an invitation to treat or an offer, as seen earlier, neither does it define what constitutes an acceptance. Regulation 11(1), however, provides that unless the parties are businesses who have agreed otherwise:

> ... where the recipient of the service [the purchaser] places his order through technological means, a service provider [the seller] shall –

> (a) acknowledge receipt of the order to the recipient of the service without undue delay and by electronic means ...

> Regulation 11(2), importantly, then states:

> (a) the order and the acknowledgement of receipt will be deemed to be received when the parties to whom they are addressed are able to access them ...

Thus the provision seems to imply that acceptance only takes place when the acknowledgement of the receipt is actually received. Such an approach is in accordance with the normal rules regarding instantaneous communication in that the acceptance is only valid when received. It should be noted that the above provisions do not apply to email communications (reg 11(3)) which continue to be plagued with the problems associated with cases like *Entores* and *Brinkibon*, above.

The termination of offers

Objective
5

So far it has been seen that, for a legally binding agreement to arise, an unconditional acceptance must be communicated and there must be the intention of being legally bound. It follows, therefore, that if the offer has ceased to exist, there can be no such acceptance. In this section relating to the fact of the agreement, we examine the ways in which an offer ceases to exist. It should also be borne in mind that, apart from the methods examined here, acceptance of an offer also terminates the offer, though to some extent this depends on the nature of the offer. Clearly, however, if *A* offers their car for sale to members of their office and *B* accepts that offer, no other member of the office can accept the offer. An offer ceases to exist in the following circumstances.

Revocation

Bilateral contracts

In *Payne* v *Cave*, it was first established that it is possible to revoke an offer at any time before the offer is accepted since no legal obligation exists until this event occurs. Any attempt to revoke an offer after acceptance must of necessity be a prima facie breach of contract. Furthermore, there is no obligation on an offeror to keep their offer open for or until a specified date or time. Thus in *Routledge* v *Grant* (1828) 4 Bing 653, it was held that where a defendant made an offer to purchase the plaintiff's house and gave him six weeks to accept the offer, he was free to revoke and withdraw his offer before the six weeks had passed. The only way the plaintiff could have held the defendant to his promise was if he had actually purchased an option, whereby the defendant would be bound by a separate, binding contract to keep his offer open for the stipulated period. Any attempt to revoke within the period in this instance would give rise to an action for breach of the option contract.

In order for the revocation to be effective, notice of the withdrawal of the offer must be communicated to the offeree. It should be noted that the postal rule as seen in the context of acceptance has no application here.

Byrne v *Van Tienhoven* (1880) 5 CPD 344

In this case, the defendants posted a letter in Cardiff on 1 October offering to sell a quantity of tinplate to the plaintiffs in New York. The offer was received by the plaintiffs on 11 October, and they immediately accepted it by telegram and confirmed their acceptance by a letter posted on 15 October. On 8 October the defendants had posted a letter withdrawing their offer but this was not received by the plaintiffs until 20 October. It was held that a contract had come into existence when the telegram was sent on 11 October and that the letter of revocation sent on 8 October had no effect on the validity of the contract since it was only effective when received on 20 October, after a legally binding contract had already come into existence.

This rule relating to communication of revocation clearly flies in the face of the earlier thinking of judges since here a contract has come into existence when the parties are patently not in agreement. The rule, nevertheless, is correct, as otherwise no one would be able to rely on any offer since it might have been revoked before it had been received by the offeree, a result which would undoubtedly lead to inconvenience and uncertainty.

There are two principal exceptions to the rule that revocation must be communicated to the offeree. First, the rule may be overturned where the revocation would have been received by the offeree but for their being negligent in some way, as, for example, by the offeree failing to inform the offeror of a change of address. This exception also raises the spectre of when communication takes place, that is, when received or when actually read by the offeree. It would be a nonsense for the offeree, for instance, knowing that a letter might contain a revocation to ignore opening that letter and reading it until they had actually sent their letter accepting the offer. The logic contained in *The Brimnes*, as already discussed, is clearly appropriate here in that communication of the revocation would be deemed to have taken place when the letter was opened in the ordinary course of business, or would have been so opened and read if the normal course of business had been followed.

A second exception occurs where an offer has been made to the general public. For example, if an offer had been placed in a newspaper it would be clearly impossible to communicate the revocation to every person who had read the offer. In these circumstances, it would seem that revocation will be effective if the offeror takes all reasonable steps to bring the notice of the revocation to all those who potentially may have read the offer. In the case of our example of the offer in the newspaper it might be that a similar-sized notice in the same newspaper on the same day might well pass this test of reasonableness. Unfortunately no English authority exists at this point but such was the decision in the American case of *Shuey* v *US*, 92 US 73 (1875).

Can an offer be terminated by the offeror sending a second offer prior to the offeree accepting the first? This point was dealt with in the Court of Appeal in the following case.

Pickfords Ltd v *Celestica Ltd* [2003] EWCA Civ 1741

The facts of the case were that Celestica Ltd ('Celestica') was an information technology company which carried on business in Stoke-on-Trent. It wished to move its place of business to Telford and approached Pickfords Ltd ('Pickfords') to carry out the removal process. Pickfords sent a fax on 13 September 2001 stating that it estimated that a total of 96,000 cubic feet of workshop and office equipment needed moving and that this would require 96 pantechnicon vehicle loads. The 'cost for the crew, fuel, vehicle, etc. to pack, load transport and unload from Stoke to Telford during a weekday will be £890'. The cost for the packing of the effects was to be £2.50 per unit and that 500 units of antistatic packs and cartons would be required. The fax then stated, 'Therefore we have an estimated budget figure to include all the above at £100,000.' (This figure included VAT.) This could be described as the 'first offer'. Pickfords then conducted a survey over a three-day period. This culminated in the sending of a second document on 27 September 2001. This was a far more detailed document and set out the process involved in managing the move. It stated that on acceptance of this offer an experienced Move Manager would be appointed. The document also stated that Pickfords undertook to do the work for a fixed price of £98,760 (plus VAT). This could be described as the 'second offer'.

The defendants then sent a fax dated 15 October 2001 stating that an invoice had been raised with reference to the fax of 13 September 2001. It stated at the bottom '(not to exceed 100K)'. Pickford's case was that a contract arose with respect to the second offer and the fax of 15 October. Celestica claimed that the contract related to the first offer and the fax of 15 October.

Pickfords claimed that the first offer was not capable of being accepted and that the second offer operated as a rejection of the first. Both these contentions were rejected at first instance. The court also held that the fax of 15 October amounted to an acceptance of the first offer since it referred back to the fax of 13 September, the first offer. On appeal Pickfords contended that the judge at first instance should have held that the second offer revoked the first offer and the judge was wrong to find that the fax of 15 October operated as an acceptance of the first offer.

Dyson LJ in the Court of Appeal stated that the only fact relied upon by Pickfords as evidence of the withdrawal of the first offer was the sending of the second offer. He considered the veracity of this contention depended on the nature between the two offers and the circumstances in which they are made. He used the example of a person asking for a quotation for work to be done and being quoted a figure of £200 per day. The offeree then asks for a fixed-price quotation and is quoted £1,500 to complete the work. Dyson LJ considered that here there were two offers and the offeree had a choice of accepting one or the other. The second quotation in the absence of something more does not operate to revoke the first. The two offers are inconsistent only in the sense that they cannot both be accepted. He considered, however, that in the case in question this was not merely a case of a difference in price and that the second offer did in fact revoke the first.

But which offer did the fax of 15 October accept? He considered that the answer to this question could only be decided by examining the three documents. He did not consider that the contents of the fax of 15 October related to the second offer. In particular, the words '(not to exceed 100K)' did not make any commercial sense if the fax was to operate as an acceptance of the second offer since this was a fixed-price offer and the two expressions are clearly inconsistent with one another. The words pointed to an acceptance of the [first] offer since it referred to a budgetary ceiling of £100,000. The problem now remained that the fax of 15 October purported to accept an offer that had been revoked. On this basis this fax operated as a counter-offer to accept the services of Pickfords on the terms of the first offer and since the work had been carried out, this counter-offer had been accepted by Pickfords. It should be noted that even if the first offer had not been revoked, the fax of 15 October would have constituted a counter-offer in any event since the words '(not to exceed 100K)' introduced a material new term to the contract. The case therefore comes down to a classic 'battle of the forms' scenario, as described earlier.

A final point relating to communication of revocation is that while the revocation must be communicated to the offeree, it is thought that it need not be communicated by the offeror. For revocation to be effective in such circumstances, however, the revocation must be communicated to the offeree via a reliable third party. Notice of the revocation would not be effective if it came to the offeree's attention by way of mere rumour or supposition. The case often quoted as being the authority for this principle is that of *Dickinson v Dodds*.

Dickinson v *Dodds* (1876) 2 Ch D 463

On 10 June, the defendant offered to sell his house to the plaintiff for £800 adding, 'This offer to be left over until Friday 12th June, 9 am.' On Thursday 11 June the defendant sold the house to someone else and that evening the plaintiff was informed of that sale to another individual named Berry. That same evening the plaintiff delivered a formal letter of acceptance to the defendant's house and followed this up with a duplicate at 7 am the next morning, that is, before the 9 am deadline. When the defendant failed to complete the contract, the plantiff sued him for a decree of specific performance. It was held by the Court of Appeal that the plaintiff should fail in his application since he was aware at the time that he accepted the offer that Dodds, the defendant, no longer intended to sell the house to him. The principle established in the case places a substantial onus on the offeree to decide whether the source of the revocation is reliable or not, or indeed the precise time at which the revocation is deemed to have been communicated to him. To a large degree, the case reflects the traditional and defunct consensus approach to establishing a legally binding agreement, but therein lies an anomaly, since there would be no consensus even if the withdrawal of the offer had not been communicated to him. A further weakness lies in the case in that the third party, Berry, subsequently became the agent of Dickinson, thus calling into question the notice of revocation being communicated by an independent third party. Perhaps, as Treitel suggests, the rule should simply be that the revocation must be communicated to the offeree by the offeror.

Unilateral contracts

It has already been seen (under 'The mode of acceptance' earlier in this chapter) that a unilateral contract occurs where a person, the promisor, binds himself to perform a stated promise when the promisee fulfils some condition stipulated by the promisor, such being the situation in our example of *Carlill v Carbolic Smoke Ball Co*.

In the context of the revocation of offers, unilateral contracts present particular difficulties because of the fact that acceptance takes place when the condition is completed. It has been established in our study of revocation that it is possible to revoke an offer at any time until it has been accepted by the offeree. In terms of unilateral contracts this rule can lead to abuse and injustice.

Example

A makes an offer stating that they will pay £1,000 to anyone who walks from Manchester Town Hall to Nelson's Column in Trafalgar Square arriving on 6 June. B sets out and arrives in Trafalgar Square on 6 June but just as B is about to touch Nelson's Column, A revokes the offer. On the basis of the general rule relating to revocation of offers A is entitled to do this.

As Goff LJ stated in *Daulia Ltd v Four Millbank Nominees Ltd*:

the true view of the unilateral contract must in general be that the offeror is entitled to require full performance of the condition that he has imposed and short of that he is not bound . . .

Such an approach is undoubtedly intolerable and unjust; and indeed, this has been recognised as such in a number of cases.

Luxor (Eastbourne) Ltd v Cooper [1941] AC 108

An owner of a piece of land promised to pay an estate agent £10,000 commission if he introduced someone who was willing to purchase the property. The agent did in fact introduce someone and a sale was agreed subject to contract. While the third party was always ready and willing to purchase the property, the owner decided not to proceed with the sale. The result of the decision was that the agent could not complete the act he was employed to do. He nevertheless claimed the £10,000 which the owner refused to pay. The agent then brought an action for breach of contract alleging that there was an implied undertaking that he would not do anything to prevent completion of the sale. The House of Lords held that the owner could revoke his offer at any time up to exchange of contract and, therefore, the agent's action failed since the commission only became payable on completion.

On the face of things, the case supports the proposition that an offer in a unilateral contract is freely revocable by the offeror until performance by the offeree. The House of Lords, however, was not so definite in its judgement, preferring to decide that *in the circumstances of the case* it would not be proper to infer an undertaking on the part of the owner not to withdraw from the sale and thereby revoke his offer. Presumably, however, if such an undertaking could be implied in a particular case the court would find such an implication justifiable and the undertaking would be binding on the offeror. In the *Luxor* case, for instance, the House of Lords would not imply such an undertaking, on the basis that the reward was very substantial for comparatively little effort on the part of the agent and therefore the agent was taken to have assumed that it was possible that the offeror would wish to withdraw from the sale. If, to effect the sale, the agent had been required to undertake an obligation or task that was substantial and onerous in comparison to the fee level promised, the House of Lords might have been prepared to imply such an undertaking.

Errington v Errington and Woods [1952] 1 KB 290

A father purchased a house in his own name and then allowed his son and daughter-in-law to live in the house provided they paid the mortgage instalments. He told them that the house would be theirs when the mortgage was paid off. The couple lived in the house and paid the instalments. They were not contractually obliged to do this, though if they did, the house would be theirs. The father eventually died and his widow claimed possession of the house. It was held that the agreement amounted to a contract which could not be revoked, provided the couple continued to pay the instalments.

Lord Denning summed up the situation as follows:

The father's promise was a unilateral contract – a promise of a house in return for their act of paying the instalments. It could not be revoked by him once the couple entered a performance of the act, but it would cease to bind him if they left it incomplete and unperformed, which they have not done . . . They have acted on the promise and neither the father nor his widow, his successor in title, can eject them in disregard of it.

While the above view was supported in *Daulia Ltd v Four Millbank Nominees Ltd*, the basis of the decisions in all three cases is conceptually elusive. Not surprisingly Lord Denning, very much the father of the modern doctrine of **promissory estoppel**, tends to rely on this as justification for the rule. The doctrine of estoppel, however, cannot provide a complete answer since its application is deficient in that there needs to be an existing legal relationship for it to apply. Very often such a relationship is not present where an offer of a unilateral contract is being revoked. Another justification for disallowing revocation of the offer once the offeree has begun to perform their side of the agreement can be found in the idea of **collateral contracts**. In other words, in fact two offers are presented in the offeror's statement. The first is the one which expressly presents itself to the offeree, and in which the offeror promises to pay once the offeree has performed the act in question. The second offer is an implied one, namely, that the offeror shall not withdraw his offer once the offeree has begun to perform the act in question. If the offeror attempts to revoke his first offer, he will be in breach of the second collateral contract. Such a view finds much favour in *Cheshire, Fifoot and Furmston*. Treitel, however, tends to favour the idea that acceptance of the offer takes place when the offeree begins to perform the act required by the offeror, thus rendering any attempt at revoking the offer impossible. The main flaw here is that a binding contract will materialise and the offeree will be in breach of contract if they fail fully to perform the act in question. It is submitted that such a consequence would be unacceptable to the offeree.

Different arguments can be found justifying the rule and it may be that there is a degree of probity in all of them. It is regrettable that the courts have been so reluctant to define the theoretical basis behind the rule that the courts will treat an offer of a unilateral contract as irrevocable once performance by the offeror has commenced.

Rejection

The rules relating to rejection have largely been dealt with in our discussion of counter-offers since these operate as a rejection of the original offer, as seen in *Hyde* v *Wrench*.

On the matter of communication, it would seem that a rejection is ineffective until it is communicated to the offeror. Treitel suggests that, this being the case, it is possible for an offeree to post a letter of rejection and subsequently accept the offer – provided the communication of the acceptance is brought to the attention of the offeror before he receives the letter of rejection. Such a conclusion would seem fair, though it would also seem to be valid to apply the postal rule to a letter of acceptance sent subsequent to the sending of the letter of rejection. Such a conclusion, however, while being legally correct, would be grossly unfair to the offeror who might, while relying on the letter of rejection received by the offeror, sell the goods (for instance) to someone else, being unaware that in fact there was a valid contract between themselves and the original offeree. The point is undecided to date.

Lapse of time

An offer cannot last indefinitely and a point must arise at some time when the offer ceases to exist. It may be that the offer is expressed to last only for a certain period and that if not accepted within that period the offer will lapse. Where no express provision is contained in the offer, it will in any event lapse after a reasonable time. What constitutes a reasonable time depends largely on the subject matter of the offer. For example, an offer to sell a quantity of perishable goods, say, tomatoes, would lapse after a fairly short period of time compared to the time reasonable for a quantity of steel. Some items, while they are not perishable in that sense, may, nevertheless, be highly volatile in other respects and this again would cause the offer to lapse in a fairly short period of time. An example may be seen in the case of *Ramsgate Victoria Hotel Co. Ltd* v *Montefiore* (1866) LR 1 Ex 109 where the defendant applied for shares on 8 June but none was allotted to him until 23 November. It was held that the company could not accept the defendant's offer to purchase the shares since that offer had lapsed. Any acceptance had to take place within a reasonable time and in the case of a highly volatile commodity such as shares, lapse occurred after a comparatively short period of time. The delay from June to November was unreasonable and therefore the action for breach of contract for failure to accept and pay for the shares failed.

Failure of a condition precedent

Apart from an offer only being effective for a stated or reasonable period of time, as discussed above, the offer may only be effective while certain conditions exist. An offer may expressly provide that it will determine on the occurrence of some condition. Any acceptance subsequent to the occurrence of the stated condition will therefore be ineffective. Such **conditions precedent** may also be implied in an offer. For example, it is implied in an offer to purchase goods that they will remain in substantially the same condition as they were in when the offer was first made.

Financings Ltd v *Stimson* [1962] 3 All ER 386

The defendant, having seen a car at the premises of the dealer, decided to buy it on *hire purchase*. He signed a form supplied by the dealer which stated that the hire purchase agreement became binding only when signed by the plaintiffs, the finance company. The defendant paid a first instalment of £70 and took the car away on 18 March. On 20 March, the defendant returned the car, dissatisfied with its performance, and stated to the dealer that he no longer wished to purchase it. On 25 March, the plaintiffs signed the agreement, thereby purporting to accept the offer of the defendant. On the night of 24/25 March the car was stolen from the premises of the dealer and badly damaged. The plaintiffs eventually sold the car and claimed damages from the defendant, who counter-claimed for his first instalment of £70. It was held that the defendant would succeed since by returning the car to the dealer the defendant had revoked his offer and there was thus no concluded contract between the parties. Further, on the facts of the case, there was an implied condition in the offer of the defendant that the car would remain in substantially the same condition until the time of acceptance. Since the damage occurred before acceptance, the plaintiffs were not in a position to accept the offer which had lapsed due to the fact that the implied condition had not been complied with.

Death

The effect of death on an offer is, unlike death itself, not quite so certain, at least where it concerns the death of the offeror. Where the contract requires the personal services of the offeror, then death will automatically terminate the offer. Thus, an offer by a film star to open a gala will clearly lapse on the death of the film star. Where, however, the contract does not require the personal services of the offeror, then it may be the case that the personal representatives will have to employ some other person to carry out those services. What is a relevant consideration here is whether notice of the death of the offeror was brought to the attention of the offeree. If the death of the offeror was brought to the attention of the offeree prior to acceptance of the offer, then the offer will cease to exist. Where the offeree has no notice of the death of the offeror, then, on acceptance, the offeror's estate will be bound by the ensuing contract.

The principles in relation to the death of the offeror can be found *obiter dicta* in **Bradbury v Morgan** (1862) 1 H & C 249. No authority exists, however, in the case of the death of the offeree, though in the context of a bilateral contract it would seem reasonable to suggest that very often the terms of the offer apply specifically to a particular offeree, and that, as a result, the death of the offeree terminates the offer.

Certainty of terms

Objective
6

Despite the fact that one can find a valid offer and acceptance leading to an agreement, the courts may nevertheless fail to find for a binding contract between the parties. Such a conclusion may be reached where one party has raised, as a defence to an action for breach of contract, the fact that some essential element has been omitted from the agreement, or that some terms are so vague that the contract as a whole is rendered unenforceable. Not surprisingly, this problem is all too common since the vast majority of contracts are negotiated and entered into by business people with no legal knowledge. It is, of course, for this very reason that standard-form contracts have been, and continue to be, so popular. Where such a device is not used, the business person is more concerned with the general round of negotiating and obtaining a contract in principle, leaving certain issues such as pricing or delivery arrangements to be negotiated at a later date.

It is the loosely drafted contract that creates the problem and here the courts are faced with a difficult task. The judge must do all they can to preserve the contract, if indeed there is one, but what they must not do is to write the contract for the parties. The question as to whether the contract is enforceable or unenforceable largely revolves around the level of vagueness, ambiguity or incompleteness in the contract for it is this which, combined with the uncertainty of the willingness of the judge to save or sacrifice the contract, creates substantial uncertainty for the parties. With this level of overall uncertainty it is impossible to draw up a precise set of rules since each case revolves very much on its own facts. It is nevertheless possible to develop a broad set of guidelines which may give some indication as to the possible direction a judge might opt for in any particular case.

The contract is uncertain but has yet to be performed

The attitude of the courts here may be seen in the case of *Scammell and Nephew Ltd* v *Ouston* [1941] AC 251, where the respondents agreed to purchase a new van from Scammell. The order was given 'on the understanding that the balance of purchase price can be had on hire purchase terms over a period of two years'. Scammell accepted the offer though the term 'hire purchase terms' was never determined. It was held that no precise meaning could be attributed to the clause as hire purchase agreements varied widely and there was thus no contract. The level of vagueness here was such as to render the contract unenforceable, since it was impossible for the court to determine either the meaning or intention of the parties with regard to the expression 'hire purchase terms'. There was, for instance, no previous course of dealings between the parties to rescue the contract, nor was there any performance of the contract which might have given the court guidance as to the meaning of the term.

Where there is no performance of the contract the courts, in the absence of any aids, will much more readily find that the contract is unenforceable. A further example of this attitude can be found in *May & Butcher* v *R* [1934] 2 KB 17n.

The contract is uncertain but performance has commenced

In this situation, the courts, as a matter of expediency, are much more likely to uphold the contract as enforceable. Perhaps it is an oversimplification of the process to suggest that expediency forces the arm of the courts to find for a contract, since very often the courts will have more information on which to resolve the uncertainty within the contract once some performance has been rendered. Nevertheless, the reluctance of the courts to unravel a contract that is partly, or perhaps even substantially, performed should not be underestimated either.

In *Hillas & Co. Ltd* v *Arcos Ltd*, the facts of which have already been considered, the court was able to determine the meaning of the option clause by reference to the previous course of dealings of the parties in the contract of which the option clause was part and parcel. Further, the position of the court was aided by the existence of well-established trade usage.

A more striking example can be seen in the following case.

Foley v *Classique Coaches Ltd* [1934] 2 KB 1

The plaintiff, who was a retail dealer in petrol, contracted to supply the defendants, who ran a coach business, with all the petrol they required 'at a price to be agreed by the parties in writing and from time to time'. No such agreement as to the price was ever concluded and three years later the defendants purported to repudiate the contract. It was held that they were not entitled to do so since in the absence of an express agreement a term would be implied that the petrol supplied by the plaintiff should be of reasonable quality and sold at a reasonable price. Undoubtedly, the fact of the contract having been performed was a major factor in the Court of Appeal's decision.

An interesting modern example of the issues arising in these cases can be seen in the following case.

Baird Textiles Holdings Ltd v *Marks & Spencer plc* [2001] EWCA Civ 274

The claimant had been a principal supplier of garments to the defendant for some 30 years. In October 1999, the defendant terminated all supply arrangements with the claimant from the end of the then current production season without warning. The claimant contended that the defendant was precluded from terminating the arrangements without reasonable notice based on the fact that there was an implied contract to acquire garments from it in such quantities and at such process prices which in all the circumstances was reasonable. There was no express contract between the parties although it was well understood between the parties that Marks & Spencer deliberately chose not to enter an express contract. The reasons for this were that Marks & Spencer did not wish to regulate any continuing or future business that would impose on them an obligation to place orders in the future or have to give reasonable notice of termination.

Judge LJ concluded that it would be unusual to imply a contract between the parties when it was clear that Marks & Spencer had deliberately avoided entering into such a contract. Morritt VC also stated that in any event the obligation on Marks & Spencer to acquire a reasonable quantity of clothes at a reasonable price was uncertain: '... there are no objective criteria by which the court could assess what would be reasonable either as to quantity or price'. He pointed out that this was not a case where there was a contract between the parties where the court is seeking to construe the terms of the contract in order to create certainty. It was in fact a case where the lack of certainty confirms the fact that there was no intention to create legal relations between the parties. It cannot be said that the conduct of the parties is consistent with the existence of a contract; indeed, the contrary was true in that the conduct of the parties pointed to the absence of an agreement. The Court of Appeal thus held that Baird Textiles had no claim in contract. The position is that all there is between the parties is a long-term business relationship but this cannot be extended any further into a contractual relationship. The basis of the contractual arrangements is based on individual orders and sales – nothing more. The relationship is only as good as the last order. There is no objective evidence of a wider relationship which the courts would have to see to establish the wider contract.

A further factor that is often taken into account by the courts in resolving problems of uncertainty is the provision for arbitration or some other means of resolving disputes within the contract. Such a clause existed in the *Foley* case and was another factor taken into account by the Court of Appeal in coming to its decision. Such a provision is always prudent if any terms, such as price or terms of delivery, are to be left open by the parties. In the past, the machinery set up by the parties for resolving disputes or such matters has nevertheless also been held to be ineffective because of the machinery itself being vague, ambiguous or defective in some other way. In *Sudbrook Trading Estate Ltd v Eggleton* [1983] 1 AC 444, the House of Lords adopted a means whereby such decisions should now be reduced. In the case there was an agreement by which a tenant could purchase his premises 'at such a price . . . as may be agreed upon by two valuers'. One valuer was to be appointed by the tenant and one by the landlord. The tenant decided to purchase his premises and appointed his valuer according to the agreement. The landlord refused to appoint the other valuer, thus nullifying the provision. The House of Lords interpreted the provision as being an agreement to sell at a fair and reasonable price to be assessed by the valuers. Since the landlord, by his conduct, had rendered this process ineffective and inoperable, the court was able to assess a price by reference to expert opinion as to what might be regarded as a fair and reasonable price.

The fact that there has been some degree of performance of the contract or that the contract contains a means of resolving any uncertainty within it does not necessarily mean that the courts will invariably treat the contract as enforceable.

British Steel Corporation v *Cleveland Bridge and Engineering Co. Ltd* [1984] 1 All ER 504

A contract was entered into concerning a major construction project; work on the project started before all the terms had been agreed, though negotiations proceeded in the expectation that a full and final agreement would eventually be forthcoming. At the heart of the negotiations were matters relating to delivery, price and certain other terms. Eventually a dispute broke out whereby BSC claimed a reasonable price for the items delivered so far, whereas CBE counter-claimed for damages for non-delivery of certain items. BSC's claim was based on a claim in *quantum meruit* and since it alleged that there was no contract between the parties, the effect would be to preclude CBE's claim. The court held that, despite the fact that substantial performance had taken place and the fact that there was a submission on CBE's part that a letter of intent sent to BSC constituted a subcontract, there was no contract in existence. It was stated that there was so much left unsaid that one could not find that a contract had been formed and, consequently, BSC could claim a reasonable sum for work done on a *quantum meruit* basis. As *Cheshire, Fifoot and Furmston* (2012) points out, the decision creates difficulties in that either party could have abandoned the project with impunity without giving notice to the other party since there was no contract – no matter how 'commercially unacceptable' the result. Further it is pointed out that the finding of no contract could present difficulties in determining whether goods delivered and accepted, but later found to be defective, could be rejected or not. Despite these difficulties and the cases already examined with regard to certainty, the case indicates that the courts still retain substantial discretion to find for no contract despite performance of the contract where the terms are uncertain. However, *G Percy Trentham Ltd* v *Archital Luxfer* Steyn LJ suggested that, where a transaction is executed, it is easier to imply a term resolving any uncertainty, or alternatively make it possible to treat as non-essential a matter not finalised in negotiations.

In executory contracts there is more likely to be a finding of uncertainty particularly where, as in the *Cleveland* case, the parties are still negotiating the terms of the contract when they start trading. It is because of this trading position that some lawyers are often tempted to look for a contract when none exists. Such a situation arose in the case of ***Whittle Movers Ltd* v *Hollywood Express Ltd*** [2009] EWCA Civ 1189, in which Hollywood, the respondent, was a subsidiary of a cinema group for which it undertook distribution and warehousing services. The distribution services were to be outsourced and therefore Hollywood invited tenders for a new subcontract and sought indicative prices for one-, three- and five-year contracts. Whittle tendered for the contract and was successful. The invitation to tender from Hollywood was expressed to be 'subject to contract' and, as such, clearly contemplated that a formal written contract would be executed. Further negotiations took place and eventually Hollywood issued a letter of intent which was signed by Whittle. The drafting of a long-term contract proceeded but, before this was actually completed and entered into, Whittle began to perform the distribution services and invoiced for them on the basis that the eventual contract was to be for five and a half years and that the pricing reflected such a long-term contract. Eventually, the parties agreed on all the terms of the contract but, before it could be signed, Hollywood was put up for sale and the contract was never signed.

Hollywood alleged that it had in fact entered into an interim contract on the same terms as that of an earlier contract it had with an earlier subcontractor and that contract could be terminated by either party giving six months' notice of termination. As such, Hollywood gave Whittle six months' notice of termination of the interim contract.

At first instance the judge held that, while no long-term contract had been entered into, Whittle was nevertheless bound by the prices that had been negotiated for a long-term contract. Whittle appealed, challenging the finding that there was no long-term contract and that an interim contract had come into existence. Instead, Whittle argued that no contract had been concluded and, following ***British Steel Corp.* v *Cleveland Bridge and Engineering Co. Ltd***, sought a restitutionary remedy on the basis that Hollywood had been unjustly enriched by being required to pay prices based on a long-term contract when the contract was of a short-term, interim duration.

The Court of Appeal allowed the appeal, stating first that the judge was correct in finding that there was no long-term contract. However, did a short-term interim contract come into existence? The Court of Appeal thought not, since it considered it was highly unlikely that the parties would have entered into an interim executory contract given that the terms were still under negotiation. The court considered that while the parties may have entered into a contract on the basis that one party would have supplied the services under the contract and the other party undertook to pay a reasonable price (as opposed to the five-year contract prices), such a contract could not have arisen where the parties were still negotiating important terms. The Court of Appeal therefore held that no contract had come into existence and that in such a case a restitutionary remedy would be available on the basis that Hollywood had been unjustly enriched. The court considered that, in such cases, it was important to analyse the terms and discover whether, in fact, the terms were still under negotiation; and, if that was the reality of the situation, the proper finding was to find that no contract existed. The court considered that it was wrong to try to force a finding of a contract, particularly when a restitutionary remedy would resolve the dispute. In this case, it was clear that all the negotiations entered into were in fact 'subject to contract' and therefore no contract could have come into existence until a formal contractual document had been signed by both parties.

Debate

Should the postal rule be abolished?

The postal rule has been subject to criticism not least that is an anachronism that has its origins in the nineteenth century and that it is an anomaly in the twenty-first century when the vast majority of contracts are entered into via many other different modes of instantaneous communication and in which the postal rule does not apply. Arguably it has been claimed that having one rule as regards communication of acceptance and indeed all forms of communication would be to provide a more coherent set of principles for the formation of an agreement. The antiquity of the rule means that it is highly unlikely that it will be overturned judicially and instead exceptions to the rule will continue to develop, as in *Holwell Securities Ltd* v *Hughes*. It should also be noted that in many jurisdictions the rule does not operate.

The justification for the rule is somewhat elusive. As we have seen, one theory is that the rule prevents the offeree accepting by post and then withdrawing his acceptance by a later, quicker mode of communication so that the letter of acceptance once received by the offeror is ineffective. The converse to this is that without the rule, the offeree would not know if he has entered into a contract of not. The truth of the matter in these circumstances is that the law has adopted an approach that fulfils a commercial expediency and really, whichever approach is adopted, one or other of the parties is bound to suffer a disadvantage. The law has therefore developed a principle that the offeror wishing to enter into the contract should bear the risk of the letter of acceptance becoming lost and, in any event having made the offer and not having received a reply, the offeror would be put on notice to chase up the matter with the offeree. In any event, the offeror is free to place conditions on the terms of his offer, for instance, 'your acceptance will only be valid when it is received by me' as in *Household Fire and Carriage Accident Insurance Co.* v *Grant and Holwell Securities Ltd* v *Hughes*. This point was also considered directly in *Manchester Diocesan Council for Education* v *Commercial and General Investments Ltd*. The position is then that if an offeror makes a stipulation that only a particular mode of acceptance is sufficient, the offeree must comply with that stipulation.

Another justification for the rule is that the Post Office acts as an agent for both the parties so that communication to the agent completes the transaction. Thus the Post Office is the agent of the offeror for delivering the offer and is also the agent for the purposes of delivering the acceptance. This is clearly incorrect as the Post Office is not an agent for those purposes and, if anything is merely an agent for the purposes of delivering the letter of acceptance and not to receive it on behalf of the offeror.

The truth of the matter is that the rule is an arbitrary one and none of the explanations really provide a satisfactory answer, though it is probably safe to say that the function of the rule in limiting the offeree's power to change his mind once he has accepted the offer provides a useful function. It can be seen that without such a principle hardship may arise. For instance, if X offers to sell Y a coat. X places no conditions on the requirement of acceptance and therefore impliedly adopts the postal rule. Y, then posts his acceptance of the offer to Y but then changes his mind and then sends a text message to X telling him to ignore his acceptance. X then sells the coat to Z on receiving the text. Could Y then change his mind again and hold X to the contract? There are several ways of looking at such a situation. Firstly, it could be that Y is in breach of contract in that he has accepted the offer and there is now a contract so his text message amounts to a breach. In such a situation it could be argued that X has accepted this breach and therefore he is now free from his obligations under the contract. Such a solution leaves X with the option to sue Y for breach if X's sale to Z is on less advantageous terms. Another way of looking at such a situation is that the contract has ended by mutual agreement.

One way of looking at the postal rule is that it provides a baseline. This baseline can then be subject to amendment by the offeror placing conditions on the mode of acceptance and setting out when the acceptance will take place. This avoids the rule and deals with such problems that might arise out of the letter being lost or misdirected. It should also be borne in mind that the courts themselves have provided an exception so that the rule does not apply where its application results in 'manifest inconvenience and absurdity' as stated in *Holwell Securities Ltd* v *Hughes*.

In 1993, the Scottish Law Commission (Scot Law Com No. 144) produced a report. 'Report of Formation of Contract: Scottish Law and the United Nations Convention on Contracts for the International Sale of Goods', in which it expressed concern over the operation of the postal rule and considered its application was inconsistent with the expectations of non-lawyers who would not expect to be bound by a contract until the acceptance of the offer had been received by them. The Scottish Law Commission advocated adoption of the Article 18 (2) and (3) of the United Nations Convention on Contracts for the International Sale of Goods (the 'Vienna Convention'):

> Article 18 (2) An acceptance of an offer becomes effective at the moment the indication of assent reaches the offeror. An acceptance is not effective if the indication of assent does not reach the offeror within the time he has fixed or, if no time is fixed, within a reasonable time, due account being taken of the circumstances of the transaction, including the rapidity of the means of communication employed by the offeror. An oral offer must be accepted immediately unless the circumstances indicate otherwise.

> Article 18 (3) However, if, by virtue of the offer or as a result of practices which the parties have established between themselves or of usage, the offeree may indicate assent by performing an act, such as one relating to the dispatch of the goods or payment of the price, without notice to the offeror, the acceptance is effective at the moment the act is performed, provided that the act is performed within the period of time laid down in the preceding paragraph.

Article 18(2) therefore provides that acceptance only becomes effective when it reaches the offeror, although it should be noted that Article 18(3) preserves the postal rule if the parties wish to adopt the rule. The provision in Article 18(2) is however tempered by Article 16(1) which provides that 'Until a contract is concluded an offer may be revoked if the revocation reaches the offeree before he has dispatched an acceptance', thus once the acceptance is sent, the offeror is unable to revoke his offer until such time as the letter of acceptance is received provided it arrives before the date fixed by the offeror.

As of May 2016, the Vienna Convention has been ratified by 85 states, however, the United Kingdom, recognised as a leading jurisdiction for the choice of law in international commercial contracts, is not a signatory on the grounds 'the government not viewing its ratification as a legislative priority, a lack of interest from business in supporting ratification, opposition from a number of large and influential organisations, a lack of public service resources, and a danger that London would lose its edge in international arbitration and litigation'.

Similar principles to the Vienna Convention are also found within UNIDROIT Principles of International Commercial Contracts (Art 2.1.6) and the Principles of European Contract Law (Art 2.202(1)).

Questions

1. What do you consider to be the advantage or disadvantages of the existing postal rule? Are the criticisms of the rule valid?

2. Are the exceptions to the postal rule now so extensive that the postal rule is now only useful as a baseline rule that the courts apply in default of the parties making their own arrangements?

3. Should England and Wales adopt such the principles set out in the international treaties?

Summary

This chapter deals with the fact of agreement and the elements necessary for establishing an agreement.

Offer

● Definition of an offer: an offer is an expression of willingness to contract on certain terms made with the intention that a binding agreement will exist once the offer is accepted.

Two types of offer

● Unilateral offers: capable of being made to the world as a whole.

● Bilateral offers: made to a specific individual or group.

Offers and invitations to treat

● Adverts: most advertisements are an invitation to treat (*Partridge* v *Crittenden*; *Harris* v *Nickerson*).

● Display of goods for sale: shop windows (*Fisher* v *Bell*); self-service displays (*Pharmaceutical Society of Great Britain* v *Boots Cash Chemists Ltd*).

● Auction sales.

● Tenders.

● Ticket cases.

Offers distinguished from requests for information

- Negotiations for the sale of land (*Harvey* v *Facey*).
- Preliminary statements (*Clifton* v *Palumbo*).
- In some circumstance, the words 'I would accept . . . ' can amount to an offer (*Bigg* v *Boyd Gibbons Ltd*).

Communication of offers

- An offer must be fully communicated to the offeree.
- An offer must be received by the offeree (*Taylor* v *Laird*).
- An offer will lapse after the passing of a reasonable period of time.

Acceptance

- Definition: 'a final unqualified expression of assent to all the terms of an offer' (Treitel).
- Two principles:
    - Acceptance must be unequivocal and unconditional.
    - The acceptance must be communicated to the offeror.

The fact of acceptance

The mode of acceptance

- An offer can be accepted in writing or verbally.
- Acceptance can be implied by conduct (*Brogden* v *Metropolitan Railway Co.* Conversely see *Weatherby* v *Banham*).
- NB: Unilateral contract and acceptance thereof by conduct (*Carlill* v *Carbolic Smoke Ball Co.*).
- An offer may state a particular requirement that must be complied with in order for acceptance to have taken place (*Western Electric Ltd* v *Welsh Development Agency*).

Counter-offers

- A counter-offer destroys the original offer (*Hyde* v *Wrench*).

Conditional acceptance

- Conditional acceptance is not full acceptance or a counter-offer.
- The parties have no intention to be legally bound until a condition has been fulfilled, e.g. 'Sold, subject to contract'.

Clarifying the terms of the offer

- Seeking clarification of the terms by making a genuine enquiry will not amount to a counter-offer (*Stevenson, Jacques & Co.* v *McLean*).

The battle of the forms

- The last form submitted wins (*Butler Machine Tool Co. Ltd* v *Ex-Cell-O Corporation (England) Ltd*).

Communication of acceptance

General rule

- Acceptance must be communicated to the other party (*Powell v Lee*). See Lord Denning, *Entores v Miles Far East Corporation*.

Exceptions to the general rule

- The effect of silence:
  - A party normally cannot accept a contract by remaining silent (*Felthouse v Bindley*).
  - NB: *Ammons v Wilson*, where the examination of the conduct of the parties established that acceptance by silence was possible.
  - NB: Unilateral offer and acceptance thereof by conduct (*Carlill v Carbolic Smoke Ball Co.*).
- The postal rule:
  - Acceptance takes place immediately the letter is validly posted (*Adams v Lindsell*; *Household Fire and Carriage Accident Insurance Co. v Grant*).
  - Valid posting is when the letter is placed into a postbox or handed to a person authorised to receive or collect letters (*Brinkibon Ltd v Stahag Stahl und Stahlwarenhandelsgesellschaft GmbH*; *Re London and Northern Bank*).
  - The postal rules can be excluded (*Household Fire and Carriage Accident Insurance Co. v Grant*; *Holwell Securities Ltd*; *Manchester Diocesan Council for Education v Commercial and General Investments Ltd*).
- Instantaneous forms of communication:
  - Telex – acceptance occurs at the place where the telex was received (*Entores v Miles Far East Corporation*).
  - A notice of withdrawal sent during office hours is effective the next working day (*The Brimnes*; *Mondial Shipping and Chartering BV v Astarte Shipping Ltd*).
- E-commerce:
  - Websites normally amount to an invitation to treat.

The termination of offers

- Acceptance of an offer also terminates the offer.

Revocation

Bilateral contracts

- An offer can be revoked at any time prior to acceptance.
- The offeror does not have to keep their offer open for or until a specified date or time (*Routledge v Grant*).
- The rule: for revocation to be effective, it must be communicated to the offeree (*Byrne v Van Tienhoven*).
- Exceptions to the rule:
  - Where revocation would be received subject to the offeree's negligence.
  - Where an offer has been made to the general public (*Shuey v US*).

Unilateral contracts

- Once a unilateral offer is made, the courts *may* imply an undertaking that the acceptor would be given a reasonable opportunity to perform the contract (*Luxor (Eastbourne) Ltd v Cooper*; *Errington v Errington and Woods*).

Rejection

- Occurs when a counter-offer is made (*Hyde v Wrench*).
- Rejections are not effective until communicated to the offeror.

Lapse of time

- An offer will lapse after the passage of a reasonable amount of time (*Ramsgate Victoria Hotel Co. Ltd v Montefiore*).

Death

- The deceased's representative should be able to accept/reject or enforce a contract that is not for the deceased's personal service.
- A contract for personal services will terminate automatically on the offeror's death.

Certainty of terms

The contract is uncertain but has yet to be performed

- Vague terms will render the contract unenforceable (*Scammell and Nephew Ltd v Ouston*).

The contract is uncertain but performance has commenced

- Vague terms are more likely to be enforced by the courts.

Further reading

Adams, 'The Battle of the Forms' (1979) 95 *Law Quarterly Review* 481

Adams and Broadsword, 'More in Expectation than Hope: The Blackpool Airport Case' (1991) 54 *Modern Law Review* 281

Austen-Baker, 'Offeree Silence and Contractual Agreement' (2006) *Common Law World Review* 354 (247)

Beatson, Burrows and Cartwright, *Anson's Law of Contract*, 30th edn (Oxford University Press, 2016)

Evans, 'The Anglo-American Mailing Rule: Some Problems of Offer and Acceptance in Contracts by Correspondence' (1966) 15 *International and Comparative Law Quarterly* 553

Fried, *Contract as Promise: A Theory of Contractual Obligations* (Harvard University Press, 1981)

Furmston, *Cheshire, Fifoot and Furmston's Law of Contract*, 16th edn (Oxford University Press, 2012)

Gower, 'Auction Sales of Goods Without Reserve' (1952) 68 *Law Quarterly Review* 457

MacQueen and Azim-Khan, 'The Argos Free TV Debacle: Two Legal Opinions' (1999) 1 *Electronic Business Law* 9

Mik, 'The Unimportance of Being "Electronic" or Popular Misconceptions about "Internet Contracting" ' (2011) 19(4) *International Journal of Law and Information Technology* 324

Mitchell and Phillips, 'The Contractual Nexus: Is Reliance Essential?' (2002) 22 *Oxford Journal of Legal Studies* 115

Morgan, 'Battle of the Forms: Restating the Orthodox', (2010) 69 *Cambridge Law Review* 230

Platt, 'Win the War but Don't Lose the Battle' (2011) *Construction Law* 22(4) 23

Smith and Atiyah, *Atiyah's Introduction to the Law of Contract, 6th edn* (Oxford University Press, 2006)

Stone, 'The Postal Rule in the Electronic Age' [1992] 12 *Student Law Review* Spring

Stone, 'Forming a Contract without Offer and Acceptance' [1994] 15 *Student Law Review* Spring

Peel, Treitel *Law of Contract*, 14th edn (Sweet and Maxwell, 2015)

Vorster, 'A Comment on the Meaning of Objectivity in Contract' (1987) 103 *Law Quarterly Review* 274

Winfield, 'Some Aspects of Offer and Acceptance' (1939) 55 *Law Quarterly Review* 499

3

Consideration

Objectives

After reading this chapter you should be able to:

1. Define and understand what is meant by the doctrine of consideration.
2. Know the differences between executed, executory and past consideration.
3. Critically evaluate the different principles applicable to the doctrine of consideration.
4. Explain that consideration must be sufficient though not necessarily adequate and the differences between the two.
5. Critically analyse the circumstances in which consideration is sufficient or insufficient.
6. Know and understand the issues regarding part payment of debt with reference to the common law rule and promissory estoppel.

Introduction

Consideration is one of the principal ingredients of an enforceable simple contract in English law. It was not always such a requirement and it is largely regarded as having originated in the sixteenth century, though the technical reasons for its evolution are not clear. One theory is that it evolved as a means of restricting the development of assumpsit, in that only promises supported by consideration could be enforced; gratuitous promises were, therefore, not enforceable. The law thus evolved in simple contracts in such a way as to enforce bargains rather than promises. The concept of **speciality contracts** evolved separately from assumpsit at a time when the law was very much more formulary in its approach. In this situation an agreement made under seal could be enforced despite the lack of consideration.

The difference between a simple contract and a speciality contract may be illustrated by reference to gifts. As we will see, consideration broadly means a quid pro quo on the part of the participants to the contract, a reciprocal giving and taking by both parties or 'something for something'. In the case of a promise by *A* to give *B* £10, this is clearly a bare gift, a *nudum pactum*, and as such is unenforceable as a simple contract since there is clearly no reciprocity between the parties. If this gift is embodied, however, in a deed, a deed being a document made under seal, then such an agreement is enforceable as a speciality contract.

In this chapter, we are thus considering what, in law, amounts to consideration that will support a simple contract. Before we approach this task, three further points need to be made. First, the question as to what constitutes consideration has to be addressed to each party's promise in relation to the contract, as each party must provide this element to enforce the contract. In other words, the validity or otherwise of consideration is assessed in relation not to the contract as a whole but to its provision by an individual participant to the contract. Second, although textbook writers often refer to this area as the doctrine of consideration, and while this might originally have been true, it is erroneous to think of it as a single concept today. Consideration has evolved into a body of rules developed by the courts in order to place limitations on the enforceability of the contracts that come before them. Third, an agreement in which consideration is lacking is not necessarily unenforceable, as we shall see in our analysis of promissory estoppel later in this chapter. Here the courts will, in certain circumstances, enforce a contract even though there is a lack of consideration. Similarly, the courts will on occasion return a finding of no contract despite the apparent existence of consideration, the basis for such a decision being that only certain types of consideration are recognised by the law. While the notion of consideration is concerned with a giving of value by both parties, only 'something of value in the eyes of the law' is regarded as amounting to consideration.

For more on sufficiency of consideration, see 'Consideration must be sufficient though not necessarily adequate', later in this chapter.

The definition of consideration

Objective
1

Consideration is the price for which the promise of the other is bought. It must be 'something of value' which is recognised by the courts as amounting to consideration. Traditionally, the doctrine of consideration has been defined in terms of either a detriment to the promisee or a benefit to the promisor. In **Currie v Misa** (1875) LR 10 Ex 153, consideration was defined as:

> A valuable consideration in the sense of the law, may consist either in some right, interest, profit or benefit accruing to one party, or some forbearance, detriment, loss or responsibility given, suffered or undertaken by the other.

This approach to defining consideration develops deficiencies when seen in contracts based purely on an exchange of promises.

Example

If A promises to buy a car from B for £2,000 and B for their part promises to sell the car to A for £2,000 there is clearly a binding contract which can be enforced, should one of the parties decide not to carry on with the contract. Until the date for performance arrives, there is clearly no detriment or benefit undertaken by either party, the consideration within the contract presenting itself via the exchange of promises made by the parties.

The definition is therefore meaningless in this context. Indeed this and other criticisms have meant that it has become preferable today to think in terms of consideration amounting to a claimant buying a defendant's promise by performing some act in return for it. Alternatively, the claimant may purchase the defendant's promise by the furnishing of a counter-promise. This modern approach was summed up by Sir Frederick Pollock (1950) in *Principles of Contract*, where he defined consideration as:

> An act or forbearance of one party, or the promise thereof, is the price for which the promise of the other is bought, and the promise thus given for value is enforceable.

This definition was approved by the House of Lords in **Dunlop Pneumatic Tyre Co. Ltd v Selfridge and Co. Ltd** [1915] AC 847 and is regarded as being more representative of the doctrine of consideration in the modern commercial contract than the nineteenth-century concept of benefit and detriment.

So far our definition has been very straightforward and simple but, as indicated earlier, it is erroneous to think of it as a single coherent principle. In truth, the definition is an expression of a body of rules or sub-principles which, together with their exceptions, make up the doctrine as we know it today. The sub-principles may be expressed as follows:

1　Consideration may be executed or executory but not past.

2　Consideration must move from the promisee but not necessarily to the promisor.

3　Consideration must be sufficient though not necessarily adequate.

Consideration may be executed or executory but not past

Executory and executed consideration

Objective
2

The above principle reflects the methods by which the claimant purchases the promise of the defendant. In **executory consideration**, the form of the consideration arises by way of a promise by the defendant in return for a promise by the claimant. In other words, the whole agreement is one which is to take place in the future. An example of this type of consideration would arise where *A* promises to purchase *B*'s car on credit, delivery to take place next week. Here both *A*'s and *B*'s considerations are to be performed in the future – it is executory. **Executed consideration** occurs when one of the parties has done all that they are required to do under the contract, that is, they have 'executed' their side of the bargain. The other party's consideration which is still unperformed remains executory in that it remains to be completed in the future.

Past consideration

The rule in English law is that 'past consideration is no consideration'. In defining consideration, we have seen that consideration for a promise has to be given in return for a promise; in other words, there has to be a causal link between the two promises in order for the contract to be enforceable. If a party makes a promise subsequent to some action carried out by the other party, then that promise can only be regarded as an expression of gratitude, a gift, and nothing more. An example of past consideration may be seen where *A* paints the outside of *B*'s house as a voluntary act while *B* is on holiday. When *B* returns from holiday *B* is pleasantly surprised by *A*'s kindness and promises to pay *A* £50. If *B* refuses to pay, can *A* claim their £50? The answer here must be that *A*'s action will fail since *A*'s consideration of painting the house is past in relation to the promise to pay made by *B* and, of course, past consideration is no consideration. Put another way, there is no causal link between the actions of *A* and *B* in that the act of painting the house was not made in response to a promise to pay for that act.

It should be noted carefully that past consideration means past in relation to the promise that the claimant is seeking to enforce and not in relation to the time at which the claimant is seeking to enforce the defendant's promise. In the above example, if *B* had promised *A* £50 if *A* painted his house, then *A* can only claim the £50 once *A* has carried out their part of the bargain, that is, their consideration is executed in that it has been carried out in response to a promise to pay by *B*. It is true, however, that *A*'s consideration here is past in that it has already been completed but here it is past in relation to the time of enforcement rather than to the promise made by *B*. Two cases traditionally illustrate this principle: ***Roscorla v Thomas*** and the modern authority of ***Re McArdle***.

Roscorla v *Thomas* (1842) 3 QB 234

In this case, the plaintiff had negotiated the purchase of a particular horse from the defendant for a certain price. Subsequent to the agreement the defendant promised the plaintiff that 'the said horse was sound and free from vice'. In fact the horse proved to be particularly vicious and the plaintiff sued for breach of the promise. It was held that his action would fail since the consideration provided by the plaintiff was already past when the promise of the defendant that the horse was sound and free from vice was made. In truth, the warranty as regards the horse was not induced by the payment made for the horse and was, as such, purely gratuitous.

Re McArdle [1951] Ch 669

By virtue of a father's will, his children were to be left his house on the death of their mother. While the mother was alive, one of the children and his wife lived in the house with her. The wife, during this period, made substantial alterations and improvements to the property. In gratitude, the children later signed a document which stated 'in consideration of your carrying out certain alterations and improvements to the property, we hereby agree that the executors shall repay to you from the estate, when distributed, the sum of £488 in settlement of the amount spent on such improvements'. The Court of Appeal held that the alterations and improvements completed before the signing of the undertaking by the children amounted to past consideration and that, when the executors refused to pay the £488, the wife was unable successfully to sue for those moneys. The wife had furnished no consideration for the promise to pay the money for the alterations and improvements.

Exceptions to the past consideration rule

The principle in *Lampleigh* v *Braithwait*

Lampleigh v *Braithwait* (1615) Hob 105

The facts of this case were that Braithwait had killed another man and asked Lampleigh to secure a pardon from the king. Lampleigh went to considerable effort and expense to secure the pardon for Braithwait who subsequently promised to pay Lampleigh £100 for his trouble. Braithwait then failed to pay the £100 and was sued on his promise by Lampleigh. Clearly on the basis of the rule relating to past consideration, the efforts of Lampleigh were in the past in relation to the promise to pay by Braithwait and therefore he should have failed in his action. The court, however, held that the original request by Braithwait in fact contained an implied promise that he would reward and reimburse Lampleigh for his efforts. Thus, the previous request and the subsequent promise were part of the same transaction and as such were enforceable against Braithwait by Lampleigh once he had secured the pardon for him.

It should be noted that the principle applies only if the claimant's services had been rendered at the defendant's request and that it was implicit that both parties must have understood that the claimant's services would have to be paid for. Further, the implication of the promise to pay normally only arises in a commercial relationship between the parties. It is often considered that the exception did not apply in the case of *Re McArdle*, above, because of the absence of a request from the defendant to his wife to maintain the property and the lack, therefore, of an implied promise to pay as a result. In truth, however, if this case had been a commercial one, an implied promise might have been found, despite the lack of a previous request.

An example of such a finding can be seen in the case of *Re Casey's Patents* [1892] 1 Ch 104, where there were joint owners of certain patent rights who wrote to the plaintiff, 'In consideration of your services as the practical manager in working our patents, we hereby agree to give you one-third share of the patents.' It was contended by the defendants that the promise was made in respect of the plaintiff's past services and therefore the plaintiff could not enforce the promise against them because he himself had supplied no consideration for it. Bowen LJ found for the plaintiff, stating that there was an implied promise that the plaintiff's services would be paid for and that the share of the patents would be regarded as such payment, despite the lack of a previous request by the defendants for the plaintiff to supply his services.

The principle in *Lampleigh* v *Braithwait* has been affirmed and restated by Lord Scarman in *Pao On* v *Lau Yiu Long* [1979] 3 All ER 65 as follows:

> An act done before the giving of a promise to make a payment or to confer some other benefit can sometimes be consideration for the promise. The act must have been done at the promisor's request, the parties must have understood that the act was to be remunerated further by a payment or the conferment of some other benefit and payment, or the conferment of a benefit must have been legally enforceable had it been promised in advance.

So far we have expressed the principle in *Lampleigh* v *Braithwait* as an exception to the rule of past consideration, and on the face of things this certainly appears to be the case. A different viewpoint is that it is not such an exception but merely reflects the normal requirement of the need for consideration. If, for example, one asks a mechanic to repair one's car, but at the time no mention is made as regards payment, this is clearly not a question of past consideration but a question of normal commercial practice. There is no question, usually at least, of the mechanic not being paid (or doing something for nothing) once the car has been fixed. What is at issue is the amount to be paid, this matter being resolved in the subsequent promise.

Statutory exceptions

1. Limitation Act 1980, s 27(5)

This provides that if a debtor acknowledges a debt it shall be deemed to accrue, for the purpose of calculating the commencement of the limitation period, from the date of the acknowledgement and not before. The acknowledgement need not necessarily be a promise to pay the debt by the debtor, though if it should take on this form the effect will still be to extend the period, despite the fact that the consideration for the promise is the antecedent debt and is thus in the past. See *Dungate* v *Dungate* [1965] 3 All ER 818 for an application of the provision. The provision does not have the effect of renewing the enforceability of a debt that is already statute-barred.

2. Bills of Exchange Act 1882, s 27

An antecedent debt, while normally regarded as past consideration, though not invariably so, will be good consideration for a bill of exchange.

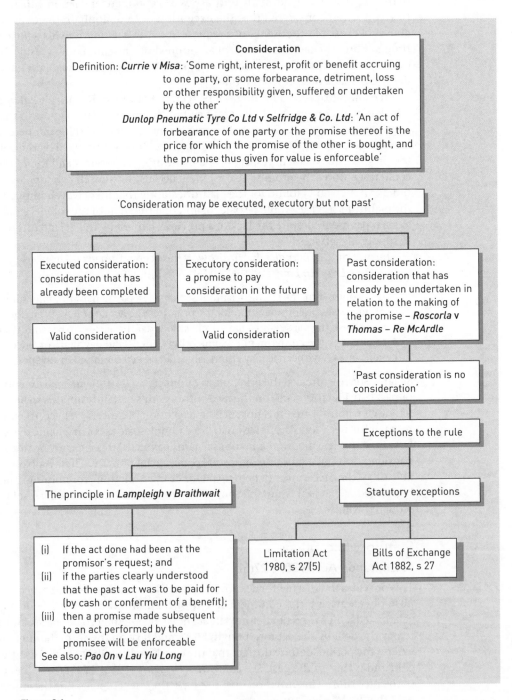

Consideration

Definition: ***Currie* v *Misa***: 'Some right, interest, profit or benefit accruing to one party, or some forbearance, detriment, loss or other responsibility given, suffered or undertaken by the other'

Dunlop Pneumatic Tyre Co Ltd* v *Selfridge & Co. Ltd: 'An act of forbearance of one party or the promise thereof is the price for which the promise of the other is bought, and the promise thus given for value is enforceable'

'Consideration may be executed, executory but not past'

Executed consideration: consideration that has already been completed

Valid consideration

Executory consideration: a promise to pay consideration in the future

Valid consideration

Past consideration: consideration that has already been undertaken in relation to the making of the promise – *Roscorla* v *Thomas* – *Re McArdle*

'Past consideration is no consideration'

Exceptions to the rule

The principle in *Lampleigh* v *Braithwait*

(i)   If the act done had been at the promisor's request; and
(ii) if the parties clearly understood that the past act was to be paid for (by cash or conferment of a benefit);
(iii) then a promise made subsequent to an act performed by the promisee will be enforceable

See also: *Pao On* v *Lau Yiu Long*

Statutory exceptions

Limitation Act 1980, s 27(5)

Bills of Exchange Act 1882, s 27

Figure 3.1

Consideration must move from the promisee though not necessarily to the promisor

Objective 3

The rule that consideration must move from the promisee means that a person can only enforce a promise made to them if they can show that they have provided consideration for that promise. An example of the principle can be seen in ***Price v Easton*** (1833) 4 B & Ad 433 where Price owed the plaintiff £13 and agreed to work for the defendant who promised to pay Price's wages to the plaintiff, but in the event failed to do so. It was held that the plaintiff could not recover the £13 from the defendant as no consideration had moved from the plaintiff.

An exchange of promises, however, can amount to consideration.

Example

If *A* promises to give *B* £5000 and *B* promises to give a car to *C*, *A* can enforce the contract against *B* if *B* fails to deliver the car to *C* since the contract between *A* and *B* is based on their promises.

In truth, the principle is a corollary of the rule requiring privity of contract between the parties to a contract. In other words, only parties to a contract can enforce the contract against the other, but in order to be a party to a contract, one must be a party to the bargain and therefore also provide consideration. The decision in ***Price v Easton*** was decided on both grounds, one judge, Lord Denman, stating that the plaintiff would not succeed as he could not 'show any consideration for the promise moving from him to the defendant'.

For more on privity of contract refer to Chapter 19.

Another judge, Littledale J, based his decision on the fact that 'no privity is shown between the plaintiff and the defendant'.

The reasonings of the two judges in ***Price v Easton*** can be seen clearly in the case of ***Tweddle v Atkinson*** (1861) 1 B & S 393 which also illustrates the second part of the principle, that consideration need not move to the promisor. In this case, the plaintiff's father and prospective father-in-law agreed with each other that they would pay the plaintiff £100 and £200 respectively in consideration of the plaintiff's intended marriage and, in fact, confirmed that agreement in writing after the marriage. The father-in-law died before he paid his £200 and the plaintiff sued the executors to recover the moneys. It was held that his action would fail as he had not furnished any consideration and he was not a party to the contract, even though it was made for his benefit. He could not enforce the contract since no consideration had moved away from him. The only person who could enforce the contract would have been the plaintiff's father, since he could show that consideration had moved away from him, though, of course, he would not benefit from the contract. It was not required of him that he show that the promisor, the father-in-law, had received the consideration but merely that something had moved away from himself. It should be noted that the Law Commission in its Report No. 242, *Privity of Contract: Contracts for the Benefit of Third Parties* (1996), has recommended that this rule be abolished as part of its reforms of the doctrine of privity of contract. The effect of such proposals being adopted would be to open up the possibility, in cases such as ***Tweddle v Atkinson***, of plaintiff third parties succeeding in their actions.

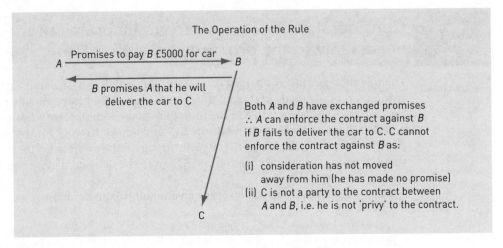

Figure 3.2

Consideration must be sufficient though not necessarily adequate

Consideration must be valuable

Objective
4

The principle we are examining here is sometimes simply referred to as a principle requiring the consideration to have some value, namely, economic value, and there is nothing errone-ous in this expression of the rule, though it fails to make the distinction between 'adequate' and 'sufficient' consideration. To the layperson there is no distinction between these terms but in a legal context the distinction is profound. The expression 'adequacy' of considera-tion is used to describe the reciprocal elements of the bargain, that is, the quid pro quo of the contract. This is the aspect that is most important to the parties to the contract since it is the factor that decides whether an individual has made a 'good' sale or purchase in eco-nomic terms. The term 'sufficiency' of consideration is the aspect that is of most concern to the lawyers since this expression describes not the economic value or otherwise of the con-sideration, but whether the consideration can exist as such in the eyes of the law as support-ing a simple contract.

Adequacy of consideration

It has been settled for many years that the courts will not make any inquiry as to whether the consideration given by the parties is adequate or not. In other words, the courts will not make a comparative economic evaluation of the consideration proffered by each party to the contract. The courts seek merely to establish that the consideration has a degree of eco-nomic value and do not inquire into the relative values of the consideration contained in the contract. The law is not concerned, barring allegations of fraud, with bad bargains where the relative values of consideration are disproportional. There is adequate consideration in a contract for the sale of a Rolls-Royce for a hairpin since both items have an economic value, albeit widely disparate, and, in the absence of fraud, there is a good contract here. A modern example of the principle can be seen in the following case.

Chappell & Co. Ltd v *Nestlé Co. Ltd* [1960] AC 87

The plaintiffs owned the copyright to a piece of music entitled 'Rockin' Shoes'. *X* made records of the tune which they sold to Nestlé, the defendants, for 4d each, who then offered them to the public for 1s 6d each plus three wrappers from Nestlé 6d chocolate bars. The wrappers were thrown away on receipt. The main object of Nestlé Ltd was to promote and sell their chocolate, though a profit was also made on the sale of the records. The plaintiffs sued the defendants for breach of copyright, relying on s 8 of the Copyright Act 1956 which provided that a person can make a record of a musical work provided it is designed for retail sale and royalties of 6 per cent 'of the ordinary retail selling price' were paid to the owner of the copyright. The defendants based their royalty fee on 1s 6d and the plaintiffs refused this on the basis that the money consideration was only part of the price and that the wrappers should also be taken into account in assessing the royalty fee. It was held that judgement should be given to the plaintiffs since the wrappers were certainly part of the consideration in that they represented an economic value, albeit one that might be very small. Lord Somervill stated:

> A contracting party can stipulate for what consideration he chooses. A peppercorn does not cease to be good consideration if it is established that the promisee does not like pepper and will throw away the corn.

A modern application of the rule can be seen in the case of **Midland Bank Trust Co. Ltd v Green** [1981] AC 513 where a father, to avoid an option granted to his son, sold a farm to his wife for £500 even though it was valued at more than £40,000. In the Court of Appeal, it was held that a sale at such an undervalued price could not amount to a sale for 'money or money's worth'. The House of Lords reversed the decision, stating that the court would not inquire into the adequacy as long as the consideration was real. There was thus a good contract between the parties.

The fact that the consideration must have an economic value means that simple love and affection cannot amount to adequate consideration. Similarly in **White v Bluett** (1853) 23 LJ Ex 36, the court held that a son's promise to stop boring his father by constantly complaining in return for his father's promise not to sue him on a promissory note was not good consideration.

Sufficiency and insufficiency of consideration

Objective 5

In discussing sufficiency of consideration we are analysing situations where a contract has been formed on the basis of a promise by one of the parties which, while being adequate in that it has an economic value, is not recognised by the law as amounting to consideration sufficient to support a simple contract. The consideration, in addition to amounting to an economic value, must be of a type recognised by law. Where a person promises to do something which they are already bound to do because the law has imposed that obligation on them, then that promise does not furnish sufficient consideration to support a simple contract. Merely repeating an obligation already imposed on a promisee amounts to a promise to do nothing at all.

The situations where the law finds the consideration to be insufficient fall into two principal categories:

1 where there is a performance of an existing obligation; and
2 where there is a promise to pay part of a debt.

Performance of existing obligations

This category may be further subdivided as follows:

1. Where a public duty is imposed by law

Very often certain persons, by their official status, or because of obligations imposed on them by the law, are obliged to carry out or do things in a certain way in order to discharge the public duties required of them. The carrying out of the public duties imposed on them by the law is not recognised by the law when it is used to support a simple contract. The leading case in this field is *Collins* v *Godefroy* (1831) 1 B & Ad 950, where the plaintiff attended and gave evidence at a civil trial by reason of a subpoena issued by the defendant. Afterwards the defendant promised to pay him a fee of six guineas. It was held that the plaintiff could not recover the moneys owed since he had furnished no consideration for the promise because he was already legally obliged to attend the trial. His consideration, in other words, was insufficient to support the promise of the defendant.

The issue of existing public duties has proved a particular problem in respect to public authorities, especially the police, over the years.

Glassbrook Bros v *Glamorgan County Council* [1925] AC 270

In this case, a colliery manager applied for police protection for his mine during a strike. He insisted that the mine could only be protected by having police officers actually billeted on the colliery premises. The police authorities considered that the colliery could be adequately protected by units of police officers patrolling the area in the vicinity of the mine, but nevertheless agreed to billet police officers at the premises provided the manager agreed to pay the specified rate. The bill for the protection amounted to £2,300, which the manager refused to pay, indicating that the police protection amounted to insufficient consideration since the police were already under an existing public duty to protect the premises. The House of Lords held that while it was true that the police were under a public duty to protect the premises, they were entitled to exercise their discretion as to the level of protection required. If the police considered that the premises would be adequately protected by an external mobile force, then any level of security over and above that, as insisted on by the manager, amounted to good and sufficient consideration to support the promise of the mine manager to pay the £2,300.

The House of Lords in the above case relied heavily on the earlier case of *England* v *Davidson* (1840) 11 Ad and El 856, where the defendant offered a reward to anyone who gave information that would lead to the conviction of a certain felon. The plaintiff, a police constable, supplied the information and claimed the reward. The defendant refused to pay and alleged in his defence that the plaintiff had done no more than the public duty imposed on him by the law to supply such information. The defendant also stated that such a contract was contrary to public policy. The basis for this is that to allow officials such as police officers to claim in circumstances where they were already under an existing public duty to act would be to risk the promotion of corruption and extortion. Both these defences were rejected by the court, the first on the ground that there were certain services a police officer was not required to render and clearly these services can amount to sufficient consideration in the proper circumstances. The second defence was rejected on the basis that to hold a contract void as being contrary to public policy requires very clear grounds for doing so and the courts do not readily accede to such a finding, particularly in cases of reward since the effect here is to encourage and promote the interests of justice.

The principles and decisions in the above two cases have also been seen in the following case.

Harris v Sheffield United Football Club Ltd [1987] 2 All ER 838

Police officers were required to be on duty within the grounds of the club when matches were being played there. The club was required to pay for 'special police services' when these were provided at the request of the club. The club refused to pay for these services on the basis that the police were merely carrying out their normal public duties in ensuring the maintenance of law and order and thus provided insufficient consideration for the promise of the club to pay for those services. The court held that the police provided more than their public duty required of them and therefore they were entitled to charge and claim for the moneys owed to them in respect of the 'special police services'.

This case, however, was distinguished in the case of **Leeds United Football Club v Chief Constable of West Yorkshire Police**.

Leeds United Football Club v Chief Constable of West Yorkshire Police [2012] EWHC 2113 (QB)

In this case, Leeds United Football Club challenged the lawfulness of charges made for the provision of 'special police services' under the Police Act 1996 on match days. The issue was whether the police were entitled to recoup from the club the costs of policing and crowd control carried out in the immediate vicinity of the club premises or whether they were confined to recovering the costs of special police services provided on land which was owned, leased or directly controlled by the club. The immediate vicinity was described as a 'footprint'. In the present case, no part of the footprint extended beyond a distance of 200 m from the club premises. It contained parts of the public highway, some parking areas, including a car park where until recently coaches would disgorge visiting fans, and the surrounding area where the Leeds United fans would confront them. It was held that police were not entitled to recoup from a football club the costs of policing and crowd control carried out on land which was in the immediate vicinity of the club but was not owned, leased or directly controlled by it.

The court heard evidence that the policing of football matches had a considerable drain on police resources as a whole, reduced the ability of the police to carry out their regular policing activities and could not be considered to be 'normal' policing activity. Previously, as can be seen from the **Harris v Sheffield United** case, football clubs would only be charged for special police services on a club's own land and the police would bear the cost of policing outside of the grounds on the basis that it fell within the traditional duty of the police to keep the peace and maintain public order. As the costs of policing escalated and there were more pressures on the use of public funds, attempts were made to try to recoup the costs from the clubs as they were responsible for hosting the matches. The result of this was that the opportunity was taken to broaden the basis of the claims by the police so as to include policing within the vicinity of the stadium, known as the 'footprint', without regard as to whether the land belonged to the club or was under its control. The expression 'footprint' had no statutory basis and indeed it was merely a pragmatic method of identifying potential 'trouble spots'. The club argued that by charging for policing beyond its own land or land that it controlled, the police were seeking payment for simply discharging their normal common law duty to keep the peace, prevent crime and protect the public.

While this submission was accurate and accorded with the common law principle there were exceptions to it, as seen in the *Glassbrook* case. This exception is now embedded in the Police Act 1996, s 25, which states:

25. – Provision of special services.

(1) The chief officer of police of a police force may provide, at the request of any person, special police services at any premises or in any locality in the police area for which the force is maintained, subject to the payment to the local policing body of charges on such scales as may be determined by that body.

The West Yorkshire Police attempted to argue that because the disputed areas were to all intents and purposes deserted on non-match days, the need for intense policing on match days implicitly meant that such policing could be categorised as 'special police services' for which they were entitled to charge. The court considered that the costs of policing within the 'footprint' fell within the normal police duty to keep the peace. Eady J referred to the case of *Reading Festival Ltd v West Yorkshire Police Authority* [2006] EWCA Civ 524 in which Scott Baker LJ had stated that 'special police services' would ordinarily require the presence of one of two key features: either the services would have been asked for but would be beyond what the police considered necessary to meet their public-duty obligations, or they would be services which, if the police did not provide them, the asker would have to provide from his own or other resources. Neither of those two features was present in the *Leeds United* case as the club had never requested services which went beyond those thought by the police to be necessary, nor were the policing requirements outside the stadium, but within the footprint, and were such as the club would have had to make provision for from its own resources.

The court considered that while s 25 indicated that special police services 'may' be provided at the request of the club, the police had discretion whether to respond to that request. On the other hand, where attendance by officers was necessary to keep the peace or to prevent violence, a common law duty arose which had to be complied with; there was thus concurrence with the decision in the *Glassbrook* case. Thus it was held that the police could not recover the costs of policing in respect of some designated 'footprint' that was not owned, leased or controlled by the relevant club. It is noticeable that the case was not principally argued on a sufficiency of consideration basis but on a public law basis. Nevertheless, the analogy is clear and no doubt because the court was using the authorities of *Glassbrook* and *Harris* a similar decision would also be reached on sufficiency of consideration grounds.

It can be seen in the above cases that the courts will very often find on a matter of public policy, rather than the presence of consideration, in deciding that there is sufficient consideration to support the promisor's promise. In some circumstances, however, the finding of good consideration on a matter of policy is not possible and, in these circumstances, the courts can go to extraordinary lengths to find for the existence of sufficient consideration. Such an instance may be seen in the following case.

Ward v *Byham* [1956] 2 All ER 318

An unmarried couple lived together from 1949 to 1954. In 1950, they had a child. However, in 1954, the man turned the woman out of their house, keeping and looking after the child. A few months later the woman, the plaintiff, requested that the child be returned to live with her. The defendant replied, offering her the child, together with £1 per week maintenance, on condition, first, that the child could decide for herself whether or not she wanted to live with her mother and, second, that the plaintiff could 'prove that she would be well looked after and happy'. The child decided that she did want to live with her mother and the defendant relinquished her to the mother for some seven months, paying the agreed £1 per week maintenance. The plaintiff then married another man and the defendant promptly ceased to make any further payments. The plaintiff sued for breach of contract and the defendant pleaded s 42 of the National Assistance Act 1948. The provision stated that the mother of an illegitimate child was bound to maintain that child. The defendant alleged that the mother had done no more than fulfil a duty imposed on her by law in return for the promise of the £1 per week maintenance, and that therefore her consideration was insufficient to support the defendant's promise of maintenance.

The Court of Appeal held that the plaintiff had exceeded the duty imposed on her by s 42 since, while the mother of an illegitimate child is bound to maintain the child, she is not necessarily bound to 'look after the child well' nor make it 'happy'. The plaintiff therefore had provided sufficient consideration for the promise of the defendant and was successful in her action.

Denning LJ significantly went further than this and stated that the defendant would be bound even if the plaintiff had done no more than the duty imposed on her by law since 'a promise to perform an existing duty, or the performance of it, should be regarded as good consideration, because it is a benefit to the person to whom it is given'. This view was not shared by other members of the court. He qualified this statement, however, in **Williams v Williams** [1957] 1 All ER 305, adding, 'so long as there is nothing in the transaction which is contrary to the public interest'.

2. Where the claimant is bound by the provisions of an existing contractual obligation owed to the defendant

A claimant provides insufficient consideration to support a promise made by the defendant if the claimant merely performs, or promises to perform, an obligation already owed by the claimant to the defendant by virtue of a previous contract made between them.

Stilk v Myrick (1809) 2 Camp 317

The plaintiff entered into a contract to sail a ship from London to the Baltic and back. During the voyage, two crew members jumped ship and subsequently the captain promised to divide the wages due to these two men between the rest of the crew since the ship was now short-handed as he had been unable to find replacements. On returning to London the captain refused to pay the extra wages and, when sued, alleged that the plaintiff had done no more than that which he was already contractually obliged to do, and that this could not therefore amount to sufficient consideration for the extra wages. The court agreed with this reasoning and found for the defendant captain.

The basis of the court's decision ignored the reasoning in an earlier decision contained in *Harris v Watson* (1791) Peake 102. The facts of this case were very similar to *Stilk v Myrick* but here the decision was based on what is known today as **economic duress**. In other words, the reason the claim was disallowed was that if an emergency arose, such as a ship being short-handed, it would otherwise be possible for the rest of the crew to 'hold a gun to the head' of the captain and demand extra money. Lord Kenyon in the *Harris* case thought that the rule was founded on the ground of public policy, while in *Stilk* Lord Ellenborough denied this and stated that the proper reasoning was that the contract was void for lack of sufficient consideration, the seaman being under an existing contractual duty. A better view may be that the rule relating to existing duties not amounting to sufficient consideration is based on the possibility of the occurrence of economic duress.

For more on duress refer to Chapter 11.

The decision in *Stilk v Myrick* might have been different if the claimant could have shown that he did something over and above his pre-existing contractual obligations.

Hartley v Ponsonby (1857) 7 E & B 872

In this case, where the facts were similar to those in *Stilk v Myrick*, the plaintiff was successful in his claim. The court, however, found that so many of the crew had deserted the ship in this case that the nature of the voyage had changed. The ship had become so short-handed that it had now become hazardous to proceed. The remaining crew had not contracted for such a voyage, and therefore they were held to be discharged from their existing contractual duties and free to make a new contract.

Both the principle in *Stilk v Myrick* and the exception propounded in *Hartley v Ponsonby* have been affirmed in *North Ocean Shipping Co. Ltd v Hyundai Construction Co. Ltd (The Atlantic Baron)* [1979] QB 705. More recently, however, the principle and the qualification to it have been subject to further discussion and analysis in *Williams v Roffey Bros & Nicholls (Contractors) Ltd*. The case requires very careful consideration since the ramifications of the decision could potentially go far beyond the boundaries of sufficiency of consideration and, indeed, raise questions about the doctrine of consideration generally.

Williams v Roffey Bros & Nicholls (Contractors) Ltd [1990] 1 All ER 512

The facts were that the defendant building contractors entered into a contract to refurbish a block of 27 flats. They subcontracted the joinery work to the plaintiff for a price of £20,000. It was an implied term of the subcontract that the plaintiff would receive interim payments for completed work. The plaintiff received £16,000 for completing work on the roof, nine flats and preliminary work on the remaining flats. This sum represented 80 per cent of the contract price though in fact the plaintiff still had far more than 20 per cent of the work to complete. The plaintiff thus found himself in financial difficulties because his initial price was too low and he had failed to supervise his workforce adequately. The defendants, who were under a penalty clause in the main contract if the work was not completed on time, became aware of the plaintiff's difficulties. The defendants agreed to pay the plaintiff an extra £10,300 based on a sum of £575 per flat on completion to ensure that he continued the work and completed the work on time. The plaintiff completed a further eight flats and the defendants made one further payment of £1,500. The plaintiff stopped work and brought an action for £10,847. The defendants denied their liability and, in particular, denied they were liable to pay any part of the £10,300 since the promise to pay these moneys was not supported by sufficient consideration from the plaintiff. The plaintiff was already under an existing contractual duty to complete the flats and as a result this could not amount to sufficient consideration to support the promise to pay the extra £10,300. Further, the defendants argued that the additional sums were only payable when the work was completed and that, as the plaintiff had left the site before this was done, he was not entitled to the extra moneys. However, both at first instance and in the Court of Appeal, it was held that the subcontractor was entitled to the contract price, less a deduction for defects.

The main argument in the case surrounded the problem of sufficiency of consideration and whether it existed to support the promise to pay the additional price of £575 per flat completed. At first instance the judge found that the contractors, the defendants, had agreed too low a price with the subcontractor and that this was clearly contrary to their interests – they would never get the job done unless they paid more money. The judge concluded that the agreement to pay the additional moneys was in both the parties' interests and that the agreement did not fail for lack of consideration. On the face of things the decision appears to be wrong since clearly on orthodox theory the subcontractor was already under an existing contractual duty to the defendants and this could not therefore amount to 'good' consideration. It may well be the case that the subcontractor had put in too low a price in his bid for the work, but it is not for the court to rewrite the contract simply because the plaintiff had made a bad bargain. It is always possible for the parties to abandon the contract by agreement and enter into a new one if they so wish. No evidence of this was forthcoming in the facts of the case.

On appeal to the Court of Appeal, the defendants indicated that they hoped to obtain three principal benefits from the agreement, namely, getting the job finished, avoiding any penalties and avoiding the trouble of engaging new carpenters. The defendants nevertheless maintained that these benefits were not benefits of law since the plaintiff was already bound by his contractual duties to carry out the contract. The Court of Appeal held that the defendants were obliged to pay the extra moneys due and that the plaintiff had provided sufficient consideration to support the promise of the defendants.

In the Court of Appeal, Glidewell LJ expressed the law in the following terms:

(i) if *A* has entered into a contract with *B* to do work for, or to supply goods or services to, *B* in return for payment by *B* and (ii) at some stage before *A* has completely performed his obligations under the contract, *B* has reason to doubt whether *A* will, or will be able to, complete his side of the bargain, and (iii) *B* thereupon promises *A* an additional payment in return for *A*'s promise to perform his contractual obligations on time and (iv) as a result of giving his promise *B* obtains in practice a benefit, or obviates a disbenefit, and (v) *B*'s promise is not given as a result of economic duress or fraud on the part of *A*, then (vi) the benefit to *B* is capable of being consideration for *B*'s promise, so that the promise will be legally binding.

On the face of things, the decision seems to go completely contrary to **Stilk v Myrick**, though Glidewell LJ was at pains to affirm the decision in that case and stated that his decision in **Williams v Roffey Bros** was merely a refinement of **Stilk v Myrick**. It will be recalled that in **Stilk v Myrick** Lord Ellenborough approved of the decision in **Harris v Watson** but not on the basis of the decision, that is, the application of public policy; instead he relied on the lack of consideration. It might be said then that the rule relating to sufficiency of consideration was a means of applying a crude notion of economic duress, which was unknown in a substantive form until recent times. If this is the case, then it may be possible to extrapolate a principle that an existing duty may be good consideration in the absence of economic duress or fraud on the part of the claimant, provided the defendant obtains a benefit in fact from the existing duty being executed. Such a proposition would also give credibility to Lord Denning's comments in **Ward v Byham** and **Williams v Williams**, above, and which appeared to be tacitly approved of in Glidewell's judgement. Further, the proposition would also support and explain the existence of the exception to the rule in **Stilk v Myrick** where a promise to perform, or the performance of, a pre-existing contractual obligation to a *third party* can be valid consideration, as expressed in **Pao On v Lao Yiu Long** and **New Zealand Shipping Co. Ltd v A M Satterthwaite & Co. Ltd, The Eurymedon** [1975] AC 154 (*see* below).

It should be noted that promissory estoppel could not be pleaded by the claimant in the case since this cannot be used as a means of bringing an action. Clearly the case could give rise to a great deal of discussion, not least an argument that the stance taken by the Court of Appeal is a move towards an adoption of a law of obligations, which is not based on the doctrine of consideration. Indeed, the role played by promissory estoppel itself, as we shall see later, takes us somewhat nearer this result. In any event, the emergence of a formal substantive doctrine of economic duress may well sound the death-knell of **Stilk v Myrick**.

The decision in *Roffey* suffers from one other major objection in that, even if it is interpreted that the obtaining of the benefit or the obviating of the disbenefit by Roffey Bros amounts to consideration for their promise to pay the extra moneys to Williams, the consideration does not move from the promisee, i.e. Williams, as required in the classical rules of consideration and contract. The decision as it stands is therefore in conflict with two very well-established principles of the doctrine of consideration and it is because of this conflict that the judgement in *Roffey* has come under increasing judicial criticism. Thus, in **South Caribbean Trading Ltd v Trafigura Beheer** [2005] 1 Lloyd's Rep 128, Colman J expressed serious doubts about the correctness of the reasoning in *Roffey*, considering that the decision is inconsistent with the long-standing rule that consideration must move from the promisee. He pointed out that in *Roffey*, Glidewell LJ had relied heavily on the **Pao On** case which involved a tripartite agreement in which a pre-existing contractual obligation to a third party could amount to valid consideration.

> ## Example
>
> If there is a promise by *A* to *B* to perform a contractual obligation that *A* already owes to *C*, this could amount to consideration as against *B*. This is correct since here for the additional promise by *A* to *B*, consideration has moved away from *A* since he has made an additional promise to perform the obligation he owes to *C*. This does not occur in a bilateral contract since *A* is only promising to *B* what he is already bound to perform under the contract. Colman J pointed out that Glidewell LJ had effectively substituted a different rule 'that the promisor must by his promise have conferred a benefit on the other party' from that of the rule that consideration must move from the promisee.

One has to be guarded in going as far as this though. The members of the Court of Appeal in *Roffey* made it very clear that the principle enunciated in the case did not go so far as to change the rule of consideration as regards the initial formation of the contract, and its application was confined to the alteration of obligations within existing contracts. This seems to be a reasonable and pragmatic approach since otherwise the requirement for consideration would amount to a fetter within commercial contracts since the commercial reality in such a context is that such contracts are altered and 'to describe one set of promises, in this context, as gratuitous, or *nudum pactum*, seems paradoxical and is prima facie implausible', per Lord Wilberforce in **The Eurymedon [1975] AC 154**. In **Dresdner Kleinwort Ltd v Atrill [2013] EWCA Civ 394,** the argument that the staff gave nothing for the promise by the bank to pay a guaranteed employment bonus and which was therefore unenforceable by the employees was roundly rejected by Elias LJ. Apart from considering that the proposition was wrong as a matter of fact in that the presence of the bonus encouraged the staff to remain at the bank, Elias LJ considered that in a pre-existing contractual relationship there was a very strong presumption that the promise to pay the bonus was intended to be legally binding and hence enforceable. Attempts to place limitations on the application can also be seen in cases such as **Re Selectmove** [1995] 2 All ER 531, as discussed later in this chapter. Not all judges have been convinced that *Roffey* does have such a narrow application, as illustrated in **Anangel Atlas Compania Naviera v IHI Co. Ltd (No. 2)** [1990] 2 Lloyd's Rep 526, and in truth it may be extremely difficult to confine the effects of *Roffey* to the very narrow circumstances in which it appears to arise.

It should be noted that the rule that consideration must move from the promisee was threatened by the Law Commission in its 1996 Report No. 242, where it recommended the abolition of the rule in furtherance of its reform of the doctrine of privity of contract, although only to the extent that it allows third parties to enforce a contract made in their favour. The requirement for consideration will still prevail in the contract between the original parties.

From a practical point of view in **Roffey**, it is somewhat perverse that, if the defendants had not taken the trouble to increase the fees owed to the claimant, they could merely have allowed him to carry on with the contract and could then have sued him for their losses under the penalty clause when the plaintiff inevitably failed to complete the work and was in breach of contract.

The problem facing the courts is clearly one of attempting to hold business persons to their promises. While the Court of Appeal in **Roffey** has attempted to do this by way of a narrow departure from normal principles, another way forward is by varying the doctrine of estoppel. As indicated earlier, this was not available in the **Roffey** case itself because of the fact that usually promissory estoppel cannot be used as initiating a course of action in that it is only available as a defence. The Australian courts have, however, attempted to enforce such promises by adopting a flexible concept of estoppel as seen in **Waltons Stores Interstate Ltd v Maher** (1988) 164 CLR 387 and **Commonwealth of Australia v Vermayen** (1990) 170 CLR 394. In New Zealand, another variation can be seen in the Court of Appeal decision of **Antons Trawling Co. Ltd v Smith** [2003] 2 NZLR 23 where reliance alone was held to be sufficient to render the alteration promise enforceable provided the claimant could demonstrate that he had acted on the promise and its terms so as to be able to claim the extra money due in the promise. These approaches to the problem at least leave the principles of consideration in contract intact.

For more on this aspect of promissory estoppel, see later in this chapter. See under 'Part-payment of debt, 1. The common law rule'.

3. Existing contractual duties owed to third parties

An existing contractual duty owed to a third party may amount to sufficient consideration in return for a promise given by the promisee. This exception is usually expressed in the context of existing contractual duties, though there appears to be no reason why it could not equally apply to existing public duties. However, such instances would be rare since such duties are largely imposed by statute.

A typical example of this exception can be seen in the case of **Shadwell v Shadwell** (1860) 9 CBNS 159, where the plaintiff's uncle wrote congratulating him on his engagement and promised to pay him £150 per annum until such time as he was earning £600 per annum as a chancery barrister. The plaintiff married and sued his uncle's executors on the promise. It was held that, even though the plaintiff was already contractually bound to marry, this was nevertheless good consideration for the uncle's promise.

For more on intention to create legal relations please refer to Chapter 4.

While **Shadwell v Shadwell** illustrates the point, it is of dubious authority not least because, as a family arrangement, it is questionable whether an intention to create a legal relationship existed or not. Further, it is doubtful whether the uncle intended the marriage to amount to consideration and, if he did not, where does the consideration lie?

The decision in **Shadwell v Shadwell** was followed in the case of **Chichester v Cobb** (1866) 14 LT 433 where the facts were somewhat, though not altogether, similar. The case which firmly establishes the principle contained in the exception is **Scotson v Pegg**.

Scotson v Pegg (1861) 6 H & N 295

The plaintiffs contracted with a third party, A, to deliver coal to A, or to the order of A. A then sold the coal to the defendant and directed the plaintiffs to deliver it to the defendant. The defendant entered into an agreement with the plaintiffs whereby, 'in consideration that the plaintiffs, at the request of the defendant, would deliver [the coal] to the defendant', the defendant promised to unload the coal at a fixed rate per day. The defendant failed to keep to his promise and, when sued for breach of contract, pleaded lack of sufficient consideration to support his promise. It was held that the defendant was liable and that the performance of an existing contractual duty could be consideration for a promise given by a third party. While the decision in the case would probably be correct today, it is deficient in that there is no definite statement as to where the consideration lies.

All three cases which tend to establish the principle have question marks hanging over them, though despite this they all positively direct us towards the principle. The question marks, however, are largely academic today and any doubts as to the probity of the principle have to be put on one side following the decision of the Privy Council in the following case.

New Zealand Shipping Co. Ltd v A M Satterthwaite & Co. Ltd, The Eurymedon [1975] AC 154

The facts of the case put simply were that the plaintiff made an offer to the defendant that if the defendant unloaded the plaintiff's goods, which the defendant was already obliged to do by virtue of a contract with a third party, the plaintiff would not hold the defendant liable for any damage to the goods. The question arose as to whether the existing contractual duty owed by the defendant to the third party could amount to consideration for the promise of the plaintiff. The majority decision of the court is best summed up in the words of Lord Wilberforce, who stated:

> An agreement to do an act which the promisor is under an existing obligation to a third party to do, may quite well amount to valid consideration and does so in the present case: the promisee obtains the benefit of a direct obligation which he can enforce. This proposition is illustrated and supported by *Scotson v Pegg* . . . which their Lordships consider to be good law.

It is of further significance that the decision in **The Eurymedon** was also supported in **Pao On v Lau Yiu Long**.

Part-payment of debt

1. The common law rule

Objective
6

We now need to consider the second area where the law considers the consideration to be insufficient. It should be said immediately that some authors treat this as part of the rules relating to existing contractual duties owed to the promisor. There is nothing wrong with this approach since here the debtor is attempting to show consideration by performing only part of what they are already contractually bound to do. It is, however, possible to distinguish this category in that what is in question here is whether some previous obligation owed has been discharged by only part of it being performed. By contrast, in the category already discussed we examined whether some new obligation could be supported by an existing contractual obligation. This difference is significant since in the previous category we were examining how the promisee could enforce the new obligations against the promisor. In the present category, we are examining how to prevent the promisor from enforcing obligations against the promisee which they, the promisor, had agreed not to so enforce. It is for this reason that promissory or equitable estoppel is so applicable to this category since, as we shall see, it can only be used as a defence to a course of action, not as a course of action itself.

The problem arising here occurs where X owes Y a sum of money and pays, or promises to pay, part of the amount owed, provided Y agrees to forgo the balance. The question now arises as to whether Y is bound by their promise. The general common law rule in English law is that all debts are payable in full and that any creditor is not bound to accept part of a debt in satisfaction of the whole amount owed.

The rule enunciated above is known as the rule in ***Pinnel's case*** (1602) 5 Co. Rep 117a, in which it was stated:

> Payment of a lesser sum on the day in satisfaction of a greater cannot be any satisfaction for the whole, because it appears to the Judges that by no possibility a lesser sum can be a satisfaction to the plaintiff for a greater sum. But the gift of a horse, hawk or robe, etc. in satisfaction is good. For it shall be intended that a horse, hawk or robe, etc. might be more beneficial to the plaintiff than the money in respect of some circumstance, or otherwise the plaintiff would not have accepted it in satisfaction . . . The payment and acceptance of parcel before the day in satisfaction of the whole would be a good satisfaction in regard to circumstance of time, for peradventure parcel of it before the day would be more beneficial to him than the whole at the day, and the value of satisfaction is not material.

Thus, while part-payment of debt is not sufficient consideration, such part-payment would be sufficient if some new element is included. The new element might be a different place of payment, or a different time, or some change in the nature of the consideration offered for satisfaction of the whole debt.

The introduction of the new element as amounting to full satisfaction of a debt is, however, subject to one qualification: the new element must be introduced at the request of the creditor, not the debtor. This factor is required to protect the creditor against a debtor who attempts to use some financial weakness of the creditor for his own purposes, or who attempts to use the threat of potential litigation on the part of the creditor as a means of reducing the amount payable.

D & C Builders Ltd v Rees [1966] 2 QB 617

The plaintiffs had done building work for the defendant for which they were owed £482. The plaintiffs pressed for payment for some six months and in fact were in dire financial straits. The defendant's wife, knowing of the financial difficulties, offered them £300 in full settlement, adding that if this was not accepted they would get nothing. The plaintiffs reluctantly agreed to this arrangement but once the cheque for £300 had cleared they sued for the balance. It was held that their claim would be successful, the Court of Appeal basing its decision on ***Pinnel's case***.

On the facts, the decision in ***D & C Builders Ltd v Rees*** is a correct application of ***Pinnel's case***, though today, with the development of the concept of economic duress, the arrangement would no doubt be void anyway. Given the development of economic duress, it is questionable whether the rule in ***Pinnel's case*** continues to serve any useful purpose, especially when it can result in inordinately unfair decisions. Such a situation occurred in the case of ***Foakes v Beer***, where the rule in ***Pinnel's case*** was nevertheless affirmed.

Foakes v Beer (1884) 9 App Cas 605

Mrs Beer had obtained judgement against Dr Foakes for £2,090 and some time later he asked for time to pay. The parties then entered a written agreement where Dr Foakes would pay £500 immediately and the balance by instalments. Mrs Beer agreed also that she would not 'take any proceedings whatever on the judgement'. The parties failed to take into account that a judgement debt carries interest from the date of the judgement. Some five years later Dr Foakes had paid the whole of the judgement debt; Mrs Beer claimed £360 for the interest on the debt. Dr Foakes refused to pay, relying on the agreement and the undertaking by Mrs Beer as a defence. It was held by the House of Lords that Mrs Beer could claim the £360, the court relying on the rule in *Pinnel's case*. Although the decision no doubt was correct in law, it has been subject to criticism, in particular from Lord Blackburn, who only reluctantly accepted the decision when confronted with powerful authorities in support of the rule in *Pinnel's case*, and commented:

> all men of business . . . do every day recognise and act on the ground that prompt payment of a part of their demand may be more beneficial to them than it would be to insist on their rights and enforce payment of the whole. Even where the debtor is perfectly solvent, and sure to pay at last, this is often so. Where the credit of the debtor is doubtful it must be more so.

How can the case of *Foakes* v *Beer* be reconciled with *D & C Builders Ltd* v *Rees?* The question is important since both decisions rest on the rule in *Pinnel's case*, though the effects are very different. In *Foakes* v *Beer*, it has been stated that the common law rule produces a harsh and unfair decision, while the application of the rule in *D & C Builders Ltd* v *Rees* is undoubtedly quite the opposite. The fact of the matter is that the circumstances of *Foakes* v *Beer* are somewhat exceptional, in that the rule in *Pinnel's case* was never formulated on the basis of the creditor acting in an unfair manner, but on the basis of an impecunious debtor attempting to wring an advantage out of the precarious financial position of the creditor by saying, 'Accept this or you won't get anything at all.' Dr Foakes was unfortunate enough to be caught by a rule which was never intended to apply to circumstances such as his own.

The rule in *Pinnel's case* continues to be good law and was reaffirmed in the Court of Appeal case of *Collier* v *P & M J Wright (Holdings) Ltd*.

Collier v *P & M J Wright (Holdings) Ltd* [2007] EWCA Civ 1329

The facts of the case were that Mr Collier ('C') was in partnership with a Mr Broadfoot ('B') and a Mr Flute ('F') and all were judgement debtors of Wright (Holdings) Ltd ('W'). C came to an arrangement with W whereby he agreed to pay one-third of the debt instalments over five years and this in fact he did. C's understanding was that the arrangement meant that he would not be liable for the remaining two-thirds of the debt and that W would pursue the other debtors separately for the outstanding amount. B and F were subsequently declared bankrupt and therefore W served a statutory demand on C for the outstanding amount. C applied to have the statutory demand set aside; however, the Court of Appeal, following *Pinnel's case* and *Foakes* v *Beer*, considered that the alleged agreement was essentially a debtor's promise to pay part of what he already owed. C attempted to set up a further exception to the rule in *Pinnel's case* by stating that the arrangement amounted to a collateral agreement between himself and W. The basis behind this was his agreement to pay part of the debt and to become severally liable for that part was a binding contract for good consideration so that C's liability for the rest of the debt was discharged. While it is true that any benefits from partial payment could be regarded in the same way as the 'horse, a hawk and a robe' argument discussed earlier, the Court of Appeal rejected this argument. Undoubtedly C would benefit from the agreement in the sense he would not be liable for any further contributions to the debt owed by B and F, but also he would lose certain benefits that he would have if he remained a joint debtor since if W decided to release B and F from the debt (because they had become bankrupt), then the effect of this would be also to discharge C automatically. He also gave up the possibility that if he predeceased B and F his liability would pass to B and F. Lady Arden considered that none of these factors could amount to good consideration since no benefit had moved to W. It follows from this that if a creditor agrees with a joint debtor to accept payment from him alone for his proportionate share, this does not result in a binding contract and thus no further exception to *Pinnel's case* arises from this position.

In the absence of an overturning of the rule in *Pinnel's case*, and with the concept of economic duress replacing this rule in cases like *D & C Builders Ltd* v *Rees*, a number of exceptions to the rule have developed. The most important of these can be found in the intervention of equity with the use of promissory estoppel.

2. The exceptions to the rule in *Pinnel's case*

There are three exceptions to the rule in *Pinnel's case*:

(a) the doctrine of promissory estoppel;

(b) cheques;

(c) **compositions with creditors**.

(a) The doctrine of promissory estoppel

The harshness of the application of the rule in *Pinnel's case*, as seen in *Foakes* v *Beer*, has been substantially mitigated by the modern development of the doctrine of **equitable estoppel**, now usually referred to as promissory estoppel in this context. The modern doctrine is founded on the following case.

Central London Property Trust Ltd v *High Trees House Ltd* [1947] KB 130

In September 1939, the plaintiffs leased a block of flats to the defendants at a ground rent of £2,500 per annum. In January 1940, many of the flats became vacant because of the prevailing war conditions and the plaintiffs reduced the ground rent to £1,250 in recognition of these factors. No time limit was fixed for the arrangement and the defendants continued to pay the reduced rent until 1945. In 1945, the flats were again full and in 1946 the receiver of the plaintiff company sought to recover the back rent for the last two quarters of 1945 and for future years. It was held by Denning J (as he then was) that the arrangement as to the reduced rent was only intended to apply while war conditions affected the letting of the flats. The flats were again full in June 1945, therefore Denning allowed the receivers to recover the full rent for the last two quarters of 1945 and for future years.

In fact, the plaintiffs were only testing their claim by suing for the last two quarters of 1945 and what they intended to do was to attempt to claim the arrears of the rent owed for the years from 1940 to June 1945, basing the claim on the rule in *Pinnel's case*. Whilst this action was not in issue in the case, Denning nevertheless turned his attention to whether such a claim would succeed. Undoubtedly, if the rule in *Pinnel's case* was applied to this problem, the plaintiffs' claim would succeed. The plaintiffs during discussion had promised to accept a lesser sum as payment for a greater sum, no consideration having been given by the defendants to support this promise and the exceptions to the rule in *Pinnel's case*, above, did not apply. Denning concluded, *obiter dicta*, that the plaintiffs would fail in such an action, relying on the operation of the doctrine of equitable estoppel as expressed in the nineteenth-century case of *Hughes* v *Metropolitan Railway Co. Ltd*.

Hughes v *Metropolitan Railway Co. Ltd* (1877) 2 App Cas 439

The appellant landlord gave his respondent tenant six months' notice to repair the premises let. Before the notice expired negotiations began between the parties for the sale of the reversion. These negotiations broke down and when the six months' notice expired the appellants brought an action for ejectment. It was held by the House of Lords that the opening of the negotiations by the appellants amounted to a promise that while they were going on, no action would be taken to enforce the notice. The tenant had done nothing to the premises because of his reliance on this promise, and thus the six months' notice ran from the date of the failure of the negotiations and not from the original date of the service of the notice. The tenant was entitled to have relief from the action to forfeit his lease. Lord Cairns stated the principle of equitable estoppel in the following terms:

> It is the first principle upon which all Courts of Equity proceed, that if parties who have entered into definite and distinct terms involving certain legal results – certain penalties or legal forfeiture – afterwards by their own act or with their own consent enter upon a course of negotiations which has the effect of leading one of the parties to suppose that the strict legal rights arising under the contract will not be enforced or will be kept in suspense, or held in abeyance, the person who otherwise might have enforced those rights will not be allowed to enforce them where it would be inequitable having regard to the dealings which have thus taken place between the parties.

On examining the *Hughes* case, Denning stated: 'I prefer to apply the principle that a promise intended to be binding, intended to be acted on and in fact acted on, is binding so far as its terms properly apply.' In *Combe* v *Combe* [1951] 2 KB 215, however, Denning J stated the doctrine of promissory estoppel in more accurate terms as:

> where one party has, by his words or conduct, made to the other a promise or assurance which was intended to affect the legal relations between them and to be acted on accordingly, then, once the other party has taken him at his word and acted on it, the one who gave the promise or assurance cannot afterwards be allowed to revert to the previous legal relations as if no such promise or assurance had been made by him, but he must accept their legal relations subject to the qualification which he himself has so introduced, even though it is not supported in point of law by any consideration, but only by his word.

Applying the doctrine as expressed by Denning, the plaintiffs in the *High Trees* case would clearly be estopped in any attempt to claim the arrears of rent from 1940 onwards.

While the doctrine of promissory estoppel, as expressed above, is fairly straightforward, there are certain aspects which emanate from the basic notion of the doctrine and which themselves can give rise to specific problems. These aspects require detailed consideration and are as follows:

1 the nature of the promise;
2 the doctrine is 'a shield not a sword';
3 whether the doctrine is suspensory or extinctive;
4 whether the promisee must act to their prejudice.

(1) *The nature of the promise.* The nature of the promise as stated in *High Trees* is that it must be clear and unequivocal. However, this alone is insufficient. Denning emphasised that there must be a clear and unequivocal promise by the promisor that he would not enforce his strict legal rights. Thus the promise must be intended to affect legal relations and not simply amount to a gratuitous privilege given to the promisee, as expressed in both *Woodhouse Israel Cocoa Ltd* v *Nigerian Produce Marketing Co. Ltd* [1972] AC 741 and *Scandinavian Trading Tanker Co. AB* v *Flota Petrolera Ecuatoriana, The Scaptrade* [1983] 2 All ER 763.

(2) *A shield not a sword.* It is well settled that the doctrine of promissory estoppel may only be used as a defence and not as a course of action, that is, it may be used as 'a shield and not a sword'. This principle was established in the case of *Combe* v *Combe* where, after a divorce, a husband promised to pay the ex-wife £100 per annum maintenance, but failed to make any payments. While she pressed him for payment, she did not in fact make any application

for maintenance to the divorce court. Nearly seven years after being awarded the decree absolute, the ex-wife brought an action for £675 representing arrears for six years nine months' maintenance. She alleged that her husband had made an unequivocal promise, intending that she would act on it and that she had in fact acted on that promise, and that the husband should therefore be estopped from going back on that promise. At first instance, the court upheld her claim but this decision was reversed in the Court of Appeal which held that the use of estoppel as a cause of action was an illegitimate extension of the principle. The reason for this rule is that to allow estoppel to be used in this manner would be completely contrary to the whole principle of the need for consideration in the law of contract since it would allow promises to be enforceable without consideration being present. Lord Denning took the opportunity to restate the position in the following way:

> The principle stated in the *High Trees* case . . . does not create new causes of action where none existed before. It only prevents a party from insisting upon his strict legal rights when it would be unjust to allow him to enforce them, having regard to the dealings which have taken place between the parties.

The principle as stated is an easy one for students to recall but it is an inaccurate statement. The principle gives the impression that only defendants can make use of promissory estoppel, but this is not necessarily the case. A claimant can rely on estoppel provided it does not form the main part of his action. *Cheshire, Fifoot and Furmston* refers back to the *Hughes* case and state that if the landlord had gone into possession, the tenant would have brought an action on the basis of the lease but used estoppel as an answer to the landlord's possible defence that he had a right to forfeit the lease. Here the principal action is based on the lease, with estoppel forming a subsidiary line of argument. Similarly if a buyer of goods stated to a seller that they would not insist on delivery of the goods according to the date in the contract, and subsequently refused to accept the goods delivered after this date because they were late, the seller could sue for breach of contract and use estoppel as a means of blocking the defence of lateness alleged by the buyer.

There have been attempts to reformulate the doctrine so as to allow actions to be based on it, chiefly by extending the principles found in the doctrine of proprietary estoppel, which does allow causes of action to be founded on such a doctrine. So far, however, these attempts have not been accepted in promissory estoppel and, in fact, were openly refuted in *Argy Trading Development Co. Ltd* v *Lapid Developments Ltd* [1977] 1 WLR 444. An attempt at pursuing such a claim arose in *Baird Textiles Holdings Ltd* v *Marks & Spencer plc* [2001] EWCA Civ 274, the facts of which have already been discussed. The claimant, apart from attempting to claim that an enforceable contract arose from conduct, also attempted to set up a claim on the basis that Marks & Spencer were estopped from denying its existence.

See Chapter 2 for the facts of *Baird Textiles Holdings Ltd v Marks & Spencer plc*.

The basis of the claim was that Marks & Spencer by its conduct in maintaining the contract induced the claimant to believe the relationship was a long-term one that could only be terminated by giving reasonable notice. Further, that during the subsistence of the contract Marks & Spencer would acquire such garments from the claimants in such quantities and at prices which in all the circumstances were reasonable and that Marks & Spencer would deal with the claimants in good faith and reasonably having regard to the objective of the relationship. In order to avoid the claim of promissory estoppel being dismissed on the basis that it was being used as a means of prosecuting an action, the counsel for the defendants attempted to rely on the Australian cases of *Waltons Stores Interstate Ltd* v *Maher* and *Commonwealth of Australia* v *Vermayen*. It was suggested that English law should follow the Australian model, which permits estoppel to create causes of actions in non-proprietary cases. This proposition was rejected by all of the judges. Morritt VC stated that promissory estoppel does not extend to enforcement of rights in the nature of the **Baird Textiles** claim. He confirmed that three decisions of the Court of Appeal – **Combe v Combe** [1951] 1 All ER 767; **Amalgamated Investment and Property Co. Ltd v Texas Commerce International Bank Ltd** [1981] 3 All ER 577; and **Western Fish Products Ltd v Penwith DC** [1981] 2 All ER 204 – all rejected the notion of estoppel in such situations. In the cases of **Combe v Combe** and **Texas Commerce**, it was stated that estoppel cannot create a cause of action; in **Western Fish Products** it was stated that proprietary or promissory estoppel may only create a cause of action if it was limited to cases involving property rights.

Thus it would seem that promissory estoppel cannot be used to set up an action except when the action is subordinate to the main part of the claimant's action, unless the Supreme Court decides to rewrite this orthodox principle in the future. Thus the **Baird Textiles** claim failed and the aphorism that promissory estoppel may 'only be used as a shield not as a sword' was affirmed.

(3) *Is the doctrine suspensory or extinctive?* In the **Hughes** case, it was seen that the rights of the landlord were merely suspended until the six months' notice from the date of the end of the negotiations for the sale of the reversion had lapsed. In **High Trees**, however, while the right to the full rent was only suspended until the ending of war conditions meant that the flats were again full, the right to the arrears of the rent lost while those conditions prevailed was effectively extinguished.

The leading case in this area is the decision of the House of Lords in **Tool Metal Manufacturing Co. Ltd v Tungsten Electric Co. Ltd**.

Tool Metal Manufacturing Co. Ltd v Tungsten Electric Co. Ltd [1955] 2 All ER 657

The appellants were the owners of a British patent and in April 1938 they contracted to give the respondents a licence to manufacture and sell certain alloys subject to the patent. The contract stipulated that if the respondent sold more than a certain quantity of the alloys, 'compensation' would be payable to the appellants. At the outbreak of the war the appellants agreed to suspend their compensation rights pending the negotiation of a new contract. The negotiations for the contract began in 1944 but soon afterwards broke down. In 1945, the respondents sued the appellants for breach of contract and they counter-claimed for the compensation payable as from 1 June 1945. The respondents' action was dismissed. In the Court of Appeal, the counter-claim by the appellants also failed since it was held that the agreement reached in 1939 operated to prevent the appellants claiming compensation until they had given reasonable notice to the respondents of their intention to revert to the terms of the original contract and that they had not given such notice to the respondents.

In September 1950, the appellants began a second action in which they claimed compensation as from 1 January 1947. The appellants alleged that their counter-claim in the first action amounted to reasonable notice of their intention to claim compensation. The claim was upheld at first instance, reversed in the Court of Appeal, whose decision in turn was reversed by the House of Lords. It is apparent from the case that the appellants' rights to arrears of compensation that had already fallen due had been extinguished and that rights to future compensation had only been suspended until such time as the agreement of 1939 had been cancelled by the appellants on giving the respondents reasonable notice of such cancellation.

Generally the view of promissory estoppel is that it is only suspensory in operation, except in cases where 'the promisee cannot resume his position', as stated by the Privy Council in **Emmanuel Ayodeji Ajayi v R T Briscoe (Nigeria) Ltd** [1964] 3 All ER 556. This approach is certainly consistent with the *Hughes* case, where the landlord clearly did not intend to give up his right to forfeit the lease for all time. If this approach is applied to *Foakes v Beer*, then the fact that Mrs Beer's right to the interest is merely suspended would be clearly offensive to equitable principles given her original undertaking. In order to reconcile this conflict, the better view would seem to be that the doctrine is suspensory, except where the promisee cannot resume his position or where there is an express or implied intention on the part of the promisor that he is giving up his rights forever. Applying such an approach to *High Trees* produces the result that rights to future rent may be revived by the giving of reasonable notice, while until such notice is given any instalments of rent at the reduced rate rendered the balance of this and other previous instalments irrecoverable and to that extent extinguished. Of course this result in *High Trees* might have been different if the promisor had indicated that the intention was only to give the promisee time to pay.

Denning in *Brikom Investments Ltd v Carr* [1979] QB 467 considered that there were certain exceptional cases where it might be impossible for the promisor to go back to his strict legal rights even though he had given reasonable notice to the promisee of his intention to do so. It is doubtful whether the courts would ever go so far as to allow the complete extinction of a promisee's strict legal rights in these circumstances, though this situation has not yet been tested in a case.

It is clear that there are considerable difficulties with this area. As Treitel points out, it is an area which is ripe for review in the House of Lords, pointing to Lord Hailsham's comment in the *Woodhouse* case, above, that the *High Trees* principle 'may need to be reviewed and reduced to a coherent body of doctrine by the courts'.

(4) *Must the promisee act to their prejudice?* It is clear from the *High Trees*, *R T Briscoe* and *Tool Metal* cases that, to invoke the doctrine of promissory estoppel, the promisee must have either acted on the promise of the promisor, or at least altered their position in reliance on the promise. It has largely been assumed that the promisee must have been prejudiced by their reliance on the promise. Indeed, one might consider that the whole *raison d'être* of promissory estoppel is the notion that it is inequitable to allow the promisor to withdraw from their promise, because that would lead to the promisee incurring some detriment. While the tenant suffered a detriment in the *Hughes* case, no such detriment or prejudice appears in the *High Trees* case.

In *W J Alan & Co. Ltd v El Nasr Export and Import Co.* [1972] 2 QB 189, Denning denied the need to prove that the promisee had suffered a detriment, and, in fact, repeated such views in *Brikom Investments Ltd v Carr*, although in both cases the other members of the Court of Appeal left the question open.

In the New Zealand case of *P v P* [1957] NZLR 854, the judge thought that the test should be based not on the position of the promisee but on 'whether it would be inequitable to allow the party seeking so to do to enforce the strict rights which he had induced the other party to believe will not be enforced'. Such an approach was also thought correct by Goff J in *Société Italo-Belge pour le Commerce et l'Industrie SA v Palm and Vegetable Oils (Malaysia) Sdn Bhd, The Post Chaser* [1982] 1 All ER 19, who insisted that all that was required to be proved was that some inequity could be shown to result by the promisor attempting to resile from his promise. He stated:

> The fundamental principle is . . . that the representor will not be allowed to enforce his rights where it would be inequitable having regard to the dealings which have thus taken place between the parties. To establish such inequity, it is not necessary to show detriment; indeed, the representee may have benefited from the representation, and yet it may be inequitable, at least without reasonable notice, for the representor to enforce his legal rights . . . But it does

not follow that in every case in which the representee has acted, or failed to act, in reliance on the representation, it will be inequitable for the representor to enforce his rights for the nature of the action or inaction may be insufficient to give rise to the equity, in which event a necessary requirement . . . for the application of the doctrine would not have been fulfilled.

Clearly this whole area is in need of review by the House of Lords since the remarks of Goff J go very much towards a view expressed by Lord Denning extra-judicially that resiling from a promise is itself inequitable and should give rise to an application of the doctrine. Such a stance is far too radical since it strikes at the heart of consideration itself. A bargain must be supported by consideration and while promissory estoppel might, correctly, be allowed as an exception to the general principle, to allow it to develop to the point of enforcing gratuitous promises generally is unacceptable at the present time.

(b) Cheques

It was stated earlier that a part-payment of debt may be good consideration if, at the creditor's request, it is made in a different form, or at a different place or time. The question that arises here is whether a cheque or other bill of exchange can amount to a different form of payment for the purposes of the exceptions to the rule in *Pinnel's case*. At one time, cheques were regarded as a different form of payment and thus formed an exception to the rule in *Pinnel's case*. This is no longer the position, as was made clear by Lord Denning in *D & C Builders Ltd v Rees*:

> No sensible distinction can be taken between payment of a lesser sum by cash and payment of it by cheque. The cheque, when given, is conditional payment. When honoured, it is actual payment. It is then just the same as cash. If a creditor is not bound when he receives a payment by cash, he should not be bound when he receives payment by cheque.

(c) Compositions with creditors

It is a common practice for a debtor who cannot pay their creditors in full to come to an arrangement with them that each will receive a percentage of the figure owed in full satisfaction of the whole of the original debts. It is clear from the rule in *Pinnel's case* that such an arrangement should not be binding on the parties to it, yet such arrangements are nevertheless upheld. The basis of their binding nature is somewhat elusive.

One theory is that the arrangements are binding since there is a contract between each and every creditor on the basis that each has promised to forgo their part of the debt. The theory is fundamentally flawed, however, since it is clear that the debtor would not be part of this contract because the debtor has provided no consideration for the creditors' promises to them.

A second approach has been to justify composition arrangements on the basis that creditors will not be allowed to go behind the agreement and sue for the balance owed to them since such action amounts to a fraud on all the parties. While such an approach can produce problems, it has tended to be adopted on the basis that it is consistent with the position as regards part-payment of debt by third parties. Such part-payment, if accepted by the creditor in settlement of the whole debt, is regarded as a good defence to a later action by the creditor against the debtor for the balance, on the basis that otherwise the creditor would be committing a fraud against the third party. The fraud arises here since the creditor is inducing a payment from the third party on the basis that they agree to discharge the debtor from the whole amount. This was the finding of the court in *Welby v Drake* (1825) 1 C & P 557, which finding has subsequently been affirmed in *Hirachand Punamchand v Temple* [1911] 2 KB 330.

A third approach can be seen in the case of **Collier v P & M J Wright (Holdings) Ltd**, the facts of which were examined earlier. In that case it was considered that where a debtor offered to pay only part of the amount he owed and the evidence suggested that the creditor had accepted that offer voluntarily and, relying on that acceptance, the debtor paid that part of the amount he owed in full, the creditor would be bound to accept the part-payment in full and final settlement by virtue of the doctrine of promissory estoppel. In such a situation the existence of promissory estoppel would extinguish the creditor's right to the full amount since it would be inequitable for him to resile from his acceptance. The debtor would of course have to demonstrate that it would be inequitable for the creditor to withdraw from his promise. Longmore LJ doubted, however, that the raising of estoppel in such a case would be sufficient to extinguish the creditor's rights. It would only operate merely to suspend those rights and he opined that agreements which attempt to forgo a creditor's rights on a permanent basis would not be construed benevolently by the courts. Both Longmore LJ and Arden LJ considered that, while the matter before them was merely an appeal from a refusal of an application to have the statutory demand set aside, the debtor in the case did present a triable issue should the matter come to court.

3. The effect of the decision in *Williams v Roffey Bros* on *Pinnel's case*

It has already been seen that the decision in **Williams v Roffey Bros and Nicholls (Contractors) Ltd** seems to withdraw from the authority laid down in **Stilk v Myrick** that the performance of, or promise to perform, an existing contractual duty owed by the party to another is no consideration for a promise from that other party and that this principle may also be applied to part-payment of debt.

> ### Example
>
> If *A* is owed £500 by *B* and agrees to take £400 in full and final settlement, this agreement is unenforceable by *B* since no consideration has been provided for *A*'s promise to accept the lower sum. *B* is under an existing contractual duty to pay the full amount and, in law at least, *A* has received no consideration or benefit in accepting less.

In relation to part-payment of debt the authority for this principle is found in **Pinnel's case** and **Foakes v Beer**. The reason for the existence of this principle in these cases is, just as in **Stilk v Myrick**, founded on the need to prevent the debtor extracting an advantage by extortion or economic duress of the type seen in **D & C Builders Ltd v Rees**. It is for this reason that the exception to the rule in **Pinnel's case**, whereby some new element is introduced, can only be brought about at the instance of the creditor. With the onset of the development of a doctrine of economic duress there would seem to be little need for the continuation of this approach.

The reasoning set out above was at least partly behind the decision in **Williams v Roffey Bros & Nicholls (Contractors) Ltd**. It will be recalled that the arguments advanced by Roffey Bros in their defence was that their promise to pay the additional moneys was unenforceable because Williams had provided no consideration for it, merely carrying out their existing contractual duties which, as stated in **Stilk v Myrick**, would be insufficient consideration for the later promise. Roffey Bros admitted that they enjoyed certain benefits from their promise to pay the extra moneys in that the work would have been completed on time and that, as a result, they would have avoided the disbenefit of having to pay penalties. Roffey Bros thus gained a *factual* benefit, though one which was not recognised in *law* in terms of the rule as stated in **Stilk v Myrick**. The Court of Appeal rejected the defence of Roffey Bros based on **Stilk v Myrick** and found for Williams, ruling that, in the absence of economic duress or fraud, where one party to a contract agrees to make a payment or convey an advantage to the other over and above the contractual obligations in order to ensure that the contract is completed on time, and that as a result obtains a benefit or avoids a disbenefit, the obtaining of that benefit could amount to consideration for their own promise to pay the extra moneys or convey the extra advantage to the other party.

The case of **Williams v Roffey Bros** was confined to a contract for goods and services but, if one accepts that the rule in **Pinnel's case** no longer serves a useful purpose in the light of the development of economic duress, this raises the question of the extent to which the decision in **Williams v Roffey Bros** could be applied to cases of part-payment of debt. Acceptance of part-payment of debt, in the absence of economic duress or fraud, may be a perfectly reasonable transaction for the creditor to enter into. The reasoning bears a close analogy to **Williams v Roffey Bros** since, whilst the creditor only receives a proportion of their moneys (or as in **Foakes v Beer** only receives them by instalments instead of in one lump sum), they also receive the benefit of avoiding having to take legal action to claim the full amount, with the possibility in the event of the bankruptcy of the debtor of only receiving a proportion of the moneys, which may be less than the amount offered by the debtor. The benefit obtained by the creditor here is clearly only a *factual* benefit since the rule in **Pinnel's case** and **Stilk v Myrick** prevents the benefit from being recognised in *law*, just as in **Williams v Roffey Bros**.

The application of the decision in **Williams v Roffey Bros** to debt situations was attempted in **Re Selectmove Ltd**.

Re Selectmove Ltd [1995] 2 All ER 531

The company entered into negotiations with the Inland Revenue concerning the payment of taxes owed. During the negotiations the company offered to pay its tax debts by instalments, the Collector of Taxes stating that he would come back to the company if the arrangement was found to be unsatisfactory. As a result, the company commenced paying the taxes owed by instalments but was then contacted by the Inland Revenue, which insisted that all the arrears of taxes should be paid immediately, otherwise it would commence winding-up proceedings against the company.

In order to avoid the winding-up petition the company argued that the case of **Williams v Roffey Bros** was authority for the proposition that promising to perform an existing obligation could amount to good consideration, provided that the promisee obtained a practical or factual benefit. They agreed that, while they were under an existing obligation to pay their arrears in taxes in full, the Inland Revenue, by accepting payment by instalments, recovered the full amount without including the cost of recovering the debt by way of legal action. The company therefore argued that this benefit was analogous to that obtained by Roffey Bros.

It was held in the Court of Appeal that the agreement to accept payment of the debt by instalments was not binding on the Inland Revenue. Their Lordships distinguished the case from that of **Williams v Roffey Bros** on the basis that the present case was concerned with an existing obligation to pay a debt, whilst the **Roffey** case was concerned with a contract for goods and services, and because of this the court was bound by the House of Lords' decision in **Foakes v Beer**. On this basis the decision is correct though it is clearly inconsistent with the decision in **Williams v Roffey Bros**.

The problem here is that the decision in *Foakes v Beer* itself ignores the realities of commercial life. Indeed, in the case itself, Lord Blackburn criticised the rule, stating that part-payment of a debt was sometimes more beneficial to the creditor than strictly insisting on compliance with his legal rights. An example of this can clearly be seen in compositions with creditors and can be seen in the facts of *Re Selectmove* itself. Surely it was better for the Inland Revenue to receive the full amount, albeit by instalments, than to take immediate action for the whole sum, with the possibility of only receiving a proportion of the moneys owed?

Until the rule in *Foakes v Beer* is overturned in the Supreme Court the present inconsistent position will remain. It should, of course, be remembered that the rule in *Foakes v Beer* will continue to be tempered by the doctrine of promissory estoppel. Two further points should be noted: first, if the rule in *Pinnel's case* as stated in *Foakes v Beer* is eventually overruled, agreements in relation to part-payment of debt will only be enforceable in the absence of economic duress or fraud as in *Williams v Roffey Bros*; second, the doctrine of promissory estoppel will be of significantly less importance in this situation.

A further aspect to the decision is that it is surprising that the Court of Appeal did not attempt to distinguish the case on the basis that in *Re Selectmove* the company, i.e. the debtor, had approached the Inland Revenue. The exceptions to the rule in *Pinnel's case* are all based on the fact that it is the creditor, i.e. the person receiving the factual benefit, who should make the approach to the debtor, in order to avoid the possibility of economic duress arising from the debtor. Similarly in *Williams v Roffey Bros*, the approach was made by Roffey Bros, again the party obtaining the factual benefit. It should also be noted that there was no indication that the Inland Revenue had accepted the arrangement. The fact that the creditor was the Inland Revenue may also have had some influence on the decision.

Summary

Definition

- A valuable consideration in the sense of the law, may consist either in some right, interest, profit or benefit accruing to one party, or some forbearance, detriment, loss or responsibility given, suffered or undertaken by the other (*Currie v Misa*).

- An act or forbearance of one party, or the promise thereof, is the price for which the promise of the other is bought, and the promise thus given for value is enforceable (*Dunlop v Selfridge*).

The sub-principles:

Consideration may be executed or executory but not past

Executory and executed consideration

- Executory consideration: Created by the defendant's promise in return for the claimant's promise over a future agreement.

- Executed consideration: Occurs when one party has completed (executed) their side of the bargain but the other party's consideration is still unperformed (executory).

Past consideration

- 'Past consideration is no consideration' (e.g. **Roscorla v Thomas**; **Re McArdle**).

Exceptions to the past consideration rule

The principle in Lampleigh v Braithwait

Statutory exceptions

- Limitation Act 1980, s 27(5).
- Bills of Exchange Act 1882, s 27.

Consideration must move from the promisee though not necessarily to the promisor

- The claimant can only enforce the defendant's promise if they can demonstrate their consideration for that promise (**Price v Easton**).
- Only parties to a contract can enforce the contract against the other (**Tweddle v Atkinson**).

Consideration must be sufficient though not necessarily adequate

Consideration must be valuable

- This should be an adequate and sufficient economic value.

Adequacy of consideration

- The courts seek to establish that the consideration has some economic value.
- The courts will not inquire as to the adequacy of the consideration given by the parties.

Sufficiency of consideration

- A formed agreement (contract) that has an adequate economic value may not have sufficient legal consideration to support a contract.

Insufficient consideration 1: performance of existing obligations

- Where a public duty is imposed by law.
- Where the claimant is bound by the provisions of an existing contractual obligation owed to the defendant.
- Existing contractual duties owed to third parties.

Insufficient consideration 2: part-payment of debt

- The common law rule:
  - All debts are payable in full.
  - A creditor does not have to accept satisfaction of part of a debt in satisfaction of the whole debt (**Pinnel's case**).
  - A creditor alone may choose to accept a lesser sum in part-payment of the debt.
  - If the debtor places the creditor under economic duress to accept a lesser sum then the courts will award the full amount (**D & C Builders Ltd v Rees**).

- The claimant may recover the interest on a debt while making an undertaking not to sue for the moneys owed (*Foakes* v *Beer*).

- Paying additional consideration to one party to prevent a greater disadvantage happening to the other party for completing the same work is acceptable (*Williams* v *Roffey Bros*).

- The exceptions to the rule in *Pinnel's case*:
  (a) The doctrine of promissory estoppel:
    - Established by Denning J in *Central London Property Trust Ltd* v *High Trees House Ltd*.
    - Promissory estoppel can be subdivided as follows:
      1 the nature of the promise;
      2 the doctrine is 'a shield not a sword';
      3 whether the doctrine is suspensory or extinctive;
      4 whether the promisee must act to their prejudice.
  (b) Cheques.
  (c) Compositions with creditors.

Further reading

Atiyah, 'Consideration: A Restatement', *Essays on Contract* (Oxford University Press, 1990)

Beatson, Burrows and Cartwright, *Anson's Law of Contract*, 30th edn (Oxford University Press, 2016)

Brinkworth and Powell, 'Contract and Consideration: A New Commercial Reality?' (1991) 12 *Business Law Review* 5

Coote, 'Consideration and Variations: A Different Solution' (2004) 120 *Law Quarterly Review* 19

Coote, 'Variations sans consideration' (2011) 27 *Journal of Contract Law* 185

Denning, 'Recent Developments in the Doctrine of Consideration' (1952) 15 *Modern Law Review* 1

Furmston, *Cheshire, Fifoot and Furmston's Law of Contract*, 16th edn (Oxford University Press, 2012)

Hird and Blair, 'Minding Your Own Business – *Williams* v *Roffey* Revisited: Consideration Reconsidered' [1996] *Journal of Business Law* 254

Hooley, 'Consideration and Existing Duty' [1991] *Journal of Business Law* 19

Jackson, 'How Many Kinds of Estoppel?' [1982] *The Conveyancer and Property Lawyer* 450

Noble, 'For Your Consideration' (1991) 141 *New Law Journal* 1529

Peel, 'Part Payment of Debt Is No Consideration' (1994) 110 *Law Quarterly Review* 353

Pollock, *Principles of Contract*, 13th edn (Stevens, 1950)

Smith and Atiyah, *Atiyah's Introduction to the Law of Contract*, 6th edn (Oxford University Press, 2006)

Peel, Treitel *Law of Contract*, 14th edn (Sweet and Maxwell, 2015)

4

Intention to create legal relations

Objectives

After reading this chapter you should be able to:

1. Know and understand the different presumptions appertaining to intention to create legal relations regarding social and domestic arrangements.

2. Know and understand the different presumptions appertaining to intention to create legal relations regarding commercial agreements.

Introduction

So far it has been seen that a contract must contain an element of agreement supported by consideration. The mere presence, however, of these elements does not necessarily mean that a legally binding contract has come into existence.

The modern law of contract has an underlying philosophy based on the will of the participants, and if they do not consent to the creation of a legal relationship, then no contract that is legally enforceable will emanate from the relationship of the parties. As Atkin LJ expressed it in the case of **_Balfour_ v _Balfour_** [1919] 2 KB 571: 'In respect of these promises each house is a domain into which the King's writ does not seek to run'.

On the face of things, then, the rule appears very simple and straightforward but, as every student of the law of contract should now be starting to realise, this is rarely the case in this subject. It is clear that serious legal, administrative and economic problems could result if, in every dispute concerning a contract, an intention to create a legal relationship had to be proved.

The general principles to be applied by the courts when determining whether the parties have made an enforceable agreement have been summarised by the Supreme Court in **_RTS Flexible Systems Ltd_ v _Molkerei Alois Muller GmbH_** [2010] 3 All ER1, where Lord Clarke said:

> Whether there is a binding contract between the parties and, if so, upon what terms depends upon what they have agreed. It depends not upon their subjective state of mind, but upon a consideration of what was communicated between them by words or conduct, and whether that leads objectively to a conclusion that they intended to create legal relations and had agreed upon all the terms which they regarded or the law requires as essential for the formation

of legally binding relations. Even if certain terms of economic or other significance to the parties have not been finalised, an objective appraisal of their words and conduct may lead to the conclusion that they did not intend agreement of such terms to be a precondition to a concluded and legally binding agreement.

The courts have thus assumed a more restrictive and pragmatic approach to this problem based on the presumed intentions of the parties. In commercial matters, the courts presume that the parties intend to create a legal relationship, while in agreements of a social or domestic nature no such presumption is made. In either case, however, the presumption may be overturned by actual evidence to the contrary. Usually the burden of rebutting this presumption is very high   indeed, one is not just attempting to overturn a straightforward legal rule, but a legal rule with judicial policy at its foundation, the policy being that the law should not interfere in respect of such transactions.

Social and domestic arrangements

Objective 1

Most social and domestic arrangements do not amount to binding contracts since they are not intended to be such. To agree to take a friend out for a meal or a drink is clearly not intended to confer on the friend a right of action before the courts should one fail to carry out one's commitment. Cases that amount to social/domestic arrangements tend to fall into two broad areas:

Family arrangements

Balfour v *Balfour* [1919] 2 KB 571

This case forms a leading authority in this area. In the case, a husband, who was a civil servant based in Sri Lanka, brought his wife to England. Eventually he had to return but his wife had to stay in England for medical reasons. He agreed to pay her £30 per month maintenance during his absence. When he failed to pay the allowance, she sued. Her action failed on two grounds: first, she had not provided any consideration for the £30 per month and, second, the parties had no intention of creating a legally binding agreement. The court stated that where the parties were husband and wife, the burden was on the plaintiff, the wife, to rebut the presumption that there was no intention to create a contract.

It should be noted that agreements between husband and wife can, from time to time, produce legally binding consequences.

Merritt v *Merritt* [1970] 1 WLR 1121

The husband left the matrimonial home to live with another woman. At a meeting with his wife he agreed in writing to pay her £40 per month maintenance from which she had to repay the mortgage and, when the repayment was completed, to transfer the house into her sole ownership. The wife did in fact pay off the mortgage but the husband then refused to transfer the house to her. The Court of Appeal held that there was an intention to create a legal relationship and therefore held the husband to his agreement. The reasoning enunciated in the Court of Appeal was based largely on the fact that the agreement took place in response to a marital breakdown. In *Balfour*, on the other hand, the arrangements were made on the basis of an amicable agreement. The *Merritt* case illustrates the point that the courts will take all factors into account in deciding the existence or non-existence of the intention to create a legal relationship.

Further, the case of **Pettit v Pettit** [1970] AC 777 also serves as a warning to those who read too much into the principles in the **Balfour** case, where Lord Diplock stated:

> It would in my view, be erroneous to extend the presumption accepted in **Balfour v Balfour** that mutual promises between a man and wife in relation to their domestic arrangements are prima facie not intended by either to be legally enforceable to a presumption that NO legal consequences should flow from acts done by them in performance of mutual promises with respect to the acquisition, improvement or addition to real or personal property – for this would be to intend what is impossible in Law.

Similar problems of intention also occur in relations between parents and children.

Jones v Padavatton [1969] 1 WLR 328

A mother agreed with her daughter that if the latter gave up her job in the USA and read for the Bar in England, the mother would pay her an allowance of $200 a month. On this basis the daughter came to England and began her legal studies in November 1962. In 1964, the mother bought a house for £6,000, whereupon the earlier agreement was now varied so that the daughter, instead of receiving her allowance, would live in part of the house and let the rest, using the rent to cover expenses and her maintenance. In 1967, the parties had an argument and as a consequence the mother brought an action for the possession of the house. The mother based her claim on the allegation that the agreement was not made with the intention of creating a legal relationship. A majority of the Court of Appeal held that there was no intention to create a legal relationship between the parties and gave the mother possession of the house. Lord Salmon agreed with the decision but arrived at it on different grounds. He considered that the first agreement was a binding contract that was intended to last for a reasonable time in order to allow the daughter to pass her Bar Finals. When five years had gone by and she had still not passed them, he considered that the contract had lapsed. The second agreement concerning the possession of the house he considered to be so ambiguous and uncertain as to be incapable of being described as a contract. Lord Salmon based his decision regarding the first agreement on the fact that he thought it inconceivable for the daughter to give up a lucrative job without there existing an enforceable promise of financial support.

Other social arrangements

Questions such as those discussed above may also occur in agreements other than those between husband and wife and parent and child, that is, in everyday social arrangements. Similarly, the presumption is against a finding of an intention to create a legal relationship, though this may also be rebutted by evidence to the contrary. A factor that can be very influential here is the notion of **mutuality**.

Simpkins v Pays [1955] 3 All ER 10

The defendant owned a house in which she lived with her granddaughter and the plaintiff, a paying lodger. The three regularly took part in a competition in a Sunday newspaper. While the entries were entered under the defendant's name, all of them contributed to the competition, though there was no regular arrangement as to the payment of postage and other expenses. One week the entry was successful but the defendant refused to pay the plaintiff his share of the prize and claimed that there was no intention to create a legally binding relationship. It was held that the plaintiff was entitled to his share, the judge stating that there was sufficient 'mutuality in the arrangements between the parties' to establish a legally binding agreement to share any prize that might be won.

Commercial agreements

Objective
2

In these types of agreements, there is a strong presumption that there is an intention to create a legally binding relationship. This presumption can, of course, be rebutted, but in fact very strong evidence is required to do this and in *Bowerman v Association of British Travel Agents Ltd* [1996] CLC 451, it was stated that one would need expressly to exclude the presumption of a legal relationship to have that effect. In addition, in *University of Plymouth v European Language Centre* [2009] EWCA Civ 784, it was held that it was necessary to consider the background of the parties to determine if a legal relationship had been entered into. In that case there had been a degree of trust arising over seven years with regard to teaching accommodation and facilities, though the detail of the arrangement was negotiated on an annual basis and set out in a formal contract. Nevertheless, on examining the background, the Court of Appeal held that there was no legal relationship between the parties. One way of rebutting the presumption is by inserting an express declaration to this effect in a written statement. In *Appleson v H Littlewood Ltd* [1939] 1 All ER 464 and in *Jones v Vernon's Pools Ltd* [1938] 2 All ER 626, the plaintiffs in both cases attempted to claim moneys which they alleged had been won in a football pool. The words 'Binding in honour only' were contained on each coupon. It was held that the words were sufficient to rebut the presumption and the plaintiffs thus failed in their action.

The decisions in the *Littlewood's* and *Vernon's* cases are not difficult to understand given the nature of the transactions, which could hardly be said to arise from the harsh world of commercial bargaining. A remarkable case that does, however, so emanate is that of *Rose and Frank Co. v J R Crompton and Bros*.

Rose and Frank Co. v J R Crompton and Bros [1925] AC 445

In this case, an English company agreed to sell certain carbon copy materials in the USA through a New York-based firm. The transaction, which was made in writing, gave the plaintiffs the sole rights to market and sell the products in the USA and Canada for a period of three years with an option to extend the period. The document contained a clause, which was described as an 'Honourable Pledge Clause', and which provided: 'This arrangement is not entered into . . . as a formal or legal agreement and shall not be subject to legal jurisdiction to the law courts either of the United States or England.' The original agreement began in July 1913 but at the end of the three-year period the option to extend was exercised; as a result the agreement was to last until March 1920. In 1919, the English defendants terminated the agreement and failed to give appropriate notice as required by the agreement, and also refused to fulfil orders received by them prior to their decision to terminate the agreement.

The Court of Appeal decided that with regard to the orders already received there arose a separate and binding contract which the defendants were bound to fulfil. With respect to the grant of the selling rights, the court found that as the parties had specifically declared that the document was not to bring about legally binding consequences, then none could exist; as a result there was no obligation to give orders or to receive them, though once they were given and accepted, the defendants were bound to execute the order.

While the case gives effect to the intentions of the parties as expressed in the written memorandum and no doubt produces a fair result as regards the orders already received, the decision in the Court of Appeal fails to address satisfactorily two problems, both of which were raised at first instance. First, how can the clause bind the parties if there is no binding contract as alleged by the clause itself? This is obviously illogical and while the end result may be said to be justifiable where the contract is entered into by business people negotiating at arm's length, serious problems might result if such clauses were to become part and parcel of a standard-form contract imposed on an unwary or weaker party. Second, the clause would appear to be void in any event as being contrary to public policy in that it purports to oust the jurisdiction of the courts. This principle is a fundamental element of the common law and seems to have been sidestepped by the argument that it only operates where the contract was intended to be legally binding in the first place. As Atiyah points out in *An Introduction to the Law of Contract*, such a distinction appears to be highly artificial.

Despite these reservations it must always be clear that the parties are free to define their liabilities in any agreement they enter into. Thus Lloyd LJ in **Pagnan SpA v Feed Products Ltd** [1987] 2 Lloyd's Rep 601 outlined and explained the several positions which parties might take:

(1) Even if the parties have reached agreement on all the terms of the proposed contract, nevertheless they may intend that the contract shall not become binding until some further condition has been fulfilled. That is the ordinary 'subject to contract' case.

(2) Alternatively, they may intend that the contract shall not become binding until some further term or terms have been agreed; see **Love and Stewart v Instone**, where the parties failed to agree the intended strike clause, and **Hussey v Horne-Payne**, where Lord Selborne said at p. 323:

> ... The observation has often been made, that a contract established by letters may sometimes bind parties who, when they wrote those letters, did not imagine that they were finally settling the terms of the agreement by which they were to be bound; and it appears to me that no such contract ought to be held established, even by letters which would otherwise be sufficient for the purpose, if it is clear, upon the facts, that there were other conditions of the intended contract, beyond and besides those expressed in the letters, which were still in a state of negotiation only, *and without the settlement of which the parties had no idea of concluding any agreement.*

(3) Conversely, the parties may intend to be bound forthwith even though there are further terms still to be agreed or some further formality to be fulfilled (see **Love and Stewart v Instone per Lord Loreburn** at p. 476).

(4) If the parties fail to reach agreement on such further terms, the existing contract is not invalidated unless the failure to reach agreement on such further terms renders the contract as a whole unworkable or void for uncertainty.

(5) It is sometimes said that the parties must agree on the essential terms and that it is only matters of detail which can be left over. This may be misleading, since the word 'essential' in that context is ambiguous. If by 'essential' one means a term without which the contract cannot be enforced, then the statement is true: the law cannot enforce an incomplete contract. If by 'essential' one means a term which the parties have agreed to be essential for the formation of a binding contract, then the statement is tautologous. If by 'essential' one means only a term which the Court regards as important as opposed to a term which the Court regards as less important or a matter of detail, the statement is untrue. It is for the parties to decide whether they wish to be bound and, if so, by what terms, whether important or unimportant. It is the parties who are, in the memorable phrase coined by the Judge, 'the masters of their contractual fate'. Of course, the more important the term is, the less likely it is that the parties will have left it for future decision. But there is no legal obstacle which stands in the way of the parties agreeing to be bound now while deferring important matters to be agreed later. It happens every day when parties enter into the so-called heads of agreement.

Similarly Andrew Smith J in *Maple Leaf Macro Volatility Master Fund* v *Rouvroy* [2009] 1 Lloyd's Rep 475 commented in this context:

> However, there are circumstances in which the parties to what would objectively be held to be contractual are not legally bound by it under English law. If the other parties actually and reasonably believed that the defendants intended to make a contract, there would be a concluded contract, but not if the other parties knew or would reasonably have believed that that was not the defendants' intention and not, in my judgement, if the other parties had simply formed no view one way or the other as to whether the defendants so intended.

Despite the decision in the *Rose and Frank* case, it still remains a strong presumption in commercial agreements that there is an intention to create a legally binding contract. This is particularly true in the case of parties to a commercial contract where part or all of the contract has been performed. Thus in *Trentham Ltd* v *Archital Luxfer* [1993] 1 Lloyd's Rep 25 Steyn LJ observed:

> The fact that a transaction has been performed on both sides will often make it unrealistic to argue that there was no intention to enter into legal relation. It will often make it difficult to submit that the contract is void for vagueness or uncertainty. Specifically, the fact that the transaction is executed makes it easier to imply a term resolving any uncertainty, or, alternatively, it may make it possible to treat a matter not finalised in negotiations as inessential . . . Clearly, similar considerations may sometimes be relevant in partly executed transactions.

Some care needs to be exercised here since it is clear that Lord Steyn's observations should not be taken as saying that it follows from the fact that work has been performed that the parties must have entered into a binding contract, though this will be a relevant factor. Whether the court will conclude that a binding contract was made will depend upon all the circumstances of the case as seen in *RTS Flexible Systems Ltd* v *Molkerei Alois Muller* above and in *Edmonds* v *Lawson* [2000] QB 501; [2000] 2 WLR 1091 where Lord Bingham CJ at para 21 stated:

> Whether the parties intended to enter into legally binding relations is an issue to be determined objectively and not by enquiring into their respective states of mind. The context is all important.

The initial presumption of the courts, however, will be to find for a binding contract in a commercial relationship and the burden of overturning the presumption lies with the party attempting to overturn it.

In *Dhanani* v *Crasnianski* [2011] EWHC 926 (Comm), the claimant (Dhanani) and the defendant (Crasnianski) had signed a letter and term sheet under which it was envisaged that the defendant would provide the claimant with €50 million, which would be invested in a private equity fund to be managed by the claimant. The relations between the two became strained and, three months after the documents were signed, the defendant informed Dhanani that 'the deal was off'. The claimant argued that the signed letter and term sheet evidenced a binding agreement on each party to do its part to set up a fund; the object to which both parties were obliged to work was the setting up of a fund with defined characteristics, and although there were outstanding matters of detail, they could be agreed or, failing agreement, resolved by them during what was known as 'the soft launch'. The defendant argued that the letter and term sheet did not evidence a binding agreement; there was no intent to create legal relations and the agreement was too vague to be enforceable, being no more than an agreement to agree. It was held that the parties had an intention, assessed objectively, to create legal relations. The reasonable business person would have understood the signed letter and term sheet as being legally binding. The wording of the letter acknowledged that the exact structure of the fund remained to be defined and that several legal documents remained to be drafted and agreed, but the reasonable business person would have understood that the main terms of the fund had been agreed in the term sheet and that each party was obliged to do their part to bring about the formation of that fund.

Edwards v *Skyways Ltd* [1964] 1 All ER 494

The plaintiff was employed as an airline pilot when the defendants, his employers, informed him that they were making him redundant and gave him three months' notice. By virtue of his contract, the plaintiff was a member of the defendants' contributory pension fund which entitled him to one of two options on leaving their service. He could either take his contributions out of the fund or receive a paid-up pension which would take effect when he was 50 years of age. The plaintiff's professional association, negotiating on his behalf, agreed with the defendants that if the plaintiff chose the first option the defendants would make him an ex gratia payment equal to the defendants' contribution to the fund. The plaintiff accepted the agreement and chose to withdraw his contributions. The defendants then paid him his total contributions but refused to make the ex gratia payment. The plaintiff sued for breach of contract and won. The judge stated that the words ex gratia did not give rise to a negative contract agreement but simply meant that the employers did not admit to any pre-existing legal liability on their part. They failed to discharge the burden of overturning the presumption that there was an intention to create a legal relationship and were thus liable to make the payment.

See Chapter 2 for the facts of **Dresdner Kleinwort Ltd v Atrill.**

In **Dresdner Kleinwort Ltd v Atrill** [2013] EWCA Civ 394, it was argued that the contract for the guaranteed employment bonus pool was unenforceable as there was no intention to create legal relations between the company and its employees. The bank argued that whilst the burden of proof in overturning the presumption of an intention to create legal relations in a commercial context lay on the party seeking to overturn it, this burden only related to situations where there was a bilateral contract not, as in this case, to a unilateral contract. This was rejected by the judge at first instance relying on the observations of Megaw J in **Edwards v Skyways** that the onus of proving there was a lack of intention to create legal relations lay with the bank. The Court of Appeal concurred with this view with Elias LJ, expressing the opinion that it did not matter whether the contract was a bilateral or a unilateral one, particularly where the parties are already in a contractual relationship. He stated that the starting premise is 'that where a term is being introduced into a pre-existing contractual relationship, there will be a strong presumption that it is intended to be legally binding'.

A development in this area has been the emergence of the so-called letters of comfort. A **letter of comfort** is a letter or memorandum usually written by a holding company to a lender about to lend money to a subsidiary of the holding company so as to reassure the lender of the financial viability of the subsidiary. Such letters are not guarantees in that the holding company is not willing to enter into a legally binding financial commitment. The possible reasons for adopting such a stance could be that the amount of the guarantee exceeds the financial commitments embodied in the articles of association of the holding company or the presence of such a financial commitment in the accounts of the holding company would have an adverse effect on its own affairs. The leading case in this area is that of **Kleinwort Benson Ltd v Malaysia Mining Corporation Bhd.**

Kleinwort Benson Ltd v *Malaysia Mining Corporation Bhd* [1989] 1 All ER 785

The plaintiff bank had agreed a loan facility to the wholly owned subsidiary of MMC, MMC Metals Ltd, which was trading in tin on the London Metal Exchange. The bank was not willing to lend the money simply on the basis of MMC Metals' creditworthiness and called on MMC itself to guarantee the loan. MMC replied to this proposal that it was not its policy to guarantee the loans of its subsidiaries. After considerable negotiations MMC agreed to issue a letter of comfort in which it stated, *inter alia*, 'It is our policy to ensure that the business of MMC Metals Ltd is at all times in a position to meet its liabilities to you.' KB agreed to accept the letter of comfort but on the basis that a higher rate of interest would be charged. Eventually the world tin market collapsed, leaving MMC Metals insolvent. The plaintiff claimed the balance of the moneys owed from the parent company, the defendant.

At first instance, the case was treated as one dealing with an intention to create a legal relationship, the judge finding that since this was a highly commercial agreement, a contractual obligation existed on the part of the defendants. The judge relied heavily on the decision in the *Skyways* case, stating that in a business context an intention to create a legal relationship was presumed and that the onus of proving a contrary assertion lay on the party making it, in this case MMC. He found that MMC had not discharged this burden and they were therefore bound to meet the liabilities of MMC Metals.

The Court of Appeal disagreed with the judge at first instance and stated that the *Skyways* case concerned a promise supported by consideration and therefore had no application to the present case. The question that had to be asked was whether the clause conveyed an express intention to create a legal relationship in that it contained within it a contractual promise. The court found that it merely conveyed a statement as to present intention and was carefully drafted so as not to contain a statement as to future conduct. The appeal of MMC was thus allowed. Nevertheless, some care has to be exercised with the case in two respects: first, the case turns very much on the court's interpretation of the clause in question, and the absence of express words indicating a promise does not necessarily prevent a statement from amounting to a contractual promise. Second, the clause in question would not be devoid of all legal effect if in fact it amounted to a fraudulent misrepresentation of the existing position.

This decision has, however, been subject to criticism and in the Supreme Court of New South Wales case of *Banque Bruxelles Lambert SA* v *Australian National Industries* (1989) 21 NSWLR 502 Rogers CJ stated:

> There should be no room in the proper flow of commerce for some purgatory where statements made by business men, after hard bargaining and made to induce another business person to enter into a business transaction would, without any express statement to that effect, reside in a twilight zone of merely honourable engagement. The whole thrust of the law today is to attempt to give proper effect to commercial transactions.

A further exception to the presumption of an intention to create a legal relationship in commercial agreements lies in the case of advertisements. In order to protect advertisers who make flamboyant claims regarding the products advertised, the law assumes that there is no intention to create a legal relationship, thus preventing some disappointed individual who finds the claims exaggerated from taking any action. Such exaggerated claims are referred to as mere 'puffs', in that they 'puff' up the product in order to make it more attractive and thereby induce consumers to purchase it. Very often such claims are gross exaggerations and no one really expects the products to produce the effects envisaged by the advertiser. Contemporary examples are very often visual and would appear to hope, for instance, to persuade the public to buy a certain brand of coffee to experience some unlikely romantic liaison for which a beer that reaches the parts the others cannot reach would also be required at some stage of the evening. In the past, slogans were very much the forte of the advertising agency, for example: 'Daz washes whiter than white!' Probably the more exaggerated the claim, the safer the advertiser is, since if the claim appears to have some semblance of credibility, the more likely it is to have a contractual effect that is legally enforceable. The case of *Carlill v Carbolic Smoke Ball Co.* [1893] 1 QB 256 provides a classic example of such a case.

See Chapter 2 for *Carlill v Carbolic Smoke Ball Co.*

The existence of an intention to create a legal relationship may also denied by statute since, if there is a statutory obligation to enter into an agreement, the terms of which are laid down in the statute, there is in fact no contract, as held in *W v Essex County Council* [1998] 3 All ER 111 with regard to fostering agreements under the Children Act 1989. Similarly by virtue of the Trade Union and Labour Relations (Consolidation) Act 1992, s 179 collective agreements between unions and one or more employers to regulate the terms and conditions of employment are conclusively presumed not to have been intended to be legally binding unless they are in writing and contain a statement that the parties intend the agreement to be legally binding.

Difficulties with regard to employment law and intentions to create legal relations have in the past been a problem with regard to the relationship of the clergy with their church since in the past the courts have held that there is no such contract of employment in such a relationship. Thus, in *President of the Methodist Conference v Parfitt* [1984] QB 368, a Methodist minister was dismissed by the governing body of the Methodist Church after disciplinary proceedings had been taken against him in the Church court. He contended that he had been unfairly dismissed and applied to an industrial tribunal for relief. The Church contended that he fell outside the jurisdiction of a tribunal since he was not employed under a contract of service. The tribunal held that he was. The Church's appeal was dismissed by the Employment Appeal Tribunal and the Church appealed to the High Court which allowed the appeal. It was stated that in all the circumstances, especially having regard to the doctrinal standards of the Church and the spiritual nature of both the act of his admission as a minister and the functions of a Methodist minister, it was clear that the parties had not intended to create binding legal relations either at the time he was ordained or when he accepted the invitation to join the circuit of the Methodist Church. Thus he did not have a contract of service with the Church and so the tribunal had no jurisdiction to hear his complaint.

In *Davies v Presbyterian Church of Wales* [1986] 1 WLR 323, the House of Lords followed the decision in Parfitt. In this case a pastor was inducted in accordance with the Book of Order and Rules of the Presbyterian Church in Wales. The pastorate was of indeterminate time and not subject to determination by notice. The book of rules provided for him to be paid a stipend and have a manse free of rent and rates from the Church's fund. Payments were only made from the fund to the extent that resources permitted. The pastor was dismissed from his pastorate and claimed to be employed by the Church under a contract of employment and that he had been unfairly dismissed. He subsequently appealed against the decision of the Court of Appeal that there was no contract of employment. The House of Lords held that while it was possible for a person to carry out spiritual duties under a contract of employment, in the present case there was no contract between the pastor and the Church. No contractual duties were imposed upon him and he devoted his whole life to his religion and had answered and accepted the call of the pastorate to attend their spiritual affairs. His duties were dictated by his conscience, not by contract. The Church was not contractually bound to pay a stipend to the pastor and discharge the expenses of the manse.

In *Percy v Church of Scotland Board of National Mission* [2005] UKHL 73. The House of Lords held in this case that a minister's claim against the Church for sex discrimination under the Sex Discrimination Act 1975, s 82(1) was not a spiritual matter under the Church of Scotland Act 1921, s 3 and as such the Church did not have exclusive jurisdiction to deal with the claim. Notwithstanding the religious nature of the services Percy was engaged to provide, she was employed by the Church under a contract personally to execute work within the meaning in s 82(1) of the 1975 Act. Lord Nicholls stated that: 'It is time to recognise that employment arrangements between a church and its ministers should not be lightly taken as intended to have no legal effect' so that its ministers were denied protection. The court considered that her rights and duties were defined by her contract, not by the office to which she was appointed. The intention of the provisions in the 1921 Act was that in matters spiritual the Church and its courts had exclusive jurisdiction. The expression 'matters spiritual' was not defined but on any ordinary understanding of that expression, if the Church authorities entered into a contract of employment with one of its ministers, the exercise of statutory rights attached to the contract would not be regarded as a spiritual matter. A sex discrimination claim would not be regarded as a spiritual matter as the foundation of the claim was a contract and the rights and obligations created by such a contract were, of their nature, not spiritual matters but matters of a civil nature.

Summary

- An intention to form legal relations is a fundamental component of any contract.
- A contract is not enforceable if the parties lack an intention to form legal relations.

Social and domestic arrangements

- Most social and domestic arrangements are not intended to amount to a binding contract.

Family arrangements

- Family arrangements for the payment of maintenance between husband and wife cannot form a contract (***Balfour* v *Balfour***).
- The burden is on the claimant to rebut the presumption that there was no intention to create a contract (***Merritt* v *Merritt***).
- The burden has to be rebutted when examining intention of the parties where they are between parents and children (***Jones* v *Padavatton***).

Other social arrangements

- Jointly taking part in a competition and sharing the prize amounts to a binding contract (***Simpkins* v *Pays***).

Commercial agreements

- In commercial transactions there is a presumption that there is an intention to create a legally binding relationship (***Edwards* v *Skyways Ltd***).
- This presumption can be rebutted by express words to the contrary (***Appleson* v *H Littlewood Ltd*; *Jones* v *Vernon's Pools Ltd***).
- Gentlemen's agreements: Honourable Pledge Clauses will not give rise to an intention to create a contract (***Rose and Frank Co.* v *J R Crompton and Bros***).

- Letters of comfort: Letters of this type aim to pacify and reassure a nervous third party entering into a contract with a subsidiary of a parent company without the parent company attracting liability for any breach (***Kleinwort Benson Ltd v Malaysia Mining Corporation Bhd***).
- Advertisements:
  - The law protects advertisers who exaggerate their product by assuming that there is no intention to create a legal relationship.
  - This presumption can be rebutted depending on how exaggerated the claims are (***Carlill v Carbolic Smoke Ball Co.***).

Further reading

Beale, Bishop and Furmston, *Contract – Cases and Materials*, 4th edn (Butterworths, 2001)

Beatson, Burrows and Cartwright, *Anson's Law of Contract*, 30th edn (Oxford University Press, 2016)

Brown, 'The Letter of Comfort: Placebo or Promise?' [1990] *Journal of Business Law* 281

Furmston, *Cheshire, Fifoot and Furmston's Law of Contract*, 16th edn (Oxford University Press, 2012)

Hedley, 'Keeping Contract in its Place: *Balfour* v *Balfour* and the Enforceability of Informal Agreements' (1985) 5 *Oxford Journal of Legal Studies* 391

Hepple, 'Intention to Create Legal Relations' [1970] *Cambridge Law Journal* 122

Smith and Atiyah, *Atiyah's Introduction to the Law of Contract*, 6th edn (Oxford University Press, 2006)

Peel, Treitel *Law of Contract*, 14th edn (Sweet and Maxwell, 2015)

Capacity

Objectives

After reading this chapter you should be able to:

1. Explain the capacity of natural persons in various circumstances, particularly minors.
2. Understand when minors' contracts are regarded as binding.
3. Understand the circumstances in which minors' contracts are held to be voidable.
4. Understand the remedy of restitution in minors' contracts.
5. Explain the rules relating to the capacity of corporations in the law of contract.

The scope of this chapter

Prima facie the law assumes that all parties to a contract have the power to enter into that contract. However, the law places restrictions on the ability of a number of groups of persons to enter into contractual relations. The idea of restrictions on contractual **capacity** belies the underlying reasoning behind the notion of capacity to contract since the aim of the law is to protect rather than to restrict. The approach taken by the law depends on whether the person is a natural person or an artificial person, that is, a corporation.

The capacity of natural persons

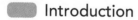 ### Introduction

Objective
1

The traditional role model of the natural person entering into contractual relations is that of the sane, sober and adult male individual. Deviation from this model immediately raises questions as to the ability of the individual to negotiate the responsibilities thrust upon him or her. Thankfully the incapacity of females, in particular, married women, to enter into contracts has disappeared in law despite the persistence of social prejudice, though protection is still imposed on drunks or those suffering from mental impairment or disability due to age.

Drunks

A contract is **voidable** if drunkenness prevents an individual from understanding the transaction they have entered into and the other party is aware of their level of intoxication, though this latter situation rarely arises since it must be virtually impossible for a person to be so drunk as not to know what they are doing without this factor being obvious to the other party. It should be noted that a drunk will be liable to pay a reasonable price for items considered necessaries (*see* below for the meaning of this term) and in any event will be liable on the contract should they ratify it on becoming sober.

Mentally disordered persons

The Mental Health Act 1983 has now been replaced by the Mental Capacity Act 2005. By s.2(1) a person lacks capacity if "he is unable to make a decision for himself in relation to the matter" at the time the contract is made. By s.2(2) it is irrelevant if the mental impairment is permanent or temporary. By s.2(4) any question as to whether a person lacks capacity is decided on the balance of probabilities; however a lack of capacity cannot be established merely by reference to a person's age or appearance, or any conditions or aspect of his behaviour, which might lead others to make unjustified assumptions about his capacity. By s.3(1) impairment may be an inability:

(a) to understand the information relevant to the decision,

(b) to retain that information,

(c) to use or weigh that information as part of the process of making the decision, or

(d) to communicate his decision (whether by talking, using sign language or any other means).

Necessaries

If the other party is aware of the incapacity then the contract is voidable at the disordered person's option. The disordered person is however liable under the Mental Health Act 2005 s.7(1). This provides that if necessary goods or services are supplied to a person who lacks capacity to contract for the supply, he must pay a reasonable price for them. By s.7(2) "necessary" means suitable to a person's condition in life and to his actual requirements at the time when the goods or services are supplied. Where the other party is unaware of the incapacity then the contract is valid and the other party is not limited in his action to recovering a reasonable price but the contract price.

Minors

Introduction

The Family Law Reform Act 1969, s 1, provides that any person below the age of 18 is classed as a minor (very often referred to as an 'infant' in older cases). As already stated, despite the petulant views of youth, the aim of the law here is to protect rather than restrict, and this includes not only protecting minors from entering into unfair contracts, but also protecting adults in their dealings with minors, provided they act in a fair and reasonable manner. The result is that minors' contracts are regarded as binding or voidable, depending on the circumstances.

Contracts regarded as binding on minors

1. Contracts for necessaries

Objective 2

From the earliest times of the common law, minors have been obliged to pay for goods or services necessary to maintain them in their particular station of life. It is important to note that necessary goods are not the same as necessities. A silk blouse may be necessary for the daughter of a millionaire, but this is hardly a necessity since one made of a cheaper material would do equally as well, as of course it must for the daughter of a process worker, for instance.

The rules relating to necessary goods are contained in s 3(3) of the Sale of Goods Act 1979, which provides that an infant must pay a reasonable price for 'necessaries'. Necessaries are defined as goods 'suitable to the condition in life of the minor and to his actual requirements at the time of the sale and delivery'. The effect is that a claimant wishing to enforce such a contract has to establish three points:

1 that the goods are capable of being necessaries;

2 that the minor has not already been adequately supplied with such items at the time of their delivery;

3 the supplier must show that the goods have been sold and delivered.

Whether the goods are *capable of being necessaries* is a question of law. Thus in **Ryder v Wombwell** (1868) LR 4 Exch 32, it was held by the jury that a pair of cuff-links worth £25 and an antique goblet worth £15 could amount to necessaries for an infant with an income of £500 per year. The court, however, set the verdict aside on the fact that the evidence could not properly justify such a finding.

The second point which must be established is whether the minor has not been already *adequately supplied with such items* at the time of their delivery. In other words, the supplier must show that the items are de facto necessary to the minor. In **Nash v Inman** [1908] 2 KB 1, for instance, a Savile Row tailor attempted to recover £122 16s 6d for items (which included 11 fancy waistcoats at £2 2s each) supplied to an undergraduate. The action failed as it was shown that the minor was already adequately supplied with clothes and therefore those supplied by the tailor could not amount to necessaries.

The third matter required for the enforcement of such a contract is that the supplier must show that the *goods have been sold and delivered.* An executory contract would thus appear to be unenforceable; in other words, can an infant who has agreed to buy goods which have yet to be delivered repudiate the contract? The answer is inconclusive since, while s 3(3) talks in terms of the goods having been delivered, that is, executed, and indeed in **Nash v Inman** it was thought that the minor was liable because he had been supplied with the goods, in **Roberts v Gray** [1913] 1 KB 520 an executory contract was held to be binding. This case was concerned with a contract for education, but it is difficult to comprehend why such a contract should be treated differently and Treitel indicates that there should be no distinction between the two categories of contract. In any event, the 1979 Act seems to be quite definite that the contract must be executed.

Even if the supplier should satisfy the above requirements, a contract may still be void if its terms are harsh and onerous to the infant.

Fawcett v *Smethurst* (1914) 84 LJ KB 473

In this case, a minor hired a car in order to transport some luggage; prima facie the contract of hire was a necessary but nevertheless it was held to be void since it was considered that a term rendering the minor absolutely liable for any damage to the car whether or not caused by his neglect was harsh and onerous. It should be noted before we proceed any further that the minor need only pay a reasonable price, not necessarily the contract price, for goods or services found to be necessaries.

2. Beneficial contracts of service

The rules here again have their foundations in the common law and are essentially the same as for goods, though here executory contracts may be enforceable.

A beneficial contract of service, such as a contract of apprenticeship, education or employment, is prima facie binding on a minor, provided it is substantially for the minor's benefit. The *whole* contract must be assessed because even though one or more stipulations may be regarded as prejudicial, this does not invalidate the contract. Adverse terms have to be expected in service agreements to a certain extent. The question to be considered is whether, in the light of an assessment of the surrounding circumstances, the contract can be said to favour the minor.

Clements v *LNWR* [1894] 2 QB 482

In this case, the minor joined the railway as a porter and agreed to join the company's own insurance scheme, which meant that he relinquished his rights to sue under the Employers' Liability Act 1880 should he ever suffer personal injury while so employed. The insurance scheme was more favourable than the Act in that it provided for compensation for more types of accidents, though the level of compensation was lower than was provided in the Act. It was held that the agreement was, on balance, of benefit to the infant and therefore valid and binding.

De Francesco v *Barnum* (1890) 45 Ch D 430

On the other hand, in this case, a 14-year-old girl was apprenticed to the plaintiff for seven years in order to be taught stage dancing. The deed signed stated that she was to be at the total disposal of the plaintiff; she would not be paid unless he employed her, which he was not bound to do, nor was he bound to maintain her. It was agreed that she would be paid 9d per evening performance and 6d per matinee for the first three years, after which her pay rose to 1s 0d per evening performance and 6d per matinee. It was further agreed that she could not accept any professional engagement without his consent, and that she was also required to obtain his consent if she wished to marry. Not least, the plaintiff could terminate her contract without notice when he wished. It should come as no surprise that the court held that the contract was unduly harsh and onerous and as a result was unenforceable.

A progressively wider notion of a beneficial contract of service has emerged in recent times. Thus in *Doyle* v *White City Stadium* [1935] 1 KB 110, it was held that a contract between a minor professional boxer and the British Boxing Board of Control which stated that he would lose his purse if he was disqualified was valid in that it not only encouraged clean fighting but encouraged the proficiency of the infant in the art of boxing. The case was thus decided on similar principles to the *De Francesco* case even though it was not strictly speaking a contract of employment. A further widening of the types of contracts covered by the term 'beneficial contract of service' can be seen in *Chaplin v Leslie Frewin (Publishers) Ltd* [1966] Ch 71 where the minor agreed, in return for royalties on the book which would be published, to tell his life story to a publishing company. It was held that the contract was analogous to a contract of service and binding on the minor.

In *Proform Sports Management Ltd v Proactive Sports Management Ltd* [2006] EWHC 2903 (Ch), Wayne Rooney entered into a player representation agreement with the claimants, Proform Sports Management Ltd ('Proform'), under which he appointed them to act as his agents and to represent him in all matters with regard to his work as a footballer. At the time of the contract Rooney was 15 years old and was a trainee at Everton Football Club. Under the Football Association Rule he was not allowed to become a professional footballer until he was 17 years old. Proform sought damages from Proactive Sports Management Ltd ('Proactive') in that Proform alleged that Proactive had unlawfully interfered with the contract and procured a breach of the contract by Rooney. In considering this question the court also considered whether Rooney's contract was binding as a beneficial contract of service. Hodge J identified the two questions to be answered in deciding the question. First, whether the contract between Rooney and Proform fell within the class of contracts analogous to contracts for necessaries and contracts of employment, apprenticeship or education. Second, if the first question was answered positively, the court had to consider whether the particular contract was beneficial to Rooney. The burden of proving these two questions lay on the party seeking to uphold the contract, Proform in this case. The judge considered that a player representation agreement did not fall within, nor was it analogous to, a contract for necessaries, or apprenticeship, education or employment. Unlike his contract with Everton Football Club, under the contract with Proform he did not undertake duties that were *essential* to the player's training or his livelihood, nor did they enable him to earn a living or advance his skills as a professional footballer.

Just because a contract is beneficial to a minor, does it become binding on him? The contract must fall within or be analogous to a contract for necessaries or a contract of employment, apprenticeship or education. Since Rooney's contract fell outside those categories, it was not binding on him. Could Proactive therefore be liable for unlawfully interfering with and procuring a breach of the contract by Rooney? The court considered that even if Proactive were responsible in procuring the breach of the agreement with Proform, it stands to reason that they could not be liable since the Proform agreement was not binding on Rooney in any event as he was free to avoid the contract.

Voidable contracts

Objective 3

Two classes of contract are described as voidable at common law: those by which the minor acquires an interest in some subject matter of a permanent nature (such as contracts to take a lease, to buy shares or to enter a partnership) and a residual class of contracts, which will be described below.

Contracts of the first type are valid and binding on the minor unless they choose to repudiate the contract within the minority or within a reasonable time of acquiring majority. Until the minor decides to repudiate the contract, they will be liable on the terms of the contract. In a lease, for instance, they will be liable for breach of any covenants, while in a contract for the purchase of shares, the minor will continue to be liable for any calls made on them for any amounts outstanding on the shares.

Since the minor is free to repudiate these contracts during infancy or within a reasonable time thereafter, the question arises as to what constitutes a reasonable time. The answer here largely depends on the facts of the particular case. In *Edwards v Carter* [1893] AC 360, it was held that a minor who purported to repudiate an agreement to pay £1,500 to trustees under a marriage settlement some four years after attaining majority would not be allowed to do so.

While a minor who repudiates a voidable contract is no longer liable to honour any obligations arising in the future, it is not settled whether they will be free from those that have already accrued at the time of the repudiation. The authorities support two viewpoints: first, that the repudiation is the equivalent of **rescission** and is therefore retrospective in operation; and second, that repudiation does not have a retrospective operation and that the minor remains liable on such obligations. *Cheshire, Fifoot and Furmston* tends to suggest that the better view is that the second should prevail although the position is unclear.

Looking at the other side of the coin, we find that a minor who attempts to recover any moneys, having repudiated the contract, has to show that they have suffered a total failure of consideration. In *Steinberg v Scala* [1923] 2 Ch 452, the plaintiff, a minor, had applied for shares in a company and had paid the amounts due on allotment and on a subsequent first call. She was not paid any dividends, nor did she attend any meetings. The shares never increased in value. Some 18 months after the shares had been allotted to her, she sought to repudiate the contract and reclaim all that she had paid for the shares. Her action failed since the company had fulfilled its side of the bargain in that it had allotted her shares on the basis of the payments made to them, and there was, therefore, no total failure of consideration.

The second class of voidable contracts is really a residual class of contracts that fail to come within the heads already discussed. The major example of such a contract is a trading contract, that is, a contract entered into by an infant during the course of their trade or profession. In reality, such contracts will now be quite rare, given the reduction of the age of majority. In common law, such contracts only became binding if the minor ratified the contract on attaining majority. While this position was altered by the Infants Relief Act 1874, this Act has now itself been repealed by the Minors' Contracts Act 1987. The position now is that the common law rules have become re-established. Thus a minor, after attaining majority, has the option to ratify contracts that are unenforceable against them or voidable.

To ratify the contract, the minor may simply make a unilateral confirmation of an earlier promise made during their minority. Previously, by s 2 of the Infants Relief Act 1874, in order to be bound, the former minor had to make a new contract relating to the subject matter of the old contract on attaining majority.

Section 5 of the Betting and Loans (Infants) Act 1892 provided that a new contract entered into by a minor, after attaining majority, to pay a debt due under a void loan contracted in infancy, was itself void. This provision is now repealed by s 1 of the 1987 Act, with the result that any new agreement to repay a loan advanced during minority is now effective and binding.

The tortious liability of minors

It is possible for a tortious act to be at the same time a breach of contract. For instance, a person may induce another to enter a contract with them by making a fraudulent statement of fact, i.e. the tort of deceit. The law therefore seeks to prevent an adult from evading a minor's immunity from contractual liability by expressing an action in tortious terms on the basis that this amounts to an indirect enforcement of an invalid contract. However, an action in tort will only be barred if the wrongful act committed by the infant is of a type that is contemplated by the contract.

The point is illustrated in the following cases. In *Jennings* v *Rundall* (1799) 8 Term Rep 335, a minor who hired a horse for riding but injured it by excessive and improper use was held not to be liable in negligence. In *Burnard* v *Haggis* (1863) 14 CBNS 45, a minor who was specifically barred from jumping his hired horse was held to be liable for injuries caused when he ignored the restriction. A more modern application of the rule can be seen in *Ballett* v *Mingay* [1943] KB 281, where an infant who had borrowed audio equipment and without authority had lent it to a friend was held liable in the tort of detinue when he failed to return it.

The rule that a minor is not generally liable in tort where the tortious act was within the contemplation of a void contract also applies where the infant commits a tort in procuring the contract. Thus in *A Leslie Ltd* v *Sheill* [1914] 3 KB 607, a minor could not be sued in deceit by inducing an adult to lend him money while fraudulently misrepresenting his age.

Restitution

Objective 4

For more on restitution refer to Chapter 18.

It can be seen in cases like *Leslie* v *Sheill* that an adult could conceivably be left without a remedy if the strict letter of the common law was adhered to. To offset this unfairness, equity has developed a doctrine of **restitution** which applies the principle that an infant should not be allowed to be enriched by their own fraud. Three situations need to be considered:

1 The minor has obtained goods by fraud and still remains in possession of them. Restitution will be ordered in such cases.

2 The minor has obtained goods by fraud but has sold or exchanged them. The position here is unsettled and while the case of *Stocks* v *Wilson* [1913] 2 KB 235 takes the view that the infant is accountable for the proceeds, *Leslie* v *Sheill* supports the contrary view.

3 The minor has obtained a loan by fraud. It is clear here that the minor will be liable to account for any of the actual banknotes still in their possession, though it is unsettled whether any items purchased with the moneys lent are recoverable. It seems probable that relief would be granted to the adult provided this does not diminish the minor's resources below what they were prior to the transaction obtained by fraud.

Apart from, and in addition to, the equitable remedy of restitution it is possible for relief to be obtained under the Minors' Contracts Act 1987. By s 3(1), where the contract is unenforceable against a person because they were a minor at that time, or where the minor repudiates the contract, the court has the power where it thinks it is 'just and equitable to do so' to require the minor to return the property, or property representing that which was acquired, to the claimant.

It is envisaged that the courts, rather than rely on the equitable doctrine of restitution, will choose s 3(1) as the main remedy in these circumstances and, indeed, there are good reasons for their doing so. First, there is no requirement as to fraud; and second, s 3(1) extends to property representing that acquired under the contract, an aspect which was open to doubt in the equitable remedy of restitution. The discretion given to the courts in s 3(1) will present few problems where the 'property acquired . . . under the contract' is still in the minor's possession. In relation, however, to exercising discretion over 'property representing it' there may still be some problems in certain circumstances, as, for example, if the 'property acquired' is sold and the proceeds paid into a bank account from which a further item is bought (also possibly under an unenforceable contract). Despite the changes wrought by the 1987 Act, if the minor has consumed or disposed of the goods or the proceeds, they cannot be required to compensate the other party.

Like the remedy of restitution, the new remedy is also discretionary, and in the appropriate circumstances it may still be wiser for the claimant to rely on remedies in **quasi-contract,** which have been specifically preserved in s 3(2) of the Act. This remedy has the advantage of being a common law remedy and therefore available as of right.

Guarantees

The Infants Relief Act 1874 rendered guarantees invalid because the main contract itself was absolutely void. Section 2 of the 1987 Act repealed this provision so that a guarantor will now be liable for the infant's contractual obligation even though it is unenforceable or the infant has repudiated their contractual obligation. This provision does not apply to necessaries because the minor is obliged to pay a reasonable price for these in any event.

Section 2 does not affect the entitlement of the guarantor to recover their losses against the minor and here they are in exactly the same position as any other creditor of the minor.

The effect of an actual guarantee of a contractual obligation very largely depends on the terms of the guarantee. It may still be possible for the guarantee itself to be rendered unenforceable, but not on the ground that the contractual obligation was unenforceable or repudiated by the minor.

The capacity of corporations

Types of corporations

Objective 5

There are two broad categories of corporations:

Chartered corporations

Such corporations, which are a creature of the common law, can only be created by royal charter. Today this form of corporation is used almost entirely for non-trading bodies such as the BBC and the Bank of England. Generally they have the same capacity as a private individual, though if a chartered corporation makes a contract that it is not authorised to by virtue of its charter, the charter itself may be revoked. Any unauthorised contract will remain valid.

Statutory corporations

Most corporations today are created either by statute or under the authority of a statute. Of these the vast majority are commercial corporations created by incorporation under the Companies Act 2006 and its predecessors, and they may take the form of either public or private companies, limited by shares or by guarantee.

The doctrine of *ultra vires*

The doctrine of ***ultra vires*** limits the capacity of a company to enter into certain contracts in that if a company enters into a contract which it is beyond the company's power to enter, then that contract is deemed to be void. If the corporation is created by statute, then the limits of the corporation's powers are set out in the relevant Act of Parliament. If the corporation is created under the Companies Act 1985, then the limitations on the company's powers are set out in the objects clause in the memorandum of association, which is a public document that has to be filed with the Registrar of Companies when the company is registered on its creation. Since the passing of the Companies Act 2006, s 28, the provisions relating to aspects of clauses are now treated as part of the company's articles of association.

Central to the doctrine of *ultra vires* is the need to protect three groups of people: investors, creditors and third parties dealing with the company. The nature of this protection arises by means of informing interested persons of the purpose or purposes for which the company was formed, by allowing them to investigate the objects clause of the memorandum of association and as a result having actual notice of the objects of the company. On the face of things this concept is sound, although closer examination reveals the protection afforded to be illusory since anyone dealing with the company was deemed to have constructive notice of the contents of the objects clause. In other words, a person would be deemed to have read the objects clause even if they had never heard of the existence of such a document as the memorandum of association! The effect of this is that if the company was acting beyond the purposes afforded to it by the objects clause, any person dealing with the company would be deemed to know that the actions of the company were *ultra vires*, whether they had read the objects clause or not. The only way to ensure that the company was acting within its powers was to obtain a copy of the memorandum but, of course, it is totally unrealistic to expect a person to obtain from the Registrar of Companies the memoranda of every company they may do business with. It is at this point that the trap is sprung on the unsuspecting, since if it transpired that the company was acting outside its powers, then the contract would be void and neither could enforce the contract against the other. The reason for this, as far as investors, creditors and third parties are concerned, is that they are deemed to know the objects of the company and, as a result, to know that the company is acting outside those objects.

Ashbury Railway Carriage Co. Ltd v *Riche* (1875) LR 7 HL 653

In this case, the company was formed with the object of carrying on business as mechanical engineers and to make and sell all kinds of railway plant and rolling stock. The directors contracted to assign a concession they had bought for the construction of a railway in Belgium to a Belgian company. The company, however, was not formed for the purpose of constructing railways by virtue of the objects clause and thus the contract was void on the grounds that the contract was *ultra vires* the company. Furthermore, the situation could not even be saved by the majority of members passing a resolution ratifying the contract. Thus the action by the Belgian company for breach of contract failed since it was deemed to have constructive notice of the objects of the company and, as a result, should have known that the company was not entitled to be involved in such a transaction.

An *ultra vires* act prior to the Companies Act 1989 (see below) could never be ratified by the shareholders, nor could such an act be enforced by a third party even if they could prove that they were unaware of the *ultra vires* nature of the company's transaction. The point is well illustrated by the following case.

Re Jon Beauforte Ltd [1953] Ch 131

In this case, the objects clause of the company authorised it to make clothing, yet it decided to start a new venture manufacturing veneered panels instead. The company ordered coke for use in the manufacturing process of the new business on headed notepaper which described the company as veneered panel manufacturers. The new business venture was not a success and the company went into liquidation. The coke suppliers failed in their action to recover the moneys owed to them. Clearly the letterhead per se did not give evidence of the fact that the company was involved in an *ultra vires* activity, but it did inform the supplier of the actual use to which the coke was to be put. Coupled with this was the fact that the supplier had constructive notice of the objects clause in the memorandum and the two factors when considered together gave a clear indication that the coke was being used for an illegitimate purpose. This resulted in the contract being rendered *ultra vires* and void, so that the supplier was unable to recover the debt owed to him. The result might have been different if the letterhead had not given any indication of the use to which the coke would be put, since the supplier could have claimed that the coke might have been put to a legitimate use.

Items which can have a general use within a company also give rise to problems in the context of the doctrine of *ultra vires,* since they may be put to both legitimate and illegitimate uses. Loans of money especially fall into this category, though it should be noted that a loan can never amount to an object of a company. While the power to raise loans may be given in the objects clause, that is all it is, a power – a means for the company to achieve its objects and nothing more. In ***Introductions Ltd* v *National Provincial Bank Ltd*** [1970] Ch 199, the company was formed to provide entertainment and accommodation during the Festival of Britain. The company then decided to go into pig breeding and obtained a loan from the bank for that purpose. The bank's contention that the borrowing of money could be an object of the company was rejected by the Court of Appeal. The court stated that the power to borrow was merely a means by which a company achieved its objects and that therefore it had to be used for the furtherance of a lawful object, which of course pig breeding was not, thus the loan was *ultra vires* and void.

The decision in the ***Introductions*** case has been challenged in the case of ***Rolled Steel Products (Holdings) Ltd* v *British Steel Corporation*** [1985] 3 All ER 1016, where it was held that the borrowing of money in such circumstances was *intra vires* the company but *ultra vires* the powers of the directors, who could then be rendered liable to the company for borrowing money for an improper purpose. If the ***Introductions*** case was decided on this basis, the bank would have been able to recover the money from the company (that is, the loan would have been *intra vires* the company), though the company would have been entitled to claim an indemnity from the directors for any losses sustained. It should be noted that the decision in the ***Rolled Steel*** case has been the subject of serious criticism. However, further consideration of the case is beyond the scope of this work.

The doctrine of *ultra vires* is now largely irrelevant since the Companies Act 2006, s 31(1) provides that unless a company's articles specifically restrict the objects of the company, its objects will be unrestricted.

Avoiding the effects of the doctrine of *ultra vires*

It can be seen from the discussions above that the doctrine of *ultra vires* fails to protect the very people it was designed to give protection to. The doctrine also has a further negative effect in that it stultifies the ability of companies to expand their operations into areas which are not within the ambit of their objects clauses. The effect of this was to motivate business persons and their legal advisers to devise methods of avoiding the effects of the *ultra vires* doctrine. These methods were eventually so effective that the doctrine started to have little significance in the operational management of companies. While these devices aided companies, third parties were still very much at risk but this was remedied by the passing of the European Communities Act 1972, s 9(1).

This provision was later re-enacted in s 35 of the Companies Act 1985, which provided:

1 In favour of a person dealing with a company in good faith, any transaction decided on by the directors shall be deemed to be one which it is within the capacity of the company to enter into, and the power of the directors to bind the company shall be deemed to be free of any limitations under the memorandum of articles.

2 A party to a transaction so decided on is not bound to enquire as to the capacity of the company to enter into it or as to any such limitation on the powers of the directors and is presumed to have acted in good faith unless the contrary is proved.

The above provision was replaced by a new s 35 enacted by s 108 of the Companies Act 1989 and therefore it must be stressed that any consideration of the old s 35 is largely historical. Nevertheless it is of interest to see how it applied, since this gives some insight into the workings of the provision.

The above provision had two principal effects: first, if the conditions in the section were satisfied, a company could not raise *ultra vires* as a defence against an outsider; and, second, registration of the memorandum of association no longer amounted to constructive notice of its contents to the whole world. It was the actual notice of the third party that became important. Had this provision been in force at the time of the decision in *Re Jon Beauforte,* its effect would have been to allow the coke supplier to recover the sums owed to him.

The old s 35 nevertheless had its limitations, for it did not aid the company, only third parties, and therefore companies were not able to enforce their own *ultra vires* contracts. The provision did not prevent a shareholder from obtaining an injunction to restrain the directors from making an *ultra vires* contract, nor did it absolve directors from liability for losses caused to the company by the entering into of an *ultra vires* contract.

It will also be noted that the third party must have acted in good faith and that the provision excluded anyone who knew, or ought to have known, that the transaction was *ultra vires*. In *International Sales and Agencies Ltd* v *Marcus* [1982] 3 All ER 551, however, it was suggested that a person, acting reasonably and honestly, who knew the contents of the objects clause but had failed to realise that it had the effect of prohibiting the company from making the contract, could nevertheless be regarded as acting in good faith.

Section 35 applied only where the transaction had been decided on by the directors, or a single director who had been given actual authority by their co-directors to act.

Companies Acts 1989 and 2006

The 1989 Act made substantial changes to the scope of the lawful actions of a company, the degree of protection offered to third parties, the duties of directors and the rights of shareholders with respect to *ultra vires* transactions. Despite recommendations going back to the report of the Cohen Committee in 1945 and the report of the Jenkins Committee in 1962, both of which called for the abolition of the *ultra vires* rule, the Act failed to go quite as far as that. For all intents and purposes, however, this was the effect of the Act except in certain very limited circumstances.

Section 35 of the Companies Act 1985, as substituted by s 108 of the 1989 Act, dealt with three aspects of the doctrine of *ultra vires;* however, this area has now been subject to modification by ss 39 and 40 of the Companies Act 2006.

The capacity of the company

Section 35 of the 1985 Act (as modified) provided that the validity of an act done by a company cannot be called into question on the basis that it is beyond the capacity of the company. The result is that a company could no longer be limited by the contents of its memorandum and therefore third parties were protected from the effects of the doctrine of *ultra vires* and could enforce such transactions against the company. While the company may also enforce a transaction entered into against a third party, a shareholder was able to restrain a company from entering into an *ultra vires* contract by way of an injunction (s 35(2)). By virtue of s 35(3) it still remained the duty of the directors to comply with any limitations on their powers contained in the memorandum or articles of association. Any actions by the directors which, but for the operation of s 35(1) above, would be *ultra vires* the company can now be ratified by the members by way of a special resolution.

The 2006 Act goes a great deal further than this and in s 39(1) it provides:

> The validity of an Act done by a company shall not be called into question on the ground of lack of capacity by reason of anything in the company's constitution.

The 2006 Act does not contain the equivalent provisions in s 35(2) and s 35(3) since it was considered that the fact that companies may now have unrestricted objects and the fact that s 171 places a specific duty on directors to abide by the company's constitution makes these provisions unnecessary.

Section 171 provides:

> A director of a company must –
>
> (a) act in accordance with the company's constitution, and
> (b) only exercise powers for the purposes for which they are conferred.

The 1989 Act also relaxed the general approach to the construction of objects clauses and s 110 of the 1989 Act provided that it was possible for a company's objects clause to state simply that it 'is to carry on business as a general commercial company'. Such a clause had the effect of creating a general commercial company which would find it virtually impossible to fall foul of the *ultra vires* doctrine. It now became easier for a company to alter its objects to incorporate such a general objects clause, though a special resolution was still required to do this. Minorities opposed to such a change were offered some protection, in that they had the right to apply to the court to have the alteration cancelled. In such a case the alteration could not take effect without the confirmation of the court.

The capacity of directors

Whilst the provisions contained in s 35A (inserted by the Companies Act 1989, s 108(1)) are largely outside the ambit of this text in that they relate to the powers of the directors to bind the company, the provision has some relevance since its effect is to extend and clarify the protection contained in the old s 35 as enacted by the 1985 Act. The effect is that a third party's position will not be prejudiced by knowing that the directors are acting beyond their powers. Thus mere knowledge that the directors are so acting will not amount to bad faith. These provisions are now restated in the 2006 Act by s 40(1) and (2). The 1989 Act was very imprecise here since there is no definition of bad faith, though it is thought that it amounted to a fraudulent act or possibly assisting the directors in the abuse of their powers. The 2006 Act provides no help at all and the existing provision is simply restated in s 40(2)(b)(iii).

Shareholders will still be able to restrain directors from committing any act which is beyond their powers, though it will not be possible to take such proceedings where the directors act in order to carry out some pre-existing legal obligation. The section does not have any effect on any liability incurred by the directors, or any other person, by reason of the directors exceeding their powers. These provisions are now again restated in s 40(4) and (5) of the 2006 Act.

The capacity of the company and third parties

By virtue of s 40(2)(b)(i) (replacing s 35B of the Companies Act 1985) a party to a transaction with a company is no longer obliged to 'enquire as to any limitation on the power of the directors to bind the company or authorise others to do so'. Originally s 35B also provided that a 'party to a transaction with a company is not bound to enquire as to whether it is permitted by the company's memorandum'; however, since company objects no longer affect the company's capacity to act, this part is no longer necessary and has been excluded from the provision. It should also be noted that s 142 of the Companies Act 1989 abolishes the doctrine of constructive notice in this context, except in certain limited instances.

The changes wrought on the doctrine of *ultra vires* by the 2006 Act have largely meant that the doctrine is mostly irrelevant now as regards the capacity of the company to enter into contracts. It should be noted, however, that ss 39 and 40 do not apply to charitable companies (s 42) unless the external party dealing with the company was unaware at the time that the act was done that the company was a charity, or the company received full consideration in respect of the act done and the external party was unaware that the act in question was beyond the company's capacity or beyond the powers of the directors. The reason the changes have been restricted is that Parliament still considers the specialised purpose of such companies should preclude them from enjoying the same freedom from the effects of the doctrine of *ultra vires* as that afforded to other types of companies.

Summary

The capacity of natural persons
Drunks

- A contract is voidable if:
  (i) drunkenness prevents an individual from understanding the transaction he has entered into; and
  (ii) the other party is aware of his level of intoxication.
- Drunks are liable to pay a reasonable price for items considered necessaries.
- When drunks are sober, they can ratify a contract and be sued upon it if a breach occurs.

Mentally disordered persons
- Those certified insane.
- Those not certified as insane.

Minors

- The Family Law Reform Act 1969, s 1: any person under 18 is a minor.
- Minors' contracts are binding or voidable, depending on the circumstances.

Contracts regarded as binding on minors

- Contracts for necessaries.
- Definition of necessaries: Goods 'suitable to the condition in life of the minor and to his actual requirements at the time of the sale and delivery'.
- A claimant wanting to enforce a contract has to establish:
  1 that the goods are capable of being necessaries;
  2 that the minor has not already been adequately supplied with such items at the time of their delivery;
  3 that the goods have been sold and delivered.
- Beneficial contracts of service:
- Examples of a beneficial contract of service: apprenticeship, education and employment.
- Such contracts are binding on minors if they are substantially for their benefit.

Voidable contracts

- Are enforceable on the minor unless he chooses to repudiate.
- Repudiation should be while the child is a minor or within a *reasonable time* of their acquiring majority.
- What is a *reasonable time* depends on the facts (NB: *Edwards* v *Carter* for an unsuccessful repudiation).

The tortious liability of minors

- A child may be liable for committing a tortious act at the same time as a breach of contract (*Burnard* v *Haggis; Ballett* v *Mingay;* conversely *see Jennings* v *Rundall*).

Restitution

- Equity introduced this doctrine to mitigate the harshness of the common law decisions that an adult could not recover the proceeds from a child if that child had committed a fraud upon him for his own benefit.
- Minors' Contracts Act 1987, s 3(1) – Court has power where it is *just and equitable* to make the child return or account for the property.

Guarantees

- Minors' Contracts Act 1987, s 2 – A guarantor will now be liable for the infant's contractual obligation even though it is unenforceable or the infant has repudiated his contractual obligation. NB: s 2 does not apply to necessaries.

The capacity of corporations

The two types of corporations

1. Chartered corporations

2. Statutory corporations

- Companies formed (incorporated) in accordance with the Companies Act 1985 (now Companies Act 2006).
- Companies can be public or private companies, limited by shares or by guarantee.

The doctrine of *ultra vires*

- Prevents a company from acting beyond its powers (authority).
- A company must act within the limits of its constitution, i.e. the object clause contained in the memorandum of association.

Avoiding the effects of the doctrine of ultra vires

- Companies Act 1985, s 35 (as amended by Companies Act 1989, s 108), now replaced by Companies Act 2006, ss 39 and 40, which deal with these aspects of *ultra vires*.

The capacity of the company – Companies Act 2006

- A company is not limited by anything in the company's constitution – s 39(1).
- A company director must act in accordance with the company's constitution – s 171.

The capacity of directors – Companies Act 2006, s 40

- Third parties are not prejudiced if they know that the directors are acting beyond their powers – s 40(1) and s 40(2).
- Shareholders will still be able to restrain directors from committing any act which is beyond their powers – s 40(4) and s 40(5).

The capacity of the company and third parties – Companies Act 2006, s 40(2)(b)(i)

- Third parties no longer have to enquire as to any limitation on the power of the directors to bind the company or authorise others to do so.

Further reading

Beatson, Burrows and Cartwright, *Anson's Law of Contract*, 30th edn (Oxford University Press, 2016)

Furmston, *Cheshire, Fifoot and Furmston's Law of Contract*, 16th edn (Oxford University Press, 2012)

Hudson, 'Mental Incapacity Revisited' [1986] *The Conveyancer and Property Lawyer* 178

Smith and Atiyah, *Atiyah's Introduction to the Law of Contract*, 6th edn (Oxford University Press, 2006)

Peel, Treitel *Law of Contract*, 14th edn (Sweet and Maxwell, 2015)

Formalities

Introduction

Objective 1

The general requirements for a simple contract have now been assessed. One of the popular misconceptions of the layperson is that for there to be a legally binding contract, there must be a properly drafted document full of incomprehensible language, sealed with red molten wax into which the long-suffering parties have, somewhat painfully, plunged their fingers or, if they were lucky enough to have one, a seal ring. Nothing is, of course, further from the truth since the vast majority of contracts are made informally, either orally or by conduct or sometimes in writing. Obviously in commercial contracts, where the terms may be very extensive, it is highly desirable to have those terms set down in writing in a formal document in case any dispute should occur. The same is also true where the contract involves very large amounts of money and thereby carries an inordinate degree of risk. There are many reasons why the parties to a contract want to have the terms set out in a formal document, though the important fact to remember is that there is no legal requirement on them to do so, subject of course to a number of exceptions.

The exceptions occur where the law considers that the nature of the contract requires it to be certain, or where the transaction is such that the parties to it are in need of protection, as in hire purchase agreements. The degree of formality required generally reflects the relative importance of the contract. Three categories of contract may be discerned:

1 contracts required to be made by deed;
2 contracts required to be in writing;
3 contracts required to be evidenced in writing.

Contracts required to be made by deed

Objective
2

Nowadays the dramatic, almost ceremonial procedure of sealing a document with molten wax has, for the most part, been replaced by the more practical, though less impressive, fixing of a self-adhesive wafer of red paper. The requirement that a certain transaction must be made under seal is for the most part a euphemism for the requirement that it must be contained in a deed. All deeds must be 'signed, sealed and delivered', but it is not the sealing of the document that makes the deed binding, rather it is the signature of the party making the deed, by virtue of s 73 of the Law of Property Act 1925. More recently, this provision was indirectly reinforced by the Law of Property (Miscellaneous Provisions) Act 1989, s 1(1)(b), which provided that, 'Any rule of law which . . . requires a seal for the valid execution of an instrument as a deed by an individual . . . is abolished.' Given the abolition of the need for a seal, how does one know whether the document is a deed or not? The answer to this question lies in s 1(2) and (3) of the 1989 Act.

Section 1(2) states:

An instrument shall not be a deed unless –

(a) it makes it clear on its face that it is intended to be a deed by the party making it or, as the case may be, by the parties to it (whether by describing itself as a deed or expressing itself to be executed or signed as a deed or otherwise); and

(b) it is validly executed as a deed by that person or, as the case may be, one or more of those parties.

Any instrument that is expressed to be by deed is sufficient for s 1(2)(a). Very often instruments begin, not by expressing themselves to be by deed, but by expressing the purpose or nature of the instrument itself, as, for example, 'This Conveyance . . . ' or 'This Underlease . . . ' If this practice is to continue, then the intention that the document is to be a deed must be indicated somewhere else within the document. For the most part, this intention will be shown by the document being signed and witnessed 'as a deed'.

Section 1(3) states:

An instrument is validly executed as a deed by an individual if, and only if

(a) it is signed –

    (i) by him in the presence of a witness who attests the signature; or

    (ii) at his direction and in his presence and the presence of two witnesses who each attest the signature; and

    (iii) it is delivered as a deed by him or a person authorised to do so on his behalf.

Quite clearly if the provisions of s 1(3) are not complied with, then the purported deed will be void.

The most common type of transaction that requires a deed is the conveyance of a legal estate in land by virtue of s 52(1) of the Law of Property Act 1925. Further, by s 54(2), a deed is required to create a legal lease of more than three years. A deed can also be used to turn a bare or gratuitous promise into a legally binding enforceable obligation, its use in this respect evolving separately from the doctrine of consideration.

Contracts required to be in writing

Generally

Objective
3

Apart from those contracts requiring to be by deed, some contracts are required to be set out in writing in order to be enforceable. There are many examples of such contracts but by far the most important until recently are contracts governed by the Consumer Credit Act 1974 (as amended by the Consumer Credit Act 2006), which requires that certain regulated agreements, such as hire purchase and credit sales agreements, are 'not properly executed' unless in the form prescribed by regulation under the Act.

Failure to comply with the requirement of being in writing has the general effect of rendering the contract unenforceable. In the case of the Consumer Credit Act 1974, however, an agreement that is not properly executed can nevertheless be enforced against a debtor on an order of the court. No such order can be made if the agreement has not been signed by the debtor, or if he has not been given a copy of the agreement or notice of his right to cancel.

Contracts for the sale or other disposition of an interest in land

The Law of Property (Miscellaneous Provisions) Act 1989 now presents probably the most important category of contracts that are required to be in writing. Prior to this Act, s 40 of the Law of Property Act 1925 provided:

(1) No action may be brought upon any contract for the sale or other disposition of any interest in land, unless the agreement upon which such action is brought, or some memorandum or note thereof is in writing, and signed by the party to be charged or by some other person thereunto by him lawfully authorised.

(2) This section applies to contracts whether made before or after the commencement of this Act and does not affect the law relating to part performance, or sale by the court.

The result of this provision was that the contract had to be evidenced by some note or memorandum in which there had to be an adequate identification of the parties to the contract, together with a description of the subject matter. Further, the nature of the consideration had to be indicated and the memorandum had to include any other terms deemed material by the parties. The memorandum was required to be signed by the party to be charged, that is, the party against whom it was sought to enforce the contract.

It was possible for the memorandum to be made up from two or more documents, provided that a document signed by the claimant existed, that there was sufficient reference in that document to a second document, and that the two, when read together, formed a complete memorandum. One further feature, and one that could and did cause substantial problems, as seen in *Law* v *Jones* [1974] Ch 112 and *Tiverton Estates Ltd* v *Wearwell Ltd* [1975] Ch 146, was the fact that the memorandum need not have been deliberately prepared as a memorandum and indeed may have been made inadvertently.

Section 40 did not provide that contracts for the sale or other disposition of an interest in land could not be created orally, but merely that such a contract was unenforceable by action unless there was a memorandum containing the information required by s 40(1). The only way to save a contract not just evidenced in writing was to bring the contract within the doctrine of part-performance as contained in s 40(2), and this was not always easy to do.

Section 2(1) of the 1989 Act now provides:

A contract for the sale or other disposition of an interest in land can only be made in writing and only by incorporating all the terms which the parties have expressly agreed in one document or, where contracts are exchanged, in each.

The requirements of s 2(1) are far more formal and the problems that arose in **Law v Jones** and **Tiverton Estates Ltd v Wearwell Ltd** will no longer arise, since the contract for the sale or other disposition of an interest in land can only be made in writing, not just evidenced in writing. The change in effect is dramatic; no longer would a contract be merely unenforceable unless it was in writing – now it would be void for non-compliance. Further, there is no longer the possibility of the agreement being saved by the doctrine of part-performance since the whole of s 40, which includes that doctrine, is repealed.

The requirements as to the actual content of s 2 contracts or other dispositions are also more formal. All the terms which the parties have expressly agreed must be incorporated in one document or, where contracts are exchanged, in each (s 2(1)). It is, however, possible to incorporate the terms in a document either by having them set out in that document or by reference to some other document (s 2(2)), thus allowing for the possibility of joinder. Further, the document incorporating the terms or, where contracts are exchanged, one of the documents incorporating them (but not necessarily the same one) must be signed by or on behalf of each party to the contract (s 2(3)). There is an obviously important difference here between s 2 and s 40(1) in that s 40(1) only required the contract to be signed by one party – 'the party to be charged' – while s 2 requires the contract to be signed by each party. The aim here is to redress the somewhat unfair situation which existed previously whereby, prior to the enactment of s 2, a party, once they had received a s 40(1) memorandum signed by the other party, could enforce the contract even though they themselves had not signed any written evidence of the contract and thus could not have it enforced against them.

As has already been stated, it is clear that a contract under s 2 must contain all the terms which the parties have expressly agreed and thus the omission of such a term will be prima facie fatal. A similar problem also existed in relation to s 40(1), as pointed out by Professor Pettit in 'Farewell Section 40' [1989] *The Conveyancer and Property Lawyer* 431 at 435, in that a defendant could defeat a claim simply by producing evidence of a term that had been omitted. In **Farrell v Green** (1974) 232 EG 587, Pennycuick V-C qualified this by stating *obiter* that if the omitted term expressly agreed between the parties is one which would have been implied by the court in any event, then the omission of the term would not be fatal to the enforceability of the contract. Possibly this exception would not apply in the case of s 2 contracts since the requirements of the section are strict – all the express terms must be in writing. Any parol (oral) variations of a written contract would also not be valid and would be ineffective.

Having examined some of the issues surrounding the construction of s 2, we must now assess the effects of the repeal of s 40 and its replacement by s 2 on the exercise of equitable jurisdiction. Such jurisdiction was previously exercised where there had been an informal contract for the sale or other disposition of an interest in land. It is a well-recognised equitable principle that 'equity looks to the intention and not to the form', and thus it is clear that s 2 is likely to have a significant effect on this concept.

The role adopted by equity is that where there has been a failure to use a deed in the creation of a legal interest as required by s 52(1) of the Law of Property Act 1925, equity regarded this as a contract to create such an interest, which it would then enforce by way of a decree of specific performance. Presumably such contracts must now be in writing to comply with s 2(1). The possible effects of such a conclusion could be extensive when analysed in the context of transactions, such as leases and options.

Leases

In order to create a legal lease, a deed is required; however, where the deed was imperfect, equity would treat the lease as a contract to grant a lease, provided the requirements of s 40 were complied with. Similarly, if the lease was granted orally, equity would treat this as a contract to grant a lease, though here a sufficient act of part-performance was required. Such was the doctrine in *Parker* v *Taswell* (1858) 2 De G & J 559. Since part-performance under s 40(2) has been repealed, it is clear that there must be a s 2 contract in order to establish an equitable lease under the doctrine in *Walsh* v *Lonsdale* (1882) 21 Ch D 9. At best, even if the imperfect grant of a lease could be interpreted as complying with s 2, the establishment of equitable leases by this method must inevitably be restricted.

The problems indicated in the application of *Walsh* v *Lonsdale* do not, however, stop at leases since over the years the principles contained in the doctrine have been applied by analogy to other interests such as easements and mortgages.

A further problem that can occur with leases revolves around the exceptions to the requirements of s 2(1) which are set out in s 2(5). Section 2(5)(a) provides that s 2 does not apply to 'a contract to grant such a lease as is mentioned in s 54(2) of the Law of Property Act 1925'.

Section 54(2) in turn provides that:

> Nothing in the foregoing provisions of this part of this Act shall affect the creation by parol of leases taking effect in possession for a term not exceeding three years (whether or not the lessee is given power to extend the term) at the best rent which can be reasonably obtained without taking a fine.

The effect of the provision is that a grant of a lease for not more than three years would take effect as a legal lease despite the absence of a deed, provided the lease took effect immediately.

Such a lease would result even if there was a complete lack of formality and it was created orally. If, however, the lease did not take effect immediately, then it would take effect as a contract to create a lease and it had to comply with s 40(1) and (2), be evidenced in writing or be supported by a sufficient act of part-performance. Since s 2 has now repealed s 40, parties negotiating such short leases should be warned of the possible danger that any agreement reached might be legally binding although it is made orally. Clearly such agreements should be qualified by words such as 'subject to a written contract being drawn up'. Time-honoured words such as 'subject to contract' are probably not sufficient because the oral agreement will be binding as a contract in any event.

Options

An option to purchase is described in *Beesly* v *Hallwood Estates Ltd* [1960] 1 WLR 549 as an offer to sell which 'the grantor is contractually precluded from withdrawing so long as the option remains exercisable'. The contract to purchase then takes place when the grantor is given notice of the exercise of the option. As indicated in *Pritchard* v *Briggs* [1980] Ch 338, the option itself does not form a contract, though it does create an immediate equitable interest in favour of the grantee as soon the option is granted, since the grantee has a right to call for the conveyance of the land to themselves, whether the grantor consents or not. Since the right of the grantee is an equitable interest in the land, then surely the notice exercising this right must comply with the s 2 requirements?

Spiro v *Glencrown Properties Ltd and Another* [1991] 1 All ER 600

In this case, it was held that while the grant of an option depended on contractual agreement and required compliance with s 2, the exercise of the power was a unilateral act and did not require such compliance. An option was described as 'a conditional contract . . . which the grantee is entitled to convert into a concluded contract of purchase'. Since the *grant* of the option did comply with s 2, it was held that there was no need for the *exercise* of the option to comply since 'it would destroy the very purpose of the option if the purchaser had to obtain the vendor's countersignature to the notice by which it was exercised'. It was also stated that 'the purpose of s 2 was to prescribe the formalities for recording the parties' consent. It followed that the grant of the option was the only "contract for the sale . . . of an interest or other disposition of an interest in land"'.

The decision would seem to be dubious since, while it may be correct in its explanation of the legal effects of the granting and exercise of options, it is wrong in principle when read in the context of the 1989 Act. The authorities are clear that the right of the grantee to exercise the right of option is an equitable interest in the land, and while the exercise of this right is not a contract of sale, it does fall within the ambit of the expression 'other disposition' for the purpose of s 2.

The 1989 Act is based on the recommendation of the Law Commission Report No. 164 (1987), in which the Law Commission indicated that, while non-compliance with s 2 would render the 'contract of sale or other disposition' void, the parties would not be without a remedy; it saw no cause to fear that the repeal of s 40 and its replacement by s 2 should inhibit the courts in the exercise of equitable jurisdiction in order to do justice between individuals in 'otherwise hard cases'. Remarkably the Law Commission, while indicating the importance of complying with the s 2 formalities, appeared to be recommending that the courts exercise equitable discretion in avoiding the worst effects of s 2. The provision thus takes on the mantle of a latter-day Statute of Frauds (*see* below), with the Law Commission advocating the use of equitable discretion to prevent it from being used as 'an engine of fraud'.

Among the possible remedies advocated in the report are remedies in tort (for example, negligence or deceit), actions for restitution or in quasi-contract, on a *quantum meruit* or total failure of consideration basis, and also actions based on the concept of collateral contract. The Law Commission seemed strongly to advocate the use of promissory or proprietary estoppel as an equitable remedy, while the Act itself in s 2(5) protected the creation and operation of resulting, implied and constructive trusts.

For more on restitution and quasi-contract refer to Chapter 18.

A further equitable remedy specifically preserved in the 1989 Act is **rectification.** This provision is found in s 2(4):

Where a contract for the sale or other disposition of an interest in land satisfies the conditions of this section by reason only of rectification of one or more documents in pursuance of an order of a court, the contract shall come into being, or be deemed to have come into being, at such time as may be specified in the order.

At one time it was thought that for rectification to apply there had to be a valid concluded contract; since this would not be the case if a term was omitted by virtue of s 2, the document could not, of course, be rectified. This principle, however, would seem to have been overturned in *Joscelyne* **v** *Nissen* [1970] 2 QB 86 which, as was pointed out in the Law Commission report, established that there does not have to be a prior valid contract, but merely a prior agreement or a common intention to contract coupled with convincing proof that the written agreement does not adequately reflect the terms of the agreement.

One problem with rectification, as identified by the Law Commission, was the fact that it was retrospective in operation. The effect of this could be that third-party rights occurring between the time of contracting and rectification could be either validated or invalidated as a consequence of rectification. The Act thus reflects the Law Commission's concern and gives discretion to the court as to the effective date of rectification.

With such equitable remedies being suggested, it is difficult to understand why the doctrine of part-performance has been repealed. It would seem that there is an attempt to remove the ability of equity to intervene on the basis of a contractual analysis of informality. Further, the Law Commission is assuming that a court would be willing to exercise its equitable jurisdiction. The exercise of such jurisdiction was not forthcoming in **Midland Bank Trust Co. Ltd v Green** [1981] AC 513 where the court applied only the strict wording of the Land Charges Act 1972. A similar approach might well be taken with the Law of Property (Miscellaneous Provisions) Act 1989, with the adoption of an attitude that the Act requires the contract to be in writing and therefore in writing it must be, and if Parliament had intended that equity would have some part to play, then express provision should have been made for it within the body of the Act.

Clearly it is difficult to predict how the courts will apply the Act and all one can do at the moment is to wait for cases to come before the courts.

Contracts required to be evidenced in writing

Introduction

Objective
4

With the repeal of s 40 of the Law of Property Act 1925, the only types of contracts now required to be evidenced in writing are contracts of guarantee. A guarantee may be defined as a promise made by one individual to another whereby the first agrees to meet the liabilities/debts owed by a third party to the second, should the third party be unable to meet those liabilities/debts.

Contracts of guarantee are governed by s 4 of the Statute of Frauds 1677, an Act that tended to promote fraud rather than prevent it because it was so badly drafted. Indeed, such was its notoriety that it was described by Lord Wright as an 'extemporaneous excrescence on the common law'. Originally the Act governed some six classes of contract but four classes were repealed by the Law Reform (Enforcement of Contracts) Act 1954 and contracts for the sale or other dispositions of an interest in land have met the fate already detailed above.

Section 4 of the Statute of Frauds

Section 4 provides:

> No action shall be brought . . . whereby to charge the defendant upon any special promise to answer for the debt, default or miscarriage of another person, unless there is written evidence of the agreement.

The formal requirements of contracts of guarantee falling within s 4 are very similar to those formerly required by s 40(1) of the Law of Property Act 1925, in that they must be evidenced by some note or memorandum in writing and signed by the party to be charged, that is, the person against whom the contract is being enforced. The note or memorandum must contain all the material terms, that is, identify the parties and describe the subject

For more on part performance refer to Chapter 13.

matter and the nature of the consideration, and any other terms deemed material by the parties. The doctrine of part-performance has no application in such contracts. Failure to comply with the requirements of s 4 renders the contract unenforceable.

At one time it was considered that the provision was confined to contractual liability, in particular, guarantees arising out of a pre-existing debt, since it was considered that the terms 'debt, default or miscarriage' were synonymous.

Kirkham v *Marter* (1819) 2 B & Ald 613

In this case, the scope of guarantees required to be evidenced in writing was extended to cover tortious liability. In the case the defendant's son rode the plaintiff's horse, with his permission, so aggressively that he killed the horse. As a result of this action he was liable in tort to the plaintiff, who then threatened to sue him. At this point the defendant promised the plaintiff that he would compensate the plaintiff if he promised not to pursue the claim against his son. This was accepted by the plaintiff, but in fact the defendant failed to pay. The defendant pleaded the Statute of Frauds as a defence, stating that his promise, to be binding, had to be evidenced in writing as required by the Act. The plaintiff argued that the Act did not apply to guarantees regarding tortious liability, that it applied only to pre-existing debts, and these were not required to be evidenced in writing. It was held that the statute was not confined to cases of contract since the father had promised 'to answer for the *miscarriage* of another' (emphasis added). For the father to be liable on his promise, the guarantee had to be evidenced in writing and, as it was not, the defendant escaped liability. The court considered that the term 'miscarriage' meant a wrongful act, and this interpretation brought guarantees in relation to tortious acts within the reach of the provision.

Some further difficulties that can arise in relation to guarantees and s 4 can be seen in the case, of ***Actionstrength Ltd*** **v** ***International Glass Engineering*** [2003] UKHL 17. In this case the second defendant, Saint-Gobain Glass, wanted to build a new glass factory in Yorkshire with Inglen, the first defendant, being the main construction contractor. The claimant Actionstrength entered into a contract with Inglen to provide construction workers for the site. The arrangement was that Actionstrength would pay the workers and then be reimbursed by Inglen. Inglen fell behind with these payments and Actionstrength threatened to withdraw its workforce from the site. Following a site meeting Actionstrength alleged that Saint-Gobain had stated that if Actionstrength maintained its workforce on the site, Saint-Gobain would ensure that Actionstrength would be paid. As a result Actionstrength retained the workforce at the site for another month in which time Inglen's indebtedness grew by a factor of five. Actionstrength then sued Inglen and Saint-Gobain obtaining summary judgement against Inglen which then went into liquidation. This left Actionstrength with an action against Saint-Gobain on the guarantee; however, Saint-Gobain argued that even if Actionstrength's version of events were true, the guarantee had been made orally and was not enforceable since it was not evidenced in writing as required by the Statute of Frauds 1677, s 4.

In the Court of Appeal, Actionstrength argued that the promise made by Saint-Gobain was not a guarantee and therefore there was no need for compliance with s 4. This argument was rejected by the Court of Appeal. Actionstrength then appealed to the House of Lords, accepting that the promise was not a guarantee but arguing that Saint-Gobain were estopped from relying on the argument put forward regarding the guarantee in that it was unconscionable in all the circumstances for Saint-Gobain to rely on s 4. This argument was rejected by the House of Lords. Lord Bingham referred to the case of ***Amalgamated Investment and***

Property Co. Ltd v *Texas Commerce International Bank Ltd* [1982] QB 84 where a party was indeed estopped from disputing the effect of a guarantee. This case provided that three questions should be asked:

1 What is the assumption which the claimant (Actionstrength) has made?
2 Did Saint-Gobain induce or encourage the making of that assumption?
3 Is it in all the circumstances unconscionable for Saint-Gobain to place reliance on s 4?

The third question had to be asked after the first two. Lord Bingham considered that it was clear that the first question could easily be answered from the facts in that the claimant clearly believed that it was to benefit from Saint-Gobain's guarantee. He thought, however, that the second question was fatal to Actionstrength's claim. He stated:

> in seeking to show inducement or encouragement Actionstrength can rely on nothing beyond the oral agreement of Saint-Gobain which, in the absence of writing, is rendered unenforceable by s 4. There was no representation by Saint-Gobain that it would honour the agreement despite the absence of writing, or that it was not a contract of guarantee, or that it would confirm the agreement in writing. Nor did Saint-Gobain make any payment direct to Actionstrength which could arguably be relied on as affirming the oral agreement or inducing Actionstrength to go on supplying labour.

It can be seen clearly that if Actionstrength's claim had been allowed, then any oral guarantee would be upheld because of the effect of the estoppel and this would result in s 4 being rendered ineffective, despite the fact that Parliament has seen fit to retain the requirement of the Statute of Frauds in relation to guarantees. While the decision is undoubtedly correct, it is questionable whether the provision should operate in commercial cases like this. The original intention behind s 4 was to protect the 'small man', in that there was danger that inexperienced people could be led into obligations that they did not fully understand with the result that unscrupulous persons could orally assert that credit was given on the faith of a guarantee that the guarantor had no intention of entering into. Saint-Gobain certainly did not fall into this category and it was in their interests to ensure that Actionstrength maintained its workforce on the site since the withdrawal could only result in the factory not being completed, with the consequent extra costs and loss of profits. By the same token, of course, it could be said of Actionstrength that it was either naïve or badly advised in not obtaining the written evidence required by s 4.

There are certain circumstances in which there is no requirement for the contract to be in writing within s 4.

Promises made to third-party debtors

No requirement of evidence in writing arises where the promise to pay the debt is made to the third-party debtor. The promise of the guarantor must be made to the creditor, as stated in *Eastwood* v *Kenyon* (1840) 11 A & E 438.

Indemnities

Section 4 applies only where the guarantor assumes secondary liability; in other words, the guarantee is not to pay the debts of the debtor in any event, but only where the debtor fails to meet their obligations. In situations where the guarantor assumes primary liability, this is not a guarantee but an indemnity, arising out of a promise to meet the losses of the creditor from the principal contract.

The practical difference between indemnities and guarantees can be seen in the case of ***Birkmyr v Darnell*** (1704) 1 Salk 27. In the case it was stated that should two persons go into a shop and one of them decide to buy something, at which point the other says to the shop-keeper, 'Let him have the goods; if he does not pay you, I will', this will amount to a guar-antee and is void without writing by virtue of the Statute of Frauds. However, if he says:' "Let him have the goods, I will be your paymaster" or "I will see you paid", this is an undertaking for himself and he shall be intended to be the very buyer and the other to act but as his serv-ant', this is an indemnity. It is not always possible to have such a clear-cut situation and the court must decide whether primary or secondary liability has been assumed by the defend-ant. A further application of the principles can be seen in ***Mountstephen v Lakeman.***

Mountstephen v *Lakeman* (1871) LR 7 QB 196

The defendant was chairman of the Brixham Local Board of Health. A surveyor to the Board proposed to the plaintiff, a builder, that he should make the connections between the drains of certain houses and the main sewer. The plaintiff then asked what arrangements were being made to pay him, at which point the defendant asked him what his objections were to doing the work, to which the plaintiff replied, 'I have none, if you or the Board will order the work or become responsible for the payment.' The defendant replied to this by saying, 'Go on Mountstephen, and do the work, and I will see you paid.' The plaintiff completed the work but the Board refused to pay him on the basis that it had not made any agreement with him. The plaintiff then sued the defendant chairman, who alleged that his state-ment amounted to a guarantee which had to comply with s 4 of the Statute of Frauds and that since this had not been complied with, he assumed no liability for the debt. It was held that because the Board had not contracted for the work, there was no debt of another person to answer for. As a result, the defendant was the only debtor. His promise amounted to an assumption of primary liability which fell outside the statute and he was thus liable on the debt.

A modern application of these principles can be seen in the case of ***Associated British Ports* v *Ferryways NV*** [2009] EWCA Civ 189, where F operated a roll-on roll-off ferry ser-vice. Handling charges for loading and unloading units carried by F were agreed with P, which provided port facilities under a contract that was to last from 2003 to 2024. M was a company in the same group as F and agreed by letter (the 'letter agreement') that M would ensure that F met its contractual obligations under the 2003 contract. In particular, M assumed responsibility for ensuring, for seven years from the date of the letter, that F had 'sufficient funds to fulfil and meet all duties, commitments and liabilities entered into and/or incurred by reason of the 2003 agreement as and when they fell due and promptly fulfilled and met all such duties, commitments and liabilities'. Subsequently disputes arose between P and F which resulted in both parties concluding a 'time-to-pay agree-ment', which took the form of a supplementary memorandum to the 2003 agreement. Following further disputes, P sought to recover sums due from F under the 2003 agreement and from M under the letter agreement.

The judge at first instance gave judgement for P against F for damages to be assessed but dismissed the claim against M. The judge considered that the letter agreement was a guar-antee that gave rise to secondary liability but that its enforceability had been discharged as a result of the time-to-pay agreement. The judge considered that the undertaking to make sure the company would have the money to meet its contractual obligations was in effect a promise to answer for the debts of another, i.e. a guarantee within the Statute of Frauds

1677, s 4. P appealed, submitting that M's liability was not contingent or secondary and that the words 'at all times' used in the letter agreement pointed to a primary liability giving rise to an immediate and continuing obligation. Furthermore, in the alternative P also submitted that the letter of agreement was a binding letter of comfort and, therefore, any liability would not be discharged by the time-to-pay agreement.

In the Court of Appeal, P's appeal was dismissed. Kay LJ gave the leading judgement, which the other members concurred with. He stated that whether a document was a guarantee or an indemnity, or whether it imposed a secondary or a primary liability, depended on the 'true construction of the actual words in which the promise was expressed' as stated by Lord Diplock in *Moschi* v *Lep Air Services Ltd* [1973] AC 331. It was simply not possible to reach the conclusion suggested by P by focusing on the words 'at all times'. The obligation in the letter was a 'see-to-it' obligation; that is, M would see to it that F performed its obligations under the 2003 agreement and, if F could not meet its liabilities to P as and when they fell due (the primary liability), then the secondary liability of M would arise by way of guarantee. That would have been sufficient to protect P but for the legal significance of the subsequent time-to-pay agreement. Kay LJ stated that P would have been protected if the letter had included the common provision found in guarantees whereby a subsequent variation or time-to-pay agreement between the creditor and the debtor was expressed not to discharge the guarantee; however, such a provision was absent from the letter agreement. The court therefore held that the judge at first instance was correct to conclude that the letter agreement was indeed a guarantee though one which failed because of the presence of the subsequent time-to-pay agreement.

With regard to P's alternative submission, that the letter agreement was a binding letter of comfort, the court concluded that since the letter agreement did not give rise to a primary liability, then this must also fail. A document expressed to be a letter of comfort would usually not give rise to legal obligations and is essentially a letter of encouragement made by one party to another who is contemplating whether or not to lend money to a third party. Essentially such letters of comfort do not give rise to binding contractual promises and really only represent statements of an existing fact. Sometimes they can impose binding obligations but this has to be decided as a matter of construction by ascertaining what the common intentions of the parties are by reference to the terms of the documents and the surrounding circumstances as set out by the Court of Appeal in *Kleinwort Benson Ltd* v *Malaysia Mining Corp. Bhd* [1989] 1 WLR 379. In this case, the Court of Appeal did not consider that the letter agreement amounted to a binding letter of comfort.

The guarantee is part of a larger transaction

Section 4 has no application where the guarantee forms part of a larger transaction. The guarantee must therefore stand alone. The courts have developed this exception to s 4 in two ways:

1. *Del credere* agents

A *del credere* agent guarantees, usually in exchange for extra commission, the solvency of any customers or clients whom they introduce to the principal and with whom the principal enters into a contract. The agent promises to pay the principal, should the client fail to do so. The object behind such a relationship is to aid the principal to sell and promote their products, while at the same time allowing the agent to make a more substantial commission. The result of such a relationship is that the courts regard this undoubted guarantee as part of a wider transaction and thereby free from the requirements of s 4, though the reasoning is hard to justify.

2. Protection of property

A further exception has been developed in cases where a defendant offers a guarantee in order to protect a proprietary interest which they have in certain goods or property held by a third party. The type of situation that might arise is where the guarantor buys certain items from a seller, though the items are, in fact, held by a third party as security for an outstanding debt owed by the seller to that third party. The guarantor in these circumstances might approach the third party and negotiate the release of the goods to themselves, provided they guarantee the debt of the seller. In these circumstances, the guarantee is regarded as being outside the reach of the Statute of Frauds and will be binding despite the lack of evidence in writing. An example of such a situation may be seen in the case of *Fitzgerald* v *Dressler* (1859) 7 CBNS 374.

Summary

Contracts required to be made by deed

- Law of Property (Miscellaneous Provisions) Act 1989, s 1(1)(b) abolishes the need to have a deed sealed.
- What is a deed? – LP(MP)A 1989, s 1(2) states:

  An instrument shall not be a deed unless –

  (a) it makes it clear on its face that it is intended to be a deed by the party making it or, as the case may be, by the parties to it (whether by describing itself as a deed or expressing itself to be executed or signed as a deed or otherwise); and
  (b) it is validly executed as a deed by that person or, as the case may be, one or more of those parties.

- Deed – execution, signing and witnessing – LP(MP)A 1989, s 1(3) states:

  An instrument is validly executed as a deed by an individual if, and only if,

  (a) it is signed –
      (i) by him in the presence of a witness who attests the signature; or
      (ii) at his direction and in his presence and the presence of two witnesses who each attest the signature; and
      (iii) it is delivered as a deed by him or a person authorised to do so on his behalf.

Contracts required to be in writing
Generally

- Agreements for consumer credit under the Consumer Credit Act 1974.
- Failure to comply with the Act renders the agreement unenforceable.

Contracts for the sale or other disposition of an interest in land

- LP(MP)A, s 2 repeals the Law of Property Act 1925, s 40 which required such contracts to be *evidenced* in writing. Such contracts must now be in writing.

Contracts required to be evidenced in writing

Guarantees

- Only contracts of guarantee need to be evidenced in writing.
- Definition of a guarantee:

  a promise made by one individual to another whereby the first agrees to meet the liabilities/debts owed by a third party to the second, should the third party be unable to meet those liabilities/debts.

- Contracts of guarantee are governed by s 4 of the Statute of Frauds 1677.

Promises made to third-party debtors

- The promise of the guarantor must be made to the creditor (*Eastwood v Kenyon*).

Indemnities

The guarantee is part of a larger transaction

- There are two exceptions to s 4:
  - (i) *Del credere* agents.
  - (ii) Protection of property.

Further reading

Beatson, Burrows and Cartwright, *Anson's Law of Contract,* 30th edn (Oxford University Press, 2016)

Burn, *Cheshire and Burn's Modern Law of Real Property,* 15th edn (Butterworths, 1994)

Dumbill, 'Spiro: The Easy Option' (1991) 141 *New Law Journal* 124

Furmston, *Cheshire, Fifoot and Furmston's Law of Contract,* 16th edn (Oxford University Press, 2012)

Howell, 'Informal Conveyances and Section 2 of the Law of Property (Miscellaneous Provisions) Act 1989' [1990] *The Conveyancer and Property Lawyer* 441

Law Commission, *Formalities for Contracts for Sale etc. of Land,* Report No. 164 (1987)

Petitt, 'Farewell Section 40' [1989] *The Conveyancer and Property Lawyer* 431

Smith and Atiyah, *Atiyah's Introduction to the Law of Contract,* 6th edn (Oxford University Press, 2006)

Peel, Treitel *Law of Contract,* 14th edn (Sweet and Maxwell, 2015)

Part 2

The contents of the contract

7

The terms of the contract

Objectives

After reading this chapter you should be able to:

1. Understand and explain how express terms are incorporated into contracts.

2. Explain and understand the principles involved in the construction of contractual terms and the influence of the Parol Evidence Rule.

3. Understand and explain how implied terms are incorporated into contracts with reference to terms implied as a matter of fact (with particular reference to the 'officious bystander' test and the 'business efficacy' test)

4. Understand and explain how implied terms are incorporated into contracts with reference to terms implied by law and by statute.

5. Understand and explain how implied terms are incorporated into contracts with reference to terms implied by statute with particular reference to the Consumer Rights Act 2015, the Sale of Goods Act 1979 and the Consumer Contracts (Information, Cancellation and Additional Charges) Regulations 2013.

6. Explain the role of good faith in the law of contract.

7. Know and understand the differences between warranties, conditions and innominate terms.

Introduction

Having analysed the basic requirements for a simple contract, we must of course examine what the parties have actually agreed to undertake in the contract. In commercial contracts, the obligations agreed to by the parties are reduced to a formal written document, while for most of the public a mere oral agreement is sufficient. The terms in these contracts have then been expressly agreed by the parties, but this is not the whole story since the law, either by statute or by trade usage, may imply further terms into such contracts. In addition, a court may imply into any contract any terms which the court thinks necessary to give commercial efficacy to the contract, or where the court considers that a particular term would have been included in the contract but for an oversight on the part of the parties to it.

In addition to the contents of a contract one has also to assess what effect a breach of a particular term will have on the ability of the parties to terminate the contract or to claim damages. The effect of the breach largely revolves around the importance attached to a particular term, since it is clear that not all terms are of equal importance.

The final consideration in this aspect of the law of contract concerns the ability of the parties to limit or exclude their liability for breach of contract.

The ability of the parties to limit or exclude their liability for breach of contract will be discussed in Chapter 8.

Express terms

Objective 1

A contract may be agreed upon either orally or in writing, or both. If a dispute arises out of an oral contract, the role of the judge is to discern what the parties have agreed upon from the evidence put before the court. The finding of the judge here is clearly one of fact.

Where the contract has been reduced to writing, the actual contents of the contract present little difficulty for the judge since they are apparent from the document or documents submitted. The role of the judge here is to decide issues concerning the interpretation of a particular term or terms *within the contractual document*. It is this last aspect that is important since the courts confine the agreement reached by the parties to the written document and, in the main, refuse to allow evidence by one of the parties that they did not agree to a particular term or that the document misinterprets their original intentions, especially if they have signed the document.

From the above it can be seen that the problems confronting the courts with regard to express terms can be reduced to two. First, to what extent are any statements made by the parties terms of the contract and, second, to what extent may the parties adduce evidence other than that contained in the document in order to prove that the document misstates their original intentions?

Incorporation of statements as terms of the contract

Simply because the parties have entered into discussions, either orally or in writing, it does not necessarily mean that any conclusions reached from those discussions are automatically terms of the contract. A distinction has to be made between statements which merely amount to representations and those that amount to terms of the contract. A term of a contract is an expression of a willingness by the parties to agree to abide by that obligation and breach of it will enable the parties to sue for breach of contract. A representation, often referred to as a 'mere representation', is only an inducement to persuade the other party to enter into the contract, but it is not a term of the agreement and no action lies for breach of contract if it is not complied with, though of course a dual liability may arise if there is a misrepresentation and the representation contained within it also becomes a term. This is not to say a representation is devoid of legal effect, since clearly one could not allow an individual to make all sorts of untrue statements simply to induce the other party to enter into a legally binding contract and yet not bear responsibility for the untruths. Thus where a person makes an untrue statement which induces the other party to enter into a contract they will be liable for **misrepresentation**, though here the action lies either in the tort of deceit or under the Misrepresentation Act 1967, or for innocent misrepresentation, depending on the degree of culpability of the representor.

The Consumer Rights Act 2015 has also had an impact on the issue of terms versus representations. Section 50 of the CRA provides that every contract to supply a service is treated as including a term with regards to anything said or written to the consumer by or on behalf of the trader, provided the information supplied is taken into account by the consumer whether to enter into the contract or as regards any decision about the service after entering into the contract. Further, any information provided by the trader under the requirements of the Consumer Contracts (Information, Cancellation and Additional Charges) Regulations 2013 (SI 2013/3134) Schedules 1 and 2 is to be treated as included as a term of the contract by regs 9,10 or 13.

For more on misrepresentation refer to Chapter 9.

The problem that thus confronts the courts is whether a statement is a term or a 'mere representation'. The distinction is not easy to make but the effect, as we have seen, is crucial. In order to make the distinction the courts adopt an objective analysis of the intentions of the parties, that is, what would a reasonable man consider to be the intentions of the parties in relation to a particular statement given the circumstances present in the case? While this test appears simple enough, it is not so easy to apply and substantial numbers of cases have resulted from attempts to apply it. A result of this is that the courts have developed several aids to help determine the outcome of the test and to attempt to produce a degree of coherence within the law, though not always successfully. The aids adopted may be broken down as follows.

Timing

The lapse of time between the making of the statement and the entering into of the contract may be relevant in determining whether the statement is a term or a representation.

Bannerman v *White* (1861) 10 CBNS 844

In this case, the parties negotiated for the sale of hops. Prior to the negotiations the defendants had indicated that they did not wish to purchase hops which had been treated with sulphur. When the plaintiff produced samples, the defendants again inquired whether sulphur had been used and they were assured that it had not. It then transpired that five acres out of a total of some 300 acres had been so treated. The defendants then repudiated the contract. The defendants argued that they had stressed the importance of their need for untreated hops and that since the seller must have known about the treatment of the five acres this was a term of the contract which allowed them to repudiate the contract should it be broken. The plaintiff, however, contended that the question regarding this non-use of sulphur had arisen in preliminary negotiations and was not therefore a term of the contract. The jury, however, found that the seller's statement was understood by both the parties to be part of the contract and that the defendants were entitled to repudiate it. This conclusion was then affirmed on appeal.

A more modern application of the principle can be seen in the following case.

Routledge v *McKay* [1954] 1 All ER 855

A motorcycle was first registered in 1930 but when a new registration book was issued the date of the original registration was given as 9 September 1941. In 1949, the seller, who was not responsible for the incorrect entry, stated, in response to a question by the buyer, that it was a late 1941 or early 1942 model. One week later the buyer and seller entered into a contract of sale. The note of the contract made no mention of the date of the motorcycle. The buyer claimed damages for breach of warranty. It was held that the interval between the negotiations and the entering into of the contract was too wide for a relationship between the two to be established. Consequently the incorrect statement was a representation and not a term of the contract and the claim for breach of warranty failed.

Reduction of the contract into writing

It may be that there has been an oral agreement but that this is later reduced into a written document. If a statement made orally between the parties is not included in the written document the inference drawn by the courts is that the statement was not intended to be a term of the contract but a mere representation. The case of **Routledge v McKay** above is a clear illustration of the principle since the note of the agreement made no mention of the date of the machine, the assumption being that if this was regarded as a significant factor in the sale the parties would have ensured its inclusion in the note. This position is also consistent with the attitude of the courts to bind the parties within the four corners of a written agreement, and to disallow the adducing of evidence of further terms outside the written agreement into the contract. In **Birch v Paramount Estates Ltd** (1956) 16 EG 396, however, the defendants made a statement regarding the quality of a house that was being sold. The written contract made no reference to the statement. The Court of Appeal nevertheless regarded this statement as a contractual term, though in this case the defendants were held to have special knowledge, which is a separate factor in itself in determining the status of a particular term (*see* below).

The importance of the statement

A statement may be regarded as a term of the contract if such importance is attached to it that the injured party would not have entered into the contract but for this statement. An example of the application of this guideline has already been seen in **Bannerman v White** above, since there was no question of the defendants entering into the contract if the hops had been treated with sulphur. Indeed, the defendants stated that they would not even have bothered to ask the price if they had known that sulphur had been used in cultivating the hops.

A similar approach can also be seen in **Couchman v Hill** [1947] 1 All ER 103 where the plaintiff bought a heifer at an auction. The catalogue described the heifer as being 'unserved'. The conditions of sale provided that the auctioneers did not warrant the condition or description of any animal auctioned. Prior to the sale, while the heifer was in the ring, the plaintiff asked the auctioneer to confirm that the animal was unserved, and this he did. Eight weeks after the sale the heifer died as a result of carrying a calf at too young an age. It was held that the statement that the heifer was 'unserved' amounted to a warranty, that is, a term of the contract, which overrode the auctioneers' conditions of sale. It was clear that the plaintiff placed such importance on the statement that he would not have bid for the animal had he known the truth of its condition. He could therefore claim damages.

The two cases stated above have, however, to be contrasted with the case of **Oscar Chess Ltd v Williams**.

Oscar Chess Ltd v Williams [1957] 1 All ER 325

Here the defendants sold a car to the plaintiffs, who were motor dealers, for £290. They described the car as a 1948 Morris 10, which they honestly believed to be the case since this fact was also confirmed by the registration book. Some six months later the plaintiffs discovered that the car was in fact a 1939 model and therefore sued for damages on the basis of a breach of warranty. It was held that their action should fail since the court, after considering all the facts, came to the conclusion and found that the defendants had no intention of binding themselves by way of a contractual obligation as to the veracity of the date of registration of the vehicle. The defendants, the court decided, had made an innocent misrepresentation as to the date when the vehicle was first registered.

Special knowledge or skill

The court is more willing to regard a statement as amounting to a term of the contract where a representor has some special knowledge or skill that places them in a stronger position of discovering the truth of the matter. The principle has already been seen in *Birch v Paramount Estates* (above), where the defendants were regarded as holding out to the plaintiffs that they had particular knowledge to the extent that the plaintiff considered that there was no need to make a check on the information supplied by the defendants. A further example can be seen in *Schawel v Read* [1913] 2 IR 81 in which the plaintiff, who was seeking a stallion for stud purposes, examined a horse which was potentially suitable. Soon after the plaintiff commenced the examination, the defendant interrupted, saying, 'You need not look for anything: the horse is perfectly sound', whereupon the plaintiff stopped his examination. A few days after this incident a price was agreed and three weeks later the purchase was completed. The horse proved to be unfit for stud purposes and the plaintiff sued for breach of contract, the defendant arguing that he had made a mere representation. The statement was held to be a term of the contract since the court not only considered that the representation had taken place at the time of the sale but that the defendant, who was the owner of the horse, clearly had special knowledge as to its condition.

The application of the special knowledge or skill criterion by the courts is best illustrated by a comparison of the cases of *Oscar Chess Ltd v Williams* and *Dick Bentley Productions Ltd v Harold Smith (Motors) Ltd* [1965] 2 All ER 65. The facts of *Oscar Chess* have already been discussed above, but it is necessary to recall that the statement regarding the age of the vehicle was held not to be a term of the contract. That decision continues to represent something of an absurdity in that a statement of such importance was not regarded as a term of the contract. Two of the criteria already discussed pointed to such a fact, in that the statement was made at the time of the contract and that the contract had not been reduced to writing and, therefore, no question arose in relation to the possibility of an oral statement being overridden by a written document. Both these factors weighed in favour of the plaintiff. However, the Court of Appeal was swayed by the argument that while the defendant seller had no actual knowledge of the first year of registration of the vehicle, the plaintiff buyers were experienced car dealers and, as such, possessed the knowledge, experience and means of determining the true age of the vehicle. Put another way, the plaintiffs, knowing that the seller was not well versed in such matters, coupled with the fact that he had not acted negligently in relation to the date of first registration, were not entitled to assume that the defendant seller had assumed responsibility for the accuracy of the date.

Dick Bentley Productions Ltd v Harold Smith (Motors) Ltd [1965] 2 All ER 65

A motor dealer made an untrue statement to a private purchaser that a car had done only 20,000 miles since being fitted with a new engine and gearbox. In fact the car had done nearly 100,000 miles. The purchaser eventually found the car to be unsuitable and the mileage untrue. The purchaser sued for breach of contract. The Court of Appeal held that the statement was a term of the contract since the defendants were clearly better placed to know the truth of the statement than the plaintiff, who thus was successful in his claim for damages.

The problem that now arises is how to reconcile the decisions in the two cases. Lord Denning was of the opinion in *Dick Bentley* that the final decision as to whether the statement was a term or a mere representation was based on the presence or absence of fault in relation to the accuracy of the statement. In *Dick Bentley*, the defendants were at fault in relation to the number of miles since they were in a position to know the true position or at least to find out, and thus the statement was a term of the contract. In *Oscar Chess*, negligence was not present as to the truth of the statement, but also the defendant seller, not being involved in the motor trade, was not in a position to confirm the date of first registration. It is, however, naive to reduce the comparison to the presence or absence of negligence, and in any event why should this be a decisive factor in determining whether a statement is a term or a representation? The answer may well lie in Lord Denning's view in *Dick Bentley* that prima facie a statement that induces a contract should be considered a warranty. If, however, the entering into of a contract is induced by an untrue statement made either fraudulently or negligently, then the statement amounts to either a negligent or a **fraudulent misrepresentation**. The effect of such a finding would be to allow the innocent party not only to claim damages but also to rescind the contract.

For more on this aspect of misrepresentation refer to Chapter 9.

If, on the other hand, the statement is made innocently and not negligently, then in practical terms it is important for the statement to be incorporated into the contract as a term of it, since the innocent party would be able to sue for breach of contract and, at the very least, claim damages. Such a remedy would not be available to the innocent party if the statement was held to be a mere representation since here they would have to sue for innocent misrepresentation, which only gives rise to the remedy of rescission – and this may be barred in certain circumstances, such as an undue delay in claiming for it, as in *Oscar Chess*. Whilst the courts may award damages in lieu of rescission under s 2(2) of the Misrepresentation Act 1967, they cannot do so where the remedy of rescission is itself lost. Although it seems likely that the taking of fault into account when assessing whether an inaccurate statement amounts to a breach of a term or a misrepresentation will produce what appear to be inconsistent decisions, as seen above, this method of assessment nevertheless produces an equitable solution if the reasoning above is applied.

The parol evidence rule

Having discussed the extent to which statements made by the parties have become either mere representations or terms of a contract, we must now see to what degree the parties may adduce evidence other than that agreed in the document. The basic rule here is known as the '**parol evidence rule**' which provides that generally evidence will not be admitted which seeks to add, vary or contradict the terms of a written contract and for this reason it is sometimes referred to as the 'exclusionary rule'. The use of the word 'parol' is somewhat deceptive since it applies not only to oral evidence but also to any other extrinsic evidence that seeks to have the above effect. The rule, in fact, reinforces the objective nature of the modern contract in that the law is not so much concerned with the actual intentions of the parties as with their manifest intentions as expressed within the four corners of the contractual document. The result of such an approach was to prevent a party from adducing evidence that the signed and written agreement did not contain the whole agreement. Thus in *Jacobs v Batavia and General Plantations Trust* [1924] 1 Ch 287 it was stated that:

> parol evidence will not be admitted to prove that some particular term, which had been verbally agreed upon, had been omitted (by design or otherwise) from a written instrument constituting a valid and operative contract between the parties.

Two principal reasons can be seen for this approach. First, one might argue that if the parties have gone to considerable lengths to negotiate and reduce a contract into writing, then why has the term in question been omitted? The only answer might be that the omitted part was never intended to be a term of the contract. Second, if terms can be added to the written contract, the effect will be to introduce uncertainty in the agreement and into the law itself, since it would not then be possible for the courts, the parties or other third parties thereby to rely on the written contract.

The parol evidence rule was originally applied by the courts as a strict rule and, indeed, as we have already seen in Chapter 6, certain types of contract in relation to land had to be contained within some sort of writing. The rule, however, began to be undermined by the fact that it did not apply to partly written and partly oral contracts and the fact that it began to be regarded as a presumption rather than a strict rule of law. Thus in *Gillespie Bros & Co.* **v** *Cheney, Eggar and Co.* [1896] 2 QB 59, Lord Russell stated:

> Although when the parties arrive at a definite written contract the implication or presumption is very strong that such a contract is intended to contain all the terms of their bargain, it is a presumption only, and it is open to either of the parties to allege that there was, in addition to what appears in the written agreement, an antecedent express stipulation not intended by the parties to be excluded, but intended to continue in force with the express written agreement.

As a result of this change of attitude, the number of exceptions to the rule continued to grow, to the extent that in 1976 the Law Commission (Working Paper No 70) proposed that what was left of the rule should be abolished. This legislation has not been forthcoming. In any event, in 1986, the Law Commission, in *Law of Contract: The Parol Evidence Rule*, Report No 154, stated that legislation was no longer necessary since the rule no longer existed. Despite this statement it is important to know the exceptions which have caused the demise of the 'rule'; however, **collateral contracts** will be considered separately later in this chapter.

Before examining the exceptions it should be noted that the parol evidence or exclusionary rule has been the subject of extensive discussion in the courts when it comes to the construction of contracts since once written terms are incorporated into a contract it remains to be seen how they are construed or interpreted by the parties. Following on from the case of *Chartbrook Ltd* **v** *Persimmon Homes Ltd* [2009] UKHL 38 and Lord Hoffmann's seminal judgement, there has been a wide ranging discussion as to what evidence can be used by the courts in construing contracts. In practice, the lines between incorporation of terms and the construction of terms are fairly blurred but for convenience and to aid understanding of this challenging area the examination of the principles of construction have been separated and can be seen later on in this chapter in the section on The Construction of Contracts and the Parole Evidence/Exclusionary Rule.

Custom

The parol evidence rule does not prevent the parties adducing evidence of a custom or trade usage, which will result in terms being added to the contract.

Non-operation

There is no objection to extrinsic evidence being offered that indicates that the parties had agreed that the contract would not operate until some specific event occurs, despite the fact that prima facie a valid enforceable contract had been entered into. The basis behind this exception, if that is the correct expression, is that the written contract is not varied or supplemented in any way, but simply that its operation is suspended. In *Pym* **v** *Campbell* (1856) 6 E & B 370, the parties negotiated for the sale of a share of a patent. The contract was in writing but the parties agreed orally that the contract would not operate until the patent had been examined and verified by a third party. It was held that parol evidence as to the oral arrangement would be admitted.

Invalidity

The parol evidence rule does not forbid the adducing of evidence that calls into question the validity of the written agreement, such as lack of capacity, mistake or misrepresentation.

Incompleteness

A further exception to the rule occurs where the court finds that the written contract was not intended to amount to a complete reflection of the agreement entered into by the parties. Where the court comes to such a finding then it will permit extrinsic evidence of the rest of the contract to be adduced by the parties. In coming to such a finding the court has reference to the intentions of the parties. The courts nowadays generally infer that the parties did not intend that the written contract was to be final and conclusive, but that it was to be read alongside any oral arrangements made between the parties. An example is the case of ***Couchman*** v ***Hill*** above, where it was held that the oral assurance given by the auctioneer that the heifer was unserved was part and parcel of the written conditions of sale. The following case summary shows a somewhat more modern case illustrating the principle.

J Evans and Son (Portsmouth) Ltd v *Andrea Merzario Ltd* [1976] 2 All ER 930

The plaintiffs were in business shipping machinery from Italy, using the defendant carriers for this purpose, conducting the business on the standard conditions used by the forwarding trade. Prior to 1967, the machinery was shipped on trailers and because of the risk of corrosion it was agreed that both the machinery and the trailers would always be carried below deck. In 1967, the defendants changed over to containers and, during discussions, they assured the plaintiffs that their goods would continue to be stowed below deck. On this basis the plaintiffs continued to use the defendants as their carriers on the written standard conditions, but these standard conditions permitted the defendants to have the goods stowed on deck. Some time later a container with goods belonging to the plaintiffs was washed overboard in heavy seas after being stowed on deck. In an action for breach of contract, the Court of Appeal held that the defendants could not rely solely on the written standard conditions and permitted the plaintiffs to raise evidence as regards the oral discussions and subsequent assurance. It was clear that the parties did not intend that the written standard conditions would form the complete basis of the ensuing contracts.

The actual reasons behind this decision in the Court of Appeal are interesting in that two approaches were adopted in arriving at the decision. Roskill and Lane LJJ considered that the contract was one which was both written and oral and therefore free from the influence of the parol evidence rule. Lord Denning, however, considered that the oral agreement amounted to a second contract, a collateral contract. With respect to the arguments of Lord Denning supporting the collateral contract approach, Roskill LJ stated:

That phrase is normally only applicable where the original promise was external to the main contract, the main contract being a contract in writing, so that usually parol evidence cannot be given to contradict the terms of the written contract . . . But the doctrine, as it seems to me, has little or no application where one is not concerned with a contract in writing (with respect I cannot accept counsel for the defendants' argument that there was here a contract in writing) but with a contract which, as I think, was partly oral, partly by writing and partly by conduct. In such a case, the Court does not require to have recourse to lawyers' devices such as collateral oral warranty in order to seek to adduce evidence which would not otherwise be admissible. The Court is entitled to look at and should look at all the evidence from start to finish in order to see what the bargain was that was struck between the parties.

The two approaches made no difference to the result, but the fact that Lord Denning's approach produces two contracts rather than a single partly written and partly oral one, as in Roskill and Lane LJJ's reasoning, may be significant in other cases. In contracts for the sale of land which, under the Law of Property (Miscellaneous Provisions) Act 1989, s 2, are required to be in writing, the oral collateral contract of Lord Denning could not be included in the sale. It is, however, important to note that this Act specifically preserves the equitable remedy of rectification, which could be used to incorporate terms from an oral contract. It should also be noted that the contract could also contain a merger clause, the effect of which would be to provide that the written contract was intended to contain the entire terms of the agreement specifically excluding the inference of a single partly written and partly oral contract.

Collateral contracts

The device of the collateral contract has been known to the law for well over 100 years, yet its rise to importance in recent times means that a student of the law of contract who ignores it does so at their peril. The collateral contract has particular significance in relation to the status of terms and has provided a substantial exception to the parol evidence rule. Its use also arises in relation to exemption clauses and privity of contract.

The concept was summed up by Lord Moulton in *Heilbut, Symons & Co.* v *Buckleton* [1913] AC 30 when he stated:

> It is evident, both on principle and on authority, that there may be a contract the consideration for which is the making of some other contract, 'If you will make such and such a contract, I will give you one hundred pounds', is in every sense of the word a complete legal contract. It is collateral to the main contract, but each has an independent existence, and they do not differ in respect of their possessing to the full the character and status of a contract.

It remains to examine its use in relation to terms and the parol evidence rule.

Terms or mere representations

If a court considers that a statement does not amount to a term but a mere representation in the principal contract, it may find that it nevertheless amounts to a term of a collateral contract, that is, that there is an implied secondary contract running alongside the principal one. The approach is supported by a number of cases: for example, *City and Westminster Properties (1934) Ltd* v *Mudd* [1958] 2 All ER 733, where the defendant had rented the plaintiffs' shop for some six years. Annexed to the shop was a room in which the defendant used to sleep, as the plaintiffs knew well. The lease came up for renewal and the plaintiffs inserted a new clause that restricted the use of the shop to 'showrooms, workrooms and offices only'. Such a clause would obviously prevent the defendant from sleeping on the premises so he asked whether he could continue the practice, to which the plaintiffs agreed. On this understanding the defendant signed the lease, though when he did sleep on the premises the plaintiffs brought an action seeking forfeiture of the lease for breach of covenant. It was held that the promise not to enforce the clause against him was a collateral contract which he could claim as a defence to the action for breach of covenant.

The use of the collateral contract to incorporate a statement as a term of a contract, as seen in the *Mudd* case above, has a useful spin-off in that it does away with the need for the claimant to frame his claim in an action for misrepresentation which might be complex. It is primarily for this reason that the use of the collateral contract device has increased over the years despite the fact that Lord Moulton and the rest of the House of Lords in the *Heilbut* case considered it should be used very sparingly. This trend towards its use can be seen in

Esso Petroleum Co. Ltd v *Mardon* [1976] 2 All ER 5, where the Court of Appeal not only found for the existence of negligent misrepresentation but also for the presence of a collateral warranty as to the accuracy and reliability of an estimate for the annual sales of petrol at a garage.

The parol evidence rule

It has already been noted that the collateral contract device may be used to avoid the parol evidence rule. Originally, the parol evidence contained in the collateral contract had to be independent of the principal contract, that is, the collateral contract could not alter or add terms to the original contract, nor was it supposed to contradict the terms of that contract. It has been seen in the *Mudd* case that the courts will now allow the collateral contract device to be used to give effect to such changes. It may be that the original limitations as described above were formed on a false assumption, but if one takes the idea of the collateral contract giving effect to an agreement independent of the principal contract, there does not appear to be any compelling reason why the collateral contract should not add to, vary or contradict the principal one. If anything, the limitations placed on the collateral contract should revolve around the need to prove the existence of a legally binding agreement supported by consideration.

Entire agreement clauses

See Chapter 13 for performance of the contract.

Before leaving express terms it is useful to have regard to a particular type of clause – the entire agreement clause. An 'entire' contract arises where a person's contractual obligations are conditional on the other party performing his side of the bargain. This type of situation is concerned with performance of the contract. An entire agreement clause, however, is completely different in that it forms part of the contract itself and provides that the contractual document is intended to contain the entirety of the contract entered into between the parties. Essentially it is an acknowledgement that any promises or undertakings entered into before the contract are encompassed within the contract itself, so that individual parties cannot later allege that they have relied on any promises or undertakings not contained within the contract. Thus in *Inntrepreneur Pub Co.* v *East Crown Ltd* [2000] 2 Lloyd's Rep 611 Lightman J thus stated that the purpose of an entire agreement clause

> . . . is to preclude a party to a written agreement from threshing through the undergrowth and finding in the course of negotiations some (chance) remark or statement (often long forgotten or difficult to recall or explain) on which to found a claim such as the present to the existence of a collateral warranty. The entire agreement clause obviates the occasion for any such search and the peril to the contracting parties posed by the need which may arise in its absence to conduct such a search. For such a clause constitutes a binding agreement between the parties that the full contractual terms are to be found in the document containing the clause and not elsewhere, and that accordingly any promises or assurances made in the course of the negotiations (which in the absence of such a clause might have effect as a collateral warranty) shall have no contractual force, save insofar as they are reflected and given effect in that document.

It has been suggested that an entire agreement clause would not prevent an allegation that there is a collateral contract from being adduced on the basis that collateral contracts provide a substantial exception to the parole evidence rule. Lightman J, however, following the Court of Appeal decision in *Deepak* v *ICI [1999] 1 Lloyds Rep 387*, considered that an entire agreement clause deprived a collateral contract or warranty of legal effect stating:

> where the formula of words used in the clause is abbreviated to an acknowledgement by the parties that the Agreement constitutes the entire agreement between them . . . it constitutes

For more on
exemption clauses,
see Chapter 8.

an agreement that the full contractual terms to which the parties agree to bind themselves are to be found in the Agreement and nowhere else and that what might otherwise constitute a side agreement or collateral warranty shall be void of legal effect. That can be the only purpose of the provision.

The Construction of Contracts and the Parol Evidence/Exclusionary Rule

Objective 2

Once written terms have been incorporated into a contract (see below), they have to be construed or interpreted by the parties and the courts in the event of a dispute. For instance, in the case of exemption or limitation clauses, it may have to be determined whether the clause has the effect of exempting or limiting the liability which a party seeks to exclude or limit. The process of construction or interpretation is clearly of fundamental importance not least because many of the disputes in contract law arise from the parties disputing the terms of the contract – or at least their interpretation of them. Much of the role of the lawyer, particularly the commercial lawyer, is spent drafting the contract so that the intentions of the parties that they consider important are correctly set out within the contract. In the case of standard form contracts, this invariably means setting out the terms which the provider of the goods or services wishes to impose on the customer, hence the notion of contracts of adhesion. Within this process of drafting invariably the lawyer has to take into account restrictions that the law places on the insertion of certain terms, such as exclusion clauses. Finally, the lawyer has to take into account the principles which the courts have evolved in construing a contract since a contract must embody certainty, and failure here will almost certainly result in one or other of the parties finding itself in breach of the terms of the contract. Nowhere is the act of drafting more important than in commercial contracts where the courts take the view that the parties to such contracts have the benefit of lawyers and as such take a strict view when construing such contracts.

Construing contracts: the literal approach v the contextual approach

In the past, the courts in construing a contract have adopted a literal approach to interpretation, that is, the courts interpret the contract according to their ordinary plain meaning without reference to any extrinsic evidence of the background to the transaction, providing of course that such a method of interpretation does not lead to ambiguity or does not lead to any manifest absurdity. Thus in *Lovell and Christmas Ltd* v *Wall* (1911) 104 LT 85 Cozens-Hardy MR stated:

> If there is one principle more clearly established than another in English law it is surely this: It is for the court to construe a written document. It is irrelevant and improper to ask what the parties, prior to the execution of the instrument, intended or understood. What is the meaning of the language that they have used therein? That is the problem, and the only problem. In saying that, I do not mean to assert that no evidence can be admitted. Indeed, the contrary is clear. If a deed relates to Black Acre, you may have evidence to show what are the parcels. If a document is in a foreign language, you may have an interpreter. If it contains technical terms, an expert may explain them. If, according to the custom of a trade or the usage of the market, a word has acquired a secondary meaning, evidence may be given to prove it . . . But unless the case can be brought within some or one of these exceptions, it is the duty of the court, which is presumed to understand the English language, to construe the document according to the

ordinary grammatical meaning of the words used therein, and without reference to anything which has previously passed between the parties to it.

The effect of such a literal approach is that the courts will look exactly at the ordinary meaning of the words no matter what the intention of the parties.

As we have seen, in applying this test the courts have traditionally limited themselves to looking within the 'four corners' of the agreement and applying a 'rule' that words should be given their 'natural and ordinary meaning'. This reflects the parol evidence rule and the fact that the courts do not readily accept that parties to the contract have made linguistic mistakes, particularly where the contract has been formulated within a formal document.

The duty of the court then is to discover the mutual intentions without reference to any contradictory evidence that may be provided by the parties so that the court has no preconceptions in arriving at an interpretation of the contractual terms and the responsibilities of the parties under the contract. The consequence of this approach is that the parties are not permitted to give direct evidence of their intentions which vary from the terms of the contact – the so-called exclusionary rule. The reason for this is that the courts considered that it is only the document itself which evinces the consensus of the parties. Nevertheless, this approach has been subject to some revision since it is clearly not appropriate to attribute to the parties intentions which they did not intend, particularly where the parties have a difference of views as to the interpretation of their contract. The problem with this approach is that it divorces the interpretation process from the context in which the parties actually negotiate their contract. The result is that the courts have moved to a purposive approach to interpretation, in much the same way as courts use this approach with regard to the interpretation of statutes and statutory instruments. The question is then to what extent are the courts entitled to look at the overall background giving rise to the contract and their pre-contractual negotiations? This change of emphasis could be seen in the case of *Prenn* v *Simmonds* [1971] 1 WLR 1381.

In *Prenn* v *Simmonds*, one of the parties contended that it was permissible to look at prior negotiations as an aid to the construction of the written agreement. The House of Lords decided that such evidence in construing a contract should be confined to the 'factual background known to the parties at or before the date of the contract as including evidence of the "genesis" and objectively the "aim" of the transaction'. Lord Wilberforce went on to state:

> The time has long passed when agreements, even those under seal, were isolated from the matrix of facts in which they were set and interpreted purely on internal linguistic considerations . . . We must . . . inquire beyond the language and see what the circumstances were with reference to which the words were used, and the object, appearing from those circumstances, which the person using them had in view. Moreover . . . it has been clear enough that evidence of mutually known facts may be admitted to identify the meaning of a descriptive term.

Whilst the approach of Lord Wilberforce demonstrates a relaxation of the hitherto literal rule, some qualifications to this approach have emerged. In *Schuler AG* v *Wickman Machine Tool Sales Ltd* [1974] AC 235, it was held that the subsequent conduct of the parties would not be admissible to aid the construction of a contract since this type of conduct was referable more to what the parties had intended to say rather than as to what they actually said, although this type of conduct may be used to show the very existence of the contract.

In *Reardon Smith Line Ltd* v *Yngvar Hansen-Tangen* [1976] 1 WLR 989, however, Lord Wilberforce revisited the trend towards a purposive or contextual approach. He stated:

> No contracts are made in a vacuum: there is always a setting in which they have to be placed. The nature of what is legitimate to have regard to is usually described as 'the surrounding

circumstances' but this phrase is imprecise: it can be illustrated but hardly defined. In a commercial contract it is certainly right that the court should know the commercial purpose of the contract and this in turn presupposes knowledge of the genesis of the transaction, the background, the context, the market in which the parties are operating.

Lord Wilberforce, however, considered that evidence from prior negotiations would not be admissible, not because of legal principle but because such evidence is largely unhelpful, aside from helping to provide a factual background, since the court is charged with interpreting the contract in a document arrived at by consensus and, of course, in prior negotiations very often no consensus may have been achieved. From this point the law moved along using both the literal and purposive approaches in varying degrees depending on the case until Lord Hoffman's seminal judgement in *Investors Compensation Scheme Ltd* v *West Bromwich Building Society* [1998] 1 WLR 896.

Lord Hoffman's seminal re-statement of interpretation of contracts: the contextual approach

In *Investors Compensation Scheme Ltd* v *West Bromwich Building Society* [1998] 1 WLR 896, Lord Hoffmann went further in the development of a contextual approach than that seen in *Prenn* v *Simmonds* and *Reardon Smith Line Ltd* v *Yngvar Hansen-Tangen* and stated that, apart from prior negotiations and declarations of subjective intent, the 'factual background includes absolutely everything available to the parties that might reasonably affect how the terminology within the document would be understood by a reasonable person and which a reasonable person would regard as relevant'. In his judgement, however, he provided a re-statement of the principles on which contracts can be construed. He stated (at pp. 912–913):

> My Lords, I will say at once that I prefer the approach of the judge. But I think I should preface my explanation of my reasons with some general remarks about the principles by which contractual documents are nowadays construed. I do not think that the fundamental change which has overtaken this branch of the law, particularly as a result of the speeches of Lord Wilberforce in **Prenn v Simmonds** [1971] 1 W.L.R. 1381, 1384–1386 and **Reardon Smith Line Ltd**. v **Yngvar Hansen-Tangen** [1976] 1 W.L.R. 989, is always sufficiently appreciated. The result has been, subject to one important exception, to assimilate the way in which such documents are interpreted by judges to the common sense principles by which any serious utterance would be interpreted in ordinary life. Almost all the old intellectual baggage of 'legal' interpretation has been discarded. The principles may be summarised as follows.

> (1) Interpretation is the ascertainment of the meaning which the document would convey to a reasonable person having all the background knowledge which would reasonably have been available to the parties in the situation in which they were at the time of the contract.
> (2) The background was famously referred to by Lord Wilberforce as the 'matrix of fact', but this phrase is, if anything, an understated description of what the background may include. Subject to the requirement that it should have been reasonably available to the parties and to the exception to be mentioned next, it includes absolutely anything which would have affected the way in which the language of the document would have been understood by a reasonable man.
> (3) The law excludes from the admissible background the previous negotiations of the parties and their declarations of subjective intent. They are admissible only in an action for

rectification. The law makes this distinction for reasons of practical policy and, in this respect only, legal interpretation differs from the way we would interpret utterances in ordinary life. The boundaries of this exception are in some respects unclear. But this is not the occasion on which to explore them.

(4) The meaning which a document (or any other utterance) would convey to a reasonable man is not the same thing as the meaning of its words. The meaning of words is a matter of dictionaries and grammars; the meaning of the document is what the parties using those words against the relevant background would reasonably have been understood to mean. The background may not merely enable the reasonable man to choose between the possible meanings of words which are ambiguous but even (as occasionally happens in ordinary life) to conclude that the parties must, for whatever reason, have used the wrong words or syntax: see *Mannai Investment Co. Ltd* v *Eagle Star Life Assurance Co. Ltd* [1997] AC 749.

(5) The 'rule' that words should be given their 'natural and ordinary meaning' reflects the common sense proposition that we do not easily accept that people have made linguistic mistakes, particularly in formal documents. On the other hand, if one would nevertheless conclude from the background that something must have gone wrong with the language, the law does not require judges to attribute to the parties an intention which they plainly could not have had. Lord Diplock made this point more vigorously when he said in *Antaios Compania Naviera SA* v *Salen Rederierna AB* [1985] AC 191, 201: 'if detailed semantic and syntactical analysis of words in a commercial contract is going to lead to a conclusion that flouts business commonsense, it must be made to yield to business commonsense'.

From this re-statement there emerge six principles that set out the approach to the interpretation of contracts and which projects Lord Hoffman's dicta case of *Investors Compensation Scheme Ltd* v *West Bromwich Building Society* as one of the most prominent cases in the law of contract in the modern era. To this extent it is worthwhile examining each component in more detail.

'Old intellectual baggage' and evolution

From the very start of his re-statement Lord Hoffman did not purport to deliver some new revolutionary concept of the approach to be taken when construing a contract but considered the fundamental change was already arising in cases such as *Prenn* v *Simmonds* and *Reardon Smith Line Ltd* v *Yngvar Hansen-Tangen* and to this extent he regarded that he simply built on the judgements of Lord Wilberforce in those case. In that respect he considered that the process of interpretation had evolved naturally, however, he sought to divest the principles of interpretation from the wealth of authority that had built up over many years, if not centuries. To that extent he was critical of the citing of many eighteenth- and nineteenth-century cases by counsel in *Bank of Credit and Commerce International SA* v *Ali* [2001] UKHL 8. He stated:

> The disappearance of artificial rules for the construction of exemption clauses seems to me in accordance with the general trend in matters of construction, which has been to try to assimilate judicial techniques of construction to those which would be used by a reasonable speaker of the language in the interpretation of any serious utterance in ordinary life. In *Investors Compensation Scheme Ltd* v *West Bromwich Building Society* [1998] 1 WLR 896, 912, I said with the concurrence of three other members of the House: 'Almost all the old intellectual baggage of 'legal' interpretation has been discarded'. But if Mr Allen's submissions on the rules of construction are accepted, a substantial piece of baggage will have been retrieved. Lord Keeper Henley's ghost (*Salkeld* v *Vernon*, 1 Eden 64) will have struck back.

Lord Hoffman therefore with reference to **Prenn v Simmonds** and **Reardon Smith Line Ltd v Yngvar Hansen-Tangen** 'appeared to be "drawing a line in the sand"' for the future of interpretation of contracts and the principles by which this process is undertaken and for the courts to turn their backs the old intellectual baggage of 'legal' interpretation. The problem here is that this not very easily applied, particularly with reference to exemption clauses. Originally in the nineteenth century it was unusual for commercial documents to be subject to the normal rules of construction; however, in the twentieth century, rules evolved but in a very different way from the general interpretation of contractual terms thus he stated, 'It was not to promote certainty of construction but to remedy the unfairness which exemption clauses could create'. Lord Hoffman referred to the judgement of Lord Denning in **George Mitchell (Chesterhall) Ltd v Finney Lock Seeds Ltd** [1983] QB 284 in which Lord Denning stated at 296–297:

> None of you nowadays will remember the trouble we had—when I was called to the Bar—with exemption clauses. They were printed in small print on the back of tickets and order forms and invoices. They were contained in catalogues or timetables. They were held to be binding on any person who took them without objection. No one ever did object. He never read them or knew what was in them. No matter how unreasonable they were, he was bound. All this was done in the name of 'freedom of contract.' But the freedom was all on the side of the big concern which had the use of the printing press. No freedom for the little man who took the ticket or order form or invoice. The big concern said, 'Take it or leave it.' The little man had no option but to take it. The big concern could and did exempt itself from liability in its own interest without regard to the little man. It got away with it time after time. When the courts said to the big concern, 'You must put it in clear words,' the big concern had no hesitation in doing so. It knew well that the little man would never read the exemption clauses or understand them. . .
>
> Faced with this abuse of power—by the strong against the weak—by the use of the small print of the conditions—the judges did what they could to put a curb upon it. They still had before them the idol, 'freedom of contract'. They still knelt down and worshipped it, but they concealed under their cloaks a secret weapon. They used it to stab the idol in the back. This weapon was called 'the true construction of the contract'. They used it with great skill and ingenuity. They used it so as to depart from the natural meaning of the words of the exemption clause and to put upon them a strained and unnatural construction. In case after case, they said that the words were not strong enough to give the big concern exemption from liability; or that in the circumstances the big concern was not entitled to rely on the exemption clause. If a ship deviated from the contractual voyage, the owner could not rely on the exemption clause. If a warehouseman stored the goods in the wrong warehouse, he could not pray in aid the limitation clause. If the seller supplied goods different in kind from those contracted for, he could not rely on any exemption from liability. If a shipowner delivered goods to a person without production of the bill of lading, he could not escape responsibility by reference to an exemption clause. In short, whenever the wide words—in their natural meaning—would give rise to an unreasonable result, the judges either rejected them as repugnant to the main purpose of the contract, or else cut them down to size in order to produce a reasonable result.'

Similarly Lord Hoffman referred to the judgement of Lord Wilberforce in **Photo Production Ltd v Securicor Transport Ltd** [1980] AC 827 who stated at p. 843:

> There was a large number of problems, productive of injustice, in which it was worse than unsatisfactory to leave exception clauses to operate. Lord Reid referred to these in **Suisse Atlantique Société d'Armement Maritime SA v NV Rotterdamsche Kolen Centrale** [1967] 1 AC 361, 406, pointing out at the same time that the doctrine of fundamental breach was a dubious

specific. But since then Parliament has taken a hand: it has passed the Unfair Contract Terms Act 1977. This Act applies to consumer contracts and those based on standard terms and enables exception clauses to be applied with regard to what is just and reasonable. It is significant that Parliament refrained from legislating over the whole field of contract. After this Act, in commercial matters generally, when the parties are not of unequal bargaining power, and when risks are normally borne by insurance, not only is the case for judicial intervention undemonstrated, but there is everything to be said, and this seems to have been Parliament's intention, for leaving the parties free to apportion the risks as they think fit and for respecting their decisions.

Lord Hoffman considered that such judicial intervention amounted to judicial creativity of a type that almost amounted to judicial legislation in which the use of the rules of construction amounted to a 'desperate remedy' needed to remedy 'widespread injustice'. He therefore concluded that there was much to be said for applying the ordinary rules of construction to exemption clauses.

The problem here is that there are a number of rules applicable to exemption clauses that are deeply rooted here. Is it Lord Hoffman's intention that his re-statement will effectively overrule these decisions? It seems so but there is a level of uncertainty here, though it is true to say that the principles in his re-statement have been applied in the construction of exemption clauses as evidenced in *National Westminster Bank plc* v *Utrecht-America Finance Co* [2001] EWCA Civ 658. Whilst Lord Hoffman's re-statement is often considered in this way there are limits to its application. Thus, for example, Lord Neuberger in the context of implied terms in *Marks and Spencer plc* v *BNP Paribas Securities Services Trust Company (Jersey) Ltd* [2015] UKSC 72 stated:

> Of course, it is fair to say that the factors to be taken into account on an issue of construction, namely the words used in the contract, the surrounding circumstances known to both parties at the time of the contract, business common sense, and the reasonable reader or reasonable parties, are also taken into account on an issue of implication. However, that does not mean that the exercise of implication should be properly classified as part of the exercise of interpretation, let alone that it should be carried out at the same time as interpretation. When one is implying a term or a phrase, one is not construing words, as the words to be implied are *ex hypothesi* not there to be construed; and to speak of construing the contract as a whole, including the implied terms, is not helpful, not least because it begs the question as to what construction actually means in this context.

Principle 1 An Objective Test

The basic tenet of construction within Lord Hoffman's first principle is that the courts must discover the intentions of the parties and that this is discovered by way of an objective test. Thus Lord Hoffmann in *Chartbrook Ltd* v *Persimmon Homes Ltd* [2009] UKHL 38 in determining this question stated:

> It is agreed that the question is what a reasonable person having all the background knowledge which would have been available to the parties would have understood them to be using the language in the contract to mean.

The point was also considered in *Rainy Sky SA* v *Kookmin Bank* [2011] UKSC 50 where Lord Clarke agreed with the dicta of Lord Hoffmann in *Chartbrook Ltd* v *Persimmon Homes Ltd* [2009] UKHL 38 and in the cases of *Mannai Investment Co. Ltd* v *Eagle Star Life Assurance*

Co. Ltd [1997] AC 749, *Investors Compensation Scheme Ltd* v *West Bromwich Building Society* [1998] 1 WLR 896 and concurring with the view of Lord Neuberger in *Pink Floyd Music Ltd* v *EMI Records Ltd* [2010] EWCA Civ 1429, stated:

> The ultimate aim of interpreting such a provision is to determine what the parties to the contract meant by it. And that involves ascertaining what a reasonable person would have understood the parties to the contract to have meant.

It should be emphasised that the objective test is determined by what a reasonable man would have understood the *expressed* intentions of the parties to be in the context of the contract not the desired intentions of the parties since this would be to apply a subjective test. The point was reinforced in *Proctor & Gamble Co* v *Svenska Cellulosa Aktiebolaget SCA* [2012] EWCA Civ 1413 where Rix LJ stated:

> In English law we have eschewed asking what the parties have actually intended, thinking that the question of contractual intention is to be derived objectively from their agreement, and that when it comes to a dispute the question of actual intention is likely to be submerged in wishful thinking.

Principle 2 The matrix of fact

In (2) above, when Lord Hoffmann stated that the 'matrix of fact' is 'subject to the requirement that it should have been reasonably available to the parties', this is an objective position, not requiring actual knowledge and furthermore it includes both parties. Thus Lord Hoffmann stated:

> It would be contrary to basic principles of construction for the meaning of a document to be affected by the facts which were known to one party but not reasonably available to the other.

The expression 'matrix fact' first arose in the case of *Prenn* v *Simmonds* and has been subject to the criticism that the concept is particularly wide and could give rise to problems in determining as to what this matrix comprises in individual cases, however, the basic task of the court was summed up in *Rank Enterprises* v *Gerard* [2000] 1 All ER (Comm) 449 by Mance LJ as being:

> to construe the documents in a manner that reflects the mutual intentions of [the parties], against a background of the transaction as a whole, looking for the meaning which the language used . . . would convey to a reasonable person, having all the background knowledge which would reasonably have been available to the parties . . . but excluding previous negotiations and evidence of subjective intent.

On the face of things, therefore, literalism has been overtaken by contextualism, but is there any limit on the width of the admissible background that can be referred to? Does Lord Hoffman really mean that the 'matrix of fact' is to be discerned by including 'absolutely anything which would have affected the way in which the language of the document would have been understood by a reasonable man'? In *Bank of Credit and Commerce International SA (in liquidation)* v *Ali* [2001] UKHL 8, Lord Hoffmann stated:

> I did not think it necessary to emphasise that I meant anything which a reasonable man would have regarded as relevant. I was merely saying that there is no conceptual limit to what can be regarded as background. It is not, for example, confined to the factual background but can include the state of the law . . . I was certainly not encouraging a trawl through 'background'

which could not have made a reasonable person think that the parties must have departed from conventional usage.

Principle 3 The exclusionary rule

In this third principle, Lord Hoffman provided a limitation on the type of background knowledge that a reasonable man is able to draw down upon to discover the expressed intention of the parties, and reinforced the fact that the test is an objective one by excluding all declarations of subjective intent. Clearly therefore he resiled from including 'absolutely anything which would have affected the way in which the language of the document'. The latter part of this exclusion is not all surprising given the objective nature of the process of construing the contract. Whilst Lord Hoffman acknowledged that the 'boundaries of this exception are in some respects unclear' it became apparent that the position of pre-contractual negotiations appeared to fall within the exclusionary rule.

The position of such pre-contractual negotiations was considered in *Chartbrook Ltd* v *Persimmon Homes Ltd* [2009] UKHL 38. In that case the appellant developer (P) entered an agreement with the respondent (C) under which P was to develop C's land. Under the agreement P was to obtain planning permission, construct a development on the site and then sell the properties. The price payable by P under the agreement included an 'Additional Residential Payment' (ARP) defined as '23.4 per cent of the price achieved for each Residential Unit in excess of the Minimum Guaranteed Residential Unit Value less the Costs and Incentives'. When the development was completed, a dispute arose as to what was the true construction of the wording in agreement as to how the ARP was to be calculated. P contended that this sum amounted to £897,051, whilst C contested that the correct sum was £4,484,862 and brought proceedings for the balance. In support of their construction of the term of the contract, P sought to rely on documents which were part of the pre-contractual negotiations. Alternatively, the defendants counter-claimed for rectification of the contract to accord with what they claimed to be the parties' common agreement. The judge at first instance and the Court of Appeal (by a majority), applying a literal approach to the construction of the document, held that evidence of the pre-contractual negotiations was not admissible, particularly when an express definition was contained within the contract. In the Court of Appeal, Lawrence Collins LJ considered that the commercial background to the case should be the correct means of construing the contract rather than the literal approach.

On appeal to the House of Lords, P argued that account should be taken of the pre-contractual negotiations. P submitted that the rule in *Prenn* v *Simmonds* that pre-contractual negotiations were inadmissible in construing a contract was illogical and prevented a court from putting itself in the position of the parties and ascertaining their true intent. P also submitted that the judge and the Court of Appeal had misunderstood the principles on which rectification could be decreed.

The House of Lords, with Lord Hoffmann giving the leading judgement, considered that the rule is that pre-contractual negotiations should be excluded as inadmissible simply because they were usually irrelevant to the question which the court had to decide and anyway were often highly subjective and for this reason offended the principle of objectivity in the interpretative process. Thus Lord Hoffman commented at para 39:

> Whereas the surrounding circumstances are, by definition, objective facts, which will usually be uncontroversial, statements in the course of pre-contractual negotiations will be drenched in subjectivity and may, if oral, be very much in dispute.

The House of Lords, however, considered that it was not necessarily inconsistent to admit evidence of previous negotiations in some situations. Thus Lord Hoffmann stated:

I do, however, accept that it would not be inconsistent with the English objective theory of contractual interpretation to admit evidence of previous communications between the parties as part of the background which may throw light upon what they meant by the language they used. The general rule, as I said in *Bank of Credit and Commerce International SA* v *Ali* [2002] 1 AC 251, 269, is that there are no conceptual limits to what can properly be regarded as background. Prima facie, therefore, the negotiations are potentially relevant background. They may be inadmissible simply because they are irrelevant to the question which the court has to decide, namely, what the parties would reasonably be taken to have meant by the language which they finally adopted to express their agreement. For the reasons given by Lord Wilberforce, that will usually be the case. But not always. In exceptional cases, as Lord Nicholls has forcibly argued, a rule that prior negotiations are always inadmissible will prevent the court from giving effect to what a reasonable man in the position of the parties would have taken them to have meant . . . The rule excludes evidence of what was said or done during the course of negotiating the agreement for the purpose of drawing inferences about what the contract meant. It does not exclude the use of such evidence for other purposes: for example, to establish that a fact which may be relevant as background was known to the parties, or to support a claim for rectification or estoppel. These are not exceptions to the rule. They operate outside it.

The principle is that parties should reasonably have been expected to transfer the conclusions of their pre-contract negotiations into the written expressed agreement. This principle had been well established for many years and expressed in the case of *Prenn* v *Simmonds*. In that case Lord Wilberforce justified the rule as follows:

The reason for not admitting evidence of these exchanges is not a technical one or even mainly one of convenience, (though the attempt to admit it did greatly prolong the case and add to its expense). It is simply that such evidence is unhelpful. By the nature of things, where negotiations are difficult, the parties' positions, with each passing letter, are changing and until the final agreement, though converging, still divergent. It is only the final document which records a consensus. If the previous documents use different expressions, how does construction of those expressions, itself a doubtful process, help on the construction of the contractual words? If the same expressions are used, nothing is gained by looking back: indeed, something may be lost since the relevant surrounding circumstances may be different. And at this stage there is no consensus of the parties to appeal to. It may be said that previous documents may be looked at to explain the aims of the parties. In a limited sense this is true: the commercial, or business object, of the transaction, objectively ascertained, may be a surrounding fact. Cardozo J. thought so in the *Utica Bank* case. And if it can be shown that one interpretation completely frustrates that object, to the extent of rendering the contract futile, that may be a strong argument for an alternative interpretation, if that can reasonably be found. But beyond that it may be difficult to go: it may be a matter of degree, or of judgement, how far one interpretation, or another, gives effect to a common intention: the parties, indeed, may be pursuing that intention with differing emphasis, and hoping to achieve it to an extent which may differ, and in different ways. The words used may, and often do, represent a formula which means different things to each side, yet may be accepted because that is the only way to get 'agreement' and in the hope that disputes will not arise. The only course then can be to try to ascertain the 'natural' meaning. Far more, and indeed totally, dangerous is it to admit evidence of one party's objective – even if this is known to the other party. However strongly pursued this may be, the other party may only be willing to give it partial recognition, and in a world of give and take, men often have to be satisfied with less than they want. So, again, it would be a matter of speculation how far the common intention was that the particular objective should be realised.

Their Lordships in *Chartbrook* considered that if they departed from this principle the result would be uncertainty where there were disputes as to interpretation in contracts. Pre-contract negotiations were, by their nature, subjective and based upon a particular individual's recollection and did not necessarily reflect the provisional consensus of the parties that was a precursor to the drafting of the final document. Furthermore, their Lordships did not consider there were grounds to depart from the decision in *Prenn v Simmonds*.

On a wider front, however, the question is raised as to whether the courts have abandoned the 'four corners' approach so that they will look at pre-contractual negotiations and the overall background of the contract in reconciling differing interpretations by the parties. In *Chartbrook Ltd v Persimmon Homes Ltd* [2009] UKHL 38, Lord Hoffmann still considered the general rule to be applicable and did not think there had been a departure from this 'exclusionary rule', adding also that 'there is no clearly established case for departure' from the rule. Lord Hoffmann considered that in some situations there is clearly something wrong with the language between the parties and considered it to be wrong that a court should attempt to attribute to the parties intention that which a reasonable person would not have understood them to mean. He considered that it requires a strong case to persuade a court to be persuaded that something had gone so wrong that it should depart from the exclusionary rule regarding extrinsic evidence and that it would not be inconsistent with the traditional objective theory of contractual interpretation to admit evidence of previous communications between the parties as part of the background that might throw light the language used by the parties. Whilst he considered that there was no established case for a departure from the exclusionary rule, he did, however, consider there are cases a departure from the exclusionary can be justified on 'pragmatic grounds'.

It is clear then that Lord Hoffmann was not resiling from the exclusionary rule but merely qualifying its application in certain exceptional cases. In this respect he approved of Brightman J's judgement in *East v Pantiles (Plant Hire) Ltd* (1981) 263 EG 61 that in appropriate cases where there was clear mistake on the face of the instrument and it was clear what correction ought to be made to cure the mistake, then the correction should be made as a matter of construction and in this regard the court is not confined to reading the document without regard to its background or context. Not to be able to look at the pre-contractual negotiations would mean that the court would not be in the same position as the parties in order to discern what the parties themselves meant in the contract, which would be essential in ascertaining the correct interpretation of the contract.

Outside of Lord Hoffmann's guidance the principles, allowing departure from the exclusionary rule, do not form the basis of a structured doctrine and no doubt such a doctrine is still evolving. This was recognised by Baroness Hale in *Chartbrook* when she stated: 'The courts . . . are able to achieve step by step changes which can distinguish cases in which evidence is "helpful" from cases in which it is not.' It is, however, possible to discern certain situations in which extrinsic evidence may be referred to, for instance, in some situations it can be seen that the parties have applied words or phrases in an unconventional context or where they have used phrases in ways that have an unconventional meaning. In such a situation the court is entitled to use evidence of previous negotiations in order to discern the actual meaning intended by the parties. This is sometimes referred to as the private dictionary principle, however, this cannot be used where the court has to adjudicate between two conventional meanings.

It will be noticed that Lord Hoffman did provide some limitations on the scope of the exclusionary rule as relating to pre-contract negotiations. He considered that there were two legitimate safety devices that could prevent any injustice arising out of the exclusionary rule – rectification (see p. 185) and estoppel by convention (see p. 185). In relation to the latter he explained that if the parties had negotiated an agreement based upon a common assumption that certain words would bear a specific meaning, then they may be estopped from contending that the words should be given a different meaning. He considered that these remedies lay outside of the exclusionary rule since, '. . . as a matter of construction, the agreement does not have the meaning for which the party seeking rectification or raising an estoppel contends'. That such evidence is not an exception to the exclusionary rule but operated outside it was affirmed in the Supreme Court in *Oceanbulk Shipping and Trading SA v TMT Asia Ltd* [2010] UKSC 44 where Lord Clarke commented:

> Trial judges frequently have to distinguish between material which forms part of the pre-contractual negotiations which is part of the factual matrix and therefore admissible as an aid to interpretation and material which forms part of the pre-contractual negotiations but which is not part of the factual matrix and is not therefore admissible. This is often a straightforward task but sometimes it is not.

It follows from this that any subjective facts contained within the pre-contract negotiations are inadmissible as part of the interpretative process but objective facts are so admissible confirming Lord Hoffman's earlier comment in *Chartbrook* at para 39 as stated earlier.

Principle 4 The meaning of words is to be interpreted contextually not literally

Lord Hoffman's fourth principle provides that the meaning which a document conveys to a reasonable man is not necessarily the same thing as the meaning of its words. He stated that whilst the meaning of words is a matter of dictionaries, the meaning of a document is what the parties using those words against the relevant background would reasonably have been understood to mean. The background may not merely enable the reasonable man to choose between the possible meanings of words which are ambiguous but even, as in life, to conclude that the parties must, for whatever reason, have used the wrong words or syntax.

In addressing this issue, the courts have attempted to take an approach that makes for certainty, in other words, applying an ordinary and natural meaning to the words; however, at other times the courts have attempted to apply a meaning which applies a sensible commercial meaning to the words. This is clearly problematical since in many commercial contracts the lawyers have honed the wording of a contractual document with the idea of certainty in mind and that the courts will apply the terminology precisely according to the ordinary and natural meaning of the words as in *Mannai Investment Co. Ltd v Eagle Star Life Assurance Co. Ltd* [1997] AC 749.

Principle 5 The presumption that people do not easily make linguistic mistakes

The effect of the fourth principle ties in neatly with Lord Hoffman's fifth principle in that words should be given their 'natural and ordinary meaning' since in formal legal documents it is commonsense that the courts should not easily accept that people have made linguistic mistakes from which they can escape. To do otherwise would create uncertainty and in a commercial context the approach should be to hold businessmen to their bargain. Lord Hoffman tempered this principle by saying that if one can conclude from the background or matrix of facts that something has gone wrong with the language then the courts should not attribute an interpretation that the parties could not have had. He reinforced this principle by reference to Lord Diplock's dicta in ***Antaios Compania Naviera SA* v *Salen Rederierna AB*** [1985] AC 191, 201 when he stated: 'if detailed semantic and syntactical analysis of words in a commercial contract is going to lead to a conclusion that flouts business commonsense, it must be made to yield to business commonsense.'

'Business common sense'

It is important that in many cases something has not gone wrong with the language and in these cases the starting point in interpretation under Lord Hoffman's fifth principle begins with a court seeking out the natural meaning of the word rather than an immediate default to an examination of the words so as to give effect to 'business common sense'. The great problem with the courts having reference to sound 'business common sense' is that there is no objective measure as to what this actually means and to that extent the concept is vague. The objective approach allows the courts to apply a level of discretion so as to arrive at a solution to a dispute between the parties where the language of a contract has more than one meaning, whilst at the same time ensuring that it does not re-write the contract.

If the language of the contract leads the court to conclude that a particular construction is correct, the court must give effect to that no matter 'how surprising or unreasonable the result may be'. This clearly makes good sense since there is no consensus as to what 'business common sense' actually means and indeed this has be borne out by the significant number of cases coming before the courts involving contractual interpretation arising out of the decision in ***West Bromwich***.

The point was raised again in the Supreme Court in ***Arnold* v *Britton*** [2015] UKSC 36 where there were 21 lessees who held 99-year leases of chalets on a leisure park owned by the respondent landlord. There were 91 chalets in total on the site. The 21 leases in question had been granted between 1977 and 1991. Each contained a covenant whereby a lessee had to pay an annual service charge and, whilst there were some variations in the leases, typically each lessee had covenanted to pay 'a proportionate part' of the cost of the provision of the services The cost was, expressed to be £90 in the first year, rising by 10 per cent each year thereafter, that is an increase that rose by a compound rate of 10 per cent in each succeeding year.

Although the lease required all the leases to be subject to identical or similar obligations, the leases of the other 70 chalets, which had been granted before 1977, were subject to a service charge increase only once every three years. The issue that arose was whether the leases provided for a fixed service charge of £90 with a yearly increase of 10 per cent, or whether it meant that the lessees had to pay a fair proportion of the cost of providing the services, up to a maximum of £90 in the first year, that maximum figure rising by 10 per cent each year thereafter. The issue on this appeal was whether the respondent's interpretation of this clause was correct. The reason for this is that it was contended that the respondent's construction of the terms of the lease resulted in such an increasingly absurdly high annual service charge in the later years of each of the 25 leases that it could not be correct and argued that, properly read, each service charge clause in the 25 leases required a lessee to pay a fair proportion of the lessor's costs of providing the services, subject to a maximum, which is £90 in the first year of the term, and increases every year by 10 per cent on a compound basis. In effect the appellants argued that the words 'up to' should be read into the clause. The appellants also argued that the clauses in their leases meant that the lessor could not recover more by way of service charge than could be recovered under each of the first 70 leases.

The Supreme Court dismissed the appeal with Lord Neuberger giving the leading judgement. He set out four factors that are relevant to the construction of contracts. Firstly, when a written contract is interpreted, the court had to identify the parties' intention by reference to what a reasonable person having all the relevant background knowledge would understand the term to mean following the decision in ***Chartbrook***. The court had to focus on the meaning of the words in their context and in the light of the natural meaning of the clause; any other relevant provisions; the overall purpose of the clause and the lease; the facts and circumstances known by the parties at the time; and business common sense. Secondly, business common sense was not to undercut the importance of the actual words used and that the less clear the words, the more ready the court would be to depart from their natural meaning; however, that did not mean that the court should look for drafting errors in order to facilitate a departure from the natural meaning. Thirdly, business common sense was not to be invoked retrospectively, just because, for example, a contract had worked out badly for one of the parties. Fourthly, a court was not to reject the natural meaning of a term simply because it seemed imprudent for the parties to have agreed it so that a court could only take into account facts or circumstances known to both parties when the contract was made.

The decision is of particular importance since it sets out clearly that the starting point in construing a contract is to examine the language used and if this is clear and unambiguous the courts will not interfere in the bargain struck between the parties. Importantly, it also qualifies the point at which business common sense becomes relevant in the interpretative process i.e. when there are clear drafting problems or ambiguity within the terms of the contract.

'Something has gone wrong with the language'

The House of Lords in ***Chartbrook*** allowed P's appeal in that, whilst it was unusual for a court to accept that a linguistic mistake had been made in formal documents, if the context and background led the court to believe that something had gone wrong with the language of a contract, 'the law did not require a court to attribute to the parties an intention which a reasonable person would not have understood them to have had' (per Lord Hoffmann). Equally, however, Lord Hoffman cautioned that 'it requires a strong case to persuade the court that something must have gone wrong with the language' in order to justify a meaning which departs from the words actually used. Their Lordships considered that to construe the ARP provision according to the normal rules of syntax made no commercial sense. In arriving at its judgement, the House of Lords referred to the case of ***East v Pantiles (Plant Hire) Ltd*** (1981) 263 EG 61, where Brightman LJ set out the conditions required for what he termed 'correction of mistakes by construction':

> Two conditions must be satisfied: first, there must be a clear mistake on the face of the instrument; secondly, it must be clear what correction ought to be made in order to cure the mistake. If those conditions are satisfied, then the correction is made as a matter of construction.

Lord Hoffmann accepted this principle subject to two qualifications. First, 'correction of mistakes by construction' is not a separate branch of the law but part of the process of interpreting an agreement so as to get as close as possible to the meaning intended by the parties. It is not 'a summary version of an action for rectification'. Secondly, in deciding whether there was clear mistake the court is not confined to reading the document without regard to its background or context. Lord Hoffmann concluded:

> What is clear . . . is that there is not, so to speak, a limit to the amount of red ink or verbal rearrangement or correction which the court is allowed. All that is required is that it should be clear that something has gone wrong with the language and that it should be clear what a reasonable person would have understood the parties to have meant. In my opinion, both of these requirements are satisfied.

On this basis the House of Lords considered that the decision in the Court of Appeal was wrong and that the definition of the ARP clause in the contract was ambiguous and obviously defective. Clearly 'something must have gone wrong with the language' and thus the House of Lords considered that to interpret the definition in accordance with the ordinary rules of syntax as per the decisions at first instance and in the Court of Appeal made no commercial sense. Such an approach would not accord with what a reasonable person having all the background knowledge available to the parties would have understood the parties to mean. The House of Lords, taking into consideration the background and context but not the pre-contractual negotiations, and applying the established principles of construction, held that C's construction could not be upheld, and the construction put forward by P was more appropriate, so that the sum of £897,051 was the appropriate amount to be paid under the contract.

The point was re-iterated in **Pink Floyd Music Ltd v EMI Records Ltd** [2010] EWCA Civ 1429, where Lord Neuberger stated:

> '. . . as Lord Hoffmann also made clear in **Investors Compensation** [1998] 1 WLR 896, there is a difference between cases of ambiguity, which may result in giving the words a meaning they can naturally bear, even if it is not their prima facie most natural meaning, and cases of mistake, which may result from concluding that the parties made a mistake and used the wrong words or syntax'. However, he emphasised the court does 'not readily accept that people have made mistakes in formal documents' — **Chartbrook** [2009] 1 AC 1101, para 23. He also pointed out in paragraph 20, that, as the court, and therefore the notional reasonable person, cannot take into account the antecedent negotiations, the fact that the natural meaning of the words appears to produce 'a bad bargain' for one of the parties or an 'unduly favourable' result for another, is not enough to justify the conclusion that something has gone wrong. One is normally looking for an outcome which is 'arbitrary' or 'irrational', before a mistake argument will run . . . approving the analysis of Brightman LJ in **East v Pantiles (Plant Hire) Ltd** (1981) 263 EG 61, as refined by Carnwath LJ in **KPMG LLP v Network Rail Infrastructure Ltd** [2007] Bus LR 1336).

Where words have more than one meaning

The issues surrounding interpretation of contractual terms also arose in **Rainy Sky SA and others v Kookmin Bank** [2011] UKSC 50. The facts of the case were that the claimants purchased six shipbuilding contracts under which they agreed to pay pre-delivery instalments. The contract provided that the claimants were entitled to a refund of the total sums paid by the claimants should the shipbuilder, *inter alia*, become insolvent. There was a condition precedent to the payment of the first instalment that the shipbuilder would deliver to the claimants refund guarantees relating to the first and subsequent instalments. Kookmin Bank agreed to guarantee the payments by way of 'advance delivery bonds'. Under paragraph 3 of the terms of the bond the bank undertook to pay 'all such sums due [to the claimants] under the Contract'. Paragraph 2 stated:

> Pursuant to the terms of the Contract, you are entitled, upon your rejection of the Vessel in accordance with the terms of the Contract, your termination, cancellation or rescission of the Contract or upon a Total Loss of the Vessel, to repayment of the pre-delivery instalments of the Contract Price paid by you prior to such termination or a Total Loss of the Vessel (as the case may be) and the value of the Buyer's Supplies delivered to the Shipyard.

When the shipbuilder became insolvent, the claimants sought to enforce the advance payment bond in order to recover the pre-delivery instalments on the basis that the act of insolvency was an event that entitled the claimants to recover the instalments. The ship-builder refused to pay. The claimants then wrote to the bank demanding repayment of the pre-delivery instalments since the purpose of the bond was to guarantee the refund of the pre-delivery instalments. The bank argued that the expression 'such sums' referred back to the sums referred to in paragraph 2 so that the guarantee did not extend to an insolvency event. The claimants, however, considered that the expression 'such sums' referred to paragraph 3 so that the guarantee did in fact cover an insolvency event.

At first instance the judge rejected the arguments put forward by the bank but in the Court of Appeal that decision was overturned by a majority of the Court of Appeal. The claimants appealed to the Supreme Court which allowed the appeal, with Lord Clarke giving the leading judgement with Lords Phillips, Mance, Kerr and Wilson concurring. Lord Clarke considered that the language used by the parties to a contract often had more than one meaning. He considered that the exercise of construction of a contract was essentially one unitary process in which a court had to consider the language used and ascertain what a reasonable person, being a person who had all the background knowledge which would reasonably have been available to the parties in the situation in which they were at the time of the contract would have understood the parties to have meant. The court had to have regard to all the surrounding circumstances and, thus, if there were more than two possible constructions the court was entitled to prefer a construction that was consistent with business common sense and then reject the other. Lord Clarke considered that paragraph 3 had two possible constructions but that he preferred the views of the claimants since that was consistent with the purpose of the bonds since it was the most likely that the security of the advanced payment bonds would be need in such a situation.

Rectification

While the written agreement is intended to reflect the intentions of the parties, it may be that the written document has done this inaccurately. Clearly this is more of a problem where the individuals themselves have attempted to draft the document, though this situation may also arise where a professional adviser or lawyer has been given inaccurate information or where that professional lacks competence. In such an instance one of the parties may apply to the court to have the document rectified in order to reflect the true intentions of the parties or the true state of affairs. The effect of the order is to amend the document retrospectively so that it states what it should have stated all along. Parol evidence is admissible here to support the application to rectify so that the exclusionary rule is avoided. Rectification commonly arises where there has been either a common or unilateral mistake in the drafting of the contract.

See Chapter 10 for a further discussion of the rectification of mistakes.

Estoppel by convention

Lord Steyn in the House of Lords in ***Republic of India v India Steamship Co.*** [1998] AC 878 Lord Steyn in the House of Lords provided a succinct statement of the modern law regarding this form of estoppel stating:

> It is settled that an estoppel by convention may arise where parties to a transaction act on an assumed state of facts or law, the assumption being either shared by them both or made by one and acquiesced in by the other. The effect of estoppel by convention is to preclude a party from denying the assumed facts or law if it would be unjust to allow him to go back on the assumption . . . It is not enough that each of the two parties act on an assumption not communicated to the other. But it was rightly accepted by counsel for both parties that a concluded agreement is not a requirement for an estoppel by convention.

The criteria necessary to establish estoppel by convention were considered by the Court of Appeal in ***ING Bank NV*** v ***Ros Roca SA*** [2011] EWCA Civ 353 where Carnwath LJ, with Rix LJ and Stanley Burton LJ concurring, decided the issue of construction of the contract in question by reference to estoppel by convention. Rix LJ considered that the two conditions established by Lord Hoffmann is confined to cases 'where the contractual language carries its own error within its own terms, as understood in context'. He thought that more often than not a contract will work perfectly well but there is a flaw in that the contract does not provide for a particular eventuality so that it may not be possible for the courts to find a solution within the 'four walls' of the contract itself. In this context he considered there was a danger of the courts seeking to remake contracts on the basis of what the courts consider to be reasonable or more sensible. Rix LJ warned against ***Chartbrook Ltd*** v ***Persimmon Homes Ltd*** being taken as providing an 'open sesame for the reconstructing the parties' contract but an opportunity to remedy by construction a clear error of language which could not have been intended.' On the other hand, he considered that:

> . . . the doctrine of estoppel is a flexible doctrine which can take account of . . . the honest and responsible interaction of business parties to a contract. Where there is room for disagreement as to the meaning or effect of a contract but the parties have clearly chosen (or purported to choose) their own understanding of it and have dealt with one another on the basis of that understanding, whether that mutuality is found in a common assumption, or in acquiescence, or in one party's reliance on another's representation, the doctrine of estoppel allows the court in a proper case to give effect to the parties' objectively ascertainable and mutual dealings with one another.

On this basis, like rectification, the doctrine of estoppel avoids the problems attached to the exclusionary rule and provides that the application of Lord Hoffmann's criteria in ***Chartbrook Ltd*** v ***Persimmon Homes Ltd*** is confined to very limited circumstances and should not be taken as a re-writing of the parole evidence rule.

Implied terms

Objective
3

The vast majority of the primary obligations of the parties to a contract will normally be expressed within the contract itself, but it is of course possible for the parties to overlook certain primary obligations or, in fact, to fail to recognise all the eventualities that might flow from the execution of the contract. In these circumstances, terms may be implied into the contract in order to make up for the omissions of the parties. The role of the courts in this process clearly contradicts the classical theory of contract which was based on the concept of the contract as a reflection of the will of the parties, independently and freely entered into. In order to avoid this contradictory stance the courts proceeded by way of fiction, in that when they implied terms into the contract they were merely giving effect to the unexpressed will of the parties by making up for their omissions within the contract. Eventually the courts began to go beyond this fiction by implying terms irrespective of the presumed intentions of the parties. At this point there is a profound separation of the nature of the implied term since, while the earlier fiction used by the courts implied terms as a matter of fact into a particular contract, the latter role of the courts was to imply certain terms into all contracts of a particular nature, the result being that the term is now implied as a matter of law.

Whether the term is implied as a matter of fact or law, the role of the courts is subject to two reservations. First, as we have already seen in Chapter 2, the contract must be certain and the court will not attempt to write the contract for the parties. Thus if there are a substantial number of omissions the courts may well find that the contract in question is void for uncertainty. Second, if the parties have produced a written contract which is very detailed the courts may also be reluctant to interfere, regarding the contract as being definitive as to the intentions of the parties, though the courts may be persuaded to imply a term into the contract where the term in question is one imposed generally by the law in the situation occurring in the case in question. The point here though is that the courts will not imply a term into a contract simply because it is reasonable to do so to make the contract better or fairer. In order to imply a term into a contract, it must be shown that the term is necessary. Thus, when Lord Denning in *Liverpool City Council v Irwin* [1976] 2 All ER 39 attempted to extend the circumstances in which terms could be implied into a contract on the grounds that it would be reasonable to do so in that the contract would be better for its inclusion, his approach was roundly rejected by the House of Lords, Lord Cross stating:

See later for the facts of this case.

> it is not enough for the court to say that the suggested term is a reasonable one, the presence of which would make the contract a better or fairer one; it must be able to say that the insertion of the terms is necessary to give—as it is put—'business efficacy' to the contract and that if its absence had been pointed out at the time both parties—assuming them to have been reasonable men—would have agreed without hesitation to its insertion.

This principle was re-affirmed in *Dear v Jackson* [2013] EWCA Civ 89 where there was a term that the shareholders of a company could appoint a director, however, there was a provision in the articles of the company that permitted the directors of the company to remove a director from office. Jackson, the director involved, argued that the provision in the articles undermined his entitlement to be re-appointed.

The judge at first instance found that there was an implied term in the contract which prevented the directors from removing Jackson as a director, save in specified circumstances. In his judgement the judge at first instance stated:

> Although necessity continues (save perhaps in relation to terms implied by law) to be a condition for the implication of terms, necessity to give business efficacy is not the only relevant type of necessity. The express terms of an agreement may work perfectly well in the sense that both parties can perform their express obligations, but the consequences would contradict what a reasonable person would understand the contract to mean. In such a case an implied term is necessary to spell out what the contact actually means.

It was alleged that this 'smacked' of a potential re-writing of contracts in order to achieve 'a 'sensible' or 'reasonable commercial result'. It was submitted that such an approach ran counter to the decision of the House of Lords in *Liverpool City Council v Irwin* [1977] AC 239 in which any idea of a mere perception of 'reasonableness', as a touchstone of the implication of contractual terms, was rejected.

The Court of Appeal rejected the approach of the judge at first instance, since the contractual purpose identified by Jackson in the contract that he should be a director of the company might have been in his mind as his commercial purpose, however, in objective terms that was not the only possibility for identifying the need to imply a term into the contract. It was not obvious that the parties would have agreed the proposed implied terms and as such would involve an improper re-writing of the agreement since it would subject them to merely one view of the most sensible solution for resolving the problem in the contract. Thus a term can only be implied if the court is 'satisfied that is what the contract actually means'. In other words, the term must be so necessary that it can be identified when construing the contract and cannot be implied if there is uncertainty as to whether both the parties would have agreed to the term which has been omitted from the contract or the term is too imprecise as in *Shell (UK) Ltd v Lostock Garages Ltd [1976] 1 WLR 1187*.

So far we have considered the case where the courts have implied terms into the contract, but one must not ignore the fact that Parliament itself, by means of a statute, imposes terms into certain types of contracts. Very often the role undertaken by Parliament is to protect certain types of parties to a contract and is recognition of the fact that the classical idea of freedom of contract is very often a nonsense. Uppermost in the mind of Parliament here is the consumer, the lone individual, who quite clearly has little protection from the vagaries of commerce. Parliament will thus impose certain terms, thereby giving the individual consumer certain rights within the contract which would otherwise no doubt be omitted by businesses, given their superior bargaining position.

The circumstances in which a term will be implied into a contract has thus been summarised by Lady Hale in *Geys* v *Société Générale* [2013] 1 AC 523 as follows:

> In this connection, it is important to distinguish between two different kinds of implied terms. First, there are those terms which are implied into a particular contract because, on its proper construction, the parties must have intended to include them . . . Such terms are only implied where it is necessary to give business efficacy to the particular contract in question. Second, there are those terms which are implied into a class of contractual relationship, such as that between landlord and tenant or between employer and employee, where the parties may have left a good deal unsaid, but the courts have implied the term as a necessary incident of the relationship concerned, unless the parties have expressly excluded it . . .

In line with Lady Hale's classification of implied terms we will now look at terms implied as a matter of fact before proceeding to examine terms implied as a matter of law.

Terms implied as a matter of fact

Terms implied as fact are those which are imputed from the implied intentions of the parties and arise where the parties to the contract forget to include a particular term or where the contract is so badly drafted that a particular term is omitted from being incorporated into the contract. It must be emphasised the process of implying a term into a contract can only begin to arise once the court has construed the express terms of the contract in line with the principles already considered on page 000 et seq. Thus in *Marks and Spencer plc* v *BNP Baribas Securities Services Trust Co (Jersey) Ltd* [2015] UKSC 72 Lord Neuberger at (at 28) stated:

> In most, possibly all, disputes about whether a term should be implied into a contract, it is only after the process of construing the express words is complete that the issue of an implied term falls to be considered. Until one has decided what the parties have expressly agreed, it is difficult to see how one can set about deciding whether a term should be implied and, if so, what term. This appeal is just such a case. Further, given that it is a cardinal rule that no term can be implied into a contract if it contradicts an express term, it would seem logically to follow that, until the express terms of a contract have been construed, it is, at least normally, not sensibly possible to decide whether a further term should be implied. Having said that . . . in some cases it could conceivably be appropriate to reconsider the interpretation of the express terms of a contract once one has decided whether to imply a term, but, even if that is right, it does not alter the fact that the express terms of a contract must be interpreted before one can consider any question of implication.

Traditionally the tests employed for implying a term into a contact as a matter of fact either had to satisfy the 'officious bystander' test or the 'business efficacy test'.

The 'officious bystander' test

This is the classic test to determine whether a term can be implied into a contract. There have been many attempts at defining the test but the one that has survived the test of time and is often quoted is that of MacKinnon LJ in ***Shirlaw* v *Southern Foundries (1926) Ltd*** [1939] 2 KB 206 where he stated:

> Prima facie that which in any contract is left to be implied and need not be expressed is something so obvious that it goes without saying; so that if, while the parties were making their bargain an officious bystander were to suggest some express provision for it in their agreement, they would testily suppress him with a common 'Oh, of course.'

On the face of things the test appears to be a subjective one in that the test appears to be contextualised by reference to how the parties respond to the question posed; however, this is not the case and in ***Equitable Life Assurance Society* v *Hyman*** [2002] 1 AC 408 it was stated that the test does not depend on the actual intention of the parties being proven. The notion that 'it goes without saying' demonstrates that this expression is just another way of asking the reasonable person what he would understand the contract to mean given the state of knowledge of the parties which provides the context or background for the purposes of construing the contract. Thus the rule cannot be applied if one of the parties is unaware of the term that it is sought to imply into the contract. The principle can be seen in the case of ***Spring* v *National Amalgamated Stevedores and Dockers Society*** [1956] 2 All ER 221.

Spring v *National Amalgamated Stevedores and Dockers Society* [1956] 2 All ER 221

The defendants and the union had agreed in 1939 on certain rules which governed the transfer of members from one union to another. This agreement had become known as the 'Bridlington Agreement'. In 1955, the defendants admitted the plaintiff to their union in breach of the agreement, although the plaintiff was completely unaware of the rules contained in the Bridlington Agreement. The breach of the rules was reported to a committee of the Trades Union Congress (TUC), which ordered the union to expel the plaintiff from its membership. When the union attempted to do this the plaintiff sued them for breach of contract, seeking an injunction restraining the expulsion. The union argued that a term should be included in the contract that the terms of the Bridlington Agreement had to be complied with. The court rejected this suggestion and granted the injunction. The reason for the rejection of the argument of the defendants was based on the reply the plaintiff would have given had a bystander asked whether the Bridlington Agreement had been included in the contract. In this case, the plaintiff would have replied, 'What's that?' rather than the 'Of course' as required by the officious bystander test enunciated by MacKinnon LJ. A term cannot be implied if an individual is unaware of the term it is sought to imply into the contract.

Another situation in which an attempt at implying a term fails is where there is uncertainty as to whether both the parties would have agreed to the term which has been omitted from the contract. This again demonstrates the objective nature of the officious bystander test. This can be seen in the case of ***Shell (UK) Ltd* v *Lostock Garages Ltd*** [1976] 1 WLR 1187.

Shell (UK) Ltd v *Lostock Garages Ltd* [1976] 1 WLR 1187

A written contract provided that Shell should supply petrol and oil to the defendants, who reciprocally agreed to buy such products only from Shell. A price war subsequently developed during which Shell reduced the price of petrol to other neighbouring garages, and this resulted in the plaintiff having to trade at a loss. The plaintiff attempted to have a term implied into the contract that Shell would not 'abnormally discriminate' against the plaintiff. The Court of Appeal refused the plaintiff's application on the basis that the term was not a necessary term that Shell would never have agreed to and, anyway, the term was too vague and uncertain.

Lord Hoffmann in **Belize** considered that the decision in **Shell (UK) Ltd v Lostock Garages**, that the term would not be implied because it was vague and uncertain and that Shell would never have agreed to the term, was simply another way of stating that a reasonable man would not have understood that to be what the instrument meant. Lord Hoffman considered that the means by which a term is implied into a contract as a matter of fact is an objective process and was not 'dependent on proof of an actual intention of the parties' though the knowledge of the parties may be relevant as a backdrop as part of the construction of the contract. Lord Hoffmann was therefore restating the process of implying terms as a matter of fact to a rule of construction that should apply an objective process as opposed to the subjective one, however, this approach, as we shall see, was itself subject to further consideration in the case of **Marks and Spencer plc v BNP Baribas Securities Services Trust Co (Jersey) Ltd** [2015] UKSC 72, where it was subject to a critical review by the Supreme Court.

It should be noted that if the parties have divergent views about a proposed term, this will also cause the officious bystander test to fail since it is clear that a reasonable person could not conclude that the parties would have agreed to such a term in the face of those divergent views. The case of **Luxor (Eastbourne) Ltd v Cooper** provides an example of such a situation. Here an estate agent was employed by the defendant to sell some property, promising to pay the agent commission if he completed a sale. In fact, the defendant himself was able to conclude a sale of the property. The court held that no term could be implied that the defendant could not refuse to sell to a person obtained by the agent since the court could not be satisfied that the defendant would have agreed to the inclusion of such a term. Viscount Simon considered this accorded with the objective nature of the test since on a true construction of the contract, the agent accepted the risk of the defendant refusing to sell to a person introduced by the agent.

The 'business efficacy' test

In this second test, the courts may attempt to imply a term that renders the business contract effective. This test, was described by Lord Wright in **Luxor (Eastbourne) Ltd v Cooper** as a term which 'can be predicated that it 'goes without saying,' some term not expressed but necessary to give the transaction such business efficacy as the parties must have intended'.

An application of the business efficacy test can be seen in the case of **The Moorcock** (1889) 14 PD 64.

The Moorcock (1889) 14 PD 64

The defendant owners of a wharf contracted to allow the plaintiff owner of a ship, The Moorcock, to discharge it at their jetty provided he paid landing charges. The jetty extended into the Thames and both parties were aware that the ship would be grounded at low tide. While the ship was unloading, the tide went out and the ship settled on to a ridge of rock beneath the mud, breaking its back. The plaintiff sued for the damage sustained by the ship. The defendants argued that they had not guaranteed the safety of the anchorage and, further, the river bed by the jetty was not vested in them. The Court of Appeal nevertheless found the defendants to be liable on the basis that there was an implied undertaking given to the plaintiff at the time of contracting that the anchorage would, so far as reasonable care could provide, be in such a condition as not to endanger the vessel.

In that case Bowen LJ stated:

An implied warranty . . . is in all cases founded upon the presumed intention of the parties, and upon reason. The implication which the law draws from what must obviously have been the intention of the parties, the law draws with the object of giving efficacy to the transaction and preventing such a failure of consideration as cannot have been within the contemplation of either side.

In order for a term to be implied, it must be obvious and necessary to give business efficacy to the agreement, and thus only those the absence of which would render the contract incomplete will be implied. Effectively, therefore, a term will be implied as a matter of fact because the term is necessary to make to make the contract work or at the very least the contract cannot be performed as the parties intended to without the inclusion of the term.

Similarly in *Reigate* v *Union Manufacturing Co (Ramsbottom) Ltd* [1918] 1 KB 592, Scrutton LJ stated: 'a term can only be implied if it is necessary in the business sense to give efficacy to the contract', adding that a term would only be implied if 'it is such a term that it can confidently be said that if at the time the contract was negotiated' the parties were asked what would happen if a certain event occurred, and both the parties would have responded 'Of course, so and so will happen; we did not trouble to say that: it is too clear.'

The officious bystander test and the business efficacy test, whilst often appearing to be separate, stand-alone tests, in fact, overlap and in truth both are expressions of the same principles that are used to imply a term into a contract as a matter of fact. Essentially a term will be implied if it satisfies the test of business necessity as more recently affirmed in *Geys* v *Société Générale* [2013] 1 AC 523 para 55 and *Arnold* v *Britton* [2015] 2 WLR 1593 para 112. Thus Lord Simon in the case of *BP Refinery (Westernport) Pty Ltd* v *Shire of Hastings* (1977) 180 CLR 266, explained the conditions required to imply a term as a matter of fact into a contract as:

> (1) it must be reasonable and equitable; (2) it must be necessary to give business efficacy to the contract, so that no term will be implied if the contract is effective without it; (3) it must be so obvious that 'it goes without saying'; (4) it must be capable of clear expression; (5) it must not contradict any express term of the contract.

Lord Hoffmann, however, in *Attorney General of Belize* v *Belize Telecom Ltd* [2009] UKPC 10 considered that Lord Simon's conditions should not be regarded as a series of independent tests that each have to be met. He considered that they were in fact different ways in which judges have previously 'tried to express the central idea that the proposed implied term must spell out what the contract actually means, or in which they have explained why they did not think that it did so'.

Lord Hoffmann considered that there is only one question that determines the implication of a term as a matter of fact, thus:

> . . . in every case in which it is said that some provision ought to be implied in an instrument, the question for the court is whether such a provision would spell out in express words what the instrument, read against the relevant background, would reasonably be understood to mean.

Lord Hoffmann considered that the previous tests effectively applied a subjective approach and that this gave rise to a distraction from the requirement for an objective construction of the contract based on what the contract was reasonably understood to mean. Indeed he stressed that the question as to how the actual parties would react to any proposed amendment was irrelevant. The basis behind implying a term as a matter of fact should revolve around an examination of the contract in order to discover what it is understood to mean by a reasonable person with knowledge of the relevant commercial background with that person considering if a construction of the contract failed to express the intentions of the parties. Lord Hoffmann therefore based the approach on the same principles he adopted in

Investors Compensation Scheme v *West Bromwich* [1998] 1 WLR 896 in order to re-base 'the doctrine of implied terms within the principles of contractual interpretation'.

Lord Hoffmann's new formulation of a single implied term test was subsequently applied in the Court of Appeal in *Mediterranean Salvage and Towage Ltd* v *Seamar Trading and Commerce Inc. (The Reborn)* [2009] EWCA Civ 531 where Lord Clarke MR, giving the leading judgement, reinforced the need to show necessity to imply a term. Simply showing it would be reasonable is not sufficient and, of course, this would take us to Lord Denning's proposition in *Liverpool City Council* v *Irwin* which was firmly rebuked in the House of Lords. Lord Clarke therefore reinforced the central question for the implication of a term, 'Is it necessary to make the contract work?'.

Mediterranean Salvage and Towage Ltd v *Seamar Trading and Commerce Inc (The Reborn)* [2009] EWCA Civ 531

The facts of *The Reborn* are remarkably similar to those in *The Moorcock* above. The dispute arose out of a dispute between the owners of a vessel and charterers who had agreed a voyage charterparty for loading at Chekka, Lebanon, and discharging the cargo at Algiers. The vessel suffered damage at Chekka during loading by virtue of a hidden projection under the water penetrating the hull at the berth nominated by the charterers as required by the charterparty. The parties did not dispute that: (1) Chekka was the agreed load port; (2) it was for the charterers to nominate the berth at which the vessel was to be loaded; and (3) there was no express warranty of safety in respect of either the port or the berth. The owners of the vessel, however, argued that the charterparty was subject to an implied term that the charterers must nominate a *safe* berth at the agreed load port.

The Court of Appeal found that the arguments of the owners to be inconsistent with clause 20 of the charter. By that clause the owners had guaranteed and warranted that upon arrival at the loading port the vessel would comply with all restrictions of the port, including its berths and approaches, and that they had satisfied themselves to their full satisfaction with and about Chekka's specifications and restrictions before entering into the charterparty. The owners were therefore accepting that the charterers had a right to elect a berth of their choice. It was, accordingly, not necessary to imply the suggested term in order to make the contract work. The charterers had not agreed to accept the risk of the berth being unsafe because of hidden dangers. The decision of the Court of Appeal affirmed the single broad ('expansive') approach of Lord Hoffmann who had emphasised that the principle of implying terms into a contract is not something to be undertaken lightly. Lord Hoffmann had made the point in *Belize* that implying terms as fact normally arises where the contract does not expressly provide for what is to happen when some event occurs. The usual inference, however, is that nothing happens so that the loss lies where it falls and the express provisions of the contract continue since, if the parties had intended something would happen on the occurrence of an event, then the contract would have said so. The Court of Appeal in *The Reborn* nevertheless reinforced the importance of necessity within the new test and demonstrated that Lord Hoffmann's reformulation does not open the way to a lower threshold of reasonableness with regards to implying terms as fact. Lord Hoffmann's approach and unification of the older tests for implying terms as fact into a contract now sit comfortably with his decision in *Investors Compensation Scheme* v *West Bromwich* regarding construction of contracts.

In *SNCB Holding* v *UBS AG* [2012] EWHC 2044 (Comm), Cooke J applied the decision in *Attorney General of Belize* v *Belize Telecom Ltd* [2009] UKPC 10, [2009] 1 WLR 1988 and followed that of *Mediterranean Salvage & Towage Ltd v Seamar Trading & Commerce Inc (The Reborn)* [2009] EWCA Civ 531. He affirmed [62] that the test to be applied is that the proposed implied term must spell out what the contract actually means. He went on to say:

> . . . that the implied term must be 'reasonable and equitable' or 'necessary to give business efficacy to the contract' or 'so obvious that it goes without saying', that it must be 'capable of clear expression' and that it 'must not contradict any express term of the contract' is to add nothing to the central idea that the proposed implied term must spell out what the contract actually means. Though these formulations may assist in considering whether or not it does so, there are dangers in taking them as the litmus test.

This clearly confirms the approach of Lord Hoffmann in *Belize*. Cooke J, however, [65] then went on to describe the approach that should be taken for implying terms as a matter of fact post-*Belize*. He stated that with regard to the business efficacy formulation:

> . . . it is not enough for a court to consider that the implied term expresses what it would have been reasonable for the parties to agree to; the court must be satisfied that it is what the contract actually means. Whilst the contract may be workable in the sense that both parties can perform their express obligations without the implication of the term, the implication is necessary 'to give effect to the reasonable expectations of the parties' in the situation in question, because this is what the contract taken as a whole must, on its proper reading, be taken to mean. Although it is not necessary in Lord Hoffmann's view for the need for an implied term to be immediately apparent on a superficial consideration of the terms of the contract against the relevant background, it must be obvious, after a careful consideration of the express terms and the background, that only one answer is consistent with the rest of the document and this must be the meaning of the contract.

Similarly in *Torre Asset Funding Ltd v Royal Bank of Scotland plc* [2013] EWHC 2670; [2013] WLR (D) 343 (Comm) Sale J stated that any term that was sought to be implied had to be sufficiently precise in order that it could operate with reasonable certainty. Failing this, it would be difficult for the parties to infer on an objective basis that they really intended that the contract should contain that term.

Recently the single broad ('expansive') approach of Lord Hoffmann has been cast into doubt by the Supreme Court decision of *Marks and Spencer plc v BNP Baribas Securities Services Trust Co (Jersey) Ltd* [2015] UKSC 72.

Marks and Spencer plc v BNP Baribas Securities Services Trust Co (Jersey) Ltd [2015] UKSC 72.

The facts of this case were that there was a lease entered into between Marks and Spencer plc ('M') with BNP Baribas Securities Services Ltd ('B'). The term of the lease was to run until 2 February 2018. Rent was payable quarterly in advance on the usual quarter days. M however exercised a right to terminate the lease under a break clause so that the lease terminated on 24 January 2012. Notice given under the break clause was only be effective if there were no arrears of rent owing and that a break premium of one year's rent was paid. M paid the basic rent in full for the quarter starting on 25 December 2011 and ending on 24 March 2012, together with the break premium. M then demanded that the rent for the period 25 January to 24 March 2012 be repaid. B, the landlord refused to make repay the rent and M commenced proceedings to recover the rent for the said period, a car parking fee, insurance charge and service charge for the post-termination period. There was no term in the lease that entitled M to the repayment it claimed and therefore M argued that such a term should be implied into the lease.

The judge at first instance held that a term should be implied into the lease to the effect that M was entitled to those sums. The Supreme Court held that the lease was very detailed and had been drawn up by expert commercial property solicitors. It held that it was well established principle that rent that is a paid in advance cannot be apportioned on a time basis at common law. Whilst this position had been altered by the Apportionment Act 1870 s 2 this only applied to rent paid in arrears and not to rent paid in advance as in this case. In that event the Supreme Court held that it would be wrong to imply a term into the lease that M was entitled to a refund of rent paid in advance on exercising its break clause, though the same could not be said for the service fees claimed which were capable of being apportioned.

The Supreme Court stated that in a commercial contract a term will only be implied if it is necessary to give business efficacy to the contract or that the term was obvious that it goes without saying that the term should be implied. During the course of its judgement the Supreme Court explicitly rejected Lord Hoffman's approach and affirmed the approach taken by Lord Simon in *BP Refinery (Westernport) Pty Ltd* v *Shire of Hastings* (1977) 180 CLR 266, thus Lord Neuberger (who gave the leading judgement with Lords Hodge and Sumption concurring) stated (at 21):

> It could be dangerous to reformulate the principles, but I would add six comments on the summary given by Lord Simon in *BP Refinery*. . . First, in *Equitable Life Assurance Society v Hyman* [2002] 1 AC 408, 459, Lord Steyn rightly observed that the implication of a term was 'not critically dependent on proof of an actual intention of the parties' when negotiating the contract. If one approaches the question by reference to what the parties would have agreed, one is not strictly concerned with the hypothetical answer of the actual parties, but with that of notional reasonable people in the position of the parties at the time at which they were contracting. Secondly, a term should not be implied into a detailed commercial contract merely because it appears fair or merely because one considers that the parties would have agreed it if it had been suggested to them. Those are necessary but not sufficient grounds for including a term. However, and thirdly, it is questionable whether Lord Simon's first requirement, reasonableness and equitableness, will usually, if ever, add anything: if a term satisfies the other requirements, it is hard to think that it would not be reasonable and equitable. Fourthly, as Lord Hoffmann I think suggested in *Attorney General of Belize* v *Belize Telecom Ltd* [2009] 1 WLR 1988, para 27, although Lord Simon's requirements are otherwise cumulative, I would accept that business necessity and obviousness, his second and third requirements, can be alternatives in the sense that only one of them needs to be satisfied, although I suspect that in practice it would be a rare case where only one of those two requirements would be satisfied. Fifthly, if one approaches the issue by reference to the officious bystander, it is 'vital to formulate the question to be posed by [him] with the utmost care', to quote from Lewison, *The Interpretation of Contracts* 5th ed (2011), para 6.09. Sixthly, necessity for business efficacy involves a value judgement. It is rightly common ground on this appeal that the test is not one of 'absolute necessity', not least because the necessity is judged by reference to business efficacy. It may well be that a more helpful way of putting Lord Simon's second requirement is, as suggested by Lord Sumption in argument, that a term can only be implied if, without the term, the contract would lack commercial or practical coherence.

Lord Neuberger considered Lord Hoffman's judgement in *Belize* in which he stated that the process of implying terms into a contract was 'part of the exercise of the construction, or interpretation, of the contract'. In that judgement Lord Hoffman had stated at (para 21) that there '. . . is only one question: is that what the instrument, read as a whole against the relevant background, would reasonably be understood to mean?'. Lord Neuberger made two points about Lord Hoffman's approach. Firstly, he stated that the notion that a term will be implied, if a reasonable reader of the contract, knowing the background of the contract, would understand the need for the term to be implied, provided the reasonable reader is treated as reading the contract at the time when it was made. Secondly, the reader would recognise the term to be so obvious as to go without saying or to be necessary for business efficacy. Thus Lord Neuberger makes the point that the question as to whether a term can be implied is to be judged at the date the contract is entered into. The second proviso is, however, crucial since otherwise Lord Hoffman's comment may be taken as stating that reasonableness is a sufficient ground for implying a term into a contract. Lords Neuberger, Sumption and Hodge rejected this formulation, stating that the test remains one of necessity so that a term will only 'be implied if, without the term, the contract would lack commercial or practical coherence' (para 21) or whether it is necessary 'in order to make the contract work' (para 77). Effectively therefore the Supreme Court reaffirmed the traditional officious bystander and business efficacy tests as stated in *The Moorcock* and *Shirlaw and Southern Foundries Ltd* and the approach taken by Lord Simon in *BP Refinery (Westernport) Pty Ltd* v *Shire of Hastings* (1977) 180 CLR 266.

The Supreme Court went on to consider Lord Hoffman's proposition that 'the process of implying a term is part of the exercise of interpretation' and that implying a term was 'one of construction of the agreement as a whole in its commercial setting'. The Supreme Court cast doubt on this proposition and considered that the process of implication was not one that can be properly classified as forming part of the exercise of interpretation. Thus Lord Neuberger stated (para 27):

> When one is implying a term or a phrase, one is not construing words, as the words to be implied are *ex hypothesi* not there to be construed; and to speak of construing the contract as a whole, including the implied terms, is not helpful, not least because it begs the question as to what construction actually means in this context.

This must be correct since it is only after the contract has been construed that one can begin to consider what term should be implied and whether it is appropriate to do so since the 'cardinal rule' is that a term cannot be implied if it contradicts an express term. The logic is therefore circular since the express terms can only be discerned once the process of construction has taken place. The Supreme Court considered that Lord Hoffman's observations were open to more than one interpretation and in some areas his interpretations were wrong in law. The conclusion therefore was that Lord Hoffman's observations 'should henceforth be treated as a characteristically inspired discussion rather than authoritative guidance on the law of implied terms'.

The comments made by the Supreme Court in *Marks and Spencer plc* v *BNP Baribas Securities Services Trust Co (Jersey) Ltd* were given a second airing in the Supreme Court in *Trump International Golf Club Scotland Ltd* v *The Scottish Ministers* [2015] UKSC 74. In this case Lord Hodge, who gave the leading judgement, reaffirmed the principle that interpretation of a contract is not the same as the implication of terms. He stated that interpretation is the precursor to implication that forms the context in which the law considers whether or not to imply terms into the contract, 'where the court concludes from its interpretation of the words used in the document that it must have been intended that the document would have a certain effect, although the words to give it that effect are absent'. Lord Hodge did not go so far as to overrule *Belize*, however, he clearly, by referring to *Marks and Spencer*, demonstrated his disapproval of *Belize*.

Lord Mance was not quite as so forthright, however. He referred to Lord Neuberger's position in *Marks and Spencer* that whether an implication is necessary to give business efficacy must be judged objectively, in the light of the provisions of the contract as a whole and the surrounding circumstances at the time when the contract is made. He observed (at para 42):

> I would not encourage advocates or courts to adopt too rigid or sequential an approach to the processes of consideration of the express terms and of consideration of the possibility of an implication. Without derogating from the requirement to construe any contract as a whole, particular provisions of a contract may, I think, give rise to a necessary implication, which, once recognised, will itself throw light on the scope and meaning of other express provisions of the contract.

Lord Mance concluded his judgement that, broadly speaking, the processes of considering express terms and the possibility of terms being implied all form part of an overall, iterative process of objectively construing the contract as a whole. Whilst Lord Mance therefore takes a 'softer' approach than Lord Neuberger, it is clear that both *Marks and Spencer* and *Trump* indicate a clear return to the old tests established in *The Moorcock* and *Shirlaw* v *Southern Foundries* so that in order to imply a term into a contract, it must be shown that the term is necessary to make the contract work.

Terms implied as a matter of law

By the courts

Objective
4

So far we have seen that terms implied as a matter of fact are based on the idea that such a term emanates from the common implied intention of the parties to the contract. Terms implied by law are obligations that arise within the contract irrespective of the intentions of the parties or the facts of a particular case. Here terms are implied where the law wishes to insert common terms into certain categories of contracts so that once a term is implied by law and the courts find for its existence in the particular circumstances of a case, then that case becomes the authority for the inclusion of the term in all subsequent cases in contracts relating to that category. An important example of this process arose in the following case.

Liverpool City Council v *Irwin* [1976] 2 All ER 39

The Council had let flats in a tower block to the tenants. While the tenancy agreements imposed obligations on the tenants, they were silent as to the obligations of the Council as regards the maintenance of the building. Lifts regularly broke down and rubbish chutes blocked with the result that the appellant decided to withhold his rent as a protest against the Council's failure properly to maintain the building. The Council brought an action to seek possession of the appellant's flat, and he counter-claimed that the Council were acting in breach of an implied obligation properly to maintain the building. The term could not be implied as a matter of fact since it did not satisfy the officious bystander test nor was it reasonably necessary to give business efficacy to the contract. However, the House of Lords implied the term as a matter of law. There was a duty on a landlord 'to take reasonable care to keep in reasonable repair and usability' the common areas of the building, such as lifts, stairways, corridors and rubbish chutes, and so on. Lord Cross thought that the test to be applied in making a decision to imply a particular term into all contracts of a specific type was whether in the general run of such cases the term in question would be one which it would be reasonable to insert.

In order to imply a term as a matter of law the courts will have regard to duties which prima facie occur in certain types of contracts. The courts will therefore often be guided by matters of policy that affect particular types of contracts and to this extent issues of fairness and reasonableness may be considered in whether to imply a term of not. It was suggested in *Scally* v *Southern Health and Social Services Board* [1992] 1 AC 294 that the test of implication of a term should be one of necessity not reasonableness. Care needs to be exercised with this expression since it is not the same as that where terms are implied as a matter of fact as seen above. There the term is implied as necessary to give business efficacy to the contract, whilst here the term is implied as being necessary to a particular and definable type of contractual relationship. For instance, terms implied by law commonly arise in contracts of employment, for example, a term that an employee will be faithful to the employer and obey reasonable instructions. On their part, employers impliedly promise to pay the employees' wages and treat the employees with the respect necessary to maintain the trust and confidence required in the relationship as in *Malik* v *Bank of Credit and Commerce International SA* [1997] 3 All ER 1. Here the term is not implied as necessary to give business efficacy to this particular contract but was implied as it was a necessary aspect in any contract of employment.

In *Crossley* v *Faithful & Gould Holdings Ltd* [2004] 4 All ER 447, the Court of Appeal rejected an argument that a contract of employment should contain an implied term that an employer should take reasonable care of an employee's economic well-being. The court considered that a test of 'necessity' in considering whether or not to imply standard terms into contracts of employment was not always helpful. The court considered that it was better to recognise that the existence and scope of such terms raise questions of 'reasonableness, fairness and the balancing of competing policy considerations'.

Other examples of terms implied by law can be seen in contracts for the supply of services it was held in *Wong Mee Wan* v *Kwan Kin Travel Services Ltd* [1995] 4 All ER 745 that if a tour operator agrees that certain service will be supplied, whether by it or others, a term will be implied that those services will be carried out with reasonable care and skill. Similarly in agency contracts there is an implied fiduciary duty: *Imageview Management Ltd* v *Jack* [2009] EWCA Civ 63.

The fact that many contracts contain similar or identical terms does not necessarily mean that it is appropriate to imply a term by operation of law. In *Ashmore* v *Corporation of Lloyd's (No 2)* [1992] 2 Lloyd's Rep 620, it was held that imply a term there had to be a broad category or relationship, such as employee/employer, principal/agent, landlord/tenant in which it is possible to say that certain obligations could be regarded as 'typical' for a term to be implied.

By statute

Objective 5

Over the years obligations which have been formally implied into contracts by the courts have very often been given statutory authority. It is, of course, impossible to trace all such instances and therefore our discussion of terms implied by statute is limited to, *inter alia*, contracts for the sale of goods and the standard of care in relation to contracts for services. It must be borne in mind that terms implied in such circumstances are a mere example as to legislative intervention.

The Consumer Rights Act 2015

Introduction

The basic common law position as regards sale of goods contracts is one of 'buyer beware' or 'caveat emptor', however, this principle has now largely been subsumed by way of implied terms contained within a body of legislation principally the Sale of Goods Act 1979 and the Supply of Goods and Services Act 1982. Both Acts have been subject to amendment by the Sale and Supply of Goods Act 1994. Originally these Acts applied to most contracts for the sale of goods and services, though their application was more limited in relation to sales in the course of a business between businesses or where a contract of sale was otherwise entered into by a person dealing not as a consumer. In such situations such terms, subject to the Unfair Contract Terms Act 1977 (see Chapter 8), were either incapable of being excluded or limited or were capable of being excluded or limited by the express agreement of the parties and subject to the Court being satisfied that the exclusion or limitation satisfied the test of reasonableness. Thus in relation to consumer contracts the ability of sellers to exclude the terms implied by these pieces of legislation was prevented.

In relation to consumer contracts, the legislative intervention has now been subject to radical reform in that the bedrock of consumer rights is now contained within the Consumer Rights Act 2015 ('CRA'). This change became necessary as the law relating to consumer protection became extremely confused, fragmented, and unnecessarily complex as a result of various pieces of legislation by way of Acts of Parliament, Regulations and the onset of European Directives and not least the fact that the law had failed to keep up with technological advances. The effect of the piecemeal nature of the various legislative enactments has meant that there developed overlapping pieces of legislation that contain significant inconsistencies. The CRA is therefore is designed to enact one piece of legislation that will consolidate the current legislation on the rights of consumers in relation to goods, services, digital content and the law relating to unfair contract terms in consumer contracts. The CRA also implements certain European Directives such as Directive 99/44/EC of the European Parliament and Council on aspects of the sale of consumer goods and associated guarantees, Directive 93/13/EEC of the Council on unfair terms in consumer contracts and some provisions of Directive 2011/83/EU of the European Parliament and Council on consumer rights. The CRA is divided into three parts with Part 1 dealing with goods, services and digital content; Part 2 dealing with unfair contract terms; and Part 3 dealing with matters such as trading standards regulations and competition regulation, which is beyond the remit of this book. The CRA will also apply to the financial services sector, though again this is outside of the remit of this book.

As we have noted, the intention behind the CRA is to consolidate and bring together consumer rights so as to harmonise the existing provisions to provide a single approach to consumer contracts entered into between businesses and consumers ('B2C'). For other types of contracts, such as business to business ('B2B') and consumer to consumer ('C2C'), the existing legislation will remain in force. The CRA will therefore have a different impact depending on the scope of the existing legislation, thus, for example, in the Supply of Goods and Services Act 1982 the business to consumer provisions will now be found in the CRA, however, the 1982 Act will be amended so that it only covers B2B and C2C contracts. In the Sale of Goods Act 1979 B2C contracts will mainly be supplanted by the CRA, however, matters, such as when the property in the goods passes, will remain within the 1979 Act. B2B and C2C contracts for the sale of goods will remain within the 1979 Act. The Supply of Goods and Services Act 1982 will be replaced by the CRA in the case of B2C contracts and the Act will be amended so that it only relates to B2B and C2C contracts. The Sale and Supply of Goods Act 1994, which amended the Sale of Goods Act 1979 and the Supply of Goods and Services Act 1982, will be replaced by the CRA. The Sale and Supply of Goods to Consumer Regulations 2002 are revoked since the CRA implements Directive 99/44/EC, from which the 2002 Regulations are derived.

Clearly therefore the CRA makes significant changes to the overall structure as to how consumer rights will be dealt with under the legislative regime and at the same time harmonising the different national and EU provisions. The CRA therefore will show up a sharp divergence with respect to implied terms in consumer and business contracts. It is, however, useful at this juncture to remind ourselves that in relation to (B2C) contracts the CRA will apply; whilst in B2B and private C2C contracts, or other contracts falling outside the CRA, the Sale of Goods Act 1979 and the Supply of Goods and Services Act 1982 will continue to apply. It is therefore vital that a contract is correctly identified from the start since this determines the appropriate legislative regime.

Definitions within the CRA

Part 1 of the CRA applies where there is an agreement between a trader and a consumer for the trader to supply goods (Chapter 2), digital content (Chapter 3) and services (Chapter 4) if the agreement is a contract. It is of no consequence how the contract is made whether oral, written or implied by the conduct of the trader and the consumer or if there is a combination of these. It should be noted that each chapter will apply even if the contract covers something covered by another chapter so that if there is a mixed contract, for instance, if the contract is one for goods and services or services and digital contract, the CRA will still apply.

The starting point for determining whether a contract falls within the CRA is found within s 1 and s 2 of the CRA. Section 1 provides where there is an agreement between a trader and a consumer for the trader to supply goods, digital content or services, if the agreement is a contract.

Section 2 provides key definitions of certain terms within the Bill and the intention here is to align these terms across the broad spectrum of consumer law. Section 2(2) provides that a 'trader' means a person acting for purposes relating to that person's trade, business, craft or profession, whether acting personally or through another person acting in the trader's name or on the trader's behalf. A 'person' here includes not just natural persons but also includes companies, charities and arms of government. Thus if these types of bodies are acting for purposes relating to the trade, craft or profession they will fall within the definition of 'trader'. It will be noticed that 'not-for-profit' organisations such as charities, mutual or co-operatives also fall within this definition so that if a charity shop is selling clothes, for instance, the Act will apply to these types of organisations.

Section 2(3) defines a 'consumer' as meaning an 'individual acting for purposes that are wholly or mainly outside that individual's trade, business, craft or profession'. A trader claiming that an individual was not acting for purposes wholly or mainly outside the individual's trade, business, craft or profession must prove it (s 2(4)). This definition is important since the definition of a 'consumer' has previously not been consistently defined across the previous legislative framework. This change is consistent with the recommendations of the Law Commission's 2013 Unfair Terms in Consumer Contract: Advice to the Department of Business and Innovation and Skills March 2013 in which it was stated:

> We recommend that the definition of a consumer should be consistent across the new consumer legislation being considered by BIS [Department of Business, Innovation and Skills]. The new definition is likely to be narrower than the definition of 'dealing as a consumer' in UCTA, but the loss of protection for businesses will be negligible. A consistent definition will introduce much needed simplification.

In the Committee Stage in the House of Commons there was an attempt to include 'micro-businesses' i.e. those with fewer than ten employees, however, this was rejected by the Government in that, following the wide consultation about the Bill, it was considered unreasonable to put such business on the same footing as consumers. The Minister stated that the Bill was designed to relate to business-to-consumer relationships and that the regulations implementing the CRD should define 'consumer' in the same way. This amendment whilst pressed to a division in the Committee Stage was defeated.

The main restriction within s 2(3) is that it only applies to individuals, i.e. natural persons, who 'are acting for purposes wholly or mainly outside the individuals' trade, business craft or profession'. The effect therefore is that if a person buys a car that is primarily for private use outside of the purchaser's business, then the fact that he uses it for some business purposes will not preclude that purchaser from being a consumer. On the other hand, if the purchaser buys a computer for use in his business but nevertheless uses it for some private purposes, then this will not fall within a purchase by a consumer. This situation encompasses the problem associated with cases such *R&B Customs Brokers Co Ltd v United Dominions Trust Ltd* [1988] 1 All ER 847 and *Stevenson v Rogers* [1999] 1 All ER 613. The Law Commission in its Consultation Paper No 166 Unfair Terms in Contracts considered that a person who makes a contract to obtain goods or services 'related to' even though not 'in the course of' his business should be treated as dealing as a business and not as a consumer. This approach seems to tie in more consistently with the decision in *Stevenson v Rogers* so that a wide interpretation has been adopted in terms of when a person is acting as a consumer. There is good reason for this since it may well be impossible for a trader to be able to distinguish between a person acting in the course of a business or as a consumer whether a company or an individual. The fact that the definition of a consumer requires that he or she must be an individual automatically eliminates the possibility of a company falling within the protection. Further to gain the protection, the individual must be able to demonstrate that his purposes are wholly or mainly outside of the individual's trade, business, craft or profession.

Certain types of contracts are excluded from the definition of a consumer so that under s 2(5) a person is not a consumer in relation to a sales contract

> . . . if—(a) the goods are second hand goods sold at public auction, and (b) individuals have the opportunity of attending the sale in person.

By s 2(7) 'business' includes the activities of any government department or local or public authority. By s 2(8) 'goods' means any tangible moveable items, but that includes water, gas and electricity if and only if they are put up for supply in a limited volume or set quantity, whilst 'Digital content' means data which are produced and supplied in digital form.

It should be noted that the CRA does not talk in terms of 'implied' terms but instead it states that certain obligations are 'included'. The effect is the same so that even if the parties do not expressly include the terms they are included in any event. It is also noticeable that the CRA does not distinguish between contracts of sale and contracts to supply that gave rise to the Sale of Goods Act 1979 and the Supply of Goods and Services Act 1982. Whilst the Sale of Goods Act 1979 applied wholly to contracts of sale, the 1982 Act applied to contracts for the transfer of ownership of goods. Such transfers amounted neither to contracts for the sale of goods nor to hire purchase agreements and thus applied to contracts for the exchange of goods, such contracts not amounting to contracts for the sale of goods because of the lack of a money consideration. Both types of contract now fall with the expression 'supply' within the CRA.

Another important feature of the CRA is that it does not designate the terms included in B2C contracts as conditions or warranties. The result of this is that effect of any breach is now determined by the provisions of the CRA rather than the common law. The distinction between a condition and a warranty is discussed more fully later in this chapter.

Terms implied in contracts within the CRA

As we have noted, the intention behind the Consumer Rights Act is to consolidate and bring together consumer rights so as to harmonise the existing provisions to provide a single approach to consumer contracts entered into between businesses and consumers ('B2C').

As we will see for other types of contracts, such as business to business ('B2B') and consumer to consumer ('C2C'), the existing legislation contained within the Sale of Goods Act 1979 and the Supply and Goods and Services Act 1982 will remain in force so that there will now be a sharp divergence with respect to implied terms in consumer and business contracts.

Consumer contracts for goods, digital content and services – Part 1

Chapter 1 The Background and Application of Part 1

This Part applies where there is an agreement between a trader and a consumer for the trader to supply goods (Chapter 2), digital content (Chapter 3) and services (Chapter 4) if the agreement is a contract.

As already indicated s 2(2) provides that a 'trader' means a person acting for purposes relating to that person's trade, business, craft or profession, whether acting personally or through another person acting in the trader's name or on the trader's behalf. A 'person' here includes not just natural persons but also includes companies, charities and arms of government. Thus if these types of bodies are acting for purposes relating to the trade, craft or profession, they will fall within the definition of 'trader'. It will be noticed that 'not-for-profit' organisations such as charities, mutual or co-operatives also fall within this definition so that if a charity shop is selling clothes, for instance, the Bill will apply to these types of organisations.

To re-iterate, s 2(3) defines a 'consumer' means an 'individual acting for purposes that are wholly or mainly outside that individual's trade, business, craft or profession'. A trader claiming that an individual was not acting for purposes wholly or mainly outside the individual's trade, business, craft or profession must prove it (s 2(4)).

Chapter 2 Contracts for the supply of goods

In Chapter 2, a contract for a trader to supply goods to a consumer applies only if the contract is one of the following:

1 a sales contract;

2 a contract for the hire of goods;

3 a hire-purchase agreement;

4 a contract for the transfer of goods.

Each of these different types of contracts is defined in Sections 5–8. Certain types of contracts are, however, specifically excluded in s 3(3), thus Chapter 2 (Goods) does not apply to:

1 A contract for a trader to supply coins or notes to a consumer for use as currency. The reference to currency should be noted here since it means that coins, for instance, supplied to a collector will be covered by the Act.

2 A contract for goods to be sold by way of execution or otherwise by authority of law. This excludes from the definition of goods items sold in situations such as a sale by an official under a legal authority to satisfy a debt (e.g. an official authorised to sell off property of a bankrupt).

3 A contract intended to operate as a mortgage, pledge, charge or other security.

4 A contract made by deed and for which the only consideration is the presumed consideration imported by the deed. Thus a contract lacking consideration will only be enforceable if it is made as a deed.

Rights of consumers within the ambit of Chapter 2

Chapter 2 sets out the rights of consumers within the Consumer Rights Act and provides statutory remedies for breach of those rights. The rights are set out as implied terms rather than as 'conditions' of the contract or 'warranties' which are features of the current legislation. Presently most of the statutory implied terms are categorised as conditions, breach of which enables the consumer to choose either to treat the contract as terminated, or to affirm the contract and claim damages as in ***Poussard*** v ***Spiers and Pond*** (1876) 1 QBD 410. Warranties, on the other hand, are regarded as minor terms, breach of which only gives the claimant the right to claim damages as in ***Bettini*** v ***Gye*** (1876) 1 QBD 183.

A full explanation of the difference between conditions and warranties can be found later in this chapter.

In 2010, the Department for Business, Innovation and Skills ('BIS') commissioned a report, entitled 'Consolidation and Simplification of UK Consumer Law' to examine how existing consumer law might be consolidated and simplified to make it more accessible to consumers, business and their advisers. The report recommended that the remedies for goods should be made clearer and more accessible by incorporating them into a single piece of legislation and aligning the remedies as much as possible. The reason for this is that many consumers, even if they are aware of their rights under the current legislation, were vague as to what their rights were. The CRA therefore attempts to provide a clearer regime setting out the remedies available for breach of the implied terms without reference to the notions of conditions and warranties as set out at common law; however, it aligns the remedies depending on whether the breach arises in relations to goods, service or digital content.

The implied terms in relation to goods are:

1 Section 9: Goods to be of Satisfactory Quality. This section provides that goods supplied under a contract to supply goods must be of satisfactory quality. It details aspects of quality which may be considered when assessing whether the goods are satisfactory, i.e. fitness for the purposes for which goods of that kind are usually supplied, appearance and finish, freedom from minor defects, safety and durability. This provision only gives an indication of such aspects, not an exhaustive list. It can be seen that this provision largely corresponds with similar existing provisions such as s 14(2) of the Sale of Goods Act, etc. The section provides that the test of whether or not the quality of the goods is satisfactory is determined by what a reasonable person would expect of the goods in question, taking into consideration all the relevant circumstances, including any description, the price and any public statements by the trader or producer or their representatives, such as statements made in advertisements or on the labels of goods. Thus it would be expected that a lower standard of quality would be expected of cheap goods when compared to similar goods that were more expensive. If, however, the consumer is made aware of a particular defect before making the contract, then that defect will not be grounds for finding the goods to be unsatisfactory. If the consumer examined the goods before making the contract, then a defect which should have been revealed by the examination will not be grounds for finding the goods to be unsatisfactory. If the goods were supplied by sample (even if the consumer did not actually examine the sample), then a defect which should have been revealed by a reasonable examination of the sample will not be grounds for finding the goods to be unsatisfactory.

2 Section 10: Goods to be fit for particular purpose. This clause provides that if a consumer acquires goods for a specific purpose and has made this purpose known to the trader beforehand, the goods must be fit for that purpose unless the consumer does not rely – or it would be unreasonable for the consumer to rely – on the skill or judgement of the trader. It can be seen that this provision largely corresponds with similar existing provisions such as s 14(3) of the Sale of Goods Act, etc.

3   Section 11: Goods to be as described. This section provides that where goods are supplied by description, the goods must be as described. Goods can be supplied by description even if they are available for the consumer to see and select, for example, on the shelves of a shop. This clause corresponds to s 13 Sale of Goods Act, etc.

4   Section 12: Other pre-contract information included in contract. This section provides that any other information provided by the trader which is of a category mentioned in Consumer Contracts (Information, Cancellation and Additional Charges) Regulations 2013 (SI 2013/3134), such as information on the trader's name and address, but which does not relate to main characteristics of the goods so does not fall under Section 11, also forms part of the contract between the trader and the consumer.

5   Section 13: Goods to match a sample. Under this section if a consumer enters into a contract for goods on the basis of a sample, the final goods delivered must match the sample in terms of quality and appearance. This differs from Section 14 below (Goods to match a model seen or examined) in that a sample is usually only a representative part of the whole goods in question. It will apply, for instance, if a consumer is purchasing some new custom-made curtains and relies on a swatch of different designs, materials, etc. then the final made-up curtains must accord with the fabric chosen from the swatch.

6   Section 14: Goods to match a model seen or examined. This section provides that if the trader displays or provides a model of the goods in question, then the goods received should match that model, with the exception that any differences specifically brought to the consumer's attention before the contract is made would not breach this protection. So, for instance, if the consumer sees a washing machine on display on the shop floor, then, when a washing machine is retrieved from the warehouse, this machine must correspond with the version on the shop floor, unless any differences were brought to the attention of the consumer.

7   Section 15: Installation as part of conformity of the goods with the contract. Where goods are both supplied and installed by a trader (or the installation is done under that same trader's responsibility), if the installation service is done incorrectly, then the goods remedies apply, with the exception of the short-term right to reject under ss 20 and 22.

8   Section 16: Goods not conforming to contract if digital content does not conform. Section 16 provides that where goods and digital content are supplied together in one product (e.g. where digital content is supplied on a disk), the section makes it clear that if the digital content rights are not met, then this will mean the goods are substandard and the consumer has the right to the full range of goods remedies (including the short-term right to reject).

9   Section 17: Trader to have right to supply the goods etc. This section provides protection to the consumer by making it a term of the contract that the trader must have the right to sell or transfer the goods or to transfer possession of them, at the time when the transfer of ownership or possession takes place. Clearly if the sale, transfer or hire takes effect immediately, then the trader will need to have this right at the time the contract is made. In other cases, the parties may agree that the goods will be sold, transferred or hired at a later time so the provision requires the trader to have these rights at tat later time. This section therefore broadly corresponds to s 12 Sale of Goods Act s.12 etc. The general rule is that ownership transfers when the parties intend it to pass and that intention is determined by what has taken place between the trader and the consumer and the circumstances of the case. Section 17(2) provides that the goods must be free of any charge or encumbrance so that no other person should have rights over the goods unless this is

disclosed to the consumer before the entry into the contract. The consumer is therefore entitled to enjoy quiet possession of the goods except insofar as that enjoyment may be disturbed by a person entitled to do so and those entitlements are made known to the consumer prior to the contract. Similarly in relation to the hire of goods, Section 17(3) provides that the consumer is entitled to quiet possession for the period of the hire except insofar as any entitlement of a third party is made known to the consumer before entering into the hire contract. It should be noted that this clause does not affect the protection afforded to private purchasers of motor vehicles under the Hire Purchase Act 1964 s 2.

See Chapter 10 for more about protection of private purchasers of motor vehicles under the Hire Purchase Act.

10 Section 18: No other requirement to treat term about quality or fitness as included. This section corresponds to s 14(1) of the SGA, but now applies to contracts between a trader and consumer. As with the SGA s14(1), this section provides that, unless there is an express term concerning the quality of the goods or the goods' fitness for a particular purpose, the contract should not be treated as including any such terms, other than those set out in ss 9, 10, 13 and (where it applies) 16.

Chapter 3 Contracts for the supply of digital content

Chapter 3 concerns contracts where a trader agrees to supply digital content to a consumer. 'Digital content' is defined in s 2(9) (Key definitions) as 'data which are produced and supplied in digital form' it therefore includes software, music, computer games and applications or 'apps' supplied under contract from a trader to a consumer. It includes data that is largely or wholly stored and processed remotely, such as software supplied via cloud computing, as well as digital content that is transmitted to the consumer's device so that they can interact with the digital content product that they have purchased. The definition of digital content would also cover the digital content supplied to a consumer as the result of a service which produced bespoke digital content, such as the production of a website design. It should be noted that there is one important exception contained in s 33(4) in that the CRA does not apply merely because the trader supplies a service by which digital content reaches the consumer, thus contracts for the supply of the Internet or a mobile phone service do not fall within the protection of the CRA.

It was seen necessary to include specific regulation for digital content since it was not clear whether digital content could be classified as goods or services or something completely different, apart from the fact it was unclear what, if any, legal rights a consumer had if the digital content proved defective or if it did not provide the consumer with what he or she considered they were purchasing. The CRA has therefore has been drafted in such a way that 'digital products should be treated exactly as physical goods, so far as that is possible' (Bradgate, 2010).

Section 33 (1) provides that Chapter 3 applies to contracts where a trader has agreed to supply digital content to a consumer for which the consumer pays a price, however, s 33(2) goes further and provides that this chapter will cover the situation where the digital content is supplied free with goods or services or other digital content for which the consumer pays a price and where it is not generally available to a consumer unless they have paid a price for the goods, services or other digital content. The references to the 'price' in (1) and (2) includes situations where the consumer pays for the digital content by way of a voucher, virtual currency (such as 'bitcoins') or a gift voucher that was originally paid for by money. This would cover not just traditional gift vouchers but also the position in some computer games where the consumer purchases tokens or 'jewels' to be traded for further digital content.

Rights of consumers within the ambit of Chapter 3

Chapter 3 sets out the rights of consumers within the CRA and provides statutory remedies for breach of those rights. The rights are, as in Chapter 2, set out as implied terms rather than as 'conditions' of the contract or 'warranties'.

1 Section 34: Digital content to be of satisfactory quality. Digital content sold to consumers must be of satisfactory quality according to the expectations of a reasonable person. There are several different factors that will affect whether the quality expectations of a reasonable person are met. These are any description of the digital content, the price paid and its state and condition, as well as any other relevant circumstances. The quality standard is therefore flexible in order to take into account the many different types of digital content thus, for example, the reasonable expectations of quality for a £2.99 app would not be as high as for one worth £15.99. Subsection (3) provides that the state and condition of the digital content are always an aspect of quality and also sets out other matters that can be aspects of quality, i.e. fitness for the purposes for which the type of digital content in question is usually supplied; freedom from minor defects, safety and durability (e.g. the lifespan of the digital content). A reasonable person's expectations as to quality are likely to vary according to the nature of the content and some aspects of quality, for example, a consumer would expect a downloaded film to be able to play once downloaded, however, a complex computer game might be expected to contain minor computer 'bugs'. Thus the matter of satisfactory quality in respect of minor defects will depend on reasonable expectations as to quality. Section 34(3) therefore provides that:

> The quality of digital content includes its state and condition; and the following aspects (among others) are in appropriate cases aspects of the quality of digital content—
>
> (a) fitness for all the purposes for which digital content of that kind is usually supplied;
> (b) freedom from minor defects;
> (c) safety;
> (d) durability.

2 It should be noted that the term contained in subsection (1) does not cover anything which makes the quality of the digital content unsatisfactory. Thus, for instance, there will be no breach if the trader specifically draws the attention of the consumer to matters which might render the digital content unsatisfactory or where the consumer examines the digital content or a trial version so that any defects rendering the digital content unsatisfactory would have been apparent on a reasonable examination. Digital content will not be in breach of this clause if the consumer was made aware of the aspect of the digital content that makes it unsatisfactory before the contract was concluded because it was specifically drawn to the consumer's attention or would have been apparent from inspection of the digital content or a trial version. These provisions therefore correspond with the provisions relating to the supply of goods in s 9.

3 Clause 35: Digital content to be fit for a particular purpose. If the consumer specifies that the digital content will be used for a particular purpose, then the digital content must be fit for that particular purpose. This section therefore corresponds to the implied terms relating to goods in s 10. The section provides that the consumer must make it known to the trader the purpose for which the digital content is intended so that the trader must be aware of the consumer's intentions.

4 Section 36: Digital content to be as described. The right for digital content to be as described is similar to the right for goods (s 10). This right is important in the digital content context since consumers may not be able to view the digital content before buying the full version. Even when the digital content matches a trial version, if it does not meet the description, then the supply of the digital content will be in breach of this provision.

5 Section 37: Other pre-contract information included in the contract. This provides that where the Consumer Contracts (Information, Cancellation and Additional Charges) Regulations 2013 require a trader to provide information to the consumer, such as information on the trader's name and address, before the contract becomes binding, the provision of that information is now to be treated as a term of the contract.

6 Section 38: No other requirement to treat term about quality or fitness as included. This provision makes it clear that no other terms about quality or fitness can be implied into the contract unless a term is expressly agreed, again, this equates with the SGA s 14(1) and the CRA s 18.

7 Section 39: Supply by transmission and facilities for continued transmission. This provision applies where in order to access digital content, it is transmitted to the consumer (for example, where digital content is bought or used via the internet or through a satellite transmission) and makes it clear that digital content must be of satisfactory quality, fit for a particular purpose and as described at the point when it reaches either the consumer's device or, if earlier, a trader with whom the consumer has contracted, such as an internet service provider or mobile network operator.

8 Section 40: Quality, fitness and description of content supplied subject to modifications. This reflects a unique issue for digital content in that manufacturers and traders are technically able to change or update digital content after the initial provision of the digital content. This may be set out in the terms and conditions of the licence. Very commonly this might apply to anti-virus software, for instance, where the product may be updated to take into account new viruses, etc. Usually this is to the benefit of consumers since it might include important updates to the digital content. Requiring consent for every update would create problems for business, both due to the logistics of contacting every consumer and getting their consent and the problems that would arise when some consumers do not accept updates. This might result in many different versions of software being in circulation and could lead to unnecessary disputes with consumers when digital content stops working due to lack of updates. The effect of this section is that a trader (or third party) is not prevented from updating digital content without the consumer's consent as long as the contract stated that such updates would be supplied. In any updates the digital content must still meet the quality rights (i.e. it must still be of satisfactory quality, be fit for purpose and match the description given). Subsection (2) makes clear that the time period for bringing a claim begins when the digital content was first supplied notwithstanding the fact that the modification itself must have occurred some time after the original supply. This means that any claim for breach of this provision must be brought within 6 years of the date the digital content was first supplied. It is for a consumer to prove that the digital content is faulty. Where a consumer has not identified a fault (and therefore not requested a repair or replacement), but a general update is sent in any case to the consumer, this does not necessarily mean that the quality rights are breached nor that the update constitutes a repair or replacement.

9 Section 41: Trader's right to supply digital content. A trader must have the right to supply the digital content to the consumer. Often where a consumer buys digital content from a trader, there will be other traders who have rights over the digital content. This is particularly important as regards the intellectual property rights to the digital content. Clearly there is a difference here from implied terms regarding goods since often the trader does not pass on the intellectual property rights, unlike the rights of ownership in goods. For instance, if one purchases music from the internet, the supplier cannot sell the intellectual property rights in the music. The result is that the consumer only

purchases a limited use of the content. Usually the trader passes on a limited right to use the digital content in certain defined circumstances so that the ownership of any rights to the digital content usually will remain with the rights holder (usually the originator of the digital content). If the trader does not have the right to supply the digital content at all, the consumer will be entitled to a refund (Section 45) such a scenario may arise with the purchase of music from a 'pirate' provider of digital music.

Chapter 4 Contracts where a trader supplies a service to a consumer

Essentially this chapter deals with contracts where a trader provides a consumer with a service and thus if the contract is broken, the trader stands liable for breach of contract. Previously, the Supply of Goods and Services Act gave some protection for persons in receipt of services, whether or not they were consumers, so that a business supplier of a service must provide that service with 'reasonable care and skill' and, if the time and charge have not been agreed, the service must be provided within a 'reasonable time' and at a 'reasonable charge'. This was done by stating that such matters are implied terms of the contract unless they are excluded. The Supply of Goods and Services Act 1982 did not provide for any statutory remedies where there is a breach of these implied terms.

Chapter 4 is the CRA equivalent of the Supply of Goods and Services Act 1982 as it applies to the provision of services. It provides that in such a situation the consumer is entitled to request (and the trader must offer) that the trader re-performs the service or subsequently offers a reduction in the price of the service, or that the consumer is entitled to recover their costs as a result of the breach. These are referred to as the 'statutory remedies'. The entitlement to the statutory remedies does not prevent the consumer from claiming other remedies available under general contract law such as a right to claim damages or termination of the contract. Furthermore, the trader cannot, in effect, limit its liability for less than the contract price.

Chapter 4 applies to all service sectors except where they are expressly excluded, thus the chapter does not cover contracts of employment or apprenticeships and, where there is legislation that gives more detailed provision about rights or duties of particular services, that legislation will take precedence over the provisions in this chapter. It should be noted that sectors such as financial and gambling services are exempt from these provisions.

Section 48 sets out the contracts that are covered by this chapter, however, as stated earlier, the chapter largely follows the corresponding provisions of the Supply of Goods and Services Act 1982 except that the chapter is only concerned with where a trader supplies a service to a consumer.

Rights of consumers within the ambit of Chapter 4

1 Section 49: Service to be performed with reasonable care and skill. This section corresponds to s 13 of the Supply of Goods and Services Act 1982 but, as with all the provisions in the Act it removes the legalistic reference to an 'implied term' that is in the Supply of Goods and Services Act 1982 and simply says that every contract where a trader supplies a service to a consumer includes a term that the service must be performed with reasonable care and skill. The standard of care that the trader must meet in s 49 is the same as that in Supply of Goods and Services Act 1982 s 13 so that if reasonable skill and care are not exercised, the trader will be deemed to be in breach of contract. It should be noted that, as previously, the notion of 'reasonable care and skill' focuses on the way a service has been carried out, and not the end result. The effect therefore is that if a trader has not

provided a service with reasonable care and skill, they will be in breach of this right, whatever the end result. This provision does not include a definition of 'reasonable care and skill', with the effect that the standard is flexible between commercial sectors and industries. It should also be noted that the price paid for the service may be a factor in determining the level of care and skill that needs to be exercised in order for the service to be 'reasonable'.

2 Section 50: Information about the trader or service to be binding. This is a new provision and there is no corresponding provision in the Supply of Goods and Services Act 1982. There are two reasons why this provision has been introduced:

(i) There may be a detriment to a consumer if the trader says something to the consumer, which the consumer then relies on, but which the trader later does not comply with. Whilst it may be the case that, on a proper legal construction these statements are validly incorporated into the contract as express terms, a trader may attempt to argue that they are not contractually bound by the statement. Thus every contract to supply a service is to be treated as containing a term of the contract that *anything* said or written to the consumer by the trader if it is taken into account by the consumer whether or not to enter into the contract must be complied with by the trader.

(ii) For certain contracts, the Consumer Contracts (Information, Cancellation and Additional Charges) Regulations 2013 in regs. 9,10 or 11 requires certain information, such as the main characteristics of the goods or services, the identity of the trader (such as the trader's trading name), the geographical address at which the trader is established and the trader's telephone number, etc. to be provided by the trader. To enable enforcement of those Regulations, the CRA makes clear that these pieces of information will form part of the contract which cannot be altered unless the parties expressly agree otherwise.

An example of the effect of these provisions can be seen where a consumer invites a trader to his home where a contract is agreed for the erection and fitting of a garden fence surrounding the consumer's garden. The consumer then chooses that trader to erect the fence. On completing the work the trader then tells the consumer that it is up to him to creosote the fence himself. In such a situation the trader will not have complied with the information it gave the consumer, and which the consumer had taken into account when entering into the contract. Under the 2013 Regulations, the trader must give the consumer the 'main characteristics' of the service and the service must comply with those characteristics. This is in addition to the right that the service must generally comply with any information given to the consumer by the trader which the consumer takes into account when deciding to enter into the contract. It will be interesting to see how this provision interacts with the law on misrepresentation. The main point with the provision is that the information provided by the trader becomes a term of the contract.

3 Section 51: Reasonable price to be paid for a service. This provision corresponds with s 15 of the Supply of Goods and Services Act 1982 but updates the language in line with the rest of Part 1. Usually a contract will set out the price for the service, and indeed the 2013 Regulations require traders (apart from those excluded) to provide information about the price before the consumer is bound by the contract. In some situations the consumer will have paid the price for the service in advance and clearly here the consumer will know the price anyway, however, if the price is not known, then this provision states that the consumer will only be required to pay a reasonable price. The question as to what a reasonable price is a question of fact.

4 Section 52: Service to be performed within a reasonable time. This provision corresponds with that contained in s 14 of Supply of Goods and Services Act 1982. Where a time for performance of the service has not been agreed, this provision gives the consumer the right to have the service provided within a reasonable time after the contract is agreed.

5 Section 53: Relation to other law on contract terms. Again, this provision has its counterpart in the Supply of Goods and Services Act 1982, in this case, s 16. The basis behind this provision is that some contracts for services are regulated by certain sector-specific legislation, such as in financial services. The effect of this provision is that sector-specific legislation will sit alongside this chapter.

The provision preserves any existing enactments or rules of law which impose stricter duties than those imposed by ss 49 and 50. 'Rules of law' means a rule of the common law. Further, where Parliament has provided for legislation for a particular service, then those provisions will take precedence over those in the CRA. This will include not only primary legislation but also secondary legislation.

Undoubtedly the Consumer Rights Act 2015 provides a significant leap forward in terms of consumer contracts and for the first time sets out specific remedies for breaches committed by traders whilst previously this had been something of a 'grey' area. The CRA maintains the rights of the consumer to claim damages on common law principles in the normal way, however, it will be interesting to see how the courts will apply this, given the CRA now contains 'included' terms that are not defined in terms of conditions or warranties and thus appear to fall into the category of innominate terms which will be discussed later in this chapter. The CRA is also to be welcomed since it removes some of the contradictions and inconsistencies that existed between the various pieces of legislation, both domestic and EU, that had grown organically over a long period of time. The overall effect of the CRA is to produce a single regime for the protection of consumers, though the dichotomy arising from the different legal regimes for B2C and B2B contracts now makes the landscape of terms implied by statute a more complex one.

Terms implied in contracts outside of the CRA

As we have already stated, contracts outside of the CRA, primarily B2B and C2C contracts, will continue to be regulated by the Sale of Goods Act 1979 (sales of goods), the Supply of Goods (Implied Terms) Act 1973 (hire purchase) and the Supply of Goods and Services Act 1982 (supply of goods, hire of goods and supply of services). We will now look at the nature of these implied terms in such contracts.

Terms implied under the Sale of Goods Act 1979

Implied term as to title – s 12

By s 12(1) in a contract of sale, other than one to which subsection (3) below applies, there is an implied term on the part of the seller that in the case of a sale he has a right to sell the goods, and in the case of an agreement to sell, he will have such a right at the time when the property is to pass. By s 12(5A) this implied term is designated as a condition.

Further in s 12(2) in a contract of sale there are two further implied terms that by s 12(5A) these terms are designated as warranties:

(a) The goods are free, and will remain free until the time when the property is to pass, from any charge or encumbrance not disclosed or known to the buyer before the contract is made.

TABLE 7.1 Terms implied by statute – A Summary

B2C Contracts	B2B Contracts
Consumer Rights Act 2015 Part 1	**Sale of Goods Act 1979**
Applies as between a "trader" and a "consumer"	**Contracts for the Sale of Goods**
Definitions: "Trader" – A person acting for purposes relating to that person's trade, business craft or profession . . ." (s.2(2)) "Consumer" – "An individual acting for purposes that are wholly or mainly outside that individual's trade business or profession" (s.2(3)).	s.12 – Implied term as to title s.13 – Implied term as to description *Beale v Turner* *Harlingdon and Leinster Enterprises Lltd v Christopher Hull Fine Art Ltd* s.14 (2) – Implied term as to satisfactory quality *Rogers v Parish (Scarborough) Ltd* *Bernstein v Pamsons Motors Ltd* *Bartlett v Sydney Marcus Ltd* *Wilson v Rickett Cockerell Ltd* s.14(3) – Implied term as to fitness for purpose *Godley v Perry* s.15 – Implied term as to sample
Chapter 2 – Contracts for the Supply of Goods s.9 – To be of satisfactory quality s.10 – To be fit for particular purpose s.11 – To to be as described s.12 – Pre-contract information included in the contract s.13 – To match sample s.14 – To match model s.15 – Installation of goods – goods remedies may apply s.16 – Goods that include digital contract s.17 – Trader to have the right to supply the goods	
	Supply of Goods (Implied Terms) Act 1973
	Contracts of Hire purchase s.8 – Implied term as to title when goods are to pass s.9 – Implied term as to description s.10 – Implied terms as to quality of fitness s.11 – Implied term as to sample
Chapter 3 – Contracts for the Supply of Digital Content "Digital content" definition – s.2(9): "Data which are produced and supplied in a digital form" e.g. music, software, films etc. s.34 – To be of satisfactory quality s.35 – To be fit for particular purpose s.36 – To be as described s.37 – Pre-contract information included in the contract s.38 – Except as provided in ss.34/35 no other requirement re quality or fitness is included unless expressly included. s.39 – Supply by transmission – fitness and quality s.40 – Quality, fitness, description subject to modifications s.41 – Trader to have the right to supply digital content	**Supply of Goods and Services Act 1982** **Supply of Goods** s.2 – Title s.3 – Description s.4(2) – Satisfactory quality s.4(5) – Fitness for purpose s.5 – Sample **Hire of Goods** s.7 – Title s.8 – Description s.9(2) – Satisfactory quality s.9(4) – Fitness for purpose s.10 – Sample
Chapter 4 – Contracts where a Trader Supplies a Service s.49 – Service to be performed with reasonable care and skill s.50 – Information about the trader or service to be binding s.51 – A reasonable price to be paid for the service s.52 – Service to be performed within a reasonable time s.53 – Relation to other law on contract terms – sector specific legislation to sit alongside this Chapter.	**Supply of Services** s.13 – To be carried out with reasonable care and skill s.14 – To be carried out within a reasonable time s.15 – A reasonable price to be paid for the service

(b) The buyer will enjoy quiet possession of the goods except so far as it may be disturbed by the owner or other person entitled to the benefit of any charge or encumbrance so disclosed or known.

By s12(3) and (4) there is an implied term that where it appears from the contract, or is to be inferred from its circumstances, an intention that the seller should transfer only such title as he or a third person may have then only such title will be transferred. The effect therefore is that the seller is able to include an express term that he will only pass a limited title and indeed such an intention may be inferred. The passing of such a limited title either of the seller or a third party (for instance, where goods are being sold by an auctioneer on behalf of third party) does not wholly exonerate both from the requirement that the buyer's implied term that he is entitled to quiet possession of the goods – s12(5).

Both the implied terms in s12(4) and (5) are designated as warranties under s12(5A).

Rowland v Divall [1923] 2 KB 500

A buyer of a car found out that it had in fact been stolen and as a result he had to return it to the true owner. He sued on the implied condition and it was held that he was entitled to recover the full price he had paid for the car, despite the fact that he had used the car for some four months and as a result the car was worth less than he had paid for it. The logic is simple, in that he had paid to become the full owner of the vehicle and since he had not acquired this ownership, he was entitled to recover his full purchase price, despite the depreciation of the car during the period that it was in his possession.

Implied term as to description – s 13

Where there is a contract for the sale of goods by description, there is an implied term that the goods will correspond with the description. By s13(1A) this implied term is designated as a condition.

In **Beale v Taylor** [1967] 1 WLR 1193, a private motorist advertised his car for sale as a 'Herald convertible, white, 1961, twin carbs'. The buyer, another private motorist, later discovered that the car was in fact a composite of two cars and that only the rear half corresponded with the description given by the seller, who was unaware of the true situation. It was held that even though the buyer had inspected the car, he had nevertheless at least partly relied on the description, so that it was a sale by description and that the seller was liable under s 13.

Before a breach of s 13 can arise in order for a sale to be by description, the description has to be of some influence in the sale in order for the description to be a contractual term so that the buyer has entered into the contract in reliance upon the description. Thus in **Harlingdon & Leinster Enterprises Ltd v Christopher Hull Fine Art Ltd** [1992] 1 QB 564, there was a sale of a painting by Gabriele Münter. Both the seller and the purchaser were specialist art dealers who had inspected the painting prior to the sale. The purchaser paid £6000 for the painting which turned out to be a fake worth no more than £100. The Court of Appeal found that the purchaser had not relied on the description within the sale catalogue but rather had relied on their own judgement as regards the attribution attached to the painting and as such there was no breach of the implied condition under s 13. Slade LJ stated:

> where a question arises whether a sale of goods was one by description, the presence or absence of reliance on the description may be very relevant in so far as it throws light on the intentions of the parties at the time of the contract. If there was no such reliance by the purchaser, this may be powerful evidence that the parties did not contemplate that the authenticity of the description should constitute a term of the contract; in other words, that they contemplated that the purchaser would be buying the goods as they were. If, on the other hand, there was such reliance (as in **Varley v Whipp** [1900] 1 QB 513, where the purchaser had never seen the goods) this may be equally powerful evidence that it was contemplated by both parties that the correctness of the description would be a term of the contract (so as to bring it within s 13(1)).

It should be noted that a sale of unascertained goods will always be a sale by description.

If the sale is by sample as well as by description it is not sufficient that the bulk of the goods corresponds with the sample if the goods do not also correspond with the description.

Implied term as to satisfactory quality

The starting point in examining the implied term that goods are to be of a satisfactory quality is that there is no such implied term about the quality or fitness for any particular purpose of goods supplied under a contract of sale. The premise here then is one of caveat emptor. Having said that, this principle is subject to the qualification that goods sold in the course of a business are to be of satisfactory quality, thus the Sale of Goods Act 1979 s 14 provides:

(1) Where the seller sells goods in the course of a business, there is an implied term that the goods supplied under the contract are of satisfactory quality.

(2) For the purposes of this Act, goods are of satisfactory quality if they meet the standard that a reasonable person would regard as satisfactory, taking account of any description of the goods, the price (if relevant) and all the other relevant circumstances.

(3) For the purposes of this Act, the quality of goods includes their state and condition and the following (among others) are in appropriate cases aspects of the quality of goods –

(a) fitness for all the purposes for which goods of the kind in question are commonly supplied;

(b) appearance and finish;

(c) freedom from minor defects;

(d) safety; and

(e) durability;

(4) The term implied by subsection (2) above does not extend to any matter making the quality of goods unsatisfactory –

(a) which is specifically drawn to the buyer's attention before the contract is made;

(b) where the buyer examines the goods before the contract is made, which that examination ought to reveal; or

(c) in the case of a contract for sale by sample, which would have been apparent on a reasonable examination of the sample.

By s 14(6) the terms implied by in subsection (2) above are conditions. The provision imposes an objective test and reforms the law previously contained in the Sale of Goods Act 1979, s 14(2), which provided that, where the seller sells goods in the course of a business, there is an implied condition that the goods supplied under the contract are of merchantable quality.

The term 'merchantable quality' was defined in s 14(6) of the Sale of Goods Act 1979 as follows:

> Goods of any kind are of merchantable quality within the meaning of subsection (2) above if they are as fit for the purpose or purposes for which goods of that kind are commonly bought as it is reasonable to expect having regard to any description applied to them, the price (if relevant) and all other relevant circumstances.

The problem with the expression 'satisfactory quality' in the amended Sale of Goods Act s 14(2) was that it provide little guidance as to how the satisfactory nature of the goods was to be assessed. The question here is to what extent the old 'merchantable quality' law can be used to provide guidance as to the new 'satisfactory quality' law.

In *Rogers v Parish (Scarborough) Ltd* [1987] 2 All ER 232, Mustill LJ regarded it to be inappropriate to refer to previous law but in the absence of any guidelines and with that qualification always in mind, it is useful to review the previous law to obtain a better understanding of some of the issues that may arise and, further, it must be borne in mind that the question of satisfactory quality, just as with merchantable quality, depends largely upon the circumstances of a particular case. In looking at the previous law also bear in mind that the cases often involve sales to consumers and these cases would no longer be considered under the Sale of Goods Act 1979 but under the CRA.

Firstly, very often the physical characteristics of the goods would determine whether the goods were of merchantable quality, although this was not always the case. A low-priced product described as 'seconds', 'shop-soiled' or 'second-hand' may have indicated a lower quality and therefore a finding that it was nevertheless of satisfactory or merchantable quality. On the other hand, higher-priced goods variously described as 'luxury', 'deluxe' or 'premier' would have given an expectation of a higher quality and produced a finding of unsatisfactory or unmerchantability even though there was only the slightest blemish on the product. Thus in *Rogers v Parish (Scarborough) Ltd* [1987] 2 All ER 232 itself, the claimant bought a new Range Rover that suffered from a number of minor defects such as a misfiring engine, an oil leak, scratches to the paintwork and a noisy gearbox. The Court of Appeal held that the vehicle was not of merchantable quality despite the fact that the defects were capable of being repaired. Similarly, in *Shine v General Guarantee Corporation* [1988] 1 All ER 911, where the plaintiff bought a second-hand sports car, a Fiat X-19, which at some point had been submerged in water so that the manufacturer's anti-corrosion warranty was invalid, it was held that the vehicle was not of merchantable quality. Here the Court of Appeal placed particular emphasis on the description of the vehicle, stating that the buyer considered that:

> he was buying an enthusiast's car, a car of the mileage shown and at the sort of price cars of that age and condition could be expected to fetch, a car described as 'a nice car, good runner, no problems . . . ' What he in fact was buying for the same price was . . . potentially a 'rogue car' and irrespective of its condition it was one which no member of the public, knowing the facts, would touch with a barge pole unless they could get it at a substantially reduced price.

Secondly, apart from the description and price, the consequences of a defect could also be a relevant factor in determining whether a product was of merchantable quality or not. Thus in **Bernstein v Pamsons Motors (Golders Green) Ltd** [1987] 2 All ER 220, the claimant bought a new car which, within three weeks of delivery and having only travelled 140 miles, suffered from a seized-up engine. This was caused by a drop of sealant blocking up the lubrication system. Repairs were carried out free of charge but the claimant refused to take the car back and asked for the return of his money. The defendants argued that the car was still usable and therefore of merchantable quality. Rougier J stated that the purchaser of a new car was entitled to expect more, though how much more depended on a number of factors. One was the intractability of a defect which was difficult to find and rectify, since here the person acquired not so much a car as a running battle with a defective machine. Another factor was the time it took to repair the defect and it was not relevant that the repair was done free of charge to the purchaser under the vendor's warranty. Another factor was the price and in that respect he considered that a mere blemish on a Rolls-Royce might render it unmerchantable, while on a more modest car it would not have this effect. He stated finally that, whilst the car had been repaired, there was a possibility that the effect of the engine seizure could have transmitted stress to other parts of the engine and created some 'knock-on damage'. While a buyer of a new car had to put up with some teething problems and have them repaired, a defect of the type that occurred in this case went far beyond what a buyer has to accept, and therefore the car was not of merchantable quality. Rougier J also stated that a relevant factor in arriving at his decision was that the car, though driveable prior to the engine seizure, was not safe since the seizure could have occurred in the fast lane of a motorway with devastating consequences.

Thirdly, clearly one cannot expect second-hand goods to be as good as new ones, though even here these goods must meet a certain standard. The case of **Bartlett v Sidney Marcus Ltd** illustrates the point. The facts of the case were that a purchaser of a car was informed that the clutch of the car he was considering purchasing was defective. The sellers offered to either repair the clutch or reduce the price of the car by £25, the buyer opting for the latter. After driving 300 miles the purchaser had to replace the clutch at a cost of £45 more than was initially anticipated. It was held that the car was of merchantable quality since the car was not unfit for its purpose merely because the defect proved to be more serious than was originally thought. Lord Denning considered that the car was usable though not perfect. Denning's opinion was that one must expect a second-hand car to be less than perfect.

Section 14(2) catches not only the goods themselves but also the packaging or anything else supplied with the goods, as illustrated in the case of **Wilson v Rickett Cockerell & Co. Ltd** [1954] 1 QB 598. In this case, the claimant purchased a ton of 'Coalite', a type of smokeless solid fuel, however, unknown to either party, a detonator from the mine had somehow found its way into the batch delivered. The claimant then put the 'Coalite' on his fire. The defendant was held liable for the resulting explosion. The defendant's argument that there was nothing wrong with the 'Coalite' itself was rejected.

Finally, it should be noticed that the condition contained within s 14(2) is excluded as regards any matter making the quality of goods unsatisfactory where any defects are specifically drawn to the buyer's attention before the contract is made or where the buyer examines the goods before the contract is made and that that examination ought to have revealed the defects. Similarly in the case of a contract of sale that is concluded by reference to a sample, the condition is excluded if a reasonable sample of the sample should have revealed any defect in the goods.

Implied term as to fitness for purpose

In a B2B contract by the Sale of Goods Act 1979 s 14(3) where the seller sells goods and the buyer either expressly or impliedly makes known to the seller any particular purpose for which the goods are being bought by s 14(6), there is an implied condition that the goods supplied under the contract are reasonably fit for that purpose, whether or not that is a purpose for which goods of that type are commonly supplied. Thus if two businessmen enter into a contract it is of course still possible that one relies on the skill and judgement of the seller. The implied condition does not operate, however, where the buyer does not rely, or it is unreasonable to rely, on the skill or judgement of the seller or a credit broker. It follows that if one is going to use the goods for an abnormal purpose, then to gain the protection of the provision one should make known to the seller what that purpose is.

In order to claim, the buyer must demonstrate that he or she has relied on the seller's skill or judgement. Such reliance is not required, however, for a claim under s 14(2) – satisfactory quality. The effect therefore is that if the goods are fit for all purposes for which such goods are commonly sold, they will be of satisfactory quality despite the fact they may not be fit for any special or unusual purpose. On the other hand, if the goods are not fit for some of the purposes for which goods of that type are commonly supplied, then the goods will not be of satisfactory quality. Sellers who know that the goods in question are not fit for some of the purposes for which goods of that nature are commonly supplied must ensure the description of the goods excludes such common purposes or at the very least publicise this fact. The burden of risk for any goods not proving satisfactory for any common purposes lies with the seller.

The operation of s 14(2) and (3) are not mutually exclusive and it is possible for the seller to be liable for breach of the condition within the same framework of fact. A pre-CRA example can be seen in the case of *Godley* v *Perry* [1960] 1 WLR 9 where the defendant sold a plastic catapult to the plaintiff, who was a boy of six years of age. When the boy used the catapult it broke, blinding him in his left eye. It was held that the defendant was liable both under s 14(2) – merchantable quality – and s 14(3) – that the catapult was not fit for the purpose for which it was sold.

Implied term as to sample

By s 15 a contract for sale by sample arises where there is an express or implied term to that effect in the contract. Where a sale is agreed to be by sample two terms are implied into the contract. First, the bulk must, with regard to quality, correspond with the sample – s 15(2) a, and secondly, goods must be free of any defect which would not be apparent on reasonable examination of he sample – s 15(2)b. By s 15(3) both the implied terms in s 15(2) are conditions.

The second implied term condition was of particular relevance in the case of *Godley* v *Perry*, above, since the retailer joined the wholesaler into the action by way of this provision, and indeed the wholesaler did the same with the importer of the catapults. We have seen that the retailer was found liable to the boy but could the wholesaler and importer be found liable? The retailer argued that both should also be found liable for breach of the condition of satisfactory quality in the contract of sale by sample since it was alleged that a reasonable examination of the catapult would have revealed its defects. It was held that the expression reasonable examination was to be construed by reference to the commonsense standards of everyday life and one was not expected to put the item in question under some bizarre tests. The wholesaler and importer were also found to be liable.

Supply of Goods (Implied Terms) Act 1973

The Supply of Goods (Implied Terms) Act 1973 (as amended by the Consumer Credit Act 1974) also imposes implied terms where there is a hire purchase agreement. Thus in a general sense the terms implied here are very similar to those found in the Sale of Goods Act 1979 amended to take into account the hire purchase nature of the transaction. Thus in relation to the matter of title, s 8(1) provides that there is an implied term that the creditor will have a right to sell the goods at the time when the property is to pass; and that the goods are free, and will remain free until the time when the property is to pass, from any charge or encumbrance not disclosed or known to the hirer. Furthermore, there is an implied term that the hirer will enjoy quiet possession of the goods unless that is disturbed by any person entitled to the benefit of any charge or encumbrance that is disclosed to the hirer.

Other than the implied terms as to title, terms are also implied as to the goods corresponding with description (s 9), being of satisfactory quality (s 10(2)), that the goods supplied under the agreement are reasonably fit for that purpose (s 10(3)) and that the goods will correspond with any sample in so far as the bulk delivered should correspond with the sample and that the hirer shall have a reasonable opportunity of comparing the bulk with the sample and that the goods will be free from any defect(s 11), which would not be apparent on reasonable examination of the sample.

Terms implied under the Supply of Goods and Services Act 1982

Contracts for the supply of goods

The 1982 Act applies to contracts for the transfer of ownership of goods in relation to B2B and C2C contracts since these are outside the CRA. Such transfer amounts neither to contracts for the sale of goods nor to hire purchase agreements. The Act thus applies to contracts for the exchange of goods, such contracts not amounting to contracts for the sale of goods because of the lack of a money consideration. Similarly, the Act will apply to a contract of service where, though goods are transferred, the main element is the purchase of a service. An example may be where a painter is employed to paint a person's portrait; here the main element of the contract amounts to the purchase of a skill or service but nevertheless goods are transferred within the contract.

The implied terms applied to the goods transferred or hired under the contracts described above are exactly the same as those found in the Sale of Goods Act 1979; thus for the transfer of goods they cover: title (s 2), description (s3), satisfactory quality (s 4(2)), fitness for purpose (s 4(4)(5)) and sample (s 5); and for the hire of goods they cover: title (s 7), description (s 8), satisfactory quality (s 9(2)), fitness for purpose (s 9(4)(5)) and sample (s 10) title.

Contracts for the supply of services

Further terms are implied in the 1982 Act where a supplier has agreed to carry out a service, with the exception of contracts of employment or apprenticeship. In such contracts, which may arise in relation to contracts for the sale of goods or hire purchase agreements, there is an implied term that the supplier, acting in the course of a business, will carry out the service with reasonable care and skill (s 13).

There is also an implied term that the supplier acting in the course of a business will carry out the service within a reasonable time, this being based on a question of fact, unless the contract fixes a time or the time for the carrying out of the service is determinable by some arrangement within the contract itself or some previous course of dealing (s 14). Finally, where the consideration due under the contract is not determined by the contract, or by some arrangement within the contract, or some previous course of dealing, the person supplied with the service will have to pay a reasonable charge, this being based on a question of fact (s 15).

The Consumer Contracts (Information, Cancellation and Additional Charges) Regulations 2013

The onset of the global market via the internet has given rise to a whole new way of buying goods and services. Not surprisingly, therefore, there have been moves to extend statutory protection for consumers into this new market environment. With the development of the Single European Market it also comes as no surprise that the European Union has moved towards making provision for consumer protection on a pan-European basis. This protection arose in the form of the Distance Selling Directive (Directive 97/7/EC), which was originally implemented in the United Kingdom in the form of the Consumer Protection (Distance Selling) Regulations 2000. Since 13 June 2014 these regulations have been replaced by the Consumer Contracts (Information, Cancellation and Additional Charges) Regulations 2013 which implements the Consumer Rights Directive (CRD) 2011/83/EU, which in itself repealed and replaced the European Distance Selling Directive 97/7/EC. The Consumer Protection (Distance Selling) Regulations 2000 still apply as regards contracts entered into prior to 13th June 2013.

The intention behind the regulations is to protect consumers in respect of contracts negotiated away from the trader's business premises. The regulations apply not only to distance contracts concluded via the internet but also provide that the means of distance communication contracts covered by the Regulations includes letters, press advertising with an order form, catalogues, telephone contracts with or without human intervention, radio, electronic mail (email), fax machines and television (by way of teleshopping) but not vending machines or other automated commercial premises. Thus the regulations apply at any time when there is no simultaneous physical presence of the consumer and the supplier. It should be noted, however, that the regulations are not confined in their scope to 'off-premises contracts' and some of the regulations apply also to 'on-premises contracts'.

The regulations apply to consumer contracts and traders, as defined by reg. 4; however, certain contracts are excluded, such as gambling contracts and banking services, by reg. 6. The regulations require that certain information (the 'informational requirements') must be given to the consumer prior to the conclusion of the contract. For on-premises contracts the information to be provided is set out in Schedule 1. With regards to these types of contracts, the regulations do not apply to contracts which involve a day-to-day transaction and is performed immediately at the time the contract is entered into – reg. 9(2). With regards to such contracts it is important to notice that any information given by the trader is to be treated as a term of the contract – reg. 9(4) and that any change to any of the information made before entering into the contract or later, is not effective unless expressly agreed between the consumer and the trader – reg. 9(5).

For off-premises and distance contracts the information requirements are set out in Schedule 2.

The rights to cancel regulations are set out in Part 3 of the regulations. Certain contracts are excluded from this part, such as passenger transport services – reg. 27. In particular Part 3 does not apply to off-premises contracts for which the price to be paid by the consumer is not more than £42. There are limitations on the right to cancel so that contracts for goods or services for which the price is dependent on the fluctuations in the financial market that cannot be controlled by the trader are excluded – reg. 28. Other than these exclusions the consumer may cancel an off-premises or distance contract at any time in the cancellation period without giving a reason and without incurring any liability, except, for instance, where enhanced delivery is chosen by the consumer; or where the consumer has diminished the value of the goods by handling them – reg. 29(1). The cancellation period begins when the contract is entered into and ends at the end of 14 days after the date on which the goods come into the physical possession of the consumer or such other person identified by the consumer to take possession of them (but not the carrier) – reg. 30(2) and (3). It should be noted that the cancellation period is extended if the trader fails to provide the consumer with the requisite informational as to his or her rights to cancel. Thus if the trader provides the information within 12 months beginning with the first day of the above 14-day period, the cancellation period ends at the end of 14 days after the consumer receives the information – reg. 31(2), otherwise the cancellation period ends at the end of 12 months after the day on which it would have ended under reg. 30 above.

Terms implied by custom

It is, of course, possible that terms may be implied into a contract by way of custom or trade usage. In *Hutton* v *Warren* (1836) 1 M & W 466, a tenant proved, by virtue of local custom, that on quitting in accordance with the notice issued by the landlord, he was entitled to an allowance for seeds and labour he had expended on the land.

Good faith as a contractual term

Objective 6

Before leaving our consideration of express and implied terms it is important to consider the issue of good faith in the law of contract. On the face of things it might seem obvious that the law requires parties to act in good faith and in the failure of an express term to this effect then the law must a priori require imply such conduct on the part of the parties.

Traditionally English law has been hostile to a general duty of good faith between contracting parties and developed a somewhat ad hoc approach, finding solutions to particular situations as and when they arose. Thus, in some contracts the notion of good faith is well established such as in contracts of insurance, contracts of employment and other fiduciary contracts. Further the notion of good faith has infiltrated from the European Union, thus the implementation of European Directive 93/13 on unfair terms in consumer contracts gave rise to the Unfair Terms in Consumer Contracts Regulations 1994, which were then contained in the Unfair Terms in Consumer Contracts Regulations 1999.

Thus, reg 5(1) of the 1999 Regulations provides:

A contractual term which has not been individually negotiated shall be regarded as unfair if, contrary to the requirement of good faith, it causes a significant imbalance in the parties' rights and obligations arising under the contract to the detriment of the consumer.

The requirement of good faith is now found within the Consumer Rights Act 2015 s62(4) and (6) so that a term or notice is regarded as unfair 'contrary to the requirement of good faith, it causes a significant imbalance in the parties' rights and obligations under the contract to the detriment of the consumer'. These provisions also set out factors that a court should take into account when determining whether a term is fair, notably that it should consider the specific circumstances existing when the term was agreed, other terms in the contract and the nature of the subject matter of the contract. This assessment is known as the 'fairness test' which is considered in more detail in Chapter 8.

Increasingly, however, in some other common law jurisdictions the notion of general duties of good faith has become more widely recognised and, while this has not found a footing in English law, the principle and its general application were nevertheless discussed in the case of *Yam Seng Pte Ltd v International Trade Corp Ltd* [2013] EWHC 111 (QB). In this case, International Trade Corp Ltd ('ITC'), the defendant was a company registered in England and in January 2009 it invited Yam Seng Pte Ltd ('YSP'), a company incorporated in Singapore, to enter into negotiations for a distribution agreement with regard to perfumes, fragrances and toiletries. ITC stated that it had recently signed a licence agreement with regards to the products it sought to distribute. In fact ITC only signed that agreement in May 2009, about the same time as the distribution agreement with YSP was entered into. The distribution agreement was to last for 30 months, however, YSP terminated the agreement after 15 months, alleging that ITC had failed to ship orders promptly, failed to make the products available, refused to supply certain products once YSP had marketed them, undercut prices in agreements with third parties and provide false information during the currency of the contract in the knowledge that YSP would rely on that information. In essence, the allegation by YSP was that ITC had failed to act in good faith. YSP brought an action for breach of contract and further alleged misrepresentation in that YSP had been induced to enter into the contract by virtue of the fact that ITC stated that it was licensed to distribute the products when it was not so licensed.

Whilst the court was required to make findings as regards each of the alleged breaches in order to determine whether they amounted to repudiatory breaches of contract that justified YSP in terminating the contract, the primary matter was whether a duty of good faith was capable of being implied into the law of contract. It was held by Leggatt J that the English contract law did not, historically, recognise a general duty to perform contracts in good faith referring to the decision of Lord Bingham in *Interfoto Picture Library Ltd v Stiletto Visual Programmes Ltd* [1989] QB 433 where he stated:

> In many civil law systems, and perhaps in most legal systems outside the common law world, the law of obligations recognises and enforces an overriding principle that in making and carrying out contracts parties should act in good faith. This does not simply mean that they should not deceive each other, a principle which any legal system must recognise; its effect is perhaps most aptly conveyed by such metaphorical colloquialisms as 'playing fair', 'coming clean' or 'putting one's cards face upwards on the table'. It is in essence a principle of fair and open dealing . . . English law has, characteristically, committed itself to no such overriding principle but has developed piecemeal solutions in response to demonstrated problems of unfairness.

The *Interfoto* case is itself an example of the courts applying the 'piecemeal' approach in that the decision required that onerous or oppressive terms in a contract have to be specifically drawn to the attention of the person on whom such a term is to be imposed or at least be given prominence within the contractual document either by way of bold or red typescript. Indeed, Denning MR also pointed to this higher degree of notice in *Spurling v Bradshaw* [1956] 2 All ER 121 where he stated, 'Some clauses I have seen would have to be printed in red ink on the face of the document with a red hand pointing to it before notice could be held to be sufficient'.

Leggatt J also referred to the case of *Walford* v *Miles* [1992] 2 AC 128 where Lord Ackner stated that a duty to negotiate in good faith is 'inherently repugnant to the adversarial position of the parties when involved in negotiations' and 'unworkable in practice'. That case was concerned, however, with the position of negotiating parties and not with the duties of parties who have entered into a contract and thereby undertaken obligations to each other. Leggatt J considered that there were three main reasons for this hostility. Firstly, as referred by Lord Bingham, the preferred method of proceeding in English law is to respond to particular situations rather than enforcing broad overarching principles. Secondly, English law is said to embody an ethos of individualism, whereby the parties are free to pursue their own self-interest not only in negotiating but also in performing contracts provided they do not act in breach of a term of the contract. Thirdly, there is a fear that recognising a general requirement of good faith in the performance of contracts would create uncertainty since it would be vague and subjective.

Leggatt J, however, recognised the influence of the principle of good faith from European systems which derived from Roman law and which had found its way into EU legislations such as the UTCCR as discussed. He also accepted that the existence of a contractual duty of good faith and fair dealing had been recognised in the United States and Australia and was cautiously gaining ground in Canada, though not in New Zealand. Leggatt J recognised the incidence of good faith in particular situations as discussed above, however, he did not consider that such a duty had reached the point that such a duty could be implied as a matter of law.

Leggatt J, however, went further and considered whether such a duty could be implied into a contract based on the presumed intentions of the parties. Certainly such terms could be implied as a matter of fact where a term is so obvious that it goes without saying that the term is necessary to give business efficacy to the contract. In *Attorney General for Belize* v *Belize Telecom Ltd* [2009] 1 WLR 1988, however, Lord Hoffmann considered that the traditional criteria should not be regarded as a set of independent tests but rather as different ways of approaching what is ultimately a question of construction, that is, what would the contract, read as a whole against the relevant background, reasonably be understood to mean? He also reiterated the principles set by Lord Hoffman in *Investors Compensation Scheme Ltd* v *West Bromwich Building Society* [1998] 1 WLR 896 in which it was stated that the construction of a contract is to be made against the background of unstated shared understandings and that the breadth of the relevant background has no conceptual limits. He considered that the relevant background includes not only matters of fact known to the parties but also 'shared values and norms of behaviour', stating:

> Some of these are norms that command general social acceptance; others may be specific to a particular trade or commercial activity; others may be more specific still, arising from features of the particular contractual relationship. Many such norms are naturally taken for granted by the parties when making any contract without being spelt out in the document recording their agreement. A paradigm example of a general norm which underlies almost all contractual relationships is an expectation of honesty. That expectation is essential to commerce, which depends critically on trust. Yet it is seldom, if ever, made the subject of an express contractual obligation. Indeed if a party in negotiating the terms of a contract were to seek to include a provision which expressly required the other party to act honestly, the very fact of doing so might well damage the parties' relationship by the lack of trust which this would signify.

The judge also considered that commerce takes place against a background of honesty and that this was recognised in *HIH Casualty* v *Chase Manhattan Bank* [2003] 2 Lloyds Rep 61 where Lord Bingham stated:

> Parties entering into a commercial contract . . . will assume the honesty and good faith of the other; absent such an assumption they would not deal.

Equally Lord Hoffmann observed:

. . . in the absence of words which expressly refer to dishonesty, it goes without saying that underlying the contractual arrangements of the parties there will be a common assumption that the persons involved will behave honestly.

Clearly making a false statement with the intention of deceiving someone is dishonest in any context, however, it may also be regarded as dishonest where there is conduct falling short of a lie, such as deliberately avoiding giving an answer, or being evasive. Traditionally, English law draws a sharp distinction between fiduciary relationships, which impose onerous obligations to disclose information, and other contractual relationships where there are no such obligations. Leggatt J considered that dichotomy to be too simplistic stating that some contracts do not fit into this model, for instance, those that involve a longer term relationship between the parties in which they make a substantial commitment, Such 'relational' contracts he argued required 'a high degree of communication, cooperation and predictable performance based on mutual trust'. These contracts involved expectations of loyalty, which were often not legislated for in the express terms of the contract, but were implicit in the parties' understanding, and were necessary to give business efficacy to the arrangements. Examples of such 'relational contracts' included joint venture agreements, franchise agreements and long-term distributorship agreements. He stated that whilst the test of good faith was sensitive to context it was nevertheless was objective, depending not on a party's perception of whether conduct was improper, but on whether the conduct would be regarded as commercially unacceptable by reasonable and honest people, applying the decision in **Royal Brunei Airlines Sdn Bhd v Tan** [1995] 2 AC 378.

Thus Leggatt J considered that as a matter of construction it would be hard to envisage any contract that would not require an underlying requirement of honesty in the performance of the contract and to that extent it goes without saying that such a requirement is necessary to give business efficacy to a commercial transaction.

Leggatt J considered that whilst there was traditional English hostility towards a doctrine of good faith in the performance of contracts there was nothing novel or foreign in English law in recognising an implied duty of good faith in the performance of a contract. He considered that the reluctance of English law to recognise an implied duty on contracting parties to deal with each other in good faith was misplaced for a number of reasons:

1 Since the duty of good faith is heavily dependent on context and is established through the process of construing the contract, its recognition is consistent with the case by case approach adopted by the common law.

2 The basis of the duty of good faith is the presumed intention of the parties and the meaning of their contract, and that its recognition is not an illegitimate restriction on the freedom of the parties to pursue their own interests.

3 A further consequence of the fact that the duty is based on the parties' presumed intention is that it is open to the parties to modify the scope of the duty by the express terms of their contract and, in principle at least, to exclude it altogether, though it is hardly conceivable that parties would seek to expressly exclude a core requirement to act honestly.

4 He saw no objection to describing the duty as one of good faith and 'fair dealing'. What constitutes fair dealing is defined by the contract and by those standards of conduct to which, objectively, the parties must reasonably have assumed compliance without the need to state them. He considered that the advantage of including reference to fair

dealing is that it draws attention to the fact that the standard is objective and distinguishes the relevant concept of good faith from other senses in which the expression 'good faith' is used in fiduciary contracts.

5 Whilst English law may be less willing than some other legal systems to interpret the duty of good faith as requiring openness of the kind described by Bingham LJ in the *Interfoto* case, this should be seen as a difference of opinion, which may reflect different cultural norms, about what constitutes good faith and fair dealing in some contractual contexts rather than a refusal to recognise that good faith and fair dealing are required.

6 He considered that the fear that the recognition of a duty of good faith will create excessive uncertainty is unjustified. He did not consider that there was anything unduly vague or unworkable about the concept. Its application involves no more uncertainty than is inherent in the process of contractual interpretation in any event.

Leggatt J subsequently held that ITC was in repudiatory breach of contract in two respects:

1 In signifying its intention to use another distributor for the toiletry products in breach of the exclusivity granted to YSP, and having refused, in breach of its contractual obligation, to supply the toiletries to YSP

and

2 In providing false information during the currency of the contract in the knowledge that YPS would rely on that information.

In respect of the alternative claim in misrepresentation Leggatt J also found for YPS under the Misrepresentation Act 1967 s 2(1).

The case of *Yam Seng Pte Ltd v International Trade Corp Ltd* [2013] EWHC 111 (QB) has been considered in two further cases, namely, *Hamsard 3147 Ltd (t/a Mini Mode Childrenswear) v Boots UK Ltd* [2013] EWHC 3251 (Pat) and *TSG Building Services Plc v South Anglia Housing Ltd* [2013] EWHC 1151 (TCC); [2013] BLR 484.

In *Hamsard*, the company had contracted to provide Boots with its own brand of childrenswear. Boots terminated the contract and *Hamsard* sued alleging that Boots had breached an implied duty of good faith by virtue of the fact that Boots had failed to maximise the net profits generated under the contract to the benefit of both the parties by cancelling some of the orders and destroying some unsold stock after the contract had been terminated. *Hamsard* relied on the decision in *Yam Seng Pte Ltd v International Trade Corp Ltd* [2013] EWHC 111 (QB), however, Norris J stated:

> I do not regard the decision in *Yam Seng Pte Ltd v International Trade Corporation* as authority for the proposition that in commercial contracts it may be taken to be the presumed intention of the parties that there is a general obligation of 'good faith'. I readily accept that there will generally be an implied term not to do anything to frustrate the purpose of the contract. But I do not accept that there is to be routinely implied some positive obligation upon a contracting party to subordinate its own commercial interests to those of the other contracting party.

That seems clear enough though one has to question whether an implied duty not to do anything to frustrate the contract is removed from Leggatt J's argument that there is an implied duty as regards honesty and good faith of the parties in relation to the operation of the contract.

In **TSG Building Services Plc v South Anglia Housing Ltd** [2013] EWHC 1151 (TCC), [2013] BLR 484 TSG entered into a contract with South Anglia Housing Ltd ('SAH') to provide gas servicing and other associated works. The written contract which came into effect on 1 July 2009 was for four years. Clause 1.1 proved that the team members of both parties were to work together 'in the spirit of trust, fairness and mutual co-operation'. The contract, by Clause 13.3, was capable of termination by either party on the giving of three months' notice. SAH then exercised its right to terminate the contract and TSG sued for breach of contract. TSG alleged, firstly, that Clause 13.3 was to be construed in the light of Clause 1.1 so that the right to terminate had to be exercised in good faith and, secondly, in the exercise of the right to terminate under Clause 13.3, there was in any event an implied duty to act in good faith. The court held that commercial contracts had to be interpreted on a contextual basis and that Clause 1.1 was confined to issues identified within the clause and that its contextual interpretation was not concerned with the right to terminate under Clause 13.3. Secondly, the court held that there was no implied term that Clause 13.3 could only be exercised in good faith since such a term would be inconsistent with the wording of Clause 13.3 which was unconstrained. In considering the case of **Yam Seng Pte Ltd v International Trade Corp Ltd** [2013] EWHC 111 (QB) Akenhead J stated:

> Because cases and contracts are sensitive to context, I would not draw any principle from this extremely illuminating and interesting judgement which is of general application to all commercial contracts.

A further case involving an express term that imposes a duty to act in good faith on the parties is that of **Mid Essex Hospital Service NHS Trust v Compass Group UK and Ireland Ltd (t/a Medirest)** [2013] EWCA Civ 200. The facts of the case were that Mid Essex Hospital Service NHS Trust ('the Trust') entered into a contract for the provision of catering and cleaning services with a contractor, Medirest, over a period of seven years. One term of the contract provided that:

> The Trust and the Contractor will co-operate with each other in good faith and will take all reasonable action as is necessary for the efficient transmission of information and instructions and to enable the Trust . . . to derive the full benefit of the Contract.

The contract also contained a mechanism that enabled the Trust to award 'service point failures' whereby the Trust could calculate deductions from payments to Medirest for any performance failures. Subsequently the Trust identified a number of service failures and as a result deducted more than half the payments for a particular six-month period. It was common ground that the Trust had awarded excessive service point failures and had deducted an excessive amount from the payments to Medirest, however, the parties could not agree on what the correct figures should be. Both parties claimed that they had terminated the contract.

At first instance the judge found that the Trust had breached its obligation to act in good faith and that it had breached an implied term not to act in an irrational, capricious or arbitrary manner with respect to its discretionary powers under the contract to make deductions. The Trust appealed on the basis that the judge was wrong to find that it had discretion to award service failure points and make deductions from the payments to Medirest.

The Court of Appeal allowed the appeal, finding that there was no discretion as regards the award of service failure points incurred and as to what deductions to make, however, once the calculations had been made, then the Trust had a discretion as to how many points to award and what deductions to make, which could be less than the contract provided for. The Trust could not be criticised from exercising its full contractual rights and taking the full amount or taking less as its discretion allowed. There was thus no need to imply a term that the Trust would not act in an arbitrary, irrational or capricious manner since if the Trust awarded more points or deducted more than it was entitled to that would amount to a breach of an express term of the contract and thus the judge at first instance was wrong on this point.

With regards the clause requiring the parties' obligation to act in good faith the Court of Appeal took a narrow view on this. Medirest attempted to claim that the clause meant that there was, firstly, a general duty of good faith, that is the Trust and Medirest 'will co-operate with each other in good faith'; and secondly, 'Will take all reasonable action as necessary . . . '. The Court of Appeal considered this as incorrect and preferred the Trust's construction of the term, that is, 'The Trust and the Contractor will co-operate with each other in good faith and will take all reasonable action as is necessary . . . '. The effect of this is that there is no general duty of good faith but that the clause meant 'that the parties will work together honestly endeavouring to achieve the two stated purposes' per Jackson LJ at 112. Jackson LJ referring to **Manifest Shipping Co Ltd v Uni-Polaris Shipping Co Ltd** [2001] UKHL 1, [2003] 1 AC 469 and **Street v Derbyshire Unemployed Workers' Centre** [2004] EWCA Civ 964, [2005] ICR 97 considered that the expression 'good faith', shorn of context, meant nothing more that 'honesty'. Once context is added, however, the construction of the term 'good faith' requires further elaboration. Jackson LJ approved the interpretation given by Auld LJ in **Street v Derbyshire Unemployed Workers' Centre** in which he stated:

> Shorn of context, the words 'in good faith' have a core meaning of honesty. Introduce context, and it calls for further elaboration. Thus in the context of a claim or representation, the sole issue as to honesty may just turn on its truth. But even where the content of the statement is true or reasonably believed by its maker to be true, an issue of honesty may still creep in according to whether it is made with sincerity of intention for which the Act provides protection or for an ulterior and, say, malicious, purpose. The term is to be found in many statutory and common-law contexts, and because they are necessarily conditioned by their context, it is dangerous to apply judicial attempts at definition in one context to that of another.

As we have already seen earlier on in this chapter, the notion of context and background knowledge in terms of the construction of contracts is extremely important but what it also indicates is that there is no overarching principle of good faith in the law of contract – context is everything here. Jackson LJ was clear at 105 'that there is no general doctrine of "good faith" in English contract law, although a duty of good faith is implied by law as an incident of certain categories of contract' and that 'if the parties wish to impose such a duty they must do so expressly'.

At the end of the day the Court of Appeal found that the Trust's breach of contract in awarding an excessive number of service failure points did not amount to a material breach. It found that Medirest was not entitled to terminate the contract and the Trust was entitled to pursue its claim for financial relief.

The classification of contractual terms

Warranties and conditions

Objective 7

It will have been seen in our analysis of terms implied by statute in B2B contracts that terms may be divided into two types, warranties and conditions, which have differing degrees of importance. The same is also true of other terms, whether expressly agreed upon by the parties or implied by the courts. A **condition** is regarded as a major term of the contract, i.e. one which goes to the very root of the contract. If a party to a contract breaks a condition the consequence is serious since it entitles the other party not only to sue for damages but also to terminate the contract. The injured party, however, does have the option of affirming the contract and simply claiming damages if they so wish. A **warranty** is regarded as a minor term of a contract, i.e. one which imposes a term that is merely ancillary to the main thrust of the contract and ordinarily merely gives the injured party the right to sue for damages only.

Until the Insurance Act 2015, rather confusingly, a warranty in a contract of insurance was regarded as a major term, with all the rights appropriate to such a term should a breach occur just as if the term was a condition. The result of this was a breach of a warranty in an insurance contract discharged the insurer from liability completely from that point onwards, even if the breach was remedied (Marine Insurance Act 1906 s33(2) and (3)). Section 10 of the Insurance Act 2015 repeals these statutory rules and any common law equivalents. Section 10 does not replace the definition of warranties which must be complied with whether the warranty is material to the risk or not. The effect of s10(2) is that a breach of warranty suspends the insurer's liability from the time of the breach until such time as the breach is remedied, so that the insurer has no liability for anything that occurs during that period of suspension. Once the breach is remedied, then the insurer will be liable for any losses occurring. With this regard, however, some breaches may be incapable of being remedied, for instance, if the warranty requires something to be done by a particular deadline date and that deadline is missed, then the insured could never cease to be in breach the contract. This situation is addressed in the Act so that by s10(5)a and s10(6) this type of breach will be remedied if the warranty is eventually complied albeit after the deadline.

> For more on damages refer to Chapter 16.

In ***Poussard* v *Spiers and Pond*** (1876) 1 QBD 410, an actress was employed to play the leading role in an operetta for the season. In fact, she was unable to take up her role until a week after the season had begun, with the result that the producers had to engage a substitute. When she eventually appeared they refused her services and purported to terminate the contract. The actress sued for breach of contract and lost her case. It was held that since the opening night of the operetta was regarded as of the utmost importance, her absence amounted to a breach of condition which entitled the producers to terminate the contract.

A contrasting illustration of the difference between conditions and warranties may be seen in the case of ***Bettini* v *Gye*** (1876) 1 QBD 183 where a singer was also engaged to perform for a whole season at various theatres. Part of the contract required him to appear six days before the start of the season for rehearsals, but in fact he arrived only three days in advance. The producers sought to treat the singer's absence as breach of a condition and thereby considered this gave them the right to terminate the contract. The singer sued for breach of contract and was successful. The court held that the terms regarding the rehearsals were merely ancillary to the main part of the contract and thus amounted to a warranty only. The producers, while being entitled to sue for damages, were not entitled to terminate the contract.

The right to terminate a contract for breach of condition is modified in relation to non-consumer contracts for the sale of goods by the Sale and Supply of Goods Act 1994, s 4(1), which inserts a new section, s 15A, into the Sale of Goods Act 1979. This states:

15A. – (1) Where in the case of a contract of sale –

(a) the buyer would, apart from this subsection, have the right to reject goods by reason of a breach on the part of the seller of a term implied by Sections 13, 14 or 15 above; but

(b) the breach is so slight that it would be unreasonable for him to reject them, then, if the buyer does not deal as consumer, the breach is not to be treated as a breach of condition but may be treated as a breach of warranty.

Section 15A(2) provides that s 15A(1) will apply unless a contrary intention appears in, or is implied from, the contract. Section 15A(3) further provides that the burden of proof is on the seller to show that the breach falls within subsection (1)(b).

Innominate terms

The distinction between conditions and warranties arises out of the relative importance attached to the terms when considered against the total background of the contract. Very often the parties to a contract may expressly agree to designate a term as a condition or warranty as an indication of the emphasis they wish to place on the importance of the term within the contract. Similarly, the law itself may give an indication of the importance of a term either by means of a statute, as in the case of the implied terms contained in the Sale of Goods Act 1979 for instance, or by means of a judicial decision as to the status of a particular term. In recent years, however, where no expression of the status of a particular term has arisen out of the agreement from whatever source, the courts have taken to classifying the term as an '**innominate term**' (referred to by some authorities as an '**intermediate term**'). The effects of a breach of an innominate term do not depend on the status of the term in the contract when it is entered into but on the effects of a breach of the term in the contract. The concept of the innominate term first arose in the following case.

Hong Kong Fir Shipping Co. Ltd v *Kawasaki Kisen Kaisha Ltd* [1962] 1 All ER 474

The defendants had chartered a ship from the plaintiffs for two years. The charterparty contained a term which required the plaintiffs to provide a ship which was 'in every way fitted for ordinary cargo service'. It transpired that the engine room crew were incompetent and that the ship was in a poor state of repair. In fact the plaintiffs openly admitted that the ship was unseaworthy. As a result of these factors some 20 weeks' use of the ship was lost and the defendants claimed to treat the contract as terminated for breach of condition. The plaintiffs claimed that the breach only entitled the defendants to sue for damages. The plaintiffs succeeded in their action against the defendants for wrongful termination. Lord Diplock stated:

> The problem in this case is, in my view, neither solved nor soluble by debating whether the shipowner's express or implied undertaking to tender a seaworthy ship is a 'condition' or a 'warranty' . . . There are many contractual undertakings of a more complex character which cannot be categorised as being 'conditions' or 'warranties' . . . Of such undertakings all that can be predicted is that some breaches will, and others will not, give rise to an event which will deprive the party not in default of substantially the whole benefit which it was intended that he should obtain from the contract; and the legal consequences of the breach of such an undertaking, unless provided for expressly in the contract, depend on the nature of the event to which the breach gives rise and do not follow automatically from a prior classification of the undertaking as a 'condition' or a 'warranty'.

Where a term is found by the court to be an innominate term the rights of an innocent party in the event of a breach are found by applying the test as to whether they have been substantially deprived of the whole of the benefit which it was intended they should obtain from the contract. If they have been so deprived then they will be entitled to terminate the contract and sue for damages; if not, they can claim damages only: see also ***Wuhan Ocean***

Economic and Technical Cooperation Co Ltd v *Schiffahrts-Gesellschaft Hansa Murcia mbH & Co KG* [2012] EWHC 3104 (Comm).

Effectively, therefore, the distinction between conditions and innominate terms lies in whether a breach of term is a repudiatory or non-repudiatory. Clearly breach of a condition will amount to a repudiatory breach of contract; however, where a term is not a condition then the *Hong Kong Fir* test will apply. An innominate term only becomes repudiatory if a breach deprives substantially deprives the injured party of the whole of the benefit of the contract. This has led to the suggestion that (except in the case of express warranties) there is no need to consider the terms of a contract in tripartite terms – conditions, warranties and innominate terms – and that terms should be simply classified as repudiatory or non-repudiatory. This was the approach taken in *Ampurius Nu Homes Holdings Ltd* v *Telford Homes (Creekside) Ltd* [2013] EWCA Civ 577, [2013] 4 All ER 377. Such an approach, however, was rejected by Sir Terence Etherton in *Urban I (Blonk Street) Ltd* v *Ayres* [2013] EWCA Civ 816 in which he stated:

It is necessary to distinguish between three types of contractual time provision. There are those which are conditions in the technical sense that any breach of them, however slight, is a repudiatory breach of contract which entitles the other party to terminate the contract immediately; those which are warranties in the technical sense that any breach of them, however serious, will only ever entitle the other party to damages and not to terminate the contract; and those which are so-called innominate terms, breach of which will only be a repudiation of the contract entitling the other party to terminate the contract if the breach deprives him or her of substantially the whole benefit which it was intended they should obtain from the contract or, in simpler language, which goes to the root of the contract: *Hong Kong Fir Shipping Co. Ltd* at 69 to 70. It is a matter to be determined on ordinary principles of contractual interpretation into which of those categories the term falls.

On this basis, there is still therefore a case to be made for a tripartite approach to the classification of terms with warranties standing out as terms that can never give rise to a repudiation of the contract, conditions that will always give rise to such an outcome and innominate terms which may give rise to such an outcome depending on the outcome of the *Hong Kong Fir* test. This seems to be an appropriate, more certain and on the face of things more logical way of classifying terms.

The decision in the *Hong Kong Fir* case does create a certain level of uncertainty since the parties will not know what their rights are in relation to a breach of contract until an action is brought before the court. Of course the parties can expressly state within the contract itself what the consequences of breaking a particular term would be and, indeed, it would be in their interests to do so. The absence of such express intentions nevertheless creates substantial problems, so much so that there have been attempts to limit the scope of the concept of the innominate term by the courts themselves. Such an attempt can be seen in the case of *Maredelanto Compania Naviera SA* v *Bergbau-Handel GmbH (The Mihalis Angelos)* [1970] 3 All ER 125.

Maredelanto Compania Naviers SA v *Bergbau-Handel GmbH (The Mihalis Angelos)* [1970] 3 All ER 125

A charterparty was entered into on 25 May 1965 providing that the ship in question would be 'expected to be ready to load under this charter about 1 July 1965 at Haiphong'. The charter also provided that should the ship 'not be ready to load on or before 20 July 1965' the charterers would be able to cancel the contract. In fact the ship was unable to be at Haiphong at this date and it transpired that the owners knew the ship would not be available on this date when they entered into the charter. The charterers purported to terminate the contract and the owners sued for breach of contract. Although the court was pressed to adopt the approach taken in the *Hong Kong Fir* case it declined to do so. The opinion was formed that the classic approach of labelling a term as a condition or warranty was still valid and, in fact, desirable in order to establish a level of certainty in such cases. It is clearly undesirable on a matter of commercial exigency to expect a charterer of a ship to have to delay the transportation of a cargo because the owners have failed to comply with the date of expected readiness to load, especially when the owners knew full well on the signing of the charter that that date could not realistically be met. Furthermore, it is unfair effectively to prevent a charterer from terminating the contract and chartering another ship on the basis of the possibility that the decision might be challenged by a legal action for breach of contract by the owners.

The point is summed up well by Megaw LJ:

One of the important elements of the law is predictability. At any rate in commercial law there are obvious and substantial advantages in having, where possible, a firm and definite rule for a particular class of legal relationship . . . It is surely much better both for shipowners and charterers (and incidentally for their advisers) when a contractual obligation of this nature is under consideration—and still more when they are faced with the necessity of an urgent decision as to the effects of a suspected breach of it—to be able to say categorically: 'If a breach is proved, then the charterer can put an end to the contract.'

The approach taken in *The Mihalis Angelos* was approved of and adopted by both the Court of Appeal and the House of Lords in *Bunge Corporation v Tradax Export SA* [1981] 2 All ER 513 where the status of an 'expected readiness to load' clause was again questioned. Both courts had no hesitation in stating that this was a condition and rejected attempts to persuade them to apply the *Hong Kong Fir* test. Lord Wilberforce stated that to find otherwise 'would fatally remove from a vital provision in the contract that certainty which is the most indispensable quality of mercantile contracts'.

The decision of a court to adopt the traditional or the *Hong Kong Fir* approach is driven by several considerations. The most important of these by far is the need for certainty and this takes on even more importance where a term is a fairly standard one, always found in particular types of contract. The 'expected readiness to load' clause in the above cases is a good example of such a term since it is common to all charterparties and one which is commonly broken. It is thus desirable to have a high level of certainty with regard to such a clause. The same considerations do not arise to the same degree where the contract is non-standard or a 'one-off' contract. Here the prime consideration may be one of doing what is just between the parties, and the innominate term concept usually achieves a greater level of fairness in such a situation. The reason for this is that parties to a contract may attempt to terminate the contract for breach of condition when they have no real justification other than purely economic or commercial motives. The choice open to the courts then is usually governed by a judicial impression of a need to achieve either certainty or fair play.

One must not assume from the above that the concept of the innominate term has been rejected by the courts. This is most certainly not so and the above cases merely qualify its use. The application of the concept can be seen in *Cehave NV v Bremer Handelsgesellschaft GmbH, The Hansa Nord* [1975] 3 All ER 739, where a cargo of citrus pellets was sold to a buyer in Rotterdam. The contract provided for 'shipment to be made in good condition'. Part of the cargo was not transported and the buyer then purported to reject the whole cargo, even though there was nothing wrong with the pellets themselves. In fact the rejected cargo, when eventually sold by the Rotterdam Court, was ultimately bought by the original buyers at a greatly reduced price, and this probably reflects the true reason for rejecting the cargo in the first place. The buyers attempted to persuade the court that the *Hong Kong Fir* approach was inappropriate since the Sale of Goods Act 1979 by implication envisaged that all terms in such contracts should be classified as conditions or warranties. The court rejected this contention and applied the *Hong Kong Fir* test, stating that the consequences of the breach were not so serious as to allow the buyer to reject the whole cargo; they had not been deprived of substantially what they had contracted for.

The reasoning in *The Hansa Nord* case was confirmed in *Reardon Smith Line Ltd* v *Yng-var Hansen-Tangen* [1976] 3 All ER 570 by the House of Lords. There is, however, still a level of debate as to when the *Hong Kong Fir* test is applied and in the case of *Valilas* v *Januzj* [2014] EWCA Civ 436 the Court of Appeal was divided as to whether the test was met. In that case a dentist (A) used the premises owned by another dentist (B) on a facilities contract whereby A paid half of the income derived from an NHS contract. When A failed to make the monthly payments B terminated the contract. At first instance it was held that B had wrongfully terminated the contract and B appealed. The majority of the Court of Appeal did not accept that it was a condition of the contract that A should make his monthly payments on time since the time of payment was not of the essence within the contract.

Lord Underhill (who gave the dissenting judgement) affirmed that time of payment is not generally of the essence of a commercial contract unless the parties have either expressly or impliedly agreed that it should be. That was not the case here and therefore the term amounted to an innominate term. In these circumstances the question to be asked is whether B had been deprived of 'substantially the whole benefit which it was the intention of the parties as expressed in the contract that he should obtain as the consideration for performing [his] undertakings', the test propounded by Diplock LJ in *Hong Kong Fir Shipping Co Ltd* v *Kawasaki Kisen Kaisha Ltd* [1962] 2 QB 26. The problem, however, was determining whether a party had in fact been deprived of substantially the whole of the benefit he was to receive under the contract. In this regard, Lord Underhill stated that 'the essential question is whether the breach or breaches are such as to justify the summary termination of the contract by the other party, having regard to all the circumstances'. In determining this question Lord Underhill referred to the judgement of Lord Wilberforce in *Federal Commerce & Navigation Co Ltd* v *Molena Alpha Inc. (The Nanfri)* [1979] AC 757, at pp. 778–9 where he said:

> Was this breach, or threatened breach, repudiatory or not? I shall not set out at any length the numerous authorities on anticipatory breach: this is one of the more perspicuous branches of the law of contract and the modern position is clear. The form of the critical question may differ slightly as it is put in relation to varying situations: '. . . an intimation of an intention to abandon and altogether to refuse performance of the contract . . . ' or 'evince an intention no longer to be bound by the contract . . . ' (*Freeth v Burr* (1874) L.R. 9 C.P. 208 , 213, per Lord Coleridge C.J.)
>
> I do not say that it is necessary to show that the party alleged to have repudiated should have an actual intention not to fulfil the contract. He may intend in fact to fulfil it, but may be determined to do so only in a manner substantially inconsistent with his obligations, and not in any other way' (*Ross T. Smyth & Co. Ltd.* v *T. D. Bailey, Son & Co.* [1940] 3 All E.R. 60, 72, per Lord Wright) such as to deprive 'the charterers of substantially the whole benefit which it was the intention of the parties . . . . that the charterers should obtain from the further performance of their own contractual undertakings' (*Hong Kong Fir Shipping Co. Ltd.* v *Kawasaki Kisen Kaisha Ltd.* [1962] 2 Q.B. 26, 72, per Diplock L.J.).

> To constitute repudiation, the threatened breach must be such as to deprive the injured party of a substantial part of the benefit to which he is entitled under the contract . . . . Will the consequences of the breach be such that it would be unfair to the injured party to hold him to the contract and leave him to his remedy in damages . . . ?' (**Decro-Wall International S.A. v Practitioners in Marketing Ltd.** [1971] 1 W.L.R. 361 , 380, per Buckley L.J.).

> The difference in expression between these two last formulations does not, in my opinion, reflect a divergence of principle, but arises from and is related to the particular contract under consideration: they represent, in other words, applications to different contracts, of the common principle that, to amount to repudiation a breach must go to the root of the contract.'

Lord Underhill, however, pointed out that the reference to breaches 'going to the root of the contract' was not a particularly helpful assessment in answering the **Hong Kong Fir** question. In this regard he referred to the judgement of Lewison LJ in **Ampurius Nu Homes Holdings Ltd v Telford Homes (Creekside) Ltd** who stated.

> The trouble with expressing important propositions of English law in metaphorical terms is that it is difficult to be sure what they mean. As the High Court of Australia majority judgement pointed out in **Koompahtoo Local Aboriginal Land Council v Sanpine Pty Ltd** [2007] HCA 61 (2007) 82 AJLR 345 at [54] to describe a breach as 'going to the root of the contract' is: '. . . a conclusory description that takes account of the nature of the contract and the relationship it creates, the nature of the term, the kind and degree of the breach, and the consequences of the breach for the other party.'

Similarly Lord Underhill referred to Hale LJ in **Rice v Great Yarmouth** [2001] LGLR 41 who stated at para. 35:

> The question for the court . . . in any case like this is whether the cumulative effect of the breaches of contract complained of is so serious as to justify the innocent party in bringing the contract to an end. The technical label is 'repudiatory' but that is just a label to describe the consequence which may flow.

Lord Underhill therefore concluded that the essential question is whether the breach or breaches are such as to justify the summary termination of the contract by the other party, having regard to all the circumstances and that those circumstances will in principle include all the matters identified by the High Court of Australia in the passage quoted by Lewison LJ in **Telford Homes** above. In the light of that he found that since A had made a deliberate choice to depart from the agreed arrangements as regards his primary obligations under the contract, this amounted to a repudiatory breach. He stated that whilst the claimant appeared to be continuing to 'affirm' the contract, he was in truth departing from it and that it was a well-established principle that a declared intention by a party to fulfil a contract but in a manner substantially inconsistent with his obligations and not in any other way amounts to a renunciation of the contract, or at least an anticipatory breach so that the other party is entitled to jump first and treat the contract as at an end and recover damages.

Lord Justice Floyd and Lady Justice Arden gave the majority decision and agreed that it is generally correct that a declared intention by a party to perform a contract in a manner which is substantially inconsistent with his obligations may amount to a renunciation of the contract. They stated, however, that this is not a special rule applicable to deviations from contractual performance that provides that every such deviation gives rise to a right in the opposite party to terminate. Whether a breach or threatened breach gives rise to a right to terminate involves a multi-factorial assessment involving the nature of the contract and the relationship it creates, the nature of the term, the kind and degree of the breach and the consequences of the breach for the injured party (as per the judgement of Lewison LJ in ***Ampurius Nu Homes Holdings Ltd v Telford Homes (Creekside) Ltd***). Both Floyd LJ and Arden LJ considered that the effect of A's past and threatened future breaches of contract could not be said to deprive B of substantially the whole benefit of the contract. Whilst it was true that B would be deprived of monthly payment he would in the end receive what he was entitled to. This position is one that is very different from that where A had refused to perform his side of the bargain altogether – this would be a repudiatory breach. The court stated, as in ***Decro-Wall International SA v Practitioners in Marketing Ltd** [1971] 2 All ER 216*, that where the contract itself does not stipulate expressly or by implication what is to be the result of the breach of its terms: 'the courts must look to the practical results of the breach in order to decide whether it goes to the root of the contract' (per Lord Simon). The effect therefore is that if B is to establish that the consequences of the breach were so serious as to substantially deprive him of the benefit he would receive under the contract then the burden of proof was on him to establish this which B had failed to do in this case.

Conclusion

Having examined the relative importance of contractual terms and the different approaches used to assess an innocent party's rights where a breach of contract arises, we shall now take an overview of the choices and possibilities that might confront that individual.

First, the parties can always expressly state what the effects of a breach of a particular term may be. If the contract specifically gives the innocent party the right to terminate the contract then the courts will allow that right to be exercised.

Second, if the contract does not expressly provide a right to terminate the contract it may be that such a right is implied. For example, in ***Schuler AG v Wickman Machine Tool Sales Ltd*** [1974] AC 235, it was stated by the House of Lords that the use of the expression 'condition' would tend to indicate a right of the innocent party to terminate the contract, whilst the use of the expression 'warranty' would tend to indicate only a right to recover damages.

Third, if the right to terminate is not implied from the description ascribed to a term then it may be implied from the operation of law. This may arise through statute, as in the case of the implied conditions and warranties contained in the Sale of Goods Act 1979. It may also arise from judicial impression, as in the case ***The Mihalis Angelos***, which established that all 'expected readiness to load' clauses contained in charterparties will be regarded by the courts as conditions, thus achieving considerable certainty as to the position of the innocent party.

Lastly, where the status of a term is not ascribed from the operation of some rule of law then one must ask the ***Hong Kong Fir*** question, namely: 'Has the innocent party been deprived substantially of what it was intended that he should receive under the contract?' If the answer to this question is in the affirmative he can terminate the contract; if not, he may only claim damages and has no right to terminate. The question as to whether the innocent party has been substantially deprived of the benefit it was intended he would receive under the contract involves a multi-factorial assessment involving the nature of the contract and the relationship it creates, the nature of the term, the kind and degree of the breach and the consequences of the breach for the injured party: ***Ampurius Nu Homes Holdings Ltd v Telford Homes (Creekside) Ltd)***.

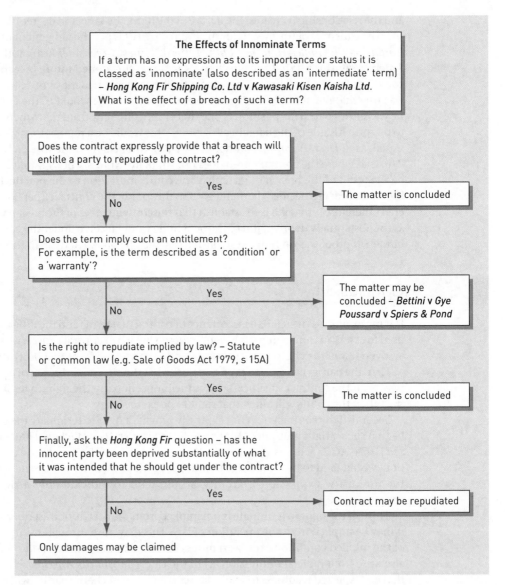

The Effects of Innominate Terms
If a term has no expression as to its importance or status it is classed as 'innominate' (also described as an 'intermediate' term) – *Hong Kong Fir Shipping Co. Ltd* v *Kawasaki Kisen Kaisha Ltd*. What is the effect of a breach of such a term?

Does the contract expressly provide that a breach will entitle a party to repudiate the contract?

Yes → The matter is concluded

No ↓

Does the term imply such an entitlement? For example, is the term described as a 'condition' or a 'warranty'?

Yes → The matter may be concluded – *Bettini* v *Gye* *Poussard* v *Spiers & Pond*

No ↓

Is the right to repudiate implied by law? – Statute or common law (e.g. Sale of Goods Act 1979, s 15A)

Yes → The matter is concluded

No ↓

Finally, ask the *Hong Kong Fir* question – has the innocent party been deprived substantially of what it was intended that he should get under the contract?

Yes → Contract may be repudiated

No ↓

Only damages may be claimed

Figure 7.1

Debate

How prominent is the business common sense criteria in the interpretation of contractual terms?

Where does business common sense lie in the dimension of judicial contractual construction?. Does, for instance, the natural meaning of a word or words simply amount to common sense no matter 'how surprising or unreasonable the result may be' or on a different level does the natural meaning yield to common sense? Alternatively, does business common sense simply form one dimension of the matrix of fact that provides the background that a reasonable person is able to ascertain what a reasonable person would have understood the parties to the contract to have meant? Where the natural meaning of the words are unambiguous, then Lord Hoffman appears to prefer the latter approach; however, he also contemplated that the matrix of fact background could also be used where there is a 'semantic' or 'syntactical' error in the words and it is this that has given rise to the plethora of cases and arguments that seem to point towards business common sense becoming predominant in the construction of contracts. It is this predominance that latterly has given rise to some concern with the result there has been a shift towards an attitude that it is the natural meaning of the words that should have primacy over the business common sense principle. Thus in *Proctor & Gamble Co* v *Svenska Cellulosa Aktiebolaget SCA* [2012] EWCA Civ 1413, Moore-Blick LJ stated:

> I entirely agree that if a clause is reasonably capable of bearing two possible meanings (and is therefore ambiguous), the court should prefer that which better accords with the overall objective of the contract or with good commercial sense, but the starting point must be the words the parties have used to express their intention and in the case of a carefully drafted agreement of the present kind the court must take care not to fall into the trap of re-writing the contract in order to produce what it considers to be a more reasonable meaning.

In the light of *Arnold* v *Britton*, the approach taken in *Rainy Sky* now appears to be incorrect in that in the former case the principle is that if the contract is unambiguous the court must first construe the natural meaning of the words and apply this to the contract and that it is inappropriate to consider the notion of business common sense before assessing whether there is any ambiguity. *Arnold* v *Britton* is therefore authority for the fact that interpretation is not the 'unitary process' suggested by Lords Clarke but an incremental stepped process. No doubt there is good reason for that since the notion of business common sense is a good deal less precise and uncertain. There are, however, cases which suggest that rather than this incremental approach the correct approach is an iterative process so that any provision is considered in the light of various meanings that may be attributed to the words and then against the other provisions within the overall document and examining the commercial consequences. By this process the court is then able to discover whether there is any problem with the language or whether any ambiguity exists. The effect therefore is that the initial interpretation of the language is not assessed within the natural meaning of the words as required by *Arnold* v *Britton*. Such an approach was advocated in *Napier Park European Credit Opportunities Fund Ltd* v *Harbourmaster Pre-rata CLO 2 BV* [2014] EWCA Civ 984 where Lewison LJ stated:

> 'The approach to the interpretation of a tradable financial instrument of this kind was authoritatively considered by the Supreme Court in *Re Sigma Finance Corp* [2009] UKSC 2; [2010] 1 All ER 571. In that case Lord Mance, approving Lord Neuberger's dissenting judgement in the Court of Appeal, said at [12]: 'Lord Neuberger was right to observe that the resolution of an issue of interpretation in a case like the present is an iterative process, involving 'checking each of the rival meanings against other provisions of the document and investigating its commercial consequences.'
>
> The iterative process thus described is not confined to textual analysis and comparison. It extends also to placing the rival interpretations within their commercial setting

and investigating (or at any rate evaluating) their commercial consequences . That is not to say that in a case like this the commercial setting should be derived from considerations outside the four corners of the contractual documents.'

This approach is an unusual one since it seems to suggest that the commercial context is examined as part of the process of assessing the natural meaning of the word. Should an ambiguity be found, then the next step is to analyse the different meanings in the context of their commercial sense and apply the appropriate construction. This approach, whilst an iterative one, appears to stand on all fours with the decision in *Rainy Sky* and adopts the unitary process of interpretation asserted there. That said such an analysis now sits uneasily with the process set out in *Arnold v Britton* but which now must be regarded as the authoritative approach.

Questions

1. Is business common sense merely part of the matrix of facts or is business common sense only to be invoked if the natural meaning of word produces an interpretation that cannot be sustained?
2. Is a unitary or stepped approach correct?

Summary

Express terms

- Can be agreed upon either orally or in writing, or both.
- Court to decide issues of interpretation of the terms *within the contractual document.*

Incorporation of statements as terms of the contract

- Distinctions should be made between terms and representations.

  CRA 2015 s50

Timing

- *Bannerman* v *White*
- *Routledge* v *McKay*

Reduction of the contract into writing

- *Routledge* v *McKay*

The importance of the statement

- *Couchman* v *Hill*
- *Oscar Chess Ltd* v *Williams*

Special knowledge or skill

- ***Oscar Chess Ltd* v *Williams***
- ***Dick Bentley Productions Ltd* v *Harold Smith (Motors) Ltd***

The parol evidence rule

- Generally, evidence will not be admitted which seeks to add, vary or contradict the terms of a written contract.

Exceptions to parol evidence

- Custom
- Non-operation
- Invalidity
- Incompleteness

Collateral contracts

Terms or mere representations

- ***City and Westminster Properties (1934) Ltd* v *Mudd***
- The parol evidence rule

Entire agreement clauses

- ***Inntrepreneur Pub Co* v *East Crown Ltd***

The construction of contracts and the parole evidence/exclusionary rule

Construing contracts – the literal approach v the contextual approach

In the past, the courts in construing a contract adopted a literal approach to interpretation, that is the courts interpret the contract according to their ordinary plain meaning without reference to any extrinsic evidence of the background to the transaction providing of course that such a method of interpretation does not lead to ambiguity or does not lead to any manifest absurdity.

- ***Lovell and Christmas Ltd* v *Wall***

The exclusionary rule

- ***Prenn* v *Simmonds***
- ***Reardon Smith Line Ltd* v *Yngvar Hansen-Tangen***

Lord Hoffman's seminal re-statement of interpretation of contracts—the contextual approach

• ***Investors Compensation Scheme Ltd* v *West Bromwich Building Society***

Lord Hoffmann went further in the development of a contextual approach and stated that, apart from prior negotiations and declarations of subjective intent, the 'factual background includes absolutely everything available to the parties that might reasonably affect how the terminology within the document would be understood by a reasonable person and which a reasonable person would regard as relevant'. After discussing some of the old law he set out five principles.

1 Principle 1 – An objective test

2 Principle 2 – The matrix of fact

3 Principle 3 – The exclusionary rule

4 Principle 4 – The meaning of words is to be interpreted contextually not literally

5 Principle 5 – The presumption that people do not easily make linguistic mistakes

- 'Old Intellectual Baggage' and Evolution
- 'Business Common Sense'
- 'Something has gone wrong with the language'
- Where words have more than one meaning
- Rectification
- Estoppel by convention

Implied terms

- Can be implied by the courts or implied by statute
  - *Liverpool City Council* v *Irwin*
  - *Dear* v *Jackson*
  - *Shell (UK) Ltd* v *Lostock Garages Ltd*
  - *Geys* v *Société Générale*
- Terms implied as a matter of fact
  - *Marks and Spencer plc* v *BNP Baribas Securities Services Trust Co (Jersey) Ltd*
- The 'officious bystander test'
  - The 'business efficacy' test
- Terms implied as a matter of law
  - By the courts
  - *Liverpool City Council* v *Irwin*
  - By statute
  - The Consumer Rights Act 2015
  - Definitions within the CRA
  - Terms implied in Contracts within the CRA
  - Consumer contracts for goods, digital content and services – Part 1

1 Chapter 1 – The Background and Application of Part 1

2 Chapter 2 – Contracts for the supply of goods

3 Chapter 3 – Contracts for the supply of digital content

4 Chapter 4 – Contracts where a trader supplies a service to a consumer

Terms implied in contracts outside of the CRA

● Terms implied under the Sale of Goods Act 1979

● Terms implied under the Supply of Goods and Services Act 1982

● The Consumer Contracts (Information, Cancellation and Additional Charges) Regulations 2013

● Terms implied by custom

Good faith as a contractual term

● *Yam Seng Pte Ltd v International Trade Corp Ltd*

● *Interfoto Picture Library Ltd v Stiletto Visual Programmes Ltd*

● *Attorney General for Belize v Belize Telecom Ltd*

● *Investors Compensation Scheme Ltd v West Bromwich Building Society*

● *TSG Building Services Plc v South Anglia Housing Ltd*

● *Mid Essex Hospital Service NHS Trust v Compass Group UK and Ireland Ltd (t/a Medirest)*

The classification of contractual terms
Warranties and conditions

● *Poussard v Spiers and Pond*

● *Bettini v Gye*

● *Maredelanto Compania Naviera SA v Bergbau-Handel GmbH (The Mihalis Angelos)*

● *Cehave NV v Bremer Handelsgesellschaft GmbH, The Hansa Nord*

● *Reardon Smith Line Ltd v Yngvar Hansen-Tangen*

● *Valilas v Januzj*

Innominate terms

● *Hong Kong Fir Shipping Co Ltd v Kawasaki Kisen Kaisha Ltd*

● *Ampurius Nu Homes Holdings Ltd v Telford Homes (Creekside) Ltd*

● *Urban I (Blonk Street) Ltd v Ayres*

Further reading

Beatson, Burrows and Cartwright, *Anson's Law of Contract*, 30th edn (Oxford University Press, 2016)

Bojeczuk, 'When is a Condition not a Condition?' [1987] *Journal of Business Law* 353

Bradgate, 'Unreasonable Standard Terms' (1997) 60 *Modern Law Review* 582

Bradgate, 'Consumer rights in digital products: A research report prepared for the UK Department for Business, Innovation and Skills', Institute for Commercial Law Studies, Sheffield and BIS (2010)

Davies, 'Recent Developments in the Law of Implied Terms' (2010) *Lloyd's Maritime and Commercial Law Quarterly* 140

Davies, 'The Meaning of Commercial Contracts' in Davies and Pila (eds), *The Jurisprudence of Lord Hoffman* (Hart Publishing, 2015)

Furmston, *Cheshire, Fifoot and Furmston's Law of Contract*, 16th edn (Oxford University Press, 2012)

Grabiner QC, Lord, 'The Iterative Process of Contractual Interpretation' (2012) 128 *Law Quarterly Review* 41

Grant, 'Unfair Terms Set On Vacation' (2004) 154 *New Law Journal* 486

Law Commission, *The Parol Evidence Rule*, Report No 154 (1986)

Law Commission, *The Parol Evidence Rule*, Working Paper No 70 (1976)

Leggatt, Hon Sir George, 'Making Sense of Contracts—The Rational Choice Theory', (2015) 131 *Law Quarterly Review* 454

Low and Loi, 'The Many Tests for Terms Implied in Fact' (2009) 125 *Law Quarterly Review* 561

McLauchlan, 'Commonsense Principles of Interpretation and Rectification' (2010) 126 *Law Quarterly Review* 8

Macdonald, 'The Duty to Give Notice of Unusual Contract Terms' [1988] *Journal of Business Law* 375

Merkin and Gürses, 'Insurance Contracts after the Insurance Act 2015' (2016) 132 *Law Quarterly Review* 445

Nicholls, Lord, 'My Kingdom for a Horse: The Meaning of Words', (2005) 121 *Law Quarterly Review* 577

Peden, 'Policy Concerns Behind Implications of Terms in Law' (2001) 117 *Law Quarterly Review* 459

Phang, 'Implied Terms Revisited' [1990] *Journal of Business Law* 394

Phang, 'Implied Terms Again' [1994] *Journal of Business Law* 255

Phang, 'Implied Terms, Business Efficacy and the Officious Bystander—A Modern History' (1998) *Journal of Business Law* 1

Smith, Atiyah's *Introduction to the Law of Contract*, 6th edn (Oxford University Press, 2006)

Steyn QC, Lord, 'Contract law: Fulfilling the reasonable expectations of honest men' (1997) 113 *Law Quarterly Review* 433

Peel, Treitel *Law of Contract*, 14th edn (Sweet and Maxwell, 2015)

Whittaker, 'Good Faith, Implied terms and Commercial Contracts' (2012) 129 *Law Quarterly Review* 463

8

Exemption Clauses

Objectives

After reading this chapter you should be able to:

1. Know the difference between exemption clauses and limitation clauses.

2. Know and explain how exemption clauses are incorporated into contracts, particularly incorporation by notice and previous courses of dealings.

3. Know and understand how exemption clauses are construed.

4. Critically analyse the problems associated with exempting liability for fundamental breach of contract.

5. Understand the factors that limit the effectiveness of exemption clauses, particularly the statutory limitations on exemption clauses.

6. Know and understand the effects of the Unfair Contract Terms Act 1977 with regard to non-consumer contracts.

7. Know and understand the effects of the Consumer Rights Act 2015 with regard to non-consumer contracts and contracts in the course of a business.

Introduction

Objective 1

Exemption clauses are those which seek to enable one of the parties to a contract to exclude their liability. **Limitation clauses**, although governed by the same principles, seek to restrict the liability of a particular individual. These clauses are not by any means new since they arose from the development of the standard-form contract during the Industrial Revolution. Therein lies the great problem with exemption clauses in modern times since, while they developed during the golden age of the development of the law of contract when laissez-faire principles reigned, as did the notion of equality of bargaining power, the emphasis in the twentieth and twenty-first centuries was upon the need to protect the consumer and the realisation that equality of bargaining power is, to a large degree, a myth.

In order to balance these two diametrically opposed positions the courts have attempted to limit the use of exemption clauses. First, just as with other clauses which the parties wish to form part of the contract, the party relying on the exemption clause will have to show that the clause amounts to a term of the contract. Second, the exemption clause, in order to protect the party relying on it, has to be constructed in such a way that it actually deals with the loss or damage that has occurred. Finally, in addition to this prescriptive approach, the law has introduced other measures designed to restrict or prevent the operation of exemption clauses in certain circumstances.

Incorporation of the exclusion clause into the contract

Objective
2

This is illustrated in Chapter 7.

A party to a contract who seeks to rely on the protection of an exemption clause has to be able to show that it has become incorporated into the contract. There are three ways in which the person may be able to do this.

Incorporation by signature

Should a party sign a contractual document they will be prima facie bound by the terms of that contract, even if they have failed to read that document, unless they have been induced to sign by virtue of some misrepresentation or fraudulent conduct. The general principle is well illustrated by the case of *L'Estrange* v *Graucob* [1934] 2 KB 394, where the plaintiff purchased an automatic vending machine. The purchase was made on terms set out in a document stated to be a 'Sales Agreement'. A number of the terms were set out in what was described by the court as 'legible, but regrettably small print'. The plaintiff signed the 'agreement' but did not bother to read it. It was held that the plaintiff was bound by the terms of the agreement, so that the **exclusion clause** contained in it meant that the defendants were not liable on the basis that the machine was not fit for the purpose for which it was sold.

The importance of signing a contract and the binding nature of it can also be seen in the case of *Peekay Intermark Ltd* v *ANZ Banking Group Ltd* [2006] EWCA 1551. The facts of this case were that the respondent (P) was an experienced customer of the appellant bank (B). P was a company that was used as an investment vehicle by its shareholders. P alleged that it had been given informal information over the telephone about a particular investment product and claimed that this amounted to a misrepresentation that had induced P into entering into a contract which it had signed. The terms of the written contract described the product differently from that of the information given in the telephone call. The question before the court was whether the misrepresentation operated despite the fact that the contract had been signed. B submitted that whatever information P was given in the telephone conversation, even if that was a misrepresentation, that was dispelled by the fact that P must have been aware of the final terms and conditions in the written contract, whether or not that he had actually read them. P could not therefore argue that it had been induced to enter into the contract by any representations made in the previous conversations.

At first instance the judge held that there was in fact a misrepresentation and that this prevailed since he considered that P was entitled to assume that the written contract contained the same description of the product given in the telephone conversation. The Court of Appeal disagreed. It considered that P was an experienced investor and whilst the description of the product in the telephone conversation was not such as to enable P to obtain a very clear understanding of the precise nature of the investment, if P had read the final terms and conditions P would have been alerted to the fact that the documents related to an investment which was something fundamentally different from what it had been expecting. Whether a person had been induced by any misrepresentation to enter into a contract was a question of fact. It was open to the defendant to show that the claimant was aware of the true facts and therefore was not induced by the misrepresentation to act as he did. The true position relating to the terms of the contract appeared on the face of the documents and that by signing the contract P was not entitled to say it did not understand the nature of the transaction described in the final written terms.

One final point about signatures is that by way of the Electronic Communications Act 2000 s 7, implementing elements of the Electronic Signatures Directive 1999/93/EC, electronic signatures have the same function and effect as written signatures.

Incorporation by notice

A party to a contract may be bound by its terms provided reasonable notice of those terms is brought to the party's attention, despite the fact that the contractual document has not been signed. What is reasonable here depends on a number of factors.

The document must be a contractual document

The exemption clauses contained in an unsigned document will fail to form part of a contract if it was never intended that the document was to have such an effect. If the person to whom the document was given knew that the document was to be a contractual one or the handing of the document to that individual could be regarded as having given them reasonable notice of the fact that it contained terms and conditions, that person may be bound by any exemption clauses contained in the document.

The test of whether a document has contractual force or not depends on a reasonable person test, that is, an objective test. In other words, would a reasonable person have assumed that the document was to be a contractual document? The description thus given to the document is not necessarily equivocal as to its effect in law. A document described as a 'receipt', for instance, is not necessarily precluded from having contractual force if the objective test above is decided in the affirmative.

Chapelton v *Barry UDC* [1940] KB 532

In this case, the plaintiff was given a ticket, on hiring a deckchair. He did not read the ticket, which stated on its back that the Council would not be liable for any damage or injuries suffered to the hirer while using the chair. The canvas on one of the chairs was defective and he claimed damages for injuries which resulted from the defect. It was held that the ticket was not a contractual document but a mere voucher or receipt which no reasonable man could regard as otherwise. The exemption clause did not thereby afford the local authority with a defence to the action.

What degree of notice is required?

If the unsigned document is to be regarded as being an integral part of the contract, reasonable notice of the exemption clause must be brought to the attention of the other party. This test was first formulated in the following case.

Parker v *South Eastern Railway Company* (1877) 2 CPD 416

In this case, a bag was left at a left luggage office. The plaintiff paid the fee, for which he was given a ticket which contained a limitation clause on the back. When the plaintiff attempted to reclaim his bag

> it could not be found. He attempted to claim the value of the bag and contents which exceeded the limit stipulated on the ticket. The railway company attempted to rely on the clause which the plaintiff claimed to be ignorant of. The Court of Appeal held that for the company to be able to rely on the clause it had to show that reasonable steps had been taken to bring the clause to the notice of the plaintiff. Since the company could not show this it was held that it could not rely on the clause. It is clear that merely handing over a ticket with an exclusion clause printed on it is insufficient since it may not be intended that the ticket will have a contractual force, as was also the case in **Chapelton v Barry UDC**.

The objective test formulated in the *Parker* case nevertheless has to be applied within the facts of the particular case.

Thompson v L M & S Railway Company [1930] 1 KB 41

> In this case, the plaintiff, who was illiterate, was handed an excursion ticket which stated that the ticket was issued subject to the defendant's conditions as stated in the company's timetables, which excluded liability for injury. The plaintiff suffered injuries on her journey and claimed for damages. It was held that her claim must fail. The fact that she could not read did not alter the position that she was bound by the contract since it was held that reasonable notice of the exemption clause had been brought to her attention.

It follows from the above two cases that whether or not reasonable steps have been taken to bring a party's attention to the existence of the exemption clause revolves around two questions: (1) Have adequate steps been taken to bring notice of the clause to the attention of the other party? (2) What is the nature of the exemption clause?

1. Adequate steps?

Clearly, if a notice is contained in a contractual document then that is normally enough for the exemption clause to become part of the contract. It is interesting that in **Thompson v L M & S Railway Company** the ticket had on its face 'See back' and on the back there was a statement that for the conditions of sale of the ticket the purchaser had to have reference to the railway company's timetable. The conditions contained in the timetable contained an exemption clause that appears on page 552. The Court of Appeal held that despite her illiteracy the company had done everything required to take reasonable steps to bring the conditions to the attention of the claimant. It was sufficient if the company had done what was reasonable to bring notice of the conditions to the ordinary literate passenger. Thus once the passenger had been made aware by way of the ticket that there were conditions they were put on notice and it was the passenger's responsibility to check the terms and conditions before travelling. Of course hardly any travelling member of the public bought the timetable but that makes no difference as Lord Denning commented in **Thornton v Shoe Lane Parking Ltd** [1971] QB 163:

> These cases were based on the theory that the customer, on being handed the ticket, could refuse it and decline to enter into a contract on those terms. He could ask for his money back. The theory was, of course, a fiction. No customer in a thousand ever read the conditions. If he had stopped to do so he would have missed the train.

The position no doubt would have been different if the company had been aware of the claimant's disability since simply handing over the ticket to a person who the company knew could not read would clearly not have been reasonable notice of the clause. Treitel suggests that this would also be the case if the party relying on the clause knew that the other did not speak the language in which the clause is expressed or if the passenger was blind. This position has been affirmed in ***Harvey* v *Ventilatoren-Fabrik Oelde GmbH*** (1988) Tr LR 138.

It should also be noted that the fact that the ticket or document refers to another document does not prevent the notice from being reasonable. Reasonable notice does not mean that the terms and conditions have to be contained within the contractual document. This point has recently been considered in ***O'Brien* v *MGN Ltd*** [2001] EWCA Civ 1279.

O'Brien v *MGN Ltd* [2001] EWCA Civ 1279

The facts of the case were that the claimant purchased a Sunday newspaper that contained a 'scratch-card' game that related to a competition being held during the following week in the *Daily Mirror*. The claimant's card revealed two 'windows' displaying £50,000 in each. The next week the claimant bought a copy of the *Daily Mirror* and in accordance with the 'rules' rang the 'hotline' and was told that the prize for that day was £50,000 and the claimant then believed he had won that amount. The intention behind the game was that there were only to be one or two £50,000 prizes each week but due to an error on the part of the defendant organisers there were 1,452 other £50,000 prize-winners that week. The organisers therefore attempted to rely on Rule 5 of the competition rules which stated that 'should more prizes be claimed than are available in any prize category for any reason, a simple draw will take place for the prize'. The claimant was not successful in the subsequent draw for the £50,000 and only received £33.99p. The claimant alleged that this amounted to a breach of contract. The scratchcard he received when he bought the Sunday paper stated: 'Full rules and how to claim – see *Daily Mirror*'. The *Daily Mirror* itself stated, 'Normal Mirror Group rules apply'. Whilst the rules were printed in various Mirror Group newspapers not every edition carried these rules. The issue was therefore whether the rules were incorporated into the contract entered into by the claimant.

The judge at first instance considered that the claimant's telephone call constituted an acceptance of an offer made in the *Daily Mirror* on that day; however, he held that the claimant was bound by Rule 5. Whilst the judge considered it highly unlikely that the claimant had read the rules when these had been published in the Mirror Group newspapers at various times, he was nevertheless bound by them since the reference to the rules was regarded as adequate notice of the rules. The fact that the claimant had ignored them in the past was of no consequence.

The Court of Appeal upheld the decision at first instance that the rules and conditions governing a newspaper's scratchcard games were incorporated into the contract despite the fact that they had not been published in the newspaper in full on the day of the game in question. The fact that the scratchcard itself made reference to the terms and conditions and that these were available in back issues of the newspaper or could be obtained from the newspaper or via its website was held to be sufficient.

The terms and conditions must be capable of being referred to. In ***Sterling Hydraulics Ltd* v *Dichtomatik Ltd*** [2007] 1 Lloyd's Rep 8, the defendant's acknowledgement of the order of the claimant purchaser stated, 'Delivery based on our General Terms of Sale' on the bottom of a blank page that contained no terms and conditions. The defendant then claimed that the contract was based on those terms and conditions that had been provided when goods had been supplied in earlier contracts. Reference to such standard terms was not in itself fatal to the defendant's defence when the goods proved defective; however, the fact that these terms were not made available at all at the time of the current contract was fatal since the court found that the terms had not been incorporated into the contract and as such did not amount to 'adequate notice'. The claimant had never received a copy of the defendant's terms and conditions on this or any previous occasion except when orders were delivered. Furthermore, the court pointed out that the defendant's faxed acknowledgements that purported to incorporate the terms did not refer to terms 'on the reverse' or 'overleaf', but simply to the defendant's 'General Terms of Sale'. The court found that in previous dealings between the parties it was always the case that the claimant had sent its terms and conditions to the defendant. The defendant had never objected to those terms and it had never sent a copy of its own terms and conditions back with any acknowledgement of an order. Any terms and conditions sent by the defendant had only been sent on delivery of the goods which is of course too late to be incorporated into the contract.

Sterling Hydraulics Ltd v *Dichtomatik Ltd* was also examined in Chapter 2 in the context of the 'battle of the forms'.

A further development in relation to incorporation can be seen in the case of *Impala Warehousng and Logistics (Shanghai) Co Ltd* v *Wanxiang Resources (Singapore) Pte Ltd* [2015] EWHC 811 (Comm) where it was held that standard terms and conditions on a website were sufficient to incorporate the terms into a contract, provided that the party seeking to rely on the conditions had done what was reasonably sufficient to give the other parties notice of the conditions. In this case, the first page of a Warehouse Certificate stated that the certificate and all disputes arising were subject to the terms and conditions of Impala. At the bottom of the page the reader was then invited to refer to the reverse page for additional conditions. On the reverse the reader was then referred to Impala's web-site for its terms and conditions; the webpage then contained the terms and conditions. The court held that the holder of the warehouse certificate knew that the certificate was subject to Impala's terms and conditions, he was then referred to the reverse of the certificate where he was then told where to find the terms and conditions. It was held that these steps were reasonably sufficient to give the holder notice of the conditions.

2. The nature of the exemption clause

A further aspect of assessing if reasonable notice of an exemption clause has been given arises where the clause is particularly onerous or unusual. In these circumstances a higher degree of notice is required in order to satisfy the reasonableness test. Very often, in order to satisfy the test, the other party's attention has to be specifically drawn to the terms incorporating the exemption clauses, or at the very least due prominence has to be given to such clauses. In *Thornton* v *Shoe Lane Parking Ltd* [1971] QB 163, it was held that while a motorist could anticipate a clause purporting to exclude liability for loss or damage to his vehicle, this was not true of a clause which purported to exclude liability for personal injury caused by negligence. The consequence of this finding was that the owner of the car park, in order to exclude liability for personal injury, would have to take special precautions to draw the term to the attention of customers using the car park. Such a conclusion has also been affirmed by Lord Denning in *Spurling* v *Bradshaw* [1956] 2 All ER 121 where he stated: 'Some clauses I have seen would need to be printed in red ink on the face of the document with a red hand pointing to it before the notice could be held to be sufficient.'

The case of *Interfoto Picture Library Ltd* v *Stiletto Visual Programmes Ltd* [1988] 1 All ER 348, while not involving exemption or limitation clauses, but onerous penalty terms, is a further example. Here the court decided that it was not sufficient for such terms to be incorporated into the contract via the standard printed contract. The onerous terms should be given prominence within the document with bold or red type, or indeed by having a special note drawing the other party's attention to the clauses.

The question then arises as to when is a term regarded as harsh or onerous? This is always a question of fact to be decided in each case. One of the arguments of the claimant in *O'Brien v MGN Ltd* [2001] EWCA Civ 1279 was that the effect of the telephone call was to turn 'winners into losers' and as such was a harsh and onerous term that as a result should have been given greater prominence. The claimant alleged that the defendants had failed to take sufficient steps to draw his attention to the clause and therefore he was not bound by the rule. Hale LJ and Potter LJ considered that whilst Rule 5 did in fact turn 'winners into losers' the rule could not by any normal use of language be regarded as 'onerous'. Hale LJ in particular distinguished the rule from the clause in the *Interfoto* case which imposed severe penalties on the defendant. She also distinguished the rule from the clause in *Thornton* v *Shoe Lane Parking* since this clause attempted to exclude liability for personal injury caused by negligence. As Hale LJ indicated, all that Rule 5 did was to deprive the claimant from a windfall for very little in return.

Is it necessary for a party to show that the particular clause in question is itself onerous or unusual or is it necessary to demonstrate that a clause of this type be onerous or unusual? In *AEG (UK) Ltd* v *Logic Resource Ltd* [1996] CLC 265, the majority of the Court of Appeal held that a clause which stated that a purchaser when returning defective goods had to do so at their own expense could only be incorporated into the contract if 'fairly and reasonably brought to the attention' of the purchaser since their lordships considered the clause to be both onerous *and* unusual. Hobhouse LJ considered this approach to be incorrect and considered the proper approach should be to look at the 'type of clause' and then to consider whether the particular clause was onerous and harsh in the context of this 'type of clause'. He stated:

> . . . it is necessary before excluding the incorporation of the clause *in limine* to consider the type of clause it is. Is it a clause of the type which you would expect to find in the printed conditions? If it is, then it is only in the most exceptional circumstances that a party will be able to say that it was not adequately brought to his notice by standard words of incorporation.

Hobhouse LJ considered the clause in question to be of a type which is ordinarily found in contracts for the sale of goods and per se is not unusual; however, the clause in this particular contract had been unreasonably drafted and afforded the seller greater protection than was reasonable or 'anyway reasonable without some special justification'. Thus Hobhouse LJ considered that first it is necessary to consider the type of clause in question and, if it is considered to be one that is not to be expected in the printed conditions referred to, then go to the question of incorporation. He considered that a wide range of clauses are commonly incorporated into contracts by general words and that if every contract was assessed to see if the clauses were usual and desirable in a particular contract then the contractual relationship between the parties would be distorted, as would the ordinary mechanisms for making contracts. He considered this would introduce uncertainty into the law of contract.

In *Ocean Chemical Transport Inc.* v *Exnor Craggs Ltd* [2000] 1 All ER (Comm) 519, the Court of Appeal rejected the approach of Hobhouse LJ in the *AEG* case. In that case Evans LJ stated:

> It seems to me that the question of incorporation must always depend upon the meaning and effect of the clause in question. It may be that the type of clause is relevant. It may be that the

effect of the particular clause in the particular case is relevant. That, of course, was the division of opinion in the AEG case . . . I would prefer to put the matter more broadly and to say that the question is whether the defendants have discharged the duty which lies upon them of bringing the existence of the clause upon which they rely to the notice of the other party in the circumstances of the particular case.

This approach was accepted by the other judges in the *Ocean Chemical* case and the position now appears to be clear that it is the particular clause that has to be onerous or unusual, not the 'type of clause'. This is a sound way forward since it is consistent with the approach taken in the *Interfoto* and *Thornton v Shoe Lane* cases.

The *Ocean Chemical* case is also good authority for the proposition that it is unnecessary to show that the clause is both onerous *and* unusual. In the earlier case of *HIH Casualty and General Insurance Ltd v New Hampshire Insurance Co.* [2001] EWCA Civ 735, it was considered that both requirements had to be demonstrated. More recently in the case of *Sumukan Ltd v Commonwealth Secretariat* [2007] EWCA Civ 243, the Court of Appeal appears to have affirmed that the clause needs to be either onerous *or* unusual.

When was notice of the exemption clause given?

In order for the exemption clause to be a term of the contract the reasonable steps to bring notice of the clause to the other party must be taken before or at the time of contracting. The classic case involving this requirement is that of *Olley v Marlborough Court Ltd*.

Olley v *Marlborough Court Ltd* [1949] 1 All ER 127

A husband and wife booked into a hotel and paid for one week's stay in advance. They went to the room allotted to them where they found a notice stating that 'the proprietors will not hold themselves responsible for articles lost or stolen unless handed to the manageress for safe custody'. The wife had a number of valuable fur coats which she left in the room and which were subsequently stolen. When sued in negligence the defendants sought to incorporate the exemption clause into the contract. The Court of Appeal decided that the contract had already been entered into before the notice of the exemption clause had been brought to the plaintiff's attention. It was therefore not contemporaneous with the making of the contract and thus not incorporated into it so that the defendants could not rely on it for protection.

Lord Denning, who also sat in *Olley v Marlborough Court Ltd*, applied similar reasoning in the case of *Thornton v Shoe Lane Parking Ltd* [1971] 1 All ER 686, where it was held that the owner of a ticket machine at an automatic car park made an offer when he held the machine out as being ready to receive money and that this offer was accepted when a customer placed his money in the slot, the contract being formed at this point. Since the contract was already in existence when the ticket was issued, any terms and conditions expressed or referred to on the ticket came too late and were not part of the contract. The defendant proprietor of the car park could not therefore rely on the protection of the exemption clause.

In the era of contracts via the Internet, great care must be taken in constructing websites so that notice of any exemption clauses is given to a person entering into a contract. With the possibility of a purchaser being able to jump pages by way of links, it is necessary to ensure that the page including the exemption clauses is not capable of being bypassed by such links. The consequences of this arising may mean that a contracting party will not be bound by any exemption clause.

Incorporation by a previous course of dealings

The courts may infer notice of an exemption clause in a contract where there has been a previous course of dealings between the parties in which exclusion clauses have been part of a contract, either by virtue of the document being a signed document or by virtue of reasonable notice of the clause being brought to the parties' attention. The possibility of such an inference can be seen to operate in the case of **Spurling v Bradshaw** [1956] 2 All ER 121, where the defendant and plaintiffs had previously dealt with each other for a number of years. The defendant delivered eight barrels of orange juice to the plaintiffs for storage, later receiving an acknowledgement of the deposit of the goods which exempted the plaintiffs 'from any loss or damage occasioned by negligence, wrongful act or default' either of themselves or their servants. When some time later the defendant went to collect the barrels he found them empty and thus refused to pay the storage charges. When sued for the charges he counterclaimed for negligence, though the plaintiffs defended this action on the basis of the exemption clause. The defendant, for his part, attempted to maintain that the notice of the exemption clause was not contemporaneous with the making of the contract and as such could not form part of the contract. The defendant admitted that in his previous course of dealings with the plaintiffs he had been sent such a document though he had never bothered to read it. The terms and conditions were held to be part and parcel of the present agreement by virtue of the previous course of dealings that had taken place between the parties.

The notion of a previous course of dealing is relatively difficult to define, though it is certain that it must be a consistent course of dealings.

McCutcheon v *David MacBrayne Ltd* [1964] 1 All ER 430

The respondents operated ferries between the Scottish mainland and islands; the appellant asked a relative, a Mr McSporran, to have his car transported to the mainland. McSporran paid the freight charge and received a receipt. The ship sank due to the respondents' servants' negligence and the vehicle was a total write-off, for which the appellant sought compensation. The respondents' liability was excluded under the terms of their printed conditions, to which reference was made on the receipt, as well as being displayed in the respondents' offices. Neither the appellant nor McSporran had read the notices and McSporran had not bothered to read the receipt. The purser had also failed to ask McSporran to sign a risk note, which included the conditions, even though one had been prepared for him to sign. Such notes had been signed on previous occasions by the appellant and McSporran, but not on every occasion, and even then they had not read them, though they knew such notes contained conditions. It was held that the appellant would succeed since the receipt and the notices did not form part of the oral contract, in that the receipt had come after the contract had been entered into and the respondents had not done what was reasonably sufficient to bring the notices displayed in the office to the attention of the appellant or McSporran. There had not been a consistent course of dealings which would allow the conditions to be implied into the contract. Lord Hodson commented:

> The course of dealing on earlier occasions is often relevant in determining contractual relations, but does not assist when, as here, there was on the part of the respondents a departure from an earlier course in that they omitted to ask the appellant's agent to sign the document by which they would have obtained protection.

It can be seen in the above case that a long consistent course of dealings did not apply because the usual steps taken to incorporate the conditions into the contract had not been taken or applied consistently. A similar view was taken in *Sterling Hydraulics Ltd v Dichtomatik Ltd* [2006] EWHC 2004 (QB) where it was stated that where it was alleged that a previous course of dealing existed, it had to be demonstrated that the dealings had to be consistent and unequivocal as regards the terms and conditions to be incorporated.

Terms and conditions may nevertheless be incorporated into a contract if the parties were aware of them even though, on the occasion in question, they had not formed part of the contract, as in *Hardwick Game Farm v Suffolk Agricultural Association* [1969] 2 AC 31. In that case a similar contract had been entered into three or four times a month before the contract in question. The usual steps taken to incorporate the terms into the contract were not carried out, but the court held it was sufficient to show that the parties knew and intended the terms to form part of the agreement.

In *Circle Freight International Ltd v Medeast Gulf Exports Ltd* [1988] 2 Lloyd's Rep 427, there was a course of dealing that consisted of eleven contracts in the previous six months. On each occasion the contract had been made orally by telephone but the invoice for the carriage charges, which were sent at a later date, stated that all business was transacted by the carrier under the current conditions of the Institute of Freight Forwarders, a copy of which was available on request. A copy was never requested. The consignor's managing director accepted that he knew that carriers by road often dealt on standard terms which addressed questions of risk of loss or damage, but said that he had not noticed the reference to the IFF conditions in the invoices sent after each of the contracts had been concluded.

The Court of Appeal held that the IFF conditions were incorporated into the contract. The consignor's managing director knew that some terms applied and that forwarding agents might impose terms which would frequently deal with risk, but never asked for a copy of the terms. In addition, he said that the terms were not particularly onerous or unusual. Taylor LJ stated:

> ... I consider that reasonable notice of the terms was given by the plaintiffs. Putting it another way, I consider that the defendant's conduct in continuing the course of business after at least 11 notices of the terms and omitting to request a sight of them would have led and did lead the plaintiffs reasonably to believe the defendants accepted their terms. In those circumstances it is irrelevant that in fact [the managing director] did not read the notices.'

Whatever a court's view regarding the need for consistency, it is certain that there has to be a course of dealings and this cannot be established if the parties have only contracted with each other on a few occasions over a lengthy period of time. This is a matter for the court to decide as a question of fact.

In *Capes (Hatherden)Ltd v Western Arable Services Ltd* [2010] 1 Lloyd's Rep 477, Havelock-Allan QC considered a course of dealing that consisted of four contracts in one year, with an interval of five months between the last of them and the two contracts that were the subject of the dispute. On each of the initial four contracts, which were made orally, the buyer received the contract note from the seller. It was in a standard printed form headed with the seller's address and logo. It set out in boxes the details of the order: for example, the purchaser, the account number, description of the goods, quantity, price, quality, and so on. Underneath the boxes was printed wording which included the following: 'Terms: AIC Contract No 1/04 for grain and pulses'. This was a reference to standard terms produced by the Agricultural Industries Confederation ('AIC'). The buyer was not required to respond positively to the contract note (e.g. by signing and returning a copy) and he did not notice the reference to Contract 1/04. Havelock-Allan QC stated:

> In my judgement these facts are right on the borderline. If there had been any persuasive evidence, either that the terms of Contract 1/04 were the usual terms on which grain merchants purchase grain from UK producers, or that Mr. Capes knew that grain merchants commonly employed standard terms which provided for disputes to be settled by arbitration, I would have been likely to hold that Contract 1/04 was incorporated. In the absence of such evidence, I do not think that the previous contracts justify the conclusion that the AIC terms were incorporated. To put it another way, the limited course of dealing between the parties is not in my view such that an impartial observer would conclude that the parties had reached a common understanding that Contract 1/04 applied.

In *Transformers and Rectifiers Ltd v Need Ltd* [2015] EWHC 269 (TCC), the facts of which have already been considered in Chapter 2, Edwards-Stuart J that where the parties are relying on a previous course of dealing in order to incorporate terms and conditions, the previous course of dealings do not have to be extensive and, indeed, three or four occasions over a relatively short period of time would suffice.

In *Hollier v Rambler Motors (AMC) Ltd* [1972] QB 71, it was held that contacting on three or four occasions over a five-year period was insufficient to establish a course of dealing. It was stated, however, that one exception for the need for a course of dealing arises where an exemption clause is implied into the contract by way of a general course of dealing that amounts to a trade usage or custom. Whilst previously such an approach might have arisen by reason of an assumption that it must have been the intention of the parties to incorporate such terms, similar to terms implied as a matter of fact; today it would seem that terms implied in this way are a means of incorporating standardised terms and are more akin to terms implied by law. An example of such a process can be seen in *British Crane Hire Corporation Ltd v Ipswich Plant Hire Ltd* [1975] QB 303. In this case the plaintiff and defendant were both engaged in the business of hiring out earth-moving equipment. The defendant, however, was also involved in drainage work on marshy ground and urgently requiring a crane. He agreed to hire a crane from plaintiff and, whilst the terms of payment were agreed, no mention was made of the plaintiff's conditions of hire. The plaintiff sent the defendant a copy of the conditions which provided, *inter alia*, that the hirer would be responsible for all expenses arising out of the crane's use. Before the defendant signed the form containing the conditions, the crane sank into the marsh through no fault of the defendant. The plaintiff claimed the cost of recovering the crane according to the Contractors' Plant Association terms which were incorporated into the contract by way of the two previous transactions between the parties. Lord Denning considered that two previous transactions would be sufficient to set up a previous course of dealings. He referred to the judgement of Salmond LJ in *Hollier v Rambler Motors (A.M.C.) Ltd. [1972] 2 Q.B. 71* in which he stated that he 'knew of no case in which it has been decided or even argued that a term could be implied into an oral contract on the strength of a course of dealing (if it can be so called) which consisted at the most of three or four transactions over a period of five years'.

Lord Denning considered that the *Hollier* case involved a private individual who was not of equal bargaining power with the defendants who had repaired his car on three or four previous occasions in which the individual had signed contract with conditions attached. In that case the terms were not incorporated into the contract. Lord Denning,

Incorporation of terms into a contract

Signature

Once a party has signed the document then prima facie they are bound by it even if they have not read it:
L'Estrange v Graucob

Effect of misrepresentation
If a person is induced to sign a document by way of a misrepresentation then a defendant cannot rely on the exemption clause:
Curtis v Chemical Cleaning and Dyeing Co. Ltd

By notice

The document must be a contractual document
Would a reasonable person have assumed the document is a contractual document (cf a receipt)?
Chapelton v Barry UDC

What degree of notice is required?
Reasonable steps must be taken to bring the clause to the notice of the plaintiff:
Parker v South Eastern Railway Co.
Blind or illiterate?
See *Thompson v LM & S Railway Co.*

When was notice of the exemption clause given?
Notice must be given before or at the time of contracting:
Olley v Marlborough Court Hotel Ltd

If the exemption clause is particularly onerous or unusual then a higher degree of notice is required to satisfy the test of reasonableness:
Thornton v Shoe Lane Ltd
Spurling v Bradshaw – 'red hand' notice
Interfoto Picture Library v Stiletto Visual Programmes Ltd
Ocean Chemical Transport Inc. v Exnor Craggs Ltd

Course of dealings

Incorporation by way of a consistent course of dealings:
Spurling v Bradshaw
McCutcheon v MacBrayne

Actual knowledge of the exemption clause despite lack of signature or notice:
Hardwick Game Farm v Suffolk Agricultural Association

No course of dealings but the parties of equal bargaining power:
British Crane Hire Corp Ltd v Ipswich Plant Hire Ltd

Figure 8.1

however, stated that in the case before him, the parties were both in the trade and were of equal bargaining power. Each was a firm of plant hirers who hired out plant. The defendants themselves knew that firms in the plant-hiring trade always imposed conditions in regard to the hiring of plant: and that their conditions were on much the same lines. and P claimed from D the cost of recovering the crane. It was held that the plaintiff's claim should be allowed and that the plaintiff's condition of hire applied. Lord Denning stated:

> From that evidence it is clear that both parties knew quite well that conditions were habitually imposed by the supplier of these machines: and both parties knew the substance of those conditions. In particular that if the crane sank in soft ground, it was the hirer's job to recover it: and that there was an indemnity clause. In these circumstances, I think the conditions on the form should be regarded as incorporated into the contract. I would not put it so much on the course of dealing, but rather on the common understanding which is to be derived from the conduct of the parties, namely, that the hiring was to be on the terms of the plaintiffs' usual conditions.

Construing exemption clauses

As stated at the start of this chapter, one of the tasks confronting the courts over the past 150 years has been the need to balance the principle of the equality of bargaining power with the notion of consumer protection. One of the means by which this task has been accomplished may be seen in the way the courts have construed exemption clauses coming before them. The courts have approached this problem in three ways.

Exemption clauses are to be construed *contra proferentem*

The rule here is that exemption clauses are construed against the party relying on them. The result of this is that if the clause fails to deal with a particular matter then it is deemed not to cover that matter. The case of *Baldry* v *Marshall* [1925] 1 KB 260 provides an example of this process where the defendant car dealers were asked to supply a car 'suitable for touring purposes'. The dealer recommended a Bugatti which proved eminently unsuitable for the required use. The plaintiff rejected the car and claimed to recover the price. The contract contained a clause excluding 'guarantees or warranties, statutory or otherwise'. The court held that the stipulation as to the suitability of the car was a condition, not a guarantee or a warranty, and as such was not covered by the exemption clause.

The attitude of the court in the above case was clearly to construe the clause against the person seeking to rely on it. A further example can be seen in *Andrews Bros (Bournemouth) Ltd* v *Singer and Co.* [1934] 1 KB 17 where there was a contract to purchase 'new Singer cars'. The contract contained a clause which excluded 'all conditions, warranties and liabilities implied by statute, common law or otherwise'. One of the cars delivered by the dealer was a used car and when sued for damages he attempted to rely on the exemption clause. The Court of Appeal held that the term regarding 'new Singer cars' was an express term and thus the exemption clause, which only excluded liability for implied terms, did not protect the dealer.

It should be noted that the application of the **contra proferentem rule** is not restricted to exemption clauses.

Vaswani v Italian Motor Cars Ltd [1996] 1 WLR 270 (PC)

In this case, the sellers agreed to sell a Ferrari car to the buyer for £179,500. The car had to be specially ordered and a deposit of £44,875, representing 25 per cent of the purchase price, had to be paid with the order, which would be forfeited if the buyer did not go through with the sale. The contract provided that the price could be altered by the sellers in certain circumstances: for example, where the exact model ordered was unavailable, because of changes in import duties and fluctuations in currency exchange rates, etc. The circumstances were set out in conditions 4 and 5. The crucial clause, which was stated in red, provided:

> The price appearing upon this document is based upon the manufacturer's current price, specification and present freight and exchange rates. The price is subject to adjustment should there be any change in the manufacturer's current price or freight rates prior to shipment or should there be any change in exchange rates prior to delivery or in any of the other cases set out in conditions 4 and 5 on the reverse hereof and the price ruling at the date of delivery will be invoiced.

When the car arrived in Hong Kong, the sellers sent the buyer a message at the beginning of June 1990 that the car was ready for delivery when the balance of £168,141 was paid. This in fact meant that the price of the car had risen to £213,800. The buyer did not at first question the price increase but was less than enthusiastic about completing the transaction, probably because he had left Hong Kong and did not intend to return to live there. The sellers insisted that the transaction should proceed but, despite the buyer assuring them that he would make performance, he failed to do so. Eventually on 6 July 1990 the sellers sent a fax message stating that unless completion took place on 10 July 1990 the sellers would treat the contract as at an end and the buyer would forfeit his deposit. The buyer failed to complete by that date and the buyer was told that his deposit had been forfeited and that the sellers would dispose of the car elsewhere and that the buyer would be liable for any losses that the sellers suffered. The case revolved around two issues: first, whether the sellers were entitled to demand payment of the increased price; and, second, whether the sellers had repudiated the contract.

It was held by the Privy Council that the sellers had erroneously increased the price. On a proper construction of the contract the sellers were not entitled to demand an increase in price based on their price list at the date of delivery, whatever had occurred. They could only increase the price within conditions 4 and 5 so that it reflected increases in their own costs to which they had become subjected by the circumstances specified in the red printed clause. Thus the amount demanded exceeded the amount which was properly due under the contract. Since the clause in red provided apparently two inconsistent criteria for fixing the price, a strict interpretation was given to the clause whereby the seller was only allowed to increase the price where its own costs were affected. The interpretation given was to be *contra proferentem* to the sellers and in favour of the buyer.

On the second question it was held that the conduct of the sellers was not inconsistent with their wish to continue the contract, in spite of the fact that the price was incorrect. The sellers therefore had not repudiated the contract and it was the buyer who had failed to perform and clearly indicated that he had no intention of making the payment due. Thus the buyer had repudiated the contract and the sellers were entitled to keep the deposit. No doubt today such variation in price clauses would also be subject to the Consumer Rights Act 2015 (CRA) which repealed the Unfair Terms in Consumer Contracts Regulations 1999. By s 62(4) of the CRA, if such a term is unfair and contrary to the requirement of good faith in that it causes a significant imbalance in the parties' rights and obligations under the contract to the detriment of the consumer then such a clause could be struck down.

Exempting liability for fundamental breach of contract

Objective 4

The processes analysed here are really only particular applications of the *contra proferentem* rule discussed above. Even in the golden age of contract in the nineteenth century, when the notion of equality of bargaining power allowed the parties to exclude themselves from various aspects of their contractual liability, the courts were reluctant to allow a party to exclude themself from serious or fundamental breaches of the contract. The approach of the courts to this process of limiting the effect of exemption clauses took two distinct lines: first, an exemption clause which sought to exclude a serious breach of contract was to be construed narrowly in order to reduce the protection offered by the clause; second, the courts developed a substantive rule of law that exemption clauses that sought to exclude liability for fundamental breach would be ineffective. An example of the first approach by the courts can be seen in the case of *Karsales (Harrow) Ltd* v *Wallis*.

Karsales (Harrow) Ltd v *Wallis* [1956] 1 WLR 936

The defendant, having inspected a second-hand car and found it to be in good order, decided to buy it on hire purchase terms. The hire purchase agreement contained a clause which stated that 'no condition or warranty that the vehicle is roadworthy or as to its condition or fitness for any purpose is given by the owner or implied therein'. The car was eventually delivered one night and, while it appeared to be the car the defendant had inspected, daylight revealed the car to be a mere shell. The cylinder head and pistons were broken, valves were burnt out; in short, it was incapable of propulsion. Not surprisingly the defendant refused to accept the car or pay the hire purchase instalments and, when eventually sued, pointed to the condition of the car. The plaintiffs in turn attempted to rely on the clause. The Court of Appeal held that there had been a fundamental and substantial deviation between the thing contracted for and that which was actually delivered. In such circumstances the plaintiffs could not avail themselves of the clause and judgement was given to the defendant.

The position of the court may be seen in the statement of Lord Wilberforce in the later case of *Suisse Atlantique Société d'Armement Maritime SA* v *NV Rotterdamsche Kolen Centrale* [1966] 2 All ER 61:

> Since the contracting parties could hardly have been supposed to contemplate such a misperformance or to have provided against it without destroying the whole contractual substratum, there is no difficulty here in holding exception clauses to be inapplicable.

This approach by the courts is very common in relation to the carriage of goods by sea where the route to be taken by a ship is usually regarded as fundamental. The result is that any deviation from the route will have the effect of preventing the shipowner from relying on the benefit of an exemption clause contained in the contract. An example of such a case may be seen in *Glyn* v *Margetson* [1893] AC 351 where there was a contract to ship oranges from Malaga to Liverpool. In fact the contract gave the carrier a wide discretion to deviate from his route, but this was held not to protect him when the ship first set a course east from Malaga, then returned to Malaga before making for Liverpool. It was held that the clause was limited to the 'main object and intent' of the contract, which was to sail from Malaga to Liverpool, though the contract permitted the carrier to deviate from this course, provided the deviation was en route for Liverpool. Sailing east was clearly not within such 'object and intent' and therefore the carrier was liable for the deterioration in the condition of the cargo.

The second approach of the courts to fundamental breaches of contract has been the development of a substantive rule that rendered exemption clauses invalid. There has been extensive debate as to whether such a rule exists as a substantive rule of law or merely as a rule of construction. It should be borne in mind that by a fundamental breach one means not a simple breach of condition but one that goes to the very core of the contract itself. Whether a particular breach is regarded as fundamental or not rests upon the facts of the particular case, the onus of proof lying on the party alleging the fundamental breach to prove it, as in **Hunt and Winterbotham (West of England) Ltd v BRS (Parcels) Ltd** [1962] 1 All ER 111.

If the court finds that a fundamental breach has occurred it has to decide whether the exemption clause is sufficiently specific to either exclude or limit a party's liability for the breach. A divergence of approach arises here between consumer and commercial contracts. In a consumer contract the courts apply the doctrine of fundamental breach as a substantive rule of law, so that an exemption clause could not exclude or limit liability for such a breach, whatever the intention of the parties. In a commercial contract, however, the doctrine was applied merely as a rule of construction; that is, an assessment was made of the intentions of the parties and if it was intended that the clause should exclude liability in the case of such a breach then the court would give effect to that intention. In the latter instance the parties were regarded as being of equal bargaining strength and having contracted at arm's length, and therefore it was correct to allow them to allocate their risks as they wished.

The above position regarding the doctrine of fundamental breach was sustained until the **Suisse Atlantique** case in 1966 when the House of Lords considered this divergence of approach to be incorrect and that the proper view was that the doctrine was a rule of construction only, whatever the status of the contract.

Viscount Dilhorne stated:

> In my view, it is not right to say that the law prohibits and nullifies a clause exempting or limiting liability for a fundamental breach or breach of a fundamental term. Such a rule would involve a restriction on freedom of contract and in the older cases I can find no trace of it.

While the other members of the House of Lords concurred with Viscount Dilhorne's statement, all of these statements were only *obiter dicta*. This, together with the fact that it was questionable whether the case was one involving a fundamental breach at all considerably weakened the effect of the case on the doctrine. The Court of Appeal under Lord Denning did not take too kindly to this move by the House of Lords, their dislike of the decision revolving around the fact that it tended to weaken their ability to protect consumers. The result was that through a series of decisions they reworked the doctrine so that it once again existed as a substantive rule of law. The case of **Harbutt's 'Plasticine' Ltd v Wayne Tank and Pump Co. Ltd** [1970] 1 QB 447 is an example of this.

The passing of the Unfair Contract Terms Act 1977 rendered the position of the Court of Appeal obsolete since consumers were now protected by the provisions of the Act. Where the Act did not apply in commercial contracts, the view that the parties should again be free to allocate their liabilities under the contract by way of exemption clauses again came into vogue. In 1980 the reversal to this position was confirmed by the House of Lords in **Photo Production Ltd v Securicor Transport Ltd** [1980] AC 827 where Lord Wilberforce stated:

> It is significant that Parliament refrained from legislating over the whole field of contract. After this Act, in commercial matters generally, when the parties are not of unequal bargaining power, and when risks are normally borne by insurance, not only is the case for judicial intervention undemonstrated, but there is everything to be said, and this seems to have been

Parliament's intention, for leaving the parties free to apportion the risks as they think fit and for respecting their decisions.

The decision of the House of Lords in the *Photo Production* case has since been affirmed by the House of Lords in *George Mitchell (Chesterhall) Ltd* v *Finney Lock Seeds* [1983] 2 AC 803. The position at common law is that whether an exemption clause protects a party when a breach occurs depends on the construction of the clause, having regard to the degree of risk assumed by the parties to the contract and the possibility of the risk being offset by insurance.

An interesting first instance decision on this matter arises in the case of *Internet Broadcasting Corp Ltd (t/a NETTV)* v *MAR LLC (t/a MARHedge)* [2009] EWHC 844 (Ch) where the court was required to interpret an exclusion clause in a joint venture contract for Internet broadcasting which stated that neither party would be liable to the other for any damage to software, damage to or loss of data, loss of profit, anticipated profit, revenues, anticipated savings, goodwill or business opportunity, or for any indirect or consequential loss or damage. A year after the agreement was signed the defendant gave notice purporting to terminate the contract with immediate effect. The defendant admitted that there had been a wrongful repudiatory termination of the contract but relied on the exclusion clause to protect it from liability in respect of loss of profits by the claimant. The defendant argued provided the clause was not repugnant, and left open an ability to sue for some substantial loss, it was to be given its literal meaning. In this case, the defendant argued that this would cover a deliberate repudiatory breach of contract. The court held that the starting point in interpreting the clause was that it was not intended to cover a deliberate repudiatory breach of contract and that to arrive at such a position very strong words would be required to persuade a court that the parties intended to cover such a case. Pointing to a literal meaning was not enough and, further, any reasonable businessman reading the exclusion clause in the contract with a view to assessing whether an insurable risk existed would recognise that the clause would not extend to a risk that was either uninsurable or likely to be uninsurable. Thus the literal meaning of the exclusion clause would defeat the main purpose of the contract. The clause therefore did not exclude liability for a deliberate repudiatory breach in the instant case.

Exempting liability for negligence

One aspect of the *contra proferentem* rule is that it regards exemption clauses as excluding liability in respect of contractual duties only. It is always possible that while a claimant may have contractual rights against a defendant they might also have rights in tort, usually negligence. The effect here is, of course, to give the claimant an additional remedy should an exemption clause operate to protect the defendant in respect of their contractual duties. The defendant for their part would, in these circumstances, be prudent to express the exemption clause in the widest possible terms, so that their liability in tort is also covered. Because of the operation of the *contra proferentem* rule, however, the defendant must generally expressly refer to negligence within the exemption clause, although the rule will be satisfied if the clause is nevertheless wide enough to cover liability for negligence: for example, by exempting a party from 'all liability whatsoever' as in *White* v *Blackmore* [1972] 2 QB 651.

The main problem that occurs in this context is where the exemption clause is ambiguous, since here the defendant is prima facie liable in both contract and tort because the clause will be construed in such a way as to exclude contractual liability only, very specific language being required to exclude liability in tort. This was so in the following case.

White v John Warwick & Co. Ltd [1953] 2 All ER 1021

The plaintiff hired a bicycle from the defendant but, while he was riding it, the seat tipped forward thereby injuring him. The hire contract stated, 'nothing in this agreement shall render the owners liable for any personal injury'. It was held that while the clause was sufficient to exclude liability in contract for the defendant supplying a defective bicycle, it was not sufficient to exclude liability in negligence. The plaintiff thus succeeded in his claim in tort. *See also* **Alderslade v Hendon Laundry Ltd** [1945] 1 KB 189 (CA).

The requirement for the clause to be explicit in the face of ambiguity is also important even if liability could not arise in any way but negligence.

Hollier v Rambler Motors (AMC) Ltd [1972] QB 71

The plaintiff agreed to have his car towed to the defendants' garage for repairs. The car was subsequently totally destroyed by a fire that broke out at the garage as a result of the defendants' negligence. The contract contained a term which stated that 'the company is not responsible for damage caused by fire to customers' cars on the premises'. The Court of Appeal concluded that the defendants would only be liable for fire if it was caused by their negligence, though it was possible for the exemption clause to be read as a warning that the defendants were not liable for loss caused by fire which was *not* due to their negligence. The court concluded that there was a sufficient degree of ambiguity to disallow the defendants from relying on the clause.

Other factors limiting the effectiveness of exemption clauses

Objective 5

So far we have seen how exemption clauses may be limited in their effectiveness because of the way they are constructed and interpreted. Even if an exemption clause when properly construed covers the losses or damages that have occurred there are further limitations on its effectiveness. The limitations divide into two groups: common law and statutory limitations.

Common law limitations on exemption clauses

Misrepresentation

For more on misrepresentation refer to Chapter 9.

An exemption clause will be held to be ineffective in affording protection to the person relying on it should that person or his agent, such as an employee, misrepresent the extent of the clause to the other party.

Curtis v Chemical Cleaning and Dyeing Co. Ltd [1951] 1 KB 805

The plaintiff took a dress to the defendants for cleaning. She was given a receipt to sign and she asked what it was for. She was told that it was to exempt the defendants from certain types of damage, in particular damage to beads and sequins. On this basis she signed the receipt. In fact the clause was a general exemption in that it excluded liability for 'any damage, howsoever arising'. When the dress was returned it was found to be badly stained, whereupon the defendants claimed the protection of the clause. It was held that the plaintiff could succeed and that the defendants could not rely on the clause since the court found that the plaintiff had been induced to sign the document by the misrepresentation as to the extent of the clause.

Third parties

For more on privity of contract refer to Chapter 19.

Where an exclusion clause is deemed to be effective, it is so only with regard to the actual parties to the contract. At common law any third parties to the contract cannot rely on the clause for protection. This rule is consistent with the doctrine of **privity of contract**. The application of the doctrine in this context can be seen in the following case.

Adler v Dickson [1954] 3 All ER 397

A sailing ticket issued to the plaintiff provided:

Passengers . . . are carried at passengers' entire risk . . . The Company will not be responsible for and shall be exempt from all liability in respect of any . . . injury . . . of any passenger . . . whether such injury . . . shall occur on land, on shipboard or elsewhere . . . and whether the same shall arise from or be occasioned by the negligence of the Company's servants . . . in the discharge of their duties, or whether by the negligence of other persons directly or indirectly . . . in the employment or service of the company . . . under any circumstances whatsoever . . .

The plaintiff was injured when a gangway was moved while she was walking up it to board the SS *Himalaya*. She brought an action for negligence, not against the shipping company, but against the captain and boatswain of the ship. It was held by the Court of Appeal that the clause offered protection only to the company and nobody else, and thus the plaintiff was successful in her claim against the two individuals.

A more modern example of the principle can be seen in *Scruttons Ltd v Midland Silicones Ltd* where similar reasoning was employed by the judges in the House of Lords.

Scruttons Ltd v Midland Silicones Ltd [1962] 1 All ER 1

In this case, a drum containing chemicals was shipped to New York on a ship owned by United States Lines to the order of the plaintiffs. The bill of lading contained a limitation clause which restricted the carriers', the shipowners', liability to US$500. The defendants were stevedores contracted to United States Lines in London on terms which purported to include the benefit of the limitation clause. The plaintiffs were unaware of the contract between the stevedore defendants and the carriers. The drum of chemicals was damaged because of the negligence of the stevedores, the damage amounting to US$593. The plaintiffs sued in negligence but the defendants attempted to rely on the limitation clause in the bill of lading for protection. It was held by the House of Lords that the plaintiffs would succeed and that the stevedores could not rely on the clause since they were not parties to the bill of lading.

Criticism of this case is dealt with more fully in Chapter 19.

Not surprisingly, attempts have been made to avoid this effect of the doctrine of privity of contract. An elaborate attempt at achieving this can be found in the Privy Council case of *New Zealand Shipping Co. Ltd v A M Satterthwaite & Co. Ltd, The Eurymedon* [1975] AC 154, where it was held that the benefit of an exemption clause can be claimed by a stevedore provided the contract of carriage was explicit as to the fact that the stevedore was intended to be protected by the contract and that the shipowner/carrier made it clear that he was contracting as agent for the stevedore, as well as himself. In addition the carrier had to have the authority of the stevedore to contract on his behalf and there had to be some consideration moving from the stevedore. It was held that these factors were present and as a result judgement was given for the defendant stevedores. The case has, however, been subject to substantial criticism.

The effects of the Contracts (Rights of Third Parties) Act 1999, s 6(5), should not be ignored here since this provides that third parties may now take advantage of a term excluding or limiting their liabilities where this contract is one for the carriage of goods by sea, road, rail or air. This provision therefore allows carriers to exclude or limit the liabilities of their servants, agents and independent contractors employed in the loading or unloading of ships. Thus the convoluted mechanism employed in cases such as *The Eurymedon* will now disappear.

Overriding oral undertaking

It is possible for an exemption clause contained in a written document to be overridden by an express inconsistent undertaking given before or at the time of contracting. An example of such an overriding undertaking can be seen in *J Evans & Son (Portsmouth) Ltd v Andrea Merzario Ltd* [1976] 1 WLR 1078.

This case was already discussed in Chapter 7.

Collateral contracts

Such contracts may prevent a party seeking to rely on an exemption clause from doing so.

Webster v *Higgin* [1948] 2 All ER 127

The defendant was considering purchasing a motor vehicle from the plaintiff garage proprietor on hire purchase. During the course of the negotiations the plaintiff's agent stated to the defendant: 'If you buy the Hillman we will guarantee that it is in good condition.' The defendant then decided to sign the hire purchase agreement which contained the following exemption clause: 'no warranty, condition, description or representation as to the state or quality of the vehicle is given or implied'. The car, when delivered, was later described by Lord Green as 'nothing but a mass of second-hand and dilapidated ironmongery'. Not surprisingly the defendant refused to accept the car or to pay the hire purchase instalments. The plaintiff sued to recover the vehicle and the instalments that had fallen due. If the exemption clause contained in the hire purchase agreement had stood alone then the defendant would have been precluded from pleading the state of the car as a defence to the action. He might have claimed that there had been a fundamental breach of contract, though this was not alleged in the case. Instead the defendant alleged that there had been two contracts entered into. He stated that the hire purchase agreement had been preceded by another contract whereby the condition of the vehicle had been guaranteed in return for the defendant promising to sign the hire purchase agreement. The Court of Appeal gave judgement to the defendant on the basis of the collateral contract that preceded the hire purchase agreement. The court found that the collateral contract had been broken and this entitled the defendant to treat the hire purchase agreement as at an end, enabling him to reclaim his deposit and the instalments already paid.

Statutory limitations on exemption clauses and unfair terms

Introduction

There have been many instances where Parliament has intervened to restrict or curtail the operation of exemption clauses. For example, s 151 of the Road Traffic Act 1960, now embodied in s 29 of the Public Passenger Vehicles Act 1981, makes it void to negate or restrict the liability of a person in respect of the death or bodily injury to a passenger while being carried in, or alighting from, a vehicle. A similar provision also exists in the Road Traffic Act 1988 which renders ineffective any antecedent agreement or undertaking (whether this is intended to be legally binding or not) to restrict the liability of the user of a motor vehicle towards a passenger. The Secretary of State has the power to curtail undesirable types of business activity.

In the Misrepresentation Act 1967, s 3, any provision in an agreement to exclude or restrict liability for a misrepresentation is effective only if the court considers the exemption or limitation clause to be fair and reasonable.

It can be seen that the different Acts have taken two broadly different approaches to exemption clauses, either to make them totally ineffective or to subject them to a test of reasonableness. The Unfair Contract Terms Act 1977 (UCTA) adopts both approaches and represents by far the biggest incursion by Parliament into controlling the use of exemption clauses and applies to a very wide range of contracts. Until the Consumer Rights Act 2015 (CRA), UCTA applied across B2B and B2C contracts so that, in relation to the latter, implied terms in relation to the sale of goods in consumer contracts could be overridden by virtue of the Sale of Goods Act 1979 s 55. Following the CRA or UCTA, the Sale of Goods Act 1979 s 55 no longer applies to consumer contracts, which are now governed by Part 2 of the CRA.

Unfair Contract Terms Act 1977 – Exemption Clauses in Non-Consumer Contracts (B2B)

Objective 6

This Act is of the utmost importance in relation to the control of exemption and limitation clauses in non-consumer contracts and the reader may therefore ask why it should be considered towards the end of this section dealing with the contents of contracts. The reason for its somewhat ignominious position is that its provisions have to be read in conjunction with the existing law and thus the Act cannot be fully understood until this aspect has first been dealt with.

Clearly the Act cuts a deep furrow right across the doctrine of freedom of contract, but some degree of care is required here since the Act does not set up a general legal structure that deals with all exemption and limitation clauses in every context. The Act does not establish general regulatory measures based on a concept of fairness but declares certain types of clauses to be totally ineffective while others are to be subject to a requirement of reasonableness.

It also needs to be established from the very start that the title of the Act is most misleading. In the first place, the Act applies to liability arising both in contract and in tort and, second, it applies to exemption and limitation clauses contained in any contractual term or notice. The Act will thus apply equally to a situation where an exemption clause is contained in a contract or to one arising where no contract is entered into, such as an exemption clause displayed in a free car park. It should also be noted that the Act applies to terms which modify expected contractual obligations; thus in ***Smith v Eric S. Bush*** [1990] 1 AC 831, the House of Lords held that a disclaimer clause in a mortgage valuation that stated that the valuation was given with no acceptance of responsibility also fell within the ambit of the Act. Apart from the operation of the CRA, which we will discuss later, certain types of contracts are specifically excluded from the operation of UCTA. These are:

1 contracts of insurance (including contracts of annuity);

2 contracts relating to the creation, transfer or termination of interests in land;

3 contracts relating to the creation, transfer or termination of rights or interests in intellectual property such as patents, trade marks, copyrights, and the like;

4 contracts relating to the formation or dissolution of a company or the constitution or rights or obligations of its members;

5 contracts relating to the creation or transfer of securities or of any right or interest therein;

6 contracts of marine salvage or towage; or charterparties of ships or hovercraft or of carriage of goods by sea, by ship or hovercraft, with the exception of liability arising by virtue of s 2(1) below, or in favour of a person acting as a consumer;

7   international supply contracts, as defined in s 26 of the Act;

8   ss 2–7 of the Act do not apply where, in an international contract, the parties agree to adopt English law as 'the proper law of the contract' (s 27).

(The last two provisions were brought in to preserve mercantile legal practice.)

1. 'Business liability'

The Act only applies to actions in contract and tort arising in relation to 'business liability'. This is defined by s 1(3) as: 'liability for breach of obligations or duties arising – (a) from things done or to be done by a person in the course of a business (whether his own business or another's); or (b) from the occupation of premises used for business purposes of the occupier'.

A 'business' is stated by s 14 to include a profession and the activities of any government department or local or public authority, nor is it necessary for the business activity to be carried on with a view to making a profit.

One further point should be noted in relation to the definition concerns the situation where a consumer holds himself out as acting in the course of business in s 12(1)(b). It would seem rather unusual for a consumer to jeopardise their protection under the CRA by taking such an action. The type of scenario possibly envisaged here is where a consumer, having acquired access to a wholesaler, represents themselves as acting in the course of a particular trade or business in order to acquire goods at a 'trade' price.

2. Liability arising in negligence

As has already been stated, the Act deals with liability arising under the tort of negligence by virtue of s 2. 'Negligence' is, however, defined by s 1(1) as a breach:

1   of any obligation arising from the express or implied terms of a contract, to take reasonable care or exercise reasonable skill in the performance of the contract;

2   of any common law duty to take reasonable care or exercise reasonable skill (but not any stricter duty);

3   of the common duty of care imposed by the Occupiers' Liability Act 1957.

This provision clearly relates to negligence as it arises in tort but also to that arising in contractual relations.

Section 2(1) provides that a person cannot by virtue of a contractual term or notice exclude or limit their liability in negligence for death or personal injury caused to another. Thus s 2(1) states:

> A person cannot by reference to any contract term or to a notice given to persons generally or to particular persons exclude or restrict his liability for death or personal injury resulting from negligence.

In respect of loss or damage caused by negligence other than that causing death or personal injury, a person cannot exclude or restrict their liability except insofar as the term or notice satisfies the requirement of reasonableness. Thus s 2(2) states:

> 'In the case of other loss or damage, a person cannot so exclude or restrict his liability for negligence except in so far as the term or notice satisfies the requirement of reasonableness.

It is of particular importance that this section does not apply to a term or a notice in consumer contracts by s 2(4), which is consistent with the fact that that UCTA no longer applies to a consumer contracts which now fall squarely within the CRA 2015.

3. Liability arising in contract

In relation to attempts to exclude liability in a contract, UCTA applies in two ways: (a) to terms that attempt to restrict liability in relation to implied statutory obligations in relation to the sale or supply of goods (UCTA ss 6 and 7); and (b) terms that attempt to exclude or limit liability for breaches of strict contractual liabilities whereas between the contracting parties one of them deals on the other's written standard terms of business (UCTA s 3).

a Excluding/restricting liability in relation to implied statutory terms.

UCTA s 6 applies to all liability and is not merely concerned with liability incurred in the course of a business, as defined by s1(3), but includes liabilities arising under any contract of sale of goods or hire-purchase agreement by way of s 6(4) and thus would extend to C2C contracts but not B2C contracts since these now fall within the Consumer Rights Act 2015. The way UCTA handles excluding restricting liability in relation to implied statutory terms is to render some as incapable of being excluded or restricted, whilst others are subject to the requirement of reasonableness.

Implied terms that cannot be excluded or restricted are the seller's implied undertaking as to title under the Sale of Goods Act 1979 s 12 and the similar provisions as to title contained within the Supply of Goods (Implied Terms) Act 1973 s 8 (relating to hire purchase). Similarly, liability for breach of the obligations under the Supply of Goods and Services Act 1982 s 2, where the possession or ownership of goods passes under or in pursuance of a contract not governed by the law of sale of goods or hire-purchase, for example, transfers of goods or contracts of hire, with regards to the implied terms as to title, cannot also be excluded or restricted by reference to any such term – UCTA s 7(3A).

With regards to the other implied terms under the Sale of Goods Act 1979, i.e. ss 13, 14 or 15 (relating to description, quality and sample) and the corresponding provisions relating to hire purchase in the Supply of Goods (Implied Terms) Act 1973 ss 9, 10, 11, liability cannot be excluded or restricted by reference to a contract term or notice, except in so far as the term satisfies the requirement of reasonableness contained within s 11 – UCTA 6(1A).

In relation to terms implied by the Supply of Goods and Services Act 1982, then any liability with respect to the goods' correspondence with description or sample, or their quality or fitness for any particular purpose (i.e. ss 2–15) , cannot be excluded or restricted by reference to such a term except in so far as the term satisfies the requirement of reasonableness in s11 – UCTA s 7(1A).

b Excluding or restricting liability on the other's written standard terms of business.

Section 3 provides a more general control of exclusion and limitation clauses, which can apply in addition to ss 6 and 7 above. The provision relates whereas between the contracting parties one of them deals on the other's standard terms of business. As against that party, the other cannot by reference to any contract term:

(a) when he himself is in breach of contract exclude or restrict any liability of his in respect of the breach; or

(b) claim to be entitled –

(i) to render a contractual performance substantially different from that which was reasonably expected of him; or

(ii) in respect of the whole or any part of his contractual obligation, to render no performance at all.

except in so far as (in any of the cases mentioned above in this subsection) the contract term satisfies the requirement of reasonableness.

Paragraph (a) above is relatively straightforward, however, paragraph (b) is a little more problematic in the sense that it appears to apply where there has been no breach of contract at all, but arises where a party seeks to rely on a term to deliver up something 'substantially different' from what he contracted to perform or even to render no performance under the contract at all. The difficulty as to how paragraph (i) operates was noted in the case of *Axa Sun Life Services plc v Campbell Martin* [2011] EWCA Civ 133 where Stanley Burnton LJ considered that the provision was aimed at the small print contained within a contract that allows a party to provide something different from that set out in the principal part of the contract. He gave as an example where a holiday operator reserved the right to vary the date, destination or flight times of holidays booked with them. Such clauses are allowed under the Act though they are subject to the test of reasonableness. The operation of paragraph (ii) is a rather puzzling provision since presumably 'to render no performance at all' amounts to a total failure of consideration. Further, if a contract gives a party free rein whether to perform the contract or not, then arguably he is not under any contractual obligation with the consequence that the requirement of reasonableness need not be satisfied.

Another issue with s 3 is that there is no definition of what is meant by the 'other's written standard terms of business'. This gives rise to the question of what a standard term contract is. At what point does a standard term contract become an individual contract, for instance? The point is problematical since many contracts are standard form contracts but require certain details to be filled in, such as quantities, etc.; the question therefore is whether the filling in of such details converts the standard form contract into a individualised contract outside of the provisions of s 3. In *Yuanda (UK) Co Ltd v WW Gear Construction Ltd* [2010] EWHC 720, it was stated that a standard form contract arises where conditions have to be standard in the sense that these are the conditions a company uses for all, or nearly all, of its contracts, apart from where blanks have to be filled in. Then again, in *Salvage Association v CAP Financial Services Ltd* [1995] FSR 654, it was stated that whether a contract is a standard form contract revolves around the extent of negotiations and variation that might take place around a standard form contract and to the extent that the actual contract between the parties moves away from the standard form contract. It is, however, important that it is not the presence of the negotiations that is important but the extent of those negotiations. In that case Forbes J. considered the question was one of context and to that extent he set out a non-exhaustive list of factors that should be considered when determining whether, as a matter of fact, it continues to be correct to describe the terms of the contract eventually agreed as the standard terms of business of the party originally putting them forward. Those factors are as follows: (i) the degree to which the standard terms are considered by the other party as part of the process of agreeing the terms of the contract; (ii) the degree to which the standard terms are 'imposed on the other party'; (iii) the relative bargaining power of the parties; (iv) the degree to which the party putting forward the standard terms is prepared to entertain negotiations with regard to the terms of the contract generally and the standard terms in particular; (v) the extent and nature of any agreed alterations to the standard terms made as a result of the negotiations; and (vi) the extent and duration of the negotiations. In *St Albans City and District Council v International Computers Ltd* [1996] 4 All ER 481, the Court of Appeal, however, was less concerned about contextual factors and considered the question was whether the parties ultimately dealt on the terms on offer regardless of whether negotiations had preceded the entering into of the contract. Arguable the distinction is one of whether the parties dealt on the standard terms, not whether the terms themselves were standard.

Then again, the test of whether a contract is a standard form contract might revolve around whether there have been 'material variations' made to the standard form contract prior to the parties entering into it as stated in **_Watford Electronics Ltd v Sanderson CFL Ltd_** [2000] 2 All ER (Comm) 984.

Despite the absence of any definition of the expression 'written standard terms of business' the Law Commission Report, Unfair Terms in Contracts, (Law Com No 292) para 4.57 resiled from providing a more precise definition stating that 'For all its faults, the phrase 'deals on the other party's written standard terms of business' is as good as any that can be achieved'.

4. Exempting liability for misrepresentation

Section 8 of UCTA amends the Misrepresentation Act 1967, s 3, and thus any term which seeks to exclude or restrict liability for misrepresentation is now subject to the requirement of reasonableness (see below). Section 3 as amended by the Unfair Contract Terms Act 1977 s 8 provides:

A broader consideration of exemption clauses in the context of misrepresentation is dealt with more fully in Chapter 9.

> If a contract contains a term which would exclude or restrict: a) any liability to which a party to a contract may be subject by reason of any misrepresentation made by him before the contract was made; or b) any remedy available to another party to the contract by reason of such a misrepresentation, that term shall be of no effect except insofar as it satisfies the requirement of reasonableness as stated in s 11(1) of the Unfair Contract Terms Act 1977; and it is for those claiming that the term satisfies that requirement to show that it does.

5. The requirement of reasonableness

It can be seen that the requirement of reasonableness stands at the core of the operation of the Act. One of the great problems with such a concept is that of actually defining what is reasonable. It is of course impractical simply to produce this requirement and leave it to the courts to formulate guidelines, and in any event the requirement could vary considerably from one case to another. The Act predicts such problems and not only attempts to explain what the requirement is but lays down guidelines for the application of the requirement.

Section 11 provides what the requirement of reasonableness is in various situations. It provides:

1 In relation to a contract term, the requirement of reasonableness for the purposes of this Part of this Act, Section 3 of the Misrepresentation Act 1967. . . is that the term shall have been a fair and reasonable one to be included having regard to the circumstances which were, or ought reasonably to have been, known to or in the contemplation of the parties when the contract was made.

2 In determining for the purposes of Section 6 or 7 above whether a contract term satisfies the requirement of reasonableness, regard shall be had in particular to the matters specified in Schedule 2 to this Act; but this subsection does not prevent the court or arbitrator from holding, in accordance with any rule of law, that a term which purports to exclude or restrict any relevant liability is not a term of the contract.

3 In relation to a notice (not being a notice having contractual effect), the requirement of reasonableness under this Act is that it should be fair and reasonable to allow reliance on it, having regard to all the circumstances obtaining when the liability arose or (but for the notice) would have arisen.

4 Where by reference to a contract term or notice a person seeks to restrict liability to a specified sum of money, and the question arises (under this or any other Act) whether the term or notice satisfies the requirement of reasonableness, regard shall be had in particular (but without prejudice to subsection (2) above in the case of contract terms) to –

(i) the resources which he could expect to be available to him for the purpose of meeting the liability should it arise; and

(ii) how far it was open to him to cover himself by insurance.

5 It is for those claiming that a contract term or notice satisfies the requirement of reasonableness to show that it does.

While it can be seen that s 11 itself provides some guidelines as to the application of the requirement of reasonableness, particularly s 11(4) (although this relates to limitation clauses only), these are only of a general nature.

In examining how the courts assess what is reasonable or not it should be first of all noticed that they may only take into account 'circumstances which were, or ought reasonably to have been, known to or in the contemplation of the parties *when the contract was made*'. Accordingly, it was held in *Stewart Gill Ltd v Horatio Myer and Co. Ltd* [1992] 2 All ER 257 (CA) that the courts determine the applicability of an exclusion clause when liability arises but retrospectively assess its reasonableness at the date the contract was made. Secondly, the burden of proving that a clause is reasonable rests on the person seeking to rely on the clause.

Since reasonableness is not specifically defined in the Act, the courts have a wide discretion to determine this issue, taking into account the circumstances of a particular case, though not circumstances that arise after the contract, such as the seriousness of the breach. The result of this 'hands-off' approach by the legislature is that the courts will have to refer to guidelines built up by way of judicial precedent.

One problem with relying on judicial impression for providing guidelines is that, although the Act has now been in operation for over 35 years, there is still a relative paucity of cases so that relying on a network of judicial guidelines is very much a hit and miss affair. This is particularly true of business contracts since in the *Photo Production* case a rebuttable presumption that the requirement of reasonableness was redundant was established, although this is considered to be a weak presumption. Thus Lord Wilberforce stated:

> in commercial matters generally, when the parties are not of unequal bargaining power, and when the risks are normally borne by insurance, not only is the case of judicial intervention undemonstrated, but there is everything to be said, and this seems to have been Parliament's intention, for leaving the parties free to apportion the risks as they think fit and for respecting their decisions.

Judicial guidelines are, of course, quite diverse and of necessity relate to the facts of particular cases; nevertheless they do provide broad points of reference which a judge may take into account. Thus, in the *Photo Production* case the question as to who is in a better position to insure against a risk was held to be a relevant consideration in assessing whether or not an exemption clause was reasonable or not. It will be noticed that s 11(4) could not be relied on for authority here since this relates only to limitation clauses, not exemption clauses.

In *Levison v Patent Steam Carpet Cleaning Co. Ltd* [1977] 3 WLR 90, the Court of Appeal considered that the clarity of a term was an important consideration, deciding that a clause stating 'All merchandise is expressly accepted at the owner's risk' was 'in the context of [the] contract, insufficiently clear or strong' to exclude liability in respect of a fundamental breach of contract. Again, in *Stag Line Ltd v Tyne Ship Repair Group Ltd* [1984] 2 Lloyd's Rep 211, it was considered that terms expressed in small print or using complex terminology may be considered to be unreasonable. Such an approach is consistent with Lord Denning's dicta in *Thornton* v *Shoe Lane Parking Ltd* and *Spurling* v *Bradshaw* when he discussed the incorporation of such terms into contracts. These considerations will be particularly relevant in consumer contracts, as in the *Levison* case. It should also be noted that in *Stag Line Ltd* v *Tyne Ship Repair Group Ltd* Orr LJ thought that it was easier to establish that a clause is reasonable when it merely attempted to limit liability rather than to exclude it altogether.

The only specific guidelines in the Act that relate to the requirement of reasonableness are to be found in Sch 2. However, these guidelines are limited to the requirement of reasonableness as it applies to ss 6(3), 7(3) and 7(4).

Schedule 2 provides:

The matters to which regard is to be had in particular for the purposes of sections 6(3), 7(3) and 7(4), 20 and 21 are any of the following which appear to be relevant –

(a) the strength of the bargaining positions of the parties relative to each other, taking into account (among other things) alternative means by which the customer's requirements could have been met;

(b) whether the customer received an inducement to agree to the term, or in accepting it had an opportunity of entering into a similar contract with other persons, but without having to accept a similar term;

(c) whether the customer knew or ought reasonably to have known of the existence and extent of the term (having regard, among other things, to any custom of the trade and any previous course of dealing between the parties);

(d) where the term excludes or restricts any relevant liability if some condition is not complied with, whether it was reasonable at the time of the contract to expect that compliance with that condition would be practicable;

(e) whether the goods were manufactured, processed or adapted to the special order of the customer.

An early case in which the requirements of reasonableness and the guidelines were considered is that of *R W Green Ltd* v *Cade Bros Farm*. It should be noted that the case was based on the provisions of the Supply of Goods (Implied Terms) Act 1973, though these are not significantly different from the relevant provisions of the 1977 Act.

R W Green Ltd v *Cade Bros Farm* [1978] 1 Lloyd's Rep 602

The facts were that there was a contract on standard written terms for the sale of seed potatoes from the potato merchants to the farmers. A clause in the contract purported to exclude liability if the buyers failed to give notice of any defects within three days of the delivery of the potatoes. Yet another clause purported to restrict the liability of the merchants to that of the contract price in respect of consequential loss. The potatoes were planted and when they had come through were found to be infected with a virus.

It was held by Griffiths J that the limitation clause in respect of the consequential loss was found to be reasonable on the basis of grounds (a) and (c) quoted above. This term had been in operation for many years and had been discussed and approved between the National Association of Seed Potato Merchants and the National Farmers' Union. As regards the exemption clause the judge found this to be unreasonable. Whilst he agreed that the clause might be reasonable as regards apparent defects, this was not the case in relation to a hidden defect such as a virus.

While the guidelines in Sch 2 are confined within the Act to ss 6(3), 7(3) and 7(4), there is evidence that the courts are willing to use them in deciding whether a particular clause is reasonable or not, as indicated in the *Levison* case (where the relative strengths of the parties were considered, although this factor did not prove decisive in the decision); and in *Woodman* v *Photo Trade Processing Ltd* (1981) 131 NLJ 933 (where the alternative means by which a customer's needs could have been met were regarded as a relevant factor). In *Flamar Interocean Ltd* v *Denmac Ltd (The Flamar Pride)* [1990] 1 Lloyd's Rep 434, Potter J stated:

> There is no requirement that Schedule 2 matters should be taken into account in dealing with reasonableness for the purpose of s 3, but it seems reasonable to do so.

In *Edmund Murray Ltd* v *BSP International Foundations Ltd* (1992) 33 Con LR 1, where in a business contract guarantees were offered to the purchaser on the basis that all other express and implied terms were excluded from the contract, the Court of Appeal simply applied the Sch 2 guidelines.

George Mitchell (Chesterhall) Ltd v Finney Lock Seeds Ltd [1983] 2 AC 803

The plaintiff farmers ordered 30 lb of cabbage seed from the sellers. The seed arrived with invoices amounting to £201.60 containing a limitation clause restricting the liability of the sellers to either replacing the seed or repaying the contract price. The farmers planted the seed which produced a useless crop when it grew, thereby causing the farmers to suffer losses amounting to some £61,000. The sellers sought to rely on the limitation clause. The House of Lords found that the clause was unreasonable, relying substantially on the fact that the suppliers very often made ex gratia payments in cases they regarded as justified, rather than rely on the clause. This conduct was regarded as indicative of the fact that the suppliers themselves did not consider their own terms to be reasonable. Second, the House of Lords considered that it was unreasonable to allow the suppliers to rely on the clause when the breach was a result of their own negligence. Third, their Lordships considered that the seller could have insured against claims resulting from the supply of defective seed and that this would not have significantly increased the contract price. Thus the plaintiffs could claim damages for their losses and were not restricted by the defendants' limitation clause.

The *George Mitchell* case was not based on the provisions of the 1977 Act but on s 55(3) of the Sale of Goods Act 1979 which contained a test of reasonableness similar to that contained in the Unfair Contract Terms Act 1977. The *George Mitchell* case is nevertheless of use in providing extra-statutory guidelines in assessing whether a clause is reasonable or not.

The House of Lords has also made an assessment of the requirement of reasonableness in relation to a clause purporting to exclude liability for negligence in two cases: *Smith* v *Eric S Bush (A Firm)* and *Harris* v *Wyre Forest District Council* which were handled as joint appeals. The two cases are of particular interest since while the facts are not so dissimilar from each other, they were decided differently by the Court of Appeal.

Smith v Eric S Bush (A Firm) and Harris v Wyre Forest District Council [1990] 1 AC 831

The plaintiff had applied to a building society for a mortgage, signing the application form which required the plaintiff to pay a fee of £38.89 for a survey valuation report from the defendants, a firm of surveyors. The application form stated that the plaintiff would be given a copy of the survey report and the valuation contained in it. The form contained an exemption clause to the effect that neither the building society nor the surveyor warranted the accuracy of the report and that no responsibility would be accepted for any inaccuracy contained within it. Eventually the plaintiff was supplied with a copy of the report in which the terms of the exemption clause were also repeated. The report valued the property at £16,500 and stated that no essential repairs were required to be done. The plaintiff did not obtain an independent survey but chose to rely on the contents of the report supplied by the defendants, eventually purchasing the property for £18,000 after accepting an advance of £3,500 from the building society. The defendants, in producing the report, had noticed that a number of chimney breasts had been removed but had not inspected whether or not the chimneys above had been adequately supported. Some one-and-a-half years later the chimneys collapsed, causing considerable damage to the property. The plaintiff sued the defendants in negligence, who sought to rely on the exemption clause as a defence. At first instance it was held that the defendants were liable. They appealed to the Court of Appeal who affirmed the first instance decision and held that the exemption clause did not satisfy the requirement of reasonableness within the Unfair Contract Terms Act 1977. The defendants appealed to the House of Lords.

In the *Harris* case, the facts were very similar except that the application form contained an exemption clause to the effect that the local authority would not accept any responsibility for the contents of the survey and valuation report and that the report produced by the surveyors engaged by the local authority was confidential and intended only to be for the benefit of the local authority. The plaintiff was warned to obtain his own independent survey, although he did not do so, preferring to rely on the report supplied to the local authority. Some three years later it transpired that the property was subject to subsidence and that repairs costing more than the purchase price were required. The plaintiff sued the local authority and the firm of surveyors in negligence, claiming that even if the exemption clause was sufficiently wide to cover such liability, it was nevertheless ineffective since it did not comply with the requirement of reasonableness under s 2(2) of the Unfair Contract Terms Act 1977. At first instance the judge decided in favour of the plaintiff. The defendants appealed to the Court of Appeal which reversed the first instance decision. The Court decided that the right to claim under the principles contained in ***Hedley Byrne & Co. Ltd v Heller and Partners Ltd*** [1964] AC 465 whereby a person may be liable for a negligent misstatement, applied only where the person making the statement had assumed responsibility for that statement. The Court of Appeal considered the effect of the exemption clause in the present case was to prevent responsibility from arising in the first instance and that since s 2(2) applied only where a duty of care already existed, the exemption clause was not subject to the requirement of reasonableness.

See Chapter 9 for Hedley Byrne & Co. Ltd v Heller and Partners Ltd.

The decision of the Court of Appeal in the ***Harris*** case was clearly very alarming since it would enable a major provision of the Unfair Contract Terms Act 1977, namely s 2(2), to be circumvented simply by constructing an exemption clause in such a way as to prevent a duty of care from arising in the first place.

The House of Lords dismissed the appeal by the valuer in the ***Smith*** case and allowed the appeal by the plaintiff purchaser in the ***Harris*** case. Their Lordships found that the surveyors/valuers in each of the cases clearly did owe a duty to take care within the principles of the ***Hedley Byrne*** case, approving the case of ***Yianni v Edwin Evans & Sons*** [1982] QB 438, and that both the exemption clauses were subject to the requirement of reasonableness contained in s 2(2). In considering the requirement of reasonableness Lord Griffiths drew attention to the four matters which should always be considered when determining the reasonableness of a clause. These were:

1 'Were the parties of equal bargaining power'?

2 'How far was it reasonably practicable for independent advice to be obtained taking into account the costs and time that may be taken up in obtaining such advice'? His Lordship

drew attention to the fact that such consideration could be of great importance to the first-time buyer with limited resources, though this would diminish as the price of the house and the resources available to the purchaser increase proportionately.

3 'How difficult is the task being undertaken for which liability is being excluded'? In the two cases the surveyors were only required to exercise such reasonable degree of care and skill as is normally required of such professional people. The result might have been different if they had been subject to a burden in excess of that particular duty.

4 'What are the practical consequences of the decision on the question of reasonableness'? The purchasers in the two cases were exposed to potentially very substantial losses which they would be unlikely to insure against. The surveyors on the other hand could easily offset their potential losses if found liable by means of professional indemnity insurance. This was an important aspect of the case since it made the concept of insurance an important consideration in assessing the requirement of reasonableness in cases involving exemption clauses. Insurance as a guideline to reasonableness is not to be found in Sch 2 to the 1977 Act but is to be found in s 11(4) which, as we have seen, relates only to limitation clauses.

A case that illustrates the approach of Lord Griffiths in his application of the requirement of reasonableness is that of *St Albans City and District Council v International Computers Ltd*.

St Albans City and District Council v International Computers Ltd (1996) The Times, 14 August (CA)

The facts of the case were that a local authority suffered serious financial losses to the extent of £1,314,846 as a result of an error in a computer program purchased from the defendants. The company's standard terms and conditions in its contract contained a limitation clause that limited its liability to £100,000 unless the 1977 Act applied. The court found that, by the Unfair Contract Terms Act 1977, s 3, a party who was in breach of contract could not rely on a term restricting liability in respect of that breach except where the term satisfied the requirement of reasonableness. In order to fall within s 3 the plaintiffs had to show that they had contracted on the defendants' 'written standard terms of business', which on the facts they were able to do. The court also found that either s 6 or s 7 applied. The court did not think that it mattered which of these two sections applied, since it considered that the relevant provisions were identical for all practical purposes. In relation to these provisions the court stated that regard had to be paid to the five matters within Sch 2 in deciding whether the requirement of reasonableness was fulfilled or not. Since the term in the defendants' contract was a limitation clause, s 11(4) applied, and in deciding the requirement here of reasonableness, regard had to be paid to the defendants' resources to meet potential liability and how far it was open to them to obtain insurance cover.

Taking all these factors into account, the court decided that the determining factors were: first, the parties were of unequal bargaining power; second, the defendants had not justified the figure of £100,000 in the limitation clause, which the court considered to be small in relation to the potential risk and the loss actually sustained; third, the defendants were insured for an aggregate sum of £50 million worldwide; and, fourth, the practical consequences. In relation to the last factor Scott Baker J thought that this followed on from the third and produced the question as to who was better able to bear the loss of the size in question, the local authority or the company? He thought that the company was well able to insure and pass the premium on to its customers. On the other hand, if the loss fell on the local authority, the losses would ultimately be borne by the local population either by way of reduced council services or by increased local taxation. He considered that it was not unreasonable that he who made the profit should carry the risk. He decided that the practical consequences favoured the local authority and that these factors outweighed the fact that local authorities, like businesspeople, should be free to negotiate their own contracts with their eyes open. The defendants failed therefore to discharge the burden imposed on them by the Act of proving that the limitation clause was a reasonable one.

The defendants appealed. However, the Court of Appeal affirmed the first instance decision that the requirement of reasonableness had not been satisfied in relation to the limitation clause. Nourse LJ adopted and applied the principles set out in *George Mitchell* v *Finney Lock Seeds Ltd*, although St Albans City and District Council was not fully successful in its action since it was held that it could not recover £484,000 in respect of community charges not received as a result of the defective computer program. The reason for this was that the Court of Appeal considered that this sum could be recovered by way of an additional charge being made of chargepayers the following year. The Council was, however, entitled to receive £685,000 for the increase in the local government precept that it had to pay out to Hertfordshire County Council since this could not be recovered from a third party – the chargepayers.

The case is important not just in relation to the court's use of the question of insurance in assessing the requirement of reasonableness, but also from the fact that the court (at first instance) took the contract price into account. The court considered that the limitation clause of £100,000 was small in relation to the overall contract price, the potential risk involved and the losses actually sustained. While it may be the case that a court would uphold a limitation clause as being reasonable if it was limited to the contract price, this may not always follow, since the actual losses may be substantially more than the contract price. The *George Mitchell* case is a good example here as the contract price of the seeds was a mere £201.60, while the losses amounted to £61,000.

The *St Albans* case is a clear indication that simply limiting liability to some arbitrary figure on the contract without regard to the possible loss will almost certainly lead to a limitation clause being struck down as being unreasonable. A serious attempt must be made to calibrate the risks that may arise under the contract. Coupled with this the party relying on a limitations clause should assess the question of insurance and who should insure against the loss in a realistic manner, in accordance with the nature of the contract. Any excess imposed by an insurance company might also be a relevant factor in determining the level of liability set out in a limitation clause.

In the *Photo Production* case it was stated by Lord Wilberforce that:

> in commercial matters generally, when the parties are not of unequal bargaining power, and when the risks are normally borne by insurance, not only is the case of judicial intervention undemonstrated, but there is everything to be said . . . for leaving the parties free to apportion the risks as they think fit and for respecting their decisions.

This statement has been taken as creating a policy that in contracts between businesspeople there was a rebuttable presumption that the requirement of reasonableness was redundant. There is now clear evidence that the courts favour a non-interventionist approach in relation to striking down exemption clauses on the grounds of reasonableness in a commercial context. The *Schenkers* case below is one example but the trend could also be seen in *Monarch Airlines Ltd* v *London Luton Airport Ltd* [1997] CLC 698 where a clause to exclude liability for unintentional damage to aircraft by the airport authorities was held to be reasonable. In these and subsequent cases it is clear that the fact the contracts are entered into by experienced businesspersons and therefore deemed to be of equal bargaining power is a significant fact that the courts take into account. In *Watford Electronics Ltd* v *Sanderson CFL Ltd* [2001] EWCA Civ 317, the Court of Appeal stated that a clause in the defendant's standard terms and conditions exempting liability for indirect and consequential losses, together with a clause limiting general loss to the price of the contract, were reasonable given that the contract had been negotiated by businessmen of equal bargaining power. The court emphasised that unless there is clear evidence that one party has taken an unfair advantage of the other or the term is so unreasonable that it could not have been properly considered by the other party the courts will not interfere. Chadwick LJ stated:

> Where experienced businessmen representing substantial companies of equal bargaining power negotiate an agreement, they may be taken to have had regard to the matters known to them. They should, in my view, be taken to be the best judge of the commercial fairness of the agreement which they have made; including the fairness of each of the terms in that agreement. They should be taken to be the best judge on the question whether the terms are reasonable. The court should not assume that either is likely to commit his company to an agreement which he thinks is unfair, or which he thinks includes unreasonable terms. Unless satisfied that one party has, in effect, taken unfair advantage of the other – or that the term is so unreasonable that it cannot have been understood or considered – the court should not interfere . . .

A similar approach was taken in *Granville Oil and Chemicals Ltd* v *Davies Turner and Co. Ltd* [2003] EWCA Civ 570 where the appellants were an international freight forwarding company, whilst the respondents manufactured and exported paint products. The appellants agreed to carry a consignment of paint from Kuwait to the respondent's warehouse in Rotherham. The contract was a standard British International Freight Association contract that contained a term that any claims under the contract had to be made in writing and within 14 days (clause 30A). A second term required that any legal action under the contract had to be brought within nine months of the event giving rise to the cause of action. 'All risks' insurance cover was provided by the appellants for the transit of the goods from Kuwait. The goods were damaged in transit and the respondents made a claim in writing within 14 days so as to comply with clause 30A and the appellants then made a claim under the insurance policy on behalf of the respondents; however, the underwriters rejected the claim. The appellants did not inform the respondents about the claim being rejected until one day before the nine-month time limit set out in clause 30B. The respondents only began their legal proceedings nearly three months after the nine-month time limit had expired, alleging breach of contract for the damage to the goods and failure to provide insurance. At first instance the judge considered that clause 30B failed to satisfy the requirement of reasonableness under UCTA, s 11 since he considered it could be used to conceal facts giving rise to a cause of action giving rise to a fraud.

The Court of Appeal disagreed with the judge at first instance that the clause could be used to conceal fraud and considered that the clause was a fair and reasonable one at the time the contract was entered into. The Court of Appeal considered that the contract was a commercial one made between businessmen who could have contracted on other terms and made their insurance arrangements. The parties were of equal bargaining power and the respondents should have known of the time bar, which had been sufficiently brought to their attention. The court considered the nine-month period to be a reasonable one as this allowed any losses or damage to be established on delivery of the goods and this provided the respondents with time to consider bringing the proceedings. With regard to the claim for failure to insure the court stated that the appellants had acted as agents for the respondents in providing insurance and the making of any subsequent claim on their behalf. The fact that the appellants had not informed the respondents that there was no insurance cover amounted to a breach of duty and this breach of duty was an ongoing breach. Thus the time limit for claiming for breach of a failure to insure would, under clause 30B, only begin to run once they had been informed of the fact that there was no insurance cover. The court therefore considered the time limit in relation to this claim was fair and reasonable. Echoing the comments of Chadwick LJ in *Watford Electronics Ltd* Gibson LJ stated:

> Generally speaking, where a party well able to look after itself enters into a commercial contract and, with the full knowledge of all the relevant circumstances, willingly accepts the terms of the contract which provides for the apportionment of the financial risks of that transaction, I think it is very likely that those terms will be held to be fair and reasonable.

Similarly, Tucker LJ stated:

> The 1977 Act obviously plays a very important role in protecting vulnerable consumers from the effects of draconian contract terms. But I am less enthusiastic about its intrusion into contracts between commercial parties of equal bargaining strengths, who should be considered capable of being able to make contracts of their choosing and expect to be bound by their terms.

The practice of non-intervention in commercial contracts where the parties were of equal bargaining power has also been followed in the cases of *Frans Maas (UK) Ltd* v *Samsung Electronics (UK) Ltd* [2004] EWHC 1502 (Comm) and *Sterling Hydraulics Ltd* v *Dichtomatik Ltd* [2007] 1 Lloyd's Rep 8. It should be noted that where the parties are not of equal bargaining power the courts can and do overturn exemption clauses as being unreasonable. An example of such a decision arose in *Motours Ltd* v *Euroball (West Kent) Ltd* [2003] EWHC 614 (QB) where the judge considered that a clause excluding liability for consequential losses was unreasonable on the basis that the parties were not of equal bargaining power and the terms of the contract had not been negotiated. However, it is worth being reminded that the question of reasonableness is really a matter of discretion and considering a whole range of circumstances. This results in a reluctance of appellate courts to overturn first instance decisions. This was forthrightly put by Lord Bridge in *George Mitchell* v *Finney Lock Seeds* where he stated:

> It may, therefore, be appropriate to consider how an original decision as to what is 'fair and reasonable' made in the application of any of these provisions should be approached by an appellate court. It would not be accurate to describe such a decision as an exercise of discretion. But a decision under any of the provisions referred to will have this in common with the exercise of a discretion, that, in having regard to the various matters to which the modified section 55(5) of the Act of 1979, or section 11 of the Act of 1977 direct attention, the court must entertain a whole range of considerations, put them in the scales on one side or the other, and decide at the end of the day on which side the balance comes down. There will sometimes be room for a legitimate difference of judicial opinion as to what the answer should be, where it will be impossible to say that one view is demonstrably wrong and the other demonstrably right. It must follow, in my view, that, when asked to review such a decision on appeal, the appellate court should treat the original decision with the utmost respect and refrain from interference with it unless satisfied that it proceeded upon some erroneous principle or was plainly and obviously wrong.

An application of this approach can possibly be seen in *Regus (UK) Ltd* v *Epcot Solutions Ltd* [2008] EWCA Civ 361.

Regus (UK) Ltd v *Epcot Solutions Ltd* [2008] EWCA Civ 361

The facts of the case were that Regus Ltd provided serviced office accommodation in a building near to Heathrow in which Epcot had taken space. Regus subsequently closed the building and relocated Epcot to another building it owned at Stockley Park. This relocation process gave rise to a claim for relocation expenses. Epcot complained that the air conditioning system at the new location was inadequate and therefore withheld fees due to Regus. This gave rise to Regus' action against Epcot for its fees. Regus' standard terms set out in clause 23(3) provided that Regus would 'not in any circumstances have any liability for loss of business, loss of profits, loss of anticipated savings, loss of or damage to data, third party claims or any consequential loss'. Furthermore, clause 23(4) provided that R's liability would in any event be capped at 125 per cent of the fees or £50,000, whichever was higher. Epcot claimed that the exemption clause under clause 23(3) and the limitation clause under clause 23(4) were unreasonable and unenforceable under the Unfair Contract Terms Act 1977. The judge at first instance found that the air conditioning was indeed defective so that Regus was in breach of contract. Clause 23 in principle and as a whole was unreasonable in that it excluded any remedy at all and on that basis was unreasonable and unenforceable under the 1977 Act. Epcot, however, also claimed that even if clause 23(3) left room for a remedy by way of a reduction in the fees paid by Epcot to Regus, it still failed the statutory requirement of reasonableness because the clause operated 'in any circumstances' including circumstances in which the loss had been caused by a deliberate act of Regus. Epcot submitted that Regus' refusal to repair the air conditioning amounted to a deliberate act in an attempt to cut costs. Regus appealed.

The Court of Appeal upheld the appeal since Epcot conceded that clause 23 did allow for a remedy based on fees being reduced to take into account the loss in the value of services provided by Regus. Thus the judge had been wrong to find that clause 23 was unreasonable because it left Epcot with no remedy for the lack of air conditioning. The loss suffered by Epcot could be measured by assessing how much less valuable the same services would have been if the offices had not been air conditioned or had only been partially air conditioned. Epcot had alleged that despite this the clause was still unreasonable because the clause operated 'in any circumstances' and thus excluded liability for losses caused by deliberate acts or even fraud. The Court of Appeal refuted the interpretation that clause 23 was intended to cover liability for fraud, malice or anything akin to these types of misconduct. Certainly the decision by Regus not to repair the air conditioning system was a deliberate act but it was not one that was calculated to harm its customers. Whilst the actions of Regus may be regarded as negligent, this was not a dishonest or malicious act.

Following on from Lord Bridge's comment above, the Court of Appeal was satisfied that the trial judge had 'proceeded upon some erroneous principle or was plainly and obviously wrong' and thus felt able to look again at the question of reasonableness in relation to the clause. The Court of Appeal considered that in principle it was entirely reasonable for Regus to restrict damages for loss of profits and consequential losses from the categories of loss for which it would become liable when in breach of contract. On the question of inequality of bargaining power the court considered that the history of negotiations made it clear that no such inequality existed between the parties. Epcot's chief executive was 'an intelligent and experienced businessman' who was fully aware of Regus' standard terms and conditions of business. He had previously contracted on similar terms and, indeed, had used similar standard terms and conditions in Epcot's business previously. Epcot could have used other premises and had previously done so. Regus did not have a local monopoly as regards such business premises. The Court of Appeal also noted that Regus had advised its customers to take out their own insurance against business losses and that this was a logical way of proceeding since it was impossible for Regus to assess the type and level of losses that could be sustained by its various customers. Furthermore, it was more economical for their customers to arrange their own insurance and in any event if Regus did take out such insurance the cost would be passed on to their customers anyway. The Court of Appeal therefore considered that clause 23(3) met the requirement of reasonableness.

Apart from the issue of the reasonableness of clause 23(3) there was one other issue that was the subject of appeal. In the first instance decision the trial judge had held that it was not open for the court to sever a clause that failed to comply with the Unfair Contract Terms Act 1977. This was important since it meant that the judge accepted Epcot's contention that the whole clause, both the exemption and limitation elements, stood or fell together under the requirement of reasonableness. In the Court of Appeal, Epcot conceded that clause 23(4) was severable, the intention being to make the upper limit of £50,000 operative at least since if the two sub-clauses stood together then they would have no claim under clause 23(4). The Court of Appeal considered that clause 23(4) was an independent clause and as a limitation clause had a different purpose from the exemption clause. The Court of Appeal followed the decision in *Watford Electronics Ltd v Sanderson CFL Ltd* [2001] EWCA Civ 317 where the Court of Appeal held that where clauses consisted of two distinct terms the requirement of reasonableness had to be considered in relation to each of them. The Court of Appeal in *Regus* concluded that the limitation clause, rather than an exemption clause, served a different purpose. It was an independent clause and entirely reasonable.

The *Regus* case again reinforces the non-interventionist approach that the courts take in commercial contracts and makes an exclusion clause in such a contract highly unlikely to be struck down for want of the requirement of reasonableness.

Another area where a reluctance to intervene also seems set to continue is in relation to standard-form contracts that are based on trade practice. Such contracts have usually evolved over many years and are normally regarded as balanced and fair. It should also be borne in mind that such contracts often operate internationally, and therefore for a court to interfere with such a contract in holding that a particular clause is unreasonable is likely to have very wide implications. Such a situation can be seen in the *Granville Oil* case, above; however, the following case also provides an example.

Overland Shoes Ltd v *Schenkers Ltd* [1998] 1 Lloyd's Rep 498

Schenkers Ltd were worldwide freight carriers and had entered into a contract to transport a consignment of shoes that Overland Shoes Ltd ('Overland') were importing from China. The contract was based on the standard terms and conditions of the British International Freight Association and included a 'no set-off' clause, as follows: '23A: The customers [Overland] shall pay to the company [Schenkers] in cash or as otherwise agreed all sums immediately when due, without reduction or deferment on account of any claim, counter claim or set off.'

In 1995, Schenkers claimed certain freight charges from Overland, which sought to set off against the sums which Schenkers owed with regard to VAT. Schenkers refused to allow this set-off, pointing out clause 23A. Overland alleged that this clause was an exclusion clause and that it was unreasonable under the Unfair Contract Terms Act 1977 and therefore unenforceable. Overland argued that the no set-off clause was manifestly unjust and that over a long period of trading the clause had rarely been applied in practice. Overland also pointed to the fact that there was inequality of bargaining power between the parties. Schenkers responded that in carrying out the contract a high level of disbursements had to be made and that this justified the inclusion of the clause.

It was held that the no set-off clause fell within s 3 as extended by s 13 (*see* below), as established in *Stewart Gill Ltd* v *Horatio Myer & Co. Ltd* [1992] 2 All ER 257, and was therefore subject to the requirement of reasonableness. The Court of Appeal considered that Schenkers Ltd had satisfied this requirement on the basis that the clause was in common use and well known in the shipping industry. It was a clause that was used by many trade associations around the world and was recognised as being well balanced, fair and reasonable. The level of disbursements which Schenkers had to pay within the contract, whilst not conclusive, was a factor in deciding the reasonableness of a clause. The court considered that trade custom was an important factor to take into account where the inequality of bargaining power between the parties was insignificant. The court distinguished the decision in *George Mitchell (Chesterhall) Ltd* v *Finney Lock Seeds Ltd* as regards the application of the clause in practice. The fact that the clause was rarely applied was of no significance. On this basis the Court of Appeal appears to have missed the point in the *George Mitchell* case. It was not the fact that the clause was never applied that was significant, but the fact that it was applied inconsistently. The clause in the *George Mitchell* case was applied in some cases but not applied in others where the sellers considered that a farmer's claim was 'genuine' and 'justified'.

The decision clearly provides additional criteria, which a court may take into account in deciding whether the requirement of reasonableness has been satisfied or not. The case contains one word of warning, however, first set out by Lord Bridge in the *George Mitchell* case:

> It may, therefore, be appropriate to consider how an original decision as to what is 'fair and reasonable' made in the application of any of these provisions should be approached by an appellate court . . . in my view when asked to review such a decision on appeal, the appellate court should treat the original decision with utmost respect and refrain from interference with it unless satisfied that it proceeded upon some erroneous principle or was plainly and obviously wrong.

On this basis careful consideration should be given to an appeal based on a trial judge's decision as to whether the requirement of reasonableness has been satisfied or not. It would seem that the prospects for success are, to say the least, very limited.

The non-interventionist policy of the courts in commercial contracts is not an absolute one and the courts do consider the nature of the risks in the contract, particularly with regard to the incidence of insurance, and indeed the nature of the contracts themselves in arriving at a decision as to whether a term is reasonable or not. In relation to the former the courts are willing to strike exemption clauses where the courts consider that the allocation of risk under the contract is unreasonable. In *Overseas Medical Supplies Ltd* v *Orient Transport Services Ltd* [1999] CLC 1243, the claimant contracted with a firm of freight forwarders to transport certain equipment to Iran. It was the responsibility of the defendant to arrange insurance. When the claimant attempted to claim for the loss of the equipment the defendant attempted to use a limitation clause in the contract to limit its liability to approximately £600, the loss sustained by the claimant being £8,590. At first instance it was considered that the limitation clause was reasonable though not in respect of liability for breach of contract for failure to provide insurance. The Court of Appeal agreed since the effect of the clause was that the claimant lost both the opportunity to recover the losses from the defendant and the opportunity to claim under the insurance policy.

Similarly, in *Britvic Soft Drinks* v *Messer UK Ltd* [2002] EWCA Civ 548, the Court of Appeal considered that an attempt to exclude liability for the supply of contaminated carbon dioxide gas to be used in the manufacture of soft drinks was unreasonable in that the contamination itself was not an issue that would have been contemplated. Similarly, in *Bacardi-Martini Beverages Ltd* v *Thomas Hardy Packaging* [2002] 2 Lloyd's Rep 379, it was considered that where loss occurred due to a manufacturing error a supplier should not be able to simply avoid liability and transfer the risk to the purchaser. Clearly the risk is completely outside the control of the purchaser in these circumstances and therefore to transfer the risk in this way is largely regarded as unreasonable. Again the position is not a strict one since the nature of the contract may determine the approach of the courts. It seems that in certain industries there is almost a trade usage as to where liability will lie. Of particular note here is the computing industry where it is fully accepted that significant consequential losses may arise from faulty software, which is notoriously difficult to develop without faults arising. Thus in *SAM Business Systems Ltd v Hedley and Co.* [2003] 1 All ER (Comm) 465, the judge upheld the exclusion clause for consequential losses as being reasonable, justifying this on the basis of the supplier remaining liable for direct losses, although this was subject to a limitation clause confining the loss to the price of the software. This type of commercial arrangement was usual and well known in the computer software industry where defects were not uncommon and thus it was considered appropriate and reasonable to limit liability for direct losses and to exclude liability for consequential losses in this way.

Before leaving the discussion of the requirement of reasonableness, it should be noted that in relation to limitation clauses the clause must state clearly and unambiguously the scope of the limitation. In other words, the *contra proferentem* rule will apply. A case which applies the principle in this context is that of *Bovis Construction (Scotland) Ltd v Whatlings Construction Ltd* [1995] NPC 153 (HL), where there was a contract for the construction of a concert hall in Glasgow. The contract between the plaintiffs (the main contractors) and the defendants (subcontractors) was contained in a printed form and a number of letters. In the contract there was agreement to limit the defendants' liability to £100,000 for 'time-related costs'.

The defendants were eventually given notice by the plaintiffs that they did not consider the defendants' work to have been carried out with due diligence and terminated the contract. Subsequently the plaintiffs brought an action for breach of contract, claiming damages amounting to £2,741,000. The defendants sought to rely on the limitation clause limiting their liability to £100,000.

At first instance the defendants' argument was upheld, but this decision was overturned by the Court of Appeal. The defendants then appealed to the House of Lords. The case in the House of Lords turned on the interpretation of the limitation clause. Their Lordships affirmed the principle that limitation clauses had to state 'clearly and unambiguously' what the scope of the limitation was. The House of Lords also confirmed that limitation clauses were not to be construed as strictly as exemption clauses, following Lord Wilberforce's comments in *Ailsa Craig Fishing Co. Ltd v Malvern Fishing Co. Ltd* [1983] 1 All ER 101 when he stated:

> Clauses of limitation are not to be regarded by the court with the same hostility as clauses of exclusion, this is because they must be related to other contractual terms, in particular to the risks to which the defending party may be exposed, the remuneration he receives and possibly also the opportunity of the other party to insure.

On this basis the House of Lords took the view that a clause that limited liability in respect of 'time-related costs' was not wide enough to cover losses that resulted from a repudiatory breach of contract. The clause was only intended to cover losses that arose from delays in the *time* of performance of the contract, not from breaches that in fact amounted to 'non-performance'. Thus their Lordships found that the losses sustained by the plaintiffs fell outside the scope of the limitation clauses and they were therefore entitled to recover damages for all their losses.

For more on performance of a contract, refer to Chapter 13.

6. Anti-evasion provisions

The Act has four anti-evasion provisions within it designed to prevent the Act from being circumvented. The first – unreasonable indemnity clauses falling under s 4 – has already been considered above. The others are secondary contracts, choice of law clauses and varieties of exemption clauses.

(a) Secondary contracts (s 10)

This provides:

> A person is not bound by any contract term prejudicing or taking away rights of his which arise under, or in connection with the performance of, another contract, so far as those rights extend to the enforcement of another's liability which this Part of this Act prevents that other from excluding or restricting.

While the terminology seems somewhat obscure, the provision appears to apply where two related contracts are entered into, the second attempting indirectly to exclude liability in respect of rights which a person could have enforced directly in the first contract.

(b) Choice of law clauses (s 27(2))

One method of evading the provisions of the Act could be to nominate the laws of a foreign country as being the proper law applying to the contract – where the laws of that country contain no rules governing the use of exemption clauses, or where that other country's rules are less strict. Section 27(2) provides:

> This Act has effect notwithstanding any contract term which applies or purports to apply the law of some country outside the United Kingdom, where (either or both) –
>
> (a) the terms appear to the court, or arbitrator or arbiter to have been imposed wholly or mainly for the purpose of enabling the party imposing it to evade the operation of this Act; or
>
> (b) in the making of the contract one of the parties dealt as consumer, and he was then habitually resident in the United Kingdom, and the essential steps necessary for the making of the contract were taken there, whether by him or by others on his behalf.

(c) Varieties of exemption clauses (s 13)

This states:

1 To the extent that this Part of this Act prevents the exclusion or restriction of any liability it also prevents –
   (a) making the liability or its enforcement subject to restrictive or onerous conditions;
   (b) excluding or restricting any right or remedy in respect of the liability, or subjecting a person to any prejudice in consequence of his pursuing any such right or remedy;
   (c) excluding or restricting rules of evidence or procedure; and (to that extent) Sections 2 and 5 to 7 also prevent excluding or restricting liability by reference to terms and notices which exclude or restrict the relevant obligation or duty.

2 But an agreement in writing to submit present or future differences to arbitration is not to be treated under this Part of this Act as excluding or restricting any liability.

B2B Contracts

Consumer Rights Act 2015

Terms/Notices Rendered Totally Ineffective	Terms Notices subject to the Requirement of Reasonableness

Negligence – s 2(1)
Liability for death or bodily injury caused by negligence cannot be excluded or restricted by any contractual term or notice.

Negligence – s 2(2)
Liability for loss or damage, other than death or bodily injury cannot be excluded or restricted by any contractual term or notice except in so far as the term or notice satisfies the requirment of reasonableness.

Sale of goods/Hire Purchase – s 6(1)
The implied terms as to title (SOGA 1979 s 12); SG(IT)A 1973 s 8) cannot be excluded or restricted by any contractual term or notice.

Sale of goods/Hire purchase – s 6(1A)
Liability for breach of the obligations arising from SGA 1979 ss13, 14 or 15 of the 1979 Act (implied terms as to description, quality or sample, or the SG(IT) 1973 ss 9, 10 or 11 of the 1973 Act (the corresponding terms hire purchase), cannot be excluded or restricted by reference to a contract term except in so far as the term satisfies the requirement of reasonableness.

Contracts for transfer of goods/hire– s 7(3A)
SSGA 1982 s2 implied term as to title where the possession or ownership of goods passes under or in pursuance of a contract not governed by the law relating to the sale of goods or hire purchase, for example transfer of goods or hire, cannot be excluded or restricted by reference to any contract term.

Contracts for transfer of goods/hire – s 7(1A)
Implied terms as to decription, quality and sample under the SSGA 1982 ss 2-15 cannot be excluded or restricted by reference to such a term except in so far as the term satisfies the requirement of reasonableness.

Contracts for transfer of goods/hire – s 7(1A)
Implied terms as to decription, quality and sample under the SSGA 1982 ss 2–15 cannot be excluded or restricted by reference to such a term except in so far as the term satisfies the requirement of reasonableness

Liability arising in contract – s 3
As between the contracting parties where one of them deals on the other's written standard terms of business then against that party, the other cannot by reference to any contract term –

(a) when himself in breach of contract, exclude or restrict any liability of his in respect of the breach; or

(b) claim to be entitled –

   (i) to render a contractual performance substantially different from that which was reasonably expected of him, or

   (ii) in respect of the whole or any part of his contractual obligation, to render no performance at all,

Except in so far as (in any of the cases mentioned above in this subsection) the contract term satisfies the requirement of reasonableness.

No definition of "standard terms of business" but see *Yuanda (UK) Co Ltd v WW Gear Construction Ltd* *Salvage Association v CAP Financial Services Ltd*

Misrepresentation – s 8
This substitutes the Misrepresentation Act 1967 s 3 so that any term or notice that seeks to exclude liabiloity for misrepresentation or any remedy by reason of any contractual term or notice has no effect except in so far that it satisfies the requirement of reasonableness.

Figure 8.2

On the face of things it seems strange that Parliament in producing an Act that seeks to control the use of exemption and limitation clauses did not actually define what these are within the Act. The undoubted reason for this and the consequent drafting of s 13 is to curtail the ingenuity of drafters of contracts. For instance, in the case of **Phillips Products v Hyland** [1987] 2 All ER 620 (CA), as discussed earlier, it was seen how an exemption clause was dressed up as an indemnity clause. Similarly, in **Smith v Eric S Bush (A Firm)** [1990] 1 AC 831, it was claimed that the disclaimer contained in the mortgage application form did not provide a defence for a breach of the surveyor's duty of care but prevented the duty of care from arising in the first place. This was therefore an attempt not only to exclude s 2 but also to circumvent the Act in its entirety. The defendants were therefore attempting to set up an exemption clause not as a defensive measure but to prevent a primary obligation arising in the first place, thereby placing the clause outside the Act, an attempt that was resoundingly rejected by the House of Lords.

The way in which s 13 widens the scope of the Act was also considered in **Stewart Gill Ltd v Horatio Myer and Co. Ltd** [1992] 2 All ER 257 (CA) where Lord Donaldson summed up the position by stating:

> It is a trite fact (as contrasted by trite law) that there are more ways than one of killing a cat. Section 13 addresses this problem.

Consumer Rights Act 2015 Part 2 – Unfair Terms in Consumer Contracts (B2C)

Introduction and history

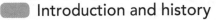

Objective 7

The first inroad into the regulation of unfair terms in consumer contract arose out of the European Directive 93/13 on unfair terms in consumer contracts adopted by the Council of Ministers in 1993. This Directive was first implemented by way of the Unfair Terms in Consumer Contracts Regulations 1994.The 1994 Regulations were subsequently repealed and replaced by the Unfair Terms in Consumer Contracts Regulations 1999 (UTCCR). Neither of these two sets of regulations made any attempt to reconcile the overlaps and conflicts that arose between the regulations, the common law UCTA. The result was that the law regulating unfair terms became unnecessarily complicated and difficult to understand since the two had similar, but not identical effects, whilst using different terminology. This has resulted in a highly technical legal regime that was confusing to consumers and businesses alike. One reason for this confusion is that the UTCCR made use of European concepts that were largely alien to English law and were often confusing in their own right. At the same time the case levelled against UCTA was that it used unnecessarily complex language that taxed even lawyers never mind the poor layperson!

In 2001, the Department of Trade and Industry asked the Law Commission to rewrite the law of unfair contract terms so that it provided a clearer and more accessible single regime. This culminated in the Law Commission publishing its report *Unfair Terms in Consumer Contracts* in February 2005 (Law Com No. 292).

In arriving at its report the Law Commission also provided a draft Act ('Act') that rewrote the law in such a way that, not only did it envelope UCTA and UTCCR, but also it provided a legal framework that covered England and Wales, Northern Ireland and Scotland. The report, therefore, *inter alia*, set out to provide a unified regime for consumer contracts and provisions for the preservation of protection given by UCTA in business contracts, and extended protection against unfair terms to small businesses and not just consumers.

The recommendations of the Law Commission were largely accepted by the government; however, any progress towards reform was postponed pending the European Union's Consumer Rights Directive (CRD) 2011/83/EU ('CRD'). In fact the CRD made only minor adjustments to the law in this area, nevertheless the Department of Business, Innovation and Skills asked the Law Commission to review its previous recommendations contained in its 2005 report in the light of the CRD. The Law Commission subsequently published an Issues Paper in July 2012, 'Unfair Terms in Consumer Contracts – a new approach'. This and the following consultation culminated in the Law Commission issuing its advice paper: 'Unfair Consumer Contracts Advice to the Department for Business, Innovation and Skills (March 2013)'. Following this on Thursday 23 January 2014 the Consumer Rights Act was finally introduced to the House of Commons and subsequently the Consumer Rights Act 2015 was enacted in March 2015, coming into effect in October 2015.

The intention of the Act is therefore to reform and consolidate the vast majority of UK consumer law, including provisions relating to the supply of goods, the supply of services, unfair contract terms, defective digital content and enforcement powers. The reforms relating to supply of goods, digital content and services are contained within Part 1 of the Act which we discussed in Chapter 7. As regards exemption clauses and unfair terms the Act drew together the law governing exemption clauses and unfair terms in consumer contracts into a single legislative regime contained within Part 2 of the Act. It is important to note that much of the case law that applied to the UTCCR is equally applicable since much of the language used in Directive 93/13 and the UTCCR is largely preserved within the CRA Part 2.

The Application of the CRA 2015 Part 2

As already indicated the aim of Part 2 ss 61–76 of the Act is to clarify and consolidate the existing legislation on unfair terms as they apply to consumers.

Contracts and Notices Covered by Part 2

Section 61 sets out the scope of Part of the CRA as follows:

1　This Part applies to a contract between a trader and a consumer.

2　This does not include a contract of employment or apprenticeship.

3　A contract to which this Part applies is referred to in this Part as a 'consumer contract'.

4　This Part applies to a notice to the extent that it –

- relates to rights or obligations as between a trader and a consumer; or
- purports to exclude or restrict a trader's liability to a consumer.

5　This does not include a notice relating to rights, obligations or liabilities as between an employer and an employee.

6　It does not matter for the purposes of subsection (4) whether the notice is expressed to apply to a consumer, as long as it is reasonable to assume it is intended to be seen or heard by a consumer.

7　A notice to which this Part applies is referred to in this Part as a 'consumer notice'.

8　In this section, 'notice' includes an announcement, whether or not in writing, and any other communication or purported communication.

The Act therefore applies to contracts between a 'trader' and a 'consumer'. These expressions are the same as for Part 1 of the Act, so that a 'trader' is defined in s 2(2) as a 'person acting for purposes relating to that person's trade, business, craft or profession, whether acting personally or through another person acting in the trader's name or on the trader's behalf'. A 'consumer' is defined in s 2(3) means an 'individual acting for purposes that are wholly or mainly outside that individual's trade, business, craft or profession'. Clearly the expression 'individual' means that limited companies and partnerships are excluded from the operation of Part 2; however, on the face of things a sole trader will also be an individual but of course in order to gain the protection of the Act the individual has to be acting outside of that 'individual's trade, business, craft or profession'. It should be noted, however, that if a trader alleges that 'an individual was not acting for purposes wholly or mainly outside the individual's trade, business, craft or profession', then the trader, by s 2(4), must prove it. The question that arises here is whether there is a difference in terms of an individual having protection within the CRA, if he is acting outside of his business –s 2(3) or whether he is not acting wholly or mainly outside of his business, i.e. acting exclusively for business purposes under s 2(4)? The 'wholly or mainly' label seems to be covering situations where a contract may be partly private and partly business purposes. The Law Commission in its report Unfair Terms in Contracts, Law, Com 292 at para 3.38 recommended that, in the case of an individual entering into a contract for 'mixed partly private and partly business purposes', it should be left to the court to determine the main, or predominant, purpose of the contract and hence whether it is a consumer contract. The effect therefore is that if an individual purchases a car for such mixed purpose, then it is for the court to decide what the 'predominant purposes' and therefore whether or not the individual is a consumer. Thus the circumstances as already examined in *Peter Symmons & Co.* v *Cook, R & B Customs Brokers Co. Ltd* v *United Dominions Trust Ltd* and *Stevenson* v *Rogers* above are clearly pertinent in this context. In *Overy* v *Paypal (Europe) Ltd* [2012] EWHC 2659 (QB), however, it was held that a contract would be only be treated as being outside of a person's trade or business if the business purpose was insignificant or negligible and the contract was centred mainly on satisfying a consumer need. The purpose underpinning the contract therefore becomes important. The judge, however, stressed that in this case the representations made at the time of the opening of the contract were significant in coming to a conclusion that the consumer in that case was acting for business purposes. In other cases, if it can be established that the predominant purpose was for consumer use, then the conclusion is that the consumer will have the benefit of the CRA. Clearly the decision is for the court in the circumstances of the particular case.

Agency situations can bring about particular difficulties is deciding whether or not an individual is a consumer. In *Domsalla (t/a Domsalla Building Services)* v *Dyason* [2007] All ER 255, the defendant's house had burnt down and his insurers accepted liability to rebuild and reinstate the property. The insurers appointed a firm to act as contract administrator and loss adjuster. On the advice of that firm the defendant signed a contract as 'agent' with the building contractor, the claimant. It was argued that as the defendant was acting as an agent for the insurance company, he could not be a consumer within the UTCCR. It was held that the defendant as 'agent' undertook personal liabilities and was liable to the builder claimant both as principal and agent and therefore fell within the protection of the UTCCR. It must be said, however, that in the majority of cases where a consumer acts as an agent for a non-consumer, then the contract will not normally be regarded as a consumer contract.

Domsalla (t/a Domsalla Building Services) v Dyason is discussed later in this chapter.

Terms and notices within the ambit of the CRA

Section 61 sets out the scope of Part 2 of the Act and covers 'consumer contracts' between a trader and a consumer that relate to their rights and obligations or which purport to exclude or restrict the trader's liability to a consumer. The expression 'consumer contracts' also includes consumer notices that are both contractual and non-contractual consumer notices. For this purpose a 'consumer notice' includes any announcement or other communication, whether or not in writing (s 61(8)), which it is reasonable to assume is intended to be seen or heard by a consumer (s 61(6)). Non-contractual consumer notices (e.g. a sign in a car park) do not require an exchange of consideration as required in a contract. By s 61(2) and (5), contracts of employment are not covered by these provisions as these have their own specific legislative regime. It follows therefore that the CRA applies to any consumer contracts or notices other than contracts and notices falling within the employment exclusion. The CRA could therefore apply to contracts relating to land: *London Borough of Newham* v *Khatan* [2004] EWCA Civ 55.

Whilst s 61 sets out the range of consumer contracts and notices to which the Part 2 applies, one should notice that by s 73 Part 2 is disapplied so that the CRA does not apply to a term of a contract, or to a notice, to the extent that it reflects mandatory statutory or regulatory provisions (s 73(1)a). Thus, for instance, the implied terms in Part 1 (such as satisfactory quality, etc.) cannot by definition be declared to be unfair and, indeed, by s 31 such implied terms are entrenched so that they cannot be excluded or restricted. Similarly provisions or principles of an international convention to which the United Kingdom or the EU is a party also cannot be deemed to be unfair (s 73(1)b.

In some consumer contracts the parties may attempt to avoid the provisions of the CRA by opting for the governing law to be the law of a country or territory other than a European Economic Area state. In such a situation, s 74 provides that where the consumer contract has a close connection with the UK, Part 2 will continue to apply despite that choice.

The basic principles within Part 2 – Section 62

The Act provides general rules regarding fairness in contract terms and notices and as such it is very much broader in application than UCTA which is confined to exemption and limitation clauses. Thus, Part 2 applies to any term that might be considered unfair, such as penalty clauses, as well as unfair exemption or limitation clauses. Part 2 therefore seeks to regulate unfair terms generally and its ambit is not restricted to those contained within Schedule 2 Part 1.

The regulation of unfair terms is to be found within s 62 which provides:

1 An unfair term of a consumer contract is not binding on the consumer.

2 An unfair consumer notice is not binding on the consumer.

3 This does not prevent the consumer from relying on the term or notice if the consumer chooses to do so.

4 A term is unfair if, contrary to the requirement of good faith, it causes a significant imbalance in the parties' rights and obligations under the contract to the detriment of the consumer.

5 Whether a term is fair is to be determined –
   (a) taking into account the nature of the subject matter of the contract; and
   (b) by reference to all the circumstances existing when the term was agreed and to all of the other terms of the contract or of any other contract on which it depends.

6 A notice is unfair if, contrary to the requirement of good faith, it causes a significant imbalance in the parties' rights and obligations to the detriment of the consumer.

7 Whether a notice is fair is to be determined –

- taking into account the nature of the subject matter of the notice; and
- by reference to all the circumstances existing when the rights or obligations to which it relates arose and to the terms of any contract on which it depends.

8 This section does not affect the operation of –

(a) Section 31 (exclusion of liability: goods contracts);

(b) Section 47 (exclusion of liability: digital content contracts);

(c) Section 57 (exclusion of liability: services contracts); or

(d) Section 65 (exclusion of negligence liability).

Section 62(1) and (2) begins by setting out the consequences of a term or notice that is found to be unfair. It should be noted, however, that the provision does not render the contract as not binding and indeed by s 67 where a term of a consumer contract is not binding on the consumer as a result of Part 2, the contract continues, so far as practicable, to have effect in every other respect. Furthermore, even if a term is unfair, s 62(3) provides that the consumer is free to continue to rely on the term or notice if the consumer chooses to do so. A court is not able to rewrite a contract or notice.

Our examination of unfair terms will now move to examining how a term or notice is assessed for unfairness before considering terms or notices that are excluded from this process despite appearing to fall within the ambit of the Act.

Assessing whether a contract term is unfair

The heart of Part 2 is found within s 62(4):

> A term is unfair if, contrary to the requirement of good faith, it causes a significant imbalance in the parties' rights and obligations under the contract to the detriment of the consumer.

The provision amounts to quite a radical change to the original test contained within reg 5(1) of UTCCR 1999 which stated that:

> A contractual term which has not been individually negotiated shall be regarded as unfair if, contrary to the requirement of good faith, it causes a significant imbalance in the parties' rights and obligations arising under the contract to the detriment of the consumer.

Thus the Regulations, unlike the Act, are limited in their application to standard-form contracts. The change in the CRA reflects the broadening out of the test so that it extends beyond standard terms, though arguably it may be difficult to prove that a term or notice is unfair if it has been individually negotiated. The change, however, does away with the possibility of an argument developing as to whether or not a term or notice was individually negotiated.

The key expressions within s 62(4) are 'the requirement of good faith' and 'significant imbalance'. The difficulty with these two expressions is that, not only are the two expressions vague, there is a lack of clarity as to the relationship between them so, for instance, are these two separate requirements or are they two components by which unfairness is measured? Directive 93/13 provides no guidance on this matter, however, one view is that 'significant imbalance' is the threshold for determining unfairness but whether or not the imbalance is significant or not is determined by reference to the requirement of good faith.

In this situation, good faith is placed on a 'substantive' footing so that it forms part of the assessment of significant imbalance in terms of the substance and performance of the contract. This seems preferential to the alternative view that the finding of a significant imbalance automatically results in the term as not meeting the requirement of good faith. Such a view essentially renders the requirement of good faith as unnecessary to the overall assessment of whether there is a significant imbalance. In this situation therefore, good faith is essentially a 'procedural' consideration that assesses the manner in which the contract is formed. Clearly this could not have been the intention, however, there is some assistance available in the Preamble to Directive 93/13 in which Recital 16 states that the requirement of good faith is satisfied by the trader dealing equitable and fairly with the consumer whose legitimate interests must be taken into account. On the other hand, it might be argued that good faith has two functions. In Beatson and Friedmann, *Good Faith and Fault in Contract Law*, Professor Beatson in Chapter 9 at p.245, 'Legislative Control of Fairness: The Directive on Unfair Terms in Consumer Contracts' makes the following comment:

> I suspect that good faith has a double operation. First it has a procedural aspect. It will require the supplier to consider the consumer's interests. However, a clause which might be unfair if it came as a surprise may be upheld if the business took steps to bring it to the consumer's attention and to explain it. Secondly, it has a substantive content; some clauses may cause such an imbalance that they should always be treated as contrary to good faith and therefore unfair.

The problem with the concept of good faith is that English law has traditionally been hostile to a general duty of good faith between the contracting parties and instead developed an ad hoc approach to the concept, for instance, it arose in contracts of insurance, employment law and of course in equity where it is founded on principles of unconscionability. The concept of good faith is a creature of continental legal systems, though it is beginning to gain ground in some common law systems, thus, in the United States, the idea of unconscionability arises in order to prevent oppressive or unfair surprises within contracts by way of the Uniform Commercial Code.

Originally in the UTCCR 1994, reg 4(3) stated that in assessing whether a term satisfied the requirement of good faith, regard had to be made to the guiding factors in Schedule 2 so that regard had to be made to:

(a) the strength of the bargaining position of the parties;

(b) whether the consumer had an inducement to agree to the term;

(c) whether the goods or services were sold or supplied to the special order of the consumer; and

(d) the extent to which the seller or supplier has dealt fairly and equitably with the consumer.

Schedule 2 therefore repeated Recital 16 but without reference to the legitimate interests of the consumer, however, the guidance in Schedule 2 was not repeated in the UTCCR 1999 and were not repeated in the CRA either. However, s 62(5) of the CRA does provide some guidance in that it states:

Whether a term is fair is to be determined –

(1) taking into account the nature of the subject matter of the contract; and
(2) by reference to all the circumstances existing when the term was agreed and to all of the other terms of the contract or of any other contract on which it depends.

A similar provision operates in relation to consumer notices by s 62(7).

The first case to consider unfairness in the context of good faith and significant imbalance is that of **Director General of Fair Trading v First National Bank** [2001] 3 WLR 1297 (HL).

Director General of Fair Trading v First National Bank [2001] 3 WLR 1297 (HL)

This case was brought under the 1994 Regulations which, as already noted, have now been superseded by the 1999 Regulations and subsequently by the CRA. The case itself concerned the First National Bank, which was a major lender in the consumer credit market and has large numbers of individuals as clients to whom it has lent money on credit terms. These agreements were made on standard form contracts. One term in this contract, clause 8, stated that if a borrower was in default on his or her loan and the bank obtained judgement against that individual regarding outstanding payments due, the interest at the contract rate on the loan would continue to run until the debt had been paid in full. Regulation 8 of the 1994 Regulations (which became reg 10 of the 1999 Regulations now CRA 2015 s 70 and Schedule 3) charged the Director General of Fair Trading with considering whether any complaint made to him as to whether any contract drawn up for general use was unfair and if necessary to apply for an injunction restraining the use of the unfair term in contracts to be entered into with consumers. The Director General brought his action within this remit.

In the Court of Appeal, the court considered that the term was unfair within reg 4 1994 Regulations (becoming reg 5 in the 1999 Regulations now CRA 2015 s 62). The Court of Appeal also found that the term was not a 'core term' within reg 3(2)b of UTCCR (which became reg 6(2)b UTCCR 1999, now s 64(1) of the CRA 2015), which we will discuss later. The bank then appealed to the House of Lords.

We will consider this aspect of the appeal later in this chapter under 'Terms or notice excluded from the assessment of unfairness'.

The case is important since it is the first case that deals with the application of the 'good faith' requirement in deciding whether a term is unfair or not, a feature of the Regulations that is largely alien in the context of English law.

The bank's case was brought on two fronts. First, it stated that the term fell outside the Regulations because it concerned 'the adequacy of the price or remuneration as against the goods or services sold or supplied' (reg 3(2)(b)).

The second basis of the bank's appeal was that the term was not unfair in that it did not contravene 'the requirement of good faith' and did not cause 'a significant imbalance in the parties' rights and obligations under the contract to the detriment of the consumer'. The real problem here was how the test of good faith was to be applied. As stated earlier, this concept is an alien one in English law in this context and indeed it has a variable interpretation across the European Union. The intention in the original European Directive was to set out a uniform test, which Lord Bingham considered to be clear and not reasonably capable of differing interpretations. He stated that a term is unfair if it causes a significant imbalance in the parties' rights and obligations under the contract to the detriment of the consumer or to such an extent that it is contrary to the requirement of good faith. The 'significant imbalance' is caused if a term 'is so weighted in favour of the supplier so as to tilt the parties' rights and obligations under the contract significantly in his favour'.

The terms illustrated in Schedule 3 provide good examples of terms that may be regarded as unfair in this context. In order to decide if the term creates a significant imbalance, one has to look at the contract as a whole and the imbalance has to be one to the consumer, not the supplier, who is assumed to be the stronger party. Terms which operate to the disadvantage of the consumer should be given due prominence, a feature that is not unfamiliar from the cases of *Spurling v Bradshaw*, *Thornton v Shoe Lane Parking Ltd* and *Interfoto Picture Library Ltd v Stiletto Visual Programmes Ltd*. Lord Bingham continued:

> Fair dealing requires that a supplier should not, whether deliberately or unconsciously, take advantage of the consumer's necessity, indigence, lack of experience, unfamiliarity with the subject matter of the contract, weak bargaining position or any other factor listed or analogous to those listed in Schedule 2 of the regulations.

Lord Bingham, with the other Law Lords concurring, did not consider the term to be unfair in that it caused a significant imbalance in the parties' rights and obligations under the contract to the detriment of the consumer in a manner that contravened the requirement of good faith. The essential bargain in such a contract is that the bank will lend money to a borrower who agrees to repay the principal over a period of time with interest. Neither the lender nor the borrower envisages that the bank will forgo any part of this consideration and, indeed, if this was the case, banks would not lend money at all. The absence of such a term would cause an imbalance to the detriment of the lender, whilst the presence of the term is not detrimental to the consumer since the obligation is clearly and unambiguously expressed in the contract. If anything, their Lordships considered that it was the underlying legal regime which created the problem in that courts were not able to require interest to be paid on judgement debts arising from such contracts, which is possible in Scotland. It may be that this case will lead to a change in the County Court Rules to allow such interest to be paid on judgement debts. Lord Bingham also drew attention to the fact that the Consumer Credit Act 1974, which was developed for the purpose of protecting consumers in credit transactions, did not attempt to legislate against post-judgement interest. He stated that such a prohibition would have been included in the Act if it had been recognised as 'a necessary or desirable form of protection'. He therefore concluded that the term could not 'be stigmatised as unfair on the ground that it violates or undermines a statutory regime enacted for the protection of consumers'.

This position has now been rectified by the Consumer Credit Act 2006, s 17 which inserts s 130A into the Consumer Credit Act 1974. This regulates the situation where a creditor wants to recover post-judgement interest from a debtor (including hirers) in connection with a sum that is required to be paid under a judgement. This requires the creditor to give notice to the debtor of his intention to recover such interest and must give the debtor further such notices at intervals of not more than six months. The debtor will have no liability to pay interest when the creditor has not provided such notice.

On the matter of good faith and its relationship to significant imbalance, Lord Bingham stated (para 17):

> The requirement of significant imbalance is met if a term is so weighted in favour of the supplier as to tilt the parties' rights and obligations under the contract significantly in his favour. This may be by the granting to the supplier of a beneficial option or discretion or power, or by the imposing on the consumer of a disadvantageous burden or risk or duty. The illustrative terms set out in Schedule 3 to the regulations provide very good examples of terms which may be regarded as unfair; whether a given term is or is not to be so regarded depends on whether it causes a significant imbalance in the parties' rights and obligations under the contract. This involves looking at the contract as a whole. But the imbalance must be to the detriment of the consumer; a significant imbalance to the detriment of the supplier, assumed to be the stronger party, is not a mischief which the regulations seek to address. The requirement of good faith in this context is one of fair and open dealing. Openness requires that the terms should be expressed fully, clearly and legibly, containing no concealed pitfalls or traps. Appropriate

prominence should be given to terms which might operate disadvantageously to the customer. Fair dealing requires that a supplier should not, whether deliberately or unconsciously, take advantage of the consumer's necessity, indigence, lack of experience, unfamiliarity with the subject matter of the contract, weak bargaining position or any other factor listed in or analogous to those listed in Schedule 2 of the regulations. Good faith in this context is not an artificial or technical concept; nor, since Lord Mansfield was its champion, is it a concept wholly unfamiliar to British lawyers. It looks to good standards of commercial morality and practice. Regulation 4(1) lays down a composite test, covering both the making and the substance of the contract, and must be applied bearing clearly in mind the objective which the regulations are designed to promote.

On first reading, Lord Bingham appears to have largely based his interpretation of 'good faith' and judgement on the issue of procedural unfairness; however, when Lord Bingham's statement above is broadened out, one can see that the concept of 'fair and open dealing', together with the requirement that there should not be a significant imbalance between the parties, extends 'good faith' to one of 'substantive unfairness within the contract'.

This position is reinforced when one also considers the judgement of Lord Steyn, who also rejected the idea that good faith is confined to procedural unfairness stating (at para 36): 'Any purely procedural or even predominantly procedural interpretation of the requirement of good faith must be rejected.'

From these two judgements it may be seen therefore that 'good faith' as far as it influences whether there has been a 'significant imbalance' may relate to both procedural and substantive issues. Lord Bingham talks of unconscionability both in relation to 'both the making and the substance of the contract'.

The other expression in deciding whether a contractual term or notice is unfair is that of 'significant imbalance'. Whilst this requirement is rather more straightforward than that of 'good faith', nevertheless even here the precise meaning of the expression is left vague. It is, however, important that there must be a *significant* imbalance in the term or notice for it to be rendered unfair, as indicated in *Office of Fair Trading v Ashbourne Management Services Ltd* [2011] EWHC 1237 (Ch) by Kitchin J at para 174. It is apparent that, unlike the 'good faith' requirement, that the assessment of significant imbalance is rooted in substantive unfairness and not procedural unfairness. Thus in *Director General of Fair Trading v First National Bank* [2001] 3 WLR 1297 (HL), Lord Bingham stated:

> But the language used in expressing the test, so far as applicable in this case, is in my opinion clear and not reasonably capable of differing interpretations. A term falling within the scope of the regulations is unfair if it causes a significant imbalance in the parties' rights and obligations under the contract to the detriment of the consumer in a manner or to an extent which is contrary to the requirement of good faith.

Lord Steyn, however, was not so convinced to pigeonhole the concept in this way and considered that there was an overlap between this concept and good faith, pointing to the fact that the two concepts should not be viewed independently of each other. Lord Millett was of the same opinion, indicating that in assessing the fairness of a term or notice, a more holistic approach should be taken, stating (at para 54):

> A contractual term in a consumer contract is unfair if 'contrary to the requirement of good faith [it] causes a significant imbalance in the parties' rights and obligations under the contract to the detriment of the consumer'. There can be no one single test of this. It is obviously useful to assess the impact of an impugned term on the parties' rights and obligations by comparing the effect of the contract with the term and the effect it would have without it. But the inquiry

cannot stop there. It may also be necessary to consider the effect of the inclusion of the term on the substance or core of the transaction; whether if it were drawn to his attention, the consumer would be likely to be surprised by it; whether the term is a standard term, not merely in similar non-negotiable consumer contracts, but in commercial contracts freely negotiated between parties acting on level terms and at arms' length; and whether, in such cases, the party adversely affected by the inclusion of the term or his lawyer might reasonably be expected to object to its inclusion and press for its deletion. The list is not necessarily exhaustive; other approaches may sometimes be more appropriate.

The conclusion is that the concepts of 'significant imbalance' and 'good faith' have been left deliberately vague so that a more fluid approach to the assessment of whether or not a term is unfair can be arrived at by examining the procedural and substantive elements of the contract as a whole. This inter-relationship can be seen by reference to in Recital 16 of the Preamble to the Unfair Terms Directive which explains:

> Whereas the assessment, according to the general criteria chosen, of the unfair character of the terms, in particular in sale or supply activities of a public nature providing collective services which take account of solidarity among users, must be supplemented by a means of making an overall evaluation of the different interests involved; whereas this constitutes the requirement of good faith, particular regard shall be had to the strength of the bargaining position of the parties, whether the consumer had an inducement to agree to the term and whether the goods or services were sold or supplied to the special order of the consumer; whereas the requirement of good faith may be satisfied by the seller or the buyer where he deals fairly and equitably with the other party whose legitimate interests he has to take into account.

Following from this it can be seen that unfairness is to be assessed by way of the subject matter of the contract, the terms contained within the contract and the processes that took place in the formation of the contract.

The guidance provided in s 62(5) and (7) by its very nature is very general and again points to the fluid nature by which the courts are able to deduct unfairness in the particular circumstances of a case; however, s 63(1) provides that Part 1 of Schedule 2 contains an indicative and non-exhaustive list of terms of consumer contracts that may be regarded as unfair (the 'grey list'). This section and Schedule 2 are based on Unfair Terms in Consumer Contracts Directive 93/13/EEC. The terms on the list are not automatically unfair, but may be used to assist a court when considering the application of the fairness test in Section 62 to a particular case. Terms on the 'grey list' are assessable for fairness even if they would otherwise qualify for an exemption under s 64 (see below) and may be assessable for unfairness even if they are 'transparent' and 'prominent' under s 64. Equally, terms not found on the list in the Schedule may be found by a court to be unfair by application of the fairness test.

The list is of considerable length providing some twenty terms that may be regarded as unfair as follows:

1 A term which has the object or effect of excluding or limiting the trader's liability in the event of the death of or personal injury to the consumer resulting from an act or omission of the trader. This does not include a term which is of no effect by virtue of Section 65 (exclusion for negligence liability).

2 A term which has the object or effect of inappropriately excluding or limiting the legal rights of the consumer in relation to the trader or another party in the event of total or partial non-performance or inadequate performance by the trader of any of the contractual obligations, including the option of offsetting a debt owed to the trader against any claim which the consumer may have against the trader.

3   A term which has the object or effect of making an agreement binding on the consumer in a case where the provision of services by the trader is subject to a condition whose realisation depends on the trader's will alone.

4   A term which has the object or effect of permitting the trader to retain sums paid by the consumer where the consumer decides not to conclude or perform the contract, without providing for the consumer to receive compensation of an equivalent amount from the trader where the trader is the party cancelling the contract.

5   A term which has the object or effect of requiring that, where the consumer decides not to conclude or perform the contract, the consumer must pay the trader a disproportionately high sum in compensation or for services which have not been supplied.

6   A term which has the object or effect of requiring a consumer who fails to fulfil his obligations under the contract to pay a disproportionately high sum in compensation.

7   A term which has the object or effect of authorising the trader to dissolve the contract on a discretionary basis where the same facility is not granted to the consumer, or permitting the trader to retain the sums paid for services not yet supplied by the trader where it is the trader who dissolves the contract.

8   A term which has the object or effect of enabling the trader to terminate a contract of indeterminate duration without reasonable notice except where there are serious grounds for doing so. This is subject to paragraphs 21 (financial services) and 24 (sale of securities, foreign currency, etc.).

9   A term which has the object or effect of automatically extending a contract of fixed duration where the consumer does not indicate otherwise, when the deadline fixed for the consumer to express a desire not to extend the contract is unreasonably early.

10   A term which has the object or effect of irrevocably binding the consumer to terms with which the consumer has had no real opportunity of becoming acquainted before the conclusion of the contract.

11   A term which has the object or effect of enabling the trader to alter the terms of the contract unilaterally without a valid reason which is specified in the contract. This is subject to paragraphs 22 (financial services), 23 (contracts which last indefinitely) and 24 (sale of securities, foreign currency, etc.).

12   A term which has the object or effect of permitting the trader to determine the characteristics of the subject matter of the contract after the consumer has become bound by it. This is subject to paragraph 23 (contracts which last indefinitely).

13   A term which has the object or effect of enabling the trader to alter unilaterally without a valid reason any characteristics of the goods, digital content or services to be provided.

14   A term which has the object or effect of giving the trader the discretion to decide the price payable under the contract after the consumer has become bound by it, where no price or method of determining the price is agreed when the consumer becomes bound. This is subject to paragraphs 23 (contracts which last indefinitely), 24 (sale of securities, foreign currency, etc.) and 25 (price index clauses).

15   A term which has the object or effect of permitting a trader to increase the price of goods, digital content or services without giving the consumer the right to cancel the contract if the final price is too high in relation to the price agreed when the contract was concluded. This is subject to paragraphs 24 (sale of securities, foreign currency, etc.) and 25 (price index clauses).

16   A term which has the object or effect of giving the trader the right to determine whether the goods, digital content or services supplied are in conformity with the contract, or giving the trader the exclusive right to interpret any term of the contract.

17   A term which has the object or effect of limiting the trader's obligation to respect commitments undertaken by the trader's agents or making the trader's commitments subject to compliance with a particular formality.

18   A term which has the object or effect of obliging the consumer to fulfil all of the consumer's obligations where the trader does not perform the trader's obligations.

19   A term which has the object or effect of allowing the trader to transfer the trader's rights and obligations under the contract, where this may reduce the guarantees for the consumer, without the consumer's agreement.

20   A term which has the object or effect of excluding or hindering the consumer's right to take legal action or exercise any other legal remedy, in particular by –

    (a) requiring the consumer to take disputes exclusively to arbitration not covered by legal provisions;

    (b) unduly restricting the evidence available to the consumer; or

    (c) imposing on the consumer a burden of proof which, according to the applicable law, should lie with another party to the contract.

The terms contained in Schedule 2 appear to break down into two broad areas: first, those that equate with such exempting or limiting terms that are already controlled by the Unfair Contract Terms Act 1977, for example, terms that exempt or limit liability for death or bodily injury within s 2 of the Act; second, the Schedule sets out terms that are outside the scope of the Act, for example, terms relating to penalty clauses (para 5), or those which allow a seller or supplier unilaterally to change the terms of a contract without a valid reason, though it may be argued that the latter example (para 11), could fall under s 3 of the Act (i.e. excluding or limiting liability for breach of contract) and are therefore subject to the test of reasonableness in s11.

Overall then, there appears to be a considerable amount guidance as to what contractual terms or notices may be regarded as unfair by the courts; however, at the end of the day a finding of unfairness amounts to a finding of fact; one further indicator of imbalance contrary to the requirement of good faith can be found in the European Court of Justice case of ***Mohamed Aziz v Caixa d'Estalvis de Catalunya, Tarragona i Manresa (Catalunyacaixa) (Case C-415/11)*** [2013] 3 CMLR 89 where it was stated:

> . . . in order to assess whether the imbalance arises 'contrary to the requirement of good faith', it must be determined whether the seller or supplier, dealing fairly and equitably with the consumer, could reasonably assume that the consumer would have agreed to the term concerned in individual contract negotiations.

Following the decision in ***Director General of Fair Trading v First National Bank*** [2001] 3 WLR 1297 (HL) there have been a number of cases in which the issue of unfairness has been considered. Other cases on this point have now appeared before the courts.

Bryen and Langley Ltd v Boston [2005] EWCA Civ 973

The defendant purchased two flats with the intention of converting them into one. He invited the claimant builders to tender for the work, the tender documents envisaging that the contract would be entered into on the Joint Contracts Tribunal (JCT) standard form. The defendant's quantity surveyor sent a letter to the claimant confirming that the defendant intended to engage the building firm for the building work. The surveyor stated that the contract would be drawn up under the JCT form. A dispute arose over how much the claimant was to be paid. The dispute went to adjudication. The defendant claimed that the JCT form did not form part of the contract and that therefore the adjudicator had no jurisdiction in the matter. The adjudicator held otherwise and made a substantive award in the firm's favour. The defendant appealed. The judge held that the JCT form had not been incorporated into the contract and ruled in the defendant's favour but rejected the defendant's submission that the adjudication provisions were unfair for the purposes of the Unfair Terms in Consumer Contracts Regulations 1999. The claimant appealed.

The basis of the appeal was whether the contract had incorporated the JCT form and, if it had, was the defendant bound by the adjudication provisions? The defendant argued he was not bound and that the provisions were unenforceable by way of the Unfair Terms in Consumer Contracts Regulations 1999.

The Court of Appeal held that the JCT form had been incorporated into the contract. The court also decided that the contract was not unfair by reason of the regulations. The basis of the decision was whether the provisions contained in the JCT form had been imposed on him. The court thought not since the defendant had the opportunity to influence the terms of the contract by way of the invitation to tender. It was not up to the claimant to ensure that the defendant knew what he was doing and furthermore he had a professional working for and advising him. It should be remembered that it was the surveyor acting on behalf of the defendant who stated that the contract would be drawn up under the JCT form. The court found that there had been no lack of openness, fair dealing or good faith in the manner by which the contract had been arrived at or entered into.

Is there an expectation that a consumer such as the defendant in this case should have actually read the terms of the contract? The answer appears to be no and anyway the defendant was receiving expert advice. Furthermore, if he had chosen to adopt the JCT form, then surely it was up to him to be informed of the terms. In such circumstances there is not a 'significant imbalance' in favour of the builder and the presumption in reg 5(2) that the terms have not been individually negotiated will be overturned. There was no question of the defendant not being able to influence the substance of the terms; he had in fact imposed the terms himself.

A similar decision was arrived at in *Westminster Building Co. Ltd* v *Beckingham* [2004] EWHC 138, TCC. The facts were very similar in that a consumer had engaged builders to renovate his property and the terms of the contract had been decided upon by Beckingham's agents who were chartered surveyors. Thus in common with *Bryen and Langley Ltd* v *Boston* [2005] EWCA Civ 973, Beckingham had received competent and objective advice as to the existence and effect of the adjudication clause before he proffered and entered into the contract. The builders did nothing more than accept the terms offered to them and were under no obligation to advise Beckingham of the terms and effects of the adjudication clause contained within them. In any event, the terms were not individually negotiated but stated in plain and intelligible language. The court held therefore that the adjudication clause did not contravene the requirement of good faith in reg 5(1). Similar reasoning was also presented in the case of *Lovell Projects Ltd* v *Legg* [2003] 1 BLR 452.

These cases can be contrasted with that of *Picardi* v *Cuniberti* [2002] EWHC 2923 (TCC), where a lay client engaged an architect on Royal Institute of British Architects (RIBA) terms. The court held that the adjudication provisions were unfair in that they should have been brought to the attention of the client since they required the client to compulsorily follow a particular course of action that would have resulted in irrecoverable costs being incurred in the event of a dispute. The terms had also been imposed by the architect. These factors resulted in the court finding that there was a significant imbalance to the detriment of the client and that the client was therefore not bound by the adjudication provision.

Domsalla (t/a Domsalla Building Services) v Dyason [2007] All ER 255

The defendant's house had burnt down and his insurers accepted liability to rebuild and reinstate the property. The insurers appointed a firm to act as contract administrator and loss adjuster. The defendant signed a contract as 'agent' on the advice of that firm with the building contractor, the claimant. The defendant signed a form authorising the firm to instruct the claimant directly and a second form agreeing to the insurers paying the claimant directly. Disputes arose about defects and delays in the building works with the result that the defendant withheld part of the contract price. The claimant referred the matter to JCT adjudication. The defendant claimed that the requirement under the contract was to issue withholding notices before deducting sums for defects and delays and the adjudication provisions were unfair within the meaning of the 1999 Regulations and thus were not binding on him by virtue of reg 8. The adjudicator rejected these contentions and awarded the claimant its claims for the work completed in full. The defendant appealed on three grounds: (1) there was no adjudication clause incorporated into the contract; (2) the adjudication and withholding notice clauses were not binding on him; and (3) the decision of the adjudicator was unenforceable due to a breach of the rule of natural justice by the adjudicator.

In reaching its decision the court considered the case of **Bryen and Langley Ltd v Boston** and found that the adjudication provisions within the JCT contract did not cause a significant imbalance in the parties' rights and obligations, even if proffered by the claimant in circumstances that would make it procedurally unfair for the claimant to rely on them. The adjudication provisions provided for a cheap, rapid and temporary legal process to determine the rights of the parties. Essentially it was a summary judgement that could be undertaken economically and speedily and that, whilst the adjudicator was not necessarily a lawyer, he was a person who had relevant professional training for the determination of construction disputes. A legal background was not an essential prerequisite of a fair and impartial procedure. In any event any decision could be overturned later on. The judge therefore concluded that the adjudication provisions were not rendered unfair by the UTCCR because the provisions did not substantially alter the parties' rights and obligations, though he did consider it was potentially unfair for the claimant to rely on the adjudication provisions.

In relation to the withholding clause the court did consider this clause to be unfair on several grounds: (1) the defendant had no say in selecting the clause and was given no advice on its existence, meaning or effect, nor was he shown or had any opportunity to consider the contract conditions prior to him having to sign the contract; (2) the defendant had no say in the making of any payments since all these were to be made by the insurers and furthermore he was not entitled to issue any withholding notices; (3) the defendant's entitlement under the contract was to receive a reinstated home rebuilt with good workmanship under the terms of the contract and any subsequent claims for breach of contract would be made in the defendant's name, though for the benefit of the insurers; (4) the claimant could sue the insurers directly or indirectly through the defendant using the adjudication provisions within the contract; (5) if the defendant became personally liable under the contract, the effect of the withholding provisions could substantially affect his rights since these provisions could only be exercised by the insurers; (6) the defendant was in the position of involuntary employer under the contract since the insurers had insisted that he act as their agent; and (7) the claimants could still rely on their right to suspend work and proceed against the insurers – the rights of the claimants were not adversely affected if the withholding provisions were held not to be binding, whilst the defendant's rights would have been substantially affected if the clause remained effective against him. The court thus held the withholding clause was unfair to and not binding on the defendant, falling within Schedule 2, paragraphs (b), (i), (o) and (q) of the 1999 Regulations.

More recently the issue of unfairness arose in the case of **ParkingEye Ltd v Beavis** [2015] UKSC 67

Parkingeye Ltd v Beavis [2015] UKSC 67

In the case, Mr Beavis parked his car in a free car park at a retail park but overstayed the maximum time of two hours by one hour with the result that he was liable to pay a charge of £85. The notice displaying this information was accepted as being reasonably large, prominent and legible so that any reasonable user of the car park would have had notice of the terms and would have had an opportunity to read them. Mr Beavis refused to pay the £85 charge maintaining that the notice which sought to impose the charge was an unfair term within Regulation 5(1) of UTCCR 1999 which, as we have seen, provides:

> A contractual term which has not been individually negotiated shall be regarded as unfair if, contrary to the requirement of good faith, it causes a significant imbalance in the parties' rights and obligations arising under the contract, to the detriment of the consumer.

The Supreme Court held that the charge was not an unfair term within the UTCCR 1999. Their Lordships (Toulson LJ dissenting) considered that the charge had two objectives: managing the efficient use of parking space in the interests of the nearby retail outlets and of their customers; and the need to provide an income stream to enable ParkingEye to meet the costs of operating the scheme and of course to make a profit. Their Lordships considered that these objectives were perfectly reasonable and that ParkingEye had a legitimate interest in charging overstaying motorists and that the charge was not out of all proportion, which extended beyond the recovery of any loss. There was no reason to suppose that £85 was out of all proportion to ParkingEye's interests. Their Lordships observed that motorists regularly used the car park, knew of the charge and regarded that this was an acceptable price for the convenience of parking. They considered that this was some evidence of the reasonableness of the term. Just because they overlooked the time they had parked there did not render the charge excessive or unconscionable.

Lords Neuberger and Sumption (with Lord Carnworth in agreement) found that the term imposing the charge was not unfair and that the term did not exclude any right which the consumer may be said to enjoy under the general law or by statute. They stated that whilst Mr Beavis would not have been liable in the absence of the agreement on the charge to ParkingEye, he would have been liable to the landowner for trespass though that would have been limited to the occupation value of the parking space. In that respect there was an imbalance in the parties' rights, however, that imbalance did not arise 'contrary to the requirement of good faith' simply because ParkingEye and the landlord to whom ParkingEye was providing the service had a legitimate interest in imposing a liability on Mr Beavis which was in excess of the damages that would have been recoverable at common law for trespass.

It was also contended by Mr Beavis that ParkingEye could not reasonably assume that customers such as Mr Beavis in individual negotiations would have agreed to the charges in ParkingEye's scheme. Referring to the guidance supplied in **Mohamed Aziz v Caixa d'Estalvis de Catalunya, Tarragona i Manresa (Catalunyacaixa) (Case C-415/11)** [2013] 3 CMLR 89 their Lordships considered that other customers in Mr Beavis's position if individually negotiating the contract and if asked about the terms would no doubt have been very satisfied with the provision of two hours free parking. They might have asked that the payment for overstaying be graduated, however, if confronted with the legitimate interests of the landowner and ParkingEye, but their Lordships were not confident that other customers would have refused the risk of having to pay £85 for overstaying. Lord Toulson dissented from this view and did not consider that ParkingEye had adduced sufficient evidence that other customers would agree to the payment of £85. He considered this to be a substantial amount of money given it was payable even if a customer overstayed by as little as one minute. The majority, however, considered that even if the amount payable was higher than could be obtained in an action for trespass, it was not disproportionately high and justifiable and not contrary to the requirement of good faith.

Before moving on to discuss terms or notices that are excluded from the test of unfairness in s 62(4), it should be noted that s 62(8) does not affect the operation of s 31 (exclusion of liability: goods contracts); s47 (exclusion of liability: digital content contracts); s 57 (exclusion of liability: services contracts); or s 65 (exclusion of negligence liability). Thus if one considers s 31, this provides that any term which seeks to exclude a trader's liability for breach of his obligation to supply goods of a satisfactory quality is not valid. In such a situation if a trader does indeed seek to exclude such liability and contends that the term is fair within the ambit of s 62(4), then s 62(8) prevents him from making such a contention.

Terms or notice excluded from the assessment of unfairness – s 64

The CRA 2015 s 64 provides a description of the terms in a contract that are exempt from being assessed under the fairness test and the conditions under which that exemption applies. Originally these were to be found in reg 3 of the UTCCR 1994 and then reg 6 of the UTCCR 1999. Section 64 now provides:

1 A term of a consumer contract may not be assessed for fairness under section 62 to the extent that –

  (a) it specifies the main subject matter of the contract; or

  (b) the assessment is of the appropriateness of the price payable under the contract by comparison with the goods, digital content or services supplied under it.

2 Subsection (1) excludes a term from an assessment under Section 62 only if it is transparent and prominent.

3 A term is transparent for the purposes of this Part if it is expressed in plain and intelligible language and (in the case of a written term) is legible.

4 A term is prominent for the purposes of this section if it is brought to the consumer's attention in such a way that an average consumer would be aware of the term.

5 In subsection (4) 'average consumer' means a consumer who is reasonably well-informed, observant and circumspect.

6 This section does not apply to a term of a contract listed in Part 1 of Schedule 2.

Thus s 64 provides that a term may NOT be assessed for fairness if it: relates to the 'main subject matter of the contract' (usually the goods, services or digital content being purchased) (s 64(1)a); or the 'assessment is of the appropriateness (usually the level) of the price payable under the contract'. These areas have become to be known as the 'core provisions' or 'core terms'.

The role of s 64(1) is to identify the terms that are capable of being exempt from assessment for unfairness under s 62, but this is then qualified by s 64(2) so that to qualify for exemption, the terms must be 'transparent and prominent'. If the term is not transparent and prominent (e.g. if it is in the 'small print'), it is assessable for fairness. If the term is transparent and prominent, it is exempt from assessment for fairness. This provision therefore replaces regulation 6(2) of the UTCCR in which there was a requirement that the term must be in 'plain intelligible language'. It will be noted, however, that the 'plain intelligible language' requirement has not been totally removed since it now re-appears in s 64(3) but here it applies as an aspect of transparency. The expression 'prominent' means that the term must be brought to the consumer's attention in such a way that an 'average' consumer who is 'reasonably well-informed, observant and circumspect' would be aware of the term; s 64(4) and (5).

It follows from this that if a term is a core provision within s 64(1)a because it specifies the main subject matter of the contract and is transparent, is expressed in plain intelligible language, and is brought to the attention of the consumer in such a way that an 'average consumer would be aware of the term', then the term is cannot be subject to the test of unfairness under s 62. The case of **Bankers Insurance Co Ltd v South** [2003] EWHC 380 QB provides a good example as to how this operates. In this case South, who was going on holiday to Cyprus, purchased holiday insurance to cover the trip. The policy contained within it a clause that excluded the company from liability arising from accidents 'involving your ownership or possession of any . . . motorized waterborne craft'. Subsequently whilst South was driving a jet ski, he was involved in an accident in which he and another person (the second defendant) suffered serious injuries. The second defendant sued South who claimed under his insurance policy. The insurance company maintained that it was not liable to indemnify South. The company maintained that as the exclusion clause was expressed in clear intelligible language and it was a core provision in that it related to the subject matter of the contract term (within reg 6(2) of the UTCCR 1999) the clause could not be assessed for fairness. This was upheld by the court and therefore the accident was excluded from the policy.

The ambit of Section s 64(1)b is a great deal more difficult to assess, not least because of the decisions that have arisen out of its predecessors – reg 3(2) UTCCR 1994 and reg 6(2)b UTCCR 1999. Regulation 6(2)b differs slightly from s 64(1)b in that it states that a term may not be assessed for fairness if the term relates 'to the adequacy of the price or remuneration, as against the goods or services supplied in exchange'. In examining the effect of this provision it is important to have regard to the cases of **Director General of Fair Trading v First National Bank** [2001] 3 WLR 1297 (HL) and **Office of Fair Trading v Abbey National plc** [2009] UKSC 6.

The facts of the case of **Director General of Fair Trading v First National Bank** have been considered earlier; however, some further explanation is required to place the dispute in the context of terms that are not subject to the test of fairness under reg 3(2)b of UTCCR 1994. Normally judgement debts carry interest and in that context if a lender obtains judgement against a debtor, the lender will obtain interest on the debt pursuant to statute. Thus the loan agreement in effect becomes merged into the judgement and the debtor pays interest at the statutory rate of interest, not the contract rate. However, a qualification has to be made here in that agreements that are within the ambit of the Consumer Credit Act 1974 fall outside the statutory interest provisions. The effect of this is that the debtor would have to repay only the judgement debt and that no more interest could be levied against him by the lender. In effect, the debtor now has an interest-free loan on the debt! This is particularly important in this context because a court has the power to require the judgement debt to be paid over a period of several years if it thinks fit. For this reason lenders imposed a condition within the contract that interest at the contract rate would continue to run after judgement. Debtors therefore could see a significant advantage disappearing here and it is this provision that the Director General of Fair Trading objected to and considered to be an unfair term within reg 4(1) UTCCR 1994. Therefore the matter was referred to the Director General of Fair Trading who brought the case and where in the Court of Appeal it was found that Clause 8 was indeed unfair. The implications of the decision in the Court of Appeal alarmed lenders, which prompted the appeal to the House of Lords.

The nature of the bank's appeal was that Clause 8 fell within reg 3(2) and, in particular, reg 3(2)b UTCCR 1994, in that it concerned the adequacy of the price or remuneration, as against the goods or services sold or supplied and as such no assessment could be made as to the fairness of the term. This argument was rejected by the House of Lords. Lord Steyn in particular stated that Clause 8 was essentially a default provision that only came into operation on the default of the consumer prescribing the remedies of the bank on such an occurrence. Clause 8 therefore was a subsidiary term and as such fell outside reg 3(2)a which related to the main subject of the contract. This avenue of defence was therefore closed to the bank. Lord Steyn considered that reg 3(2) as a whole had to be given a restrictive interpretation otherwise the whole purpose of the regulations would be frustrated 'by endless formalistic arguments as to whether a provision is a definitional or an exclusionary provision'. Turning his attention to reg 3(2)(b) dealing with 'the adequacy of the price of remuneration', he considered this must also be subject to the test of fairness and given a restrictive interpretation. He stated:

> After all, in a broad sense all terms of the contract are in some way related to the price or remuneration. That is not what is intended . . . It would be a gaping hole in the system if such clauses were not subject to the fairness requirement. For these further reasons I would reject the argument of the bank that regulation 3(2), and in particular 3(2)(b), take clause 8 outside the scope of the regulations.

The effect therefore is that reg 3(2) has to be construed restrictively otherwise traders would simply draft their contracts to fall within the provision so that these terms or notices will be excluded from the assessment of fairness and thereby subvert the intentions behind this regulatory scheme.

In this case it was clear that Clause 8 being a default position did in fact fall outside reg 3(2) and to that extent the decision is clearly correct; however, as the case of *Office of Fair Trading* v *Abbey National plc* [2009] UKSC 6 shows, traders can successfully bring their terms within this provision (or their equivalent in UTCCR 1999) so that their terms stand outside the regime for the assessment of fairness.

In the case of *Office of Fair Trading* v *Abbey National plc* [2009] UKSC 6 the OFT wished to investigate the fairness of banks to levy certain charges comprising unpaid item charges, paid item charges, over-draft excess charges and guaranteed paid item charges ('the relevant charges'). These charges ('Relevant Charges') had been a long-running sore with members of the public, who regarded the size of the charges levied on customers taking *unauthorised* overdrafts from the banks as unfair and disproportionate. Banking customers entered into contracts for an overall package of banking facilities, described as on a 'free-if-in-credit' basis. The OFT argued that this indicated that this suggested the agreement to pay Relevant Charges cannot be regarded as the or a part of the price or remuneration in exchange for which banking facilities are supplied and as such fell outside reg 6(2)b. The banks contended that the clear corollary of 'free-if-in-credit' is that the services provided will not be free if the customer is not in credit. They then posed the question as to what other price or remuneration there is, if not the Relevant Charges. The banks contended that such an investigation for fairness of the Relevant Charges was limited by the effect of reg 6(2) UTCCR 1999.

It must be emphasised that, on appeal, the Court of Appeal was not considering whether the system of charging personal current account customers adopted by UK banks was per se unfair but whether the relevant charges constituted 'the price or remuneration, as against the services supplied in exchange' within the meaning of reg 6(2)(b). The court held that the Relevant Charges were ancillary in nature and not part of the core bargain between bank and customer and that the fairness of the charges fell to be assessed by the OFT for fairness.

The banks appealed to the Supreme Court, which allowed the appeal finding that the Court of Appeal was wrong to find that reg 6(2)(b) did not apply to charges that were ancillary to the core contract between a bank and a customer. Their Lordships considered that any monetary price or remuneration payable under the contract would naturally fall within the language of reg 6(2)(b), though the regulation had to be applied restrictively and not every monetary term fell within reg 6(2)b. In this case, however, the Supreme Court re-stated the point that the Directive and Regulations applied only to terms which had not been individually negotiated. The Supreme Court, rather surprisingly, considered that bank charges levied on personal current account customers in respect of unauthorised overdrafts, including unpaid item charges and other related charges, constituted part of the price or remuneration for the banking services provided and, insofar as the terms giving rise to the charges were in plain intelligible language, no assessment under the 1999 Regulations of the fairness of those terms could be undertaken by the OFT as regards the adequacy of the charges, as opposed to any services supplied by virtue of the operation of reg 6(2)b.

The Supreme Court therefore rejected the decision in *First National* that there was a distinction between ancillary sums or terms and those that represented the core provisions of the contract. As Lord Walker (at para 41) indicated that reg 6(2)b contains no indication that only essential price or remuneration is relevant and that 'Any monetary price or remuneration payable under the contract would naturally fall within the language of paragraph (b)'. Similarly Lord Phillips stated (at para 78):

> I can see no justification for excluding from the application of Regulation 6(2) price or remuneration on the ground that it is 'ancillary or incidental price or remuneration'. If it is possible to identify such price or remuneration as being paid in exchange for services, even if the services are fringe or optional extras, Regulation 6(2) will preclude an attack on the price or remuneration in question if it is based on the contention that it was excessive by comparison with the services for which it was exchanged. If, on analysis, the charges are not given in exchange for individual services but are part of a package of different ways of charging for a package of varied services, this does not mean that they are not price or remuneration for the purpose of Regulation 6(2).

The problem that remains is how to reconcile these two decisions since it seems that the Supreme Court in *Abbey National* has overturned its own decision in *First National*. Judging from Lord Walker's dicta in *Abbey National* apparently not, thus (at para 43) he stated:

> 'This House's decision in First National Bank shows that not every term that is in some way linked to monetary consideration falls within Regulation 6(2)(b). Paras (d), (e), (f) and (l) of the 'grey list' in Schedule 2 to the 1999 Regulations are an illustration of that. But the relevant term in First National Bank was a default provision. Traders ought not to be able to outflank consumers by 'drafting themselves' into a position where they can take advantage of a default provision. But . . . the Court can and will be astute to prevent that. In First National Bank Lord Steyn indicated that what is now Regulation 6(2) should be construed restrictively, and Lord Bingham said that it should be limited to terms 'falling squarely within it'. I respectfully agree. But in my opinion the Relevant Terms and the Relevant Charges do fall squarely within Regulation 6(2)(b).

The effect therefore is that ancillary provisions or 'default provisions' will continue to remain outside of the ambit of s 6(2)b and will be subject to assessment for fairness.

A further case that has arisen in relation to the scope of s 6(2)b is that of *Office of Fair Trading* v *Asbourne Management Services Ltd* [2011] EWHC 1237 (Ch) where the Office of Fair Trading challenged a series of terms in a number of standard form contracts for gym membership, *inter alia*, on the ground that they were unfair within the meaning of the

Unfair Terms in Consumer Contracts Regulations 1999 ('UTCCR'). Ashbourne Management Services Ltd ('AMS') was a company which carried on the business of recruiting members for gym and health and fitness clubs, providing standard form contracts for their use and collecting payments from members under those contracts. AMS advised gym clubs to adopt agreements with specified minimum membership that ranged from periods of 12 months up to 36 months. These contracts carried with them no or little possibility of cancellation without incurring liability. Members who wanted to terminate their agreements before the end of the minimum periods were described as 'defaulters'. These members were dealt with by registering or threatening to register their default of their breach of contract with a credit reference agency. Following complaints from consumers, the OFT investigated AMS's business practices and considered them to be unfair. The OFT therefore sought declarations to that effect and also injunctions restraining AMS from using its standard form contracts and also restraining the company from relying on any unfair terms in their existing contracts.

The OFT contended, *inter alia*, that the terms in AMS's agreements providing for a minimum membership period were unfair within the meaning of the UTCCR Reg 5(1) in that a contractual term 'which has not been individually negotiated shall be regarded as unfair if, contrary to the requirement of good faith, it causes a significant imbalance in the parties' rights and obligations arising under the contract to the detriment of the consumer'. Schedule 2 of the regulations sets out a list of terms which may be regarded as unfair.

The OFT also contended that AMS's standard form agreements were not expressed in plain intelligible language contrary to reg 7. In this regard the OFT contended that the agreements did not plainly set out that a member would have to make payments for the whole of the minimum period; that there was no statement as to a member's overall liability under the contract; that there was no clear explanation that a member who terminated the agreement early would have to pay all the payments that would have been incurred over the remaining period of the minimum term of the agreement; and that there were differences in the terminology used in the body of the agreement and the conditions set out on the reverse of the agreement.

AMS contended that within reg 6(2) certain provisions are not subject to the fairness test, provided they were expressed in plain intelligible language. Provisions which define the main subject matter of the contract fall within this limitation. AMS therefore argued that a provision which defines the period that the consumer can use the facilities is a defining aspect of the obligations of the gym and therefore this prohibited an assessment as to whether a provision was fair. The OFT countered this argument by stating that whilst gym membership and the right to use the facilities did form the main subject matter of the agreement, the issue of the period of time of the minimum membership did not. Thus the OFT argued that reg 6(2)(a) which states: 'In so far as it is in plain intelligible language, the assessment of fairness of a term shall not relate – (a) to the definition of the main subject matter of the contract', did not apply and that therefore the fairness of the term could be assessed.

On the matter of fairness, the judge considered that the provisions that provided for a minimum membership were so weighted as to cause a significant imbalance in the rights and obligations of the parties and that this was contrary to good faith. It was not possible for a gym member to anticipate all events which might make the continued use of a gym impractical or unaffordable. AMS's agreements did not address the tendency of the average consumer to overestimate the use he would make of gym facilities and, indeed, that he was likely not to attend at all after two or three months. He considered that AMS's business policy, in advising clubs to adopt agreements with minimum membership periods, was designed and calculated to take advantage of the naivety and inexperience of the average consumer using gym clubs and the agreements contained a trap into which the average consumer was likely to fall.

Whilst the judge found that the term providing for a minimum period was a core term and therefore fell within the scope of reg 6(2), he did not consider that this precluded any assessment of the fairness of the term. He considered the fairness of the term did not relate to the definition of the main subject matter of the contract but to the consequences of early termination by the gym members. In this way he avoided the ambit of reg 6(2) and could question the fairness of the term and, accordingly, found the minimum period term to be unfair and contrary to the UTCCR 1999.

Finally, the question has to be asked, what is the impact of the decisions of *First National* and *Abbey National* on the scope of s 64(1)b of the CRA? It appears that whilst the language has changed from 'adequate' in reg 6(2)b to 'appropriate' in s 64(1)b, this has had little impact on the decisions in *First National* and *Abbey National*. In any event, Lord Mance in *Abbey National* at [para 94] considered the two expressions to be synonymous stating that 'adequacy' means 'appropriateness or reasonableness'. The main change arises in s 64(2) which states that s 64(1) only excludes a term from an assessment under s 62 only if it is 'transparent and prominent'. This appears to be a stricter requirement than 'plain intelligible language' more exacting requirement than reg 6(2). Reflecting the case law then, the effect of s 64(1) is that if a term concerns other aspects of the price (not the amount), such as the time of the payment, then the term may be assessed for fairness under s 62. On the other hand, the price itself cannot be assessed for fairness as it falls within s 64(1)b, providing it is 'transparent or prominent' within s 64(2).

Example

If a consumer enters into a contract for a hotel room at £200 per night, a court cannot look at whether it is fair to pay that amount of money, providing it is transparent and prominent, but it may look at, say, any cancellation charges.

Bar on exclusion or restriction of negligence liability – s 65 and s 66

Section 65 repeats UCTA s 2(1) in that a trader cannot, in a consumer contract or consumer notice, exclude or limit liability for death or personal injury resulting from negligence. It should be noted that in some circumstances a person is aware of a risk but chooses to ignore it and as such is deemed to have consented to the risk, however, s 65(2) provides that a person cannot be assumed to have consented to the risk simply by agreeing to or having knowledge of a term in a consumer contract or consumer notice that limits a trader's liability for negligence. This is an important change from the UTCCR 1999 since terms or notices that sought to restrict or limit liability for death or bodily injury in negligence were not automatically barred but subject to the fairness test in s 62. It follows from this that for terms or notices excluding liability for other loss or damage, i.e. other than death or bodily injury, then such terms or notices will be subject to the fairness test.

It should be noted that there are some exceptions to the operation of s 65 contained within s 66. Thus s 65 does not apply to contracts of insurance, any contract so far as it relates to the creation or transfer of an interest in land or to the liability of an occupier of premises to a person who obtains access to the premises for recreational purposes if a person suffers loss or damage because of the dangerous state of the premises, for instance.

The effect of a term or notice being unfair – s 67

Section 67 reflects regulation 8(2) of the UTCCR in that whilst a court may find a particular term to be unfair and thus render it not binding on the consumer, it may not be in the interests of the consumer for the entire contract not to be binding, therefore, in so far as is practical, a contract may continue even if one or more terms within it are deemed unfair. The fact that this is only possible 'as far as practicable' reflects the fact that if a term is so fundamental to the contract, then the consequence may be that the contract as a whole will fail. This also generally reflects the position of severance in illegal contracts where it is possible grammatically and where it is appropriate on public policy issues.

Severance is dealt with more fully in Chapter 12.

Terms and notices must be transparent – s 68

Whilst it can be seen that the Act focuses on providing that a contract term must be fair, and how that is to be determined, s 68(1) imposes an additional requirement on the trader in that it now 'must ensure that a written term of a consumer contract, or a consumer notice in writing, is transparent'. Section 68(2) provides that a consumer notice is transparent for the purposes of subsection (1) if it is expressed in plain and intelligible language and it is legible. This clause reflects regulation 7(1) of the UTCCRs and is designed to deal with the issues arising out of the 'small print'. The Act provides no consequence if a term or notice is in breach of this provision so, presumably, this is a matter which is considered as part of the assessment of fairness. This provision clearly bears a close resemblance to Denning's 'red-hand test' in *Spurling v Bradshaw*. There also seems to be a close analogy with the decision in *Interfoto Picture Library Ltd v Stilletto Visual Programmes Ltd* as regards the legibility issue since small print may well raise a legibility issue particularly if the terms or notices are regarded as harsh or onerous.

Contra proferentem – s 69

The Act encompasses the *contra proferentem* rule and recognises that contract terms or notices can be ambiguous and capable of different interpretations, particularly if they are not in writing. Section 69 therefore provides that in such a situation the interpretation that is most beneficial to the consumer rather than the trader is to be adopted. This section reflects regulation 7(2) of the UTCCRs.

The enforcement of the law on unfair contract terms – s 70

Article 7(1) of EU Directive 93/13 provides that Member States have to ensure that 'adequate and effective means exist to prevent the continued use of unfair terms in contracts concluded with consumers'. Thus Member States are required to provide some mechanism whereby alleged unfair contract terms can be challenged by some body, person or persons, other than a consumer, in civil litigation. No guidance was given in the Directive as to the form that such a mechanism should take, except insofar as Art 7(2) provides that there must be a means by which any person or body that has a legitimate interest in protecting consumers can challenge that 'contractual terms drawn up for general use are unfair'. This was looked upon with some anticipation by bodies such as the Consumers' Association who may have considered that the Directive gave them a substantial weapon in challenging the standard form contracts of bodies such as British Rail, or trade associations. Package holiday firms and banks also appeared to be potential targets of the new Directive. Article 7, as implemented by reg 8 in the 1994 Regulations, immediately doused the expectations of consumer protection groups since the right to take action on behalf of consumers was vested in the Director General of Fair Trading. This position has now been amended by the 1999 Regulations which in Sch 1 give other regulatory bodies the power to seek an injunction against anyone using or recommending the use of unfair terms.

The provisions of the CRA 2015 now give effect to Article 7 of Directive 93/17. These are found in s 70 which simply provides that the regulation and enforcement of the law on unfair contracts terms are now in the hands of the Competition and Markets Authority ('CMA'), rather than the Office of Fair Trading. Other 'regulators' are provided for in Schedule 3 and these include any local weights and measures authority in Great Britain, Information Commissioner, the Office of Rail Regulation, the Gas and Markets Authority, the Water Services Authority, the Office of Rail Regulation and the Consumers' Association.

The functions of the CMA and the other regulators are conferred in Schedule 3 whilst the investigatory powers of these bodies are contained within Schedule 5. Schedule 3 applies to a term of a consumer contract, a term proposed for use in a consumer contract, a term which a third party recommends for use in a consumer contract, or a consumer notice. Thus any regulator may consider a complaint made in relation Part 2 of the CRA; however, if the regulator is a body other than the CMA, then it must notify the CMA of its intention to do so. By para 3 a regulator may apply for an injunction in order to prevent the use or proposed use of term or notice that purports to exclude or restrict liability in respect of the entrenched rights contained in ss 31, 47, 57 and 65(1) (i.e. exclusions or restrictions for goods contracts, digital content contracts, service contracts and business liability for death or personal injury caused by negligence). A regulator may also seek an injunction against any person recommending the use or proposed use of such terms or notices and so the regulator may use this provision against trade associations recommending the use of standard form contracts that contain unfair terms.

Paragraph 3 clarifies the fact that a regulator may apply for an injunction in respect of current or proposed contracts so that the type of challenges seen in *Office of Fair Trading v Foxtons Ltd* [2009] EWCA Civ 288 will be avoided. In UTCCR 1999 reg 10 which empowered the Director General of Fair Trading to make general challenges, the relationship of those challenges to existing contracts already entered into, as opposed to future contracts, has always been a moot point. In that case the OFT brought proceedings against Foxtons Ltd, which operated as estate agents, challenging the fairness of terms within its standard form contracts. These terms entitled Foxtons to make certain charges relating to transactions between a landlord and tenant, despite the fact that Foxtons had played no part in the transactions or negotiations. The judge distinguished between a general challenge, which a body such as the OFT could make, and the challenge that an individual could make if sued. He held that Foxtons should not be prevented from enforcing individual contracts already entered into, as the circumstances of those contracts might establish that the relevant term was fair, even if, on the general challenge, the term had been held unfair. The OFT argued that the language of Directive 93/13, which the 1999 Regulations implemented, supported the view that general challenges were directed not only to future contracts but also to existing contracts. Foxtons argued that the court lacked the jurisdiction to grant declarations in a case where the parties before the court were not the parties to the contracts in which the terms appeared. In arriving at his decision, the judge had regard to reg 6(1), which states that in an individual challenge the court assesses the unfairness of a term by looking 'at the time of the conclusion of the contract, to all the circumstances attending the conclusion of the contract and to all the other terms of the contract. . . '. The judge considered it was not possible to have regard to these matters in a general challenge by a body such as the OFT.

The OFT appealed against the judge's decision and it was held in the Court of Appeal that Article 7 of the Directive was clearly intended to cover existing as well as future contracts, and thus an issue on a general challenge could be the fairness of a term in a current contract. Waller LJ stated:

> It would be quite inadequate protection to consumers if a court on a general challenge, having found a term as used in current contracts to be unfair, had no power to prevent the supplier or seller from continuing to enforce that term in current contracts. As the European Court of Justice, and indeed Lord Steyn in ***Director General of Fair Trading v First National Bank plc*** [2001] UKHL 52, [2002] 1 AC 481, recognised, 'the system of pre-emptive challenges is a more effective way of preventing the continuing use of unfair terms . . . than *ex casu* actions' . . . It is therefore most unlikely that the Directive intended that a general challenge should not relate to a standard term in current contracts and did not intend the courts of member states to have power to prevent continued reliance on that term by a supplier or service provider against a consumer.

Under para 3(6) ,a regulator is entitled to apply for an injunction in relation to a term or notice irrespective of whether it has received a complaint about the term or notice from a member of the public, so that a regulator has the ability to act pre-emptively. It should be noted, however, that before a regulator other than the CMA makes an application under para 3 above then, by para 4 that regulator must notify the CMA that it intends to do so and may not commence an application within 14 days of that notification (unless the CMA agrees otherwise).

By para 6, the CMA is entitled to consider any undertakings given to the CMA from any person against whom it has applied or is considering applying for an injunction. Such undertakings may provide that the person subject to the application or the proposed application will comply with certain conditions about the terms or notices specified in the undertaking. This enables the CMA and the person involved in the application to avoid what may become protracted and expensive litigation.

Duty of the court to consider the fairness of a term – s 71

The Act provides guidance as to how the unfair contract terms are to be enforced, thus s 1 71 provides that it is the duty of the court to consider the fairness of the term, even if the parties do not specifically ask the court to do so. This is qualified, however, in that the courts do not have to look at the unfairness of a term if the court does not have sufficient legal or factual information to do so. It should be noted that the requirement that terms should be fair also extends to contracts agreed in addition to the original contract, whether or not they are contracts between a trader and a consumer (as in ***Office of Fair Trading v Foxtons Ltd***). This provides additional protection for consumers, by ensuring that any agreements made after, before or in addition to the signing of a contract are also covered by these rules.

B2C Contracts

Consumer Rights Act 2015 Part 2

Application

Applies to contractual terms and notices bertween a trader and a consumer (not employment contracts)

Basic Principles – s 62

CRA provides general rules regarding fairness in cosnumer contracts or notices and includes ANY term that may be unfair, for example, exemption/limitation/penalty clauses. Thus:

S 62(1) & (2)	Any unfair term or notice is not binding on a consumer; however, a consumer can rely on the term if he/she wishes – s 62(3)
S 62(4) & (6)	A term or notice is unfair if contrary to good faith it causes a significant imbalance in the parties rights and obligations under the contract to the detriment of the consumer.
S 62(5) & (7)	Whether a term or notice is unfair is determined by: – Taking into account the nature of the subject matter of the term or notice, AND – By reference to all the circumstances existing when the contractual term was agreed and all the other terms of the contract or any other contract on which it depends.rights and obligations, or – By reference to all the circumstances existing when the rights and obligations to which the notice relates arose and to the terms of any contract on which it depends,

Meaning of "good faith" – *Director General of Fair Trading* v *First National Bank*

Further guidance on the operation of s 62(5) and (7) is provided in s 63 and Schedule 3 – the "grey list".

Section 64 - Certain terms are excluded for the assessment of fairness:

1 Terms specifying the main subject matter of the contract or where the assessment of fairness involves assessing the fairness of the price.
2 In order to be excluded from assesssment the term must be:
"Transparent" – expressed in plain inteligible language – s 64(3), AND
"Prominent" – brought to the consumer's attention in a way that the average consumer would be aware of the term – s 64(4).*ParkingEye Ltd v Beavis*

Section 65 – Negligence

In a consumer contract/notice a trader cannot exclude or restrict liability for death or bodily injury except in contracts of insurance/contracts to create or transfer an interest in land/ in relation to occupier's liability – s 66.

Section 67 – Effect of an unfair term or notice

A term or notice that is found to be unfair is not binding on the consumer.

Section 68 - Transparency

This is an additional requirment in that a trader must ensure that 'a written term of a consumer contract, or a consumer notice in writing , is transparent', that is it must be in plain intelligible language and legible. Compare with Denning's 'red-hand test' in *Spurling* v *Bradshaw* and *Interfoto Picture Library Ltd* v *Stilletto Visual Programmes Ltd* . The Act provides no consequence for a term in breach of this provision.

Section 69 – Contra Proferentem

Where a contractual term or notice is ambiguous, then the interpretation most beneficial to the consumer is adopted.

Section 70 – Enforcement of the law on unfair terms

Regulation and enforcement are now in the hands of the Competition and Markets Authority + other regulators

Section 71 – Duty of the court to consider the fairness of a term

The duty arises even if the parties do not ask the court to do so, provided there is sufficient information.

Figure 8.3

Summary

Incorporation of the exclusion clause into the contract

The party relying on the exclusion clause has to show that it has become incorporated into the contract.

Incorporation by signature

- *L'Estrange* v *Graucob*

Incorporation by notice

The document must be a contractual document

- *Chapelton* v *Barry UDC*

What degree of notice is required?

If the unsigned document is to be regarded as being an integral part of the contract, reasonable notice of the exemption clause must be brought to the attention of the other party.

- *Parker* v *South Eastern Railway Company*
- *Thompson* v *L M & S Railway Company*

Adequacy?

- *Thornton* v *Shoe Lane Parking Ltd*
- *O'Brien* v *MGN Ltd*
- *Sterling Hydraulics* v *Dichtomatic Ltd*
- *Impala Warehousng and Logistics (Shanghai) Co Ltd* v *Wanxiang Resources (Singapore) Pte Ltd*

The nature of the exemption clause

- *Interfoto Picture Library Ltd* v *Stiletto Visual Programmes Ltd*
- *AEG (UK) Ltd* v *Logic Resource Ltd*
- *Ocean Chemical Transport Inc.* v *Exnor Craggs Ltd*

When was notice of the exemption clause given?

Reasonable steps must be taken before entering the contract to bring the clause to the notice of the other party.

- *Olley* v *Marlborough Court Hotel*

Incorporation by a previous course of dealing

A frequent course of dealings may incorporate a term:

- *Spurling* v *Bradshaw*
- *McCutcheon* v *David MacBrayne Ltd*
- *Sterling Hydraulics Ltd* v *Dichtomatik Ltd*
- *Hardwick Game Farm* v *Suffolk Agricultural Association*

- *Circle Freight International Ltd v Medeast Gulf Exports Ltd 7*
- *Capes (Hatherden) Ltd v Western Arable Services Ltd*
- *Transformers and Rectifiers Ltd v Need Ltd*
- *Hollier v Rambler Motors (AMC) Ltd*
- *British Crane Hire Corporation Ltd v Ipswich Plant Hire Ltd*

Construing exemption clauses
Exemption clauses are to be construed *contra proferentem*

- *Vaswani v Italian Motor Cars Ltd*
- Consumer Rights Act 2015 s 62(4)

Exempting liability for fundamental breach of contract

- *Karsales (Harrow) Ltd v Wallis*
- *Suisse Atlantique Société d'Armement Maritime SA v NV Rotterdamsche Kolen Centrale*
- *Photo Production Ltd v Securicor Transport Ltd*
- *Internet Broadcasting Corp Ltd (t/a NETTV) v MAR LLC (t/a MARHedge)*

Exempting liability for negligence

- A claim is possible in tort even though a contract excluded liability for negligence (*White v John Warwick & Co Ltd*).
- A clause must be explicit in the face of ambiguity (*Hollier v Rambler Motors (AMC) Ltd*).

Other factors limiting the effectiveness of exemption clauses
Common law limitations on exemption clauses
Misrepresentation

- An exclusion clause is not enforceable where its extent is misrepresented to the other party (*Curtis v Chemical Cleaning and Dyeing Co. Ltd*).

Third parties

- Third parties cannot rely on an exclusion clause for protection as it offends the principle of privity of contract (*Scruttons Ltd v Midland Silicones Ltd*).
- NB: *The Eurymedon* on where privity rule was circumvented.
- Note also how the Contracts (Rights of Third Parties) Act 1999 circumvents the privity rule.

Overriding oral undertaking

- A written exclusion clause can be overridden by verbal undertaking given before or at the time of contracting (*J Evans & Son (Portsmouth) Ltd v Andrea Merzario Ltd*).

Collateral contracts

- May prevent a party from relying on an exclusion clause (***Webster* v *Higgin***)

Statutory limitations on exemption clauses and unfair terms

Unfair Contract Terms Act 1977- Exemption Clauses in Non-Consumer Contracts (B2B)

This applies to:

- Liability arising both in contract and in tort, and exemption and limitation clauses contained in any contractual term or notice.
- UCTA does *NOT* apply to contracts relating to:

  - insurance;
  - land;
  - intellectual property;
  - formations or dissolutions of companies;
  - creations or transfers of securities;
  - contracts of marine salvage or towage or charterparties;
  - international supply contracts where the adoption of English law as 'the proper law of the contract' (s 27).

'Business liability'

- The Act only applies to actions in contract and tort arising in relation to 'business liability'.

Liability arising in negligence

'Negligence' is, however, defined by s 1(1) as a breach:

(a) of any obligation arising from the express or implied terms of a contract, to take reasonable care or exercise reasonable skill in the performance of the contract;

(b) of any common law duty to take reasonable care or exercise reasonable skill (but not any stricter duty);

(c) of the common duty of care imposed by the Occupiers' Liability Act 1957.

Liability arising in contract

In relation to attempts to exclude liability in contract UCTA applies on two ways:

1. to terms that attempt to restrict liability in relation to implied statutory obligations in relation to the sale of supply of goods (UCTA ss 6 and 7);

2. to terms that attempt to exclude or limit liability for breaches of strict contractual liabilities whereas between contracting parties one of them deals ... on the other's written standard terms of business (UCTA s 3).

Exempting liability for misrepresentation

Section 8 of UCTA amends the Misrepresentation Act 1967, s 3, and thus any term which seeks to exclude or restrict liability for misrepresentation is now subject to the requirement of reasonableness.

The requirement of reasonableness

Section 11 provides guidelines for the application of reasonableness. The courts take into account:

1 The 'circumstances which were, or ought reasonably to have been, known to or in the contemplation of the parties when the contract was made'.

2 The burden of proving that a clause is reasonable rests on the person seeking to rely on the clause.
   (NB: *George Mitchell (Chesterhall) Ltd* v *Finney Lock Seeds Ltd* for extra-statutory guidelines for assessing reasonableness).

Schedule 2: Factors to be taken into account when assessing reasonableness:

1 Were the parties of equal bargaining power?

2 How far was it reasonably practicable for independent advice to be obtained taking into account the costs and time that may be taken up in obtaining such advice?

3 How difficult is the task being undertaken for which liability is being excluded?

4 What are the practical consequences of the decision on the question of reasonableness?

Consumer Rights Act 2015 Part 2 – Unfair Terms in Consumer Contracts (B2C)

The Act therefore applies to contracts between a 'trader' and a 'consumer'. These expressions are the same as for Part 1 of the Act, so that a 'trader' is defined in s 2(2) as a 'person acting for purposes relating to that person's trade, business, craft or profession, whether acting personally or through another person acting in the trader's name or on the trader's behalf'. A 'consumer' is defined in s 2(3) means an 'individual acting for purposes that are wholly or mainly outside that individual's trade, business, craft or profession'.

Further reading

Adams and Brownsword, 'The Unfair Contract Terms Act: A Decade of Discretion' (1988) 104 *Law Quarterly Review* 94

Beatson, Burrows and Cartwright, *Anson's Law of Contract*, 30th edn (Oxford University Press, 2016)

Beatson and Friedmann, *Good Faith and Fault in Contract Law* (Oxford University Press, 1995)

Bright, 'Winning the Battle Against Unfair Contract Terms' (2000) 20 *Legal Studies* 331

Brown and Chandler, 'Unreasonableness and the Unfair Contract Terms Act' (1993) 109 *Law Quarterly Review* 41

Furmston, *Cheshire, Fifoot and Furmston's Law of Contract*, 16th edn (Oxford University Press, 2012)

Law Commission, *Unfair Terms in Contracts*, Consultation Paper No 166 (2002)

Law Commission, 'Unfair Terms in Contracts', Report No 292 (2005)

Law Commission, Issues Paper, 'Unfair Terms in Consumer Contracts: A New Approach' (July 2012)

Law Commission, 'Unfair Consumer Contracts: Advice to Department of Business, Innovation and Skills' (March 2013)

Lawson, 'Limits to the Unfair Contract Terms Act' (2006) 27 *Business Law Review* 202

Lawson, *Exclusion Clauses and Unfair Contract Terms*, 10th edn (Sweet & Maxwell, 2011)

Macdonald, 'Incorporation of Contract Terms by a "Consistent Course of Dealing"' (1988) 8 *Legal Studies* 48

Macdonald, 'Exclusion Clauses: The Ambit of S 13(1) of the Unfair Contract Terms Act 1977' (1992) 12 *Legal Studies* 277

Macdonald, 'In the Course of a Business – A Fresh Examination' (1999) 3 *Web Journal of Current Legal Issues*

Macdonald, 'Scope and Fairness of the Unfair Terms in Consumer Contract Regulations: *Director General of Fair Trading* v *First National Bank*' (2002) 65 *Modern Law Review* 763

Macdonald, 'Unifying Unfair Terms Legislation' (2004) 67 *Modern Law Review* 69

Macdonald, *Exemption Clauses and Unfair Terms*, 2nd edn (Tottel Publishing, 2006)

Macmillan, 'Evolution or Revolution? Unfair Terms in Consumer Contracts' [2002] *Cambridge Law Journal* 22

Morgan, 'Bank Charges and the Unfair Terms in Consumer Contract Regulations 1999: The End of the Road for Consumers?' (2010) *Lloyd's Maritime and Commercial Law Quarterly* 208

Palmer, 'Limiting Liability for Negligence' (1982) 45 *Modern Law Review* 322

Palmer, 'Clarifying the Unfair Contract Terms Act 1977' (1986) 7 *Business Law Review* 57

Peel, 'Reasonable Exemption Clauses' (2001) 117 *Law Quarterly Review* 545

Smith, Atiyah's *Introduction to the Law of Contract*, 6th edn (Oxford University Press, 2006)

Spencer, 'Signature, Consent, and the Rule in *L'Estrange* v *Graucob*' (1974) 32 *Cambridge Law Journal* 104

Peel, Treitel *Law of Contract*, 14th edn (Sweet and Maxwell, 2015)

Wood, 'Proposals for Reform of the Law on Unfair Contract Terms – First Reactions to the Report of the Law Commission and the Scottish Law Commission' (2005) 5 *Business Law Review* 110

Part 3

Factors that vitiate a contract

Misrepresentation

Objectives

After reading this chapter you should be able to:

1. Define what comprises a misrepresentation.
2. Understand the nature of a misrepresentation so as to be able to distinguish between statements of fact and statements of law, opinion and intention.
3. Explain how a party is induced into a contract in terms of the materiality of the misrepresentation, reliance on the misrepresentation and the awareness of the representee as to the misrepresentation of fact.
4. Understand the nature of misrepresentations.
5. Know and understand the effects of the Consumer Insurance (Disclosure and Representations) Act 2012.
6. Know and understand the remedies available for the different types of misrepresentations.
7. Explain how liability for a misrepresentation may be excluded.

Introduction

Objective 1

Prior to the making of a contract, the parties often make statements to each other with the intention of inducing the other party to make the contract. Some of these statements may well be translated into terms of the contract, breach of which will give the innocent party certain rights in an action for breach of contract, depending on either the relative importance or status of the term within the contract or the seriousness of the consequences of its breach. Some statements, however, will not themselves become terms of the contract but remain as 'mere representations', that is, statements of fact which are intended only to induce the other party to enter into the contract. The process of discerning between statements which are terms and those that are 'mere representations' may not be an easy one, as seen earlier in *Oscar Chess* v *Williams* [1957] 1 All ER 325. A further point should be noted here in that whilst a representation may become a term the opposite is also true in that a term may provide evidence of a representation and this would of course allow the representee to claim the remedies available under misrepresentation. At one time it might have been important to establish a breach of a term rather than a misrepresentation since, with the exception of fraudulent misrepresentation; the remedies for breach of contract were more generous. This is no longer the case since the passing of the Misrepresentation Act 1967.

Of itself a breach of a mere representation is not actionable and it may amount to nothing more than a trade 'puff'. Should the 'mere representation' turn out to be a false statement, however, calculated to induce a party to enter into a contract, then an action may lie in the law of tort for misrepresentation, the effect of which is to render the contract voidable, giving the injured party a possibility of either rescinding the contract or claiming damages, or both. The Misrepresentation Act 1967 s 1 provides that where a person, the representee, has entered into a contract after a misrepresentation has been made to him and the misrepresentation has either become a term of the contract and/or the contract has been performed, then his entitlement to claim rescission is preserved despite the fact that the misrepresentation has become a term and/or the contract has been performed. More will be said about remedies later.

A misrepresentation may be defined then as a false statement of fact that induces another to enter into a contract. The representor's intentions when they made the contract are irrelevant, although this may influence what type of misrepresentation is claimed by the misrepresentee.

The nature of the inducement

Objective 2

As our definition indicates, the false statement must be a statement of fact. It is extremely important to distinguish between statements that are statements of fact and those which are merely statements of law, opinion or intention.

Statements of law

Formerly it was always considered that a statement of law could not amount to a misrepresentation. The rule was thought to be justifiable on the basis that the law is equally accessible to everyone and if a person is not sure as to the state of the law they should seek the advice of their own legal adviser. The rule revolved around the principle of *ignorantia juris non excusat* or 'ignorance of the law is no excuse'. In other words, everyone is presumed to know the law; therefore, a misrepresentation of law could not amount to a vitiating factor.

The distinction between statements of law and statements of fact are not easy to discern from each other. Clearly, statements relating to the contents and meaning of an Act of Parliament or Statutory Instrument are statements of law. The position is not so clear in relation to other documents since, while the meaning of the nature of a particular document might be a statement of law, a statement as to its contents might be a statement of fact. For example, a statement that all contracts for the sale or other disposition of an interest in land must be in writing to be enforceable is a statement of law. A statement that the contract for the sale of land between A and B is in writing and is therefore enforceable is a statement of fact in that it is declaratory of the rights of the parties to the contract.

For more on mistakes of law refer to Chapter 10.

The rule that a statement of law could not amount to a misrepresentation now appears to have been overruled by the House of Lords in **Kleinwort Benson Ltd v Lincoln City Council** [1999] 2 AC 349 where it was held that money paid under a mistake of law could now be recoverable. The result of this is that money paid under a mistake of law is now to be treated on the same basis as money paid under a mistake of fact. This ruling, however, also has repercussions for the rule that misrepresentations of law are generally not actionable.

These repercussions can be seen in the case *Pankhania* v *Hackney London Borough Council* [2002] EWHC 2441 (Ch). The facts of the case were that the claimant had bid in an auction for some commercial property which was partly occupied by a car park operated by NCP Car Parks Ltd ('NCP'). The allegation of the claimant was that he had been induced into the contract to purchase the property as a result of a misrepresentation in the auction catalogue. The basis of his claim was that the catalogue indicated that NCP occupied the premises as a contractual licensee and therefore could be given three months' notice to quit. In fact, NCP was a business tenant and therefore protected under the Landlord and Tenant Act 1954. The claimant sought damages based on the costs incurred to buy out NCP's tenancy in order to obtain vacant possession of the whole premises. The defendants claimed that the misrepresentation was one of law and therefore not actionable because of the well-established rule that misrepresentations of law were not actionable. It was held that since the *Kleinwort Benson* case, just as mistakes of law were now actionable, so misrepresentations of law were also actionable. The judge stated:

> I have concluded that the 'misrepresentation of law' rule has not survived the decision in *Kleinwort Benson Ltd* v *Lincoln City Council* . . . [its] historical origin is an offshoot of the 'mistake of law' rule, created by analogy with it, and the two are logically interdependent. Both are ground in the maxim '*ignorantia juris non excusat*' [ignorance of the law is no excuse], a tag whose dubious utility would have been enhanced had it gone on to explain who was not excused, and from what.

The case is not without difficulty, though, since arguably there is not misrepresentation of law but a statement of law as applied to the particular facts of the case, as illustrated above. Such representations have traditionally been actionable anyway and this appears to cast doubt on the reasoning behind the decision, though, having said that, there is no question that the rule that a misrepresentation of law is not actionable now has to be open to doubt. Essentially the misrepresentation here is one as to private rights as opposed to law. A similar position to the *Pankhania* case can be seen in mistake in *Solle* v *Butcher* [1950] 1 KB 671 where a mistake as to whether a property was controlled by the Rent Acts, which therefore affected the maximum rent that could be charged, was held to be a mistake of fact (i.e. 'private rights'), not a mistake as to law. It should also be noted, however, that some observers consider that this rule exists because statements of law must of necessity be mere statements of opinion as to the state of the law and as such not actionable on that basis (see below). This issue has yet to be considered by the courts but presumably the same distinctions as discussed above will have to be taken into account, the difference being that if a statement is found to be one of opinion only then will there be no actionable cause.

For more on
Solle v *Butcher*
see Chapter 10.

Statements of opinion

Cheshire, Fifoot and Furmston (2012) defines a statement of opinion as a 'statement of a belief based on grounds incapable of actual proof'. The point is easily illustrated by the following case.

Bisset v *Wilkinson* [1927] AC 177

The vendor of a farm in New Zealand, when asked about the number of sheep the farm could sustain, declared that in his judgement it would support 2,000 sheep. In fact the farm had never held sheep and thus it was held that the statement could amount to nothing more than an honest statement of opinion and not a statement of fact. The action for misrepresentation thus failed.

The rule that a statement of opinion cannot form the basis of an action in misrepresentation may nevertheless be overturned if it can be shown that a reasonable man in possession of the same knowledge as the representor could not have honestly held such an opinion. In such a circumstance the statement will be regarded as one of fact rather than one of opinion. In **Smith v Land and House Property Corporation** (1884) 28 ChD 7, a vendor described his property as being 'let to Mr Frederick Fleck (a most desirable tenant) . . . thus offering a first class investment'. In fact, the tenant was in arrears with his rent at the time of the sale and soon after it he declared his bankruptcy. The purchasers refused to complete the sale on finding out the truth and were sued for specific performance of the contract. The court held that since the vendor was in the position to know the true facts of the situation his statement could not be regarded as one of opinion but as one of fact. The decision in the **Smith** case was affirmed in the case of **Esso Petroleum Co. Ltd v Mardon**, which distinguished **Bisset v Wilkinson**.

Esso Petroleum Co. Ltd v Mardon [1976] 2 All ER 5

Esso represented to a prospective purchaser of a petrol station that was being built that it was likely that possible sales of petrol could reach 200,000 gallons a year. In fact the local authority refused planning permission for the proposed layout of the garage, so that the pumps had to be placed to the rear of the site with an entrance via a back street. Despite these changes the market researchers at Esso confirmed that the selling capability of the garage would not be affected and on this basis the defendant bought the petrol station with the help of a loan from Esso. The garage sold a maximum of only 78,000 gallons and as a result incurred such losses that the purchaser could not afford to repay Esso the instalments on the loan. Esso sued to repossess the petrol station and the defendant counter-claimed on the basis of negligent misrepresentation and breach of contract. Esso argued that their estimate as to the maximum sales was one of opinion, since, as in the **Bisset** case, there had never been a petrol station at this location before and therefore any statement as to the potential sales could only be an expression of opinion. The Court of Appeal rejected this contention and found the statement as to the maximum sales to be one of fact. In contrast to the **Bisset** case, Esso had substantial experience and skill in the form of their market research analysts as to the potential sales a petrol station in such a location could expect to achieve. In the circumstances they had failed to exercise reasonable care and skill in relation to the potential sales of the petrol station in question and were thus held to be liable to the defendants. In the **Bisset** case, the parties were of equal bargaining strength and thus both were able to formulate their own opinions as to the maximum number of sheep the farm could support.

A more recent example of the principle can be seen in the case of **Cherrilow Ltd v Richard Butler-Creagh** [2011] EWHC 2525 (QB) in which Cherrilow Ltd ('C') claimed that it was induced to purchase a large property at Henley-on-Thames reputedly built by Sir Christopher Wren by way of dishonest representations made by Richard Butler-Creagh ('B'). The property was owned by a religious group known as the Marian Fathers and B had successfully bid to purchase the property from them. He then negotiated an exclusivity agreement with the group whereby he was required to proceed with the purchase 'as soon as reasonably practicable'. He agreed that if he was not able to proceed with the purchase he should inform them immediately. B then showed Ms Hersham around the property with a view to purchasing it via Cherrilow Ltd, a company set up at Ms Hersham's request.

C alleged that B had made a number of misrepresentations. First, he alleged that he had an exclusive right to purchase the property and develop the property so that no one else could approach the Marian Fathers. Second, that B valued the property at £22.5 million when in fact its market value was closer to £10 million. Third, that the property could be redeveloped into a hotel with residential units within 26 months and this development would net a profit of £32 million. B also claimed that he had 25 years' experience as a property developer and that the purchase had to be completed urgently as there were other purchasers interested in the property.

B argued that the representations did not induce C into the contract to purchase the property and in any event C had suffered no loss. He also counter-claimed on grounds of undue enrichment because C had not paid him for his services. He also claimed that Ms Hersham owed him a £5 million fee for allowing Ms Hersham to take advantage of the exclusivity agreement he had with the Marian Fathers. It was held that C's claim for fraudulent misrepresentation succeeded and B's claim for the £5 million failed.

While the case has three aspects with regard to actions in misrepresentation, with regard to the distinction between statements of fact and statements of opinion it was held that if a reasonable man could not have honestly held the opinion made then the statement will be regarded as a statement of fact not opinion. The court held that B had no genuine belief in the valuation he placed upon the property since he had no grounds to believe that a purchaser would be willing to pay £22.5 million. Thus the court held that C was induced to purchase the property on the basis of B's valuation.

Statements of intention

Often a promise to do something in the future may not only amount to consideration in a contract but also comprise a term of the contract. Failure to carry out the promise in such circumstances will amount to a breach of contract. A mere representation as to future conduct is not actionable either as a breach of contract or as a misrepresentation since such statements do not amount to statements of fact. A statement of intention that induces a person to enter into a contract is, however, actionable as a misrepresentation of fact where it can be shown that the maker knew that their promise would not be carried out.

Edgington v Fitzmaurice (1885) 29 ChD 459

The directors of a company issued a prospectus inviting subscriptions for debentures. The money raised from the loan capital arising from the sale of the debentures was, according to the prospectus, to be used to complete alterations to the company's premises, to purchase horses and vans and to develop the business. The plaintiff advanced money in the wrong belief that debenture holders would have a charge over the company's premises. The object of raising the loan capital was in fact to enable the company to pay off pressing debts. It was held that the plaintiff could rescind the contract because there was found to be a misrepresentation of fact. The company directors had not simply made a promise as to the future use of the money which they may or may not have fulfilled, but consciously told an untruth in order to induce members of the public to subscribe to the debentures. Bowen LJ justified the decision as follows:

> The state of a man's mind is as much a fact as the state of his digestion. It is true that it is very difficult to prove what the state of a man's mind at a particular time is, but if it can be ascertained it is as much a fact as anything else. A misrepresentation as to the state of a man's mind is, therefore, a misstatement of fact.

Silence as a misrepresentation of fact

As a general rule silence cannot amount to a misrepresentation since there is no duty to disclose facts which may influence a person not to enter into a contract. This rule has its origins in the classical theory of contract where the notion of freedom to contract and equality of bargaining power reigned supreme.

There are, however, three exceptions to the above rule.

Change of circumstances

Where a statement is made which is true at the time but subsequently becomes untrue to the knowledge of the representor before the contract is made, then a failure by the representor to inform the representee of the change of circumstances will amount to a misrepresentation. This is qualified, however, in that if the context makes it clear to a reasonable representee that the representor accepts no responsibility either for the statement or for reviewing the statement, then no misrepresentation will arise. Thus where a representor knows that the subsequent events or circumstances render a statement to become untrue, they are under a duty to disclose the change of circumstances. The reasoning behind such a principle is that representations are treated as continuing until the contract between the parties is actually concluded.

With v *O'Flanagan* [1936] Ch 575

A doctor was negotiating the sale of his practice and made certain representations regarding the income that could be earned from it. At the time the misrepresentation was made the figures were true. Subsequently the doctor fell ill so that the income earned from the practice decreased substantially. The reduction was not made known to the purchaser, who purchased the practice on the basis of the original earnings. When the purchaser discovered the true state of affairs he sought to rescind the contract. It was held that the purchaser should succeed in his action for rescission on the grounds of misrepresentation, as the doctor should have declared the change of circumstances.

As a general rule, there is no obligation to disclose a change in one's intentions. The principle can be seen in **Wales v Wadham** 1977 1 WLR 199 where during proceedings for a divorce the husband entered into an agreement to pay his wife £17000 provided she agreed not to pursue proceedings for maintenance. During the proceedings the wife repeatedly stated that she would not re-marry; however, by the time of the agreement the wife had changed her mind but did not disclose her change of intention to her former husband. On discovering his former wife's change of intention, he brought proceedings for the agreement to be set aside on the basis that he would not have consented had he known the true facts. His application failed since the court held that the wife was under no obligation to communicate her change of intention since her original intention was honestly held at the time of the agreement and thus did not amount to a representation of fact. That said, in **Jenkins v Livesey (formerly Jenkins)** [1985] AC 424 where the facts were broadly similar, the House of Lords overruled the decision in **Wales v Wadham** stating a court could not properly exercise its discretion unless it was provided with correct, complete, and up-to-date information. Each party was under a duty to make full and frank disclosure of all material facts to the other party and to the court. The House of Lords stated that the wife's remarriage is one of the 'circumstances of the case' contained in the Matrimonial Causes Act 1973 for consideration by the court with regard to consent orders so the change of circumstances should have been disclosed. Failure to do so meant that the consent order should be set aside.

A similar point was made in **Inclusive Technology v Williamson** [2009] EWCA Civ 718 where a landlord served a statutory termination notice on his tenant under the Landlord and Tenant Act 1975 on the basis that he wanted to refurbish the premises and that the refurbishment could not be carried out whilst the tenant remained in occupation of the premises. He later changed his mind and decided to potstone the work 'until the circumstances were right'. The landlord did not inform the tenant of his change of intentions. The tenant, believing he had to quit the premises, arranged a lease on some alternative premises. At first instance the judge found that the landlord's original representation did not amount to a representation that the landlord would not change his mind and, secondly, the landlord had not concealed his intentions since 'concealment' required the landlord to do something consciously and deliberately which the landlord had not done. The Court of Appeal found that the relevant provisions of the Landlord and Tenant Act 1975 was intended to encourage fair dealing between the parties and as regards the disposition of legal rights the landlord was placed in a special position in that this was determined by reference to his subjective intentions. The result was that the representations made by the landlord gave rise to a continuing obligation in that 'there was a specific transaction, a specific purpose and a specific timeframe'. The result was that the continuing representation became false and became a misrepresentation since there was a duty to communicate a change of mind.

The decision in **Inclusive** *Technology* **v** *Williamson* accords with the decision in ***Spice Girls Ltd* v *Aprilia World Service BV*** [2002] EWCA Civ 15 where Aprilia, a motorcycle manufacturer, entered into a contract to sponsor a tour by the pop group Spice Girls. The substance of the contract was agreed on 4 March 1998. Subsequently on 30 March 1998 a fax was sent to Aprilia confirming the commitment of the Spice Girls to the arrangements. Further, on 4 May all five of the Spice Girls took part in a photo shoot promoting Aprilia and the agreement signed on 6 May 1998 described the Spice Girls as 'currently consisting' of the five named members. The agreement provided that Aprilia pay £400,000 by three instalments, two of which had already been paid, and £112,500 as a non-returnable advance against royalties payable in respect of motor scooters manufactured and sold by the Aprilia Group bearing the name Sonic Spice. On 31 May 1998, it was announced that Ms Geri Halliwell, professionally known as Ginger Spice, had left the Spice Girls on 27 May 1998. It subsequently transpired that Ms Halliwell had informed the other four members of the group on 3 and 9 March that she would be leaving the group. This intention was reaffirmed on 25 April. Aprilia as part of its defence to an action for breach of contract for non-payment of the remaining instalment alleged that it had been induced into the contract by way of a material misrepresentation, namely, the fax dated 30 March 1998 described the group as 'currently consisting' of the five members.

In the Court of Appeal, Lord Chadwick stated that whilst it is a well-established principle that a representation must be one of fact, representations as to the future or of opinion also may contain implied representations. Once a representation has been made it is likely to have continuing effect in that it will continue until the transaction is complete or at least ceases to operate on the mind of the representee. The effect of this is that whilst the representation is continuing and the representor discovers the untruth of the representation he is under a duty to communicate this to the representee, as he would in any change of circumstances. On this basis the Court of Appeal held that nothing had been done to correct the continuing representation in this case and that the Spice Girls had induced the contract by misrepresentation in breach of the Misrepresentation Act 1967 s 2(1). In arriving at his judgement Lord Chadwick referred to the dicta of Romer LJ in **With v O'Flanagan** where he stated:

> If A with a view to inducing B to enter into a contract makes a representation as to a material fact, then if at a later date and before the contract is actually entered into, owing to a change of circumstances, the representation then made would to the knowledge of A be untrue, and B subsequently enters into the contract in ignorance of that change of circumstances and

relying upon that representation, A cannot hold B to the bargain. There is ample authority for that statement and, indeed, I doubt myself whether any authority is necessary, it being, it seems to me, so obviously consistent with the plainest principles of equity.

The principle therefore seems to be reaffirmed. It is, however, unclear if the duty extends to statements of opinion, i.e. if one held an opinion, which as we have seen is not a statement of fact, and one's opinion changes, is there a duty to disclose this to the representee and, if there is such a duty, would this become a statement of fact and be actionable if the change of opinion is not disclosed?

The statement made is only half the truth

A representor must take care not to mislead the representee by revealing only part of the circumstances prevailing. In other words, the representor must not suppress anything disadvantageous which may be considered relevant by the representee.

In *Dimmock v Hallett* (1866) LR 2 Ch App 21, a landlord selling property which he disclosed in the negotiation as fully let was under a duty to reveal that in fact the tenants had served notice to quit on the representor landlord.

Confidential/fiduciary relationships

A fiduciary relationship exists where a person has placed a confidence in another person, whereby that person, having been privy to such information, is under a duty not to disclose information gained from such a relationship. Such relationships exist between a trustee and a beneficiary, or a doctor and their patient, or a solicitor and their client.

A fiduciary relationship also arises in certain types of contract irrespective of the nature of the relationship between the parties, where one party has the sole access to information forming the basis of the contract. Such contracts are known as contracts of *uberrimae fidei* (utmost good faith). An example of a common contract *uberrimae fidei* is a contract of insurance.

British insurance law developed during the eighteenth and nineteenth centuries, and was partly codified by the Marine Insurance Act 1906. While this Act applies to marine insurance, the courts have applied its provisions across all types of insurance, particularly consumer insurance contracts. The justification for this is that the 1906 Act in fact codifies the common law. The 1906 Act, ss 17 and 18 provide that a contract of insurance is a contract of *uberrimae fidei* and that if that is not observed by either party, the contract may be avoided by the other party. Thus, a person must disclose every matter that is material to a prudent insurer's decision to insure at all or, if the insurer will insure, what premiums will be charged. A failure to declare such matters allows the insurer to avoid the contract and refuse all claims under it, even where the insured person is not aware of what the insurer would consider material.

The issue of contracts of *uberrimae fidei* in contracts of insurance have changed as regards consumers by way of the Consumer Insurance (Disclosure and Representations) Act 2012. The purpose of the Act is to update the law relating to pre-contractual disclosure and misrepresentations and to this extent it gives effect, with minor modifications, to the recommendations set out in the Law Commission and the Scottish Law Commission's 2009 joint report *Consumer Insurance Law: Pre-Contract Disclosure and Misrepresentation* (Law Com No 319; Scot Law Com No 219).

This Act replaces the duty to volunteer material information and provides instead that consumers have a duty to take reasonable care not to make a misrepresentation during re-contractual negotiations. If a consumer breaches this duty and this misrepresentation induces the insurer to enter the contract, the insurer will have a remedy. By s 1, a 'consumer' means an individual who enters into a consumer insurance contract or proposes to do so in the future. Also by s 1, a 'consumer insurance contract' means a contract of insurance between:

1 an individual who enters into the contract wholly or mainly for purposes unrelated to the individual's trade, business or profession; and

2 a person who carries on the business of insurance and who becomes a party to the contract by way of that business (whether or not in accordance with permission for the purposes of the Financial Services and Markets Act 2000).

The nature of the insurer's remedy depends on the nature of the consumer's misrepresentation. If a consumer makes a deliberate or reckless misrepresentation, the Act permits the insurer to treat the contract as if it never existed and refuse all claims. If, when answering questions posed by an insurer, a consumer answers carelessly, the Act provides that the insurer may have a remedy according to whether it would have entered into the contract on different terms. If it would not have entered into the contract at all it may refuse all claims but it must return the premiums paid. If it would have entered into the contract on different terms, the contract may be taken to include those different terms. If the premium would have been higher this may have consequences for the amount of any claim. If the consumer acts with reasonable care, the insurer must pay the claim in full.

In relation to non-consumer contracts, the issue of *uberrimae fidei* is now also dealt with in the Insurance Act 2015. The aim of the Act is to update and replace the existing duty on non-consumer policyholders to disclose risk information to insurers before entering into an insurance contract, i.e. the principle of *uberrimae fidei*. This principle is found within the Marine Insurance Act 1906 s 17 which provides that insurance contracts are contracts based upon the utmost good faith. It goes on to say that, 'if the utmost good faith be not observed by either party, the contract may be avoided by the other party'. The common law mirrors this provision in relation to non-marine insurance.

In s 14 (1) of the Insurance Act 2015, it is stated that any rule of law that permits a party to a contract of insurance to avoid the contract on the ground that the principle of utmost good faith has not been observed by the other party is abolished. The effect therefore is that whilst the remedy for breach of *uberrimae fidei* has disappeared, the principle remains but only as an interpretative principle. The Act, however, redefines the principle in s 3 in that a person seeking insurance must make a fair presentation of the risk to the insurer, i.e. 'the duty of fair presentation'. This is defined in s 3(3) in that a fair presentation of risk is one which makes the disclosure 'in a manner which would be reasonably clear and accessible to a prudent insurer' (s 3(3)b), and, 'in which every material representation as to a matter of fact is substantially correct, and every material representation as to a matter of expectation or belief is made in good faith' (s 3(3)c).

The disclosure required under the Act is set out in s 3(4) is that of every material circumstance which the insured knows or ought to know – s 3(4)a. Failing that, the disclosure must give the insurer sufficient information that puts a prudent insurer on notice that it needs to make further enquiries for the purposes of revealing the material circumstances – s 3(4)b. Having said that, s 3(5) provides that the insured is not required to disclose a circumstance that diminishes the risk, a circumstance which the insurer knows or is presumed to know or anything for which the insurer waives information.

A 'material circumstance' is defined in s 7. 'Circumstance' is defined as including 'any communication made to, or information received by the insured' – s 7(2); whilst ' material' is that which would 'influence the judgement of a prudent insurer in determining whether to take the risk and, if so, on what terms' – s 7(3). Thus a material circumstance may be any special or unusual risk or any concerns which prompted the insured to seek insurance cover for the risk. Similarly it would also include anything which an insurer in a particular type of field of insurance, e.g. shipping, plant and machinery, etc. would generally understand to be something which would arise under a fair presentation of the risks involved in that type of insurance. It should, however, be noted that a material representation as to a matter of fact is regarded as correct if a prudent insurer would not consider the difference between what is presented and what is actually correct to be material.

Importantly, the Act introduces a new system of proportionate remedies where the 'duty of fair presentation' has been breached. Thus the single remedy of avoidance of the contract that existed previously is replaced. Thus in s 8 in such circumstances the insured only has a remedy if the insurer can show that but for the breach the insurer would not have entered into a contract of insurance at all or, if he would have done so, this would be done on different terms. Where the insurer has a remedy against the insured, this is referred to as a 'qualifying breach' – s 8(3). By s 8(4), a qualifying beach is one which is either deliberate or reckless, or neither deliberate nor reckless. By s 8(5) a qualifying breach is deliberate or reckless if the insured knew that it was in breach of the duty of fair presentation, or did not care whether or not it was in breach of that duty. It is for the insurer to show that the qualifying breach was deliberate or careless. The remedies are set out in Schedule 1 so that by para 2, if a qualifying breach was deliberate or reckless, the insurer may avoid the contract and refuse all claims and, further, need not return any of the premiums paid. Where there is no qualifying breach but the insurer would not have entered into the contract on any terms, the insurer may avoid the contract and refuse all claims, but must in that event return the premiums paid – para 4. On the other hand, by para 5, if the insurer would have entered into the contract, but on different terms (other than terms relating to the premium), the contract is to be treated as if it had been entered into on those different terms, assuming the insurer so requires. Further, if the insurer would have entered into the contract (whether the terms relating to matters other than the premium would have been the same or different), but would have charged a higher premium, the insurer may reduce the amount to be paid on the claim by a proportionate amount.

One further point should be noted in relation to the duty to disclose is that by the Fraud Act 2006 s 3 a failure to discharge that duty and disclose the information amounts to a criminal offence if there was an intention to make a gain or cause loss to another – s 3.

The fact of the inducement

Objective
3

Our definition of a misrepresentation indicates that the statement of fact must have induced the innocent party to enter the contract. In order to prove the inducement we must take certain factors into consideration.

The misrepresentation must be material

The misrepresentation, to be actionable, must be important enough to influence a reasonable person in considering whether or not to enter into a contract, or on what terms they are prepared to enter into the contract. As we have already seen above, the Insurance Act 2015 also contains a materiality requirement in consumer insurance contracts so that the insured must disclose material circumstances that puts the prudent insurer on notice that further enquiries may be required for the purpose of revealing the material circumstances, materiality being circumstances which would 'influence the judgement of a prudent insurer in determining whether to take the risk and, if so, on what terms' (s 7(3)).

It should be noted that an objective test is applied here and, thus, even if the representor does not consider the false statement to be material, it may nevertheless be held to be so as affirmed by the House of Lords in *Pan Atlantic Insurance Co. Ltd v Pine Top Insurance Co. Ltd* [1995] 1 AC 501. It is also true of course that a lie which has no impact on misrepresentee is not good enough. Even in the law of insurance a material misrepresentation or non-disclosure in the making of the contract, whether honest or dishonest, will not give rise to a right of avoidance unless it induced the insurer to accept the risk or to do so on the particular terms: *Pan Atlantic Insurance Co Ltd v Pine Top Insurance Co Ltd* [1995] 1 AC 501 and *Versloot Dredging BV v HDI Gerling Industrie Versicherung AG* [2016] UKSC 45.

The objective approach to testing materiality is important because it is largely this factor which distinguishes this rule from the need for reliance on the misrepresentation, which is discussed below. In deciding whether a person has relied on a misrepresentation one examines the actual state of the representee's mind with regard to the false statement at the time they enter into the contract. Materiality, on the other hand, rests on the importance of an untrue statement to the reasonable person of business when deciding whether or not to enter into a contract.

JEB Fasteners Ltd v Marks Bloom & Co. [1983] 1 All ER 583

The plaintiffs decided to launch a takeover of a company for the purpose of obtaining the services of two directors. The plaintiffs inspected the accounts of the company but these were inaccurate because of the negligence of the defendant firm of accountants. While the accounts were regarded as a material misrepresentation the plaintiffs' action failed as they had not relied on the accounts. This conclusion was reached since the principal objective of the plaintiffs was not to acquire the company for commercial reasons but to secure the services of the two directors in question. The case therefore represents a good illustration of the distinction between reliance and materiality.

Nevertheless, the requirement of materiality has more recently been called into question in the case of *Museprime Properties Ltd v Adhill Properties Ltd* [1990] 36 EG 114 where there was a sale by auction of three properties. During the auction certain representations were made to the effect that a rent review was outstanding and that it was still possible for the purchaser to negotiate higher rents. In fact, new rents had already been fixed for the next review period. The plaintiffs sued to have the contract rescinded on the grounds of misrepresentation. The defendants argued, *inter alia*, that they could not do so because the misrepresentation was not material since no reasonable bidder would have allowed such a misrepresentation to affect his bid. The court held that the materiality was not determined objectively on the basis of whether a reasonable person would have been induced to enter into the contract. It was sufficient if the purchaser could show that he was actually affected by the representation.

It is considered that the test of reasonableness in relation to materiality was only important in relation to the representee proving to the court that they had in fact been induced by the misrepresentation. In other words, the more unreasonable the misrepresentation, the more difficult it will be for the representee to prove that they were actually induced by the statement. Thus, if the representor had made the statement in good faith and the representation would not have influenced a reasonable person, then the representee may find it exceedingly difficult to prove that the statement was in fact material to their decision.

In *Downs* v *Chappell* [1996] 3 All ER 344, the Court of Appeal confirmed that a misrepresentation is material when its tendency, or its natural and probable result, is to induce the representee to act on the faith of it in the kind of way in which they are proved to have in fact acted. The test remains an objective one – would the reasonable person have been induced to enter into the contract by the representation? Once materiality is proved by this test and it is shown that the misrepresentee has been induced into the contract as a matter of fact, the misrepresentee does not have to prove causation since this has been done by proving both materiality and inducement. On this basis it is wrong to go on and ask if the claimant would have entered into the contract had they been told the truth since, of course, they had never been told the truth.

Even if the representee can show that they were actually influenced by the statement, it may be that a court would not award them rescission but only nominal damages in such a situation.

It should be noted that all statements are deemed material where a contract expressly provides for this. Contracts of insurance, for instance, commonly provide that statements made in proposal forms are deemed to be material, no matter how minor or trivial they may be.

Reliance and inducement

The misrepresentation must have induced the misrepresentee to enter into the contract

In other words, the person to whom the misrepresentation is made must have taken cognisance of the statement so that it influences them in the making of the decision to enter into the contract. Thus the person to whom the representation was made must have relied on the statement in that it induced them to enter the contract. Inducement is a question of fact, not one of law, thus Hobhouse LJ in *Downs* v *Chappell* [1997] 1 WLR 426 stated that 'for a plaintiff to succeed in the tort of deceit of deceit it is necessary for him to prove that (1) the representation was fraudulent, (2) it was material and (3) it induced the plaintiff to act to his detriment'. He added that 'As regards inducement, this is a question of fact . . . '.

Various expressions have been used to describe the test of inducement, so, for instance, it must have been the 'effective cause' of entering into the contract or must have 'materially contributed' to the decision to enter the contract. Essentially the test is the 'but for' test, that is, had the representation not been made to them, the representee would not have entered into the contract or would have done so on different terms, as held in *Raiffeisen Zentralbank Osterreich AG* v *Royal Bank of Scotland plc* [2010] EWHC 1392 in which Clarke LJ followed the decision in *Pan Atlantic Insurance co Ltd* v *Pine Top Insurance Co Ltd* [1995] 1 AC 501 where the House of Lords stated that an insurer must not only demonstrate that the information that had not been disclosed was material but also that the insurer was induced to enter into the contract. Even in the law of deceit under fraudulent misrepresentation:

> it is fundamental that the representee must have acted on the misrepresentation. If he would have done the same thing even in the absence of the misrepresentation, a claim based on it will fail. The same position applies where there is a claim under an insurance policy where the insurer rejects the claim and purports to rescind a contract for misrepresentation, fraudulent or otherwise. Thus, if an insurer were to settle a claim by agreement and then discover that that he had been told a lie in the course of the claim process, he would have to show that his agreement was influenced by the lie in order to rescind it. A lie which had no impact on him would not be good enough.

Per Lord Sumption in *Versloot Dredging BV and Another* v *HDI Gerling Industrie Versi-cherung AG* [2016] UKSC 45(29).

> ## Example
>
> *X* is offered a car for £2,500 and is told by *Y* that the car has done only 20,000 miles but in fact it has done 40,000 miles. Here there is a clear misrepresentation, but one which is actionable only if *X* has been induced into the contract by the statement as to the mileage of the car. If *X* is not bothered about the mileage or in fact chooses the car because of its colour, age or model, then they will have no action for misrepresentation.

Attwood v *Small* (1838) 6 Cl & Fin 232

> The appellant negotiated the sale of certain mines and works to the respondents. The respondents asked questions regarding the capacity of the mine and subsequently had the appellant's answers confirmed by the reports of their own mining engineers. Some six months after the sale the respondents discovered that the answers supplied by the appellant were inaccurate and claimed to rescind the contract for misrepresentation. It was held that their action would fail since the respondents had not relied on the statements made by the appellant but on the reports of their own mining engineers.

A person is not precluded from claiming in misrepresentation merely because they relied on other factors as well as the false statement. As we have already seen in the case of *Edgington* v *Fitzmaurice*, above, the plaintiff there relied not only on the false statements made in the prospectus but also on his own, wrong assumption that subscribing to the debenture would give him a charge over the company's property. He was nevertheless held to be entitled to rescind the contract for misrepresentation.

On the other hand, in *Peekay Intermark Ltd* v *Australia and New Zealand Banking Group Ltd* [2006] EWCA Civ 386, the facts of which have already been stated in Chapter 8, it was held that incorrect investment information given over the telephone in an informal conversation could not amount to an inducement as the claimant was an experienced investor. He had been induced to sign the contract not by anything the bank has told him orally but as a result of his own assumptions. Whatever information the investor was given in the telephone conversations, even if it was a misrepresentation, was dispelled by the fact that he must have been aware of the final terms and conditions, whether or not he had read them of the contract so that any information given in the telephone conversation could not have amounted to a misrepresentation. He had simply assumed that the information in the telephone conversation corresponded with the investment information in the written contract.

The test therefore is not based on whether the misrepresentee relied exclusively on the misrepresentations made to him. Whilst it is necessary to prove that the representations played a significant role in entering into the contract, it is not necessary to prove that the representations played a decisive role in inducing the representee to enter into the contract. This in *Dadourian Group International Inc.* v *Simms* [2009] EWCA Civ 169, Arden LJ stated:

> (1) it is a question of fact whether a representee has been induced to enter into a transaction by a material misrepresentation intended by the representor to be relied upon by the representee; (2) if the misrepresentation is of such a nature that it would be likely to play a part in

the decision of a reasonable person to enter into a transaction it will be presumed that it did so unless the representor satisfies the court to the contrary (see Morritt LJ in **Barton v County NatWest Limited** [1999] Lloyd's Rep Banking 408 at 421, paragraph 58); (3) *the misrepresentation does not have to be the sole inducement for the representee to be able to rely on it: it is enough if the misrepresentation plays a real and substantial part, albeit not a decisive part, in inducing the representee to act*; (4) the presumption of inducement is rebutted by the representor showing that the misrepresentation did not play a real and substantial part in the representee's decision to enter into the transaction; the representor does not have to go so far as to show that the misrepresentation played no part at all; and (5) the issue is to be decided by the court on a balance of probabilities on the whole of the evidence before it. [Emphasis added]

This test was also approved of in **Taberna Europe CDO II Plc v Selskabet (Formerly Roskilde Bank A/S) (In Bankruptcy)** [2015] EWHC 871 (Comm). Further support can also be found in **Standard Chartered Bank Ltd v Pakistan National Shipping Corporation Ltd (Nos 2 and 4)** [2003] 1 AC 959 in which Lord Hoffman stated in the context of fraudulent misrepresentation:

> if a fraudulent representation is relied upon, in the sense that the claimant would not have parted with his money if he had known that it was false, it does not matter that he also had some other negligent or irrational belief about another matter and, but for that belief, would not have parted with his money either. The law simply ignores the other reasons why he paid.

Similarly Morritt VC in **Spice Girls Ltd v Aprilia World Service BV** [2002] EWCA Civ 15 commented, 'It is sufficient that the misrepresentation is a material inducement, it does not have to be the only one . . . '.

Truth known to the representee?

A person cannot claim in misrepresentation if, in fact, they were aware of the untruth of the statement of fact before or at the time of entering into the contract. Clearly if the representee is aware of the untruth of the statement, then it would be very difficult to establish that he had been induced to enter into the contract or that he had suffered loss as a result. The burden of proof that the representee knew of the untruth of the statement lies with the representor, who cannot establish this merely by showing that the representee had the means of discovering the falsehood. Clearly it would be nonsensical to allow a person to make a false statement and then to escape liability by stating that the representee should have discovered the untruth because they had the means to do so. The point can be seen in the following case.

Redgrave v *Hurd* (1881) 20 ChD 1

A solicitor was induced to buy a practice on the basis of an innocent misrepresentation as to the value of the practice and the property attached to it. The solicitor had the accounts made available to him though he did not examine them. It was held that he was able to rescind the contract despite the fact that the accounts would have revealed the untruth of the statements made to him.

It would appear that in cases involving negligent misrepresentation it is possible that it may be reasonable for a representee to make use of an opportunity to discover the truth of a representation, with the effect that failure to do so will defeat the claim, or at least raise a spectre of contributory negligence (see below). Such a possibility was indicated in the case of **Smith v Eric S Bush** [1990] 1 AC 831 where the plaintiffs, who were purchasing a house, relied on a negligently prepared survey carried out by the surveyors engaged by their lender. They would have discovered the truth about the property if they had engaged their own surveyor. However, the House of Lords stated that where the value of a house was modest, it was unlikely that such purchasers would engage their own surveyor and, indeed, it was not reasonable for them to do so. The case thus followed *Redgrave v Hurd* in that their failure to engage their own surveyor did not prevent them from taking action. However, if the house was of a substantial value or comprised commercial property, the House of Lords indicated that the position would have been different and failure to take the opportunity to discover the truth of a state of affairs would have prevented them from taking action. It is, however, uncertain whether the same principles could be applied to cases of innocent misrepresentation. Presumably the decision in *Redgrave v Hurd* will still stand since, as Treitel points out, 'there is actual, and reasonable, reliance on the misrepresentation in such a case'.

In *Cherrilow Ltd v Richard Butler-Creagh*, the facts of which have already been discussed above, the representor, Richard Butler-Creagh (B), argued that Ms Hersham (C) should not have relied on his statements and should have sought her own valuation and enquiries about the property. He therefore sought to rely on the principle that to claim misrepresentation Ms Hersham must have relied on the statement so that it induced her to enter into the contract and that a person cannot claim in misrepresentation if he was aware of the untruth of the statement of fact. The burden of proof lies with the representor, B, to show that the representee knew of the untruth of the statement. The representor cannot discharge this burden by stating that the representee should have discovered the nature of the falsehood: *Redgrave v Hurd*. In the case Eady J stated:

> The justification for this aspect of legal policy is especially evident in a case such as this, where the defendant has made representations as to urgency, specifically with a view to discouraging independent checks being made on his claims.

Whilst a person cannot claim in misrepresentation if they were aware of the untruth of the statement of fact before or at the time of entering into the contract, does the converse apply in that in order to show the requisite influence by or reliance on the misrepresentation a defrauded representee has to prove that he believed the misrepresentation was true? The point was considered in the Supreme Court in *Hayward v Zurich Insurance Co plc* [2016] UKSC 48.

Hayward v Zurich Insurance Co plc [2016] UKSC 48

The facts of the case were that the respondent injured his back as a result of an accident at work. The effect of this was that his ability to work was seriously impaired and he suffered from continuous back pain. He sued his employer and Zurich Insurance then conducted the defence on behalf of the employer. Part of the evidence in the defence was a video showing the respondent undertaking heavy work at home and as a result it was alleged that he had exaggerated the extent and seriousness of his injury. Eventually the dispute was settled with Zurich agreeing to pay £134,973 in full and final settlement of the claim. Two years later the respondent's neighbours contacted the employer saying that they believed that the respondent had fully recovered from the accident at least a year before the date of the settlement. Zurich then brought an action alleging fraudulent misrepresentation with respect that the respondent had misled the insurance company with regard to the extent of his injuries with a view to securing a larger claim. The judge at first instance set the settlement agreement aside reducing the damages to £14,720. The respondent appealed against the decision to set the settlement agreement aside, though crucially did not contest the facts or the assessment of the damages.

In relation to the matter of reliance the judge (at para 2.5) stated:

Lastly, of course, it is necessary that the employer/Zurich should *rely* on the representations and suffer loss as a result. Here an interesting (and apparently unresolved) question of principle arises. In the ordinary case, sale of goods, for example, reliance by the purchaser is effectively equivalent to his *belief in the truth* of the statement; if he believes the goods are as represented, he will be relying on the representation (and acting on it by his purchase) and if not, not. In the litigation context the position is different. In such a situation, the party to whom the representation is made is by no means likely to believe it to be true at the pre-trial stage. At the very least, statements made in the course of litigation will be viewed with healthy scepticism and weighed against the other material available. Often the other party will not be sure, even then, whether the statement is in fact true, and will mainly concern himself with how likely it is to be accepted by the court. Sometimes (a staged road traffic 'accident', for example) the other party may actually be certain from his own direct knowledge that the statement is a deliberate lie. But even then he and his advisers cannot choose to ignore it; they must still take into account the risk that it will be believed by the judge at trial. This situation is quite different from a proposed purchase, where if in doubt one can simply walk away. For these reasons, it appears to me that the many dicta relied on by [the respondent], to the effect that liability requires that the representation must be believed by the other party, are not applicable to a case like the present. The formulation adopted by the editors of *Clerk and Lindsell*, 20th ed (2010), at 18–34 fits the case better; 'The claimant must have been *influenced* by the misrepresentation'.

Effectively Zurich would have a healthy scepticism about the truth of the respondent's disabilities. The video evidence was damning but even in the face of this, the respondent continued with the false claims. Whilst Zurich was aware, at the time of the settlement, that there was a real possibility of fraud, nevertheless the deliberate continuing misrepresentations influenced Zurich in making a higher level of settlement and thus the judge considered the conditions required for setting aside the settlement were met.

The Court of Appeal reversed that decision. In arriving at their decision, Underhill, Briggs and King LJJ rejected the principles set out by the judge at first instance because of the state of mind of Zurich at the time the settlement was made.

In the appeal to the Supreme Court, the main issue arose in relation to the matter of reliance. The issue was whether, in order to show the requisite influence or reliance on the misrepresentation, it was necessary to prove that the defrauded misrepresentee believed that the misrepresentations were true. The Supreme Court thought not. Lord Clarke, giving the leading judgement, considered that whilst it must be shown that a defendant made a materially false representation which was intended and did induce the representee to act to its detriment, i.e. he has been influenced by the misrepresentation; it was not necessary as a matter of law to prove that the representee believed that the representation was true. Lord Clarke considered that in some circumstances the state of mind of the representee may be relevant in that if he did not believe the statement to be true, he may be faced with some difficulty in establishing that he was induced into the contract. Lord Clarke agreed with the judge at first instance that reliance on a statement by the representee is effectively equivalent to a *belief in the truth* of the statement; however, whilst one may infer that a representee who believes a misrepresentation has been induced to rely on it, the absence of a belief does not mean that there has been no inducement. Once it is established that a false statement is material, in that it is likely to induce a contract and the representee subsequently enters a contract, then it is an inference fact, not one of law, that he was influenced by the misrepresentation and that this is particularly strong in cases of fraudulent misrepresentation. There is thus a **'presumption of inducement'** particularly in cases where there is an intention to induce a contract by means of fraud. If it had to be shown that the representee actually believed in the misrepresentation, then there would be no need to have such a presumption. The presumption of inducement is a difficult one to rebut although there is an inconsistency in the authorities as to how this test is formulated, for instance, is it necessary to prove that the misrepresentation played 'no part at all' in the entering of the contract by the representee or whether it did not play a 'real and substantive part'?. Lord Clarke considered that the orthodox view on this point was contained in the case of **Sharland** v **Sharland** [2015] 3 WLR 10 in which Lady Hale, following **Smith** v **Kay** (1859) VII HLC 749, stated, '. . . a party who has practised deception with a view to a particular end, which has been attained by it, cannot be allowed to deny its materiality'. Similarly, in **Downs** v **Chappell** [1996] 3 All ER 344, Hobhouse LJ stated:

> The judge was wrong to ask how they [the representees] would have acted if they had been told the truth. They were never told the truth. They were told lies in order to induce them to enter into the contract. The lies were material and successful . . . The judge should have concluded that the plaintiff's had proved their case on causation . . .

Further, in **BP Exploration Operating Co Ltd** v **Chevron Shipping Co** [2003] 1 AC 197 Lord Millett stated:

> The representor must have decided to make the misrepresentation because he or she judged that the truth or silence would not, or might not, serve their purposes or serve them so well. In doing so they fashioned an evidentiary weapon against themselves, and the court should not subject the victim to 'what if' inquiries which the representor was not prepared to risk at the time.

The Supreme Court allowed the appeal, finding that, firstly, it was not necessary for the defrauded representee to prove that it was induced into a contract or a settlement because it believed the misrepresentations were true and, secondly, that an inducement is found if the fact of the misrepresentations was a material cause of the defrauded representee entering into a contract or a settlement.

Representee unaware of the misrepresentation?

As already indicated, the misrepresentation, to be actionable, must have acted on the mind of the representee. It follows therefore that if the representee is unaware of the misrepresentation, they cannot take action on the basis of it. Thus in **Ex Parte Briggs** (1859) 28 LJ Ch 50, a purchaser of shares in a company could not rescind the contract on the basis of false reports as to the state of the financial affairs of the company because he could not prove that he had actually read or been aware of the contents of the reports before or at the time he purchased the shares.

The issue about a misrepresentation not being actionable if the representee is unaware of the misrepresentation is subject to one qualification, as can be seen in the Supreme Court decision in **Cramaso LLP** v **Ogilvie-Grant** [2014] UKSC 9. In this case a businessman, Mr Erskine, was interested in taking the lease of a grouse moor in Scotland. The owners of the moor over which commercial shooting of grouse took place had recognised that a significant investment was required to increase the number of grouse on the moor but were unwilling to undertake that investment themselves. The owners thus decided to lease the moor to a tenant. Mr Erskine learned that the lease might be available but did not pursue the matter. The owners then entered into negotiations with another potential tenant, X, but that person was concerned about the possible over-shooting of the moor in the 2006 shooting season. The owners sought to reassure X by way of an email sent on 4 August 2006 about the capacity of the moor to bear the shooting planned for later that year. In that regard, they produced information about the estimated number of grouse on the moor. However, the counts that were carried out were not representative of the moor as a whole, as they were taken from parts of the moor which were considered to be the most heavily populated by grouse. As a result, the estimated grouse population, as stated in the email, was well in excess of the actual population. X then decided not to pursue with the transaction. Mr Erskine was then contacted and invited to pursue an interest in the moor. After taking part in a shoot Mr Erskine also expressed his concern about the grouse population on the moors. The owners' agent then sent Mr Erskine the information contained in the email to X on 4 August. In October, Mr Erskine decided to proceed with the transaction which was to be concluded in the name of Cramaso LLP, which would take the lease. The lease was signed, however, Mr Erskine then discovered that the counting areas were not representative of the moor as a whole, that the grouse population was smaller than he had been led to believe and that the population would take longer to recover. He considered that he had been deliberately misled by the email of 4 August 2006 in order to induce him to take the lease.

Their Lordships heard the case as an appeal from the Inner House of the Court of Session. Whilst the case is a Scottish case, the law is essentially the same as in England and Wales. Their Lordships considered that there had been a material misrepresentation but that the owners' representative had acted honestly but negligently as he had been aware of Mr Erskine's concern about the grouse population and there was no basis for the representations he had made and had not checked the facts. Their Lordships concurred with the Lord Ordinary, Lord Hodge, that the misrepresentation was not a fraudulent misrepresentation. The Inner House had found that Mr Erskine was the directing mind of Cramaso LLP and had entered into the contract in reliance of the negligent misrepresentation contained in the email prior to Cramaso LLP's formation, however, the Lord Ordinary held that Cramaso LLP could not recover damages as it did not exist when the email was sent. The Inner House held that whilst a duty of care could be owed to a person not in existence when the contract was made there was no duty owed to Cramaso LLP as there was insufficient proximity between the owners and Cramaso LLP. The issue for the Supreme Court was whether there had been a continuing representation which was capable of remaining effective until the contract had been concluded by Cramaso LLP.

Their Lordships allowed the appeal by Cramaso LLP, stating that in appropriate circumstances the law could impose a continuing responsibility on a representor making a pre-contract representation where there was an interval between the making of the contract and the conclusion of a contract in reliance on the representation. In this case, the Supreme Court found that the representation in the email was of a continuing nature for so long as Mr Erskine remained a prospective contracting party. Lord Reed stated:

> The law relating to the effect of representations upon a contract proceeds on the basis that a representation made in the course of pre-contractual discussions may produce a misapprehension in the mind of the other party which continues so as to have a causative effect at the time when the contract is concluded. It is on that basis that a misrepresentation may lead to the setting aside of the contract as being vitiated by error or fraud.

Whether a representation is to be treated as continuing depends on the facts of the individual case, however, a misrepresentation will cease to have continuing effect if it is withdrawn, lapses or because the representee discovers the truth of the state of affairs before the contract is entered into as seen in *Redgrave v Hurd* and *Cherrilow Ltd v Richard Butler-Creagh* above. It should be noted that continuing responsibility also remains where there is a representation which is true but becomes false by the time the contract is entered into, as in *Shankland & Co v Robinson & Co* 1920 SC (HL) 103, for example.

The issue that arose was whether the representation remained of a continuing nature after the identity of the contracting party had changed, in this case Cramaso Ltd, so that the owners had a responsibility to Cramaso LLP for the accuracy of the information contained in the email. This was a novel point for which no authority was cited to the court. The Supreme Court considered that, in the circumstances drawn from the conduct of the parties, the representation continued to have a causative effect. The owners therefore had responsibility for the accuracy of the information contained in the email even though the contracting party was not the original representee and could not have known of the representation in that it had not been formed at the date of the email to Mr Erskine. Again Lord Reed stated:

> Where the inference to be drawn is that a representation continued to be made until the contract was concluded, it may also be inferred that the risk of harm being suffered as a result of reliance upon it, in the event that it was inaccurate, continued to be foreseeable. In such circumstances, the representor may be taken to have assumed responsibility for the accuracy of the representation towards the contracting party who relied upon it, even though that person was not the original representee.

Thus the change in identity of the prospective contracting party did not affect the continuing nature of the representation nor its consequences: *Briess* v *Woolley* [1954] AC 333. It was clearly foreseeable by the owners that during the negotiations that Cramaso LLP would be the vehicle for Mr Erskine's investment so that it continued to be foreseeable that the representation would induce Cramaso LLP to enter into the contract and that they had failed in their duty of care to Cramaso LLP.

The nature of the misrepresentation

Objective 4

The remedies available for misrepresentation vary according to the nature of the misrepresentation alleged. In this section, therefore, we will look at the nature of the various types of misrepresentation and the particular remedies available for each, and in the next section we will look at the various factors which may affect the remedies themselves or their availability.

Originally at common law only two types of misrepresentation were recognised: fraudulent and innocent. However, we have seen over the years the development of negligent misrepresentation at common law under *Hedley Byrne & Co. Ltd* v *Heller & Partners Ltd* [1964] AC 465 and in statute by virtue of the Misrepresentation Act 1967, s 2(1).

Fraudulent misrepresentation

In *Derry* v *Peek* (1889) 14 App Cas 337, Lord Herschell set out the necessary criteria to prove fraudulent misrepresentation. He stated:

> First, in order to sustain an action in deceit, there must be proof of fraud and nothing short of that will suffice. Secondly, fraud is proved when it is shown that a false representation has been made (1) knowingly, (2) without belief in its truth, or (3) recklessly, careless whether it be true or false.

Thus in order to establish a claim for fraudulent misrepresentation/deceit it is necessary for a claimant to prove that the representations were made dishonestly in that the defendant (a) knew that he was making the statement that the court finds him to have made; and (b) had conscious knowledge of the facts alleged to render the statement false.

With regard to (a), it is necessary for the claimant to identify the representation made and to show that the representor/knew what he was saying. It is not sufficient that the representation was false in a sense which the representor did not understand or intend it to bear. With regard to (b), the claimant must show that the defendant knew that he was not telling the truth.

In *AIC Ltd* v *ITS Testing Services (UK) Ltd* (*The Kriti Palm*) [2007] 1 All ER (Comm) 667, Rix LJ restated the principles:

> As for the element of dishonesty, the leading cases are replete with statements of its vital importance and of warnings against watering down this ingredient into something akin to negligence, however gross. The standard direction is still that of Lord Herschell in *Derry* v *Peek* (1889) 14 App Cas 337.

Carelessness of itself does not amount to dishonesty, but where a person acts recklessly it is open for the court to find dishonesty in that the person could not reasonably have believed in the truth of their statement. Great care needs to be exercised here since the terms 'careless' and 'recklessly' are today very often regarded as synonymous with negligence, and negligence must never be confused with fraud. Fraudulent misrepresentation is a dishonest statement but it is not necessarily dishonest to state a belief that would not convince a reasonable person, though this may, of course, amount to a negligent misstatement. Thus a statement made recklessly or carelessly may only amount to evidence of fraud, though if the maker of the statement believes it to be true then they cannot be liable for a fraudulent misrepresentation. This position was affirmed in *Thomas Witter Ltd* v *TBP Industries Ltd* [1996] 2 All ER 573 (ChD) where it was stated that damages cannot be claimed in deceit on the basis of recklessness alone since the basis of deceit is dishonesty. To establish fraudulent misrepresentation in these circumstances it had to be shown that the recklessness of the defendant was such that it amounted to a disregard for the truth so that they could be regarded as having acted fraudulently.

In effect, therefore, recklessness is a species of dishonest knowledge since in both instances there is an absence of a belief in the truth of a statement. For this reason, in order to establish fraud, proof is required with respect to both knowledge and recklessness. Thus in *Angus* v *Clifford* [1891] 2 Ch 449 Bowen LJ stated:

> Not caring, in that context, did not mean not taking care, it meant indifference to the truth, the moral obliquity of which consists in a wilful disregard of the importance of truth, and unless you keep it clear that that is the true meaning of the term, you are constantly in danger of confusing the evidence from which the inference of dishonesty in the mind is to be drawn – evidence which consists in a great many cases of gross want of caution – with the inference of fraud, or of dishonesty itself, which has to be drawn after you have weighed all the evidence.

Similarly in *Armstrong* v *Strain* [1951] 1 TLR 856, Devlin J stated this about the knowledge that is required:

> A man may be said to know a fact when once he has been told it and pigeon-holed it somewhere in his brain where it is more or less accessible in case of need. In another sense of the word a man knows a fact only when he is fully conscious of it. For an action of deceit there must be knowledge in the narrower sense; and conscious knowledge of falsity must always amount to wickedness and dishonesty. When Judges say, therefore, that wickedness and dishonesty must be present, they are not requiring a new ingredient for the tort of deceit so much as describing the sort of knowledge which is necessary.

These requirements were reiterated in *AIC Ltd v ITS Testing Services (UK) Ltd* by Buxton LJ:

> Where knowledge of a fact held by the speaker is relied on to make his statement deceitful, he must be 'fully conscious' of that fact and have conscious knowledge of the falsity of his statement: *Armstrong v Strain* at p. 871, per Devlin J.

Proving that the representor has made a fraudulent misrepresentation by suing in the tort of deceit is not easy since a claimant who alleges deceit, while they have to prove their case on the balance of probabilities, has a higher burden of proof. In *Smith New Court Securities Ltd v Citibank NA* [1997] AC 254, on appeal from *Smith New Court v Scrimgeour Vickers (Asset Management) Ltd* [1994] 1 W.L.R. 1271 Lord Steyn agreed with counsel stating:

> . . . the undisputed proposition [is] that while as a matter of law fraud only has to be proved to the civil standard, proof to that standard must necessarily take into account the consideration that the more serious the allegation is, the greater the proof is needed to persuade a court that it can be satisfied that the allegation is established. In other words, the very gravity of an allegation of fraud is a circumstance which has to be weighed in the scale in deciding as to the balance of probabilities.

Further, in *AIC Ltd v ITS Testing Services (UK) Ltd*, Rix LJ stated:

> Moreover, whether it is in the matter of identifying the relevant misstatement or in the finding of a dishonest mind, it is necessary to bear in mind the heightened burden of proof which bears on the claimant, as discussed in cases from *Hornal v Neuberger Products Ltd* [1957] 1 QB 247 to *In re H (Minors)* [1996] AC 563. In the latter case, Lord Nicholls of Birkenhead said this (at 586):
>
> > 'Built into the preponderance of probability standard is a generous degree of flexibility in respect of the seriousness of the allegation. Although the result is much the same, this does not mean that where a serious allegation is in issue the standard of proof required is higher. It means only that the inherent probability or improbability of an event is itself a matter to be taken into account when weighing the probabilities and deciding whether, on balance, the event occurred. The more improbable the event, the stronger must be the evidence that it did occur before, on the balance of probability, its occurrence will be established.'

In addition, in terms of discharging the burden of proof for fraudulent misrepresentation, it was held in *Ticket2final OU v Wigan Athletic AFC Ltd* [2015] EWHC 61b (Ch) that although the standard of proof for fraudulent misrepresentation was the normal civil standard of proof, the 'very allegation of fraud is a circumstance which has to be weighed in the scale of deciding as to the balance of probabilities'.

One further matter relating to fraudulent misrepresentation is that it is possible for a fraudulent misrepresentation may arise not just in terms of inducing a contract but also in relation to a post-contract situation, where a party to a contract fabricates or exaggerates a claim under the contract. In such a situation the misrepresentee may use the fraudulent claim to avoid a liability under the contract. Such a situation commonly arises within a contract of insurance where the insured will fabricate or exaggerate the claim under the policy and in such circumstances the insurer may attempt to prevent the insured from claiming under the policy ('the fraudulent claim rule'). The rule is found within the Marine Insurance Act 1906 s 17 which states:

> 'Insurance is *uberrimae fidei*
>
> 17 A contract of marine insurance is a contract based upon the utmost good faith, and, if the utmost good faith be not observed by either party, the contract may be avoided by the other party'.

The authority for the rule at common law can also be found in the case of ***Britton v Royal Insurance Co*** (1866) 4 F & F 905 where Willes J stated:

> A fire insurance, he said, is a contract of indemnity; that is, it is a contract to indemnify the assured against the consequences of a fire, provided it is not wilful. Of course, if the assured set fire to his house, he could not recover. That is clear. But it is not less clear that, even supposing it were not wilful, yet as it is a contract of indemnity only, that is, a contract to recoup the insured the value of the property destroyed by fire, if the claim is fraudulent, it is defeated altogether. That is, suppose the insured made a claim for twice the amount insured and lost, thus seeking to put the office off its guard, and in the result to recover more than he is entitled to, that would be a wilful fraud, and the consequence is that he could not recover anything. This is a defence quite different from that of wilful arson. It gives the go-by to the origin of the fire, and it amounts to this — that the assured took advantage of the fire to make a fraudulent claim. The law upon such a case is in accordance with justice, and also with sound policy. The law is, that a person who has made such a fraudulent claim could not be permitted to recover at all. The contract of insurance is one of perfect good faith on both sides, and it is most important that such good faith should be maintained. It is the common practice to insert in fire-policies conditions that they shall be void in the event of a fraudulent claim; and there was such a condition in the present case. Such a condition is only in accordance with legal principle and sound policy.

The simple rationale was set out by Lord Hobhouse's words in ***Manifest Shipping Co. Ltd.* v *Uni-Polaris Shipping Co. Ltd. (The 'Star Sea')* [2001] 2 WLR 170**: 'The fraudulent insured must not be allowed to think: if the fraud is successful, then I will gain; if it is unsuccessful, I will lose nothing'. The policy of the law to discourage fraudulent claims being made was also set out in ***Galloway* v *Guardian Royal Exchange (UK) Ltd.* [1999]** LRLR 209 where Millett LJ declared that the fraudulent claims rule was 'a necessary and salutary rule which deserves to be better known by the public' and one which he 'would be most unwilling to dilute ... in any way'.

The rationale for the common law rule regarding fraudulently exaggerated claims has arisen in a wider context where fraudulent devices are used to promote an insurance claim. Very often the insured employs a fraudulent device to support a claim as a matter of expediency because he is unsure that his claim will succeed. If the fraudulent device is successful, the insured wins either because the insurer pays up on the policy or, more rarely, where he wins at trial as regards his claim. On the other hand, if the lie is detected, then at common law the whole claim and indeed the insurance policy itself are forfeit since as a matter of policy since the insured should not be allowed to think he will lose nothing by using a fraudulent device – there must be an incentive not to lie.

The problem that arises is, what is the relationship between the common law rule and s 17 and their different effects? Section 17 gives rise to an automatic right of forfeiture for the insurer, however, the effect of the common law principle is not to give such an automatic right to what is quite a draconian outcome in the case of s 17. In ***Versloot Dredging***, Lord Sumption considered that whilst the rule originated in the realms of insurance law and is a manifestation of the duty of utmost good faith, that the rule must be regarded as a 'term implied or inferred by law so that it falls with the general principles of the law of contract.

In ***Versloot Dredging BV* v *HI Gerling Industrie Versicherung*** AG [2016] UKSC 45, the Supreme Court by a majority decision of nine judges (Lord Mance dissenting) held that the fraudulent claims rule should not apply where the insured makes use of fraudulent devices or collateral lies where the claim is justified and the lie has no relevance to the insurer's liability.

Versloot Dredging BV v HI Gerling Industrie Versicherung AG [2016] UKSC 45

In this case, a ship's engine room flooded, causing the engine to be damaged beyond repair, leading to the shipowner claiming under the policy. Initially the cause of the flood was unclear, however, the shipowner stated that whilst the bilge alarm had sounded, the crew was unable to control the flood because of the rolling of the ship in heavy seas. This statement was untrue and in fact the true cause was that; first, the crew had negligently failed to close a sea valve on an emergency fire pump; second, earlier contractors had failed to make sure that the engine room bulkheads were properly sealed; and third, there were defects in the engine room pumping system.

The Supreme Court held that the fraudulent claim rule applied where the whole claim was fabricated and also where the claim was justified but dishonestly exaggerated and in such an instance the insurer was not liable even for those parts of the claim that were justified under the terms of the policy. In such circumstances, the insured was attempting to get something to which he was not entitled. The insured is also not entitled to any part of the claim that was honestly made, since here the law did not permit the honest part of the claim to be severed form the dishonest part. The Supreme Court, however, went on to consider whether the fraudulent claim rule applied where the claim was justified but was dishonestly embellished with a view to either securing the acceptance of the insurer for the claim or securing the faster payment of the claim. Such embellishments are called 'fraudulent devices' or, more accurately 'collateral lies'. A collateral lie arises is a claim or statement which has no relevance to the insured's right to recover under the policy, in other words, as Lord Clarke describes;

> The critical point is that, in the case of a collateral lie . . . the insured is trying to obtain no more than the law regards as his entitlement and the lie is irrelevant to the existence or amount of that entitlement. Such a lie is thus immaterial to the claim. As Lord Sumption puts it, the lie is dishonest but the claim is not.

Whilst the fraudulent claim rule was legitimate in terms of deterring fraud, in the case of collateral lie, the Supreme Court did not consider it justifiable to apply the rule in such a case. The insured gains nothing from the collateral lie in terms of the legitimacy of his claim and the insurers also lose nothing since they are liable under the policy in any event.

In *Versloot Dredging* and in *The Aegeon* (among others), the issue of materiality was considered in terms of the application of the common law rule and so placing it outside of the ambit of s 17. Thus in order to use the fraudulent claim rule, it would have to be shown that the effect of the fraudulent device was material to the claim in order for an insurer to avoid the claim. This materiality device was set out by analogy with materiality in terms inducing a contract by way of a misrepresentation when entering into a contract. Lord Sumption considered that materiality was irrelevant when divorced from inducement, as in the case of a claim under a policy. There is no question of inducement here and, in any event, if a statement has no impact on the insurer 'why should it matter what impact it might objectively have been expected to have?' per Lord Sumption at para 34. Lord Sumption at para 36 set out the principles for dealing with fraudulent devices and collateral lies as follows:

> . . . the fraudulent claims rule applies to a wholly fabricated claim. It applies to an exaggerated claim. It applies even to the genuine part of an exaggerated claim if the whole is to be regarded as a single claim, as it must be. But it does not apply to a lie which the true facts, once admitted or ascertained, show to have been immaterial to the insured's right to recover. It is true that the moral character of the insured's lie is in no way mitigated by the fact that it turns out to

have been unnecessary. But there are principled limits to the role which a claimant's immorality can play in defeating his legitimate civil claims. These limits have been applied outside the realm of insurance ever since the failure two centuries ago of Lord Mansfield's attempt to introduce a general duty of good faith in the law of contract. Ultimately, however, even the law of insurance is concerned more with controlling the impact of a breach of good faith on the risk than with the punishment of misconduct. The extension of the fraudulent claims rule to lies which are found to be irrelevant to the recoverability of the claim is a step too far. It is disproportionately harsh to the insured and goes further than any legitimate commercial interest of the insurer can justify . . . In my opinion, it is not the law.

Likewise, Lord Toulson stated:

I agree . . . that the lie told in the latter case may be 'material' to the insured's conduct, in that it may induce the insurer to accept the claim; but, if so, the insurer will have been induced to pay what it was liable to pay, and the insured will have gained no more than his legal entitlement. I agree with Lord Sumption that such a lie should not be regarded as 'material' in the same sense as a lie which goes to the existence or amount of the insured's entitlement. It is aptly described as collateral, or irrelevant to the existence and amount of the insurer's liability. In that critical sense it is immaterial to the parties' respective rights and obligations.

In the case itself it was found that whilst one of the directors had made an untrue statement as regards the alarm sounding, the statement was made when the director was frustrated that the insurers were not paying up immediately and were intended to reassure the insurers that the ship was not unseaworthy and that its alarms were functioning correctly. As it happened, the false statements made no difference to the claim since the entry of the water was not altered by the operation of the bilge alarm. As such the statements by the director amounted to a collateral lie and the insurers were not able to rely on the fraudulent claim rule to avoid the claim.

With regards to the operation of the Marine Insurance Act 1906 s 17, it must be now borne in mind that consumer insurance contracts are now dealt with by the Consumer Insurance (Disclosure and Representations) Act 2012 and, in the case of both consumer and commercial contracts, the Insurance Act 2015 now applies, both of which abolish s 17. The effect of the statutes is to separate the duty of good faith from the law relating to fraudulent claims. The Insurance Act 2015 s 12 now deals with fraudulent claims and preserves the rule that a fraudulent claimant will recover nothing, including any unexaggerated element. It takes the opportunity to limit the right of the insurer to avoid the whole policy but leaves open the scope of the fraudulent claims rule, and in particular leave open the issue as to whether it extends to fraudulent devices.

Of course, any allegation of dishonesty is likely to be hotly disputed. Failure to prove it may result in an action in defamation so the decision to pursue such an action should never be taken lightly. These factors and the difficulty of proving fraudulent misrepresentation mean that an action under s 2(1) of the Misrepresentation Act 1967 (below) is often more advisable.

As a postscript, one might wonder why Lord Herschell referred to carelessness in his definition in *Derry* v *Peek*. Clearly it cannot per se amount to fraudulent conduct in today's terms. This is really an issue of history. When Lord Herschell delivered his judgement in 1889 there was no such thing as negligent misrepresentation at common law – the law had to wait another 75 years until the case of *Hedley Byrne & Co. Ltd* v *Heller & Partners Ltd* for that to arise. In that intervening period the only way a person could bring an action with respect to a 'careless' misrepresentation was to bring it within the judgement in *Derry* v *Peek*, something which is not appropriate today because of the onset of negligent misrepresentation at common law under *Hedley Byrne*. As can be seen below, *Hedley Byrne* has its limitations both in terms of application and in terms of where the burden of proof lies, so that most actions for negligent misrepresentation today are brought within the terms of the Misrepresentation Act 1967 which has significant procedural advantages.

Common law negligent misrepresentation

The case of *Hedley Byrne & Co. Ltd* v *Heller & Partners Ltd* fundamentally changed the nature of misrepresentation, which until then was based on the principle that all misrepresentations that were not fraudulent were in fact innocent misrepresentations. The decision in *Hedley Byrne* extended the common law tort of negligence to cover negligent misstatements that result in loss.

Hedley Byrne & Co. Ltd v Heller & Partners Ltd [1964] AC 645

The facts of the case were that the plaintiffs had been asked for credit by a particular company and decided to ask for advice as to the financial standing of the company from the company's own bankers, the defendants. The defendants, who were aware of the purpose behind the plaintiffs' request, stated carelessly that the company was financially sound. The House of Lords decided that while the defendants owed the plaintiffs a duty to take care, they were not liable because of a disclaimer enclosed with the credit reference which stated that the advice was given 'without responsibility'.

The decision established that a representor had a duty of care to do all that is reasonable to make sure that their statement is accurate irrespective of the existence of a fiduciary or contractual relationship. The duty arose in any situation where there was a 'special relationship' between the parties. Unfortunately the House of Lords was not very specific as to what a 'special relationship' was. Certainly there was no need for a direct contractual link between the parties, though there had to be a sufficient degree of proximity between the parties for the action to be sustained, a principle reaffirmed in *Caparo Industries plc* v *Dickman and Others* [1990] 1 All ER 568.

At first, it was thought that the degree of proximity between the parties arose only between professional people whose business involved the giving of advice to clients, such as solicitors, accountants and surveyors (see *Yianni* v *Edwin Evans & Son* [1982] QB 438), estate agents (see *McCullagh* v *Lane Fox and Partners Ltd* [1995] EGCS 195 (CA)) and barristers (see *Rondel* v *Worsley* [1969] 1 AC 191). This approach was confirmed by the Privy Council in *Mutual Life and Citizens' Insurance Co. Ltd* v *Evatt* [1971] AC 793, though rejected in *Esso Petroleum Co. Ltd* v *Mardon*, above. In the latter case, it was held that a special relationship also exists in a purely commercial transaction where the representor has superior knowledge and experience to that of the representee and where it is reasonable for the representee to rely on the statements made to them by the representor. Lord Denning MR stated the principle as follows:

> if a man, who has or professes to have special knowledge or skill, makes a representation by virtue thereof to another – be it advice, information or opinion – with the intention of inducing him to enter into a contract with him, he is under a duty to use reasonable care to see that the representation is correct, and that the advice, information or opinion is reliable. If he negligently gives unsound advice or misleading information or expresses an erroneous opinion, and thereby induces the other side to enter into a contract with him, he is liable in damages.

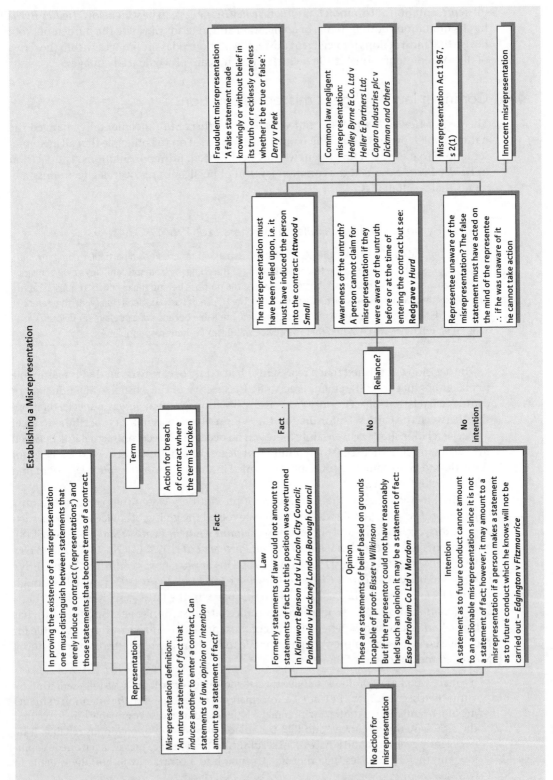

Figure 9.1

Ormrod LJ pointed out, however, that liability would not have arisen in a case where a representor could assume that the representee would seek the advice of their own professional advisers.

It is more difficult to bring a claim for negligent misrepresentation at common law than to bring an action under s 2(1) of the Misrepresentation Act 1967 (see below). The burden of proof lies on the representee who must prove not only the existence of the so-called special relationship but also the existence of a duty of care and its breach, coupled with resulting and foreseeable loss. Such an action does have one advantage, though, since it is not limited to actions in respect of misrepresentations that induce a contract.

Misrepresentation Act 1967, s 2(1)

Section 2(1) provides:

> Where a person has entered into a contract after a misrepresentation has been made to him by another party thereto and as a result thereof he has suffered loss, then, if the person making the misrepresentation would be liable to damages in respect thereof had the misrepresentation been made fraudulently, that person shall be so liable notwithstanding that the misrepresentation was not made fraudulently, unless he proves that he had reasonable grounds to believe and did believe up to the time the contract was made that the facts represented were true.

Immediately it will be seen that there are significant differences between this and negligent misrepresentation at common law. First, there is no need to prove a 'special relationship'; second, the misrepresentation must result in a contract being entered into; third, the burden of proof is reversed so that the representor is liable unless 'he had reasonable grounds to believe and did believe up to the time the contract was made that the facts represented were true' (the 'innocence defence').

Clearly the provision imposes a form of liability for negligent misrepresentation; this is subject to the special conditions stated above which make actions under this provision far more desirable for the representee, in that they have a procedural advantage given the reversed burden of proof. It should be stressed that a contract must result between the representor and the representee. Provided a contract results, the vast majority of actions will be framed within this provision.

Innocent misrepresentation

Prior to *Hedley Byrne* v *Heller* this type of misrepresentation encompassed all misrepresentations that were not fraudulent. Given the developments since *Hedley Byrne*, this category of misrepresentation is confined to those that are wholly innocent. It should be noted, however, that in *Thomas Witter Ltd* v *TBP Industries Ltd* it was stated that should an action fail under s 2(1) because of the operation of the 'innocence defence', then it was still possible for the claimant to plead innocent misrepresentation successfully with all its consequent remedies.

Consumer Insurance (Disclosure and Representations) Act 2012

Objective 5

The Law Commission and the Scottish Law Commission's 2009 joint report *Consumer Insurance Law: Pre-Contract Disclosure and Misrepresentation* (Law Com No. 319; Scot Law

Com No 219), in proposing their draft Bill in developing this Act, made it clear that the concept of a misrepresentation should be interpreted according to common law principles. It has been seen above that this Act has stripped away from consumer insurance contracts the concept of *uberrimae fidei* so that a misrepresentation is only actionable if it is 'material', in that it would influence the judgement of a hypothetical prudent underwriter. It is therefore enough if an insurer can show that it was induced by the misrepresentation, and that a reasonable consumer would not have made it. Section 2(2) of the Act imposes on the consumer a duty to take reasonable care not to make a misrepresentation to the insurer. This removes the consumer's duty to volunteer information to the insurer and requires consumers to answer an insurer's questions honestly and to take reasonable care that their replies are accurate and complete. Previously insurers sat back and relied on consumers to tell them everything that they need to know in deciding whether to insure at all or as to what premiums they would charge. The problem with this is that many consumers are unaware that they are required to volunteer information and in any event even if they know that they are under a duty to disclose they may have no idea what is relevant to the insurer.

The Law Commission report referred to the case of ***Lambert* v *Co-operative Insurance Society Ltd*** [1975] 2 Lloyd's Rep 485 as an example of the problems associated with the duty to disclose information. In this case Mrs Lambert insured her family's jewellery. However, in the proposal form the insurer did not ask about her husband's previous convictions and she did not mention them. Even the judge, Mackenna J, commented that Mrs Lambert was unlikely to have thought that it was necessary to disclose the distressing fact of a recent conviction by her husband when she was subsequently renewing the policy. Later Mrs Lambert claimed £311 for lost jewellery; the insurer avoided the policy on the ground that she did not disclose the conviction. The Court of Appeal held that the insurer was entitled to do so under the rules of law set out in the Marine Insurance Act 1906. The conviction was a material circumstance, which would have influenced a prudent insurer. It did not matter that a person in Mrs Lambert's position would not have realised this. The law was clear, though clearly not fair.

If consumers do provide insurers with information which was not asked for, they must do so honestly and carefully. Further, where a contract of insurance is being renewed, as often happens in the case of car or home insurance contracts, a failure by the consumer to comply with an insurer's request to confirm or amend particulars previously given is also capable of being a misrepresentation (s 2(3)). The Act makes no specific reference to renewals since technically these are new contracts. However, the section covers statements that are incomplete and this often arises in renewal contracts where a consumer is asked to confirm or amend any information that the consumer has previously supplied to the insurer. Furthermore, a failure to supply information can of itself be capable of being a misrepresentation under this provision.

The Act goes further than simply setting out the duties of consumers but also provides an explanation as to what is meant by 'reasonable care' in s 3(1) where it states that, 'Whether or not a consumer has taken reasonable care not to make a misrepresentation is to be determined in the light of all the relevant circumstances'. In s 3(2), the Act also provides examples of the types of circumstances that might be taken into account; thus a court will have regard to:

1   the type of consumer insurance contract in question, and its target market;

2   any relevant explanatory material or publicity produced or authorised by the insurer;

3   how clear, and how specific, the insurer's questions were;

4 in the case of a failure to respond to the insurer's questions in connection with the renewal or variation of a consumer insurance contract, how clearly the insurer communicated the importance of answering those questions (or the possible consequences of failing to do so);

5 whether or not an agent was acting for the consumer.

The standard of care required is that of a reasonable consumer, thus imposing an objective test. However, if the insurer was, or ought to have been, aware of any particular characteristics or circumstances of the actual consumer, those are to be taken into account. Interestingly, s 3(5) provides that if a consumer makes a dishonest misrepresentation this is always to be taken as showing a breach of the duty to take reasonable care when making disclosures to the insurer. This provision is necessary because the objective test imposed looks at the characteristics of the reasonable consumer and does not take into account any subjective characteristics of a particular consumer. This provision therefore takes into account the consumer who has more than usual knowledge and acts dishonestly while on the other hand the 'normal' consumer might well have made a reasonable mistake about the same issues. The issue of dishonesty or otherwise does, however, affect the type of remedy available to the insurer where there is a breach of the duty to take reasonable care.

It is not enough for the insurer to show that the consumer was simply in breach of the duty to take reasonable care under s 2(2) since s 4 also requires the insurer to demonstrate on the balance of probabilities that without the misrepresentation the insurer would not have entered into the contract at all or would have done so on different terms. This provision therefore ties in with the requirement as regards the need for the misrepresentation to induce the insurer to enter into the contract, as seen in *Pan Atlantic Insurance Co. Ltd* v *Pine Top Insurance Co. Ltd* and followed in *Raiffeisen Zentralbank Osterreich AG v Royal Bank of Scotland plc*. It will be noticed that the requirement that the misrepresentation must influence the decision of a hypothetical prudent insurer whether to enter into the contract is done away with in s 4. The requirement now is that the insurer which is a party to the contract must show it relied on the misrepresentation whether or not a hypothetical insurer would have done so.

Section 4(2) also provides that the misrepresentation for which the insurer has a remedy against the consumer must be a 'qualifying misrepresentation'. This expression is defined in s 5(1) as either '(a) deliberate or reckless, or (b) careless'. One may immediately see the resonance with Lord Herschell's definition in *Derry* v *Peek* here. Section 5(2) provides:

A qualifying misrepresentation is deliberate or reckless if the consumer –

1 knew that it was untrue or misleading, or did not care whether or not it was untrue or misleading; and

2 knew that the matter to which the misrepresentation related was relevant to the insurer, or did not care whether or not it was relevant to the insurer.

Thus a consumer acts recklessly if they act without care or regard for the truth. On the other hand, a consumer who makes a statement genuinely believing it to be true but without taking sufficient care to check the truth of their statement will be regarded as acting carelessly. It is for the insurer to prove that a misrepresentation was deliberate or reckless. Having said this, in s 5(5) there are two presumptions set out so that unless the contrary is shown it is presumed that a consumer has the knowledge of a reasonable consumer and, secondly, it is presumed that the consumer knew that a matter asked about by the insurer in a clear and specific question was of relevance to the insurer. The effect of these presumptions is to reverse the burden of proof so that if an insurer asks a clear and specific question which a reasonable consumer would understand then the insurer does not have to prove that the consumer acted deliberately or recklessly. In such a case, it is up to the consumer to demonstrate that they did not know the answer or did not understand the question.

Example

Mrs A is going on holiday and takes out holiday insurance. One of the questions asks if she had ever suffered asthma. She replies that she has not, although three years ago she suffered from asthma related to a bout of severe hay fever and had been diagnosed and treated by her doctor for the condition. During her holiday she does in fact suffer from an asthmatic attack and the insurance company seeks to avoid the contract on the basis for her pre-existing medical condition. The question is a clear and specific one and thus the insurance company is relieved of the burden of proving that Mrs A acted deliberately or recklessly since most reasonable people would know that they had suffered from asthma. The burden is now with Mrs A to show that she did not know she had suffered from asthma or did not understand the question. For instance, in Mrs A's case she might have confused her previous attack with hay fever unless she can prove that she did not understand the question.

The different types of misrepresentation are an important feature of the Act since the Act itself sets out the remedies for the different types of misrepresentation. These remedies are set out in Sch 1 to the Act. Where the misrepresentation is honest and reasonable the insurer has no remedy and must pay the claim.

In the case of misrepresentations that are careless the insurer has a compensatory remedy in that the remedies of the insurer are based on what the insurer would have done if the consumer had complied with the duty set out in s 2(2). Thus if the insurer would not have entered into the consumer insurance contract on any terms the insurer is able to avoid the contract and refuse the claim, though here the premiums must be repaid. On the other hand, if the insurer would have entered into the contract but on different terms the contract is treated as if it had been entered into on those terms if the insurer so requires. Furthermore, if the insurer would have entered into the contract, whether the terms are the same or different, but a higher premium would have been charged, the insurer is entitled to reduce the amount to be paid on the claim proportionately based on the difference between the premium charged as against the higher premium.

Where the misrepresentation is deliberate or reckless the insurer may avoid the contract, refuse all claims and is not obliged to return any of the premiums 'except to the extent that it would be unfair to the consumer to retain them'. There is no definition as to what is 'unfair' in the Act. However, the Law Commission considered that the ability of the insurer to retain premiums demonstrated society's disapproval of deliberate and reckless behaviour and that it was important to send a strong message that such behaviour was unacceptable. The Law Commission did, however, accept that this rule could be overly harsh, particularly in joint policies where one policyholder makes a deliberate misrepresentation while the other acts honestly and reasonably. The Law Commission therefore considered that insurers should have the ability to keep any premiums paid but that the courts or Financial Ombudsman Service should have discretion to order that some or all of the premiums are returned to the consumer.

Section 10 of the Act prevents insurers from giving themselves greater rights to reject claims for non-disclosure and misrepresentation by adding terms to this effect to their contracts so that consumers are placed in a worse position as regards disclosures and misrepresentations made by the consumer to the insurer before the contract is entered into or varied. Similarly it is not possible for insurers to introduce terms into a contract that places consumers in a worse position as regards their remedies for qualifying misrepresentations. It should be noted that s 10 has no application with regard to terms that require consumers to give insurers information during the course of the contract, since such terms are caught by the Unfair Terms in Consumer Contracts Regulations 1999 and would need to be fair as within the terms of those regulations in any event.

The Act also intervenes to prevent terms known as 'basis of the contract' clauses. In these clauses, the insurer adds a declaration to a proposal form or policy stating that the consumer warrants the accuracy of all the answers given, or that such answers 'form the basis of the contract'. This has the legal effect of turning representations into warranties. As we have already seen in Chapter 7, a 'warranty' in a contract of insurance has a special status and is regarded as a major term of the contract, the equivalent of a condition, not a minor or subsidiary term. Furthermore, in the Marine Insurance Act 1906, s 33(3) it is stated that a 'warranty . . . is a condition which must be exactly complied with, whether it be material to the risk or not. The effect of this is that once the insurer has shown that the consumer has warranted the truth of the representation, the insurer can avoid the policy for any mistake, however trivial or unimportant. The effect of such a clause can be devastating to a claim, as can be seen in the case of **Dawsons Ltd v Bonnin** [1922] 2 AC 413. In this case, a furniture removal firm took out insurance on a lorry. The firm filled out a proposal form, giving its business address in central Glasgow. The form asked where the lorry was usually parked, the firm inadvertently wrote 'above address'. In fact, the lorry was usually parked in the outskirts. The firm argued that this fact was not material as it did not increase the risk and indeed probably reduced it. The form, however, had contained a declaration that the proposal 'shall be the basis of the contract'. The House of Lords held that this had the effect of converting the statements into warranties. Thus it did not matter whether the mistake was material or not. The insurer could use any mistake on the form to refuse all claims under the policy.

Such 'basis of the contract' clauses have been the subject of criticism for many years, not least because few consumers would understand the significance of 'warranties' or 'basis of the contract' clauses. The Law Commission was unclear as to why insurers should be permitted to refuse claims because of trivial or immaterial mistakes on application forms. While in the course of their enquiries the Law Commissioners found there to be agreement amongst insurers not to refuse claims for immaterial errors, as a matter of strict law a court could uphold such a clause against a consumer. The Act therefore provides in s 6 that such a representation made by a consumer in connection with a proposed consumer insurance contract or a proposed variation to such a contract is not capable of being converted into a warranty.

The Consumer Insurance (Disclosure and Representations) Act 2012 goes a great deal of the way in providing a structured approach to reforming the issues of disclosures and misrepresentations made by consumers when entering into consumer insurance contracts and in this respect the Act is very narrow in its scope. Importantly, it is transparent and lucid in what it is trying to achieve – more than can be said with many of the insurance policies that insurers publish! The Act also deals with agents and with group insurance in much the same way and on the face of things appears to clarify and remedy many of the mysteries and defects surrounding disclosures and misrepresentations in such contracts. Time alone will tell how insurers themselves will react to the Act but the signs are that many operate already with many of the terms of the Act and therefore compliance will not, or should not, be a major issue for many.

The remedies available for misrepresentation

Rescission and indemnity

Rescission

Objective
6 The general rule is that the effect of misrepresentation is to render the contract voidable, **not** void, and thus the contract is still valid and subsisting until the representee decides to set it aside. Of course, the representee may decide to carry on with the contract, that is, to affirm it. A representee may affirm the contract either by expressing the intention to do so or by simply performing such an act as would indicate to a reasonable person that the representee intends to proceed with the contract.

A further remedy available to the representee is to cease the performance of the contract and allow themselves to become liable for breach of contract, then raise the misrepresentation as a defence to the action for breach. This occurs commonly where a person fails to declare matters of importance when filling in a proposal form to an insurance company. As we have already seen (above), such contracts are contracts of *uberrimae fidei* and therefore a person (other than a person entering into a 'consumer insurance contract' and falling within the ambit of the Consumer Insurance (Disclosure and Representations) Act 2012 as set out above) is bound to declare matters of interest to a prudent insurer. The insurer on finding out about the omission may rescind the contract. Very often insurers will refuse to return any premiums paid, but if sued for their return may successfully raise the misrepresentation as a defence to the action. Misrepresentation thus acts as a bar to an order for a decree of specific performance of the contract.

As an alternative to the above approaches the representee may decide to rescind the contract, which they may simply do by making clear to the other party that they no longer consider themself bound by the contract. Once the representee has elected to treat the contract as either rescinded or affirmed then they cannot retract from that election. If they delay in making the election they will be deemed to have affirmed since, as we shall see later, delay defeats equity and since rescission is an equitable remedy the representee will be precluded from claiming.

While the communication to the representor of the representee's election to rescind the contract is crucial, this communication is relaxed in two instances.

First, it may be that the representor cannot be contacted so that communication of the election is impossible, as where a person making a fraudulent misrepresentation to acquire goods makes off with them and disappears. In such circumstances, all that the representee is required to do to effect rescission is to show by some overt act that they intend to rescind.

Car and Universal Finance Co. Ltd v Caldwell [1964] 1 All ER 290

A car was sold and delivered to a rogue whose cheque was dishonoured the next day, by which time the rogue and the car had disappeared. In order to attempt to recover the car the owner informed the police and the Automobile Association. The rogue then sold the car to a garage which knew that the rogue had a defective title to the vehicle. The garage subsequently sold the car to a buyer who purchased the car in good faith. It was held that the owner, by informing the police and the Automobile Association, had made it clear that he sought to rescind the contract, with the result that the rogue no longer had title to the goods so that no title could pass to the garage or to the innocent buyer, and the latter had to return the car to the owner.

Second, if the representee seizes or otherwise retakes possession of the goods from the representor, this action of itself amounts to rescission and there is no requirement for the representee to communicate the election to rescind formally.

So far we have been considering the exercise of rescission out of court but it is possible, and indeed desirable in some cases, to apply to the court for a formal order of rescission. Such a situation might arise where a representee has been induced to buy shares by way of a misrepresentation. Since the representee has paid money to the representor it is useless to think in terms of repossessing the moneys paid, and while it may be possible to declare one's intention to rescind to the other party this is unlikely to have any great effect. In the sale of goods, the reason for informing the rogue of one's election or informing the police, etc. is often to prevent title being passed to some third party, but this is not the case with money. Whatever one's motives for applying for a formal order, it should be noted that even here rescission is regarded as an act of the representee, and the result is that the rescission takes effect from the date of the communication of the application of the order to the representor rather than from the award of the order by the court.

As stated earlier, the effect of misrepresentation is to render the contract *voidable not void* and a claim for rescission requires that the parties should be restored to their original positions. It follows that if this so-called *restitutio in integrum* cannot be achieved, then rescission is not possible. There must be an ability to give counter-restitution as well since it must always be borne in mind that the logic of rescission is to place the parties back in the same position they would have been in had there been no contract as held in *Erlanger* v *New Sombrero Phosphate Co.* (1878) 3 App Cas 1218. This requires some qualification, however, since in *Halpern* v *Halpern* [2007] EWCA Civ 291, it was stated by the Court of Appeal that 'the primary obligation may not always be the need to restore both parties to their previous positions'. Thus, whilst the parties may can be substantially returned to their *status quo ante*, the representee might have incurred other expenses which would not necessarily figure in the mutual handing back of what each party has received under the contract. In fraudulent misrepresentation, this presented no problem since damages were available at common law for this type of misrepresentation and the expense element was often included within the damages element. In innocent misrepresentation, however, damages were not available at common law and thus the courts, to make an award for such expenses incurred, had to manipulate the rules so as to produce a substantial return of the parties to their *status quo ante*. The courts achieved this by making an award, not of damages, but of an indemnity, whereby the representee was awarded a sum that equated with expenses or obligations necessarily incurred as a result of the representation. The point is that in exercising its discretion to award rescission, the courts will not allow minor imperfections to prevent the award of rescission.

It should be noted with regard to rescission is that it is available for *any* type of misrepresentation.

One final point is that it must be remembered that in relation to fraudulent claims, following *Versloot Dredging BV* v *HI Gerling Industrie Versicherung* AG [2016] UKSC 45, the Supreme Court held that the fraudulent claims rule should not apply where the insured makes use of fraudulent devices or collateral lies where the claim is justified and the lie has no relevance to the insurer's liability. The result is that an insurer cannot avoid the claim in such circumstances.

Indemnity

As already stated, an indemnity is a means whereby, as part of the process of *restitutio in integrum*, the representee can recover expenses necessarily incurred by the creation of the contract induced as a result of the misrepresentation. It is important that an indemnity is not confused with a person's common law right to damages. The distinction may be seen in the case of **Whittington v Seale-Hayne**.

Whittington v Seale-Hayne (1900) 82 LT 49

In this case, the plaintiffs were lessees of premises which they used for breeding poultry. They alleged that they were induced to take up the lease because of representations made by the defendant's agents that the premises were in a sanitary condition and in a good state of repair. They further alleged that as a consequence of the premises being in an insanitary condition their farm manager and his family became seriously ill and that much of the poultry either died or became valueless for breeding purposes. The local authority also condemned the premises as being unfit for human habitation because of defective drainage. The plaintiffs claimed that they were entitled to an indemnity as regards the losses in respect of the stock and the medical expenses of the farm manager and his family since these were incurred as a consequence of entering into the contract. It was held that the claim would fail as it really amounted to a claim for damages, which could not be awarded for an innocent misrepresentation. The plaintiffs were, however, entitled to those expenses which were incurred as a requirement of entering into the lease, such as rent, rates and repairs. The contract did not require the plaintiffs to appoint a manager so the expenses claimed in respect of his medical condition were not an expense necessarily incurred by the contract. Similarly the contract did not require the farm to be used as a poultry farm and therefore these expenses also were not necessarily incurred by the contract.

Bars to the remedy of rescission

A person may be barred from exercising the remedy of rescission in four circumstances.

1. Affirmation

We have already seen that when a person elects to affirm the contract that election cannot be retracted and rescission will cease to be available to the representee. It should, however, be remembered that the election may be made expressly or made impliedly by conduct and that, further, **affirmation** can only take place if the representee knows of the truth of the situation. As regards the latter, mere rumours or vague hints as to the untruth of the representations made are not regarded as discovery of the truth.

An example of affirmation can be seen in the following case.

Long v Lloyd [1958] 1 WLR 753

The vendor of a lorry falsely stated that it was in good condition and the vehicle was subsequently purchased by the plaintiff. After the first journey some defects were found, but when they were pointed out to the defendant he offered to meet half the costs of the repairs and this offer was accepted by the plaintiff. The following day on the second journey the lorry broke down and serious defects were discovered to the extent that it was unroadworthy. The defendant's representations as regards the vehicle were clearly untrue, though honestly made, and the plaintiff sought to rescind the contract for innocent misrepresentation. It was held that by accepting the offer of assistance with the repairs after the first journey the plaintiff had accepted the lorry and therefore lost any rights he may have had to rescind the contract.

2. Lapse of time

Rescission is not barred by lapse of time where the misrepresentation is fraudulent; it simply provides evidence of affirmation of the contract. In this type of misrepresentation, time only becomes relevant from the discovery of the truth of the misrepresentation. Similarly, once the misrepresentation has been discovered, any time spent negotiating a solution to the dispute does not count towards debarring a claim.

In misrepresentations other than fraudulent misrepresentations, the rule is that rescission must take place within a reasonable time, even though there is no evidence of an intention to affirm the contract.

Leaf v *International Galleries* [1950] 1 All ER 693

The plaintiff bought a painting after accepting it to be a genuine Constable on the basis of misrepresentation made by the defendants. Five years after the sale the plaintiff discovered that the painting was not by Constable and sought to rescind the contract on the grounds of innocent misrepresentation. It was held that his right to rescind was barred. Even though there was no evidence that the plaintiff had affirmed the contract the lapse of time nevertheless debarred him from his remedy.

On the other hand, in ***Salt* v *Stratstone Specialist Ltd (t/a Stratstone Cadillac Newcastle)*** [2015] EWCA Civ 745, it seems to have come to a very different notion of what is a reasonable time since the Court of Appeal considered that delay would not always be a bar to seeking rescission as it had been in ***Leaf*** v ***International Galleries***.

Salt v *Stratstone Specialist Ltd (t/a Stratstone Cadillac Newcastle)* [2015] EWCA Civ 745

In 2007, the appellant sold a luxury sports car to the respondent (Salt) for £21,895 describing it as 'brand new'. In fact, the car was not brand new since, whilst it had not been registered at the time of purchase, the car had been delivered to the appellant two years previously and in that period had had various repairs carried out upon it. Various defects emerged after the respondent took delivery of the car and, whilst the appellant repaired some of them, the respondent eventually rejected the car in September 2008, asking for his money back, claiming the car was not of merchantable quality. The appellant refused to return the money. When it eventually emerged that the car was not new, the respondent claimed misrepresentation and rescission.

The district judge found that the respondent would not have bought the car without the appellant's misrepresentation as to it being brand new, however, *inter alia*, he decided that he could not make an order for rescission as there had been a considerable lapse of time since the date of the original sale, and that the respondent's remedy was limited to damages in lieu of rescission under the Misrepresentation Act 1967 s 2(2).

The respondent appealed to the High Court which allowed his appeal, with the judge finding that it was possible to allow rescission and, on the time issue, considered the delay was not so long as to bar rescission. The appellant appealed to the Court of Appeal, again, on various grounds including the issue as regards time, alleging that a delay of nearly four years between the contract of sale and the application for rescission operated to bar relief just as it had been in *Leaf*.

In the Court of Appeal the appeal was dismissed. The court found that the respondent had only become aware of the misrepresentation and the possibility when the disclosure of documents in the case revealed that the car was not new. Longmore LJ considered that lapse of time on its own could not be a bar to rescission and pointed out that the respondent only became aware of the misrepresentation following the disclosure of documents and that most of the subsequent delay was a result of the litigation process and the appellant's refusal to take the car back and return the price paid.

3. Where *restitutio in integrum* has become impossible

The basis of the remedy of rescission is that of restitution, that is, a mutual handing-back of what has been given and received under the contract. The principle, then, is that rescission cannot take place if the parties cannot be returned substantially to their original positions. Clearly there should be no problem if the representee merely has to hand back money received, but the position may be very different with other types of property or benefits received. One example could be if the representee has been induced to purchase a car by the misrepresentation but, prior to the exercise of rescission, they have had an accident and written it off. Similarly, the benefit received might have deteriorated in value, as in a sale of shares induced by a misrepresentation where prior to the exercise of rescission the value of the shares had fallen substantially, as in *Armstrong* v *Jackson* [1917] 2 KB 822. Still further, rescission would not be possible if the representee had consumed the goods misrepresented to them.

In *Salt* v *Stratstone Specialist Ltd (t/a Stratstone Cadillac Newcastle)* [2015] EWCA Civ 745, the facts of which have already been examined at earlier, the District Judge held that he could not order rescission as *restitutio in integrum* was impossible, since the car had now been registered and could not be returned as an unregistered car. In the High Court, it was held that it was possible to return the parties to their original positions since the car still existed; the fact of registration could not be a bar to rescission; and any difference in the car's value should be at the risk of the misrepresentor not the misrepresentee. The Court of Appeal with Longmore LJ agreed with that decision. The car had been unregistered prior to the sale and registered in the respondent's name following the sale and they did not agree that returning a registered car would be 'returning a registered car would be to return something different from the article [the respondent] bought'. Longmore LJ stated, 'If that were right, it would always be impossible to rescind a contract for a car which was wrongly said to be new. I cannot accept that; registration is a legal concept which does not change the physical entity that a car is'.

Of course, there are various degrees by which the property or benefits might have changed. At common law the rule relating to rescission was strict in the sense that the restitution had to be precise. Equity was not so strict and it allowed rescission if the property or benefit returned was substantially the same as when it was received, minor changes being compensatable by damages in all but innocent misrepresentations. The same is also true where the representee has enhanced the value of the item received, since here they may be able to claim the cost of such enhancement as damages, though not (as stated earlier) for innocent misrepresentation.

This issue also arose in *Stratstone* since the District Judge considered that because a car is a depreciating asset and that rescission would constitute a prejudice to Stratstone. The Court of Appeal considered that it would be comparatively easy to compensate Stratstone, the appellant, for that prejudice. Another point made by the District Judge was that the respondent had had the benfit of using the car, although intermittently because of the problems with it. Longmore LJ considered that neither depreciation nor intermittent enjoyment should be regarded as reasons for saying that restitution is impossible. He stated, 'It has always been the case that a court of equity, contemplating rescission, could order an account and/or an inquiry to determine the terms on which restitution should be made'.

4. The intervention of third parties

In a broad sense this bar to the right of rescission is really only an extension of the principles discussed in (3) above. Here the right to rescind will be lost if an innocent third party acquires the subject matter of the contract in good faith and for value. The situation commonly arises in a case of fraudulent misrepresentation where a person is induced to sell certain items to the representor by fraud. If the representor sells the items to an innocent third party then the remedy of rescission will be barred by the acquisition of title to the goods by the third party. It can be seen, as in *Car and Universal Finance Co. Ltd* v *Caldwell*, for instance, that it is extremely important for the representee to exercise the right of rescission as soon as possible after discovering the fraud, since this will preclude a third party from acquiring the title to the subject matter of the contract and enable the representee to recover the goods from the third party by way of an action in the tort of conversion.

> This area is dealt with more fully in Chapter 10 under unilateral mistake as to identity.

Damages in lieu of rescission

Before we proceed to analyse fully the remedy of damages in relation to misrepresentation, it needs to be pointed out that the right of rescission may be lost where the court decides to exercise its discretion under s 2(2) of the Misrepresentation Act 1967 and award damages in lieu of rescission. Section 2(2) provides:

> Where a person has entered into a contract after a misrepresentation has been made to him otherwise than fraudulently, and he would be entitled by reason of the misrepresentation to rescind the contract, then, if it is claimed in any of the proceedings arising out of the contract, that the contract ought to be or has been rescinded, the court or arbitrator may declare the contract subsisting and award damages in lieu of rescission, if of the opinion that it would be equitable to do so, having regard to the nature of the misrepresentation and the loss that would be caused by it if the contract were upheld, as well as to the loss that rescission would cause the other party.

It is important to note that the discretion to award damages in lieu of rescission cannot be exercised in relation to fraudulent misrepresentation. The reason for this can be found in the general reasoning for the introduction of the s 2(2) discretion, which is to extinguish the use of rescission in cases where the consequences of the misrepresentation are trivial and where damages would provide an adequate remedy. This reasoning for this is sound since the effect of rescission can be serious in that there must be a handing back of money paid and goods received since the contract ceases to have a legal effect: *William Sindall plc* v *Cambridgeshire County Council* [1994] 1 WLR 1016 (CA). This poses a particular problem in innocent misrepresentation where the only remedy available is rescission and therefore the Act permits the court to award damages in lieu of rescission in an appropriate case. Fraud, however, is never regarded as trivial and thus the discretion does not arise in that type of misrepresentation.

In *William Sindall*, Lord Hoffmann at pp. 1036–1037 examined the three criteria set out in s 2(2) that a court should take into account in deciding whether or not to exercise its discretion:

1 The nature of the misrepresentation.

   The court must consider the nature of the misrepresentation that is the court must consider the importance of the representation in relation to the subject matter of the transaction. Lord Hoffmann provided an example stating that

> ... in the context of a £5m sale of land, a misrepresentation which would have cost £18,000 to put right and was unlikely seriously to have interfered with the development or resale of the property was a matter of relatively minor importance.

2 The loss to be sustained by the representee if rescission is not allowed.

The court must have regard to 'the loss that would be caused by [the misrepresentation] if the contract were upheld'. In other words, the court must have regard to the effects on the misrepresentee if it were not allowed to rescind the contract. Lord Hoffmann stated that the section speaks in terms of loss suffered rather than damages recoverable but clearly contemplates that if the contract is upheld; such loss will be compensated by an award of damages. Thus he stated that Section 2(2) gives a power to award damages in circumstances in which no damages would previously have been recoverable. Furthermore, such damages will be compensation for loss caused by the misrepresentation, whether it was negligent or not. He considered this is made clear by s 2(3), which provides:

> Damages may be awarded under subsection (2) of this section whether or not he is liable to damages under subsection (1) thereof, but where he is so liable any award under subsection (2) shall be taken into account in assessing his liability under the said subsection (1).

Lord Hoffmann stated that damages under s 2(2) amounted to damages for the misrepresentation and raised the matter as to how those damages should be measured. He stated that this is a matter for inquiry by the court, however, the court in the exercise of its discretion needs to know whether damages under s 2(2) would be an adequate remedy and to be able to compare such damages with the loss which rescission would cause to the misrepresentor.

He stated that the measure will not necessarily be the same as an award of damages under s 2(1) which is the same as for fraudulent misrepresentation – 'all loss caused by the plaintiff having been induced to enter into the contract'. Thus the misrepresentor will have to pay damages to compensate for the loss of the bargain (the difference between the price paid and the value of the thing sold, plus any damages for consequential losses suffered by entering into the contract).

3 The loss to the representor resulting from rescission. The court must take into account the effect of rescission on the misrepresentor since s 2(2) was enacted because it was thought that hardship may be caused to the misrepresentor if that person was deprived of the whole benefit of the bargain on account of some minor misrepresentation. Lord Hoffmann considered that it could not possibly have been intended that the exercise of discretion to award damages in lieu of rescission under s 2(2) would have the same effect as this.

Another important aspect of s 2(2) is that it applies only where a person 'would be entitled by reason of the misrepresentation to rescind the contract'. The effect of this is that if a person's entitlement to claim rescission is barred by one of the factors discussed above then the court cannot exercise its discretion in relation to an award of damages under s 2(2). In the case of innocent misrepresentation, this may of course result in the representee being without any remedy, with the exception of claiming indemnity.

In *Thomas Witter Ltd* v *TBP Industries Ltd* [1996] 2 All ER 573 (ChD), it was suggested that the power to award damages under s 2(2) does not depend on an existing right to rescission but only on the right having existed in the past. Certainly Jacob J considered that the power to award damages under s 2(2) does not depend upon an existing right to rescission but only that such a right 'having existed in the past'. There may be some sympathy with such a view in that as a matter of policy there seems to be no reason why the operation of one of the bars to rescission should restrict the discretion to award damages. For instance, while it may be inappropriate to allow rescission where the contract has been affirmed or third-party rights have intervened, there seems to be no reason why this should prevent a court from making an award of damages. A reading of s 2(2), however, seems to indicate that the reasoning of the court is incorrect. Section 2(2) operates only where, on the facts, the representee 'would be entitled by reason of the misrepresentation to rescind the contract'. On this wording it would appear that the representee must still be able to avail themselves of rescission at the time they bring the action. This would clearly not be the case if one of the factors that bar a person's right to rescission exists.

Apparently the decision of Jacob J in *Thomas Witter* arose from evidence that whilst the Act was proceeding through Parliament, Sir Dingle Foot, the Solicitor General, had made a statement that the unavailability of rescission would not prevent an award of damages. Be that as it may, it was not followed in *Floods* v *Shand Construction* [2000] BRL 81 where HHJ Lloyd QC refused to follow *Thomas Witter* on the ground that the meaning of the Act was only too clear that damages would not be available unless the claimant was entitled by reason of the misrepresentation to rescind the contract.

This position was followed in *Zanzibar* v *British Aerospace (Lancaster House) Ltd* (2000) *The Times*, 23 March. The action arose out of the purchase of a corporate jet from British Aerospace by the Zanzibar government in 1992. The thrust of the action was that Zanzibar had been induced to purchase the jet by virtue of representations made by British Aerospace as to the type of the jet and its airworthiness, which were untrue. Zanzibar claimed to be entitled to rescission or, alternatively, damages under s 2(2) of the Misrepresentation Act 1967. It was held that the effect of Zanzibar's delay in applying for rescission meant that the right had been lost and that the necessary consequence of this was that the right to damages in lieu of rescission had also been lost.

Furthermore, in *Pankhania* v *London Borough of Hackney [2002] EWHC 2441 (Ch)*, the court also followed the decisions in *Floods* and *Zanzibar*. All the decisions on this point have been considered at first instance level; however, the point was considered in the Court of Appeal in *Salt* v *Stratstone Specialist Ltd (t/a Stratstone Cadillac Newcastle)* [2015] EWCA Civ 745 where Longmore LJ considered the wording of the statute. The words are 'if it is claimed . . . that the contract ought to be or has been rescinded, the court . . . may declare the contract subsisting and award damages in lieu of rescission'. He considered that the words 'in lieu of rescission' must carry with it the implication that rescission is available (or was available at the time the contract was rescinded). He considered that if rescission is not available because, for instance. 'the contract has been affirmed, third party rights have intervened, an excessive time has elapsed or restitution has become impossible, rescission is not available', then damages cannot be awarded in lieu of rescission.

Oblique authority for this proposition may also be found by analogy in *Law Debenture Trust Corporation plc* v *Ural Caspian Oil Corporation Ltd and Others* [1993] 2 All ER 355, where Hoffmann J considered that damages could not be awarded in lieu of injunctive relief by virtue of the Supreme Court Act 1981 (now Senior Courts Act 1981), s 50, if injunctive relief itself was unavailable.

A further case illustrating the principles is that of *Harsten Developments Ltd* v *Bleaken* [2012] EWHC 2704 (Ch). This case concerned the sale of a parcel of land in 2007, which had planning permission, between two existing plots. The vendors, who owned the parcel of land and one of the adjoining lots of land, misrepresented the extent of the boundary around the parcel of land for the 'infill' development as well as other misrepresentations. The claimant developer sought to have the contract rescinded. The court considered that rescission was available to the developer despite the fact that it had re-applied for the planning permission. The court did not consider that it had affirmed the contract in doing this since it was unaware of its ability to rescind the contract at that time. The court then went on to consider whether it should award damages in lieu of rescission under s 2(2). The court considered that the misrepresentations made by the vendors were significant and serious with the effect that the parcel of land purchased by the developer was different from that which they believed they were buying and in this respect the court distinguished the position from that which occurred in the *William Sindall* case.

The court considered the three criteria set out in s 2(2). In relation to the first the judge considered that it was clear that the misrepresentations meant that the land transferred was substantially different in terms of quantity and quality from what the developer had been led to expect. In terms of the second requirement it is clear that the developer would suffer adverse consequences if the decision was to refuse rescission. It was clear that the developer did not want the land since it had purchased at the top of the market and that the market value of the land had now fallen by a substantial amount. If rescission was refused then the developer would retain the land but would be entitled to damages from the vendors calculated in accordance with s 2(3). If the judge were to allow rescission then the developer would re-transfer the land to the vendors who would have to repay the purchase money plus interest plus damages under s 2(1). The judge considered that the ordinary remedy for misrepresentation is rescission and given the significance of the misrepresentations in this case he was not persuaded that it would be equitable to deny the developers the remedy of rescission. Morgan J considered the issue of lapse of time from late 2007 to the case coming to court and whether this would militate against rescission. He considered that such lapse of time is material when considering the operation of s 2(2), however, in this case, rather surprisingly no argument was submitted by the vendors on this point.

The court in the *Thomas Witter* case also addressed the issue of the effects where damages under s 2(1) were not available because the defendant had proved that 'he had reasonable grounds to believe and did believe up to the time the contract was made that the facts represented were true', i.e. the so-called innocence defence. If this were the case, then presumably the defendant could still be liable for innocent misrepresentation, entitling the claimant to apply for rescission, although they could be granted damages in lieu of this remedy under s 2(2).

In deciding whether or not to exercise its discretion, the court thus has to take into account the degree of seriousness of the breach and the likely consequences of the exercise of the discretion on the representee and the representor, particularly in cases involving an innocent misrepresentation where the degree of loss is minimal.

Damages for misrepresentation

Fraudulent misrepresentation

Damages are available at common law for fraudulent misrepresentation, the measure being a tortious one since the claim is based on the tort of deceit. The difference between a tortious measure and a contractual one is that, in the latter, the principle behind the award is to place the injured party in the same position they would have been in had the contract been completed. A tortious measure is based on the principle of placing the injured party in the same position they would have been in had the wrongful act not been committed.

While the measure of damages in tort is limited by the concept of **remoteness of damages**, that is, that one is only liable for damages that are reasonably foreseeable, this has no application in fraud where the damages are awarded on a causation basis. Lord Denning in *Doyle* v *Olby (Ironmongers) Ltd* [1969] 2 QB 158 stated the position to be as follows:

'In contract, the damages are limited to what may reasonably be supposed to have been in the contemplation of the parties. In fraud, they are not so limited. The defendant is bound to make reparation for all the actual damages directly flowing from the fraudulent inducement. The person who has been defrauded is entitled to say: 'I would not have entered into this bargain at all but for your representation. Owing to your fraud, I have not only lost all the money I paid you, but, what is more, I have been put to a large amount of extra expense as well and suffered this or that extra damages.' All such damages can be recovered: and it does not lie in the mouth of the fraudulent person to say that they could not reasonably have been foreseen.

The decision in *Doyle* v *Olby (Ironmongers) Ltd* was affirmed in *Smith New Court Securities Ltd* v *Citibank NA* [1997] AC 254 *(aka Smith New Court Securities Ltd* v *Scrimgeour Vickers (Asset Management) Ltd* [1996] 4 All ER 769) where *Smith New Court Securities Ltd* ('SNS') was induced to purchase shares in a company based on the fraudulent misrepresentation of the broker to the defendant ('SV'). Subsequently a fraud was perpetrated against the company by a third party, causing the value of the shares to slump. SNS had purchased the shares as a long-term investment but had purchased the shares at a price that was more than the market value, even as at the date of the contract. The result of this was that there was no possibility of reselling the shares at a price that would enable SNS to recover its original investment. At first instance the judge awarded the sum of £10,764,005, being the difference between the price paid by SNS and the true value of the shares based on all the facts known about the company at the time of purchase. In the Court of Appeal, the sum of £1,196,010 was substituted on the basis that SNS's loss on selling the shares was not foreseeable and that the value should be assessed according to the circumstances and the date they bought the shares. Both SNS and SV appealed to the House of Lords.

The question before the House of Lords was whether SNS could recover the difference between the price paid for the shares and the eventual price for which SNS sold them, which reflected the value of the company following the massive fraud that had taken place, or whether SNS could only recover the difference between the price paid and the value of the shares at the date of the contract. If the measure of damages was based on the first means of computation, then such a measure would take into account the catastrophic loss which was a directly consequence of the fraudulent misrepresentation of the defendant. The basis behind such a measurement was that SNS would not have been exposed to the risk but for the inducement arising from the fraudulent misrepresentation. If the measure of damages was based on the latter, i.e. the transaction date, the computation would not of course have reflected the fraud that had taken place which had not been discovered at that point in time.

The House of Lords allowed SNS's appeal stating that the defendant was liable for all losses directly flowing from the fraudulently induced transaction even if they were not foreseeable. The normal rule for the assessment of damages is that the loss is to be assessed at the date of the transaction; however, this rule was flexible and would not normally 'be applied where to do so would prevent [the misrepresentee] obtaining full compensation', for instance, where the misrepresentation had continued after the date of the transaction or where the claimant had become locked into the property as a result of fraud. The House of Lords held that consequential losses could also be recovered, although in such a situation a claimant would be obliged to do whatever was reasonable to mitigate the loss once they became aware of the fraud. The House of Lords held that SNS were to be put in the position that they would have been in had misrepresentation not occurred.

Lord Browne-Wilkinson set out the principles to be applied in assessing the damages payable where a contract has been induced by a fraudulent misrepresentation. He stated that: first, a defendant is bound to make reparation for all the damage that directly flowed from the transaction; second, although such damage need not be foreseeable, it must have been directly caused by the transaction, i.e. there must be a causative link; third, in assessing the damages credit must be given for any benefits a claimant may have received from the transaction and that their entitlement to the full price paid would be reduced by this amount; fourth, as a general rule the benefits received by the claimant would include the market value of the goods acquired by them as at the date of acquisition, but this rule would not be applied where it would prevent the claimant from receiving full compensation for the wrong suffered; fifth, the circumstances in which the general rule would not apply could not be fully stated – however, it would not apply in two circumstances: (a) where the misrepresentation had continued to operate after the date the asset was acquired, or (b) the circumstances were such that the claimant was locked into the property by reason of the fraud; sixth, the claimant was entitled to recover consequential losses caused by the transaction; and seventh, the claimant had taken all reasonable steps to mitigate their losses once they had discovered the fraud.

In *OMV Petrom SA* v *Glencore International AG* [2016] EWCA Civ 778, the purchaser contracted for the shipment of crude oil from the defendant, the contract stipulating that the crude oil would be Iranian Heavy and GOSM grade. The shipment documents confirmed that the oil being shipped was of these grades but these documents were false since some of the crude shipped consisted of other grades of crude oil. The judge at first instance held that the purchaser had a claim in deceit. The purchaser claimed that the measure of damages should be the difference between the price paid for the cargoes and the actual value of the shipments that were delivered. The defendant claimed that the proper measure of damages should be the difference in value between the lower value of the yield derived from refining the blends actually delivered and the higher yield that would have resulted in crude if the correct grades of crude oil had been delivered. At first instance, applying the principles set out in *Smith New Court*, the judge adopted the purchaser's valuation approach. The judge found that the clamant was entitled to be compensated for its loss by placing it in the same position it would have been in had the false statements not been made, but taking into account the benefit received by the claimant, that is the price paid for the crude oil that was delivered. The effect therefore was that the damages should be the price paid but credit was to be given for the actual value of the oil at the date of purchase. It was irrelevant what the purchaser chose to do with the crude oil.

In the Court of Appeal, the defendant's appeal was dismissed and the judge's assessment of damage affirmed. The Court of Appeal stated that the basic damages were the price paid less the benefits received as a result of the contract, the value to be assessed at the date of its acquisition. In this instance the relevant date was the bill of lading date. The Court of Appeal considered that crude oil cargoes were unique and therefore had to be valued by way of the total cost, insurance and the freight value of the component crude oils. Thus the damages recoverable were the difference by which the price paid exceeded that value and that the judge was correct in ejecting the defendant's comparative yield approach. Such an approach relied on a hypothetical and approximate assessment of the relative yields. Further, such an approach would allow the defendant to retain part of its fraudulently obtained profits.

The result is that the court will award damages for all losses including consequential losses. It is this factor, the lure of heavier damages, that may encourage representees to pursue a claim under fraudulent misrepresentation and, conversely, it deters representors from making a fraudulent misrepresentation.

The decision in *Smith New Court Securities Ltd* v *Citibank NA* [1997] AC 254 is not an inevitable result. In *East* v *Maurer* [1991] 2 All ER 733, the Court of Appeal stated that the 'reparation for all actual damage' as indicated by Lord Denning would include loss of profits. The assessment of loss of profits, however, was to be made on a tortious basis. The result is that the assessment of damages for loss of profits caused by a fraudulent misrepresentation must be based on the level of profits that might have been expected had the false representation not been made, rather than on the basis of a contractual warranty. The effect of such an approach may well result in the amount of damages to be awarded for loss of profits being reduced, as indeed they were in this case.

There are some limitations on the ability of a claimant to recover all loss that flows from the breach; for instance, one cannot simply incur expenditure and express this as a loss flowing from the fraudulent misrepresentation. As Eady J pointed out in *Cherrilow Ltd* v *Richard Butler-Creagh*, it is necessary to demonstrate that the expenditure was necessary or reasonable in order to mitigate one's losses. In any event, Eady J held that Cherrilow Ltd was entitled to recover not only the difference between the value of the property at the date of the exchange and what was eventually paid for it, but also the consequential losses that arose such as stamp duty, borrowing costs as well as reasonable running and staffing costs. Eady J stated:

> One cannot simply spend money in a situation of this kind and express it as a loss flowing from the actionable misrepresentations. It is said that the money has been spent with nothing to show for it. It needs, however, to be demonstrated that it was necessary or reasonable to spend the money to mitigate loss or to preserve the relevant asset. It is surely appropriate to demonstrate that the claimant in question has had to spend the money, not merely as a matter of choice, but as a result of being placed wrongfully in a particular predicament as a result of the misrepresentation(s) comprising the cause of action.

Negligent misrepresentation at common law

Clearly the measure of damages here is based on a tortious measure and is thus subject to the test of remoteness, that is, damages which are reasonably foreseeable.

Negligent misrepresentation under s 2(1)

As with s 2(2), there is no specific statement as to the measure of damages to be applied though the wording clearly suggests that a tortious measure is intended. In *Watts* v *Spence* [1976] Ch 165, a contractual measure was used, but it would seem settled that this is wrong since, in *André et Cie SA* v *Ets Michel Blanc et Fils* [1977] 2 Lloyd's Rep 166 and later in *Sharneyford Supplies Ltd* v *Edge* [1985] 1 All ER 976, it was decided that a correct measure was one based on tort.

Having decided that a tortious measure is appropriate, we must next ask whether the measure is based on negligence or on the tort of deceit. As we have already seen, damages under the tort of deceit are wider, being based on causation and not being limited to those which may be reasonably foreseen as in negligence. While there has been considerable debate over this question in the past, the Court of Appeal in *Royscot Trust Ltd* v *Rogerson* [1991] 3 All ER 294 stated that s 2(1) was clear in that the correct measure was that based on the tort of deceit. Balcombe LJ stated that the plaintiff was entitled to recover all losses even if those losses were unforeseeable, provided they were not otherwise too remote.

It may be the case that the decision in *Royscot Trust Ltd* v *Rogerson* will not ultimately decide this issue. In *Smith New Court Securities Ltd* v *Citibank NA*, Lord Steyn questioned whether it was correct to 'treat a person who was morally innocent as if he were guilty of fraud when it comes to the measure of damages'. The point was not developed, however, since it was irrelevant to the facts of the case. Lord Steyn did nevertheless clarify the distinction between an action under s 2(1) and one under fraudulent misrepresentation. He stated that in an action under s 2(1) the recoverable loss does not go beyond the consequences that arise from the negligent misrepresentation. It can be seen immediately that this is narrower than the principle in *Doyle* v *Olby (Ironmongers) Ltd*, where the claimant is entitled to recover all loss flowing directly from the fraudulently induced contract, provided there is a causative link between the statement and the loss.

The difference between the calculation of damages in tort and the calculation in contract can be seen in the case of *Naughton and Another* v *O'Callaghan*.

Naughton and Another v O'Callaghan [1990] 3 All ER 191

The facts of the case were that in September 1981 the plaintiffs bought a thoroughbred yearling for 26,000 guineas from the Newmarket sales. The horse was trained in England and Ireland for two seasons but was unplaced in all the races it was entered for. The horse's lack of success meant that its value fell to £11,500. In June 1983, it was discovered that the horse's pedigree had been incorrectly described in the sales catalogue because of an error at the stud farm where the horse was foaled. Subsequent to this discovery further expenses were incurred and the following year the plaintiff purchasers purported to repudiate the contract, seeking the purchase price and training fees and expenses amounting to £14,734. Judgement was entered by default against the defendants and the stud farm. In assessing the damages, evidence was produced that if the yearling had been correctly described it would only have fetched approximately 23,000 guineas at the sale. The defendants and the stud farm contended that the plaintiffs had bought a horse of practically the same value as the one they had intended to buy and that therefore they were only entitled to the difference in value. Further, they contended that they were not liable for the training fees and other expenses since such expenses would have been incurred whatever horse had been purchased.

It was held that the correct measure of damages was the difference between the purchase price and the value of the horse at the time of the discovery of the misrepresentation, *not* the difference between the purchase price and the horse's actual value at the time it was purchased. As regards the expenses, it was decided that the plaintiffs were entitled to these since the plaintiffs were entitled to say that this was not the horse they thought they had bought and, as such, was not a horse that they would have spent money on training or keeping. The expenses were moneys spent in reliance on the misrepresentation. In other words, plaintiffs are entitled to be put into the same position they would have been in had they not entered into the transaction.

Innocent misrepresentation

Damages are not recoverable for innocent misrepresentation unless the court decides to exercise its discretion under s 2(2) and award damages in lieu of rescission. The measure of damages for this is discussed below.

The measure of damages under s 2(2)

As with s 2(1) this provision gives no express indication as to the measure of damages though both Treitel (2011) and *Cheshire, Fifoot and Furmston* (2012) indicate that the measure should be somewhat lower than those that may be awarded under s 2(1). There are two reasons for

Table 9.1 Summary of the remedies available for misrepresentation

Rescission + Indemnity (available for all types of misrepresentation)	
Note the bars to rescission: 1 Affirmation 2 Lapse of time 3 Restitution impossible 4 Intervention of third parties 5 Discretion to award damages under the Misrepresentation Act 1967, s 2(2)	
Damages	
Fraudulent misrepresentation	Damages here are based on the tort of deceit, that is, on causation; therefore, damages are available for all loss, including consequential loss, providing there is a causative link: ***Doyle* v *Olby (Ironmongers) Ltd***; ***Smith New Court Securities Ltd* v *Citibank NA*** [1997] AC 254; ***East* v *Maurer*.**
Negligent misrepresentation at common law	Damages are based on a tortious measure as found in the common law tort of negligence and thus only loss that is reasonably foreseeable may be recovered provided there is a 'special relationship' between the parties: ***H-edley Byrne & Co. Ltd* v *Heller & Partners Ltd*; *Caparo Industries plc* v *Dickman and Others*.** Burden of proof is on the misrepresentee.
Negligent misrepresentation under the Misrepresentation Act 1967, s 2(1)	No measure of damages is specified in s 2(1) but ***Royscot Trust Ltd* v *Rogerson*** indicated that damages here are based on the tort of deceit – see above. This was questioned in ***Smith New Court Securities Ltd* v *Citibank NA*** and it was stated that in an action under s 2(1) the recoverable loss does not go beyond the consequences that arise from negligent misrepresentation – narrower than in ***Doyle* v *Olby (Ironmongers) Ltd*** above. Burden of proof is on the misrepresentor to prove he was NOT negligent – a procedural advantage for the innocent party.
Innocent misrepresentation	Damages are not recoverable unless the court exercises its discretion under s 2(2). Not the same measure as s 2(1) since s 2(3) states this. ***William Sindall plc* v *Cambridgeshire County Council*** indicates a measure that compensates a claimant 'for the difference in value between what the plaintiff was misled into believing that he was acquiring and the value of what in fact he received'. Consequential losses not available.
Remedies where the misrepresentation is also a term of the contract	
Condition	Damages + Rescission
Warranty	Damages only
Innominate term	The *Hong Kong Fir* test applies: Has the party been substantially deprived of the whole of the benefit he would receive under the contract?

See Chapter 7 for more on the *Hong Kong Fir* test.

this proposition. First, s 2(3) tends to suggest that a lower measure be adopted. Section 2(3) provides:

> Damages may be awarded against a person under subsection (2) of this section whether or not he is liable to damages under subsection (1) thereof, but where he is so liable any award under

the said subsection (2) shall be taken into account in assessing his liability under the said subsection (1).

Second, damages under s 2(2) are to be awarded in lieu of rescission and since the purpose of this remedy is to effect a restitution between what the representee handed over and what the representee received then the damages awarded under s 2(2) should reflect such a measure. Such a measure would therefore preclude sums representing consequential losses.

Surprisingly, there has been very little judicial consideration of the measure of damages under s 2(2). The issue has, however, been discussed in *William Sindall plc v Cambridgeshire County Council* [1994] 1 WLR 1016 (CA), where both Hoffmann LJ and Evans LJ concurred that the measure is different from that which arises under s 2(1) since s 2(3) indicates this. They considered that the measure should be an amount that compensates the plaintiff 'for the loss he has suffered on account of the property not having been what it was represented to be'. Evans LJ was a little more explicit and stated that the measure of damages should be based on 'the difference in value between what the plaintiff was misled into believing that he was acquiring, and the value of what in fact he received'. This measure was to be calculated at the time of the contract and consequential losses should not be taken into account.

Contributory negligence

To what extent may contributory negligence operate, in relation to misrepresentation, so as to reduce the misrepresentee's damages? In *Gran Gelato Ltd v Richcliff (Group) Ltd* [1992] 1 All ER 865, the defendant had given the plaintiff an under-lease for ten years in 1984. The head lease contained a break clause which was exercisable on the giving of 12 months' notice, expiring on or after June 1989. Neither Gran Gelato nor its solicitors was aware of this restriction. In reply to an enquiry, the defendant's solicitors had stated that there were no such rights in the head lease that would affect the tenant's enjoyment of the property 'to the lessor's knowledge'. In 1988, the lessor of the head lease exercised the break clause in order to redevelop the property. The plaintiff brought an action for misrepresentation under s 2(1) and for negligent misstatement at common law, i.e. under *Hedley Byrne and Co. Ltd v Heller & Partners Ltd*. The defendant claimed that the plaintiff was contributorily negligent in not asking for and examining the head lease. The plaintiff argued that the Law Reform (Contributory Negligence) Act 1945, s 1, did not apply to a claim for damages under s 2(1) of the 1967 Act. The question that arose is that whilst the Act applies to common law negligent misstatement, could it also apply to s 2(1)? Nicholls VC stated: that liability under the Misrepresentation Act 1967 was essentially founded on negligence, in the sense that the defendant, the representor, did not have reasonable grounds to believe that the facts represented were true. It was held that the 1945 Act applied to both the claim under s 2(1) and for negligent misstatement at common law since both types of action were essentially tortious actions. Thus Nicholls VC stated:

> ... in short, liability under the Misrepresentation Act 1967 is essentially founded on negligence, in the sense that the defendant, the representor, did not have reasonable grounds to believe that the facts represented were true ... This being so, it would be very odd if the defence of contributory negligence were not available to a claim under that Act. It would be very odd if contributory negligence were available as a defence to a claim for damages based on a breach of a duty to take care in and about the making of a particular representation, but not available to a claim for damages under the Act in respect of the same representation.

In arriving at this conclusion, Nicholls VC referred to the Court of Appeal decision in *Forsikringsaktieselskapet Vesta v Butcher* [1989] A.C. 852 where the court held that the

1945 Act applied to a case where there was a claim for damages for negligence at common law, together with a claim in contract to the same effect. In this case, O'Connor LJ adopted the view expressed in the New Zealand case of *Rowe* v *Turner Hopkins & Partners* [1980] 2 N.Z.L.R. 550 where Pritchard J, regarding the New Zealand equivalent of the 1945 Act, stated:

> I therefore conclude, in the absence of any clear authority to the contrary, that the first limb of the definition of section 2 determines the meaning of the word 'fault as it relates to the plaintiff's cause of action: that accordingly, the Contributory Negligence Act cannot apply unless the cause of action is founded on some act or omission on the part of the defendant which gives rise to liability in tort: that if the defendant's conduct meets that criterion, the Act can apply – whether or not the same conduct is also actionable in contract.

Nicholls VC considered that the conclusion to be drawn from the *Vesta* case is that where there are concurrent claims in negligence in tort and in contract, the 1945 Act applies. By analogy therefore, where there are concurrent claims both in negligent misstatement and under s 2(1), the 1945 Act will equally apply. Nicholls VC considered that 'fault' within the 1945 Act was wide enough to encompass the 1967 Act. The decision was based on the fact that there was a concurrent liability under both s 2(1) and common law negligent misstatement under the principle in *Hedley Byrne and Co. Ltd* v *Heller & Partners Ltd*. On the facts, however, it was decided that it was not just and equitable to make a reduction in damages when the representor had intended or should be taken as intended that the representee should act in reliance on the answers which had been given to his questions.

It may happen, however, that a defendant is liable under s 2(1) alone so that there is no concurrent liability with common law negligent misstatement, for instance, because the claimant has not proceeded on this. The problem here is that damages under s 2(1) are assessed in the same way as damages are assessed in fraud. In *Alliance & Leicester Building Society* v *Edgestop Ltd* [1994] 2 All ER 38, however, Mummery J considered that contributory negligence has no application in the case of fraudulent misrepresentation. This decision clearly distinguishes that of *Gran Gelato* and may be considered as affirming the decision of Lord Jessel MR in *Redgrave* v *Hurd* (1881) 20 ChD 1, in which he stated: 'Nothing can be plainer, I take it, on the authorities in equity than that the effect of false representation is not got rid of on the ground that the person to whom it was made has been guilty of negligence.' This decision therefore poses a particular problem since, presumably, contributory negligence should not then be applied to s 2(1). The reasoning is that damages under s 2(1) are based on the fiction of fraud as held in *Royscot Trust Ltd* v *Rogerson* [1991] 2 QB 297 and if contributory negligence cannot be pleaded for fraudulent misrepresentation, then it cannot by the same token be pleaded for s 2(1) since the assessment of damages is the same. The effect therefore would be to indirectly overturn Nicholls VC's reasoning that contributory negligence can apply if s 2(1) is pleaded on its own. How can this apparent conflict be resolved? One answer to this problem may lie in Lord Steyn's opinion that damages under s 2(1) are to be assessed on the narrower principle that recoverable loss is limited to the foreseeable consequences that arise from the negligent misrepresentation, rather than the 'all loss' principle in *Doyle* v *Olby (Ironmongers) Ltd*. If that approach is taken, then consistency should arise between the various authorities.

In *Standard Chartered Bank* v *Pakistan National Shipping Corporation* [2003] 1 AC 959, however, Lord Hoffmann concurred with the view of Mummery J that there is no common law defence of contributory negligence in cases of fraudulent misrepresentation, and stated that it follows that no apportionment of damages under the 1945 Act is therefore possible. Again, the reasoning appears to be based on an application of the rule in *Redgrave* v *Hurd*. The basis of a contributory negligence claim is that a claimant could, with reasonable care, have discovered that the representation was untrue and in *Redgrave* v *Hurd* the court held that it would be incorrect for a person to make a false statement and then escape liability by stating that the representee could have discovered the truth. It should be noted, however, that in relation to s 2(1) Lord Hoffman appeared to approve of Nicholls VC's comments in *Gran Gelato* that, in principle, a defence of contributory negligence should be available for a claim for damages under s 2(1).i.

On the face of things, therefore, it appears that if a claim is framed under s 2(1) alone, then a claimant may avoid the apportionment, despite the claimant possibly having a valid claim at common law negligent misstatement under *Hedley Byrne and Co. Ltd v Heller & Partners Ltd*. This point arose in *Taberna Europe CDO II Plc v Selskabet (Formerly Roskilde Bank A/S) (In Bankruptcy)* [2015] EWHC 871 (Comm). It was alleged that the claim for damages under s 2(1) could be reduced on the basis that by not taking out specialist market advice, relying on investment information that was out of date and failing to undertake a proper assessment of the capitalisation of the bank amounted to contributory negligence.

On behalf of the investor, it was argued contributory negligence could not reduce damages awarded under s 2(1) where there was no additional claim under negligent misstatement at common law, though in fact the investor had originally claimed under both heads but later dropped the latter one. This is of course a potential strategic approach to the action since if contributory negligence is not available under s 2(1), and only applied where there is a concurrent action with negligent misstatement at common law, which was not the case, the investor's damages could not be reduced by reason of the contributory negligence. This argument was rejected by the judge, stating that there was no reason why contributory negligence could not apply. Eder J considered stated:

> ... it does not seem to me that the question as to whether a defendant can rely upon the 1945 Act should depend on the happenstance as to whether the claimant advances a claim based on a breach of a concurrent duty of care. Rather, the question should, in my judgement, depend on whether or not there is or would be concurrent liability.

Thus where the representations arise in circumstances that give rise to a conclusion that a claim under the common law duty of care for negligent misstatement could also be generated then it follows that any misrepresentation giving rise to liability under s 2(1) makes available the defence of contributory negligence under the 1945 Act. Thus it is not necessary to found that by establishing a concurrent duty of care, a single duty of care under s 2(1) would suffice, provided a concurrent liability could be established.

Exclusion of liability for misrepresentation

Objective 7

See Chapter 8 for exemption clauses.

While exemption clauses have already been discussed with regard to the incorporation of exemption clauses and the statutory control of them, there are particular issues relating to the exclusion of liability that need to be addressed in a wider context. The earlier analysis of exemption clauses was largely concerned with the exempting of liability with respect to contractual liability; however, it is possible to frame an exemption clause in such a way as to exclude liability for statements that induce a party to enter into a contract. Here the exemption is often framed in such a way as to avoid liability in its broadest sense by excluding or limiting the remedies for misrepresentation which might include damages or the right to rescind the contract itself where an operative misrepresentation has occurred. The control of such exemption clauses may arise not just by statute as in the Unfair Contract Terms Act 1977 and the Unfair Terms in Consumer Contracts Regulations 1999, but also by way of common law controls imposed by the courts.

Controls imposed at common law

Fraud

The first and fundamental restriction on the use of exemption clauses is that the courts will not allow an exemption clause to operate so as to exclude liability for fraudulent misrepresentation. In *HIH Casualty and General Insurance Ltd* v *Chase Manhattan Bank* [2003] UKHL 6, Chase was advancing substantial sums to finance the making of future films. If the films proved successful and generated any profits, then Chase would expect to recoup its outlay from the profits. On the other hand, if a film was not successful and made no profits, then Chase would seek to recover its outlay from an insurance policy and without such security Chase would not have lent any money at all. The issues between the parties centred around the correct interpretation of a 'Truth of Statement' clause, contained in the policy, which provided that Chase would have no duty to make any representation, warranty or disclosure of any nature. Further, that Chase would have no liability for any information provided by other parties and that any information provided by or non-disclosure by other parties, including their agents, Heaths (Chase's brokers), would not be a ground for avoidance of obligations under the policy.

The House of Lords held that the insurers were entitled in law to avoid/rescind the contracts on the grounds of fraudulent misrepresentation or fraudulent non-disclosure by Heaths, as agent for Chase, and to damages for fraudulent representation or fraudulent non-disclosure by Heaths. The truth of statement clause in the policy did, however, prevent the insurers from avoiding the policy on the ground of innocent or negligent misrepresentation by Heaths. Liability for fraudulent misrepresentation, however, was not excluded since each party to a contract assumes the honesty and good faith of the other. Lord Bingham stated, 'It is clear that the law, on public policy grounds, does not permit a contracting party to exclude liability for his own fraud in inducing the making of the contract'.

Entire agreement clauses

For more on entire agreement clauses refer to Chapter 7.

It was seen earlier that an entire agreement clause is essentially an acknowledgement that any promises or undertakings entered into before the contract are encompassed within the contract itself, so that individual parties cannot later allege that they have relied on any promises or undertakings not contained within the contract as per Lightman J in *Inntrepreneur Pub Co.* v *East Crown Ltd* [2000] 2 Lloyd's Rep 611.

Attempts have been made to make use of entire agreement clauses, to prevent the consideration of all statements and representations made during the negotiations to be eliminated from being actionable. In *AXA Sun Life Services plc* v *Campbell Martin Ltd* [2011] EWCA Civ 133, it was held that an entire agreement clause did not exclude any liability for misrepresentations as to matters that were not the subject of the terms of the agreement. The Court of Appeal therefore followed *Deepak* v *ICI* [1999] 1 Lloyd's Rep 387, where it was stated that while entire agreement clauses excluded collateral warranties, they did not exclude misrepresentations. Of course an entire agreement clause could be constructed in such a way as to exclude liability for misrepresentations. In *Springwell Navigation Corporation* v *JP Morgan Chase Bank* [2010] EWCA Civ 1221, the court, confirming its decision in *Peekay Intermark Ltd* v *ANZ Banking Group Ltd* [2006] EWCA 1551, stated that a clause acknowledging that no representations had been made is effectively an exclusion of any liability in misrepresentation. The position in *Springwell* was confirmed by Lady Justice Gloster in *Shoreline Housing Partnership Limited* v *Mears Limited* [2013] EWCA Civ 639 in which she stated [17] '. . . the Court of Appeal held in *Springwell* . . . the doctrine of freedom of contract allows parties to agree that, at the time they enter into the contract, a representation-free state of affairs exists, even if, in reality, that is not the case and prior representations have been indeed been made that might ground an estoppel'. If that is the case, such a clause would be subject to the Misrepresentation Act 1967, s 3, which provides that any term that seeks to exclude or restrict liability for misrepresentation will be subject to the requirement of reasonableness under the Unfair Contract Terms Act 1977, s 11(1).

For more on the requirement of reasonableness, refer to Chapter 8.

Non-reliance clauses

As we have already seen, in order to make a claim in misrepresentation, the person to whom the misrepresentation has been made must show that the statement influenced them in making the decision to enter into the contract. It follows from this that a party may avoid liability by providing that the other party has not relied on any representations made to them prior to entering into the contract.

That is one level at which a non-reliance clause operates. However, it can also be explained by way of establishing an evidential or contractual estoppel. In *EA Grimstead & Son Ltd* v *McGarrigan* (unreported, 27 October 1999), Chadwick LJ stated:

> In my view an acknowledgement of non-reliance . . . is capable of operating as an evidential estoppel. It is apt to prevent the party who has given the acknowledgement from asserting in subsequent litigation against the party to whom it has been given that it is not true. That seems to me to be a proper use of an acknowledgement of this nature, which, as Mr Justice Jacob pointed out in the *Thomas Witter* case [*Thomas Witter Ltd* v *TBP Industries Ltd*], has become a common feature of professionally drawn commercial contracts.

In *Watford Electronics Ltd* v *Sanderson CFL Ltd* [2001] 1 All ER (Comm) 696, Chadwick LJ stated that an acknowledgement of non-reliance does not purport to prevent a party from proving that a representation was made, nor that it was false. What it in fact seeks to do is to prevent the person to whom the representation was made from asserting that he relied upon it. If it is to have that effect, it is necessary to set up a contractual estoppel by establishing the criteria set out by the Court of Appeal in *Lowe* v *Lombank Ltd* [1960] 1 WLR 196 that a representor cannot found an estoppel based on a non-reliance clause signed by the representee unless the representor can show:

1 That it is clear and unambiguous.

2 That the representee intended that the representor should act upon the statements as regards non-reliance or at least so conduct himself so that a reasonable man in the position of the representor would take the representation to be true and believe that it was meant that he should act upon it.

3 That the representor in fact believed the non-reliance statements to be true and was induced by such belief to act upon it.

In *Watford*, Chadwick LJ recognised that attempting to prove such requirements may present insuperable difficulties since they often arise in the representor's standard form contract and yet the non-reliance clause is being used to claim that the representee has asserted their non-reliance so that they are estopped from proving that they relied on the representations made to him. He stated:

> it may be impossible for a party who has made representations which he intended should be relied upon to satisfy the court that he entered into the contract in the belief that a statement by the other party that he had not relied upon those representations was true.

The difficulties in establishing a contractual estoppel were acknowledged in the case of *Peekay Intermark Ltd* v *ANZ Banking Group Ltd* where Moore-Bick LJ considered that there was no reason in principle why parties to a contract should not agree that a certain state of affairs should form the basis for the transaction, whether it be the case or not. He considered that it is common in certain kinds of contracts to include an express acknowledgement by each of the parties that they have not been induced to enter the contract by any representations other than those contained in the contract itself. He could see no reason in principle why it should not be possible for the parties to an agreement to give up any right to assert that they were induced to enter into the contract by way of misrepresentation, provided that the parties made that intention clear. He considered, however, that this gave rise to a different type of estoppel, a contractual estoppel, which arose simply on the grounds of the parties agreeing the basis on which the contract was made and the non-reliance clause simply preventing them from denying the terms of the contract. Moore-Bick LJ's approach has a tendency to avoid the difficulties presented by evidential estoppel since it tends to treat the contract as it stands on face value rather than requiring an investigation of what has taken place as required in *EA Grimstead & Son Ltd* v *McGarrigan*. This was acknowledged in *Trident Turboprop (Dublin) Ltd* v *First Flight Couriers Ltd* [2008] EWHC 1686 (Comm) where Aikens J considered a clause which stated 'the Lessor has not and shall not be deemed to have made any warranties or representations, express or implied, about the Aircraft . . .' and concluded that such a provision could be relied upon to defeat a defence in misrepresentation since the parties had agreed that their contract was based on the absence of any representations.

In *Raiffeisen Zentralbank Osterreich AG* v *Royal Bank of Scotland plc*, Clarke J rejected the argument that contractual estoppel could not apply to past facts, stating:

> The distinction between past and present facts is not without difficulty. If a party agrees that he is entering into a contract in reliance on three identified representations which are the only representations that have been made to him, his agreement may be said to relate partly to the present (his reliance at the moment of contract) and partly to the past (what he has been told). It would be somewhat curious if such an agreement operated as a contractual estoppel only in respect of the claimant's agreement as to what he relied on at the moment of contracting but not in respect of his agreement as to the limits of what he had been told . . . I do not regard myself as bound by *Lowe* v *Lombank* to conclude that an agreement that no representations have been made or relied on (or as to any other past fact) can never amount to a contractual estoppel. There is no intrinsic reason why that should be so. There is good reason for allowing businessmen to agree with each other the basis of fact (including past fact) upon which they are to do business.

Controls imposed by statute

The common law controls on exemption clauses have to be considered in the wider context of the statutory controls, particularly the Misrepresentation Act 1967, s 3 as substituted by Unfair Contract Terms Act 1977, s 8 and the Consumer Rights Act 2015 Schedule 4 para 1. Section 3 now reads:

(1) If a contract contains a term which would exclude or restrict –
   (a) any liability to which a party to a contract may be subject by reason of any misrepresentation made by him before the contract was made; or
   (b) any remedy available to another party to the contract by reason of such a misrepresentation:

that term shall be of no effect except in so far as it satisfies the requirement of reasonableness as stated in section 11(1) of the Unfair Contract Terms Act 1977; and it is for those claiming that the term satisfies that requirement to show that it does.

(2) This section does not apply to a term in a consumer contract within the meaning of Part 2 of the Consumer Rights Act 2015 (but see the provision made about such contracts in section 62 of that Act).

The first thing to notice about s 3 is that it no longer applies in relation to consumer contracts, i.e. B2C contracts. In relation to consumer contracts any term seeking to exclude liability or limit liability for misrepresentation is assessed by the fairness test in s 62, that is, a term is unfair if, contrary to the requirement of good faith, it causes a significant imbalance in the parties' rights and obligations under the contract to the detriment of the consumer. This is determined by taking into account the nature of the subject matter of the contract, and by reference to all the circumstances existing when the term was agreed and to all of the other terms of the contract or of any other contract on which it depends.

In relation to non-consumer contracts, i.e. B2B contracts s 3 renders ineffective any clause that seeks to exclude or limit liability or a remedy for pre-contractual misrepresentations, unless the clause satisfied the requirement of reasonableness under the Unfair Contract Terms Act, s 11(1) (see Chapter 8). It should be noted, however, that in relation to negligent misrepresentation under *Hedley Byrne* v *Heller*, this is subject to the Unfair Contract Terms Act 1977, s 2(2) which provides that in respect of loss or damage caused by negligence other than that by causing death or personal injury a person cannot exclude or restrict their liability except in so far as the term or notice satisfies the requirement of reasonableness.

Parties to a contract may agree that a particular state of affairs is to be the basis upon which they are contracting, regardless of whether or not that state of affairs is true. As we have seen above, there is a line of cases that establish that such an agreement may give rise to a contractual estoppel and thus preclude the assertion of facts inconsistent with those that have been agreed to form the basis of the contract. If that is done, the question arises as to whether or not the agreement constitutes an attempted exclusion of liability for misrepresentation to which s 3 of the Misrepresentation Act 1967 applies.

In *William Sindall Plc* v *Cambridgeshire County Council*, property was sold under a contract which incorporated the National Conditions of Sale (20th edn), including condition 14 and special condition 17, which stated:

14. Without prejudice to the duty of the vendor to disclose all latent easements and latent liabilities known to the vendor to affect the property, the property is sold subject to any rights of way and water, rights of common and other rights, easements, quasi-easements, liabilities and pubic rights affecting the same.

17. The purchaser shall be deemed to purchase with full notice of and subject to:

. . . (e) all easements, quasi-easements rights and privileges (whether of a public or private nature) now affecting the property but without any obligation on the part of the vendor to define the same.

Hoffmann LJ, with other members of the Court of Appeal in agreement, held that the judge had been wrong to treat those conditions as exclusion clauses which had to satisfy the test of reasonableness in accordance with s 3. He stated:

In my judgement they are nothing of the kind. Section 3 deals with provisions which exclude or restrict a party's liability for 'any misrepresentation made by him before the contract was made'. The clauses in question do not exclude a liability for misrepresentation but go to the question of whether there was a misrepresentation in the first place. They qualify the obligations to convey as beneficial owner and give vacant possession and therefore qualify any representation which could be implied from having undertaken those obligations.

Section 3 poses a particular set of problems where the clause seeks to prevent a misrepresentation occurring at all, as may occur in the case of entire agreement and non-reliance clauses, since it might be considered that such clauses do not amount to exclusion or limitation clauses and thus fall outside the ambit of s 3. As seen above, in *Springwell Navigation Corporation* v *JP Morgan Chase Bank*, the court, confirming its decision in *Peekay Intermark Ltd* v *ANZ Banking Group Ltd*, stated that such clauses are effectively exclusion clauses and therefore fall within s 3. A clause acknowledging that no representations had been made is effectively an exclusion of any liability in misrepresentation.

The question as to whether a non-reliance clause falls within s 3 and amounts to an attempt at excluding or limiting liability largely comes down to one of construction. The Court of Appeal in *Cremdean Properties Ltd* v *Nash* [1977] EG 63 considered that one should look at the substance of the clause and not just its form. The facts of the case were that the plaintiffs claimed rescission of contracts for sale of two properties, alleging innocent misrepresentation of the area of lettable office space. The defendant relied on a notice of disclaimer for the accuracy of particulars and a provision that no misdescription shall annul the sale. The plaintiffs argued that the notice was invalid because of the Misrepresentation Act 1967, s 3. The Court of Appeal rejected the defendant's argument that the effect of the clause was that no representation had been made at all. The court also questioned whether a clause that was effective in providing that no representations had been made could sit outside of s 3. Thus, while Bridge LJ considered that the notice 'did not amount even to a purported annulment of the existence of any representation', he stated he would:

> go further and say that if the ingenuity of the draftsman could devise language which would have that effect, I am extremely doubtful whether the court would allow it to operate so as to defeat section 3. Supposing the vendor included a clause which the purchaser was required to, and did, agree to in some terms as 'notwithstanding any statement of fact included in these particulars the vendor shall be conclusively determined to have made no representation within the meaning of the Misrepresentation Act 1967', I should have thought that that was only a form of words, the intended and actual effect of which was to exclude or restrict liability, and I should not have thought that the courts would have been ready to allow such ingenuity in the form of language to defeat the plain purpose at which section 3 is aimed.

Scarman LJ agreed, stating:

> in particular with the observations that my Lord made about the submissions put to the court . . . Nevertheless, the case for the appellant does have an audacity and a simple logic which I confess I find attractive. It runs thus: a statement is not a representation unless it is also a statement that what is stated is true. If in context a statement contains no assertion express or implied that its content is accurate, there is no representation. Ergo, there can be no misrepresentation; ergo, the Misrepresentation Act 1967 cannot apply to it. Humpty Dumpty would have fallen for this argument. If we were to fall for it, the Misrepresentation Act would be dashed to pieces, which not all the King's lawyers could put together again.

Scarman LJ also held that the notice, fairly construed, was:

> a warning to the would-be purchaser to check the facts; that is to say, not to rely on [the representation]. It is because the statement contains the representation that the warning is given. Since the statement was false, there was a false representation; the Act therefore applies.

The court thus considered that if a representation has been made but the clause attempted to provide there was no reliance, as required in *Redgrave* v *Hurd* and *Attwood* v *Small*, the clause will be subject to s 3 and to the requirement of reasonableness under s 11(1). Such an approach was also adopted by Aikins J in *Trident Turboprop (Dublin) Ltd* v *First Flight Couriers Ltd*, where he stated that if the clause in question expressly contemplates that the representee would, but for the clause, have rights in respect of representations and was therefore purported to restrict or exclude liability for misrepresentations, then it would fall within s 3 and be subject to the requirement of reasonableness as set out in the Unfair Contract Terms Act 1977, s 11(1).

This broad approach was not taken in the earlier case of *Overbrooke Estates Ltd* v *Glencombe Properties Ltd* [1974] 1 WLR 1335 where the plaintiffs brought an action for specific performance of a contract for the sale of land entered into by the defendants, who had successfully bid for the land at an auction. The general conditions of sale applying to the auction, which were supplied to the defendants beforehand, provided that the auctioneers had no authority to give any representation or warranty relating to the property. Prior to the auction the defendants asked the auctioneer whether the local authority had any plans for the land or whether there was any possible scheme for the compulsory purchase of the land and the auctioneers assured them that this was not the case. After the auction the defendants found that the land was likely to be included in a slum-clearance programme and refused to complete the sale, claiming that the auctioneers, as agents for the plaintiffs, had made a misrepresentation. The plaintiffs denied that the auctioneers, by virtue of the general conditions of sale, had any authority to make a representation. It was held that the plaintiffs, as principal, were not liable for the acts of the auctioneers, as agent, committed beyond the scope of the auctioneers' authority where those limits were communicated to the defendants. Importantly, the court also held that the clause limiting the auctioneers' authority did not fall within the ambit of s 3, which did not affect the plaintiffs' right to restrict the authority of their agents, the auctioneers. Brightman J considered that it was necessary to look at the restrictions on the authority of an agent before deciding if the plaintiff had made a misrepresentation. In this case, the defendants knew or ought to have known from the general conditions of sale that nothing told them by the auctioneers could bind the plaintiffs. The fact that the conditions of sale did not amount to an exclusion clause meant that it was outside of the Misrepresentation Act 1967 s 3.

Undoubtedly, the case of *Overbrooke Estates Ltd* v *Glencombe Properties Ltd* takes a narrow view as to the type of clauses that are subject to s 3 and the decision is no doubt correct on the facts. The approach in *Cremdean*, however, is much broader and tends to look behind the clause at what the clause is attempting to do in substance and not just its form so that if the court considers that without the clause there would be an actionable misrepresentation then the clause in question will fall within s 3.

There is, however, an important difference between a clause that makes clear that no representation is being made and one which purports to exclude a representation that has been made. In *IFE Fund SA* v *Goldman Sachs International* [2006] EWHC 2887 (Comm), Toulson J provided two examples illustrating the difference between the two. He firstly gave the example of the seller of a car who says to a buyer 'I have serviced the car since it was new, it has had only one owner and the clock reading is accurate'. Toulson J considered that a statement that would amount to a representation and would continue to be so even if the seller had added the words 'but those statements are not statements on which you can rely'. On the other hand, if the seller of the car had said 'The clock reading is 20,000 miles, but I have no knowledge whether the reading is true or false' the position would be different because the qualifying words could not fairly be regarded as an attempt to exclude liability for a false representation arising from the first half of the sentence.

In *Raiffeisen Zentralbank Osterreich AG* v *Royal Bank of Scotland plc*, Clarke J provided a version of Toulson J's example:

> The dealer says '*I have serviced the car since it was new, it has had only one owner and the clock reading is accurate*'. He is not fraudulent but mistaken, carelessly confusing one car for another, in relation to which the statement is true. Relying on his statement the buyer purchases the car. Without it he would not have done so. The car has had several owners, no known service history, and the clock reading is substantially inaccurate. The contract of sale provides (in one of many paragraphs on the back of the form which the buyer does not read and to which his attention is not directed) that the buyer is entering into the contract on the basis that no representations have been made to, or relied on by, the purchaser. In that example there has been a clear statement of fact, on a matter said to be within the representor's personal knowledge, which was in fact intended to induce the contract, upon which the purchaser in fact relied, which is false. If section 3 has no application in respect of a contractual estoppel there is no further control mechanism on its operation, which does not require detrimental reliance. The seller (and any other similar seller) may, subject to any applicable consumer protection laws, make non-fraudulent misrepresentations of that type with impunity.

Clarke J considered that s 3 was applicable to such a set of circumstances since the purchaser would reasonably consider the statement made by the dealer to be a representation, which it was intended he would rely on and in fact he did rely on. The clause clearly seeks to avoid liability for what, without the clause, would be a clear liability in misrepresentation. The situation might be different in the unlikely scenario that before he contracts the buyer sees the clause and, eyes wide open, agrees that he is not relying on what he may have been told. Such a conclusion is consistent with the decision at first instance in *Cremdean*, that if there is a misrepresentation, any clause, whatever its form, which excludes liability is within the mischief of s 3. It is also consistent with the comments in the Court of Appeal that clever draftsmanship will not be allowed to annul the existence of any representation so as to exclude the operation of s 3 and therefore undermine the purpose of that provision.

The essential issue therefore is whether the clause in question has the effect of precluding any representation being made because there is no statement of fact or opinion being made since there is no assumption of responsibility for the statement. Thus in *Springwell*, Gloster J found that the effect of the particular clauses was to preclude any representation, whether of fact or opinion, being made at all because Springwell and JP Morgan Chase had contracted on the express basis that Springwell was taking its own decision to enter into the transactions, independently and without reliance on the bank, and because the latter was not assuming any responsibility for statements of fact or opinion that were made. There is no actionable misrepresentation, for example, if the statement states 'the clock says 20,000 but I do not know whether that is true': this is clearly not actionable as there is no assumption of responsibility.

The position, however, is very different if there is essentially in substance an attempt to exclude or limit liability. Thus Clarke J stated: 'Per contra, to tell the man in the street that the car you are selling him is perfect and then agree that the basis of your contract is that no representations have been made or relied on, may be nothing more than an attempt retrospectively to alter the character and effect of what has gone before, and in substance an attempt to exclude or restrict liability' and would be caught by s 3. Clearly the lesson to be learned is that clauses need to be drafted carefully since there is no reason why 'suitably drafted clauses' that have the effect of indicating that no representations are being made or can be relied upon may avoid being caught by s 3.

Debate

Versloot Dredging – The dissenting judgement of Lord Mance

In many respects the fact that Lord Mance provided the dissenting judgement in *Versloot Dredging* is somewhat surprising given that in *Agapitos v Agnew (The 'Aegeon')* [2002] EWCA Civ 247 he gave a considered opinion as to whether 'as a matter of policy, the underlying rationale of the fraudulent claim principle should extend to invalidate not merely the whole of a claim where part proves otherwise good, but the whole of a claim where the whole proves good'.

In that judgement Mance LJ commenced by setting out the accepted principle in the older common law cases (particularly, *Levy v Baillie (1831)* 7 Bing. 349 , *Goulstone v Royal Insurance Co.* (1858) 1 F & F 276 and *Britton v Royal Insurance Co.* (1866) 4 F & F 905) stood for a rule of law to the effect that an insured who has made a fraudulent claim forfeits any lesser claim which he could properly have made. *The Aegeon*, as in the case of *Versloot*, was concerned with the scope and effects of the post-contractual duty of good faith.

He concluded that the use of a fraudulent device did give rise to a defence to the insurer with respect to a claim; however, he stated:

> In the context of use of a fraudulent device or means, one can contemplate the possibility of an obviously irrelevant lie – one which, whatever the insured may have thought, could not sensibly have had any significant impact on any insurer or judge. Tentatively, I would suggest that the courts should only apply the fraudulent claim rule to the use of fraudulent devices or means which would, if believed, have tended, objectively but prior to any final determination at trial of the parties' rights, to yield a not insignificant improvement in the insured's prospects – whether they be prospects of obtaining a settlement, or a better settlement, or of winning at trial.

In *Versloot Dredging*, however, he considered that insurance is about assessing risk and the settlement of claims with both processes relying on good faith. He considered that to 'suggest that a lie which the insured felt necessary to promote settlement of a claim is immaterial or "collateral" if years later it can be shown that it was after all unnecessary to tell it mistakes the nature of the business and the relationship'. He considered that materiality is an essential component since the collateral lie is told to influence an underwriter's decision to settle the claim and therefore it must act as an inducement to that regard. He considered that to suggest that a lie that is told to promote a claim is immaterial to the respective rights and obligations of the parties just because the lie was unnecessary is a 'charter for the untruth'. He thought that such a situation overlooks the need for integrity on both sides and that in any event a lie is told for one purpose and that is to obtain an advantage based on a false premise.

In Lord Mance's opinion, he considered that the approach taken by the majority would distort the claims process in two ways: Firstly, if the fraudulent device is undiscovered, then that could lead to the recovery of a bad or exaggerated claim, and; secondly, if the fraudulent device is discovered, the claims process will have been distorted by reason of the time and cost involved in unveiling the fraud and ascertaining its implications. He considered that it made little sense to adopt a stance adopting a principle in which that 'the lie is dishonest, but the claim is not' and allowing the claim. He considered that 'abolishing the fraudulent devices rule means that claimants pursuing a bad, exaggerated or questionable claim can tell lies with virtual impunity' and that the same logic applies equally to fraudulent devices as it does to fraudulent claims generally. He completed his judgement by concurring with the view of Lord Hobhouse in *Manifest Shipping Co Ltd v Uni-Polaris Insurance Co Ltd (The 'Star Sea')* [2003] 1 AC 469 at para 62:

> The fraudulent insured must not be allowed to think: 'if the fraud is successful, then I will gain; if it is unsuccessful, I will lose nothing'.

Questions

- Do you consider that Lord Mance is correct in that the approach taken by the majority is a 'charter for the untruth'?
- Do you consider that materiality is a sound process for determining the impact of a fraudulent device or collateral lie for the purpose of assessing whether or not the insurer can rescind the contract or reduce the claim?
- As a person seeking insurance or paying for insurance. are you happy with such a judgement in that if insured persons lie or exaggerate their claims and this conduct is undiscovered. then your insurance premiums are likely to rise?
- What advice would you give to an insurer following this judgement?

Summary

- A misrepresentation may be defined as a false statement of fact that induces another to enter into a contract.
- Terms v representations (*Oscar Chess v Williams*).

The nature of the inducement

- The untrue statement must be one of fact that induced the other party to enter the contract.

Statements of law

- Now treated as the same as a statement of fact (*Kleinwort Benson Ltd v Lincoln City Council*; *Pankhania v Hackney London Borough Council*).

Statements of opinion

- Honest statements of opinion will not amount to a misrepresentation (*Bisset v Wilkinson*; *Esso Petroleum Co. Ltd v Mardon*).

Statements of intention

- A mere representation as to future conduct is not actionable either as a breach of contract or as a misrepresentation (*Edgington v Fitzmaurice)*.

Silence as a misrepresentation of fact

- Silence cannot amount to a misrepresentation.
- The three exceptions:
  1. Change of circumstances.
     - (a) *With v O'Flanagan*
     - (b) *Wales v Wadham*
     - (c) *Inclusive Technology v Williamson*
     - (d) *Spice Girls Ltd v Aprilia World Service BV.*
  2. The statement made is only half the truth.
     - (a) *Dimmock v Hallett.*
  3. Confidential/fiduciary relationships.
     Contracts of *uberrimae fidei*
     - (a) Consumer Insurance (Disclosure and Representations) Act 2012
     - (b) Insurance Act 2015.

The fact of the inducement

- To prove the inducement we must take certain factors into consideration.

The misrepresentation must be material

- *Pan Atlantic Insurance Co Ltd v Pine Top Insurance Co Ltd*
- *Versloot Dredging BV v HDI Gerling Industrie Versicherung.*
- *JEB Fasteners Ltd v Marks Bloom & Co*
- *Museprime Properties Ltd v Adhill Properties Ltd*
- *Downs v Chappell.*

Reliance and inducement

The misrepresentation must have induced the misrepresentee to enter into the contract.

- *Downs v Chappell*
- *Raiffeisen Zentralbank Osterreich AG v Royal Bank of Scotland plc*
- *Pan Atlantic Insurance Co Ltd v Pine Top Insurance Co Ltd*
- *Versloot Dredging BV v HDI Gerling Industrie Versicherung*
- *Attwood v Small*
- *Peekay Intermark Ltd v Australia and New Zealand Banking Group Ltd*
- *Dadourian Group International Inc. v Simms.*

Truth known to the representee?

- The representor has to prove that the representee knew of the untrue statement.
  - *Redgrave v Hurd*
  - *Hayward v Zurich Insurance Co plc*
  - *BP Exploration Operating Co Ltd v Chevron Shipping Co.*

Representee unaware of the misrepresentation?

- If the representee is unaware of the misrepresentation they cannot take action on the basis of it.
  - *Ex Parte Briggs*
  - *Cramaso LLP v Ogilvie-Grant*.

The nature of the misrepresentation

Fraudulent misrepresentation

- Definition: A 'false statement made knowingly or without belief in its truth or recklessly careless whether it be true or false' (*Derry v Peek*)
- A statement made recklessly or carelessly may only amount to evidence of fraud, though if the maker of the statement believes it to be true then they cannot be liable for a fraudulent misrepresentation (*AIC Ltd v ITS Testing Services (UK) Ltd (The Kriti Palm); Thomas Witter Ltd v TBP Industries Ltd*)
- Proving deceit has a higher burden of proof: (*Smith New Court Securities Ltd v Citibank NA); Ticket2final OU v Wigan Athletic AFC Ltd*)
- The Fraudulent Claims Rule (*Britton v Royal Insurance Co; Manifest Shipping Co. Ltd. v Uni-Polaris Shipping Co. Ltd. (The 'Star Sea'); Galloway v Guardian Royal Exchange (UK) Ltd; Versloot Dredging BV v HI Gerling Industrie Versicherung AG*).

Common law negligent misrepresentation

- *Hedley Byrne & Co. Ltd v Heller & Partners Ltd*

  1 A representor had a duty of care to do all that is reasonable to make sure that his statement is accurate.
  2 Imposed a duty arising from a 'special relationship'.

Misrepresentation Act 1967, s 2(1)

- Distinction between s 2(1) and negligent misrepresentation at common law.

  1 No need to prove a 'special relationship'.
  2 The misrepresentation must result in a contract being entered into.
  3 The burden of proof is reversed so that the representor is liable unless 'he had reasonable grounds to believe and did believe up to the time the contract was made that the facts represented were true'.

Innocent misrepresentation

- Covers wholly innocent misrepresentations
  - Consumer Insurance (Disclosure and Representations) Act 2012.

The remedies available for misrepresentation

Rescission and indemnity

Rescission

- The effect of misrepresentation renders the contract voidable, *not* void.
- A representee may affirm the contract by expressing their intention to do so or by conduct.
- A representee can use misrepresentation as a defence by allowing themselves to become liable for breach of contract.
- The representee may rescind the contract by making clear to the representor that they no longer consider themselves bound.
- Failure to rescind a contract will mean that it is affirmed.
- Rescission is available for *any* type of misrepresentation.

Indemnity

- Allows the representee to recover expenses incurred by the creation of the contract as a result of the misrepresentation.
- An indemnity is not the same as damages (*Whittington* **v** *Seale-Hayne*)

Bars to the remedy of rescission

A person may be barred from exercising the remedy of rescission in four circumstances:

- Affirmation
- Lapse of time (*Leaf* **v** *International Galleries*; *Salt* **v** *Stratstone Specialist Ltd (t/a Stratstone Cadillac Newcastle)*)
- Where *restitutio in integrum* has become impossible (*Salt* **v** *Stratstone Specialist Ltd (t/a Stratstone Cadillac Newcastle)*)
- The intervention of third parties (*Car and Universal Finance Co. Ltd v Caldwell*).

Damages in lieu of rescission

- The right of rescission may be lost where the court decides to exercise its discretion under s 2(2) and award damages in lieu of rescission.
- NB: the discretion to award damages in lieu of rescission cannot be exercised in relation to fraudulent misrepresentation (*William Sindall plc* **v** *Cambridgeshire County Council*)
- Section 2(2) applies only where a person 'would be entitled by reason of the misrepresentation to rescind the contract' (*Thomas Witter Ltd* **v** *TBP Industries Ltd*; *Floods* **v** *Shand Construction*; *Zanzibar* **v** *British Aerospace (Lancaster House) Ltd*; *Pankhania* **v** *London Borough of Hackney*; *Salt* **v** *Stratstone Specialist Ltd (t/a Stratstone Cadillac Newcastle)*)
- In deciding whether or not to exercise its discretion the court has to take into account the degree of seriousness of the breach and the likely consequences of the exercise of the discretion on the representee and the representor, particularly in cases involving an innocent misrepresentation where the degree of loss is minimal.

Damages for misrepresentation

Fraudulent misrepresentation

- Damages are available at common law for fraudulent misrepresentation, the measure being a tortious one since the claim is based on the tort of deceit (**Doyle v Olby (Ironmongers) Ltd; Smith New Court Securities Ltd v Citibank NA; OMV Petrom SA v Glencore International AG**).

Negligent misrepresentation at common law

- Damages based on remoteness (**Hedley Byrne v Heller**).

Negligent misrepresentation under s 2(1)

- Measure of damages suggests that a tortious application is needed (**André et Cie SA v Ets Michel Blanc et Fils; Sharneyford Supplies Ltd v Edge); Royscot Trust Ltd v Rogerson; Smith New Court Securities Ltd v Citibank NA**).

Innocent misrepresentation

- Damages are not recoverable unless the court decides to exercise its discretion under s 2(2) and award damages in lieu of rescission.
- The measure of damages under s 2(2).
- This provision gives no express indication as to the measure of damages.
- Suggestions are that damages are less than in s 2(1) for two reasons:
  1 Section 2(3) provides:
  2 Damages may be awarded against a person under subsection (2) of this section whether or not he is liable to damages under subsection (1) thereof, but where he is so liable any award under the said subsection (2) shall be taken into account in assessing his liability under the said subsection (1).
  3 Damages under s 2(2) are to be awarded in lieu of rescission.

Contributory negligence

- **Gran Gelato Ltd v Richcliff (Group) Ltd**
- **Standard Chartered Bank v Pakistan National Shipping Corporation**
- **Taberna Europe CDO II Plc v Selskabet (Formerly Roskilde Bank A/S) (In Bankruptcy).**

Exclusion of liability for misrepresentation

- Controls imposed at common law
  - Fraud (**HIH Casualty and General Insurance Ltd v Chase Manhattan Bank**)
- Entire agreement clauses (**Inntrepreneur Pub Co. v East Crown Ltd; AXA Sun Life Services plc v Campbell Martin Ltd; Springwell Navigation Corporation v JP Morgan Chase Bank; Peekay Intermark Ltd v ANZ Banking Group Ltd; Shoreline Housing Partnership Limited v Mears Limited**)

- Non-reliance clauses (*EA Grimstead & Son Ltd* v *McGarrigan*; *Watford Electronics Ltd* v *Sanderson CFL Ltd*; *Lowe* v *Lombank Ltd*; *Peekay Intermark Ltd* v *ANZ Banking Group Ltd*; *Trident Turboprop (Dublin) Ltd* v *First Flight Couriers Ltd* ; *Raiffeisen Zentralbank Osterreich AG* v *Royal Bank of Scotland plc*).

Controls imposed by statute

- Misrepresentation Act 1967, s 3 as substituted by Unfair Contract Terms Act 1977, s 8 and the Consumer Rights Act 2015 Schedule 4 para 1.

Further reading

Beale, 'Damages in Lieu of Rescission for Misrepresentation' (1995) 111 *Law Quarterly Review* 60

Beale, 'Points on Misrepresentation' (1995) 111 *Law Quarterly Review* 385

Beatson, Burrows and Cartwright, *Anson's Law of Contract*, 30th edn (Oxford University Press, 2016)

Bigwood, 'Pre-Contractual Misrepresentation and the Limits of the Principle in *With* v *O'Flanagan*' [2005] *Cambridge Law Review* 94

Brinkworth and Powell, 'Fraudulent Misrepresentation: Dead or Simply Resting?' (1992) 13 *Business Law Review* 3

Furmston, *Cheshire, Fifoot and Furmston's Law of Contract*, 16th edn (Oxford University Press, 2012)

Handley, Hon KR, 'Causation in Misrepresentation' (2015) *Law Quarterly Review* 275

Mitchell, 'Loss of a Chance in Deceit' (2009) 125 *Law Quarterly Review* 561

Smith and Atiyah, *Atiyah's Introduction to the Law of Contract*, 6th edn (Oxford University Press, 2006)

Spencer, Bower and Turner, *The Law of Actionable Misrepresentation*, 3rd edn (Butterworths, 1974)

Peel, Treitel *Law of Contract*, 14th edn (Sweet and Maxwell, 2015)

Trukhtanov, 'Misrepresentation of Non-Reliance as a Defence' (2009) 125 *Law Quarterly Review* 648

Trukhtanov, 'Exclusion of Liability for Pre-Contractual Misrepresentation: A Setback' (2011) 127 *Law Quarterly Review* 345

Vaughan, 'Misrepresentation after 'Humming Bird': Not a Turkey' (1988) 85 *Law Society Gazette* 28

10

Mistake

Objectives

After reading this chapter you should be able to:

1. Understand the nature of mistake as a vitiating factor, how an 'operative' mistake arises and that the effect of an operative mistake is to render a contract void *ab initio*.

2. Recognise the different types of mistake at common law, the incidence of mistake of law and how the effect of this differs from a mistake of fact.

3. Recognise and understand the nature of common initial mistakes, how these arise and the effects both on the parties to the contract and third parties.

4. Recognise and understand the nature of consensus mistakes (i.e. mutual mistakes and unilateral mistakes), how these arise and the effects of each both on the parties to the contract and third parties.

5. Appreciate the nature of mistake in equity and how this differs from mistake at common law, with particular reference to the remedies of rescission, rectification and specific performance.

6. Know and understand mistake as to the nature of the document signed or *non est factum*.

Introduction

Objective 1

The nineteenth-century history of contractual obligation was covered in Chapter 1.

In the nineteenth century, the theory of contractual obligation was based on that of *consensus ad idem*. The courts were willing to intervene if it could be shown that the contract lacked consensus, on the basis that genuine consent to the agreement was non-existent. This being the case the courts would find that there was no valid contract, thereby relieving the parties of their rights and liabilities under the contract.

The twentieth century saw a marked change in the willingness of the courts to allow a mistake of the parties to vitiate the existence of a contract. The courts began to realise that many contracts coming before them where mistake was alleged were for the most part commercial contracts entered into by business people at arm's length. The attitude of the judiciary was that such people ought to be held to the bargain they had freely entered into and that, initially, the power lay with these individuals to draft their contracts in such a way as to account for factors that might only come to light after the contract was entered into.

A further aspect that promoted the change of attitude was the effect on third parties of the finding of mistake at common law. At common law where a mistake was found to exist, the finding would be that the contract was void *ab initio*, that is, the common law refused to recognise the existence of a contract at all. The effect of this was that if goods were sold to an individual under a contract which was void for mistake then no title to the goods would pass to the other party, and they would then have to return them to the seller.

Between the parties to the alleged contract this created no significant problem. However, if the party who had 'purchased' the goods had sold them to a third party then that third party could be compelled to return the goods to the seller. The reason for this was that if the purchaser did not acquire title to the goods then no title could be passed from the purchaser to the third party. The principle is summed up in the maxim ***nemo dat quod non habet***, that is, no one has power to transfer the ownership of that which they do not own. The result was that a third party's rights to title could be prejudiced by a mistake in a prior contract, the existence of which they may not even be aware of. Thus a third party could be compelled to return goods to the original seller, while at the same time being left with no or very limited rights against the person who had sold the goods.

The constraints that the courts placed on their finding for an operative mistake were clearly well justified in view of the above factors, yet, nevertheless, instances did arise where it was unjustifiable to hold the parties to their contracts. The courts thus evolved an equitable doctrine of mistake where the contract was held not to be void *ab initio* but voidable, thus preserving at least some of the rights of an innocent third party, though not always so.

It should be noted that for a mistake to be an operative one the mistake must be one relating to a fundamental, underlying fact that existed at the moment the contract was entered into. This was so in the following case.

Amalgamated Investment and Property Co. Ltd v *John Walker and Sons Ltd* [1976] 3 All ER 509

A contract was entered into for the purchase of a warehouse which the purchasers wished to redevelop and for which redevelopment both parties knew that planning consent would be required. In the pre-contract enquiries the purchasers asked the vendors whether the building was designated as a building of special architectural interest. This was important because it would render the obtaining of planning consent substantially more difficult. The vendors answered in the negative, a statement which was true on 14 August 1973. In fact later, unknown to both parties, the Department of the Environment decided to give the building such a designation as from 25 September 1973. The parties actually signed their contracts on that date and the purchasers were informed by the Department of the Environment of the change of designation on 26 September 1973. The purchasers claimed that the contract should be rescinded for mistake. The Court of Appeal refused the application on the basis that on the date of the contract both parties believed the property to have no such designation and that since that was in fact the case at that time, there had been no mistake.

The case also illustrates another important point in that there are often great similarities between mistake and misrepresentation. While this latter concept was not pleaded in the case, it is not too difficult to see why very often claims will arise mainly in relation to misrepresentation rather than to mistake.

Given the two divergent approaches of the common law and equity to mistake it is logical and convenient to divide our study of mistake into these two areas.

Mistake at common law

The courts at common law have become reluctant to grant relief for mistake for the reasons already indicated, but they could be persuaded to find the contract void *ab initio* if satisfied that the mistake was one which was fundamental to the contract. Such a fundamental mistake can occur in two broad ways.

First, a mistake may arise where the parties have entered into a contract on an assumption that a certain state of affairs exists but which it is subsequently discovered does not exist. In this type of mistake there is an undoubted agreement between the parties, but they have both made the same or a **common mistake** as to a fundamental fact on which the agreement is based. This is referred to as *common initial mistake* in what follows.

Example

A agrees to charter a ship from B but at the time of the charter neither A nor B were aware that the ship had already sunk during a storm. Here there is a common initial mistake as to a fundamental fact on which the agreement had been made, that is, the ship existed and was able to take cargo.

Second, a mistake may arise in relation to the terms of the agreement and this may preclude the formation of an agreement. This is a mistake that precludes the *consensus ad idem* of the parties. Such a mistake might arise where the parties are at cross-purposes with one another, as, for example, where A is offering one thing, whilst B is accepting something else. This type of mistake will be referred to as mutual mistake.

Example

A offers to sell a Ford Galaxy GL to B. B accepts believing he is buying a Ford Galaxy GLX. Here both the parties are at cross-purposes as to what they are buying and selling.

Another type of mistake may arise where only one party makes a fundamental mistake of fact as to a term of the agreement, the other party being aware, or being presumed to be aware, of the mistake being made by the first individual. This type of mistake will be referred to as unilateral mistake.

Example

A accepts an offer to sell goods to B who pretends to be X. A only intends to deal with X as the identity of X is of fundamental importance to him. B is aware that A is entering into the contract under this mistake. Since only A is making the mistake there is therefore a unilateral mistake as there is no *consensus ad idem*.

Mutual and unilateral mistake will be grouped in our examination of mistake in contract under the heading consensus mistake.

One word of warning needs to be made at this point in that the terms common, mutual and unilateral mistake are used interchangeably by different authors, particularly the first two terms. No confusion should arise, however, if one bears in mind the circumstances in which each arises rather than simply relying on the label given to each type by the different authors.

One last point that should be noted is that in all types of mistake, however labelled or described, the mistake must be a fundamental mistake of either fact or law.

Mistakes of law

While it is firmly established that mistakes of fact can render a contract void, for many years it was considered that mistakes of law did not have the same effect, a principle affirmed in *Westdeutsche Landesbank Girozentrale* v *Islington Borough Council* [1996] AC 669. This is no longer the case, however, following the landmark case of *Kleinwort Benson* v *Lincoln City Council* [1999] 2 AC 349 where the House of Lords held that money paid under a mistake of law could now be recoverable. The result of this is that money paid under a mistake of law is now to be treated on the same basis as money paid under a mistake of fact.

In *Brennan* v *Bolt Burdan* [2004] EWCA Civ 1017, it was held by the Court of Appeal that a mistake of law could render a contract void. The facts of the case were that Miss Brennan, a local authority tenant, sought damages for personal injury sustained by breathing in carbon monoxide fumes from a faulty boiler. She entered into a compromise agreement in the belief that she had brought her action out of time and withdrew her claim. Subsequent to this a legal precedent was overruled by the Court of Appeal and Miss Brennan argued that the compromise agreement was void for mistake in that the parties had been mistaken as regards her action being out of time. The Court of Appeal held that a change in the law was a risk that all parties had to accept and that in any event this was not a true mistake of law at all but more a state of doubt. It was considered that the compromise agreement which was possible to perform was a matter of give and take which should not be lightly set aside. The case, however, indicates that the courts have now accepted that mistakes of law can render a contract void.

The general reluctance of the common law to recognise mistake as a vitiating factor invariably gave rise to an equitable doctrine that was more flexible, discretionary and provided that a contract was voidable rather than void *ab initio*. It is perhaps not surprising therefore that the basis of recovery lies within the law of restitution where an overriding principle preventing recovery of money irrespective of the justice of the case is clearly a contradiction to the concept of undue enrichment. The change wrought by the *Kleinwort Benson* case, while confined to money paid under a mistake of law, is thought to be capable of applying to other areas as well; for instance, it has been extended into the area of misrepresentation in the case of *Pankhania* v *London Borough of Hackney* [2002] EWHC 2441. Similarly, in the House of Lords decision in *Deutsche Morgan Grenfell Group plc* v *Inland Revenue Commissioners* [2006] UKHL 49 their Lordships confirmed that there existed a common law right to restitution of unlawfully demanded tax paid under a mistake of law.

For more on the law of restitution and mistakes of law refer to Chapter 18.

The extent of the change in this area of the law is still very much uncertain and embryonic. In the fullness of time the legal principles applicable to mistakes of law and mistakes of fact may become fully integrated. At the moment at least, relief for mistakes of law is confined to the recovery of money paid under a mistake of law.

Common initial mistake

Objective 3

To reiterate, this type of mistake arises commonly where the parties make a mistake that a certain state of affairs – on which the agreement is based – exists, but which it is subsequently discovered does not exist. Clearly if, unknown to both parties, a fact which is fundamental to the agreement either never existed or ceased to exist prior to the entering into of the contract then no contract can arise and therefore any agreement entered into is void *ab initio*.

It is important to emphasise that the state of affairs must cease to exist prior to the entering into of the contract. Should the state of affairs actually exist at the time the contract is entered into, but then subsequently cease to exist, the contract will be binding, though it may be discharged for subsequent impossibility under the doctrine of **frustration**. The doctrine of frustration will be examined in Part 4 and it is well to bear in mind the difference between initial mistake and subsequent impossibility when reading Chapter 15 on frustration.

For more on the doctrination of frustration and initial/subsequent impossibility refer to Chapter 15.

One should point out that initial mistake rarely causes a contract to fail at common law and while it has generally been left to equity to provide a remedy for this type of mistake the position in equity has now been subject to scrutiny in the case of *Great Peace Shipping Ltd v Tsavliris Salvage (International) Ltd* [2002] 4 All ER 689 to the extent that this means of action is now closed. This is dealt with later on in this chapter. Nevertheless, the common law has seen fit to attempt to intervene in three circumstances but before considering these in detail one must be aware that the doctrine of common mistake is strict so that if a mistake is found to be attributable to one party or if the contract actually provides for the risk of mistake within the terms of the contract then the doctrine will not operate.

Mistake as to the existence of the subject matter

This type of mistake is often referred to as *res extincta* and it arises where, unknown to both the parties, the subject matter of the contract had ceased to exist at the time the contract was entered into. This principle also has support in the form of the Sale of Goods Act 1979, s 6, which provides:

> Where there is a contract for the sale of specific goods, and the goods without the knowledge of the seller have perished at the time when the contract was made, the contract is void.

The application of the principle can be seen in the following case.

Couturier v *Hastie* (1856) HL Cas 673

The plaintiff merchants sold a cargo of Indian corn to the defendant. Unbeknown to either party, a few days before the contract was made, the cargo, which was on board a ship, had overheated and started to ferment, and as a result the captain had sold the cargo in order to prevent it from deteriorating further. The buyer contended that since the subject matter of the contract, the corn, had ceased to exist prior to the entering into of the contract, then the contract was void and he was not liable to pay the price. The vendor, however, argued that the contract was based on the handing over of the shipping documents and that the defendant had not simply bought a cargo of corn but a whole venture in which he took all the risks regarding the shipment of the cargo. It was held by the House of Lords that the purchaser was not bound to pay for the cargo. The contract contemplated that the goods sold actually existed, and, since they did not, the seller could not be required to deliver the goods, nor the buyer to pay for them. Lord Cranworth stated:

> The whole question turns upon the construction of the contract . . . Looking to the contract itself alone, it appears to me clearly that what the parties contemplated, those who bought and those who sold, was that there was an existing something to be sold and bought . . . The contract plainly imparts that there was something which was to be sold at the time of the contract, and something to be purchased. No such thing existing . . . there must be judgement . . . for the defendants.

One of the problems with the use of this case to illustrate mistake as to the existence of the subject matter is that nowhere in the judgement is mistake mentioned, let alone discussed. Furthermore, the contract was not held to be void at all, the judgement being based on the fact that since the seller was unable to produce the goods, he was unable to recover the price for them. The result of such a decision is that in reality this was not a case based on *res extincta* but one based on a total failure of consideration, where the question as to whether the contract is a nullity or valid would not arise. The reasoning is clear in that, if the cargo has ceased to exist then it cannot be delivered, in which case the seller can neither claim the contract price from the purchaser, nor, indeed, retain any moneys paid. The position, however, becomes very different if the action becomes that of the purchaser who claims for non-delivery of the goods. This might easily have been the case in *Couturier v Hastie* if it had been regarded as simply a case of a sale of specific goods from the outset, rather than an attempt by the seller to claim that it was a sale of a venture. Whether the purchaser can claim here depends largely on the terms of the contract. The position of the purchaser can be seen in the Australian case of *McRae v Commonwealth Disposals Commission*.

McRae v Commonwealth Disposals Commission (1951) 84 CLR 377

The Commission, the defendants, invited tenders for the sale of a wreck of an oil tanker which was said to be lying on the Jourmand Reef. The plaintiff, the successful bidder, was unable to find the reef on the marine charts and therefore asked for the ship's position, and this he was duly given. The plaintiff then spent a considerable sum of money equipping a salvage operation but, on arriving at the position given, found there was no tanker, nor had there ever been such a tanker. The plaintiff sued for breach of contract and this was resisted by the defendants who claimed the contract was void for *res extincta* on the basis of *Couturier v Hastie*.

The plea of the defendants was accepted by the court at first instance but rejected on appeal to the High Court in which Dixon and Fullagar JJ decided that *Couturier* provided authority for the existence of *res extincta*. They stated that the case did not concern itself with the validity of the contract, being based on the existence of a total failure of consideration, but the court did consider the situation where the validity of the contract could be called into question. It was stated that this might arise if the purchaser had brought the action for non-delivery in *Couturier*. In this context, Dixon and Fullagar JJ stated:

If it had so arisen, we think that the real question would have been whether the contract was subject to an implied condition precedent that the goods were in existence. Prima facie, one would think, there would be no such implied condition precedent, the position being simply that the vendor promised that the goods were in existence ...

In the *McRae* case, no such implied condition precedent arose, nor was it required, since the buyers clearly relied on an assertion made by the defendants that the tanker existed. It was not a case, as would have arisen in *Couturier*, had the purchaser brought the action, of a contract being entered into on the basis of a common assumption of fact as to the existence of the subject matter being a condition precedent to the entering into of that contract. In *McRae*, the defendants had contracted on the clear basis that the tanker existed and therefore were liable for breach of contract.

The actual basis of *Couturier v Hastie* remains open and several theories have been expounded by as many commentators as to what this basis is. As was shown above, the decision could amount to authority either as to the existence of a common mistake as to the existence of the subject matter; or a case providing an example of a total failure of consideration; or a case involving an implied condition precedent as to the existence of the subject matter. Whatever that basis is, it would seem extreme to suggest that the analysis of the decision in *McRae* results in the questioning of the existence of *res extincta* itself as a legal concept. Both Dixon and Fullagar JJ acknowledge the fact that in *Couturier*, Coleridge J in the Court of Exchequer Chamber and Cranworth LJ in the House of Lords talk in terms of the judgement turning 'entirely on the reading of the contract'.

The true position is probably as stated by Beatson (2010) when he comments:

> When properly construed, the contract may indicate that the seller assumed responsibility for the non-existence of the subject matter. This was so in *McRae*'s case, where the seller was held to have guaranteed the existence of the tanker. Or it may indicate that the buyer took the risk that the subject matter might not exist and undertook to pay in any event. This was the point at issue in *Couturier* v *Hastie*, where the House of Lords was called upon to decide whether or not the buyer had purchased merely the expectation that the cargo would arrive.

As in many areas of the law of contract, the whole question is ultimately reduced to deciding who should bear the loss in a contract based on the assumption that certain facts exist when they do not. In deciding the issue one asks if either party had accepted responsibility for the existence of the assumed facts. If one party did so, then clearly that is the end of the matter and the action lies for breach of contract against that individual. If neither party has assumed responsibility under the contract then ultimately the court has to decide whether either party can be regarded as having taken the risk. The court may consider, and it is submitted that this is a rare occurrence, that neither party can be regarded as having assumed the risk. Should this be the case the contract will be void for common mistake. This process of questioning would seem to have the support of Steyn J in *Associated Japanese Bank (International) Ltd* v *Crédit du Nord SA* [1988] 3 All ER 902, which is discussed more fully below, where he states:

> Logically, before one can turn to the rules as to mistake . . . one must first determine whether the contract itself, by express or implied condition precedent or otherwise, provides who bears the risk of the relevant mistake. It is at this hurdle that many pleas of mistake will either fail or prove to have been unnecessary. Only if the contract is silent on the point is there scope for invoking mistake.

A factor that complicates the above summary is the existence of s 6 of the Sale of Goods Act 1979. This provision gives statutory authority for what was commonly assumed to be the position in *Couturier* v *Hastie* regarding the common mistake as to the existence of the subject matter of the contract. In *McRae*, the judges considered that the provision (which was then contained in the Sale of Goods Act 1893, s 6) did not apply to that case since the provision talks in terms of goods having perished and since the tanker in *McRae* never existed in the first place the facts of the case fell outside the provision.

In relation to s 6, Smith and Atiyah (2006) argue that the provision amounts only to a prima facie rule which may be overturned by the express agreement of the parties. There is no suggestion whatsoever that Parliament intended this within the Act and therefore the assertion by Atiyah must be considered guardedly, though he is undoubtedly correct in the light of the above that s 6 is something of an anachronism today. See also Treitel (2011) and Beatson (2010) on this point.

Mistake as to title

This type of mistake is sometimes referred to as *res sua*. It is described by Lord Atkin in *Bell v Lever Bros* [1932] AC 161 as follows:

> Corresponding to mistake as to the existence of the subject-matter is mistake as to title in cases where, unknown to the parties, the buyer is already the owner of that which the seller purports to sell to him. The parties intended to effectuate a transfer of ownership: such a transfer is impossible: the stipulation is *naturali ratione inutilis*.

An example of this type of mistake may be seen in the following case.

Cooper v Phibbs (1867) LR 2 HL 149

An individual agreed to lease a fishery from another. Unbeknown to either party the purchaser already owned the fishery. In fact the case was not decided on common law principles at all, the court granting rescission of the contract, though Lord Atkin considered the contract to be void for *res sua* when he discussed the case in **Bell v Lever Bros**.

The principle so far seems very straightforward, but one must be careful not to jump to conclusions and immediately think in terms of invoking the principle. In many contracts the seller often warrants that they do have title, in which case the proper action is to sue for breach of contract. In contracts for the sale of goods, in particular, s 12(1) of the Sale of Goods Act 1979 implies a condition that in such contracts the seller has the right to sell or that in executory contracts they will have the right to sell at the time when the property is to pass.

Mistake as to quality only arises where there is neither an implied condition nor a warranty as to title. At the same time title must be regarded as an integral part of the contract to the extent that the contract becomes meaningless without it.

Mistake as to the quality of the subject matter of the contract

The question that arises here is whether it is possible for the contract to be void on the basis that the subject matter of the contract does not have the quality it is thought to have by the parties to the contract. The leading case on this area is that of **Bell v Lever Bros**.

Bell v Lever Bros [1932] AC 161

The appellant was employed on a fixed-term contract as chairman of a subsidiary company of the respondents. The respondents decided to amalgamate the subsidiary with another company so that the appellant's services were no longer required, despite the fact that there was a substantial period of time of his contract to run. The respondents paid the appellant compensation amounting to £50,000 for the early termination of his contract. It later transpired that the appellant had been involved in certain speculative deals which would have entitled the respondents to dismiss the appellant summarily without compensation. Neither party had considered this as a possibility when the contract terminating his employment was entered into. The respondents, on discovering the truth, sought to have the contract rescinded and the moneys paid returned. At first instance it was acknowledged that the appellant did not fraudulently conceal his breach of duty and did not consider it as a relevant factor when the severance agreement was being entered into. It was found that there was a mistake as to a fundamental fact that would enable the respondents to avoid the contract and recover the compensation money. The fundamental fact in question was that both parties assumed that the contract was one that could be terminated with compensation, whereas it was capable of being terminated without such compensation being payable. This decision was affirmed by the Court of Appeal who found that Lever Bros had clearly contracted under a fundamental mistake.

In the House of Lords it was held, by a majority decision, that the contract was valid and binding. Lord Atkin's judgement is generally regarded as being the principal one. He concluded that 'it would be wrong to decide that an agreement to terminate a definite specified contract is void if it turns out that the contract had already been broken and could have been terminated otherwise'. He stated that Lever Bros got what they bargained for, that is, early release from the contract (the similarity of reasoning in **Saunders v Anglia Building Society** [1970] 3 All ER 961 under *non est factum* should be noted here).

He thought it was irrelevant that they could have arrived at a similar conclusion by some other means or that if they had known the true facts they would not have entered into the contract at all.

Both Lord Atkin and Lord Thankerton, who also considered there to be no mistake, went further and discussed the circumstances in which common mistake might arise. They considered that for an operative mistake to arise there had to be a mistake as to a fundamental assumption on which the contract was based and which *both* parties considered to be the basis of the agreement. As Lord Thankerton stated, mistake as to the subject matter of the contract 'can only properly relate to something which both must have necessarily accepted in their minds as an essential and integral element of the subject matter'. He considered that this test was not satisfied in the case since there was nothing to indicate that Bell regarded the validity of the original contract as vital to that of the severance contract – only Lever Bros considered this to be 'essential and integral' and therefore there was no common mistake.

Lord Atkin expressed, at least initially, an equally wide test. He stated:

> Mistake as to quality of the thing contracted for raises more difficult questions. In such a case a mistake will not affect assent unless it is the mistake of both parties, and is as to the existence of some quality which makes the thing without the quality essentially different from the thing as it was believed to be.

In isolation the test is very clear, but the waters have become muddy by the fact that this test was discussed in the context of *res extincta* and *res sua*, not mistake as to quality. Further, Lord Atkin later on in his judgement produces a more restrictive test whereby the question is posed: 'Does the state of the new facts destroy the identity of the subject-matter as it was in the original state of facts'?

The inconsistencies set out have produced much debate as to whether **Bell v Lever Bros** is authority for a separate concept of mistake as to quality or not. The fact that there was no finding as to this type of mistake in the case has caused much debate as to when this type of mistake will arise since the facts of **Bell** seem to fall within the first broad test enunciated by Lord Atkin. One hypothesis put forward by *Cheshire, Fifoot and Furmston* (2012) is that since there was no finding as to mistake as to quality in **Bell v Lever Bros** within the tests of Lord Atkin, it follows that it is difficult to come to such a finding in any case, and that therefore the test confines mistake to that of the subject matter of the contract only: 'the only false assumption sufficiently fundamental to rank as operative mistake is the assumption that the very subject matter of the contract is in existence'.

On this basis *Cheshire, Fifoot and Furmston* cast doubt on whether common mistake as to the quality of the thing contracted for exists at all in law, and if it does it must be a very rare bird indeed! Further, they point to later cases as supporting their proposition, notably that of **Solle v Butcher** [1950] 1 KB 671 where the parties negotiated for the lease of a flat. There was a mistaken belief that the rent was not subject to the control of the Rent Acts and it was agreed that the rent should be fixed at £250 per annum. Later it was discovered that the flat was subject to a controlled rent of £140 per annum and the plaintiff claimed to recover the overpayments made as a result of his living in the flat for two years after entering into the contract. The defendant counter-claimed that the contract was void for mistake. It was held that the contract was not void for mistake, though it could be agreed, and was in *Cheshire, Fifoot and Furmston*, that this was a case clearly falling within Lord Thankerton's expression of mistake as being something 'which both must necessarily have accepted in their minds as an essential and integral element of the subject matter'. The majority of the Court of Appeal, however, held that the contract could be rescinded on equitable principles (see 'Mistake in equity', below).

Further evidence was also produced in the form of **Leaf v International Galleries**.

Leaf v *International Galleries* [1950] 1 All ER 693

It will be recalled that in this case the parties contracted for the sale and purchase of a picture which both mistakenly believed to be by Constable. The plaintiff based his claim in misrepresentation, but what would the result have been if the plaintiff had claimed as to common mistake as to the quality of the thing contracted for? This case would seem to fall squarely within Lord Atkin's test, that is, 'it is the mistake of both parties, and is as to the existence of some quality which makes the thing without the quality essentially different from the thing as it was believed to be'. The Court of Appeal did not consider the facts to amount to a mistake within the definition. Almost certainly Lord Atkin would have come to a similar conclusion since in *Bell* **v** *Lever Bros* he set out a series of examples where he thought there would be no operative mistake. One example bore remarkable similarity to the *Leaf* case:

A buys a picture from B; both A and B believe it to be the work of an old master, and a high price is paid. It turns out to be a modern copy. A has no remedy in the absence of representation or warranty.

Lord Atkin's argument here no doubt is that *A* thinks that they are buying a painting from *B* and that was what they got, a painting, therefore there is no mistake. Treitel, however, considers this to be erroneous. He also quotes an example of where *A* purchases a painting from *B* for £5 million which both believe to be a Rembrandt. On the completion of the contract if one were to ask *A* what he has bought he will reply that he has bought 'a Rembrandt' not 'a painting'. If it transpires that the painting is not a Rembrandt then quite clearly there is fundamental common mistake as to the quality of the thing contracted for. Treitel considers that this contract is void despite Lord Atkin's comment and the *dicta* in *Leaf* **v** *International Galleries*. This debate has been the subject of much scrutiny by Steyn J in *Associated Japanese Bank (International) Ltd* **v** *Crédit du Nord SA*.

Associated Japanese Bank (International) Ltd v *Crédit du Nord SA* [1988] 3 All ER 902

The facts were that a fraudster, Jack Bennett, entered into a sale and lease-back transaction with the plaintiff bank. The bank agreed to buy four precision engineering machines for £1 million and then to lease them back to him, but before doing so required a guarantor, the defendant bank agreeing to this position. The whole arrangement was a fraud by Jack Bennett since the machines did not exist at all, and on receiving the £1 million he disappeared and made no attempt to keep up the repayments. The plaintiff bank then attempted to enforce the guarantee against the defendants. The defendants claimed that the transaction was void since it was based on four specific pieces of equipment which both believed to exist but which in reality did not.

On the face of things this appears to be a case based on *res extincta* and has all the hallmarks of the *McRae* case since Jack Bennett was actually guaranteeing that the machines existed, as did the Commission with regard to the tanker in *McRae*. In the *Associated Japanese Bank* case, however, the party alleging the mistake, the defendants, were not guaranteeing the existence of the machines. They had entered the guarantee contract on the basis that the machines did in fact exist, a conclusion which they had apparently reached from their discussions with Bennett. The subject matter of the contract was not therefore the machines themselves but the obligations undertaken by Bennett and in particular his representation that the machines actually existed. Steyn J dismissed the claim and found the defendants to be not liable on the basis that he considered that the guarantee was based on an express condition precedent that the machines did in fact exist and that if such an express term did not exist there was an implied term to that effect. He did, however, also consider the issue of common mistake and concluded, following Lord Atkin in *Bell* **v** *Lever Bros*, that the contract would be void on the basis that the subject matter of the guarantee was 'essentially different from what it was reasonably believed to be'. He then concluded that 'for both parties the guarantee of obligations under a lease with non-existent machines was essentially different from a guarantee of a lease with four machines which both parties at the time of the contract believed to exist'.

Steyn J in the course of his judgement made a close examination of **Bell v Lever Bros** and of the proposition set out in *Cheshire, Fifoot and Furmston*. He considered the analysis by the latter to be 'too simplistic' and that the actual decision in **Bell v Lever Bros** was founded on the particular facts of the case. He considered that the courts should attempt to uphold rather than destroy apparent contracts although this did not preclude the possibility of mistake. He considered that the common law rules regarding mistake as to the quality of the subject matter were designed to cope with unexpected and wholly exceptional circumstances that occur within contracts. He stated that for a plea of mistake to be operative in this context it had to be a mistake of both the parties and, given this, the judgements of Lords Atkin and Thankerton were to be regarded as the *ratio decidendi* of **Bell v Lever Bros**. He considered that mistake as to quality could produce a nullity in a contract but confined it to the test enunciated by Lord Atkin, that is, a mistake will not affect assent unless it is 'as to the existence of some quality which makes the thing without the quality essentially different from the thing as it was believed to be'. Steyn J concluded that the tests for common mistake as to the subject matter and that of common mistake as to quality could be reduced to one single principle: 'the mistake must render the subject matter of the contract essentially and radically different from the subject matter which the parties believed to exist'. The use of the term 'subject matter' here apparently encompassed both types of mistake.

Steyn J added a final qualification in that a party seeking to rely on the mistake had to show that he had reasonable grounds for his belief that gave rise to the mistake. This qualification is useful since it produces an approach that is consistent with that of equity, where the fault of either party precludes the quality of equitable relief. He was at pains to point out that this last qualification was not based on notions of estoppel or negligence but 'simply because policy and good sense dictate that positive rule regarding common mistake should be so qualified'.

The decision in the **Associated Japanese Bank** case has been affirmed in **Great Peace Shipping Ltd v Tsavliris Salvage (International) Ltd**.

Great Peace Shipping Ltd v Tsavliris Salvage (International) Ltd [2002] 4 All ER 689

The facts of the case were that a ship, the *Cape Providence*, suffered severe structural damage whilst in the South Indian Ocean and was in danger of sinking. The ship owners engaged the defendants to salvage the vessel; however, a tug they engaged to carry out the salvage was four to five days from the sinking vessel. Fearing the ship would sink with the loss of the crew, the defendants asked its brokers to locate a ship near to the stricken vessel which would assist, if necessary, with the evacuation of the crew. The brokers consulted a reputable organisation, Ocean Routes, which provided weather forecasting information to the shipping industry and received reports of vessels at sea, for the location of vessels in the vicinity of the *Cape Providence*. The names of four vessels were provided and the broker was informed that the nearest ship was the *Great Peace*, a vessel owned by the claimants. It was estimated that the *Great Peace* was within 12 hours' sailing of the *Cape Providence*. However, this position was wrong. On the basis of the position of the ship given to them, the defendants entered into a contract with the claimants to hire the *Great Peace* for a minimum of five days. It later transpired that the *Great Peace* was several hundred miles from the *Cape Providence*. The defendants therefore cancelled the contract and refused to pay for any hire. The claimants therefore sued, claiming five days' hire. The defendants argued, first, that the contract was void at common law for a fundamental mistake, or, second, that the contract was voidable in equity for common mistake. This second issue will be dealt with in 'Mistake in equity', below.

With regard to the first issue, the case turned on the question of whether the mistake as to the distance apart of the two vessels had the effect that the services that the *Great Peace* was to provide were something essentially different from that which the parties had agreed. The Court of Appeal concluded that the analysis of Lord Atkin and Lord Thankerton in ***Bell v Lever Bros*** was correct and endorsed the comments of Steyn J in ***Associated Japanese Bank***, and that to establish mistake as to the quality of the subject matter the mistake must render the contract essentially and radically different from the subject matter which the parties believed to exist and that this was not present. The mistake as to the distance between the two vessels did not render the services to be provided by the claimants' vessel essentially different from what the parties had agreed.

The judgement is important since it emphasises the need to consider the terms of the contract and its surrounding circumstances in order to determine whether or not the parties themselves had allocated the risk under the contract. An example of this can be seen in ***McRae v Commonwealth Disposals Commission***, the facts of which have already been considered above. It will be recalled that here there was no mistake because the defendants were deemed to have promised that the tanker in the case actually existed. The risk of the tanker not existing had been clearly placed in the court of the defendants and they could not therefore escape liability on the basis that the contract was void for mistake.

In ***Great Peace***, the claimants were not aware of any condition precedent as to the distances between the two ships by the defendants. This was of vital importance to the defendants but not to the claimants, who had simply agreed to charter a ship to the defendants and they were therefore entitled to their five-day hire fee. They had fulfilled their part of the bargain. Furthermore this bargain could not be nullified by mistake. The fact that the *Great Peace* was further away from the *Cape Providence* did not in their eyes render the contract 'essentially and radically different'. It should also be borne in mind that both Lord Atkin and Lord Thankerton had stressed in ***Bell v Lever Bros*** that a mistake had to be the mistake of both parties and here it was the mistake of the defendants only.

Lord Phillips in ***Great Peace*** provided a statement as to the criteria needed to establish a common mistake as to quality. He stated:

> the following elements must be present if common mistake is to avoid a contract: (i) there must be a common assumption as to the existence of a state of affairs; (ii) there must be no warranty by either party that that state of affairs exists; (iii) the non-existence of the state of affairs must not be attributable to the fault of either party; (iv) the non-existence of the state of affairs must render performance of the contract impossible; (v) the state of affairs may be the existence, or a vital attribute, of the consideration to be provided or circumstances which must subsist if performance of the contractual adventure is to be possible.

Lord Phillips thought the second and third factors were exemplified by the decision in the ***McRae v Commonwealth Disposals Commission*** case since in that case the assumption that the tanker existed was created by the Commission without any reasonable grounds for believing it was true. Lord Phillips approved of the judgements of Dixon and Fullagar JJ in that case which considered that whether impossibility of performance discharged obligations under the contract depended on the construction of the contract and, anyway, if this was not correct, they stated that:

> a party cannot rely on mutual mistake where the mistake consists of a belief which is, on the one hand, entertained by him without any reasonable ground, and, on the other hand, deliberately induced by him in the mind of the other party.

Dixon and Fullagar JJ considered that on a proper construction the contract contained a promise that the tanker existed but considered that if the doctrine of mistake was to be applied:

> then the Commission cannot in this case rely on any mistake as avoiding the contract, because any mistake was induced by the serious fault of their own servants, who asserted the existence of a tanker recklessly and without any reasonable ground.

Lord Phillips considered this to be the correct approach and that the doctrine of mistake fills a gap where the parties enter into a contract that proves impossible to perform without the fault of either party and they have not either expressly or impliedly dealt with their rights and obligations within the contract themselves. This also concurs with the approach of Steyn J in the *Associated Japanese Bank* case, as stated earlier.

Lord Phillips considered, therefore, that once a court has determined that unforeseen circumstances have occurred that have resulted in the contract becoming impossible to perform it is then necessary, on the construction of the contract, to determine if one or other party has assumed responsibility for the risk that it might not be possible to perform the contract. If that is the case then no recourse to the doctrine of mistake is required – the construction of the contract determines the outcome. This also accords with the notion that the law should uphold contracts in the first instance and concurs with the view of Steyn J. As Lord Phillips stated:

> Supervening events which defeat the contractual adventure will frequently not be the responsibility of either party. Where, however, the parties agree that something shall be done which is impossible at the time of making the agreement, it is much more likely that, on true construction of the agreement, one or other will have undertaken responsibility for the mistaken state of affairs. This may well explain why cases where contracts have been found to be void in consequence of common mistake are few and far between.

It is clear from the above that instances of common mistake as to quality are going to be very exceptional. The cases seen until now have concerned mistake of fact but in cases where mistakes of law arise, particular problems may arise in the context of common mistakes as to quality and *res extincta*.

In the case of *Brennan v Bolt Burdan*, the facts of which have already been considered, the Court of Appeal held that this was not a case involving impossibility of performance since at all times the compromise agreement was capable of performance and, as such, that put it beyond the decision of *Great Peace* and common mistake. The court considered that there could not be an operative mistake where there is doubt as to the law. A state of doubt was considered to be different from that of a mistake since a person who pays when in doubt of the law assumes the risk that he may be wrong. The Court of Appeal thought that it was possible for a compromise agreement to be void for a mistake of law, though it could not envisage how the test in *Great Peace* could operate in such a scenario. Sedley LJ considered that perhaps another test was required in the case of mistakes of law. He considered that a test which reflected that in *Great Peace* was required, that is, had the parties, when negotiating the contract, known then what the law states now, would there still have been an intelligible basis for the agreement? He thought this came close to the issue in *Great Peace*, that is, is there 'a common assumption (in that case one of fact) which renders the service that will be provided if the contract is performed something different from the performance that the parties contemplated'? He thought his proposed test also echoed the question posed by Lord Atkin in *Bell* v *Lever Bros*: 'Does the state of the new facts destroy the identity of the subject matter as it was in the original state of facts if for "facts" one reads "law"?'.

Another case involving compromise agreements is that of *Kyle Bay Ltd (t/a Astons Nightclub)* v *Underwriters Subscribing under Policy No. 019057/08/01*.

Kyle Bay Ltd (t/a Astons Nightclub) v *Underwriters Subscribing under Policy No. 019057/08/01* [2007] EWCA Civ 57

The facts of the case were that Kyle Bay Ltd ('K Ltd') had operated a nightclub and had taken out insurance cover from the defendant. A fire ensued and, on claiming, K Ltd found that the cover was different from that requested by them. They were advised to enter into a compromise agreement for £205,000, which was about one-third less than the amount they would have been able to claim had the cover they had envisaged actually been entered into. Later on it transpired that the type of policy and cover they had originally requested had actually been in place and K Ltd could have claimed the full amount. This meant that the compromise agreement and settlement had been entered into by mistake. K Ltd sought to have the agreement overturned and declared void on the basis of mistake.

At first instance the judge found that the settlement had been entered into on the basis of a mistake, but held that the mistake was not of a nature to justify vitiation of the agreement. The Court of Appeal dismissed K Ltd's appeal and stated that the judge had been correct to dismiss the claim in so far as it was based on common mistake. It was appropriate to apply the test in the *Associated Japanese Bank* and *Great Peace* cases. The mistake in the case did not render what the parties believed to be the subject matter of the agreement 'essentially and radically different' from what it was. K Ltd's mistake was that they were getting one type of cover as opposed to another type and, while the difference between the actual and assumed subject matter of the agreement could be characterised as significant, it was not an 'essential and radical' difference. It was considered that what was wrongly assumed was a detail, and that this did not go to the validity of the policy. While K Ltd received a third less than it should have done, which was a significant amount, this could not fairly be characterised as an 'essentially or radically' different sum from its entitlement.

In *Bell* v *Lever Bros*, Lord Atkin suggested that another basis for common mistake was the notion that a contract may be void because of an implied term that the validity of the contract depends on the existence of a certain state of affairs at the time of the contract and during its performance and that this implied term was of fundamental importance. In *Great Peace*, this implied term approach was rejected, just as it has been in the doctrine of frustration (see Chapter 15), and, as we have seen, the case established that common mistake is now founded on 'a rule of law under which, if it transpires that one or both of the parties have agreed to do something which it is impossible to perform, no obligation arises out of that agreement'. Lord Phillips considered it was unrealistic and inappropriate for the court in *Great Peace* to make inquiries as to whether the parties had included a term that provided that a contract would not exist in certain circumstances. It will be recalled that the second element in Lord Phillips's criteria stated that for a common mistake to exist there must be 'no warranty by either party that a state of affairs existed'. Thus a court, in considering whether a common mistake existed, must have regard as to what the parties expressly agreed would be performed. If, therefore, the parties included such a term in the contract that a particular state of affairs exists then this would preclude the operation of a common mistake.

This was the position in *McRae v Commonwealth Disposals Commission* where there was a term in the contract that warranted the existence of the tanker on the Jourmand Reef. This particular approach was also supported by Steyn J in the *Associated Japanese Bank* case.

The position, therefore, is that once the court has determined that a contract is impossible to perform because of unforeseen circumstances, the court must then consider if one of the parties has, either expressly or impliedly, undertaken responsibility to accept the risk for the mistake. If that is the case then a plea of common mistake will not be allowed. This approach can be seen in the case of *Graves v Graves*.

Graves v Graves [2007] EWCA Civ 660

The facts of **Graves v Graves** were that the parties had been married for five years when they got divorced. As part of the divorce a 'clean break' settlement order was made by consent under which Mr Graves had to pay his wife a substantial amount of capital, together with £300 per month by way of maintenance. Subsequently Mr Graves agreed that his ex-wife and children could return to the former matrimonial home and thereafter Mrs Graves lived in a series of houses owned either by Mr Graves alone or by Mr and Mrs Graves jointly. In June 2003, Mr Graves transferred his half-share of a house in Fleet to his wife for £8,500. Under the agreement Mrs Graves waived the children's future maintenance, which at the time was assessed as having a value of £50,000. Later the wife ran into financial difficulties and was unable to pay the mortgage repayments on the house and so she sold the house in 2004. Mr Graves then agreed that Mrs Graves could live in another house owned by him. An assured shorthold tenancy was entered into by the parties whereby Mrs Graves would pay a deposit of £12,000 and a monthly rent of £1,150. Mr Graves, however, was concerned as to his ex-wife's ability to pay the rent, particularly as he was no longer paying any maintenance to her. The tenancy had been entered into on the basis that Mrs Graves would be entitled to housing benefit from the local council. Whilst the local authority had initially indicated that she would be entitled to such benefit it transpired that she was not in fact entitled to it. Mrs Graves now found herself in a situation where she had paid nearly all her capital to Mr Graves and had no money to pay the rent. Mr Graves then brought proceedings for possession of the house and Mrs Graves in her defence argued that the tenancy agreement was void on the grounds of mistake or, alternatively, had been frustrated.

At first instance the judge considered that the requisite elements set out by Lord Phillips in *Great Peace* were present and therefore the tenancy agreement was void for common mistake. He found that there was a common assumption by both parties that housing benefit would be available to pay most of the rent and that neither party had made any warranty that the contract had been entered into on that basis. Neither party was at fault in believing the housing benefit would be made since both Mr and Mrs Graves had made separate enquiries about this prior to Mrs Graves moving into the premises. Finally, the judge considered that the tenancy had become impossible because of the non-payment of the housing benefit in that the purpose of the contract was to provide Mrs Graves and her children with an affordable home given that access to both income and capital was very limited. The result of this reasoning was that the tenancy agreement was void for common mistake and, as a consequence, Mrs Graves was a trespasser and Mr Graves was entitled to possession.

In the Court of Appeal, it was held that the tenancy agreement was not void for common mistake. It was contended by Mr Graves that his wife had warranted that she would receive the housing benefit and could pay the rent. In the court Thomas LJ gave the leading judgement and stated that the starting point was to look at the nature of the agreement and whether the contract itself had made provision as to who should bear the risk of the relevant mistake as per the *dicta* of Steyn J in *Associated Japanese Bank*. Thomas LJ considered that neither Mr nor Mrs Graves assumed any risk as to the housing benefit. Mr Graves knew his wife could not pay the rent without the housing benefit, while Mrs Graves knew Mr Graves would never have allowed her to occupy the house without the housing benefit being available. Thus the basis of the agreement was that Mr Graves would provide a house and his wife would be able to live in it on the basis of most of the rent being met by the housing benefit. Thomas LJ considered that there was an implied condition in the contract that if the housing benefit ceased to be payable then the tenancy would also end. He stated that on the basis of *Bell* v *Lever Bros* such a condition could only be implied if the 'effect of the new state of facts [that is the lack of housing benefit] was such that performance of the agreement was impossible or the agreement was something different in kind from the agreement in the original state of facts'. In *Bell* v *Lever Bros*, Lord Atkin considered that such a term could only be implied if it were necessary since otherwise this would undermine contractual certainty and allow the courts to rewrite a contract. This caution of course accords with that seen in the application of the 'officious bystander' test. Thomas LJ considered that it was not impossible for Mrs Graves to pay her rent – 'inability to perform a contract because of impecuniosity does not make performance impossible'; however, the agreement was made on the basis that most of the rent would be paid by way of the housing benefit. It was clear in his mind that the basis for the agreement was one that did not exist because of the absence of the housing benefit and therefore he considered that the agreement was different in kind to that originally contemplated. Thomas LJ therefore thought that these were circumstances in which a condition would be implied into the agreement to the effect that the tenancy would come to an end if the housing benefit was not payable. Thus the tenancy was determined on the basis of the implied condition and therefore it was unnecessary to consider the issue as to whether the contract was void for mistake or frustration.

For more on the 'officious bystander' test, refer to Chapter 7.

From *Graves* v *Graves* it can be seen that the implied term approach as set out by Lord Atkin in *Bell* v *Lever Bros* is still a valid way of proceeding even though Lord Phillips in *Great Peace* considered that this was not the correct way forward, finding that common mistake existed by way of a rule of law rather than a rule of construction. Nevertheless, it can be seen that even with Lord Phillips's criteria the implied term approach still has some validity providing the new state of facts is such that performance of the contract is impossible or, alternatively, the agreement is something different in kind from the agreement in the original state of facts; however, such implied terms 'are to be no more than are necessary for giving business efficacy to the transaction . . . ' (*per* Lord Atkin).

The further application of Lord Phillips' criteria in *Great Peace* can also be seen in the following case.

Dany Lions Ltd v *Bristol Cars Ltd* [2013] EWHC 2997 (QB)

Dany Lions Ltd ('D') owned a very rare vintage car. D had been in email communication with Bristol Cars Ltd ('B') about B undertaking extensive restoration work on the vehicle. In one message B had set out the work it proposed to do to the car, including the fitting of an automatic gearbox. B stated that the price would be £153,000 which would be paid by D making a first payment of £50,000, a second of £40,000, and a final one of the 'balance of the invoice price'. In any event, B did not carry out the works and thus D commenced proceedings for alleged breach of contract. B argued that the contract was void for common mistake because it was based on the parties' fundamental mistaken view that it would be possible to convert D's car to automatic transmission without affecting its full functionality, or alternatively, that the contract had been frustrated when the parties realised that it would not be possible to carry out the conversion.

It was held that B had agreed to adapt the engine; not that it would agree to see if the adoption of an automatic gearbox was possible. The starting point for considering B's arguments based on common mistake and frustration was that B had assumed a positive liability to achieve a result, that is fit an automatic gearbox. B's case was not that it would be impossible to fit an automatic gearbox but that in fitting it the car's functionality would have been impaired. Whilst that might have been the case, it did not relieve B of its obligation to satisfy its contractual liability. On a proper construction of B's email, which amounted to the offer to do the works, it had warranted that it would be possible to fit an automatic gearbox.

Was there a common assumption as to the existence of a state of affairs such as to give rise to a mistake? In arriving at a decision Seymour J referred to Lord Phillips' criteria in *Great Peace*. In applying these principles Seymour J thought there was no mistake since B had assumed a contractual obligation to supply and fit an automatic gearbox. As regards the second requirement – 'there must be no warranty by either party that that state of affairs exists' – Seymour J found that B had warranted that it could supply and fit an automatic gearbox to the car in question on the terms of the contract. Seymour J did not think it necessary to consider the third element.

As regards the fourth element: 'The non-existence of the state of affairs must render the contract impossible', Seymour J considered this element to be important since that element was not present in the case. Even assuming that the ability, or not, of B to supply and fit an automatic gearbox in the car amounted to a state of affairs, and even assuming that there was a common assumption as to the existence of such a state of affairs, the inability of the defendant to perform its contractual obligation without adverse consequences for the performance of the car did not render performance of the contract impossible. The greater part of the contract was wholly unaffected by whether the automatic gearbox could be supplied and fitted or not. The supply and fitting of the automatic gearbox were but one element in a much more extensive range of works which B agreed to undertake.

As regards the fifth element above, whilst the supply and fitting of the automatic gearbox were obviously an important part of the work, it was not fundamental to the whole contract such as to render impossible the performance of the contractual obligations of the defendant, other than in relation to the supply and fitting of the automatic gearbox, even if one assumed in favour of B that that was the actual position.

Seymour J therefore concluded that the matters needed to be demonstrated to justify the conclusion that the contract was void on the ground of common mistake had not been demonstrated. Seymour J also rejected B's defence of frustration on the basis that this was based upon essentially the same matters of mistake as regards the state of affairs at the date of the contract, albeit in frustration the existence of the state of affairs only came into force at some point after the making of the contract.

Consensus mistake

Objective 4

It has already been stated that this type of mistake arises because there is a mistake as to the terms of the contract. The effect of this is to preclude an agreement from arising, that is, there is a lack of *consensus ad idem*.

There are two basic categories, mutual mistakes and unilateral mistakes, though prima facie these types of mistake do not render the contract void unless the mistake induces the contract and constitutes a mistake of fact which is fundamental to the contract.

Mutual mistake

This type of mistake occurs where the parties are at cross-purposes where, to use the example given above, *A* is offering one thing while *B* is accepting something else. It is clear in such a circumstance that the contract is void because the offer and acceptance of *A* and *B* respectively do not coincide.

An example of the above principles can be seen in the following case.

Raffles v *Wichelhaus* (1864) 2 H & C 906

The defendants had agreed to purchase '125 bales of Surat cotton . . . to arrive ex *Peerless* from Bombay'. From the agreement it appeared that the defendants thought they were purchasing a cargo of cotton from the SS *Peerless* which had set sail from Bombay in October. In fact the plaintiffs thought they had sold a cargo of cotton on another ship called the SS *Peerless* which had set sail from Bombay in December. It was held that the contract was void for a fundamental mistake of fact that had prevented the formation of agreement – the offer and acceptance of the parties had failed to coincide.

In order to establish a mutual mistake one has to show that there is such a degree of ambiguity that it is impossible, on applying the objective test of a reasonable person, that the parties intended to be bound by one set of terms or the other. If, on an objective view, the parties could only have come to a single, common understanding of the terms of the contract then they will be bound by the contract, despite the actual view of a party that they were mistaken as to the terms. The test was expressed by Blackburn J in *Smith v Hughes* (1871) LR 6 QB 597. He stated:

> If whatever a man's real intention may be, he so conducts himself that a reasonable man would believe that he was assenting to the terms proposed by the other party, and that other party upon that belief enters into a contract with him, the man thus conducting himself would be equally bound as if he intended to agree to the other party's terms.

The application of the objective test approach can be plainly seen when the case of *Scriven Bros & Co.* v *Hindley & Co.* is compared with that of *Smith* v *Hughes* (above).

Scriven Bros & Co. v *Hindley & Co.* [1913] 3 KB 564

The defendants wanted to purchase a quantity of hemp being sold at auction by the plaintiffs. Two lots were put up for sale from the same ship; however, one lot consisted of hemp and one of tow, though the identification marks on the bales were precisely the same. Closer examination would have revealed the distinction, but the defendants, having inspected the first lot and found it to contain hemp, immediately mistakenly considered that the other lot also contained hemp. The auction catalogue itself did not reveal the distinction and as a result the defendant paid a high price for a lot thought to contain hemp but in fact containing tow, which would normally have attracted a far lower price. The auctioneer at the time of the sale realised that the defendants had made a mistake, but one which related to the market value of tow rather than as to the nature of the lot per se. The defendants refused to pay, alleging mutual mistake. On applying the objective test the court found that one could not state with any degree of certainty which commodity formed the basis of the contract since it was clear that a reasonable person would have been misled as to the nature of each lot. The contract was thus held to be void for mistake.

Smith v *Hughes* (1871) LR 6 QB 597

In this case, the defendant, a racehorse owner, wished to purchase a quantity of oats. A sample of the oats was inspected and the defendant agreed to purchase the whole amount. When the oats were delivered, it was discovered they were 'green', that is, that season's oats. The defendant refused to pay for them, saying he thought he was buying 'old', or the last season's oats. When sued for the price, the defendant argued that the contract was void for mistake. The court held that on an objective test basis there was a valid contract. On a finding of fact the seller had not misrepresented the oats as being old, nor was there any suggestion that there was a term of the contract to this effect. The purchaser could not establish mistake on the basis of the fact that he had been careless and as a result misled himself as to the nature of the oats.

A further matter that may be seen to operate in these two cases is that of negligence. It is possible to discern a line of authority that appears to present evidence of an underlying policy that the courts will find for mistake, or not, as the case may be, because of the negligence of one of the protagonists to the contract. Thus in the *Scriven* case, the contract was held to be void, not only on the basis of a lack of consensus, but also because the mistake was in effect promoted by the inaccurate or incomplete description attached to the two lots in the catalogue. Thus Lawrence J stated: '[A] contract cannot arise when the person seeking to enforce it has by his own negligence, or by that of those for whom he is responsible, caused or contributed to cause, the mistake.' In the *Smith* case, however, the purchaser, who was no doubt mistaken as to what he thought he was purchasing, was nevertheless held to his bargain, bad though it was, because his mistake was carelessly self-induced. Certainly in the latter case this line of reasoning conforms to the common law notion of *caveat emptor* and is seen in the judgement of Cockburn CJ when he states:

> I take the true rule to be, that where a specific article is offered for sale, without express warranty, or without circumstances from which the law will imply a warranty . . . and the buyer has full opportunity of inspecting and forming his own judgement, if he chooses to act on his own judgement, the rule *caveat emptor* applies . . . The buyer persuaded himself they were old oats, when they were not so . . . He was himself to blame.

In both cases, carelessness precludes the rights of a party from arising and must therefore be regarded as a relevant consideration in applying the objective test as to whether he has entered into a contract or not.

Unilateral mistake

In this type of mistake the objective test discussed above is replaced with a subjective one since we are concerned here with a situation in which one party is actually aware of the other party's mistake. This type of mistake arises directly out of the classical analysis of contract in that where one party contracts on the basis of a mistake as to the nature of a promise made by the other party and that other party is aware of the mistake of the first, the contract is void for there is no conjoining link between the offer and the acceptance of the parties concerned.

It should be noted carefully that for this type of mistake to operate there must be a fundamental mistake as to the nature of the promise made by the other party – a mistake as to quality will not suffice. The mistake must also be one which induces the other party to enter into the contract. It should also be borne in mind that, as with other types of mistake, the overwhelming presumption is to find for the existence of a valid and binding contract. It is for the person seeking to avoid the contract to rebut this presumption. This burden of proof is indeed an onerous one and the reported instances of this being done are few and far between.

The instances of unilateral mistake fall into two categories: mistake as to the terms of the contract and mistake as to the identity of the person contracted with.

1. Mistake as to the terms of the contract

Such a mistake will arise where one party makes an offer to another and they are aware that that other person is fundamentally mistaken as to the nature of the promise contained in the offer.

An example is the case of **Hartog v Colin and Shields** [1939] 3 All ER 566 where the defendant mistakenly offered to sell a number of hareskins, the price to be determined at a certain sum per pound, an offer which the plaintiffs accepted. In fact, preliminary negotiations had been concluded on the basis that the skins would be sold at a certain sum per piece, which accorded with normal trade usage. The plaintiffs attempted to enforce the contract on the basis of a price per pound since this was financially advantageous to them. It was held the plaintiffs could not do so since they must have known when they accepted the offer that the defendant had made a mistake.

It should be stated that this type of mistake is now very rare indeed. The common law rule of *caveat emptor* and the development of statutory provisions relating to consumer protection have substantially reduced the need to plead this type of mistake.

2. Mistake as to the identity of the person contracted with

A contract may become a nullity where a party is mistaken as to the identity of the person contracted with and the other party is aware of that mistake. It should be stressed that the question of the other party's identity must be of fundamental importance to the innocent party for the type of mistake to operate. It is a question of fact as to whether the identity of the other party is fundamental or not. It is for the person seeking to have the contract set aside for mistake to rebut this presumption. As with other types of mistake the presumption is that there exists a valid contract between the parties to the contract.

The last point is particularly important in this type of mistake, which is perhaps the most common of all alleged mistakes. Related to this point is the fact that the courts have in mind the protection of third parties who may be adversely affected by the finding of a contract being void *ab initio* for mistake, as was indicated at the start of this chapter. The courts, however, are often faced with a conflict of interest since frequently the problem of identity arises because a rogue misrepresents their identity to obtain goods from the innocent party. The balance that the courts have to make between mistake as to identity, fraudulent misrepresentation and the rights of innocent third parties produces some interesting results.

Example

The typical situation that arises occurs where A accepts an offer to sell goods to B, who pretends to be X. B, having obtained the goods, now sells them to an innocent third party, Z. At this point B usually disappears although, even if they can be traced, any rights that A has against them are very often worthless since such rogues are usually 'men of straw'. A's action will therefore be framed in terms of an action in the tort of conversion against Z, alleging that they, A, have a better title to the goods than Z. In order to prove the case A will attempt to prove that the contract with B is void *ab initio* for mistake as to identity. If A is able to do this then it follows that B never acquired good title to the goods, in which case, they cannot convey good title to Z – *nemo dat quod non habet* – so Z will have to surrender the goods to A. Z's action here will lie against B for breach of the implied condition as to title under s 12 of the Sale of Goods Act 1979.

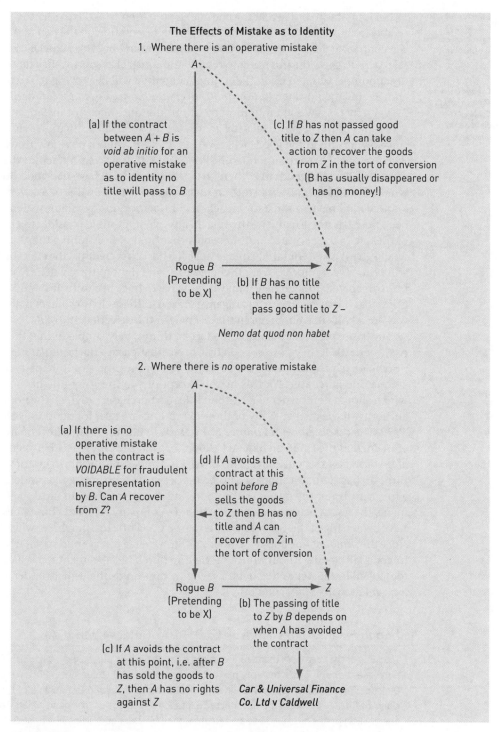

The Effects of Mistake as to Identity

1. Where there is an operative mistake

A

(a) If the contract between A + B is *void ab initio* for an operative mistake as to identity no title will pass to B

(c) If B has not passed good title to Z then A can take action to recover the goods from Z in the tort of conversion (B has usually disappeared or has no money!)

Rogue B (Pretending to be X) → Z

(b) If B has no title then he cannot pass good title to Z –

Nemo dat quod non habet

2. Where there is *no* operative mistake

A

(a) If there is no operative mistake then the contract is *VOIDABLE* for fraudulent misrepresentation by B. Can A recover from Z?

(d) If A avoids the contract at this point *before B* sells the goods to Z then B has no title and A can recover from Z in the tort of conversion

Rogue B (Pretending to be X) → Z

(b) The passing of title to Z by B depends on when A has avoided the contract

(c) If A avoids the contract at this point, i.e. after B has sold the goods to Z, then A has no rights against Z

Car & Universal Finance Co. Ltd v *Caldwell*

Figure 10.1

For more on
fraudulent
misrepresentation
see Chapter 9.

*Car and Universal
Finance Co. Ltd v
Caldwell* ???is
discussed in
Chapter 9.

If *A* is unable to prove that the contract is void for mistake as to identity, *A* will generally be able to show that there is a fraudulent misrepresentation on the part of *B* and this renders the contract voidable. In these circumstances, timing becomes crucial, since here *A* must take steps to show the intention to rescind the contract as soon as they have discovered the deception perpetrated upon them. Invariably they will be seeking to rescind out of court and, as already indicated in ***Car and Universal Finance Co. Ltd* v *Caldwell*** [1964] 1 All ER 290, *A* may display such intention by informing the police, for instance. If *A* manages to avoid the contract *before B* sells the goods to *Z* then the same situation as for mistake exists, since ownership in the goods will revert to *A* and *B* will not have any title to convey to *Z*, who again will have to surrender the goods to *A*. If, however, *A* rescinds the contract only *after B* has sold the goods to *Z*, then up to this point *B* will have had good title to the goods which *B* will have transferred to *Z*. In such a case, *A* will be unable to recover the goods from *Z* and would have to sue *B* for breach of contract for non-payment which, as has already been noted, is not usually worthwhile. In any event *A* should consider tracing the proceeds of the sale to the bank accounts or some other fund of *B*, assuming they have one! Tracing would give *A* a procedural advantage since if *B* has other creditors the effect of a tracing order will be to give *A* priority over other creditors. The right to trace will be lost if the fund has been dissipated, though here it may be possible to trace in equity. It should also be borne in mind that *A* may be able to trace against *Z* even in these circumstances if *A* can show that *Z* was not a bona fide purchaser in that *Z* knew of the defective title of *B*.

The basic rule as set out is, on the face of things, very simple in that the seller can only pass good title if they possess good title in the first place – the *nemo dat* rule. Of course this principle can produce some very unfair results for the innocent third party, even if they are a bona fide purchaser. For this reason exceptions to the strict rule have been developed which allow a non-owner to pass good title to a purchaser provided the non-owner has the authority of the owner. Many of these exceptions are now found in the Sale of Goods Act 1979. The case of ***Shogun Finance Ltd* v *Hudson*** illustrates the effect of another example contained in the Hire Purchase Act 1964, s 27, and the differences between void and voidable contracts as set out above. This provision applies specifically to motor vehicles held on hire purchase terms. It should be noted that a person who buys goods under a hire purchase agreement is not the owner of the goods but merely hires them until the last payment is made, the goods being owned by the finance company. Thus the hirer does not normally have ownership of the goods to be able to pass good title to a purchaser when they sell them since the *nemo dat* rule applies. Under s 27, however, a private purchaser, who, while acting in good faith and without notice of the hire purchase agreement, buys a car from a seller (described in the Act as the 'debtor') who in turn holds the vehicle under a hire purchase agreement, will obtain good title.

Shogun Finance Ltd v *Hudson* (2001) The Times, 4 July (CA)

The facts of the case were that a rogue visited a car dealer and purchased a Mitsubishi Shogun on hire purchase terms. In order to verify his identity he produced a stolen driving licence in the name of Mr Patel. The dealer contacted Shogun Finance Ltd, the claimant, requesting finance for 'Mr Patel'. The claimant finance company then conducted a finance search against the name of 'Mr Patel' and subsequently accepted a hire purchase agreement signed by the rogue, giving him finance to purchase the car. The rogue then paid a deposit of 10 per cent and drove the car away. The rogue sold the car to Mr Hudson, the defendant. The rogue then disappeared and the finance company brought an action for conversion from Hudson, who claimed that he had acquired good title to the car under the Hire

Purchase Act 1964, s 27. Under this provision, where a private purchaser buys a motor vehicle from someone who has it subject to a hire-purchase agreement or conditional sale agreement and does not yet properly own the vehicle (because it is still under the hire-purchase or conditional sale agreement), then, if the private purchaser is a purchaser in good faith and without notice of the hire-purchase agreement or conditional sale agreement, the transaction is treated as if the person selling the vehicle did properly own it. The County Court gave judgement in favour of the claimant finance company and Hudson appealed.

The Court of Appeal, by a majority, dismissed the appeal, stating that s 27 of the Hire Purchase Act 1964 only protects a purchaser from a 'debtor' and the question then arose as to whether the rogue was in fact the 'debtor'. The court was divided on this issue, Dyson LJ and Brooke LJ deciding that the rogue, having forged Mr Patel's signature, was not the debtor – this was Mr Patel himself. The agreement could not be enforced against Mr Patel since the fact that his signature had been forged precluded this. Their Lordships relied on a rather peculiar judgement in *Hector* v *Lyons* (1988) P & CR 156, which stated the principle that in a written contract the identities of the parties are established by the names on the contract. The problem with the use of the case in this context is that it really is not relevant to an action involving a seller and a third party, as in this case and as pointed out by Sedley LJ, who gave the dissenting judgement.

The Court of Appeal also considered the issue of unilateral mistake as to identity. As can be seen later, it is easier to prove unilateral mistake where the parties are not in each other's presence (*inter absentes*). Dyson LJ stated that the identity of the hirer was of crucial importance to the finance company in that it only intended to deal with Mr Patel. The claimant company was therefore able to show that the hire purchase agreement between themselves and the rogue was void for unilateral mistake and therefore Hudson could not rely on s 27. Since the rogue would not have had ownership of the car under the hire purchase agreement, he could not pass good title to Hudson.

The Court of Appeal decision was upheld in the House of Lords (Lords Nicholls and Millett dissenting) ([2004] 1 All ER 215). Lord Hobhouse gave the leading judgement and stated that the relevant question is whether the rogue was the debtor under the hire purchase agreement relating to the car. Mr Hudson considered he was, while the finance company considered otherwise. He stated that the agreement emphasised that the customer/hirer could only be the person named on the front of the document; that the agreement was the written agreement contained in the written document; the offer being accepted by the creditor is that contained in the written document, that is the offer of Mr Patel; that for the offer to be made the form had to have been signed by Mr Patel; and most importantly the question in issue revolves around the construction of the written document alone.

Taking each point in turn, Lord Hobhouse considered that the document referred to nobody else but Mr Patel. The finance company was only willing to do business with the person identified in the written document and no one else. This is what the rogue expected since the company was willing to deal with Mr Patel but not with the rogue. Lord Hobhouse considered that Sedley LJ in the Court of Appeal was wrong in concluding that this was a case of a rogue using an alias 'to disguise the purchaser rather than to deceive the vendor as seen in the case of *King's Norton Metal Co. Ltd* v *Edridge, Merrett & Co. Ltd*' (see below). Thus it is Mr Patel who is the debtor, not the rogue.

Of course it is not disputed that the rogue had no authority to deal on behalf of Mr Patel, nor that he was Mr Patel. Mr Hudson dealt with this issue by stating that it was the rogue that came into the showroom, not Mr Patel. Mr Patel knew nothing of the agreement, had not signed the agreement and therefore Mr Patel could not be the debtor. Lord Hobhouse considered that this was an attempt to adduce oral evidence in order to overturn a written agreement. He did not consider that this was possible where a party is specifically named in the agreement. In arriving at this conclusion he also referred to the case of *Hector* v *Lyons*

(1988) 58 P & CR 156, referred to in the Court of Appeal. It is useful to look at this case in more detail in order to understand the position more clearly.

The case concerned the purchase of a piece of land in which Mr Hector Senior negotiated with Mrs Lyons. Originally they negotiated over the telephone and then on a face-to-face basis. In fact Mr Hector Senior was negotiating on behalf of his son because he was under age. In due course Mr Hector Senior instructed his solicitors to act for him in his son's name and in due course contracts were signed and exchanged. The name of Mr Hector Junior was given as the purchaser and Mr Hector Senior signed in his son's name. Mrs Lyons then failed to complete the sale and Mr Hector Senior brought an action for specific performance in his own name. His action failed on the basis that there was no contract with Mr Hector Senior. The identity of the parties was established by the names in the contract – Mrs Lyons and Mr Hector Junior – as held by Lords Woolf and Browne-Wilkinson.

Mr Hudson in **Shogun** contended that this decision was wrong and should be overruled; however, Lords Hobhouse, Phillips and Walker considered the decision to be correct. Lord Browne-Wilkinson in **Hector v Lyons** was very clear about the distinction between contracts concluded in a face-to-face sale and those concluded in writing. In a face-to-face sale he stated that the law is well established in that the mere fact that the vendor is under a misapprehension as to the identity of the person in front of them does not in itself render the contract void for mistake. This type of mistake is one as to the attributes of the person with whom they are dealing – a mistake as to creditworthiness – which may render the contract voidable for misrepresentation. The only time a contract becomes void for a mistake as to identity is when the identity of the person contracted with is 'of a direct and important materiality in inducing the vendor to enter into the contract'. He went on to state:

> In my judgement the principle [there enunciated] has no application to a case such as the present where the contract is wholly in writing. There the identity of the vendor and of the purchaser is established by the names of the parties included in the written contract. Once those names are there in the contract, the only question for the court is to identify who they are.

Lord Woolf concurred with this position:

> Parties to the contract are normally to be ascertained from the document or documents containing the contract. There can be limited circumstances where it is possible to allow oral evidence to be given in relation to a written contract, but those circumstances are recognised as being exceptional and should, in my view, be strictly confined.

Where does this leave Mr Hudson? Since Mr Patel was named in the agreement he was a party to it. The delivery of the car to the rogue was wrongful since the dealer only had the authority of the finance company to deliver it to Mr Patel and no one else. Delivering the car to the rogue was a tortious act, even though the dealer had acted under an innocent mistake induced by the fraud of the rogue. The exception contained in the Hire Purchase Act 1964, s 27 only protects a purchaser from a debtor. The debtor here is Mr Patel, but of course he did not sell the car to Mr Hudson. This was done by the rogue. Essentially the rogue was a thief, who had no title to the car and could not therefore confer any title on Mr Hudson – *nemo dat quod non habet*. Mr Hudson was therefore liable to the finance company for the value of the car.

In order to prove unilateral mistake as to identity, the person alleging mistake must prove *each* of the following:

1 an intention to deal with some other person;

2 that the other party knew of this intention;

3 that the identity was of fundamental importance;

4 that reasonable steps had been taken to verify the identity.

One has to show that there was *an intention to deal with some other person* than the one with whom they appear to have made the contract. In other words, it has to be shown that there is confusion between two identities. The point is well illustrated by the following case.

King's Norton Metal Co. Ltd v Edridge, Merrett & Co. Ltd (1897) 14 TLR 98

A rogue by the name of Wallis set up a business under the name of Hallam & Co. with the sole purpose of defrauding the plaintiffs. He had letterheads drawn up and printed which depicted the firm as being one of some substance. He then obtained goods from the plaintiffs after sending an order on one of the sheets of letterheaded notepaper. Wallis then sold the goods to the defendants, who bought them in good faith. The plaintiffs now sued the defendants alleging that the contract with Hallam & Co. was void for mistake and that no title could be conveyed to the defendants. It was held that their action should fail since there was no mistake as to identity – they had intended to contract with Hallam & Co. and that was whom they had in fact contracted with. The plaintiffs failed to show that there was some other person with whom they had intended to do business; the court therefore rejected their claim.

The mistaken party must prove that *the other party was aware of the above intention*. Usually there is little problem in proving this since, where mistake as to identity is pleaded, it is usually the result of a fraud being perpetrated on the mistaken party. It is clear that one cannot present oneself as a party to a contract knowing that the other party had no intention of entering into a contract with that person. It follows from this that an offer can only be accepted by the party to whom it is addressed. The case of **Boulton v Jones** illustrates the point and provides a rare example of a case in which no fraudulent misrepresentation arose.

Boulton v Jones (1957) 2 H & N 564

The facts were that the plaintiff, Boulton, had bought the business belonging to Brocklehurst. The defendant, Jones, had formerly dealt with Brocklehurst with whom he had a running account. One feature of the business relationship between Jones and Brocklehurst was that Jones could set against the account moneys owed to him by Brocklehurst. Jones sent an order for goods from Brocklehurst but on the day the order was received the business was sold to Boulton, who executed the order. When Jones was presented with the bill he refused to pay since he had intended the order to go to Brocklehurst so that he could set off against the value of the order moneys owed to him by Brocklehurst. It was held that Jones was not liable for the price.

The actual basis for the decision in **Boulton v Jones** is ambiguous in that it could be based on either unilateral or mutual mistake. If the decision is based on unilateral mistake then it is undoubtedly correct, but if based on mutual mistake then it is highly questionable. In mutual mistake the finding of mistake in the contract is assessed in objective terms rather than subjectively as in unilateral mistake. Translated into a test the question that has to be asked is whether the reasonable person in the position of the offeree would have considered the offer to be intended for them, *not* whether the offeror intended to deal with the person to whom the offer was made. On this basis a reasonable person would no doubt have concluded that the identity of the seller was a matter of indifference to the purchaser. Such a conclusion would result in there being no *operative* mistake, and thus Jones would have been bound by the contract despite the fact that he could prove that he had made a mistake. The point is affirmed in *Upton-on-Severn RDC v Powell* [1942] 1 All ER 220.

In order to prove mistake the party alleging it must show that at the time of contracting *the identity of the person they were dealing with was of fundamental and crucial importance to them*. This is not easy to prove since the mistaken party clearly has to produce evidence of the fact from their conduct before or at the time of contracting. In these circumstances such individuals are generally mistaken more as to the attributes of the person they are dealing with, such as creditworthiness, rather than as to identity. Further it should be noted that it is usually easier to prove this where the parties contract *inter absentes*, for example, by post. Where the parties contract *inter praesentes*, for example, in a shop, the presumption is that the mistaken party intends to deal with the person before them, whoever they are, and very strong evidence indeed is required to rebut the presumption.

Can a person deal with another *inter absentes* but actually contract *inter praesentes* via an agent? In *Shogun Finance Ltd v Hudson* above, Sedley LJ, who gave the leading judgement, thought so. While the majority of the Court of Appeal considered that the contract was made *inter absentes* between the rogue and the finance company, Sedley LJ considered that the car dealer acted as the finance company's agent. The dealer, he said, was the finance company's eyes and ears for the purposes of establishing the rogue's identity, faxing his driving licence and obtaining his signature of the hire purchase agreement. This, Sedley LJ stated, 'amounted to face-to-face dealing as if they had been carried out at the [finance company's] office'. While this is only a dissenting judgement it is nevertheless a credible conclusion in arrangements of this nature.

If we look at cases involving alleged mistake, *inter absentes* first of all, in the case of *King's Norton Metal Co.*, the facts of which have already been discussed, it is clear that the party alleging mistake was not mistaken as to the identity of the person they had contracted with. They were merely mistaken as to the creditworthiness of that party. They thought they were contracting with a solvent and substantial business as portrayed on the letterhead, not some insolvent rogue. They were ready and willing to deal with anyone and were concerned not as to the identity per se but as to whether they would get paid on the contract. The case can be contrasted with that of *Cundy v Lindsay*.

Cundy v Lindsay (1878) 3 App Cas 459

A rogue set up a business by the name of Blenkarn at 37 Wood Street and sent an order for goods to the plaintiffs. The order was signed by the rogue in such a way that it looked like the name Blenkiron and Co. which traded at 123 Wood Street, a firm which the plaintiffs knew to be highly respectable. The plaintiffs accepted the order and despatched them to 'Messrs Blenkiron and Co., 37 Wood Street'. The rogue, having received the goods, sold them to the defendants, who took the goods in good faith. The plaintiffs now attempted to recover the goods from the defendants in conversion. The House of Lords held that they would succeed in their action in that they had intended only to contract with Blenkiron and Co. and nobody else and that the identity of the person they were to contract with was of fundamental and crucial importance at the time of entering into the contract. The position was summed up by Lord Cairns:

> I ask the question, how is it possible to imagine that in that state of things any contract could have arisen between the Respondents and Blenkarn, the dishonest man? Of him they knew nothing, and of him they never thought. With him they never intended to deal. Their minds never even for an instant of time rested on him, and as between him and them there was no consensus of mind which could lead to any agreement or any contract whatsoever.

In *Cundy* v *Lindsay* there was clearly confusion as to which of two distinct entities had been contracted with. In the *King's Norton* case this was not apparent since there existed only one entity, Hallam & Co. On this basis, then, to establish mistake it is not enough for the party alleging mistake merely to show that they did not intend to contract with a particular individual. They must show also that they intended instead to contract with some other person capable of being identified, though it may be questionable whether this person must actually exist or whether the person may remain completely fictitious.

Turning our attention to cases where the parties are *inter praesentes* we find, as already indicated, that it is particularly difficult to refute the presumption that the party alleging mistake intended to deal with the person in front of them. As a result, successful actions are fairly rare. One of the early cases exemplifying this problem is that of *Phillips* v *Brooks Ltd*.

Phillips v *Brooks Ltd* [1919] 2 KB 243

The facts of the case were that a rogue named North entered the jewellery shop owned by the plaintiff and selected some pearls valued at £2,500 and a ring valued at £450. He then proceeded to write out a cheque and as he did so stated, 'You see who I am, I am Sir George Bullough', giving an address in St James's Square. The plaintiff had heard of Sir George Bullough and on checking the telephone directory confirmed the address given. The plaintiff then asked if he would like to take the articles with him, to which the rogue replied, 'You had better have the cheque cleared first, but I should like to take the ring, as it is my wife's birthday tomorrow.' The plaintiff let North take the ring, and North then pawned it to the defendant, who took it in good faith. The plaintiff, on discovering the fraud, now sued the pawnbroker defendant in conversion, alleging that the contract was void for mistake. It was of course imperative that he successfully establish mistake since otherwise the contract would only be voidable for fraudulent misrepresentation, in which case the contract would be valid until disaffirmed and rescinded by the plaintiff jeweller. In such a case the plaintiff would not be able to recover the ring from the defendant since the rescission would have come after the goods and the ownership to them were transferred to the defendant pawnbroker, thereby leaving the plaintiff with a worthless claim against the rogue North.

It was held that while the jeweller believed he was dealing with Sir George Bullough he would in fact have contracted with anyone present in the shop. Evidence of this decision can be seen in the fact that the contract had already been completed when the question of identity arose. The rogue had selected the items and offered to buy them. The plaintiff had accepted the offer and the rogue was writing out the cheque in payment for the goods when the question of identity arose. The identity of the person in front of the jeweller was not of fundamental or of crucial importance before or at the time of contracting. The jeweller thus failed in his action in conversion against the defendant.

Two other cases also illustrate the problems that arise in this context. The first is that of *Ingram* v *Little* [1960] 3 All ER 332, where two sisters jointly owned a car which they advertised for sale. A rogue called and agreed with one of the sisters to purchase the car for £717. When he proffered a cheque for the amount the sister adamantly refused to accept it, whereupon the rogue stated that he was P G M Hutchinson and that he had substantial business interests. Whilst the discussions were taking place the other sister checked the name and address of P G M Hutchinson in the telephone directory which seemed to corroborate his story. The sisters then agreed to let him have the car and accept his cheque. The cheque was subsequently dishonoured and the rogue, who was of course not P G M Hutchinson, sold the car to a third party who purchased the vehicle in good faith. The plaintiffs sued the defendant in conversion, alleging that the contract was void for mistake as to the identity and succeeded. The case, however, is largely regarded as being at best decided on the facts of the particular case and at worst, wrongly decided. It is suggested that in fact the latter is the only appropriate description of the case. It has been clearly established that the mistake as to identity must be of fundamental or crucial importance before or at the time of contracting to be operative. In this case the contract was complete, the sale agreed, and it was only when the rogue proffered a cheque that the question of identity arose. There may have been a dispute as to the mode of payment but identity was not at issue until this point.

The second case is that of *Lewis* v *Averay* [1971] 3 All ER 907 where the facts were very similar to those of *Ingram* v *Little*. Here again the plaintiff was the owner of a car that he wished to sell, and to do so he advertised it in the local newspaper. A rogue arranged to see the car and on doing so offered to buy it at the stated price. The plaintiff accepted the offer and the rogue then wrote out a cheque signing it 'R A Green'. The rogue asked if he could take the car straightaway but at this the plaintiff became hesitant and did not want to part with the car until the cheque had cleared. The plaintiff asked the rogue whether he had some evidence as to his identity. The rogue produced a pass to Pinewood Studios as proof that he was Richard Greene, the well-known actor. The plaintiff, on examining the pass, allowed the rogue to take the car. The rogue then sold the car to an innocent third party and the cheque was subsequently dishonoured. The plaintiff then claimed the goods from the third party in conversion on the basis that the contract between himself and the rogue was void for mistake as to identity.

The Court of Appeal held that his action must fail since the plaintiff intended to deal with the person in front of him irrespective of his identity and that the contract was subsequently only voidable for fraudulent misrepresentation. Since the plaintiff had disaffirmed the contract only after the third party had purchased the car, the third party acquired a good title in the vehicle. Megaw LJ based his decision on the traditional analysis that the identity of the rogue was not of fundamental and crucial importance before or at the time of contracting and only became relevant when the rogue paid by cheque and wanted the car immediately. Lord Denning MR arrived at the same decision though on a somewhat different basis. He considered that the fine distinction between identity and attributes, or creditworthiness, and the time when the identity became important was to miss the point of the principle of mistake, which was ultimately to protect innocent third party purchasers. He considered that the effect of mistake as to identity was not to render the contract void but merely voidable, 'that is, liable to be set aside at the instance of the mistaken person, so long as he does so before third parties have in good faith acquired rights under it'. There would appear to be considerable merit in such an approach since the cases clearly tend to reflect this situation in any event.

The following is a rather more modern case that deals with the distinction between identity and attributes.

Citibank NA v Brown Shipley & Co. Ltd; Midland Bank plc v Brown Shipley & Co. Ltd [1991] 2 All ER 690

Here a rogue claimed to be a signatory on a company account held with the plaintiff bank. The rogue telephoned the defendant bank and asked to purchase some foreign currency which he would pay for by a banker's draft drawn on the company account held by the plaintiff. The rogue then telephoned the plaintiff requesting the banker's draft, which it handed to a 'messenger' whom the plaintiff thought was from the company. In exchange for the draft, a forged letter of authority was given. The draft was then paid to the defendant who, after confirming that the draft had in fact been issued by the plaintiff in the ordinary course of business, paid the cash to the rogue. In due course the defendant presented the draft to the plaintiff bank and was subsequently paid. When the fraud was eventually discovered, the plaintiff bank brought an action to recover the value of the draft from the defendant. The action was based on the allegation that title had never passed to the defendant bank as it could not derive a good title from the rogue and that there was no contract between the two banks. The court held that the fact that the plaintiff had mistakenly dealt with a rogue instead of the company which the plaintiff bank thought they were dealing with did not prevent the formation of a contract between the two banks. The court agreed that the rogue had no title because of mistaken identity but they found that he was a 'mere conduit'. Title did not pass from the rogue to the defendant. The important factor was the identity of the paying bank, the defendant, and that there was no mistake here.

The party alleging mistake must last of all show that they have taken *reasonable steps to attempt to verify the identity* of the person with whom they are about to contract. This requirement must be shown whether or not the contract is made *inter absentes* or *inter praesentes*.

In *Shogun Finance Ltd* v *Hudson*, Lords Phillips and Walker, however, considered that the present law as to mistake as to identity was correct. The presumption was that in a contract made face to face (and possibly in telephone conversations) the offer (or in an appropriate case the acceptance) was made to the person present whoever he or she was, as in *Phillips* v *Brooks*. They considered that *Ingram* v *Little* was wrongly decided, something which lawyers for many years have considered to be the case. The presumption, however, did not apply in written contracts, since the offer and acceptance was derived from the written correspondence. In such cases, where the rogue passes himself or herself off as an existing individual or company of reputable standing, the offer is intended to be with the individual or the company, not the rogue, as held in *Cundy* v *Lindsay*. Lord Hobhouse, however, did not consider mistake as to identity to be an issue in the case, basing his judgement on the issue of the construction of a written contract.

The dissenting judges, Lords Nicholls and Millett, considered that it was unsatisfactory to decide the issues by reference to the mode by which the contract was concluded. The notion that there was a difference between mistake as to identity and mistake as to attributes was untenable and the face-to-face presumption should be abolished. A person should be deemed 'to intend to contract with the person with whom he is actually dealing, whatever mode of communication' (*per* Lord Nicholls). On this basis both their Lordships considered that *Cundy* v *Lindsay* was wrongly decided and should no longer be followed. In some respects the arguments put forward by Lords Nicholls and Millett are attractive propositions since here the vendor will bear the loss. This is considered to be fair since, given that the vendor and third party are both innocent, the vendor is not only usually better able to bear the loss but also it is the vendor who has taken the risk of parting with the goods without recovering payment for them.

Mistake in equity

Objective 5

It has been seen that the effect of mistake at common law is to render the contract void *ab initio*, whereas mistake in equity has the effect of merely rendering the contract voidable. Furthermore, equity is generally prepared to come to such a conclusion despite the fact that the common law itself might refuse to intervene. Thus in *Solle* v *Butcher* Lord Denning stated:

> Let me next consider mistakes which render the contract voidable, that is liable to be set aside on some equitable ground. Whilst pre-supposing that a contract was good at law, or at any rate not void, this court of equity would often relieve a party from the consequences of his own mistake, so long as it could do so without injustice to third parties. The court had power to set aside the contract whenever it was of the opinion that it was unconscionable for the other party to avail himself of the legal advantage which he has obtained . . .

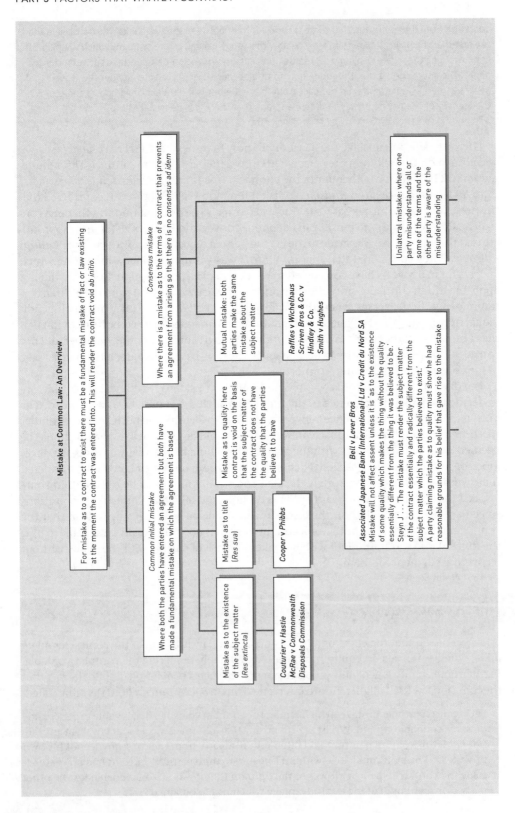

Mistake at Common Law: An Overview

For mistake as to a contract to exist there must be a fundamental mistake of fact or law existing at the moment the contract was entered into. This will render the contract void *ab initio*.

Common initial mistake

Where both the parties have entered an agreement but *both* have made a fundamental mistake on which the agreement is based

Mistake as to the existence of the subject matter (*Res extincta*)

Couturier v Hastie
McRae v Commonwealth Disposals Commission

Mistake as to title (*Res sua*)

Cooper v Phibbs

Mistake as to quality: here contract is void on the basis that the subject matter of the contract does not have the quality that the parties believe it to have

Bell v Lever Bros
Associated Japanese Bank (International) Ltd v Credit du Nord SA
Mistake will not affect assent unless it is as to the existence of some quality which makes the thing without the quality essentially different from the thing it was believed to be.'
Steyn J '. . . The mistake must render the subject matter of the contract essentially and radically different from the subject matter which the parties believed to exist.'
A party claiming mistake as to quality must show he had reasonable grounds for his belief that gave rise to the mistake

Consensus mistake

Where there is a mistake as to the terms of a contract that prevents an agreement from arising so that there is no *consensus ad idem*

Mutual mistake: both parties make the same mistake about the subject matter

Raffles v Wichelhaus
Scriven Bros & Co. v Hindley & Co.
Smith v Hughes

Unilateral mistake: where one party misunderstands all or some of the terms and the other party is aware of the misunderstanding

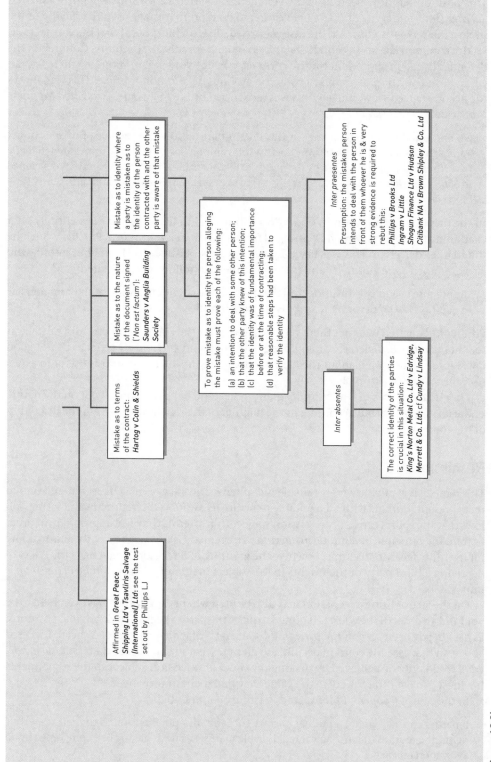

Figure 10.2b

This position has now been subject to challenge in *Great Peace Shipping Ltd* v *Tsavliris Salvage (International) Ltd*. As stated earlier in relation to mistake as to the quality of the subject matter of the contract, the case was based, first, on the ground that the contract was void at common law and, second, that it was voidable for mistake in equity. Counsel for the defendants had proposed that if the contract was not void at common law there was an equitable jurisdiction to grant rescission on grounds of common mistake. This was always the acknowledged view; indeed, this was recognised by Steyn J in the *Associated Japanese Bank* case where he stated:

> No one could fairly suggest that in this difficult area of the law there is only one correct approach or solution. But a narrow doctrine of common law mistake (as enunciated in *Bell* v *Lever Bros Ltd*), supplemented by the more flexible doctrine of mistake in equity (as developed in *Solle* v *Butcher* and later cases), seems to me to be an entirely sensible and satisfactory state of the law.

In the first instance decision in *Great Peace*, Toulson J took a different view entirely after examining the basis on which Denning LJ formed his decision in *Solle* v *Butcher*, which he found to be defective. This was taken up by the Court of Appeal by Lord Phillips MR, who also examined *Solle* v *Butcher* and the many cases that followed it. He stated:

> the premise of equity's intrusion into the effects of the common law is that the common law in question is seen in the particular case to work injustice.

Phillips MR queried whether there was a legal basis for the equitable doctrine of mistake as set out in *Solle* v *Butcher*. He disapproved of the decision and considered it to be not good law. More will be stated about this decision later but for the moment it is useful to assess how mistake in equity evolved.

The circumstances in which equity grants relief tend to be categorised not on the nature of the mistake per se but according to the manner of the relief that is within the discretion of the court.

Rescission

This remedy is available widely outside the sphere of mistake, as may be seen in relation to misrepresentation. As with all equitable remedies its award is discretionary and it thus follows that the courts can apply rescission subject to any terms they feel appropriate in order to fulfil the principle of *restitutio in integrum*. The remedy is lost where a party fails to apply for it within a reasonable time, or where the granting of rescission would have the effect of depriving a third party of their rights in the subject matter or where *restitutio in integrum* is impossible.

On the face of things, rescission may also be used where the contract has been held to be void and an order of the court is required to place the parties back in their original positions, as has already been seen in *Cooper* v *Phibbs*, the facts of which have already been discussed above. In that case the court in deciding to grant rescission considered that *restitutio in integrum* could only be achieved by making the order of rescission subject to the respondents having a lien over the fishery to the value they had spent improving it.

In the case of *Cooper* v *Phibbs*, Lord Westbury commented:

> If parties contract under a mutual mistake [*sic*] and misapprehension as to their respective rights, the result is that the agreement is liable to be set aside as having been proceeded upon a common mistake.

The effect of the case is thus often upheld as providing a general authority for the use of rescission in cases of a common and material mistake irrespective of the presence of *res extincta* or *res sua*. The case of **Huddersfield Banking Co. Ltd v Henry Lister & Son Ltd** also provides authority for this proposition.

Huddersfield Banking Co. Ltd v *Henry Lister & Son Ltd* [1895] 2 Ch 273

The defendant's company had mortgaged its mills and the fixtures contained in them to the bank. Eventually the company went into insolvent liquidation. The bank claimed that it was entitled to 35 looms in the mills on the basis that since these were bolted to the floor they represented fixtures and thus fell within their security for the loans. If this was the case they could not fall into the hands of the Official Receiver to be sold to pay off the general creditors. On touring the factory premises, the agent of the bank and of the liquidator found that the looms were not in fact bolted to the floor and thus fell outside the fixtures capable of being claimed by the bank. The bank therefore gave a consent order for the looms to be sold. It then became apparent that the looms had in fact been bolted to the floor but had been wrongfully disconnected by some unauthorised person. The bank immediately applied for the consent order to be rescinded. The court held that the order had been made on the basis of a common and mutual mistake and gave an order for rescission. Lord Kay stated:

> It seems to me that, both on principle and on authority, when once the Court finds that an agreement has been come to between parties who were under a common mistake of a material fact, the Court may set it aside, and the Court has ample jurisdiction to set aside the order founded upon that agreement.

A similar decision was arrived at in **Solle v Butcher** where, as we have already seen, the contract was not held to be void for common mistake at common law. In equity, however, it was decided that the lease should be set aside. If equity had allowed the contract to be void, as in common law, this would clearly have resulted in an inequitable solution as far as the tenant was concerned since he would be dispossessed of his lease. The court thus offered him a choice of either surrendering the lease or continuing it but on the basis of paying the full rent allowable, which would have been £250 once statutory notices allowing for the increase had been served. The decision was similar in **Grist v Bailey** [1966] 2 All ER 875, where the mistake, while not being fundamental enough to render the contract void at common law, was sufficiently fundamental to render the contract voidable in equity.

The problem with the above cases is that they are difficult to reconcile with the case of **Bell v Lever Bros**, where the contract was held to be valid and binding rather than void at common law or voidable in equity. Following the case of **Associated Japanese Bank (International) Ltd v Crédit du Nord** it may be possible to find that in **Bell** the contract should have been void at common law. Failing this, why should it not have been held to be voidable in equity?

The latter point was considered in the case of **Magee v Pennine Insurance Co. Ltd** [1969] 2 All ER 891 in which the plaintiff bought a car on hire purchase terms for his son. At the time of purchase a proposal form for the insurance of the vehicle was filled out by the manager, who made several errors amounting to innocent misrepresentation. Some time later the car was written off in an accident and the plaintiff claimed £600, though he agreed to accept a lesser sum of £385 after negotiations with the defendant. The defendant then discovered the misrepresentations and claimed to repudiate the agreement. The majority of the Court of Appeal found that the agreement had been reached on the basis of a common mistake though not one that was so fundamental as to render the contract void at common law, as in **Bell v Lever Bros**. The court, however, considered that the mistake was sufficiently fundamental to render the contract voidable in equity, though no terms were imposed on the parties. Lord Winn dissented and considered the case no different from *Bell v Lever Bros* and as such it should be regarded as binding. Lord Denning MR reconciled the decision in *Magee* with *Bell* by stating that there was an underlying doctrine of equity, which was never expressly referred to in *Bell*, that allowed equity a discretion to set a contract aside on the basis of a common mistake as to quality. Such a proposition is somewhat radical given the stature of the judges sitting in the *Bell* case since, if such a doctrine existed, then surely such judges would have referred to it. The view put forward by many commentators is that such a doctrine is a figment of Lord Denning's lively and radical legal imagination.

So far we have been considering the effect of rescission in the context of shared mistakes, that is, those arising in both mutual mistake and common mistake. In assessing the intervention of equity in unilateral mistake in relation to the exercise of rescission, we find that there also arises a level of doubt as to the circumstances in which equity will exercise its discretion. One view is that such discretion should only be exercised where there has been some misrepresentation or fraudulent conduct by the other party. Another view is that rescission is available in a unilateral mistake where the other party is guilty of conduct, that would make any insistence on their part that the contract be performed inequitable.

The Court of Appeal decision in *Riverplate Properties Ltd v Pau* [1975] Ch 133 tended to suggest the first narrower approach and held that equitable relief was not available simply on the ground of unilateral mistake unless the party against whom relief was being sought knew that the other party had contracted under a mistake. The case tended to lean against the establishment of a general doctrine of equitable relief in mistake, whereby the court would exercise its discretionary jurisdiction where the circumstances of the case and justice demanded it. Such a proposition was suggested in *Solle v Butcher* by Lord Denning when he stated:

> It is now clear that a contract will be set aside if the mistake of one party has been induced by a material misrepresentation of the other, even though it was not fraudulent or fundamental; or if one party, knowing that the other is mistaken about the terms of the offer, or the identity of the person by whom it is made, lets him remain under his delusion and concludes a contract on the mistaken terms instead of pointing out the mistake . . . A contract is also liable in equity to be set aside if the parties were under a common misapprehension either as to facts or as to their relative and respective rights, provided that the misapprehension was fundamental, and that the party seeking to set it aside was not himself at fault.

It is, however, fair to say that Lord Denning's proposals provided a degree of flexibility that is highly desirable when balancing the interests of the contracting parties together with those of third parties. Indeed, in the *Associated Japanese Bank* case, Steyn J, as stated, concurred with this view.

In *William Sindall plc v Cambridgeshire County Council* [1994] 1 WLR 1016, Evans LJ considered that there existed 'a category of mistake which is "fundamental", so as to permit the equitable remedy of rescission, which was wider than the kind of "serious and radical" mistake that rendered the agreement void and of no effect in law'. He suggested that the difference between these two types of mistake lay in the fact that mistake at common law is confined to those types of mistake that have regard to the subject matter of the contract. Mistake in equity, however, he considered to be a wider concept that arose where the mistake was sufficiently 'fundamental' as regards a material fact and that this category appeared to have unlimited application. This wider notion of mistake in equity was not accepted in *Clarion Ltd v National Provident Institution* [2000] 2 All ER 265, where Rimer J considered that while equity may relieve a party from an unconscionable bargain, it was ordinarily no part of the function of equity to provide relief from a bad bargain. Thus equity only extended to modify relief when the nature of a party's mistake related to the contract's subject matter or terms, and not to the commercial consequences of the contract irrespective of whether this mistake was 'fundamental' or not.

It is clear that the basis of mistake in equity is the subject of substantial confusion and that its whole rationale required reviewing. This long-awaited review took place in the Court of Appeal in *Great Peace Shipping Ltd* v *Tsavliris Salvage (International) Ltd*. The leading judgement was delivered by Lord Phillips MR, who considered the extent to which Denning's doctrine stood alongside the decision in *Bell* v *Lever Bros*. He considered that Denning's doctrine was based on an error that arose in the case of *Cooper* v *Phibbs* by Lord Westbury. It will be recalled that Lord Westbury stated:

> If parties contract under a mutual mistake [*sic*] and misapprehension as to their respective rights, the result is that the agreement is liable to be set aside as having been proceeded upon a common mistake.

This comment was considered by the Court of Appeal in the decision in *Bell* v *Lever Bros*. Here Lords Scrutton and Lawrence considered that, while Lord Westbury's comment was generally correct, he should not have stated that the agreement was 'liable to be set aside' but should have stated that it was *void*. In other words, the effect of the mistake is that the agreement fails to become a contract at all. Lord Phillips considered that it was for this reason that when *Bell* came before the House of Lords the notion of an equitable doctrine was not considered. There was no awareness of an equitable doctrine at all, only that mistake at common law rendered the contract void. Indeed, this was affirmed by Lord Atkin who also, while agreeing with Lord Westbury's statement, commented that the only error in it was that mistake would render the contract void not voidable.

In *Great Peace*, Lord Phillips, having summarised the relevant sections of the various judgements of the House of Lords, stated:

> We do not find it conceivable that the House of Lords overlooked an equitable right in *Bell* v *Lever Bros Ltd* to rescind the agreement, notwithstanding that the agreement was not void for mistake at common law. The jurisprudence established no such right.

Lord Phillips then turned his analysis to the decision in *Solle* v *Butcher*, the facts of which have already been considered earlier. In this case, Bucknill LJ considered there was a mistake of fact and that this mistake was of fundamental importance that allowed the contract to be rescinded under the principles set out in *Cooper* v *Phibbs*. Jenkins LJ, however, considered that the mistake was not one of fact at all but one of law and that there was no right of rescission based on an error of law at that time. Lord Denning, however, considered that there was no mistake as to the quality of the subject matter at common law that would render the contract void. He identified the effect of common mistake at common law in *Bell* v *Lever Bros Ltd* in the following way:

> The correct interpretation of that case, in my mind, is that, once a contract has been made, that is to say, once the parties, whatever their inmost states of mind, have to all outward appearances agreed with sufficient certainty in the same terms on the same subject matter, then the contract is good unless and until it is set aside for failure of some condition on which the existence of the contract depends, or for fraud, or on some equitable ground. Neither party can rely on his own mistake to say it was a nullity from the beginning, no matter that it was a mistake which to his mind was fundamental, and no matter that the other party knew he was under a mistake. *A fortiori*, if the other party did not know of the mistake, but shared it. The cases where goods have perished at the time of sale, or belong to the buyer, are really contracts

which are not void for mistake but are void by reason of an implied condition precedent, because the contract proceeded on the basic assumption that it was possible of performance.

Thus Denning held that in **Solle v Butcher** there was a contract since the parties had agreed the same terms in relation to the same subject matter and that, while there was a fundamental mistake, this was not one that could cause the contract to be void at common law. He then turned to equity and considered that it was possible for the court to set the contract aside or rescind it where it was unconscionable for a party to take advantage of it:

> A contract is also liable in equity to be set aside if the parties were under a common misapprehension either as to the facts or as to their relative and respective rights, provided that the misapprehension was fundamental and that the party seeking to set it aside was not himself at fault.

On this basis Denning ordered the lease in **Solle** to be set aside since there was a 'common misapprehension that was fundamental', relying on **Cooper v Phibbs**. In **Great Peace**, Lord Phillips considered that **Cooper v Phibbs** did not establish an equitable jurisdiction for common mistake in circumstances that fell short of those that allowed the common law to find the agreement was void. He considered and concurred with Toulson J, the judge at first instance, that Denning was using **Cooper v Phibbs** to avoid the decision in **Bell v Lever Bros** so as to grant equitable relief. He expressed some sympathy with Denning's approach:

> We can understand why the decision in **Bell v Lever Bros** did not find favour with Denning LJ. An equitable jurisdiction to grant rescission on terms where a common fundamental mistake has induced a contract gives greater flexibility than a doctrine of common law which holds the contract void in such circumstances.

Nevertheless, Lord Phillips considered that **Solle v Butcher** and the cases that followed it could not stand alongside **Bell v Lever Bros**, disapproved of it and considered it to be not good law. He concluded that there is scope for legislation to give greater flexibility to the law on mistake. On this basis it seems that the equitable doctrine of mistake is a highly questionable one and that it does indeed seem to be a product of Denning's radical legal imagination. This position has not been universally approved and in the Canadian Court of Appeal case of **Miller Paving Ltd v B Gottardo Construction Ltd** (2007) ONCA 422 Goudge JA stated:

> The loss of flexibility needed to correct unjust enrichment results in widely diverse circumstances that would come from eliminating the equitable doctrine of common mistake would, I think, be a backward step.

Whether this view will be translated back into English law remains to be seen and no doubt the issue must be brought before the House of Lords in order to determine the issue once and for all. It does seem that **Great Peace** takes away part of the armoury that allows the courts a flexible means of providing a remedy where unjust enrichment materialises.

Rectification

1. The Principles

The equitable remedy of rectification arises where a written document does not represent the common intentions of the parties. As in all equitable remedies, the exercise of it by the courts is discretionary. It should be noted that the remedy does not lie where there is a mistake as to the subject matter of the contract but where there is an error on the face of the record. It is thus erroneous to talk in terms of rectification of a contract since the remedy allows only alteration of the instrument reflecting the contract.

In *Swainland Builders Ltd v Freehold Properties Ltd* [2002] 2 EGLR 71, Gibson LJ set out the requirements of rectification for common mistake as follows:

The party seeking rectification must show that:

(1) the parties had a common continuing intention, whether or not amounting to an agreement, in respect of a particular matter in the instrument to be rectified;
(2) there was an outward expression of accord;
(3) the intention continued at the time of the execution of the instrument sought to be rectified;
(4) by mistake, the instrument did not reflect that common intention.

In addition to these requirements for rectification to be appropriate there must be convincing proof that the concluded agreement does not represent the common intention of the parties: *Crane v Hegeman-Harris Co.* [1939] 1 All ER 662. This summary by Gibson LJ was affirmed and supported by Lord Hoffmann and the other members of the House of Lords in *Chartbrook Ltd v Persimmon Homes Ltd* [2009] UKHL 38 within their *obiter* judgements since the issue of rectification was not in issue in that case.

At one time there was a requirement that the parties must have reached an 'antecedent agreement' on all the terms before a court would grant rectification. However, in *Joscelyne v Nissen* [1970] 2 QB 86, it was held that it was sufficient if there was a common continuing intention as to part of the contract and that this existed up to the time the agreement was reduced into writing.

The facts of *Joscelyne v Nissen* were that the plaintiff sought to have the written contract, whereby he made over his car-hire business to his daughter, rectified. It had been expressly agreed that in return for the business she would pay certain coal, gas and electricity bills. This agreement was not contained in the written document and when the daughter failed to pay these bills the plaintiff sought a declaration that she should do so and that the written document should be rectified to this effect.

The Court of Appeal held that the agreement should be rectified despite the fact that prior to the written contract being executed no antecedent agreement had been concluded. The court stated that, in order to obtain rectification, some outward sign of a common intention was evident. In this case, the father could show that, up to the contract being executed, both parties were agreed that the daughter would pay the bills.

In *Daventry District Council v Daventry and District Housing Ltd* [2011] EWCA 1153, the appellant local authority (DDC) had entered into a contract to transfer its housing stock to the respondent (DDH), a 'registered social housing landlord'. The negotiations were complex with regards the amount DDH would pay since the calculation involved a number of elements, one of which that DDH would make good a deficit of £2.4 million in DDC's pension fund for the housing department staff who would be transferred to DDH. Version 1 of the contract provided that DDH was to pay the pension deficit. DDH's negotiator nevertheless believed that DDC would be paying the deficit, this resulted in DDH being led to believe that DDC would be paying the deficit since the negotiator presented Version 1 as meaning that DDH would not have to pay the pension deficit. The eventual transfer contract had a clause inserted (at the insistence of DDH's bank) that provided that DDC would pay the deficit, though DDC's representatives did not notice this clause in the final document. DDC alleged that this contract should have provided for DDH to pay it and claimed for rectification of the contract so as to conform with the agreement as embodied in Version 1 on the ground of mutual mistake.

At first instance ([2010] EWHC 1935) it was confirmed that for rectification to be appropriate there must be convincing proof that the concluded instrument does not represent the common intention of the parties. In establishing this failure, Lord Hoffmann in **Chartbrook Ltd v Persimmon Homes Ltd** [2009] UKHL 38 stated that evidence of continuing intention had to be assessed objectively, that is by reference as to what a reasonable person would have considered to be the intentions of the parties and not what the parties themselves understood their intentions to be. Vos J stated that it was clear that in looking for the common intention of the parties one is concerned with what, objectively speaking, one would regard as that intention. He stated that whilst the parties' subjective intention may be relevant to establishing what the parties' objective intentions were, such evidence was to be given lesser weight where the intentions of the parties is contained within the documentation, as in this case. He considered that the claim for rectification for mutual mistake must fail since the crucial ingredient of the common intention of the parties did not extend to the transfer contract.

DDC appealed and in the Court of Appeal it was stated that DDH did not share DDC's mistaken belief that under the transfer contract the pension deficit would be paid by DDH. There was, however, a mistaken belief by both DDC and DDH that the transfer contract was consistent with the original version of the contract, though they had diametrically opposite reasons for their shared mistaken belief in that DDC believed DDH was paying the deficit and DDH believed that DDC was paying the deficit. Clearly the shared mistaken belief of the parties existed at the time the contract was executed. The Court of Appeal decided (with Etherton LJ dissenting) that DDC was entitled to have the transfer contract rectified on the basis of mutual mistake since both DDH and DDC both believed that the transfer document gave effect to Version 1 and they had both been in agreement on that document, although their understanding of the document was diametrically opposite to each other. In terms of a finding of common intention Neuberger MR considered that on an objective basis DDH was not departing from the Version 1 prior agreement and to this extent there was a common intention present, though it was making a mistake. Etherton LJ did not agree and considered that on an objective basis DDH by the time of entering into the transfer contract had indicated to DDC that it was contracting on a different basis and to that extent there was no common intention present to justify rectification of the contract. It must be remembered that rectification is discretionary and awarded on the basis of equitable principles and in this regard the Court of Appeal did not consider it unfair to rectify the transfer contract so as to require DDH to pay the pension deficit because of the actions of its representative who was aware that the parties were entering into the contract at cross-purposes to one another and to that extent had acted unconscionably.

The test applied in **Daventry** has also been applied in the case of **Liberty Mercian Ltd v Cuddy Civil Engineering Ltd** [2013] EWHC 2688. In this case, Liberty entered into a contract for the construction of a new retail plateau for the future construction of a supermarket. A tender form for the works had been completed naming the contractor as 'Cuddy Group' ('CDDL'). This was the trading name of the second defendant which was a company carrying on the business as a construction and civil engineering company. L sent CDDL a letter of intent and subsequently CDDL commenced work on site. Liberty's solicitors then conducted an Internet search and discovered the name of the first defendant, Cuddy Civil Engineering Ltd ('CCEL'), which was a dormant company that had the same shareholders and directors as CDDL. The solicitors then informed the supermarket operator ('S') that the contractor on the construction was to be CCEL. Whilst a warranty was entered into between Liberty, S and CCEL, CDDL nevertheless continued to work on the site and was paid for the work completed as per the invoices submitted to Liberty. Eventually a contract was executed that named CCEL as the contractor. CCEL was happy to go along with that arrangement in order to finalise the contract. The construction project suffered from a variety of problems so that eventually Liberty terminated the contract because there was a failure to remedy defects in the works. CCEL accepted the notice of termination, treating it as a repudiatory breach of contract. Liberty then commenced proceedings against CCEL seeking a declaration that under the contract CCEL was obliged to deliver a parent company guarantee, performance bond and deeds of warranty and that these had never been provided. Liberty then contested that there had been a mistake in identifying CCEL as the contractor and that the contract should be rectified naming CDDL instead.

Liberty attempted to make use of various devices to bring about this change on the issue of rectification for mutual mistake. *Inter alia* Romer J, firstly, considered that the background evidence clearly pointed to the parties intending that the contractor was to be CDDL. He found that L had failed to demonstrate that the naming of CCEL as the contractor in the contractual documentation was a 'misnomer' which was capable of being corrected as a matter of construction. Having regard to the matrix of facts Romer J did not consider that the reference to CCEL could be considered as a mistake. On an objective analysis of the facts there was nothing to demonstrate that the request to have CCEL named in the contract had been mistake. Romer J therfore applied the decision in *Chartbrook Ltd v Persimmon Homes Ltd* [2009] UKHL 38, [2009] 1 AC 1101.

Secondly, Romer J considered that since there was no common continuing intention there had been no mutual mistake and to this degree, following *Daventry*, there was no question of rectification being available. Clearly there had been a mistake in confusing CDDL with CCEL but an objective observer would have concluded that it was the common intention of the parties that the contractor was to be CCEL not CDDL irrespective of which company was actually carrying out the works. The effect therefore was that objectively speaking, there was no mistake.

The principle that there must be some 'outward expression of accord' was stated in *Munt v Beasley* [2006] EWCA Civ 370 to be 'an evidential factor, rather than a strict legal requirement in all cases of rectification' so that it does require the disputed term to be expressly mentioned in the document. While there must be clear evidence for a court to apply rectification, it is possible for the term to be implied provided there is some material evidence that the instrument does not reflect the agreement of the parties. In *Daventry*, Etherton LJ at para 80 considered that the requirements of 'common continuing intention' and 'outward expression of accord' are not separate conditions 'but two sides of the same coin, since an uncommunicated inward intention is irrelevant'. Etherton LJ suggested that Gibson LJ's statement of the requirements for rectification for mutual mistake in *Swainland Builders Ltd v Freehold Properties Ltd* [2002] 2 EGLR 71 can be rephrased as (1) the parties had a common continuing intention, whether or not amounting to an agreement, in respect of a particular matter in the instrument to be rectified; (2) which existed at the time of execution of the instrument sought to be rectified; (3) such common continuing intention to be established objectively, that is to say by reference to what an objective observer would have thought the intentions of the parties to be; and (4) by mistake the instrument did not reflect that common intention. It is suggested that this produces a clearer statement of the requirements needed to establish rectification for mutual mistake.

It follows from the discussions above that if on an objective basis the parties **did** in fact agree that the instrument reflects the intentions of the parties, but one party considers that the meaning of the words has been mistaken, then rectification is unavailable. The point was made by Denning LJ in *Frederick E Rose (London) Ltd* v *William H Pim Jnr & Co Ltd* [1953] 2 QB 450:

> Rectification is concerned with contracts and documents, not with intentions. In order to get rectification it is necessary to show that the parties were in complete agreement on the terms of their contract, but by an error wrote them down wrongly; and in this regard, in order to ascertain the terms of their contract, you do not look into the inner minds of the parties – into their intentions – any more than you do in the formation of any other contract. You look at their outward acts, that is, at what they said or wrote to one another in coming to their agreement, and then compare it with the document which they have signed. If you can predicate with certainty what their contract was, and that it is, by a common mistake, wrongly expressed in the document, then you rectify the document; but nothing less will suffice.

Similarly in *Etablissements George et Paul Levy* v *Adderley Navigation Co. Panama SA (The Olympic Pride)* [1980] 2 Lloyd's Rep 67 Mustill J stated at p 72:

> The prior transaction may consist either of a concluded agreement or of a continuing common intention. In the latter event, the intention must have been objectively manifested. It is the words and acts of the parties demonstrating their intention, not the inward thoughts of the parties, which matter.

Thus in looking for the common intention of the parties the courts are concerned with what, objectively, the intentions of the parties are from the way they have expressed themselves. That is not to say that the parties' subjective intentions are not relevant, they may well be, but only to the extent of assessing what objectively the parties are taken to have intended and which the document failed to give effect. Subjective evidence, however, carries little weight where the prior consensus of the parties is expressed in writing and can be gleaned from the documents.

2. Rectification where the instrument fails to reflect the intention of only one party – unilateral mistake

In relation to common mistake it is important that the issue of rectification relates to the common intention of the parties, not to the individual intention of one of them. In other words, to obtain rectification, a party must be able to demonstrate that there is a literal disparity between what was agreed and what was recorded and that the executed instrument has failed to reflect the intentions of both parties. In relation to unilateral mistake in *A Roberts & Co. Ltd* v *Leicestershire County Council* [1961] 2 All ER 545 it was held that the remedy could be used where a mistaken claimant could show that a term, beneficial to himself, which both parties had intended to be included in the document, had been omitted and that the other party knew of the omission at the time of the document being executed. This latter point has been reaffirmed in *Agip SpA* v *Navigazione Alta Italia SpA* [1984] 1 Lloyd's Rep 353.

The requirements for rectification for unilateral mistake were set out by Buckley LJ in *Thomas Bates Ltd* v *Wyndham's (Lingerie) Ltd* [1981] 1 WLR 505, affirmed in the Court of Appeal in *George Wimpey UK Ltd* v *VIC Construction Ltd* [2005] EWCA Civ 77, in the following terms:

> For this doctrine – that is to say the doctrine of *A Roberts & Co. Ltd* v *Leicestershire County Council* – to apply, I think it must be shown: first, that one party A erroneously believed that the document sought to be rectified contained a particular term or provision, or possibly did not contain a particular term or provision which, mistakenly it did contain; secondly, that the other party B was aware of the omission or the inclusion and that it was due to a mistake on

the part of A; thirdly, that B has omitted to draw the mistake to the notice of A. And I think there must be a fourth element involved, namely, that the mistake must be one calculated to benefit B. If these requirements are satisfied, the court may regard it as inequitable to allow B to resist rectification to give effect to A's intention on the ground that the mistake was not, at the time of the execution of the document, a mutual mistake.

Thus rectification for unilateral mistake will be allowed provided it can be shown that the non-mistaken party (B) knew of the mistake but had not drawn it to the attention of the mistaken party (A), provided that there is some inequitable benefit to B. This knowledge of the non-mistaken party does not necessarily have to be actual knowledge. The conduct of the non-mistaken party could amount to wilfully shutting one's eyes to the mistake, or wilfully and recklessly failing to make those enquiries that an honest, reasonable man would make, as stated by Lightman J in *Rowallan Group Ltd* v *Edgehill Portfolio No. 1 Ltd* [2007] EWHC 32 (Ch), following *George Wimpey UK Ltd* v *VIC Construction Ltd*. In *Riverplate Properties Ltd* v *Pau* it was said that the non-mistaken party B had to be guilty of some sort of 'sharp practice' but this was denied in *Thomas Bates Ltd* v *Wyndham's (Lingerie) Ltd*, where it was stated that all that has to be shown is that B's conduct is inequitable in some way. Broadly speaking, therefore, it has to be shown that B's conduct is unconscionable. Clearly this would arise if B had been guilty of some fraud or misrepresentation, or where the conditions for an estoppel have arisen.

The problem of establishing actual knowledge and unconscionable conduct means that it is not difficult to see that the remedy of rectification with regard to a unilateral mistake is difficult to prove. Thus in *Liberty Mercian Ltd v Cuddy Civil Engineering Ltd* [2013] EWHC 2688, Liberty could not establish rectification for unilateral mistake since there was no evidence that the defendants had either actual knowledge or wilfully shut their eyes to the obvious or wilfully and recklessly failed to make the enquiries which an honest and reasonable person would make so that it had acted in an unconscionable manner.

One final point as regards rectification is that, as with all other equitable remedies, the acquisition by a third party of rights under the written contract or where there has been a lapse of time in applying for the remedy will cause the remedy to be lost.

Refusal of specific performance

If a person refuses to perform their side of the bargain it is open to the other party to apply to a court of equity for a decree of specific performance to compel that person to carry out their contractual obligations. Since this remedy, like the others, was discretionary, the court would refuse to grant such a decree where the common law remedy of damages was regarded as adequate redress, as it very often was, except where the goods could be regarded as unique goods. Specific performance could, however, also be refused where one of the parties has contracted under such a mistake that it would be regarded as inequitable to compel them to carry out their contractual obligations. The effect of this, then, is to prevent a contract being enforced in circumstances where a mistake is insufficient to render the contract void *ab initio* at common law.

For more on specific performance refer to Chapter 17.

In *Webster* v *Cecil* (1861) 30 Beav 62, the plaintiff was offered several plots of land by the defendant for £1,250. Soon after sending the offer the defendant realised that he should have stated the price as £2,250 and informed the plaintiff immediately. Unfortunately his revocation arrived too late as the plaintiff had already accepted the offer. The court refused to give the plaintiff a decree of specific performance since it decided that he must have been aware of the defendant's mistake as he (the defendant) had already refused an offer of £2,000 from the plaintiff.

Mistake as to the nature of the document signed

Objective 6

This category of mistake forms a separate and distinct category of mistake at common law. Cases arising in this type of mistake might occur where a person is induced by a false statement made by some other person to sign a written contract that is fundamentally different from the one they thought they were signing. While the person inducing the signing may well be a party to the contract it might be the case that they are a third party to the contract.

Example

X by some fundamental statement induces Y to sign a guarantee of Y's indebtedness to X's bank, Z. If Z attempts to enforce the guarantee against Y, Y may attempt to avoid liability on the basis of mistake as to the nature of the document signed. It is obvious here that X is not a party to the contract between Y and Z. It is this feature that separates this type of mistake from the others.

See Chapter 8 for L'Estrange v Graucob.

Traditionally this type of mistake was often referred to as ***non est factum***, literally translated as 'it is not my deed'. The rule originated as a limited defence to the proposition that a person was bound by any document signed by that person, as we have seen in ***L'Estrange* v *Graucob*** [1934] 2 KB 394. In fact the rule developed in medieval times when few people could read or write and were thus dependent on others accurately to describe the contents and meaning of a deed. Thus if the terms of a deed were read or explained in such a way that the deed did not in fact represent the true intention of the signor, the signor could escape liability on the basis that they would not have signed had the true situation been revealed to them.

The growth of literacy as educational opportunities increased raised serious doubts as to whether the plea continued to exist. In the nineteenth century, however, the scope of the plea was widened to include persons who had been tricked into signing a document which they would not have signed had they understood its true nature. The scope of the plea thus widened to include persons who were of low intelligence or mentally infirm, as well as blind persons. Persons of full capacity and literacy cannot generally rely on *non est factum*. The modern leading authority on *non est factum* is ***Saunders* v *Anglia Building Society*** (formerly known as ***Gallie* v *Lee***).

Saunders v *Anglia Building Society* [1970] 3 All ER 961

The plaintiff was an elderly widow who had decided to give the title deeds of her house to her nephew, so that he could use the property as security for a loan in order to go into business. The widow made one stipulation, which was that whatever he did she would be allowed to live in the house for the rest of her life. A document was prepared by a friend of the nephew's, Lee, who was a dishonest managing clerk, whereby the property was to be assigned to the nephew. In fact the document prepared by Lee was a deed of conveyance giving effect to a sale of the property to Lee for £3,000, though this sum was never paid. At the time the deed was signed by Mrs Gallie, she had broken her glasses and thus relied on Lee's explanation of the nature of the document. Lee then mortgaged the property to the building society but never repaid any of the mortgage instalments.

On discovering the truth of the matter the plaintiff sought a declaration that the conveyance of the property was void on the ground of *non est factum*. She alleged that she had signed the document under a fundamental mistake as to its nature. She thought that she was signing a deed of gift to her nephew, while what she in fact signed was a deed of conveyance to Lee.

It was held by the House of Lords, affirming the earlier decision of the Court of Appeal, that her plea would fail. While on the face of things, the two documents appear to be very different, the court thought that in assessing whether the nature of the document was different, one had to have regard to the 'object of the exercise'. The object of the exercise in assigning the property to the nephew was to enable him to use it as security to raise money by way of a secured loan. Their Lordships considered that this object would also have been arrived at had Lee acted honestly. There was thus no difference in the nature of the document Mrs Gallie signed and what she thought she was signing.

The case of **Saunders v Anglia Building Society**, however, established that three principles had to be proved before the defence would apply. First, the plea can only rarely be relied upon by a person of full age and capacity; such a person will generally be bound by the document. Generally in order to succeed one has to show that one is signing under some disability, such as illiteracy, blindness or senility. Second, the person relying on the defence has to show that the document signed was different in nature from the one they thought they were signing within the concept of *non est factum* as discussed above. Lastly, the person attempting to rely on the defence has to show that they were not careless in signing and that they took all reasonable precautions to ascertain the contents and significance of the document to be signed.

It has to be stated that *non est factum* is rarely pleaded and even more rarely is it successful. For an example, see **Lloyds Bank plc v Waterhouse** [1991] Fam Law 23.

Summary

Mistake at common law

- A contract is void *ab initio* if the mistake was fundamental to the contract.

Common initial mistake

- Where the parties enter a contract wrongly believing that the subject exists.
- If the subject has never existed or ceased to exist prior to the entering into of the contract then no contract can arise and therefore any agreement entered into is void *ab initio*.

Mistake as to the existence of the subject matter (res extincta)

- Occurs where, unknown to both the parties, the subject matter of the contract had ceased to exist at the time the contract was entered into. See **Couturier v Hastie** – fermenting corn (NB: this case was based on lack of consideration and not mistake).

Mistake as to title (res sua)

Definition:

- '. . . unknown to the parties, the buyer is already the owner of that which the seller purports to sell to him' (**Bell v Lever Bros**).
- Rescission allowed for rental of a fishery owned by the lessee (**Cooper v Phibbs**).

Mistake as to the quality of the subject matter of the contract

- This means mistake as to the bargaining.
- For mistake as to the quality to arise, the mistake must be as to a fundamental assumption on which the contract was based and must be a mistake of both parties (***Bell v Lever Brothers***; ***Leaf v International Galleries***; ***Associated Japanese Bank (International) Ltd v Crédit du Nord SA***).

Consensus mistake

- Happens where there is a mistake as to the terms of the contract.
- Stops an agreement from arising as there is a lack of *consensus ad idem*.
- The two basic categories are (i) mutual and (ii) unilateral mistakes.

Mutual mistake

- Occurs where the parties are at cross-purposes, e.g. two ships with the same name (***Raffles v Wichelhaus***).
- To establish a mutual mistake there must be such a degree of ambiguity that it is impossible, on applying the objective test of a reasonable man, that the parties intended to be bound by one set of terms or the other.

Unilateral mistake

- This test is subjective and *not* objective. One party is actually aware of the other party's mistake.
- There must be a fundamental mistake as to the nature of the promise made by the other party – a mistake as to quality will not suffice.
- The mistake must induce the other party to enter into the contract.
- The person seeking to avoid the contract has to rebut the presumption.
- Three types of unilateral mistake:

  1 Mistake as to the terms of the contract:
   - Where the offeror is aware that the acceptor is fundamentally mistaken as to the nature of the promise contained in the offer, e.g. sale of hareskins – per lb or per skin? (***Hartog v Colin and Shields***).
  2 Mistake as to the identity of the person contracted with:
   - A contract may become a nullity where a party is mistaken as to the identity of the person contracted with and the other party is aware of that mistake. ***Shogun Finance Ltd v Hudson***.
   - In order to prove unilateral mistake as to identity, the person alleging mistake must prove each of the following:
     (a) an intention to deal with some other person;
     (b) that the other party knew of this intention;
     (c) that the identity was of fundamental importance;
     (d) that reasonable steps had been taken to verify the identity.
   - He has to show that there was *an intention to deal with some other person* than the one with whom he appears to have made the contract (***King's Norton Metal Co. Ltd v Edridge, Merrett & Co. Ltd***).

    – The mistaken party must prove that the other party was aware of the above intention.

    – Trading with a person at a distance:

      (a) The correct identity of the parties is crucial when trading at a distance.

      (b) Rogue misleading as to his identity those who intend to deal with some other person may allow for recovery (***Cundy* v *Lindsay***; contrast with ***King's Norton Metal Co. Ltd* v *Edridge, Merrett & Co. Ltd***).

    – Trading with a person face to face:

    – Presumption – the mistaken party intends to deal with the person in front of them whoever he is and very strong evidence indeed is required to rebut the presumption (***Phillips* v *Brooks Ltd*; *Shogun Finance Ltd* v *Hudson***).

3 Mistake as to the nature of the document signed:

    – *non est factum*, 'it is not my deed'. Limited defence for a person who was bound, having signed a document.

    – ***Saunders* v *Anglia Building Society***.

Mistake in equity

● Mistake in equity renders a contract voidable (***Solle* v *Butcher***).

● This decision is thought to be wrong in law (***Great Peace Shipping Ltd* v *Tsavliris Salvage (International) Ltd***).

Further reading

Atiyah, '*Couturier* v *Hastie* and the Sale of Non-Existent Goods' (1957) 78 *Law Quarterly Review* 340

Beatson, Burrows and Cartwright, *Anson's Law of Contract*, 30th edn (Oxford University Press, 2016)

Cartwright, '*Solle* v *Butcher* and the Doctrine of Mistake in Contract' (1987) 103 *Law Quarterly Review* 594

Dabbs, 'The Risk of Mistake in Contract' (2002) 152 *New Law Journal* 1654

Furmston, *Cheshire, Fifoot and Furmston's Law of Contract*, 16th edn (Oxford University Press, 2012)

Hare, 'Identity Mistakes: A Lost Opportunity' (2004) 67 *Modern Law Review* 993

Kramer, 'Common Mistake and the Abolition of the Equitable Doctrine' [2003] *Student Law Review*, Spring

McLauchlan, 'Mistake of Identity and Contract Formation' (2005) 21 *Journal of Contract Law* 1

McLauchlan, 'The "Drastic" Remedy of Rectification for Unilateral Mistake' (2008) 124 *Law Quarterly Review* 608

McLauchlan, 'Commonsense Principles of Interpretation and Rectification?' (2010) 126 *Law Quarterly Review* 8

Macmillan, 'How Temptation Led to Mistake: An Explanation of *Bell* v *Lever Bros Ltd*' (2003) 119 *Law Quarterly Review* 625

Macmillan, 'Mistake as to Identity Clarified?' (2004) 120 *Law Quarterly Review* 369

Macmillan, 'Rogues, Swindlers and Cheats: The Development of Mistake of Identity in English Contract Law' [2005] *Cambridge Law Journal* 711

Macmillan, *Mistakes in Contract Law* (Hart Publishing, 2010)

Pawlowski, 'Common Mistake: *Law* v *Equity*' (2002) 152 *New Law Journal* 132

Phang, 'Common Mistake in English Law: The Proposed Merger of Common Law and Equity' (1990) 9 *Legal Studies* 291

Phang, 'Mistake in Contract Law – Two Recent Cases' [2002] *Cambridge Law Journal* 272

Phang, 'Controversy in Common Mistake' (2003) *Conveyancer and Property Lawyer* 247

Smith, 'Rectification of Contracts for Common Mistake, *Joscelyne* v *Nissen* and Subjective States of Mind' (2007) *Law Quarterly Review* 116

Smith and Atiyah, *Atiyah's Introduction to the Law of Contract*, 6th edn (Oxford University Press, 2006)

Tettenborn, 'Agreements, Common Mistake and the Purpose of Contract' (2011) 27 *Journal of Contract Law* 91

Peel, Treitel *Law of Contract*, 14th edn (Sweet and Maxwell, 2015)

11

Duress, undue influence and inequality of bargaining power

Objectives

After reading this chapter you should be able to:

1. Understand and explain the common law doctrine of duress.

2. Understand and explain the equitable doctrine of undue influence.

3. Recognise the circumstances in which actual undue influence arises and identify its different categories.

4. Understand the requirement of 'manifest' disadvantage and transactions 'calling for an explanation'.

5. Explain the effect of undue influence on third parties and understand how creditors avoid being fixed with constructive notice of the principal debtor's misrepresentations.

6. Know and understand the effects of undue influence on a contract.

7. Understand Lord Denning's wider concept of equitable intervention where there is inequality of bargaining power.

Introduction

The essence of an agreement and hence a legally binding contract is founded upon the parties giving their free consent to be bound by the terms of the agreement. It follows that where a party is coerced into a contract by threats or undue pressure that stifles the principle of free consent, that individual should not be bound by that contract. Both the common law and equity concurred in this fact, the common law through its strict doctrine of **duress** and equity through the doctrine of **undue influence**, which had a wider sphere of operation than duress. Mere inequality of bargaining power is, as a general rule, insufficient to vitiate a contract entered into, though in more recent years Lord Denning attempted to develop a general concept under this heading whereby relief would be given to an individual who had not entered into a contract as a free agent. Finally, statute has intervened to protect individuals in certain types of contracts.

The common law doctrine of duress

The early doctrine

Objective
1

Duress at common law relates to contracts induced by violence or the threat of violence. The act or threatened act must be illegal in that it may amount to either a tort or a crime. It follows that if the threatened act is one which would otherwise be lawful then this cannot amount to duress (as, for example, a threat of lawful imprisonment as in **Williams v Bayley** (1866) LR 1 HL 200). The effect of duress at common law is to render the contract voidable.

At common law it was always considered that duress had to be directed against the person and that a threat to goods could not amount to duress. It follows that in **Skeate v Beale** (1840) 11 A & E 983, a promise given in return for goods that had been unlawfully detained was held to be valid. This principle has been criticised, however, and in **Maskell v Horner** [1915] 3 KB 106 it was held that money that had been paid in order to recover goods unlawfully detained could itself be recovered on the basis of money had and received under the law of restitution.

The notion of duress not including duress to goods has also been the subject of a great deal of criticism in more recent years when there has arisen a wider concept of economic duress. An early example of this being recognised was the case of **D & C Builders Ltd v Rees** [1966] 2 QB 617 which has already been examined in the context of sufficiency of consideration. In that case Lord Denning considered that the actions of the wife had amounted to improper pressure in order to compel the building firm to accept a sum substantially less than the one they were truly owed. In such a situation Lord Denning refused to exercise estoppel because of the wife's inequitable actions since she knew the builders needed the money. The case thus amounted to a crude but crucial step towards the development of the wider doctrine of economic duress.

Economic duress

A more formal doctrine of economic duress began to emerge in the case of *Occidental Worldwide Investment Corporation v Skibs A/S Avanti, The Sibeon and The Sibotre*.

Occidental Worldwide Investment Corporation v Skibs A/S Avanti, The Sibeon and The Sibotre [1976] 1 Lloyd's Rep 293

There was a worldwide recession in the shipping industry with the result that the charter rates had fallen substantially. The charterers of two ships renegotiated the rates of the charters, having warned the owners that they would become insolvent unless this was done, although it was shown that the existing rates would probably not have had this effect on the charterers. They also stated that should action be taken against them for breach of contract no benefit would accrue to the owners since they, the charterers, had insignificant assets against which a claim could be made. The charterers were also cognisant of the fact that, should the charterers break their contract, the owners would be highly unlikely to be able to re-charter the vessels given the depth of the recession. This would result in the ships being laid up and the owners themselves would probably be forced into liquidation. This was a grossly pessimistic outlook, but nevertheless the defendants, the owners, agreed to reduce their hire rates. Later they withdrew both ships from the charters. The charterers sued claiming that the contract had been wrongly repudiated, while the owners claimed that they had renegotiated the charters only because of the duress placed upon them by the charterers. It was held that the owners' claim for duress would fail. Kerr J rejected the early doctrine of duress that was based simply on a threat of physical violence. He stated:

> I do not think that English law is as limited . . . For instance, if I should be compelled to sign a lease or some other contract for a nominal but legally sufficient consideration under an imminent threat of having my house burnt down or a valuable picture slashed, though without any threat of physical violence to anyone, I do not think that the law would uphold the agreement. I think that a plea of coercion or compulsion would be available in such cases . . .

In this statement Kerr J unlocked the door to the development of a notion of economic duress, albeit that he had not pushed the door wide open. He was cautious, stating that mere commercial pressure was inadequate to set up the defence. He considered that there had to be such a degree of coercion of will that the other party was deprived of their ability freely to consent. How was this test to be satisfied? Kerr J identified two questions that had to be asked before the test could be satisfied. First, did the victim protest at the time of the demand and, second, did the victim regard the transaction as closed or did they intend to repudiate the new agreement?

Kerr J stated thus:

> But even assuming, as I think, that our law is open to further development in relation to contracts concluded under some form of compulsion not amounting to duress to the person, the court must in every case at least be satisfied that the consent of the other party was overborne by compulsion so as to deprive him of any *animus contrahendi*. This would depend on the facts of each case. One relevant factor would be whether the party relying on the duress made any protest at the time or shortly thereafter. Another would be to consider whether or not he treated the settlement as closing the transaction in question and as binding upon him, or whether he made it clear that he regarded the position as still open . . . the facts of the present case fall a long way short of the test which would in law be required to make good a defence of compulsion or duress. Believing the statements about the charterers' financial state . . . [the owners] made no protest about having to conclude [the contract] . . . [the owners] regarded the agreement then reached as binding and sought to uphold it in the subsequent arbitration . . . [they were] acting under great pressure, but only commercial pressure, and not under anything which could in law be regarded as a coercion of will so as to vitiate consent. I therefore hold that the plea of duress fails.

The tests propounded by Kerr J were considered more fully in the following case.

North Ocean Shipping Co. Ltd v Hyundai Construction Co. Ltd, The Atlantic Baron [1979] QB 705

The facts of the case were that the defendants had agreed to build a tanker for the plaintiffs at a price to be payable in five instalments in dollars. The plaintiffs paid the first instalment but then the dollar suffered a 10 per cent drop in the international money market. The defendants demanded a 10 per cent increase in the contract price, stating that they would not complete the ship unless this was forthcoming. At the time the defendants were not aware that this threat was particularly damaging to the plaintiffs since they had an agreement to charter the ship when it was completed. The plaintiffs agreed to pay the extra money despite the fact that, as they pointed out to the defendants, they were not legally obliged to do so. Eventually all four of the further instalments were paid, increased by 10 per cent, and the plaintiffs took delivery of the ship. Eight months later the plaintiffs sought to recover the extra moneys paid, but failed in their action. While Mocatta J considered that this was a case of economic duress, he held that they would be unable to recover since their delay in seeking the recovery of the extra moneys paid amounted to affirmation of the contract, even if they had no intention of affirming the contract as such.

In *Barton v Armstrong* [1976] AC 104, Lord Wilberforce and Lord Simon of Glaisdale said at 121:

> in life . . . many acts are done under pressure, sometimes overwhelming pressure, so that one can say that the actor had no choice but to act. Absence of choice in this sense does not negate consent in law: for this the pressure must be one of a kind which the law does not regard as legitimate.

This statement was approved of by Lord Scarman in the case of *Pao On v Lau Yiu Long* [1979] 3 All ER 65 in which Lord Scarman identified that economic duress required two elements: firstly, pressure amounting to 'coercion of will that vitiates consent' and secondly, pressure or threat that is illegitimate. To a large degree, this analysis affirms the analysis of Kerr J in *The Sibeon and The Sibotre*. More recently in *D S N D Subsea Ltd (formerly D S N D Oceantech Ltd) v Petroleum Geo Services ASA* [2000] BLR 530 Dyson J stated at 131:

> The ingredients of actionable duress are that there must be pressure, (a) whose practical effect is that there is compulsion on, or a lack of practical choice for, the victim, (b) which is illegitimate, and (c) which is a significant cause inducing the claimant to enter into the contract.

It is useful to examine these two elements in more detail.

Pressure amounting to coercion of will

With regard to the matter of coercion of will Lord Scarman stated:

> there is nothing contrary to principle in recognising economic duress as a factor which may render a contract voidable provided always that the basis of such recognition is that it must amount to a coercion of will, which vitiates consent. It must be shown that the payment made on the contract entered into was not a voluntary act.

Further, in assessing whether or not a coercion of will had taken place, he stated:

> it is material to inquire whether the person alleged to have been coerced did or did not protest; whether, at the time he was allegedly coerced into making a contract, he did or did not have an alternative course open to him such as an adequate legal remedy; whether he was independently advised; and whether, after entering the contract, he took steps to avoid it.

The judgement presents a significant problem when it talks in terms of the payment made or the contract entered into 'not [being] a voluntary act'. Quite clearly if one does agree to a situation like this, then such an act must of necessity be a voluntary act since the party coerced must have formed an intention to enter the situation. Scarman LJ's statement is thus an oversimplification and fails to address this aspect of his judgement in enough detail. He would have done better to express it not as a voluntary act but as a voluntary submission compelled by the fact of no other available course of action.

The notion that economic duress is founded upon the vitiation of consent so that the entry into the agreement is involuntary has been strongly criticised, principally because the victims of duress are fully aware that they are entering into an agreement and of course in doing so intentionally submit to the transaction. The question arose in the case of *Universe Tankships Inc. of Monrovia v International Transport Workers' Federation (The Universe Sentinel)* [1983] 1 AC 366 where both Lord Scarman and Lord Diplock recognised the criticism and concluded that economic duress may arise where there is an intentional submission to the inevitable and that the pressure used to secure such submission was illegitimate in that there was a suppression of the will of the victim. Since *The Universe Sentinel* the coercion of will requirement has been re-adjusted in terms of the victim having 'no realistic choice' but to submit to the agreement in a number of subsequent cases. The position can be seen in *Atlas Express Ltd v Kafco (Importers and Distributors) Ltd* [1989] 1 Al ER 641.

Atlas Express Ltd v Kafco (Importers and Distributors) Ltd [1989] 1 All ER 641

The facts of this case were that the plaintiffs, a firm of road hauliers, contracted with the defendants to deliver cartons of basketware to branches of Woolworths throughout the United Kingdom. Prior to entering into the contract a manager of the plaintiffs, having inspected the cartons, estimated that each load would comprise between 400 and 600 cartons. On this basis he agreed a contract rate of £1.10 per carton. The first load fell well below his estimations, comprising only 200 cartons. The manager then went back to the defendants and stated that his firm would be unable to transport any more loads unless the defendants agreed to a minimum price of £440 per load. The defendants were a small concern that were heavily dependent on their contract with Woolworths and were unable to find another carrier willing to transport their goods, and so they reluctantly agreed to pay the minimum charge. The defendants later refused to pay the minimum charge and when sued claimed economic duress as a defence. It was held that where a defendant had no alternative but to accept revised terms that were detrimental to its interests, this amounted to economic duress that vitiated the apparent consent to the renegotiated terms.

Similarly in *Adam Opel GmbH v Mitras Automotive (UK) Ltd* [2007] EWHC 3205 (QB) where there was a threat to stop supplying automotive components unless an increased price was paid amounted to duress on the basis that there were no alternative suppliers. The claimants therefore had no realistic choice in the matter other than close down the production line.

Pressure or threat that is illegitimate

The second requirement for economic duress set out in *Pao On v Lau Yiu Long* is that the pressure or threat must be illegitimate. One of the difficulties here is being able to test the difference between legitimate and illegitimate pressure and where the line is drawn between the two.

Universe Tankships Inc. of Monrovia v International Transport Workers' Federation (The Universe Sentinel) [1983] 1 AC 366

In this case, the plaintiff's vessel, *The Universe Sentinel* was 'blacked' by the defendant trade union. The 'blacking' operated as an instruction to the tugmen not to operate their tugs to assist and manoeuvre the vessel, which was in breach of their contract of employment. The defendants demanded that the plaintiffs pay $80,000 to the crew by way of back-pay and also contribute $6,840 to the union's welfare fund. These monies were paid by the defendants in order to release their vessel but then sought to recover the money paid to the welfare fund. The defendants conceded that the money was paid under economic duress but maintained that they were entitled to retain the money as they enjoyed immunity conferred by the Trade Union and Labour Relations Act 1974 s 13.

In arriving at its decision the House of Lords recognised the difficulties that can arise in testing the difference between illegitimate and legitimate pressure. A majority of the House of Lords held that the defendants did not enjoy the immunity that was asserted and therefore the money paid to the welfare fund was recoverable. It was considered that there was a distinction to be made between commercial pressure and economic duress arising in the field of industrial relations. Thus Lord Diplock stated:

> Commercial pressure, in some degree, exists wherever one party to a commercial transaction is in a stronger bargaining position than the other party. It is not, however, in my view, necessary, nor would it be appropriate in the instant appeal, to enter into the general question of the kinds of circumstances, if any, in which commercial pressure, even though it amounts to a coercion of the will of a party in the weaker bargaining position, may be treated as legitimate and, accordingly, as not giving rise to any legal right of redress. In the instant appeal the economic duress complained of was exercised in the field of industrial relations to which very special considerations apply.

The majority of their Lordships considered that the Trade Union and Labour Relations Act 1974 was confined to bestowing immunity from liability in tort and did not provide immunity in any other type of action. Their Lordships considered that economic duress to induce another person to part with property or money is not a tort per se within the ambit of the Act. It was considered that economic duress gives rise to an action for restitution of property or money exacted under the duress and the right to avoid the contract that the claimant had been induced into. Their Lordships considered that extending the concept of economic duress and the restitutionary remedy flowing from it into the realm of industrial relations was not appropriate. It was stated that 'public policy requires that the line should be drawn between what kind of commercial pressure by a trade union upon an employer in the field of industrial relations ought to be treated as legitimised despite the fact that the will of the employer is thereby coerced, and what kind of commercial pressure in that field does amount to economic duress that entitles the employer victim to restitutionary remedies' (per Lord Diplock). The effect therefore was that the legislations did not 'legitimise' the actions of the trade union so that the pressure exercised fell within the realms of economic duress so that the claimant was able to avoid the contract and recover the money paid.

The minority in the House of Lords (Scarman LJ and Brandon LJ) considered that the union did enjoy immunity and protection by the Trade Union and Labour Relations Act 1974; however, they considered that even a lawful threat could amount to being illegitimate if it was used for an illegitimate purpose, such as blackmail.

Lord Scarman stated at 400 and 401:

> . . . in life, including the life of commerce and finance, many acts are done 'under pressure, sometimes overwhelming pressure': but they are not necessarily done under duress. That depends on whether the circumstances are such that the law regards the pressure as legitimate.
>
> In determining what is legitimate two matters may have to be considered. The first is as to the nature of the pressure. In many cases this will be decisive, though not in every case and so the second question may have to be considered, namely, the nature of the demand which the pressure is applied to support.
>
> The origin of the doctrine of duress in threats to life or limb, or to property, suggests strongly that the law regards the threat of unlawful action as illegitimate, whatever the demand. Duress can, of course, exist even if the threat is one of lawful action: whether it does so depends upon the nature of the demand. Blackmail is often a demand supported by a threat to do what is lawful, e.g. to report criminal conduct to the police. In many cases, therefore, 'What [one] has to justify is not the threat, but the demand . . . ': see per Lord Atkin in *Thorne v Motor Trade Association* [1937] AC 797, 806.

Lord Scarman therefore identified two elements in deciding the legitimacy or otherwise of the demand – 'the nature of the pressure', which will often be decisive, but failing that 'the nature of the demand'. The effect therefore is that whilst action which is unlawful will clearly be illegitimate, action which is lawful does not necessarily indicate that the action is legitimate, as can be seen from Lord Scarman's example in the case of blackmail.

In *Alec Lobb (Garages) Ltd* v *Total Oil Great Britain Ltd* [1983] 1 WLR 87 on the other hand, the Court of Appeal stated that no duress could arise where legitimate rights were threatened, however, these views of the Court of Appeal have now given way to those of the House of Lords and this seems to be confirmed in the case of *CTN Cash and Carry Ltd* v *Gallaher Ltd* [1994] 4 All ER 714, where the Court of Appeal confirmed that a lawful act coupled with a demand for payment may amount to economic duress. The court, however, qualified this view by stating that it would be difficult, though not impossible, to maintain such a claim in the context of two trading companies dealing at arm's length in a commercial transaction, particularly if the party making the threat was acting in the bona fide belief that its demand was valid and legitimate. The court considered that the development of the so-called lawful act duress in pursuing a bona fide claim in a commercial context would create an undesirable level of uncertainty in the commercial bargaining environment.

The observations of Lord Scarman were also considered in the case of *R* v *HM Attorney-General for England and Wales* [2003] UKPC 22. In this case, a former member of the SAS alleged that he had been subject to duress when signing a contract preventing him from disclosing information relating to the work of the United Kingdom Special Forces after he left the SAS. He alleged that the duress arose when he had been told that if he refused to sign the contract, he would be returned to his old regiment. It was held that the soldier had not been subject to duress since the Crown was entitled to transfer a member of the SAS to another unit and thus the threat of returning him to his old regiment had been lawful. Furthermore, the Privy Council found that the Ministry of Defence had acted legitimately in introducing confidentiality contracts and that it was entitled to regard anyone unwilling to accept the confidentiality obligation as unsuitable for a role in the SAS so that the demand to sign the contract supported by the threat of a return to the individual's old regiment could be justified.

An example of a case involving illegitimate pressure is that of *Vantage Navigation Corporation* v *Suhail and Saud Bahawn Building Materials LLC (The Alev)*.

Vantage Navigation Corporation v Suhail and Saud Bahawn Building Materials LLC (The Alev) [1989] 1 Lloyd's Rep 138

The facts of the case were that a ship, *The Alev*, was chartered to carry a cargo of steel. The defendants had an interest in the cargo. The charterers of the ship in fact had substantial financial problems, with the result that they defaulted in paying instalments under the terms of the charterparty to the shipowners, the plaintiffs. This default rendered the plaintiffs, by virtue of the bill of lading, liable to carry the cargo to its destination at considerable loss to themselves. In order to offset some of the losses, the plaintiffs entered into negotiations with the defendants, with the result that a contract was entered into whereby the defendants would bear the port costs (together with some other costs) and agreed not to detain or arrest the ship while it was in port. This agreement was reached in part by the plaintiffs threatening not to transport the cargo. In fact, when the ship entered port and began unloading its cargo, the defendants arrested the ship and, in defence to a claim for breach of contract by the plaintiffs, pleaded economic duress. It was held that the contract could be avoided by the defendants on the basis of economic duress. The court held that the threat to refuse to transport the cargo was illegal, that the plaintiffs knew this and, as a result, the contract was voidable.

The grounds for economic duress have continued to be picked over and analysed in a number of subsequent cases, thus in *Carillion Construction Ltd* v *Felix (UK) Ltd* [2001]

BLR 1 it was held that the threats to withhold deliveries, when under a contractual duty to prevent delays, amounted to illegitimate pressure and therefore to economic duress.

Similarly the principles were considered again in *Kolmar Group AG v Traxpo Enterprises Pvt Ltd* [2010] EWHC 113 where the contract involved the purchase of methanol at an agreed price by Kolmar from Traxpo. Kolmar then intended to sell the methanol on to an important customer. Traxpo then refused to supply the quantity that it had contracted to deliver at the agreed price. Kolmar was as a result placed in a position in which it had no choice but to submit to Traxpo's demands for further payment and then hope to claim redress at a later date. The court found that Kolmar had only agreed to increase the price to be paid and reduce the amount under the contract as a result of illegitimate pressure amounting to economic duress by Traxpo. This left Kolmar with no practical choice but to agree to pay the increased price for such methanol as it did eventually receive. The court in arriving at its decision applied principles set out in *D S N D Subsea Ltd (formerly D S N D Oceantech Ltd) v Petroleum Geo Services ASA* [2000] BLR 530 where Dyson J stated at 131:

> In determining whether there has been illegitimate pressure, the court takes into account a range of factors. These include whether there has been an actual or threatened breach of contract; whether the person allegedly exerting the pressure has acted in good or bad faith; whether the victim had any realistic practical alternative but to submit to the pressure; whether the victim protested at the time; and whether he affirmed and sought to rely on the contract. These are all relevant factors. Illegitimate pressure must be distinguished from the rough and tumble of the pressures of normal commercial bargaining

The principles were again demonstrated in *Progress Bulk Carriers Ltd v Tube City IMS LLC (The Cenk Kaptanoglu)* [2012] EWHC 273 (Comm). It was held that the actions of the appellant that was in repudiatory breach could amount to illegitimate pressure despite the fact that the actions were not in themselves illegal. In that case the appellant, Progress Bulk Carriers Ltd, a shipowner ('P') appealed against a decision of arbitrators that a settlement agreement between the parties was voidable for duress because P's conduct amounted to the illegitimate pressure required to establish duress in law. P chartered its vessel to Tube City IMS LLC, the respondent ('T'), in order to transport a cargo from the US to China. The charter did not give any right to substitute the vessel for another but nevertheless P fixed the vessel to another charterer without informing T. P was therefore in repudiatory breach of the charter; however, T did not accept that breach as terminating the contract. P conceded that it had made a mistake and said that it would find an alternative vessel and would compensate T for all damages resulting from its failure to provide the contracted vessel. T accepted a substitute vessel with a discount on the freight rate but sought to reserve its rights in respect of all claims for damage arising out of breach of the charter. T's sale contract was amended with a reduced price for the cargo and a later shipment date. P then made a 'take it or leave it' offer requiring acceptance of the vessel with the reduction of the freight rate but with T's agreement to waive all claims for loss and damage. T accepted that arrangement under protest.

P argued that T had failed to mitigate by not going into the market and obtain another vessel. The arbitrators found that there was no failure to mitigate since T was assured that a new vessel would be found and that T was entitled to believe a new vessel would be forthcoming but as the days passed they were increasingly driven into a corner. When a substitute vessel was found, T had no choice but to accept the vessel on a full and final, take it or leave it offer so that T's agreement to waive its claims was procured by economic duress.

The issue on appeal was whether P's conduct amounted to the illegitimate pressure required to establish duress. P submitted that economic duress only operated if the victim was subjected to pressure by unlawful action; alternatively, if conduct which was lawful could amount to the requisite illegitimate pressure, the bar had to be set very high and required conduct on a par with that which the law expressly recognised as illegal or criminal, and that the facts found by the arbitrators could not amount to 'illegitimate pressure'.

The court dismissed P's appeal. Whilst the arbitrators exonerated P from any illegal or criminal conduct, they found that P was in repudiatory breach of the charter. The arbitrators found that it was not legitimate for P to produce the 'take it or leave it' offer, having put T into the position it was in by reason of its own breach and subsequent conduct. Referring to *Pao On v Lau Yiu Long* [1979] 3 All ER 65, *Universe Tankships Inc. of Monrovia v International Transport Workers Federation (The Universe Sentinel)* [1983] J 1 AC 366 and considering the width of the doctrine of economic duress in *CTN Cash and Carry Ltd v Gallaher Ltd* [1994] 4 All ER 714, the Court of Appeal stated that it was clear from the authorities that 'illegitimate pressure' could be constituted by conduct which was not in itself unlawful, although it would be an unusual case in such a circumstance, particularly in the case of two parties dealing at arm's length in a commercial environment. The court stated that a past unlawful act, as well as a threat of a future unlawful act could, in appropriate circumstances, amount to 'illegitimate pressure'.

The court considered that P's submissions overlooked the fact that its repudiatory breach was the root cause of the problem and that its continuing conduct was designed to put T in a position where it had no option but to accept the settlement agreement in order to ship the cargo to China and avoid further losses on the sale contract to the Chinese receiver. The pressure created by P in its demand for a waiver of rights by T had to be seen in the light of its repudiatory breach and in the light of its subsequent conduct, including its refusal to comply with the assurances it had previously given about providing a substitute vessel and paying full compensation in respect of that breach.

A further consideration in determining whether a threatened breach of contract is illegitimate is the presence or otherwise of bad faith. This was not a relevant matter in *The Atlantic Baron* and in *The Sibeon and The Sibotre* Kerr J did not consider that bad faith as relevant at all. In *Huyton SA v Peter Cremer GmbH & C0* [1999] 1 Lloyd's Rep 620, it was suggested that bad faith ought to be a pre-condition to relief. Mance J, however, would not go that far stating:

> The law will of course be cautious about re-opening an apparent compromise made in good faith on both sides . . . on the other hand, [it is] difficult to accept that illegitimate pressure applied by a party who believes bona fide in his case could never give grounds for relief against an apparent compromise

Whilst it might be argued that bad faith is not an essential ingredient and no more than a factor that could make a court more likely to find that a party's conduct is illegitimate, in *Kolmar* Clarke J qualified this, stating:

> a threat to break a contract will generally be regarded as illegitimate, particularly where the defendant must know that it would be in breach of contract if the threat were implemented

This appears to represent the current state of the law, though there is no clear position as to the relevance of good or bad faith other than the general principle that English law does not distinguish between the two in the context of a breach of contract.

The protestations of the victim?

Another matter that needs to be considered in the context of economic duress is the question of the protestations of the victim. In the case of *North Ocean Shipping Co. Ltd* v

Hyundai Construction Co. Ltd, The Atlantic Baron [1979] QB 705 whilst the judgement of Mocatta J undoubtedly gave additional support to the test propounded by Kerr J for a doctrine of economic duress, the judgement also produced a serious deficiency in the concept of economic duress as stated by Kerr J. The problem is that the victim was placed on the horns of a dilemma. If the victim protests too vehemently, the other party will walk away from the contract, leaving the victim economically disadvantaged, despite their right to sue for breach of contract. A mild protest, however, may be read by the courts as not being sufficient to repudiate the contract and will be regarded as affirmation of the contract. Further if the victim fails to refute the contract quickly they will be regarded as having affirmed the contract and will be bound by it. In *The Atlantic Baron* case itself, the eight months delay by the plaintiff in seeking to recover the monies paid was regarded as fatal to their claim for economic duress as this was regarded as an affirmation of the contract.

The difficulties as regards the actions of the innocent party were recognised in the case of *Kolmar Group AG v Traxpo Enterprises Pvt Ltd* [2010] EWHC 113 where Clarke J stated that it was established that

> ... the presence, or absence, of protest, may be of some relevance when considering whether the threat had coercive effect. But, even the total absence of protest does not mean that the payment was voluntary.

In *DSND Subsea*, however, the fact that there were no protestations by the victim clearly had a bearing on the decision and as such it is difficult to envisage a claim for economic duress being successfully pleaded without the victim demonstrating that they were being subject to duress by way of some degree of protest. The timing of this depends on the circumstances of the case though there has to be some degree of immediacy. As we have seen in *The Atlantic Baron* eight months was too long, though in *Borelli v Ting* [2010] UKPC 21 a claim for economic duress was upheld some years after the compelling event. One further point to be noted in this context is whether the duress is of a continuing nature as in *Antonio v Antonio* [2010] EWHC 1199 (QB). In this case, Mrs Antonio had a valuable business and was in the process of separating from her husband. Before they totally split up, her husband placed pressure on his wife to enter into a shareholders agreement so that they would be joint owners of the business. Threats and intimidation continued for two years when the husband violently assaulted Mrs Antonio. Mrs Antonio then issued proceedings to claim that she had entered into the agreement under duress. It was held that Mrs Antonio's principal reason for entering into the agreement was the threats and intimidation at the hands of her husband and that she was otherwise reluctant, which was apparent to all those present at the meeting in which she agreed to enter into the agreement. The fact that two years had elapsed following the date on which she had entered into the agreement did not mean that she had affirmed the contract, as the duress had continued during that time.

Causation

The party asserting duress carries the burden of proving causation, and must prove that the duress '... has constituted a significant cause inducing the plaintiff to enter into the relevant contract'; per Goff LJ in *Dimskal Shipping Co SA v International Transport Workers Federation (The Evia Luck)* [1992] 2 AC 152 at 165 affirming the comments of Lord Wilberforce and Lord Simon in *Barton v Armstrong* [1976] AC 104. The position was also summed up by Mance J in *Huyton SA v Peter Cremer GmbH & CO* [1999] 1 Lloyd's Rep 620 in the following terms:

> The minimum basic test of subjective causation in economic duress ought, it appears to me, to be a 'but for' test. The illegitimate pressure must have been such as actually caused

the making of the agreement, in the sense that it would not otherwise have been made either at all or, at least, in the terms in which it was made. In that sense, the pressure must have been decisive or clinching.

The party alleging the economic duress is thus therefore required to prove that he would not have entered into the contract but for (the 'but for' test) the improper or illegitimate pressure place upon him.

Conclusion

In *Lupofresh Limited* v *Sapporo Breweries Limited (A company incorporated under the laws of Japan)* [2013] EWCA Civ 948, Tomlinson LJ stated, 'economic duress is an emerging doctrine, the bounds of which can by no means be regarded as yet settled'. As has no doubt become apparent, it is clear that the law as regards economic duress is very uncertain and this probably arises because the boundaries of the doctrine are still being formed. As the cases indicate, the doctrine is well on the way to developing some established principles but there is still some way to go. The law has moved on from the initial requirements of only having to prove a suppression of will and voluntary consent to the transaction by the victim, however, the law is still in an unsatisfactory state. As Tomlinson LJ indicates, the truth of the matter is that the doctrine of economic duress is still evolving and is some way off being formulated into a hard set of principles.

The effects of duress

It should be noted that duress and economic duress render a contract voidable and as such the proper remedy is rescission, this being affirmed in *The Universe Sentinel*. As already seen in misrepresentation, this remedy may be lost by lapse of time, the intervention of third-party rights and by affirmation, as seen in *The Atlantic Baron*, above. In order for rescission to be available, *restitutio in integrum* or counter-restitution must be available. It is not available if it is no longer possible to restore the parties to substantially the same positions they were in before the contract was made. This principle was affirmed in *Halpern* v *Halpern* [2007]: the parties had been engaged in a dispute over an inheritance. This was then settled on the basis of a compromise agreement. When the claimants sought damages for breach of this agreement, the defendants alleged that it had been entered into under duress. Certain documents had been destroyed as part of the compromise agreement. The High Court held that since these documents could not be restored to the claimants, the right to rescind the agreement for duress had been lost. In the Court of Appeal a more flexible approach was taken. The court noted that in a related context (*Erlanger* v *New Sombrero Phosphate Co* [1873]) the House of Lords had held that the courts may do *'what is practically just, though it cannot restore the parties precisely to the state they were in before the contract'*. The same approach should apply to duress, so that the exact result will depend on the circumstances of the particular case. In *Halpern*, this meant that a decision as to whether a remedy for duress could be granted would depend on the nature and effect of any improper pressure used, and the identity and significance of the documents destroyed. These issues would need to be determined at trial. The court rejected the strict rule applied by the High Court that there could be no restitution without full counter-restitution.

The equitable doctrine of undue influence

Objective
2

Equity has always been more flexible in the way it grants or refuses relief. While the common law required concepts to be strictly defined, this was never the case in equity which, partly because it was discretionary and partly because it acted according to the principles of good conscience, developed concepts that fell short of the requirements of the common law. It was originally defined in *Allcard* v *Skinner* (1887) 36 ChD 145 as some unfair and improper conduct, some coercion from outside, some overreaching, some form of cheating and generally, though not always, some personal advantage obtained by the guilty party. An instance of such a concept is undue influence, where equity would grant relief from a contract that had been entered into because improper pressure had been placed on one of the parties.

With regard to undue influence, the courts will intervene where a relationship between the two parties has been exploited by one party in order to gain an unfair advantage. It follows that the exploitation can arise where there is an abuse of a particular confidence placed in a party or where that party is in a position of dominance over the victim. It should be stressed, however, that with regard to the latter category, it was held in *Goldsworthy* v *Brickell* [1987] 1 All ER 853 that domination is not a prerequisite of undue influence and that this was merely an example of conduct that might amount to undue influence. In the case of *Bank of Credit and Commerce International SA* v *Aboody* [1990] 1 QB 923 it was held that whatever category of undue influence is alleged it is a requirement that the transaction entered into must have been to the manifest disadvantage of the victim, though this must now be read in the light of the House of Lords' decision in *Barclays Bank plc* v *O'Brien and Another* [1993] 4 All ER 417, *CIBC Mortgages plc* v *Pitt* [1993] 4 All ER 433 and more recently in the case of *Royal Bank of Scotland* v *Etridge (No. 2)* [2001] 4 All ER 449 ('*Etridge No. 2*').

In classifying the different categories of undue influence, it should be noted that undue influence may be either actual or presumed. In *BCCI* v *Aboody* the Court of Appeal adopted the following classification:

1 Class 1: actual undue influence;

2 Class 2: presumed undue influence, which had two sub-classifications.

In *O'Brien* the Class 2 presumed undue influence was further recognised as being subdivided into types 2A and 2B. This classification was also broadly recognised in *Etridge No. 2* where Lord Nicholls stated:

> Equity identified broadly two forms of unacceptable conduct. The first comprises overt acts of improper pressure or coercion such as unlawful threats . . . The second form arises out of a relationship between two persons where one has acquired over another a measure of influence, or ascendancy, of which the ascendant person then takes unfair advantage . . . In cases of this latter nature the influence one person has over another provides scope for misuse without any acts of persuasion. The relationship between the two individuals may be such that, without more, one of them is disposed to agree a course of action proposed by the other. Typically this occurs when one person places trust in another to look after his affairs and interests, and the latter betrays this trust by preferring his own interests. He abuses the influence he has acquired.

On this basis one can begin to examine the nature of undue influence by dividing the subject into two areas: actual and presumed undue influence. It should be noted, however, that Lord Nicholls did not approve of this way of classifying undue influence on the basis that he considered it tended to confuse the issues of definition and the requirements of evidence or proof. Moreover, he disapproved of dividing presumed undue influence into two further subdivisions stating that this tended to 'add mystery rather than illumination'. The reasoning behind this re-evaluation is that the expression 'presumed' relates to an evidential requirement and did not point to a conclusion that there was 'undue' influence. Whether or not influence is undue is a factor that has to be evidentially ascertained from the facts. Bearing in mind this reservation, it is nevertheless a convenient tool in understanding the concept of undue influence to divide the concept into two: actual and presumed undue influence.

Actual undue influence

Objective 3

In this classification it is necessary for the claimant to prove affirmatively that the wrong-doer exerted undue influence on the complainant to enter into a particular transaction which is thus impugned. This type of undue influence arises where there is no special relationship between the parties so that there is no abuse of a particular confidence.

The leading case on this area is that of *Williams* v *Bayley* where a father, to save his son from being prosecuted and possibly transported for giving his bank promissory notes on which he had forged his father's signature, was forced to give security for the debts of the son. It was held that the father's agreement had been extracted by virtue of undue influence being exerted on the father. The agreements were held to be invalid.

Other examples of such undue influence include taking advantage of persons acting under religious delusions, as in *Norton* v *Reilly* (1764) 2 Eden 286; or a young man's mentor influencing him to incur liabilities, as in *Smith* v *Kay* (1859) 7 HLC 750.

In *National Westminster Bank plc* v *Morgan* [1985] 1 All ER 821, it was held that in presumed undue influence (i.e. formerly Class 2 undue influence) a claim to set a transaction aside for undue influence could not succeed unless the claimant could prove that the transaction was manifestly disadvantageous. This requirement was taken up and applied to cases of actual undue influence (i.e. formerly Class 1 undue influence) by the Court of Appeal in *BCCI* v *Aboody*. In *CIBC* v *Pitt*, Lord Browne-Wilkinson did not agree with *Aboody* and considered the requirement that the undue influence had to be manifestly disadvantageous as laid down in *Morgan* had no application to cases of actual undue influence. He stated:

> Actual undue influence is a species of fraud. Like any other victim of fraud, a person who has been induced by undue influence to carry out a transaction which he did not freely and knowingly enter into is entitled to have that transaction set aside as of right . . . A man guilty of fraud is no more entitled to argue that the transaction was beneficial to the person defrauded than a man who has procured a transaction by misrepresentation. The effect of the wrongdoer's conduct is to prevent the wronged party from bringing a free will and properly informed mind to bear on the proposed transaction, which accordingly must be set aside in equity as a matter of justice.

Thus, where there is no special relationship and the claimant proves actual undue influence, they are not under a further burden of proving that the transaction induced by this undue influence was manifestly disadvantageous to them and they may have it set aside as of right. *Etridge No. 2*, however, makes it clear that the undue influence, while not being manifestly disadvantageous, must not be innocuous. The onus of proof is, however, on the claimant to prove the presence of undue influence. This position was affirmed by the House of Lords in *Etridge No. 2*, where it was stated that the question as to whether a transaction has been brought about by the exercise of undue influence is one of fact. The evidence to discharge this burden of proof depends on various factors, such as the nature of the alleged undue influence, the personalities of the parties, their relationship to one another, the 'extent to which the transaction cannot readily be accounted for by the ordinary motives of ordinary persons in that relationship, and all the circumstances of the case'. This is the general rule regarding the burden of proving the existence of undue influence.

However, it is not sufficient simply to show 'influence'. The claimant must prove that the influence has been 'undue' as well. In **Dunbar Bank plc v Nadeem and Another** [1998] 3 All ER 876, it was stated *obiter* that it is not enough simply to show that one party dominated another, but that there had to be an actual unfair advantage exacted over the victim. In this case the Court of Appeal decided that there was no actual undue influence since there was a 'clear finding that Mr Nadeem did not take unfair advantage of his position. Seen through his eyes, the transaction was obviously beneficial to his wife and was intended to be for her benefit.' This approach, however, had the great danger of being too subjective as regards the intentions of the dominant party. Simply because the dominating party considers the transaction to be of benefit to the victim, should this necessarily be so? There is a certain arrogance in assuming that the dominating party knows what is beneficial or advantageous for the victim. The test set out in **Etridge No. 2** provides a more objective assessment of what is 'undue'.

This type of undue influence is becoming much more rare today since there is a continuing blurring of this area with duress. For example, in **Flower v Sadler** (1882) 10 QBD 572, a promise to pay a sum of money extracted by the threat of criminal prosecution was held to be invalid for undue influence. Today such conduct would no doubt fall within the ambit of duress. Similarly, the case of **Williams v Bayley** would probably be considered to be a case of duress today.

Presumed undue influence

As stated earlier, the Court of Appeal in **BCCI v Aboody**, approved by the House of Lords in **O'Brien** and **Etridge No. 2**, established that a confidential relationship could arise in two ways, thus creating two sub-classes:

Class 2A Presumed undue influence

Certain types of relationship automatically presume the existence of undue influence: for instance, the relationship between trustee and beneficiary (**Benningfield v Baxter** (1886) 12 App Cas 167); solicitor and client (**Wright v Carter** [1903] 1 Ch 27); parent and child (**Powell v Powell** [1900] 1 Ch 243); religious leader or adviser and disciple or parishioner (**Allcard v Skinner**).

The use of the expression 'presumption' here is one which describes the shift in the evidential burden of proof on the question of fact. The claimant has to show, first, that there is a relationship of trust or confidence between themselves and the wrongdoer and, second, the existence of a transaction which calls for an explanation.

On proof of these two matters there is an inference that the transaction has arisen from undue influence and the evidential burden of proof shifts to the defendant to provide evidence that counters the presumption. Not every type of fiduciary relationship gives rise to such a presumption since it has to be shown that the confidence placed in the wrongdoer gives that person some authority over the victim or that it creates an obligation on the wrongdoer to offer or recommend the victim to seek independent advice. The person in whom the confidence is reposed is in such a position that that person has an obvious opportunity of enhancing their position, to the extent that they must prove that they have not exercised their position of influence in that manner.

There is thus no need for the victim to prove that undue influence has actually taken place, since all they have to do is to prove that a confidential relationship has arisen and that the transaction itself calls for an explanation. Once the victim has done that a rebuttable evidential presumption of undue influence automatically arises at law. The burden of proof then shifts to the wrongdoer to prove that the victim entered into the transaction of their own volition, for instance by showing that the victim had received independent advice. The court in turn then has to draw 'the appropriate inferences of fact upon a balanced consideration of the whole of the evidence at the end of the trial in which the burden of proof rested upon the plaintiff' (*per* Lord Nicholls in *Etridge No. 2*). The second requirement therefore is an evidential presumption which can be rebutted by the so-called wrongdoer.

In *Etridge No. 2*, it was considered that it was only in Class 2A undue influence that a true presumption of influence arises. It was stated that 'the law has adopted a sternly protective attitude' towards the types of relationship described above where one party acquires influence over another vulnerable person. It is sufficient for the claimant to prove the existence of such a relationship and that the transaction 'calls for an explanation'. 'Alternatively the claimant must demonstrate that the transaction is not one that is readily explicable by the relationship of the parties'. The second presumption found in Class 2A undue influence is a necessary constraint on the width of this type of undue influence. Thus Lord Nicholls stated in *Etridge No. 2*:

> The second pre-requisite . . . is good sense. It is a necessary limitation upon the width of the first requisite. It would be absurd for the law to presume that every gift by a child to a parent, or every transaction between a client and his solicitor or between a patient and his doctor, was brought about by undue influence unless the contrary is affirmatively proved . . . The last would be rightly opened to ridicule, for transactions such as these are unexceptionable. They do not suggest that something may be amiss. So something more is needed before the law reverses the burden of proof, something which calls for an explanation.

Despite the definitive statements by Lord Nicholls, individual cases continue to throw up anomalies, such as that of *Leeder* v *Stevens* [2005] EWCA Civ 50. The facts of the case are that Denis Stevens, a married man, for many years had an affair with Maureen Leeder. Maureen owned a house worth £70,000 subject to a mortgage of £5,000. The couple discussed marriage and, as part of these discussions, Denis offered to pay off the mortgage in return for which the house would be transferred into joint names. Subsequently, Maureen agreed to the transaction and the house was transferred into joint names as tenants in common in equal shares. At the time of the transfer a Deed of Trust was drawn up under which either party could force a sale of the property subject to a right of pre-emption (a right of first refusal). Soon after the transfer Denis forced a sale and Maureen argued that the Deed of Trust should be set aside on the grounds of undue influence. Her action failed at first instance and she appealed to the Court of Appeal.

It was held that this was a case of presumed undue influence and that there was no evidential reason to rebut it. The decision is remarkable in that in *Etridge No. 2* it was clearly stated that the presumption of undue influence can only arise in two situations: first, where the relationship is one in which the law presumes the existence of undue influence; second, that the wrongdoer has acquired an influence over a vulnerable party so that the existence of the relationship 'calls for an explanation'. The Court of Appeal considered that the relationship which exists between an engaged couple falls within the type of relationship that presumes undue influence. The court considered that the relationship between Denis and Maureen was analogous to that position. This decision appears to be at odds with *Etridge No. 2* itself since it was held in the House of Lords that a presumption of undue influence does not apply to a husband and wife relationship. If that is the case then it is clearly anomalous that such a presumption should exist in the case of an engaged couple. This would mean that their relationship in terms of presumed undue influence would change, possibly for the worse, simply because they became married. Furthermore, the relationship of an engaged couple did not fall within Lord Nicholls's examples of relationships that give rise to presumed undue influence in *Etridge No. 2*. The decision also appears to contradict the earlier Court of Appeal decision in *Zamet v Hyman* [1961] 3 All ER 933 where the court considered that the presumption of undue influence would not arise in the case of engaged couples unless the transaction was clearly unfavourable to the party attempting to avoid the transaction or, in modern parlance, the transaction 'calls for an explanation'.

Class 2B Presumed undue influence

Where there is no special relationship that falls within Class 2A giving rise to an automatic presumption of undue influence, it may nevertheless be the case that the victim can prove the existence of a relationship in which they have placed a trust and confidence in the wrongdoer as a fact. The victim will therefore be able to have the transaction set aside merely by proving that they have placed a trust and confidence in the wrongdoer, without the need to prove that an actual undue influence arose.

The husband and wife relationship is a good example of a category of relationship within Class 2B that does not exist per se but which has to be proved as a fact. This was established in *Howes v Bishop* [1909] 2 KB 390 and *Bank of Montreal v Stuart* [1911] AC 120, and again confirmed in *Midland Bank plc v Shephard* [1988] 3 All ER 17. In *Kingsnorth Trust Ltd v Bell* [1986] 1 All ER 423, the wife was able to prove undue influence as a fact where the husband was regarded as an agent of the bank in procuring the agreement of the wife to a particular transaction. Similarly, in *BCCI v Aboody*, a wife was able to avoid liability to the bank in respect of a surety transaction, which she was induced to enter by her husband, on the basis that the bank had notice, actual or constructive, of the husband's actions in either exercising undue influence over his wife or misrepresenting the extent of his indebtedness to the bank.

But why doesn't the relationship fall into Class 2A? In *Yerkey v Jones* (1939) 63 CLR 649, Dixon J explained that the courts were not blind to the opportunities that a husband may have in unfairly influencing the decisions of his wife. The actions of a wife, however, could also arise from motives of affection or some other such reason and there was nothing strange or unusual in that. Thus while there is no presumption of undue influence in such a relationship the court will note, as a matter of fact, the opportunities a husband may have in abusing his wife's confidence in him. This is taken into account alongside all the other evidence put forward in the case.

While the cases which cause most concern arise out of the husband and wife relationship, Class 2B undue influence may arise in any transaction where the victim can prove as a fact that when he or she entered into a transaction there was a relationship of trust and confidence between the victim and the wrongdoer. This being done, a court will presume that the victim has been subject to undue influence.

Lloyds Bank Ltd v Bundy [1975] QB 326

The defendant was an elderly farmer whose only asset comprised a farmhouse that was also his home. The defendant shared the same bank as his son and his son's company. The company ran into financial difficulties and so the defendant gave a guarantee in respect of the company to the bank, the guarantee being secured by a charge over the farmhouse. In fact the fortunes of the company failed to improve and the defendant was then approached by his son and the manager of the bank, who informed him that the bank was unwilling to continue to support the company without additional security. In response to this approach, and without seeking independent advice, the defendant extended the guarantee and with it the charge over his property. Eventually a receiver was appointed in respect to the company and as a result the bank sought to enforce its security against the farmhouse. The defendant pleaded undue influence based on the fact that there was a long-standing relationship between himself and the bank, and as such he had placed confidence in it in that he looked to the bank for financial advice. Clearly the bank in having a financial interest in the company could not present itself as being able to give independent financial advice. It was incumbent upon the bank to advise the defendant to seek such advice, which they failed to do, and therefore could not rebut the presumption of undue influence.

It has to be stated that the **Bundy** case is a somewhat exceptional one and turns on its own facts, since the presumption of undue influence does not normally arise between banks and their customers.

National Westminster Bank plc v Morgan [1985] 1 All ER 821

A husband and wife were the joint owners of the family home which was mortgaged to a building society. The husband became unable to meet the mortgage repayments because his business began to fail. When the building society began to take proceedings for possession of the property in order to enforce the mortgage, the husband decided to seek new finance from the bank, which had agreed to help. The bank manager then called at the family home to have the relevant documents executed by the wife, who did not receive any independent legal advice before signing the new mortgage. Although the husband was initially present the wife insisted that she wished to discuss the mortgage with the bank manager privately. During her discussions with the manager she stated that she had little confidence in her husband's business ventures and that she did not want the legal charge to cover her husband's business liabilities. The manager assured her, incorrectly, that the legal charge would cover only the refinancing of the mortgage and that it did not extend to the business liabilities. The financial difficulties of the husband and wife continued and they again fell into arrears with the mortgage repayments, although the husband's business was not in debt to the bank. The bank sought to enforce their security on the charge by seeking possession of the property. Soon afterwards the husband died. The wife then appealed against the order for possession on the grounds that the mortgage had been obtained by virtue of undue influence and therefore the legal charge should be set aside. The Court of Appeal allowed her appeal but she failed in the House of Lords.

The House of Lords rejected the contention that undue influence arose simply out of the relationship of the parties and that the presence of such undue influence allowed the transaction to be set on one side. Lord Scarman (who delivered the only judgement) referred to the judgement of Sir Eric Sachs in **Lloyds Bank Ltd v Bundy** where he considered that undue influence does not simply arise because of the relationship of banker and client, as in a simple case of the bank going about its normal duties where it is, for instance, obtaining a guarantee and in the course of that explains the legal effect of the guarantee and the sums involved. For the presumption of undue influence to arise the bank must normally 'cross the line' into the area of confidentiality. Lord Scarman did not approve of the latter expression, preferring to find whether or not a dominating influence was present by a 'meticulous examination of the facts', an expression used by Sir Eric Sachs in determining whether or not an area of confidentiality had been crossed into. He considered that on the facts the bank had not exercised a dominant influence over the wife.

Lord Scarman decided that on a 'meticulous examination of the facts' the bank in the **Morgan** case had not crossed the line to where a presumption of undue influence existed.

In any event he considered that the presence of this presumption was not of itself sufficient. He stated that one also had to show that the transaction was of itself wrongful in that it constituted a manifest disadvantage to the person influenced. He found that the transaction had not been unfair to the wife; indeed, quite the contrary, since it had allowed Mr and Mrs Morgan to stay in their house on terms that were not substantially different from those of the building society. The transaction, if anything, was to their advantage and thus the bank had no duty to ensure that Mrs Morgan received independent advice.

But what of the effect of *Etridge No. 2* on this analysis of presumed undue influence? *Etridge No. 2* provides authority that presumed undue influence merely shifts the evidential burden of proof from the claimant to the wrongdoer. It is *not* a presumption that undue influence exists per se, but rather that the burden of explaining why the transaction was not caused by undue influence is shifted to the wrongdoer. The wrongdoer may therefore dispel any notion of undue influence by producing evidence that the transaction had been properly entered into. Thus the 'presumption' of undue influence, either by way of a 'relationship' (as in Class 2A cases) or demonstrating a relationship of trust and confidence (as in Class 2B cases), arises in circumstances that require 'explanation', for instance because the transaction is manifestly disadvantageous. This then shifts the burden of proof on to the wrongdoer to provide an explanation for the transaction. If the wrongdoer is unable to discharge this burden of proof by providing an explanation then undue influence will be found to exist.

From this it may be seen that the difference between the 'old' Class 2A and 2B categories is that in the former the relationship of trust and confidence cannot be disputed. In the latter the wrongdoer is entitled to provide evidence that no such relationship existed, which in turn means it is unnecessary to provide an explanation for the transaction.

The requirement of 'manifest disadvantage' and transactions 'calling for an explanation'

Objective
4

To what extent is 'manifest disadvantage' a necessary prerequisite to establishing presumed undue influence? As already stated, there are two prerequisites that bring about a shift in the evidential burden of proof. To reiterate, the first is that the complainant must have placed a trust and confidence in the other party, or that the other party had influence over the complainant. The second prerequisite is that the transaction is not one which is explicable by the relationship of the parties to each other. In the past this second prerequisite was proved by the complainant proving the transaction was to his or her manifest disadvantage. This, as seen in *Morgan*, was therefore a significant factor in limiting the application of undue influence. The courts would nevertheless enforce a transaction where the potential benefits outweighed the disadvantages.

The requirement to prove manifest disadvantage is a contentious one and has been much criticised. It appears to derive from the case of *Allcard v Skinner*, where Lindley LJ indicated that the mere existence of influence was not enough – it had to be undue. In the case of small gifts to a person standing in a relationship to the donor some proof of influence had to be shown. Lindley LJ continued:

> if the gift is so large as not to be reasonably accounted for on the ground of friendship, relationship, charity, or other ordinary motives on which ordinary men act, the burden is upon the donee to support the gift.

This was followed in *Goldsworthy v Brickell* [1987] Ch 378 by Nourse LJ, who stated:

> the presumption of [undue influence] is not perfected and remains inoperative until the party who has ceded the trust and confidence makes a gift so large, or enters into a transaction so improvident, as not to be reasonably accounted for on the ground of friendship, relationship, charity or other ordinary motives on which men act. Although influence might have been presumed beforehand, it is only then that it is presumed to have been undue.

Thus, the intention behind this prerequisite is to limit the first prerequisite so that undue influence does not arise from innocuous transactions that take place within the trust and confidence relationship. Not to do so would mean that every transaction between persons in such a relationship, such as children and parents, patient and doctor, client and solicitor and so on, stood to be overturned on grounds of undue influence. Something more is required before a court will reverse the burden of proof. There must be a transaction that requires an 'explanation' as to why the weaker party entered into the transaction. As Nicholls LJ in *Etridge No. 2* indicates:

> the greater the disadvantage to the vulnerable person, the more cogent must be the explanation before the presumption will be regarded as rebutted.

Lord Nicholls considered that the label 'manifest disadvantage', as used by Lord Scarman in explaining the second prerequisite, was too limited and gave rise to misunderstandings; indeed, he considered that it was not being used in a manner intended by Lord Scarman. In the context of a wife guaranteeing her husband's debts, one had to consider whether such a transaction by which she not only guaranteed the debts but charged her share of the matrimonial home was to her manifest disadvantage. He stated that in the narrow sense such a transaction is clearly or 'manifestly' disadvantageous to the wife. She undertakes a 'serious financial obligation' for which 'she personally receives practically nothing'. However, in the wider sense there are advantages to the wife in embarking on such a transaction. If the husband's business is the provider of the main income, the wife has an interest in supporting her husband.

Lord Nicholls considered neither the narrow nor the wider interpretations to be correct in deciding whether or not the transaction is disadvantageous to the wife. He considered that the label 'manifest disadvantage' should be abandoned in favour of the test set out by Lindley LJ in *Allcard v Skinner*, above, and adopted by Lord Scarman in *Morgan*.

In relation to husband and wife cases, Lord Nicholls considered that, in the ordinary course of things, a guarantee by the wife should not be regarded as a transaction that is explicable only on the basis that it has been procured by undue influence on the part of the husband, unless there is proof to the contrary. The fact that wives enter into such transactions with a pessimistic view of the outcome does not provide prima facie evidence of undue influence. His conclusion is salutary:

> Wives frequently enter into such transactions. There are good and sufficient reasons why they are willing to do so, despite the risks involved for them and their families. They may be enthusiastic. They may not. They may be less optimistic than their husbands about the prospects of the husbands' businesses. They may be anxious, perhaps exceedingly so. But this is a far cry from saying that such transactions are to be regarded as prima facie evidence of the exercise of undue influence by their husbands.

Lord Nicholls states this situation as applying 'in the ordinary course of things' and he acknowledges that there are cases where a husband deliberately misleads his wife as to the proposed transaction, so that he prefers his own interests to those of his wife's. Here the husband abuses his position and the influence he has over his wife and 'fails to discharge the obligation of candour and fairness he owes a wife who is looking to him to make the major financial decisions'.

Rebutting the presumption – what is the effect of independent advice?

While it has been seen that the presumption of undue influence may be rebutted by the person having the dominating influence showing that the other party had had access to independent advice or at least been in a position to exercise free judgement, such advice is not always successful in saving the situation. It must be competent advice and made in the knowledge of all the facts of the case: *Inche Noriah v Shaik Allie Bin Omar* [1929] AC 127.

The weight the court must place on the advice depends on the circumstances. Ordinarily, advice from a solicitor or a financial adviser might normally be expected to make the complainant aware of the nature of the transaction about to be entered into. This does not necessarily preclude undue influence since a person who is aware of the nature of the transaction may still be acting under the influence of another. Whether or not independent advice precludes the effects of undue influence is a question of fact to be decided by reference to the evidence of the facts of the case.

The effect of undue influence on third parties

Objective 5

So far the examination of undue influence has been looked at in the context of where the victim is attempting to avoid a transaction entered into with the wrongdoer. However, as alluded to above, it sometimes arises, particularly in the context of a husband and wife relationship, that the victim is persuaded to enter into a guarantee or surety contract with a bank or some other creditor on the basis of some undue influence, misrepresentation or other legal wrong, not by the bank or creditor, but by some third party, for instance a husband. The question arises, therefore, to what extent that undue influence will affect the transaction between the victim and the bank/creditor? If one adopts the usual rule of privity of contract, the actions of the wrongdoer should have no effect on the transaction; however, in certain instances the courts have allowed the victim to have the transaction set aside.

The law whereby creditors have been affected by the actions of the wrongdoer and thus unable to enforce the surety contract/guarantee has evolved in three phases that encompass different approaches – agency, special equity and the doctrine of notice. The first two have now been laid to rest and rejected in *Barclays Bank plc v O'Brien* where Lord Browne-Wilkinson considered the correct approach in protecting the interests of wives was by way of a more wide-ranging doctrine of notice.

Barclays Bank plc v O'Brien [1993] 4 All ER 417

Mr O'Brien wanted to increase the overdraft facility of a company in which he was a shareholder. The bank agreed a loan of £120,000 that was to be guaranteed by Mr O'Brien, his liability in turn being secured by a second charge over the matrimonial home, which was jointly owned by Mr O'Brien and his wife. The bank manager gave instructions for the relevant documents to be prepared, including a legal charge to be signed by both Mr O'Brien and his wife, together with a guarantee to be signed by the husband alone. Instructions were also given that both Mr O'Brien and his wife should be advised as to the nature of the transactions and that, if they had any doubts, they should obtain independent advice. These instructions were not complied with and subsequently both husband and wife signed the documents without reading them. The company's indebtedness then increased beyond the agreed limit and the bank took proceedings to enforce its security against the husband and wife. In her defence the wife contended that her husband had put undue pressure on her to sign the surety agreement and, second, that her husband had misrepresented the effect of the legal charge in that she believed it was limited to a sum of £60,000 over three weeks.

The judge at first instance, and the Court of Appeal and House of Lords, dismissed the wife's contention that she had been subject to undue influence by her husband and therefore the case turned on the misrepresentation of the husband as to the extent and the duration of the liability and whether the bank's ability to enforce the surety contract against the wife was prejudiced by the actions of her husband.

On the facts, the bank was aware that the parties were husband and wife and thus was put on notice as to the circumstances in which the wife would have been asked to stand as surety. The bank failed to warn the wife of the risks she ran in entering into the surety contract or as to her potential liability in respect of her husband's debts. Furthermore, the bank had not advised her to seek independent legal advice. On this basis the bank was fixed with constructive notice of the misrepresentation made by the husband to induce his wife into the surety contract and therefore the wife was entitled to have the legal charge on the matrimonial home securing her husband's liability to the bank set aside.

Lord Browne-Wilkinson thus considered that the key to whether a creditor is bound by the wrongdoings of the principal debtor, and thereby unable to enforce security as a guarantor or surety, lay in whether the creditor had actual or constructive notice of the equitable right of the surety to have the transaction set aside on the basis of the debtor's wrongdoings. He stated that 'the doctrine of notice lies at the heart of equity' and 'provides the key to finding a principled basis for the law'. He went on to state that where there are two innocent parties, both of whom enjoy rights, the earlier right prevails against the later one if the holder of that later right has actual notice of the earlier one or has constructive notice of it and would have discovered it by making proper inquiries. Translating this to the husband and wife scenario, where the wife has agreed to stand as surety for the debts of her husband by virtue of some undue influence or misrepresentation, then the creditor will be deemed to have constructive notice of the equitable right of the wife to have the surety agreement set aside, provided the circumstances are such as to put the creditor on inquiry. Lord Browne-Wilkinson thus applied the equitable maxim, since undue influence is an equitable doctrine, that 'where the equities are equal the first in time prevails'. Thus since the first equity is the wife's and the second equity belongs to the bank, the wife's interest should prevail. In *Barclays Bank plc* v *Boulter* [1997] 2 All ER 1002, however, it was held that the burden of proof lies on the bank to prove that it did not have constructive notice of the undue influence or misrepresentation. It is not incumbent on the surety to prove that the bank does have constructive notice.

Lord Browne-Wilkinson considered that it was at this point that the special position of wives became important since, even today, many wives place a confidence and trust in their husbands in relation to their financial affairs. Thus the relationship between a husband and wife in these circumstances gave rise to an 'invalidating tendency' which meant that a wife was in a better position to be able to establish Class 2B presumed undue influence by her husband. The informality of the dealings between a husband and his wife meant that there was a higher likelihood of the husband misrepresenting the liability of the undertaking to the wife in order to secure her assent to the surety contract. His Lordship considered that the informality of the business dealings between a husband and his wife would be sufficient to put a creditor on notice if two factors are satisfied:

1 the transaction is on its face not to the financial advantage of the wife; and

2 there is a substantial risk in transactions of that kind that, in procuring the wife to act as surety, the husband has committed a legal or equitable wrong that entitles the wife to set aside the transaction.

Thus where a creditor is put on inquiry it is incumbent on him to ensure that the wife's consent to act as surety has been properly obtained, since otherwise he will be deemed to have constructive notice of the wife's right to have the surety agreement set aside, on the basis of either undue influence or misrepresentation. This position has now been affirmed by the House of Lords in *Etridge No. 2* where it was stated that 'a bank should take steps to ensure that it is not affected by any claim the wife may have that her signature . . . was procured by the undue influence or other wrong of her husband'.

But what of the situation outside the husband and wife relationship? Lord Browne-Wilkinson stated that the special position of wives does not arise out of the status of the husband and wife relationship but out of the emotional ties that arise within that relationship. These emotional ties also arise in the case of cohabitees, whether of a heterosexual or homosexual nature. Where the creditor knows that a surety or guarantor is cohabiting with the principal debtor, the nature of the surety contract and the relationship of the parties means that the possibility of undue influence or misrepresentation can be inferred, with the consequence that the creditor will have constructive notice of the equitable right of the surety to have the transaction set aside, just as in the husband and wife situation.

Of course, these principles are not confined to cohabitees but will arise in any situation where a creditor is aware that the surety places a confidence and trust in the principal debtor. Lord Browne-Wilkinson gave an example of this type of relationship in the following case.

Avon Finance Co. Ltd v *Bridges* [1985] 2 All ER 281

In this case, a son persuaded his parents to act as surety for his debts by means of a misrepresentation. It was held that the surety contract was unenforceable by the finance company, *inter alia*, because the finance company had knowledge of the trust the parents reposed in their son with regard to their financial dealings. One may discern a difference of approach here since there would appear to be a requirement to prove actual knowledge by the creditor of the confidence and trust reposed in the debtor by the surety, while in the cohabitee scenario undue influence or misrepresentation may be inferred.

The problem now remained as to how creditors could avoid the consequences set out above. Lord Browne-Wilkinson considered that the answer to this question lies in good banking practice by the various financial institutions. He stated:

Where one cohabitee has entered into an obligation to stand as surety for the debts of the other cohabitee and the creditor is aware that they are cohabitees: (1) the surety obligation will be valid and enforceable by the creditor unless the suretyship was procured by the undue influence, misrepresentation or other legal wrong of the principal debtor; (2) if there has been undue influence, misrepresentation or other legal wrong by the principal debtor, unless the creditor has taken reasonable steps to satisfy himself that the surety entered into the obligation freely and in knowledge of the true facts, the creditor will be unable to enforce the surety obligation because he will be fixed with constructive notice of the surety's right to set aside the transaction; (3) unless there are special exceptional circumstances, a creditor will have taken such reasonable steps to avoid being fixed with constructive notice if the creditor warns the surety (at a meeting not attended by the principal debtor) of the amount of her potential liability and of the risks involved and advises the surety to take independent legal advice.

By 'reasonable steps' he considered that financial institutions could lend in confidence on the basis of a surety contract provided the surety is warned, independently of the principal debtor, of the extent of his or her liability and the risks involved. Furthermore, the surety should be advised to seek independent advice. His Lordship also considered that notices in the documentation did not provide an adequate warning, no matter what prominence such warnings are given, since very often such written warnings were not read by potential sureties or they were intercepted by the principal debtor. There is thus a legal requirement on financial institutions to explain the matters indicated above to the potential surety in a personal interview from which the principal debtor is excluded.

Despite the fact that a creditor took the above precautions, Lord Browne-Wilkinson referred to 'exceptional circumstances' that would still cause the transaction to fail. What sort of 'exceptional circumstances' did he envisage? His Lordship did not give explicit examples but it would appear that such circumstances may arise if the creditor had knowledge of facts that made the presence of undue influence highly likely rather than a mere possibility. In such a situation the transaction would be set aside unless the creditor ensured that the innocent party was *actually* independently advised.

Avoiding constructive notice

The case of *O'Brien* contained within it procedures that are required to be taken by creditors when entering surety transactions in order to avoid being fixed with constructive notice of the principal debtor's misrepresentations, undue influence or other wrongdoing. Lord Browne-Wilkinson considered these procedures to be good banking practice. To reiterate, the following procedures had to be taken by the creditor:

1 There is a legal requirement that the innocent party is called in for a personal interview. It is important that the principal debtor is excluded from this interview. Written advice is not regarded as being adequate.

2 The extent of the proposed liability of the innocent party (the potential surety) should be explained at the interview.

3 The risks of entering into the transaction should be explained.

4 The innocent party should be encouraged to seek independent legal advice.

Clearly the procedures are designed to ensure that the innocent party is given a maximum degree of protection; however, the question arises as to whether the procedures are to be regarded as best practice guidelines rather than hard-and-fast rules.

In *Massey v Midland Bank plc* [1995] 1 All ER 929, Steyn LJ made two observations here: first, the guidance given did not need to be exhaustive to satisfy the *O'Brien* requirements; second, the guidance requirements in *O'Brien* should not be applied mechanically. This position accords with that set out in the earlier decision of *Bank of Baroda v Shah* [1988] 3 All ER 24, where it was stated that the bank can assume that the solicitor is honest and competent and that any conflict between the solicitor and the wife is not one for the bank to concern itself with. This position was also affirmed in the Court of Appeal decision in *Banco Exterior Internacional v Mann* [1995] 1 All ER 936.

The principles applied in these were followed and extended in the subsequent cases of the **Bank of Baroda v Rayarel** [1995] 2 FLR 376 (CA) and **Halifax Mortgage Services Ltd v Stepsky** [1996] 2 All ER 277. In the former it was held that where a surety was advised by a solicitor acting for the alleged wrongdoer, the bank was entitled to assume that the surety had been properly advised as to the nature and extent of the transaction. It was also stated that it was a matter for the solicitor to decide if there was a conflict of interest. In **Stepsky**, the solicitor was acting for the wife, the husband and the building society. The Court of Appeal decided that the knowledge gained from the husband relating to the true purpose of the loan could not be imputed to the building society since the knowledge had been gained prior to the appointment of the solicitor by the building society.

The issue of whether a bank has taken 'reasonable steps' to avoid constructive notice by ensuring that the surety has obtained independent legal advice continued to be blurred by subsequent cases.

Barclays Bank plc v Thomson [1997] 4 All ER 816

A bank instructed a solicitor to act on its behalf for the purpose of ensuring that the wife received independent legal advice as to her liabilities under a charge in the bank's favour; the bank was entitled to rely on the solicitor's assurance that he had discharged his duty and given her professional independent advice. This was so even where the solicitor was also acting for both the bank and the husband. It was stated that deficiency in the advice given by the solicitor could not be imputed to the bank. On the other hand, in **Royal Bank of Scotland v Etridge** [1997] 3 All ER 628 it was held that the bank was not discharged of its duty to take reasonable steps to ensure that the wife received independent advice simply by the fact that the solicitor had signed a certificate stating that the nature and effect of the transaction had been explained to her. This was because the wife had signed the charge in the presence of the husband; she regarded the solicitor as employed by her husband; and, lastly, the solicitor had been appointed by the bank and was therefore regarded as being an agent of the bank. The case thus distinguished the cases of **Massey** and **Mann**.

Undoubtedly, the contradictory decisions in these two cases are unsatisfactory and produced further uncertainty and confusion in this increasingly complex area of the law. The case of **Royal Bank of Scotland v Etridge** was followed by the case of **Crédit Lyonnais Bank Nederland NV v Burch** [1997] 1 All ER 144 (CA), which applied a principle first set out by Lord Browne-Wilkinson in **O'Brien**. He stated that in an exceptional case a creditor may be so aware of the fact of undue influence by the third party wrongdoer that it would be inadequate for the creditor simply to advise the wife/surety to obtain independent advice; the creditor must insist upon it so that independent advice is actually received. The case is also authority for the proposition that if the transaction is one for an unlimited guarantee then it must be regarded as onerous. In such circumstances the solicitor is bound to inquire as to the nature of any onerous clauses. If the solicitor does discover such clauses they should advise their client not to enter into the transaction. If the client persists in carrying on with the transaction, the solicitor should then refuse to act any further for the client, unless satisfied that the transaction is one which, given the overall circumstances, the client should sensibly enter into free from improper pressure.

In both the **Massey** and **Mann** cases the Court of Appeal considered that the **O'Brien** principles set out by Lord Browne-Wilkinson were not exhaustive ones that had to be applied in all cases. Both Steyn LJ (in the **Massey** case) and Morritt LJ (in the **Mann** case), considered the principles in *O'Brien* to be simply an indication of 'best practice'. Thus Steyn LJ stated:

> The guidance ought not to be mechanically applied . . . It is the substance that matters.

Morritt LJ stated:

> I do not understand Lord Browne-Wilkinson to be laying down for the future the only steps to be taken which will avoid a bank being fixed with constructive notice of the rights of the wife, rather he is pointing out . . . best practice.

On this basis, the absence of a private meeting will not necessarily be fatal to the agreement, provided the overall objective of the guidelines is met in ensuring that the innocent party is made sufficiently aware of the consequences of entering into the proposed transaction so that the undue influence, misrepresentation or other wrong committed by the principal debtor is counteracted.

It cannot be doubted that the decisions in the *Massey* and *Mann* cases considerably weakened the ability of sureties to have transactions set aside following *Barclays Bank plc* v *O'Brien*. Conflicting decisions in subsequent cases such as *Etridge* and *Thomson* exacerbated the situation. The result was a growing uncertainty that made it almost impossible at times for either the banks or sureties to predict the outcome of their respective positions. The problem appeared to be that the banks and other financial institutions involved in lending money adopted a variety of different practices believing that these met the *O'Brien* principles. The other problem was that at times the courts also seemed to produce equally varied responses. If the *O'Brien* guidelines were to be viewed as 'best practice' then the confusion being created by subsequent decisions was making the law so confused and unpredictable that it could only be labelled as 'worst practice'.

Into this picture came the case of *Royal Bank of Scotland* v *Etridge (No. 2)*. As indicated earlier, the leading judgement in the House of Lords was delivered by Lord Nicholls. He first of all directed his attention to the criticisms that had been made of the decision in *O'Brien*. He reiterated the process in which the doctrine of constructive notice had been applied by Lord Browne-Wilkinson in *O'Brien*. Usually a bank that takes a guarantee from the wife of a customer will be completely ignorant of any undue influence that might be brought to bear in order to compel her concurrence with the loan arrangements. As we have seen, Lord Browne-Wilkinson used constructive notice as a means of putting the creditor on notice of the wife's rights unless the creditor has taken reasonable steps to satisfy themselves that the wife's agreement has been properly obtained.

As Lord Nicholls pointed out, this is an unusual use of constructive notice in that the law does not impose an obligation on one party to check whether the other's agreement was obtained by undue influence. Usually in a situation such as a surety transaction where there are three persons involved, the wife only avoids liability if it can be shown that the bank has been a party to the conduct that caused the wife to enter into the transaction. What *O'Brien* essentially does is to introduce a concept that the bank will lose the benefit of a contract if it 'ought' to have known that the other's concurrence has been procured by the misconduct of the third party.

Another unusual feature of constructive notice as applied in *O'Brien* was considered by Lord Nicholls. Under conventional principles a person is deemed to have constructive notice of a prior right when they do not actually know of the prior right but would have learned of it had they made those inquiries that a reasonably prudent purchaser would have made. In *O'Brien*, however, the bank is not required to make such inquiries. The decision merely sets out the steps to be taken by the bank to reduce or eliminate the risks incurred by the wife entering into a transaction by way of some misrepresentation or undue influence by her husband. The steps here are to *minimise* the risk, not *discover* if the husband has exerted influence over his wife by misrepresentation or undue influence. Thus in establishing guidelines as to when a bank is put on inquiry, the use of the expression 'constructive notice' is not technically correct since a bank is not required to make such inquiries but to ensure that the risk of undue influence being exerted upon the wife has been reduced.

Lord Nicholls then set out some principles and guidelines regarding the position of lenders and the duties of solicitors in advising wives in transactions where a wife proposed to charge her share of the matrimonial home as security for a loan to her husband or a company within which the husband operates his business.

1. When is the bank put on inquiry?

A bank is put on inquiry when a wife offers to stand as surety for her husband's debts. This arises from the fact that the transaction is not, on the face of things, to the wife's financial advantage. Further, in such transactions there is a substantial risk that the husband has committed a wrong that would entitle the wife to set the transaction aside. These two factors provide the underlying rationale for the bank to be put on inquiry. Both do not, however, have to be proved before the bank is put on inquiry.

The above principles apply not just in the case of married couples, but also in the case of unmarried couples, whether homosexual or heterosexual, where the bank is aware of the relationship. Couples do not have to be cohabiting, thus affirming the decision in *Massey*, above, nor indeed does there have to be a sexual relationship. Lord Nicholls in *Etridge No. 2* considered that banks will always be put on inquiry in all cases where there is a non-commercial relationship between the surety and the debtor, referring to this as the 'wider principle'. Thus he stated:

> the only practical way forward is to regard banks as 'put on inquiry' in every case where the relationship between the surety and the debtor is non-commercial. The creditor must always take reasonable steps to bring home to the individual guarantor the risks he is running by standing surety. As a measure of protection, this is valuable. But, in all conscience, it is a modest burden for banks and other lenders. It is no more than is reasonably to be expected of a creditor who is taking a guarantee from an individual. If the bank or other creditor does not take these steps, it is deemed to have notice of any claim the guarantor may have that the transaction was procured by undue influence or misrepresentation on the part of the debtor.

Lord Nicholls therefore suggests that in any non-commercial situation a bank/lender must assume that it is put on inquiry and must take appropriate action to avoid being fixed with constructive notice.

In *First National Bank plc* v *Achampong* [2003] EWCA Civ 487, a wife attempted to establish that a bank was put on inquiry because the loan had been made to benefit her husband's business and that she had received no benefit from the loan. The Court of Appeal considered it was unnecessary to inquire into the latter two matters and considered that undue influence arose on the basis of the 'wider principle' as set out above.

The bank is also put on inquiry if the wife acts as surety for the debts of a company whose shares are held by the wife and her husband, even where the wife is a director or company secretary. Lord Nicholls did not consider this type of situation to be a joint loan since shareholders' interests and the identity of directors did provide an accurate guide as to who had de facto control of the company's business. The case of *Bank of Cyprus (London) Ltd* v *Markou* [1999] 2 All ER 707 provides an example of such circumstances.

2. What steps should the bank take when put on inquiry?

When a bank has been put on inquiry it need only take such reasonable steps as is necessary to satisfy itself that the practical implications of the proposed transaction have been brought home to the wife in a meaningful way. Lord Nicholls states:

> The furthest a bank can be expected to go is to take reasonable steps to satisfy itself that the wife has had brought home to her, in a meaningful way, the practical implications of the proposed transaction. This does not wholly eliminate the risk of undue influence or misrepresentation. But it does mean that a wife enters into a transaction with her eyes open so far as the basic elements of the transaction are concerned.

There is no requirement on a bank to discharge its responsibility by having a personal meeting with the wife – provided a suitable alternative means of communicating the necessary information to her is used. Lord Nicholls considered that the risk of litigation ensuing by having a personal meeting with the wife was high and that it was not unreasonable for the bank to insist that she receive advice from an independent financial adviser. Ordinarily it is reasonable for a bank to rely upon confirmation from a solicitor that they have given the wife appropriate advice. It would not, however, be reasonable if the bank knows that the solicitor has not duly advised the wife or from the facts the bank knows that the wife has not received appropriate advice. Normally the deficiencies in the advice provided by the solicitor are a matter between the wife and the solicitor. The solicitor is regarded as acting solely for the wife and is not an agent of the bank. Thus the quality of the advice given is a matter between the wife and the solicitor.

In assessing what steps the bank should take when put on inquiry, Lord Nicholls considered that many of the cases already discussed featured the wife becoming involved at a very late stage of the transaction between the bank and the husband. She often had little opportunity to express a view on the identity of the solicitor who advised her. She was often unaware that the purpose of the interview was for the solicitor to confirm to the bank the fact that she had received advice. It was not unusual for the solicitor to act for both the wife and her husband.

Lord Nicholls considered that in future transactions banks should take the following steps when looking for the protection of legal advice given to the wife by the solicitor. He considered that the bank should take steps to check directly with the wife the name of the solicitor she wishes to act for her. The bank should also communicate directly with the wife informing her that, for its own protection, it will require confirmation by the solicitor acting for her that they have fully explained to her the nature of the documents and the practical implications the transaction may have for her. She should be informed that the purpose of this requirement is that she should not be able to dispute that she is legally bound by the documents once she has signed them. She should be asked to nominate a solicitor whom she is willing to instruct to advise her, separately from her husband, and act for her in giving the necessary confirmation to the bank. She should be informed that, if she wishes, the solicitor may be the same solicitor as is acting for her husband in the transaction. If the solicitor is already acting for both herself and her husband, she should also be asked whether she would prefer that a different solicitor should act for her regarding the bank's requirement for confirmation from a solicitor. The bank should not proceed with the transaction unless it has received an appropriate response from the wife directly.

Since the bank's representatives are likely to have a better idea of the husband's financial affairs than the solicitor, the bank must provide the solicitor with the financial information necessary to provide an explanation to the wife, unless the bank is willing to take on the role itself. In practice, it will probably become usual for banks to supply the solicitor with the necessary financial information. The information required will largely depend on the facts of the case. Ordinarily this will include information on the purpose for which the loan is required, the husband's current level of indebtedness, the amount of his current overdraft facility, and the amount and terms of any new facility. If the bank's requirement for security arises from a written application by the husband for a facility, a copy of the application should be sent to the solicitor. Of course the bank would need to obtain the consent of the husband for this confidential information to be circulated, but if this consent is not forthcoming the transaction would not be able to proceed.

If the bank suspects that the wife has been misled by her husband or is not acting of her own free will, the bank must inform the wife's solicitor of the facts giving rise to that belief or suspicion.

The bank should in every case obtain from the wife's solicitor a written confirmation to the effect above. It should be noted that the steps set out will apply only to future transactions. In respect to past transactions, the bank will usually be regarded as having discharged its obligations if the solicitor acting for the wife has given the bank confirmation to the effect that they have brought home to the wife the risks she is running in acting as surety in the transaction.

In future, banks should regulate their affairs on the basis that they are put on inquiry in every case where the relationship between the surety and the debtor is not a commercial one. A bank must always take care therefore to ensure that reasonable steps are taken to inform the individual guarantor as to the risks she is taking by acting as surety. If the bank or other creditor does not take such steps it will be deemed to have any notice of any claim the guarantor may have that the transaction was procured by undue influence or misrepresentation on the part of the debtor.

3. What are the responsibilities of the solicitor in advising the wife?

It must always be remembered that the solicitor is acting solely for the wife and is not an agent of the bank. The solicitor will need to explain to the wife the purpose for which they have become involved. They should also advise the wife that their involvement may be used by the bank to counter any suggestion that she has been compelled to enter the transaction by the husband or that she has not properly understood the implications of the proposed transaction. The solicitor will need to obtain confirmation from the wife that she wishes them to act for her in the matter and to advise her on the legal and practical implications of the proposed transaction. Once the instruction has been obtained from the wife, the content of the advice provided by the solicitor will be dictated by the facts of the case.

As a minimum the solicitor would typically be expected to cover the following matters:

1 The solicitor will need to explain the nature of the documents and the practical consequences these will have for the wife if she signs them. The solicitor should draw her attention to the fact that she could lose her home if her husband's business fails to prosper.

2 The solicitor should advise her that her home may be her only substantial asset, as well as the family home, and that she could be made bankrupt.

3 The solicitor will need to point out the seriousness of the risks involved.

4 The wife should be told the purpose of the new lending facility – its amount and principal terms. She should be informed that the bank may increase the loan facility, change its terms, or grant a new facility without further reference to her. She should be told the extent of her liability under the guarantee.

5 The solicitor should discuss the wife's financial means, including her understanding of the property to be charged, and whether the wife or her husband have any other assets out of which payment can be made if the husband's business fails.

6 The solicitor should explain clearly to the wife that she has a choice whether or not to enter the arrangement and the decision is hers alone. In explaining this choice the solicitor should discuss the current financial position, including the amount of the husband's present indebtedness and the amount of his current overdraft facility.

7 The solicitor should check whether the wife wishes to proceed. They should ask if she is content for the solicitor to write to the bank confirming that they have explained the nature of the documents and the practical implications they may have for her. They should also ask if she would prefer the solicitor to negotiate with the bank on the terms of the transaction, for instance, the sequence in which various securities are called in or the level of her liability. The solicitor should not give any confirmation to the bank without the wife's authority.

The solicitor's meeting with the wife should take place in a face-to-face meeting without the husband being present. The solicitor's explanations should be in non-technical language in order to ensure that the wife has a clear understanding of her position. The interview should not be regarded as a formality since the solicitor has an important task to perform in such transactions.

The solicitor must ensure that they obtain from the bank any information necessary. If the bank fails to provide this information, then the solicitor must decline to provide the confirmation required by the bank. It is not, however, the solicitor's role to veto the transaction by declining to provide the confirmation. The solicitor's role is to explain the documents to the wife and the risks involved. If the solicitor considers that the transaction is not in the best interests of the wife they should tell her so. Ultimately, the decision whether or not to enter into the transaction is the wife's, not the solicitor's, since the wife may have her own reasons for entering into a transaction that might be regarded as unwise. If it is clearly apparent that the wife is being seriously wronged, then the proper action for the solicitor is to decline to act for her.

Can the solicitor act for the husband or the bank and the wife at the same time? As seen earlier, this has been a vexed question that has arisen over the years. Lord Nicholls considered that a clear and simple rule was required to provide an answer to this question. He considered it was confusing to use a rule based on whether the bank deals directly with the husband and the wife, or whether the bank deals with the solicitors acting for the husband and the wife, as seen in **Bank of Baroda v Rayarel**. He considered that some balance was required here depending on the circumstances. Thus, some factors clearly pointed to the need for the solicitor to act for the wife alone. For example, a wife may be inhibited in discussing the transaction with a solicitor who is also acting for her husband, as in **Banco Exterior Internacional v Mann**, above. A solicitor may not be able to give the same single-minded attention to the wife's interests as they would if they were acting solely for her. Lord Nicholls considered that as a matter of general understanding 'independent advice' would suggest that the solicitor should not be acting within the same transaction for the person who is the source of any undue influence.

Lord Nicholls thought that there was nothing inherently wrong in the solicitor also acting for the bank or the husband and the wife, provided it is in the wife's best interests and no conflicts of duty or interests arise. For instance, the costs of the transaction may be lower than if the solicitor acts for her solely; the wife may be happier being advised by the family solicitor; sometimes the solicitor who knows the husband and wife and their histories may be better placed to give advice than a solicitor who is a complete stranger.

Lord Nicholls considered that the advantages attached to the solicitor acting for both parties outweighed independent advice being applied prescriptively to each party. Once the solicitor receives instructions from the wife the solicitor assumes legal and professional responsibilities directed towards her alone and is concerned only with her interests. In every case the solicitor must consider whether there is any conflict of interest or duty and decide whether it is in the wife's best interests for them to accept instructions from her. The House of Lords, however, did recognise that there could be some circumstances where a solicitor should decline to act for the wife and refuse to supply the bank with confirmation that the wife had been advised appropriately. The court stated that such circumstances arose in 'exceptional cases where it is obvious that the wife is being grievously wronged'. The case of **Crédit Lyonnais Bank Nederland NV v Burch** is often cited as an example here.

The facts were that Mrs Burch was only a modestly paid employee who, despite having no financial interest in a company, was persuaded to act as surety for the company's debts by way of a second charge on her small flat. The flat was valued at £100,000 and was already subject to a charge of £30,000. The second charge exposed her to unlimited liability for an unlimited period of time. At the time she entered into the second charge she was not aware that the current level of indebtedness of the company would have meant that she would have lost her home and incurred a personal debt of £200,000. Clearly this was a transaction which not only was manifestly to her disadvantage but was one which shocked 'the conscience of the court'.

The House of Lords' decision in **Etridge No. 2** now provides for a coherent process for dealing with surety arrangements. It should be noted that the principles apply to any lender embarking on such a transaction – it is not confined to banks. Effectively both lenders and solicitors have now put on notice that married couples must no longer be considered as a single unit, but as two separate individuals who may have conflicting interests. It is to be hoped that this decision will also put to bed the catalogue of confusion that has arisen since the decision in **O'Brien**.

The effects of undue influence

Objective 6

For more on restitution refer to Chapter 18.

The effect of undue influence on a contract is to render it voidable rather than void. It follows that the victim must take steps to avoid the contract by rescinding it. As in other instances where rescission is the remedy it may be lost where *restitutio in integrum* is impossible, or where the contract has been affirmed or where a bona fide third party has acquired the title to any property sold.

It should be noted that restitution does not have to be precise but merely substantial, as in **O'Sullivan v Management and Music Ltd** [1985] QB 428. In **TSB Bank plc v Camfield** [1995] 1 All ER 951, however, it was stated that where rescission is ordered the whole transaction is to be set aside (*restitutio in integrum*). In that case the wife was persuaded by her husband to charge her beneficial interest as security for a loan facility for the husband's business. The husband, on the basis of an innocent misrepresentation, falsely told his wife that the maximum liability on the loan would be £15,000, being his share of a £30,000 loan to himself and his partner. In fact the charge was an unlimited one. It was held that the charge should be set aside in its entirety and that the wife was not required to make restitution of even the £15,000 she thought the charge amounted to. The basis of the decision was that the wife would not have agreed to the transaction at all had she known that the charge was to secure unlimited liability. In *Newbiggin v Adam* (1886) 34 ChD 582, Bowen LJ described the principle in the following terms:

> There ought, as it appears to me, to be a giving back and a taking back on both sides, including the giving back and taking back of the obligations which the contract has created, as well as the giving back and taking back of the advantages.

This principle is important since it is designed to prevent unjust enrichment arising. In *Camfield*, however, the wife obtained no benefit whatsoever and therefore the principle had no application as regards the wife since she had nothing to give back. By the same token it would be wrong to impose terms on any relief that she sought.

But what of the situation where a benefit is obtained? At what level should the restitution be assessed? At first instance in *Dunbar Bank plc v Nadeem and Another* [1997] 2 All ER 253, while finding that undue influence was present, the judge refused to set the transaction aside unconditionally, as occurred in *Camfield*. He found that case to be quite different because there the wife received no benefit from the transaction. Relying on *Erlanger v New Sombrero Phosphate Co.* (1878) 3 App Cas 1218, he concluded that there could be no setting aside of the transaction unless Mrs Nadeem accounted to the bank for the benefit she received from the money advanced. Since she had received a half-share in the home, the question arose as to whether she should refund either the full amount of the loan or half that plus interest. The judge concluded that the latter should be repaid since otherwise the wife would be funding her husband's share of the loan and interest in the home. In the Court of Appeal it was stated that the judge at first instance was wrong in principle to impose the condition he did. Millett LJ considered that there were two agreements. The first was made between Mr Nadeem and his wife, that he would give her a half-interest in the home on the basis that she would join him in charging the property with the moneys advanced by the bank to effect the purchase. Thus Mrs Nadeem would get a beneficial interest or share in the property. The second transaction was between Mr and Mrs Nadeem and the bank on the terms set out in a letter describing the loan facility.

On the basis of the two agreements Mrs Nadeem obtained, first, an interest in the property and, second, a loan advance of £260,000 on the basis that £210,000 would be used to purchase the property, which she and her husband would charge to the bank to secure the repayment of the loan moneys. In relation to the second agreement there was no question of Mrs Nadeem getting a free-standing loan to do with what she wanted. The loan had to be applied for the purpose of acquiring the property.

In assessing the level of restitution it is necessary to consider the level of Mrs Nadeem's enrichment since it is this which restitution seeks to redress. Millett LJ and Morritt LJ held that this should not be based on the money advanced but on the interest she obtained in the property by way of the loan because this was the extent of her enrichment. They thus concluded that in having the legal charge discharged as against her she should restore the beneficial interest to her husband. It should be noted that her obligation to restore the beneficial interest was not an obligation to restore it to the bank since it was not derived from the bank. The consequence of the beneficial interest being restored to the husband would mean that the whole beneficial interest would come within his charge to the bank. A further consequence, however, would be that the wife would have no defence to claims for possession of the property brought by the bank in order to recoup the loan.

Problems can arise where restitution is ordered but the value of the property in question has changed. Such a situation arose in the case of *Cheese v Thomas*.

Cheese v *Thomas* [1994] 1 WLR 129

In this case, the plaintiff (Cheese) bought a house with his great-nephew (Thomas) for £83,000. The money for the purchase was raised by the plaintiff contributing £43,000 and the defendant £40,000 by way of a mortgage on the property for that amount. The house was purchased in the defendant's name, though it was agreed that the plaintiff would have sole use of the house for the rest of his life. It was further agreed that on the plaintiff's death the house would belong to the defendant exclusively. Eventually the plaintiff became worried that the defendant was not paying the mortgage repayments, conduct which inevitably would have placed his interest in the property at risk. The plaintiff thus sought to have the arrangement set aside on the basis of undue influence.

The judge at first instance ruled that the agreement could be set aside for undue influence. Normally, where restitution is ordered, the plaintiff should have been able to recover his full £43,000 contribution since the principle behind this remedy is that the parties should be restored to their original positions. In this case, however, the house was sold for £55,400, i.e. a £27,600 loss. Should the plaintiff receive his £43,000 in full or only a proportion of it to reflect the loss sustained on the sale of the property? The Court of Appeal held that it was appropriate that the loss should be shared since each party had contributed to the purchase of a house in which each would have an interest. Further, the defendant's personal conduct was not found to be open to criticism – he had acted as an 'innocent fiduciary' rather than in some unconscionable manner. Presumably the result of this decision is that if the parties can show that they have an interest in the property then, if the property has been sold at a profit, the parties would have likewise been entitled to a share of the profit.

Inequality of bargaining power

Objective
7

In ***Lloyds Bank Ltd* v *Bundy***, Lord Denning MR propounded a wider doctrine of equitable intervention whereby relief would be given where some unfair advantage had been obtained of a party to a transaction because of a substantial difference in the bargaining powers between the parties.

Lord Denning, rather than formulate a judgement in terms of undue influence, decided, having examined various categories of unconscionable bargains, to base his decision on a general theory that the courts could, and should in this case, give relief where the parties were of substantially unequal bargaining strengths. He stated the theory in the following terms:

> Gathering all together, I would suggest that through all these instances there runs a single thread. They rest on 'inequality of bargaining power'. By virtue of it, the English law gives relief to one who, without independent advice, enters into a contract upon terms which are very unfair or transfers of property for a consideration which is grossly inadequate, when his bargaining power is grievously impaired by reason of his own needs or desires, or by his own ignorance or infirmity coupled with undue influences or pressures brought to bear on him by or for the benefit of the other.

The other members of the Court of Appeal, while expressing sympathy with the view of Lord Denning, did not see fit to follow it and based their decisions on an orthodox application of the principles to be found in the doctrine of undue influence. Further, Lord Denning's approach was not followed in ***National Westminster Bank Ltd* v *Morgan*** by Lord Scarman, who stated:

> The fact of an unequal bargain will, of course, be a relevant feature in some cases of undue influence. But it can never become an appropriate basis of principle of an equitable doctrine

which is concerned with transactions 'not to be reasonably accounted for on the ground of friendship, relationship, charity or other ordinary motives on which ordinary men act' (Lindley LJ in *Allcard* v *Skinner*).

To set up a general doctrine of inequality of bargaining power, Lord Scarman further stated, would require a legislative enactment. Such a doctrine does exist within the United States Uniform Commercial Code, but the only indications of the United Kingdom Parliament moving in this direction have been in very specific instances of hire purchase and consumer protection legislation. For instance, the Consumer Credit Act 2006, s 19 (amending the Consumer Credit Act 1974 by inserting a new s 140A into the 1974 Act) allows the court to adjust a credit agreement if the court decides that the relationship between the creditor and the debtor arising out of the agreement is unfair to the debtor because of any of the terms of the agreement, the manner in which the creditor has exercised or enforced their rights under the agreement, or any other thing done (or not done) by or on behalf of the creditor either before or after the making of the agreement. The Consumer Credit Act 2006, s 20 also inserts a new s 140B into the 1974 Act that gives the courts powers to regulate unfair relationships. Thus, *inter alia*, the court can require the creditor or any associate or former associate to repay in whole or in part any sum paid by the debtor. The court can reduce or discharge any sum payable by the debtor and set aside any duty imposed on the debtor or on a surety by virtue of the agreement. The court may also direct the return to a surety of any property provided by them for the purposes of the security and, finally, the court can alter the terms of the agreement. Further, there are criminal sanctions available under the Fair Trading Act 1973, s 17, in situations where a business practice subjects consumers to undue pressure.

The Unfair Terms in Consumer Contracts Regulations 1999, also introduced a concept of unfairness in the law by virtue of reg 5(1) of the 1999 Regulations:

> A contractual term which has not been individually negotiated shall be regarded as unfair if, contrary to the requirement of good faith, it causes a significant imbalance in the parties' rights and obligations arising under the contract to the detriment of the consumer.

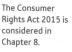

The Consumer Rights Act 2015 is considered in Chapter 8.

This provision has now been replaced by the Consumer Rights Act 2015 s 62(4) which provides for a very similar provision:

> A term is unfair if, contrary to the requirement of good faith, it causes a significant imbalance in the parties' rights and obligations under the contract to the detriment of the consumer.

A similar provision is found within s 62(6) to cover consumer notices. It should be noted, however, that the Act, unlike the UTCCR, is not limited in its application to standard-form contracts. The change reflects the broadening out of the test so that it extends beyond standard terms, though arguably it may be difficult to prove that a term or notice is unfair if it has been individually negotiated. The change, however, does away with the possibility of an argument developing as to whether or not a term or notice was individually negotiated.

The Act continues to provide for a general concept of fairness by imposing a requirement of 'good faith'. The Act requires that the assessment of the unfair nature of a term or consumer notice should be made by taking into account the nature of the subject matter of the contract, and by reference to all the circumstances existing when the term was agreed and to all of the other terms of the contract or of any other contract on which it depends – s 62(5) and (7).

This guidance by its very nature is very general and again points to the fluid nature by which the courts are able to deduct unfairness in the particular circumstances of a case; however, s 63(1) provides that Part 1 of Schedule 2 contains an indicative and non-exhaustive list of terms of consumer contracts that may be regarded as unfair (the 'grey list'). This section and Schedule 2 are based on Unfair Terms in Consumer Contracts Directive 93/13/ EEC. The terms on the list are not automatically unfair, but may be used to assist a court when considering the application of the fairness test in s 62 to a particular case.

The issues relating to fairness have been considered in the case of **Director General of Fair Trading v First National Bank plc** [2001] 3 WLR 1297 (HL), which was considered in more detail in Chapter 8.

While Lord Denning's views have been virtually dismissed by the courts, some academics have expressed some sympathy with his exposition of a general doctrine. Nevertheless it seems highly unlikely such an approach will be adopted since it is all too easy to deal with cases on the traditional basis of duress (including economic duress) and undue influence. Further, Lord Denning's general doctrine is far too wide and is marked by an absence of governing principles within it, since inequality of bargaining power can exist in a vast number of cases and it is inconceivable that each one of these could be avoided on this basis. There can be a world of difference between a case where a party exercises a superior bargaining position over another and a case where that person's bargaining power is impaired, thus putting the other party in a superior position. The superior or weaker position may also arise from the effects of a completely external commercial source. Lastly, Lord Denning failed to make clear that it is not the fact of inequality of bargaining power that will render a contract voidable, but a state of affairs whereby a party in a superior position has abused that position to the detriment of the weaker individual.

The European Unfair Commercial Practices Directive 2005/29/EC (OJ L 149/22) also made an o impact on the law relating to unfair practices, seeking to achieve a high level of consumer protection by approximating the law and regulations of Member States as regards unfair commercial practices that harm consumers' economic interests. The provisions relating to the enforcement of the law of unfair terms are now also contained within the Consumer Rights Act 2015 and provide a mechanism whereby alleged unfair terms can be challenged by some body, person or persons, other than a consumer, in civil litigation. No guidance was given in the Directive as to the form that such a mechanism should take, except insofar as Art 7(2) provided that there must be a means by which any person or body that has a legitimate interest in protecting consumers can challenge that 'contractual terms drawn up for general use are unfair'. The provisions for allowing this are contained in s 70 and Schedules 3 and 5, which are again considered more fully in Chapter 8.

Summary

The common law concept of duress

- Duress relates to contracts induced by violence or the threat of violence.
- The act or threatened act must be illegal:
  - it may amount to either a tort or a crime;
  - the threat must be directed at a person.
- NB: Lawful threats cannot be duress. (Lawful imprisonment as in **Williams v Bayley**.)
- Duress renders the contract voidable.
- Threat to goods cannot amount to duress (**Maskell v Horner**).
- Economic duress. **D & C Builders Ltd v Rees; Atlas Express Ltd v Kafco (Importers and Distributors) Ltd; Vantage Navigation Corporation v Suhail and Saud Bahawn Building Materials LLC (The Alev).**

The equitable concept of undue influence

- The transaction entered must be of manifest disadvantage to the victim – *Bank of Credit and Commerce International SA v Aboody*.
- *Royal Bank of Scotland v Etridge (No. 2)* confirmed the two types of undue influence:

  1 Class 1: actual undue influence.
  2 Class 2: presumed undue influence, which had two sub-classifications:
     - Class 2A. Overt acts of improper pressure or coercion such as unlawful threats . . .
     - Class 2B. Interparty relationships where one has acquired a measure of influence, or ascendancy over another and then takes unfair advantage . . .

Class 1: Actual undue influence

- Occurs where there is no special relationship between the parties so that there is no abuse of a particular confidence.
- The claimant must prove that the transaction was manifestly disadvantageous.
- *National Westminster Bank plc v Morgan*.
- The exercise of undue influence is one of fact.

Class 2: Presumed undue influence

2A Presumed undue influence

Examples of automatic presumed undue influence:

- trustee and beneficiary – *Benningfield v Baxter*;
- solicitor and client – *Wright v Carter*;
- parent and child – *Powell v Powell*;
- religious leader/adviser and disciple/parishioner – *Allcard v Skinner*.

The claimant must show:

1 a relationship of trust or confidence exists between themselves and the wrongdoer, and
2 the existence of a transaction which calls for an explanation.

NB: The victim need not prove that the undue influence has actually taken place; all they have to prove is that a confidential relationship has arisen and that the transaction itself calls for an explanation.

In *Etridge No. 2* it was considered that it was only in Class 2A undue influence that there was a true presumption of influence.

2B Presumed undue influence

Example:

- Husband and wife relationships: *Midland Bank plc v Shephard*.

  The burden of proof:

- The victim will be able to set aside a transaction by proving as of fact that they have placed a trust and confidence in the wrongdoer, without the need to prove that an actual undue influence arose.
- *Etridge No. 2* provides authority that presumed undue influence merely shifts the evidential burden of proof from the claimant to the wrongdoer.

- It is not a presumption that undue influence exists per se, but rather that the burden of explaining why the transaction was not caused by undue influence is shifted to the wrongdoer.

The effect of undue influence on third parties

Example:

- Informal business dealings between a husband and wife would be sufficient to put a creditor on constructive notice if two factors are satisfied:

  (a) the transaction is on its face not to the financial advantage of the wife; and
  (b) there is a substantial risk in transactions of that kind that, in procuring the wife to act as surety, the husband has committed a legal or equitable wrong.

Avoiding constructive notice

- A bank must take reasonable steps to avoid constructive notice by ensuring that the innocent party has obtained independent legal advice (*Royal Bank of Scotland* v *Etridge (No. 2)*).

  (a) When is the bank put on inquiry?
  (b) What steps should the bank take when put on inquiry?
  (c) What are the responsibilities of the solicitor in advising the wife? The House of Lords decision in *Etridge No. 2* now provides for a coherent process for dealing with surety arrangements.

The effects of undue influence

- The effect of undue influence on a contract is to render it voidable rather than void.
- The victim must take steps to avoid the contract by rescinding it.
- Rescission may be lost where *restitutio in integrum* is impossible, or where the contract has been affirmed or where a bona fide third party has acquired the title to any property sold to him.
- Restitution does not have to be precise but merely substantial (*O'Sullivan* v *Management and Music Ltd*).

Inequality of bargaining power

- Lord Denning MR proposed a wider doctrine of equitable intervention in *Lloyds Bank Ltd* v *Bundy* where relief would be given where some unfair advantage had been obtained of a party to a transaction because of a substantial difference in the bargaining powers between the parties. This has been disapproved of by the English courts in *National Westminster Bank Ltd* v *Morgan* by Lord Scarman.
- The European Unfair Commercial Practices Directive 2005/29/EC.

Further reading

Atiyah, 'Economic Duress and the Overborne Will' (1982) 98 *Law Quarterly Review* 197

Beatson, Burrows and Cartwright, *Anson's Law of Contract*, 30th edn (Oxford University Press, 2016)

Bigwood, 'Undue Influence in the House of Lords: Principles and Proof' (2002) 65 *Modern Law Review* 435

Chen-Wishart, 'Loss Sharing, Undue Influence and Manifest Disadvantage' (1993) 110 *Law Quarterly Review* 173

Doyle, 'Borrowing Under the Influence' (1994) 15 *Business Law Review* 6

Furmston, *Cheshire, Fifoot and Furmston's Law of Contract*, 16th edn (Oxford University Press, 2012)

Korotana, 'Undue Influence in the Context of the Residential Mortgage Transaction' (2000) 21 *Business Law Review* 226

Levy, 'Under Duress' (2006) 156 *New Law Journal* 936

Nash, 'A Killer Contract' (2006) 156 *New Law Journal* 280

Pawlowski and Greer, 'Constructive Notice and Independent Legal Advice: A Study of Lending Institution Practice' [2001] *Conveyancer and Property Lawyer* 229

Phang and Tijo, 'The Uncertain Boundaries of Undue Influence' [2002] *Lloyd's Maritime and Commercial Law Quarterly* 231

Smith and Atiyah, *Atiyah's Introduction to the Law of Contract*, 6th edn (Oxford University Press, 2006)

Tamblyn, 'Causation and Bad Faith in Economic Duress' (2011) 27 *Journal of Contract Law* 140

Thal, 'The Inequality of Bargaining Power Doctrine: The Problem of Defining Contractual Unfairness' (1988) 8 *Oxford Journal of Legal Studies* 17

Tiplady, 'The Judicial Control of Contractual Unfairness' (1983) 46 *Modern Law Review* 601

Peel, Treitel *Law of Contract*, 14th edn (Sweet and Maxwell, 2015)

Wong, 'Revisiting *Barclays Bank* v *O'Brien* and Independent Legal Advice for Vulnerable Sureties' [2002] *Journal of Business Law* 439

Illegality

Objectives

After reading this chapter you should be able to:

1. Know and understand how illegal contracts are classified.

2. Recognise the effects of illegal acts that are illegal by statute.

3. Understand the circumstances that render a contract illegal at common law.

4. Know and understand the effects of illegality.

5. Be aware of the recommendations of the Law Commission and the need to reform the illegality defence.

6. Understand the effects of contracts that are in restraint of trade and the circumstances when these arise.

7. Understand and apply the means by which parties recover money or property in illegal contracts and how the courts apply severance.

8. Understand the circumstances in which the doctrine of severance can be applied.

Introduction

Oliver Cromwell's assertion of the state of English land law in the seventeenth century that it was an 'ungodly jumble' would also be most apt when applied to this area of the law of contract today. The area is a minefield for the student of the subject since it has little in the way of uniform structure and what there is produces tremendous inconsistencies. Students may therefore be forewarned by the words of A. P. Herbert in *Uncommon Law* (1989) who says of the effect of the law relating to lotteries and gaming, 'This department of the law is a labyrinth of which Parliament and the Courts may well be proud!' Similarly in *Parkingeye Ltd v Somerfield Stores Ltd* [2012] EWCA Civ 1338 at para 28, Sir Robin Jacob stated 'illegality and the law of contract is notoriously knotty territory' and in fact it is one of the least satisfactory parts of the law of contract. Thrown into this mêlée is the *coup de grâce* for many people studying this area in that the terms 'illegal', 'void' and 'unenforceable' are not used consistently by the judges and are often used interchangeably. Thus Etherton LJ put it this way in *Les Laboratoires Servier v Apotex Inc* [2012] EWCA Civ 593:

It is not necessary in order to resolve this appeal to undertake a comprehensive analysis of the decided cases. Such an exercise would in any event be complex, very lengthy and in large part unrewarding. The decisions inevitably turn on their own particular facts. The statements of law or principle they contain are not all consistent or easily reconciled. The jurisprudence in this area has been an evolving one, but its evolution has not followed a consistent pattern.

This topic concerns the fundamental principle that the courts will not enforce contracts that are considered to be **illegal**. Although this principle seems simple enough, the problem is that illegality as a concept covers a multitude of sins. While it is clearly illegal to commission the murder of another, at the same time, at the other end of the spectrum, it is also illegal to commission the theft of a toy from a shop or commit some other minor transgression. Thus there is a wide disparity in the seriousness of **illegal contracts**, but the question arises as to whether the various illegal acts should all have the same degree of effect on the contract. In addition to the problems of reconciling the differences that arise in this broad spectrum there looms the spectre of decisions based on the notion of public policy. Thus a transaction is also regarded as illegal where the conduct involved is one which the court regards as being contrary to the public interest even though the conduct itself is not actually unlawful.

The centrality of public policy to the issue of illegality is borne out by the observation of Lord Wright in **Vita Food Products Inc v Unus Shipping Co**. [1939] AC 277:

> Each case has to be considered on its merits. Nor must it be forgotten that the rule by which contracts not expressly forbidden by statute or declared to be void are in proper cases nullified for disobedience to a statute is a rule of public policy only, and public policy understood in a wider sense may at times be better served by refusing to nullify a bargain save on serious and sufficient grounds.

The classification of illegality

Objective
1

Following on from the above, it is possible to divide the incidence of illegality into two broad categories: (1) contracts that involve the commission of a legal wrong, and (2) transactions which are contrary to public policy. In many of the decisions in the cases dealing with illegality much is sometimes made of two general principles summed up in the expressions *ex turpi causa non oritur actio* or 'no action arises from an unworthy cause' and *in pari delicto, potior est conditio defendentis* or 'where the guilt is shared the defendant's position is stronger'. To apply the principles rigidly would clearly cause injustice to parties in some cases and therefore the courts have seen fit to step outside of these rules to arrive at a preferred outcome. This has resulted in a body of law that is inconsistent, often incomprehensible and lacking in certainty – indeed, the very antithesis of what a good legal system should represent.

Authors have attempted to classify the circumstances of illegality in many ways, and rarely satisfactorily, since it is a truism to state that the circumstances of illegality probably defy classification in terms of conceptual analysis. In the Law Commission's *Report on the Illegality Defence* (Law Com. No. 320, 2010) it was stated that the principle of illegality in the law of contract is:

> a body of law made up of an intricate web of tangled rules that are difficult to ascertain and distinguish. Neither litigants not their advisers are able to predict with confidence which particular line of authority the court may follow.

When contracts that involve the commission of a legal wrong are examined, it can be seen that this category in turn also falls into two broad categories: breaches of statutory provisions; and crimes or civil wrongs that arise at common law. Contracts involving transactions that are contrary to public policy covers the type of activity that the law disapproves of as not being in the interests of the public. There are very many examples of these types of transactions so this work will deal with what is probably a very broad selection, though they are categories which are widely recognised.

In this work it has been decided to treat the subject matter under two categories – where an act is illegal by statute and where an act is illegal at common law – though this is subdivided into contracts for the commission of an act that is wrong at common law and contracts that are contrary to public policy. It should be noted that these categories are to some degree arbitrary and must be seen merely as vehicles for providing a descriptive analysis of the law rather than as forming conceptual boundaries.

Acts illegal by statute

Where the contract is prohibited by statute

Objective 2

Where a contract is expressly declared to be prohibited in a statute then there is little doubt that Parliament intended that the contract could not be enforced. An example of such a case is *Cope v Rowlands* (1836) 2 M & W 149, below. Where the statute is silent on the point, then it is for the court to interpret the relevant provisions so as to determine whether the legislation impliedly renders the contract unenforceable by either or both parties. It should be noted that while the statute in question may involve a criminal offence, this is not necessarily the case for an implied statutory prohibition to apply.

In *Re Mahmoud and Ispahani* [1921] 2 KB 716, the Seeds, Oils and Fats Order 1919 prohibited the dealing in linseed oil without a licence from the Food Controller. The plaintiff had a licence to deal in linseed oil with other such licensed dealers. He agreed to sell linseed oil to the defendant and asked him if he held a licence to deal in such oils. The defendant stated that he did, but that was a fraudulent misrepresentation. The defendant subsequently refused to accept the delivery of the linseed oil on the basis that he in fact did not have a licence. The plaintiff sued for damages for non-acceptance. Despite the fact that the plaintiff was unaware that the contract was illegal when the contract was made, it was held that his action would fail. The Court of Appeal stated that the legislation was clear and unequivocal that such contracts were impliedly prohibited by statute and unenforceable.

Frequently, statutes expressly specify the effects that a breach of a particular Act of Parliament has on a contract today. The principle can also be seen in the case of *Mohamed v Alaga & Co. (a firm)* [2000] 1 WLR 1815, where a firm of solicitors agreed to pay to an individual (M) a fee for introducing refugees requiring legal services to the firm. The payments were to be taken from the legal aid paid to the firm, such payments being expressly prohibited by the Solicitors Practice Rules 1990. M was not aware of the illegality. It was held that public policy prevented recovery for these services either by way of an action for breach of contract or under the law of restitution. The Court of Appeal, however, allowed M to amend his claim so that he could claim on a *quantum meruit* basis for interpreting services, since fees for these were allowable under the legislation. The fact that M was not aware of the breach and the fact that public policy did not preclude him for claiming for his interpretation services was central to this approach.

Contracts performed in an unlawful manner

Illegality may have two principal effects on a contract and the distinction between the two is of the utmost importance. First, a contract may be regarded as illegal if the actual creation of the contract itself is prohibited. The position here is that the contract is void *ab initio*. Thus in *Cope* v *Rowlands* it was provided by statute that anyone acting as a broker in the City of London had to have a licence or pay £25 to the City for any transaction conducted without such a licence. The plaintiff was an unlicensed broker, and when he sued the defendant for his commission in buying and selling the defendant's stock it was held that the action must fail. Parker B stated:

> The legislature had in view, as one object, the benefit and security of the public in those important transactions which are negotiated by brokers. The clause, therefore, which imposes a penalty, must be taken . . . to imply a prohibition of all unadmitted persons to act as brokers, and consequently to prohibit, by necessary inference, all contracts which such persons make for compensation to themselves for so acting.

Second, a contract may be created lawfully but nevertheless be illegal because of the way in which it is performed. In such a situation the validity or invalidity of the contract is not nearly so decisive. In *Anderson Ltd* v *Daniel* [1924] 1 KB 138, there was a statutory requirement that vendors of artificial fertilisers had to state on their invoice the chemical breakdown of the fertiliser. In the contract in question the vendors had sold 10 tons of fertiliser to the defendants but failed to comply with the statutory requirement. When the defendants failed to pay, the plaintiffs sued for the price, but were met with the defence that the contract was unenforceable due to statutory invalidity. It was held that the plaintiffs would lose in their action since the court stated that where a contract is lawful in its inception but illegal in its execution, then the plaintiff vendors would be unable to rely on their contractual rights. In *Shaw* v *Groom* [1970] 2 QB 504, however, it was held that where a landlord had failed to give his tenant a rent book, thereby committing an offence, he could nevertheless claim the rent owed by the tenant. The aim of the legislation here was to punish the landlord rather than to render the lease invalid, which would clearly be detrimental to the tenant.

The test for deciding which approach to take was stated in *St John Shipping Corporation* v *Joseph Rank Ltd*.

St John Shipping Corporation v *Joseph Rank Ltd* [1956] 3 All ER 683

The defendants withheld part of the freight due to the plaintiffs on the basis that while carrying the cargo the master of the ship had overloaded the ship contrary to the Merchant Shipping Act 1932. The defendants contended that the plaintiffs in an action for the freight withheld could not enforce a contract that had been performed in an illegal manner. The court held that the plaintiffs could succeed, stating that the test in deciding the validity or invalidity was based on the question as to whether the statute intended to penalise the conduct of the offending party or to invalidate the contract itself. Here the court held that the statute did not interfere with the rights and remedies arising under the ordinary law of contract. If a statute does not expressly provide for a contractual claim to be unenforceable then the courts should not imply that it does so. As Lord Devlin, who was then a High Court judge, stated:

> I think that a court ought to be very slow to hold that a statute intends to interfere with the rights and remedies given by the ordinary law of contract. Caution in this respect is, I think, especially necessary in these times when so much of commercial life is governed by regulations of one sort or another, which may easily be broken without wicked intent.

An example of this approach may be seen in the case of **Hughes v Asset Managers plc** [1995] 3 All ER 669 (CA) where the appellants paid £3 million to the respondents so that they could purchase shares for the appellants. A month later the market fell and the appellants instructed the respondents to sell the shares, which they did at a loss of £1 million. The appellants sued for the recovery of the loss on the grounds, *inter alia*, that although the respondents were licensed to deal in securities by virtue of the Prevention of Fraud (Investments) Act 1958, s 1, the person who made the agreements on behalf of the respondents did not at the time hold a representative's licence as required by s 1(1)(b). As a result the appellants alleged that the agreements were a nullity since the Act prohibited unlicensed persons from dealing in securities.

It was held by the Court of Appeal that the 1958 Act was designed to protect the public by imposing criminal sanctions on those, whether as principals or agents, who dealt in securities without a licence. The public interest was fully met by the imposition of the sanctions. The Act was not directed towards the deals themselves nor against the parties to the deals, but against the employee/agent making the deal. The words of the Act did not show any parliamentary intention that the deals entered into via an unlicensed dealer would be struck down and thereby rendered ineffective. The appellants' claim was therefore rejected.

It may also be seen that the courts often adopt a more relaxed attitude where the innocent party is attempting to enforce the contract, but is unaware of an illegal act perpetrated by the other party. This was so in **Archbold's (Freightage) Ltd v S Spanglett Ltd** [1961] 1 All ER 417 where the defendants agreed to carry the goods of the plaintiff, who was unaware that the defendants did not have the requisite licence required by statute for such a transaction. The goods were stolen in transit and the plaintiff sued for compensation for the loss. It was held that he could succeed since the contract itself was not illegal in its inception and in any event the plaintiff was unaware of the illegal performance of the contract by the defendants.

A different attitude may, however, result where the innocent party condoned or otherwise participated in the illegal performance of the contract. This was so in **Ashmore, Benson, Pease & Co. Ltd v A V Dawson Ltd** [1973] 1 WLR 828 where the plaintiffs engaged the defendant road hauliers to carry a 25-ton tube to a port. The transport manager of the plaintiffs helped to supervise the loading of the tube on to the lorry, which had a maximum load weight of 20 tons. On the journey to the port the lorry overturned, damaging the tube. The plaintiffs sued to recover the losses resulting from the damage to the tube. It was held that the plaintiffs' action must fail since the transport manager had participated in the illegal performance of the contract.

There is clearly a public interest in the court not appearing to reward wrongdoing or condone a breach of the law. But where, as in **Parkingeye Ltd v Somerfield Stores Ltd** [2012] EWCA Civ 1338, both parties were complicit in the illegality; denial of one party's claim on that ground will be to give an unjustified benefit to the other. The rule that where both parties are equally at fault the defendant should prevail may be right in more serious cases (on the ground that the court should, in effect, wash its hands of the dispute), but may be a disproportionately severe response in less serious cases, especially where the parties did not appreciate that they were acting contrary to the law. There is a public interest in doing justice between the parties and, as Lord Wright said, in nullifying a bargain only on serious and sufficient grounds.

Parkingeye Ltd v Somerfield Stores Ltd [2012] EWCA Civ 1338

In the case the appellant, Somerfield Stores Ltd (S), had entered into a 15-month contract with Parkingeye Ltd (P) whereby P was to install and operate a monitoring and control system in a number of S's supermarket car parks. S allowed its customers a certain amount of free parking time, and levied a charge on overstayers. P's system read the registration numbers of vehicles using the car parks and recorded how long each was parked. P then sent overstayers a series of pro-forma letters demanding payment of the charge. Although the contract with S did not prescribe the form of those letters, they had nevertheless been approved by S before the contract was entered into. P received no payment from S but was entitled to retain all the overstay charges it collected. S terminated the contract after some six months, by which time the system had been installed in 17 of its car parks.

P claimed damages for loss of revenue resulting from the early termination of the contract. S defended the claim on the ground of illegality, claiming that one of P's pro-forma letters was deceptive and used illegal means to induce overstayers to pay. It argued that even though the overstayers were liable to pay, the deception tainted the whole contract and public policy required that it should be held unenforceable as a whole.

At first instance the judge rejected that defence. He found that the letter sent out by P contained serious and deliberate falsehoods, and found that P was guilty of the tort of deceit in respect of it. The judge, however, was not satisfied that P had had, at the time of the execution of the contract, a firm and settled intention to act in an unlawful manner. He found that insofar as there had been an agreement on the form of the third letter, that agreement was collateral to the main contract, which in itself was free from illegality.

S appealed against the rejection of its defence of illegality to an action for repudiatory breach of contract brought against it by P. In its appeal, S relied on a principle expressed in *Colen v Cebrian (UK) Ltd* [2003] EWCA Civ 1676. This stated that a contract was unenforceable if, at the time of its formation, one of the parties had the intention of performing it in an unlawful manner. The Court of Appeal considered that this principle could not be read as applying to any intended illegality of performance no matter how peripheral or partial. The Court of Appeal considered that in *Colen* the court was not considering a case like the one before it where the intention was limited to only a partial and minor mode of performance, and which was qualified in that it could be changed at any time, and indeed would have been changed had the illegality been pointed out. The Court of Appeal stated that the law was not in a straitjacket in that once it was shown that illegality of any sort was intended from the start that unenforceability would automatically result. The Court of Appeal in considering the scope of principle set out in *Colen* and *St John Shipping Corp v Joseph Rank Ltd* [1957] 1 QB 267 stated that a number of factors had to be considered: Firstly, the object and intent of the party seeking to enforce the contract; secondly, the gravity of the illegality and how central it was in the context of the contract and the claim; and, thirdly, the nature of the illegality. In *St John Shipping Corporation v Joseph Rank Ltd* [1957] 1 QB 267 at p 283, Devlin J stated as a general principle that:

> . . . a contract which is entered into with the object of committing an illegal act is unenforceable. The application of this principle depends upon proof of the intent, at the time the contract was made, to break the law; if the intent is mutual the contract is not enforceable at all, and, if unilateral, it is unenforceable at the suit of the party who is proved to have it.

However, one can see the justice of treating a party who deliberately sets out to break the law in a serious respect, such as overloading a vessel, differently from a party who breaks the law without meaning to do so or in a way which may be minor and indeed Devlin J had such differences in mind as he later stated:

> Persons who deliberately set out to break the law cannot expect to be aided in a court of justice, but it is a different matter when the law is unwittingly broken. To nullify a bargain in such circumstances frequently means that in a case – perhaps of such triviality no authority would have felt it worthwhile to prosecute – a seller, because he cannot enforce his civil rights, may forfeit a sum vastly in excess of any penalty that a criminal court would impose; and the sum forfeited will not go into the public purse but into the pockets of someone who is lucky enough to pick up the windfall or astute enough to have contrived to get it. It is questionable how far this contributes to public morality.

See later section in this chapter on The Law Commission and the reform of the illegality defence.

The Court of Appeal considered that the effect of illegality revolved around the centrality and illegality in the context of the contract and the claim. In looking at this matter it referred to the Law Commission's Consultative Report (No. 189), *The Illegality Defence* (2009) in which it was stated:

> However, it clearly cannot be in every case that where a contract is unlawfully performed, even where this was the original intention, that the offending party loses his or her remedies. Such a proposition would result in the widespread forfeiture of contractual remedies as a result of minor and incidental transgressions. Although there is general agreement on this point amongst academic commentators, there is surprisingly little authority.

The Court of Appeal held that the contract between S and P was not all or nothing, legal or illegal, as regards its performance or intended performance. The contract was never intended to be carried out in an illegal manner and that the contract envisaged continuous performance over a period of time. The court found that the contract was always intended to be carried out in a lawful manner and that if the principle invoked by S was accepted this would lead to a disproportionate result that P would be left with no remedy to recover revenue that would have been wholly lawful. P had no fixed intention to act unlawfully and the illegality that arose was incidental to only part of the contract and was not central to the contract as a whole. The proper course of action by S once it had become aware of the objectionable nature of the letter sent out by P was to draw it to P's attention and require P to perform the contract in a lawful manner. Toulson LJ considered there was no justice in S having the option of either behaving in that way or, if it preferred, of repudiating the contract. This would give S a windfall reward for its own previous illegality. If S's argument is taken to its logical conclusion, on appreciating that the letter was objectionable, it could have kept the point up its sleeve until P had installed all the monitoring equipment at its car parks which it required, and then terminated the contract at whatever moment best suited its commercial interest, so enabling it to keep for itself all subsequent payments by users of the car parks who overstayed. To borrow Devlin J's phrase, that would not contribute to public morality. In summary, the disallowance of P's claim on the ground of illegality is not compelled by the authorities, and it would not be a just and proportionate response to the illegality.

The Court of Appeal considered that the judge was correct in rejecting S's illegality defence for wrongful repudiation of the contract.

In other situations, an Act may impliedly indicate that the contract will not be rendered ineffective, in that the main sanction of the Act is directed towards the participants to the agreement, as in *Hughes* v *Asset Managers plc*, above. Where a statute only impliedly declares a contract to be prohibited then the court must examine the Act to find the intention of Parliament in respect of the effects of the prohibition on the contract.

Acts illegal at common law

Objective 3

The concept of a contract being illegal at common law is extremely wide and has its origins in the idea that a contract would not be upheld if its effect was contrary to the common good or it was injurious to society generally. The presence of such a concept in the nineteenth century and the early part of the twentieth century is rather contradictory to the idea of freedom of contract. While the courts supported this idea, they recognised the need to qualify it so that contracts that were regarded as abhorrent or prejudicial to the interests of the community would not be upheld. Very often the decisions in cases falling within this area of concern were declared invalid by the judges on the basis of a vague notion of public policy, a concept which, of course, may cover a multitude of sins.

One of the great problems with the concept of public policy is that it is vague and has extremely wide borders. Even in the nineteenth century it had its critics. Thus Burrough J in *Richardson v Mellish* (1924) 2 Bing 229 stated: 'I, for one, protest . . . against arguing too strongly upon public policy; – it is a very unruly horse, and when you get astride it you never know where it will carry you.' Further, Lord Jessel MR in *Printing and Numerical Registering Co. v Sampson* (1875) LR 19 Eq 462 counselled caution with its use. Lord Denning MR chose not to be reticent in handling the thorny stem of public policy and presented a reply to Burrough J in *Enderby Town FC Ltd v The Football Association Ltd* [1971] Ch 591 when he stated: 'With a good man in the saddle, the unruly horse can be kept in control. It can jump over obstacles.' The result has been something of a renaissance of public policy in recent times, though this is not perhaps so unusual since the concept lacks continuity. What one generation considers necessary for the common good is not necessarily true of the next generation, so it is inevitable that every so often a brush will make a clean sweep of areas that have, in the past, been subject to public policy and no doubt will introduce the concept to new aspects of commercial and social life.

Before we proceed to analyse in depth contracts contrary to public policy, a word about the organisation of the topic within this text would seem necessary. Some authors, including *Cheshire, Fifoot and Furmston*, discuss this area in two parts, namely, contracts illegal on grounds of public policy and contracts void on grounds of public policy. However, there is some disagreement as to which types of contracts are considered illegal and which are considered void. In particular, as was indicated in the introduction to this chapter, authors cannot agree on the effects of contracts being illegal or void at common law. In any event such a classification, as Treitel indicates, is an oversimplification since the effects of such contracts vary so much that it is almost impossible to group them under these two headings. In this work the contracts will be divided into contracts for the commission of an act that is wrong at common law and contracts which are contrary to public policy. However, it must again be stated that such a classification has been adopted in order to aid understanding of the subject matter rather than to place the contracts discussed into watertight compartments. With respect to contracts contrary to public policy, contracts in **restraint of trade** will be treated separately since this area of public policy is not only particularly important, but also somewhat lengthy.

Contracts for the commission of an act that is wrong at common law

It is clear that a contract to commit a crime must itself be illegal and the courts will not enforce such a contract. In *Bigos v Bousted* [1951] 1 All ER 92, it was held that a contract that was contrary to exchange control regulations would be unenforceable. Similarly, it is well established that a person cannot benefit from their own crime. Thus in **Beresford v Royal Insurance Co. Ltd** [1937] 2 KB 197, it was held that the relatives of a person who had committed suicide could not claim under a life insurance policy, even though the insurance allowed a claim in such circumstances, provided the suicide (which was a crime at this time) did not occur within two years of the making of the policy. The court considered that to allow a claim to succeed would be to allow the deceased to provide for his relatives via a criminal act. The principle, however, must be treated guardedly since there are a great many statutory offences today which often do not require a guilty intention to secure conviction. In such cases it would be harsh to apply a general rule that no one can benefit from their crime. It should be noted that in the field of motoring insurance it is still possible for an insured person to claim against their policy despite the fact that their actions might amount to a crime or incur civil liability, or both. In order for such a claim to be upheld, however, the act of the driver must not be a deliberate act but a negligent or reckless one, as was held in **Tinline v White Cross Insurance Association Ltd** [1921] 3 KB 327.

A contract will also be illegal if it has as its object the deliberate commission of a civil wrong. Thus a contract to commit an assault was held to be void in **Allen v Rescous** (1677) 2 Lev 174. Where, however, there is an unintentional commission of a civil wrong it would seem that if both the parties are unaware of the illegality then the contract is enforceable by and against each other. If, however, one party knows the contract to be illegal then it would seem that only the innocent party can enforce the contract.

Not surprisingly a contract to defraud the HM Revenue & Customs or a rating/polling authority whether national or local is clearly illegal. Thus in **Alexander v Rayson** [1936] 1 KB 169 there was a lease of a flat in Piccadilly. The rent was £450 per annum but the lease provided that certain other services were to be provided. The 'other services' were detailed in a second document and the defendant had to pay another £750 per annum for these services. A dispute arose and the defendant refused to pay the moneys due under the agreement. When sued the defendant stated that the object of having two documents was to deceive the local authority as to the rent payable since the calculation of the rateable value, and hence the rates, depended on the rent payable. The Court of Appeal held that the plaintiff would not be entitled to recover the moneys owed if the purpose of the two documents was indeed to perpetrate such a fraud.

Contracts contrary to public policy

Contracts prejudicial to the administration of justice

Such contracts are nearly always void and illegal no matter how slight the transgression. There are many examples of the application of this rule: for instance, an agreement not to proceed with divorce proceedings as in **Cooper v Willis** (1906) 22 TLR 582, an agreement by a wife that she would not apply for maintenance in divorce proceedings as in **Hyman v Hyman** [1929] AC 601, or an agreement by a witness not to give evidence as in **Harmony Shipping Co. SA v Davis** [1979] 3 All ER 177.

It is, of course, most important that the exercise of the criminal law should not be capable of being suppressed by virtue of some private agreement. The courts will not hesitate to declare such a contract illegal and void where the agreement results in the withdrawal of a prosecution of a crime. In some cases, however, the courts will allow the question of liability to be compromised by agreement provided the offence is not one which is contrary to public interest. Thus in cases of libel, which may be the subject of a private suit or a criminal prosecution, an agreement compromising a prosecution may well be upheld since the choice of civil or criminal proceedings lies in the hands of the injured party. A similar situation arises in cases involving assault as seen in **Keir v Leeman** (1846) 9 QB 371. Although in this case it was held that the compromise was void, nevertheless Lord Denman CJ stated that normally a compromise is lawful where the criminal offence is one which also gives rise to civil liability. He stated that compromise is not possible where the offence involves the public interest. The case was not simply a case of assault but involved the public offence of riot and an assault on a public officer (a sheriff's officer) carrying out his duties.

So far our examination of contracts that are prejudicial to the administration of justice has been concerned with the situation where a party attempts by means of a contract to prevent the force of the law being brought against himself. There are, however, two categories of contract which the law regards as unlawful since they tend to promote litigation resulting in actions that are not brought in good faith and may be regarded as speculative. It is regarded as contrary to public policy to allow a person to sell their right of action to another or, in fact, to allow a person to incite the bringing of litigation.

The two categories of contracts falling within this area are known as **maintenance** and **champerty**. A contract of maintenance arises when a person encourages and supports a course of litigation in which they have no interest. Such contracts will, however, be valid if they can show that they have just cause or excuse in promoting and supporting the litigation. Thus in **Martell v Consett Iron Co. Ltd** [1955] Ch 363, the action of a fishing club in supporting a riparian owner against the pollution of a river was held not to be a contract of maintenance.

Champerty is a contract in which a person is given assistance in bringing an action, either financially or by the provision of evidence, in return for a share in the rewards arising from the action, if successful. In **Trendtex Trading Corporation v Crédit Suisse** [1982] AC 679 (HL), Lord Wilberforce stated, at p. 694:

> [champerty] . . . involves trafficking in litigation – a type of transaction which, under English law, is contrary to public policy. I take the definition of 'champerty' . . . is a particular kind of maintenance, namely maintenance of an action in consideration of a promise to give the maintainer a share in the proceeds or subject matter of the action.

Originally both maintenance and champerty gave rise to both criminal and tortious liability but both have now been abolished by the Criminal Law Act 1967, ss 13 and 14. In relation to whether such contracts are treated as contrary to public policy or otherwise illegal, s 14(2) of this Act specifically preserves champerty as a rule of public policy that is capable of rendering a contract as unenforceable:

> The abolition of criminal and civil liability under the law of England and Wales for maintenance and champerty shall not affect any rule of that law as to the cases in which a contract is to be treated as contrary to public policy or otherwise illegal.

In **Factortame Ltd v Secretary of State for the Environment, Transport and the Regions (No. 2)** [2002] EWCA Civ 932, Lord Phillips stated that, because the principle is based on public policy, the law had to be kept continuously under review as public policy changes. Such a situation has been seen to have arisen by the introduction of conditional fee or 'no win no fee' agreements by the Courts and Legal Services Act 1990, s 58, as amended by the Access to Justice Act 1999. This means that, while previously officers of the court (solicitors) have had to be inhibited as a matter of public policy from putting themselves in a position where their personal interest conflicted with that of the court, this is no longer an absolute requirement. In certain situations the law expressly restricts the circumstances in which contracts in support of litigation are lawful, as in conditional fee agreements, and in these circumstances there is a clear indication as to the limits of public policy. In other circumstances, however, the courts have to look at the facts and consider whether, in the words of Lord Denning in *Re Trepca Mines Ltd (Application of Radomir Nicola Pachitch (Pasic))* [1962] 3 All ER 351, 'the champertous maintainer [has been] tempted, for his own personal gain, to inflame the damages, to suppress evidence, or even to suborn witnesses' so as to undermine the administration of justice. Thus for a contract to be champertous it must be in the nature of an agreement which undermines the legal process of litigation by way of providing the expert involved in the case with a significant financial interest in the outcome of the litigation.

Picton Jones & Co. v *Arcadia Developments* [1989] 3 EG 85

The plaintiffs, a firm of chartered surveyors, agreed to act for the defendants in their attempt to acquire some amusement arcades. The contract required the plaintiffs to make applications for gaming licences and planning permission, but their fees were only to be payable 'in the event of ultimate success'. The plaintiffs successfully carried out their part of the contract but when they pressed the defendants for their fee they were told that the contract was one of champerty and unenforceable. Further they maintained that such a method of dealing was contrary to the rules of the plaintiffs' professional body and as such contrary to public policy and void. With regard to the latter defence it was held that an action that is contrary to the rules of a professional association was not necessarily illegal at law. With regard to the allegation that the contract was one of champerty it was held that such contracts only applied to the outcome of litigation. The plaintiffs were thus successful.

A rather more conventional case involving champerty is that of *Simpson v Norfolk and Norwich University Hospital Trust* [2011] EWCA Civ 1149. The claimant's (S) late husband had contracted a hospital-acquired infection while dying from cancer in hospital. The infection had not contributed towards his death, but S believed that the defendant trust had failed properly to control the spread of infections and wanted to force it to confront its shortcomings. Another patient had also issued proceedings against the trust after contracting the same infection. He assigned his claim to S for £1 and S pursued it in her own name and for her own benefit. A district judge struck out the claim on the ground that a bare right to litigate was incapable of assignment. On appeal, it was held that the claim was of a personal nature and therefore incapable of assignment. It was further held that even if the claim was capable of assignment, S did not have the necessary interest to support a valid assignment.

The issues that arose before the Court of Appeal were whether it was possible to assign a cause of action in tort for damages for personal injury, and, secondly whether such an assignment would be void for public policy reasons. The Court of Appeal held that while a right to recover compensation for personal injury caused by negligence was a form of property that could properly be regarded as a 'legal thing in action' within the meaning of the Law of Property Act 1925, s 136 and therefore capable of being assigned, a personal chose in action was not so capable. In this case the assignment of the action was not a personal chose in action since the obligation to pay compensation arose by operation of the law and was not therefore personal in the sense that it depended on the identity of the claimant. In any event the claimant failed in her action since the law did not recognise an assignment of a right to litigate that was unsupported by an interest sufficient to justify an assignee's pursuit of proceedings for their own benefit on grounds of public policy. The assignment of a cause of action for the purposes of enabling the assignee to make a profit out of the litigation would generally be void as 'savouring of champerty', thus following *Trendtex Trading Corp*.

v *Crédit Suisse*. Thus while S had honourable motives in bringing the action she did not have a sufficient interest in the other patient's claim to support the assignment of a bare right of action and was therefore guilty of 'wanton and officious intermeddling' with the disputes of others. The Court of Appeal considered that the law on maintenance and champerty was open to further development as perceptions of public interest changed and it was not possible to state definitively what might constitute a sufficient interest to support the assignment of a cause of action in tort for personal injury. The court nevertheless considered that it was not in the public interest to encourage litigation whose principal object was not to obtain a remedy for a legal wrong, but to pursue a different object namely, in the present case, a campaign against the Trust.

It should be noted that for an agreement to be champertous it must undermine the English judicial system and litigation. Thus a champertous agreement made in England is valid if it relates to litigation in a country where champerty is lawful. The cases of *Re Trepca Mines Ltd* and more recently *Papera Traders Co. Ltd v Hyundai Merchant Marine Co. Ltd* [2002] 2 All ER (Comm) 1083 clearly illustrate this point. This also indicates clearly that one is not dealing with an overriding matter of public policy which strikes down wherever such an agreement is made or performed.

Contracts calculated to oust the jurisdiction of the courts

Such contracts have for many years been regarded as contrary to public policy and void. There is, however, no objection to a contract that requires the parties to attempt to resolve their dispute by reference to arbitration, provided there is no attempt to deprive the parties of their right to have their case heard before the ordinary courts of law.

Arbitration

It is not unusual for a right to take such action to be the subject of a condition precedent in the contract, whereby an arbitration award must first be made before the cause of action can be placed before the ordinary courts of law. Such a clause is known as a '*Scott* v *Avery*' **clause** and is not per se regarded as ousting the jurisdiction of the courts.

The Arbitration Act 1996, which governs the rules regarding this area, specifically allows for an appeal to the court to challenge an award made in arbitration proceedings on the ground of some serious material irregularity affecting the tribunal, the proceedings or the award (s 68(1)). Section 68(2) sets out various matters that a court is to consider as constituting a serious irregularity. Broadly, these are matters that will cause substantial injustice to the applicant, for instance, where the tribunal exceeds its powers, or fails to conduct the proceedings in accordance with the procedure agreed by the parties, or the tribunal fails to deal with the issues put before it.

Section 69(1) allows for an appeal to the court on a question of law arising out of an award made in arbitral proceedings. This right of appeal is limited in that it can only be brought where all the parties agree to the appeal proceedings or where the leave of the court has been obtained (s 69(2)). Such leave is only granted if the court is satisfied according to the criteria set out in s 69(3):

1 that the determination of the question will substantially affect the rights of one or more of the parties;

2 that the question is one which the tribunal was asked to determine, that on the basis of the findings of fact in the award –

   (i) the decision of the tribunal on the question is obviously wrong; or

> (ii) the question is one of general public importance and the decision of the tribunal is at least open to serious doubt; and

3 that, despite the agreement of the parties to resolve the matter by arbitration, it is just and proper in all the circumstances for the court to determine the question.

Such a right of appeal is subject to the overriding proviso that the parties may expressly agree to exclude the jurisdiction of the court. Further, the right of appeal under ss 68 and 69 may not be brought if the applicant or appellant has not first exhausted any available appeal or review within the arbitration process itself (s 70(2)).

Nuptial agreements and maintenance

Originally ante- and post-nuptial agreements were unenforceable on the basis that agreements for *future* separation in marriage were contrary to public policy on the basis that they undermined the sanctity of marriage. That rule was essentially swept away in the case of ***Radmacher v Granatino*** [2010] UKSC 42, although to the extent that such agreements oust the jurisdiction of the courts they are still contrary to public policy. The courts may take such agreements into account when considering their powers in relation to ancillary relief under the Matrimonial Causes Act 1973, Part II in divorce, nullity or judicial separation proceedings. It is incorrect to talk of such agreements being 'enforceable' since, while the courts are bound to have regard to them, they are still not bound to give effect to them. It should be noted that post-nuptial agreements are not contrary to public policy as held in *Macleod v MacLeod* [2008] UKPC 64.

As we have seen in the case of contracts prejudicial to the administration of justice, where a spouse promises to pay an allowance to another in the course of separation or matrimonial proceedings in return for the other spouse promising not to apply to the court for maintenance, it was held by the House of Lords in ***Hyman v Hyman*** that the agreement did not prevent the other spouse from applying for such maintenance. The court considered that a 'wife's right to future maintenance is a matter of public concern which she cannot barter away' and as such the contract was illegal. The corollary of this is that if the first spouse fails to pay the allowance that he or she promised this also could not be enforced because it was illegal, as held in ***Bennett v Bennett*** [1952] 1 KB 249. By the Matrimonial Causes Act 1973, s 34, however, if the agreement is in writing, an action can be brought to enforce a promised allowance, even though a provision that purports to restrict any right to apply to the court for an order for financial arrangements, such as a maintenance agreement, is void. It should nevertheless be noted that by s 35 the court has a power to revoke or alter such an agreement. Further it was held in ***Edgar v Edgar*** [1980] 1 WLR 1410 that the court must take the agreement into account when considering its powers to award ancillary relief.

Contracts tending to corrupt the public service

It is clear that the public has a substantial interest in the negation of activities which tend to corrupt the administration of the state, whether at a central or a local level, or which fetter the performance of public officers in exercising their duties. The object of the law here is clear in that it seeks to prevent the sale of public offices or the diversion of the salaries accruing to such offices by way of either assignment or mortgage. The reason for this latter point is thought to arise from the notion that should public officers assign their salaries, they will be open to the possibility of poverty which may lead them to compromise their positions. One wonders how such a principle has escaped the attention of public service pay negotiators in recent years!

Contracts prejudicial to the status of marriage and the family

The action for breach of promise to marry was abolished by the Law Reform (Miscellaneous Provisions) Act 1970, s 1, but even when such contracts existed it was void as contrary to public policy for an individual to enter into a contract to marry while being already married.

This being the starting point it is fairly easy to arrive at the point whereby a separation agreement made between parties still living together or contemplating marriage is also void as being inconsistent with the status and sanctity of marriage. Where the parties to the marriage are already separated, the sanctity of the matrimonial state is no longer in jeopardy and agreements providing for separation here are valid. It should be noted that where the parties have separated but have become reconciled, any agreement providing for the possibility of future separation will also be valid, as held in *Macmahon* v *Macmahon* [1913] 1 IR 428. The apparent logic in finding such agreements to be valid is that unless such an agreement is arrived at, the possibility of a reconciliation may be prejudiced.

A further type of contract that may arise in this context is the contract in restraint of marriage. Marriage has a peculiar position in the law and can itself amount to consideration. Historically much of the sanctity afforded to it revolves around the transmission of estates and interests in land. Given this state of affairs it is not surprising that a contract that unjustifiably restricts a person's ability to marry is void as contrary to public policy. Where the restraint is only partial, in that it is for a limited duration or where it merely limits the class or type of person that may or may not marry, then it is possible for the contract to be valid. Under the latter limitation, however, the persons capable or not of being married must be so small or large, as the case may be, as to render the ability to marry or not illusory. Further, a contract is not invalid if it operates not to restrain but merely to deter marriage, as, for example, an allowance of £500 per month until *X* marries.

The rule whereby a contract is void on the grounds of public policy also extends to the relationship between parent and child. Today there are statutory restrictions on agreements made between parents who are not living together as to parental rights and duties, in that such agreements to be enforceable must be for the benefit of the child. One statute providing such restrictions is the Guardianship Act 1973.

Sexually immoral contracts

Traditionally the law does not render any immoral contracts void as being contrary to public policy, except those promoting sexual immorality. Many of the rules found in the common law revolve around the promotion of cohabitation. Contracts in this area have been held to be illegal and void, a conclusion which is not surprising given the attitude of the common law to marriage, above. It is, however, a somewhat dated attitude given the present morality of society with regard to such matters. It was held in *Benyon* v *Nettleford* (1850) 3 Mac & G 94 that a promise by a man for a woman to become his mistress was illegal. However, it is not uncommon today to find unmarried couples making agreements as regards the purchase of houses and the distribution of their income within the relationship. There would seem to be nothing wrong in principle in these agreements being binding.

Clearly contracts involving prostitutes are void and unenforceable. It is thus highly unlikely that a prostitute could sue for her fees, though prostitution per se is not illegal, unlike the act of soliciting for clients by a prostitute. In *Pearce* v *Brooks* (1866) LR 1 Ex 213, a prostitute was held not to be liable for the charges arising from the hire of a carriage to be used for the purpose of soliciting. Presumably the same would also apply to the hire of a room or a flat for such purposes. However, a contract to hire a room, flat or house to an unmarried couple would be enforceable. The undoubted change in moral principles may well present the courts faced with such situations with something of a dilemma. This change can be seen in the case of ***Armhouse Lee Ltd v Chappell*** (1996) *The Times*, 7 August (CA), where the defendants placed advertisements in a magazine publicising a telephone sex line and sex dating. When they were sued by the publishers for the cost of the advertisements, the defendants resisted the claim on the basis that the advertisements were immoral and illegal. At first instance the judge found for the plaintiffs and the defendants appealed. The Court of Appeal rejected the argument that such contracts were unenforceable on the grounds of public policy. It was stated that 'it was undesirable in such a case, involving an area regarded as the province of the criminal law, for individual judges exercising a civil jurisdiction to impose their own moral attitudes'. The court therefore upheld the decision of the judge at first instance; however, the decision of the Court of Appeal would seem to indicate that sexually immoral contracts should no longer be regarded as unenforceable, except where the immoral conduct amounts to or involves a criminal offence.

The effects of illegality

The general effect

Objective 4

As was indicated at the start of the chapter, the expression 'illegal' covers a multitude of sins, some serious, some minor. It was also stated that the effect of illegality is widely disparate and not always consistent.

The fundamental rule of the courts was stated as long ago as the eighteenth century when Lord Mansfield declared in ***Holman v Johnson*** (1775) 1 Cowp 341: that no person who is aware of an illegality within a contract can enforce it, thus:

> No court will lend its aid to a man who founds his cause of action on an immoral or an illegal act. If, from the plaintiff's own stating or otherwise, the cause of action appears to arise *ex turpi causa*, or the transgression of a positive law of this country, there the court says that he has no right to be assisted. It is upon that ground the court goes; not for the sake of the defendant, but because they will not lend their aid to such a plaintiff. So if the plaintiff and defendant were to change sides, and the defendant was to bring his action against the plaintiff, the latter would then have the advantage of it; for where both are equally in fault . . .

Illegality has the potential to provide a defence to civil claims of all sorts, whether relating to contract, property, tort or unjust enrichment, and in a wide variety of circumstances. The basis behind the rule is that English law has a repugnance of claims that are founded on a defendant's own illegal or immoral acts. Thus the rule provides that no person who is aware of an illegality within a contract can enforce it and, furthermore, any money or property transferred under that contract is irrecoverable. Since illegality is founded on public policy, such a rule is apparently sound in this context, but with regard to the parties themselves it produces great difficulties, mainly because it provides a defence to a defendant who may not merit such protection. The result of the rule is that the principle of illegality is available to both parties, whatever the rights and wrongs of their respective situations. Thus a claimant cannot base their claim on an illegal contract, though they may be able to do so if they can find an additional ground not based on the illegality. Further, a claimant will not succeed where they are seen to benefit from the illegality.

The problem with the illegality principle is that it is unclear to what extent it applies where the object of the contract includes an element which is unlawful with regard to some aspect, or, where the contract involves some performance that is unlawful but in either case the illegality is not central to the contract. For instance, in *St John Shipping Corpn* v *Joseph Rank Ltd* [1957] 1 QB 267, the claim was for freight under a charterparty. In the course of taking on bunkers, the vessel was overloaded and the master thereby committed an offence, for which he was prosecuted and fined £1,200. The extra freight earned by the overloading was £2,295 and to that extent the ship owners stood to profit from their wrong. The cargo owners refused to pay that part of the freight, pleading that the illegal actions of the ship-owners provided them with a defence to the claim for the extra amount. Devlin J rejected their defence. He held that since the goods had been delivered safely, the ship owners had proved all that they were required to do. He was not prepared to construe the statute impos-ing the illegality as having the effect of making the contract prohibited. If it had been oth-erwise, the shipowners would not have been entitled to any freight and would therefore have suffered an additional penalty, much greater than that provided for by Parliament, for conduct which might have been unintentional. Thus at 288 Devlin J said:

> If a contract has as its whole object the doing of the very act which the statute prohibits, it can be argued that you can hardly make sense of a statute which forbids an act and yet permits to be made a contract to do it; that is a clear implication. But unless you get a clear implication of that sort, I think that a court ought to be very slow to hold that a statute intends to interfere with the rights and remedies given by the ordinary law of contract. Caution in this respect is, I think, especially necessary in these times when so much of commercial life is governed by regulations of one sort or another, which may easily be broken without wicked intent.

By comparison in *Ashmore, Benson, Pease and Co Ltd* v *Dawson* [1973] 1 WLR 828, the Court of Appeal adopted a different approach. In this case, manufacturers of heavy engineer-ing equipment entered into a contract of carriage with the road hauliers. There was nothing inherently illegal in the formation of the contract, but the hauliers overloaded the vehicles which were to transport the load, in breach of road traffic regulations, and one of the lorries toppled over during the journey as a result of the driver's negligence. The manufacturers' transport manager was present when the goods were loaded and was aware of the overload-ing. A claim by the manufacturers for the cost of repair of the damaged load was rejected on grounds of illegality. The Court of Appeal did not follow the analysis set out by *St John Shipping* case and simply held that since the manufacturers had participated in the illegal performance of the contract they were barred from suing on it.

The difference in approaches of the courts in the above cases demonstrates the inconsist-encies that have arisen in the application of the principle and it is for this reason this area of law has become somewhat notorious in the administration of justice with regards to civil claims. The operation of the principle, however, is one of great complexity. Since the cases display an array of contradictory judgements, it is extremely difficult to discern any pattern with regards to the application of the illegality principle and indeed the courts have also struggled to develop a coherent approach. In recent years there have been attempts at resolv-ing this matter from *Tinsley v Milligan* [1993] 3 WLR 126, the Law Commission report, *The Illegality Defence* (Law Com. No. 320) (2010) and finally to the important Supreme Court decision of *Patel v Mirza* [2016] UKSC 42; however, before doing so, it is worth examining how the rule has been applied in a number of scenarios, though it must be emphasised that the decisions, whilst justifiable on their own terms, often lack transparency and appear unpredictable, as Lord Toulson stated in *Patel* v *Mirza* [2016] UKSC 42. (at para 3):

> Take the law of contract. A contract may be prohibited by a statute; or it may be entered into for an illegal or immoral purpose, which may be that of one or both parties; or performance

according to its terms may involve the commission of an offence; or it may be intended by one or both parties to be performed in a way which will involve the commission of an offence; or an unlawful act may be committed in the course of its performance. The application of the doctrine of illegality to each of these different situations has caused a good deal of uncertainty, complexity and sometimes inconsistency.

Public policy is a dominant feature within judicial reasoning in deciding cases concerning illegality so that the courts traditionally will not grant relief in cases where to do so would amount to aiding and abetting a criminal act, an action amounting to an affront to public conscience. This was indicated in *Thackerell* v *Barclays Bank plc* [1986] 1 All ER 676 and affirmed by the Court of Appeal in *Saunders* v *Edwards* [1987] 2 All ER 651. The effect of this 'affront to public conscience' approach can be seen in the following case.

Howard v *Shirlstar Container Transport Ltd* [1990] 3 All ER 366

The plaintiff, a pilot, made a contract to recover an aircraft that had been impounded in Nigeria. The contract was illegal in that it was not so much a 'rescue' mission as a mission to steal the aircraft from under the noses of the Nigerian authorities. When he had successfully completed the contract, the defendants refused to pay; when sued, they raised the question of illegality as a defence. Even though the effect of his claim succeeding would have been to allow the plaintiff to benefit from an illegal act, the court decided that his claim should succeed since the conscience of the court in the opinion of Slaughter LJ was not compromised. While this decision has been described and praised as the adoption of a 'pragmatic approach', it does not seem calculated to produce certainty within the law.

The issue of the affront to public conscience approach arose again in the important case of *Tinsley* v *Milligan*.

Tinsley v *Milligan* [1993] 3 WLR 126

The facts of the case were that a lesbian couple bought a house together using their joint money, but having done that the house was registered in Tinsley's name only. The basis behind this conduct was to allow Milligan to claim social security benefits which she would not otherwise be entitled to. The couple eventually argued and fell out and Tinsley sought to evict her former partner, Milligan, from the property. Milligan claimed that she was entitled to half the purchase money of the house, the beneficial interest, by way of her contributions to the purchase price by way of a resulting trust, which is an equitable principle. Tinsley argued that Milligan was not entitled to that share because she had behaved illegally as regards her claim for the social security payments.

The majority of the Court of Appeal decided in favour of Milligan by applying a test based on whether it would be an affront to public conscience to grant relief. Thus Nicholls LJ stated:

The court should keep in mind that the underlying principle is the so-called public conscience test. The court must weigh, or balance, the adverse consequences of granting relief against the adverse consequences of refusing relief. The ultimate decision calls for a value judgement . . . I have no doubt that far from it being an affront to public conscience to grant relief in this case, it would be an affront to the public conscience not to do so. Right-thinking people would not consider that condemnation of the parties' fraudulent activities ought to have the consequence of permitting the plaintiff to retain the defendant's half share of this house.

Nicholls LJ considered, therefore, that the mere presence of fraud or illegality should not automatically mean that relief should not be granted. He thought that, in deciding where the equitable balance lay, the court should take into account the nature and seriousness of the illegality, the extent to which

> failure to enforce the claim would result in unjust enrichment, the extent to which enforcement would encourage others to act in an illegal manner and the overall culpability of the parties. This was the majority decision of the Court of Appeal with Gibson LJ dissenting. While Gibson LJ thought that upholding the resulting trust would produce a fairer result, he considered that the proper principle should be that equity should not give effect to an equitable remedy based on an unlawful transaction, i.e. 'he who comes to equity must come with clean hands'.

The House of Lords unanimously rejected the Court of Appeal's public conscience test, i.e. whether it would be an affront to public conscience to grant relief for the illegality rule but by a majority of three to two upheld the Court of Appeal's decision. Lord Browne-Wilkinson, who gave the leading judgement, stated that the starting point was that title to property can pass by way of an unlawful transaction; but held that a court would not assist an owner to recover property if he had to rely on his own illegality to prove his title – a distinction that had been recognised in ***Bowmakers Ltd* v *Barnet Instrument Ltd*** [1945] KB 65. Lord Browne-Wilkinson therefore held that attempting to assess whether the public conscience would be 'affronted by recognising rights created by illegal transactions' was improper. Lord Browne-Wilkinson held that it was enough for Milligan to show that she had contributed to the purchase of the property and that there was a common understanding that the parties were joint owners and that she did not have to explain why the property had been put into Miss Tinsley's sole name. On the other hand, he considered that the result would have been different if the relationship between Tinsley and Milligan had been one of mother and daughter and each had contributed to the purchase price. In such a situation the presumption of advancement would have applied in favour of the daughter. In order to rebut the presumption, the mother would have had to rely on the illegal nature of the transaction and her claim would therefore have been defeated by the doctrine of illegality.

The majority of the House of Lords therefore came to a decision with reference to the so-called reliance principle, that is, if a claimant needs to 'rely on' or bring evidence relating to the illegality to prove his or her claim, then the claim will fail. Their Lordships considered that a person may recover money or property under an illegal contract if that person can establish his right or title to the property without relying on the contract or on its illegal nature. Thus in this case Milligan won because she could establish her claim by virtue of the resulting trust and she did not have to rely either on an illegal contract (because she already owned the property under the resulting trust) or on the illegal conduct in order to establish her claim. Thus Lord Browne-Wilkinson stated:

> A party to an illegality can recover by virtue of a legal or equitable property interest if, but only if, he can establish his title without relying on his own illegality.

Lord Browne-Wilkinson acknowledged that this approach was a procedural one stating:

> The effect of illegality is not substantive but procedural. The question therefore is, 'In what circumstances will equity refuse to enforce equitable rights which undoubtedly exist?'

Both Lord Goff and Lord Keith gave dissenting judgements in the House of Lords, preferring to base their judgements on traditional principles, not least that, irrespective of how the resulting trusts arose, whether based on an illegality or not, a court of equity should not intervene to assist someone who transfers property into the hands of another as part of an illegal act in order to establish an equitable claim to the property. Lord Goff did not consider it appropriate for the courts to introduce a discretion based on an affront to public conscience test in order to grant relief. To decide otherwise would be to introduce uncertainty, since each court would have to decide where the equitable balance lay on the facts of individual cases, though he recognised the hardship that might arise out of his approach.

As Lord Goff recognised, one of the problems arising from the reliance principle is that it is selective in whom it will benefit since, in other circumstances, the presumption of advancement may apply and a very different result could arise. Until its abolition by the Equality Act 2010, s 199, the concept of the presumption of advancement was really an outdated anomaly within the law of trusts but one which nevertheless continued to have a modern impact. The presumption of advancement applied where a husband or father gave, or 'advanced', money or property to his wife or children. The presumption did not operate in relation to a man and his mistress and here a resulting trust would apply and, as we have seen in *Tinsley* v *Milligan*, here the man could recover his money or property, any underlying illegality not affecting his claim since this arose by way of the resulting trust.

In such a situation he could not rely on the principle of resulting trust that we saw in *Tinsley* v *Milligan*. The husband/father was deemed to have made a gift of the property to his wife or children. If the husband or father was to recover his property, he had to first overturn the presumption in order to establish a resulting trust. If his gift was made to achieve an illegal purpose, for instance, to evade paying taxes, his claim would 'rely' on the presence of the illegality and therefore he was prevented from recovering because of the underlying illegality. The case of *Chettiar* v *Chettiar* [1962] AC 294 is a good example where a father transferred land to his son, recording a payment by the son which was not in fact made. The idea behind the transaction was to deceive the authorities that the father had less land than he had in order to avoid restrictions for the production of rubber. The Privy Council dismissed his claim that the son held the land on trust for him since for the father to overturn the presumption of advancement he would have had to rely on the illegal nature of the purpose for the transaction in the first place.

The decision on *Tinsley* v *Milligan* has been the subject of much criticism, not so much the result but for the reasoning contained within it and we will return to this later on when we examine the future of illegality.

The public conscience test historically has not been totally devoid of legal authority thereby allowing an innocent party to succeed in a claim. It may be that the contract itself is lawful but there is an intention to use it to further some illegal purpose or where one of the parties intends to perform it in some illegal manner. Here the innocent party will be able to recover damages or what is due to them under the contract, provided they were unaware of the illegal intention of the other party as in *Bloxsome* v *Williams* (1824) 3 B& C 232, though here it was the subject matter of the contract that was illegal. In *Cowan* v *Milbourn* (1867) LR 2 Ex 230, it was also stated that if they discover the illegality before the transaction is performed then the innocent party can withdraw from the contract. An innocent party who discovers the illegality part of the way through performing the contract may withdraw from the contract and sue on a *quantum meruit* basis.

It should be borne in mind that a party to a contract will not be regarded as innocent if, while being fully aware of the facts, they are not aware of the illegality within the contract because they are ignorant of the law. Ignorance of the law is no excuse (*ignorantia juris neminem excusat*), thus in *J M Allan (Merchandising) Ltd* v *Cloke* [1963] 2 All ER 258, it was held that the fees for the hiring of a roulette wheel for purposes of a game that was illegal under the Betting and Gaming Act 1960 were not recoverable, despite the fact that both parties were unaware of the illegal nature of the game. As a postscript it should be noted that, whilst before the Gambling Act 2005, a gambling agreement was not unlawful, in the sense that nobody broke the law simply by entering into it, it was beyond the reach of the law in the sense that obligations under the contract could not be enforced by civil proceedings. The Gambling Act 2005 has altered this position, making gambling contracts enforceable.

It was seen in our earlier examination of acts declared illegal that a contract either expressly or impliedly prohibited by statute was void and unenforceable. In such a situation the innocent party is not necessarily precluded from obtaining a remedy since it may be that they have been induced into the contract by some misrepresentation. Had such an action been adopted in *Re Mahmoud and Ispahani* the result might have been different. Further it may be possible to avoid the effects of the illegality by alleging the existence of a collateral contract. Thus in *Strongman (1945) Ltd* v *Sincock* [1955] 2 QB 525 the plaintiffs, who were builders, contracted to modernise some houses for the defendant architect. At that time, due to shortages of materials, it was illegal to do such work without a licence. The plaintiffs were told by the defendant that he would obtain the necessary licences, but in fact he failed to do so. The defendant failed to pay for the work and when sued pleaded that the contract was void and unenforceable on the grounds that it was illegal. The court nevertheless held that there existed a collateral contract based on the promise of the defendant to obtain the appropriate licences and since he had failed to do so, he was liable in damages. There are limits to the use of this device since the finding and enforcing of a collateral contract must not equate with the enforcement of the illegal contract. It may be, however, that an action could be sustained in misrepresentation despite such a finding, though of course the measure of damages would be different. Presumably the use of the fiction of collateral contracts would be subject to the 'public conscience' criterion.

An explanation of collateral contracts can be found in Chapter 2.

Recovery of money or property

For more on the topic of quasi-contracts and the law of restitution, refer to Chapter 18.

It has been seen in *Holman* v *Johnson*, above, that one effect of illegality was to render any money or property irrecoverable, just as a person is not allowed to benefit from an illegal contract, as we saw in *Beresford* v *Royal Insurance Co. Ltd*, above. In such a case even claims in quasi-contract, restitution and undue enrichment cannot be maintained. There are, however, three broad situations in which the courts have allowed the parties to be relieved of the effect of the doctrine of illegality within a contract.

Where the parties are not *in pari delicto*

The Latin maxim *in pari delicto, potior est conditio defendentis* provides that when the parties are equally blameworthy, the defendant has the stronger position. Thus where the parties are not equally in the wrong, it may be possible for the less 'blameworthy' party to recover any property transferred or moneys paid under the contract. This result may arise where the statute rendering the contract illegal is designed to give protection to a particular class of individuals, of whom the less guilty party forms a part. Thus under the Rent Act 1977, s 125 allows a premium to secure a lease to be recovered where such a premium could not be lawfully required. This position also applies even if the tenant was a knowing party to a contract to evade the Rent Acts. This was so in *Kiriri Cotton Co. Ltd* v *Dewani* [1960] AC 192, where a landlord's acceptance of a premium from the plaintiff to secure a flat was illegal, though the relevant statute did not allow for the recovery of such a premium. The court found that the plaintiff had little choice but to accept the terms of the landlord, who fully intended to exploit the deficiencies in the legislation. In these circumstances the plaintiff could recover the premium paid despite its illegality.

The same criteria also apply where the less culpable party has been induced to enter the contract by virtue of some fraud or undue pressure by the other party. In *Hughes* v *Liverpool*

Victoria Legal Friendly Society [1916] 2 KB 482, the plaintiff was induced by the fraudulent misrepresentation of the defendant's agent to take out a number of insurance policies against the lives of persons in whom she had no insurable interest, on the basis that such policies were valid and legal. In fact such policies were illegal and void, but nevertheless she could recover the premiums paid in respect of the policies. There is also authority that moneys or property may also be recovered in similar circumstances where the defendant stands in a fiduciary relationship to the claimant.

Where the illegal contract has been withdrawn from

Money paid or property transferred under an illegal contract may be recovered if the contract did not take effect because of the claimant's decision to withdraw from it. Here the claimant relies on the doctrine of *locus poenitentiae*, meaning he is claiming to withdraw from the contract during a 'time for repentance'. In *Kearley v Thomson* (1890) 24 QBD 742, it was stated that recovery ceases to be possible once the illegal purpose has commenced, whether or not it is completed. This decision overturns an earlier one where it was suggested that recovery will be allowed provided withdrawal occurs before the illegal purpose is carried out. It is suggested that *Kearley v Thomson* now represents the true position.

In order to claim recovery under this head it must also be shown that the withdrawal from the contract is voluntary. If the execution of the contract is frustrated by the other party failing to carry out their side of the bargain, or where there is some other reason whereby withdrawal occurs other than by a voluntary act, then recovery will not be allowed. This was the case in *Bigos v Bousted* in which, as we have already seen, there was an illegal contract to avoid the provisions of the Exchange Control Act 1947. The plaintiffs claimed that they could recover a share certificate deposited with the defendants as security for Italian currency because the currency was never forthcoming. It was held that the certificate could not be recovered because there was no voluntary withdrawal but merely a frustration of the contract by the defendant.

It is not necessary that true repentance of the illegal scheme is required and it is sufficient, as in *Tribe v Tribe*, below, that the fact that the scheme is no longer required is sufficient to raise the exception. Forced withdrawal from the illegal scheme is, however, not sufficient to raise the exception. In *Q v Q* [2008] EWHC 1874 (Fam), *dicta* suggested that illegal purpose should be broadly defined and that, as soon as any steps are taken towards its accomplishment, then the withdrawal exception cannot be utilised.

A slightly different variation to the above principles can be seen in *Tribe v Tribe* [1995] 4 All ER 236. In this case a father transferred shares in his company to his son after a landlord made a substantial claim against the father with respect to the dilapidation of the business premises. The father's motives for this was that he was worried that the landlord's claim would harm the financial viability of the business so that he would have to sell it to pay the landlord's claim. The objective behind the transfer of the shares to the son was to convince the landlord that he, the father, no longer held shares in the business to sell in order to meet the claim. In the end the claim was settled and the landlord was never made aware of the share transfer. The father now demanded the return of his shares from the son, who refused to return them. The father alleged that the son was always aware that he had to transfer the shares back to the father when he demanded their return. The father argued that he retained property rights in the shares, a 'beneficial interest', which he concealed from his creditors. The son argued that his father could not use the unlawful purpose to support his claim to rebut the presumption of advancement. The son argued that there was a general rule of public policy that prevented such evidence from being used. At first instance the court held that the father's claim would succeed since the attempt by the father to deceive his creditors never materialised and therefore the son held the shares on a resulting trust and would have to return them to his father. The son's appeal was dismissed by the Court of Appeal agreeing with the judge at first instance that where a presumption of advancement arose evidence of an unlawful purpose that had not been carried through could be heard.

At one level the decision appears just, in that the son had taken the shares knowing the reason behind the transfer and that it was always the intention of the father that he would retain his beneficial interest. On another level, however, it could be argued that the father had indeed entered into and executed a transfer of the shares for an illegal purpose, though it could be argued, as indeed the father did, that the transfer was not necessarily connected to the illegal intention.

The decision in **Tribe v Tribe** was followed in the case of **Patel v Mirza** [2014] EWCA Civ 1047 where the facts of the cases was that Mirza was a foreign exchange broker who offered Patel and their mutual friend X an opportunity to use his spread-betting account to bet on the movement of Royal Bank of Scotland (RBS) shares. Patel paid Mirza more than £600,000 on hearing that Mirza had contacts with the bank who could supply advance inside information about a statement anticipated to be made by the Chancellor of the Exchequer about the Government's investment in the bank, which would affect the bank's share prices. The plan was that Mirza would use Patel's money, along with his own, to bet on the Investor's Gold Index on movements in the quoted share price over a specified period using insider information. Patel's case was that Mirza did not place the bets because the Government statement never materialised, and that the money was supposed to be repaid but that it was mistakenly paid to X instead. Patel was unable to recover the money from X. Patel maintained that the money was recoverable from Mirza as money paid for a consideration that had wholly failed, and/or that it was held by Mirza on trust for Patel. Mirza's case was that the money had been received for the purpose of speculative trading in RBS shares.

The court at first instance had held that Patel's claim was barred by illegality since the case was founded on an illegal agreement that sought to take advantage of insider information. The judge, applying the *locus poenitentiae* doctrine, stated that the position would have been different if Patel had withdrawn from the agreement before its implementation became frustrated, but he had not done that.

The issues for the appeal were whether; Firstly, Patel was entitled to recover the money without relying on the fact that it was paid to M under an illegal agreement for insider dealing; secondly, it was open to Patel to recover money paid under the illegal agreement in circumstances where he neither repudiated nor withdrew from the agreement before its performance but where its performance then became frustrated.

The Court of Appeal held that Patel should succeed in his appeal. The Court of Appeal considered, firstly, that it was clear that Patel was positively relying on the illegal agreement in order to make good his claim for the return of the money for undue enrichment. Patel's case, however, ran into the rule that on grounds of public policy that no person who is aware of or reliant on an illegality can enforce it and furthermore any money or property transferred is irrecoverable, following, **Holman v Johnson**.

Secondly, the court considered that if, before Patel had learnt that the venture could not be carried out because the insider information was not forthcoming, he had repudiated and withdrawn from the agreement, he would have been entitled to sue for and recover his money even though he would have had to plead the illegal arrangement under which he had paid it over, thereby following **Taylor v Bowers** (1876) 1 Q.B.D. 291 in which it was held that withdrawal was allowed before completion of the contract. The court found that in such a situation he would have fallen squarely within the principle that permitted a claimant to rely on an illegal arrangement provided that he had voluntarily withdrawn from it before it had been carried into effect. It made no difference that Patel's withdrawal from the illegal agreement was not because he had changed his mind and no longer wished to participate but because the agreement was no longer capable of being performed at all. The Court of Appeal held that to distinguish between cases where the withdrawal was from an illegal agreement that was no longer needed for the purpose for which it was designed and cases that could not be or were not going to be performed, was unattractive. The court stated that such a distinction would depend on holding that genuine repentance on the part of the withdrawer was required, which it was not, thereby applying the decision in *Tribe* v *Tribe*. The Court of Appeal did not, however, follow *Bigos* v *Bousted*. The Court of Appeal found that, as in *Tribe* v *Tribe*, voluntary withdrawal from an illegal agreement when it had ceased to be needed was sufficient to entitle a claimant to recover. It stated that it would be an odd distinction if a claimant was not entitled to recover by relying on an illegal agreement that was not, and could not be, performed. It was held that to recognise such a distinction would require proof of a true sense of penitence, something that following *Tribe* v *Tribe* was not required or expected of the successful claimant.

Mirza appealed to the Supreme Court [2016] UKSC 42 where it was held that his appeal would be dismissed and Patel was entitled to restitution of the £620,000 he had paid to Mirza. In the Supreme Court a root and branch examination of the illegality doctrine was conducted which we discuss later in this chapter.

Where the illegal contract is not relied on for recovery

Here the recovery of goods transferred is not based on the illegal nature of the contract but on the existence of a proprietary interest in the goods. In other words, the claimant is relying on the fact that they retain some title to the property transferred. This being the case it is clear that recovery will not be allowed in a contract for the sale of goods, since here the property in the goods passes on sale, unless, of course, the seller has retained title by virtue of a *Romalpa* or retention of title clause. For the most part, however, recovery is limited to circumstances whereby something less than full ownership is delivered up to the other party, such as that found under a hire purchase agreement or lease. Thus in *Bowmakers Ltd* v *Barnet Instruments Ltd* [1945] KB 65 the defendants came into the possession of certain machine tools under an illegal hire purchase agreement. They failed to pay the instalments and in fact, contrary to their rights under the agreement, sold some of the tools. The plaintiffs sued under the tort of conversion to recover the value of the tools on the basis of asserting the proprietary rights they retained in the tools. They based their claim purely on the rules of hire purchase and bailment, making no reference to the illegality of the transaction. On this basis the court upheld their claim. If, however, they had made reference to the illegality of the transaction then the claim would probably have been rejected since it would have indicated that they were not relying on their proprietary rights but on the illegality.

The decision has been subject to criticism since it is apparent that in pursuing the claim in conversion they must have had to rely on the contract – which was, of course, void and unenforceable for illegality. The position appears to be that when the courts consider the proprietary consequences of an illegal contract the issues of illegality are ignored, though it should be noted that the Court of Appeal in *Bowmakers Ltd* v *Barnet Instruments Ltd* distinguished its decision from the earlier one of *Taylor* v *Chester* [1945] KB 65, where the plaintiff deposited half a banknote as security for the payment of food and drink he had consumed in a brothel. He then sought to recover the half note relying on his proprietary interest in it. He failed to do so since in order to overturn the defence that the half note had been validly deposited he would be 'obliged to set forth the immoral and illegal character of the contract upon which the half-note had been deposited'. It was therefore impossible for him to recover except through the medium and by the aid of an illegal transaction to which he was himself a party.

It has been suggested that the difference between the two cases is that, in *Bowmaker*, rights retained by the transferor are being enforced after entering into an illegal contract, which is allowed, while in *Taylor* v *Chester* the plaintiff is attempting to enforce rights created by the illegal contract, which is not permissible. On the face of things, though, it is difficult to make out a case in *Bowmaker* that the plaintiff is not in fact enforcing rights created by the illegal contract.

The Law Commission and the reform of the illegality defence

Objective 5

The intervention of the Law Commission arose principally out of the case of the House of Lords decision in *Tinsley* v *Milligan*, which was examined above. In *Tinsley* v *Milligan*, Lord Goff called for the Law Commission to examine the whole area of the so-called illegality defence. As a result, the wide-ranging difficulties associated with the issue of illegality in the law of contracts (and other areas) subsequently became the subject of a review by the Law Commission in 2010 in its report, *The Illegality Defence* (Law Com. No. 320). This report proved to be a difficult one to accomplish for the Law Commission and it arose out of three consultative documents. The first, *Illegal Transactions: The Effect of Illegality on Contracts and Trusts* (Law Consultation Paper No. 154) in 1999, in which the law relating to the doctrine of illegality as it operates in contract and trusts was examined. The second consultation paper, *The Illegality Defence in Tort* (Law Consultation Paper No. 160) was published in 2001 and examined the law relating to illegality and tort. Following from these consultation documents, the Law Commission published a third consultation report entitled *The Illegality Defence* in 2009 (Law Consultation Paper No. 189). The reason for the third consultative document was that, because of the length of time from the 1999 and 2001 consultative documents, the Law Commission decided to consult further on its recommendations. It was from its findings in the 2009 consultative document that the final 2010 report emerged.

Clearly the extent of the consultation work carried out by the Law Commission is a good indicator of the difficulty it had in drawing together the strands of illegality and its effects. However, it must be emphasised that not all of the study was directed at the law of contract and it also included the use of the illegality defence in the law of tort, unjust enrichment and the law of trusts.

The Law Commission in its consultative document *Illegal Transactions: The Effect of Illegality on Contracts and Trusts* (Law Consultation Paper No. 154) in 1999 came to two principal conclusions: first, the reliance principle as set out in *Tinsley* v *Milligan* should be abandoned; and, second, the courts should have the discretion to take into account the effects of the illegality when making their decisions. The Law Commission considered that the technical and complex rules governing the effects of illegality in the law of contract and trusts should be replaced by a 'discretion'. Under that discretion the court could decide 'whether or not to enforce an illegal transaction, to recognise that property rights have been transferred or created by it, or to allow benefits conferred under it to be recovered'. It proposed that illegality should be allowed to continue to provide a defence to a claim for a breach of contract and that it would not be allowed to be used as a cause of action except in cases of withdrawal from the illegal act (*locus poenitentiae*).

The Law Commission did not consider that the courts should have an open-ended discretion to produce what it considers to be a 'just' solution, since it considered that the discretion should be more structured in order to promote greater certainty. The Law Commission therefore proposed a statutory discretion which a court should take account of in exercising its discretion. A court should take into account the following:

> (i) the seriousness of the illegality involved; (ii) the knowledge and intention of the party seeking to enforce the illegal transaction, seeking the recognition of legal or equitable rights under it, or seeking to recover benefits conferred under it; (iii) whether refusing to allow standard rights and remedies would deter illegality; (iv) whether refusing to allow standard rights and remedies would further the purpose of the rule which rendered the transaction illegal; and (v) whether refusing to allow standard rights and remedies would be proportionate to the illegality involved.

The Law Commission did not consider that it was appropriate for the courts to be able to use the discretion to override the express provisions of a statute where a statute had expressly provided what the effect of illegality on a transaction should be.

It was considered that the proposals had two advantages. First, a court would be able to reach its decision on the facts of a case using open and explicit reasoning that gave full effect to the relevance of the illegality on the transaction. Second, it considered the proposals would be more likely to result in illegality being used less so as to deny a claimant his or her usual rights or remedies. Thus the Law Commission considered that illegality could only be used as a defence where there was a clear and justifiable public interest reason for it to do so.

In its 2010 report the Law Commission resiled from its previous recommendation for the introduction of a statutory discretion, as set out above. The Law Commission recognised that the body of case law that had sprung up was an intricate web of tangled decisions that created uncertainty in the law. The Commission, however, acknowledged that it was rare for courts to reach an 'unjust' result and that, for the most part, the courts applied the illegality defence in a fair manner. It considered that in most cases the illegality defence was applied according to the policies that underpin its use. The Commission, however, considered that the courts did not articulate the policy reasons behind their decisions very well. This resulted in decisions that were not as transparent as they could have been and it was rare for the courts to refer to the policy reasons that justified their decisions in their judgements. The Commission considered that the decision in *Tinsley* v *Milligan* and the cases following it exemplified problems relating to arbitrariness, uncertainty and the potential for injustice. It considered that in that case the question whether the illegality affected the recognition or enforcement of the trust depended not on the merits of the parties, nor the policies underlying the illegality defence, but on a procedural issue. Moreover the effect of applying the reliance principle in cases involving the presumption of advancement gave that presumption an overriding importance which it was never intended to have. It led to uncertainty because there was much confusion over what exactly amounted to 'reliance', particularly when the claimant was seeking to establish an equitable interest under a constructive trust. It had the potential to force the court into unjust decisions because, by focusing on procedural matters, the reliance principle precluded the court from paying attention to the policies that justified the existence of the defence, or taking into account such matters as the seriousness of the illegality and the value of the interest at stake.

The Commission therefore recommended that in future the courts should consider whether the illegality defence can be justified on the basis of the policies that underlie the defence, base their decisions on those policies and refer to them openly so as to come to a transparent decision. The Law Commission considered that the courts were moving in this direction in any event and referred to two House of Lords decisions as evidence of this: *Gray* v *Thames Trains* [2009] UKHL 33 and *Stone & Rolls* v *Moore Stephens (a firm)* [2009] UKHL 39.

The case of *Gray* v *Thames Trains* illustrates the use of the illegality defence in the law of tort and therefore it may be said to have limited relevance to the law of contract. It is, however, useful to see how the principles set out in the Law Commission report were applied here. The facts of the case were that the claimant (G) sustained minor injuries in the Ladbroke Grove rail crash in London and as a result suffered post-traumatic stress disorder that led to a dramatic change in his personality. He became unemployed and after two years stabbed a stranger to death. He was convicted of manslaughter on the grounds of diminished responsibility. He then claimed damages for his loss of earnings from the date of the crash but also claimed general damages for his detention, conviction, feelings of guilt plus an indemnity against any actions that might be brought against him by any relatives of his victim. The defendant admitted liability for the crash and G's loss of earnings up to the date of the killing but not for earnings after that date or the general damages. It was not disputed that, but for the rail crash, G would not have suffered psychiatric damage and killed someone.

It was held by the House of Lords that, as a matter of public policy based on the principle of *ex turpi causa*, G was precluded from recovering compensation either for losses suffered in consequence of his own criminal act or for damage that was the consequence of a sentence imposed on him for a criminal act. On this basis, a claimant who had committed manslaughter as a result of psychological problems and post-traumatic stress disorder caused by the negligence of a third party could not recover general damages and loss of earnings arising from his crime. Lord Hoffmann explained, with Phillips LJ and Scott LJ concurring, that the illegality defence in this context existed in a narrow form and in a wider form. Lord Hoffmann stated that the narrow form provides that:

> You cannot recover for damage which flows directly from loss of liberty or fine or other punishment lawfully imposed upon you in consequence of your unlawful act.

Their Lordships considered that such an approach was important for consistency, since as a matter of penal policy it would be inconsistent for the law to award compensation for damage that has resulted from the law imposing a penalty. This meant that G could not recover compensation for his loss of earnings after the date of the killing nor general damages for conviction and detention.

The wider form of the rule is that a 'person cannot recover compensation for loss suffered as a consequence of your own criminal act' and, as a consequence, G was precluded from recovering general damages for his conviction, detention, feelings of guilt and an indemnity against claims brought by the dependants of the victim. Lord Hoffmann did not consider the expression *ex turpi causa* to be useful. He considered it more appropriate to draw a distinction between cases where, although the damage would not have happened but for the tortious act of the defendant, it was in fact caused by the criminal act of the claimant; and cases where, although the damage would not have happened without the criminal act of the claimant, it was in fact caused by the tortious act of the defendant.

In terms of the illegality defence generally, however, Lord Hoffmann considered that it is a defence based on several policy justifications and that these could vary in different circumstances. Thus he did not find any discussions around the reliance principle in *Tinsley* v *Milligan* useful in this case. All the judges rejected the notion that the reliance principle can be applied mechanically as a formal test and reinforced the principle that, at least in the law of tort, the illegality defence must be justified in terms of public policy and that a range of factors would determine whether those policy factors would apply, thus the seriousness of the offence or the mental state of a claimant may deliver a different set of results.

The judgement in *Gray* v *Thames Trains* mirrors very much what the Law Commission was attempting to achieve in its 2010 report and it was fairly easy to extract principles from the case.

The House of Lords decision involving the illegality defence in *Stone & Rolls Ltd* v *Moore Stephens* was not so clear-cut. The facts of the case were that Stone & Rolls (R) was managed and effectively controlled by a Mr Stojevic (S), who used the company as a vehicle for defrauding banks. Moore Stephens (M) acted as auditors for R. An action was brought against R and S for deceit and both were found to be liable but, as a result of that judgement, R went into liquidation. R brought an action against M for negligence in that it failed to detect the fraudulent activities of S. M accepted that it owed a duty of care to R but contested that R's action should fail, in that the fraud itself was committed by R. M stated that S's fraudulent acts as the controller of R were directly attributable to R. M relied, *inter alia*, on the illegality defence in that R would have to rely on the illegal acts of S to prove its claim, i.e. the reliance defence.

The majority of the House of Lords held that the acts of S should be attributable to R and therefore S's illegal acts would bar the claim by R. Of the majority, Lord Phillips stated that the illegality defence should not be applied automatically and, while he held that the illegality defence applied, it was because M's duty did not extend to creditors but only to the company and its shareholders. Since these had acted fraudulently, they could not take advantage of M's duty to them. With regard to the illegality defence, though, Lord Phillips stated:

> I do not believe that it is right to proceed on the basis that the reliance test can automatically be applied as a rule of thumb. It is necessary to give consideration to the policy underlying the *ex turpi causa* in order to decide whether this defence is bound to defeat [Stone & Rolls's] claim.

Thus, according to Lord Phillips, the essential issue was that, in applying *ex turpi causa*, one should look behind the company to discover whose interests the relevant duty was intended to protect. The sole person for whose benefit such duty was owed was S, who was responsible for the fraud and therefore, in those circumstances, *ex turpi causa* provided a defence to the claim.

Of the minority judges, Lord Scott considered that the illegality defence had no application, since M's duty applied only to the company and the shareholders and therefore if R succeeded in its claim the only beneficiaries would be the creditors of R, to whom M owed no duty of care. Lord Mance decided the case on other issues.

One other interesting aspect of the case was the attempt by R to raise what has become known as the 'very thing' principle. The principle is that where a defendant (M) is under a duty to prevent a claimant (R) from committing an illegal act and the claimant goes on to commit that act, the claimant should always have a remedy against the defendant since to decide otherwise would be to render the duty invalid. Thus in *Stone & Rolls Ltd* v *Moore Stephens*, it was argued that the 'very thing' the auditors were employed to prevent was the commission of a fraud. Thus M could not rely on the fraud they were employed to prevent as a means of avoiding the liability they owed to R for breach of their duty. Clearly the use of such a principle would effectively trump the use of the illegality defence by M. All their Lordships, except Scott LJ, rejected the use of this principle in this way. Their Lordships agreed that the 'very thing' principle was a principle of causation and could not operate to neutralise the illegality defence.

In *Stone & Rolls Ltd* v *Moore Stephens* their Lordships all stressed the importance that the illegality defence should not be applied in a mechanistic manner and that the policies underlying the defence should be considered.

The Law Commission considered that this approach and that adopted in **Gray v Thames Trains** signalled an important new era in the use of the illegality/reliance defence in that there is a movement away from the mechanistic application of the defence as seen previously. The Commission recognised that the courts were now more willing to explore the relevant policies that lie at the heart of the defence; further, that the courts were now also more willing to consider the importance of the links between the illegality and the claim itself, together with the seriousness of the illegal act. The Law Commission also considered that, in the law of contract, tort and unjust enrichment, the courts had applied the illegality doctrine in a fair and appropriate way and often applied the correct policy decision. At the end of the day, the Law Commission considered that, in the face of that shift in approach by the courts towards a more transparent process in their judgements, no legislative reform was required, nevertheless, the Law Commission's report laid bare differences of opinion regarding the processes for the application of the illegality principle.

Clearly then the illegality defence is one of great complexity with cases not being capable of being reconciled with one another. Such a conclusion was reached by Etherton LJ in the Court of Appeal in **Les Laboratoires Servier v Apotex Inc** [2012] EWCA Civ 593, who stated:

> It is not necessary in order to resolve this appeal to undertake a comprehensive analysis of the decided cases. Such an exercise would in any event be complex, very lengthy and in large part unrewarding. The decisions inevitably turn on their own particular facts. The statements of law or principle they contain are not all consistent or easily reconciled. The jurisprudence in this area has been an evolving one, but its evolution has not followed a consistent pattern.

This view was reiterated in **ParkingEye Ltd v Somerfield Stores Ltd** [2012] EWCA Civ 1338 where Sir Robin Jacob considered that 'illegality and the law of contract is a notoriously knotty territory' and indeed Toulson LJ considered this was 'a mild way to describe it' and that 'it is one of the least satisfactory parts of the law of contract'. Toulson LJ acknowledged that the 'fundamental reason why illegality is a difficult topic is that the doctrine is founded on public policy, and public policy not infrequently gives rise to conflicting considerations'. As an example, he referred to the judgement of Lord Wright in **Vita Food Products Inc v Unus Shipping Co** [1939] AC 277, where he stated:

> Each case has to be considered on its merits. Nor must it be forgotten that the rule by which contracts not expressly forbidden by statute or declared to be void are in proper cases nullified for disobedience to a statute is a rule of public policy only, and public policy understood in a wider sense may at times be better served by refusing to nullify a bargain save on serious and sufficient grounds.

Toulson LJ considered that there was a public interest in the court not appearing to reward wrong doing or condone a breach of the law. But where both parties were complicit in the illegality, denial of one party's claim on that ground would in effect give an unjustified benefit to the other. He stated that '

> the rule that where both parties are equally at fault, the defendant should prevail may be right in more serious cases (on the ground that the court should, in effect, wash its hands of the dispute), but may be a disproportionately severe response in less serious cases, especially where the parties did not appreciate that they were acting contrary to the law. There is a public interest in doing justice between the parties and, as Lord Wright said, in nullifying a bargain only on serious and sufficient grounds.

Toulson LJ, however, warned against a mechanistic approach to the issue. He considered that whilst it is in the interests of commercial certainty to have fixed rules in the law of contract, in the area of illegality 'experience has shown that it is better to recognise that there may be conflicting considerations that the rules need to be developed and applied in a way which enables the court to balance them fairly'. In achieving this balance he considered that and

> Rather than having over-complex rules which are indiscriminate in theory but less so in practice, it is better and more honest that the court should look openly at the underlying policy factors and reach a balanced judgement in each case for reasons articulated by it. This is not to suggest that a list of policy factors should become a complete substitute for the rules about illegality in the law of contract which the courts have developed, but rather that those rules are to be developed and applied with the degree of flexibility necessary to give proper effect to the underlying policy factors.

In arriving at that conclusion he endorsed Etherton LJ's comment in *Les Laboratoires Servier v Apotex Inc [2012] EWCA Civ 593* that:

> ... what is required in each case is an intensive analysis of the particular facts and of the proper application of the various policy considerations underlying the illegality principle so as to produce a just and proportionate response to the illegality. This is not the same as an unbridled discretion.

The flexible but balanced approach was considered by the Supreme Court in *Hounga v Allen* [2014] UKSC 47.

Hounga v Allen [2014] UKSC 47

The facts of the case Hounga was a 14-year-old Nigerian national who had agreed to come to the United Kingdom to work for the defendant as an au pair. In order to gain entry to the UK she agreed to take on a false identity. Hounga overstayed her visa and against this background suffered serious abuse at the hands of the defendant. The defendant also threatened to reveal the girl's illegal presence in the UK if she complained and stated that she would be imprisoned if the authorities discovered her illegal entry into the UK.. After an altercation the defendant threw Hounga out of the house and dismissed her. Hounga brought a claim for unlawful discrimination under the Race Relations Act 1976 which was upheld by the employment tribunal, which awarded her damages. The Court of Appeal set the order of the employment tribunal aside on the basis that the illegal contract of employment was material to her complaint and that to uphold would amount to a condonation of the illegality. Hounga, the claimant appealed to the Supreme Court.

The Supreme Court by a majority (Lords Hughes and Carnwath dissenting in part) allowed the appeal. The Supreme Court considered that the reliance test, that is the rule that the claimant had to rely on the illegality, had been criticised for its arbitrary application and that it was correct that the operation of the rule should be softened by reference to the public policy considerations that surround the application of the principle on the facts of this case. The Supreme Court considered that the illegality defence rested upon the foundation of public policy and as such it was necessary to ask 'what is the aspect of public policy which founds the defence'? and then 'is there another aspect of public policy to which application of the defence would run counter'?. In answer to the first question Lord Wilson drew down on the Canadian case of *Hall v Hebert* [1993] 2 SCR 159 which addressed the issue in the context of the law of tort and in which McLachlin J stated.

> My own view is that courts should be allowed to bar recovery in tort on the ground of the plaintiff's immoral or illegal conduct only in very limited circumstances. The basis of this

power, as I see it, lies in duty of the courts to preserve the integrity of the legal system, and is exercisable only where this concern is in issue. This concern is in issue where a damage award in a civil suit would, in effect, allow a person to profit from illegal or wrongful conduct, or would permit an evasion or rebate of a penalty prescribed by the criminal law. The idea common to these instances is that the law refuses to give by its right hand what it takes away by its left hand. It follows from this that, as a general rule, the *ex turpi causa* principle will not operate in tort to deny damages for personal injury, since tort suits will generally be based on a claim for compensation, and will not seek damages as profit for illegal or immoral acts.

In addressing the policy considerations or preserving the integrity of the legal system, the majority of the Supreme Court considered that applying the illegality defence to bar the claim for compensation could have the effect of encouraging employers to enter illegal contracts of employment safe in the belief that they could discriminate against their employees with impunity. Balanced against this, the court considered that the award by the employment tribunal did not allow the claimant to benefit from her wrongdoing since the award was compensation for her injury to feelings from her dismissal; the award to not allow for the evasion of a criminal penalty; and, the award would not have encouraged other persons in the claimant's position to enter into such illegal contract. The Supreme Court therefore concluded that the considerations of public policy in favour of applying the defence barely existed on the facts of this case.

On the second question, the Supreme Court held that the Court of Appeal's decision ran counter to a further issue of public policy that arose in the case in that to allow the claimant's case to be defeated by the illegality defence would breach the UK's obligations under the European Convention on Action against Trafficking in Human Beings 2005. The Supreme Court therefore decided that the public policy underpinning the illegality defence had to give way to the UK's public policy obligations against trafficking. The minority of the Supreme Court argued the point in another way in that the proximity between the claimant's immigration offences and her claim for discrimination were insufficient to sustain the illegality defence by the defendants.

In *Les Laboratoires Servier v Apotex Inc [2014] UKSC 55*, a differently constituted Supreme Court from the Hounga case disapproved of the flexible approach set out in in the Court of Appeal and the decision in *ParkingEye Ltd v Somerfield Stores Ltd*. The court considered that the illegality defence was a rule of law not a mere discretionary power and was based on public policy not on the merits of the respective claims of parties to a dispute, thus following *Tinsley v Milligan*. Thus to rely on the subjective facts of particular cases introduced a discretionary process that was contrary to established legal principle. As Lord Sumption stated, 'two features of this area of law have been characteristic of it from the outset. First, it is a rule of law and not a mere discretionary power. Secondly, it is based on public policy, and not on the perceived balance of merits between the parties to any particular dispute.'

Similarly the court disapproved of the proposed public conscience test set out by the Law Commission in 'The Illegality Defence: A Consultative Report (2009)' (Consultation Paper 189). It was considered that this approach was inconsistent with the decision in *Tinsley* v *Milligan* and as a result made the law uncertain.

The Supreme Court considered that rule arises out of *ex turpi cause non oritur* action ('no action arises from an unworthy cause') and that therefore, as a starting point, one has to identify the unworthy cause or the 'turpitude' and what acts constitute this for the purposes of the defence. Lord Sumption considered that 'turpitude' conjures up a criminal offence and that whilst Lord Mansfield in *Holman* v *Johnson* referred to 'immoral or illegal' acts, this meant acts that engage the 'interests of the state or as we would put it today, the public interest'. Lord Sumption therefore considered that illegality defence:

> where it arises, it arises in the public interest, irrespective of the interests or rights of the parties. It is because the public has its own interest in conduct giving rise to the illegality defence that the judge may be bound to take the point of his own motion, contrary to the ordinary principle in adversarial litigation. In some contexts, notably the invalidity of contracts prohibited by law, the *ex turpi causa* principle can be analysed as part of the substantive law governing the parties' rights. The contract is void, and any right derived from it is non-existent. But in general, although described as a defence, it is in reality a rule of judicial abstention. It means that rather than regulating the consequences of an illegal act (for example by restoring the parties to the status quo ante, in the same way as upon the rescission of a contract) the courts withhold judicial remedies, leaving the loss to lie where it falls. This is so even in a contractual context, when the court is invited to determine the financial consequence of a contract's voidness for illegality. The *ex turpi causa* principle precludes the judge from performing his ordinary adjudicative function in a case where that would lend the authority of the state to the enforcement of an illegal transaction or to the determination of the legal consequences of an illegal act.

The effect therefore is that 'turpitude' refers to criminal or quasi-criminal acts on the basis that it is only those acts that engage the public interests. On the other hand, torts (other than those involving dishonesty), breaches of contract, and statutory and other civil wrongs, offended against private, rather than public interests and there was no reason to depart from ordinary remedies of corrective justice. It is clear then that the Supreme Court is attempting to distinguish between civil liabilities, which do not offend the public interest because they do not carry the necessary moral turpitude to trigger the illegality. Thus in order for the defence to operate, there must be a connection between the illegal act and the claim and as such the correct approach to the illegality defence is that set out in **Tinsley v Milligan**. This can be reconciled in **Hounga** since in that case because there was no connection the claimant was able to claim and the illegality defence could not operate.

The difficulty that is now left is that we now have two conflicting Supreme Court decisions (given within a month of each other!), one with the 'policy-based flexible/balanced approach' (**ParkingEye** and **Hounga**) and the other following the 'rule-based reliance principle' (**Tinsley**). Thus following these two decisions the law as regards the illegality defence appears to have been left in a highly unsatisfactory and uncertain state; however, the status of the decision in **Tinsley** was the subject of further discussion in the Supreme Court in **Bilta (UK) Ltd v Nazir (No 2)** [2015] UKSC 23. Lord Neuberger considered that the debate on the topic involved a 'spectrum of views'. He did not consider that this case was the correct forum for a full discussion of the rule since the material facts of the case did not provide the context for that discussion. The result was that neither he nor the majority of the court expressed a particular view.

The opportunity for a full discussion arose in the Supreme Court in **Patel v Mirza** [2016] UKSC 42. The facts of this case were examined earlier in this chapter in which Patel succeeded in his appeal from the court of first instance. The Court of Appeal found that whilst Patel ran into the rule that no party to a contract who is aware of or reliant on an illegality can enforce it and furthermore any money or property transferred is irrecoverable, following, **Holman v Johnson**, the principle permitted a claimant to rely on an illegal arrangement provided that he had voluntarily withdrawn from it before it had been carried into effect. Mirza then appealed to the Supreme Court where his appeal was unanimously dismissed.

In the Supreme Court Lord Toulson gave the lead judgement, with Lady Hale, Lord Kerr, Lord Wilson and Lord Hodge concurring with his judgement. Lords Neuberger, Mance,

Clarke and Sumption concurred with the result but by a different process of reasoning. The fact that the constituted Supreme Court comprised nine law lords gives an indication of the importance of the decision. The essence of the issues in *Patel v Mirza* revolved around whether Lord Mansfield's maxim in *Holman v Johnson* precludes a party to a contract tainted with illegality from recovering money paid under a contract from the other party on the basis of unjust enrichment. One side of the argument is that such an approach does not advance the public policy underlying the maxim, 'once the underlying policy is properly understood'. The other side of the argument is that such an approach is that a court must not assist a party who has engaged in any type of illegality.

Lord Toulson in his judgement reviewed the authorities surrounding the illegality principle and the fact that there was a sharp divide of opinion about the proper approach to the rule and whether it should be 'on the one hand, a strictly rule-based approach [or], on the other hand, a more flexible approach by which the court would look at the policies underlying the doctrine and decide whether they militated in favour of the defence, taking into account a range of potentially relevant factors'. Neither approach was resolved in the case of *Bilta (UK) Ltd v Nazir (No 2)*, though Lord Neuberger considered that the difference should be resolved as soon as possible, when it was appropriate to do so.

In arriving at his decision Lord Toulson referred to Lord Goff's observations in *Attorney General v Guardian Newspapers Ltd (No 2)* [1990] 1 AC 109, 286,the Spycatcher case, that the 'statement that a man shall not be allowed to profit from his own wrong is in very general terms, and does not of itself provide any sure guidance to the solution of a problem in any particular case'. He considered that a narrow meaning should be given to profit and agreed with the reasoning of McLachlin J in *Hall v Hebert* [1993] 2 SCR 159 where she expressed the view that the rationale that a claimant not being allowed to profit from his or her own wrongdoing

> does not fully explain why particular claims have been rejected, and that it may have the undesirable effect of tempting judges to focus on whether the plaintiff is 'getting something' out of the wrongdoing, rather than on the question whether allowing recovery for something which was illegal would produce inconsistency and disharmony in the law, and so cause damage to the integrity of the legal system.

Whilst this expression does not address what is meant by 'inconsistency and disharmony', he did not see this as a weakness, he stated:

> It is not a matter which can be determined mechanistically. So how is the court to determine the matter if not by some mechanistic process? In answer to that question I would say that one cannot judge whether allowing a claim which is in some way tainted by illegality would be contrary to the public interest, because it would be harmful to the integrity of the legal system, without a) considering the underlying purpose of the prohibition which has been transgressed, b) considering conversely any other relevant public policies which may be rendered ineffective or less effective by denial of the claim, and c) keeping in mind the possibility of overkill unless the law is applied with a due sense of proportionality. We are, after all, in the area of public policy. That trio of necessary considerations can be found in the case law.

Clearly it is important to take into account the purpose of the relevant prohibition, for instance, the relevant statutory context, as are countervailing public interest considerations of the type seen in *Hounga v Allen*. Similarly in terms of the overkill dangers, Lord Toulson referred to the dicta of Bingham LJ who stated:

> Where issues of illegality are raised, the courts have (as it seems to me) to steer a middle course between two unacceptable positions. On the one hand it is unacceptable that any court of law

should aid or lend its authority to a party seeking to pursue or enforce an object or agreement which the law prohibits. On the other hand, it is unacceptable that the court should, on the first indication of unlawfulness affecting any aspect of a transaction, draw up its skirts and refuse all assistance to the plaintiff, no matter how serious his loss nor how disproportionate his loss to the unlawfulness of his conduct.

With regards to the disproportionate nature of the loss, this can be clearly seen in *Tinsley v Milligan*; here it would have been disproportionate to have prevented her from enforcing her equitable interest in the property and conversely to have left Miss Tinsley unjustly enriched. In determining whether it would be disproportionate to refuse relief to a claimant who would otherwise be entitled, as a matter of public policy, various factors may be relevant, such as the degree to which the conduct was serious or contrary to public policy; the degree to which the conduct of the claimant was central to the contract or its performance; the seriousness of the denial of enforcement of the contract for the claimant; the degree to which the denial of enforcement will operate as a deterrent towards conduct that is illegal or contrary to public policy, the degree to which the conduct was intentional, and the respective culpability of the parties. Lord Toulson resiled from laying down a proscriptive or definitive list of factors that, as a matter of public policy, might be relevant but insisted that the integrity and harmony of the law require flexibility.

In adopting the 'range of factors' approach Lord Toulson addressed the critics of such an approach who consider that this creates an unacceptable level of uncertainty. He argued that the current position is in any event 'riven by uncertainty' and unpredictability, particularly as to how courts reach a decision in the quest for a just and reasonable result. In his judgement Lord Toulson had examined the position in other jurisdictions that had a flexible approach and he found that there was no evidence that this approach was the source of serious problems. Finally, whilst there are areas where the law requires certainty, for instance, in mercantile transactions, the same considerations did not apply in the same way when the parties contemplate unlawful activity.

Lord Toulson considered that the reliance rule as laid down in *Bowmakers* and *Tinsley v Milligan* should no longer be followed. He stated that:

> the essential rationale of the illegality doctrine is that it would be contrary to the public interest to enforce a claim if to do so would be harmful to the integrity of the legal system (or, possibly, certain aspects of public morality, the boundaries of which have never been made entirely clear and which do not arise for consideration in this case).

In assessing whether the public interest would be harmed, he stated that it is necessary

> a) to consider the underlying purpose of the prohibition which has been transgressed and whether that purpose will be enhanced by denial of the claim, b) to consider any other relevant public policy on which the denial of the claim may have an impact and c) to consider whether denial of the claim would be a proportionate response to the illegality, bearing in mind that punishment is a matter for the criminal courts.

He thought that within that framework various factors may be relevant. He was adamant, however, that a court is not free to decide a case in an undisciplined manner. He considered that the 'public interest is best served by a principled and transparent assessment of the considerations identified, rather by than the application of a formal approach capable of producing results which may appear arbitrary, unjust or disproportionate'.

Lord Kerr wrote a concurring judgement. He considered Lord Toulson's judgement outlined a structured approach to what had hitherto been an 'intractable problem' and that this was the preferred path to follow. He considered that the flexible approach, if properly applied, would promote, rather than detract from, consistency in the law. It also had the added advantage of avoiding the need to devise piecemeal and contrived exceptions to previous formulations of the illegality rule. He stated that the rule-based reliance approach had failed to deliver on what some have claimed to be its principal virtues, i.e. ease of application and predictability of outcome and that the facts of *Patel v Mirza* exemplified the point. In terms of those who claim the reliance rule provided a predictability of outcome, he questioned whether predictability should be given such weight in circumstances where the claimant and defendant have entered into an agreement that is plainly illegal. Whilst certainty and predictability are a laudable aim, 'it is not a premium to which those engaged in disreputable conduct can claim automatic entitlement'.

Lord Neuberger was not attracted to the approach suggested by Lord Toulson, however, at the end of the day, he considered that this approach provides reliable and helpful guidance. He considered that where a claim based on a contract involves illegal activity (whether or not the illegal activity has been wholly, partly or not at all undertaken), the court should, when deciding how to take into account the impact of the illegality on the claim, bear in mind the need for integrity and consistency in the justice system, and in particular, (a) the policy behind the illegality, (b) any other public policy issues, and (c) the need for proportionality. Whilst Lord Neuberger's analysis might have been slightly different from Lord Toulson's, he did not think there was any significant difference in practice and agreed with Lord Toulson's framework for arriving at an outcome.

Lord Mance, Lord Clarke and Lord Sumption considered that there was no basis for substituting the clear-cut principles set out in *Holman v Johnson* and *Hall v Hebert* which were founded on the need to maintain the integrity of the law. They considered that the range of factors approach, as advocated by Lord Toulson, did not offer the same degree of coherence or certainty. Lord Mance did not consider that the illegality doctrine should be generally rewritten. The difficulties with the reliance principle as set out by Lord Toulson as regards the enforcement of contract have not led to any real difficulty in achieving just solutions, 'certainly not to such difficulty as to justify tearing up the existing law and starting again'. He did not consider the new range of factors approach, 'over and above statutory purpose and effect, would avoid similar analysis of statutory policy'.

Lord Clarke, along with Lord Mance and Lord Sumption, considered that the appeal should be dismissed but not on the basis of the application of the illegality doctrine, whether in its orthodox form or under the revised range of factors approach, but on the basis of undue enrichment. Lord Sumption considered that the rule in *Holman v Johnson* arose automatically and by operation of law and that when it did arise, a right to restitution followed in principle from the legal ineffectiveness of the contract. Such an analysis therefore avoided a contrived result arising from an analysis of a range of factors. He considered that 'the Rule is consistent with authority and with policy and renders the outcome in cases of contracts involving illegality and the maxim *ex turpi causa non oritur action* relatively clear and certain'. On this Mr Patel would in any event be entitled to restitution of the £620,000 on the basis that Mr Mirza would otherwise be unjustly enriched.

It is apparent therefore that on a majority of the Supreme Court decision in *Patel v Mirza* that the reliance principle as originally set out in *Holman v Johnson* and applied in the much-criticised case of *Tinsley v Milligan* has undergone a significant revision. Whilst it has not moved towards a wholly discretionary process, it has at least addressed the indiscriminate effect of the rule which Lord Goff recognised as being the cause of potential injustice. Whether or not this will make for transparent and principled decision making in this area of law is for time to tell. There is an argument that the revised doctrine will make matters worse in that it may not offer the necessary degree of coherence or certainty. The decision is not without its detractors as seen in the judgements of Lord Clarke, Lord Mance and Lord Sumption who, whilst arriving at the same decision, do so in a different manner by way of the law of restitution. Their position is a principled one, considering the rule that the orthodox rule maintains certainty and that where a claimant cannot recover on the basis of illegality, he does in any event have access to redress by way of restitution and unjust enrichment. The decision in **Patel v Mirza** does not preclude this avenue of redress and it seems there is no reason to suggest that if Lord Toulson's range of factors approach fails to provide a solution, then a claimant cannot fall back on equitable principles with the law of restitution.

Contracts in restraint of trade

General principles

Objective 6

Such contracts are prima facie void as being contrary to public policy, which intervenes on two grounds. First, the common law seeks to protect an individual from negotiating away his livelihood to another, possibly contractually stronger, party, particularly where the restraint is a general one. Second, the law understood, even in the earliest days of the doctrine in the sixteenth century, that it was not in the public interest for the state to be deprived of a valuable benefit in allowing a person to be restricted in carrying out his lawful trade or business. It is possible that the degree of interference in such contracts may be closely associated with the prevailing economic theory of the day, as regards the encouragement or discouragement of competition, though as Beatson, *Anson's Law of Contract*, emphasises, there are no judicial authorities pointing out such fluctuations of policy.

Contracts in restraint of trade are defined in *Cheshire, Fifoot and Furmston* as:

> A contract in restraint of trade is one by which a party restricts his future liberty to carry on his trade, business or profession in such manner and with such persons as he chooses.

The modern doctrine of restraint of trade is to be found in the case of **Nordenfelt v Maxim Nordenfelt Guns and Ammunition Co**.

Nordenfelt v Maxim Nordenfelt Guns and Ammunition Co. [1894] AC 535

A machine-gun manufacturer sold his business and agreed in the contract of sale to restrict his future activities in that business worldwide for 25 years. The covenant was held to be valid and binding, even though prior to this case the general principle was that general restraints of this nature were prima facie void, while partial restraints were prima facie valid. The leading judgement in the case comes from Lord MacNaghten who stated:

> The true view at the present time I think, is this: The public have an interest in every person's carrying on his trade freely: so has the individual. All interference with individual liberty of action in trading, and all restraints of trade of themselves, if there is nothing more, are contrary to public policy, and therefore void. That is the general rule. But there are exceptions: restraints of trade and interference with individual liberty of action may be justified by the special circumstances of a particular case. It is a sufficient justification, and indeed it is the only justification, if the restriction is reasonable – reasonable, that is, in reference to the interests of the parties concerned and reasonable in reference to the interests of the public, so framed and so guarded as to afford adequate protection to the party in whose favour it is imposed, while at the same time it is in no way injurious to the public.

The result of this decision, together with a number of other later ones, is that the doctrine of restraint of trade can be reduced to a number of principles. First, all contracts in restraint of trade are prima facie void. Second, it is a matter of law for the court to decide whether any special factors exist which may or may not justify the restraint. If the view is taken that such special factors do not justify the restraint then the contract will be void as being contrary to public policy. Third, however, if the special circumstances do point to the restraint being valid, then it must be reasonable not only as regards the parties to the contracting, but also as regards the interests of the public. Lastly, the burden of proving that the restraint is reasonable lies on the party alleging it to be so. If that burden is satisfied, then it is always open for the party attempting to avoid the restraint to prove that the restraint is, in any event, contrary to the public interest and therefore void on this basis.

The above principles are now well established where the contract is in restraint of trade, though the obvious qualification is that the contract must be regarded as being in restraint of trade in the first place. In *Esso Petroleum Co. Ltd* v *Harper's Garage (Stourport) Ltd* [1968] AC 269 Lord Wilberforce stated:

> It is not to be supposed, or encouraged, that a bare allegation that a contract limits a trader's freedom of action exposes a party suing on it to the burden of justification. There will always be certain categories of contracts as to which it can be said, with some degree of certainty, that the 'doctrine' does or does not apply to them. Positively, there are likely to be certain sensitive areas as to which the law will require in every case the tests of reasonableness to be passed; such as . . . contracts between employer and employee as regards the period after the employment has ceased. Negatively . . . there will be types of contracts as to which the law should be prepared to say with some confidence that they do not enter into the field of restraint of trade at all.

The court must therefore decide whether the contract is in restraint of trade before considering the reasonableness or not of the restraint.

Reasonableness of the restraint

Reasonableness as regards the parties to the contract

A covenant found to be in restraint of trade can only be regarded as reasonable if it is designed only to protect the legitimate interests of the covenantee. While the basis for such a finding will undoubtedly vary from case to case, in *Herbert Morris Ltd* v *Saxelby* [1916] AC 688 Lord Shaw identified two types of contracts which illustrate the types of interests capable of being protected by a covenant in restraint of trade. First, in contracts for the sale of a business, together with its goodwill, it is clearly proper for the purchaser to restrain the vendor from acting in competition with the business just sold to the purchaser since the goodwill is a proprietary interest legitimately capable of protection. Second, in contracts of employment an employer, while not legitimately able to prevent a former employee from acting in competition with the employer, is able to prevent the former employee from making use of trade secrets acquired during a period of employment. Similarly, the employer can prevent a former employee from soliciting the former employer's customers. In these two examples one can clearly see that the law is attempting to balance the rights of the individual and the requirements of the state in respect of trade.

Once it has been established that there is a legitimate interest capable of being protected it has to be remembered that the courts will only allow the covenantor to impose such a restraint that will do no more than protect their interest. If the covenant is excessive then it will be void. In assessing the reasonableness of the restraint the court will have regard to its nature, area and duration (see below). Lastly the covenantee has to show that the restraint must be reasonable as regards both parties at the time of contracting. The effect is that the question of reasonableness is one which is directed towards the contract as a whole, and a contract will not be held to be reasonable if it is found to be unreasonable as regards one of the parties.

Reasonableness as regards the public interest

Contracts that are void as being unreasonable as regards the public interest are extremely uncommon. One such example is that of **Wyatt v Kreglinger and Fernau** [1933] 1 KB 793 where the defendants promised the plaintiff a pension provided that he would not compete against them in the wool trade. The plaintiff eventually agreed and the pension was paid for nearly nine years, when the defendants then refused to pay. The plaintiff sued for breach of contract. The defendants denied there was a contract and stated that in any event such a contract was void since it was an unreasonable restraint of trade. The Court of Appeal held for the defendants and agreed that the restraint was too wide and in any event it was contrary to the public interest. One must, however, wonder to what degree the public was affected by this restraint. The decision would seem to stretch the notion of public interest beyond the realms of reality.

It is, however, possible to see a public interest element if a person's skills are in short supply. Here the public interest lies in the general availability of the individual's skills to the wider economy rather than the skills provided by the individual per se. Here the restraint is invalid as contrary to the public interest even though the restraint against the individual is legitimate.

Other factors influencing the degree of reasonableness

The courts will also consider the following factors in deciding whether or not the covenant is reasonable:

1 the duration of the restraint;
2 the area of the restraint.

The restraint of trade covenant will be struck down if it is found to be unreasonably extensive as to its *duration*. It is clear that an employee's connections with their former employer's customers must wane in time, and, similarly, one cannot protect one's trade secrets indefinitely. The question of duration is largely one of fact, depending on the nature of the business. Thus in the **Nordenfelt** case 25 years was upheld as being reasonable. It is nevertheless possible for the restraint to last indefinitely as in **Fitch v Dewes** [1921] 2 AC 158, where a covenant by a solicitor's clerk that he would not practise within seven miles of Tamworth town hall was held to be reasonable, even though it was for an unlimited duration. The court considered that this restraint did no more than protect the legitimate interests of the solicitor, given the knowledge acquired by the clerk in respect to the clients of his former employer. On the face of things, however, this period seems excessive and the decision should probably be considered to be exceptional.

The covenant must not be excessive in respect of the *area* to which the restraint applies. Again in the **Nordenfelt** case a worldwide ban was appropriate given the reputation of the covenantor in that business. In **Forster & Sons Ltd v Suggett** (1918) 35 TLR 87 a covenant by a works manager, who had acquired knowledge of a secret glass-making process, not to engage in glass-making anywhere within the United Kingdom was held to be reasonable. On the other hand, in **Mason v Provident Clothing and Supply Co.** [1913] AC 724 a covenant by a canvasser not to work in a similar trade or business within 25 miles of London was held to be unreasonable given the covenantor's limited sphere of influence in his employment.

The construction of covenants in restraint of trade

In considering whether or not a contract is void as being contrary to public policy, the task of the court is to construe the contract in order to determine the nature and the extent of the restraint contemplated by the parties in the circumstances of the situation at the time. If the restraint of trade clause is too wide then it will be void; however, in arriving at this conclusion the courts will apply a literal interpretation to the clause and, in common with the general tenets of contract law, the court will not redraft the clause for the parties to make the clause reasonable. Sometimes it is possible to see what the parties had in mind although the wording of the clause does not reflect those objectives; nevertheless, the court will apply the literal meaning. A good example of this is the case of **Home Counties Dairies Ltd** v **Skilton** [1970] 1 All ER 1227, where a milkman agreed 'not at any time during the period of one year after the determination of his employment . . . either on his own account or as a representative or agent of any person or company, to serve or sell milk or dairy produce to . . . any person or company'. Clearly the expression 'dairy produce' includes butter and cheese and therefore the contract would preclude him from taking employment as a grocer's assistant where the grocer traded in those products. The Court of Appeal held that, while the parties had not contemplated such a restraint, this was the effect of the literal interpretation of the clause and it was held that the restraint was valid.

The literal approach set out above has not always been followed. In **Littlewoods Organisation Ltd** v **Harris** [1977] 1 WLR 1472 the Court of Appeal took a more flexible approach to the construction of restraint of trade clauses. In this case Harris was employed by Littlewoods and agreed as part of his contract that he would not, if he left the company, go to work for its rival Great Universal Stores (GUS) for a period of 12 months. Harris was privy to many of the strategic policy decisions behind the running of the Littlewoods mail order business and therefore had an important role. The business of Littlewoods was confined to the mail order business within the United Kingdom whilst GUS was a multinational firm whose business was wider than that of the mail order business. The Court of Appeal held that the application of the clause should be construed so as only to apply to the UK mail order business, since this was the interest that the parties had only intended to protect even though on a literal interpretation the clause itself was very much broader than this. This decision was not welcomed by the whole court and Browne LJ stated: 'rewriting [the clause] so as to make enforceable that which would otherwise be unenforceable . . . I think that this is something which this court cannot do'.

Maybe it is possible that the decision can be countenanced on the basis that this restraint in the **Littlewoods** case applied to a particular competitor as opposed to a general restraint; however, the decision of the Court of Appeal has not been totally accepted, as can be seen in the case of **J A Mont (UK) Ltd** v **Mills**.

J A Mont (UK) Ltd v Mills [1993] IRLR 173

The defendant was a man aged 43 who had been employed for 20 years in the paper tissue industry. It was the only work he knew and he had risen to become marketing and managing director of the company. In 1991 that company amalgamated with the plaintiffs and he became redundant. In 1992 he entered into a severance agreement with the plaintiffs in which he was paid a year's salary and released from working for them for 12 months. This agreement was subject to a restriction that he was not to join another company in the paper tissue industry within one year of leaving the plaintiff's employment.

The defendant contended that the restraint was unreasonable as being too wide in that it not only operated worldwide but also restrained him from being involved in the paper tissue industry in any capacity at all. It was held at first instance that an interlocutory injunction should be granted in that there was a possibility that the defendant could have used confidential information in his new position. The judge, however, stated that the parties should cooperate with each other in drafting the restraint of trade clause in more reasonable terms. The plaintiffs contended that the judge should have construed the clause as being reasonable.

The Court of Appeal (Simon Brown LJ giving the leading judgement) found that there was no attempt to draft the covenant in terms that restrained the defendant from using confidential information, which was the only legitimate way in which the defendant could be restrained should he obtain future employment in the paper tissue industry. The Court of Appeal decided that as a matter of policy it would not attempt to discover whether there was any implicit limitation in the clause that rendered the clause narrower and, therefore, reasonable such that it could be enforced by injunction.

The Court of Appeal by the above decision took a highly restrictive view of its ability to construe restraint of trade clauses. However, the Court of Appeal in *Hanover Insurance Brokers Ltd and Christchurch Insurance Brokers Ltd v Schapiro* indicated that a rather more liberal approach should be taken in construing such clauses.

Hanover Insurance Brokers Ltd and Christchurch Insurance Brokers Ltd v Schapiro [1994] IRLR 82

The facts of the case were that the business of Hanover Insurance Brokers Ltd (the first plaintiffs) was sold to Christchurch Insurance Brokers Ltd (the second plaintiffs) in June 1993. The defendants were all employees of the first plaintiffs (HIB); indeed three of the defendants were also directors of HIB, who all resigned once the sale had been completed. It was alleged by the plaintiffs that the defendants were attempting to solicit clients and employees of HIB both prior to and after leaving the employment of HIB. These activities were explicitly forbidden by a restrictive covenant in their contracts of employment. Subsequently the plaintiffs obtained an *ex parte* injunction (now called a without notice injunction) against the defendants, which they then attempted to get discharged.

There was a difference in the wording between the restrictive covenants in the contracts of the first and second defendants and those of the third and fourth. In the latter the covenants were expressed to protect not only HIB, but also Hanover Acceptances Ltd (which was the holding company of HIB) and any of its subsidiaries. In the former the operation of the covenants was expressed to protect only HIB itself. The third and fourth defendants argued that by further restricting the non-solicitation of clients to Hanover Acceptances Ltd and its subsidiaries, there was an attempt to impose far wider protection than was necessary and that the clause was thus void for being an unreasonable restraint of trade. Their reasoning was based on the argument that the restrictive covenant could also operate in fields of economic activity other than the insurance brokerage business. The plaintiffs argued that the court should adopt a purposive approach to its construction of the clause, so that a narrow interpretation could be given to the clause in order that it reflect the intention of the parties, thereby rendering the clause enforceable.

Both the judge at first instance and the Court of Appeal considered that the only true intention of the parties was to restrict the defendants in soliciting insurance broking clients. Since HIB was the only subsidiary involved in this activity the court decided that the parties only intended to protect the clients of this company, and therefore by applying this purposive approach the clause was enforceable to this degree. In arriving at this decision the Court of Appeal referred to *Littlewoods Organisation Ltd v Harris*, where the Court of Appeal decided that a clause stating 'Great Universal Stores Ltd or any company subsidiary thereto' limited the protection of the clause to that part of the plaintiffs' business activities to which they were reasonably entitled.

It should be noted that the decision of the Court of Appeal in the *Schapiro* case took place in relation to interim proceedings. The court considered that the cases of *J A Mont Ltd* and *Littlewoods* needed to be reconciled in a full hearing.

It would appear that while the traditional approach of the courts of not rewriting restraint of trade clauses persists, in principle at least, the courts are willing to provide a more relaxed approach to rewriting a clause in order to provide a commercial logic to the contract by enforcing the perceived intentions of the parties. Such an approach can be seen in the case of *ChipsAway International Ltd v Errol Kerr* [2009] EWCA Civ 320. The facts of the case are that ChipsAway had rights to a system for repairing bodywork on cars, as well as providing paints and other products used in the system. ChipsAway franchised the system and the supply of the products to others but was not actually involved in the repairing process itself. ChipsAway and Kerr (K) entered into a franchise arrangement in 2002. As part of that agreement, K agreed that, for a period of 12 months following termination of the agreement for whatever reason, he would not, without ChipsAway's prior written consent, 'be engaged in any capacity in any business which competes with the business (as carried on at the date of termination . . .) within the territory'. At the end of the franchise period, K informed ChipsAway that he did not wish to continue with the franchise. Nevertheless he continued to undertake bodywork repairs to cars at his premises. He did not use ChipsAway's name or products in carrying out the repairs. ChipsAway brought an action against K, stating that by carrying on bodywork repairs in the same area as the former franchise territory K was in breach of the restraint of trade clause even though ChipsAway did not have a franchisee in the territory nor was it contemplating appointing one.

At first instance the judge considered that the clause was a nonsense since, when read with the agreement, it appeared to state that K could not engage in any business that competed with K – in other words, it appeared to say that he could not compete with himself. The judge concluded that in order to avoid such a conclusion it was necessary to depart from the literal meaning of the words in order to arrive at an interpretation that gave effect to the underlying intention behind the restraint of trade clause. The judge therefore modified the clause to the effect that K was restrained from engaging in any business which competed with a franchise business that was 'a successor to or otherwise has the characteristics of' the business conducted by K as part of the franchise agreement at the time of its termination. The court therefore held that, following the termination of a franchise agreement, K was not acting in breach of a restrictive covenant by operating his own car care business where the claimant had no businesses in the area with which the franchisee could compete. The court stated that the position would have been different if the claimant had appointed a new franchisee in the territory, or did so within the 12-month term of the covenant. There was no breach of the covenant unless and until that happened. The crucial words in the covenant were 'which competes' and referred to competing on the facts as they were, not to the possibility that competing might begin to happen in the future if the facts changed.

ChipsAway appealed and the Court of Appeal has overturned the judgement of the lower court, making it clear that contracts should be construed according to their ordinary meaning and give effect to the obvious business intentions of the parties. In this case it stated that the apparent intention of the restrictive covenant was to prevent former franchisees such as K from engaging in any business which competed with that of the franchisor for the period of 12 months after termination of the franchise agreement. The court considered that the purpose of the clause was to protect the goodwill of ChipsAway in that territory and allow it adequate time to find a new franchisee and that it was irrelevant to the operation of the provision that the franchisor did not look for one.

The application of covenants in restraint of trade in various situations

The categories of contract discussed below are merely examples of the application of such covenants. The categories of restraint are never closed.

1. Contracts of employment

Covenants restraining an employee while actually engaged by their employer cannot usually be called into question since the employer can require an employee to maintain confidentiality in the course of their employment. Similarly, in contracts of employment an employer can demand that an employee does not act in competition to the employer's business. In these circumstances the doctrine of restraint of trade has no bearing on the validity or otherwise of the restraint.

It is only after an employee has left the covenantee's employment that the doctrine comes to bear. It has already been stated that an employer has a legitimate interest in protecting confidential information or preventing a former employee from soliciting customers so as to protect the goodwill of the employer's business. It is not legitimate, however, to prevent the former employee from exercising a personal trade or skill, even though that may have been acquired during the period of employment, as in an apprenticeship, for instance.

An interesting variation on this theme arose in *Hanover Insurance Brokers Ltd and Christchurch Insurance Brokers Ltd v Schapiro*, as already discussed. One of the arguments put forward by the first defendant, who was the former chairman of HIB, was that he should not be restricted from soliciting clients that he brought to HIB when he began working there. In putting forward this argument he relied on the following case.

M & S Drapers (A Firm) v *Reynolds* [1957] 1 WLR 9

A sales representative, when taking up employment with the plaintiffs, brought with him customers from his previous employment. On joining the plaintiffs he entered into a contract that contained a restrictive covenant which stated that on terminating his employment with the firm he would not, for the period of five years, solicit former customers on whom he had called during his employment. It was held that the clause was unenforceable in that the duration of the restraint was unreasonable.

The Court of Appeal in *Hanover* distinguished that case from that of *M & S Drapers* on the basis that in the latter case it was considered that a sales representative's customer connections amounted to the equivalent of his tools of the trade, so that he could not be unreasonably deprived of them. In *Hanover*, however, the Court of Appeal considered that one of the reasons for employing the first defendant was the fact that he would bring clients into the business of the company; indeed, his salary reflected this commitment. The Court of Appeal therefore dismissed the arguments put forward by the first defendant.

One other aspect of the *Hanover* case that is relevant in the context of restraints in contracts of employment arose in relation to the third and fourth defendants, who argued that the restraint was unreasonable since it prevented them from soliciting clients with whom they had had no contract while employed by HIB. In arriving at its decision the Court of Appeal considered two apparently conflicting Court of Appeal cases: *G W Plowman & Son Ltd* v *Ash* and *Marley Tile Co.* v *Johnson* [1982] IRLR 75.

G W Plowman & Son Ltd v Ash [1964] 1 WLR 568

The defendant, a sales representative, was employed under a contract that contained a restrictive covenant that he would not, for two years after the termination of his contract, solicit any farmer or market gardener who had been a customer of his employers at any time during the course of the defendant's contract. The defendant argued that this clause was too wide in that it sought to restrain him from soliciting customers who were not known to him. The court rejected this argument since it considered that he could easily avoid innocently breaching the covenant by simply asking a potential customer whether or not he had been a customer of the plaintiffs. If the answer was in the affirmative he could then avoid attempting to solicit business from that customer.

In *Marley Tile* there was a similar covenant against soliciting or dealing with former customers, but on this occasion the Court of Appeal held that this clause was too wide and unenforceable. The court found that of the 2,500 customers of the plaintiffs, the defendant could only have known or come into contact with a small proportion of them. In considering this case, though, it has to be noted that the restraining clause was wider than that in the *G W Plowman* case in two respects: first, the restriction prevented the defendant not only from soliciting former customers, but also from dealing with them; second, the restriction attempted to restrain the defendant from engaging in activities other than those for which he had been employed by the plaintiffs.

In the *Hanover* case, Dillon LJ, in considering *G W Plowman* and *Marley Tile*, thought that the decisions in these cases clearly showed that every case has to be decided on its own facts. His Lordship therefore resiled from making a decision, since in dealing with interim proceedings the full facts were not known to him, i.e. he was not aware of what proportion of HIB's clients the defendants had contact with. This was not the problem in another case on this issue, *Austin Knight (UK) Ltd* v *Hinds* [1994] FSR 52, where Vinelott J had detailed knowledge of the extent of the employee's knowledge about her employer's clients. This information showed that she knew only a third of the clients and therefore Vinelott J distinguished the case before him from *G W Plowman*. The basis of the decision was that it is an unreasonable restraint of trade to prevent a defendant from approaching or dealing with customers of a former employer whom the defendant had no knowledge of or contact with during his or her employment.

The distinction between a personal skill or knowledge and confidential information obtained during employment can be exceedingly difficult to make, especially since 'knowhow' is not widely regarded as a commodity in its own right. In *Leng & Co. Ltd* v *Andrews* [1909] 1 Ch 763 a journalist covenanted not to work for any other newspaper within 20 miles of Sheffield. The principle behind the covenant was to protect so-called sources of information. It was held that such interests could not be protected.

In *Rock Refrigeration Ltd* v *Jones* [1997] 1 All ER 1, it was held by the Court of Appeal that a restrictive covenant purporting to restrain an employee from working for a competitor would be extinguished where the employer committed a repudiatory breach of contract that was accepted by the employee as terminating the contract.

2. Contracts for the sale of a business

Covenants in restraint of trade are far more likely to be upheld where they are contained in a contract for the sale of a business. It should be borne in mind, however, that restraints attempting to prevent competition per se are not valid, since there must be shown to be a legitimate interest worthy of protection. It follows from this that the restraint can only protect the legitimate interests of the business actually sold. This being the case, in ***British Reinforced Concrete Engineering Co. Ltd* v *Schelff* [1921] 2 Ch 563** a manufacturer of a specialised road improvement product could not be restrained from engaging in the manufacture or sale of road reinforcements generally when he sold the business to the plaintiffs. The sale of the business concerned the specialised product only and therefore the restraint could curb his activities only in relation to that product.

Very often the restraint is designed to protect the goodwill that may be purchased with the business and this does, of course, form a proprietary interest capable of protection, though, again, regard must be had to the area and duration of the restraint in assessing its reasonableness.

3. Exclusive trading

Such contracts commonly arise where a manufacturer, or sometimes a wholesaler, attempts to restrict the retailer in a method of distribution or pricing policy or simply to tie the retailer so closely to the chain of supply that they are prevented from selling similar goods produced by competing manufacturers or distributed by competing wholesalers. Such agreements are traditionally termed '**solus agreements**', or, more recently, 'vertical agreements'. Technically there is no difference between the two in that they generally take the form of a person entering into an agreement to purchase all requirements as regards certain types of goods from a particular manufacturer. Alternatively, they may be required to sell all that they produce of a particular item to an individual buyer. The leading case in this area is that of ***Esso Petroleum Co. Ltd* v *Harper's Garage (Stourport) Ltd*.**

Esso Petroleum Co. Ltd v *Harper's Garage (Stourport) Ltd* [1967] 1 All ER 699

> The respondent owners of two garages entered a solus agreement with the appellants whereby they contracted to purchase all their petrol from the appellants. The agreement was to last for four years and five months in respect of one garage, during which the owners would receive a discount in the price of petrol purchased from the appellants. In respect of the second garage the 'tie' was to last for 21 years in return for a mortgage of £7,000 but covenants in the second agreement stated that they had also to comply with covenants contained in the agreement made in respect of the first contract. Further, the respondents were not entitled to redeem the 21-year mortgage before the end of the term of the mortgage. When the respondents started to sell another brand of petrol they were sued by the appellants. The respondents argued that they were not bound by the contracts since they were an unreasonable restraint of trade.

The House of Lords held that both transactions fell within the doctrine of restraint of trade and were thus prima facie void. Their Lordships decided that there was nothing unlawful per se in a solus agreement since very often both parties benefited from the transaction. One party benefited from acquiring a chain of distribution which made the supply of its products efficient and economical. On the other hand, the other party, the respondents in this case, gained by acquiring extra capital finance and a preferential wholesale price. On this basis there were clearly interests that merited protection. Nevertheless the restrictions could only be enforced if they could be reasonable, not only between the parties, but also as regards the public interest. With regard to the first agreement they found that it was reasonable since it protected a legitimate interest of the parties and at the same time it was not contrary to the public interest. The court, however, decided that such agreements would become unreasonable if they operated for an excessive period and in this regard considered the second agreement to be unreasonable and void.

The stance taken by the House of Lords with regard to the second agreement is also consistent with the general principle in relation to the law of mortgages. Here equity will not allow a 'clog or fetter' on the equity of redemption. Any attempt to postpone the right of redemption or to render it illusory is void here. The court, however, stated that the doctrine of restraint of trade still applied even though it crossed into the field of land law. Their Lordships then adopted an unusual stance and stated that the doctrine did not apply where the restriction was applied to covenants contained in leases or conveyances of land. Thus if one purchases a garage, for instance, or takes a lease of such a garage and the oil company imposes covenants akin to those found in the *Harper's Garage* case, then such restrictions will be prima facie valid. This presumption as to validity will only be rebutted if it can be shown that the restrictions are contrary to the public interest, as stated in ***Cleveland Petroleum Co. Ltd* v *Dartstone Ltd*** [1969] 1 All ER 201, where the Court of Appeal considered that to find otherwise would be to allow the doctrine of restraint of trade to be sidestepped by the adoption of a conveyancing device.

An attempt to make use of the above distinction between a person who is already in possession of their business premises entering into a solus agreement, thereby surrendering rights, and a person who enters into restrictions as they acquire their business premises can be seen in the case of ***Alec Lobb (Garages) Ltd* v *Total Oil Great Britain Ltd*** [1983] 1 WLR 87 where the plaintiff company was a petrol filling station. In 1969 it found itself in financial difficulties and turned to the defendants for help. This help took the form of the defendants taking a 51-year lease of the garage forecourt for £35,000 plus a nominal rent. There was an immediate lease-back arrangement whereby the directors of the plaintiff company acquired a 21-year sub-lease at a rent of £2,500 per annum, together with a solus clause whereby the plaintiffs agreed to buy all their petrol from the defendants. The reason the sub-lease was granted to the two directors of the plaintiff company was to avoid the solus clause being challenged, since if the clause was contained in what might be considered a separate transaction, namely the sub-lease, it would not be subject to the doctrine of restraint of trade.

The plaintiff company relied on an earlier decision of the Privy Council in ***Amoco Australia Pty Ltd* v *Rocca Bros Motor Engineering Co. Pty Ltd*** [1975] AC 561 that a lease and a lease-back were held to be a single transaction, and that since the result of the solus clause was to render the sub-lease unenforceable, the effect was to render both transactions, that is, the lease and the sub-lease, unenforceable. This decision was followed in the *Alec Lobb* case, although the effect of the solus clause was not quite so fundamental as to render both transactions unenforceable. The Court of Appeal decided that the solus clause was severable from the sub-lease, with the result that both the lease and the sub-lease were upheld as valid but without the benefit of the solus clause.

4. Anti-competitive agreements and abuse of a dominant position

Despite the fact that the public interest must be considered in assessing the validity of an agreement in restraint of trade, most cases decide the validity of the restraint in such agreements by reference to their reasonableness as regards the parties. The result is that it is possible for restraints to go unchecked despite the fact that the public may be adversely affected by such an agreement. Since the validity is decided as a matter of private law should the case come to court (which it may not do, of course), there is no possibility of such restraints being challenged by third parties. The result of this state of affairs was the intervention of Parliament by the passing of, first, the Monopolies and Restrictive Practices (Inquiry and Control) Act 1948. Subsequently a series of other statutes impacted upon **cartel** and monopoly activities. The Competition Act 1998 reformed the whole regime in these areas to bring United Kingdom law into line, from 1 March 2000, with Arts 81 and 82 of the Treaty of Rome. The Enterprise Act 2002 has made significant changes to competition law enforcement and rights in the United Kingdom.

In general terms the Competition Act outlaws any agreements, business practices and conduct that damage competition. Chapter I of the Act prohibits agreements between undertakings, decisions by associations of undertakings, and concerted practices which prevent, restrict or distort competition or are intended to do so, and which may affect trade within the United Kingdom. Chapter II prohibits the abuse by one or more undertakings of a dominant position in a market which may affect trade within the United Kingdom.

Under the Act, the Office of Fair Trading has powers to investigate undertakings suspected of being involved in anti-competitive activities. Breach of either prohibition may result in an order to terminate or amend the offending agreement or to cease the offending conduct. Additionally, undertakings found to have infringed either prohibition may be liable to a penalty of up to 10 per cent of their turnover in the United Kingdom. There is the possibility of appeal to the Competition Appeal Tribunal against the Office of Fair Trading's findings and penalties. Of particular importance to contract law is the fact that parts of any agreement found to infringe the Chapter I prohibition are null and void and therefore cannot be enforced. In addition, third parties who consider that they have been harmed as a result of any unlawful agreement, practice, or conduct may have a claim for damages in the courts or before the Competition Appeal Tribunal.

Many types of 'cartel' agreement may be caught by the Chapter I prohibition and the Act lists specific examples. These include agreeing to: fix prices or other trading conditions; limit or control production, markets, technical development or investment; share markets or supply sources; apply different trading conditions to equivalent transactions, thereby placing some parties at a competitive disadvantage; and make contracts subject to unrelated conditions. Abuse of a dominant position under the Chapter II prohibition includes: imposing unfair purchase or selling prices; limiting production, markets or technical development to the prejudice of consumers; applying different trading conditions to equivalent transactions, thereby placing certain parties at a competitive disadvantage; and attaching unrelated supplementary conditions to contracts.

It is important to note that the Competition Act does provide for exemption of certain agreements from the Chapter I prohibition and that certain categories of agreement and conduct are specifically excluded from the scope of the Act.

5. Commercial agency agreements

The Commercial Agents (Council Directive) Regulations 1993 control the use of restraint of trade clauses in commercial agency agreements. Regulation 20(1) provides that restraint of trade clauses in this context will only be valid if they are expressed in writing and are limited to the geographical area and/or group of customers and to the kind of goods covered by the agency contract. Furthermore, reg 20(2) provides that the restraint of trade clause must not last for more than two years after the termination of the agency contract. It should be noted that reg 20(3) preserves other enactments and rules of law and thus it would seem that, as regards the application of the Regulations in English law, the requirement that restraint of trade clauses have to be reasonable as between the parties is still a necessity for such clauses to be valid.

6. Other situations

Contracts that incorporate covenants in restraint of trade are found in many other situations, though of course the same principles apply. Two cases which illustrate the flexibility of the law in dealing with restraints are *Schroeder Music Publishing Co. Ltd v Macaulay* and *Panayiotou v Sony Music International (UK) Ltd*, where the principles were extended to service contracts.

Schroeder Music Publishing Co. Ltd v *Macaulay* [1974] 1 WLR 1308

Macaulay, an unknown songwriter, entered into a contract with Schroeder. The contract, which was a standard-form contract, was very much in Schroeder's favour in that it engaged Macaulay's services for five years during which time he assigned full copyright for all his compositions to Schroeder, which was not obliged to publish or promote any of his work. Further, if Macaulay's royalties exceeded £5,000 the contract was to be automatically extended for a further five years. Schroeder was free to terminate the agreement at any time with one month's notice, whilst Macaulay had no such right. Macaulay subsequently alleged that the contract was an unreasonable restraint of trade and void.

It was held by the House of Lords that the agreement fell within the doctrine of restraint of trade and that it was unreasonable and therefore void. It was agreed in the case that the contract was in a standard form that was widely used and that there was never any indication that it caused injustice. Lord Reid acknowledged that while full weight should be given to standard-form contracts established by way of commercial practice, this did not apply where the parties were not bargaining on equal terms. He further stated:

> Any contract by which a person engages to give his exclusive services to another for a period necessarily involves extensive restriction during that period of the common law right to exercise any lawful activity he chooses in such manner he thinks best. Normally the doctrine of restraint of trade has no application to such restrictions: they require no justification. But if contractual restrictions appear to be unnecessary or to be reasonably capable of enforcement in an oppressive manner, then they must be justified before they can be enforced.

Lord Reid considered on this basis that the restraint was unreasonable. Macaulay was bound to assign the fruits of his endeavours to Schroeder for five years, but what did Schroeder have to do in return? The answer to this question was simply, 'nothing'. It did not have to publish the songs, and if it did not Macaulay got nothing by way of remuneration, nor was there anything he could do about this. Lord Reid considered that 'the public interest requires in the interest both of the public and of the individual that everyone should be free so far as practicable to earn a living and to give to the public the fruits of his particular abilities'.

Panayiotou v *Sony Music International (UK) Ltd* [1994] 1 All ER 755

In this case a different decision was arrived at. The facts were that in 1983 the plaintiff, George Michael, and Andrew Ridgeley, comprising the pop group 'Wham!', sought to have their recording contract with Inner Vision declared void on the basis that it was in restraint of trade. This dispute was subsequently compromised by agreement and Wham! entered into a new contract with CBS in 1984. In 1987 George Michael became established as a successful solo artist, and in 1988 a new contract was entered into so as to give effect to his 'superstar' status. Also in 1988 CBS was taken over by Sony. The 1988 agreement was renegotiated in 1990 so as to improve the plaintiff's financial terms still further. In 1991 George Michael wished to change his personal and musical image and in so doing became dissatisfied with Sony. He sought to have the 1988 agreement declared void and unenforceable as an unreasonable restraint of trade and not in his interest.

It was held that it would be incorrect to treat the 1988 agreement as separate from the 1984 agreement since it was a renegotiation of that agreement. The court regarded the 1984 agreement as enforceable and that it would be contrary to public policy to find otherwise. This conclusion was based on the reasoning that it was in the public interest to uphold proper and genuine compromises. If it were possible for the plaintiff to challenge the compromise of the restraint of trade dispute with Inner Vision on the basis that the compromise itself was in restraint of trade, then any restraint of trade dispute could never be compromised by the substitution of a new agreement as had occurred in this case. No improper pressure had been placed on George Michael to enter into the agreement and, unlike in Macaulay's case, he had the benefit of being advised by a person who was regarded as being one of the most experienced and toughest negotiators in the business. It followed from this that these arguments could not be used as against the 1988 agreement, which did not therefore attract the doctrine of restraint of trade. It would be unfair and unconscionable to allow George Michael to assert that the 1988 agreement was unenforceable. Furthermore, there was no evidence to suggest that the 1988 agreement was detrimental to George Michael's interests.

In considering contracts in restraint of trade it should be noted that the doctrine can apply in contracts despite the fact that rights under the contract are ancillary to a person's actual occupation. The principle can be seen in the case of **Proactive Sports Management v Rooney** [2011] EWCA Civ 1444. The facts of the case were that Wayne Rooney, a famous professional football player, set up a company, Stoneygate 48 Ltd ('Stoneygate'), and then assigned his 'image rights' to it. Stoneygate then appointed the appellant sports agency ('Proactive') to act as its agent by what is known as an image rights representation agreement. Proactive thereby became responsible for, amongst other things, negotiating contracts with third parties for exploiting rights such as endorsement contracts, for instance, allowing Rooney's picture to be used for advertising sportswear. The agreement was for eight years and in consideration for its services Stoneygate would pay Proactive 20 per cent commission of the gross sum payable under any contracts, such as promotional, endorsement or advertisement contracts. In addition, Proactive also acted for Wayne Rooney's wife, Colleen, on similar terms without any written agreement. All went very well for five years until Rooney fell out with Proactive. Stoneygate and Wayne Rooney then purported to terminate the agreement and appointed Triple S Ltd ('S') in its place. Proactive treated the termination as a repudiatory breach of contract. Stoneygate made no more payments of commission and therefore Proactive brought an action for unpaid commission. The case revolved around the financial implications of the termination and whether there was any contract between Proactive and Mrs Rooney, and, if so, on what terms as to commission.

At first instance the judge held that the doctrine of restraint of trade applied to the agreement since it imposed very substantial restraints upon Rooney's freedom to exploit his earning capacity over a very lengthy period. Rooney was only 17 when he entered into the agreement and both he and his parents were unsophisticated in legal and commercial matters. Furthermore they did not receive independent legal advice prior to entering into the agreement. The judge considered that Proactive had failed to demonstrate that the restrictions were reasonable and as such the agreement was unenforceable. On this basis Proactive was not entitled to commission on sums paid to Stoneygate by third parties in respect of endorsement contracts that had been negotiated by Proactive but not paid at the time the contract was terminated.

Proactive appealed, submitting that where it had procured an endorsement contract for Wayne Rooney its entitlement to commission arose and was payable even if the payment was received after the termination of the agreement. Proactive also appealed on the basis that the agreement did not give rise to doctrine of restraint of trade since Wayne Rooney's trade was a footballer and the agreement did not relate to that activity but to his ability to earn supplementary income and was ancillary to that activity. Proactive argued that the agreement was neither unfair nor oppressive.

In the Court of Appeal it was held in relation to the first point raised by Proactive that it was the procurement of an endorsement contract that gave rise to the liability to pay any commission. The court considered that the contract stated that the commission became due when any sums of money became 'payable' not when any sums were received. Proactive was therefore entitled to commission on payments made by third parties after the agreement had been terminated with respect to contracts negotiated by Proactive prior to termination.

With regard to the restraint of trade issue, the Court of Appeal, with Arden LJ giving the leading judgement, referring to the case of *Panayiotou* v *Sony Music Entertainment Ltd*, considered that there are two stages in arriving at the conclusion as to whether a contract is in restraint of trade or not. First, the court has to address the question as to whether the contract is one to which the doctrine of restraint of trade applies at all and, second, if that is the case, whether the restraint is reasonable. Lady Arden considered that the line between the two stages was not clear-cut, and that 'the analysis has to be an iterative one between them. In particular, the matters that might be raised under the second stage might also be relevant to the question whether the doctrine of restraint of trade is engaged at all.' Lady Arden, referring to both *Esso Petroleum Ltd* v *Harper's Garage (Stourport) Ltd* [1968] AC 269 and *Schroeder Music Publishing Co. Ltd* v *Macaulay*, considered that the doctrine is clearly engaged by contracts that restrict the whole of a person's services and which are oppressive. Since the contract in question was one for the appointment of Proactive as Stoneygate's sole and exclusive agent, and thus restricted the whole activity of exploiting Wayne Rooney's image rights, it fell within the doctrine.

In arriving at this conclusion Lady Arden found that the question of restraint of trade had to be considered by reference to the terms of the agreement when executed. The fact that there had been substantial financial rewards on all sides was not a justification. The court agreed that while the image rights were ancillary to Wayne Rooney's occupation as footballer, such rights were capable of being protected under the doctrine of restraint of trade. While the fact that such rights are ancillary might reduce the effects of the restriction, this did not of itself put the agreement outside of the doctrine of restraint of trade. Lady Arden pointed out that the boundary between contracts that are contrary to public policy as being in restraint of trade and which will not be enforced, and contracts that contain acceptable restrictions, is an uncertain and porous one. Lady Arden, however, in referring to *Esso Petroleum Ltd* v *Harper's Garage (Stourport) Ltd* [1968] AC 269, stated that it is impossible to define the circumstances in which a contract falls within the doctrine. However, referring to Lord Reid in that case, she stated that the doctrine could apply to any contract that restricted a person's ability to trade that was out of the norm, thus normal commercial contracts would be outside of the doctrine.

As seen above in *Schroeder Music Publishing Co. Ltd* v *Macaulay*, Lord Reid analysed the doctrine as one based on oppression. Lord Diplock, however, expressed the matter differently. He concluded that the right question to be asked was whether the contract was unfair:

> So I would hold that the question to be answered as respects a contract in restraint of trade of the kind with which this appeal is concerned is: 'Was the bargain fair?' The test of fairness is,

no doubt, whether the restrictions are both reasonably necessary for the protection of the legitimate interests of the promisee and commensurate with the benefits secured to the promisor under the contract. For the purpose of this test all the provisions of the contract must be taken into consideration.

It was agreed that there was essentially no difference between these statements by the counsel in the Rooney case. The question in the Rooney case therefore was whether the agreement was 'oppressive' and that this question is to be answered by an evaluation of all the factors. In this case Rooney was only 17 when he entered into the agreement, neither he, nor his parents, received independent legal advice and none was offered by Proactive even though the company was warned beforehand that they should advise Rooney to obtain such advice. Lady Arden considered that it was this lack of independent legal advice that underscored the inequality of bargaining power between the parties and predisposed the agreement to a finding that it was one-sided, unfair or oppressive. The length of the agreement was long considering the average span of a footballer's career and indeed was much longer than the norm. It was found that Proactive wished to have a long contract because of the stellar potential of Wayne Rooney and that this was based on a desire to restrict him from going elsewhere, not a desire justifiably to protect some legitimate interest of its own, to create stability and facilitate continuity and better planning. Lady Arden, with Lord Justice Sullivan and Lord Justice Gross concurring found the contract to be in restraint of trade.

The effects of the finding in the case are interesting since, as we have seen above, Proactive was therefore entitled to commission on payments made by third parties after the agreement had been terminated with respect to contracts negotiated by Proactive prior to termination. The well-established effect of a finding that a contract was in restraint of trade is that once a party has withdrawn from the contract it is unenforceable. This resulted in Proactive not being able to enforce its contractual right to commission due under the agreement before or after the date that Stoneygate refused to abide by it. Thus in order to obtain its remedy Proactive would have to claim in restitution on a *quantum meruit* basis.

For more on claims in *quantum meruit*, refer to Chapter 18.

Severance

Generally

Objective 7

Severance amounts to the removal of the illegal elements of the contract, leaving behind a valid and enforceable agreement. The application of severance is particularly important in contracts in restraint of trade, enabling an objectionable restraint to be removed. There are, of course, limitations on the principle since, as we have seen in relation to implied terms, it is not for the court to rewrite the contract for the parties in order to produce something entirely different from what they intended. Should it be impossible to sever the objectionable parts of the contract so as to leave a contract that is capable of being carried out, then the whole contract will be void and unenforceable.

Before we assess the specific rules relating to the application of severance it should be noted that severance can only be used where it is consistent with the rule of public policy that renders the contract illegal in the first place. In **Napier v National Business Agency Ltd** [1951] 2 All ER 264 there was a contract in which an employee's wages were supplemented with an inflated figure for expenses far beyond those which he would normally incur. This arrangement was arrived at with the sole aim of defrauding HM Revenue & Customs. It was held that the contract was so tainted with illegality that the court refused to apply severance, with the result that the whole contract was vitiated. The employee could not recover wages owed to him despite the fact that he withdrew his claims in respect of 'expenses' outstanding. It should also be noted that severance is not permitted if the contract involves serious moral turpitude such as the deliberate commission of a serious criminal offence. See **Bennett v Bennett**.

The requirements necessary for the exercise of severance

The 'blue pencil' rule

The effect of this rule is that an objectionable part of a contract can be severed only where it leaves the remaining part verbally and grammatically correct and capable of standing alone. A case commonly quoted as an example of this rule is that of *Goldsoll v Goldman* [1915] 1 Ch 292 where a defendant sold his imitation jewellery business to the plaintiff, at the same time agreeing that he would not, for a period of two years, deal in real or imitation jewellery in the United Kingdom, France, the USA, Russia or within 25 miles of Potsdammerstrasse, Berlin, or St Stefans Kirche, Vienna, either on his own account or jointly. It was held by the Court of Appeal that the restraint was valid notwithstanding that the area of the restraint was too extensive. They therefore removed the restriction as to real jewellery and confined the area of the restraint to the United Kingdom.

The illegality must not comprise the main part of the contract

The objectionable part of the contract must not form the main part of the contract since the effect of severance would be to remove a central aspect of the contract. This is expressed by Beatson (2010) in terms of the severance effectively reducing the consideration within the contract. The effect would be to compel the other party to continue with a bargain that represents far less than originally contracted for.

Bennett v Bennett [1952] 1 KB 249

In this case, a wife petitioned for a divorce, claiming maintenance for herself and her son. Prior to the hearing for the decree nisi she entered a deed with her husband whereby she agreed to withdraw the application for maintenance in return for the husband paying an annuity to her and the son and, at the same time, conveying certain property to the wife. The husband did not keep to the arrangement and was sued by the wife. The court found that the covenant entered into by the wife not to apply for maintenance was contrary to public policy and void. Severance of the offending covenant was considered but it was found that this played a central part in the agreement – it effectively represented the consideration for the agreement – therefore severance was not feasible. The agreement was thus held to be unenforceable and void, so that the wife could not claim the annuity.

The agreement must not be altered by the act of severance

It was stated in *Attwood v Lamont* by Lord Sterndale MR that the operation of severance must not 'alter entirely the scope and intention of the agreement'.

Attwood v Lamont [1920] 3 KB 571

The plaintiff operated a general outfitter's business, in Kidderminster, which was divided into different departments. The defendant had been employed as a tailor and cutter in the tailoring department. His contract of service contained a restraint of trade clause whereby he agreed that he would not, at any time, be concerned in the trade or business of a 'tailor, dressmaker, general draper, milliner, hatter, haberdasher, gentlemen's, ladies' or children's outfitter' within 10 miles of the plaintiff's store. It was held by the Divisional Court that the clause was too wide but that it could become enforceable by the severing of all the trades except that of tailor. The Court of Appeal also found the clause to be too wide in that it sought to restrain the defendant from trades in which he had not been employed. The court, however, refused to apply severance, stating that this was not possible where the covenant formed a single covenant, which they found to be the situation here, rather than a 'combination of several distinct covenants'.

The basis of the Court of Appeal's decision seems to be that severance would have altered the entire nature of the covenant. The original covenant was intended to protect the entire business, while severance would have had the effect of protecting only that part of the business, namely tailoring, in which the defendant had been employed. In other words, the Court of Appeal considered the covenant to be entire, standing or falling in that entirety.

The case is extremely difficult to reconcile with *Goldsoll* v *Goldman*, which in many respects is virtually identical. On the face of things it would appear that the idea of dividing covenants into those which are entire and those which are several is unsatisfactory. Each case should be examined on its own facts and a decision made as to whether the effect of severance is to alter the scope and intention of the agreement.

Summary

The classification of illegality

Acts illegal by statute

Where the contract is prohibited by statute

- Where a contract is expressly or impliedly declared to be prohibited in a statute then there is little doubt that Parliament intended that the contract could not be enforced
- Re Mahmoud and Ispahani

The unlawful manner of performance

- Illegality may have two principal effects:

  1 A contract may be regarded as illegal if the actual creation of the contract itself is prohibited. Result – void *ab initio* (*Cope* v *Rowlands*)
  2 A contract may be created lawfully but nevertheless be illegal because of the way in which it is performed (*Anderson Ltd* v *Daniel*; *St John Shipping Corporation* v *Joseph Rank Ltd*; *Parkingeye Ltd* v *Somerfield Stores Ltd*.)

Acts illegal at common law

- Where the courts will not uphold a contract if its effect was contrary to the common good or it was injurious to society generally.

Contracts for the commission of an act that is wrong at common law

- **Bigos v Bousteadib**; *Beresford* v *Royal Insurance Co. Ltd*

Contracts contrary to public policy

- Contracts prejudicial to the administration of justice.
- Maintenance and champerty (*Trendtex Trading Corporation v Crédit Suisse; Factortame Ltd v Secretary of State for the Environment, Transport and the Regions (No. 2); Picton Jones & Co v Arcadia Developments*)
- Contracts calculated to oust the jurisdiction of the courts.
- Contracts tending to corrupt the public service.
- Contracts prejudicial to the status of marriage and the family.
- Sexually immoral contracts (*Pearce v Brooks; Armhouse Lee Ltd v Chappell*)

The effects of illegality

The general effect

- An illegal contract cannot be enforced.
- The rule: 'no person who is aware of an illegality within a contract can enforce it' (*Holman v Johnson*)
- Money or property transferred under an illegal contract is irrecoverable.
- The defence of illegality is available to both parties regardless of their situations.
- A claimant cannot succeed if they are to benefit from the illegality.
- How does illegality operate where a contract includes an illegal principle that it not central to the contract? (*St John Shipping Corpn v Joseph Rank Ltd; Ashmore, Benson, Pease and Co Ltd v Dawson; Tinsley v Milligan; Patel v Mirza*)
- No relief is available where to do so aids and abets a criminal act (*Thackerell v Barclays Bank plc; Saunders v Edwards; Howard v Shirlstar Container Transport Ltd; Tinsley v Milligan; Bowmakers Ltd v Barnet Instrument Ltd*)
- An innocent party can withdraw before the transaction is performed if the contract is illegal. Likewise if part performed (*Cowan v Milbourn; J M Allan (Merchandising) Ltd v Cloke*)
- Illegality may be avoided by using a collateral contract (*Re Mahmoud and Ispahani; Strongman (1945) Ltd v Sincock*)

Recovery of money or property

- Illegality renders any money or property irrecoverable just as a person is not allowed to benefit (*Beresford v Royal Insurance Co. Ltd.*
- There are three situations where the parties will be relieved of the illegal nature of the contract:
  1. Where the parties are not in *pari delicto* (*Kiriri Cotton Co. Ltd v Dewani*)
  2. Where the illegal contract has been withdrawn from (*Kearley v Thomson; Bigos v Bousted; Tribe v Tribe; Patel v Mirza*)
  3. Where the illegal contract is not relied on for recovery.

The Law Commission and the reform of the illegality defence

- *Tinsley* v *Milligan*
- *Gray* v *Thames Trains*
- *Stone & Rolls* v *Moore Stephens (a firm)*
- *Hounga* v *Allen*
- *Bilta (UK) Ltd* v *Nazir (No 2)*

Contracts in restraint of trade

- *Nordenfelt* v *Maxim Nordenfelt Guns and Ammunition Co.*

General principles

- Such contracts are prima facie void as being contrary to public policy on two grounds:
  1 The common law seeks to protect an individual from negotiating away their livelihood.
  2 It is not in the public interest for the state to be deprived of a valuable benefit in allowing a person to be restricted in carrying out their lawful trade or business.
- The doctrine of restraint of trade can be reduced to a number of principles.
  1 All contracts in restraint of trade are prima facie void.
  2 The courts decide whether any special factors exist which may or may not justify the restraint.
  3 If the special circumstances do point to the restraint being valid, then it must be reasonable not only as regards the parties to the contracting, but also as regards the interests of the public.
  4 The burden of proving that the restraint is reasonable lies on the party alleging it to be so.
- The court must therefore decide whether the contract is in restraint of trade before considering the reasonableness or not of the restraint (*Esso Petroleum Co. Ltd* v *Harper's Garage (Stourport) Ltd*)

Reasonableness of the restraint

- Reasonableness as regards the parties to the contract.
- Reasonableness as regards the public interest.
- Other factors influencing the degree of reasonableness.
- The courts will also consider the following factors in deciding whether or not the covenant is reasonable:

  1 the duration of the restraint;
  2 the area of the restraint.

The construction of covenants in restraint of trade

- The construction of covenants and Hanover Insurance Brokers Ltd and Christchurch Insurance Brokers Ltd v Schapiro for a more liberal application (*ChipsAway International Ltd* v *Errol Kerr*)

The application of covenants in restraint of trade in various situations

- The categories of restraint are never closed.
- Contracts of employment.
- Contracts for the sale of a business.
- Exclusive trading.

Severance

Generally

- Severance removes the illegal elements of the contract, leaving behind a valid and enforceable agreement.
- Severance can only be used where it is consistent with public policy that renders the contract illegal in the first place (***Napier*** v ***National Business Agency Ltd***).

The requirements necessary for the exercise of severance

- The 'blue pencil' rule.
- The illegality must not comprise the main part of the contract.
- The agreement must not be altered by the act of severance (***Attwood*** v ***Lamont***)

Further reading

Barnett and George, 'Post-employment Restrictive Covenants' (2002) 152 *New Law Journal* 1849

Beatson, Burrows and Cartwright, *Anson's Law of Contract*, 30th edn (Oxford University Press, 2016)

Buckley, 'Illegal Transactions: Chaos or Discretion?' (2000) 20 *Legal Studies* 155

Buckley, *Illegality and Public Policy* (Sweet & Maxwell, 2002)

Davies, 'The Illegality Defence: Two Steps Forward, One step Back?' [2009] *The Conveyancer and Property Lawyer* 182

Davies, 'The Illegality Defence and Public Policy' (2009) 125 *Law Quarterly Review* 556

Enonchong, 'Title Claims and Illegal Transactions' (1995) 111 *Law Quarterly Review* 135

Furmston, *Cheshire, Fifoot and Furmston's Law of Contract*, 16th edn (Oxford University Press, 2012)

Herbert, *Uncommon Law* (Methuen, 1989)

Jefferson, 'Evading the Doctrine of Restraint of Trade' (1990) 134 *Solicitors Journal* 532

Law Commission, 'Illegal transactions: The Effect of Illegality on Contracts and Trusts Law', Consultation Paper No. 154 (1999)

Law Commission, 'The Illegality Defence', Consultative Report No. 189 (2009)

Smith and Atiyah, *Atiyah's Introduction to the Law of Contract*, 6th edn (Oxford University Press, 2006)

Strauss, 'Ex Turpi Causa Oritur Actio', (2016) 132 *Law Quarterly Review* 236

Peel, Treitel *Law of Contract*, 14th edn (Sweet and Maxwell, 2015)

Wynn-Evans, 'Restrictive Covenants and Confidential Information – Some Recent Cases' (1997) 18 *Business Law Review* 247

Part 4

Discharge of contracts

Discharge by performance and breach

Objectives

After reading this chapter you should be able to:

1. Understand how contracts are discharged by performance with particular reference to mitigation of the strict performance rule and time of performance.
2. Understand the different circumstances in which a breach of contract arises.
3. Know and understand the effects of breach on a contract and when the right to treat a contract as discharged arises and when it is lost.

Performance

Introduction

Objective 1

The basic rule in relation to performance of a contract is that it must be carried out strictly in accordance with the terms of the contract. Failure to do so will entitle the innocent party to allege that the contract has not been performed and will give them the right to claim damages or to repudiate the contract and treat themselves as discharged from it, as well as entitling them to claim damages (as we saw in Chapter 7). In the case of *Re Moore & Co.* v *Landauer & Co.* [1921] 2 KB 519 there was a contract for the sale of tins of canned fruit which were to be packed in cases of 30 tins. On delivery it was found that a number of the cases contained only 24 tins. It was held that the defendants could reject the entire consignment even though the total number of tins delivered was correct.

Arcos Ltd v *E A Ronaasen & Son* [1933] AC 470

In this case there was a contract for a consignment of wooden staves to be used in barrel making, described in the contract as being half an inch thick. At the time of delivery the price of timber had fallen, and this meant that it was in the interests of the purchaser to be able to reject the cargo, since he could then renegotiate the contract at a lower price or go elsewhere for the timber. When the timber was measured it was found that most of it was 9–16 of an inch thick, though this difference would not have had any effect on the usefulness of the timber. The purchaser nevertheless was held to be entitled to reject the cargo. Lord Atkin stated the position in the following terms:

> A ton does not mean about a ton, or a yard about a yard. Still less when you descend to minute measurements does half-an-inch mean about half-an-inch. If a seller wants a margin he must, and in my experience does, stipulate for it . . . No doubt there may be microscopic deviations which businessmen and therefore lawyers will ignore . . . But apart from the consideration the right view is that the condition of the contract must be strictly performed.

The position maintained by Lord Atkin needs qualifying in two ways. First, and Lord Atkin hints at this qualification in the above passage, the law will not take notice of 'microscopic' deviations. This practice is sometimes expressed in the maxim *de minimis non curat lex*, though even where the deviation is minimal the innocent party may still reject where the contract expressly provides for precise performance. Second, in *Reardon Smith Line Ltd* v *Yngvar Hansen-Tangen* [1976] 1 WLR 989 there was a reaction against an over-excessive exercise of the right to rescind the contract. In a contract for the sale of goods by description, words which merely identify the goods may not be regarded as being part of the description, thus preventing a breach of condition from arising. In the case there was a charter of a tanker ship that was under construction. Since the ship had not been named, it was described as 'Yard No. 354 at Osaka'. In fact, the ship was not built at this place, though it met the contractual specifications and was built under the control of Osaka. The tanker market collapsed and the charterers sought to repudiate the contract. It was held that they could not do so since the phrase 'Yard No. 354 at Osaka' was only a means of identifying the ship and a substitute for a name, not a description of the ship. Lord Wilberforce commented on the *Landauer* and *Ronaasen* cases, stating that their decisions were 'excessively technical and due for fresh examination in this House'.

Despite the above means of limiting the strict approach to performance it should be borne in mind that the approach does have some statutory authority in certain circumstances. In contracts for the sale of goods, the Sale of Goods Act 1979, s 30(1), provides that 'where the seller delivers to the buyer a quantity of goods less than he contracted to sell, the buyer may reject them, but if the buyer accepts the goods so delivered he must pay for them at the contract rate'. Conversely, s 30(2) states that 'where the seller delivers to the buyer a quantity of goods larger than he contracted to sell, the buyer may accept the goods included in the contract and reject the rest, or he may reject the whole'. However, s 4(2) of the Sale and Supply of Goods Act 1994 now provides for an additional provision to be inserted into s 30 of the Sale of Goods Act 1979. The new provision states:

(2A) A buyer who does not deal as a consumer may not –

    (a) where the seller delivers a quantity of goods less than he contracted to sell, reject the goods under subsection (1) above, or

    (b) where the seller delivers a quantity of goods larger than he contracted to sell, reject the whole under subsection (2) above,

if the shortfall or, as the case may be, excess is so slight that it would be unreasonable for him to do so.

By s 30(2B) it is for the seller to show that a shortfall or excess is so slight that it would be unreasonable for them to reject the goods. There is thus now a statutory basis for the *de minimis* **rule** in non-consumer contracts.

It should be noted that under the Consumer Rights Act 2015 s 25 there is a corresponding provision to s 30, however, s 25 is not limited to sales contracts though it only applies insofar as it relates to trader to consumer contracts Section 25(1) provides that the consumer may reject the goods if the wrong quantity is delivered, but if they choose to accept the goods then they must pay the contract rate for what they receive. By s 25(2), if more is delivered than was contracted for, the consumer has the additional option to reject the excess and keep the contracted amount which must be paid for at the contracted rate – s 25(3) . Where the section entitles the consumer to reject goods any entitlement for the consumer to treat the contract as at an end depends on the terms of the contract and the circumstances of the case – s 25(4). By s 25(5), the consumer rejects goods under this section by indicating to the trader that the consumer is rejecting the goods, which may be something the consumer says or does, but it must be clear enough to be understood by the trader. These provisions do not prevent the consumer claiming damages, where it is open to the consumer to do so, however, the provision is subject to any usage of trade, special agreement, or course of dealing between the parties – s 25(8).

The right to reject will still exist where there is a breach of the implied conditions that arise under the 1979 Act. In the context described above, s 13 (implied condition as to description) is particularly appropriate, especially in a contract for the sale of unascertained goods, since these are invariably sales by description. One should be aware, however, that in non-consumer sales, s 15A of the Sale of Goods Act 1979 (as inserted by s 4(1) of the Sale and Supply of Goods Act 1994) limits the right to reject for a breach of condition where the breach is so slight that it would be unreasonable for the buyer to reject the goods, subject to contrary intention either express or implied in the contract. Similar provisions are to be found within the Consumer Rights Act 2015 as regards consumer contracts, though here the right to reject relates to breach of the implied terms set out in Chapter 7.

For more on implied conditions, refer to Chapter 7.

The strict rule relating to performance is also relevant in what may be described as 'entire' contracts. In such contracts a person's contractual obligations are conditional on the other party performing their side of the contract completely and entirely.

Cutter v Powell (1756) 6 Term R 320

In this case, there was a contract by a seaman to serve on a ship bound from Jamaica to Liverpool. He was to be paid 30 guineas 'provided he proceeds, continues and does his duty . . . from hence to the port of Liverpool'. Unfortunately he died at sea prior to reaching Liverpool. The defendants refused to pay for the work he had completed prior to his death and were sued by the administratrix. It was held that her action would fail since the terms of the contract meant that he would be paid only if he sailed the ship to Liverpool and since he did not do so, no pay was owed.

In *Hoenig v Isaacs* [1952] 2 All ER 176 Lord Denning MR gave valuable guidance as to when a contract constitutes an entire contract. He said this:

In determining this issue the first question is whether, on the true construction of the contract, entire performance was a condition precedent to payment. It was a lump sum contract, but that does not mean that entire performance was a condition precedent to payment.

When a contract provides for a specific sum to be paid on completion of specified work, the courts lean against a construction of the contract which would deprive the contractor of any payment at all simply because there are some defects or omissions. The promise to complete the work is, therefore, construed as a term of the contract, but not as a condition.

. . . It is, of course always open to the parties by express words to make entire performance a condition precedent.

The application of the rule requiring strict performance is particularly harsh when seen in the light of *Cutter* v *Powell* above, and for this reason the courts have developed several rules which have mitigated the effects of the general rule. An application of the conditions laid down by Lord Denning can be seen in the case of *Smales* v *Lea and Kemsley* [2011] EWCA Civ 1325.

Mitigating the strict performance rule

The doctrine of substantial performance

In many respects this doctrine is really an offshoot of the *de minimis* rule outlined above. It arises where a person in fully performing their side of the bargain hopes that they have done all they were required to do under the contract, or supplied everything they were supposed to supply, but there are nevertheless minor defects in the performance of the contract. In such a case the court will find that the person has substantially performed their side of the contract and allow them to claim the contract price, less an amount by which the value of the contract has been diminished by the breach. Clearly such a solution is more equitable since it protects the interests of the innocent party while allowing the individual concerned an amount for work actually completed. If such a position was not adopted by the courts it could well mean that many sound businesses could be drawn into insolvency by virtue of minor breaches of contract. In any event it is unfair to allow a party to take the substantial benefit of the contract while at the same time escaping liability to pay for that benefit by reason of minor, technical breaches of the contract.

Clearly this area of performance is closely linked to the remedy of damages for breach of warranty or breach of an innominate term under the principle in *Hong Kong Fir Shipping Co. Ltd* v *Kawasaki Kisen Kaisha Ltd* [1962] 1 All ER 474, since in both situations it might be considered that there is substantial performance. An example of the application may be seen in the following case.

Hoenig v Isaacs [1952] 2 All ER 176

In this case, there was a contract by the plaintiff to decorate and furnish the defendant's flat for £750. The defendant alleged that the workmanship was poor and defective but paid £400. The plaintiff sued for the balance. The court found that there were defects in the work but that these could be cured for some £55, and thus awarded the plaintiff the full amount of the contract less the cost of putting right the defects and, of course, the amount already paid.

Partial performance

It may happen that an individual only partially performs their side of the contract yet nevertheless the other party, rather than reject the work, decides to accept the work that has actually been done. In these circumstances the promisee will be obliged to pay for the work done on a *quantum meruit* basis. It should be borne in mind that the promisee has complete discretion as to whether to accept the partial performance or not.

Sumpter v Hedges [1898] 1 QB 673

The plaintiff, who had agreed to erect certain buildings for the defendant, could not claim on a *quantum meruit* basis for work completed before he abandoned the contract. The defendant had gone on to the premises and completed the work himself, making use of materials left on the site by the plaintiff. The defendant had no option but to complete the buildings, though the plaintiff could recover for the materials used by the defendant since the defendant had the option of using those materials or not. Since he had decided to use them, the court held that he should pay a reasonable price for them.

Tender of performance

To offer a tender to perform is regarded as equivalent to actual performance. It is clearly wrong to allow the promisee to avoid a contract for non-performance where the promisee has refused to accept the offer of performance. Where such a situation arises it is open to the promisor to treat the refusal as discharging them from any further obligations under the contract. The promisor is also entitled to raise the promisee's refusal to accept their offer of performance as a defence to an action by the promisee for breach of contract.

Startup v *Macdonald* (1843) 6 Man & G 593

The parties had contracted for the sale of 10 tons of linseed oil, which was to be delivered 'within the last fourteen days of March'. The plaintiffs delivered the oil at 8.30 pm on 31 March, a Saturday. The defendant refused to accept delivery and it was held that the plaintiffs were able to recover damages for the non-acceptance of the delivery of the oil. This decision needs, however, to be qualified in the context of the modern law contained in the Sale of Goods Act 1979, s 29(5), whereby 'Demand or tender of delivery may be treated as ineffectual unless made at a reasonable hour; and what is a reasonable hour is a question of fact.'

So far **tender of performance** has been examined in the context of performance of a service or delivery of goods. Performance may also be tendered by the payment of money. Where money is proffered for tender of performance but refused by the promisee, it should be borne in mind that the promisor is not discharged from the debt and must remain willing and ready to discharge the debt, and that any special terms regarding payment must be complied with. Should the promisor tender payment and this is refused, they should wait until they are sued on the debt and then pay the moneys owed into court, raising the offer of payment as a defence to the action brought by the promisee. This will result in the promisee recovering the debt and no more, while the promisor will be entitled to claim legal costs.

It may also arise that the promisor commences performance of the contract but is subsequently prevented from completing it because of the fault or actions of the promisee. In such a situation the promisor will be able to sue for breach of contract and gain damages on a *quantum meruit* basis for work actually completed. In ***Planché* v *Colburn*** (1831) 8 Bing 14, where the defendants had embarked on the publication of a series of books entitled *The Juvenile Library*, the plaintiff was engaged to write a volume on ancient armour and costume for £100, the sum being payable on completion of the manuscript. When he had researched and written part of the book, the defendants abandoned the project. It was held that the plaintiff had accepted the abandonment of the project as discharging the contract, and that therefore he was entitled to be paid for the work actually completed at the acceptance of the breach. The court therefore awarded him £50 for his work.

Divisible contracts

The means of mitigating the rule requiring strict performance of a contract, as discussed above, have also been augmented by the development by the courts of a distinction between entire and divisible contracts. A **divisible contract** may be defined as a contract in which partial performance attracts an obligation to provide payment of part of the consideration. Such a state of affairs may be expressly provided for in the contract, where, for instance, large quantities of a particular commodity may be required. Here it could be agreed that the promisor will be paid for each ton of the commodity delivered or that a proportion of the contract price is payable on the delivery of each instalment of the item in question. If the promisor fails to complete the whole contract he will nevertheless be entitled to a proportion of the moneys owed under the contract.

A further example of such a contract arises in contracts of employment where the terms of the contract state that a particular worker is to be paid weekly. If this term had applied to a case such as *Cutter v Powell*, the administratrix would have been able to claim the seaman's wages for each week of work completed before his death. Whether a contract is entire or divisible depends on the intentions of the parties as discovered by the courts.

The time of performance

At common law, time was regarded as being 'of the essence' in a contract, unless the parties had agreed otherwise. Equity did not, however, regard time as being of the essence and would apply equitable remedies to the contract even where there was a failure to comply with the time fixed for completion of the contract.

The position is now governed by the Law of Property Act 1925, s 41, which provides:

> Stipulations in a contract, as to time or otherwise, which according to rules of equity are not deemed to be or to have become of the essence of the contract, are also construed and have effect at law in accordance with the same rules.

The result of this provision is to fuse the rules of equity and those of the common law, producing the effect that if time is not of the essence there arises only a right to damages rather than a right to terminate the contract, as was held in *Raineri v Miles* [1981] AC 1050.

Equity did, however, regard time as being of the essence in three situations, stated in *Halsbury's Laws of England* (2012, 5th edn, Vol. 22) para 502 to be where:

1 the parties expressly stipulate that conditions as to time must be strictly complied with; or

2 the nature of the subject of the contract or the surrounding circumstances show that time should be considered to be of the essence; or

3 a party who has been subjected to unreasonable delay gives notice to the party in default making time of the essence.

This statement of law has been stated to be correct and confirmed by the House of Lords in *United Scientific Holdings Ltd v Burnley Borough Council* [1978] AC 904 and in *Bunge Corporation v Tradax Export SA* [1981] 2 All ER 513.

See Chapter 14 for Charles Rickards Ltd v Oppenheim.

It is possible on the basis of the above for time in a contract to be initially not of the essence but to become so on the giving of reasonable notice. The case of *Charles Rickards Ltd v Oppenheim* [1950] 1 All ER 420, more fully discussed later provides authority for this point. When does the right to give such notice arise? The Court of Appeal in *British and Commonwealth Holdings plc v Quadrex Holdings Inc.* [1989] 3 All ER 492 considered that before an innocent party could give such notice there had to be an unreasonable delay in the performance of the contract. This requires some qualification where a specific date for performance is given in the contract, albeit that the time is not stated as being of the essence. In *Behzadi v Shaftesbury Hotels Ltd* [1991] 2 All ER 477 the Court of Appeal stated that reasonable notice could be given making time of the essence as soon as the contractual date for performance had passed.

Where time is of the essence in a contract then any delay will amount to repudiation of the contract.

Union Eagle Ltd v Golden Achievement Ltd [1997] 2 All ER 215

The appellant entered into a written contract to purchase a flat in Hong Kong for $HK4.2 million from the respondent vendor. A deposit of 10 per cent was paid and the date for completion of the contract was set as 30 September 1991 before 5 pm. Time was stated to be of the essence and non-compliance would result in the deposit being absolutely forfeited 'as and for liquidated damages (and not a penalty)'. The appellant was 10 minutes late in tendering the cheques and the relevant documents required to complete the purchase. The vendor's solicitor refused to accept the cheques and the documents and informed the purchaser that the contract had been rescinded and the deposit forfeited. The purchaser appealed to the Privy Council, contending that he was entitled to specific performance of the contract and entitled to relief against forfeiture in respect of both the agreement and the deposit. It was held by the Privy Council that, in the absence of a waiver of the breach of contract by the vendor, the court would not grant an order of specific performance where there was a rescission of a contract for sale of land because of a failure to comply with an essential condition as to time. The court held that the purpose of the condition and the right to rescind was to give the vendor the certainty of knowledge that he could resell the property which, in a rising property market, was 'a valuable and volatile right'.

Where a contract specifies that it is performed within a reasonable time, it was held in **Hick v Raymond & Reid** [1893] AC 22 the party on whom that obligation rests fulfils the obligation, notwithstanding protracted delay, so long as the delay is attributable to causes beyond his control and he has neither acted negligently nor unreasonably. This approach was elaborated on by Kay LJ in **Peregrine Systems Ltd v Steria Ltd** [2005] EWCA Civ 239 (with whom the other members of the Court of Appeal agreed) as follows:

The consideration of whether there has been a breach of an obligation to perform within a reasonable time is not limited to what the parties contemplated or ought to have foreseen at the time of the contract. In my judgement, the correct interpretation of authorities such as **Hick v Raymond & Reid [1893] AC 22** is that adopted by His Honour Judge Richard Seymour QC in **Astea (UK) Ltd v Time Group Ltd** [2003] EWHC 725, [2003] All ER (D) 212, where he said that the question whether a reasonable time has been exceeded is:

'a broad consideration, with the benefit of hindsight, and viewed from the time at which one party contends that a reasonable time for performance has been exceeded, of what would, in all the circumstances which are by then known to have happened, have been a reasonable time for performance. That broad consideration is likely to include taking into account any estimate given by the performing party of how long it would take him to perform; whether that estimate has been exceeded and, if so, in what circumstances; whether the party for whose benefit the relevant obligation was to be performed needed to participate in the performance, actively, in the sense of collaborating in what was needed to be done, or passively, in the sense of being in a position to receive performance, or not at all; whether it was necessary for third parties to collaborate with the performing party in order to enable it to perform; and what exactly was the cause, or were the causes of the delay to performance. The list is not intended to be exhaustive.'

Thus even if a contract requires a party to complete the contract within a reasonable time, the fact that the parties had contemplated at some earlier stage that completion would take place does not necessarily mean that a failure to complete by that time would involve a breach of the obligation to complete within a reasonable time. Thus whether a contract has been completed within a reasonable time is highly fact sensitive: **Urban I (Blonk Street) Ltd v Ayres** [2013] EWCA Civ 816.

Time of performance is also important in consumer contracts conducted by means of distance communications. The Consumer Rights Act 2015 s 28 provides that, unless the parties agree otherwise, contracts must be performed within 30 days, taking effect after the day in which the consumer sent the order to the supplier. If the supplier is unable to perform the contract because the goods or services are unavailable within the period for performance, they are required to inform the consumer of this and return any sums paid by or on behalf of the consumer. The reimbursement must take place as soon as possible and in any event no later than 30 days commencing with the day after the day on which the period for performance expired. If the contract is not performed within the period for performance it is treated as if it had not been made. The consumer may of course take action against the supplier for breach of contract for non-performance in the usual way as already described above.

Breach

Objective 2

Where a person fails to perform their side of the contract then, subject to the mitigating factors, they will be in breach of contract. A breach of contract will always give rise to a claim for damages, no matter how minor or serious the nature of the breach. Whether an innocent party is also entitled to treat the contract as at an end, so that they can treat the contract as discharged, depends on whether the breach is so serious that it goes to the root of the contract, that is, there is a breach of a primary obligation, or whether the other party has repudiated the contract prior to the performance of the contract.

Breach of primary obligation

For more on breach of primary obligation and how it discharges the contract, see Chapter 7.

Where there has been a breach of a primary obligation of the contract, the innocent party may treat the contract as discharged. A primary obligation is often expressed as a condition. Such an obligation will give the parties this right if they have expressly agreed that it will do so, or where this effect is implied by the parties simply expressing a term to be a 'condition'. Such an effect may also be implied by the courts, as in *The Mihalis Angelos* [1970] 3 All ER 125, or by statute, as in the condition implied by the Sale of Goods Act 1979. Furthermore, a contract may be treated as discharged where a term is found to be an innominate term and its breach has had the effect of depriving the innocent party of substantially what it was intended that party should obtain under the contract, as in the *Hong Kong Fir Shipping* case.

In *Ampurius Nu Homes Holdings Ltd* v *Telford Homes (Creekside) Ltd* [2013] EWCA Civ 577 [2013] 4 All ER 377 the Court of Appeal examined the test as to when a repudiatory breach arises. In 2008, Telford and Ampurius entered into an agreement for a lease. Under the terms of the agreement Telford was to develop four mixed-use blocks (A, B, C and D). Ampurius would then lease the commercial units in the blocks on a 999-year lease. The target date for completion of blocks C and D was July 2010; for A and B the date was February 2011 or 'as soon as reasonably possible' after these dates. Work on blocks C and D fell behind schedule but were nevertheless completed in April 2011. Work on blocks A and B, however, was suspended because funding difficulties arose. Ampurius wrote to Telford stating that it considered the suspension of the construction work to be a repudiatory breach and reserved its right to either affirm or terminate the agreement at a later date. Unknown to Ampurius, work resumed on 4 October 2010. On 22 October 2010 Ampurius then purported to terminate the agreement because of the delay and claimed damages.

At first instance the judge held that there had been a repudiatory breach in that Ampurius had only received two of the blocks and that the suspension and delays in completing blocks A and B meant that Ampurius' efforts to market blocks C and D would be made significantly more difficult. The judge considered that the repudiation had arisen in July 2010 since he considered that this was the date on which it became clear that blocks A and B could not have been completed by the target date of February 2011. Telford appealed arguing that the judge had not assessed the benefit Ampurius would receive under the contract in order to determine whether or not the breach had substantially deprived Ampurius of the benefit of the contract but rather had focused on assessing the correct date as to when the breach became repudiatory.

The Court of Appeal upheld Telford's appeal applying the test in the *Hong Kong Fir Shipping* case. It stated that the starting point for determining when a repudiatory breach had occurred was to consider the benefit the injured party was intended to obtain from the contract and then assess whether the injured party had been substantially deprived of the whole of the benefit of the contract by reason of the breach. The Court of Appeal considered that the judge had not given adequate weight to the overall objective of the contract, that is, for Ampurius to acquire a 999-year lease of the four blocks and given too much weight to the effects on the period of marketing the blocks. The contract had envisaged that there would be a staged handover so that the effects of a seven-month delay were not so serious as to amount to a repudiatory breach. In any event the effect of a seven-month delay in the context of a 999-year lease was of minor importance. The Court of Appeal considered that the delay in marketing the development was not so serious as to substantially deprive Ampurius of the whole of the benefit of the contract, particularly as Ampurius accepted that the delay had not caused any loss. The court considered that it would be unusual for a breach that caused no loss to be repudiatory in nature and that being the case it was necessary to consider the future losses of Ampurius. The court calculated that if Ampurius had delayed the marketing of blocks C and D until the construction of blocks A and B had caught up it would have incurred losses of £100,000, which was eminently capable of being compensated. This loss, however, when measured against the overall development cost of £100 million and a purchase price for the blocks of £8 million was not so serious as to cause Ampurius to be substantially deprived of the benefit of the contract.

The Court of Appeal held that if a breach was remedied before the injured party purported to terminate the contract the fact that the breach was remedied was a factor to be taken into account. Similarly if there was a delay in the performance of a continuing contractual obligation it may be possible for the delay to be made up by increased performance. The judge therefore should have considered the *Hong Kong Fir* test at the date of the purported termination, i.e. 22 October. By that date work on blocks A and B had restarted and thus the judge could not have come to the conclusion that at the date of termination that the actual and reasonably foreseeable effects of Telford's breach had been to deprive Ampurius of substantially the whole benefit of the contract. Accordingly, what fell to be considered was the position as at the date when the injured party purported to terminate the contract.

The decision in *Ampurius Nu Homes Holdings Ltd v Telford Homes (Creekside) Ltd* was applied in *Urban I (Blonk Street) Ltd v Ayres* [2013] EWCA Civ 816. In this case the focus was in relation to an implied term as regards the completion of a construction contract. The facts of the case were that in 2007, Urban I (Blonk Street) Ltd entered into a written contract with Mr and Mrs Ayres granting them a 125-year lease of an apartment in its new development. The contract did not specify a fixed completion date, although the target date for completion was December 2008. Mr and Mrs Ayres received a mortgage offer on the basis that the mortgage had to commence in December. The build suffered from various delays so that the completion date moved into 2009. In March 2009, Mr and Mrs Ayres wrote to Urban terminating the contract due to unreasonable delay on the basis that there was an implied term in the contract that completion would take place within a reasonable time. The apartment was eventually finished in July 2009 at which point Urban served a notice on Mr and Mrs Ayres to complete within 10 days on 1 September 2009 and following this Urban then sought specific performance against Mr and Mrs Ayres, together with a claim for damages for late completion. Mr and Mrs Ayres served a counterclaim alleging that Urban had wrongfully refused to perform the contract and had therefore repudiated it. They alleged that their mortgage offer had expired and they sought the return of their deposit.

At first instance the judge found that the overall delay by Urban was such as to amount to a repudiation of the contract entitling Mr and Mrs Ayres to refuse to complete. Urban appealed stating that since the building contract was a 'design and build' contract and as such it had limited control over the delays of contractors and that a reasonable time for completing the apartment would have been after Mr and Mrs Ayres' letter of March 2009.

The Court of Appeal allowed the appeal. It stated that the trial judge was correct that, in the absence of any express stipulated date, it was an implied term of the contract that completion of the apartment, and the subsequent completion of the contract, was to be within a reasonable time. The judge had correctly identified the implied term as being an innominate term. Contractual completion was to take place at the latest 10 days after a reasonable time for building of the apartment had elapsed. The Court of Appeal found that the judge had not correctly identified that date considering it had elapsed by the date of Mr and Mrs Ayres' letter in March 2009. Sir Thomas Etherton stated:

> The reason why it was important to identify the contractual completion date was that, being an innominate term, and the respondents never having served a notice to complete on the appellant, the respondents only became entitled to terminate the contract thereafter (1) if and when it ceased to be equitable to grant the appellant specific performance, and (2) which is probably the same date, if and when the delay was such as to go to the root of the Contract, that is to say it deprived the respondents of substantially the whole benefit which it was intended they should have under the Contract; or alternatively, (3) the appellant showed that it had no intention of carrying out the contract or, at any event, only to do so in a manner substantially inconsistent with the appellant's contractual obligations such as to deprive the respondents of substantially the whole benefit which it was intended they should receive under the Contract.

He stated that the reasonable time for completion was highly fact-sensitive but that where a term is to be performed within a reasonable time the party on who that obligation rests fulfils the obligation, notwithstanding any protracted delay, provided the delay is attributable to causes beyond his control and he has acted nether negligently nor unreasonably. It was clear that Urban was not in repudiatory breach of the contract by March 2009 since it would only be repudiatory if it went to the root of the contract at that date. The delay of one month, between the earliest possible date for contractual completion and A's purported termination of the contract in March 2009, could not possibly be said to have deprived Mr and Mrs Ayres of substantially the whole benefit of the contract, which was a 125-year lease. The court therefore followed the Court of Appeal decision in *Ampurius Nu Homes Holdings Ltd* v *Telford Homes (Creekside) Ltd* [2013] EWCA Civ 577, [2013] 4 All ER 377.

Repudiation prior to performance of the contract

The types of breaches that have been discussed so far are those that have arisen by virtue of the fact that a party has not performed the contract in compliance with the terms of the contract when the time for performance has arrived. It may, however, occur that a party may indicate, either expressly or impliedly, by words or conduct, that they do not intend to honour their obligations under the contract. Such a repudiation is known as an **anticipatory breach**. The legal basis behind anticipatory breach is a somewhat elusive one; some commentators consider it is based on an implied term that the contract will be completed whilst others consider it is based on the notion that it arises by way of a breach of the contract as yet to fall due. In essence, it is a pragmatic approach to dealing with a situation in which it is pointless for the innocent party waiting for the date of performance of the contract to fall in before taking steps to mitigate his loss. In this regard Lord Mustill in 'The Golden Victory – Some Reflections' (2008) stated:

> . . . the common law has never succeeded in finding a solution which is both theoretically sound and capable of producing sensible results in practice. The attempt was, to all intents and purposes, given up a long time ago, and the courts have been content to employ that powerful but dangerous weapon of the common law, a fiction. . . . in the field of anticipatory repudiation, a breach was simply assumed to have occurred when the repudiatory conduct took place . . . The concept of anticipatory breach cannot be rationalised, but must be seen as a piece of positive law, firmly established but not anchored in or deducible from the ordinary course of the law of contract.

In a similar vein, Lord Sumption in **Bunge Sa v Nidera BV** [2015]UKSC 43 (at 12) stated:

> Anticipatory breach of contract, probably more accurately referred to as 'renunciation', is a concept which can be traced back to the earliest years of the common law . . . In its modern form it is a response to the pragmatic concern of Victorian judges to avoid the waste of economic resources implicit in any inflexible rule which required the parties to go through the motions of performing a contract which was for practical purposes dead.

An example of an explicit repudiation can be seen in **Hochester v De La Tour** (1853) 2 E & B 678 where the defendant entered into a contract in April to employ the plaintiff in June as a courier. In May he wrote stating that he no longer required the plaintiff's services. The plaintiff brought his action prior to the date on which he was supposed to start work and succeeded. He was entitled to elect to treat the contract as discharged immediately and to sue for damages although the date of performance had not arisen.

An example of an implied repudiation may be seen in **Frost v Knight** (1872) LR 7 Exch 111 where the defendant promised to marry the plaintiff as soon as his father died. When the defendant retracted his promise by breaking off the engagement prior to his father's death, it was held that the plaintiff could immediately sue for damages for breach of contract, although the father was still alive.

Some care needs to be taken in deciding whether or not the anticipatory breach amounts to repudiation since it needs to be established beyond reasonable doubt from the circumstances of the case that the other party does not intend to perform their side of the contract. Thus in **Freeth v Barr** (1874) LR 9 CP 208, Keating J stated:

> It is not a mere refusal or omission of one of the contracting parties to do something which he ought to do, that will justify the other in repudiating the contract; but there must be an absolute refusal to perform his part of the contract.

Similarly Lord Selbourne in *Mersey Steel and Iron Co.* v *Naylor Benzon & Co.* (1884) 9 App Cas 434 stated:

> You must look at the actual circumstances of the case in order to see whether one party to the contract is relieved from its future performance by the conduct of the other; you must examine what that conduct is so as to see whether it amounts to a renunciation, to an absolute refusal to perform the contract . . . and whether the other party may accept it as a reason for not performing his part.

While an express intention may well be taken as amounting to repudiation, it is always possible, just as where the repudiation is implied, that a misinterpretation may arise. If the innocent party treats such an anticipatory breach as an actual breach and treats the contract as at an end they would render themselves in anticipatory breach no matter that the motives in taking such action were in good faith, as is illustrated in the *Hong Kong Fir Shipping* case. In *Federal Commerce and Navigation Co. Ltd* v *Molena Alpha Inc.* [1979] 1 All ER 307, a charter authorised the charterer to sign bills of lading stating that cargo had been prepaid. During the dispute the shipowners withdrew the authority of the charterers to sign the bills of lading so that the charterers were unable to issue bills of lading. Without these bills they would be unable to operate the ship. The shipowners believed they were entitled to take such action, but the charterers claimed that the action by the shipowners amounted to a wrongful repudiation of the contract. The House of Lords agreed with the charterers since, even though the owners believed that they could take such action, this belief could not be reconciled with the disastrous effects of such a course of action on the business of the charterer.

The decision in the *Molena Alpha* case was, however, thrown open to doubt a year later by the House of Lords' decision in *Woodar Investment Development Ltd* v *Wimpey Construction (UK) Ltd*.

Woodar Investment Development Ltd v *Wimpey Construction (UK) Ltd* [1980] 1 All ER 571

In this case there was a contract for the sale of land which allowed Wimpey, the purchasers, to rescind the contract should proceedings compulsorily to purchase the property commence before the completion of the sale. On the date the contract was signed, the local authority had already commenced compulsory purchase proceedings in respect of part of the land. In the meantime the state of the market had changed, with land prices becoming depressed, so Wimpey wanted to escape from the contract. Just as in the *Molena Alpha* case, Wimpey took legal advice and proposed to Woodar that they should renegotiate the contract, but that if these negotiations failed, they would rescind the contract. Woodar alleged that Wimpey had no right to take such action, at which point Wimpey wrote back rescinding the contract because they alleged that the contract had become discharged by way of the local authority's action. Woodar then alleged that the action of Wimpey amounted to repudiation which they (Woodar) had accepted and that they were therefore entitled to claim damages. The House of Lords held that Wimpey had not repudiated the contract.

Lord Wilberforce stated:

> So far from repudiating the contract, Wimpey were relying on it and invoking one of its provisions, to which both parties had given their consent. And unless the invocation of that provision were totally abusive or lacking in good faith (neither of which is contended for), the fact that it has proved wrong in law cannot turn it into repudiation . . . the proposition that a party who takes action relying simply on the terms of the contract, and not manifesting by his conduct an ulterior intention to abandon it, is not to be treated as repudiating it . . .

Lord Wilberforce went further:

> I would only add that it would be a regrettable development of the law of contract to hold that a party who bona fide relies upon an express stipulation in a contract in order to rescind or terminate a contract should, by that fact alone, be treated as having repudiated his contractual obligations if he turns out to be mistaken as to his rights. Repudiation is a drastic conclusion which should only be held to arise in clear cases of a refusal, in a matter going to the root of the contract, to perform contractual obligations. To uphold the respondents' contentions in this case would represent an undesirable extension of the doctrine.

On the facts of that case the majority of the House of Lords felt able to conclude that, despite the unqualified terms of the notice, the circumstances in which it was given did not manifest an intention to refuse further performance. The time for performance had not arisen, Woodar needed to serve a notice in order to reserve its position, and the discussions between the parties had proceeded on the basis that the service of a notice was not to be regarded as a hostile act, and that the entitlement or otherwise of Woodar to serve the notice would be determined by the court, to which Woodar would apply, by whose decision both parties would abide.

On the basis of this judgement it would seem that if a party is mistaken as to their rights, then this, provided they have acted in good faith, cannot amount to a repudiation of the contract. Lord Wilberforce was thus effectively drawing a distinction between a threatened breach, which would result in serious consequences for the other party, as in the *Molena Alpha* case, and a situation where a party exercised what they erroneously, but in good faith, believed to be a right under the contract, as in the *Woodar* case. This point has also been approved in the Privy Council decision in *Vaswani v Italian Motor Cars Ltd* [1996] 1 WLR 270 (PC).

The decision in the case is a majority one, with Lord Salmon and Lord Russell dissenting, alleging that the case was identical to that of *Molena Alpha*. Lord Salmon stated that he was entirely unable to agree with the proposition that Wimpey's notice of rescission was consistent either with the intention to preserve or abandon the contract. He regarded that the notice was served with the clearly expressed intention of bringing the contract to an end, particularly as it was accompanied by a letter describing the contract as '*now discharged by the enclosed notice*'. He also said that, if the notice of rescission did not demonstrate an intention to be no longer bound by the contract and therefore amount to a repudiation, he could not imagine what would; further, that he did not understand how Wimpey's honest belief in a bad point of law (as to the validity of their notice) could in any way avail them. Lord Russell held that if a party to a contract purports to rescind and renounce it on grounds that are not justified in law, there can *never* be circumstances in which the party rescinding the contract can dispute the repudiatory quality of his action. Lord Salmon and Lord Russell stated that in both the cases, one party was determined to depart from the terms of the contract on the basis that the contract entitled them to do so, though this view of the contract was an erroneous one.

While the decision of the majority was undoubtedly at odds with the proposition set out in *Federal Commerce and Navigation Co. Ltd v Molena Alpha Inc.*, that it is no defence to a party who has repudiated a contract to say that he acted in good faith under a mistaken understanding of the law, it may be possible to reconcile the two cases. In *Molena Alpha* the repudiation consisted of an act – the instruction of the master not to sign prepaid bills of lading – which had the immediate effect of substantially depriving the charterers of virtually the whole benefit of the charter since the issue of such bills was essential to the maintenance of the charterers' trade. By contrast, the notice of termination in *Woodar* did not have that or a similar consequence. In addition *Cheshire, Fifoot and Furmston* (2012) points to three distinguishing factors between the cases. First, in *Woodar*, the sellers could have waited and tested the correctness of their view of the contract by legal process rather than take immediate action. Second, in *Woodar*, the time for completion was some way off and if Wimpey had refused to complete on this basis, their conduct would have amounted to repudiation. Third, in the *Molena Alpha* case, the breach was anticipatory but the gap between repudiation and performance was short and thus greater pressure was placed on the charterers. That these differences exist cannot be doubted but in practical terms it leaves the parties, such as the charterers and Woodar, in an impossible position of having to make a qualitative decision as to whether a repudiation is based on a bona fide mistake as to rights contained in the contract, as in *Woodar*, or whether it is based on a decision by the other party not to carry on with the performance of the contract. On such a view it might be better to confine the decision in *Woodar* to the circumstances of that particular case.

In *Vaswani v Italian Motors*, the facts of which have already been referred to in Chapter 8, Lord Woolf in the Privy Council stated:

> While therefore here the request for the payment of an excessive price would not in itself amount to a repudiation, if the conduct relied on went beyond the assertion of a genuinely held view of the effect of the contract the conduct could amount to a repudiation. This is the position if the conduct is inconsistent with the continuance of the contract.

Lord Woolf concurred with Lord Wilberforce's view in *Molena Alpha* that 'If a party's conduct is such as to amount to a threatened repudiatory breach, his subjective desire to maintain the contract cannot prevent the other party from drawing the consequences of his actions.' Lord Woolf went further and stated that 'Nor is conduct, if it is repudiatory, excused because it occurs in consequence of legal advice as may be the case with the sellers' actions in this case' thus confirming Lord Denning's dicta in *Woodar*:

> I have yet to learn that a party who breaks a contract can excuse himself by saying that he did it on the advice of his lawyers: or that he was under an honest misapprehension . . . I would go by the principle . . . that if the party's conduct objectively considered in its impact on the other party is such as to evince an intention no longer to be bound by his contractual obligations, then it is open to the other party to accept his repudiation and treat the contract as discharged from that time onwards.

Whatever view that one may take with regard to the consistency or otherwise of *Molena Alpha* and *Woodar*, what is certain, as Lord Wilberforce stated in *Woodar*, is that 'Repudiation is a drastic conclusion which should only be held to arise in clear cases of a refusal, in a matter going to the root of the contract, to perform contractual obligations.' Thus the repudiation must be of a nature that it must amount to a breach of condition.

A further hazard in this context by way of implied acceptance or repudiation is seen in the *Vitol SA v Norelf Ltd (The Santa Clara)* case.

Vitol SA v Norelf Ltd (The Santa Clara) [1996] 3 All ER 193

The facts of the case were that there was a contract for the sale of a cargo of propane to be shipped from Houston at a price of $400 per tonne. The contract provided that a bill of lading had to be tendered by the seller immediately after the loading of the cargo. Prior to the loading on 8 March the buyer sent a telex to the seller stating that they were repudiating the contract and rejecting the goods. This was held by the arbitrator to be a wrongful anticipatory breach that amounted to a repudiatory breach. Following the telex the seller did not attempt to perform the contract. A few days later the seller resold the cargo for $180 per tonne. On 9 August the seller sent a letter to the buyer claiming the difference between the contract price and the resale price. The arbitrator found for the seller by deciding that the buyer's wrongful repudiation had been accepted as ending the contract by the seller not taking steps to perform the contract. The buyer appealed to the High Court.

In the High Court, Phillips J found that there was no reason why an acceptance of an anticipatory breach by one party could not arise either by words or conduct, provided these made it clear that the innocent party was responding to the repudiation by treating the contract as at an end. The court considered that while it might be more difficult to indicate acceptance of the repudiation solely on the basis of conduct, it was possible for this to arise if an innocent party did something completely incompatible with their own performance, or by simply not performing their own contractual obligations. Phillips J considered that there was an analogy to be drawn here with offer and acceptance in the formation of a contract.

The buyer appealed to the Court of Appeal which held that an innocent party's election to accept a repudiation by the other party must be clear and unequivocal. The court thus held that mere non-performance of the contract by the innocent party after the repudiation could not amount to a clear acceptance of the repudiation. The reason for this is that, while it is possible that a failure to perform one's obligations may amount to acceptance of the repudiation, it is also possible that this is simply evidence of indecision or inadvertence by the innocent party. Further, the inaction could also be evidence of the innocent party merely being confused as to what their rights under the contract are. In other words, the court, also drawing on the offer and acceptance analogy, was stating that silence cannot amount to acceptance, either of an offer or of a repudiation.

The decision of the Court of Appeal raised serious implications with respect to implied acceptance of repudiation, since the decision did not go further and explain the practical results of the decision on the parties, other than that the buyer was not required to pay the damages awarded by the arbitrator. If, however, one accepted that the decision was correct and that acceptance of a repudiation has to be clear and unequivocal, then why was the letter of 9 August not treated as an implied but unequivocal acceptance of the repudiation? If such a letter is not sufficient, then it would seem that hardly anything less than express acceptance will suffice. A possible answer as to why the letter was not considered sufficient may lie in the fact that this amounted to an unreasonable delay in communicating the acceptance of the repudiation. The analogy with offer and acceptance becomes extremely tenuous in this context. It seems peculiar to argue that if one delays in accepting a repudiation, the contract can still be regarded as subsisting!

Other difficulties lie with the decision of the Court of Appeal; for instance, if the implied repudiation is regarded as equivocal and therefore ineffective, then surely the resale by the seller must itself amount to repudiation of the contract. The question then arises, who can sue whom? If the seller fails to deliver the goods on the contract date, they are presumably liable for breach of a primary obligation under the contract. There would appear to be nothing to stop the buyer from renouncing their earlier statement (i.e. their anticipatory breach) indicating that they do not intend to proceed with the contract and from treating the contract as still subsisting. The buyer would then be free to sue the seller for breach, but if this were to be correct there is no doubt that it could apply in other situations where one party's breach amounts to repudiation of the contract. It could apply, for instance, where a party is in breach of a condition or where the breach is such that it would substantially deprive the innocent party (i.e. the seller in the present case) of the benefits they would receive under the contract, or where in fact the party's actions amount to an actual breach of contract by virtue of their repudiation of the contract.

It can be seen that very substantial practical difficulties arise from the Court of Appeal decision and no doubt there was a sigh of relief when the seller appealed to the House of Lords, who reversed the decision of the Court of Appeal. Their Lordships, Lord Nolan giving the leading judgement, found that as a matter of law mere failure to perform a contractual obligation was capable of amounting to acceptance of an anticipatory repudiation by an aggrieved party (the seller), depending on the particular circumstances of the case and the contractual relationship entered into. The inference drawn by the arbitrator that the seller had elected to treat the contract as at an end and the communication of it by the failure to tender the bill of lading, which was a precondition to payment, was a question of fact that remained within the sole and exclusive jurisdiction of the arbitrator. The act of acceptance of the repudiation requires no particular form. All that is necessary is for the communication or the aggrieved party's conduct to be an unequivocal and clear indication of his election to treat the contract as at an end. Nor does the indication have to come from the aggrieved party personally; all that is required is for the election to come to the repudiating party's attention, whether by an agent, authorised or unauthorised, or some other third party.

Lord Nolan rejected the analogy of offer and acceptance put forward by Nourse LJ in the Court of Appeal. While it is true, as we have already seen, that an offer cannot be accepted by silence, there are exceptions to this rule – for instance in unilateral contracts where the need for communication of acceptance is impliedly waived by the offeror.

A difficult question regarding repudiation arises in relation to contracts for the sale of goods where delivery is made by instalments, each instalment being paid for separately. Whether a failure to make or pay for an instalment amounts to repudiation largely depends on the terms of the contract and the circumstances in which the failure arises. In *Maple Flock Co. Ltd v Universal Furniture Producers (Wembley) Ltd* [1934] 1 KB 148 it was stated by Lord Hewart in the Court of Appeal that:

> the main tests to be considered . . . are, first, the ratio quantitatively which the breach bears to the contract as a whole, and secondly, the degree of probability or improbability that such a breach will be repeated.

The principle contained in *Maple Flock* seems also to have been adopted in *Decro-Wall International SA v Practitioners in Marketing Ltd* [1971] 2 All ER 216 in that not just any breach of contract can be regarded as repudiation, but only those which deprive the injured party of a substantial benefit of what it was intended they should receive under the contract. In the case the defendants were sole dealers for the plaintiffs in the United Kingdom, but as they were short of working capital they were often late in paying for goods received from the plaintiffs. This caused inconvenience to the plaintiffs in that they had to pay interest to the bank when payments were not made promptly, though there was no question that they would ultimately be paid. On the face of things the Court of Appeal found that such a situation would almost certainly continue but found that the delays in payment could not amount to repudiation since they were not sufficiently serious as to bring the whole contract to an end. Buckley LJ suggested that the test to be applied was whether:

> the consequences of the breach be such that it would be unfair to the injured party to hold him to the contract and leave him to the remedy in damages as and when a breach or breaches may occur? If this would be so, then repudiation has taken place.

The process was affirmed in the House of Lords in *Afovos Shipping Co. SA v Pagnan and Lli, The Afovos* [1983] 1 All ER 449 where it was stated that the treatment of an anticipatory breach as repudiation could arise only if the breach related to a primary obligation or a fundamental breach.

The effects of breach

The right to affirm the contract

Objective
3

Where a party to a contract is in breach of a primary obligation or where the party is guilty of conduct that amounts to repudiation then this will not bring about the automatic termination of the contract, and the innocent party is free to treat the contract as still subsisting. Where such a situation applies in a contract for the sale of goods, the seller remains liable to deliver the goods in accordance with the contract, while the buyer remains liable to accept delivery and pay for the goods. Both parties also retain their right to sue on the contract.

In a situation where there has been an anticipatory breach of contract and the innocent party elects to affirm the contract, they are still required to perform their own obligations under the contract, but face the danger that, should they subsequently become guilty of a breach of contract, the other party may escape liability. This point was discussed in the following case.

Fercometal SARL v Mediterranean Shipping Co. SA (The Simona) [1989] AC 788

A charterparty was entered into in June 1982 whereby the shipowner agreed to take a cargo of steel coils from Durban to Bilbao. The charterparty contained an 'expected readiness to load' clause which entitled the charterers to cancel the charterparty should the ship not be ready to load on or before 9 July. On 2 July the shipowners asked for an extension to the expected readiness-to-load date as they wanted to load another cargo first and this meant that the ship would not be ready until 13 July. On receiving this request the charterers immediately cancelled the charterparty and chartered another vessel. The shipowners did not accept the repudiation and on 5 July gave notice to the charterers that the ship would be ready to load on 8 July. When the vessel subsequently arrived in Durban on that date, the shipowners gave notice that the ship was now ready to load. In fact this was not the case so the charterers rejected the notice and proceeded to load the cargo onto the second vessel. The shipowners brought an action for dead-freight.

In the arbitration proceedings that followed, the arbitrator upheld the shipowners' claim on the basis that the wrongful repudiation of the charterers relieved the shipowners from complying with their own obligations. The effect was that the shipowners' failure to tender the ship ready to load on time did not prevent them from recovering damages for wrongful repudiation by the charterers. On appeal this decision was set aside, though on further appeal to the Court of Appeal it was held that the unaccepted wrongful repudiation of the charterers did not prevent them from cancelling the contract when the shipowners failed to tender the vessel ready to load on 9 July.

The shipowners subsequently appealed to the House of Lords. Their Lordships confirmed the position that where a party wrongfully repudiated a contract, the innocent party could elect to affirm or treat the contract as discharged, subject to the criteria already discussed. If they elected to affirm the contract they were obliged to comply with their own contractual obligations under the contract. If an innocent party subsequently failed to comply with those obligations then the repudiating party could escape from their liability for wrongful repudiation. The shipowners in question having affirmed the contract were subsequently in breach of contract themselves by not tendering the vessel ready to load on 9 July and thus remained bound by the cancellation clause in the charterparty which was exercised by the charterers when the ship arrived late in Durban. The shipowners' appeal was consequently dismissed.

A further danger with affirmation lies in the possibility that a frustrating event may occur after the innocent party has affirmed the contract. Frustration will be dealt with more fully elsewhere but basically it amounts to an external event that renders the contract impossible.

The effect of frustration is automatic and radical in that it brings the contract to an end so that both parties are excused from further performance of the contract. Where an innocent party has decided to affirm a contract and there is an anticipatory breach, frustration will destroy the rights of that party to sue for the breach when the date of performance on the contract arrives. The point is well illustrated by the case of *Avery v Bowden* (1855) 5 E & B 714 where a ship was chartered to sail to the Russian Baltic port of Odessa and to take a cargo from the charterer's agent within 45 days. On the ship's arrival the agent stated that he could not provide a cargo and told the plaintiff to take the ship away. The plaintiff kept the ship at the port and repeatedly over the period in question asked the agent for a cargo and was in turn advised to take the ship away from the port. Before the 45-day period expired the Crimean War broke out and this rendered Odessa an enemy port and as a result the contract became frustrated. The effect of this was that the plaintiff lost the rights to sue for breach of contract since the frustrating event had destroyed the contract he had affirmed, together with his rights under it.

Once the innocent party has elected to affirm, or for that matter to treat the contract as discharged, the party cannot retract this election. In *Panchaud Frères SA v . . . Etablissements General Grain Co.* [1970] 1 Lloyd's Rep 53 it was held that affirmation is really a species of waiver that results in an innocent party being estopped from altering his election.

The fact that an innocent party can treat the contract as still subsisting and affirm their obligations under it so that they can go on to complete their obligations cannot be denied. In some circumstances, however, such a proposition is very unfair to the other party despite the fact that they were originally the offending party. The unfairness results from the fact that, in affirming the contract, the innocent party is entitled to continue to perform their obligations under the contract, thereby increasing their losses. There is no obligation on the innocent party to mitigate his losses, that only arises where there is a breach that gives rise to damages. Here the contract is still regarded as subsisting; there is no breach. When the date of performance arrives they can, despite having been told by the other party that they do not intend to perform the contract, use these losses as the basis of a claim for damages against the offending party.

White and Carter (Councils) Ltd v McGregor [1962] AC 413

> The appellants were suppliers of litter bins to local authorities, although the bins were paid for not by the local authorities but by businesses who had advertisements displayed on the bins. The respondents, who were proprietors of a garage, agreed to pay for advertisements on the bins for three years but on the same day that they entered into agreement they decided not to proceed and informed the appellants to that effect. The appellants refused to accept the cancellation (repudiation) and affirmed the contract even though they had at that stage taken no steps towards carrying out the contract. For the three years they prepared advertising plates, attached them to bins and displayed them throughout the locality agreed, making no attempt to mitigate their losses. At the end of the three-year period they sued for the entire contract price. It was held by a majority of the House of Lords that they were entitled to the contract price.

The decision is clearly unsatisfactory and all the judges considered that the appellants should not be allowed to succeed in such a claim, though none could find or develop a test which allowed the general rule relating to affirmation while qualifying its application in such a context. Lord Reid suggested that a claimant should not be allowed to affirm the contract and continue with it unless they could show that they had a legitimate interest, financial or otherwise, in performing the contract rather than claiming damages. Lord Reid stated:

> It may well be that, if it can be shown that a person has no legitimate interest, financial or otherwise, in performing the contract rather than claiming damages, he ought not to be

allowed to saddle the other with an additional burden with no benefit to himself. If a party has no interest to enforce a stipulation, he cannot in general enforce it: so that it might be said that, if a party has no interest to insist on a particular remedy, he ought not to be allowed to insist on it. And just as a party is not allowed to enforce a penalty, so he ought not to be allowed to penalise the other party by taking one course when another is equally advantageous to him.

At the end of the day their Lordships reiterated the basic principle that, if one party to a contract repudiates it, in the sense of making it clear to the other party that he refuses or will refuse to carry out his part of the contract, the innocent party has the option of either accepting that repudiation and suing for damages for breach of contract, or refusing to accept the repudiation and affirming the continuation of the contract. If then the innocent party can complete the contract himself, without the need for any action on the part of the contract breaker, he will be in a position to sue for the agreed price.

The decision in *White and Carter* has been heavily criticised but it would seem that Lord Reid's approach has now been accepted and indeed judicially approved of in a number of cases, though not without qualification.

In *Attica Sea Carriers Corporation* v *Ferrostaal Poseidon Bulk Reederei GmbH (The Puerto Buitrago)* [1976] 1 Lloyd's Rep 250 the charterers chartered a ship from the shipowners for 17 months. After six months the ship required significant repairs. The repairs amounted to a cost of $2m but this was not economically viable since the ship was only worth $1m. The charterers then prematurely terminated the charter and returned the ship to the shipowners. The charterers admitted liability for $400,000, however, the shipowners refused to accept the redelivery contending that the charterers were liable to pay the hire until the repairs had been carried out. The shipowners' argument was rejected finding that the obligation to repair the ship was not a pre-condition of the entitlement of the charterers to the redelivery the ship. It was not necessary for the Court of Appeal to consider the position as to whether or not the shipowners were entitle to recover the hire charges until the repairs had been carried out, nevertheless the Court of appeal considered the issues arising out of *White and Carter*. Lord Denning considered that the principle in *White and Carter* had no application whatsoever in a case where a claimant ought

> in all reason, to accept the repudiation and sue for damages provided that damages would provide an adequate remedy for any loss suffered by him

He stated that the reason was that, by suing for the money the claimant was seeking to enforce specific performance of the contract which he would not be allowed to do if damages was an adequate remedy. The other members of the Court of Appeal concurred with this view.

In *Gator Shipping Corp* v *Trans-Asiatic Oil SA (The Odenfeld)* [1978] 2 Lloyd's Rep 357 Kerr J considered that *The Puerto Buitrago* was a case in which the facts were 'extreme in their nature' and it was on this basis that it was unreasonable for the owners to seek to hold the charterers to the charter rather claim damages. He did not consider that the case provided a proposition that in a time charter if the charterer repudiated the contract for whatever reason or circumstances that the shipowners were always bound to take the ship back simply because their refusal to do so amounted to the equivalent of an order of specific performance. He did consider that the principle in *White and Carter* was a qualified one but that the entitlement of the innocent party whether or not to elect to accept repudiation would only apply in extreme cases 'where damages would be an adequate remedy and where an election to keep the contract alive would be wholly unreasonable'.

In *The Odenfeld [1978] 2 Lloyds Rep 357* Kerr J did not consider that damages would be an adequate remedy since it would be extremely difficult to assess not least because the damages would have to be assessed in relation to a prospective six and a half year period following repudiation. This was of course very different to *The Puerto Buitrago* where the damages would amount to a very small sum indeed, if any. A further factor that influenced Kerr J was that the plaintiffs in that case were in fact assignees of the owners of the ship and therefore to accept the repudiation of the defendants would be to put the plaintiffs in breach of their covenants with the owners.

In *Clea Shipping Corporation* v *Bulk Oil International Ltd, The Alaskan Trader (No. 2)* [1984] 1 All ER 129 the shipowners chartered a ship to the plaintiff charterers for twenty-four months. One year later the ship suffered from a serious engine failure that would take several months to repair, the plaintiffs therefore told the shipowners that they had no further use for the ship. The shipowners carried out the repairs at a cost of £800,000. Once the repairs were completed, the shipowners then informed the plaintiff that the ship was now ready for its use. The plaintiff considered that the charter was at an end and refused to give directions to the ship's master. The shipowners refused to accept this and kept the ship fully manned and at the disposal of the plaintiff. Since the plaintiff had paid for charter of the ship for the entire period of the charter it sought to recover the hire charges for the period from when the ship became disabled to the end of the charter period. It was held that the shipowners were entitled to recover their hire charges subject to their being liable for damages sustained by their refusal to re-take the ship. Lloyd J considered that the shipowners had no legitimate interest in claiming the hire rather than pursuing a claim for damages. Lloyd J was unable to accept the submission that Lord Reid's qualification was incorrect. He stated that Lord Reid had not defined what he meant by a 'legitimate interest', however, he stated it would be not sufficient to simply demonstrate that the innocent party was acting unreasonably. He considered that *The Puerto Buitrago* was at the very least a very strong persuasive authority in support of Lord Reid's comments in *White and Carter*. Furthermore in considering the judgement of Kerr J in *The Odenfeld* he considered that whilst Kerr J considered that *The Puerto Buitago* was an extreme case on the facts he nevertheless accepted the principle that the case was important in limiting the unfettered right of election in favour of the innocent party. Lloyd J stated:

> Whether one takes Lord Reid's language, which was adopted by Orr and Browne LJJ in *The Puerto Buitrago*, or Lord Denning MR's language in that case ('in all reason') or Kerr J's language in *The Odenfeld* ('wholly unreasonable. quite unrealistic, unreasonable and untenable'), there comes a point at which the court will cease, on general equitable principles to allow the innocent party to enforce his contract according to its strict legal terms. How one defines that point is obviously a matter of some difficulty, for it involves drawing a line between conduct which is merely unreasonable (see per Lord Reid in *White and Carter* at pages 429–430) and conduct which is wholly unreasonable (see per Kerr J in *The Odenfeld* at page 374). But however difficult it may be to define the point, that there is such a point seems to me to have been accepted both by the Court of Appeal in *The Puerto Buitrago* and by Kerr J in *The Odenfeld*.

He then went on to say:

> It seems to me that this court is bound to hold that there is some fetter, if only in extreme cases; and for want of a better way of describing that fetter, it is safest for this court to use the language of Lord Reid, which, as I have already said, was adopted by a majority of the Court of Appeal in *The Puerto Buitrago*.

In *Stocznia Gdanska SA v Latvian Shipping Co* [2001] 1 Lloyd's Rep 537 Clarke J at first instance, having considered the above authorities stated the principle as being:

> that an innocent party is entitled to continue to perform a commercial contract which has been repudiated by the other party unless he has 'no legitimate interest, financial or otherwise in performing the contract' (per Lord Reid) or he should 'in all reason' accept the repudiation (per Lord Denning) or where it would be 'wholly unreasonable' to keep the contract alive (per Mr Justice Kerr) or where it would be 'not merely unreasonable but wholly unreasonable' to do so (per Mr Justice Lloyd).

In the Court of Appeal ([2002] EWCA Civ 889) Staughton LJ stated that to be a 'legitimate interest, the innocent party must have reasonable grounds for keeping the contract open, bearing in mind also the interests of the wrongdoer'. Staughton LJ, however, did not elaborate on what the test for a legitimate interest may be.

The decisions clearly create a dilemma for the innocent party in that if they affirm but can show no legitimate interest then they will not be able to claim the full damages available – and that position is clearly fair. On the other hand, if they wrongly consider that there is an absence of a legitimate interest and decide to treat the contract as discharged, so that they can sue for their losses immediately, they may well find themselves in breach of contract should they be unable to justify that stance in accordance with the rules discussed in the last section. Nevertheless in *Ocean Marine Navigation Ltd v Koch Carbon Inc. (The Dynamic)* [2003] 2 Lloyd's Rep 693 it was considered that Lord Reid's 'legitimate interest' test, whilst clearly justifiable in order to disallow the innocent party 'to saddle the other with an additional burden with no benefit to himself' was clearly a serious matter. Simon J considered that Lord Reid's limitation should be confined to 'extreme cases' in which damages would provide an adequate remedy and that the right to elect to affirm the contract and proceed with the contract would be 'wholly unreasonable'. Simon J considered that the burden of preventing the innocent party from claiming the election to repudiate or affirm the contract lies on the party breaking the contract and that this burden cannot be discharged merely by showing the benefit to the other party is small in comparison to the loss suffered by the contract breaker. The effect of such an approach is, it is suggested, to alter the balance in favour of allowing affirmation of the contract and claiming damages as appropriate. Simon J stated that the authorities had established an exception to the general rule that the innocent party has an option whether or not to accept a repudiation, with the following characteristics:

1 The burden is on the contract breaker to show that the innocent party has no legitimate interest in performing the contract rather than claiming damages.

2 This burden is not discharged merely by showing that the benefit to the other party is small in comparison to the loss to the contract breaker.

3 The exception to the general rule applies only in extreme cases: where damages would be an adequate remedy and where an election to keep the contract alive would be unreasonable.

In *Isabella Shipowner SA v Shagang Shipping Co Ltd (The Aquafaith)* [2012] EWHC 1077 (Comm) a shipowner refused to accept early redelivery by a charterer under a long-term time charter. The ship had been chartered for a duration of 59–61 months and within the charter there was an express warranty that the ship would not be redelivered prior to the minimum period of 59 months. The charterer then redelivered the ship 94 days earlier than the minimum period, which it admitted was an anticipatory breach of the charter. The shipowner refused to accept the redelivery, affirmed the contract and claimed the hire charges for the balance of the minimum charter period. In arbitration the arbitrator held that the shipowner was required to accept the redelivery and then to offer the ship on the spot market by way of mitigation and then claim damages in respect of any losses that may be suffered. He held that the shipowner had no legitimate interest in affirming the contract.

The shipowners appealed claiming that the arbitrator was wrong to hold that the owners had no legitimate interest in refusing early redelivery and that the shipowners could only avoid the limitation on the *White and Carter* principle if they could show that the facts here constituted an exceptional case.

Cooke J rejected the argument that the shipowners had no legitimate interest in continuing to perform the contract. He considered that the arbitrator should have asked himself whether or not this was an extreme case of the kind where damages were an adequate remedy and the conduct of the owners 'was so beyond the pale that they should not be allowed to keep the contract alive'. Cooke J stated that the arbitrator was wrong to refuse the shipowners the option of affirming the contract on the basis that damages could be assessed and be available on the facts of the case. He stated that when Lord Reid's speech in *White and Carter* is read in its entirety, it was clear that the innocent party's right to elect is not shackled by the requirement to act reasonably. This is consistent with Lord Reid's judgement in *White and Carter* where he stated:

> It might be but it never has been the law that a person is only entitled to enforce his contractual rights in a reasonable way, and that a court will not support an attempt to enforce them in an unreasonable way. One reason why that is not the law is, no doubt, because it was thought that it would create too much uncertainty to require the court to decide whether it is reasonable or equitable to allow a party to enforce his full rights under a contract.

Something more is required before the courts will interfere and prevent the innocent party insisting on performance of the contract. Whereas Simon J thought the word 'wholly' in the expression 'wholly unreasonable' added nothing to the test, this was because he said that it was only in extreme cases that the limitation would operate. Cooke J stated at [44]:

> The effect of the authorities is that an innocent party will have no legitimate interest in maintaining the contract if damages are an adequate remedy and his insistence on maintaining the contract can be described as 'wholly unreasonable', 'extremely unreasonable' or, perhaps, in my words, 'perverse'.

On the decisions above it can be seen that any definition of 'legitimate interest' is somewhat elusive. By its nature the expression is equitable in nature and provides the courts with a discretion to find that the innocent party has no legitimate interest in continuing to perform the contract and hence claim the contract price, albeit this discretion is only exercised in exceptional cases. The main factor in determining the operation of the legitimate interest discretion appears to be an assessment of the wastefulness of the innocent party's continuing performance when balanced against the performance of the interest in achieving the contract price in the circumstances of the particular case. The finding that the innocent party has no legitimate interest in continuing with the contract will only arise in an exceptional case where there is shown by the party in breach that there is no 'cogent reason' for the innocent party to continue with the contract and that to do so is 'unrealistic, unreasonable and untenable' or amounts to a 'commercial absurdity'. The requirement for the maintenance of the contract to be 'wholly unreasonable' appears to be an additional factor that provides influence as to whether the innocent party can continue with performance so as to claim the contract price. For instance it might be submitted by the innocent party that damages would be an inadequate remedy because the breaching party is in financial difficulty. The innocent party therefore faces the risk that the breaching party will direct any limited funds it has to meet its obligations to other third parties and at the same time delay the payment of any sums to the innocent party. Still further it is conceivable that the breaching party could become insolvent or raise arguments to secure a discount on any loss claimed. By continuing with the contract the innocent party therefore guards against such a possibility by maintaining the contract with the ability to sue and without the risk of the breaching party raising the argument that the innocent party has failed to mitigate. A further factor will also be the balance between the innocent party's interest and those of the contract breaker. It is not sufficient for the contract breaker merely to show wastefulness in the innocent party proceeding with the contract but that on a benefit/cost basis the wastefulness of such an action is out of all proportion and excessive.

Cases where, having elected not to accept a repudiation of the contract, an innocent party will be prevented from enforcing their contractual right to keep the contract in force and sue for the contract price, namely where damages would be an adequate remedy and where the election to keep the contract alive would be 'wholly unreasonable', remain a fairly limited category. The case of *Reichman v Beveridge* illustrates that the principles in *White and Carter* are still appropriate to landlord and tenant situations.

Reichman v Beveridge [2006] EWCA Civ 1659

The facts of the case were that two tenants took a lease on office premises for a five-year term from January 2000 at a yearly rent of £23,101 payable quarterly in advance. They practised there as solicitors until February 2003, when they quit the premises, having no further use for them. In January 2004 the landlords began proceedings to recover rent arrears totalling £23,101 with VAT of £4,026.76. The tenants claimed in their defence that the landlords had failed to take steps to mitigate their loss by failing to instruct agents to market the premises, failing to accept an offer from a prospective tenant who wanted to take an assignment of the lease or a new lease and failing to accept an offer to negotiate a payment for the surrender of the lease. On the trial of a preliminary issue that defence was rejected by the district judge, whose decision was affirmed by the judge on the appeal of one of the tenants. The tenants then appealed to the Court of Appeal.

The Court of Appeal dismissed the appeal. The basis of the tenants' argument was that it was, following Lord Reid's dicta in *White and Carter*, wholly unreasonable for the landlord to elect to affirm the contract following an anticipatory breach by the tenant and that damages would be an adequate remedy; furthermore, the landlord did not have a legitimate interest to protect in affirming the contract. The court considered that it was not clear if the landlord was acting unreasonably in not taking their own steps to find a new tenant, rather than leaving it to the tenants to find a new one, or indeed in rejecting a proposal by the tenants. The Court of Appeal also considered that damages may not be an adequate remedy. The reason of the court was that, despite the contractual nature of the lease, where a tenant had abandoned the lease and failed to pay rent and other sums, if the landlords had re-let the premises they may not have received the loss of the future rent if they could only re-let the premises at a lower rent than that available under the lease. The basis behind this argument was that there was no authority in English law for the ability of a landlord to recover *future* rent, thus if the landlords had terminated the lease and then re-let at the lower rent, they were then not able to recover damages to compensate for the loss of the rent. On the other hand, if the market value for the rent had been the same or higher and the tenants had taken steps to find their own assignee or tenant and the landlords had refused to accept that assignee or new tenant then the tenants would have had a statutory remedy under the Landlord and Tenant Act 1985. On this basis the Court of Appeal considered that the landlords were not acting reasonably in not terminating the lease. The Court of Appeal considered that the principle in *White and Carter* that allowed the innocent party to affirm the contract and claim damages with no duty to mitigate was a limited one, given the acceptance of Lord Reid's qualifications; but it was a wholly justified principle in the context of landlord and tenant law.

A further limit on affirmation principle in *White and Carter* is that in certain contracts confirmation of the contract is only possible with the cooperation of the other party. If such cooperation is not forthcoming then clearly affirmation will not be possible and the innocent party must rely on an action in damages and of course make an attempt to mitigate his losses in the normal way. Such a situation often arises in contracts of employment. If an employer wrongfully dismisses an employee, that employee cannot claim that they are ready and willing to work but being prevented from doing so by the employer and that the employer is liable for all losses of wages from the date of the dismissal. The employee's only remedy is to sue immediately for damages.

In *Hounslow Borough Council v Twickenham Garden Developments Ltd*, the court considered that it was not just a question of the innocent party demonstrating that he had a legitimate interest in completing the contract but also the contract had to be capable of being completed without the cooperation of the party in breach.

Hounslow Borough Council v Twickenham Garden Developments Ltd [1971] Ch 233

The facts of the case were that Twickenham Garden Developments (TGD) was instructed to carry out some work for Hounslow Borough Council (HBC) on some land owned by the council. HBC purported to cancel the contract under a clause contained in the contract. TGD disputed whether HBC was entitled to cancel the contract in this way and continued to work on HBC's land. HBC sought an injunction to prevent TGD from trespassing on its land. TGD sought to rely on the principle in *White and Carter*, arguing that it was entitled to complete the contract. HBC argued that this case should be distinguished from *White and Carter* on the grounds that in that case the appellants had been able to go ahead and complete the contract without any cooperation from the other party. In this case, however, TGD required the cooperation of HBC, i.e. to allow TGD to go on to the land.

The court granted the injunction, stating that the principle in *White and Carter* only applied where the contract could be completed without the cooperation of the other party and that the innocent party had a legitimate interest in completing the contract. Neither of these requirements was present in this case.

The principle applies whether the co-operation of the party in breach is passive or active, thus in *Hounslow Borough Council*, Megarry J provided some elucidation of the process. He stated:

The case before me is patently one in which the contractor cannot perform the contract without any co-operation by the borough. The whole machinery of the contract is geared to acts by the architect and quantity surveyor, and it is a contract that is to be performed on the borough's land. True, the contractor already has de facto possession or control of the land; there is no question of the borough being required to do the act of admitting the contractor into possession, and so in that respect the contractor can perform the contract without any 'co-operation' by the borough. But I do not think that the point can be brushed aside so simply. Quite apart from questions of active co-operation, cases where one party is lawfully in possession of property of the other seem to me to raise issues not before the House of Lords in *White and Carter (Councils) Ltd* . v *McGregor* [1962] AC 413. Suppose that A, who owns a large and valuable painting, contracts with B, a picture restorer, to restore it over a period of three months. Before the work is begun, A receives a handsome offer from C to purchase the picture, subject to immediate delivery of the picture in its unrestored state, C having grave suspicions of B's competence. If the work of restoration is to be done in A's house, he can effectually exclude B by refusing to admit him to the house: without A's 'co-operation' to this extent B cannot perform his contract. But what if the picture stands in A's locked barn, the key of which he has lent to B so that he may come and go freely, or if the picture has been removed to B's premises? In these cases can B insist on performing his contract, even though this makes it impossible for A to accept C's offer? In the case of the barn, A's co-operation may perhaps be said to be requisite to the extent of not barring B's path to the barn or putting another lock on the door: but if the picture is on B's premises, no active co-operation by A is needed. Nevertheless, the picture is A's property, and I find it difficult to believe that Lord Reid intended to restrict the concept of 'co-operation' to active co-operation. In *White and Carter (Councils) Ltd* v *McGregor* no co-operation by the proprietor, either active or passive, was required: the contract could be performed by the agents wholly without reference to the proprietor or his property. The case was far removed from that of a property owner being forced to stand impotently aside while a perhaps ill-advised contract is executed on property of his which he has delivered into the possession of the other party, and is powerless to retrieve.

Thus if the right to payment is not dependent upon the innocent party performing his obligations under the contract, then the innocent party can claim the payment he is entitled to under the contract. Where, however, the innocent party's right to payment under the contract is dependent on that innocent party performing his contractual obligations, which he is unable to do, the other party refused to co-operate with him, then that innocent party is unable to claim his payment under the contract because his right to payment has not materialised.

In examining the right to treat the contract as discharged, one should note in the case of B2C contracts the Consumer Rights Act 2015 ss 20–22. Section 20 states there are two provisions for the right to reject : the short-term right to reject, which is subject to s 22, and the final right to reject, which is subject to s 24. Each of these rights entitles the consumer to reject the goods and treat the contract as at an end, subject to ss (20) and (21), that is the consumer is entitled, depending on the terms of the contract and the circumstances of the case, to reject the goods to which a severable obligation relates and treat that obligation as at an end. The right is exercised if the consumer indicates to the trader that the consumer is rejecting the goods and treating the contract as at an end. The indication may be something the consumer says or does, but it must be clear enough to be understood by the trader.

The right to treat the contract as discharged

The innocent party has the right to elect to accept the repudiation as discharging the contract with the result that all their future obligations under the contract come to an end, as do the obligations of the guilty party, though here their obligation to pay damages arises by operation of law, as stated in *Moschi* v *Lep Air Services Ltd* [1973] AC 331. Just as in affirmation above, once the election to accept the repudiation has been made, it is not possible to retract it.

Before proceeding, however, it should be noted that there is a critical distinction between rescission and discharge by breach. In the case of an accepted repudiatory breach, the contract had come into existence but had been put to an end or discharged. It was held in ***Howard-Jones v Tate*** [2011] EWCA Civ 1330 that acceptance of a repudiatory breach did not bring about rescission *ab initio*, thus following the decision in ***Johnson v Agnew*** [1980] AC 367. Rescission *ab initio* is very different from a failure of performance which entitles the innocent party to treat the contract as discharged. While that latter situation is sometimes referred to as 'rescission', it does not have the consequence that the contract is treated as never having come into existence but simply that the parties are absolved from future performance and the innocent party may claim damages for breach, as per ***Photo Production Ltd v Securicor Transport Ltd*** [1980] AC 827.

One refinement on the above principle arose in the case of ***Stocznia Gdynia SA v Gearbulk Holdings Ltd*** [2009] EWCA Civ 75, where it was alleged that where there was a contractual right to terminate a contract, the innocent party was precluded from terminating the contract at common law and further could not recover damages for loss of bargain. The facts of the case were that the appellant purchaser (G) had entered into contracts with S for the construction of three vessels. In fact, none of the vessels were delivered. Article 10 of the contracts provided for the price to be reduced by way of liquidated damages for delay in delivery and specified deficiencies and, provided that G had the right to terminate the contract if there was a major breach by S of its obligation, to proceed with construction of the vessel. On any such termination S had to repay any sums previously paid, with interest. While some work had commenced with regard to the first vessel, this work had in fact stopped and therefore G wrote to S terminating the contract in respect of that vessel. G then exercised its right under art 10 to recover the first instalment of the price which it had paid on signing the contract. G later took similar steps to terminate the contracts for the other two ships and to recover the first instalments for those as well. G further claimed that it was entitled to recover damages for the loss of its bargain. S said that because G had exercised its contractual right to terminate, its remedy was limited to recovery of the instalments only in accordance with the contract. An arbitrator held that S had repudiated the contracts and that the contract terms did not exclude G's rights at common law. He also rejected an argument that G had affirmed the contracts. On appeal the judge held that the contract terms were not an exclusive code preventing any claim for damages, but that G was precluded from claiming damages at common law for the repudiation of the contracts because it had affirmed the contracts by virtue of having claimed the instalments under the contract. S submitted that art 10 contained a complete contractual code which precluded any right to treat the contract as repudiated at common law or claim damages for loss of bargain at common law.

The Court of Appeal held that art 10 in the contract did not displace the right to treat the contract as repudiated. The primary purpose of that provision was to provide an agreed measure of compensation for breaches of contract by way of delay in delivery and deficiencies in capacity and performance which, although important, did not go to the root of the contract. However, the parties had also agreed that there was a point at which the delay or deficiency was so serious that G should be entitled to terminate the contract. The court considered that the parties had to be taken as having agreed that it was at that point the breach was a serious breach and one that went to the root of the contract. In those circumstances G had the right to terminate the contract with the usual consequences and it would be wrong to treat the right to terminate in accordance with the terms of the contract as different from the right to treat the contract as discharged by reason of repudiation at common law. The court further considered that art 10 did not exclude the right to recover damages for loss of bargain in the event of termination by G. It was stated that a person who exercised a contractual right of termination which arose on the other party's breach was not inevitably prevented from treating the contract as discharged and recovering damages for the loss of his bargain. The exercise by G of its right to recover the instalments of the contract price under art 10 was not to be taken as an election on G's part to affirm the contract and there was no inconsistency in recovering instalments of the price under art 10 and recovering damages for loss of bargain at common law.

Once the innocent party has decided to accept the repudiatory breach, that party is entitled to recover for the loss of the benefit that the performance would have brought. The loss of those benefits accrues at the time of the repudiation. It is not open to the repudiating party to seek to reduce the damages on the basis of some subsequent act of the innocent party that might reduce the overall benefit that would have accrued. The point can be seen in the case of *Chiemgauer Membran und Zeltbau GmbH (formerly Koch Hightex GmbH)* v *New Millennium Experience Co. Ltd (formerly Millennium Central Ltd) (No. 2)* (2001) *The Times*, 16 January. Strictly speaking, the case does not concern a repudiatory breach since the claimant had a contractual right to terminate the contract; however, the principle can nevertheless still be seen.

In July 1997, the claimant (Koch) was awarded the contract to construct the roof for the Millennium Dome. The contract permitted the defendant, the New Millennium Experience Co. Ltd (NMEC), to terminate the contract without cause provided it paid compensation calculated in accordance with a term of the contract. This term permitted Koch to claim damages for 'direct loss and/or damage'. In August 1997, NMEC exercised its right to terminate the contract without cause and subsequently Koch filed for bankruptcy under German law in August 1998. In 1999, the Court of Appeal granted Koch judgement in respect of NMEC's liability under the contract but did so without expressing any interpretation as to the meaning of the compensation clause. Koch then applied to the Chancery Division in order to find out whether: first, the expression 'direct loss and/or damage' allowed it to claim for loss of profits; and, second, whether in assessing Koch's claim the court was obliged to assume that Koch would have been able to perform the contract had it not been terminated by NMEC, notwithstanding that Koch had subsequently become insolvent.

It was held that the term 'direct loss and/or damage' had a clear and established meaning in that it equated with the first limb of *Hadley v Baxendale* (1854) 9 Exch 341 (see Chapter 16). In other words, Koch could claim for losses which arose naturally according to the usual course of things from the breach of contract. The loss of ordinary profits suffered by Koch fell squarely within this definition. It was, however, contended by NMEC that the damages should be reduced or extinguished since it was likely that Koch would have become insolvent anyway in the course of carrying out the business. On this basis Koch would have made either no profits or profits at a reduced rate as a result and that this should be taken into account when assessing the level of damages to be awarded. The court considered that this case was analogous to the situation where an innocent party accepted a defendant's repudiatory breach. In this situation the repudiating party is precluded from alleging that the innocent party would not have been able to perform the contract. The innocent party is entitled to any benefits the contract would bring on the basis that those benefits had been lost because of the breach of contract by the repudiating party. A repudiating party cannot rely on some intervening act, such as the insolvency of the innocent party, to reduce or even extinguish the right to damages. This right arose and accrued to the innocent party, Koch, as soon as the repudiating party, NMEC, repudiated the contract.

The decision to accept the repudiation and treat the contract as discharged is not one to be taken lightly since, as we have seen in cases such as *Woodar*, *Molena Alpha*, and so on, if the repudiation does not amount to a breach of a primary obligation, then there is no right to treat the contract as discharged, with the result that the innocent party themselves may be held to be in breach of contract.

What is the effect where an innocent party is entitled to refuse performance of their contractual obligations but gives the wrong reason for this refusal, albeit that they do have a justifiable reason? In *Glencore Grain Rotterdam BV v Lebanese Organisation for International Commerce* [1997] 4 All ER 514, it was held that in such circumstances an innocent party does not deprive themselves of the right to refuse performance. Furthermore, it is irrelevant whether they are aware or not that they have a justifiable reason at the time of their refusal.

This principle is, however, subject to two qualifications. First, it will not apply if the justification, known or unknown, by the innocent party could have been put right. Second, the principle does not apply if the innocent party makes some unequivocal representation to the contrary, and this is acted upon by the other party, so that it would be unjust or unfair for the innocent party to rely on their strict contractual right. The representation could take the form of a promise or some other conduct that indicates that the contract is being affirmed, as seen in *Panchaud Frères SA v . . . Etablissements General Grain Co*. The affirmation could take the form of a waiver, though in that case Lord Denning expressed it as an estoppel by conduct. He stated: 'The basis of it is that a man has so conducted himself that it would be unfair or unjust to allow him to depart from a particular state of affairs which another has taken to be settled or correct.' Later, in *V Berg & Son Ltd v Vanden Avenne-Izegem PVBA* [1977] 1 Lloyd's Rep 499, Lord Denning referred to *Panchaud Frères* 'as a case where there was a waiver by one person of his strict right – or an estoppel – whatever you like to call it – whereby a person cannot go back on something he has done'. Whether estoppel, waiver or some other conduct, the second qualification to the principle set out in *Glencore Grain* must amount to an unequivocal representation, by conduct or otherwise, which was acted upon by the other party. In *Tele2 International Card Co SA v Kub 2 Technology Ltd (formerly C3 Calling Card Co (Ireland) Ltd)* [2009] EWCA Civ 9 the Court of Appeal found that the continued performance by the defendant of the agreement for nearly a year without any protest or reserve of any kind in relation to the breach was only consistent with an election to abandon the right to terminate for that breach. It was a clear and unequivocal communication, by conduct, of the claimant's election to affirm the agreement and to abandon its right to terminate it for breach.

The loss of the right to treat the contract as discharged

In contracts for the sale of goods in a B2B contract by the Sale of Goods Act 1979, s 11(4) the buyer loses the right to repudiate the contract once they have accepted the goods. But what constitutes acceptance? This is defined in the Act as when the buyer intimates to the seller that they have accepted them (s 35(1)). If the goods have been delivered to the buyer, any act of the buyer that is inconsistent with the seller's ownership once the buyer has had the opportunity to examine the goods to ensure conformity with the contract or, in the case of a sale by sample, by comparing the bulk with the sample (s 35(2)), will suffice. The buyer is deemed to have accepted the goods when after the lapse of a reasonable time they retain the goods without intimating to the seller that they have rejected them (s 35(4)). In determining what is a reasonable time the Act states that one of the factors to be taken into account is whether the buyer has had the opportunity to examine the goods for the purposes set out in s 35(2) (see above). Further, the buyer is not deemed to have accepted the goods merely because they ask for, or agree to, their repair (s 35(6)(a)) or have the goods delivered to a sub-buyer/third party (s 35(6)(b)). Similarly, accepting delivery of part of the goods while at the same time claiming an entitlement to reject the rest does not amount to acceptance.

The operation of these principles can be seen in the case of *Clegg* v *Ollie Andersson (t/a Nordic Marine)* [2003] 2 Lloyd's Rep 32 (CA) where the defendants had contracted to purchase a new yacht from the claimants. When the yacht was delivered in August 2002, the yacht's keel was found to be substantially heavier than the manufacturer's specification. The parties entered into a protracted round of correspondence between August 2000 and March 2001 in which the effects of the overweight keel were discussed, the potential safety repercussions and the means of remedying the defect. In March, the defendant purchasers informed the seller that they were entitled to reject the yacht on the basis that there was a breach of the implied condition under the Sale of Goods Act 1979, s 14(2), in that the yacht was not of satisfactory quality. The sellers rejected the condition that the goods were not of satisfactory quality and further alleged that the buyers had lost their right to reject the goods under s 11(4) since they had intimated acceptance within the provisions of s 35(1) or, in any event, had left it too late to reject within the provisions of s 35(4).

At first instance the judge agreed with the sellers that the goods were of satisfactory quality and that the buyers had lost their right to reject by virtue of the operation of s 35(1) and (4). The buyers appealed.

In the Court of Appeal the court held that the test to determine what was satisfactory quality was whether a reasonable person would think the goods satisfactory taking into account their description, price and all other relevant circumstances. On the facts the court considered that a reasonable person would not consider the yacht to be of satisfactory quality because of the overweight keel, the adverse effect it had on the safety of the yacht and the fact that the work required to remedy the defect was more than what could be considered minimal remedial work. The buyers had therefore established a breach of s 14(2) and their right to reject the yacht by virtue of s 11(4); but had they lost this right by virtue of the operation of s 35(1) and/or s 35(4)? The Court of Appeal thought they had not, stating that time taken to ascertain the effect of any modification or repair was a relevant matter in determining the question of fact that arose in s 35(4). The court also stated that in any event s 35(6) states that a buyer does not accept the goods simply by asking for or agreeing to a repair. The court stated that it followed that a buyer did not lose his right to reject by seeking information that would enable him or her to make an informed choice between acceptance, rejection or cure. Once the sellers had supplied the information required to the buyers, the buyers had taken only three weeks to inform the sellers that they were exercising their right to reject, which was not an unreasonable amount of time. The buyers were therefore entitled to the return of their purchase price and compensation for consequential losses.

The decision in this case also overturned the heavily criticised earlier decision of *Bernstein* v *Pamson Motors (Golders Green) Ltd* [1987] 2 All ER 220 where a subjective test had been applied by Rougier J where he said of s 35:

> That section seems to me to be directed solely to what is a reasonable practical interval in commercial terms between a buyer receiving the goods and his ability to send them back, taking into consideration from his point of view the nature of the goods and their function, and from the point of view of the seller the commercial desirability of being able to close his ledger reasonably soon after the transaction was complete. The complexity of the intended function of the goods is clearly of prime consideration here. What is a reasonable time in relation to a bicycle would hardly suffice for a nuclear submarine.

In situations outside the sale of goods the loss of the right to repudiate may arise by way of a **waiver**. It is considered that for a party to waive a right to rescind they must know of their rights in that respect in the first place. This is because essentially a waiver is a type of election and as such requires knowledge. This view is supported by the case of *Peyman* v

Lanjani [1985] Ch 457 where the defendant entered into a contract for the assignment of a lease that was subject to a covenant that the lease was not to be assigned without the consent of the landlord. This consent was obtained from the landlord by way of a fraudulent misrepresentation, though the plaintiff played no part in the deception. The plaintiff, despite consulting his solicitors, was not aware that he had a right to rescind the contract and therefore, also on the advice of his solicitors, paid £10,000 to complete the transaction and went into possession. Later he consulted new solicitors who advised him that because of the defendant's deception, the plaintiff's title was defective and that he had a right to rescind the contract. The defendant argued that the plaintiff had waived his right to rescind by paying the £10,000 and going into possession. The Court of Appeal held that a person would not lose the right to rescind merely by being aware of the facts that give rise to the right to rescind; they also had to be aware of the right to rescind itself. Since he was not aware of this right he was not deemed to have waived his rights in this respect and could rescind the contract.

In consumer contracts, the Consumer Rights Act provides that the short-term right to reject under s 20(1) must be exercised within certain time limits and if these are not adhered to, the consumer loses the short-term right to reject, unless the trader and the consumer agree otherwise (s 22(1). Contracting out of the short-term right to reject is not binding on a consumer (s 22(2). The time limit set out in s 22(3) for exercising the right to reject is the end of 30 days beginning with the first day after the following has occurred:

1 ownership or (in the case of a contract for the hire of goods, a hire- purchase agreement or a conditional sales contract) possession of the goods has been transferred to the consumer,

2 the goods have been delivered, and

3 where the contract requires the trader to install the goods or take other action to enable the consumer to use them, the trader has notified the consumer that the action has been taken.

There is a proviso with regard to the short-term right to reject in that by .22(4) if the goods are of a kind that can reasonably be expected to perish after a shorter period of time, for instance, fruit, the time limit for exercising the short-term right to reject in relation to those goods is the end of that shorter period.

All these provisions are adjusted if the consumer requests or agree that the goods be replaced or repaired and in such circumstances the time limits under ss 22(3) and (4) stop running for the waiting period whilst a repair or replacement is carried out. This must be done within a reasonable time and without inconvenience to the consumer (NB: the trader must bear the necessary costs incurred in doing so, i.e. parts, labour and postage – s 23(2)b). If the goods supplied by the trader in response to that request or agreement do not conform to the contract, then the time limit for exercising the short-term right to reject is then, either 7 days after the waiting period ends, or if later, the original 30-day time limit for exercising the right, extended by the waiting period. By s 22 (8) the waiting period begins with the day the consumer requests or agrees to the repair or replacement of the goods, and ends with the day on which the consumer receives goods supplied by the trader in response to the request or agreement.

By s 23(3), the consumer cannot require the trader to repair or replace the goods if that remedy (the repair or the replacement) is either impossible or is disproportionate compared to the other remedies such as offering a refund or proving a price reduction to the consumer.

Whilst the trader must repair or replace the goods within a reasonable time and without inconvenience to the consumer, conversely the Act provides that the consumer must give the trader a reasonable time to replace or repair the goods. By s 24(5) the final right to reject the goods arises 'in one of these situations:

1 after one repair or one replacement, the goods do not conform to the contract;

2 because of s 23(3) the consumer can require neither repair nor replacement of the goods; or

3 the consumer has required the trader to repair or replace the goods, but the trader is in breach of the requirement of s 23(2)(a) to do so within a reasonable time and without significant inconvenience to the consumer.'

It should be noted that where the consumer opts for a repair or replacement and, following that, the consumer exercises his final right to reject, in some circumstances the trader may make a deduction from any refund to take into account any use that the consumer has made of the goods. There are limitations on this in the sense that such deductions cannot be made if the final right of rejection is exercised in the first six months unless the goods relate to a motor vehicle.

Summary

Performance

- A contract must be performed strictly in accordance with its terms otherwise the innocent party can claim damages or repudiate the contract (*Re Moore & Co.* v *Landauer & Co.*; *Arcos Ltd* v *E A Ronaasen & Son*).

- Non-consumers can still reject for a breach of condition – s 13 SGA.

- Non-consumers cannot reject for a breach of condition where the breach is so slight that it would be unreasonable for the buyer to reject the goods, subject to contrary intention either express or implied in the contract – s 15A.

- Consumers may exercise similar rights under the Consumer Rights Act 2015 s 25

- 'Entire' contracts – a person's contractual obligations are conditional on the other party performing their side of the contract completely and entirely (*Cutter* v *Powell*).

Mitigating the strict performance rule

The doctrine of substantial performance

- Occurs where a person makes minor defects when fully performing their side of the bargain.

- Damages – a person who substantially performs his side of the contract can claim the contract price, less an amount by which the value of the contract has been diminished by their breach (e.g. *Hoenig* v *Isaacs*).

Partial performance

- Occurs where one side partially performs their side of the contract and the other decides to accept the work done rather than reject it. The promisee will be obliged to pay for the work done on a *quantum meruit* basis. The promisee has complete discretion as to whether to accept the partial performance or not.

Tender of performance

- To offer a tender to perform is regarded as equivalent to actual performance.
- The promisee cannot avoid a contract for non-performance where they themselves have refused to accept the offer of performance (**Startup v Macdonald**).
- The promisor can sue for damages on a *quantum meruit* basis if they have started work but the promisee prevents them completing it (**Planché v Colburn**).

Divisible contracts

- Defined as a contract in which partial performance attracts an obligation to provide payment of part of the consideration.

The time of performance

- Time must be made of the essence if a party wishes to terminate the contract, otherwise only damages may be sought (**Raineri v Miles**).
- Equity considers time of the essence where:
  1. the parties expressly stipulate that conditions as to time must be strictly complied with; or
  2. the nature of the subject of the contract or the surrounding circumstances show that time should be considered to be of the essence; or
  3. a party who has been subjected to unreasonable delay gives notice to the party in default making time of the essence (**United Scientific Holdings Ltd v Burnley Borough Council**; **Bunge Corporation v Tradax Export SA**)
- Time not made of essence can become of essence on the giving of reasonable notice (**Charles Rickards Ltd v Oppenheim**).
- Before a party gives reasonable notice, there must be an unreasonable delay (**British and Commonwealth Holdings plc v Quadrex Holdings Inc.**).
- Reasonable notice can be given making time of the essence as soon as the contractual date for performance has passed (**Behzadi v Shaftesbury Hotels Ltd**).
- Where time is of the essence in a contract, then any delay will amount to repudiation of the contract (**Union Eagle Ltd v Golden Achievement Ltd**).
- Consumer Rights Act 2015 s 28 – 'unless the parties agree otherwise, contracts must be performed within 30 days, taking effect after the day in which the consumer sent his order to the supplier'.

Breach

- Occurs where a person fails to perform their side of the contract.
- A breach gives rise to a claim for damages, regardless of its severity.

Breach of primary obligation

- The innocent party may treat the contract as discharged where there has been a breach of a primary obligation of the contract.

- A primary obligation is often expressed as a condition (*The Mihalis Angelos; Hong Kong Fir Shipping; Ampurius Nu Homes Holdings Ltd v Telford Homes (Creekside) Ltd*).

Repudiation prior to performance of the contract

Anticipatory breach: occurs when a party either expressly or impliedly, by words or conduct, indicates that they do not intend to honour their obligations under the contract.

- Express anticipatory breach (*Hochester v De La Tour*).

- Implied repudiatory breach (*Frost v Knight*)

- Burden of proof for anticipatory breach is beyond reasonable doubt (*Freeth v Barr; Mersey Steel and Iron Co. v Naylor Benzon & Co; Federal Commerce and Navigation Co. Ltd v Molena Alpha Inc.; Woodar Investment Development Ltd v Wimpey Construction (UK) Ltd.*).

The effects of breach

The right to affirm the contract

- An innocent party can elect to continue with the contract or to terminate it upon a breach.

- where there has been an anticipatory breach of contract and the innocent party elects to affirm the contract, they are still required to perform their own obligations under the contract, but face the danger that, should they subsequently become guilty of a breach of contract, the other party may escape liability (*Fercometal SARL v Mediterranean Shipping Co SA (The Simona)*).

The right to treat the contract as discharged

- The innocent party has the right to elect to accept the repudiation as discharging the contract with the result that all their future obligations under the contract come to an end.

- When the acceptance of the repudiation has been made, it is not possible to retract it.

The loss of the right to treat the contract as discharged

- B2B Contracts – Sale of Goods Act 1979, s 11(4) – the buyer loses the right to repudiate the contract once he has accepted the goods. Section 35(1) states acceptance is 'when the buyer intimates to the seller that he has accepted them'.

- B2C Contracts – Consumer rights Act 2015 – consumers have a short-term right to reject of 30 days which is lost after that date. The period can be extended if the consumer asks for a replacement or repair whereupon the trader has a reasonable time to comply.

Further reading

Beatson, 'Discharge for Breach: The Position of Instalment, Deposits and Other Payments Due Before Completion' (1981) 97 *Law Quarterly Review* 389

Beatson, Burrows and Cartwright, *Anson's Law of Contract*, 30th edn (Oxford University Press, 2016)

Carter, 'Discharge as the Basis for termination for Breach of Contract' (2012) 128 *Law Quarterly Review* 283

Coote, 'Breach, Anticipatory Breach, or the Breach Anticipated' (2007) 123 *Law Quarterly Review* 503

Courtney, 'Termination of a Contract by a Party in Breach' (2008) 3 *Journal of Business Law* 226

Furmston, *Cheshire, Fifoot and Furmston's Law of Contract*, 16th edn (Oxford University Press, 2012)

Liu, 'Inferring Future Breach: Towards a Unifying Test of Anticipatory Breach of Contract' [2007] *Cambridge Law Journal* 574

Liu, 'The White and Carter Principle: A Restatement' (2011) 74 *Modern Law Review* 171

Mustill, 'The Golden Victory – Some Reflections' (2008) 124 *LQR* 569, 571–572.

Smith and Atiyah, *Atiyah's Introduction to the Law of Contract*, 6th edn (Oxford University Press, 2006)

Treitel, 'Affirmation After Repudiatory Breach' (1998) 114 *Law Quarterly Review* 22

Peel, Treitel *Law of contract*, 14th edn (Sweet and Maxwell, 2015)

14

Discharge by agreement

Objectives

After reading this chapter you should be able to:

1. Recognise what is meant by bilateral discharge and understand the forms that it may take and what is meant by 'accord and satisfaction'.
2. Understand the nature of unilateral discharge of a contract.

Introduction

The general rule here is that since contracts are created by agreement, then they may be extinguished by agreement. The rule thus stated is simple, but while the parties may agree to extinguish the contract, there is always the possibility of one of the parties reneging on the agreement and taking action against the other for breach of contract. It is therefore advisable for the parties to formulate their agreement in terms of a second contract supported by consideration. But if the agreement is contained in a deed, then no consideration will be required, regardless of whether the **discharge** is **bilateral** (i.e. where the contract is wholly or partly executory) or **unilateral** (i.e. where the contract is wholly executed by one party, but not by the other). For the most part, however, it is rare for such an agreement to be encompassed within a deed. It is therefore necessary to examine the nature of the consideration needed in the formulation of an agreement which purports to discharge a legally enforceable contract.

While until now **discharge by agreement** has been expressed in terms of bringing the contract to an end, the principles apply not only where the parties are terminating the contract, but also where they are replacing it with a new one or simply varying the terms of the agreement.

Bilateral discharge

Accord and satisfaction

Objective 1

As has already been stated, where both parties have yet to carry out their obligations under the contract, either wholly or partially, then their respective promises must be supported by consideration. This situation is often described by lawyers as '**accord and satisfaction**' – which is just mystical legal parlance for describing the need for new consideration to support the discharge agreement. It was explained in *British Russian Gazette Ltd* v *Associated Newspapers Ltd* [1933] 2 KB 616 by Scrutton LJ in the following terms:

> Accord and satisfaction is the purchase of a release from an obligation, whether arising under a contract or tort by means of any valuable consideration, not being the actual performance of the obligation itself. The accord is the agreement by which the obligation is discharged. The satisfaction is the consideration which makes the agreement operative.

For detailed discussion of consideration, see Chapter 3.

The 'satisfaction' supplied by the parties must not be something less than what was required under the original contract, as indicated in *Pinnel's case* ((1602) 5 Co Rep 117a), and must amount to sufficient consideration. In this context, however, special attention must be given to the case of *Williams* v *Roffey Bros & Nicholls (Contractors) Ltd* [1990] 1 All ER 512 since here a variation of the terms of the contract was enforceable despite the fact that the promise of the contractors was not supported by any consideration supplied by the claimants, but by the contractors obviating a disbenefit that arose because of a further obligation to a third party. Since such consideration falls well short of what is normally regarded as consideration, it may be that the law is moving away from such a doctrine, possibly towards a position whereby discharge by agreement will come to rely more on the use of promissory estoppel as a means of enforcing the agreement. The discussions that arise in and out of the case of *Re Selectmove Ltd* [1995] 2 All ER 531 should also be considered here.

For more on promissory estoppel refer to Chapter 3.

The form of discharge

Rescission and variation

Very often the problems relating to discharge revolve around the problems that arise because of the formalities required by certain types of contract. Thus it has been seen that certain contracts are required to be under seal, others to be evidenced in writing and yet others to be in writing. The rule here is that where it is intended to bring about the discharge of the contract there is no need to comply with the formalities required at law. The position is different, however, where it is intended not only to discharge the contract but also to substitute a new one since, in this situation, the formalities would have to be complied with, as indicated in *Morris* v *Baron & Co.* [1918] AC 1.

When a contract is rescinded or varied different effects can arise. The point was considered in *Compagnie Noga d'Importation et d'Exportation SA* v *Abacha* [2003] EWCA Civ 1100 where Tuckey LJ stated that the essential difference between rescission and variation is that a contract comes to an end if it is rescinded but continues if it is varied. If the rescinded contract is replaced by a new agreement, even if the terms are the same, new consideration is required and if that is forthcoming there will be sufficiency of consideration to support the new agreement. It follows from this that the case of *Stilk* v *Myrick* (1809) 2 Camp 317 has no application since that decision is based upon continuing obligations under a former agreement. Thus if *X* agrees to sell his boat to *Y* for £10,000 and later they agree to tear up the contract or rescind it and replace the contract with one in which X agrees to sell the boat to Y for £8,000, then clearly there is a valid contract here. There is sufficiency of consideration in that the mutual release and the mutual promises in the new contract will be regarded as sufficient consideration to support the initial release (the rescission) and the new contract. The position is not the same, however, if X and Y simply agree to alter the contract so that the price is £8,000 since here there is a possibility that the case of **Stilk v Myrick** does have application and there is insufficient consideration to support the variation.

For more on sufficiency of consideration refer to Chapter 3.

Waivers

The situation above is the position where the parties are entering into an agreement for their mutual advantage, but different considerations apply where the advantage is only to benefit one of the parties. Such a situation is termed a waiver and it normally arises where one party requests an alteration of the terms of the contract and the other party agrees not to insist on strict compliance with the terms of the contract, so, for example, allowing late delivery at the request of the other party. The difference between a waiver and a variation is that in the former no new contract is created; it is simply that one party is agreeing to forgo their strict legal rights. This fact points to the historical basis for the existence of waivers in that it was a method of evading the requirement of evidence in writing under the Statute of Frauds, since no new contract was being created. So desperate were the judges to avoid the effects of the Statute of Frauds that they made no attempt to justify how a purely gratuitous promise could be enforceable.

The enforcement of purely gratuitous promises in waivers still poses a conundrum for lawyers when they are attempting to justify their existence, and it is probably better simply to regard them as a form of promissory estoppel. In truth, waivers are slightly wider in application than promissory estoppel, which normally requires the promisee to alter their position in reliance on the promise of the other party; such a requirement is not necessary in waivers.

The modern authority on waivers remains ***Charles Rickards Ltd v Oppenheim.***

Charles Rickards Ltd v *Oppenheim* [1950] 1 All ER 420

A chassis for a Rolls-Royce was ordered from the plaintiffs, who later also agreed to build a body for it in 'six to seven months'. At the end of seven months the body had not been completed and the defendant agreed to wait another three months. At the end of this period it was still not ready so the defendant gave notice that if it was not ready within four weeks he would cancel the order. At the end of this period the body was still not ready so the order was cancelled. The Court of Appeal held that he was entitled to do so since, even though he had waived the stipulation as to time of delivery, he had given reasonable notice of his intention to make time of the essence. Lord Denning commented:

> Whether it be called waiver or forbearance on his part, or an agreed variation or substituted performance, does not matter. It is a kind of estoppel. By his conduct he evinced an intention to affect their legal relations. He made, in effect, a promise not to insist on his strict legal rights. That promise was intended to be acted on, and was in fact acted on. He cannot afterwards go back on it.

In fact some authorities distinguish between waivers and promissory estoppel, considering that they are related but separate doctrines that produce the same effects. Such a difference of opinion can be seen in ***Brikom Investments Ltd* v *Carr*** [1979] 2 All ER 753.

Express provision for discharge

The parties may agree either expressly or impliedly in their contract that it will become discharged should certain circumstances arise. A common example would be where the parties have agreed that the operation of some condition subsequent will have the effect of discharging the contract.

Unilateral discharge

Objective
2

Unilateral discharge usually arises where one party has fully performed their obligations under the contract, the other party having yet to do so. The situation may arise, therefore, that the first party agrees to release the other from any obligations that are yet to be performed. The problem with this type of discharge is that it is purely gratuitous and unenforceable, unless it is made by deed.

Summary

This chapter deals with the discharge of contracts by agreement. The general rule here is that since contracts are created by agreement they may be extinguished by agreement.

Bilateral discharge
Accord and satisfaction

- Where both parties have yet to carry out their obligations under the contract, either wholly or partially, then their respective promises to discharge the contract must be supported by consideration.
- The 'satisfaction' supplied by the parties:
  (i) must not be something less than what was required under the original contract (*Pinnel's case*), and
  (ii) must amount to sufficient consideration.
- NB: The effect of **Williams v Roffey Bros & Nicholls (Contractors) Ltd.**

The forms of discharge
Rescission and variation

- No formalities required to discharge the contract.
- NB: Formalities are required where a contract is to be discharged and a new one put in place (*Morris v Baron& Co.*).

Waivers

- Occur where one party requests an alteration of the terms of the contract and the other party agrees not to insist on strict compliance with the terms of the contract.

Express provision for discharge

- The parties may agree either expressly or impliedly in their contract that it will become discharged should certain circumstances arise.

Unilateral discharge

- Occurs where one party has performed their obligations under the contract, the other party having yet to do so.

Further reading

Beatson, Burrows and Cartwright, *Anson's Law of Contract*, 30th edn (Oxford University Press, 2016)

Dugdale and Yates, 'Variation, Waiver and Estoppel – A Reappraisal' (1976) 38 *Modern Law Review* 680

Furmston, *Cheshire, Fifoot and Furmston's Law of Contract*, 16th edn (Oxford University Press, 2012)

Smith and Atiyah, *Atiyah's Introduction to the Law of Contract*, 6th edn (Oxford University Press, 2006)

Peel, Treitel *Law of Contract*, 14th edn (Sweet and Maxwell, 2015)

15

Discharge by frustration

Objectives

After reading this chapter you should be able to:

1. Understand what is meant by frustration in the discharge of a contract.
2. Know the modern development of the doctrine and understand that the modern test is based on a radical change of circumstances and be able to distinguish this from a radical change in circumstances.
3. Recognise and apply the different applications of the doctrine.
4. Identify the factors that affect the operation of the doctrine.
5. Explain the legal effects of the doctrine both at common law and under the Law Reform (Frustrated Contracts) Act 1943.

Introduction

Objective
1

It has already been seen in relation to the discharge of contracts by performance that the overriding principle is that compliance with the terms of a contract is strict. This principle, however, would be grossly unfair if a promisor becomes liable for breach of contract because they are prevented from performing their side of a bargain by the occurrence of some unforeseeable event that is beyond their control. In such circumstances the law provides the promisor with the excuse that the contract has become frustrated.

Frustration is really an expression indicating that the contract, once entered into, has subsequently become impossible to perform, as opposed to the doctrine of initial impossibility in relation to mistake. The effect of frustration being proved is dramatic and radical, in that it brings about the immediate and automatic end to the contract, releasing the parties from the need to perform their obligations under it.

Mistake in relation to contracts was discussed in Chapter 10.

Originally supervening events that were beyond the control of either party had no effect on the obligations of the parties to perform their side of the contract, as we see in the case of *Paradine v Jane* (1647) Aleyn 26. Once the doctrine began to emerge, however, such was its radical impact on the contract that the courts strove to confine it within narrow limits. This confinement of the doctrine operated at two levels. First, the courts would only allow frustration to be used as a defence to an action for breach of contract where the supervening event destroyed a fundamental assumption on which the contract was based. Second, the courts recognised that contracts themselves could provide for the consequences of the occurrence of such an event. The second point gave rise to so-called *force majeure* clauses that business people commonly began to draft into their contracts in order to restrict the effects of a frustrating event.

The development of the modern doctrine

Objective
2

Just as business people could insert in their contracts express provisions dealing with frustrating events, the courts were empowered to imply terms into contracts, as we have already seen in Chapter 7. In the nineteenth century the principles of freedom of contract and equality of bargaining power were very much in vogue, with the result that the courts were most reluctant to imply terms into contracts, though they could be persuaded to do so where the gravity of their failure to intervene would produce serious consequences. It should be recalled, however, that this intervention was not made on the basis of judicial intervention but on the fiction that they were giving effect to the unexpressed wishes or intentions of the parties.

The ability of the courts to imply terms into contracts produced the breakthrough that was needed in order to develop the modern doctrine of frustration. The case which produced this result was *Taylor v Caldwell*.

Taylor v Caldwell (1863) 3 B & S 826

In this case the defendant agreed to hire a music hall to the plaintiff. After the contract was made, but prior to the day of the first concert, a fire broke out, completely destroying the music hall. By this time the plaintiffs had made extensive arrangements with regard to the productions they intended to perform. The loss of the music hall meant that their concerts had to be cancelled, resulting in substantial financial loss to the plaintiffs. The contract contained no express provisions dealing with this eventuality so the plaintiffs sued for non-performance of the contract in order to recover their losses. The defendants pleaded the destruction of the music hall through no fault of their own as a defence.

The court upheld the defence of the defendants, deciding that the principle contained in *Paradine v Jane* was confined to positive contracts. The contract in *Taylor v Caldwell* was found not to be a positive contract, where performance was guaranteed, but one that was subject to an implied condition that the hall would continue to exist until performance was due. Thus Blackburn J stated the position to be:

> that, in contracts in which performance depends on the continued existence of a given person or thing, a condition is implied that the impossibility of performance arising from the perishing of the person or thing shall excuse the performance. In none of these cases is the promise in words other than positive, nor is there any express stipulation that the destruction of the person or thing shall excuse the performance; but that excuse is by law implied, because from the nature of the contract it is apparent that the parties contracted on the basis of the continued existence of the particular person or chattel.

From this basis the doctrine of frustration began to expand, though it always relied on the basis of an implied term because of the continued fiction of equality of bargaining power. Eventually the implied term became almost as fictitious as the principle it sought to avoid, so wide was its area of application.

The fictitious nature of the implied term was discussed in **Davis Contractors Ltd v Fareham UDC** [1956] 2 All ER 145, in which both Lord Reid and Lord Radcliffe expressed dissatisfaction with the concept. Lord Radcliffe in particular thought that it was clearly illogical to imply a term into a contract. He stated:

> there is something of a logical difficulty in seeing how the parties could even impliedly have provided for something which, *ex hypothesi*, they neither expected nor foresaw.

The falsehood of the implied term concept is clearly exposed here, since in such circumstances it would be impossible to apply that other peculiar fiction in this area – the officious bystander test – since this relies, as expressed in **Shirlaw v Southern Foundries** (1926) Ltd [1939] 2 KB 206, on the parties reacting with an 'Oh, of course' to the suggestion that a particular term be contained in the contract. If the parties could not possibly have expected or foreseen the implied term expressed in **Taylor v Caldwell**, then it stands to reason they cannot fall within the officious bystander test.

For more on the 'officious bystander' test refer to Chapter 7.

This obvious inconsistency led both Lord Reid and Lord Radcliffe to find for some other basis for a doctrine of frustration. Lord Reid expressed this basis in the following terms:

> It appears to me that frustration depends, at least in most cases, not on adding any implied term but on the true construction of the terms which are, in the contract, read in the light of the nature of the contract and of the relevant surrounding circumstances when the contract was made.

Lord Radcliffe stated this position more fully:

> So, perhaps it would be simpler to say at the outset that frustration occurs whenever the law recognises that, without default of either party, a contractual obligation has become incapable of being performed because the circumstances in which performance is called for would render it a thing radically different from that which was undertaken by the contract.

Thus both Lord Reid and Lord Radcliffe stepped outside the concept of the implied term perpetuated by **Taylor v Caldwell** and found that the modern doctrine of frustration should be based on an objective rule within the law of contract that arose independently of the intentions of the parties, as formulated in cases such as **Shirlaw v Southern Foundries Ltd**. It may, of course, still be possible to base the application of frustration on an implied term today, but here it will arise as a term implied by law, an application of which was seen in **Liverpool City Council v Irwin** [1976] 2 All ER 39 in Chapter 7, where the intentions of the parties also have no relevance. Lord Wilberforce in **National Carriers Ltd v Panalpina (Northern) Ltd** [1981] AC 675 was most reluctant to repudiate the continued existence of the implied term basis, preferring to think of it as having merged into the modern test and remaining almost dormant until the circumstances require its use.

The modern test is often expressed as a 'radical change in obligations' or a 'construction' test. The court is required to construe the contract in the light of its nature and surrounding circumstances so that the obligations of the parties can be determined. Once this has been done, the court is then able to assess whether the obligations of the parties have changed because of the subsequent supervening events.

It should be noted carefully that it is not a radical change in circumstances that triggers the operation of the doctrine of frustration but a radical change in the obligations of the parties under the terms of the contract as construed by the court. As Lord Radcliffe pointed out in the **Davis Contractors** case:

> it is not hardship or inconvenience or material loss itself which calls the principle of frustration into play. There must be as well such a change in the significance of the obligation that the thing undertaken would, if performed, be a different thing from that contracted for.

Similarly, Lord Simon, in the **National Carriers Ltd** case, stated the test to be:

> Frustration of a contract takes place when there supervenes an event (without default of either party and for which the contract makes no sufficient provision) which so significantly changes the nature (not merely the expense or onerousness) of the outstanding contractual rights and/or obligations from what the parties could reasonably have contemplated at the time of its execution that it would be unjust to hold them to the literal sense of its stipulations in the new circumstances; in such a case the law declares both parties to be discharged from further performance.

Before we see how the doctrine of frustration has been applied in various types of situation, it should be noted that the test amounts to a question of law, not fact, even though the issue of fact heavily overlays the considerations of the court.

Applications of the doctrine of frustration

Objective
3

It is not possible to discuss all the circumstances in which the doctrine of frustration applies since these are obviously innumerable, but it is possible to identify certain typical situations which cover most of those in which the doctrine has arisen.

Destruction and unavailability of the subject matter of the contract

Clearly this is the most obvious situation, an example of which has already been seen in **Taylor v Caldwell** above. The death of an individual on whom the execution of the contract depends would present another example.

A similar situation also arises where the subject, though not destroyed, ceases to be available for the purposes of the contract. To a large degree the finding of frustration here revolves around the period of unavailability. If this is only a short time, then the courts might well determine that the contract still subsists, such a finding becoming less predictable the longer the period of unavailability. So, for instance, the absence of an artiste from a show for one night because of illness would almost certainly not frustrate the contract, while an absence of several weeks would. It is easy to see here how it is important for the courts to construe the contract in the light of its nature and circumstances before deciding the issue of frustration. In situations like that in the example above, the length of the overall contract balanced against the period of illness is of major consideration by the court. A case displaying a particular problem in this respect is that of **Condor v The Barron Knights Ltd**.

Condor v The Barron Knights Ltd [1966] 1 WLR 87

A contract relating to a member of a pop group contemplated that he would be able to work seven evenings a week, should this work be available. The member fell ill and was advised to work only a limited number of nights a week. In fact he ignored this advice since he considered himself sufficiently well to work to the contract, and he did so. The court nevertheless held the contract to be frustrated because it was possible that the member's health could have broken down at any time, and therefore it was necessary to employ another musician to be available to take the regular member's place should this event occur. This was, however, impracticable since it meant that the group had to rehearse twice, in order to prepare the reserve member of the group should he be needed.

The unavailability of the subject matter of the contract does not, however, always cause a contract to be frustrated. An example of this can be seen in the case of **CTI Group Incorporated v Transclear SA, The Mary Nour** [2008] EWCA Civ 856, where the Court of Appeal held that if a supplier decided not to make unascertained goods available for shipment, thereby making performance by the seller of goods to the buyer impossible, this is not of itself sufficient to frustrate the contract. The court's decision was based on the earlier case of **Blackburn Bobbin Co. Ltd v Allen and Sons Ltd** [1918] 2 KB 467, in which there was a contract whereby the defendants contracted to sell to the claimants Finnish timber. On the outbreak of the First World War, the defendants' source of the timber was cut off. The claimants themselves were not aware that the timber was imported into the United Kingdom and that no stacks were held here. The Court of Appeal held that there was no operable frustrating event since only the seller was concerned about the source of supply. Basically, the seller took the risk of his source of supply being available to perform his contract. These decisions also tie in nicely with the concept that it is not a radical change of circumstances that triggers the doctrine of frustration but a radical change in the obligations of the parties under the terms of the contract, as already examined in **Davis Contractors Ltd v Fareham UDC**.

It should be noted, however, that in both of these cases the contracts consisted of unascertained goods. The position may not be the same if a contract had been for specific goods since in this case the contract would normally have been entered into on the common assumption of the parties that the goods would be available and that this would have been fundamental to the existence of the contract.

Non-occurrence of an event central to the contract

It may happen that while it may be physically possible to carry out the contract, the non-occurrence of an event specified in the contract, on which the contract is based, renders the contract pointless. The question that arises here is whether the non-occurrence renders the object of the contract defeated and thereby frustrated. One has to distinguish here between the situation where the specified event amounts to the object of the contract and that where it amounts merely to the motive for entering into the contract in the first place.

The distinction between object and motive is clearly seen in the so-called 'Coronation cases' of **Krell v Henry** and **Herne Bay Steamboat Co. v Hutton**.

Krell v Henry [1903] 2 KB 740

The plaintiff hired a flat to the defendant for 26 and 27 June 1902. The defendant intended to use the flat in order to watch and celebrate the coronation procession of Edward VII which would pass by the flat. No mention of this purpose was made in the contract. A prepayment of one-third of the rent was made. Due to the sudden illness of the King the coronation procession was cancelled and the defendant refused to pay the balance of the rent owing. It was held that the plaintiff could not recover these moneys since the contract had been frustrated by the cancellation of the procession. The court found that the procession and the position of the flat formed the objective of the contract which was thus frustrated and discharged as a result.

Herne Bay Steamboat Co. v Hutton [1903] 2 KB 683

The defendant hired a motor launch for 28 and 29 June 1902 for the purpose of seeing the coronation naval review of the fleet at Spithead and allowing the passengers themselves the opportunity of touring the fleet. Again the review was cancelled because of the King's illness, though the fleet remained at Spithead. It was held that the defendant was bound by the contract which had not been frustrated by the cancellation of the review. The coronation review was held not to be the object of the contract but merely the motive for the hiring of the motor launch on these dates. The court based its decision on two grounds. First, it was still possible for the tour of the fleet to take place and, second, since the defendant intended to charge the passengers for the trip it was his venture and therefore he should bear the risks inherent in the venture.

Inability to comply with specified manner of performance

In commercial contracts it is common for the contract to require a party to carry out the terms of the contract in a particular manner, and if it should become impossible to comply with that specified manner then the contract will be frustrated. A distinction is made between mandatory stipulations and those which merely express an expected manner of performance. In the latter any supervening events that occur and prevent such an expected manner of performance rarely have the effect of rendering the contract frustrated.

Thus in 1956 and 1967 the closing of the Suez Canal meant that ships had to be diverted around the Cape of Good Hope in order to reach India and the Far East. This diversion obviously meant that extra costs were incurred by the shipping companies, which therefore sought to have their contracts set aside for frustration in order that they could renegotiate their freight contracts. In a number of cases, like that of *Tsakiroglou & Co. Ltd v Noblee Thorl GmbH* [1962] AC 93 and *The Eugenia* [1964] 1 All ER 161, the courts held that the contracts were not frustrated since, while the shipowners had contemplated moving their ships through the Suez Canal when pricing their freight rates, such a manner of performance of the contract was not stipulated within the contract. The fact that their costs had increased substantially over what had been contemplated did not help the shipowners since, if we recollect the words of Lord Radcliffe in the *Davis* case, 'it is not hardship or inconvenience or material loss itself which calls the principle of frustration into play'.

Unavailability

It is clear that a delay in performing the contract caused by some supervening event may also frustrate the contract. Cases that arose out of the Gulf War between Iran and Iraq (1980–88) produce an example, where ships became trapped in the Gulf by virtue of hostilities there. Of course the degree of delay is important but in cases like those of *The Evia* [1983] 1 AC 736, *The Agathon* [1982] 2 Lloyd's Rep 211, *The Wenjiang (No. 2)* [1983] 1 Lloyd's Rep 400 and *Finelvet AG v Vinava Shipping Co. Ltd*, the ships were confined for such long periods that the contracts were found to be frustrated.

Finelvet AG v Vinava Shipping Co. Ltd [1983] 2 All ER 658

The ship was a time-chartered ship which became trapped on 22 September 1980. However, the court upheld the decision of the arbitrator to find that the contract was frustrated, not on this date, but on 24 November 1980. The reasoning was that at the earlier date expert opinion considered that the war would be quickly won by Iraq, thereby reducing the period of confinement. At the time of the later date the expert opinion had changed to that of anticipating a protracted war, which clearly resulted in the contract being frustrated. The courts thus have to balance the length of time of the charter with the temporary unavailability of the vessel caused by the frustrating event. In the case of *Pioneer Shipping Ltd v BTP*

Tioxide Ltd, The Nema [1981] 2 All ER 1030, a time charter envisaged that during a nine-month period the vessel would be able to make six or seven voyages. In fact a strike at the port where the ship was being loaded meant that the number of voyages within the contract period was reduced to two. It was held that the contract was frustrated since the degree to which the contract was capable of performance was inordinately small compared to that contracted for. Lord Wright stated the position:

> If there is a reasonable probability from the nature of the interruption that it will be of an indefinite duration, they ought to be free to turn their assets, their plant and equipment and their business operations into activities which are open to them, and to be free from commitments which are struck with sterility for an uncertain future period.

One difficulty with frustration in such instances is when can one treat the contract as discharged? The delay or unavailability of the subject matter might be for a short period or a long period, but of course one does not know which. In such a situation it is possible for the courts to wait and see in order to determine the possible length of unavailability, either as a matter of fact or as a matter of inference by reference to all the circumstances surrounding the contract and the frustrating event, as we saw in the *Finelvet* case above. Thus a variety of factors may be taken into account in determining whether unavailability amounts to a frustrating event. In *Edwinton Commercial Corporation* v *Tsaviliris Russ (Worldwide Salvage and Towage) Ltd, The Sea Angel* [2007] EWCA Civ 547 Tsaviliris had chartered the vessel from the shipowners, Edwinton in order to help in salvage operations in relation to a tanker which ran aground with a cargo of light crude oil in the approaches to Karachi. The tanker was a major pollution risk. Edwinton's ship was to operate as a shuttle tanker taking off the light crude oil so as lighten the stricken tanker. The charter was for up to 20 days. After the shuttle tanker had transported its last cargo Tsaviliris gave notice of redelivery of the ship to Edwinton, however the ship was not able to leave Karachi because of its unlawful detention by the port authorities. Tsaviliris maintained that the delay caused by the ship being unlawfully detained and the time taken to secure the ship in the Pakistani courts had caused the charter to be frustrated. Edwinton submitted that the detention of the ship was a known risk which had been assumed by Tsaviliris under the charter so that the delay was not a sufficient reason to justify frustration. The Court of Appeal held that the unlawful detention was not sufficient to amount to frustration. The court considered that the timing issue was only one of a number of factors to be considered. In particular, the contract had largely been performed so that the purpose of the contract had not been frustrated. The only consequence of the detention of the ship was a financial liability to pay for the charter of the ship for a longer purpose. The risk of detention by the port authorities arising out of a salvage situation where there was a concern about pollution was in general terms foreseeable. This general risk was foreseeable by the salvage industry and to that extent it was provided for in any event by the terms of the special compensation protection and indemnity clause which was incorporated in the charter and had been invoked by Tsaviliris. In assessing whether a frustrating event had occurred Rix LJ stated at [111 and 112]:

> In my judgment, the application of the doctrine of frustration requires a multi-factorial approach. Among the factors which have to be considered are the terms of the contract itself, its matrix or context, the parties' knowledge, expectations, assumptions and contemplations, in particular as to risk, as at the time of contract, at any rate so far as these can be ascribed mutually and objectively, and then the nature of the supervening event, and the parties' reasonable and objectively ascertainable calculations as to the possibilities of future performance in the new circumstances. Since the subject matter of the doctrine of frustration

is contract, and contracts are about the allocation of risk, and since the allocation and assumption of risk is not simply a matter of express or implied provision but may also depend on less easily defined matters such as 'the contemplation of the parties', the application of the doctrine can often be a difficult one. In such circumstances, the test of 'radically different' is important: it tells us that the doctrine is not to be lightly invoked; that mere incidence of expense or delay or onerousness is not sufficient; and that there has to be as it were a break in identity between the contract as provided for and contemplated and its performance in the new circumstances.

What the 'radically different' test, however, does not in itself tell us is that the doctrine is one of justice, as has been repeatedly affirmed on the highest authority. Ultimately the application of the test cannot safely be performed without the consequences of the decision, one way or the other, being measured against the demands of justice. Part of that calculation is the consideration that the frustration of a contract may well mean that the contractual allocation of risk is reversed. A time charter is a good example. Under such a charter, the risk of delay, subject to express provision for the cessation of hire under an off-hire clause, is absolutely on the charterer. If, however, a charter is frustrated by delay, then the risk of delay is wholly reversed: the delay now falls on the owner. If the provisions of a contract in their literal sense are to make way for the absolving effect of frustration, then that must, in my judgment, be in the interests of justice and not against those interests. Since the purpose of the doctrine is to do justice, then its application cannot be divorced from considerations of justice. Those considerations are among the most important of the factors which a tribunal has to bear in mind.

This 'multifactorial approach' has since been applied in a number of cases, such as, *Islamic Republic of Iran Shipping Lines* v *Steamship Mutual Underwriting Association (Bermuda) Ltd* [2010] EWHC 2661; *ACG Acquisition XX LLC* v *Olympic Airlines SA (in liquidation)* [2012] EWHC 1070 (Comm) (approved of at [2013] EWCA Civ 369). In the latter case Teare J considered Rix LJ's 'demands of justice' approach in *The Sea Angel* in order to determine whether the contract was frustrated or did not favour the frustration of the contract. Similarly in *Bunge SA* v *Kyla Shipping Co Ltd* [2012] EWHC 3522 (Comm) and *Meli Bank plc* v *Holbud Ltd [2013]* EWHC 1506 (Comm) also affirmed Rix LJ's multifactorial approach in *The Sea Angel*.

Supervening illegality

It occasionally happens that once a contract has been entered into, the law, quite independently, may move to the position that the performance of contracts of the type entered into is illegal. The position here was simply and cogently put by Lord Macmillan in *Denny, Mott and Dickson Ltd* v *James B Fraser & Co. Ltd* [1944] 1 All ER 678. He stated: 'It is plain that a contract to do what it has become illegal to do cannot be legally enforceable.' Thus if a contract is made to ship goods to a country and it subsequently becomes illegal to import such goods then the contract becomes frustrated.

The problem of frustration in leases

The particular problem that arises with frustration in leases is that when a tenant takes a lease over property they are acquiring an estate in land that persists even if the building rented is completely destroyed by, for instance, fire or bomb damage or is completely demolished by a heavy goods vehicle. The logic is correct since, while the layperson may think in terms of renting a house, flat, warehouse or factory, the lawyer knows that one is actually leasing the land, the rent that is paid reflecting the length of the lease, the type of property and its position and location. The result is that even if the building is completely destroyed, one still has to pay the rent *on the land* leased, regardless of the fact that it merely comprises a burnt-out shell or a hole in the ground. Evidence of this state of affairs lies in the fact that when one purchases a house, for instance, it is well established that the purchaser should take out building insurance from the time the contracts are signed and exchanged, since the risk in the property passes to them at that point. Is it possible, however, to claim that the lease has been frustrated by the occurrence of such an event?

Cricklewood Property & Investment Trust Ltd v *Leighton's Investment Trust Ltd* [1945] AC 221

In this case, a plot of land was let in 1936 to the lessees for 99 years in order that they could build shops on the property. Before the lessees could begin construction the war broke out and the government subsequently passed regulations restricting such development. The effect was that the lessees could not build the shops they had covenanted to do and they thus claimed that the lease was frustrated. The House of Lords held that the doctrine of frustration did not apply, basing their decision in terms more appropriate to unavailability, as outlined above, in that the restrictions would only delay building for a comparatively short period when balanced against the full extent of the 99-year lease. Their Lordships were of divided opinions as to whether frustration could ever apply to leases. Lord Simon and Lord Wright considered it could, but only in the rather extreme circumstance where the land is engulfed by the sea. Lord Russell and Lord Goddard considered that frustration could never apply, while Lord Porter declined to express an opinion.

The position not to allow frustration in leases is, however, more than just a little illogical since if one rents a property for a particular purpose then surely if that purpose becomes impossible the doctrine should apply. Certainly frustration does exist in the case of a contractual licence to hold land since it was fully accepted in the case of ***Krell*** v ***Henry***, where the contract to rent a room for the coronation procession was held to be frustrated when the procession was cancelled. From here the argument can be taken to the point that the law would have to make a distinction between a legal lease and an equitable lease. The latter takes effect as a contract to grant a lease under the doctrine of ***Walsh*** v ***Lonsdale*** (1882) 21 ChD 9, and it could therefore be discharged by frustration, while a legal lease could not be.

The issue relating to frustration and leases would seem to be now decided by the case of ***National Carriers Ltd*** v ***Panalpina (Northern) Ltd*** where the House of Lords decided that frustration could apply to leases. They expressed the view, however, that its occurrence would be rare and probably confined to the situation where there was a joint intention that the property was to be released for a particular purpose, and that the purpose had become impossible because of events beyond the control of the parties. Lord Wilberforce stated:

> if the argument is to have reality, it must be possible to say that frustration of leases cannot occur because in any event the tenant will have that which he bargained for, namely, the leasehold estate. Certainly this may be so in many cases . . . But there may also be cases where this is not so. A man may desire possession and use of land or buildings for, and only for, some purpose in view and mutually contemplated. Why is it an answer, when he claims that this purpose is 'frustrated' to say that he has an estate if that estate is unusable and unsaleable? In such a case the lease, or the conferring of an estate, is a subsidiary means to an end, not an aim or end of itself.

The result in the case, however, was that a lease for a warehouse which had four and a half years to run was not frustrated by a street closure order that prevented the warehouse from being used for 18 months.

Factors affecting the operation of the doctrine

 ### Self-induced frustration

Objective
4

It has been seen that the basis of frustration lies in the fact that it amounts to a supervening event that is beyond the control of the parties to the contract. It follows therefore that if the event arises out of the actions of a party to the contract then the doctrine cannot be relied on.

Maritime National Fish Ltd v Ocean Trawlers Ltd [1935] AC 524

In this leading case, the appellants chartered a trawler from the respondents. The trawler was fitted with a type of net called an 'otter trawl', the use of which was illegal without a licence from the Canadian government, both the parties being aware of this fact. The appellants had four other trawlers all fitted with the same type of net. They applied for five licences but in fact were awarded only three. They had to stipulate to which trawlers the licences applied. The appellants nominated three of their own trawlers and then claimed that their charter of the trawler belonging to the respondents was discharged for frustration on the basis that no licence was forthcoming for that vessel. It was held, by the Privy Council, that their claim would fail since they could have nominated the vessel in question to have one of the licences but had declined to do so. The result was that the appellants had control of the supervening event and therefore frustration could not be relied upon as discharging the contract. Their claim was thus rejected.

The question of choice that arose in the case above with regard to the supervening event was again considered by the Court of Appeal in *J Lauritzen AS v Wijsmuller BV*.

J Lauritzen AS v Wijsmuller BV [1990] 1 Lloyd's Rep 1

In this case the plaintiffs needed to transport a drilling rig from Japan to Rotterdam. The defendant possessed two specialist transportation systems capable of performing this task, *Super Servant One* and *Super Servant Two*. The contract was open as regards which vessel could be used, though the choice of vessel rested with the defendants. In fact, although they did not mention this to the plaintiffs at the time, the defendants intended to use *Super Servant Two* for the task and allocated other tasks to the sister ship. *Super Servant Two* sank some six months before the contract was to be performed. The defendants claimed that the contract was frustrated. The plaintiffs contested this application, stating that the contract would still have been capable of being carried out but for the decision of the defendants to allocate *Super Servant One* to other tasks. The supervening event thus lay in the hands of the defendants. The Court of Appeal held that the contract was not frustrated since the loss of a vessel to the contract was due to the actions of the defendants, even if they were neither negligent nor in breach of contract.

Where the supervening event arises because of the negligent actions of one of the parties then again frustration will not be deemed to have arisen. To take an example, if the music hall fire in *Taylor v Caldwell* had arisen because of a negligent act by the owners, then they could not have pleaded frustration and would have been liable for breach of contract. Negligent actions per se will not prevent frustration from arising since the onus of proving the existence of frustration lies on the party seeking to rely on the doctrine as a means of discharging their contractual obligations.

Frustration expressly provided for in the contract

The parties may make provision for what is to happen should a particular supervening contingency occur. These clauses are the so-called *force majeure* clauses mentioned earlier. If the clause, as a matter of construction, deals with the event that has occurred, then the courts will not deem that the contract has been frustrated. The clause must be capable of dealing with any form that the contingency may take, no matter how serious, otherwise it will not prevent the operation of the doctrine of frustration. In *Jackson v Union Marine Insurance Co. Ltd* (1874) LR 10 CP 125, a ship was chartered to sail 'with all possible despatch' from Liverpool to Newport to pick up a cargo and then to proceed to San Francisco 'dangers and accidents of navigation excepted'. The ship ran aground one day out from Liverpool. The repairs took eight months to complete, during which time the charterers repudiated the contract. It was held that despite the *force majeure* clause the contract was still frustrated. Undoubtedly the clause took account of the contingency that had occurred but it was not designed to cover damages and delay of such an extensive nature. It was considered that if the contract had been upheld and a voyage to San Francisco had taken place the venture would have been entirely different commercially.

The legal effects of the doctrine of frustration

The general rule

Objective 5

See Chapter 13 for discharge by breach.

Where there is a breach of contract, the injured party has to elect whether to treat the contract as discharged by the breach or not. Such discretion does not arise in the case of discharge by frustration since, as was pointed out by the House of Lords in *Hirji Mulji v Cheong Yue Steamship Co.* [1926] AC 497, the effect of frustration is to bring about the automatic termination of all obligations incurred under the contract. In turn the effect of automatic dissolution of the contract at common law is to produce fundamental and often harsh repercussions on the parties to the contract.

The effect of frustration at common law

The effect of frustration at common law was that from the date of the supervening event the parties were released from all future contractual obligations. Any obligations that had already arisen under the contract had to be performed. This position is well illustrated by the case of *Chandler v Webster*.

Chandler v Webster [1904] 1 KB 493

In this case the defendant agreed to let a room to the plaintiff for £141 for the purpose of viewing the coronation procession. The cost of the hire was payable immediately but in fact the plaintiff paid only £100 in advance. Before he paid the balance the procession was cancelled and the contract frustrated as a result. It was held that the plaintiff could not recover the £100 but additionally he was also liable to pay the balance since the obligation to pay this had already accrued prior to the supervening event. Counsel argued that he could recover the £100 in quasi-contract (see Chapter 18) in that there had been a total failure of consideration. The Court of Appeal, however, held that this line of argument could not be sustained since the effect of frustration was not to discharge the contract *ab initio* but only from the time of the supervening event, and there was no *total* failure of consideration.

It is useful to compare the effects of frustration in the **Chandler** case with the case of **Krell v Henry** since in the latter case the obligation to pay had not accrued at the time of the supervening event. The result here was that the defendant hirer of the room was not obliged to pay anything – all his future obligations ceased to exist at the time of cancellation.

The decision in the **Chandler** case that the 'loss lies where it falls' clearly could produce extremely harsh consequences for the parties. The position was no less satisfactory for the reason that the effects on the parties were completely unpredictable and it was largely a matter of luck as to whether one walked away from the situation unscathed or not. The decision was, however, overruled by the House of Lords in **Fibrosa Spolka Akcyjna v Fairbairn Lawson Combe Barbour Ltd**.

Fibrosa Spolka Akcyjna v Fairbairn Lawson Combe Barbour Ltd [1943] AC 32

In this case the appellants ordered some machinery from the respondents for delivery to their factory in Poland, paying £1,000 in advance by virtue of the terms of the contract. In 1939 Germany invaded Poland and the contract became frustrated. The London agent for the appellants asked for the return of their £1,000 but the respondents refused on the basis that a substantial amount of time and money had already been expended on the order.

Clearly on the basis of the **Chandler** case the £1,000 would have been irrecoverable, but the House of Lords allowed the claim, which of necessity was based in quasi-contract since the contract had ceased to exist by virtue of the supervening event. The House of Lords decided that there had been a total failure of consideration, overruling the **Chandler** decision. The appellants had not received anything under the contract they had bargained for and could thus recover the moneys they had paid.

In fact the decision is really no less unsatisfactory than that of the **Chandler** case, perhaps even more so in some circumstances. Parties in the position of the respondents could, just as in the case itself, have incurred considerable expenditure in preparing the subject matter of the contract only to find that they would receive no recompense for the time and money put into fulfilling the order. To add insult to injury they might also be left with a product that was so specialised as to be unsaleable to anyone else. Such a sale would have provided them with some degree of return on the energy expended on the contract. Indeed it is very likely because of these last two points that the deposit was charged in the first place so as to underwrite the expenses to be incurred in preparing the subject matter of the contract. In truth the House of Lords had merely shifted the burden of the effects of frustration from one party to the other. The continued unsatisfactory nature of the law led to the passing of the Law Reform (Frustrated Contracts) Act 1943.

Law Reform (Frustrated Contracts) Act 1943

The operation of this Act is confined to circumstances where a contract is frustrated, although it has no effect on the decision as to whether the contract has been frustrated or not but merely deals with the consequences of frustration. The Act seeks to regulate, first, the recovery of moneys paid or payable under the contract; second, compensation payable for expenses incurred in the performance of the contract; third, the financial readjustment of the parties where one has received a valuable benefit under the contract in the absence of any prepayment.

Recovery of money paid

The position here is enacted by s 1(2) as follows:

> All sums paid or payable to any party in pursuance of the contract before the time when the parties were so discharged (in this Act referred to as 'the time of discharge') shall, in the case of sums so paid, be recoverable from him as money received by him for the use of the party by whom the sums were paid, and, in the case of sums payable, cease to be so payable.
>
> Provided that, if the party to whom the sums were so paid or so payable incurred expenses before the time of discharge in, or for the purpose of, the performance of the contract, the court may, if it considers it just to do so having regard to all the circumstances of the case, allow him to retain or, as the case may be, recover the whole or any part of the sums so paid or payable, not being an amount in excess of the expenses so incurred.

Two effects are immediately discernible from the provision. First, the decision in *Fibrosa* is confirmed in that moneys paid are recoverable despite the absence of a total failure of consideration; at the same time any moneys that are owed cease to be payable. Second, the provision regulates the position of the payee, that is, the respondents in the *Fibrosa* case, since the court now has a discretionary power to award them a sum in respect of any expenses incurred by the payee in the performance of the contract prior to the discharge of the contract. It should be noted that the payee will not get their expenses but only what the court considers to be a just sum having regard to the circumstances of the case, and in any event this will be no more than their actual expenses. An application of these principles can be seen in *Gamerco SA v ICM/Fair Warning (Agency) Ltd* [1995] 1 WLR 1226, where it was stated that where a contract is frustrated a claimant is entitled to recover payments made in advance by virtue of s 1(2), although the proviso gives the court a wide discretion to make a deduction to offset the defendant's expenses incurred prior to the time of discharge, or for the performance of the contract. It was stated that the court is not obliged to incline towards total retention by a defendant of the sums paid, nor is the court obliged to consider that the loss be equally divided between the parties.

Financial readjustment where a valuable benefit is conferred

The position here is governed by s 1(3) as follows:

> Where any party to the contract has, by reason of anything done by any other party thereto in, or for the purpose of, the performance of the contract, obtained a valuable benefit (other than a payment of money to which the last foregoing subsection applies) before the time of discharge, there shall be recoverable from him by the said other party such sum (if any), not exceeding the value of the said benefit to the party obtaining it, as the court considers just, having regard to all the circumstances of the case and, in particular –

(a) the amount of any expenses incurred before the time of discharge by the benefited party in, or for the purpose of, the performance of the contract, including any sums paid or payable by him to any other party in pursuance of the contract and retained or recoverable by that party under the last foregoing subsection, and

(b) the effect, in relation to the said benefit, of the circumstances giving rise to the frustration of the contract.

BP Exploration Co. (Libya) Ltd v Hunt (No. 2) [1979] 1 WLR 783 (decision affirmed by the House of Lords [1983] 2 AC 352)

This is the leading case on the operation of s 1(3). The facts of the case were that there was a contract between BP and Hunt for the exploration and, ultimately, the exploitation of an oil concession in Libya that was held by Hunt. BP's part of the contract was that they were to get a half-share in the concession, but that they were to provide the finance and conduct the exploration work, though their expenses would be recoverable at a rate of three-eighths of Hunt's share should oil be found until 125 per cent of their initial expenses had been recouped. In fact a large oil field was discovered and in 1967, it came on stream. In 1971, Libya expropriated Hunt's concession with the result that the contract between BP and Hunt became frustrated. At this point BP had recovered only a proportion of their expenses and thus brought an action based on s 1(3) of the 1943 Act.

Robert Goff J decided that in the method of assessing the claim under s 1(3) regard had to be paid, first, to identifying and valuing any benefit obtained and, second, to assessing what would be a just sum. In accordance with s 1(3) this sum could not exceed the valuation placed on the valuable benefit. Goff J stated that the valuable benefit should not be assessed on what had been paid out by BP in the exploration work but on the benefit received by Hunt. Hunt's benefit amounted to the value by which his concession had been enhanced but this had to be reduced, because of the effect of s 1(3)(b), by the diminution to the value of the concession caused by the expropriation. On this basis the valuable benefit obtained by Hunt amounted to the value of the oil he had received plus the amount of compensation awarded to him by the Libyan government for the expropriation. The court, however, took into account that half of this benefit was attributable to BP's efforts, and thus the valuable benefit obtained by Hunt amounted to $85 million.

Turning to the question of assessing what would be a just sum, Goff J decided that this should be calculated on the basis of what BP had actually spent on developing the concession, namely, $87 million, plus any moneys paid to Hunt, that is, $10 million, less expenses actually recovered, that is, $62 million. On this basis the just sum was $35 million and it was this figure that was recoverable by BP in full, since it did not exceed the figure for the assessment of the valuable benefit, which by s 1(3) would otherwise have restricted the amount recoverable for the just sum.

That the provision goes some way towards correcting the inequities that existed prior to the Act cannot be doubted, but the Act itself contains defects. The subsection allows recovery only where a party has received a valuable benefit which has been obtained 'before the time of discharge'. Thus, if the expropriation had taken place prior to any financial reward arising from the concession, for instance, in the form of profits from oil, BP could not have recovered anything under s 1(3) since there would have been no valuable benefit. That this is the effect of s 1(3) is not open to doubt, but very serious flaws appear in Goff J's reasoning where a party receives a valuable benefit but this is destroyed by the frustrating event. Such a situation did not arise in the *BP v Hunt* case since the valuable benefit had already accrued to Hunt at the time of the expropriation. If, however, one takes a case such as *Appleby v Myers* (1867) LR 2 CP 651 the defect becomes quickly apparent. In this case the plaintiffs had contracted to install machinery in the defendant's factory, and the defendant was to pay when the installation was complete. When some of the machinery had been installed a fire broke out, completely destroying the factory and the machinery. It was held that the contract had been frustrated. If the plaintiffs attempted to sue under s 1(2) they would receive nothing since no money was payable at the time of the frustrating event and all that they could hope to recover would be an amount for expenses.

If the plaintiff had attempted to claim under s 1(3) in respect of a valuable benefit being obtained by the defendant, he would be met by the argument that the frustrating event had destroyed this and therefore no valuable benefit accrued to the defendant in respect of which a just sum may have been recoverable in the discretion of the court. This is the position adopted by Goff J in his interpretation of s 1(3)(b). His view was that if 'the effect . . . of the circumstances giving rise to frustration of the contract' (s 1(3)(b)) was to destroy the valuable benefit then nothing could be recovered for this. This interpretation has been widely criticised both by academic lawyers in the United Kingdom and judicially in a number of Commonwealth decisions and it is certainly wrong. A cursory glance at s 1(3) indicates that the court has to assess the level of the valuable benefit before the frustrating event, that is, 'where any party . . . obtained a valuable benefit . . . before the time of the discharge'. Furthermore, s 1(3)(b) itself clearly indicates that the valuable benefit must first be assessed and then the court must consider the effect of the frustrating event, that is, 'the effect, in relation to the said benefit, of the circumstances giving rise to frustration'. The interpretation given by Goff J here is unnecessarily restrictive and it may be that his approach has been to regard the Act not as an attempt to apportion losses but as an attempt to prevent undue enrichment – and this was certainly not the original aim of the Act. Unfortunately the decision has been affirmed by the House of Lords, subject to one or two minor adjustments, and thus one will have to wait until their Lordships have the opportunity of reviewing the position in which *BP* v *Hunt* has placed the law.

A summary of the impact of the Law Reform (Frustrated Contracts) Act 1943

Effects of section 1(2)		
Money paid	⟶	Recoverable
Money payable	⟶	Ceases to be payable
Expenses incurred in the performance of the contract may be recovered at the discretion of the Court		
Effects of section 1(3)		
Any benefits obtained may have to be paid for – the court has discretion to award a 'just sum'. In the exercise of discretion the court will consider: (a) Whether benefited party has incurred expenditure to obtain benefit. (b) Whether the benefit has been reduced by the frustrating event.		
BP Exploration Co. (Libya) Ltd v *Hunt (No. 2)* [1979] 1 WLR 783; [1983] 2 AC 352		

Contracts falling outside the Act

Certain contracts fall outside the ambit of the Act. Thus s 2(3) allows the parties to contract out of its provisions where they have made express provisions regarding the effect of a frustrating event on the contract.

By virtue of s 2(4) the Act does not apply to those parts of a severable contract that have been wholly performed prior to the frustrating event. For example, if there is a contract for the installation of two machines, payment being effected when each machine is installed, and a fire breaks out that completely destroys the factory, the Act will not apply in respect of the machine that is installed and paid for. In respect of the second, partially installed machine the Act will apply and the plaintiff may succeed if the other party receives a valuable benefit, if any, in recovering a just sum for that benefit in the discretion of the court.

By s 2(5)(a) and (b) the provisions of the Act do not apply to any charterparty (except a time charterparty), carriage of goods by sea or any contract of insurance. The apparent reason for these exceptions is that they are largely concerned with the apportionment of risk themselves and should therefore lie outside the Act.

By s 2(5)(c), contracts falling within s 7 of the Sale of Goods Act 1893 (now s 7 of the Sale of Goods Act 1979), which renders void any agreement to sell specific goods whereby, without any fault on the part of the seller or buyer, the goods perish before the risks pass to the buyer, are excluded from the provisions of the 1943 Act. This exclusion is more general and does not relate only to s 7 since s 2(5)(c) also states that 'any other contract for the sale, or for the sale and delivery, of specific goods, whereby the contract is frustrated by reason of the fact that the goods have perished' is also excluded.

Summary

- Frustration is really an expression indicating that the contract, once entered into, has subsequently become impossible to perform.
- The doctrine operated at two levels:
  - the courts would only allow frustration to be used as a defence;
  - the courts recognised that contracts themselves could provide for the consequences of the occurrence of such an event (*force majeure* clauses).

The development of the modern doctrine

- Historically the courts imply terms developing the modern doctrine of frustration, e.g. destruction of a music hall (*Taylor v Caldwell*).
- The fictitious nature of the implied term was discussed in *Davis Contractors Ltd v Fareham UDC*. NB: The officious bystander test (*Shirlaw v Southern Foundries (1926) Ltd*).
- The test is a question of law, not fact, even though the issue of fact heavily overlays the considerations of the court.

Applications of the doctrine of frustration

- Destruction and unavailability of the subject matter of the contract
- Non-occurrence of an event central to the contract
- Inability to comply with specified manner of performance
- Unavailability
- Supervening illegality
- The problem of frustration in leases
- Equitable lease takes effect as a contract to grant a lease under the doctrine of *Walsh v Lonsdale* and it could therefore be discharged by frustration.

Factors affecting the operation of the doctrine
Self-induced frustration

- Frustration does not apply to an event arising out of the actions of one party to the contract.
- Negligent actions of a party will not give rise to frustration.

Frustration expressly provided for in the contract

- The parties may make provision for what is to happen should a particular supervening contingency occur (*force majeure* clauses).
- The clause must be capable of dealing with any form that the contingency may take, no matter how serious, otherwise it will not prevent the operation of the doctrine of frustration (*Jackson v Union Marine Insurance Co. Ltd*).

The legal effects of frustration

- Frustration will terminate a contract automatically (***Hirji Mulji v Cheong Yue Steamship Co.***).

The effect of frustration at common law

- From the date of the supervening event the parties are released from all future contractual obligations.
- Any obligations that had already arisen under the contract had to be performed and traditionally any loss lies where it falls (***Chandler v Webster***).
- NB: ***Fibrosa Spolka Akcyjna v Fairbairn Lawson Combe Barbour Ltd*** overruled ***Chandler***, allowing the recovery of moneys where there had been a total failure of consideration.

Law Reform (Frustrated Contracts) Act 1943

- The Act seeks to regulate:

  - recovery of moneys paid or payable under the contract (s 1(2));
  - compensation payable for expenses incurred in the performance of the contract (s 1(2));
  - financial readjustment of the parties where one has received a valuable benefit under the contract in the absence of any prepayment (s 1(3) – *BP v Hunt*).

Further reading

Battersby, 'Frustration: A Limited Future' (1990) 134 *Solicitors Journal* 354

Beatson, Burrows and Cartwright, *Anson's Law of Contract*, 30th edn (Oxford University Press, 2016)

Clark, 'Restitution and the Law Reform (Frustrated Contracts) Act 1943' (1996) *Lloyd's Maritime and Commercial Law Quarterly* 170

Furmston, *Cheshire, Fifoot and Furmston's Law of Contract*, 16th edn (Oxford University Press, 2012)

Hall, 'Frustration and the Question of Foresight' (1984) 4 *Legal Studies* 300

Haycroft and Waksman, 'Frustration and Restitution' (1984) *Journal of Business Law* 207

McKendrick, 'Self-Induced Frustration and *Force Majeure* Clauses' (1989) *Lloyd's Maritime and Commercial Law Quarterly* 3

Smith and Atiyah, *Atiyah's Introduction to the Law of Contract*, 6th edn (Oxford University Press, 2006)

Swanton, 'The Concept of Self-Induced Frustration' (1990) 2 *Journal of Contract Law* 206

Peel, Treitel *Law of Contract*, 14th edn (Sweet and Maxwell, 2015)

Treitel, *Frustration and Force Majeure*, 3rd edn (Sweet and Maxwell, 2014)

Part 5

Remedies for breach of contract

16

The common law remedy of damages

Objectives

After reading this chapter you should be able to:

1. Understand the basis on which damages for breach of contract are awarded, the difference between expectation loss and reliance loss and what is meant by restitutionary loss and actions for an agreed sum.

2. Know the difference between value and cost of cure in assessing damages as a remedy.

3. Understand how damages are assessed by reference to the market.

4. Understand the question of time in assessing an award of damages.

5. Understand the effect of tax on the assessment of damages.

6. Know and understand the limitations that apply to the availability of damages, particularly with regard to causation and the rule regarding remoteness of damages.

7. Know and understand the factors that influence the quantum of damages and be able to explain how and to what extent loss for speculative damages and non-pecuniary losses are recoverable.

Introduction

So far in our analysis of the doctrines, principles and rules that bind the law of contract we have talked in terms of enforcing contracts. In fact the notion of enforcement is somewhat erroneous since at common law the only remedy is damages or compensation for the breach of contract. Of course, the result may be the same in monetary terms but this can be far removed from the notion of forcing compliance with the terms of the contract. It is true that a party to a contract can enforce compliance via decrees of specific performance and injunctions, but these are equitable remedies available only at the discretion of the court, while damages at common law are available as of right. Nor are damages limited to circumstances where a party to the contract suffers loss because of the breach. As we have already seen, liability in breach of contract is strict and a party may claim damages, albeit only nominal damages, despite the fact that they have suffered no loss.

For more on equitable remedies refer to Chapter 17.

While a person may recover damages even where they have suffered no loss, it has to be said that the majority of claims will be in circumstances where substantial loss has been suffered. The injured party cannot recover for all loss since a causal link must be shown to exist between the loss suffered and the breach of contract. Even where this causal link exists an individual will not in any event be compelled to pay for all loss, since the losses must not be 'too remote' from the consequences of the breach. The limitations on the availability of damages for breach of contract, together with **causation** and remoteness, will form the second part of the analysis of the common law remedy of damages. The third part of this analysis will be concerned with how the damages are measured in terms of quantum (amount). Initially, however, we need to make an assessment of the basis on which the courts award damages for breach.

Assessment of the basis on which damages are awarded

General principles

Objective 1

As has been indicated already, the basis of an award of damages is to compensate the injured party for the breach of contract. It is for the innocent party to prove his loss from the breach and that notwithstanding the breach he would have been able to carry his part of the contract: *Flame SA* v *Glory Wealth Shipping PTE Ltd* [2013] EWHC 3153 (Comm). The underlying and fundamental principle here, as stated in **Robinson v Harman** (1848) 1 Ex 855, is to place the injured party in the same position they would have been in had the contract been carried out, in so far as money is able to do this. The injured party is thus claiming damages for the gains they could have reasonably expected from the execution of the contract. They are thus claiming for loss of bargain or loss of profits. Such damages are often referred to as an '**expectation loss**'.

Alternatively the injured party may decide not to claim for loss of bargain/loss of profits but for the expenses incurred because of a reliance on the contract being performed. This is often referred to as a '**reliance loss**'. The circumstances in which a party claims reliance loss may arise where the profits that they hope will materialise from the contract are too speculative or uncertain. In such circumstances the injured party may find it simpler and safer to claim any expenses incurred in performance of the contract. An example of such an instance can be seen in the following case.

Anglia Television Ltd v *Reed* [1972] 1 QB 60

The defendant, an actor, had entered into a contract with the plaintiffs to produce a film. At the last moment the defendant withdrew from the contract with the result that the plaintiffs had to abandon the whole project. They decided not to sue for expectation losses since these clearly would be purely speculative, but for loss of expenses, or reliance losses, in respect of moneys expended hiring other actors, finding locations and engaging scriptwriters. The court allowed the claim for these items of expenditure.

The *Anglia Television* case, as affirmed in **Omak Maritime Ltd v Mamola Challenger Shipping Co** [2010] EWHC 2026 (Comm), is also authority for the fact that the courts will not allow the injured party to claim for both expectation and reliance loss. Wasted expenditure cannot be recovered as damages for breach of contract where an award of damages on that basis would put the claimant in a better position than he would have been in had the contract been performed.

Thus Lord Denning MR stated:

> It seems to me that a plaintiff in such a case as this has an election: he can either claim for his loss of profits; or for wasted expenditure. But he must elect between them. He cannot claim both. If he has not suffered any loss of profits – or if he cannot prove what his profits would have been – he can claim in the alternative the expenditure which has been thrown away, that is, wasted, by reason of the breach. That is shown by *Cullinane* v *British 'Rema' Manufacturing Co. Ltd.*

The '*Rema*' case [1954] 1 QB 292, indicates that to claim both reliance loss and expectation would in effect be to compensate the claimant twice for the same loss. However, this requires qualification since such a state of affairs only exists if the expectation loss consists of gross profits which will include expenditure on the contract. There would seem to be no objection to a claimant claiming reliance loss and expectation loss where the latter consists of a claim for net profits. Unfortunately Lord Denning did not clarify this situation. The position has since been clarified in *Western Web Offset Printers Ltd* v *Independent Media Ltd*.

Western Web Offset Printers Ltd v *Independent Media Ltd* (1995) *The Times*, 10 October

The defendant wrongfully repudiated a contract under which the plaintiff was to print 48 issues of a weekly newspaper. The only issue in the case arose as to the correct measure of damages. The plaintiff claimed £–176,903 as representing the gross profit having deducted direct expenses such as paper and ink. It was argued by the defendant that the plaintiff was only entitled to net profit deducting, in addition to direct expenses, appropriate proportions of the plaintiff's labour costs and overheads. This produced a total of £38,245. The judge at first instance accepted the defendant's calculations and the plaintiff appealed.

The Court of Appeal allowed the plaintiff's appeal. It stated that the correct approach was that the loss of bargain principle should be applied. The question to be asked was, 'What loss had been caused to the plaintiff by the breach of contract?' It was noted by the court that the plaintiff had been unable to find replacement work for the loss of the contract and had thus not been able to mitigate his loss. This failure, however, was not his own fault but a result of the economic recession. The court decided that the plaintiff's 'profit and expenditure account was depreciated by the loss, not just of the notional net profit, but the availability of £176,903 to help defray its existing and inevitable overheads'. The plaintiff was therefore entitled to damages amounting to £176,903.

Whilst the claimant generally can choose whether to claim expectation loss or reliance loss, this choice may nevertheless be imposed by the court in certain situations. For instance, the courts look very warily on claims for reliance loss where the claimant has made a 'bad bargain', in that there would normally have been no profits made from the contract – because the return on the contract might not even have covered the expenses incurred, either wholly or partly.

Thus in *C & P Haulage* v *Middleton* [1983] 3 All ER 94 the court held that in the circumstances of this case there would be no recovery for reliance losses. It would clearly be wrong, though, to prevent a person from recovering for reliance loss simply on the basis that no profits were made on the contract. The court stated that reliance loss could be recovered provided that the losses claimed arose from the breach of contract and that it was anticipated that the return on the contract would have meant, under normal circumstances, that the expenditure on the contract would have been recovered. On the other hand, if it is shown that the wasted expenditure would have arisen whether or not the contract had been broken, then the courts will disallow the claim for those losses.

In *C & P Haulage* v *Middleton* [1983] 3 All ER 94 Ackner LJ, having also referred to *Cullinane* v *British Rema* and *Anglia Television* v *Reed*, said at p 1467:

> It is not the function of the courts where there is a breach of contract knowingly, as this would be the case, to put a plaintiff in a better financial position than if the contract had been properly performed.

Fox LJ agreed and noted at p 1468:

> ... while it is true that the expenditure could in a sense be said to be wasted in consequence of the breach of contract, it was equally likely to be wasted if there had been no breach, because the plaintiffs ... could terminate the licence at quite short notice. A high risk of waste was from the very first inherent in the nature of the contract itself, breach or no breach. The reality of the matter is that the waste resulted from what was, on the defendant's side, a very unsatisfactory and dangerous bargain.

As seen earlier, principles can also be seen in *Omak Maritime Ltd* v *Mamola Challenger Shipping Co.* [2010] EWHC 2026 (Comm).

Omak Maritime Ltd v *Mamola Challenger Shipping Co.* [2010] EWHC 2026 (Comm).

The charterer of a ship ('C') agreed to charter the shipowner's ('S') vessel for five years. Under the charterparty S was required to make modifications to the vessel prior to delivery. S incurred expenses in preparing the vessel for the necessary modifications to be made. It then became doubtful that C would perform the charter and eventually S treated C's conduct as a repudiatory breach of contract. The result of this is that the preparatory expenses were wasted and provided S with no residual benefit. S claimed as damages the expenses it had incurred in preparing the vessel for the charterparty. The market rate of hire was higher than the charterparty rate. The arbitrators held that since S could trade the vessel at the higher market rate it had earned or would earn under the charterparty the excess would be greater than the amount of the wasted expenditure. The arbitrators nevertheless awarded S damages for wasted expenditure. C appealed claiming that this decision was wrong in law since S had in fact suffered no loss by reason of C's breach because the market rate of hire was higher than the charter rate. S therefore had more than recuperated the losses it claimed for the breach of the charterparty. C therefore asserted that to award S more than nominal damages would be to breach the compensation principle.

Teare J reaffirmed the principles set out in the *Rema* and *Anglia Television* cases that it was permissible for a claimant to seek damages on the reliance basis rather than upon the expectancy basis in that a claimant could frame his damages claim by reference to the expenses incurred in reliance on the contract being performed instead of his expected profit. He stated that normally where damages are claimed for breach of contract on an expectancy basis both expected profits and necessary expenses are taken into account. Where, however, a claimant, such as S, had abandoned a claim for expectation losses in favour of a claim for reliance losses for expenses, he was not entitled to such damages as would place him in a better position than he would have been in had the contract been performed. Referring to *C&P Haulage* v *Middleton* [1983] 1 WLR 1461 Teare J stated that this principle was a fundamental one and provided 'a rational and sensible explanation for the view that the expectation loss principle underpinned the award of damages in wasted expenditure cases'. S's claim for loss of expenditure was based on an expectation that the charterparty would be performed and therefore it was appropriate to have regard to the position of S had the contract been performed.

Teare J stated that if it was possible for a claimant to recover the expenses he had incurred in the expectation of the contract being performed and no regard was paid to the claimant's position had the contract been performed, then the defendant was effectively underwriting the claimant's decision to enter into the contract in the first place. Thus if the claimant had made a 'bad bargain' in that his expenses exceeded his gross profit it was clearly inappropriate for the defendant to have to pay for the claimant's loss of expenses because his breach had not caused that loss. Teare J allowing the defendant's appeal stated that a claimant's expenditure is only recoverable where the likely gross profit would at least cover that expenditure.

The burden was on the defendant to show that the likely profits would not at least equal the claimant's expenditure, *CCC Films (London) Ltd* v *Impact Quadrant Films Ltd* [1985] QB 16 considered. The arbitrators' error was to regard a claim for wasted expenses and a claim for loss of profits as two separate and independent claims which could not be mixed. But the weight of authority clearly showed that both claims were illustrations of, and governed by, the fundamental principle in *Robinson* v *Harman*, which required the court to compare the claimant's position with what it would have been had the contract been performed.

The burden of proof in relation to the last matter is important since it was stated in *CCC Films (London) Ltd* v *Impact Quadrant Films Ltd* [1984] 3 All ER 298, affirmed in *Omak Maritime Ltd* v *Mamola Challenger Shipping Co* [2010] EWHC 2026 (Comm) that the onus of proof is not on the claimant to show that their reliance losses would be at least as much as their expected profits. Such a burden of proof would be almost impossible to sustain. The onus is on the defendant to show that the claimant would not have recovered their wasted expenditure even if the terms of the contract had been fully complied with, that is the burden is on the defendant to prove that the claimant had made a bad bargain and thus avoid the claimant's claim for loss of expenditure.

An example of a defendant being unable to discharge this burden of proof can be seen in *Grange* v *Quinn* [2013] EWCA Civ 24. In this case the Court of Appeal considered an appeal by Grange ('G') against an award of damages in her action for breach of contract against the Quinns ('Q') who had been found to have wrongly evicted G from her business premises after six months and ten days of a six-year lease. When the lease was executed G had paid Q a £9,950 premium for the goodwill of a business that they had carried on at the premises. After the eviction, G brought a claim for loss of profits. An expert prepared a report on the amount of profits which was unfavourable to G. She therefore abandoned her claim for loss of profits and sought instead to recover the premium she had paid. At first instance the report was not challenged by G, however, the judge found that the goodwill had no value and that in any event even if the contract had been fulfilled G would not have recovered the amount of the premium. The judge therefore awarded G nominal damages of £300. G argued that she should have been awarded the full amount of the premium, or the full amount apportioned to take into account the time she had actually spent in the premises.

The Court of Appeal, with Arden LJ dissenting, allowed G's appeal. Gloster J considered that the court in a wasted expenditure claim had to have regard as to whether a claimant might wrongly recover more than he would have had the contract been performed. Q as defendants would therefore have to demonstrate, in order to discharge the evidential burden, that G would not have recouped her wasted expenditure from the gross returns that would have been generated from the business had the contract been performed.

The evidence and the expert report did not establish that G would not have recovered the premium paid either from the gross returns from the business or from an assignment and sale of the lease and business. The report had not been produced to answer that question but instead to assess the loss of profits and the value of the business. In fact, the report contained some factual errors and taking these into account the estimated profits would have been more than sufficient for the premium to be amortised over the period of the lease and leave a surplus. There was thus no basis for the judge at first instance finding that G would never have got back her money. The Court of Appeal considered that Q had failed to establish on the balance of probabilities that G would not have recovered her wasted expenditure from the gross profits generated from the business. Thus Jackson LJ and Gloster J awarded G damages based on the purchase price of £9,950 less £871 being the benefit that G had received before the lawful eviction.

Arden LJ provided a dissenting judgement and considered that G had no right to the return of the premium. She distinguished the payment of the premium from any other expenditure which a victim of a breach of contract incurs in anticipation of enjoying the benefits of the contract i.e. the lease. The premium was paid in consideration of goodwill and the execution of the lease. The premium therefore was a cost incurred in entering into the contract and as a loss it did not emanate from the contract itself. She stated that the premium could only be recovered if it constituted wasted expenditure i.e. expenditure lost as a result of the terms of the lease and in this regard there was no loss. Expenditure lost as a result of the terms of the bargain or of adverse trading was not recoverable, and that the judge at first instance had been entitled to hold that Q had shown that the expenditure had been lost because of unprofitable trading.

The burden of proof incumbent on a defendant where a claimant makes a claim for loss of expenditure is clearly one to the advantage of the claimant. If the defendant is unable to adduce evidence to this effect then the assumption must be that the overall contract must be a good bargain, as stated by Leggatt J in *Yam Seng Pte Ltd v International trade Corp Ltd* [2013] EWHC 111 (QB).

A second situation where a claimant will be prevented from exercising the choice of expectation or reliance loss arises where the court itself considers that the claim for expectation loss is too speculative. An example of such a move by the courts occurred in *McRae v Commonwealth Disposals Commission* (1951) 84 CLR 377, where the court considered that the claim for loss of profits was incapable of calculation since there was nothing in the contract to indicate the size of the tanker in question nor the approximate quantity of oil on board. The court decided that only a claim for reliance loss would be entertained.

Restitutionary loss

It is worth noting at this point that so far we have been concerned with compensation for loss of bargain or expenses incurred. However, it is also possible to claim for the recovery of a benefit received by the defendant from the unperformed contract. Such claims are based in restitution. Claims in restitution are conceptually different from those for damages for breach of contract since the aim is to place both the parties in the same position that they were in *before* the contract had been entered into, that is, as if the contract had not been made. It should be noted that restitution is not the same as claims for reliance loss either since, while the intention in the latter is to compensate for losses sustained before the contract was entered into, it is only intended to return the claimant to the pre-contract

Claims under restitution are discussed more fully under quasi-contracts in Chapter 18.

position and not the defendant, and the latter may be left in a significantly worse position than before. Restitution, therefore, does not amount to compensation at all but a method of returning both parties to the pre-contract status quo so as to prevent a party from being unjustly enriched from the breach. In other words, the damages are used here to prevent a defendant from benefiting from the breach by making a profit. The defendant therefore will be required to '*account for profits*' to the claimant.

By now it can be seen that damages are not intended to be punitive in nature, which is to penalise a guilty defendant for any gains they may have received by way of the breach of contract. There is no concept in English law of assessing the mental state of the defendant so that compensation is payable for a deliberate breach of contract. Traditionally therefore the innocent party can recover only their actual losses and if a defendant made a profit from the breach the claimant would not be able to recover such profits. This traditional position can be seen in the following case.

Surrey County Council v *Bredero Homes Ltd* [1993] 3 All ER 705

In this case, the council had sold land to the defendant property developer. The contract required the developer to develop the land on the terms of the planning permission to build 72 houses. Once the transaction had been completed the developer obtained new planning permission that allowed the defendant to build an additional five houses on the site. This was a deliberate and calculated breach of the contract of sale to develop the site only in accordance with the terms of the original planning permission granted by the council.

The council sued for breach of contract, claiming damages for the breach. The amount of the damages claimed was the sum the council would have required the developer to pay in order to be released from the condition in the contract. It was held that the council could recover only nominal damages since it had not sustained any losses from the breach of the contract. The fact that the defendants themselves made extra profits from their deliberate breach of contract was of no consequence.

This traditional position was criticised by the Law Commission in its Consultation Paper No. 132, *Aggravated, Exemplary and Restitutionary Damages*, 1993, where it suggested that damages should be available if a defendant obtains a benefit from some deliberate wrongdoing capable of being restrained by way of injunction. Steyn LJ in **Bredero Homes** considered this to be completely unsatisfactory since injunctions were 'wholly different' from an award of damages and were discretionary in nature, while damages are available as of right for breach of contract. It is nevertheless argued that restitutionary damages calculated by reference to the contract breaker's profit would go a long way towards preventing deliberate breaches of contract.

Certainly this was a factor in the Court of Appeal awarding an order of specific performance in *Co-operative Insurance Society Ltd* v *Argyll Stores (Holdings) Ltd* [1996] 3 WLR 27 (CA), in circumstances that normally precluded such an order being given. The Court of Appeal decided that the breach of contract by the defendant could only be described as 'wanton and unreasonable' and 'gross commercial cynicism'. Since restitutionary damages were not available the Court of Appeal made an order of specific performance instead, stating that damages could not adequately compensate the claimant. Lord Hoffmann in the House of Lords rejected this approach, stating that the nature of the defendant's conduct was irrelevant and that specific performance in the circumstances required the constant supervision of the court, which precluded such an award, and thereby overturned the decision of the Court of Appeal.

The facts of the *Co-operative Insurance Society Ltd* v *Argyll Stores (Holdings) Ltd* case and the ultimate House of Lords decision are dealt with more fully in Chapter 17.

On this basis it seemed that English law was a long way from seeing the introduction of restitutionary damages for breach of contract. As already stated, Steyn LJ in *Bredero Homes* strongly disapproved of any moves towards such a development. He stated:

> The introduction of restitutionary remedies to deprive cynical contract breakers of the fruits of their breaches of contract will lead to greater uncertainty in the assessment of damages in commercial and consumer disputes. It is of paramount importance that the way in which disputes are likely to be resolved by the courts must be readily predictable. Given the premise that the aggrieved party has suffered no loss, is such a dramatic extension of restitutionary remedies justified in order to confer a windfall in each case on the aggrieved party? I think not . . . The recognition of the proposed extension will, in my view, not serve the public interest.

In some situations, however, the exploitation of a breach of contract is so cynical that a remedy is called for in that it would deter future breaches of contract. Such a remedy would revolve around the possibility of compelling the defendant to surrender their gain. Such an approach is a very different concept from the classical compensatory nature of damages for breach of contract and is clearly a break from the traditional approach.

An early authority for such an approach, however, can be seen in the case of *Wrotham Park Estate Co. Ltd* v *Parkside Homes Ltd*.

Wrotham Park Estate Co. Ltd v *Parkside Homes Ltd* [1974] 1 WLR 798

A developer acquired land that was subject to a restrictive covenant that had been imposed for the benefit of an adjoining estate and in breach of that covenant built houses on it. An injunction was sought by the estate owners but their application was unsuccessful. They were, however, awarded damages that were based upon the profits the defendant made from the breach of covenant. The damages were assessed on the basis of what the plaintiffs could have expected to gain in agreeing to relax the restrictive covenants. The award may be regarded as being in lieu of damages as permitted under the Supreme Court Act 1981 (now Senior Courts Act 1981), s 50.

For Senior Courts Act 1981 *see* Chapter 17.

Certainly this was the interpretation placed on this award by the Court of Appeal in *Bredero Homes*, although this was not available to the Court of Appeal in that case since one of the precursors to such an award is that the claimant must have applied for either injunctive relief or specific performance and such equitable relief had not been applied for in that case. Aside from that difficulty the Court of Appeal expressed reluctance to move towards a principle of restitutionary damages in the law of contract. This reluctance was in turn based on principle in that the award of damages is to compensate for loss and since the council had not suffered loss there was no entitlement to compensation.

The award of damages in lieu of equitable relief argument has, however, one fundamental drawback in that it was established in *Johnson* v *Agnew* [1980] AC 367 that the measure of damages in such circumstances is calculated on the same basis as in the common law; in the case of breach of contract this is to put the claimant in the same position he or she would have been in had the contract been completed. This position is limited in one respect, however, in that the damages claimed in lieu of the equitable relief must relate to the same breach and this could not apply where there is no right to damages at common law, such as where an injunction or specific performance is claimed for a future breach of contract, as held in *Jagger* v *Sawyer* [1995] 1 WLR 269. This position may demonstrate the true difference between *Bredero Homes* and *Wrotham Park* in that in the former there was no possibility of a future breach occurring since the defendants had by then disposed of all the houses and therefore there was no possibility of injunctive relief being granted. This was not the position, however, in **Wrotham Park**.

The position regarding restitutionary damages for breach of contract was considered again in **Attorney-General v Blake**.

Attorney-General v Blake [2001] 1 AC 268

In this case Blake was a member of the intelligence services who passed secret information to secret agents belonging to the Soviet Union. This was not only in breach of his contract of employment but also an offence under the Official Secrets Act 1911. He was subsequently convicted of espionage and sentenced to 42 years in prison. He then escaped from prison and fled to Russia where 20 years later he entered into a contract with an English publisher for the publication of his autobiography. The information he was to release in his book was no longer secret when he completed the manuscript and had it published. The disclosure, however, amounted to a further offence under the Official Secrets Act 1911 and breach of his contract of employment. The Crown of course suffered no material loss from the breach for which damages representing compensation could ordinarily have been awarded. The usual remedy in such a situation would be to restrain the breach by way of an injunction. Such a remedy should have been sought before the publication of the autobiography and this was not done; further, it was doubted whether such a remedy would have been effective in any event.

The House of Lords held by a majority that where damages were not sufficient and that injunctive relief or specific performance was unavailable, the court could 'exceptionally' exercise its discretion in requiring the defendant to account to the plaintiff for the benefits he was to receive from his breach of contract, the damages being measured with reference to the benefits received by the defendant from the breach of the plaintiff's contract. This development was partly founded on the notion that the court has discretion to award damages in lieu of injunctive relief or specific performance where the contract is of a type for which such equitable relief is unavailable. Lord Nicholls, however, went further than this and considered that equity always had discretion to require a wrongdoer to account for profits made from breaches that have already occurred. There is an interplay here between injunctions and an account for profits in that the injunction restrains future breaches and the wrongdoer is then required to account for the profits made so that the two complement each other. Furthermore, the account for profit arises even if the plaintiff has not suffered any financial loss or has been otherwise disadvantaged. The position is closely aligned to actions for breach of trust or breach of fiduciary duty where both trustees and fiduciaries are required to account for any profits made from their duties irrespective of their honesty or culpability. An example of this can be seen in the case of **Boardman v Phipps** [1967] 2 AC 46; [1966] 3 WLR 1009. The issue, however, is when does the discretion arise and when does it become exercisable?

Lord Nicholls stated that the circumstances in which the remedy to account for profits may arise is uncertain, although he considered it would only be granted in 'exceptional circumstances . . . no fixed rules can be prescribed'. He considered the criteria on which the discretion to order an account for profits may be exercised. He stated that a 'court will have regard to all the circumstances, including the subject matter of the contract, the purpose of the contractual provision which has been breached, the circumstances in which the breach occurred, the consequences of the breach and the circumstances in which relief is being sought'. He went on to state that 'a useful general guide, although not exhaustive, is whether the claimant had a legitimate interest in preventing the defendant's profit making activity and, hence, depriving him of his profit'.

An account for profits is an exceptional remedy and Lord Nicholls attempted to indicate circumstances in which such a remedy would not be appropriate. In this he concurred with the judgement of Woolf MR in the Court of Appeal who suggested three circumstances in which a departure from the normal rules of damages would not be appropriate. These are: 'the fact that the breach was cynical and deliberate; the fact that the breach enabled the defendant to enter into a more profitable contract elsewhere; and the fact that by entering into a new and more profitable contract the defendant put it out of his power to perform his contract with the plaintiff'.

Lord Woolf did, however, identify two cases in which restitutionary damages would be appropriate where compensatory damages would not apply. The first category was that of 'skimped performance', where the defendant fails to provide the full extent of services they were contracted to provide. Lord Nicholls did not think this fell within the remedy of an *account for profits* since this was capable of being remedied by a part-refund of the price, which would be the normal outcome for an action for breach of contract. The second category suggested by Lord Woolf was where a defendant obtained a profit by doing the very thing they had contracted not to do. Lord Nicholls also rejected this as an appropriate category on the basis that it was too wide to fit into the very exceptional situation that arose in the *Blake* case. He considered that to include all breaches of negative stipulations within a contract took the remedy to account for profits for breach of contract into the mainstream of contractual remedies and a liability to account is anything but that. Of course it would be useful if it could apply, for instance, in cases such as *Ruxley Electronics* (see below) where there was an issue of finding a remedy that was reasonable in that it provided a balance between the loss suffered by a claimant and the need for the defendant to pay damages that were not excessive. Here a remedy requiring the defendant to account for the saving he had made by way of 'skimped performance' would certainly provide for a remedy that was fair between the respective parties. The remedy of an account must remain an exceptional one, but in those very exceptional cases it is necessary in order to produce a just response. As Lord Nicholls stated in *Blake* (with Lords Goff, Browne-Wilkinson and Steyn concurring):

> When, exceptionally, a just response to a breach of contract so requires, the court should be able to grant the discretionary remedy of requiring the defendant to account to the plaintiff for the benefits he has received from his breach of contract. In the same way as a plaintiff's interest in performance may make it just and equitable for the court to make an order for specific performance or grant an injunction, so the plaintiff's interest in performance may make it just and equitable that the defendant should retain no benefit from his breach of contract.

Not surprisingly, lawyers have jumped at the vagueness of the principles set out by Lord Nicholls and have attempted to bring cases within the discretionary jurisdiction of the court to order an account for profits. Clearly the circumstances in which restitutionary damages in the form of an account for profits arise is extremely uncertain and very limited.

Following the case of *Blake* was that of *Esso Petroleum Co. Ltd v Niad* [2001] All ER 324, in which Niad owned a petrol station and entered into a price agreement with Esso for the supply of petrol. The purpose of the agreement was to provide support for a particular pricing regime to enable Esso to sell petrol at lower prices and remain competitive with the supermarkets. Niad charged higher prices to its customers than had been agreed, which meant that Esso provided a price support which Niad was not entitled to. Niad was, therefore, in breach of its agreement with Esso.

It was held by Morritt VC that Esso was entitled to an account of the profits Niad received by way of overcharging on the price of petrol beyond that agreed with Esso. Morritt VC applied the decision in *Blake* in that he considered that compensatory damages were inadequate because Esso could not establish what sales had been lost due to the actions of Niad.

Niad's breach undermined the 'price watch' scheme and, therefore, Esso was justified in preventing Niad from acquiring the profits from its breach. Thus Esso succeeded in claiming gain-based damages, or restitutionary damages, based on the *Blake* principle that compensatory damages were inadequate and that there was a legitimate interest to protect. On this basis, the court made an award that stripped Niad of the profits it had made.

Why are compensatory damages inadequate? In order to claim these types of damages, one has to establish a causal link between the breach and the loss. Esso could not establish that the lost sales were the result of Niad's failure to implement the 'price watch' scheme. In such a situation Esso would only be able to claim nominal damages for the breach itself on a compensatory basis. But the only way in which the actual loss could be compensated was on a restitutionary basis giving rise to damages based on the gains made by Niad – i.e. compensation for unjust enrichment or an account for profits.

A more recent case demonstrating this is that of *Experience Hendrix LLC v PPX Enterprises Inc.* [2003] EWCA Civ 323 in which there was a breach of a negative stipulation regarding the use of certain licences appertaining to the music of Jimi Hendrix. An injunction was granted as regards future breaches but the claimant wanted to claim damages for previous breaches even though there was no loss attributable to those breaches. The claimant therefore attempted to claim an account for profits on the basis of *Blake*. Mance LJ in the Court of Appeal stated that the circumstances in *Blake* were exceptional in that the case involved employment in a national security agency in which 'secret information was the lifeblood, its disclosure being a criminal offence . . . Blake had furthermore committed deliberate and repeated breaches causing untold damage . . . although the argument that Blake was a fiduciary was not pursued beyond first instance, the contractual undertaking he had given was 'closely akin to a fiduciary obligation, where an account of profits is a standard remedy in the event of breach'.'

The court held that on the facts the case of *Experience Hendrix* was not sufficiently exceptional in that it did not involve national security; nor was there any breach of a fiduciary obligation. While the claimant had a legitimate interest to protect in preventing the profit-making activity of the defendant the circumstances were not exceptional within the *Blake* criteria. The Court of Appeal in coming to this conclusion clearly had in mind the dangers of importing such a remedy into a commercial context, particularly as the court held that the defendant should pay the claimant a sum that was quantified on the basis of the cost of buying out the negative stipulation from the claimant. This accorded with the approach taken in *Wrotham Park* and since the claimant had a remedy in this form it was unnecessary to allow the principles set out in *Blake* to evolve into such a scenario.

Neither is the *Niad* case exceptional. There was, of course, evidence of a deliberate breach, but there are no issues concerning national security or a contractual relationship which was 'closely akin to a fiduciary obligation'. What appears to be occurring in the judgements is confusion between the different assessment of the damages in *Wrotham Park* and *Blake*. Both the remedies in these cases are gain-based on restitutionary damages; however, the way in which the damages are calculated is different. In *Wrotham Park* the damages are based on the cost to the defendant of buying out the benefit of the claimant's negative condition/covenant in the contract, referred to by some writers as 'transfer reversing' damages. In *Blake* the damages are gain-based on the principle of disgorgement, which requires the defendant to hand back profits improperly received in circumstances akin to a breach of fiduciary obligation.

In *Lane v O'Brien Homes Ltd* [2004] EWHC 303 there was a sale of land for residential purposes. The sale was subject to a collateral contract (as opposed to a restrictive covenant) that no more than three houses were to be built on the land. There was planning permission for this number. Several months after the sale, O'Brien obtained planning permission to build four houses on the land. Mrs Lane applied for an injunction to restrain the development in that it involved the building of four houses, not three. She was refused the injunction, although she was awarded £150,000 damages, based on the hypothetical price that O'Brien would have had to pay Mrs Lane in order to be released from the collateral contract. O'Brien then appealed.

It was held that the appeal would be dismissed in that the assessment of the damages had been correctly assessed in line with the **Wrotham Park** case. O'Brien's argument was that, since Mrs Lane had suffered no loss by the building of the fourth house, she was not entitled to any damages – there was no expectation loss. On the facts, though, the court found that Mrs Lane had suffered a loss – her right to charge O'Brien for the release from the collateral contract. Since Mrs Lane would have been prepared to negotiate a release from the collateral contract, she had lost her opportunity to bargain. This factor distinguishes the case from the **Wrotham Park** decision where it was clear that the estate owners would not have entered into negotiations over the relaxation of the restrictive covenant. Nevertheless, the criteria in **Blake** were fulfilled in that the damages were inadequate and Mrs Lane had a legitimate interest to protect. The assessment of damages based on 'transfer reversing' damages as a restitutionary remedy was correct. The more controversial aspect of the decision, however, was the fact that these damages were described as damages for loss of opportunity to bargain, which are compensatory and not restitutionary.

The decisions in Wrotham Park and Blake were also considered in **WWF World Wide Fund for Nature** v **World Wrestling Federation Entertainment** [2006] EWHC 184.

WWF World Wide Fund for Nature v World Wrestling Federation Entertainment [2006] EWHC 184

In the case a dispute arose from the World Wrestling Federation's ('F') use of the initials 'WWF' in connection with its activities. Those initials had been long used by the World Wide Fund for Nature ('N'). In 1994 the parties had entered into an agreement to compromise litigation and regulate the future use of the WWF initials. The agreement did not give N an exclusive right to the initials; however, it did substantially restrict F's use of the initials. N brought proceedings, alleging that F had broken the agreement, and claimed damages. Subsequently N sought to amend its claim so that it could claim for an account of profits on the basis of Blake. While it obtained summary judgement, it was refused an application for an account of profits. The basis behind this decision was that there was nothing of an 'exceptional character', which was a fundamental requirement for a claim on the principles set out in that case. Some years later N brought a further claim for damages, this time based on Wrotham Park in that the damages should be measured by reference to the sum that N might reasonably have demanded from F for relaxing its rights under the agreement. In deciding the preliminary issue Smith J held that damages based on this principle were recoverable. F appealed on two points: first, the remedy sought by N was either the same as or juridically similar to the relief refused by Jacob J in the original hearing and therefore was *res judicata*. The basis of this point was that both the account of profits under Blake and the damages based on Wrotham Park were both gain-based forms of relief. Second, N's attempt to claim damages based on Wrotham Park at this stage was an abuse of process since it had not entered such a plea in the earlier proceedings.

In the trial of the preliminary issue Smith J provided a thorough and comprehensive review of the authorities surrounding the issue of restitutionary damages in the law of contract. Smith J considered that the basis of the damages in **Wrotham Park** was of a compensatory nature, which is not the case. This is based on the fiction that **Wrotham**

Park is concerned with a lost opportunity of the claimant to profit from giving up the negative covenant in the contract. The fallacy in this argument is revealed when it becomes clear that the claimants never intended to relax the covenant and, therefore, no such opportunity was ever contemplated. Furthermore, the concept of the 'lost opportunity to bargain' principle was firmly rejected in *Experience Hendrix* and *Surrey CC v Bredero*.

The Court of Appeal [2007] EWCA Civ 286 allowed the appeal on the second ground and considered that N could and should have raised the claim for damages on the *Wrotham Park* principle when it sought to amend its claim for an account of the profits. To raise such a claim at this point in time was an abuse of process in that it had asked the earlier court to decide the issue on the basis that there would be no claim for damages based on the *Wrotham Park* principle. Essentially N was therefore attempting to re-establish such a claim in later proceedings when it had decided that a claim based on the *Wrotham Park* principle was unsustainable at the earlier hearing. Chadwick LJ considered that to allow the claim would be 'inconsistent with the underlying interest that there should be finality in litigation'. With respect, this is incorrect since the difference between *Wrotham Park* damages and an account of profits was not established until later in *Experience Hendrix*. Essentially the court was attempting to read back this difference to the time when N was seeking leave to amend its claim. Furthermore, the parameters and nature of *Wrotham Park* damages were uncertain at that time and one could therefore well understand why N did not raise this claim at that time.

With regard to the first ground of appeal the court affirmed the principles established in *Experience Hendrix* in that where there was a claim by a covenantee (N) for damages against a covenantor (F), who had acted in breach of a restrictive covenant, a court could award an amount assessed on the sum the court considered it would have been reasonable for the covenantor to pay and the covenantee to accept for a hypothetical release from the covenant immediately before the breach. In the light of *Experience Hendrix* the court considered that it was settled that where a covenantee claimed for an injunction and damages against a covenantor for breach of a restrictive covenant it could, in addition to awarding an injunction for future breaches, also award damages for past breaches even though the covenantee had not suffered any financial loss. The sum awarded was to be assessed on the basis (a) that the hypothetical release would have taken effect from the date immediately before the covenantor was first in breach; and (b) that the hypothetical release should be for the period ending with the date on which the injunction to restrain future breaches took effect.

The court went on, however, and stated that the damages being awarded under this process were not 'gain-based' damages but compensatory damages. Having said this, the court then accepted F's contention that the award of damages under *Wrotham Park* was juridically similar to an account for profits. This is highly questionable. In *Blake* the award of account for profits is emphatically not compensatory and patently of a restitutionary nature in that they are gain-based to prevent a defendant benefiting from a breach of contract in circumstances where the claimant suffers no loss per se, where, as Lord Nicholls stated 'it [is] just and equitable that the defendant should retain no benefit from his breach of contract'. The damages awarded in *Niad* were also based on the same premise that compensatory damages were inadequate and that there was a legitimate interest to protect, leading the court to strip Niad of the profits it had made – clearly 'gain-based' damages. The reasoning of the court appears to ignore the fact that an account for profits lies within equity on a restitutionary basis and is applied in many circumstances where a claimant does not suffer loss. *Boardman v Phipps* [1967] 2 AC 46 is a prime example of this, where a trustee was held to be accountable for profits gained from his position of trustee. The trustee had acted openly but nevertheless was required to hand his 'gains' over. The beneficiaries had suffered no loss from the trustee's breach.

There is a further contradiction within the judgement. If an account for profits is, according to Chadwick LJ, compensatory and this was refused by Jacob J, why are damages under *Wrotham Park* allowable if they also are compensatory? One answer lies in the fact that an account is 'gains based' and *Wrotham Park* compensatory. If one examines the *Wrotham Park* case, though it can be seen that the remedy in that case is also 'gains-based', the Court of Appeal expressed reluctance in introducing restitution remedies into the law of contract. It would seem, therefore, that account for profits and *Wrotham Park* damages are both founded in restitution as 'gains-based' remedies. With respect, neither are based in compensation. The lack of clarity in this judgement unfortunately requires to be resolved in another case at another time.

In summary, therefore, as an alternative to damages calculated on a conventional basis, that being to place the claimant in the same position he would have been in had the contract been performed, it is possible to award damages on the basis of a sum that might reasonably have been negotiated between the claimant and the defendant on a quid pro quo basis for the removal of say restrictive covenants as in the *Wrotham Park* case. Such damages were described by Neuberger J in *Lunn Poly Ltd v Liverpool and Lancashire Properties Ltd* [2006] 2 EGLR 29 as 'negotiating damages'. Such damages then are clearly of a compensatory nature available for breach of contract. In *Pell Frischmann Engineering Ltd v Bow Valley Iran Ltd* [2009] UKPC 45 it was stated that such damages can be linked back to damages in lieu of specific performance or an injunction, though neither of these remedies are necessary for the award either in terms of being claimed or granted. Negotiating damages do not have to be linked to breaches of proprietary rights (per Lord Walker). Negotiating damages are therefore a form of compensatory damages, thus Richards J in *Abbar v Saudi Economic and Development Co. (SEDCO) Real Estate Ltd* [2013] EWHC 1414 stated [225]:

> Negotiating damages have not, however, replaced the usual compensatory damages as the primary remedy in damages for breach of contract. It is a basis of assessment available where a breach of contract has been established but the claimant cannot establish any financial loss, assessed on the usual basis, flowing from the breach. In those circumstances, and where the defendant has proceeded to act without the consent of the claimant, justice requires that there should nonetheless be an award of substantial as opposed to nominal damages.

Richards J went on to stress that the inability to demonstrate and identify financial loss of the conventional type is a pre-condition to such an award quoting from Chadwick LJ in *WWF* in which he stated at [59]:

> When the court makes an award of damages on the *Wrotham Park* basis it does so because it is satisfied that that is a just response to circumstances in which the compensation which is the claimant's due cannot be measured (or cannot be measured solely) by reference to identifiable financial loss. Lord Nicholls' analysis in *Blake*'s case demonstrates that there are exceptional cases in which the just response to circumstances in which the compensation which is the claimant's due cannot be measured by reference to identifiable financial loss is an order which deprives the wrongdoer of all the fruits of his wrong. The circumstances in which an award of damages on the *Wrotham Park* basis may be an appropriate response, and those in which the appropriate response is an account of profits, may differ in degree. But the underlying feature, in both cases, is that the court recognises the need to compensate the claimant in circumstances where he cannot demonstrate identifiable financial loss.

The result is that *Blake* and *Wrotham Park* damages are linked with, *Blake* providing for an award on the basis of an account for profits on an exceptional basis, whilst *Wrotham Park* damages emanate from a breach that involves the defendant doing something he has promised not to do. Whilst damages in **Wrotham Park** amount to a preliminary assessment in determining the appropriate measure of the breach, damages in **Blake** are based upon the recovery of profits that the defendant has received as a result of the breach. Both awards, however, have a common basis in that they are awarded where the claimant requires compensation but in circumstances where the claimant cannot 'demonstrate identifiable financial loss' on the conventional compensatory basis.

Actions for an agreed sum

Before we embark on an analysis of the specific issues that may arise in assessing the basis on which damages are awarded, a distinction has to be drawn between actions for damages and actions for an agreed sum. The latter commonly arise where the contract provides that an agreed sum is payable in return for some performance under the contract by the other party, such as the sale of goods for a fixed price. Actions to recover the agreed price or sum are very different from actions for damages in two respects. First, such actions take the form of specific relief, though without the restrictions normally found in actions for decrees of specific performance. Second, not only does the remedy differ in nature from damages, but it also differs in respect of the limitations imposed upon its award. Such actions are truly speaking actions in debt, since a precise known sum is being claimed. The result is that claims for such sums are not subject to the limitations of remoteness, mitigation of loss and so on that are frequently imposed on awards of damages.

Difference in value and cost of cure

Objective 2

While damages for reliance losses or restitution are fairly readily quantifiable, this is not necessarily the case when trying to quantify damages for loss of bargain, that is, restoring the claimant to the same position he would have been in had the contract been performed. In assessing the damages here one of two methods may be adopted: they will be assessed either on a 'difference in value' basis or on a 'cost of cure' basis. Choosing between these two methods in itself is not as straightforward as it may appear.

In contracts for the sale of goods there is generally no problem, since where the goods are not of the correct quality, for instance, the prima facie rule is that damages are assessed on the difference in value basis, that is, 'the difference between the value of the goods . . . and the value they would have had' if the quality of the goods had been in accordance with the contract, as stated in the Sale of Goods Act 1979, s 53(3) in relation to B2B contracts. The approach here is based on the principle that the buyer can resell the goods they received and add the proceeds to the damages awarded so that they can then go out and purchase goods of the correct quality. The buyer would then be in the same position as if the contract had been performed, which of course is the general principle set out in **Robinson v Harman**. The prima facie nature of this rule, however, has to be emphasised and it may be displaced if a defect in the goods can be removed at a reasonable cost.

Other factors may also displace the principle contained in s 53(3). In **Bence Graphics International Ltd v Fasson UK Ltd** [1997] 3 WLR 205 (CA), the defendants were suppliers of vinyl film, which was used to manufacture identification numbers for bulk containers. The plaintiffs printed words or numbers on the film so it could be applied to the containers. The plaintiff used the film to manufacture decals for Sea Containers Ltd and it was an implied term that the film would survive in good legible condition for at least five years. In fact, the film started to degrade well within this period, with the result that several customers of Sea Containers complained about the poor labelling on the containers. The plaintiffs claimed the whole purchase price or alternatively for an indemnity against all claims from their customers. At the time of the claim the plaintiffs had retained some £22,000 of unused defective vinyl, but had not themselves had a claim brought against them by their own customers.

Section 53(2) of the Sale of Goods Act 1979 provides that:

> The measure of damages for breach of warranty is the estimated loss directly and naturally resulting, in the ordinary course of events, from the breach of warranty.

Section 53(4) also provides:

> The fact that the buyer has set up the breach of warranty in diminution or extinction of the price does not prevent him from maintaining an action for the same breach of warranty if he has suffered further damage.

These two subsections lay down basic principles for remoteness of damage in terms that are very similar to those used in *Hadley* v *Baxendale* (1854) 9 Exch 341 and which will be discussed more fully in the context of remoteness later on. It is, however, sufficient to state at this juncture that the rule in *Hadley* v *Baxendale* allows only for the recovery of true loss and neither more nor less. At first instance, however, the judge applied s 53(3) and found that the correct measure of damages was the difference between the value of the goods at the time of delivery and the value they would have had if they had complied with the warranty. In the Court of Appeal, however, it was decided that the correct measure of the damages was the actual losses suffered by the buyer. It was clear that both parties, at the time of entering into the contract, would have contemplated that the plaintiff would have wished to pass on to the defendants claims for damages from its own dissatisfied customers. The parties, in other words, must have contemplated that any latent defect in the vinyl film, either at the time of delivery or at the time the buyer converted it into decals, might when discovered later expose the buyer to claims for damages which he may wish to pass back to the defendant seller.

For more on the decision in *Hedley* v *Baxendale* see later in this chapter under 'Remoteness of damages'.

Where the contract is for building work the prima facie rule is that damages are assessed on a 'cost of cure' or reinstatement basis, that is, the builder will be liable for the costs of putting the defects right or completing the contract. Thus in *East Ham Borough Council* v *Bernard Sunley Ltd* [1965] 3 All ER 619 (HL), a contractor was held to be liable to replace stone panels that fell off the side of a building owing to defective fixing.

Such an approach was also suggested in *Ruxley Electronics and Construction Ltd* v *Forsyth*; *Laddingford Enclosures Ltd* v *Forsyth*, although the case again demonstrates the prima facie nature of the rules on the assessment of loss of bargain.

Ruxley Electronics and Construction Ltd v Forsyth; Laddingford Enclosures Ltd v Forsyth [1995] 3 All ER 268 (HL)

The facts of the case were that the defendant (the owner) entered into a contract with two plaintiff companies for the construction and enclosure of a swimming pool in his garden for a price of £70,178. The contract expressly provided that the maximum depth of the pool was to be 7ft 6in. When the work was completed the owner observed that the maximum depth was only 6ft 9in. Further, where people had hoped to dive in, the depth was only 6ft. The owner had paid various sums in advance but owed £39,072. The builders sued for this amount and the owner counter-claimed for breach of contract. While it was accepted that there had been a breach of contract, the judge at first instance found that the value of the pool had not been diminished by the breach and that the pool as constructed was safe to dive into. He found that the only method of curing the defect was to demolish the existing pool and construct a new one. He considered that the cost of rebuilding was wholly disproportionate to the disadvantage of having a pool of a depth shallower than that contracted for. The judge ordered that the owner should pay £40,777 to the builders. The judge, however, considered that the owner was entitled to £2,500 damages for loss of amenity.

The owner appealed, contending that the judge should have awarded damages for the breach or deducted a sum from the contract price to reflect the need for the pool to be reconstructed to the depth specified in the contract. The Court of Appeal allowed the appeal, finding that it was reasonable to award damages to take into account the cost of replacing the pool in order to make good the breach of contract, despite the fact that the pool was still usable and that the breach had not diminished the value of the pool. The plaintiffs appealed to the House of Lords, where their Lordships upheld the findings of the judge at first instance and reversed the decision of the Court of Appeal.

In deciding which measure of damages should be applied the House of Lords considered three aspects. First, the question of reasonableness in the context of reinstatement; second, the question as to the relevance of whether the owner intended to use any damages to rebuild the swimming pool if damages were awarded; and, third, the award of damages for loss of amenity, which is more fully discussed below.

With regard to the first aspect the court took the view that it was unreasonable for the owner to insist on the reconstruction of the swimming pool in order to make good the breach, the reason being that the expense of the reconstruction work would be out of all proportion to the benefit obtained. In such cases their Lordships found a claimant would be limited to the difference in value between what he had contracted for and what he had actually received. Lord Jauncey reiterated the general principle that damages were to compensate for an established loss and not to provide a gratuitous benefit, so that the reasonableness of the award is directly referable to the loss sustained. He stated that while reinstatement might be a starting point for the assessment of damages, this was subject to the qualification that it must be reasonable, having regard to the loss sustained. Thus if a claimant has suffered no loss then they may be awarded only nominal damages. Lord Lloyd considered that this principle also accords with the overall requirement that a claimant should mitigate any loss, that is, a claimant should take reasonable steps to reduce their losses, as stated by Viscount Haldane in *British Westinghouse Electric and Manufacturing Co. Ltd* v *Underground Electric Railways Co. of London Ltd* [1912] AC 673.

In applying the above criteria to the two means of assessing damages for loss of bargain, Lord Lloyd stated that if the cost of reinstatement is less than the difference in value, the measure of damages would be the cost of reinstatement. Claiming the difference in value in such circumstances would mean that a claimant is failing to mitigate the loss. Lord Lloyd, however, considered that the requirement of reasonableness went further than simply the duty to mitigate. He affirmed the principle set out by Steyn LJ in *Darlington Borough Council* v *Wiltshier Northern Ltd* [1995] 1 WLR 68, where he stated:

> in the case of a building contract, the prima facie rule is cost of cure, i.e. the cost of remedying the defect. . . But where the cost of remedying the defects involves expense out of all proportion to the benefit which could accrue from it, the court is entitled to adopt the alternative measure of the difference of the value of the works.

The problem in the *Ruxley* case, however, was that if the proper measure of damages is the difference in value and that the diminution in value is nil, then should the court not revert to an award based on the cost of reinstatement? Lord Lloyd considered that an injustice that arises by way of making an award of too little is not counterbalanced by a court making an award of too much: 'that cannot make reasonable what. . . has been found to be unreasonable'.

It was further argued in the case that this was not a commercial contract but a contract for a personal preference and that the test of what was reasonable had to have regard to those personal preferences. Lord Lloyd considered that this was correct but that such preferences could not be elevated into a separate category of damages with its own special rules. Personal preferences were to be regarded as simply another factor to be taken into account, but only where the cost of reinstatement is not unreasonable. Where the cost of reinstatement is unreasonable, as in the *Ruxley* case, a claimant is not entitled to have their personal preferences satisfied. Lord Lloyd considered that a claimant could be compensated for loss of disappointed expectations and did not consider that the law of damages was so inflexible that it could not compensate in these circumstances. He quoted from the case of *G W Atkins Ltd v Scott* (1980) 7 Const LJ 215 where Sir David Cairns in the Court of Appeal stated:

> There are many circumstances where a judge has nothing but his commonsense to guide him in fixing the quantum of damages, for instance, for pain and suffering, for the loss of pleasurable activities or for inconvenience of one kind or another.

Lord Lloyd considered that personal preference could give rise to a modest award for loss of amenity and that this amounted to another exception to the rule in *Addis v Gramophone Co. Ltd* [1909] AC 488, which will be discussed more fully later. He therefore affirmed the decision of the judge at first instance to make an award of £2,500 on this basis.

So far the question of reasonableness in the context of reinstatement has largely been confined to building contracts; however, the principles apply in a wider context. A claimant can only be placed in the same position as if the contract had been performed if it is reasonable for him to be so. The principles can also be seen in *Sealace Shipping Co. Ltd v Ocean-voice Ltd, The Alecos M* [1991] 1 Lloyd's Rep 120.

The court in *Ruxley* also considered the relevance of whether the owner, if he was awarded damages, would actually spend the damages on rebuilding the pool. Lord Lloyd stated that while the courts were not normally concerned as to what a claimant does with his damages, the question of the intention to rebuild was not irrelevant to the question of reasonableness in relation to the measure of damages to be awarded. He referred to Megarry VC in *Tito v Waddell (No. 2)* [1977] 3 All ER 129 in which he stated:

> if the plaintiff has suffered little or no monetary loss in the reduction in value of his land, and has no intention of applying any damages towards carrying out the work contracted for, or its equivalent, I cannot see why he should recover the cost of doing the work which will never be done. It would be a mere pretence to say that this cost was a loss and so should be recoverable as damages.

Thus the absence of a desire to spend the damages on rebuilding or otherwise remedying the breach can undermine the reasonableness of a claim for such damages. In the *Ruxley* case itself the owner undertook to spend any damages he would receive on rebuilding the pool; however, Lord Lloyd considered that this did not affect the principle. A claimant cannot create a loss where no loss existed simply to punish the defendant for a breach of contract.

The *Ruxley* case is important in that it restates that the general principle in the assessment of damages is that it is based on the loss which the injured party has suffered. The injured party must not be overcompensated since this is just as much an injustice as if he were insufficiently compensated. The fact that the owner had received a usable pool meant that he would be overcompensated if he received the cost of rebuilding it. On the other hand, he had not received what he had contracted for and thus the award of £2,500 for loss of amenity was undoubtedly a fair award, though this was not contested in the House of Lords. The decision is also a good indicator of the position that the courts will not shy away from making an assessment simply because it is difficult to do so and gives an indication that further exceptions to the rule in *Addis v Gramophone Co. Ltd* may emerge where the courts find this expedient.

For more on the rule in the *Addis v Gramophone Co. Ltd* case and the exceptions to it, see the section on 'Speculative damages and damages for non-pecuniary losses'.

The assessment of damages by reference to the market

Objective
3

An area where expectation losses are commonly claimed arises out of contracts for the sale of goods. The assessment of damages here depends on whether the seller is in breach of contract for non-delivery or whether it is the buyer who is in breach for non-acceptance of the goods delivered. In either case the measure of damages is dependent on the difference between the contract price and the price of the goods in the market at the time of the breach of contract.

Breach caused by non-delivery

Such a breach will occur where the seller refuses or neglects to deliver the goods to the buyer. In such a case the buyer is expected to mitigate this loss by going into the marketplace and buying goods of a similar nature, the damages being the difference between the contract price and market price, assuming that the buyer has had to pay more for the goods, otherwise they are only entitled to nominal damages. Thus the Sale of Goods Act 1979, s 51(3) states:

> Where there is an available market for the goods in question the measure of damages is *prima facie* to be ascertained by the difference between the contract price and the market or current price of the goods at the time or times when they ought to have been delivered or (if no time was fixed) at the time of refusal to deliver.

This measure, however, will change somewhat where the buyer has contracted to resell the goods and this resale is within the contemplation of the seller (see the rule in *Hadley* v *Baxendale*, below). If there is no available marketplace, then the resale price is taken as the market price and the measure of damages will thus be the difference between the contract price and the resale price, as was held in *Patrick* v *Russo-British Grain Export Co.* [1927] 2 KB 535. If there is an available marketplace, then the damages remain the same as stated in s 51(3), that is, the difference between the contract price and the market price, whether or not the resale was within the contemplation of the seller, as was held in *Williams* v *Reynolds* (1865) 6 B & S 495.

Where the delivery is late but is nevertheless accepted by the buyer, the damages have to be assessed on a different basis entirely since here the buyer's complaint is that they will only be able to resell them at a lower price than that prevailing at the time the goods should have been delivered. In such an instance the measure of damages is the difference between the market value of the goods when they ought to have been delivered and the market value when they were actually delivered. Nevertheless, it was held in *Wertheim* v *Chicoutimi Pulp Co. Ltd* [1911] AC 301 that this rule will be displaced if the goods were resold at more than their market value at the time of delivery. Here the measure of damage will be the difference between the market price at the time fixed for delivery and the price for which the goods are resold. By way of illustration, if the market price of the goods was £20 per tonne at the time fixed for delivery and £9 per tonne at the time of actual delivery, then prima facie the loss is £11 per tonne. If, however, the buyer was able to resell the goods for £15 per tonne, then according to the *Wertheim* case the measure of damages should be £5 per tonne, since otherwise, according to the court, the buyers would make a profit out of the breach. The decision has been heavily criticised (see, for instance, Treitel) since arguably the profit has been made not from the breach but the advantageous sub-sale.

Breach caused by non-acceptance

Such a breach occurs where the buyer refuses or neglects to accept delivery of the goods. In a private sale the seller can recover from the buyer the difference between the value of the goods still in their possession and the agreed sale price, subject of course to their duty to take reasonable steps to mitigate the loss by attempting to sell them elsewhere. This position can be seen in the Sale of Goods Act 1979, s 50(3) which states:

> Where there is an available market for the goods in question the measure of damages is *prima facie* to be ascertained by the difference between the contract price and the market or current price at the time or times when the goods ought to have been accepted or (if no time was fixed for acceptance) at the time of refusal to accept.

The situation is not quite so simple where the seller is a dealer. It is true that the dealer has to take reasonable steps to mitigate the loss, just as in a private sale, so that where there is an available market the loss is the difference between the contract price and the market price. The problem, however, may be that there is no difference between the contract price and the market price so that the claim will be for the loss of profits from the sale. The ability of the seller to recover such loss of profit depends, however, on the supply and demand for the goods in question.

Thompson Ltd v *Robinson (Gunmakers) Ltd* [1955] Ch 177

In this case, there was a contract for the sale of a new Vanguard car but the defendants refused to accept delivery. The defendants contested that the plaintiff dealers were only entitled to nominal damages given that there was no difference between the contract price and the market price. The plaintiffs, however, claimed their loss of profits since they maintained that given that the supply of such vehicles exceeded demand, they had sold one car less than they would normally have been able to do. It was held that the plaintiffs were entitled to their loss of profits, the judge finding that since s 50(3) was only a prima facie rule it could be displaced in such circumstances. On the other hand, in Charter v Sullivan [1957] 2 QB 117 it was held that only nominal damages could be claimed where demand exceeds supply since there the dealer, being able to sell all that he could get his hands on, had suffered no loss.

The situations described above tend to arise where there is a fixed retail price for the goods, and it may be that in the competitive market that exists today the rule in s 50(3) may be a more appropriate means of measuring the loss. Certainly the above rules do not apply to second-hand goods which do not have a fixed retail price. Such goods are unique and a failure to accept does not give rise to a claim for loss of profits here. The seller must again take reasonable steps to mitigate the loss by going into the marketplace, should a market be available; and if they sell the goods at the same or a higher price they can recover no damages from the first buyer, as held in *Lazenby Garages Ltd* v *Wright* [1976] 1 WLR 459. If the seller can sell only at a diminished price, then the damages are the difference between the contract price and the market price as provided in s 50(3).

It should be noted that if the buyer delays in accepting the goods, then by the Sale of Goods Act 1979, s 38, the seller can recover any losses resulting from that delay, together with a reasonable charge for the care and custody of the goods.

'Available market'

The expression 'available market' in s 50(3) and s 51(3) appears to have no precise definition. Various rather unconvincing attempts have been made over the years to define the expression. In *Shearson Lehman Hutton Inc.* v *Maclaine Watson & Co. Ltd (No. 2)* [1990] 3 All ER 723 Webster J, having examined several cases, summarised the position as follows:

> What, in the light of these decisions, is the meaning of 'available market'? ... Approached in this way, the answer seems to me to be: that if the seller actually offers the goods for sale there

is no available market unless there is one actual buyer on that day at a fair price; and that if there is no actual offer for sale, but only a notional or hypothetical sale for the purposes of s 50(3), there is no available market unless on that day there are in the market sufficient traders potentially in touch with each other to evidence a market in which the actual or notional seller could if he wished sell the goods.

Thus in the case of a breach by the buyer, a market arises where the seller actually offers the goods for sale and there is a buyer who offers a fair price on the day. Alternatively, there will be a market where the seller does not actually offer the goods for sale but where, nevertheless, it can be shown that there are sufficient dealers potentially in touch with one another to evince the existence of a market. Presumably a market arises on a similar basis where it is the seller who is in breach.

In *Hooper* v *Oates* [2013] 3 All ER 211 the Court of Appeal considered that in relation to sales of land the availability of a market was highly relevant in the assessment of damages. However, it stated that in such a circumstance there was hardly ever a readily available market in the sense of a new buyer being found and then able to proceed to contract immediately. The court stated that in assessing the level of damages the date of the breach was only appropriate where there was an immediate available market for the sale of the asset concerned, which would be most unlikely in the case of a sale of land. If there was no available market at the time of the breach so that the seller retained the property then the measure of damages should be calculated at the later date when the seller decided to sell and that if the market value had diminished in that time, then that loss formed part of the calculation of the damages and represented the loss suffered by the seller for which he was entitled to be compensated. The eventual resale price was likely to be the figure to be set against the contract price for assessment of damages, not because it represented the market value at the date of the breach, but because it showed what loss the seller had suffered, uncomplicated by issues of remoteness or failure to mitigate. The Court of Appeal found there was no basis of policy or principle on which to impose on H the value as at the breach date rather than the later date when, having taken steps to mitigate their loss, they eventually decided to retain the property.

The question arises as to what the position is in a sale of goods contract where there is no available market. The answer here lies within the Sale of Goods Act 1979 s 51(2) which throws the disappointed purchaser back into the rule set out in the first limb of *Hadley* v *Baxendale*. The measure of damages is therefore the loss directly and naturally arising, in the usual course of events, from the breach of contract by the seller. In order to arrive at the measure of damages, these are based on the value of the contract goods at the time and place of the breach, which can be assessed by any relevant evidence. Such an assessment does not require the goods to be sold and the evidenced adduced could, for instance, be based on the cost of the nearest equivalent goods. The buyer of course must act reasonably so as to mitigate his loss: *Hughes* v *Pendragon Sabre Ltd (t/a Porsche Centre Bolton)* [2016] EWCA Civ 18.

The question of time in assessing an award of damages

Objective 4

Damages are usually assessed as at the time the contract has been broken and this principle is evidenced by both s 50(3) and s 51(3) of the Sale of Goods Act 1979, above. This principle is only a presumption and is largely based on the fact that a claimant's obligation to take reasonable steps to mitigate their loss assumes that they will act immediately. In *Johnson* v *Agnew*, however, it was stated that the claimant does not have to take such immediate action where it is reasonable for them to take some other course of action, such as attempting to persuade the defendant to carry out their side of the bargain or to seek confirmation from the defendant that they do intend to perform. Thus Lord Wilberforce stated:

> The general principle for the assessment of damages is compensatory, i.e. that the innocent party is to be placed, so far as money can do so, in the same position as if the contract had been performed. Where the contract is one of sale, this principle normally leads to assessment of damages as at the date of the breach, a principle recognised and embodied in s 51 of the Sale of Goods Act 1893. But this is not an absolute rule; if to follow it would give rise to injustice, the court has power to fix such other date as may be appropriate in the circumstances.
>
> In cases where a breach of a contract for sale has occurred, and the innocent party reasonably continues to try to have the contract completed, it would appear to me more logical and just rather than to tie him to the date of the original breach, to assess damages as at the date when (otherwise than by his default) the contract is lost.

On this basis it would seem that the courts fully intend to give themselves substantial discretion as to the time when the assessment of damages should be made. This discretion was used in *Gardline Shipping Ltd* v *Dyson and McCarthy* (1998) (unreported). It was stated, applying *County Personnel (Employment Agency) Ltd* v *Alan R Pulver & Co.* [1987] 1 WLR 916 (as approved by *Smith New Court Securities Ltd* v *Citibank NA* [1997] AC 254 *(aka Smith New Court Ltd* v *Scrimgeour Vickers Ltd* [1996] 4 All ER 769), that while the general principle usually meant that the assessment of damages would be as at the date of the breach, this was not an absolute rule. The principle may be relaxed not only to prevent injustice to the defendant, but also to prevent injustice to the claimant, as held in *Kennedy* v *Van Emden* (1997) 74 P & CR 19. Further in *Hooper* v *Oates* [2013] 3 All ER 211 the Court of Appeal, referring to *Techno Land Improvements* v *British Leyland (UK) Ltd* [1979] 2 EGLR 27, held that the general principle did not require the court to disregard matters occurring after the breach or after the commencement of the action or even after the court's decision on liability if those matters enabled the court to fix the loss more accurately. As we saw earlier in that case the Court of Appeal considered there was no basis of policy or principle on which to impose on H the value as at the breach date rather than the later date when, having taken steps to mitigate their loss, they eventually decided to retain the property. The proper time for assessing the award of damages, at least in relation to contracts for the sale of land where there was rarely a readily available market at the time of the breach, was not the value of the property at the time of the breach but the time at which the property was eventually sold. Thus if the property had declined in value, then that diminution in value formed part of the losses sustained by the seller for which he should be compensated. Affirmation of the time of breach rule has also occurred in the case of *Golden Strait Corporation* v *Nippon Yusen Kubishka Kaisha (The Golden Victory)*.

Golden Strait Corporation v *Nippon Yusen Kubishka Kaisha (The Golden Victory)* [2007] UKHL 12 (HL)

The facts of the case were that the shipowner, the Golden Strait Corporation ('GS'), had chartered a ship to Nippon ('N') by way of a period time charterparty dated 10 July 1998. The earliest contractual date for termination of the contract was 6 December 2005. Clause 33 of the charterparty provided that if war should break out between certain countries, named as including the USA, the United Kingdom and Iraq, both GS and N would be entitled to cancel the charter. N repudiated the charter on

14 December 2001 by redelivering the ship to GS and three days later GS accepted the repudiation. By the time the consideration for the damages for the breach came to arbitration the second Gulf War had broken out. This event would have entitled N to cancel the charter had it still been current. At the time of the outbreak of the war there was an available market for ships such as the Golden Victory. The arbitrator decided that the outbreak of war in March 2003 placed a limit on the damages that could be awarded in that no damages were capable of being recovered after that date.

It fell before the House of Lords to decide, where damages for an accepted repudiation of a contract were claimed, in what circumstances could the party in breach of the contract rely on subsequent events to show that the contractual rights lost by the anticipatory breach would have been less valuable, or even valueless, by virtue of those events. GS contended that since there was an available market, loss was measured at the date of acceptance of the repudiation and that such loss was measured as the difference between the contract rate and the market rate for chartering a substitute ship for the balance of the charter period. Such an argument concurred with the formulation of the measure of damages in ***Koch Marine Inc. v d'Amica Societa di Navigazione ARL (The Elena d'Amico)*** [1980] 1 Lloyd's Rep 75 as a case where there was a wrongful repudiation of a charter by shipowners. Having referred to the general principle for the assessment of damages for breach of contract, namely *restitutio in integrum* within the limits of ***Hadley v Baxendale***, Goff J stated:

> But as in other cases, there is, I consider, a normal measure of recovery in cases of premature wrongful repudiation of a time charter by the owners, and that normal measure is that, if there is at the time of the termination of the charter-party an available market for the chartering in of a substitute vessel, the damages will generally be assessed on the basis of the difference between the contract rate for the balance of the charter-party period and the market rate for the chartering in of a substitute vessel for that period.

GS also argued that events subsequent to that date were irrelevant and that in commercial agreements the overriding consideration was certainty. N, however, argued that while the normal assessment of damages is at the date of the breach this was not an absolute rule and that the available market rule required an innocent party to mitigate his loss. Clearly any condition within a contract that would bring the contract to an end on the occurrence of a specific event always created an element of uncertainty and therefore damages had to be assessed on a causation basis.

A majority of the House of Lords dismissed the appeal by GS, stating that the outbreak of war contingency within the contract had to be taken into account when assessing the damages. The fundamental principle governing the measure of damages for breach of contract was to compensate the victim and put him in the same position as he would have been in had the contract been performed, so far as damages could accomplish that. Usually the assessment of damages at the date of the breach achieves that result, but it was for the courts to find a solution that most fairly compensates the party suffering the loss. If the contract would have terminated earlier because of a particular event, the chance of that event occurring had to be taken into account. Thus if it was certain that the terminating event would occur, the damages had to be assessed on that basis. The reasoning behind this is that the charterparty in the case had made provision (Clause 33) for the termination of the contract on the happening of a certain event, the outbreak of war. The benefit that GS was deprived of by the breach was the right to receive the hire rate during the currency of the charterparty. The occurrence of the event terminated those rights and therefore GS could not claim damages for the whole of the charterparty. To decide otherwise would have meant that GS would have received more compensation than they would have been deprived of. The House of Lords, however, recognised that the principle as stated was subject to exceptions and should not be applied mechanistically. The principle may be overridden if to do so would be to provide a more accurate measure of compensation. The majority recognised that, while certainty in commercial contracts was important, this did not take precedence over principles of law.

Lords Bingham and Walker gave dissenting judgements in this case and both considered that the value of the charterparty lost on the date of repudiation was one with four years to run and that GS should be compensated to that extent considering that certainty and predictability in contracts should not be overridden and that such a principle was a long-established one in commercial contracts. The outbreak of war was no more than a possibility and therefore they considered that at the time of the breach the contract had four years to run. Thus they considered that the damages should be assessed on the full term of the contract.

The issue of producing a calculation of damages that mirrors the actual loss of a party with regard to post-breach events can be seen in the case of *Glory Wealth Shipping Pte Ltd* v *Korea Line Corp. (The Wren)* [2011] EWHC 1819 (Comm). In this case the appellant charterers, Glory Wealth, appealed against an arbitrators' award of damages to the respondent shipowners, Korea Line, for repudiatory breach of a time charter. The vessel in question was a newbuild which was time-chartered for a minimum of 36 months. After five months Glory Wealth purported to make early redelivery following a collapse in the market. Korea Line accepted this as a repudiatory breach that entitled them to terminate the charterparty. The dispute was referred to arbitration. The parties agreed that at the time of termination there was no available market for a charter that was equivalent to the balance of the charterparty. Korea Line claimed damages on what was called a 'hybrid basis': first, by reference to actual losses on substitute fixtures the vessel had contracted in the spot market and, after the market had revived, by reference to market rates for the balance of the charter period of some two years from that time. The arbitrators decided that Korea Line was entitled to advance a claim for both actual and market damages and that there was an available market at the relevant time and, much like the opinions of Lords Bingham and Walker in *The Golden Victory*, awarded damages to Korea for the balance of the charter period on that basis.

Where there was an available market at the time of termination, damages for repudiation of a charter were normally assessed on the basis of the difference between the contract rate and the market rate for the vessel for the balance of the charterparty period: *Koch Marine Inc.* v *d'Amica Societa di Navigazione ARL (The Elena d'Amico)*. The court considered that the arbitrators were wrong to assess damages by way of the reasoning in *The Elena D'Amico*. Such an approach departed from the decision in *The Golden Victory* that damages should be awarded to put the injured party in the same financial position as if the contract had been performed i.e. where at the date of termination of the contract there was no available market for the unexpired period and when the market subsequently revived two years later, the damages were to be assessed by reference to the actual loss of the owners. The correct course was to consider Korea Line's actual losses accruing up to the contractual expiry date of the charterparty. The court considered that whilst the revival of the market is obviously relevant and, may be a factor to take into account in calculating future loss if damages fall to be assessed before the end of the contractual period, the revival of a market for the then unexpired period of the charter does not in itself provide the correct measure of damages. It should be noted, however, that the owners had managed to obtain substitute charters in the short term within the spot market and the sums obtained were relevant as regards mitigation of the post-repudiation losses and had to be considered when the actual losses were assessed.

The assessment of damages by way of *The Golden Victory* formula was also adopted in the case of *Force India Formula One Team Ltd v Etihad Airways PJSC* [2009] EWHC 2768. In this case Etihad entered into an agreement to sponsor Force India motor racing team for three seasons. One of the terms stated that Etihad was required to pay a performance related bonus. Etihad served notice of termination of the agreement arguing that First India had broken the agreement by their actions, including using another company's logo, changing the team's name and using new livery, and that its notice had constituted an acceptance of the antecedent repudiation of the agreement by First India. Etihad argued that any claim for the loss of the chance of acquiring bonus points in the second and third seasons should fail since the possibility of acquiring such bonuses was mere speculation as at the date of First India's acceptance of the repudiation. It was held that Force India should be allowed to recover damages for wrongful termination and the bonus of being the penultimate winner in the championship. In addition, applying the principles in *The Golden Victory*, as Force India had already gained points for the second and third seasons by way of the points acquired in the first season; these points amounted to bonus points which in turn gave rise to performance-related payments.

The principle in *The Golden Victory* as per the judgement in the House of Lords is not to be applied mechanistically and can be over-ridden if to do so produces a more accurate measure of the compensation to be awarded. In *Ageas (UK) Ltd v Kwik- Fit (GB) Ltd* [2014] 2178 (QB) it was held that the prima facie rule was that damages were to be assessed at the date of the breach and that only events which had occurred at that date could be taken into account, however, this principle could be departed from in appropriate cases. Thus Popplewell J stated:

> The prima facie rule, from which departure must be justified, is that damages are to be assessed at the date of breach and that only events which have occurred at that date can be taken into account.

The compensatory principle may also be effected by taking a date for the assessment of damages which was later than the date of the breach and that there was no conceptual difficulty in making use of subsequent events to provide information as to an assessment of value at an earlier date in appropriate cases so that any valuation could be made with the benefit of hindsight. This was on the basis that a judge should avail himself of all the relevant information at the time of making the award. Popplewell J stated:

> ... when assessing damages for breach of contract by reference to the value of a company or other property at the date of breach, whose value depends upon a future contingency, account can be taken of what is subsequently known about the outcome of the contingency as a result of events subsequent to the valuation date where that is necessary in order to give effect to the compensatory principle. In an appropriate case, the valuation can be made with the benefit of hindsight, taking account of what is known of the outcome of the contingency at the time that the assessment falls to be made by the court.

Popplewell J provided an example of how the compensatory rule operates with regard to subsequent events and hindsight, thus,

> In the course of argument I posited an example of the sale of a racehorse, which the seller warranted to be free from disease; its value at the date of sale was to be measured by reference to an assessment of the races it might win and its consequent stud value; at the date of sale it had a latent disease which increased the risk of it suffering a career-ending lameness at some stage; if the parties had known the true position at the date of sale the horse would have been valued at half the price because of this increased risk of lameness; by the time damages came to be

assessed, however, the horse's racing days were over and it was known that there had been no incidence of career-ending lameness despite the increased risk. Would the buyer still be able to claim half the price of the horse on the basis that its value without the benefit of hindsight was half what he paid? I am inclined to think not. By the time damages come to be assessed, it is known that the buyer received a horse which was every bit as valuable at the date of sale as the horse as warranted; with the benefit of hindsight it is known that the horse was as capable of winning the same number of races over its racing career as a horse without the latent disease. To award the buyer half the price of the horse would offend the compensatory principle and provide the buyer with a windfall.

Popplewell J, however, sounded one note of caution a note of caution about such an approach, stating that departure from the prima facie rule must not infringe the parties' own allocation of risk:

> ... it is important to keep firmly in mind any contractual allocation of risk made by the parties. Party autonomy dictates that an award of damages should not confound the allocation of risk inherent in the parties' bargain. It is not therefore sufficient merely that there is a future contingency which plays a part in the assessment. It is necessary to examine whether the eventuation of that contingency represents a risk which has been allocated by the parties as one which should fall on one or other of them. If the benefit or detriment of the contingency eventuating is a risk which has been allocated to the buyer, it is not appropriate to deprive him of any benefit which in fact ensues: it is inherent in the bargain that the buyer should receive such benefit. In *The Golden Victory* the contractual allocation of risk, in relation to the period of the charter, formed no impediment to the majority's approach to assessment of damages. The contingency was the outbreak of war, which the parties had provided for by the right to cancel conferred by clause 33. The risk of that happening had been foreseen and had been agreed to be one which if it eventuated would entitle the other party to terminate the charter. The owners had contractually undertaken the risk of such an event allowing the charterers to terminate the charterparty. Adopting an approach to the assessment of damages which took into account the eventuation of the contingency to reduce the owners' damages did not cut across the contractual allocation of risk.

The application of the rule in *The Golden Victory* to one-off contracts for the sale of goods, for instance, has been problematical. In *The Golden Victory* itself Lord Scott seemed to suggest that the principle in that case did not apply to one-off sales where there was an open market, so that in a contract for the sale of goods

> the loss caused by the breach to the seller or the buyer, as the case may be, can be measured by the difference between the contract price and the market price at the time of the breach. The seller can re-sell his goods in the market. The buyer can buy substitute goods in the market. Thereby the loss caused by the breach can be fixed.

The issue arose in the case of **Bunge SA v Nidera BV** [2015] UKSC 43 where buyers contracted to buy a large quantity of Russian milling wheat from the sellers. The contract was entered into in June 2010 with a shipping date between 23 and 30 August 2010. On 5th August, Russia applied an embargo on wheat exports taking effect between 15 August and 30 December 2010. On 9th August the sellers informed the buyers about the introduction of the embargo and cancelled the contract. This cancellation was premature and amounted to a repudiation of the contract since it was always possible that the embargo could have been lifted before the delivery dates. The buyers accepted the repudiation of the contract on 11th August 2010. The next day the sellers offered to reinstate the contract on the same terms, which the buyers rejected. The buyers sought damages of over $3 million which represented the difference between the contract price and the market price on the 11th August. At first instance the judge considered it an open question as to the applicability of the principle in *The Golden Victory* in one-off sale of goods since there was no difficulty about valuing what has been lost – 'the innocent party is compensated for the value of what he has lost at the time he loses it ... Fixing the damages by reference to market value promotes certainty and predictability, and helps inform the innocent party's decision whether or not to terminate.' The matter, however, was not fully argued at this stage. The Supreme Court overturned the decisions in the lower courts to award the substantial damages.

Two questions regarding the compensatory principle at common law arose in the case. Firstly, where there was an available market, what was the date on which the market price was to be assessed for the purposes of calculating the damages and what were the circumstances in which contingencies (other than the change in market price) should be taken into account if subsequent events showed that the contingencies would have reduced the value of the performance? It was held that the prima facie rule is that where there is an available market, the market price was the price at the contractual date for delivery. Applying the decision in *Koch Marine Inc v d'Amica Societa di Navigazione arl (The Elena d'Amico)* [1980] 1 Lloyd's Rep. 75, the Supreme Court stated that normally the injured party is required to mitigate his loss by entering into a substitute contract as soon as is reasonable after the repudiation of the contract by the other party and in such a case the damages are assessed by reference to the price paid under that contract. Thus in *Bunge* the buyers should have attempted to purchase the grain from elsewhere and so the damages would be the difference between the contract price and the price in the new contract. Where, however, a new contract was not entered into, the damages would be assessed by reference to the market price. Lord Sumption, who gave the leading judgement, stated that this, however, is a prima facie rule that did not provide an answer as to when it 'would be relevant to take into account of contingencies (other than a change in the market price) if subsequent events show that they would have reduced the value of performance, perhaps to nothing'. This leads on to the second question.

The second question gives rise to the extent that a judge should take into account any contingencies known at the date of the judge's assessment of the damages if the effect of those contingencies gave rise to the contract being lawfully terminated before or at the term of the contract. This is the compensatory principle ('the lodestar') which operated irrespective of the date at which the market price was valued. The effect of this is that in *Bunge* the Supreme Court held that the buyers could not recover the substantial damages claimed since the buyers had suffered no loss as the embargo had not been lifted and, irrespective of the wrongful repudiation on the 11th August, the sellers could have legitimately repudiated the contract on the 15th August when the embargo came into force. The Supreme Court therefore upheld the decision in *The Golden Victory* in that it was possible as part of the compensatory principle to take into account events that occurred after the repudiation of the contract with the aim of preventing the injured party recovering more than his actual losses.

In arriving at his decision Lord Sumption referred to Lord Denning's dicta in the Court of Appeal in *Maredelanto Compania Naviera SA v Bergbau-Handel GmbH (The Mihalis Angelos)* [1971] 1 QB 164 in which he stated, 'You must take into account all contingencies which might have reduced or extinguished the loss.' Lord Sumption then went on to consider the decision in *The Golden Victory* where the majority of the House of Lords considered that the over-riding principle (or 'lodestar') was the compensatory principle. Irrespective of the date as at which the market price was ascertained, it was necessary to take account of contingencies that are known to have occurred at the date of the assessment and whether the effect of those contingencies would have allowed the contract to be lawfully terminated.

Thus in the context of *The Golden Victory*, damages were on the assumption that the charter would have only lasted for another 14 months. To assess the damages for the four years left to run on the charterparty would have over-compensated GS, the shipowners. Lord Sumption explained the difference between the majority and the minority decisions in *The Golden Victory* as follows:

> The real difference between the majority and the minority turned on the question what was being valued for the purpose assessing damages. The majority were valuing the chartered service that would actually have been performed if the charterparty had not been wrongfully brought to a premature end. On that footing, the notional substitute contract, whenever it was made and at whatever market rate, would have made no difference because it would have been subject to the same war clause as the original contract . . . The minority, on the other hand, considered that one should value not the chartered service which would actually have been performed, but the charterparty itself, assessed at the time that it was terminated, by reference to the terms of a notional substitute concluded as soon as possible after the termination of the original. That would vary, not according to the actual outcome, but according to the outcomes which were perceived as possible or probable at the time that the notional substitute contract was made. The possibility or probability of war would then be factored into the price agreed in the substitute contract . . . I think that the majority's view on this point was correct. Sections 50 and 51 of the Sale of Goods Act , like the corresponding principles of the common law, are concerned with the price of the goods or services which would have been delivered under the contract. They are not concerned with the value of the contract as an article of commerce in itself. As Lord Brown observed at paras 82–83, even if the charterparty rights could have been sold for a capital sum, this was not a proper basis for assessing loss, and an assessment which proceeded as if it were would 'extend the effect of the available market rule well beyond its proper scope'.

Turning to the question as to whether *The Golden Victory* principle could not apply to one-off sales, the Supreme Court considered that there was no difference between contracts for one-off sales and the supply of goods and services over a period of time. Lord Sumption did not consider that Lord Scott in *The Golden Victory* intended to limit the application of the principle in this way, thus Lord Sumption stated:

> The leading speech for the majority, which was delivered by Lord Scott of Foscote, contains dicta which have sometimes been taken to suggest a distinction between a contract for a one-off sale and a contract for the supply of goods or services over a period of time . . . These dicta influenced both the Appeal Board and Hamblen J in the present case. But I do not think that Lord Scott was suggesting that the underlying principle was any different in the case of a one-off sale. Where the only question is the relevant date for taking the market price, the financial consequences of the breach may be said to 'crystallise' at that date. But where, after that date, some supervening event occurs which shows that neither the original contract (had it continued) nor the notional substitute contract at the market price would ever have been performed, the concept of 'crystallising' the assessment of damages at that price is unhelpful. The occurrence of the supervening event would have reduced the value of performance, possibly to nothing, even if the contract had not been wrongfully terminated and whatever the relevant market price. The nature of that problem does not differ according to whether the contract provides for a single act of performance or several successive ones. Nor, as it seems to me, is there any principled reason why the majority's solution should be any different in the two cases. If a distinction were to be made between them, it is difficult to see how *The Mihalis Angelos* , which concerned a contract for a single voyage, could have been decided as it was. As Lord Scott observed in *The Golden Victory* at para 36, the compensatory principle would be equally offended by disregarding subsequent events serving to reduce or eliminate the loss

under 'any anticipatory breach, the acceptance of which had terminated an executory contract'. The most that can be said about one-off contracts of sale is that the facts may be different. In particular, if the injured party goes into the market and enters into a substitute contract by way of mitigation, it will not necessarily be subject to the same contingencies as the original contract.

There is, however, one firm exception to the normal date of breach rule. This arises when a party is claiming damages in lieu of a decree of specific performance under the Chancery Amendment Act 1858 (otherwise known as the Lord Cairns Act). Here damages are assessed as at the date of the judgement, though it should be noted here that the damages claimed are not damages at common law.

The effect of tax on the assessment of damages

Objective 5

The principle that damages are merely designed to compensate the claimant for their actual losses means that their liability in respect of tax has to be taken into account.

British Transport Commission v Gourley [1956] AC 185

In this case there was a claim for loss of earnings that arose from personal injuries caused by negligence. The plaintiff was awarded a sum of £37,720 which represented the claim relating to loss of gross earnings. It was held by the House of Lords that the damages had to be reduced by the amount the plaintiff would have had to pay in tax in respect of that sum. Consequently the plaintiff was awarded a sum of £6,695 representing net income.

The rule in *Gourley*'s case establishes that damages will be reduced to take into account taxation only if two criteria are met:

1 the damages must represent taxable income or gains; *and*
2 the damages themselves are not taxable by HM Revenue & Customs.

As a general guide, the following are not taxable by HM Revenue & Customs:

1 *Compensation for personal injuries.* Clearly these will not generally attract the application of the rule as they do not represent taxable income or gains. Thus if the hirer of a taxi successfully claims in contract for personal injuries sustained by the taxi owner's failure to take reasonable care and is awarded £100,000, then these damages would be payable in full. Similarly, if a person suffers emotional distress from a ruined holiday or wrongful demotion then the awards here will both be payable in full since neither of these awards represents income.

2 *Compensation for loss of office up to £30,000.* The effect of the Income and Corporation Taxes Act 1988, s 148 is that the first £30,000 of any payment for loss of office, redundancy or wrongful dismissal is tax free. Any balance paid in excess of that amount is added to the recipient's income for the year and taxed at the appropriate income tax rate(s). It follows that damages for loss of office etc. up to £30,000 do not represent taxable income or gains and should be paid to the claimant in full. As damages over and above £30,000 will be taxed by HM Revenue & Customs, they should be paid to the claimant in full to avoid the possibility of double taxation. The effect is to achieve Parliament's intention by ensuring that the claimant receives the first £30,000 tax free and the excess is then taxed by HM Revenue & Customs. Thus if *A* has a fixed-term contract of employment for

one year for which they are to be paid £70,000 per annum and *A* is subsequently, in breach of contract, dismissed after six months, *A* may well successfully claim £35,000 compensation for the breach. In such a case the court will pay the first £30,000 in full to take into account s 148, whilst the remaining £5,000 will be paid in full and left to be taxed by HM Revenue & Customs itself.

Income and capital receipts of a trade, profession, office or employment (subject to the above) are taxed by HM Revenue & Customs and therefore fall outside the *Gourley* rule. Thus if *X*, a motor dealer, successfully sues a customer for loss of profit on a sale caused by the customer acting in breach of contract, *X* will receive the damages in full since they effectively represent a receipt of the trade. The damages will then be added to *X*'s gross income and duly taxed by HM Revenue & Customs. Similarly if *R* contracts to buy certain goods from *S* for £1,000 and subsequently *S* fails to deliver in breach of contract so that *R* has to buy similar goods which cost him £1,500, then *R* may claim the £500 extra expense as damages. It is suggested that *R* will be awarded this amount in full since here the amount does not represent income but increased expenditure for an asset from which *R* might have made a profit eventually.

While the logic of *Gourley* may be correct, it has been criticised in its operation since it treats damages awarded for loss of earnings arising out of personal injuries as taxable income.

Beach v *Reed Corrugated Cases Ltd* [1956] 2 All ER 652

In this case, it was estimated that an employee who had been wrongfully dismissed would have received £58,000 by way of salary over the next ten years. In fact the plaintiff had a large personal fortune and therefore his damages were reduced by reference to his tax liability in respect of both earnings and the personal fortune, despite the fact that the fortune might of course vary over that period. The plaintiff was eventually awarded £18,000, though Pilcher J admitted that this was no more than a rough estimation.

It would seem much more sensible for the courts to award the gross sum to the claimant and then allow them to make the necessary arrangements with regard to tax with HM Revenue & Customs. While the principle in *Gourley* was considered in 1958 by the Law Reform Committee, 7th Report (1958) Cmnd 501, no recommendations arose out of the discussions. In the meantime it might be more convenient for the courts to follow the decision in *Shove* v *Downs Surgical plc* [1984] 1 All ER 7, where Sheen J estimated the claimant's net loss of income after deduction of tax and to this he added an amount equivalent to income tax. A further way round the rule is to treat awards of damages for loss of earnings as loss of earning capacity since such damages are treated for tax purposes as representing losses to a capital asset and they do not attract income tax. As the law stands at the moment, however, it is possible for a defendant to rely on totally extraneous matters, such as private income, as in the *Beach* case, to reduce the damages payable by themselves, a result that is hardly just.

Limitations on the availability of damages

Causation

Objective
6

In order to claim damages the claimant must show that there is a causal link between the losses sustained and the breach of contract. The problem here is that circumstances might arise whereby a breach of contract occurs but the defendant argues that the level of loss sustained by the claimant has resulted, not from the breach of contract, but from some other intervening state of affairs.

It was stated in **Galoo Ltd and Others v Bright Grahame Murray** [1994] 1 All ER 16 that the nature of the causation necessary to establish liability for breach of contract (or in tort) was one of the most difficult areas of law. The Court of Appeal said that it was clear that if a breach of contract by a defendant was to entitle a claimant to claim damages, it must first be found to be the dominant cause of the loss. In considering whether a breach of contract was the cause of the loss or merely the occasion for the loss, a court had to arrive at that decision on the basis of common sense.

It may be the case that the loss is caused by the very nature of the contract itself so that it is this factor that results in the loss rather than the breach of contract itself.

C & P Haulage v Middleton [1983] 3 All ER 94

In this case the plaintiff hired a garage on a six-monthly contract basis for use in his business. During the operation of one such contract he decided to equip the garage to meet his own particular needs. The garage owner then, in breach of contract, terminated the contract ten weeks early and the plaintiff sued to recover his expenses in equipping the garage. It was held that his action would fail since the garage owner could legitimately have terminated the contract ten weeks later whereupon the plaintiff would have sustained his losses in any event. Clearly it was not the breach that had caused the loss but the nature of the contract he had entered into, although the breach meant that he suffered his losses somewhat earlier than was intended.

These matters were also discussed in **Young v Purdy** (1995) *The Times*, 7 November, where Leggatt LJ in the Court of Appeal stated that the common-sense test set out in the *Galoo* case was an uncertain guide in deciding whether a particular breach of duty resulted in the loss being caused. The breach of duty may be the actual cause of the loss or it may be merely an occurrence without which no loss would have been sustained, with the result that no damages would be awarded, as can be seen in the *C & P Haulage* decision.

A further situation which may break the causal link between the breach of contract and the losses suffered occurs where the loss results partly from a breach of contract and also from the intervening acts of a third party. In such circumstances the party who is in breach of contract will continue to be liable provided the actions of the third party are, on the balance of probabilities, foreseeable. Thus in **Stansbie v Troman** [1948] 2 KB 48 a painter was engaged to decorate some premises. On completion he left the house unlocked so that thieves were able to enter and burgle the premises. He was held to be liable for the value of the goods stolen since it was reasonably foreseeable that such an event might occur and that he should have guarded against the possibility by securing the premises. A case that contrasts with this position and is referred to extensively by Treitel is **Weld-Blundell v Stephens**.

Weld-Blundell v Stephens [1920] AC 956

In this case an accountant was employed to conduct an investigation into the affairs of a company. The plaintiff wrote a letter to the accountant in which he libelled a number of directors of the company in question. The letter was then negligently left in one of the company's offices by the accountant's

> partner and when found by a manager it was handed to the directors concerned. The directors subsequently brought an action in defamation and secured damages from the plaintiff who, in turn, brought an action against the accountant for breach of contract. The claim was dismissed by the House of Lords on the basis that the action in libel did not result from the breach of contract but from the unforeseeable actions of the manager.

While this case illustrates the point in question the basis for the decision has to be questionable since it is clear that the accountant owed the claimant a duty of confidentiality. Similarly, the actions of the manager are reasonably foreseeable since any employee is bound to disclose information that may be damaging to their employer's interests. Even though this reasoning would appear wrong, the case is probably correctly decided on the basis that the action in defamation was in any event independent of the contract, although it resulted from the accountant's breach of contract in the first place.

Remoteness of damages

The orthodox rule

Having established that there is a causal link between the breach and the losses sustained by the claimant it must not nevertheless be assumed that the defendant will be liable for all losses arising out of the breach. In *Hadley v Baxendale* it was held that a defendant will be liable for all types of losses that arise from the consequences of the breach which can be said to be within his contemplation, or ought to have been within his contemplation, at the time of contracting, other losses being regarded as 'too remote'. The case forms the basis of the modern law as regards remoteness and can be described as the 'orthodox rule'. However, before looking at the rule in detail it is useful to recognise from the outset that the rule has been subject to some modification following the case of *Transfield Shipping Inc.* v *Mercator Shipping Inc. (The Achilleas)* [2008] UKHL 48; [2008] 3 WLR 345. This case modified the orthodox rule so that a defendant would be liable for all types of loss for which he has 'assumed responsibility' when entering into the contract. We shall call this the 'modified rule' so as to distinguish later on in the discussions regarding remoteness. It has to be said from the outset that the application of the modified rule is restricted to exceptional cases and that, as Lord Hoffmann indicated in *The Achilleas*, 'cases of departure from the ordinary foreseeability rule based on individual circumstances will be unusual'. Suffice it to say we will commence our examination of the rules regarding remoteness by looking at the orthodox.

Hadley v Baxendale (1854) 9 Exch 341

> The plaintiffs' mill had ceased working because of a broken crankshaft. As there was no spare shaft, the broken one had to be sent to the manufacturer for use as a pattern for a new one. To this end the plaintiffs engaged the defendant carriers to transport the shaft to the manufacturers. The defendants were told what the item was, a broken shaft from a particular mill, and that the plaintiffs were the proprietors of the mill. The defendants were negligent in their delivery of the shaft and their negligence resulted in the operation of the mill being shut down for longer than would have been ordinarily necessary had there been no delay in the transit of the shaft. The plaintiffs sued for their increased loss of profits caused by the delay and were unsuccessful. In his judgement Alderson B produced what has since become known as the rule in *Hadley v Baxendale*:

> Where two parties have made a contract which one of them has broken, the damages which the other party ought to receive in respect of such a breach of contract should be such as may fairly and reasonably be considered either arising naturally, i.e. according to the usual course of things, from such breach of contract itself, or such as may reasonably be supposed to have been in the contemplation of both parties, at the time they made the contract, as the probable result of the breach of it.

It can be seen that the rule in fact has two limbs to it. Some authorities consider that there are two rules but this interpretation has largely been discounted today in favour of the notion of one rule with two limbs. The result is that there is a single test as regards the liability for damages for breach of contract based on a reasonable foresight test, and that the level of liability varies depending on the degree of knowledge that the party in breach has or is assumed to have. The effect is that the more remote the damage becomes the greater the degree of knowledge required of the guilty party. It can be seen that the two limbs represent two extremes, one dealing with normal (natural) loss, the other with abnormal (exceptional) losses. The two limbs thus comprise damage:

1 'arising naturally, i.e. according to the usual course of things, from such breach of contract itself'. This limb covers damage that is an inevitable consequence of the breach and which the defendant should have contemplated as arising from the breach, that is, the defendant is deemed to have imputed notice of this type of damage since it is a normal consequence of the breach. This type of loss is often referred to simply as 'normal' loss;

2 'such as may reasonably be supposed to have been in the contemplation of both the parties, at the time they made the contract, as the probable result of the breach of it'. This limb covers losses which would not normally be in the contemplation of the defendant as likely to result from the breach, but which they may nevertheless be liable for if they had actual knowledge of those consequences when they entered into the contract. The type of loss dealt with by this limb is usually referred to as 'special' or 'abnormal' loss.

Translating the rule into the facts of *Hadley* v *Baxendale* the court decided that the loss of profits could not be regarded as a normal loss since such loss was not an inevitable consequence of the delay, as the mill owners could well have had a spare shaft, or have one available to them, which would have prevented any loss from occurring. It could not have been contemplated by the carrier that the delay in returning the mill shaft would have meant that the mill would be standing idle. While no doubt the claimants would have anticipated that the mill would be at a standstill, this was not in the contemplation of both the parties at the time the contract was made.

If the loss of profits was not a normal loss in the contemplation of the parties as being an inevitable consequence of the breach, then it must have amounted to a 'special loss'. Could the claimants succeed here? The court again decided that they could not since this type of loss required actual knowledge on the part of the carriers that their delay would result in such losses being incurred. Since the carriers were not given actual knowledge of this potential consequence by the claimants, they could not be held liable for that consequence. If they had been given this knowledge then no doubt they would have taken steps to ensure the expeditious return of the shaft so as to limit their liability. It is therefore important that a claimant makes it clear at the time of the entry into the contract that there may be 'special losses' that might arise in the event of a breach of contract. It is not open to a claimant to avoid such a disclosure because, for instance, this might increase the contract price and then surprise the defendant with a claim far larger than the defendant anticipated when entering into the contract.

In *Hadley* it was not clear what the nature of the disclosure should be. Is it sufficient for the defendant to be simply informed about the special loss or must the defendant not only have the special loss disclosed to him but have accepted responsibility for the loss should a breach occur? In *Simpson* v *London and North Western Railway Co.* (1876) 1 QBD 274 it was held that simply informing the defendant as regards the potential loss at the commencement of the contract would suffice and this appears to be correct within the orthodox approach. On the other hand in *British Columbia Saw Mill Co.* v *Nettleship* (1868) LR 3 CP 499 it was stated that the knowledge must be brought to the attention of the defendant in such a way that the claimant reasonably believes that the defendant has accepted responsibility for the special losses that arise should a breach occur. This approach appears to be more in line with the modified approach taken by Lord Hoffmann in *Transfield Shipping Inc.* v *Mercator Shipping Inc. (The Achilleas)* [2008] UKHL 48; [2008] 3 WLR 345.

See later section for details of the modified rule.

1. The application of the orthodox approach

The rule in *Hadley* v *Baxendale* was given substantial airing by Asquith LJ in *Victoria Laundry (Windsor) Ltd* v *Newman Industries Ltd*.

Victoria Laundry (Windsor) Ltd v *Newman Industries Ltd* [1949] 2 KB 528

The facts of the case were that the plaintiffs, hoping to expand their business, bought a second-hand boiler from the defendants. At the time of contracting the boiler had yet to be dismantled but in carrying out that operation the defendants damaged it. The result of this was that it arrived at the plaintiffs 22 weeks late. The delay meant that the plaintiffs failed to reap the extra profits the new boiler would have produced. These were assessed at £16 per week. The plaintiffs also lost a lucrative dyeing contract with the Ministry of Supply, the damages for the loss of profits here being assessed at £262 per week. The plaintiffs sued for breach of contract. It was held that the plaintiffs could recover the £16 per week. The loss of profits here clearly fell within the first limb, being normal losses which the defendants must have known, at the time of entering into the contract, that the plaintiffs would sustain by their failure to deliver the boiler on time. The claim in respect of the £262 per week failed. This item was a special or abnormal loss for which the defendants would be liable only if they had actual knowledge of the possibility that such loss might occur at the time of entering into the contract. Since the plaintiffs had not told or otherwise informed the defendants of the lucrative dyeing contract, the defendants had no actual knowledge of such potential loss and were not therefore liable for this item.

Asquith LJ considered that the liability for loss depended on whether the loss was 'reasonably foreseeable as liable to result from the breach'. Thus he stated:

In cases of breach of contract the aggrieved party is only entitled to recover such part of the loss actually resulting as was at the time of the contract reasonably foreseeable as likely to result from the breach . . . In order to make the contract-breaker liable under either rule it is not necessary that he should actually have asked himself what loss is liable to result from a breach . . . It suffices that, if he had considered the question, he would, as a reasonable man, have concluded that the loss in question was liable to result . . . Nor, finally, to make the particular loss recoverable, need it be proved that on a given state of knowledge, the defendant could, as a reasonable man, foresee that a breach must necessarily result in that loss. It is enough if he could foresee it was likely so to result. It is enough . . . if the loss (or some factor without which it would not have occurred) is a 'serious possibility' or a 'real danger'. For short, we have used the word 'liable' to result. Possibly the colloquialism 'on the cards' indicates the shade of meaning with some approach to accuracy.

The test of remoteness therefore depends on the state of the defendant's knowledge and to this extent every defendant has imputed knowledge of things which occur in the usual course of things. In the case of the loss of general profits, then such loss is clearly imputed to them and are 'reasonably foreseeable as likely to result from the breach'. The same is not true of the special losses which they could not have reasonably foreseen unless they had actual knowledge of such losses at the time they entered into the contract. The defendants knew nothing of the special government contracts and therefore they were not liable for such losses.

The result of the above was that Asquith LJ seemed to suggest that the test of remoteness in contract was the same as the test applied in tort. This approach was subject to sharp rebuke from their Lordships in *Koufos* v *Czarnikow Ltd*, *The Heron II*.

Koufos v Czarnikow Ltd, The Heron II [1969] 1 AC 350

A ship was chartered to carry a cargo of sugar from Constanza to Basrah. At the time the contract was entered into the charterer intended to sell the sugar as soon as it was unloaded at Basrah. Although the shipowner was not aware of this, he was aware that there was a market for sugar at Basrah and that 'if he had thought about the matter he must have realised that at least it was not unlikely that the sugar would be sold in the market at market price upon arrival'. In fact the shipowner deviated from his route so that, in breach of contract, he arrived at Basrah nine days late during which the market price for sugar fell. It was held that the charterer was entitled to damages for the loss suffered by reason of the fall in the market price of the sugar.

Their Lordships considered that it was insufficient merely to show reasonable foreseeability of the loss. Lord Reid, in particular, considered that the question of liability turned on whether:

> on the information available to the defendant when the contract was made, he should, or the reasonable man in his position would, have realised that such loss was sufficiently likely to result from the breach of contract to make it proper to hold that the loss flowed naturally from the breach of contract or that loss of that kind should have been within his contemplation.

Lord Reid for the most part confined liability to that of loss arising naturally from the breach or loss that should have been within contemplation, that is, special loss. He considered that loss that fell within these two extremes would only occur 'in a minority of cases' and that such loss was not recoverable. He stated:

> I am satisfied that the Court did not intend that every type of damage which was reasonably foreseeable by the parties when the contract was made should either be considered as arising naturally i.e. in the usual course of things or be supposed to be in the contemplation of the parties. Indeed the decision makes it clear that a type of damage which was plainly foreseeable as a real possibility but which would only occur in a small minority of cases cannot be regarded as arising in the usual course of things or be supposed to have been within the contemplation of the parties: the parties are not supposed to contemplate as grounds for the recovery of damage any type of loss or damage which on the knowledge available to the defendant would appear to him as only likely to occur in a small minority of cases.

An application of the rule in *Hadley* v *Baxendale* can also be seen in the Scottish case of *Balfour Beatty Construction (Scotland) Ltd* v *Scottish Power plc* (1995) 71 BLR 20 where Balfour Beatty were the main contractors for the construction of a section of the Edinburgh bypass and its associated structures. In order to carry out the project it was necessary to build a concrete production plant to provide for a continuous pour of concrete. The defendants contracted to provide a temporary supply of electricity to the plant. During construction the electricity supply was interrupted which caused a break in the continuous pour process. As a result of this an aqueduct could not be constructed according to the civil engineering specifications and therefore had to be demolished and rebuilt. The plaintiffs sought to recover the costs of the demolition and reconstruction from the defendants.

The House of Lords held that the loss was too remote. It applied the principles in *Hadley* v *Baxendale* (the rule also operates in Scots law), i.e. whether the loss was of the type that might reasonably have been contemplated by the defendants at the time of the contract as a consequence of the breach. Their Lordships found there was no evidence that the defendants were aware of the need for a continuous pour process. They considered that it had always to be a question of fact what one contracting party was presumed to know about the business activities of the other. Jauncey LJ considered that there was no general rule to the effect that in all the circumstances contracting parties were presumed to have reasonable knowledge of the course of business conducted by each other, finding support for this view in the *Heron II* case. However, the simpler the activity, the more likely could it be inferred that the parties had a reasonable knowledge of each other's business activities. On the other hand, if one party was involved in complex manufacturing or construction processes, there was no reason why a supplier of a product to be used in those processes should be aware of the details of all the techniques to be used in the process and thus be aware of the effect of a failure or deficiency in the product supplied.

2. Reasonable foreseeability: contract versus tort

Lord Reid in *Heron II* went on to distinguish between foreseeability in tort and foreseeability in contract. He considered that reasonable foreseeability in tort imposed a wider liability and allowed for recovery of the most unusual losses – provided that they were reasonably foreseeable. In contract, however, he considered the situation was different since the parties were free to protect themselves in respect of unusual or special losses by specifically drawing the attention of the other party to that particular risk, thereby placing it within the contemplation of that individual. Lord Reid considered that in contract a higher degree of probability than reasonable foreseeability was required to be shown and that Asquith LJ implied this when he referred to 'loss reasonably foreseeable as liable to result from the breach'. In attempting to describe the higher degree of probability the other judges within the House of Lords produced various ways of explaining the difference in the foreseeability test in contract and in tort, though these attempts were largely spurious exercises in semantics which failed to explain the difference adequately, although four of the five members of the House considered the 'on the cards' expression of Asquith LJ to be inappropriate. Thus the judges spoke in terms that there must be a 'serious possibility' or a 'very substantial' or a 'real danger' that loss would occur. Thus in the law of contract a higher degree of probability has to be shown to satisfy the test of remoteness and that the expression 'reasonable foreseeability' in contract refers to this higher degree of probability. The decisions in the *Victoria Laundry* and *Heron II* cases were extensively considered in the Court of Appeal in *H Parsons (Livestock) Ltd* v *Uttley Ingham*.

H Parsons (Livestock) Ltd v Uttley Ingham [1978] 1 All ER 525

In this case there was a contract for the sale and installation of an animal feed hopper which was to have a ventilated top. During transit to the site the ventilation hatch had been sealed and when installation was completed the defendants forgot to open the hatch. The result was that some of the feed went mouldy and caused a rare intestinal disease to break out amongst the plaintiff's pigs, killing 254 of them. At first instance the plaintiff lost his claim for the loss of the pigs since the judge considered that such loss was not within the contemplation of the parties as the particular rare illness and the subsequent deaths of the pigs was considered to be an unlikely result of the breach at the time the contract was made. The Court of Appeal reversed this decision.

As we have seen in *Heron II*, Lord Reid and the other judges agreed that a higher degree of foreseeability is required in contract than in tort since they considered that a party to a contract is able to ensure that he can recover for all the consequences of a breach by informing the other party of any factors that increase the degree of risk. Lord Denning adopted a different solution to the problem, differentiating between economic loss, such as loss of profits, as occurred in *Victoria Laundry* and *Heron II*, and physical loss, which occurred in the *H Parsons* case. He considered that the stricter test proposed by Lord Reid was appropriate where the loss amounted to economic loss, and to some degree this view has some credence since, as pointed out by Lord Reid himself, the parties can provide for such occurrence specifically within the contract itself. In respect of physical loss, that is, personal injury or damage to property, Lord Denning considered that the test of remoteness in contract should be the same as that found in tort. In such an instance the defendant is liable for any loss which they ought reasonably to be able to foresee at the time of the breach as being a possible consequence of the breach, no matter how slight that possibility. Lord Denning in formulating a test of reasonable foreseeability therefore distinguishes between the *types* of damage suffered – physical damage following the more generous tortious test, while economic loss of the type suffered in breaches of contract following the *Heron II* test is recoverable if the loss is reasonably foreseeable as a serious possibility. The view of Lord Denning undoubtedly reconciles the particular problems of cases like *H Parsons* with those encountered in *Victoria Laundry* and *Heron II*, but it is unattractively unwieldy and has no authoritative support.

Lord Scarman did not agree with Lord Denning's dual approach although he did agree with the result in that damages should be recoverable since there was a serious possibility that harm would result. Once the type of damage is within the contemplation of the parties then the extent or degree or seriousness of the damage is irrelevant. Lord Scarman thus took a diametrically opposing view to that of the House of Lords in the *Heron II* case and was supported by Orr LJ. He stated that there was no difference between the test of remoteness in contract and that in tort. He stated that, in any event, whether it be in contract or in tort, the test of remoteness depended, not on the contemplation of the degree of injury, but simply on proof that the type of loss could reasonably have been anticipated. He stated that if the defendants had merely manufactured the defective hopper which had then been sold to a retailer, who, in turn, had resold it to the plaintiffs, then the action of the plaintiffs would have been in tort against the manufacturer. The test of remoteness here would have been based on a reasonable foreseeability test based in tort and there was no reason why this should be any different from the test that should exist in contract. The arguments of Lord Scarman make a great deal of sense and certainly make for a simpler application of the law given the concurrent liability that can arise in contract and tort.

In *Jackson v Royal Bank of Scotland plc* [2005] UKHL 3 the House of Lords confirmed that the rule of remoteness of damages in contract was governed by that which was contemplated by the parties at the commencement of the breach of the contract. The logic in making this distinction between remoteness in contract as from tort is sound. In the law of contract parties enter into their obligations from the time of contracting and therefore it is assumed that any breach of the contractual terms arises from the inception of the contract. Thus, on entering into a contract, if a party wishes to know what their liability is for breaking it that party can be advised accordingly from a simple examination of the contract. This is not the case in tort. One cannot foresee the consequences of a tortious act until the act itself occurs and it is only at this time that one can assess the likely liability.

The discussions that took place in the Court of Appeal in *H Parsons* clearly stand in the shadow of the decision in *Heron II*. For the moment at least the reasoning of Lord Reid, that liability for special loss arises only where that loss is contemplated, must persist. It has one advantage in that the strictness of the rule should encourage parties to a contract to provide information as regards the possible extent of their losses, though it is clearly inappropriate in cases such as *H Parsons*.

So far we have been examining the differences between the reasonable foreseeability tests in contract versus tort, however, nowhere do these tests come more sharply into focus than where a case arises in which there appears to be concurrent liability under both heads. One such case where this situation occurred is the case of ***Wellesley Partners LLP v Withers LLP*** [2015] EWCA Civ 1146. The facts of the case were that Wellesley Partners LLP ('WP') was a firm of headhunters which instructed a firm of solicitors, Withers LLP ('Withers') to draft a new partnership agreement which was to cover new partners. WP wanted the agreement to be drafted in such a way as to allow a new partner/investor to have the option to withdraw half its capital after 42 months. In fact, the agreement as drafted by Withers gave the investor an option to withdraw at any time within the first 41 months. The investor exercised its option and the drafting error was then revealed. WP sought damages for loss of profits it would have made by opening an office in New York, arguing that it had relied on the investment to achieve that objective and that specifically it had been unable to obtain mandates from an investment bank, Nomura, in the US which had wanted to use WP in its objective of developing and building its US activities.

The judge at first instance held that Withers had been negligent in drafting the new agreement and also that it was in breach of contract. The judge in examining the remoteness rule where there is concurrent liability in contract and in tort considered that there should only be one test and considered that where the parties were in a contractual relationship, the contractual test should prevail despite the claim being for professional negligence. He reasoned that in a contractual relationship the parties were not strangers to one another and therefore were able to make an assessment of the risks involved. The judge considered that the loss of opportunity arising from the Nomura initiative fell within the tort test of foreseeability, which was more generous to WP. On this basis the judge found, applying the tortious test, that the loss of the chance of the Nomura opportunity was a type of damage that was reasonably foreseeable and not too remote to be recovered in the tort of negligence. The judge, obiter, expressed a view that he doubted that the damages in respect of the Nomura opportunity could be recovered in contract. His reasoning was that this opportunity did not exist at the time the agreement was drafted and therefore could not have been reasonably contemplated at that time. In arriving at that opinion the judge drew an analogy with the loss of profits for the lucrative contacts in *Victoria Laundry* and the loss of profits on the charterparty in *The Achilleas* (see below).

Withers appealed, arguing that the judge had wrongly adopted the tortious test for remoteness regarding the loss of the Nomura contract stating that a contractual test should have been adopted. WP argued that the judge had wrongly categorised the loss of profits as a loss of chance claim and that, in the event that the tortious remoteness rule did not apply, then the sums for the Nomura opportunity remained recoverable as damages for breach of contract.

On the issue of remoteness the Court of Appeal considered that where contractual and tortious duties to take care in carrying out instructions exist side by side, the test for recoverability of damage for economic loss should be the same, and should be the contractual one. The reasoning behind adopting the remoteness test in contract is that the parties have the opportunity to draw special circumstances to each other's attention at the time of formation of the contract. The parties in a contractual relationship are assumed to be contracting on the basis that liability will be confined to damage of the kind which is in their reasonable contemplation. The Court of Appeal considered that it made no sense at all for the existence of the concurrent duty in tort to upset this consensus.

This decision did not result in the appeal by Withers being allowed since the damages awarded were in any event recoverable under the contractual remoteness test. The damage sustained had been of a kind that was within the reasonable contemplation of the parties. Whilst the judge found that Withers knew sufficient for it to be reasonably foreseeable that if the investor withdrew its capital WP might be prevented from earning profits in the US, on the evidence it was equally within the reasonable contemplation of the parties that it was not unlikely that this would be so. Withers were aware that WP wished to expand into the US and that the investment was the means to facilitate this in order to make profits.

The Court of Appeal distinguished the case from that of **Victoria Laundry**. Floyd LJ considered that the loss of the lucrative government contract which was unknown to the defendant was a loss of a different kind from losses of the ordinary business of a laundry. The contract breaker had no knowledge that the laundry was proposing to undertake work of this kind and would have regarded the profits on these contracts as a different and higher form of risk than the general risk of loss of profits by the laundry. By contrast, in the present case, it would be artificial to suppose that Withers being employed to draft a contract in such a way as to prevent the investor withdrawing its capital would have regarded the losses from the New York initiative as a different sort of risk. The Court of Appeal considered that the analogy with the decision in **The Achilleas** was also not persuasive. Floyd LJ stated,

> That case also turned, at least in part, on the particular commercial circumstances known to the parties at the time of formation of the contract. These included the evidence of the general understanding in the shipping market that liability was restricted to the difference between the market rate and the charter rate for the overrun period, and that any departure from this rule was likely to give rise to a real risk of serious commercial uncertainty which the industry as a whole would regard as undesirable. We are not in that territory in the present case.

The Court of Appeal therefore decided that the losses in respect of the New York initiative were recoverable.

3. The type and extent principle

We have seen that in **H Parsons** Scarman LJ and Orr LJ considered that since the type of loss was within the contemplation of the parties, the extent of the loss need not be considered. It was for that reason that the defendants were liable for the loss of the pigs since it was within the contemplation of the parties that there was a 'serious possibility' that the pigs might become ill from the defects in the hopper. This loss was within the *type* of loss contemplated by the parties. On the other hand the plaintiff could not recover for the 'loss of profit on future sales' of the pigs since this *type* of loss was not within the contemplation of the parties as being a serious possibility.

If these principles were to be translated into the case of *Victoria Laundry* then the loss of general profits are recoverable since these were of the type that were within the contemplation of the parties as being a serious possibility of occurring, though the same could not be true of the loss of the profits from the government contract.

Once the kind of damage brought about by the breach of contract is found to be of a type that is within the reasonable contemplation of the parties, whichever branch of the rule in *Hadley v Baxendale* applies, the fact that the results are far more serious than could be reasonably contemplated is immaterial, as held in *Vacwell Engineering Co. Ltd v BDH Chemicals Ltd* [1971] 1 QB 111 and affirmed in *Brown v KMR Services Ltd* [1995] 4 All ER 598.

The issues surrounding the type and extent principles can be seen more recently in *Jackson v Royal Bank of Scotland plc* where the defendant bank ('RBS') inadvertently disclosed the prices charged by an overseas supplier of dog food ('Pet Products'). Samson was the UK importer who sold on the products to a UK distributor ('Economy Bag'). Once Economy Bag discovered the extent of the mark up charged by Samson, it decided to cut out Samson as the intermediary and buy directly from Pet Products. This proved disastrous for Samson since it lost its highly lucrative contract with Economy Bag and indeed eventually went out of business. Clearly the bank was in breach of contract but to what extent could Samson recover damages for the profits it would have made from its contract with Economy Bag – over what period of time could it claim for loss of profits? The Court of Appeal considered that the damages would be limited to profits for one year as the bank would only have contemplated damages for one year. The Court of Appeal awarded damages of $45,000 for that year alone. The House of Lords considered this award to be incorrect since once it was established that the type of loss was recoverable in that it was a loss that arose naturally according to the usual course of things or was in the contemplation of the parties, then there were no limits to the extent of the loss that could be recovered, duration being a question of extent. The best estimate of the loss sustained was measured over a period of four years with a diminishing return of profits over that period and so the House of Lords reinstated the damages of $124,500.

The modified rule

It was stated earlier that the two limbs of the rule represent two extremes. However, the question remains as to the parameters of liability for loss which is something more than a natural loss and yet falls short of a special loss, actual knowledge of which has been given to the defendant. It has been seen that once the type of loss has been held to be not too remote then damages are not limited in extent. However, there have to be some limits to this principle. Just how far does the first limb of *Hadley v Baxendale* go in establishing or limiting liability for loss in terms of the type of loss? The matter was considered in the case of *Transfield Shipping Inc. v Mercator Shipping Inc. (The Achilleas)*.

The judgements in the House of Lords were not unified and, while agreed on the outcome, their Lordships adopted different approaches to their decisions. Lord Rodger and Baroness Hale adopting the orthodox approach, while Lord Hoffmann and Lord Hope took a very different view and developed what may be termed the 'modified' approach to the problem. Lord Walker took an approach very similar to that of Lord Hoffmann and Lord Hope though not expressed in the same terms.

Transfield Shipping Inc. v Mercator Shipping Inc. (The Achilleas) [2008] UKHL 48; [2008] 3 WLR 345

In this case the House of Lords reviewed the operation of the first arm of the rule in *Hadley* v *Baxendale*. The facts of the case were that Mercator Shipping ('M'), the shipowner, had chartered a ship to Transfield Shipping ('T'), for a period of five to seven months, to end no later than midnight on 2 May 2004. T notified M that the ship would be back no later. M therefore contracted to let the ship to new charterers for a period of about four to six months, promising that they could have the ship no later than 8 May 2004. The agreed price of hire was $39,500 a day. The ship was delayed on its last voyage and M did not get it back until 11 May 2004. The new charterers agreed to take the ship, but by then the market had fallen sharply and they would only take it at a reduced price of $31,500 a day. The dispute went before the arbitrators on the basis of whether T was liable to pay only for the use of the ship for the number of days that it was late at the market rate then prevailing (9 days × $31,500) or whether, as M had argued, T was liable to pay the difference between what M would have got from the new charter had the ship been returned in time and what it in fact got ($8,000 × 191 days being the period of time of the new charter). The arbitrators, by a majority, adopted the latter approach. They concluded that the loss on the new charter fell within the first rule in Hadley v Baxendale as arising 'naturally, i.e. according to the usual course of things, from such breach of contract itself' or 'normal' loss. It fell within that rule because it was damage 'of a kind which the [charterer], when he made the contract, ought to have realised was not unlikely to result from a breach of contract caused by delay in redelivery'. A dissenting arbitrator did not deny that T would have known that M would be very likely to enter into a following fixture (or charter) during the course of the charter and that late delivery might cause that fixture to be lost. However, he concluded that a reasonable man in T's position would not have understood that he was assuming liability for the risk of the type of loss in question. He stated that the general understanding in the shipping market was that liability was restricted to the difference between the market rate and the charter rate for the overrun period and that 'any departure from this rule [is] likely to give rise to a real risk of serious commercial uncertainty which the industry as a whole would regard as undesirable'. The appellant charterer (T) appealed against the decision to the Court of Appeal, which upheld the decision by the arbitrators. The appellant charterer then appealed to the House of Lords, which allowed the appeal concluding that damages should be awarded at the lower calculation.

The difficulty facing the House of Lords was that while the loss of profits by M are foreseeable within *Hadley* v *Baxendale* in that it was 'not unlikely' that a delay in returning the ship would give rise to the loss of profits claimed by M, they were all clearly of the opinion that M should not succeed for the claim for profits for 191 days. It was acknowledged by the arbitrators and the lower courts that this was not the norm in the shipping market where there was a general understanding that liability was restricted to the difference between the market value and the charter rate for the overrun period and 'any departure from this rule is likely to give rise to a real risk of serious commercial uncertainty which the industry as a whole would regard as undesirable'. Furthermore, the state of the market rates at this time was very volatile and some acknowledgement of the commercial background and circumstances had to be taken into account.

Lord Hoffmann, with Lord Hope concurring, considered that, in accepting M's submission what mattered was whether the type of loss claimed was foreseeable, that is 'not unlikely' to have arisen. The majority arbitrators had applied too crude a test, and it was an error of law to adopt it. Lord Hoffmann considered that the common basis on which the parties had contracted was essential to the rule in *Hadley* v *Baxendale* as a whole. In *Heron II* their Lordships had in mind that it was not simply a question of probability but also of what the contracting parties had to be taken to have had in mind, having regard to the nature and object of their business transaction. What mattered was whether it was the common intention of reasonable parties to a charterparty of this sort that in the event of a relatively short delay in redelivery that an extraordinary loss, measured over the whole term of the renewed fixture of 191 days, was, in the words of Lord Reid in *Heron II*, 'sufficiently likely to result from the breach of contract to make it proper to hold that the loss flowed naturally from the breach or that loss of that kind should have been within [the defaulting party's] contemplation'. The court considered that would not have been the common intention of reasonable contracting parties and it was contrary to the principle stated in *Victoria Laundry (Windsor)* v *Newman Industries*, as reaffirmed in *Heron II*, to suppose that the parties were contracting on the basis that T would be liable for any loss, however large, occasioned by a delay in redelivery in circumstances where it had no knowledge of, or control over, the new fixture entered into by M.

Lord Hoffmann and Lord Hope were clearly of the opinion that the rule in *Hadley* v *Baxendale* is more than simply a principle that 'remoteness of damages in contract is determined by. . . what at the time of the contract was reasonably foreseeable' (Lord Hope). In order to arrive at the losses for which the charterer was liable one has to consider not just the question of foreseeability but also whether the losses are of a 'type' or 'kind' which the charterer ought fairly to be taken to have accepted responsibility for. Thus while the losses suffered by M are foreseeable, in the sense that T must have known that M would have suffered loss by the charter overrun, T would not have reasonably contemplated the losses sustained by M – a reasonable man in T's position would not have understood that he was assuming liability for the risk of the type of loss in question. As Lord Hoffmann stated:

> It is generally accepted that a contracting party will be liable for damages for losses which are unforeseeably large, if loss of that type or kind fell within one or other of the rules in *Hadley* v *Baxendale* . . . But . . . a party may not be liable for foreseeable losses because they are not of a type or kind for which he can be treated as having assumed responsibility. What is the basis for deciding whether loss is of the same type or a different type? It is not a question of Platonist metaphysics. The distinction must rest upon some principle of the law of contract. In my opinion the only rational basis for the distinction is that it reflects what would have [been] reasonable [as] regarded by the contracting party as significant for the purpose of the risk he was undertaking.

Thus Lord Hoffmann developed a modification to the orthodox approach seen in *Hadley* v *Baxendale*. The claim of M in this case was a novel one. Previous cases had always assumed that the measure of damages for late delivery was the difference between the charter rate and the market rate. None of the previous authorities had dealt with the possibility of damages for the loss of a following charter; indeed it was always assumed in a number of previous cases that the measure of damages for late delivery is the difference between the charter rate and the market rate.

In arriving *at his judgement Lord Hoffmann relied heavily on the case of Banque Bruxelles Lambert SA* v *Eagle Star Insurance Co. Ltd (sub nom South Australia Asset Management Corporation* v *York Montague Ltd)* [1997] AC 191. In that case the question had arisen as to whether a valuer, who (in breach of an implied term to exercise reasonable care and skill) had negligently misinformed his client, a bank, that property to be used as security for a loan was worth significantly more than its true market value, was liable not only for the losses attributable for the deficient security but also further losses attributable to the fall in the property market. The House of Lords considered that he should not be so liable on the basis that a term implied by law that imposes a duty of care on the valuer could only render him liable to the extent that the lender, the bank, does not obtain less than the bank was reasonably entitled to expect. Furthermore, the liability of the valuer could not be extended to more than he could reasonably have thought he was undertaking. The effect of this was to exclude the liability for the fall in the property market despite the fact that those losses were foreseeable in the sense of being 'not unlikely' to arise. Those losses were therefore 'outside of the scope of liability which the parties would have reasonably considered that the valuer was undertaking' (*per* Lord Hoffmann).

Lord Hoffmann also referred to the judgement of Goff J in *Satef-Huttenes Albertus Spa* v *Paloma Tercera Shipping Co. SA (The Pegase)* [1981] Lloyd's Rep 175 in which he stated that the test was:

> ... have the facts in question come to the defendant's knowledge in such circumstances that a reasonable person in the shoes of the defendant would, if he had considered the matter at the time of making the contract, have contemplated that, in the event of a breach by him, such facts were to be taken into account when considering his responsibility for loss suffered by the plaintiff as a result of such a breach.

This position was also adopted in the later Court of Appeal case of *Mulvenna* v *Royal Bank of Scotland plc* [2003] EWCA Civ 1112 in which a property developer sought to recover loss of profits that he hoped to make from a development to be financed by the bank and which he lost by the actions of the bank in withdrawing from the loan agreement. In that case the Court of Appeal held that even if the bank knew the purpose for which the funds were to be required and that it was foreseeable that the claimant developer would suffer loss of profit if he did not receive them, the damages were not recoverable.

In this case Sir Anthony Evans provided a useful insight into why the loss of profits was not recoverable and reconciled the decision in terms of the judgements contained in *South Australia* and *The Pegase* cases. He thus stated:

> The authorities to which we were referred ... demonstrate that the concept of reasonable foreseeability is not a complete guide to the circumstances in which damages are recoverable as a matter of law. Even if the loss was reasonably foreseeable as a consequence of the breach of duty in question (or of contract, for the same principles apply), it may nevertheless be regarded as 'too remote a consequence' or not a consequence at all, and the damages claim is disallowed. In effect, the chain of consequences is cut off as a matter of law, either because it is regarded as unreasonable to impose liability for that consequence of the breach (*The Pegase* [1981] Lloyd's Rep 175, Robert Goff J), or because the scope of the duty is limited so as to exclude it (*Banque Bruxelles Lambert SA* v *Eagle Star Insurance* [1997] AC 191), or because as a matter of common sense the breach cannot be said to have caused the loss, although it may have provided the opportunity for it to occur ...

Sir Anthony Evans therefore provides us with three reasons why the damages in each of the cases were irrecoverable. It would appear that even if losses could be regarded as reasonably foreseeable they are still not recoverable since the losses were not of the type or kind for which a contracting party at the time the contract was entered into could have contemplated assuming responsibility. Essentially in the *Mulvenna* case one may argue that the losses claimed for were too speculative. Clearly the bank could not have predicted being liable for such loss of profits – even if such profits were made. Building developments often make losses and clearly it could not be in the contemplation of the bank when agreeing to a development loan that they could be liable for loss of profits that may or may not arise. As Sir Anthony Evans indicates, 'as a matter of commonsense the breach cannot be said to have caused the loss'. Equally, damages may not be recoverable if the level of loss is unpredictable in the sense that while the losses may be reasonably foreseeable, they were 'outside of the scope of liability which the parties would have reasonably considered that the valuer was undertaking', as in *South Australia*. It is suggested that this is the essence behind the decision in *The Achilleas*. Would the decision in *The Achilleas* have been different if the second charterer on not receiving the ship on time had repudiated their contract with M? Would T have been liable for the losses sustained by M from the loss of that contract? Presumably this would have been reasonably foreseeable and in the contemplation of the parties as a likely result of an overrun on the charter and, subject to mitigation of loss by M, damages would be recoverable in such an instance.

The orthodox approach and narrow ground adopted by Lord Rodger and Baroness Hale in applying the orthodox approach in *The Achilleas* found that the parties could not have reasonably contemplated that the delay in returning the ship would, in the ordinary course of things, have resulted in the owners suffering the type of loss for which they claimed damages, as Lord Rodger stated:

> I am satisfied that, when they entered into the addendum in September 2003, neither party would reasonably have contemplated that an overrun of nine days would 'in the ordinary course of things' cause the owners the kind of loss for which they claim damages. That loss was not the 'ordinary consequence' of a breach of that kind. It occurred in this case only because of the extremely volatile market conditions which produced both the owners' initial (particularly lucrative) transaction, with a third party, and the subsequent pressure on the owners to accept a lower rate for that fixture. Back in September 2003, this loss could not have been reasonably foreseen as being likely to arise out of the delay in question. It was, accordingly, too remote to give rise to a claim for damages for breach of contract.

The difficulty that is plainly apparent is that this approach produced two conflicting views since in the lower courts it was held that the shipowners could recover for 191 days, while in their judgements their Lordships came to a different conclusion. Broadly speaking they both considered that it was not within the contemplation of the parties that in the usual course of things an overrun of nine days would produce a liability for 191 days. There is nothing inherently wrong in that conclusion as it does fit within the orthodox rule. However, if they have recognised that the *type* of loss falls within the rule then surely the defendant is liable for the full extent of the loss, that is 191 days? This comes back to the point made earlier in terms of *Victoria Laundry* in that having identified that the carrier was liable for the loss of normal profits as a *type* how does one distinguish the loss of profits for the government contract?

Both Lord Rodger and Baroness Hale justified their decisions on the basis of the particular conditions prevailing. Baroness Hale appeared to have some sympathy for the decisions of the lower courts. She did make the point that the object of damages for breach of contract is to put the claimants in the position in which they would have been had the contract been properly performed. Had this contract not been broken in the way that it was, the claimants would have had the benefit of the next charter at the original rate. Putting them in the position in which they would have been had the contract been performed in accordance with its terms would therefore make them liable to pay the difference. She stated, however, that a contract breaker is not inevitably liable for all the loss which his breach has caused. Loss of this type on the facts has to be 'within the contemplation' of the parties at the time when the contract was made. However, while it is one thing to say that the losses that might arise from the late return of the ship was within the parties' contemplation as 'not unlikely', it is quite something else to find that the 'extremely volatile' conditions which brought about this particular type of loss were 'not unlikely'.

The orthodox rule versus the modified rule

To reiterate the orthodox rule with regard to normal loss, the defendant is liable for all types of loss which were, or ought to have been in the contemplation of the parties at the time the contract was made and where the losses were of a kind that the defendant, when they made the contract, ought to have realised was not unlikely to result from the breach of contract; that being the case the defendant is liable for all losses no matter how high.

This rule has previously been regarded as an external rule of law that is applicable to all contracts. However, in *The Achilleas* Lord Hoffmann questioned whether in fact this was a prima facie assumption as regards the intention of the parties that, while applicable in the vast majority of cases, could be overturned in cases in which the context, surrounding circumstances or general understanding in the relevant market shows that a party would not reasonably have been regarded as assuming responsibility for such losses. Lord Hoffmann considered this to be the correct principle since he considered that it must be wrong to hold a defendant accountable for losses for which persons entering into that particular market would not reasonably have undertaken responsibility. To that extent the orthodox approach was reformulated so that a defendant is only liable for loss for which they have 'assumed responsibility'. Lord Hoffmann considered that the case of *The Achilleas* fell within the scope of this principle. A number of factors led to such a conclusion, such as the volatility of the market. Importantly, the parties did not intend the defendant to be liable for losses that were even within his reasonable contemplation. The losses were clearly of a kind that were not unlikely to occur, but the defendant would have no way of knowing if in fact there was a follow-on charter, how long it was and the possible diminution of the charter rate. To that extent the defendant would not have 'assumed responsibility' for those losses.

It can be seen therefore that Lord Hoffmann and Lord Hope considered that the modified rule will only apply in certain exceptional cases and to that extent they did not envisage a fundamental departure from the orthodox approach. Nevertheless the decision in *The Achilleas* has introduced an element of uncertainty into the law and rather than it being used in exceptional cases there are signs that it is becoming part of the mainstream doctrine of remoteness as seen in *Supershield Ltd v Siemens Building Technologies FE Ltd* [2010] EWCA Civ 7. The case is interesting since it shows how the modified rule can have an inclusionary effect in relation to the recovery of losses as opposed to the exclusionary effect of the type seen in *The Achilleas* where the charterer was held not to be liable for the losses. In this case Toulson LJ stated:

> *Hadley v Baxendale* remains a standard rule but it has been rationalised on the basis that reflects the expectation to be imputed to the parties in the ordinary case, i.e., that a contract breaker should ordinarily be liable to the other party for damage resulting from the breach if, but only if, at the time of making the contract a reasonable person in his shoes would have had damage of that kind in mind as not unlikely to result from a breach. However, *South Australia* and *Transfield Shipping* are authority that there may be cases where the court, on examining the contract and the commercial background, decides that the standard approach would not reflect the expectation or intention reasonably to be imputed to the parties. In those two instances the effect was exclusionary; the contract breaker was held not to be liable for loss which resulted from its breach although some loss of the kind was not unlikely. But logically the same principle may have an inclusionary effect. If, on the proper analysis of the contract against its commercial background, the loss was within the scope of the duty, it cannot be regarded as too remote, even if it would not have occurred in ordinary circumstances.

Thus while *Hadley* v *Baxendale* remains the standard rule there may be cases where the court on examining the contract and the commercial background, decides that the standard approach would not reflect the expectation or intention reasonably to be imputed to the parties. While in *The Achilleas* this had an exclusionary effect, in *Supershield* it was held that on a proper analysis of the contract against the commercial background the losses caused by flooding could not be regarded as too remote even though those losses would not have ordinarily occurred in the circumstances.

In *Sylvia Shipping Co. Ltd* v *Progress Bulk Carriers Ltd* [2010] EWHC 542 (Comm) Hambden J considered that the broader 'assumed responsibility' approach found in the modified approach should only be used in 'unusual' cases where the losses were 'unquantifiable, unpredictable, uncontrollable or disproportionate'. In reality, he stated that the 'assumption of responsibility' will be applied in all cases as a means of the courts departing from the standard rule but that it is only where the case is an 'unusual' one that a different result from the standard rule in *Hadley* v *Baxendale* will arise. The uncertainty that arises from *The Achilleas* lies in the courts making a judgement that the circumstances are unusual or exceptional and to that extent the matter of assumed responsibility now sits alongside the application of the standard rule. Note, for instance, the case of *Pindell Ltd* v *Air Asia Bhd* [2010] EWHC 2516 (Comm), where the claimant lessors of an aircraft claimed damages in respect of a lost sale of an aircraft allegedly caused by late delivery. Here Tomlinson J considered that the lessee and sub-lessee of the aircraft, as reasonable contracting parties, would not, when making the contract, have had it in mind that the loss of the follow-on sale or lease was 'not unlikely' to result from the timely return of the aircraft. Further, the loss of the follow-on lease or sale in the event of late delivery was not loss of a type for which the lessee assumed responsibility.

It must be emphasised that the application of the modified rule is restricted to exceptional cases and that, as Lord Hoffmann indicated in *The Achilleas*, 'cases of departure from the ordinary foreseeability rule based on individual circumstances will be unusual'. This principle can be seen in the Court of Appeal decision in *John Grimes Partnership Ltd* v *Gubbins* [2013] EWCA Civ 37 where Gubbins ('G') had engaged the John Grime Partnership Ltd ('J') to design a road and drainage system for the development of a residential estate and obtain approval from the local authority for the road's design with a view to the local authority adopting the road when completed. J failed to complete the work by the date agreed and so G eventually engaged another engineer, who completed the designs and obtained approval 15 months after the agreed date. J successfully claimed against G for unpaid fees, but the judge also allowed G's counter-claim, which included damages for the decline in value of the development during the period for which its completion had been delayed as a result of J's breach of contract in failing to complete its work on time. J appealed on the grounds that the diminution in value loss had not been reasonably foreseeable.

The Court of Appeal held that if the type of loss, at the time of the contract, was reasonably foreseeable by J as not unlikely to result from the breach then such type of loss was not too remote, as held in *Koufos* v *C Czarnikow Ltd (The Heron II)* [1969] 1 AC 350 followed. This conclusion therefore followed the 'orthodox rule'. To depart from this approach so that a defendant would be liable for all types of loss for which he has 'assumed responsibility' when entering into the contract, according to Lord Hoffmann 'will be unusual'. Thus the Court of Appeal in *John Grimes Partnership Ltd* v *Gubbins* [2013] EWCA Civ 37 affirmed this conclusion and stated that *The Achilleas* had not brought about a major change from *Heron II*, so that if there was no express term in the contract that determined what losses the parties were liable for, then the law implied a term that provided an answer. The term implied by the courts normally accepted responsibility for the types of losses that could reasonably be foreseen at the time of contract as not unlikely to result if the contract was broken. On the other hand if there was evidence on the facts of a particular case that the nature of the contract, the commercial background and any other special circumstances rendered the implied assumption of responsibility inappropriate for the type of loss sustained, then a defendant would escape liability.

The judge at first instance had considered whether losses arising from movement in the property market were reasonably foreseeable at the time of contract as a consequence of delay by J, and had concluded that they were. He had gone on to consider whether the case was unusual so as to take it outside the more common *Hadley* v *Baxendale* approach. He expressly considered the commercial background of the contract and whether the standard approach would reflect the expectation or intention reasonably to be imputed to the parties. Thus Sir David Keene stated at 24:

> It seems to me to be right to bear in mind, as Lord Hoffmann emphasised in *The Achilleas* that one is dealing with the law of contract, where the situation is governed by what is agreed between the parties. If there is no express term dealing with what types of losses a party is accepting potential liability for if he breaks the contract, then the law in effect implies a term accepting responsibility for the types of losses which can be reasonably be foreseen at the time of the contract to be not unlikely to result if the contract is broken. But if there is evidence in a particular case that the nature of the contract and the commercial background, or indeed other relevant special circumstances, render the implied assumption or responsibility inappropriate for a type of loss, then the contract-breaker escapes liability. Such was the case in *The Achilleas*.

There had been no evidence before the judge to show that there was some general understanding or expectation in the property world that a party in J's position would not be taken to have assumed responsibility for losses arising from movement in the market where there had been delay in breach of contract. The fact that a loss was suffered because of a change in market values during the wrongful delay did not render the case out of the ordinary. The defendant's argument that the scale of the loss was disproportionate to the fee payable under the contract was unpersuasive in that such situations were not infrequent. Whilst the difference between the scale of the loss and the fee payable might be an indicator that the defendant had not undertaken such a potential liability, that in itself was insufficient to establish an absence of reasonable foreseeability. Thus the Court of Appeal held that the judge at first instance was correct in finding that there was nothing in the case to take it outside of the conventional reasonable foreseeable approach as set out in *Heron II*.

Undoubtedly the 'assumption of responsibility' approach found under the modified rule is an expression of the current reflection of the courts based on implied terms and interpretation as found in the cases of *Investors Compensation Scheme Ltd* v *West Bromwich Building Society* [1998] 1 WLR 896 and *Attorney-General of Belize* v *Belize Telecom Ltd* [2009] UKPC 10 appears to introduce an unnecessary level of complexity into the law. Indeed in the *MFM Restaurants Pte Ltd* v *Fish & Co. Restaurants Pte Ltd* [2010] SGCA 36 the Singapore Court of Appeal considered that the facts of *The Achilleas* could easily be dealt with under the orthodox rule and refused to endorse the 'assumption of responsibility' approach. Andrew Phang Boon Leong JA stated at 140:

> We . . . take this opportunity to state that the approach advocated by Lord Hoffmann in *The Achilleas* is not the law in Singapore, except to the extent that the learned lord's reliance on the concept of the assumption of responsibility by the defendant is already incorporated or embodied in both limbs in *Hadley* itself.

This decision strikes at the core of the argument in that Lord Hoffmann's assumption of responsibility is already accounted for within the orthodox rule anyway. The first limb of

Hadley v *Baxendale* provides that a defendant has an implied assumption of responsibility in that a reasonable person in the position of the defendant is taken to have assumed responsibility for losses that flow naturally from the breach. Lord Hoffmann's approach seems to suggest that the assumption of responsibility is an additional factor and is not implicit within the first limb and to this degree there is a departure from the orthodox approach. With regards to the second limb of *Hadley* we saw earlier that in *Hadley* and *Simpson* v *London and North Western Railway Co.* (1876) 1 QBD 274 it was held that simply informing the defendant so that he has actual knowledge as regards the potential loss at the commencement of the contract would suffice. Such an approach signals a very different approach from that found in *The Achilleas* and to that extent there is a departure from the orthodox rule. On the other hand if the second limb in *Hadley* is approached in the manner formulated in *British Columbia Saw Mill Co.* v *Nettleship* (1868) LR 3 CP 499 that the knowledge must be brought to the attention of the defendant in such a way that the claimant reasonably believes that the defendant has accepted responsibility for the special losses that arise should a breach occur then there is a convergence of the second limb with that of the decision in *The Achilleas*.

The Achilleas as a House of Lords decision ensures that the English courts are obliged to follow the approach taken by Lord Hoffmann and do not have the luxury of the Singaporean courts of avoiding the decision. The default position, however, is the orthodox approach in *Hadley* v *Baxendale*, that is a defendant is liable for losses which can be reasonably foreseen at the time of entry into the contract as not unlikely to result from the defendant's breach of contract. *The Achilleas* provides a means for the parties to contract out of the default position into the modified rule. As we have seen, there are two ways in which this might arise: either by the parties restricting the liability of the defendant, as in *The Achilleas* where the losses were reasonably foreseeable but the defendant had not assumed responsibility for that loss; or by increasing the liability of the defendant, as in *Supershield* where the defendant was liable for losses it would not normally have incurred having assumed responsibility for the loss.

Factors influencing the quantum of damages

Mitigation of loss

Objective 7

It has been seen how the basic concept of damages in contract, that is, to place the claimant in the same position they would have been in had the contract been carried out, is subject to the test of remoteness. However, the basic concept is also limited by the notion of **mitigation of loss**. Mitigation essentially means that a claimant will not be able to claim for losses which could have been avoided by the taking of reasonable steps to reduce those losses once the plaintiff has elected to treat the contract as at an end.

The principle may be seen in the context of a fixed-term contract of employment, say, for two years. If the employee is wrongfully dismissed four months into the contract, they cannot sit back and do nothing for the balance of the two years and then claim the full salary for the period of the contract. They must attempt to reduce the loss as far as can be expected of a reasonable person. They should, as held in *Brace* v *Calder* [1895] 2 QB 253, attempt to take up other employment, thereby reducing the losses. As stated by Haldane LC in *British Westinghouse Electric and Manufacturing Co. Ltd* v *Underground Electric Railways Co. of London Ltd*:

> I think that there are certain broad principles, which are quite well settled. The first is that, as far as possible, he who has proved a breach of a bargain to supply what he contracted to get is

to be placed as far as money can do it, in as good a situation as if the contract had been performed. The fundamental basis is thus compensation for pecuniary loss naturally flowing from the breach; but this first principle is qualified by a second, which imposes on a plaintiff the duty of taking all reasonable steps to mitigate the loss consequent on the breach, and debars him from claiming in respect of any part of the damage which is due to his neglect to take such steps.

British Westinghouse Electric and Manufacturing Co. Ltd v Underground Electric Railways Co. of London Ltd [1912] AC 673

The facts of this case were that the appellants, Westinghouse, had contracted to supply turbines to the respondents. The respondents laid down that the turbines had to meet certain specifications. While the appellants built and delivered the turbines, they never met the specifications required by the contract. In due course the respondents had to replace the turbines with those produced by a different manufacturer. The new turbines were highly efficient, so much so that they quickly paid for themselves. Nevertheless the respondents sued for the cost of purchasing and installing the new turbines.

The House of Lords held that they could not recover such costs. The respondents were required to mitigate their losses and this they had done, but so efficiently as to eliminate the costs of replacing the original turbines, and therefore nothing could be recovered as regards these losses. They were, however, entitled to compensation for the losses sustained while the inefficient turbines were being used.

In some circumstances the process of mitigation not only avoids losses but actually provides a benefit to a claimant following a breach by the other party and in these circumstances the benefit must be brought into account in assessing the claimant's loss. This point was considered in **Fulton Shipping Inc. of Panama v Globalia Business Travel (formerly Travelplan SAU) of Spain, The New Flamenco** [2015] EWCA Civ 1299. The facts of the case were that a cruise ship was subject to early redelivery in November 2007 under a time charterparty when the charter still had two years to run. There being no available chartering market on redelivery in 2007, the owners decided to sell the vessel. The price obtained was $23,765,000. If the vessel had been sold when the charter was due to come to an end in November 2009, her value would have been $7,000,000, a fall in value of $16,765,000. The question in the appeal was whether that difference constituted a benefit which, on principles of mitigation and avoidance of loss, should be brought into account in the owners' claim for the charterers' breach of contract by making an early redelivery. An arbitrator held that it should; however, Popplewell J at [2015] 1 All E R Comm 1205 held that it should not be taken into account.

The Court of Appeal held that if as part of the mitigation process that arose out of a breach of contract a claimant took action which was in the ordinary course of business, and that action provided a benefit to the claimant, then the benefit would normally be brought into account when the claimant's loss was assessed, unless the actions taken was one which was wholly independent of the relationship between the parties, thereby following the decision is **British Westinghouse**. The Court of Appeal considered the availability of a market was an important consideration in such cases and one which has statutory force in relation to the sale of goods. The measure here, as we have already seen in cases where a seller fails to deliver goods, is the difference between the contract price and the market price and this is the measure normally applied in time charterparty cases as held in **Koch Marine Inc v d'Amica Societa di Navigazione arl (The Elena d'Amico)** [1980] 1 Lloyd's Rep 75, however, these authorities only apply where there is an available market. Where there was no available market, however, the prima facie measure in hire contracts was the difference between the contractual hire and the costs of earning that hire, for instance, crew wages and fuel costs. The court, however, considered that it would not normally be reasonable for a shipowner to claim that prima facie measure if it was able to mitigate its loss by selling the vessel if an opportunity arose. It could be that the shipowner, in adopting such a course of action might make additional losses or profits, but either way these have to be taken into account since such consequences arise from the breach of contract itself, thus following the decisions in *Glory Wealth Shipping Pte Ltd v Korea Line Corp (The Wren)* [2011] EWHC 1819 (Comm) and *Zodiac Maritime Agencies Ltd v Fortescue Metals Group Ltd* [2010] EWHC 903 (Comm) Longmore LJ stated:

> The unusual facts of the instant case showed that, as well as spot chartering the vessel, an owner might equally decide to mitigate its loss by selling the vessel. If so, it was not easy to see why any benefit secured by selling the vessel should not be brought into account just as much as benefit secured by spot chartering it during the unexpired charterparty term. There was also no reason why the value of the benefit should not be calculated by reference to the difference between the value of the vessel at the time of sale and its value when the charterparty was due to expire.

It was decided therefore that whilst the doctrine of mitigation might require an owner to sell the vessel if it was returned early but, if that was the position, the owner could only recover the amount of hire after it had given credit for the sale price it could have obtained if it had sought to sell after the breach. The Court of Appeal held that the arbitrator was correct in following the principles in *Famosa Shipping Co Ltd v Armada Bulk Carriers Ltd (The Fanis)* [1994] 1 Lloyd's Rep. 633 where it was held that the question as to whether any profit or loss should be brought into account depends on whether it is sufficiently associated with the breach. There has to be a 'causal nexus' between the breach and the profits obtained and if this existed, the profits had to be taken into account as part of the mitigation process. Such a causal nexus is established by taking into account all the circumstances, including the nature and effects of the breach, the nature of the profit, the manner in which it occurred and any intervening or collateral factors which played a part in its occurrence. The establishment of a causal nexus will result in the profits being taken into account, as in this case but if that was not the case, then the profit made would not be a consequence of the breach and the shipowner would be able to take advantage of the windfall profit without it being taken into account.

Whether a claimant has taken reasonable steps to reduce their losses is a question of fact, the question revolving around whether the claimant has done everything a reasonable person might be expected to do in the ordinary course of business. From this it can be seen that the claimant is not obliged to embark upon a difficult course of action in order to mitigate any losses. Thus it was held in *Pilkington v Wood* [1953] 2 Ch 770 that the claimant was not obliged to embark upon difficult and complicated litigation. In *Zodiac Maritime Agencies Ltd v Fortescue Metals Group Ltd* [2010] EWHC 903 (Comm) it was held that the injured party is not obliged to embark on any action to mitigate that involves him in unreasonable expense or inconvenience. Similarly, in *Selvanayagam v University of the West Indies* [1983] 1 WLR 585 it was held that the claimant was not required to undergo an operation which carried a risk of post-operative complications in order to mitigate the loss. According to *Payzu Ltd v Saunders* [1919] 2 KB 581 the burden rests on the defendant to prove that the claimant has not taken reasonable steps to mitigate any losses. In this context it should be noted that provided the claimant's attempts to mitigate are reasonable at the time, it is irrelevant if they are subsequently found to be inefficient, as stated in *Gebruder Metel Mann GmbH & Co. KG v NBR (London) Ltd* [1984] 1 Lloyd's Rep 614.

White and Carter (Councils) Ltd v McGregor and *The Alaskan Trader* are discussed in Chapter 13.

The rules on mitigation present particular problems in relation to anticipatory breach since there is no duty to mitigate while the claimant treats the contract as still subsisting, as may be seen in the case of **White and Carter (Councils) Ltd v McGregor** [1962] AC 413. In this context, however, the attempts to restrict this rule as stated in **The Alaskan Trader** [1984] 1 All ER 129 should also be noted carefully. Thus the duty to mitigate in anticipatory breach arises only where the plaintiff elects to treat the contract as at an end.

There are two final points on mitigation. First, there is no duty on the claimant to mitigate. A claimant is only under a duty to take reasonable steps to mitigate the loss, and if the claimant chooses to take no steps it simply means that they will fail to be compensated for those losses which they could have avoided by the taking of reasonable steps. Second, there is no duty on an agent to mitigate their loss for the purpose of calculating their indemnity under reg 17 of the Commercial Agents (Council Directive) Regulations 1993, as held in **Moore v Piretta PTA Ltd** [1999] 1 All ER 174.

Contributory negligence

The apparent overlap between contract and tort in relation to the test of remoteness also arises in this fourth limitation on the availability of damages, contributory negligence. The limitation of contributory negligence on an award of damages in tort has been recognised for some time, initially as a complete defence to an action and latterly, since the Law Reform (Contributory Negligence) Act 1945, as a means of reducing the amount of damages that might be recovered. The question arises as to whether such a doctrine will apply equally to contract as to tort, given the different criteria by which damages are assessed in the two areas and the fact that the law of contract imposes strict liability.

The answer to the question appears to lie within ss 1(1) and 4 of the 1945 Act. Section 1(1) states:

> (1) Where any person suffers damage as the result partly of his own fault and partly of the fault of any other person or persons, a claim in respect of that damage shall not be defeated by reason of the fault of the person suffering the damage, but the damages recoverable in respect thereof shall be reduced to such extent as the court thinks just and equitable having regard to the claimant's share in the responsibility for the damage.

For liability in contract to fall within this provision it would be necessary to show that it falls within the concept of 'fault' as expressed in s 1. 'Fault' is defined in s 4, which is the interpretation section of the Act. It states:

> 'Fault' means negligence, breach of statutory duty or other act or omission which gives rise to a liability in tort or would, apart from this Act, give rise to the defence of a contributory negligence.

In deciding whether liability in contract falls within the latter part of this provision Hobhouse J in **Forsikringsaktieselskapet Vesta v Butcher** [1986] 2 All ER 488 (affirmed by the Court of Appeal [1989] 1 All ER 404) identified three possibilities: first, the defendant is in breach of their strict obligations under the contract; second, the defendant is in breach of a duty to take reasonable care which is laid down in a contract, though there is no corresponding duty in tort – for example, such a duty may arise in a contract for services; third, the defendant is in breach of a duty of care arising out of liability both in contract and in tort.

It was held in the **Butcher** case that the 1945 Act would apply only in regard to the third classification, thus allowing contributory negligence to have a bearing on the overall assessment of damages. Apparently the reason is that the defendant's liability in contract could also arise separately and independently within an action in negligence, in which, of course, the 1945 Act would apply. This position was also affirmed in **Barclays Bank plc v Fairclough Building Ltd** [1995] 1 All ER 289 (CA).

In **AB Marintrans v Comet Shipping Co. Ltd** [1985] 3 All ER 442 and **Basildon District Council v J E Lesser (Properties) Ltd** [1985] 1 All ER 20, it was stated that the 1945 Act did not apply to the first possibility since s 4 clearly placed 'fault' in the context of a claim in tort, thereby specifically excluding liability arising in contract solely from the provisions of s 1. With regard to the second possibility, Neil LJ in the **Comet Shipping** case considered that the 1945 Act applies only where the breach complained of involves a breach of a duty in tort. This view thus also excludes this category from the provisions of the 1945 Act. This reasoning is also propounded by O'Connor LJ in the **Butcher** case.

Gran Gelato Ltd v Richcliff (Group) Ltd [1992] 1 All ER 865

This case considered whether contributory negligence should operate to reduce an award of damages made under an action for breach of the Misrepresentation Act 1967, s 2(1). The facts of the case were that the defendant had given the plaintiff an underlease for ten years in 1984. The head lease contained a break clause which was exercisable on the giving of 12 months' notice, expiring on or after June 1989. Neither Gran Gelato nor its solicitors was aware of this restriction. In reply to an inquiry, the defendant's solicitors had stated that there were no such rights in the head lease that would affect the tenant's enjoyment of the property 'to the lessor's knowledge'. In 1988 the lessor of the head lease exercised the break clause in order to redevelop the property. The plaintiff brought an action for misrepresentation and for negligent misstatement. The defendant claimed that the plaintiff was contributorily negligent in not asking for and examining the head lease. The plaintiff argued that the Law Reform (Contributory Negligence) Act 1945, s 1, did not apply to a claim for damages under s 2(1) of the 1967 Act. It was held that the 1945 Act applied to both the claim under s 2(1) and that for negligent misstatement at common law. It was also stated that this would be the case if a claim was framed under s 2(1) alone, otherwise plaintiffs could avoid apportionment by bringing a claim under the Misrepresentation Act 1967. Nicholls VC considered that 'fault' within the 1945 Act was wide enough to encompass the 1967 Act. On the facts, however, it was decided that it was not just and equitable to make a reduction in damages.

For more on fraudulent misrepresentation and the case of *Redgrave* v *Hurd* refer to Chapter 9.

It should be noted that in **Alliance & Leicester Building Society v Edgestop Ltd** [1994] 2 All ER 38, Mummery J considered that contributory negligence has no application in the case of fraudulent misrepresentation. This decision clearly distinguishes the decision in **Gran Gelato** and may be considered as affirming the decision of Lord Jessel MR in **Redgrave v Hurd** (1881) 20 ChD 1 in which he stated: 'Nothing can be plainer, I take it, on the authorities in equity than that the effect of false representation is not got rid of on the ground that the person to whom it was made has been guilty of negligence.' But is it correct to place so much store in this decision? After all, contributory negligence is widely accepted as being applicable to negligent misstatements following the 1945 Act today. It is arguable that a person who has the opportunity of investigating the representations made to them, for example, by having accounts audited, should be regarded as being contributory negligent if they fail to do so. Furthermore, Lord Jessel MR makes no reference specifically to fraud. It thus appears to be somewhat dubious to use **Redgrave v Hurd** as expounding a principle that contributory negligence could be used in the case of fraudulent misrepresentation, although the circumstances in which this may arise must be very limited. One should also note the wording of s 4 of the 1945 Act, 'negligence, breach of statutory duty or other act or omission which gives rise to a liability in tort'. This does not preclude contributory negligence in fraud – the tort of deceit; quite the contrary, it states it can apply to 'liability in tort' in the generic sense of the expression.

The Law Commission proposed in Law Commission Working Paper No. 114 that the 1945 Act should apply to a breach of the strict contractual duty, although this proposal has not found favour, probably because of the need to balance the interests of the parties within the contract, particularly with regard to the equality of their bargaining power.

In 1993, the Law Commission published its report *Contributory Negligence as a Defence in Contract* (Law Com. No. 219). The Law Commission recommended that the possibility of apportionment should be rejected where there was liability for breach of a strict contractual obligation. It was stated that the reason for this conclusion related to a consideration of the position before a claimant is aware, or must be taken to be aware, of the defendant's breach of contract. If the defendant commits himself to a strict obligation regardless of fault (as arises in contract), then a claimant should be able to rely on the defendant fulfilling his obligations and should not have to take precautions against the possibility that a breach might occur. The Law Commission thus affirmed the present law and, while it considered that the rules on mitigation of loss were not a substitute for apportionment for contributory negligence, they nevertheless prevented the plaintiff from acting unreasonably once they became aware of the loss or the defendant's breach.

The Law Commission considered, however, that where a claimant suffered damage partly as a result of their own failure to take reasonable care for the protection of themself or their interests and partly as a result of the defendant's breach of a contractual duty to take reasonable care or exercise reasonable skill, apportionment should be allowed in respect of the claimant's damages. It was stated that whether a duty of reasonable care is classified as contractual or tortious does not affect the content of the duty and the Law Commission considered that the availability for apportionment should not depend on how the duty to take reasonable care is classified.

The report (which also contains a draft Bill) defines contributory negligence as a 'plaintiff's failure to take reasonable care for the protection of himself or his interests' (clause 1(1)(b) of the draft Bill). The criteria for apportionment would be the same as in the 1945 Act, i.e. the claimant's damages would be reduced by the amount the court thinks 'just and equitable having regard to the claimant's share in the responsibility for the damage' (clause 1(1) of the draft Bill). While the Law Commission allowed for the parties to contract out of contributory negligence as a defence (clause 1(2)), it also stated that, if a contract made provision for liquidated damages in the event of a breach, this amount would not be subject to a reduction on the grounds of the claimant's contributory negligence (clause 1(2)). The Law Commission also made it clear that anything done or omitted to be done by the claimant prior to entering into the contract would be disregarded for the purposes of assessing whether the damages should be reduced for contributory negligence (clause 1(3)).

As the law stands, it may nevertheless still be possible, by the use of the common law rule, to raise contributory negligence as a means of defeating a claimant's claim altogether. The effect of contributory negligence here, however, is to break the chain of causation and it is rather different conceptually since the basis here is that the claimant was solely responsible for their injury or loss, as was held in **Quinn v Burch Bros (Builders) Ltd** [1966] 2 QB 370.

Contractual provisions relating to the limitation of damages

It has been clearly demonstrated in this work that it was in the nineteenth century first and foremost that a philosophy of freedom of contract was established. Embedded in this philosophy was not only the freedom to enter into and negotiate the terms of contract, but also the right of the parties to determine the levels of compensation payable in the event of a breach. The courts therefore readily surrendered their right to make awards to the will of the parties themselves as expressed within the terms of the contract. There were substantial advantages to the judicial process by the adoption of this approach, such as savings in time and expense. Despite the adoption of this position by the courts there was no question of their completely abrogating their jurisdiction as regards awards of damages. The courts were not so naive as to think that freedom of contract and equality of bargaining power represented the same thing and would step in to regulate awards of damages despite the terms of the agreement. The regulatory nature of the courts may be encountered in two broad areas: first, in the area of **penalties**; and, second, in the regulation of **deposits** and **forfeiture clauses**.

Liquidated damages and penalties

The parties may decide to make a genuine pre-estimate of the losses they may encounter should the other party be in breach of contract and then agree that certain sums will be payable if such an event occurs. Where the sums payable are a genuine pre-estimate of loss then the courts will support claims for such sums, despite the fact that the actual losses may be more or less than the actual loss sustained by the breach. The sums agreed to be payable by the parties in these circumstances are termed 'liquidated damages'.

In some contracts, however, the sums agreed by the parties to be payable are not based on a genuine pre-estimate of the losses the parties may encounter should a breach occur. These sums are usually excessive in relation to the maximum possible losses the parties may sustain in such circumstances. Such sums, rather than being 'liquidated damages' and amounting to compensation, are termed 'penalties' and are placed in the contract as a punitive measure to hold a party *in terrorem* of (as a warning against) breaking the terms of the contract. The courts will not award sums which are considered to be penalties and will substitute a sum representing the actual losses sustained to a party by reason of the breach. The distinction between a clause providing for a genuine pre-estimate of damages and a penalty clause remains fundamental to the modern law. Whether a damages clause is a penalty falls to be decided as a matter of construction as at the time that it is agreed.

Whilst the rule is relatively easy to state, in practice, it can be difficult to apply, despite the fact that the origins of the rule go back several centuries. As Lord Neuberger and Lord Sumption in the Supreme Court in the conjoined appeals of *Cavendish Square Holding BV v Talal El Makdessi* and *ParkingEye Ltd v Beavis* [2015] UKSC 67 stated, 'the penalty rule in England is an ancient, haphazardly constructed edifice which has not weathered well'. Despite its ancient origins, the difference between a penalty clause and a liquidated damages clause, that is a genuine pre-estimate of loss, is of fundamental importance since a finding that a clause is a penalty is a 'species of agreement which the common law considers to be by its nature contrary to the policy of the law'. The effect here is that the clause is wholly unenforceable so that the innocent party is thrown back on his common law right to damages. The question of whether a clause is a penalty or one providing for a genuine pre-estimate of damages is one which is decided as a matter of construction at the time of agreement.

The modern law as regards penalties and a liquidated damages clause arises from two cases - *Clydebank Engineering and Shipbuilding Co. v Don Jose Ramos Yzquierdo y Castaneda [1905] AC 6* and *Dunlop Pneumatic Tyre Co. Ltd v New Garage and Motor Co. Ltd* [1915] AC 79; however, it is the latter that is regarded as the primary source of guidance on this matter.

Dunlop Pneumatic Tyre Co. Ltd v *New Garage and Motor Co. Ltd* [1915] AC 79

In this case a contract was entered into for the supply and purchase of tyres. The agreement was said to be a 'Price Maintenance Agreement' under which the defendants were not to sell the tyres below certain prices, not to sell to persons on a 'black' list, not to exhibit or export the tyres without consent and, finally, not to tamper with certain marks on the tyres. The defendants had to pay £5 by way of liquidated damages for every tyre cover or tube sold or offered in breach of the agreement. The defendants sold a tyre below the plaintiff's current list price, and he claimed the £5 damages. The court held that the sum amounted to liquidated damages, the reason being that, while the sum involved was disproportionate to the loss sustained, the motive behind the agreement was to prevent a price war, as this would have damaged Dunlop's selling organisation. The motive behind this clause therefore was not to hold the defendants *in terrorem* of breaking the agreement, but to maintain balance within the industry. From Dunlop's point of view this would amount to a genuine pre-estimate of their possible indirect losses.

In his judgement Lord Dunedin stated 'the various propositions' that set out the distinction between a penalty and a liquidated damages clause as follows:

1 Though the parties to a contract who use the words 'penalty' or 'liquidated damages' may prima facie be supposed to mean what they say, yet the expression used is not conclusive. The Court must find out whether the payment stipulated is in truth a penalty or liquidated damages. This doctrine may be said to be found passim in nearly every case.

2 The essence of a penalty is a payment of money stipulated as *in terrorem* of the offending party; the essence of liquidated damages is a genuine covenanted pre-estimate of damage.

3 The question whether a sum stipulated is a penalty or liquidated damages is a question of construction to be decided upon the terms and inherent circumstances of each particular contract, judged as at the time of the making of the contract, not as at the time of the breach.

4 To assist this task of construction various tests have been suggested, which if applicable to the case under consideration may prove helpful, or even conclusive. Such are:

(a) It will be held to be a penalty if the sum stipulated for is extravagant and unconscionable in amount in comparison with the greatest loss that could conceivably be proved to have followed from the breach.

(b) It will be held to be a penalty if the breach consists only in not paying a sum of money, and the sum stipulated is a sum greater than the sum which ought to have been paid. This, though one of the most ancient instances, is truly a corollary to the last test. Whether it had its historical origin in the doctrine of the common law that when A. promised to pay B. a sum of money on a certain day and did not do so, B. could only recover the sum with, in certain cases, interest, but could never recover further damages for non-timeous payment, or whether it was a survival of the time when equity reformed unconscionable bargains merely because they were unconscionable – a subject which much exercised Jessel M.R. in *Wallis* v *Smith* – is probably more interesting than material.

(c) There is a presumption (but no more) that it is a penalty when 'a single lump sum is made payable by way of compensation, on the occurrence of one or more or all of several events, some of which may occasion serious and others but trifling damage' (Lord Watson in *Lord Elphinstone* v *Monkland Iron and Coal Co.*).

On the other hand:

(d) It is no obstacle to the sum stipulated being a genuine pre-estimate of damage, that the consequences of the breach are such as to make precise pre-estimation almost an impossibility. On the contrary, that is just the situation when it is probable that pre-estimated damage was the true bargain between the parties.

This presumption is weakened if it is almost impossible to prove the actual losses that may result from the various breaches, although the fact that an accurate pre-estimation of loss is not possible will not prevent a sum from being a penalty. Thus

A rather more straightforward approach to differentiating between a liquidated damages clause and a penalty can be seen in *Lordsvale Finance plc* v *Bank of Zambia* [1996] QB 752 where Coleman J stated:

> Whether a provision is to be treated as a penalty is a matter of construction to be resolved by asking whether at the time the contract was entered into the predominant contractual function was to deter a party from breaking the contract or to compensate the innocent party for breach. That the contractual function is deterrence rather than compensatory can be deduced by comparing the amount that would be payable on breach with the loss that might be sustained if breach occurred.

The case of *Philips Hong Kong Ltd* v *Attorney-General of Hong Kong* (1993) 9 Const LJ 202 appeared to advocate a rather more flexible approach than that laid down in *Dunlop Pneumatic Tyre Co. Ltd* v *New Garage and Motor Co.* In that case Lord Dunedin stated:

> The question whether a sum stipulated is penalty or liquidated damages is a question of construction to be decided upon the terms and inherent circumstances of each particular contract, judged of as at the time of the contract not at the time of the breach.

While on this basis the clause has to be viewed objectively, the *Philips* case suggests that a court can examine what actually happened in the case to decide whether or not the clause represents a penalty or liquidated damages, since it allows an assessment to be made of what the parties expected the losses to be when the contract was made. This would allow a court to disregard a liquidated damages clause which in the particular circumstances of the case provides for a disproportionate sum in relation to the actual losses suffered, if the facts showed that the parties did not intend the clause to apply in those circumstances. This would therefore allow such clauses to stand, whereas previously, following the *Dunlop* case, they would have been entirely severed from the contract. It may be that this broader approach is confined to commercial contracts, as in the *Philips* case, since the court considered that such contracts (and clauses) are entered into by business people at arm's length who should normally be bound by what they have agreed. Such an approach would accord with the comments of Lord Roskill in *Export Credits Guarantee Department* v *Universal Oil Products Co.* [1983] 2 All ER 205 in which he stated:

> My Lords, one purpose, perhaps the main purpose, of the law relating to penalty clauses is to prevent a plaintiff recovering a sum of money in respect of a breach of contract committed by a defendant which bears little or no relationship to the loss actually suffered by the plaintiff as a result of the breach by the defendant. But it is not and never has been for the courts to relieve a party from the consequences of what may in the event prove to be an onerous or possibly even a commercially imprudent bargain.

This approach to penalty clauses in commercial contracts has been subsequently approved of in several cases, for instance, *Lordsvale Finance plc v Bank of Zambia*; *Euro London Appointments Ltd v Claessens International Ltd* [2006] 2 Lloyd's Rep 436; *M & J Polymers Ltd v Imerys Minerals Ltd* [2008] 1 Lloyd's Rep 541; *Steria Ltd v Sigma Wireless Communications Ltd* [2008] BLR 79; and *McAlpine Capital Projects Ltd v Tilebox Ltd* [2005] BLR 271, where Jackson J stated:

> Because the rule about penalties is an anomaly within the law of contract, the courts are pre-disposed, where possible, to uphold contractual terms which fix the level of damages for breach. This predisposition is even stronger in the case of commercial contracts freely entered into between parties of comparable bargaining power.

While the distinction between a pre-estimate of damages and a penalty often lies at the heart of this area of law, one has to be aware that this does not cover all the possibilities. Thus in *Lordsvale Finance plc v Bank of Zambia* Coleman J stated:

> There would . . . seem to be no reason in principle why a contractual provision, the effect of which was to increase the consideration payable under an executory contract upon the happening of a default, should be struck down as a penalty if the increase could in the circumstances be explained as commercially justifiable, provided always that its dominant purpose was not to deter the other party from breach.

This approach was also approved of by Mance LJ in *Cine Bes Film Cilik ve Yapimcilik v United International Pictures* [2003] EWCA 1669, stating that there are 'clauses which may operate on breach, but which fall into neither category, and they may be commercially justifiable'. Mance LJ considered this was a more accessible paraphrase of the concept of penalty rather than relying on statements such as '*in terrorem*'. In *Murray v Leisureplay plc* [2005] EWCA Civ 963 Lady Arden stated that the courts are not confined to the terms of the agreement in determining whether a term is a penalty or not and it was stated that the court may look at the inherent circumstances of the contract to be judged at the time the contract was entered into such as the bargaining power of the parties. This principle seems to have been followed in the Court of Appeal in *Makdessi v Cavendish Square Holdings BV*; *Team Y & R Holdings Hong Kong Ltd* [2013] EWCA Civ 1539 where the question arose as to whether the two clauses in a contract were unenforceable on the grounds that they were penal. It was argued that the appropriate test was whether the clauses had a commercial purpose and justification. The court found that the older authorities had approached the issue as a dichotomy between a genuine pre-estimate of loss, on the one hand, and a penalty on the other. The Court of Appeal considered *Dunlop Pneumatic Tyre Co. Ltd v New Garage & Motor Co Ltd* [1915] AC 79; *Lordsvale Finance Plc v Bank of Zambia* [1996] QB 752; *United International Pictures v Cine Bes Filmcilik ve Yapimcilik AS* [2003] EWCA Civ 1669, [2004] *1 CLC 401 and Jobson v Johnson* [1989] 1 WLR 1026 and decided that the test as to whether a clause was a penalty or not was whether the clause was extravagant and unconscionable and contained a predominant function of deterrence. Thus under the doctrine of penalties, the court would grant relief against the enforcement of provisions for payment where, as here, the amount was out of all proportion to the loss attributable to the breach and acted as a deterrent. The Court of Appeal considered that the criteria set out in *Dunlop* were not definitive since everything depends on the circumstances of the individual case. The criteria in *Dunlop* were merely presumptions that were capable of being rebutted. The court, however, considered that the doctrine was wider than that. It considered that whilst a payment on breach might not be a genuine pre-estimate of loss that does not necessarily mean that it is penal in operation. A court may decline to consider a clause as a penalty where there is a good commercial justification that may be a ground for deducing that deterring a breach was not the dominant purpose of the term. This conclusion is more easily arrived at if the parties are of equal bargaining power.

It was held in **Robophone Facilities Ltd v Blank** [1966] 1 WLR 1428 that the burden of proving whether a sum is a penalty lies on the party from whom the sum is being recovered. The mere fact that a clause is described in the contract as being either a 'liquidated damages' clause or a 'penalty' clause is not conclusive. Thus in **Cellulose Acetate Silk Co. Ltd v Widnes Foundry (1925) Ltd** [1933] AC 20 a pre-estimated sum of £20 per week which was payable on late performance was described in the contract as a penalty. In fact, the amount was not excessive with regard to the actual losses that would be sustained by late performance and was thus awarded, despite the designation given to the term.

The Supreme Court considered the penalty rule in conjoined appeals in the cases of **Cavendish Square Holding BV v Talal El Makdessi** and **ParkingEye Ltd v Beavis** [2015] EWCA Civ 402. In this appeal their Lordships considered the rule with Lord Neuberger and Lord Sumption stating that 'for many years the courts have struggled to apply standard tests formulated more than a century ago for relatively simple transactions to altogether more complex situations'.

The two appeals concerned two very different situations; commercial contracts and consumer contracts.

Cavendish Square Holding BV v Talal El Makdessi – Commercial Contracts

This case concerned a contract that had been negotiated over many months through highly experienced lawyers under which Makdessi was to set a multi-milllion pound controlling interest in a marketing and communications company. The price agreed largely reflected the goodwill within the business and as such the contract sought to protect this goodwill. In order to do this Makdessi agreed to certain non-competition clauses within the contract. Any breach of these terms meant that Makdessi would forfeit his right to receive some of the interim instalments and/or the final instalment (clause 5.1); furthermore Makdessi would have to sell his remaining shares at their net asset value (that is the value with no enhancement by way of the goodwill value) (clause 5.6).

Makdessi admitted breaching the non-competition provisions and as such the forfeiture and sale agreements were triggered. Makdessi alleged that the provisions were unenforceable as penalties in that they were excessive, unconscionable and did not amount to a genuine pre-estimate of the loss. Cavendish argued that the clauses were not penal in that the contract was a freely negotiated commercial contract. The purpose of the clauses was to protect the goodwill of the business which would be adversely affected by a breach of the non-completion clauses.

ParkingEye Ltd v Beavis – Consumer Contracts

In the case Mr Beavis parked his car in a free car park at a retail park but overstayed the maximum time of two hours by one hour with the result that he was liable to pay a charge of £85. The notice displaying this information was accepted as being reasonably large, prominent and legible so that any reasonable user of the car park would have had notice of the terms and would have had an opportunity to read them. Mr Beavis refused to pay the £85 charge, maintaining that the notice which sought to impose the charge was a penalty and unenforceable on the basis that the charge was not a genuine pre-estimate of the loss ParkingEye would suffer as a result of his overstaying in the car park. (Note: Mr Beavis also alleged that the term was an unfair term within the provisions of the UTCCR 1999 - this is considered in Chapter 8).

Lord Neuberger and Lord Sumption considered that Lord Dunedin's dicta in Dunlop 'had achieved the status of a quasi-statutory code in subsequent case law' and considered this to be unfortunate since Lord Dunedin only intended his four tests to be considerations in a particular case that is under consideration; they were not 'rules' as such. These tests apply perfectly adequately in consumer contracts but, as we have seen above, in commercial cases the courts have adopted a broader approach by way of 'commercial justification' for clauses that might otherwise be regarded as penalties as Coleman J pointed out in *Lordsvale Finance plc* v *Bank of Zambia* as stated earlier.

The Supreme Court made it clear that just because a sum stipulated in the contract does not amount to a genuine pre-estimate of the loss that does not necessary mean that it therefore amounts to a penalty. Thus providing the intention behind the clause is to protect the legitimate interests of the claimant and the sum involved is not completely out of all proportion, then the clause will not amount to a penalty. Lord Neuberger and Lord Sumption considered that

> the law relating to penalties has become the prisoner of artificial categorisation, itself the result of unsatisfactory distinctions: between a penalty and genuine pre-estimate of loss, and between a genuine pre-estimate of loss and a deterrent. These distinctions originate in an over-literal reading of Lord Dunedin's four tests and a tendency to treat them as almost immutable rules of general application which exhaust the field.

Lord Neuberger and Lord Sumption accepted the penalty rule amounted to an interference with freedom of contract since it undermined the certainty which parties to a contract expect of the law; however, they did not propose the abolition of the rule. They considered that in a negotiated contract between properly advised parties of comparable bargaining power, the strong presumption must be that 'the parties themselves are the best judge of what is legitimate in a provision dealing with the consequences of breach'. They described the test to be applied when distinguishing between a penalty clause and a liquidated damages clause as follows:

> The real question when a contractual provision is challenged as a penalty is whether it is penal, not whether it is a pre-estimate of loss. These are not natural opposites or mutually exclusive categories. A damages clause may be neither or both. The fact that the clause is not a pre-estimate of loss does not therefore, at any rate without more, mean that it is penal. To describe it as a deterrent (or, to use the Latin equivalent, *in terrorem*) does not add anything. A deterrent provision in a contract is simply one species of provision designed to influence the conduct of the party potentially affected. It is no different in this respect from a contractual inducement. Neither is it inherently penal or contrary to the policy of the law. The question whether it is enforceable should depend on whether the means by which the contracting party's conduct is to be influenced are 'unconscionable' or (which will usually amount to the same thing) 'extravagant' by reference to some norm.
>
> The true test is whether the impugned provision is a secondary obligation which imposes a detriment on the contract-breaker out of all proportion to any legitimate interest of the innocent party in the enforcement of the primary obligation. The innocent party can have no proper interest in simply punishing the defaulter. His interest is in performance or in some appropriate alternative to performance. In the case of a straightforward damages clause, that interest will rarely extend beyond compensation for the breach, and we therefore expect that Lord Dunedin's four tests would usually be perfectly adequate to determine its validity. But compensation is not necessarily the only legitimate interest that the innocent party may have in the performance of the defaulter's primary obligations . . . And it is recognised in the more recent decisions about commercial justification.

Two aspects of the test should be noted; Firstly, the test applying to the penalty rule is more than just an assessment as to whether it is a genuine pre-estimate of loss and its assessment is based on the broader consideration of the innocent party's interest; secondly, the penalty rule applies in relation to breaches of a party's secondary obligations, i.e. obligations that arise from a breach of the primary obligations under the contract.

Translating the test into the facts of the *Cavendish Square Holding*, the Supreme Court held that clause 5.1 amounted to a price adjustment clause that amounted to a primary obligation not a secondary obligation. The court found that Cavendish had a legitimate interest in the non-competition clause and that since the clause had been a negotiated agreement conducted by highly experienced lawyers on behalf of the parties that were negotiating at arm's length, the clause was not extortionate, exorbitant or unconscionable and as such was not a penalty. In respect of clause 5.6, the formula for assessing the price of the retained shares also amounted to a primary obligation which reflected the price they would have been prepared to pay had Makdessi remained in competition to the undertaking, though the price was not representative of the loss that was attributable to Makdessi's breach.

For a discussion of the Beavis case, see Chapter 8.

The necessity of a breach of contract?

It should be noted that the rules regarding penalties and liquidated damages are only applicable where there has been a breach of contract. Where a sum becomes payable because of the occurrence of some other event, the above rules have no application, leaving the stronger of the two parties in a position to apply and enforce what would otherwise amount to a penalty. In *Export Credits Guarantee Department* v *Universal Oil Products Co.*, Lord Roskill explained the reasoning for the principle in the following way:

> My Lords, one purpose, perhaps the main purpose, of the law relating to penalty clauses is to prevent a plaintiff recovering a sum of money in respect of a breach committed by a defendant which bears little or no relationship to the loss actually suffered by the plaintiffs as a result of the breach by the defendants. But it is not and never has been for the courts to relieve a party from the consequences of what may, in the event, prove to be an onerous or possibly even imprudent commercial bargain.

Lord Roskill's principles in *Export Credits Guarantee Department* v *Universal Oil Products Co.* were followed in *Cadogan Petroleum Holdings Ltd* v *Global Process Systems LLC* [2013] EWHC 214 (Comm). In this case Cadogan Petroleum Holdings Ltd entered into a contract with Global Process Systems LLC in 2009 for the construction of two gas stripping plants. The plants had been constructed by Global which agreed to sell them to Cadogan for use by its subsidiaries in the Ukraine. Various disputes arose between the parties and whilst proceedings had been issued, these were resolved by an agreement by which the property in the plants was vested in Cadogan and provided for Global to buy them back with a view to resale. The price of US$37.5 million was payable by instalments and property was not to pass until payment of the total price by Global. If Global failed to pay any instalment, then Cadogan had the right under the agreement to terminate without prejudice to any accrued rights arising under the agreement or its right to claim damages for breach. Global paid instalments totaling $7.5 million but did not pay further sums due. Cadogan gave notice of termination. It claimed to be entitled to retain the $7.5 million that had been paid at the date of termination and recover the further instalments, totalling $20 million, which had accrued and was payable at the date of termination. Cadogan also claimed damages for breach of contract. Global maintained that Cadogan was obliged to return the $7.5 million and that Global was not obliged to pay any further instalments.

Furthermore Global maintained that if Cadogan was entitled to those sums, Global sought relief against forfeiture. Global also claimed that if the payments made were non-refundable, so that Global forfeited those payments as a result of Global not paying the full price, then this would amount to a penalty and was unenforceable. Global also argued that Cadogan had suffered no loss and was entitled to nominal damages only, since the plants had a value of $40–48 million in any event. It was held that Cadogan would succeed in its claim since as a matter of construction the agreement made it plain that Cadogan's accrued rights under the contract were to be unaffected by the exercise of the right of termination and that such accrued rights included the right to retain the amounts already paid and to recover the outstanding payments at the date of termination. The obligation to pay the instalments was not triggered by any breach and the obligation to pay preceded and was quite independent of any breach. For this reason the payment of the instalments were not capable of being a penalty. The court stated that where a contract explicitly provided for the circumstances in which benefits would or would not be returned, as in the agreement in this case, it was not possible to found a restitutionary claim which Global was claiming. Further a penalty provision in a contract is designed to deter a party from breaching a contract and as such only takes effect when a breach occurs and as such has no application to events other than a breach of contract as stated by Lord Roskill in *Export Credits Guarantee Department* v *Universal Oil Products Co.* [1983] 2 All ER 205. On this basis, the principles as regards penalties did not apply to Global's obligations to pay the instalments which arose independently of any breach.

Whilst the rule is easy to understand when placed in such a context, nevertheless in practical terms it can operate in a perverse and illogical manner. In *Campbell Discount Ltd* v *Bridge* [1962] AC 600 Lord Denning referred to this in the following way: 'Let no one mistake the injustice of this. It means that equity commits itself to this absurd paradox: it will grant relief to a man who breaks his contract but will penalise the man who keeps it.' In that case concerning the hire purchase of a car if the hirer was conscientious and gave notice of termination of the agreement and returns the car, without falling into arrears, then he would be liable to pay the penalty sum without the benefit of any relief by way of the penalty rule. On the other hand, if he is not conscientious so that he falls into arrears and the hire purchase company seizes the car and demand the penalty, then the hirer will be able to avail himself of the penalty rule and obtain relief since in that circumstance he will be in breach of his agreement with the hire purchase company.

This so-called breach limitation was rejected in the High Court in Australia in the case of *Andrews* v *Australia and New Zealand Banking Group Ltd* (2012) 147 CLR 205 where it was held that the penalty rule is not limited to sums of money payable on a breach of contract. This approach was firmly rejected in the *Cavendish/Beavis* appeals with Lords Neuberger and Sumption stating the courts do not review the fairness of men's bargains and that 'the penalty rule regulates only the remedies available for breach of a party's primary obligations, not the primary obligations themselves'. Also stating 'there is a fundamental difference between a jurisdiction to review the fairness of a contractual obligation and a jurisdiction to regulate the remedy for its breach'.

Deposits and forfeiture clauses

Deposits are essentially the converse of penalties in that they are payable before a breach occurs, rather than after as in the case of a penalty. Deposits are normally regarded as a part-satisfaction of the contract price which may be retained should the purchaser fail to perform their side of the bargain.

Forfeiture clauses normally arise where there is a purchase of goods by instalments and the contract provides that, should the purchaser default on any instalment then they must surrender the goods, at the same time forfeiting any instalments already paid. Both deposits and forfeiture clauses are regarded as guarantees that the contract will be performed.

The normal rule in relation to deposits is that if the money has been paid and the party to whom it is paid breaks the contract, then the payer may recover the deposit either for breach of contract or in quasi-contract. Deposit moneys payable in the future usually cease to be payable.

For more on quasi-contracts refer to Chapter 18.

Where the person who has paid the deposit is in breach of contract, then one must distinguish between sums paid as a deposit and those which amount merely to prepayments made on account. As regards the latter, it has been held in *Dies v British and International Mining and Finance Corporation* [1939] 1 KB 724 that in a contract of sale the advance payments on account can be recovered, subject to any rights of set-off possessed by the seller in respect of actual losses. The reasoning can be seen in the observations of Stable J at p. 742 stated:

> In my judgement there would be a manifest defect in the law if, where a buyer had paid for his goods but was unable to accept delivery, the vendor could retain the goods and the money quite irrespective of whether the money so retained bore any relation to the amount of damage, if any, sustained as a result of the breach. The seller is already amply protected, since he can recover such damage as he has sustained and can, it seems, set off his claim for damages against the claim for the return of the purchase price.

In *Hyundai Heavy Industries Co. Ltd v Papadopoulos* [1980] 2 All ER 29, the House of Lords held that such advance payments could not be recovered. The apparent reason for the distinction is that in the latter case the prepayment on the shipbuilding contract was regarded as an unconditional payment for the work that had already been completed, while generally in contracts of sale prepayments are conditional on performance taking place subsequent to the prepayment. The position was stated by Kerr LJ in *Rover International Ltd v Cannon Film Sales Ltd (No. 3)* [1989] 3 All ER 423 as:

> The question is whether there was any consideration in the nature of part performance for which the instalment was payable, as in the *Hyundai Heavy Industries* case, or whether the instalment was payable in advance of any performance which was required from the party in default.

There does not appear to be any reason why a shipbuilding contract (as in the *Hyundai* case) should be different from any other type of contract of sale. *Cheshire, Fifoot and Furmston* (2012) suggests that the distinction can be justified in three ways: first, the *Dies* case is wrong; second, shipbuilding contracts should be viewed differently from other contracts of sale; and, third, more convincingly, it is suggested that distinction lies in the fact that in *Dies* there was a total failure of consideration but that this was not the case in *Hyundai*.

Where a person who has paid money is in breach of contract, the deposit or prepayment may be made subject to a right of forfeiture. In such circumstances the payee is entitled to keep all of the deposit despite the fact that their losses may be less than the amount of deposit paid, as stated in *Howe v Smith* (1884) 27 ChD 89. It should also be noted that if the deposit is payable but so far unforthcoming, the innocent party can (it has been held in *Damon Cia Naviera SA v Hapag-Lloyd International SA, The Blankenstein* [1985] 1 All ER 475) take action to recover the deposit. The same principles have also been held to apply to money paid as a prepayment.

It may be noticed that the effect of a payee being able to keep a deposit which in fact exceeds their losses is not very different from the effect of a penalty. Despite the similarity there is no, or little, relief available in cases of forfeiture which corresponds to that already seen in relation to penalties. Such relief as does exist tends to arise in specialist contracts, as in the termination of hire purchase and conditional sale agreements under the Consumer Credit Act 1974, s 100, or in contracts for the sale of land under the Law of Property Act 1925, s 49(2). The latter provides:

> Where the court refuses to grant specific performance of the contract, or any action for the return of a deposit, the court may, if it thinks fit, order the repayment of the deposit.

The question arises, however, as to whether relief against forfeiture can be given outside these rather specialist areas. As a starting point it is likely to be very difficult to establish a case for relief against forfeiture in a commercial context involving a freely negotiated contract and there is a strong view that the form of any such relief should generally be limited to giving the contract-breaker more time in which to pay the sum he has failed to pay on time. In equity the court will normally grant relief where the payer is overdue in the payment of instalments. Relief here as already stated normally takes the form of extending the time for payment, though occasionally the court may order the repayment of moneys paid. Relief here is dependent on the buyer being ready and willing to pay an instalment or the balance of moneys owed within a period fixed by the court, as stated in *Starside Properties Ltd* v *Mustapha* [1974] 2 All ER 567.

In *Stockloser* v *Johnson* [1954] 1 All ER 630 Lord Denning and Lord Somervell considered that there existed a more general equitable principle that gave relief against forfeiture. This principle, they thought, arose where the sum to be forfeited by reason of the forfeiture was out of all proportion to the losses sustained by the innocent party, in other words that the clause was penal in character, and that it was unconscionable for that party to retain the moneys paid. Lord Romer, however, took a far more restrictive view and considered that equity could intervene in this way only if the seller had acted in a fraudulent or unconscionable manner.

The view of Lord Romer is the one that seems to have gained prevalence in recent cases. In *Scandinavian Trading Tanker Co. AB* v *Flota Petrolera Ecuatoriana, The Scaptrade* [1983] 2 AC 694, the House of Lords held that relief against forfeiture could not be invoked by a time charterer of a ship where he had failed to pay the hire instalments on time in order to prevent the shipowner withdrawing the ship from the charterparty. The reason given was that such relief would not be granted where specific performance would not be granted and it would not normally be given in the case of a time charter, since damages are an adequate remedy where there has been a breach of such a contract. The effect of relief against forfeiture here would be tantamount to a decree of specific performance. From this it follows from the decision of the House of Lords that relief against forfeiture is available only where proprietary or possessory rights are being forfeited. In *The Scaptrade* they clearly were not, since a time charter was regarded as merely a contract for the use of a ship, that is, a contract for services. This position has recently been affirmed in *Sport International Bussum BS* v *Inter-Footwear Ltd* [1984] 2 All ER 321, though in *BICC plc* v *Bundy Corporation* [1985] 1 All ER 417 the Court of Appeal considered that such relief could extend to proprietary and possessory rights in goods, rather than being confined to contracts for the sale of land as envisaged by Lord Diplock in *The Scaptrade*. In *Cadogan Petroleum Holdings Ltd* v *Global Process Systems LLC* [2013] EWHC 214 (Comm), the facts of which have already been considered above, relief against forfeiture was not given. Eder J considered that whilst the court had jurisdiction to grant relief against forfeiture, that jurisdiction rested on equitable principles and, as stated by Denning LJ in *Stockloser v Johnson*, such relief will be granted '... *on such terms as may be just.* ...'. The contract made it clear that Cadogan's accrued rights included the right to retain accrued amounts and recover outstanding payments at the date of termination. Cadogan was prima facie entitled to the $27 million. Eder J considered that the position might have been different if the gas plants had been sold to a third party out of all proportion to the loss suffered by Cadogan or if the value of the gas plants similarly was out of all proportion to such loss. Eder J had his hands tied here since firstly the plants had not been sold and in any event the parties had agreed that he should not determine the value of the plants. In such circumstances Eder J considered that the demands of equity and justice were fully satisfied by maintaining the contractual scheme i.e. upholding Cadogan's rights to retain the sum paid of (say) US$7.5 million and to recover the further sum of US$20 million in debt. He further ordered that any further sums that might be recovered by way of sale of the Gas Plants up to a maximum of US$10 million (plus any interest to which Cadogan would be entitled) be paid to Cadogan with the balance, thus bringing the sum up to the $37.5 million contract price.

One further point in relation to relief from forfeiture needs to be made in that it is only available in respect of prepayments subject to a forfeiture clause, *not* deposits, despite the fact that the distinction between the two, as already seen, is non-existent.

Speculative damages and damages for non-pecuniary losses

The fact that damages cannot be accurately assessed is in no way a bar to the recovery of compensation, provided that they do not fall foul of the rules regarding remoteness. A clear example of this can be seen in the following case.

Chaplin v *Hicks* [1911] 2 KB 786

The plaintiff, who had entered a beauty contest and won the earlier stages, was prevented from competing in the final stages of the contest contrary to the terms of the contract. One argument levelled against the plaintiff's claim was that the loss depended on so many contingencies that it was incapable of assessment. All three members of the Court of Appeal rejected that argument. There was no doubt that the claimant had lost the opportunity to participate in the competition or the chance of winning the prize. That lost opportunity was itself a head of compensatable damage. It was held that she was entitled to a proportionate award of damages which would value what she had lost, namely the chance of winning, notwithstanding the difficulties of that might arise in assessing her losses..

In *Chaplin* v *Hicks* it was clear that the plaintiff had lost a real chance of winning the contest and as such was entitled to be compensated for that loss but, as we have already noted, it does not always follow that what may be seen as speculative damages will the courts be so obliging. It will be remembered that in *McRae* v *Commonwealth Disposals Commission* (1951) 84 CLR 377, the court considered that the claim for loss of profits was so speculative that it would only award damages for reliance losses i.e. loss of expenses only. The difference between the two cases appears to rest on whether there is a 'substantial chance' on the balance of probabilities of a claimant being able to make a profit as held in *Allied Maples Group Ltd* v *Simmons and Simmons (a firm)* [1995] 1 WLR 1602. In that case the plaintiff's claimed that it was badly advised by the defendant, in breach of contract, and that as a result the plaintiff lost the opportunity to negotiate a better deal with certain target companies in respect of an acquisition process. The Court of Appeal held that on the balance of probabilities there was a 'substantial chance' of negotiating a better deal and that this did not amount to a mere speculative chance. It was unnecessary for the plaintiff to establish successful negotiations would definitely have been concluded. All the claimant has to show is that the chance is a real or substantial one. The establishment of causation therefore is a hypothetical one and it is not expected that a claimant has to show that the particular sum he is claiming as general damages is likely to be commensurate with the precise damage which he has suffered. Once he has done that, the claimant must then show, on the balance of probabilities, that the defendant's act has caused the loss of the chance. This is the causation issue and once the claimant has shown on the balance of probabilities that he has lost the relevant chance, the valuation of the chance then becomes a question for the quantification of the damages.

In *Wellesley Partners LLP* v *Withers LLP* [2015] EWCA Civ 1146, the facts of which have already considered earlier in this chapter, the claimants Wellesley Partners LLP made a claim based on the general loss of an opportunity to make profits in a new initiative in New York with an investment bank, Nomura, and in this respect it was a different claim to that of the claim in *Allied Maples* where the loss of opportunity related to a specific claim. The Court of Appeal stated that whilst WP would need to show on the balance of probabilities that, but for the negligence complained of, they would have opened a US office, the actual loss which they claimed to have been caused by Withers was dependent on the hypothetical actions of a third party, namely, Nomura. Thus it was necessary to determine if there was a real and substantial chance of securing the Nomura contract. Summing up then, Floyd LJ stated:

> WP's case on causation, that Withers' negligence caused WP to lose the Nomura mandates, was one which depended on the hypothetical actions of Nomura, a third party. WP had, first, to prove that its own actions would have been such as to place itself in a position to obtain that work, and it had to do so on the balance of probabilities. It did so. All that remained on the issue of causation was for WP to establish whether there was a real and substantial chance that Nomura would have awarded some part of the mandates to WP. It did so. That was the beginning and end of its case on causation.

Separate from the issue of causation, however, is the issue of the quantification of the damages. It does not follow that it is no longer relevant to consider the chances that WP would have obtained the mandates. The evaluation of that chance is, however, not an issue of causation but part of the process of the quantification of damages. It would be wrong in principle to treat the conclusion on causation as if it meant that the chances of obtaining some part of the mandate were 100%. The judge was correct to reflect his view of the chances of WP obtaining the mandate in his quantification of damages. In this respect the Court of Appeal did not disturb the judge at first instance, finding that the chance of being some part of the contract was 60% and that if WP had won some part of the contract, there was a 25% chance of being appointed as the sole recruitment agency for Nomura and a 75% chance of being appointed with one or more other firms. The judge considered that the overall chance of being awarded the contract as the sole recruitment agency was 15% and a 45% chance of receiving half the contract.

While damages may be available for losses which are clearly speculative, it is equally clear that damages are not available as a punitive measure, since damages are purely compensatory in nature. Nevertheless, damages are not confined to financial loss, though it is true that in most of the cases discussed so far, the actions revolve around commercial contracts in which such losses provide the main cause of the actions. Despite the fact that damages are not confined to financial loss, the law is not as flexible as might first be supposed, since for many years the principle was that physical inconvenience had to arise from the breach and not simply mental distress, as affirmed in the case of *Addis* v *Gramophone Co. Ltd*, where loss of reputation caused by the abrupt dismissal of the plaintiff was held to be irrecoverable.

In recent years a number of cases have arisen that have undermined the principle and allowed damages for mental distress and anxiety to be claimed. This position developed out of the case of *Jarvis* v *Swans Tours Ltd* [1973] 1 QB 233 and was affirmed in *Jackson* v *Horizon Holidays Ltd* [1975] 1 WLR 1468.

In both cases the plaintiffs suffered considerable disappointment as to the quality of the holidays they had bought, which did not live up to their expectations based on the holiday brochures of the respective tour companies. In both cases the courts decided that damages for disappointment, mental anxiety and distress could be compensated. In the *Jarvis* case Lord Denning stated:

> What is the right way of assessing damages? It has often been said that on a breach of contract damages cannot be given for mental distress . . . I think those limitations are out of date. In a proper case damages for mental distress can be recovered in contract, just as damages for shock can be recovered in tort. One such case is a contract for a holiday, or any other contract to provide entertainment and enjoyment. If the contracting party breaks his contract, damages can be given for the disappointment, the distress, the upset and frustration caused by the breach. I know it is difficult to assess in terms of money, but it is no more difficult than the assessment which the courts have to make every day in personal injury cases for loss of amenities.

The *Jarvis* and *Jackson* cases produced a considerable widening of the scope for awarding damages for mental distress caused by the breach of contract. Thus in *Cox* v *Phillips Industries Ltd* [1976] 3 All ER 161 an employee was able to recover damages for distress and anxiety caused by his wrongful demotion, the judge distinguishing it from the *Addis* case on the basis that the decision there arose out of a dismissal, though why this is any the less distressing remains something of a mystery. Clearly, where the contract is of a personal nature it can be expected that there will be some degree of anxiety and distress if a breach of contract occurs. However, the principle soon expanded to cover other areas. In *Perry* v *Sidney Phillips & Son (a firm)* [1982] 3 All ER 705, for example, damages were awarded for the mental distress caused by the failure of a negligent surveyor to discover major structural defects in a dwelling house.

In recent years there has been a movement in the courts towards a considerable tightening up of awards of damages for such types of losses. Thus in *Shove* v *Downs Surgical plc* the decision in *Addis* was reaffirmed and Sheen J found that damages for mental distress caused by wrongful dismissal were irrecoverable. More importantly in *Bliss* v *South East Thames Regional Health Authority* [1985] IRLR 308, the Court of Appeal reversed the decision at first instance that the mental distress and anxiety caused by the suspension of an orthopaedic surgeon for refusing to submit to an examination by a psychiatrist was recoverable. The decision substantially overruled the *Cox* case and also reaffirmed *Addis*. In the course of their judgements, the members of the Court of Appeal confined liability for damages for mental distress to facts such as those seen in the *Jarvis* and *Jackson* cases, where the provision of comfort, pleasure or 'peace of mind' was a central feature of the contract, or, indeed, where the relief of discomfort played such a prominent role in the contract. This decision received affirmation in *Hayes* v *James and Charles Dodd (a firm)* [1990] 2 All ER 815 where Staughton LJ stated that damages could not be recovered for the distress that might result from a breach of a commercial contract. In relation to the 'peace of mind' criterion discussed in *Bliss*, Lord Staughton stated:

> it might be that the class was wider than that. But it should not include any case where the object of the contract was not comfort or pleasure or the relief of discomfort, but simply carrying on a commercial contract with a view to profit.

In *Watts* v *Morrow* [1991] 1 WLR 1421 Lord Bingham reiterated the principle that damages are not generally recoverable for 'any distress, frustration, anxiety, displeasure, vexation, tension or aggravation' caused by the breach, even though the parties contemplated that a breach would cause the parties to suffer such 'distress', etc. The reason for this is that such non-pecuniary or non-physical harm presents difficulties of measurement and proof. As the Law Commission stated in its paper *Aggravated, Exemplary and Restitutionary Damages* (1993) (Law Com. No. 132), there is 'no standard measure of assessment by reference to which the harm can be converted into monetary form'.

The *Watts* case, however, produced two exceptions to the general rule as set out above. Lord Bingham stated further:

> But the rule is not absolute. Where the very object of a contract is to provide pleasure, relaxation, peace of mind or freedom from molestation, damages will be awarded if the fruit of the contract is not provided or if the contrary result is procured instead . . . A contract to survey the condition of a house for a prospective purchaser does not, however, fall within this exceptional category. In damages not falling within this exceptional category, damages are in my view recoverable for physical inconvenience and discomfort caused by the breach and mental suffering directly related to that inconvenience and discomfort.

Thus, damages for **non-pecuniary loss** may be awarded where the object of the contract was for pleasure or where physical inconvenience flowed from the breach of contract. The first exception equates largely to the situations which occurred in the *Jarvis* and *Jackson* cases, though here there is a subtle tightening of the exception in that the 'very object' of the contract must be to provide pleasure, etc. rather than where it is simply a central feature of the contract.

The application of the first exception can be seen in the decision of the House of Lords in *Ruxley Electronics and Construction Ltd* v *Forsyth*; *Laddingford Enclosures Ltd* v *Forsyth* where it was stated that the exceptions to the rule in the *Addis* case are not closed. Lord Lloyd considered the first instance decision to award the plaintiff £2,500 for loss of amenity because of the swimming pool being built shallower than the depth stated in the contract, thereby precluding the ability of users to dive into the pool. He concurred with the judge that the contract was one 'for the provision of a pleasurable amenity', the loss of which was compensable. Lord Lloyd was of the opinion that the decision to make an award was a simple extension of the principle in the *Jarvis* and *Jackson* cases rather than another exception to the *Addis* case.

For more on the *Ruxley Electronics* case, see the section on 'Difference in value and cost of cure' earlier in this chapter.

Lord Lloyd, however, went a little further and considered the situation where damages for loss of amenity were not available, that is, the majority of cases. He gave an example of where a house is built that does not conform to some minor specification in the contract, for instance, where there is a difference in level between two rooms requiring a step. In this situation if there is no measurable difference in the value of the house contracted for and that received, and the cost of reinstatement is prohibitive, then no damages would be available. He questioned whether there was any reason why a court should not compensate the buyer for his disappointed expectations:

> Is the law of damages so inflexible . . . that it cannot find some middle ground in such a case?

Lord Lloyd referred to Sir David Cairns's judgement in *G W Atkins Ltd* v *Scott* where he stated:

> There are many circumstances where a judge has nothing but his commonsense to guide him in fixing the quantum of damages, for instance, for pain and suffering, for the loss of pleasurable activities or for inconvenience of one kind or another.

Lord Lloyd considered this could amount to an alternative basis for an award of damages for loss of amenity where the exceptions to the principle in the *Addis* case may not apply. Whether or not this approach will find general favour is open to speculation; however, in *Alexander* v *Rolls-Royce Motor Cars* (1995) *The Times*, 4 May (CA) and *Knutt* v *Bolton* (1995) 45 Con LR 127 (CA) it was stated that damages for disappointment would not be awarded where the contract was a commercial one or where pleasurable amenity was not the main purpose of the contract.

The position as regards whether the 'very object' of the contract is flexible enough to include contracts where the pleasure is merely an important feature of the contract was considered by the House of Lords in the case of *Farley* v *Skinner*.

Farley v *Skinner* [2001] 4 All ER 801

The facts of the case were that Mr Farley wanted to buy an idyllic house set in the Sussex countryside. He had hoped to retire to the house and was looking for a peaceful location. He was therefore concerned that the house did not lie on the flight path to Gatwick airport 15 miles away. If this was the case, he would not have proceeded with the purchase. He employed a surveyor to conduct a survey of the house and to investigate specifically if the property was on the flight path or not. The surveyor's report stated that he considered it 'unlikely that the property will suffer greatly from such noise'. The surveyor negligently failed to notice, however, that the house was situated close to a navigation beacon. This meant that at busy times aircraft were 'stacked up' around the beacon until given clearance to land. In reliance on the surveyor's report Mr Farley purchased the property for £420,000 and then spent another £125,000 renovating the property. On moving into the house Mr Farley found that the house was badly affected by aircraft noise. He did not, however, wish to move from the house having spent such a large amount of money renovating it and decided to 'make the best of a bad job'. He sued the surveyor for damages.

At first instance the judge found that Mr Farley had not suffered any pecuniary loss on the basis that the price paid for the house already reflected the level of aircraft noise. The judge, however, awarded Mr Farley £10,000 as compensation for his discomfort. The surveyor appealed and the Court of Appeal, by majority, allowed the appeal against the award. The court considered that the case fell outside the two exceptions stated by Lord Bingham in *Watts* v *Morrow* since, first, the facts did not support an action for an award arising out of physical inconvenience. Second, the case was outside the category where the 'very object of the contract [was] to provide pleasure, relaxation, peace of mind'. Mr Farley then appealed to the House of Lords.

Their Lordships allowed his appeal, stating that it did not matter that the object of the contract was not to provide 'pleasure, relaxation, peace of mind' provided this was an important part of the contract and that the surveyor had been specifically requested to report on the issue of aircraft noise. Their Lordships thus reinterpreted the first exception as set out in *Watts* v *Morrow*, moving it back in line with the *Jarvis* and *Jackson* cases. Lord Steyn in particular disagreed with the 'very object of the contract' criterion interpretation. He considered it was sufficient if a 'major or important object of the contract is to give pleasure, relaxation or peace of mind'. He considered it to be wrong to allow a party to a contract to recover damages if the contract had merely been to report on aircraft noise (i.e. the 'very object of the contract') but not where that issue was part of a wider contract in relation to the structure of the house as well (i.e. an important part of the contract).

Farley v *Skinner* is authority that the exception is now based on whether 'it is sufficient if a major or important object of the contract is to give pleasure, relaxation or peace of mind'. It should be noted that a surveyor's general or standard contract would not suffice here. The important issue is that the surveyor was specifically instructed to investigate the matter of aircraft noise. This exception cannot, however, apply to commercial contracts as stated by Lord Staughton above. The reason for this is that such contracts are contracts for profit and pecuniary loss has to be proved in such cases. Thus *Farley* v *Skinner* recognises that consumer contracts are generally not those for profits and that consumers enter into contracts for other motives that are not measurable in terms of pecuniary loss.

Their Lordships also examined the second exception and, indeed, some considered that Mr Farley's case fell within this exception as well. It was considered that 'physical inconvenience' should be given a broader interpretation and that it could encompass the effects of aircraft noise since this could 'be regarded as having a physical effect on him'. *Farley* v *Skinner* thus represents a significant step forward in allowing claims for damages with respect to non-pecuniary losses and provides a realistic interpretation of the two exceptions to the principle set out in *Addis*.

Debate

Should the penalty rule be abolished?

As we have seen from Lord Neuberger's and Lord Sumption's dicta in the *Cavendish/Beavis* appeals that the 'penalty rule in England is an ancient, haphazardly constructed edifice which has not weathered well, and which in the opinion of some should simply be demolished'. Why didn't the Supreme Court take the opportunity to do so? Certainly they were invited by counsel in the case to take the opportunity and equally the Supreme Court doubted the penalty rule and whether such a rule would have developed today. Lords Neuberger and Sumption set out a number of reasons why the rule continues to be necessary:

> Firstly, one of the primary arguments levelled against the rule is that there is now a growing body of statute law that is applicable to this field. The landmark legislation in this field is the Unfair Contract Terms Act 1977 though the operation of this now confined to B2B contracts and anyway the thrust of the Act very different to the role of the penalty rule which, as we have seen, is confined to the circumstances where there is a breach of contract and is applicable where the provision is 'a secondary obligation which imposes a detriment on a contract-breaker out of all proportion to any legitimate interest of the innocent party in the enforcement of a primary obligation'. The thrust of UCTA, however, is very different to the penalty rule in that it regulates exclusion and limitation clauses rather than remedies. In consumer contracts the Consumer Rights Act 2015, replacing the Unfair Terms in Consumer Contracts Regulations 1999, in Schedule 2 Part 1 provides a list of terms which may be regarded as unfair and which provides:
>
> A term which has the object or effect of requiring that, where the consumer decides not to conclude or perform the contract, the consumer must pay the trader a disproportionately high sum in compensation or for services which have not been supplied.
>
> A term which has the object or effect of requiring a consumer who fails to fulfil his obligations under the contract to pay a disproportionately high sum in compensation.

On the face of things, therefore, penalty clauses are controlled but the Act is far from a generalised form of control, not least the fact that it is confined to consumer contracts. The effect of the controls set up by the UTCCR 1999 can be seen in the *Beavis* appeal but here the £85 charge was not considered by the Supreme Court to have infringed the regulations since the charge was 'not contrary to the requirements of good faith' since ParkingEye had a legitimate interest in managing the car park for the benefit of users and the charge was necessary to protect that legitimate interest.

It should be noted that in the UTCCR 1999 the assessment of unfair terms in consumer contracts was limited to contract terms which were not individually negotiated. This limitation disappeared from the Consumer rights Act 2015 so to that extent at least the scope of regulation has been widened.

Secondly, the statutory provisions are far from comprehensive in dealing with penalty clauses and for this reason the rule continues to be necessary, particularly in non-consumer contracts. Indeed, in 1975, the Law Commission in its Working Paper No 61, 'Penalty Clauses and Forfeiture of Monies Paid', suggested that the scope of the penalty rule should be expanded much along the lines of the Australian position set out in **Andrews v Australia and New Zealand Banking Group Ltd** (2012) 147 CLR 205. Certainly Lord Mance (at para 167) considered that before any attempt is made to abolish or even radically alter the penalty rule, then a great deal more research was required before entering into such an exercise. Similarly in 1999, the Scottish Law Commission in its Report on Penalty Clauses (Scot Law Com No 171) recommended that there should continue to be judicial control over contractual penalties, whatever form they take – whether payment of money or forfeiture of money or transfer or forfeiture of property. It also recommended that judicial control should not be confined to cases where the promisor is in breach of contract following the Australian line in Andrews.

Thirdly, as Lord Hodge pointed out, there are major areas such as non-consumer contracts, notably non-consumer contracts, which are not regulated by statute and where there remains significant imbalances in the negotiating power between the parties to the contract so that such businesses have little say as to the terms of their contracts and which require some protection.

Fourthly, it can be said that the penalty rule promotes uncertainty in commercial dealings as the contracting parties may not be able to foresee the judges' value judgement on whether a particular provision is exorbitant or unconscionable. Arguably, however, because the rule is so limited, this means that parties are free to negotiate arrangements to fix the consequences of a breach occurring and this in turn has the benefit of avoiding expensive legal disputes. As Lord Mance (at para 266) stated: 'The criterion of exorbitance or unconscionableness should prevent the enforcement of only egregious contractual provisions.' Equally the proposal that the rule should not apply to commercial transactions in which the parties are of equal bargaining power and each have the benefit of professional legal advice was not welcomed in the Supreme Court. It was considered that such an application of the rule would 'risk adding to the expense of commercial disputes by requiring the court to rule on issues of fact about the bargaining power of the parties and the calibre of their respective legal advisers', per Lord Mance at para 259.

Fifthly, the penalty rule is a common feature of virtually all legal systems in the western world and therefore an 'abolition of the rule against penalties would go against the flow of legal developments both nationally and internationally', per Lord Mance at para 265. Note also the dicta of Lords Neuberger and Sumption at para 37 in this regard.

One issue with the penalty rule as it now stands is that it is subject to the fact that it can only be applied where there is a breach of contract – the so-called 'breach limitation'. The intervention is further curtailed by the fact that the rule only regulates remedies available for breach of a party's primary obligations, not the primary obligations themselves. As we noted earlier, the rule as formulated by the Supreme Court applies where the provision is 'a secondary obligation which imposes a detriment on a contract-breaker out of all proportion to any legitimate interest of the innocent party in the enforcement of a primary obligation'. The emphasis on 'secondary obligations' presents the situation that the application of the rule may depend on how the obligation is framed within the agreement. Thus, if the agreement provides that a party must do something within the contract and provides that if he does not do that act, he will have to pay a sum of money to the other party, then the obligation to pay that money is framed as a secondary obligation to which the rule will apply. On the other hand, it may be possible to frame the obligation as a primary obligation and in which case the penalty rule is avoided. Thus if the agreement does not impose an obligation to perform an act (a 'primary obligation') but nevertheless provides that he will pay a sum of money if he does not perform (a 'condition'), then the obligation becomes a conditional primary obligation, which is therefore ostensibly outside of the penalty rule since the conditional primary obligation is simply providing a contractual alternative to damages. Such a way of avoiding the rule arises from the fact that the rule only applies in the context of a breach of contract.

The effect therefore is that by careful drafting, it is possible on the face of things to circumvent the rule by disguising it as a payment conditional upon performance of a primary obligation. The distinction between the two forms, however, is not an easy one to draw. Lord Hodge, however, was clear that where parties have circumvented the rule so that the substance of the contract is that it imposes a punishment for breach of contract in the form of a disguised penalty, the courts may intervene. The principle, however, is always one of 'substance not form' as seen in *Robophone Facilities Ltd* v *Blank* [1966] 1 WLR 1428 and *Cellulose Acetate Silk Co. Ltd* v *Widnes Foundry (1925) Ltd* [1933] AC 20.

Questions

1. Do you think that the reasons provided by the Supreme Court provide sufficient reason for the maintenance of the rule against penalties?

2. Should the 'breach limitation' continue to be an over-arching principle of the penalty rule?

3. Should the rule be widened much along the lines of the Australian position set out in *Andrews* v *Australia and New Zealand Banking Group Ltd* (2012) 147 CLR 205?

4. Would you consider that 'freedom of contract' should continue to provide a universal legal value in the context of the penalty rule so that the rule should be abolished in favour of a statutory regime?

Summary

Damages may be:

(i)   Liquidated: where the parties have agreed the damage as a genuine pre-estimate of loss.

(ii) Unliquidated: where no amount has been fixed and the court decides.

Assessment of the basis on which damages are awarded

General principles

- An injured party to be in the same position they would have been in had the contract been carried out, in so far as money is able to do this (***Robinson v Harman***).
- The injured party can claim damages for loss of bargain/ profits ('expectation losses') and expenses ('reliance losses') (***Anglia Television Ltd v Reed)***

Restitutionary loss

- Damages are not intended to be punitive but compensatory.
- Claims in restitution are conceptually different from those for damages for breach of contract since the aim is to place both the parties in the same position that they were in *before* the contract had been entered into, that is, as if the contract had not been made.
- ***Surrey County Council v Bredero Homes Ltd***
- ***Wrotham Par k Estate Co. Ltd v Parkside Homes Ltd.***
- ***Johnson v Agnew***
- ***Attorney General v Blake***
- ***WWF World Wide Fund for Nature v World Wrestling Federation Entertainment***

Actions for an agreed sum

- Distinction between actions for damages and actions for an agreed sum

Difference in value and cost of cure

- In assessing the damages one of two methods may be adopted:
    (i)   a 'difference in value' basis, or
    (ii) a 'cost of cure' basis (***Ruxley Electronics and Construction Ltd v Forsyth; Laddingford Enclosures Ltd v Forsyth***)
- Mitigation of loss:
    (a) No loss = nominal damages.
    (b) A claimant should mitigate their loss by taking reasonable steps to reduce it (***British Westinghouse Electric and Manufacturing Co. Ltd v Underground Electric Railways Co. of London Ltd***)

The assessment of damages by reference to the market

- Depends on whether:
    (i)   the seller is in breach of contract for non-delivery, or
    (ii) the buyer is in breach for non-acceptance of the goods delivered.

'Available market'

- No precise definition of 'available market'.
- A market arises where the seller actually offers the goods for sale (*Shearson Lehman Hutton Inc. v Maclaine Watson & Co. Ltd (No. 2)*
- *Hooper v Oates; Hughes v Pendragon Sabre Ltd t/a Porsche Centre Bolton*)

The question of time in assessing an award of damages

- *Johnson v Agnew*
- The general principle for the assessment of damages is compensatory.
- Damages are usually assessed as at the time the contract has been broken.
- The principle may be relaxed to prevent injustice
- *Kennedy v Van Emden*
- *Golden Strait Corporation v Nippon Yusen Kubishka Kaisha (The Golden Victory).*
- *Glory Wealth Shipping Pte Ltd v Korea Line Corp. (The Wren)*
- *Koch Marine Inc. v d'Amica Societa di Navigazione ARL (The Elena d'Amico)*
- *Force India Formula One team Ltd v Etihad Airways PJSC*
- *Ageas (UK) Ltd v Kwik-Fit (GB) Ltd*
- **Bunge SA v Nidera BV**

Limitations on the availability of damages
Causation

- To claim damages a causal link between the losses sustained and the breach of contract must be shown (*Young v Purdy; C & P Haulage*).
- Break of the causal link between the breach of contract and the losses suffered occurs where the loss results partly from a breach of contract and also from the intervening acts of a third party (*Stansbie v Troman*; contrast with *Weld-Blundell v Stephens*).

Remoteness of damages

- The defendant will be liable only for losses that arise from the consequences of the breach and which can be said to be within the contemplation of the parties at the time of contracting.
- Damages under *Hadley v Baxendale*:
  - The orthodox approach
    1. Loss 'arising naturally, i.e. according to the usual course of things, from such breach of contract itself . . . '
    2. Loss 'such as may reasonably be supposed to have been in the contemplation of both the parties, at the time they made the contract, as the probable result of the breach of it'.
       - Introduction of reasonable foreseeability to damages (*Victoria Laundry (Windsor) Ltd v Newman Industries Ltd*).
       - *Koufos v Czarnikow Ltd, The Heron II*. Remoteness in contract was not the same as the test applied in tort (*Wellesley Partners LLP v Withers LLP*

(–) The modified rule (*Transfield Shipping Inc. v Mercator Shipping Inc (The Achilleas)*)

Factors influencing the quantum of damages

Mitigation of loss

- Claimant will not be able to claim for losses which they could have avoided by the taking of reasonable steps.
- Reasonable steps to mitigate losses is a question of fact (*British Westinghouse Electric and Manufacturing Co. Ltd v Underground Electric Railways Co. of London Ltd; Fulton Shipping Inc. of Panama v Globalia Business Travel (formerly Travelplan SAU) of Spain, The New Flamenco*

Contributory negligence

- Law Reform (Contributory Negligence) Act 1945 reduces the amount of damages that might be recovered if fault is proved.

Contractual provisions relating to the limitation of damages

- The parties can agree the amount of damages to be paid on a stipulated event.
- The courts will still regulate agreements regarding (i) penalty clauses and (ii) the regulation of deposits and forfeiture clauses.

Liquidated damages and penalties

- Courts support claims where the parties make a genuine attempt to pre-estimate the loss if there is a breach.
- Damages payable from genuine pre-estimates of loss are termed 'liquidated damages'.
- The courts will not award sums which are considered to be penalties.
- Penalty clauses v pre-estimate of loss clauses: how to identify the difference: (*Dunlop Pneumatic Tyre Co. Ltd v New Garage and Motor Co. Ltd* .; *Philips Hong Kong Ltd v Attorney-General of Hong Kong; Cavendish Square Holding BV v Talal El Makdessi* – Commercial contracts; *ParkingEye Ltd v Beavis* – Consumer contracts)

Deposits and forfeiture clauses

- Deposits are payable before a breach occurs and deposits are normally regarded as a part consideration which may be retained should the purchaser fail to perform their side of the bargain.
- Forfeiture clauses normally arise where there is a purchase of goods by instalments and the contract provides that should the purchaser default on any instalment then they must surrender the goods, at the same time forfeiting any instalments already paid.

Speculative damages and damages for non-pecuniary losses

- Inaccurately assessed damages do not bar the recovery of compensation, subject to remoteness (*Chaplin v Hicks; Allied Maples Group Ltd v Simmons and Simmons (a firm); Wellesley Partners LLP v Withers LLP*)

- Damages are not confined to financial loss – physical inconvenience had to arise from the breach and not simply mental distress (***Addis*** v ***Gramophone Co. Ltd.***)

- Holidays – damages for disappointment, mental anxiety and distress could be compensated (***Jarvis*** v ***Swans Tours Ltd***; ***Jackson*** v ***Horizon Holidays Ltd***; ***Farley*** v ***Skinner***)

Further reading

Beatson, Burrows and Cartwright, *Anson's Law of Contract*, 30th edn (Oxford University Press, 2016)

Bishop, 'The Choice of Remedy for Breach of Contract' (1985) 14 *Journal of Legal Studies* 299

Capper, 'Damages for Distress and Disappointment: The Limits of *Watts* v *Morrow*' (2000) 116 *Law Quarterly Review* 553

Capper, 'Damages for Distress and Disappointment – Problem Solved' (2002) 118 *Law Quarterly Review* 193

Carter and Peden, Damages Following Termination for repudiation: taking Account of Later Events', (2008) 24 *Journal of Contract Law* 145

Coote, 'Contract Damages, *Ruxley* and the Performance Interest' (1997) 56 *Cambridge Law Journal* 537

Cunningham, 'Changing Conceptions of Compensation' (2007) 66 *Cambridge Law Journal* 507

Darck, 'The Limb of Foreseeability and *The Achilleas*' (2011) 17(5) *Journal of International Maritime Law* 360

Furmston, *Cheshire, Fifoot and Furmston's Law of Contract*, 16th edn (Oxford University Press, 2012)

Hoffmann, Lord, '*The Achilleas*: Custom and Practice or Foreseeability?' (2010) 14(1) *Edinburgh Law Review* 47

Hudson, 'Penalties Limiting Damages' (1974) 90 *Law Quarterly Review* 31

Hudson, 'Penalties Limiting Damages' (1975) 91 *Law Quarterly Review* 25

Isaacs and Davies, 'The Fine Line between Liquidated Damages and Penalties' (2008) 23 *Butterworths Journal of International and Banking Law* 152

Karia and Semark, 'Remoteness in Contract, *The Achilleas* and *The Sylvia*: What does it all mean?' (2010) *Shipping and Trade Law* (May) 1

Kendrick, 'Breach of Contract and the Meaning of Loss' (1999) *Current Legal Problems* 37

Kramer, 'The New Test of Remoteness in Contract' (2009) 125 *Law Quarterly Review* 408

Law Commission Working Paper No 114, *Contributory Negligence as a Defence in Contract Law* (1990)

Law Commission Report, *Contributory Negligence as a Defence in Contract* (Law Com No 219) 1993

Lee, 'Contractual Interpretation and Remoteness', [2010] *Lloyd's Maritime and Commercial Law Quarterly* 150

Mustill, '*The Golden Victory* – Some Reflections' (2008) 124 *Law Quarterly Review* 570

McLauchlan, 'The Redundant Reliance Interest in Contract Damages', (2011) 127 *Law Quarterly Review* 23

McKendrick, 'Breach of Contract and the Meaning of Loss', [1999] 52(1) *Current Legal Problems* 37

Mustill, 'The Golden Victory – some reflections' (2008) 124 LQR 569

Naravane, 'The Implications of *Transfield* for Concurrent Liability in Tort and Contract' (2012) *Journal of Business Law* 404

O'Sullivan, 'Damages for Lost Profits for Late Redelivery: How Remote Is Too Remote?' (2009) 68(1) *Cambridge Law Journal* 34

Pearce and Halson, 'Damages for Breach of Contract: Compensation, Restitution and Vindication' (2008) 28 *Oxford Journal of Legal Studies* 73

Peel, 'Remoteness Re-Visited' (2009) 125 *Law Quarterly Review* 6

Phang, 'The Crumbling Edifice? The Award of Contractual Damages for Mental Distress' (2003) *Journal of Business Law* 341

Robertson, 'The Basis of the Remoteness Rule in Contract' (2008) 28 *Legal Studies* 172

Smith and Atiyah, *Atiyah's Introduction to the Law of Contract*, 6th edn (Oxford University Press, 2006)

Taylor, 'Expectation, Reliance and Misrepresentation' (1982) 45 *Modern Law Review* 139

Tettenborn, '*Hadley* v *Baxendale* Foreseeability: A Principle Beyond its Sell-by Date' (2007) 23 *Journal of Contract Law* 120

Trotman, 'Damage Control' (2012) 162 *New Law Journal* 134

Peel, Treitel *Law of Contract*, 14th edn (Sweet and Maxwell, 2015)

Wallace, 'Third Party Damage: No Legal Black Hole?' (1999) 115 *Law Quarterly Review* 394

Webb, 'Performance and Compensation: An Analysis of Contract Damages and Contractual Obligation' (2006) 41 *Oxford Journal of Legal Studies* 26

Yip and Goh, 'The compensatory principle: a golden victory for a new certainty', (2016) 4 *JBL* 335

17

Equitable remedies and limitation of actions

Objectives

After reading this chapter you should be able to:

1. Explain the nature of an order for specific performance and know the effect of such an order, together with the factors a court will take into account when making an order.

2. Explain the nature of the remedy of injunction, the limitations on the use of prohibitory injunctions and the ability of a court to award damages in lieu of an injunction or an order for specific performance.

3. Know and explain the different periods imposed by the Limitation Act 1980 that limit the opportunity for the injured party to take action for breach of contract.

Equitable remedies

Specific performance

The nature of the remedy

Objective 1

Specific performance is an order of the court which compels a defendant to carry out their obligations under a contract in accordance with the terms and conditions set out in the contract. Failure to comply with the order will render the defendant liable to criminal proceedings for contempt of court. The remedy is normally used to enforce positive obligations, negative ones being restrained with the use of a prohibitory injunction.

Specific performance is a remedy *in personam* and can be ordered even where the subject matter of the contract is outside the jurisdiction, provided the party subject to the order is within the jurisdiction. The remedy is awarded at the discretion of the court and it should be noted that it is only sparingly awarded, where the court considers it just and equitable to do so. The award will not be given, for instance, where its effect would be to cause hardship amounting to injustice to either party or an interested third party, as was held in *Patel v Ali.*

Patel v *Ali* [1984] Ch 283

In this case the vendor and her husband were the co-owners of a house which they had entered into a contract to sell in 1979. Completion was delayed by reason of the husband's bankruptcy. In addition the vendor contracted bone cancer which resulted in her having to have a leg amputated. These events also corresponded with the birth of their second and third children. The purchaser applied for, and was awarded, an order of specific performance, but the vendor appealed on the grounds of hardship. The vendor spoke little English and had to rely on friends and relatives for help. The effect of the decree would thus be to expose her to undue hardship. The court held that in an appropriate case relief could be given against specific performance where hardship arose once the contract had been entered into, even if the hardship itself was not related specifically to the subject matter and not caused by the plaintiff. The court decided that damages should be awarded instead of specific performance as the latter would amount to injustice, given the level of hardship that would be inflicted on the vendor.

While an application for an award of specific performance will usually be made where a breach of contract has occurred, a breach is not an essential requirement for the application of an award. The award of the order is based on the existence of a contract, together with circumstances rendering it just and equitable to make an award, as stated in **Hasham v Zenab** [1960] AC 316, where an order of specific performance was given before the contractual date for completion since the defendant was in anticipatory breach of contract.

The award of an order of specific performance is not an arbitrary one and various factors might influence a court in the granting of the order.

Factors to be considered in making an order for specific performance

1. Damages must not be an adequate remedy

If damages are an adequate remedy then an order of specific performance will not be awarded (the same principle also applying to the award of injunctions). The reason for this is that the remedies of the courts of chancery arose out of the inadequacy of the award of damages at common law. In the vast majority of contracts damages provide an adequate remedy, as, for example, in contracts for the sale of goods, where compensation will generally allow a purchaser to buy the goods elsewhere. In contracts for the sale of land, however, an order of specific performance will normally be awarded since, on just and equitable grounds, a simple award of damages would defeat the reasonable aspirations and expectations of the vendor.

Specific performance will be awarded for contracts for the sale of goods, however, where the goods in question are unique.

Example

A contract for the purchase of a valuable antique clearly would not be compensated by damages since there is no or little prospect of a buyer being able to go into the marketplace to purchase a similar item. This factor is another reason why contracts for the sale of land lend themselves readily to the award of such a remedy. Even in these circumstances the court will not make an order where the award would produce an injustice to the defendant. The principle is illustrated by the case of **Wroth v Tyler.**

Wroth v Tyler [1974] Ch 30

In this case a husband, who was the owner of a matrimonial home, entered into a contract to sell the property with vacant possession. Before completion could take place his wife, who did not want to move, registered her right of occupation under the Matrimonial Homes Act 1967 (now 1983) as a Class F landcharge against the property, and this action had the effect of placing an encumbrance on the ability of the husband to give vacant possession. The husband withdrew from the contract and the purchaser sued for an order of specific performance.

It was held by Megarry J that the purchaser should fail in his action since to compel the husband to carry out his obligation he would have had to apply to the court to terminate the wife's right of occupation. In order to do this the husband would have had to embark on difficult and uncertain litigation against his own wife, which was clearly undesirable given the fact that they were still living together. Even if he was successful in such an action, the court's decision to remove the right of occupation was in any event discretionary. Further, if the court awarded specific performance subject to the wife's right of occupation this would have entailed the purchaser obtaining an order of eviction against the husband and his daughter, thereby resulting in the break-up of the family.

The facts of *Beswick v Beswick* are given in Chapter 19.

Contracts to pay money do not usually attract an order for specific performance since damages are normally an adequate remedy here. In certain circumstances the use of such an order can be justified where there is a contract under which money has to be paid to a third party. The case of ***Beswick v Beswick*** [1968] AC 58 is an obvious and extremely good illustration of the use of specific performance in such circumstances. An award of damages to Peter Beswick's estate would have been nominal since the contract to pay the annuity in question to his widow resulted in no loss to his estate, while the annuity payable to himself ceased on his death. The most appropriate remedy, therefore, was a decree of specific performance in order to compel the defendant to comply with his obligations under the contract to the third party.

2. The requirement of mutuality

The general principle is that specific performance will not be awarded unless the order is available to both parties, that is, availability of the award is mutual. Thus in ***Flight v Bolland*** (1828) 4 Russ 298 an application for specific performance by a minor failed since the award would not have been available against the minor by the other party because of the incapacity of the applicant. The Landlord and Tenant Act 1985, s 17, provides an exception to the rule requiring mutuality. It states that the court can make an order of specific performance in respect of a landlord's covenant to keep the premises in a good state of repair despite rules of equity restricting the award of the order to 'whether based on mutuality or otherwise'.

One problem that has arisen in the past with respect to mutuality is the time at which mutuality should be present between the parties. It was suggested by Fry in *Specific Performance* (1921) that there had to be mutuality between the parties at the time an enforcement contract had been entered into. Ames, however, in *Lectures on Legal History* (1913) pointed to several exceptions to this rule, stating that the rule should be expressed as:

> Equity will not compel specific performance by a defendant if, after performance, the common law remedy of damages would be his sole security for the performance of the plaintiff's side of the contract.

The rule, however, was subject to extensive review in the case of ***Price v Strange***.

Price v *Strange* [1978] Ch 337

The facts of the case were that the defendant had contracted to grant a sub-lease to the plaintiff, provided the plaintiff did some external and internal repairs to the premises. The plaintiff did the internal repairs but, though he was ready and willing to do the external repairs, he was unable to do so because the defendant had by then done them herself at her own expense. The defendant repudiated the contract and the plaintiff claimed for an order of specific performance. At first instance the application failed since the availability of the remedy was not mutual at the date of the contract because the defendant could not have compelled the plaintiff to carry out the repairs. The decision was reversed on appeal to the Court of Appeal. Goff LJ stated that the principle of mutuality is:

> that one judges the defence of mutuality on the facts and circumstances as they exist at the hearing, albeit in the light of the whole contract of the parties in relation to the subject-matter, and in the absence of any other disqualifying circumstances, the court will grant specific performance if it can be done without injustice or unfairness to the defendant.

It should be noted that the rule regarding the need for mutuality is one which affects the discretion of the court to award specific performance. The rule does not affect the jurisdiction of the court to award damages in lieu of specific performance under the Chancery Amendment Act 1858, which will be dealt with later.

3. The exercise of discretion

As already stated, the exercise of discretion is not an arbitrary one but is exercised within certain broad parameters in order to promote justice between the parties. Should the exercise of the discretion result in injustice being wrought upon an individual then the order of specific performance will not be given. The notion that governs this aspect of the exercise of discretion is sometimes expressed in the equitable maxim, 'he who seeks equity must do equity', or rather more graphically, 'he who comes to equity must come with clean hands'.

It has been seen how hardship can prevent the exercise of equitable discretion to give an order for specific performance, and the same is also true of mistake and misrepresentation. It should be noted, however, that a defendant cannot resist the granting of an order simply because they made a mistake. As a general rule, the defendant will be held to their bargain, unless they can prove that this would lead to injustice. In **Webster v Cecil** (1861) 30 Beav 62 the vendor offered to sell some property to the purchaser for £2,250 but mistakenly wrote £1,250. The purchaser, who was aware of the mistake, immediately accepted the offer. The vendor on realising his mistake gave notice of it to the purchaser. It was held that in the circumstances he could not be compelled to carry on with the sale.

See Chapter 13 for rules relating to time in relation to performance of a contract.

The rules relating to time in relation to performance of a contract have been discussed elsewhere in this book. There it is seen that the rule in equity is that time is not of the essence in a contract and that therefore a claimant can obtain specific performance, despite the fact that they have not carried out their obligations under the contract at the time specified in the contract. Where, however, the parties have agreed that time will be of the essence then specific performance will not be awarded if the elements relating to time have not been met by the claimant. This principle applies even if time was only made of the essence by the service of notice during the ambit of the contract. Even where time is not of the essence specific performance may still be lost since the rule that 'delay defeats equity' (the **doctrine of laches**) may apply. Unreasonable delay, then, may defeat an application for equitable relief, including specific performance, but what is unreasonable depends substantially on the subject matter of the contract. At one time it was considered that specific performance had to be applied for within 12 months. However, in *Lazard Bros & Co. Ltd v Fairfield Properties (Mayfair) Ltd* (1977) 121 SJ 793, Megarry VC stated that specific performance should not be regarded as a prize to be awarded to the zealous and denied to the indolent. In that case a delay of over two years was held not to be a bar to the award of an order.

The exercise of the discretion to award specific performance is not given where the contract demands a personal service or work, for instance, in contracts of employment. The reason is that the order would require the constant supervision of the court, as was held in *Ryan v Mutual Tontine Westminster Chambers Association* [1893] 1 Ch 116 where the landlord of a flat agreed that he would appoint a porter who would be in constant attendance to maintain the common areas of the building, collect mail, and so on. The porter appointed also worked as a chef at a nearby club and was thus constantly absent. The plaintiff's action for specific performance failed since the exercise of the order would require the constant supervision of the court. It should also be noted that the courts are reluctant to order specific performance in personal contracts since as a matter of public policy it is considered undesirable to force a person to carry out obligations with another against their will.

A more modern example of the refusal of the courts to grant specific performance where the order requires the constant supervision of the court is in the House of Lords decision in *Co-operative Insurance Ltd v Argyll Stores (Holdings) Ltd.*

Co-operative Insurance Ltd v Argyll Stores (Holdings) Ltd [1997] 2 WLR 898

The facts of the case were that the plaintiffs granted the defendants a lease of a unit in a shopping centre for a term of 35 years from 1979 to operate a Safeway supermarket. The supermarket was the largest retail outlet in the centre and its presence was likely to have a substantial impact on the success of the centre and the other retail outlets as a whole. The lease contained a covenant that the defendants undertook to keep the supermarket open for retail trade during the usual hours of business in the locality.

In 1995, the supermarket was running at a loss and the defendants resolved to close it. The plaintiffs attempted to persuade them to keep the supermarket open, but when these efforts failed an order for specific performance was sought.

It was held at first instance that the application should be refused and that damages only would be awarded. The plaintiffs were successful on their appeal to the Court of Appeal, which considered that the order should be made on two grounds. First, the Court of Appeal considered that damages would not be an adequate remedy since it would be difficult to quantify the loss that flowed from the breach. Second, the Court of Appeal considered the breach to be cynical and unreasonable. The defendants appealed to the House of Lords which reversed the Court of Appeal's decision, stating that it had long been settled practice that the courts do not award specific performance of covenants to carry on business or to continue trading. Lord Hoffmann stated, in accordance with orthodox practice, that an order in such circumstances was undesirable because it required the constant supervision of the court. Further, he stated that the only way to enforce compliance if such an order was made was to initiate criminal proceedings for contempt of court. He considered such proceedings to be inappropriate in a commercial contract requiring a party to continue trading.

Lord Hoffmann was prepared to accept that an order of specific performance could be made in exceptional cases where a one-off result was required, for instance, where a landlord required a tenant to comply with a covenant to repair premises under a lease, since here compliance was easy to achieve. It is not clear, however, whether it will always be so easy to make a distinction between an award of specific performance to achieve a stated result as in this case, and an award to ensure a continued compliance with a covenant to carry on a business or trading. Further, it is questionable whether Lord Hoffmann's reasoning ignores the reality of the situation in that the order of specific performance is a commercial gambit to ensure that adequate levels of compensation should be paid. It should be noted that damages would normally be assessed on the loss of rent to the landlord, while the landlord would be seeking not just those losses but also the wider losses that might arise from the withdrawal of an 'anchor' tenant from the shopping centre. An order for specific performance would be a useful lever in securing damages for such losses from the defendants that would not otherwise be recoverable. Lord Hoffmann might have been better relying on the imprecise nature of the covenant as a reason for his refusal rather than tying the strings of the discretionary bag so tightly as to prevent the courts from adopting a flexible approach to the award of such orders.

The Court of Appeal considered the deliberate cynical conduct of the defendants to be an important issue in their award of specific performance. Lord Hoffmann rejected this argument and considered that all the defendants had done was to make a commercial decision to shut down a loss-making site and nothing else could be read into this decision.

4. 'Equity will not assist a volunteer'

In *Penn* v *Lord Baltimore* (1750) 1 Ves Sen 444, Lord Hardwicke declared that 'the court never decrees specifically without a consideration'. The requirement of consideration is a fundamental requirement for the granting of an order for specific performance, whether or not the contract is a simple one or one that is made under seal by deed.

Injunctions

The nature of the remedy

Objective
2

For more on contracts in restraint of trade refer to Chapter 12.

A further way in which a contract may be enforced is by the use of an **injunction,** which can be either prohibitory or mandatory in its application. A prohibitory injunction in the law of contract is used only to restrain a breach of a negative undertaking, for instance where the defendant has broken an agreement not to carry on a particular trade, as in *Nordenfelt* v *Maxim Nordenfelt Guns and Ammunition Co. Ltd* [1894] AC 535.

A mandatory injunction is an order to the defendant to do some positive act, such as demolishing a building, and is thus restorative in its nature. As a general rule, such injunctions arise out of tortious acts rather than contractual ones, where specific performance is used. This type of injunction is quite uncommon and is not usually issued where damages are an adequate remedy or where the injunction would require the constant supervision of the court. Generally speaking, if a mandatory injunction should be claimed in a contractual situation, it will be subject to very similar limitations to those imposed on applications for specific performance.

Limitations on the use of prohibitory injunctions

The rule that damages must be shown to be inadequate before equitable relief will be granted does not apply to prohibitory (sometimes called 'ordinary') injunctions. That is not to suppose that the courts will allow this difference to be used in order to allow a claimant to gain a benefit that they would not ordinarily be entitled to claim in an application for specific performance. The courts will thus grant the injunction only where there is an express stipulation in the contract that the defendant should not do a particular act. Thus in *Lumley* v *Wagner* (1852) 1 De GM& G 604 the defendant agreed to sing at the plaintiff's theatre over a particular period. She eventually abandoned the contract and took engagements to sing elsewhere. It was held that the plaintiff could have an injunction restraining the defendant from singing anywhere else. The negative nature of the injunction should be noted in the case, since the court could not compel the defendant to work solely for the plaintiff, though it could prevent her from working for anyone else.

The decision in *Lumley* v *Wagner* was followed in the case of *Warner Bros Inc.* v *Nelson* [1937] 1 KB 209 where the actress Bette Davis was restrained from working for anyone but the plaintiffs. Both cases have been criticised as being tantamount to forcing the defendants to work for the respective plaintiffs, an effect which in personal contracts has always been ruled against in the granting of equitable relief. Indeed, in the case of *Page One Records Ltd* v *Britton* [1968] 1 WLR 157 the courts refused to grant an injunction which would have had the effect of compelling the defendant, representing The Troggs pop group, to engage the plaintiffs as their agents and managers or to wind up the group. This approach was also followed in *Nichols Advanced Vehicle Systems Inc.* v *De Angelis* (unreported, 21 December 1979) where Oliver J considered the proper approach was that taken in the *Page One Records* case, unless the period of the contract was very short, as in *Lumley* v *Wagner*.

Lastly, it should be stated that there are no restrictions on a court granting a prohibitory injunction to prevent an employee from breaking particular terms in their contract of employment. Examples of the use of an injunction in these circumstances are *Lansing Linde Ltd* v *Kerr* [1991] 1 All ER 418 and *Lawrence David Ltd* v *Ashton* [1991] 1 All ER 385 where prohibitory injunctions were used to prevent employees from disclosing the confidential information of their employers to a business rival.

Damages in lieu of specific performance and injunction

The Chancery Amendment Act 1858 gave the court of chancery the opportunity to grant damages in lieu of specific performance or injunction. It is possible for the court to grant damages in addition to these orders, provided the claimant can show that they have suffered some special loss or damage.

The position with respect to these types of damages is now governed by the Supreme Court Act 1981, s 50. It should be noted that the damages that arise here are discretionary and that the discretion arises only where the contract is of a type for which an injunction or an order for specific performance is not available. Where the contract is of such a type then the court may exercise its discretion to award damages despite the fact that an injunction or an order for specific performance would not be given because of some discretionary reason, for example the lack of mutuality. In order for the court to exercise its discretion, however, the claimant must have applied for either an injunction or an order for specific performance.

The measure of damages under the Act is calculated on the same basis as those at common law, as held by Lord Wilberforce in *Johnson* v *Agnew* [1980] AC 367.

Limitation of actions

Limitation Act 1980

Objective
3

While equity could exercise its discretion not to grant relief under the doctrine of laches, where a claimant unreasonably delayed in applying to the court, the common law developed no such rule, although stale actions were discouraged as a matter of policy.

The Limitation Act 1980 has laid down a framework of periods within which actions must be brought or be debarred. In actions for breach of contract the following periods are laid down by the Act.

Actions founded on a simple contract

Here the action must be commenced within six years from the date on which the cause of the action accrued, by virtue of s 5. In contract the cause of action accrues from the time of the breach, rather than from the time any damage occurs, as in actions for negligence. Where the action can be framed in either contract or tort, or both, there may thus be a procedural advantage in framing the action in terms of a tortious claim.

Where the breach gives rise to personal injuries then s 11 of the Act provides that the limitation period is reduced to three years from the date on which the cause of action accrued.

Actions founded on a speciality contract

By s 8(1) an action upon a specialty contract shall not be brought after the expiration of 12 years from the date on which the cause of action accrued.

Action for an account

By s 23 an **action for an account** shall not be brought after the expiration of any time limit which is applicable to the claim which is the basis of the duty to account, that is, six years in relation to breach of contract.

The suspension of the 1980 Act by virtue of disabilities

If the claimant is under a disability, for example, is a minor or of unsound mind, when the cause of action accrued, then the limitation period does not begin to run until the disability has ceased to operate, by virtue of s 28(1). It should be noted that by s 28(2), if time under the limitation period had already started to run, then any subsequent disability has no effect on the running of time for the purposes of calculating the limitation period.

Postponement of the limitation period in cases of fraud or mistake

The position here is governed by s 32(1) of the 1980 Act which provides:

> where in the case of any action for which a period of limitation is prescribed by this Act, either –
>
> (a)   the action is based upon the fraud of the defendant; or
> (b)   any fact relevant to the plaintiff's right of action has been deliberately concealed from him by the defendant; or
> (c)   the action is for relief from the consequences of a mistake;
>
> the period of limitation shall not begin to run until the plaintiff has discovered the fraud, concealment or mistake (as the case may be) or could with reasonable diligence have discovered it.

Extension of the limitation period by acknowledgement or part-payment

It is provided by s 29(5) that:

> Where any right of action has accrued to recover –

(a) any debt or other liquidated pecuniary claim . . . and the person liable or accountable therefore acknowledges the claim or makes any payment in respect thereof, the right shall be deemed to have accrued on and not before the date of the acknowledgement or the last payment.

The result of the above provision is that if a person owes a debt to another then, every time the debtor makes a part-payment of the debt or acknowledges the debt, the limitation period begins to run afresh from the date of each part-payment or acknowledgement of the debt. By s 29(7), however, once the debt is statute-barred then the right of action cannot be revived by any acknowledgement or part-payment. An effective acknowledgement must be made in writing signed by the debtor, or their agent, and made to the other party or their agent by virtue of s 30.

Summary

Equitable remedies

Specific performance

The nature of the remedy

- Specific performance is an order of the court which compels a defendant to carry out their obligations under a contract.
- The defendant is liable to criminal proceedings for contempt of court if they fail to comply.
- Specific performance is used to enforce positive obligations.
- Negative obligations are restrained with a prohibitory injunction.
- Specific performance is an equitable remedy.
- Specific performance is not used if it causes hardship to a party or third party (*Patel v Ali*).
- The courts will not order specific performance in personal service contracts.

Factors to be considered in making an order for specific performance

- *Damages must not be an adequate remedy:* if damages are an adequate remedy, then an order of specific performance will not be awarded.
- *The requirement of mutuality:* specific performance is generally not awarded unless the order is available to both parties (*Flight v Bolland*).

Injunctions

The nature of the remedy

- Injunctions can be either prohibitory or mandatory.
- Prohibitory injunctions restrain a breach of a negative undertaking (*Nordenfelt v Maxim Nordenfelt Guns and Ammunition Co. Ltd*).
- Mandatory injunction – order to the defendant to do some positive act.

Limitations on the use of prohibitory injunctions

- The rule that damages must be shown to be inadequate before equitable relief will be granted *does not* apply to prohibitory injunctions.

Damages in lieu of specific performance and injunction

- Governed by the Supreme Court Act 1981, s 50.
- Damages that arise here are discretionary.
- Discretion arises only where the contract is of a type for which an injunction or an order for specific performance is not available.
- For the court to exercise its discretion the claimant must have applied for either an injunction or an order for specific performance.

Limitations of actions

Limitation Act 1980

- The Act provides periods in which actions must be brought or be debarred.

Actions founded on a simple contract – s 5

- Six years from the date on which the cause of the action accrued for a breach of contract.

Actions founded on a speciality contract – s 8(1)

- An action upon a speciality contract shall not be brought after the expiration of 12 years from the date on which the cause of action accrued.

Action for an account – s 23

- No claim to be brought outside the time limit.

Postponement of the limitation period in cases of fraud or mistake – s 32(1)

- Limitation begins to run when the fraud is discovered.

Extension of the limitation period by acknowledgement or part-payment

- Limitation Act 1980, s 29(5).

Further reading

Ames, *Lectures on Legal History* (Harvard University Press, 1913)

Beatson, Burrows and Cartwright, *Anson's Law of Contract,* 30th edn (Oxford University Press, 2015)

Burrows, 'Specific Performance at the Crossroads' (1984) 4 *Legal Studies* 102

Burrows, *The Law of Restitution,* 3rd edn (Oxford University Press, 2011)

Fry, *Specific Performance,* 6th edn (Stevens, 1921)

Furmston, *Cheshire, Fifoot and Furmston's Law of Contract,* 16th edn (Oxford University Press, 2012)

Kronman, 'Specific Performance' (1978) 45 *University of Chicago Law Review* 351

Phang, 'Specific Performance: Exploring the Roots of "Settled Practice"', (1998) 61 *Modern Law Review* 421

Smith and Atiyah, *Atiyah's Introduction to the Law of Contract,* 6th edn (Oxford University Press, 2006)

Spry, *The Principles of Equitable Remedies: Injunctions, Specific Performance and Equitable Remedies,* 3rd edn (Sweet & Maxwell, 1984)

Peel, Treitel *Law of Contract,* 14th edn (Sweet and Maxwell, 2015)

Quasi-contract and the law of restitution

Objectives

After reading this chapter you should be able to:

1. Understand the nature of quasi-contracts and the broader body of law known as the 'law of restitution'.

2. Understand the nature of actions to recover moneys paid where there has been a total and partial failure of consideration and know how a partial failure of consideration is converted into a total failure of consideration and how moneys can be recovered in a void contract.

3. Know how moneys paid under a mistake of law can be recovered.

4. Understand the nature of *quantum meruit* claims and how *quantum meruit* can be used within a contract.

Introduction

Objective 1

The doctrine of quasi-contract lies within a broader area of law known as the **law of restitution**. Historically, actions based in quasi-contract arose individually, though they possessed a common procedure within the now defunct forms of action. Nevertheless, it was always considered that there was some linking element between the cases which broadly fell into the category now known as quasi-contract. Eventually Lord Mansfield in **Moses v Macferlan** (1760) 2 Burr 1005 expressed the common link as being one of unjust advantage. In explaining the basis for an action for money had and received he stated that:

> This kind of equitable action, to recover back money, which ought not in justice to be kept, is very beneficial, and therefore much encouraged. It lies only for money which, *ex aequo et bono*, the defendant ought to refund: It does not lie for money paid by the plaintiff, which is claimed by him as payable in point of honour and honesty, although it could not have been recovered from him by any course of law; as in payment of a debt barred by the Statute of Limitations, or contracted during his infancy or to the extent of principal and legal interest upon a usurious contract, or for money fairly lost at play: because in all these cases, the defendant may retain it with safe conscience, though by positive law he was debarred from recovering. But it lies for money paid by mistake; or upon a consideration which happens to fail; or for money got

through imposition (express or implied); or extortion; or oppression; or an undue advantage taken of the plaintiff's situation, contrary to laws made for the protection of persons under those circumstances. *In one word, the gist of this kind of action is, that the defendant, upon the circumstances of the case, is obliged by the ties of natural justice and equity to refund the money.* (emphasis added)

Lord Mansfield saw this action as one which arose independently of an action in either contract or tort, arising as an obligation imposed by the law on the basis of natural justice. This approach did not find favour after the abolition of the forms of action, with the passing of the Common Law Procedure Act 1852, for two reasons. First, there developed a hardening of the categories into which legal obligations fell, those not being tortious of necessity being contractual, and vice versa. The result was that quasi-contractual obligations, being clearly not tortious, had to come within the law of contract. Second, since such obligations fell within the law of contract their existence within this category had to be justified in legal terms, especially as the tendency of nineteenth-century judges was to reject such nebulous concepts of natural justice. The result was that the existence of quasi-contractual obligations was justified in terms of contracts implied by law.

The implied contract approach has been subject to fierce criticism and largely rejected today in favour of a doctrine based on unjust enrichment which does not depend on the existence of a contract. In truth, quasi-contract, and the wider concept of restitution, now exist as a subject in its own right, forming the middle ground between the narrow concept of the law of contract and the wide concept of the law of obligations. Thus Lord Wright in *Fibrosa Spolka Akcyjna* v *Fairbairn Lawson Combe Barbour Ltd* [1943] AC 32 stated:

> It is clear that any civilised system of law is bound to provide remedies for cases of what has been called unjust enrichment or unjust benefit, that is to prevent a man from retaining the money of or some benefit derived from, another which is against conscience that he should keep. Such remedies in English law are generically different from remedies in contract and tort, and are now recognised to fall within the third category of the common law which has been called quasi-contract or restitution.

The broad parameters in which the courts will grant relief for unjust enrichment have been set out by Jones in *Goff and Jones: The Law of Restitution* (2002). It is stated that the principle requires three factors to be present: first, that the defendant has been enriched by some benefit given to him; second, that the enrichment has been acquired at the expense of the claimant; and, third, that the retention of the benefit by the defendant would be unfair or unjust.

While claims in quasi-contract cover myriad situations, making it difficult to classify the instances in which the remedy arises, we will conduct our study of the subject by analysing actions to recover money paid, actions for payments made under a mistake of law and claims in *quantum meruit*. Such an analysis will not cover all the situations in which restitution arises, but it will cover the use of the remedy as it arises within the law of contract.

Actions to recover moneys paid

Objective 2

An action will lie in quasi-contract to recover moneys paid under either a contract or purported contract either where there has been a total failure of consideration or where the moneys have been paid under a void contract.

Total failure of consideration

Generally

A party may recover moneys paid in anticipation that the other will perform their contractual obligations in circumstances where there has been a total failure of consideration, that is, where they have received nothing that they bargained for, even where the other party is not in breach of contract. Thus any moneys paid in advance in a contract that is subsequently frustrated, for instance, may be recovered in circumstances where there has been a total failure of consideration. The *Fibrosa* case is a typical example of the operation of quasi-contract in such a situation, where a buyer was able to recover moneys paid in advance for a contract that subsequently became impossible for the seller to carry out due to the outbreak of war. Since the buyer received no benefit from the contract there was deemed to be a total failure of consideration and it was clearly a case where the seller would have been unjustly enriched had he retained those moneys.

See Chapter 15 for more on *Fibrosa*.

Consideration in this context refers, usually, to the performance of a promise, rather than the promise itself. This distinction is important since while (as already seen in Chapter 3 in the analysis of consideration) it is possible for an exchange of promises to amount to consideration, this definition is not appropriate in this context. Clearly if a promise could amount to a consideration then there will rarely, if ever, be a total failure of consideration. The position was explained by Lord Simon in the *Fibrosa* case as:

> In the law relating to the formation of contract, the promise to do a thing may often be the consideration, but when one is considering the law of failure of consideration and of the quasi-contractual right to recover money on that ground, it is, generally speaking, not the promise which is referred to as consideration, but the performance of the promise. The money was paid to secure performance and, if performance fails, the inducement which brought about payment is not fulfilled. If this were not so, there could never be any recovery of money, for failure of consideration, by the payer of the money in return for a promise of future performance.

As Lord Simon indicates, it is not always the case that quasi-contract requires an absence of performance of a promise, since it may be that the promise itself may form the basis of the consideration. Treitel gives the example of a contract of insurance where the insured bargains for the promise of the insurer with the result that if their property is destroyed by some hazard other than that insured against, they cannot recover their premiums on the basis of a total failure of consideration since they have already enjoyed the benefit of the insurer's promise. Treitel points out that such premiums could only be recovered should the property insured be destroyed before the insurer adopts the risk via the contract. This point is also illustrated in the following case.

Stocznia Gdanska SA v Latvian Shipping Co. [1998] 1 WLR 574 (HL)

A shipyard entered into a contract to design, build and deliver a vessel to the buyers. The design and construction formed part of the consideration. The contract was subsequently rescinded by the shipyard before the ownership in the vessel passed to the buyers. It was held that the shipyard was able to refute the claim by the buyers that they were able to recover an instalment of the contract price on the grounds of failure of consideration. The test for failure of consideration did not depend on whether the promisee (the buyer) had or had not received anything under the contract, but on whether the promisor had performed any part of the contract for which the payment was due.

Partial failure of consideration

The rule here is that if a promisee has received part of the consideration due to them under the contract then they are unable to recover moneys paid in advance, as held in **Whincup v Hughes** (1871) LR 6 CP 78 where the plaintiff paid a watchmaker a premium of £24 to apprentice his son to him for six years. After one year the watchmaker died, though it was held that the plaintiff could not recover his money since the failure of the consideration was only partial. It should be noted, however, that the circumstances in this case would now be covered by the Law Reform (Frustrated Contracts) Act 1943, s 1(2), as a sum 'paid . . . in pursuance of the contract before the time when the parties were so discharged'.

Where there is a partial failure of consideration caused by a party failing wholly to perform their side of the bargain then the usual remedy is to sue for damages for breach of contract. The reason for the rule apparently is that the courts baulk at attempts to apportion the amounts due in relation to the partial performance of the contract. This rule, however, is not an absolute one and where apportionment is easy, as in the case of a divisible contract, or where the moneys paid can be divided up on a pro rata basis in relation to the performance of the contract, then partial restitution may be allowed.

Converting a partial failure into a total failure of consideration

In certain circumstances it may be possible to convert a partial failure into a total failure of consideration by the promisee returning such benefits as they have already acquired under the partial performance of the contract. Such a situation may occur where the promisee has a right to rescind the contract because the performance itself is either partial or defective. The result of the act of rescission is to produce a total failure of consideration. Such a situation arises where there has been a breach of condition which is discovered only when the goods are delivered. The breach of condition may arise either through a term of the contract or by virtue of a condition implied by statute. Thus if a purchaser pays in advance for an item in a catalogue which, when delivered, does not correspond with the description in the catalogue, then the purchaser can quite clearly rescind the contract under s 13 of the Sale of Goods Act 1979 and claim back the purchase moneys on the basis of a total failure of consideration.

For more on implied terms see Chapter 7.

Rescission depends, however, on *restitutio in integrum* and where this is not possible, then clearly there can be no total failure of consideration. Thus, for example, where there is a contract to rebuild a dilapidated vintage car that has been partially completed, it would probably not be possible for rescission to take place and the failure of performance could only remain as a partial one. The only alternative for the promisee here would be to sue for damages. One should, however, note that the principle of *restitutio in integrum* will not apply where the reason for the impossibility of rescission arises because of the very defect from which the right to rescind emanates in the first place.

Rowland v Divall [1923] 2 KB 500

The plaintiff bought a car from the defendant and used it for some four months. The plaintiff then discovered that the defendant was not the owner of the car and had no right or authority to sell it. The plaintiff sued to recover the price and succeeded. He was entitled to treat the contract as discharged as there had been a total failure of consideration. Lord Atkin stated:

> There has been a total failure of consideration, that is to say, the buyer has not got any part of that for which he paid the purchase money. He paid the money in order that he might get the property and he has not got it.

It was clear from the case that the defendant could not claim that the plaintiff had derived some consideration from the contract in that the plaintiff had used the car or that the car was not worth as much at the time of rescission because of depreciation. The plaintiff had paid the price to acquire ownership, which he had not got and it was from this defect that his right to rescind arose. The use of the car in this context was totally irrelevant to the contract for the sale of the vehicle.

In certain circumstances the use of the benefit under the contract by the promisee may, despite the above decision in **Rowland v Divall**, prevent the failure of consideration from being total.

Hunt v Silk (1804) 5 East 449

A contract for a lease provided that the landlord should carry out certain repairs, that immediate possession was to be given, that the lease be executed within ten days of the agreement and that on execution the tenant would pay the landlord £10. The tenant duly went into possession and paid the £10 in advance and prior to the lease being executed. In fact the landlord failed to carry out the repairs or execute the lease within the ten-day stipulation, and as a result the tenant vacated the premises and claimed his £10 on the basis of a total failure of consideration. The court applied the strict rule that a person receiving part of the benefit he contracted for under the contract cannot recover his moneys in quasi-contract. The tenant had occupied the premises, albeit for a short period of time, and thus he could not recover his £10, though, of course, he might have been able to claim damages for breach of contract and thus the decision is probably correct and proper in such circumstances.

In truth the **Rowland v Divall** case is a means of mitigating the rule as applied in **Hunt v Silk**. Its application in this way can result in great harshness simply because a party has received a benefit, no matter how slight. Nevertheless, the principle in **Rowland v Divall** can itself produce great unfairness.

Butterworth v Kingsway Motors Ltd [1954] 1 WLR 1286

A person who was buying a car on hire purchase, and thus had no title to the car, sold it before all the instalments had been paid. The car was then bought and sold by several persons until it was eventually sold by the defendant to the plaintiff for £1,275. The plaintiff used the car for 12 months before being told by the finance company that the car belonged to them but that he could acquire the title by paying off the final amount owing on the hire purchase agreement, a sum of £175, otherwise they would want the car returned to them. The plaintiff claimed the return of his £1,275 even though the car was now worth only £800 due to a slump in the second-hand car market. Further, eight days after the plaintiff heard from the finance company and after he had claimed the return of the £1,275 the original hirer paid off the final instalment so that the title to the vehicle should have 'fed' to the plaintiff. The court nevertheless allowed the plaintiff the full £1,275 despite the fact that the court considered his claim had little merit.

The case represents an unfair and illegitimate extension of the **Rowland v Divall** case, and has led to substantial criticism of the **Divall** case itself. Nevertheless, there is nothing wrong with the principle within it if it were to be confined to dealers who are making the purchase in order to resell the item in question and who therefore require good title. In the case of the consumer, however, it would seem that the better principle is to be found in **Hunt v Silk**, since the consumer will generally be able to maintain an action for damages for breach of contract.

Recovering moneys paid in a void contract

The basic rule here is that money paid under a void contract is recoverable, though this rule is not an absolute one and depends largely on the reason for the contract being held to be void. Thus it has been seen in the consideration of illegal contracts above that the effects can vary considerably. Suffice it to say that in cases where the contract is void for mistake then it is possible to recover moneys paid under such a contract.

Actions for payments made under a mistake of law

Objective 3

Until recently the general rule of English law was that money paid under a mistake of law, or as to the legal effect of the circumstances on which money was paid, but on a full understanding or knowledge of the facts, was irrecoverable. The rule dates back many years, though it was affirmed in 1996 in the case of **Westdeutsche Landesbank Girozentrale v Islington London Borough Council** [1996] AC 669. Despite its long pedigree the rule has been the subject of heavy criticism primarily because it allows a payee to retain moneys paid to them which would have not been so paid but for the payer's mistake of law. Further, the rule that money paid under a mistake of law was not recoverable became unpredictable, indeed often capricious, as the lines of distinction between mistakes of fact and mistakes of law became blurred.

For more on mistakes of law refer to Chapter 10.

By the early 1990s the rule that money paid under a mistake of law was irrecoverable began to be challenged in several Commonwealth jurisdictions. In 1994 the Law Commission (Law Com. No. 227) recommended that the rule should be abolished. In 1998 the House of Lords in the case of **Kleinwort Benson v Lincoln City Council** [1999] 2 AC 349 essentially did just that and declared that the rule would no longer form a part of English law.

The background to the **Kleinwort Benson** case was that at this time local authorities in England and Wales were subject to 'rate-capping' by the central government. It was in order to avoid the effects of rate-capping that several local authorities, Lincoln City Council included, became involved in transactions known as 'loan swaps'. Under such a scheme Kleinwort Benson paid a substantial amount of money to Lincoln City Council, believing such loan-swap arrangements to be legal and valid. In 1992, however, in **Hazell v Hammersmith and Fulham London Borough Council** [1992] 2 AC 1, the House of Lords held that such loan-swap schemes were *ultra vires* the local authorities and as a result were void.

Following the **Hazell** case, Kleinwort Benson claimed for the recovery of the money it had paid to the local authority under the void contract. The problem it faced was that some of the payments had been made more than six years previously and therefore the claim for restitution for mistake was statute-barred as being outside the limitation period. Kleinwort Benson, however, attempted to rely on s 32(1)(c) of the Limitation Act 1980, which provides that time does not begin to run for limitation purposes until the mistake has been discovered. Kleinwort contested that the mistake was not known until the decision in the **Hazell** case and until that case no one was aware that such schemes were void. Thus Kleinwort alleged that time only began to run from the date of this decision and as such it was entitled to bring an action in restitution to recover the money paid under the void contract. The judge at first instance rejected the claim on the basis that a restitutionary claim was unsustainable where the payment of money had been made under a mistake of law. Kleinwort appealed and the judge invoked the leapfrog procedure under the Administration of Justice Act 1969, s 12, so that the case went directly to the House of Lords.

In the House of Lords their Lordships were unanimous in deciding that the rule that money paid under a mistake of law was irrecoverable should be abolished. There was disagreement, however, as to whether the change should be brought about judicially, given that the existing rule was an embedded principle of English law. The majority clearly indicated that the rule that a payment could be recovered by way of restitution on the grounds of a mistake of law could be implemented by judicial decision. The minority of the House of Lords, while they considered that the present rule ought to be overturned, did not consider that the mistake in the case was a mistake of law at all. On this basis they did not consider it appropriate to abolish a rule if it meant that the payment in the case would then become recoverable.

What then are the principles governing the recovery of money under a mistake of law? Broadly, the principles are similar to those found in cases of mistake of fact: was there a mistake? Did the mistake cause the payment to be made? Did the payee have a right to the money paid to them? The Council in the case argued that the bank had not made a mistake of law because at the time the payment was made it was considered that 'loan-swap' arrangements were lawful. Such arrangements only became illegal and void following the decision in the *Hazell* case. The Council argued that on this basis there was no mistake of law at the time the arrangement was entered into. The bank for its part concurred with this view but argued that at the time the arrangement was entered into, the law was not settled and that this therefore allowed a mistake of law to arise that, in turn, allowed for restitution to be made.

Thus both the Council and the bank agreed that in establishing a mistake of law it was necessary to examine the law at the time of the contract. The point of difference lay in whether the law could be considered to be settled at that time. If it was not, as alleged by the bank, then a mistake of law could arise. The decision of the majority of the House of Lords, however, went a great deal further than this. Their Lordships considered that whether the law was settled at the time of the payment was irrelevant. Further, they stated that it did not matter if the law was changed after the payment had been made and that this would also give rise to a mistake of law.

This last point is astounding since it means that if a person entered into a contract and made a payment to another, say, in 1980, if there is a later decision in 2000 that overturns a principle of law which the parties had assumed to be settled law, then recovery of the payment by way of restitution is possible! Just a look at many of the situations that arise within this book where decisions of earlier cases have been overturned by the Court of Appeal or the House of Lords will give an idea of the implications of this decision. It is of course a founding principle of the common law and the notion of judicial precedent that they are based on a declaratory theory. The underlying principle in this theory, which every student of law knows, is that it declares the previous law to be erroneous and that the corrected law applies retrospectively. The basis behind this is that the newly declared law is what the law has always been and therefore the parties must have contracted under a mistake of law.

The problem that arises from this in the context of restitution under a mistake of law, as declared by the House of Lords, is that it is expecting every party to a contract to be vested with a crystal ball. Decisions to enter into a contract based upon a legal authority that has long been considered to be an absolute statement of the law, which is then subsequently overturned, must invariably give rise to a mistake of law.

Both the dissenting judges, Lord Browne-Wilkinson and Lord Lloyd, expressed surprise at the logic set out above and recognised immediately the profound effects the majority decision would have. Both considered that if the law was regarded as settled when the payment was made, but that position changed as a result of a later decision, then the payment was not made under a mistake of law. Thus Lord Lloyd stated:

> If it is right that the House of Lords can change the law by overruling a previous decision of the Court of Appeal, it must follow that a person relying on the old law was under no mistake of law at the time, and cannot claim to have been under a mistake post facto because the law is subsequently changed.

Similarly, Lord Browne-Wilkinson was equally unequivocal. He stated:

> although the decision in *Hazell*'s case is retrospective in its effect, retrospection cannot falsify history: if at the date of each payment it was settled law that local authorities had capacity to enter into swap contracts, Kleinwort were not labouring under a mistake of law at that date. The subsequent decision in *Hazell*'s case could not create a mistake where none existed at the relevant time.

Unfortunately, the Limitation Act 1980, s 32(1)(c), does not help provide a solution to the dilemma created by the decision of the House of Lords in *Kleinwort Benson*. The Act is quite clear in stating that time does not begin to run until the mistake is discovered, and in the situation in *Kleinwort Benson* this is at the time of the overruling decision. Perhaps the solution to the problem could nevertheless be found by Parliament taking the initiative and amending s 32(1)(c) in order to prevent recovery of payments in these circumstances. Some degree of caution is required here, since amending the provision so that time begins to run from the time the contract is entered into, as opposed to the discovery of the mistake, will probably have the effect of preventing bona fide claims under mistakes of fact from being brought.

The decision in *Kleinwort Benson* is undoubtedly a landmark decision, but it is considered that it is unlikely to survive in its present form. There is no doubt that defences to the application of the principle will emerge over time; indeed Lord Goff specifically stated that such defences will undoubtedly develop in future cases. One such defence is quickly apparent in that the payee will not be required to pay money if the payee has already spent the money, provided that the money was received in good faith in the first place. Such a defence is more likely to be raised where there is a long period of time between the payment of the money and the overruling precedent. It should be noted, however, that for this defence to apply, the burden of proof would be on the payee to justify the retention of the money.

For more on illegal contracts see Chapter 12.

On the issue of defences Lord Goff considered that English law contained no principle to the effect that a contract that was fully performed rendered any money paid irrecoverable. He stated that it would be incorrect to allow an *ultra vires* contract to stand merely because the contract had been fully performed. To do otherwise would be to validate a contract that was contrary to public policy on the basis that it was illegal and void.

It is also no defence for the mistaken party to claim that they honestly believed that they were entitled to retain the money paid. The House of Lords considered that such a defence would be too wide and would effectively preclude the other party from recovering money paid under a mistake of law.

One further limitation on the right of the payer to recover money paid under a mistake of law arises where the law is changed by legislation as opposed to a judicial decision. The reason for this is that in this situation there is no mistake of law at the time the payment was made. This position may be different, however, if the legislation enacted is retrospective in operation.

The decision in *Kleinwort Benson* can throw up some quite bizarre results. It has been established that where a person makes a payment on the basis of a judicial decision and believes the transaction to be valid, they may recover that payment if a later decision overrules that earlier one. But what about the losing party in the case that forms the earlier decision, could they claim in restitution for any money not recovered by them? Lord Hope in **Kleinwort Benson** emphatically declared that such a party could not so recover since they had not paid any money under a mistake of law but because the court had ordered them not to do so. An example of the application of the principles in **Kleinwort Benson** can be seen in **Nurdin and Peacock plc v D B Ramsden and Co. Ltd (No. 2)**.

Nurdin and Peacock plc v D B Ramsden and Co. Ltd (No. 2) [1999] 1 All ER 941

In this case a dispute arose out of a 25-year lease which provided for an annual rent of £207,000, an extra rent of £59,000 for years 4 and 5 and a rent review in 1995 at the end of year 5. No review took place and accordingly the rent, as per the terms of the lease, should have reverted to the sum of £207,000. Between November 1995 and February 1997 the claimant paid all the sums demanded. In April 1997 after reading the terms of the lease the claimant informed the defendant that it would pay only the lower amount and stated that it intended to set off the overpayments against future rent. Subsequently the claimant sought legal advice. The solicitors advised the claimant to continue paying the higher amount without set-off until the dispute had been resolved through arbitration or court proceedings. Furthermore the solicitors advised the claimant that if it were successful in these proceedings it would be entitled to a full refund of the excess. As a result of this advice the claimant paid rent in May 1997 at the higher rate. The claimant then sought to recover all the overpayments including that made in May 1997. The problem, however, was that the May payment was made by the claimant when it was not acting under a mistake that the higher sum was payable. On this basis the claimant had no legal right to recover the overpayment since it was aware that the payments had not been due. Nevertheless the claimant contended that it was entitled to recover the May payment. The defendant contested the claim stating that the money paid under a mistake of law could only be recovered if the payer had mistakenly believed that it was liable to make the payment.

It was held that where a claimant sought to recover money under a mistake of law, it was not required to prove that it had mistakenly believed it was liable to make the payment. It had to show that it would not have made the payment but for the mistake, that the mistake was directly related to the overpayment and/or it was connected to the relationship between the payer and the payee.

Claims in *quantum meruit*

Objective 4

A *quantum meruit* claim is defined as a claim arising where goods are supplied or services rendered by one person to another in circumstances which entitle them to be recompensed by that other by receiving a reasonable price or remuneration.

Quantum meruit claims arise in two situations:

1 by way of an action in restitution, or
2 from within a contract.

Restitutionary *quantum meruit* actions

Very often the contract will contain express terms setting out what remuneration is payable on the occurrence of certain events. In such circumstances the court has no option but to award such sums. However, it may occur that the remuneration expressly provided for does not become payable because there is no valid or subsisting contract so that a person who has provided a benefit or advantage is unable to recover a reasonable sum in payment for the benefit or advantage provided. In such a situation the appropriate question to ask is whether a defendant has been unduly enriched and if so to what extent so as to make an appropriate restitution. In some circumstances it is possible to claim on a *quantum meruit* basis despite the presence of a contract. *Quantum meruit* claims therefore can be categorised as either being outside of a contract that is a claim for unjust enrichment, or exceptionally within a contract.

Quantum meruit outside of a contract

Lord Greer in ***Craven-Ellis* v *Cannons Ltd*** [1936] 2 KB 403 explained the nature of restitutionary *quantum meruit* as:

> an interference which a rule of law imposes on the parties where work has been done or goods have been delivered under what purports to be a binding contract but is not so in fact.

In such circumstances restitutionary *quantum meruit* actions will arise independently of the existence of any promise or agreement on the basis that unjust enrichment is an independent source of rights and obligations within the law of obligations alongside the law of contract and tort, indeed. It was established in ***Banque Financière de la Cité* v *Parc (Battersea) Ltd*** [1999] 1 AC 221 where Steyn LJ in the House of Lords stated that to establish a claim in unjust enrichment four questions must be asked: (1) Has the defendant benefited or been enriched? (2) Was the enrichment at the expense of the claimant? (3) Was the enrichment unjust? (4) Are there any defences?

It was held in the Supreme Court in ***Benedetti* v *Sawiris*** [2013] UKSC 50; [2013] 3 WLR 351 that in assessing what is a reasonable sum for the purposes of quantifying an unjust enrichment an objective test is applied, that is, the sum is assessed by reference to the price a reasonable person in the defendants' position would expect to have to pay for the benefit or advantage and such a sum may be framed in terms of the market value per Clarke LJ at [15–19]:

> The circumstances in which such *quantum meruit* awards are made may be as follows.

Void contracts

An example of such a case can be seen in ***Craven-Ellis* v *Cannons Ltd*** itself.

Craven-Ellis v *Cannons Ltd* [1936] 2 KB 403

Here the plaintiff was employed as the managing director of the defendant company. By virtue of the articles of association of the company the plaintiff was required to take qualification shares within two months of taking office, failure to do so rendering him unable to act. The plaintiff failed to take up the shares but, nevertheless, the company executed an agreement under seal in which it agreed to pay the plaintiff. In fact, the resolution of the directors to affix the company's seal to the agreement was invalid, which rendered the agreement void. The plaintiff's action to recover the promised remuneration in contract must, of course, have failed since the contract was void. He could, however, succeed in *quantum meruit* for services already rendered.

Frustrated contracts

Where a contract becomes frustrated then by virtue of s 1(3) of the Law Reform (Frustrated Contracts) Act 1943 a party is able to recover such sums as the court considers just where the other party has a valuable benefit conferred on them. Clearly this would appear to be a statutory-based type of *quantum meruit*. The rule would also apply outside the 1943 Act

For more on the
doctrine of
frustration and the
effects of the Law
Reform (Frustrated
Contracts) Act 1943
refer to Chapter 15.
where work is done after the frustrating event and still carries on, with the result that it may be said that the claimant's actions are voluntary. The effect of this will be to deny them a claim in *quantum meruit*, though it is, of course, possible that a new contract will be implied, giving them a right to damages for breach of contract.

Contracts discharged by breach

Where a contract has been broken so that the innocent party can elect to treat the contract and their obligations under it as discharged, the innocent party can elect to claim in *quantum meruit* for work done rather than to sue in damages for breach of contract. It should be noted that it is only the innocent party who may claim in *quantum meruit*. The remedy is not available to those in default. Second, the breach must entitle the innocent party to treat the contract as discharged.

The use of *quantum meruit* is particularly useful in such circumstances where the actions of the party in default allow the other party to treat the contract as discharged halfway through them performing the obligations under the contract. It is clear that the innocent party could not claim the sum fixed for completing the work since it has not been completed, but *quantum meruit* allows them to claim for the reasonable value of the work actually completed. An example of *quantum meruit* in such circumstances can be seen in *Planché* v *Colburn* (1831) 8 Bing 14, where the defendants were in the process of com-piling a series of books to be entitled *The Juvenile Library*. They engaged the plaintiff to write a book on medieval costume and armour. When the plaintiff had written several chapters the series was cancelled. It was held that he was entitled to refuse the publisher's offer to publish the book separately and claim in *quantum meruit* for work completed on the book.

Services rendered in contemplation of a contract

It sometimes occurs that a party undertakes work on the basis that a formal contract will be entered into at some future time. If the contemplated contract fails to materialise then the party that has undertaken the work may claim in *quantum meruit* for the work done, as seen in the case of *British Steel Corporation* v *Cleveland Bridge and Engineering Co. Ltd* [1984] 1 All ER 504 where construction work had begun at the request of the defendants in contemplation of a contract that never materialised. Here the plaintiffs, on ceasing further performance, could claim on a *quantum meruit* basis for work carried out. This position was also affirmed in the case of *Whittle Movers Ltd* v *Hollywood Express Ltd* [2009] EWCA Civ 1189. The decision in *Cleveland Bridge*, however, was distinguished in *Regalian Properties plc* v *London Dockland Development Corporation* [1995] 1 WLR 212 where work was not carried out at the request of the defendants in the contemplation that the plaintiffs hoped to win a contract from the defendants. Further the negotiations between the parties had been carried out on a 'subject to contract' basis. The court held that the work was carried at the plaintiff's own risk and as a result the defendants had not had a benefit conferred on them so that the plaintiff was not able to recover their expenditure on a *quantum meruit* basis. The cases of *G Percy Trentham Ltd* v *Archital Luxfer* [1993] 1 Lloyd's Rep 25 and *RTS Flexible Systems Ltd* v *Molkerei Alois Muller Gmbh & Co. KG (UK Production)* [2010] UKSC 14 The decisions in these cases were fully discussed in Chapter 2. should be noted since they suggest that a broader approach to the finding for a contract should be taken, particularly where the whole or part of it is executed, and this may mean that there will be less need to rely on quasi-contract in these circumstances.

 ### The use of *quantum meruit* within a contract

Quantum meruit may arise within a contract in two situations.

Where part-performance has been accepted

Where a party in breach of contract has only partly performed the contract and the other party elects to accept that performance, then they will be required to pay for that part-performance on a *quantum meruit* basis. By accepting the partial performance the innocent party implies that they will pay a reasonable sum for such performance. The same rules also apply where the party in default completes the contract in a manner different from that contemplated by the parties originally and where the innocent party accepts such performance. It should be noted that *quantum meruit* will *not* apply where the innocent party has no option to accept either part-performance or performance in a manner different from the original contract.

Where there is an implied agreement to pay

It may be that the parties have entered into a contract but have failed to include provision for payment within the contract. In such a situation the law implies on a *quantum meruit* basis that a reasonable sum will be payable. In contracts for the sale of goods the Sale of Goods Act 1979 s.8(1) makes explicit that the price of goods need not be fixed by the contract but may be 'left to be fixed in a manner agreed by the contract, or may be determined by the course of dealing between the parties. Furthermore s 8(2) provides that when goods are bought and sold without an express agreement as to price, then the buyer must pay a reasonable price, thus giving statutory authority to the rule in such contracts. A similar provision is also contained in the Supply of Goods and Services Act 1982, s 15.

Summary

- The doctrine of quasi-contract lies within a broader area of law known as the law of restitution.
- The broad parameters in which the courts will grant relief for unjust enrichment have been set out by Jones in *Goff and Jones: The Law of Restitution* (2002):
  - (i) The defendant has been enriched by some benefit given to him.
  - (ii) The enrichment has been acquired at the expense of the claimant.
  - (iii) The retention of the benefit by the defendant would be unfair or unjust.

Actions to recover moneys paid

- An action will lie in quasi-contract to recover moneys paid under either a contract or purported contract either where there has been a total failure of consideration or where the moneys have been paid under a void contract.

Actions for payments made under a mistake of law

- Until recently, the general rule of English law was that money paid under a mistake of law, or as to the legal effect of the circumstances on which money was paid, but on a full understanding or knowledge of the facts, was irrecoverable (***Westdeutsche Landesbank Girozentrale* v *Islington London Borough Council***).
- The rule that money paid under a mistake of law was irrecoverable was abolished (***Kleinwort Benson* v *Lincoln City Council***).

- What then are the principles governing the recovery of money under a mistake of law?

    (i)   Was there a mistake?
    (ii)   Did the mistake cause the payment to be made?
    (iii)   Did the payee have a right to the money paid to them?

Claims in quantum meruit

- Defined as a claim arising 'where goods are supplied or services rendered by one person to another in circumstances which entitle him to be recompensed by that other by receiving a reasonable price or remuneration', Beatson, *Anson's Law of Contract* (2010).

Further reading

Beatson, 'Courts, Arbitrators and Restitutionary Liability for Breach of Contract' (2002) 118 *Law Quarterly Review* 377

Beatson, Burrows and Cartwright, *Anson's Law of Contract*, 30th edn (Oxford University Press, 2016)

Burrows, 'Contract, Tort and Restitution – A Satisfactory Division or Not?' (1983) 99 *Law Quarterly Review* 217

Burrows, 'Law Commission Report on Pecuniary Restitution on Breach of Contract' (1984) 47 *Modern Law Review* 76

Burrows, 'No Restitutionary Damages for Breach of Contract' (1993) *Lloyd's Maritime and Commercial Law Quarterly* 453

Burrows, *Remedies for Torts and Breach of Contract*, 3rd edn (Oxford University Press, 2004)

Burrows, *The Law of Restitution*, 3rd edn (Oxford University Press, 2011)

Campbell, 'The Extinguishing of Contract' (2004) 67 *Modern Law Review* 817

Furmston, *Cheshire, Fifoot and Furmston's Law of Contract*, 16th edn (Oxford University Press, 2012)

Jones, 'The Law of Restitution: The Past and the Future', in Burrows (ed.), *Essays on the Law of Restitution* (1991), p. 4

Jones, *Goff and Jones: The Law of Restitution*, 6th edn (Sweet & Maxwell, 2002)

Law Commission, *Law of Contract: Pecuniary Restitution on Breach of Contract*, Law Com. Report No. 121 (1983)

Smith and Atiyah, *Atiyah's Introduction to the Law of Contract*, 6th edn (Oxford University Press, 2006)

Tettenborn, *Law of Restitution in England and Ireland*, 3rd edn (Cavendish Publishing, 2001)

Peel, Treitel *Law of Contract*, 14th edn (Sweet and Maxwell, 2015)

Part 6

The rights and liabilities of third parties to the contract

19

Privity of contract

Objectives

After reading this chapter you should be able to:

1. Understand what is meant by privity of contract.

2. Know and understand the effects of the doctrine of privity of contract.

3. Explain how the doctrine of privity can be avoided by way of actions in tort and collateral contracts.

4. Know and explain the exceptions to the privity rule with specific reference to exceptions that allow third parties to claim under a contract and those that allow obligations to be imposed on third parties whether in relation to land or personal property.

5. Know and understand the criticisms of the privity rule, the proposals of the Law Commission and the effects of the Contracts (Rights of Third Parties) Act 1999.

The general rule

Objective
1

The rule in English law is that only the parties to the contract may enforce the contract against each other, even if the contract was entered into with the sole intention of benefiting or imposing liabilities on a third party. The rule was confirmed as being part of English law in the nineteenth century. However, the modern authority for the rule is said to be the decision of the House of Lords in **Dunlop Pneumatic Tyre Co. Ltd v Selfridge & Co. Ltd** [1915] AC 847 where Viscount Haldane LC stated:

> My Lords, in the law of England certain principles are fundamental. One is that only a person who is a party to a contract can sue on it. Our law knows nothing of a *jus quaesitum tertio* arising by way of contract. Such a right may be conferred by way of property, as, for example, under a trust, but it cannot be conferred on a stranger to a contract as a right to enforce the contract *in personam*. A second principle is that if a person with whom a contract not under a seal has been made is to be able to enforce it consideration must have been given by him to the promisor or to some other person at the promisor's request.

It can be seen that the rule relating to privity is closely interlinked with the rule that consideration must move from the promisee. It is sometimes stated that the rule that only a party to a contract can sue on it is a different way of stating the above rule relating to consideration, and vice versa. This is not the case and both aspects are required to be shown in order to allow a person to sue on the contract. Very often when the rule relating to consideration arises it is assumed that there was an intention to include a person as party to the contract. If one translates this into the case of *Tweddle v Atkinson* (1861) 1 B & S 393 it can be seen that even if the husband had furnished consideration for the promises of his father and father-in-law he would still not have been able to enforce the contract since the terms of the contract were not addressed to him; there was no intention to make the husband a party to the contract.

See Chapter 3 for a discussion of the facts of *Tweddle* v *Atkinson*.

The precise reasons for the presence of the rule are somewhat unclear and over the years several different theories have emerged that have attempted to explain its existence. For instance, it is considered that to impose contractual liability on a person without their consent and in an arbitrary manner strikes at the liberty of the individual. Similarly, it is considered unjust to allow a person to sue on a contract which cannot be enforced against themselves. Lastly, it is considered that gratuitous beneficiaries of a simple contract should not be entitled to enforce the contract. It may be that there is a vestige of an equitable principle in the latter point in that it is inequitable for a person who had nothing to be able to gain a benefit that is accruing to them only by way of the goodwill of the parties to the contract.

For more on the principle that consideration must move from the promisee see Chapter 3.

Whatever the reasons for the existence of the rule, it is now confirmed as part of the law though, as we shall see later, not without substantial criticism. The application of the rule can be seen in the following cases.

Dunlop Pneumatic Tyre Co. Ltd v Selfridge & Co. Ltd [1915] AC 847

The appellants sold tyres to a distributor on the basis that he would not resell them below the appellants' list price and that if the distributor sold the tyres to a trade buyer, the distributor would ensure that the trade buyer would also have the price restriction clause imposed on him. The distributor sold the tyres to Selfridge & Co. and imposed the price restriction clause in the contract and provided that Selfridge would pay £5 to Dunlop in respect of each tyre sold in breach of the price restriction clause. Selfridge sold the tyres to customers below Dunlop's list price and were sued by them in respect of each transgression and an injunction was issued restraining Selfridge from further sales of tyres below the list price. It was held that their action would fail since Dunlop had provided no consideration for Selfridge's promise. Privity of contract did not arise between Selfridge and Dunlop.

Beswick v Beswick [1968] AC 58

Peter Beswick sold his coal business to his nephew who agreed to pay £6 10s a week to Peter for the rest of his life. He further agreed that in the event of Peter predeceasing his wife, the nephew would pay the widow £5 per week for the rest of her life. On Peter's death the nephew made only one payment to the widow and refused to make any further payments. The widow sued but did so in two capacities: first, in her personal capacity as widow and beneficiary of the contract; and, second, as administratrix of her husband's estate. It was held that in respect of her personal capacity her action would fail as she was not a party to the contract and had not supplied any consideration under it. In her capacity as personal representative of Peter's estate she was successful since here she represented Peter's personal capacity rather than her own, such as it was.

The effect of the doctrine of privity of contract

The basic effect

Objective
2

Where *A* and *B* contract with the intention that *C* will be the object benefiting from the contract then *C* will be unable to sue on the contract despite the intentions of the parties, as seen in *Tweddle* v *Atkinson.* The only way in which *C* can have the contract enforced is by seeking the assistance of a promisee. Lord Denning considered in *Beswick* v *Beswick* that the third party could compel a promisee to bring the action by starting the action himself and then conjoining the promisee as co-defendant. This process was rejected by the Court of Appeal who took a traditional stance in relation to the doctrine.

The basic position as regards third parties has a particular effect in relation to consumer protection. It was seen in Chapter 7 that in contracts for the sale of goods, for instance, the parties enjoy the benefit of certain implied conditions, such as the implied condition as to satisfactory quality. If the third party receives the goods other than by way of entering into a consumer contract then they will be unable to benefit from the implied conditions and warranties imposed by the Sale of Goods Act 1979.

Contracts for the benefit of third parties do not affect the validity of the contract as

---

Example

If *C* above receives the goods by way of a birthday present and they prove not to be of satisfactory quality then *C* has no right of action against the seller since *C* is not a party to the contract. Again, *C*'s only hope is to enlist the help of the purchaser of the gift.

---

regards the parties to the contract, who may take action to enforce it in the usual way. Such action may, however, affect the position of the third party.

Actions against the promisor for damages

It is clear that a third party cannot enforce the contract against the parties to the contract. While it may be possible for the third party to persuade a party to the contract to enforce the contract, that party can recover damages only in respect of their own loss, unless they, or the third party, can bring the claim within one of the exceptions to the rule. Further, the losses recoverable by the promisee are likely to be nothing more than nominal damages. This problem can be seen in the case of *Beswick* v *Beswick* since if the widow as administratrix had sued for damages in respect of the breach of contract as it affected Peter Beswick's estate, the amount of the damages would have been purely nominal given that the payments to Peter ceased on his death.

Even if the party to the contract can recover damages for losses incurred by the third party, there is always the problem of the third party recovering those damages from the promisee. Unless there is a contract between them, there would appear to be no legal basis for such a claim.

Jackson v *Horizon Holidays Ltd* [1975] 3 All ER 92

In this case a husband booked a holiday for himself, his wife and his two children. His original booking proved to be unavailable and a substitute was found. The holiday proved to be a disaster and fell far short of what had been promised. The company admitted liability for breach of contract but appealed on the basis of the £1,100 damages awarded by the judge at first instance, since this figure was only just short of the full cost of the holiday. Lord Denning agreed that as regards the husband's losses alone the award was excessive, but that the assessment was correct as regards the loss sustained by the family as a whole. He considered that a promisee, as a matter of general principle, was entitled to recover damages on behalf of third parties who were beneficiaries of the contract entered into by the promisee and that the third parties could, in turn, compel the promisee to hand over to them such proportion of the damages as represented their losses. The other members of the court upheld the award but did not openly support Lord Denning's proposition.

Undoubtedly the decision of Lord Denning represented a substantial inroad into the doctrine of the privity of contract, but was one that was comparatively short-lived.

Woodar Investment Development Ltd v *Wimpey Construction* (UK) Ltd [1980] 1 All ER 571

The vendors had contracted to sell land to the purchasers for £850,000 for themselves and £150,000 in respect of a third party. A dispute arose between the purchasers and the vendors who brought an action for breach of contract, claiming not only the £850,000 owed to themselves but also the £150,000 owed to the third party. The House of Lords decided that the purchasers were not liable for breach of contract. Their Lordships agreed that even if the purchasers had been liable then the vendors would not have succeeded in their claim in respect of the £150,000 since this was due, not to themselves, but to a third party. The vendors had not, in other words, suffered any loss in relation to the £150,000. The House of Lords stated that the principle stated by Lord Denning was not of general application but confined to a situation where a trust arose. Nevertheless, their Lordships considered that the decision in *Jackson* v *Horizon Holidays Ltd* was a correct one, albeit based on erroneous reasoning. Unfortunately, while a number of their Lordships were highly critical of the doctrine of privity of contract, they were not prepared to present a legal rule that would allow parties to a contract to sue on behalf of a third party. Lord Wilberforce considered that the *Jackson* case was a special one that called for 'special treatment'. He stated:

> I am not prepared to dissent from the actual decision in *Jackson*. It may be supported either as a broad decision on the measure of damages or possibly an example of a type of contract, examples of which are persons contracting for family holidays, ordering meals in restaurants for a party, hiring a taxi for a group, calling for special treatments. As I suggested in *New Zealand Shipping Co. Ltd* v *A. M. Satterthwaiteb & Co. Ltd,* there are many situations of daily life which do not fit neatly into conceptual analysis, but which require some flexibility in the law of contract. *Jackson*'s case may well be one.

The decision in **Woodar** is not entirely satisfactory since rather than provide an answer to the problem of whether a party can sue on behalf of a third party and whether the third party can subsequently recover their share of the losses from the promisee, it tends to pose a problem as to when such a claim is sustainable. At the moment it can only be said that such a principle exists where a promisee, for instance, stands in a fiduciary relationship to the third party.

A footnote has to be added to the case of *Jackson* v *Horizon Holidays* and the doubtful reasoning within it in the form of the Package Travel, Package Holidays and Package Tours Regulations 1992. These Regulations make an organiser or retailer of package holidays liable to consumers, including third party beneficiaries, for the proper performance of their obligations under the contract. The Regulations only apply to 'package' holidays or travel as defined in reg 2(1). The effect of the regulation is to put the decision on a more substantial footing, giving third parties specific rights outside of the Contracts (Rights of Third Parties) Act 1999. However, *Jackson* v *Horizon Holidays* and the 1999 Act will continue to apply where a holiday falls outside the definition of a package holiday.

The promisee and specific performance

It was seen in *Beswick* v *Beswick* earlier that an action for damages by the widow as administratrix would result in only nominal damages being awarded. The claim here would be a representative action on behalf of the estate to recover any sums owed to Peter Beswick by the nephew under the contract. Since none were owed and the weekly payments to Peter were to cease on his death, the damages would only reflect a technical breach of contract. The real loss arising from the breach would be to the widow herself but, as we have already noted, as third party she could not claim in respect of this loss. The court, however, found that the widow in her capacity of administratrix could enforce the contract between the nephew and Peter Beswick by way of a decree of specific performance. The effect of the decree was to ensure that the widow in her personal capacity received the payments due to her under the contract.

The use of specific performance to enforce an undertaking in respect of a third party is not, however, without difficulties. The facts of the case were particularly beneficial to the widow in *Beswick* v *Beswick* because she had dual roles. Ordinarily the position of personal representative might reside in completely different hands from that of the third party, the result of which would be to leave the third party with the problem of persuading the personal representative to adopt the action. Further, it should be borne in mind that specific performance as an equitable remedy is a discretionary remedy.

Undertakings where the promisor promises not to sue the third party

There may arise a term in the contract between the promisee and the promisor, whereby the promisor undertakes either expressly or impliedly not to sue a third party. If the promisor reneges on the undertaking there is nothing the third party can do to restrain the action brought by the promisor since they are not a party to the contract. In such a case the promisee can obtain a stay of proceedings on the basis of the breach of the contractual undertaking by the promisor.

Snelling v *John Snelling Ltd* [1973] QB 87

In this case the need to prove an interest worthy of protection by the promisee was ignored by the court. In the case the plaintiff, together with his two brothers, were directors and creditors of the family company. Arguments arose between the brothers who therefore agreed that should any one of them resign, then that individual would forfeit all moneys owed to him by the company. Despite the agreement, which was meant to put an end to the arguments, the plaintiff resigned. The plaintiff then brought an action for the debt owed to him by the company. The plaintiff's brothers were cited as co-defendants in the action against the company. The brothers counter-claimed on the basis that the brother by resigning had forfeited his rights in respect of the debts owed to him by the company. As a third party the company could not rely on the agreement in order to avoid the debt so the brothers sought a declaration that the agreement bound the plaintiff and that his action ought to be stayed. It was held by Ormrod J that the brothers should be entitled to have the action stayed as between themselves and the plaintiff. He further held that the brothers could have the action stayed against the plaintiff as regards the company also. The judge considered that the most convenient way of dealing with this situation was to dismiss the action against the company.

The obtaining of the stay of proceedings is not always a straightforward exercise. In *Gore v Van Der Lann* [1967] 2 QB 31 it was held that the grant of a stay of proceedings was dependent on the promisee being able to show that he had an interest to protect by enforcing the undertaking against the promisor.

Clearly the *Snelling* case runs contrary to the principles contained in the *Van Der Lann* case. Treitel considers that the decision is consistent with the *Beswick* case and submits that in such a situation the most appropriate remedy is either a decree of specific performance or an injunction.

Total failure of consideration

Where the parties have entered into a contract for the benefit of a third party under which the promisee has paid money to the promisor, then, if the promisor has completely and totally failed to carry out their part of the contract, for example by delivering goods to the third party, the promisee can recover the moneys paid on the basis of a total failure of consideration under quasi-contract.

For more on quasi-contracts refer to Chapter 18.

Avoiding the doctrine of privity of contract

Actions in tort

Objective 3

The law of torts, in particular the law of negligence, has developed to give relief to third parties in certain circumstances. Thus if *X* has been given a present that has been manufactured or produced in a negligent manner so that *C* is injured or otherwise suffers loss, then *X* will have a right of action against the negligent person, as seen in *Donoghue* v *Stevenson* [1932] AC 562. Very often the action for negligence will lie against the manufacturer and thus avoids the contracting parties altogether. This is not necessarily the case, however, since if, for instance, the defect in the goods arises because the seller has stored the goods in a negligent manner then the action will lie against them rather than against the manufacturer or the wholesaler. Thus in *Donoghue* v *Stevenson* the consumer of the adulterated ginger beer did not have to rely on the support of the purchaser in an action against the seller but could take direct action against the manufacturer.

The principle in *Donoghue v Stevenson* can also be seen in the case of *Junior Books Ltd v Veitchi Co. Ltd* [1983] 1 AC 520 where the plaintiffs entered into a contract with *X* to build a warehouse. *X* employed the defendants as subcontractors for the flooring work. The defendants allegedly did this work in a negligent manner. Normally the plaintiffs would have sued *X* who, in turn, would have sued the defendants. The House of Lords held, however, that on the facts there was no reason why the plaintiffs, despite the fact that they would not suffer injury or damage as a result of the actions of the defendants, could not maintain the action against them. It is unclear why the plaintiffs took such a course of action but the case created some disquiet and the decision has been subsequently confined to the facts of the particular case. In the case of *D & F Estates Ltd v Church Commissioners for England* [1989] AC 177 the court made it clear that it would be unlikely that a plaintiff could maintain an action against a subcontractor in the future. The change of attitude probably also reflects a feeling that to allow such actions as a matter of general policy would be likely to result in a formulation of a principle that every breach of contract could arise as an action in tort where the breach had arisen as a result of the negligence of the defendant.

The use of negligence by third parties has also been curtailed to some degree by the ruling that pure economic loss cannot be claimed in an action. Since physical injury or damage is less likely to occur in a contract, the ruling places some limitations on the use of tort as a means of securing a remedy and avoiding the doctrine.

Collateral contracts

The rule of privity of contract can be avoided by the finding of a collateral contract between the third party and the promisor, who may enforce the contract for and against each other. Such contracts must comply with the normal rule of contract and each party must, as a result, provide consideration. The principle of collateral contract can be seen in the case of *Shanklin Pier Ltd v Detel Products Ltd.*

Shanklin Pier Ltd v Detel Products Ltd [1951] 2 KB 854

The plaintiffs employed contractors to repair and repaint their pier. The plaintiffs specified in the contract with the contractors that they had to use the paint manufactured by the defendants, since they had been persuaded by the defendants that the paint would last seven years despite the harsh conditions to which it would be exposed. The contractors purchased the paint from the defendants but it soon became apparent that it did not match the specification represented by the defendants to the plaintiffs. In fact the paint only lasted three months and approximately £4,000 had to be spent remedying the defects. The problem for the plaintiffs was that, since the contract for the purchase of the paint was between the contractors and the defendants, they were third parties and clearly could not recover on the basis of that contract. The court, however, found that there was a collateral contract between the plaintiffs and the defendants and that the defendants were liable to pay damages for breach of the collateral contract. One problem faced by the court was that of finding consideration for the contract. The court held that the plaintiffs had provided consideration for the defendants' undertaking as to the longevity of the paint by entering into a contract with the contractors, in which they had stipulated that the defendants' paint had to be used.

Exceptions to the doctrine of privity of contract

Objective
4

The doctrine of privity of contract has often been subject to sharp criticism, in particular by Lord Denning who considered it to be an outmoded nineteenth-century concept. The doctrine nevertheless continues to form part of the modern law, though it exists as a doctrine that is by no means absolute since the courts and Parliament have seen fit from time to time to create exceptions to the rule. One of the great problems of completely abolishing the rule is that while there is general agreement that third parties should be allowed to take action to enforce benefits due to them under a contract, the same is not true when the converse arises – where the parties to a contract wish to impose liabilities on a third party.

Exceptions allowing a third party to claim under a contract

Statutory exceptions

1. Road Traffic Act 1988

The driver of a motor vehicle is obliged to take out a policy of insurance to cover possible claims by persons suffering injury by virtue of the actions of the driver of the vehicle. The Act permits an injured third party to make a direct claim against the insurance company despite the fact that he is not a party to the contract, by virtue of s 148(7).

2. Married Women's Property Act 1882

By virtue of s 11 of this Act a husband can take out a policy of insurance on his own life for the benefit of his wife and children (and vice versa). The effect of this provision is that when the husband dies the proceeds of the policy are held on trust for the wife and the children. The result of this is that the proceeds do not fall into the estate of the husband and are thus outside the application of inheritance tax. If the insurance company does not pay out on the policy, the wife and/or the children may take direct action against the company.

3. Companies Act 2006

By virtue of s 33 (formerly Companies Act 1985, s 14) the provisions of a company's constitution bind the company and its members to the same extent as if there were covenants between the company and its shareholders and between the shareholders *inter se*. The result is that an individual shareholder can sue another shareholder on the basis of the contract contained in the memorandum and articles of association.

4. Bills of Exchange Act 1882

Negotiable instruments provide an important exception to the privity of contract rule since the debt on the face of the instrument is enforceable not only by the original party to the transaction but by anyone to whom the debt is negotiated and who is deemed to be a 'holder in due course'. By virtue of s 38(2) the holder in due course may take action not only against the original debtor on the instrument if they fail to pay, but also against any other previous signatories of the instrument who have had the debt negotiated to them. In order for the holder in due course to be able to enforce the instrument in this way, the instrument must be in a deliverable state which means that, if the instrument is made out to a named individual X, or 'to X or order', the instrument must be endorsed on to the third party by X. Where the instrument is not made out to a named individual but to the 'bearer' then the instrument is said to be a 'bearer bill' which is in a deliverable state and may be negotiated on without the need for endorsement.

5. Third Parties (Rights against Insurers) Act 2010

This Act is not concerned with conferring benefits on third parties per se but provides for rights to be transferred to a third party where an insured person is insolvent. The core purpose of the Act is to ensure that on insolvency the proceeds of insurance policies go to the purpose for which they were intended, that is to compensate an injured third party, so that they do not fall into the general funds of the insured where they may be swallowed up by the insured's general creditors.

Agency

The principle in agency is that 'he who does an act through another does it himself'. Thus if *A* contracts with *B* on behalf of *C,* then the contract that results is between *B* and *C.*

Assignment

This will be dealt with in greater detail in Chapter 20.

Trusts

If property is given to a person (the **trustee**) on trust for another (the **beneficiary**), then the former is the legal owner of the property, while the latter is said to be the equitable owner of the property. A trustee is in a fiduciary relationship to the beneficiary and this results in the trustee being under a duty to protect the property appertaining to the **trust.** Such a duty extends to the trustee taking action against a third party to the trust who is in breach of obligation to the trust. Where the trustee fails to take action the beneficiary can require the trustee to do so or alternatively have an action against the third party themselves, at the same time joining the trustee into the action as co-defendant or, if they consent, as co-claimant.

The property that may be the subject of the trust can include intangible property, known generically as a **chose in action,** which includes a right to enforce a contractual obligation. Immediately one can see that this allows the possibility of a third party enforcing a contract, if the promisor simply declares that they hold the benefit of the contract on trust for the third party. The principle can be seen in the case of *Les Affréteurs Réunis SA v Leopold Walford (London) Ltd.*

Les Affréteurs Réunis SA v Leopold Walford (London) Ltd [1919] AC 801

Walford, acting as a broker, arranged a charterparty between the owners of a ship and a charterer. The charterparty provided that the shipowners would pay commission owed to Walford by the charterers. The shipowners subsequently refused to pay Walford's commission and so he brought an action for breach of contract as beneficiary under a trust. In such circumstances it was a normal practice of the shipping industry for the charterers to sue as trustees on behalf of brokers and this practice was acknowledged by the shipowners. It was thus possible for a broker to sue in the name of a trustee promisor, namely, the charterers. From that proposition the House of Lords found that the promisor could waive that requirement thus allowing the broker beneficiary to sue in his own name.

Clearly the trust idea could have been used to drive a large hole in the doctrine of privity of contract but this was not to be. The courts limited the application of the principle by imposing the requirement that to create a trust certainty of intention must be shown clearly from the circumstances of the case. Such certainty of intention to create a trust will not be regarded as arising simply where the parties enter into a contract for the benefit of a third party. Thus Lord Greene MR stated in **Re Schebsman, Official Receiver v Cargo Superintendents (London) Ltd and Schebsman** [1944] Ch 83:

> It is not legitimate to impute into the contract the idea of a trust when the parties have given no indication that such was their intention.

Similarly, in the same case, Du Parcq LJ stated:

> It is true by the use possibly of unguarded language, a person may create a trust . . . but unless an intention to create a trust is clearly to be collected from the language used and the circumstances of the case, I think that the court ought not to be astute to discover indications of such an intention.

The above comments do not destroy the possibility of the occurrence of a constructive trust at all, but the burden of proving the certainty of intention has the effect of severely curtailing the use of this device.

The notion that a trustee can recover damages to compensate loss suffered by the beneficiaries can arise only if it was known to both parties to the contract that one of them was contracting as a trustee. Thus in **Rolls-Royce Power Engineering plc v Ricardo Consulting Engineers Ltd** [2003] EWHC 2871 (TCC) it was held that, where a subsidiary had contracted with the defendant on behalf of its parent company, the subsidiary would not be able to claim damages as a trustee. This is because the defendant was not aware at the time of the contract, nor had any reason to know, that the parent company had a direct interest in the contract. This principle follows from Lord Clyde's judgement in **Panatown Ltd v Alfred McAlpine Construction Ltd** [2000] 4 All ER 97, where he stated that the recovery of damages in such circumstances can only arise where the claimant 'expressly enters a contract as a trustee or agent'.

The rule in *Dunlop* v *Lambert*

In many respects the expression 'rule' here is somewhat of a misnomer since the case in fact provides an exception to the general principle of English law that a person cannot recover substantial compensation for breach of contract where they have suffered no loss. Thus the exception in **Dunlop v Lambert** [1839] 6 Cl & F 600, which has been affirmed in **The Albazero** [1977] AC 774, provides a remedy where no other remedy would be available for a breach of contract in circumstances where the contracting parties contemplated that a breach by one was likely to cause loss to an identified or identifiable stranger to the contract. The purpose therefore was to prevent a claim for damages from falling into a legal 'black hole'.

The rule has been applied more recently in the House of Lords in the joint appeals of **Linden Gardens Trust Ltd v Lenesta Sludge Disposals Ltd; St Martin's Property Corporation Ltd v Sir Robert McAlpine Ltd** [1994] 1 AC 85, where the so-called 'black hole' can be easily identified. Thus it arises in cases such as the **St Martin's** case where A enters into a contract with B for the erection of a building by B on land owned by C. If the building proves defective, who has the remedy against B – A or C? An application of the general rule provides that A can only recover damages for the losses sustained by A. It may be argued though that since A does not own the land or the building, no loss has been suffered and therefore A cannot recover damages as compensation. C as owner of the land and the building clearly suffers damage but, since C is not a party to the contract, there is no right of action against B. Thus the claim falls into the 'black hole' with neither A nor C being able to recover damages.

Originally the rule in **Dunlop v Lambert,** as also seen in **The Albazero,** arose in the context of contracts for the carriage of goods. Thus a consignor of goods could recover damages from a carrier for loss or damage to goods in transit, even if the goods had become the property of the consignee before the loss or damage occurred, and who had not acquired any rights to sue the carrier under the contract of carriage. The effect of the joint appeals in the **Linden Gardens** and **St Martin's** cases, however, was to extend this principle to building contracts. This meant that an employer could recover substantial damages from a contractor on the basis that the employer had contracted on behalf of the owner of the land. A further modern application of the rule can be seen in **Darlington Borough Council v Wiltshier Northern Ltd.**

Darlington Borough Council v Wiltshier Northern Ltd [1995] 1 WLR 68

The Council wished to build a new recreational centre but, to avoid some of the financial constraints, employed Morgan Grenfell (Local Authority Services) Ltd ('MG'). MG entered into contracts for the construction work with the defendants, Wiltshier Northern Ltd ('W'), for the benefit of the Council. A collateral agreement provided for MG to pay W and then the Council would reimburse MG, who would assign to the Council all rights which MG had against W.

On completion, serious defects were found to exist which would cost £2 million to remedy. At first instance it was stated that MG had no proprietary interest in the recreational centre and had suffered no loss or damage caused by the defects. The result of this was that MG could only assign rights to nominal damages for breach of contract, rather than a claim for substantial compensation for the defects. The Council was precluded by the rule of privity of contract from claiming the damages it suffered; indeed, it was agreed between the parties that the Council, as assignees of MG, could not recover any damages from W beyond those which MG could have recovered if there had been no assignment.

In the Court of Appeal Dillon LJ stated that damages for breach of contract were merely compensatory and that it remained the law that a third party could not sue for damages on a contract to which they were not a party. He affirmed the decision in **Woodar Investment Development Ltd v Wimpey Construction (UK) Ltd** [1980] 1 WLR 277 that a plaintiff could only recover for their own loss and that if a plaintiff entered into a contract with a defendant for the benefit of a third party, who was not a party to the contract, the plaintiff could not recover substantial damages from the defendant for breach of that obligation by the defendant. Dillon LJ, however, stated that it was obvious to W that the centre was being constructed for the Council and that the rule in **Dunlop v Lambert** would apply as an exception to the rule that a plaintiff could only recover damages for their own loss. The Council, as assignee, had a valid claim against W for breach of contract and the damages would be assessed on the normal basis as if the Council had employed W. Further, the Court of Appeal held that in any event MG could have recovered from W the losses of the Council, to whom it stood in a fiduciary relationship.

The rule in **Dunlop v Lambert** is subject to a proviso set out in the **The Albazero.** This states that the rule in **Dunlop v Lambert** does not apply when the parties to the original contract, the consignor and carrier, contemplated that a separate contract would come into existence between the carrier and the consignees, regulating the liabilities between them. This is because it is envisaged that the consignees would have their own right of action against the carrier. Such a right of action would preclude the consignors from suing the carrier for their own losses and those of the consignees since this would result in the carrier paying out twice.

This view was referred to as the 'narrower ground' in the **Linden Gardens** case, in that *A* only had a cause of action to recover from *B* the losses suffered by *C*. This gave rise to a second provision in that *A* was liable to account to *C* for the losses *A* had recovered.

Lord Griffiths in the **Linden Gardens** case proposed and indeed came to his decision on an entirely different ground – 'the broader ground'. This broader ground states that *A* has a right of action against *B* in their own right and that the damages may be more than nominal damages. This right of action by *A* arises despite the fact that *A* did not own the land at the time of the breach. In other words, by reason of the breach, *A* himself had suffered damage, this being the loss of the value to him of performing the contract to provide *C* with the benefit that *B* had agreed to provide – referred to as the 'performance interest'.

A use of the proviso in **The Albazero** as a defence to claim based on the rule in **Dunlop v Lambert** occurred in the following case.

Alfred McAlpine Construction Ltd v Panatown Ltd (1998) 88 BLR 67

The facts of the case were that the contractor, McAlpine, was employed by Panatown to design and build a multi-storey car park. Panatown alleged that the building when completed was so seriously defective that it would have to be demolished and rebuilt, and that McAlpine was in breach of contract. While Panatown employed McAlpine it was not the owner of the site; the owner was an associate company, Unex Investment Properties Ltd (UIPL), which was broadly speaking the developer.

On the same day that McAlpine entered into the construction contract with Panatown it also entered into a duty of care deed with UIPL. When Panatown commenced proceedings against McAlpine claiming damages for defective works, McAlpine alleged as a defence that Panatown was not entitled to recover such damages since it was not, and never had been, the owner of the site. The losses claimed by Panatown had not been incurred by Panatown but by UIPL, which was the owner and the developer of the site. On this basis McAlpine claimed that even if the breaches were proved, Panatown could claim only nominal damages since it had suffered only nominal losses. On the other hand, McAlpine also argued that UIPL could not claim damages for the defective works since it was not a party to the construction contract.

At first instance the arbitrator rejected McAlpine's defence, but the official referee on appeal reached the opposite conclusion. Panatown appealed to the Court of Appeal where the issue before the court was whether Panatown could claim substantial damages despite the fact that it was not and never had been the owner of the site.

The Court of Appeal stated that the cases of **Dunlop v Lambert, Linden Gardens Trust Ltd v Lenesta Sludge Disposals Ltd; St Martin's Property Corporation Ltd v Sir Robert McAlpine Ltd** and **Darlington Borough Council v Wiltshier Northern Ltd** were all authorities for the principle that a contracting party (*A*) could recover substantial damages for breach of contract, notwithstanding that the financial loss, which was the measure of damages, was not suffered by *A*. Further, that this right to damages existed despite the fact that the contracting party had no proprietary interest in the property. In other words, the 'broader ground' of entitlement was applied, as set out by Lord Griffiths in the **Linden Gardens** and **St Martin's** cases, allowing *A* to recover damages in respect of *A*'s 'performance interest'. The question remained, however, whether the proviso in **The Albazero** would prevent the rule in **Dunlop v Lambert** from applying, thereby precluding the claim of Panatown. In other words, did the fact that contractual rights were given to UIPL in the duty of care deed preclude Panatown's claim to substantial damages?

The court considered that the building contract clearly contemplated that the accounts would be settled between Panatown and McAlpine and that an anomaly would arise if the employer, Panatown, could not claim for the defective work. On the other hand, the duty of care deed was also clearly intended to create a separate right of action by the site/building owner against the contractor if the contractor was in breach of the terms in the duty of care deed. There was no intention within this deed, however, to prevent Panatown from receiving substantial damages for McAlpine's breach of contract.

Clearly this reasoning poses a problem in that there is a risk of a double recovery arising against McAlpine, one by Panatown and one by UIPL. It is this risk that forms the basis of the proviso set out in *The Albazero.* In the present case the double liability arose from two separate contracts. This is not to say that double liability would occur in reality since the court considered that, given that Panatown could recover substantial damages, such damages would be taken into account should UIPL make a separate claim under the duty of care deed.

The problem in the *Panatown* case was that there was one factor that was essentially different from the previous *Linden Gardens* and *St Martin's* cases. In the *Panatown* case UIPL had negotiated for and had obtained a direct contractual obligation between itself and McAlpine which was contained in the duty of care deed. This provided that McAlpine would exercise all reasonable skill, care and attention and owed a duty of care in respect of all matters within the scope of its responsibilities under the building contract to UIPL. It was the existence of this duty of care deed that formed the basis of McAlpine's appeal to the House of Lords ([2000] 4 All ER 97).

In the House of Lords it was held that if a contractor (*B*) had been in breach of a contract with an employer (*A*) to construct a building for a third party (*C*), *A* would not be able to recover substantial damages on behalf of *C* if it had been intended that *C* would have a direct cause of action against *B* to the exclusion of any substantial claim by *A*. Lord Browne-Wilkinson considered that the whole contractual matrix of the development envisaged that McAlpine's obligations could be enforced not only by Panatown, but also by UIPL and indeed any successors in title of UIPL.

Lord Browne-Wilkinson considered that the direct cause of action given to UIPL prevented any claim by Panatown on the 'narrower ground'. This is clearly correct since the whole basis of the rule in *Dunlop* v *Lambert,* as set out in *The Albazero,* was based on the fact that a remedy was provided to a third party 'where no other would be available to a person sustaining loss which under a national legal system ought to be compensated by the person who caused it'. Thus if the contractual arrangements gave a third party, UIPL, a direct right of action against the wrongdoer, McAlpine, the whole basis for the application of the rule was negated. Further, in such a situation since *C* had a direct right of action against *B*, *A* had no right to recover damages on behalf of *C*.

On 'the broader ground' Lord Browne-Wilkinson affirmed the reasoning of Lord Griffiths in the *Linden Gardens* and *St Martin's* cases in that *A* had a right of action in his own right for substantial damages with respect to the loss of his 'performance interest', namely 'the failure to provide *C* with the benefit that *B* had contracted for *C* to receive' or the cost to *A* of providing *C* with the benefit. His Lordship, however, qualified the application of this principle in that he stated that *A* would have no such right if the contract gave *C* a direct cause of action of the type given to UIPL under the duty of care deed. He stated that the critical factor was to establish *A*'s interest in the provision of his service to *C*. He considered that in the *Panatown* case the whole contractual scheme was aimed at giving UIPL and its successors a legal remedy against McAlpine for failure to perform the construction with due care. On this basis he considered that Panatown had not suffered any loss to its 'performance interest'. Any physical or pecuniary losses suffered by UIPL could be recovered by UIPL by way of its own cause of action. While UIPL had such a cause of action

Panatown had suffered no damage to its performance interest and on this basis the House of Lords distinguished the case from that of the decisions in the **Linden Gardens** and **St Martin's** cases.

It must be emphasised that the rule in **Dunlop v Lambert** is limited to situations where damage is caused to property which is transferred to a third party by one of the contracting parties. While the scope of the rule has been extended from contracts for the carriage of goods to contracts generally, it is nevertheless bound by this restriction, at least for the moment. It could not be applied to situations such as that seen in **Jackson v Horizon Holidays.**

The position seen in the **Linden Gardens** case may still arise following the passing of the Contracts (Rights of Third Parties) Act 1999. Section 4 provides that, 'Section 1 does not affect any right of the promisee to enforce any term of the contract'.

Example

In a contract between *A* and *B*, *A* will still be able to enforce the contract against *B* even where the Act also gives *C* the right to enforce the contract on one of its terms. Thus on *B*'s failure to perform a contract in favour of *C*, *A* can make any claim for damages, specific relief or an action for an agreed sum that would have been available to them at common law. Thus the Act itself is unlikely to affect the number of situations where *A* can recover damages in respect of a third party's (*C*'s) loss.

Law of Property Act 1925, s 56(1)

This provides:

> A person may take an immediate or other interest in land or other property, or the benefit of any condition, right of entry, covenant or agreement over or respecting land or other property, although he may not be named as a party to the conveyance or other instrument.

In **Beswick v Beswick** Lords Denning, Salmon and Danckwerts applied the literal rule to this provision and found that Mrs Beswick was entitled to enforce the contract in her personal capacity. They considered that s 56 formed a general exception to the doctrine of privity of contract. Their arguments revolved around the interpretation of the words 'other property' since s 205(1) of the Law of Property Act 1925 stated, in part:

> (xx) Property includes anything in action and any interest in real or personal property.

Since 'anything in action' or a chose in action, as we have already seen, can amount to a contractual obligation, the Court of Appeal proposed that s 56(1) had abolished the doctrine of privity of contract. The House of Lords rejected this proposition and unanimously held that s 56(1) did not have this effect. They added that s 205(1)(xx) was to be construed in a restrictive way so that it had no application in the law of contract.

Exceptions imposing obligations on a third party

Obligations imposed by way of interests arising in land

1. Obligations arising in leasehold land

Very often in leases the original parties, the landlord and the tenant, undertake to abide by certain conditions or covenants within the lease. These covenants are enforceable between the original parties to the lease since there exists privity of contract. Where the tenant assigns the lease to an assignee, *X*, then the landlord can continue to enforce covenants that are said to 'touch and concern' the land against *X,* as stated in ***Spencer's case*** (1583) 5 Co. Rep 16a. For his part *X* can also enforce such covenants against the landlord. There is said to be privity of estate between *X* and the landlord.

The rules that render *X* liable for breaches of covenant above are also of application where the landlord assigns their reversion to a third party, *Y,* since the original tenant can enforce covenants that have 'reference to the subject matter of the lease' against *Y,* by virtue of s 142 of the Law of Property Act 1925. For their part *Y* can also enforce covenants against the original tenant on the same basis by virtue of s 141. Again between *Y* and the original tenant there is said to exist privity of estate. The same position also applies with respect to *X* and *Y* themselves, both being able to enforce the covenants against each other even though they were not parties to the original lease, again by virtue of s 141 and s 142.

The above rules do not apply where the original tenant grants a sub-lease to a subtenant, *Z.* Although the original tenant can enforce the contracts against *Z* on the basis of privity of contract, neither this nor privity of estate exists between the original landlord or the assignee and *Z,* none of whom can enforce the covenants against each other, unless the covenant is a **restrictive covenant.** The rules regarding restrictive covenants are contained in the decision in ***Tulk v Moxhay*** which will be discussed in relation to **freehold land** below.

2. Obligations arising in freehold land

The position in relation to the enforcement of restrictive covenants in both freehold and, in certain circumstances, **leasehold land** is to be found in the rules that arose out of the decision in ***Tulk v Moxhay.***

Tulk v *Moxhay* (1848) 2 Ph 774

The facts of the case were that the plaintiff was the owner of a number of plots of land in Leicester Square. The plaintiff sold the gardens to a purchaser who entered a covenant to the effect that he would maintain the status of the gardens and that he would not build on the site. After the land in question had passed through the hands of several purchasers it came into the hands of Moxhay, the defendant. Despite the fact that Moxhay knew of the restrictive nature of the covenant in relation to the land, he nevertheless proposed to build on it. The original party could not, of course, obtain damages against Moxhay at common law for being in breach of the covenant since he was not a party to the contract with Moxhay. Instead the plaintiff sought the equitable remedy of an injunction to restrain Moxhay from building. The court issued the injunction on the basis that to allow the defendant to ignore an obligation of which he had knowledge at the time he purchased the property was contrary to the principles of equity and good conscience.

The case thus established the notion of the restrictive covenant which will be binding, not only on the original parties, but also on the third parties who later acquire the land with knowledge of the restrictive covenant. It should be noted that it is not merely because there is knowledge of a covenant that is of a restrictive nature that the doctrine will apply. In addition the person seeking the injunction (the covenantee) must show that they retained an interest in land adjoining the land being sold which was intended to benefit from the restrictive covenants.

Obligations imposed by way of interests in personal property

The problem that arises here is whether the principle as expressed in relation to covenants in land may be extended to personal property. Thus where the owner of a car agrees to hire it to an individual and then sells the car to a third party, to what extent is the third party bound by the contract of hire, assuming they have knowledge of it when they purchase the car? Is it possible for the hirer to restrain the new owner from using the car in a manner which is inconsistent with the terms of the contract of hire by way of an injunction? The answer seems to be that equity will not assist the hirer in such circumstances. Equity will normally grant an injunction only where, first, damages are inadequate and, second, the property in question is unique. In the example above it is clear that the hirer could be adequately compensated by an award of damages, unless the vehicle was unique in some way, such as a Rolls-Royce Silver Ghost which was to be used for a wedding. It is thus somewhat unlikely in the normal course of things that the courts will grant an injunction in such circumstances.

Despite the above it would appear that the courts have attempted to extend the principles seen in *Tulk* v *Moxhay* to charterparties, that is, personal property. This development was first seen in the case of *Lord Strathcona Steamship Co.* v *Dominion Coal Co. Ltd.*

Lord Strathcona Steamship Co. v Dominion Coal Co. Ltd [1926] AC 108

In this case the Dominion Coal Co. Ltd had a long-term charterparty of a ship, the *Lord Strathcona*. The owners of the ship sold it and after a series of transactions it came into the hands of the Lord Strathcona Steamship Co., the respondents, who were fully aware of the charterparty at the time of the purchase and in fact specifically agreed with the sellers to abide by it. The respondents later broke the charterparty when they refused to yield up the ship at the start of the charter period. The respondents were sued by the appellants but claimed as a defence that since they were not parties to the original charterparty they were not bound by it. The Privy Council rejected the contentions of the respondents and awarded an injunction restraining them from using the ship in a manner that was inconsistent with the charterparty.

The Privy Council applied the rules as expressed in *Tulk* v *Moxhay,* finding that the respondents were bound by the charterparty because they had notice of it at the time of purchase. This reasoning, however, has been heavily criticised since the rules in *Tulk* v *Moxhay* revolve not only around notice but also around the fact that the person attempting to enforce the restrictive covenant owns adjoining land which it was intended that the restrictive covenant should benefit. No such proprietary interest arose in the *Lord Strathcona* case since the charterer merely had a personal right to the use of the ship. This right, rather than simply an action for damages, might be enforced by an injunction where the property in question is unique. There was no indication that the *Lord Strathcona* could be regarded as unique and damages would therefore have amounted to an adequate remedy. There thus appears to be no justification for the decision, especially when a ship only amounts to personal property and is no different from the car in the above example.

In *Port Line Ltd* v *Ben Line Steamers Ltd* [1958] 2 QB 146 Lord Diplock considered the *Lord Strathcona* case to be wrongly decided and stated that a proprietary interest was an essential element in *Tulk* v *Moxhay,* an interest that was noticeably absent in the *Lord Strathcona* case.

Some judges have supported the decision in the *Lord Strathcona* case, notably Browne-Wilkinson J in *Swiss Bank Corporation* v *Lloyds Bank Ltd* [1979] Ch 548 who considered that the appellants were bound by the charterparty on the basis that they were constructive trustees of the ship and therefore obliged by equity to comply with their fiduciary obligations to the respondents. Further consideration of this aspect of privity of contract arose in the following case.

Law Debenture Trust Corporation plc v Ural Caspian Corporation Ltd and Others [1993] 2 All ER 355

The facts of the case were that the minority shareholders in the first four defendants ('the Russian companies') agreed to sell their shareholdings to Leisure Investments (Overseas) Ltd (LIO Ltd). The Russian companies were in fact English registered companies which had traded in Russia prior to the 1917 revolution and whose assets had been confiscated by the Soviet authorities without compensation. The majority shareholding was held by Shell Petroleum Co. Ltd who also agreed to accept the offer by LIO Ltd on condition that, should the Soviet authorities ever decide to pay compensation, that compensation would be applied for the benefit of the existing shareholders. In 1986 each of the Russian companies and LIO Ltd entered into covenants with the plaintiff, Law Debenture Trust Corporation plc, as trustee for the shareholders. The covenants also required the Russian companies to take whatever action was necessary to pursue the compensation claims. Further, the covenants required that, should LIO Ltd decide to dispose of its control of the companies, it would ensure that the transferee also entered into similar covenants. On this basis Shell and the minority shareholders relinquished control of the companies to LIO Ltd.

Later LIO Ltd sold the shares in the Russian companies to Hilldon Ltd but imposed no requirements in the contract that Hilldon should enter into covenants with the plaintiff. Hilldon subsequently sold its shareholdings to Caspian Resources Ltd, again without imposing the requirement that Caspian enter into the covenants with the plaintiff. In the meantime compensation amounting to some £13.2 million was paid to the Russian companies by the Soviet authorities by way of the Foreign Compensation Commission. The Russian companies then refused to pay any of the moneys received to the plaintiff.

The plaintiff subsequently sought damages from the six defendants, alleging that Hilldon (the fifth defendant) had, with knowledge of the agreements between the Russian companies and LIO Ltd, caused LIO Ltd to breach the covenants and that therefore Hilldon was, by virtue of an implied collateral contractual agreement, bound to comply with the covenants. It was also argued that the sixth defendant, Caspian, by purchasing the shares from Hilldon, with the knowledge of the previous agreements, had also caused Hilldon to breach its implied collateral obligation and was, as a result, under an implied collateral obligation itself.

Hilldon and Caspian applied for the plaintiff's statement of claim to be struck out on the basis that it disclosed no reasonable cause of action. The plaintiff then applied to have its original statement of claim amended in order to include an allegation that, since both Hilldon and Caspian took the shares with knowledge of the covenants and LIO Ltd's breach of them, they also took the burden of the covenants and were therefore under either a legal or equitable obligation to perform the covenants and could be compelled to do so by way of a mandatory (positive) injunction. Alternatively, the plaintiff argued that it should receive damages in lieu of the award of an injunction or the shares should be re-transferred to the plaintiff so that the covenants could then be enforced against LIO Ltd.

It was held that the claim against Caspian depended on whether Hilldon was under a contractual duty to the plaintiff which Caspian had caused it to break. The court, however, considered that neither Hilldon nor Caspian was party to a contract with the plaintiff, nor were there any grounds for implying a collateral contract. There was thus no arguable claim against Caspian.

The court also considered the principles set out in *De Mattos* v *Gibson* [1843–60] All ER 803, as now set out in the *Lord Strathcona* case, as affirmed in the *Swiss Bank* case, namely, that where a person acquires property from another, who has entered into a legally binding contract with a third party to use the property for a particular purpose, the person acquiring the property is bound not to use the property in a manner inconsistent with the contract, provided they had full knowledge of the contract when they acquired the property. The court admitted that neither *Lord Strathcona* nor *Swiss Bank* made it entirely clear when the above principle applied; however, the court decided to apply the principle nevertheless. It considered that the difficulty did not lie with the principle itself but with the remedy to be applied.

In his judgement, Hoffmann J considered that the principle in *De Mattos* v *Gibson* only gave rise to a possibility of an award of a prohibitory (negative) injunction, that is to restrain an acquirer of this property from doing acts which are inconsistent with the performance of the contract by the original contracting party. He stated that the principle has never allowed the imposition of a mandatory injunction to compel the acquirer of the property to carry out an obligation to perform covenants imposed on his predecessor. To support his position Hoffmann J referred to Lord Shaw in the ***Lord Strathcona*** case when he stated:

> It has sometimes been considered that *Tulk* v *Moxhay* . . . and *De Mattos* v *Gibson* . . . carried forward to and laid upon the shoulders of an alienee with notice, the obligations of the alienor, and, therefore, that the former is liable to the covenantee in specific performance as by the law of contract, and under a species of implied privity. This is not so; the remedy is a remedy in equity by way of injunction against acts inconsistent with the covenant, with notice of which the land was acquired.

He pointed out that there was not one case in which the ***De Mattos*** v ***Gibson*** principle was applied that allowed an award of a mandatory (positive) injunction, a position that was confirmed by Browne-Wilkinson J in the ***Swiss Bank*** case. He also stated that it was this point that prevented the principle in ***De Mattos,*** as applied in ***Lord Strathcona,*** from being applied in ***Port Line Ltd*** v ***Ben Line Steamers Ltd*** since there the owner was under a positive obligation to provide the vessel. Injunctive relief, therefore, was only available to prevent the purchaser from doing an inconsistent act, that is, chartering the vessel to someone else; it could not be used to compel a purchaser of the vessel to deliver it up to the charterer. Hoffmann J considered that Diplock J in ***Port Line Ltd*** was wrong in concluding that just because positive injunctive relief was not available, the principle in ***De Mattos,*** as applied in ***Lord Strathcona,*** was entirely wrong.

As regards the claim that damages could be awarded in lieu of injunctive relief by reason of the Supreme Court Act 1981 (now Senior Courts Act 1981), s 50, Hoffmann J decided that this claim could not be sustained. He reasoned that damages in these circumstances were a substitution for injunctive relief and that, since this was not available for the reasons already given, so an award of damages under s 50 could not be sustained.

Protecting third parties in exemption clauses

The question that arises here is to what extent third parties can rely on the protection of an exemption clause in a contract made between the promisor and the promisee. The principle can be seen in the following case.

Scruttons Ltd v *Midland Silicones Ltd* [1962] 1 All ER 1

In this case a shipping company had agreed to carry a drum of chemicals for the plaintiffs. The bill of lading limited the shipping company's liability to $500. The shipping company had contracted with the defendant stevedores for the latter to unload the drum, specifically stating that the defendants were to have the benefit of the limitation clause. The plaintiffs were unaware of the contract between the shipping company and the defendants. The drum was damaged to the extent of $1,800 by the negligent acts of the defendants, who were sued for this amount by the plaintiffs. The defendants claimed the protection of the limitation clause contained in the bill of lading.

It was held by the Court of Appeal and the House of Lords that the defendants should be liable for the full extent of the loss suffered. The courts held that since the defendants were not parties to the bill of lading, they could not rely on its protection. The fact that such clauses were commonplace in the commercial field did not exclude the operation of the privity rules, even in the case of an alleged implied contract between the plaintiffs and the defendants.

While the privity rule was fatal to the claim, Lord Reid stated that a third party could have the benefit of an exemption clause in agency. While this exception to the doctrine of privity will be dealt with in the next chapter, the comments of Lord Reid are worth noting. He stated:

> I can see a possibility of success of the agency argument if (first) the bill of lading makes it clear that the stevedore is intended to be protected by the provisions in it which limit liability, (secondly) the bill of lading makes it clear that the carrier, in addition to contracting for these provisions on his own behalf, is also contracting as agent for the stevedores that these provisions should apply to the stevedore, (thirdly) the carrier has authority from the stevedore to do that, or perhaps later ratification by the stevedore would suffice, and (fourthly) that any difficulties about consideration moving from the stevedore were overcome.

The arguments of the defendants pointing to the existence of an agency thus failed since Lord Reid found that there was nothing in the bill of lading that stated or implied that the parties to it intended the limitation of liability to extend to the defendant stevedores. Lord Reid's statement did not go unnoticed, however, and it led to the development of 'Himalaya' clauses, so called after the name of the ship in *Adler v Dickson* [1954] 3 All ER 397. A typical Himalaya clause may read as follows:

> Without prejudice to the foregoing, every such servant, agent and subcontractor shall have the benefit of all exceptions, limitations, provisions, conditions and liberties herein benefiting the carrier as if such provisions were expressly made for their benefit, and, in entering into this contract, the carrier, to the extent of these provisions, does so not only on [his] own behalf but also as agent and trustee for such servants, agents and subcontractors [extract from *The Mahkutai* [1996] 2 Lloyd's Rep 1].

The remarks of Lord Reid were taken into account in the following case.

New Zealand Shipping Co. Ltd v *A M Satterthwaite & Co. Ltd (The Eurymedon)* [1975] AC 154

There was a contract between a consignor and a carrier to ship drilling equipment to New Zealand. The contract contained an exemption clause exempting the carrier and its servants and agents, including any independent contractors that might be employed by the carrier from time to time, from liability in respect of damage to cargo. In respect of this exclusion it was stated that the 'carrier is acting as agent and all such persons shall to the extent be parties to the contract'. The defendants were employed as stevedores to unload the cargo and they negligently damaged the machinery. They attempted to rely on the exclusion clause in the contract between the consignor and the carrier.

It was held by the Privy Council that the stevedores could rely on the exemption clause. The first three factors set out by Lord Reid were found to be present. The case largely revolved around whether any consideration had been provided by the stevedores since, as we saw in Chapter 3 on consideration, the performance of unloading the ship was an existing contractual duty owed to the carrier. It was held that sufficient consideration had been provided by the stevedores since the court found that a promise to perform a duty to the carrier could also amount to consideration for the promise of the consignor.

The decision in *The Eurymedon* has since been affirmed in the case of *Port Jackson Stevedoring Pty Ltd* v *Salmond and Spraggon Pty (Australia) Ltd, The New York Star* [1980] 3 All ER 257, where Lord Wilberforce stated that the principle contained in Lord Reid's statement was now of general application. The principle is, however, always subject to the general principles contained in the law of agency. Thus, in *Southern Water*

Authority v *Carey* [1985] 2 All ER 1077 the attempt to bring third parties within the scope of the exemption via agency failed on the basis that the third parties (who are the principals in the matter) did not exist when the agent entered into the main contract. The principle in agency by **ratification** is that this type of agency cannot arise without there being an ascertainable **principal** at the time of the contract. Since the third parties, who were subcontractors, could not possibly have been ascertained at the time the main contract was entered into, they could not ratify the acts of the agent and thereby gain the benefit of the exemption clause. The problem of agency arising in such circumstances must clearly point to a major weakness in the use of agency to bring third parties within the ambit of an exemption clause.

The use of so-called Himalaya clauses and the acceptance of the approach set out in *The Eurymedon* and *The New York Star* as an exception to the privity of contract have to be treated somewhat guardedly. The principles as set out allow third party subcontractors only to take advantage of exclusion clauses contained in the main contract. The principles go no further than that so as to allow third parties to regard the whole contract as applying to them, since some terms can apply only where mutual agreement has taken place.

This position was discussed by Lord Goff in *The Mahkutai* [1996] 2 Lloyd's Rep 1, where the owners of a ship attempted to claim the benefit of an exclusive jurisdiction clause through the applicability of a Himalaya clause. It was alleged that the charterers of the ship had contracted as agents for the shipowners. It was stated by Lord Goff that the principles as set out in *The Eurymedon* and *The New York Star* applied only to exemptions and limitations and they had no application to exclusive jurisdiction clauses. He stated:

> Such a clause can be distinguished from terms such as exceptions and limitations in that it does not benefit only one party, but embodies a mutual agreement under which both parties agree with each other as to the relevant jurisdiction for the resolution of disputes. It is therefore a clause which creates mutual rights and obligations.

The problem in this case was that the Himalaya clause (see above) talked of 'exceptions, limitations, provisions, conditions and warranties'. Surely the expression 'provisions' would also encompass an exclusive jurisdiction clause? The Privy Council thought not and the expression was given a restricted interpretation in that it only related to terms inserted in the bill of lading for the charterer's protection. The expression could not extend to terms contained in the contract by mutual agreement.

Undoubtedly Lord Goff's reasoning makes commercial sense since, for instance, if a carrier agrees to take a cargo for the owners to a port in the USA subject to an exclusive jurisdiction clause that all disputes would be subject to English law, the bill of lading containing a Himalaya clause, it would clearly be wrong for stevedores in the USA to be able to claim the benefit of the exclusive jurisdiction clause. The stevedores have no connection whatsoever with the jurisdiction chosen by the carrier for the resolution of any disputes. The exclusive jurisdiction clause arises by way of mutual agreement between the carriers and the owners of the cargo and is not intended to benefit anyone else.

The effect of third party actions on contracts

It will have been noticed in Chapter 11 that it is possible for the actions of third parties to affect the validity of a contract between two persons. This very often occurs in the context of a husband and wife relationship where a wife is induced to enter into a contract of guarantee with a bank or some other creditor with respect to her husband's debts. If the wife is induced into the contract by the undue influence, misrepresentation or some other legal wrong of her husband, she will be entitled to rescind the contract. This therefore provides an exception to the rule of privity of contract in that a third party is, by his or her actions, able to affect the legal relationship between two parties to a contract. Previously this exception might have fallen into the category of agency, as already discussed above; however, since *Barclays Bank plc v O'Brien* [1993] 4 All ER 417, this is no longer possible as the effects of the third party's actions are now based on the doctrine of notice rather than an agency relationship.

Reform of the doctrine of privity of contract

Objective
5

The doctrine of privity of contract has been criticised, not so much with regard to the rule that no one can be made liable on a contract to which they are not a party, which is clearly correct, but for the fact that the rule prevents a third party who has an interest in a contract from enforcing it. Of course, the exceptions to the rule offset some of its major vagaries; nevertheless, it has been agreed that the doctrine ought to be abolished, or at least modified. In 1937 the Law Revision Committee (6th Interim Report, Cmd 5449) recommended that:

> Where a contract by its express terms purports to confer a benefit directly on a third party it shall be enforceable by the third party in his own name subject to any defence that would have been valid between the contracting parties.

No action was taken in response to the call for the abolition of the rule and, as seen above, in the intervening years the courts continued to exercise their imagination in finding means to avoid the rule. However, the Law Commission in its Consultation Paper No. 121, *Privity of Contract: Contracts for the Benefit of Third Parties,* 1991, again considered the need for the rule, which it referred to as 'the third party rule'.

The Consultation Paper accepted several pronouncements in decisions in the House of Lords; for instance, the case of *Murphy v Brentwood District Council* [1991] 1 AC 398 that called for the rule to be reconsidered. The Law Commission agreed with the comments of Viscount Simonds in *Scruttons Ltd v Midland Silicones Ltd* [1962] AC 446 that reform of the rule should come by legislative enactment, given that the rule is an established principle of law involving complex issues and is already circumscribed by numerous exceptions. Further, the Law Commission considered that simply widening the scope of damages available to a promisee so as to encompass loss suffered by a third party, as in *Jackson v Horizon Holidays,* was an inadequate reform of the law. It took the view that the third party here was in the hands of the promisee, who might refuse to act, thereby depriving the third party of compensation. Thus in *Beswick v Beswick,* if the executor had been someone other than Mrs Beswick herself, she might have been without a remedy had the executor declined to act.

In deciding that the third party rule should be the subject of legislative reform, the Law Commission then went on to consider what form this should take. First, it considered whether the contents of any enactment could simply be restricted to extending the exceptions to the third party rule in certain specific instances. This approach was rejected on the basis that the number and variety of exceptions had already produced a complex body of law and that the creation of further exceptions would simply further complicate the position. Second, the Law Commission considered simply abolishing the rule preventing the promisee from recovering the third party's loss in damages. This approach was rejected on the grounds already discussed above. Third, it was considered whether any enactment could provide that no third party be denied enforcement of a contract made for their benefit on the grounds of lack of privity. The Law Commission considered that such a general approach could not address in a satisfactory manner all the situations in which third party rights arise. For instance, the Law Commission considered that the problem of defining the class of third party beneficiaries would not be solved by such a piece of legislation and that it was incorrect to leave this and other complex matters to the judiciary to solve without more complete legislative guidance.

Lastly, the Law Commission considered that reform could take place by means of a full legislative scheme that defined matters such as the rights of contracting parties to modify or terminate the contract, promisor's defences and the types of remedy available to third parties. It considered that this approach had the advantages of clarity and certainty. The Law Commission considered, however, that simply giving third parties the right to enforce contracts made for their benefit would be unacceptably wide in that it would open the floodgates to litigation and leave promisors open to a potentially indeterminate class of third party claimants. In attempting to limit the position of third parties, the Law Commission considered that only allowing them to sue where it was expressly intended they should be able to do so within the contract was not sufficiently wide since it excluded the enforcement of contracts by third parties who, while it was intended that they should benefit, could not do so because there was no express term to this effect. Similarly, the Law Commission found themselves faced with the floodgates argument if third parties could sue merely because they could show that the original parties intended that they should benefit from the contract.

In order to reconcile the problems set out above, the Law Commission recommended that a third party should be able to enforce a contract in which the parties intend that the third party should receive the benefit of the promised performance and also intend to create a legal obligation enforceable by that person. Thus a third party's rights could not be inferred from the fact that they would derive a benefit from the performance of the contract. Similarly, the third party would not be able to sue on a contract that is simply made for their benefit – they would have to show that the parties intended to confer a legally enforceable obligation on them. Whether or not this intention exists is to be derived from the terms of the contract and the surrounding circumstances of the case. Thus it would not be necessary to name the beneficiary or even for the beneficiary to exist at the time the contract is made (as in the case of a pre-incorporation contract), though it has to be said that difficulties in identifying a beneficiary would presumably affect whether the parties to the contract could have intended to confer a legally enforceable obligation on a third party.

It can be seen immediately that the Law Commission considers that an objective test should be employed in determining the original parties' intentions vis-à-vis the ability of a third party to take action on the contract.

Benefits and defences

The Law Commission also considered what benefits would be conferred on third parties under the arrangements set out above. The Law Commission recommended that the rights created would arise only to the extent that the contract itself was valid and would be conditional on the other party performing their obligation under it. Thus a contract that is affected by misrepresentation, lack of formalities (where relevant) or frustration would also limit the rights of a third party. Similarly, if the promisee had failed to perform their own obligations under the contract, then the consequent rights of the third party would also be affected. The Law Commission gave an example here of an insurance policy taken out by a father in favour of his son and stated that the son could clearly not enforce the policy if his father had not paid the premiums due under it.

It was stated that, where rights are created in favour of a third party, that party should have the right not only to receive the promised performance of the contract from the promisor where that is appropriate, but also to pursue any remedies for defective performance of the contract. The Law Commission also considered that the third party would have the right to rely on terms in the contract which restrict or exclude the third party's liability as if the third party were a party to the contract.

With regard to defences, the Law Commission considered that the third party's rights would be subject to the promisor's defences, rights of set-off and counter-claims. The Law Commission, however, was undecided as to whether the promisee should be made a party to an action when the third party seeks to enforce a contract made for their benefit.

Variation and cancellation of contracts

It is clear that parties to a contract are entitled, subject to the provisions of the contract, to vary the terms of the contract or even to cancel it. The Law Commission considered that they should still be entitled to do so where third party rights arise, provided the parties expressly allow for such reservations on the rights of third parties. The Law Commission, however, was undecided as to whether variation or cancellation would be allowed where there was no such express provision. In considering this position the Law Commission examined several possibilities: thus it was considered that variation or cancellation would cease to be available once the third party adopted the contract, either expressly or by conduct; that variation or cancellation would be available until the third party accepted the contract or until they materially altered their position in reliance on the contract.

Creation of duties in third parties

The Law Commission Consultation Paper is centred on the conferment of benefits on third parties. However, the Law Commission also briefly examined the question as to whether parties to a contract could impose liabilities on third parties. It was considered that this should not be allowed except to the extent that the parties to the contract could impose conditions on the enjoyment of any benefits conferred on the third party by the contract. By way of example the Consultation Paper refers to the case of *Halsall v Brizell* [1957] Ch 169, in that it states that if a contracting party agrees to allow a third party to use a road across their land on condition that the third party keeps it in repair, the third party becomes subject to an obligation, though one that arises out of their own implied agreement rather than one that is imposed on them by the parties to the contract.

Conclusions

The proposals for reform put forward by the Law Commission answered many of the criticisms of the privity of contract rule, although the proposals themselves do create substantial difficulties in some situations – for instance, in relation to the variation and cancellation of contracts where third party rights arise. The double-intention criteria based on an objective test will tend to blur the point at which third party rights arise and, indeed, if applied to cases such as *Jackson v Horizon Holidays* may well produce a different result.

Law Commission Report No. 242, *Privity of Contract: Contracts for the Benefit of Third Parties (1996) and the Contracts (Rights of Third Parties) Act 1999*

Following on from its Consultation Paper No. 121, the Law Commission published its report, which also contained a draft Bill. The report proposed that the principle of privity of contract should no longer apply to prevent third parties from enforcing contracts that are made for their benefit. The draft Bill was introduced into Parliament in 1997 but failed to make the statute book because of the general election of that year. It was subsequently reintroduced into Parliament in December 1998 and, apart from some amendments, seeks to implement the recommendations of the Law Commission report.

The Contracts (Rights of Third Parties) Act 1999 came into force on 11 November 1999. The Act provides a major exception to the privity of contract rule – it is not a wholesale abolition of this rule, which still applies as regards imposing burdens on third parties. The Act only creates an exception to the doctrine of privity in the context of contracts for the benefits of third parties, but even here the reform is not a complete one. The traditional doctrine still applies in some situations. This is confirmed by Law Commission Report No. 242 which states:

> it is important to emphasise that, while our proposed reform will give some third parties the right to enforce contracts, there will remain many contracts where a third party stands to benefit and yet will not have a right of enforceability. Our proposed statute carries out a general and wide-ranging exception to the third party rule, but it leaves the rule intact for cases not covered by the Statute.

The Act therefore provides a statutory exception that will apply in addition to the common law exceptions already discussed. This is expressly provided for in s 7(1) which states that 'section 1 does not affect any right or remedy of a third party that exists or is available apart from this Act'. Thus, in contracts that fall outside the Act, the courts will continue to be able to make use of existing legal principles to avoid the application of the doctrine of privity of contract.

The general right of a third party to enforce contractual terms

Section 1(1) of the 1999 Act states:

> Subject to the provisions of this Act, a person who is not a party to a contract (a 'third party') may in his own right enforce a term of the contract if –
>
> (1) the contract expressly provides that he may, or
> (2) subject to subsection (2), the term purports to confer a benefit on him.

The provision therefore provides two means by which a third party can enforce a contract made for their benefit. The first requires little in the way of explanation but in relation to the second, when will a contract purport to confer a benefit on a third party? It would seem that this question has to be resolved by looking at the whole contract; although s 1(2) provides that the second means will:

> not apply if on a proper construction of the contract it appears that the parties did not intend the term to be enforceable by the third party.

On this basis it would seem that all third parties will be assumed to have the right to enforce the contract and that this right is cut down if, on a true construction of the contract, the contracting parties do not intend a third party to have the right to enforce it. The meaning of 'purports' was considered in the case of ***Prudential Assurance Co. Ltd v Ayres*** [2007] 3 All ER 946 where the court examined what was necessary to satisfy the requirements of that provision. The court considered that the expression 'purports' is different from the expression 'express' in s 1(1)(a). Lindsay J stated that the expression is defined as, *inter alia,* 'to bear as its meaning; to express, set forth, state; to mean, imply'. He thus considered that s 1(1)(b) was satisfied 'if, on a true construction of the term in question, its sense had the effect of conferring a benefit on the third party in question'. The court held that there was nothing in s 1(1)(b) which required the benefit on a third party to be the predominant purpose or intent behind the term in question. Conversely neither did s 1(1)(b) contain anything which denied applicability of s 1(1)(b) if the term conferred a benefit on someone other than a third party.

The rights of third parties are further reduced in s 1(3) since this requires that the third party must be expressly identified in the contract 'by name, as a member of a class or as answering a particular description but need not be in existence when the contract is entered into'. Thus the provisions do not give rights to third parties generally, although they establish that the third parties do not have to be in existence when the contract is made. It is therefore possible for the contracting parties to confer enforceable contractual rights on a future spouse, unborn children or companies that have yet to be incorporated.

It should be noted that s 1(3) requires that third parties' rights 'must be expressly identified in the contract by name, as a member of a class or as answering a particular description'. Thus it was held in ***Avraamides v Colwill*** [2006] EWCA Civ 1533 that there is no possibility of third party rights becoming available by way of construction or implication under a contract.

The benefits conferred on third parties must arise under a contract and not by any other means, such as a will.

White v *Jones* [1995] 2 AC 207

In this case, a person entered into a contract with his solicitor for him to draft a will. The solicitor failed to deal with the matter expeditiously so that the client died before the will had been drafted. The potential beneficiaries, who failed to gain an interest in the deceased's estate because of the lack of a will, successfully sued the solicitor in tort. Clearly they had no right to sue in contract on the basis of existing law of contract principles relating to privity of contract. Would they be able to succeed under the new provisions? The answer appears to be that they would not be able to. The contract between the solicitor and the client did not purport to confer a benefit on the potential beneficiaries as required by s 1(1)(b). In any event, if any benefit had been conferred on the beneficiaries, this would have arisen not from the contract but from the will and would therefore have been outside the ambit of the Act.

A very different perspective emerges if one analyses the case of ***Beswick v Beswick*** in the context of the Act. It will be recalled that Mr Beswick's contract with his nephew provided that the nephew should pay an annuity to Mr Beswick's widow on his death. Mrs Beswick would now have the right to sue the nephew personally since he had promised to confer a benefit on her. The nephew could only avoid liability if he could show that there was no intention between himself and his uncle that Mrs Beswick should have the right to enforce the provision in the contract. The fact that Mrs Beswick was specifically named in the contract is not of itself sufficient to confer enforceable rights on her. The contract must expressly confer (s 1(1)(a)) or purport to confer (s 1(1)(b)) benefits on her. The other feature of Mrs Beswick's case was that, unlike in ***White v Jones,*** her rights emanated from the contract, not from Mr Beswick's will.

To what extent are a third party's rights limited by the terms of the contract? This is dealt with by s 1(4) which states that a third party's right of enforcement is subject to the terms and conditions imposed by the contract. Thus a third party does not have any greater rights than the parties themselves; indeed, it is open to the parties to the contract to place limitations or conditions on the third party's rights of enforcement.

What remedies are available to the third party? This matter is dealt with in s 1(5) which provides that all the substantive remedies available to the person bringing an *action* for breach of contract are equally available to the third party seeking to enforce their rights under s 1(1). The expression 'action' is understood to mean that the third party is only entitled to remedies that a court could award. The third party is not entitled to terminate a contract for a breach since this is essentially a self-help remedy. Also since the section refers to an action for 'breach of contract' it is considered that this means that the third party cannot sue for a remedy under the law of restitution, for instance. The provision goes on to state that 'the rules relating to damages, injunctions, specific performance and other relief shall apply accordingly'. The third party's rights are limited to those they could have enjoyed if they had been a party to the contract. Thus the normal rules of law that govern such an entitlement apply equally to the third party's claim. They must mitigate their losses, they cannot claim for damages which are too remote and subject to other restrictions which apply to the remedy they are claiming. Thus the rules regarding time (the doctrine of laches) in applying for equitable remedies will have equal application. One peculiarity that could arise here is that a third party's rights to an equitable remedy, such as an order for specific performance, would be lost if such an order caused hardship or injustice to another interested third party, as in the case of ***Patel v Ali*** [1984] Ch 283. Similarly, the equitable rule that 'Equity will not assist a volunteer' will also be limited with the passing of the 1999 Act, though it will not of course be completely devoid of effect since it will continue to apply to third parties who are not within the Act, or where there is a contract that is outside its ambit.

See Chapter 17 for more on *Patel v Ali*.

Section 1(6) provides:

> Where a term of a contract excludes or limits liability in relation to any matter references in this Act to the third party enforcing the term shall be construed as references to his availing himself of the exclusion or limitation.

This provision therefore ensures that the third party can take advantage not just of their positive rights as set out in s 1(5), but also of any exclusion or limitation clauses contained within the contract.

The rights of third parties where the original parties cancel or vary the contract

One question that emerged in Law Commission Report No. 242 was whether the proposed reforms limited the rights of the original parties to the contract to exercise their freedom to cancel or vary the terms of the contract. This is of great importance since if the original parties had such unlimited rights, then a third party would not have any rights that they could confidently rely on. Whilst the original parties do still retain general rights to cancel or vary the contract, s 2 places limitations on these rights. Thus s 2(1) provides:

> where a third party has a right under section 1 to enforce a term of the contract, the parties to the contract may not, by agreement, rescind the contract, or vary it in such a way as to extinguish or alter his entitlement under that right, without his consent if –
>
> (1) the third party has communicated his assent to the term to the promisor;
> (2) the promisor is aware that the third party has relied on the term; or

(3) the promisor can reasonably be expected to have foreseen that the third party would rely on the term and the third party has in fact relied on it.

Section 2(2) provides that the assent referred to in (a) above may be by words or by conduct, although if the assent is sent by post then the postal rules are specifically excluded from operating in that the communication must be 'received by him'. It is possible to limit the effects of s 2(1) by expressly allowing a contract to be cancelled or varied without the consent of the third party. Alternatively the contract may expressly require that the third party's consent is required, but only in cases outside those stated in s 2(1)(a)–(c) above.

One of the difficulties with the general requirement that the consent of a third party is required to cancel or vary the contract arises where the third party cannot be traced or is found to be mentally incapable of giving consent. In such an instance a court may dispense with the need for consent on an application of the parties to the contract (s 2(4)). Similarly, a court may dispense with the need for consent if it cannot reasonably be ascertained whether a third party has in fact relied on the contract under s 2(1)(c) above (s 2(5)). Where a court dispenses with the need for the consent of the third party, it may impose such conditions as it thinks fit, which may include a condition that the parties to the contract pay compensation to the third party.

Defences available to the promisor

A 'promisor' is defined by s 1(7) as the 'party to the contract against whom the term is enforceable by the third party'. Such an individual may have all sorts of defences, set-offs and counter-claims available against an action by a promisee, defined in the Act as 'the party to the contract by whom the term is enforceable against the promisor'. To what extent, however, are these defences available to a promisor in an action brought against him by a third party?

Section 3(2) provides:

The promisor shall have available to him by way of defence or set-off any matter that –

(1) arises from or in connection with the contract and is relevant to the term, and
(2) would have been available to him by way of defence or set-off if the proceedings had been brought by the promisee.

Thus the promisor has available any defence or set-off which arises from or in connection with the contract and which would have been available if the promisee themselves had brought the action. On this basis a void, discharged or unenforceable contract is no more enforceable by a third party than by a promisee. Another example of the application of this provision arises where the promisor (*A*) and the promisee (*B*) enter into a contract whereby *B* will sell goods to *A*, who is to pay the purchase price to the third party (*C*). If *B* is in breach of contract by selling goods that do not meet the correct specification and *C* sues for the price, then *A* is entitled to reduce or extinguish the price payable by reason of the breach of contract. In other words, *A* is able to exercise the same rights as if *B* had brought the action.

Section 3(3) provides:

The promisor shall also have available to him by way of defence or set-off any matter if –

(1) an express term of the contract provides for it to be available to him in proceedings brought by the third party, and
(2) it would have been available to him by way of defence or set-off if the proceedings had been brought by the promisee.

This rather obscure provision allows an express term to be inserted into the contract that has the effect of making a third party's claim subject to *all* defences and set-offs that the promisor would have had against the promisee, and not just those that arise out of the contract itself.

> ## Example
>
> The promisor, A, may enter into a contract with B (the promisee) for the purchase of a car. It is agreed that A will pay the purchase price to the third party, C, when B transfers his car to A. If B owes A money by reason of some other totally unrelated contract, then they may agree to insert an express term in the contract for the sale of the car that A can set off against any claim by C the money owed by B under the unrelated contract.

Section 3(4) provides:

The promisor shall also have available to him –

(1) by way of defence or set-off any matter, and
(2) by way of counterclaim any matter not arising from the contract,

> that would have been available to him by way of defence or set-off or, as the case may be, by way of counterclaim against the third party if the third party had been a party to the contract.

This provision is intended to provide that the third party's claim, in addition to being subject to defences and set-offs that the promisor would have had in an action by the promisee, will also be subject to the defences, set-offs and counter-claims (not arising from the contract) that would have been available to the promisor had the third party been a party to the contract. Again, an example can best illustrate how this provision might operate. Thus if *A*, the promisor, enters into a contract with *B*, the promisee, to pay £1,000 to *C*, the third party, if *C* already owes *A* £400, then *A* has a right of set-off so that he will only be obliged to pay £600.

The Law Commission was presented with substantial problems with regard to this provision since, if a counter-claim against the third party arose from within the contract, the effect might have been to impose a contractual burden on the third party – something that is outside the objectives of the legislation. This provision is therefore designed to allow the promisor to offset any claim independent of the contract they may have against a third party. This might arise where the promisor was induced into the contract by way of a fraudulent or negligent misrepresentation, duress or undue influence or some other independent counter-claim that may be available against the third party.

For more on these vitiating factors refer to Chapters 9 and 11.

The rights of the promisor that are given to them in s 3(2) and (4) above may be subject to an express term in the contract making the promisor's defences, rights of set-off and counter-claims unavailable to them, by virtue of s 3(5). Third parties also are subject to a limitation under these provisions in that an action may not be brought within the ambit of s 1 if they could not have brought an action if they had been parties to the contract themselves, by virtue of s 3(6).

The Act does not purport to affect the rights of the promisee to enforce any contractual term (s 4); however, the promisor is protected from incurring double liability by virtue of s 5, which provides:

> Where under section 1 a term of the contract is enforceable by a third party, and the promisee has recovered from the promisor a sum in respect of –

(1) the third party's loss in respect of the term, or

(2) the expense to the promisee of making good to the third party the default of the promisor,

then, in any proceedings brought in reliance on that section by the third party, the court shall reduce any award to the third party to such extent as it thinks appropriate to take account of the sum recovered by the promisee.

In its deliberations the Law Commission refused to make any recommendations as to whether there should be some order of priority as between the actions of the promisee and the third party. Implicitly there is such a priority being made in s 5. There is no corresponding provision that states that where a third party takes action and receives damages, followed by an action by the promisee, the court will reduce any amount awarded to the promisee to take into account a sum recovered by the third party. The Law Commission considered that no problem should arise in this context since if the third party does recover first a promisee would be left with no outstanding corresponding loss. In any event, where a promisor does satisfy the judgement of the third party, no doubt the promisor could raise an equity in the action brought by the promisee that any judgement obtained by the promisee must be met from that given to the third party.

Excluded contracts

Not all contracts are covered by the Act and there are some notable exceptions. Section 6(1) states that s 1 confers no benefits on third parties in the case of a contract contained in a bill of exchange, promissory note or any other negotiable instrument. No benefits are conferred on third parties in the case of any contract binding on a company and its members under s 33 of the Companies Act 2006 (formerly s 14 of the Companies Act 1985).

Limitations in s 6(3) and (4) are designed to prevent a third party from enforcing a term in a contract of employment against an employee or other worker. Thus a customer of an employer would not be able to enforce a term of a contract of employment against the employee, for instance a confidentiality clause. Enforcement here lies solely with the employer. Similarly, a third party has no rights to enforce a contract for the carriage of goods by sea or a contract for the carriage of goods by road, rail or air, which are subject to the rules of the appropriate transport conventions. However, while such contracts are excluded from the Act, in s 6(5) the Act allows third parties to take advantage of a term excluding or limiting their liabilities. Thus the Act allows for the operation of so-called Himalaya clauses so that a carrier of goods will now be able to exclude or limit the liability of their servants, agents and independent contractors employed in the loading and unloading of ships.

For more on exemption clauses refer to Chapter 8.

This provision effectively reverses the decision in *Scruttons Ltd v Midland Silicones Ltd* and affirms the principles set out in *The Eurymedon* and *The New York Star*. To a limited degree the Act also appears to push the decision in *Southern Water Authority v Carey* (see above) into a backwater. It will be recalled that the agency principles set out in *The Eurymedon* and *The New York Star* were held not to apply because the third party principals were unascertainable at the time of the contract. Nowadays this is unnecessary by virtue of s 1(3) provided the third party is named or is a member of a class or answers a particular description.

It should be noticed that s 6(5) does not extend to cases such as *The Mahkutai* since, while objections to a third party acquiring rights under a contract have been removed, this does not extend to choice of law clauses. The legislation is very specific here in that it only applies to exclusion or limitation clauses.

Other provisions relating to third parties

Section 7(1) provides that 'Section 1 does not affect any right of remedy of a third party that exists or is available apart from this Act'. This provision is intended to preserve all the existing statutory and common law exceptions to the privity of contract rule. Thus a third party will still be able to rely on actions in tort or collateral contract devices in order to take action. Similarly, in appropriate cases they will be able to rely on Himalaya clauses and the law of trusts, where this is applicable. It should be noted that many of the provisions of the 1999 Act, such as ss 2 and 3, apply only where s 1 itself applies and not in any other circumstances.

Section 7(2) operates to prevent a third party from invoking s 2(2) of the Unfair Contract Terms Act (UCTA) 1977 so as to contest the validity of a clause that seeks to exclude or limit the promisor's liability under the Act to third parties for loss or damage caused by negligence, except where personal injury or death results. Thus a promisor is not restricted in excluding their liability to a third party even where apparently the term may be regarded as unreasonable were it to apply to the promisee.

By s 7(3) the provisions of the Limitation Act 1980 that apply to simple contracts and speciality contracts apply equally to actions brought by a third party, so that their action must be brought within 6 years and 12 years respectively.

> For more on UCTA 1977 refer to Chapter 8.
>
> The limitation periods for such contracts are discussed in more detail in Chapter 17.

Conclusions

The Contracts (Rights of Third Parties) Act 1999 should have a profound effect on decisions of the kind seen in *Beswick* v *Beswick, Jackson* v *Horizon Holidays* (provided the holiday falls outside the Package Travel, Package Holidays and Package Tours Regulations 1992), and *Woodar Investment Development* v *Wimpey*. In *Beswick* v *Beswick* Mrs Beswick would now be able to sue in her personal capacity and claim damages and specific performance of the contract made between her husband and her nephew for her benefit. In cases like *Jackson* v *Horizon Holidays,* third parties not covered by the 1992 Regulations will have a firmer base on which to found their actions where a holiday company has failed to meet its obligations. This is to be welcomed especially when the decision in *Jackson* v *Horizon Holidays* was of a questionable nature anyway. There is one proviso to this in that the ability of parties to exclude the provisions of the Act may render it stillborn. It is almost inconceivable that a professionally drafted agreement will allow a third party to retain a right of action or enforcement. The main dangers that arise from the Act come from s 1(1)(b) where a 'term purports to confer a benefit' on a third party since this will expose the promisor to actions from third parties which were not within their contemplation when they entered into the contract. This position is further exacerbated by the fact that the third party need not be specifically named, provided they can be identified by reference to a class or description (s 1(3)), or were in existence at the time of the contract. It is suggested therefore that in most standard-form contracts, the rights of third parties conferred by the Act will invariably be excluded.

In contracts for the carriage of goods by sea and carriage of goods by rail, air and road, where the contract is subject to the rules of the appropriate international transport convention, the Act will make a substantial mark in bringing employees, agents and subcontractors within the ambit of the promisor's exclusion clauses. Thus in cases such as *Adler* v *Dickson,* albeit this was an action for personal injuries, such provisions will have the effect of removing a promisee's alternative right of action against such third parties. In *Adler* v *Dickson* the plaintiff suffered serious injuries when she fell off a gangplank as she was boarding a ship due to the negligence of the captain and bosun. She found that she could not pursue an action against the shipping company in vicarious liability because of the presence of an exclusion clause. However, she successfully sued the captain and bosun who were not within the ambit of the company's exclusion clause. The effect of the Act would now be to draw the protection of the exclusion clause not just around the company itself but also around its employees, agent and subcontractors, but only in contracts for the carriage of goods. Thus the plaintiff would still have an action for personal injuries against the captain or bosun today, though not if her action was to recover for damage to her goods.

The Act is likely to have an important effect in certain industries. Of particular note here is the construction industry where the use of subcontractors is widespread. Actions such as those seen in *Alfred McAlpine Construction* v *Panatown* should now be placed on a somewhat simpler footing, provided always that the rights of third parties are not excluded. It may be unlikely that this would arise in such cases since the whole point of the transaction is that one party, the employer, is contracting on behalf of a third party and for their benefit.

The Act opens the way for actions by third parties in situations that were not considered by the Law Commission, such as those where the law implies a contract where certain formalities are not complied with. For instance, in the law of trusts, in order to create an express trust the person creating the trust, the settlor, must do two things. They must make a valid declaration of trust and transfer the property subject to the trust to the trustees. Failure to comply with these formalities prevents the trust from taking effect – it is said to be 'incompletely constituted' and takes effect as a contract to create a trust.

What happens if the settlor makes a valid declaration of trust but fails or refuses to hand the trust property over to the trustees? The answer to this question lies, first, as to who the contracting parties are. If the contract is made between the settlor and the beneficiaries of the trust, the beneficiaries may either claim damages, based on the value of the trust property, or enforce the contract by way of specific performance. The choice of remedy depends on the type of consideration given by the beneficiaries. However, this is a technical matter that is best left to a wider study of the law of trusts itself. The settlor and beneficiaries are the original parties to the contract so there is no problem regarding privity here. Usually the agreement is made between the settlor and the trustees for the benefit of the beneficiaries. Can the trustees take action on the contract? The answer is yes, but only with regard to the breach as it affects them as *trustees,* not on behalf of the beneficiaries. Any damages awarded would not be based on the trust property but on what fees, if any, the trustees would have been entitled to if the trust had been properly constituted. Such a sum may be a purely nominal amount. Usually the agreement or promise between the settlor and the trustees arises within a deed of trust and, since equity does not recognise a deed, the trustees are confined to an action for damages only. The trustees cannot obtain an order for specific performance since this is an equitable remedy and therefore not available to them.

Can the beneficiaries compel the trustees to obtain specific performance *on behalf* of the beneficiaries? The courts in several judgements such as *Re Pryce* [1917] 1 ChD 9 and *Re Kay* [1939] ChD 329, have always refused such applications. The reasoning in these cases is that the courts wi-ll not allow the beneficiaries to compel the trustees to seek specific performance, since this would be allowing the beneficiaries to enforce indirectly what the law would not allow them to enforce directly.

A different position will now arise following the passing of the 1999 Act since such beneficiaries will almost invariably fall within s 1 either because the trust is stated to be expressly for the benefit of the beneficiaries or because the trust purports to confer a benefit on them. Thus the provisions of the Act will have a profound effect on this area of law that was until now very settled. Of course, within the terms of the Act, it is possible to exclude the beneficiaries from being able to take action as benefiting third parties. The document that emerges will no doubt be a strange one in that it is clearly made for the benefit of third party beneficiaries and yet, within its terms, it will deny them the right to enforce the contract.

There is no doubt that the 1999 Act will also have substantial effects in law relating to landlord and tenant.

Example

The scenario that arises here concerns a situation where a landlord (*L*) gives a lease (the 'head lease') to a tenant (*T*), who then gives a sub-lease to a subtenant (*S*). Of course there is privity of contract between *L* and *T* and also between *T* and *S*. Usually the conditions or covenants in the sub-lease will be the same as those in the head lease. There is no privity of contract between *L* and *S* and therefore if *L* wishes to take action they have first to sue *T* who, in turn, would have to sue *S*. There is an exception to this rule where the covenant that has been broken is a restrictive covenant. The 1999 Act therefore seems to set up a general exception that will allow *L* to take direct action against *S*, provided it can be shown that the sub-lease is for the benefit of *L*.

There is no doubt that the 1999 Act is important and is set to change the landscape of the law of contract as it relates to the rule of privity of contract. In formal contracts, however, it is highly likely that the provisions will be excluded and therefore the Act's overall effects are going to be substantially limited. In less formal contracts the Act may make substantial inroads into the existing doctrine. Would this apply to consumer-type contracts? For instance, would the buying of a Christmas present for someone now be regarded as a contract for the benefit of a third party entitling that person to take action on the contract under the terms implied by the Sale of Goods Act 1979? The answer appears to be clearly in the affirmative. There are, however, provisos that place severe limitations on the scope of the Act in such contracts. First, in s 1(3) of the 1999 Act the third party has to be 'expressly identified in the contract by name, as a member of a class or as answering a particular description'. It is suggested that it may be unusual to do this in these types of contracts, though not beyond the realms of possibility. A more serious limitation, however, arises in s 7(4). This provides that the Act is not to give third parties any additional causes of action under any other statutory provisions. It states that 'a third party shall not . . . be treated as a party to the contract for the purposes of any other Act'. This provision would seem to preclude a third party from relying on the terms implied by the Sale of Goods Act 1979 and any other consumer legislation for that matter. Thus third parties would not be able to bring themselves within s 3 of the Unfair Contract Terms Act 1977, which applies 'as between contracting parties where one of them deals as a consumer or on the other's written standard terms of business'.

The Law Commission originally considered that the rule that consideration must move from the promisee would have to be abolished in order to accommodate the proposed reforms of the privity of contract rule. This move has not been taken on board within this piece of legislation, nor was it adopted within the Law Commission's own draft Bill despite the fact there was some concern that it may nullify their proposed reform of the privity of contract rule. It is unclear as to why this has been excluded; presumably because it was considered that the application of the legislation would not be impaired by the continuance of the rule.

Summary

The general rule

- Only the parties to the contract may enforce the contract against each other (*Dunlop Pneumatic Tyre Co. Ltd* v *Selfridge & Co. Ltd*).
- A third party cannot enforce a contract even if it was made for their benefit (*Tweddle* v *Atkinson;* NB: *Beswick* v *Beswick*).

The effect of the doctrine of privity of contract

The basic effect

- Consumers have no implied statutory rights under Sale of Goods Act 1979 if they are not a party to the contract.

Actions against the promisor for damages

- A third party could persuade the buyer to enforce the contract against the seller but the buyer will only recover damages for their own loss.
- Damages may be recoverable where a trustee acts on behalf of a beneficiary.
- The beneficiary can compel the trustee to hand over to them the proportion of damages that represent their losses (*Jackson* v *Horizon Holidays Ltd*). *Woodar Investment Development Ltd* v *Wimpey Construction (UK) Ltd* confined *Jackson* to a situation where a trust arose.
- Contracts (Rights of Third Parties) Act 1999 allows third parties to sue on a contract.

Total failure of consideration

- Where the parties have entered into a contract for the benefit of a third party, moneys can be recovered if there is a total failure of consideration by one party.

Avoiding the doctrine of privity of contract

Actions in tort

Collateral contracts

Exceptions to the doctrine of privity of contract

Exceptions allowing a third party to claim under a contract

Statutory exceptions

- Road Traffic Act 1988, s 148(7) – compulsory third party insurance.
- Married Women's Property Act 1882, s 11 – a husband's life assurance for the benefit of his wife and children.
- Companies Act 2006, s 33 (formerly Companies Act 1985, s 14) – memorandum/articles of association form a contract between the company and its shareholders and between the shareholders *inter se.*
- Bills of Exchange Act 1882 – the debt on the face of the instrument is enforceable not only by the original party to the transaction but by anyone to whom the debt is negotiated and who is deemed to be a 'holder in due course'.
- Third Parties (Rights against Insurers) Act 2010.

Agency

- The principle in agency is that 'he who does an act through another does it himself'.

Trusts

- A trustee can sue a third party on behalf of the beneficiary.
- A beneficiary can sue a third party where the trustee fails to do so (*Les Affréteurs Réunis SA v Leopold Walford (London) Ltd*).

Law of Property Act 1925, s 56(1)

- Does not abolish privity (in *Beswick v Beswick*).
- Section 205(1)(xx) is restrictive and has no application in the law of contract.

Exceptions imposing obligations on a third party

Obligations imposed by way of interests arising in land

- Obligations arising in leasehold land – *Spencer's Case.*
- Obligations arising in freehold land – *Tulk v Moxhay.*

Obligations imposed by way of interests in personal property

- *Lord Strathcona Steamship Co. v Dominion Coal Co. Ltd.*

Protecting third parties in exemption clauses

- Third parties and reliance on exemption clauses (*Scruttons Ltd v Midland Silicones Ltd*).
- Third parties can rely on exemption clauses (*New Zealand Shipping Co. Ltd v A M Satterthwaite & Co. Ltd (The Eurymedon)* affirmed *Port Jackson Stevedoring Pty Ltd v Salmond and Spraggon Pty (Australia) Ltd (The New York Star)*, *Adler v Dickson*.

The effect of third party actions on contracts

- Contracts (Rights of Third Parties) Act 1999.

The general right of a third party to enforce contractual terms

- Section 1(1) – a third party can enforce a contract made for their benefit, or when a contract confers a benefit on a third party.
- Section 1(3) – requires the third party to be expressly identified in the contract 'by name, as a member of a class or as answering a particular description but need not be in existence when the contract is entered into'.

Further reading

Adams, Beyleveld and Brownsword, 'Privity of Contract: The Benefit and Burdens of Law Reform' (1997) 60 *Modern law Review* 238

Andrews, 'Strangers to Justice No Longer – The Reversal of the Privity Rule Under the Contracts (Rights of Third Parties) Act 1999' (2001) *Cambridge Law Journal* 353

Beatson, Burrows and Cartwright, *Anson's Law of Contract*, 30th edn (Oxford University Press, 2016)

Burrows, 'Reforming Privity of Contract: Law Commission Report No 242', [1996] *Lloyd's Maritime and Commercial Law Quarterly* 467

Coote, 'The Performance Interest, Panatown, and the Problem of Loss' (2001) 117 *Law Quarterly Review* 81

Flannigan, 'The End of an Era (Error)' (1987) 103 *Law Quarterly Review* 564

Furmston, *Cheshire, Fifoot and Furmston's Law of Contract,* 16th edn (Oxford University Press, 2012)

Law Commission Consultation Paper No. 121, *Privity of Contract: Contracts for the Benefit of Third Parties,* 1991,

Law Commission Report No. 242, *Privity of Contract: Contracts for the Benefit of Third Parties* (1996)

Macmillan, 'A Birthday Present for Lord Denning: The Contracts (Rights of Third Parties) Act 1999' (2000) 63 *Modern Law Review* 721

Phang, 'On Justification and Method in Law Reform: The Contracts (Rights of Third Parties) Act 1999', (2002) 18 *Journal of Contract Law* 32

Reynolds, 'Privity of Contract, the Boundaries of Categories and the Limits of Judicial Function' (1989) 105 *Law Quarterly Review* 1

Smith and Atiyah, *Atiyah's Introduction to the Law of Contract,* 6th edn (Oxford University Press, 2006)

Stevens, 'The Contracts (Rights of Third Parties) Act 1999', (2004) 120 *Law Quarterly Review* 292

Stone, 'Privity – The New Legislation' (1999) 27 *Student Law Review* 19

Treitel, 'Damages in Respect of a Third Party's Loss' (1998) 114 *Law Quarterly Review* 527

Peel, Treitel *Law of Contract,* 14th edn (Sweet and Maxwell, 2015)

Unberath, 'Third Party Losses and Black Holes: Another View' (1999) 115 *Law Quarterly Review* 535

Wallace, 'Third Party Damage: No Legal Black Hole' (1999) 115 *Law Quarterly Review* 394

20

Assignment of contractual rights

Objectives

After reading this chapter you should be able to:

1. Know how contractual rights may be assigned both at common law and in equity.

2. Know the requirements needed for a voluntary assignment of contractual rights at common law.

3. Know the requirements needed for a voluntary assignment of contractual rights in equity.

4. Understand the principles applicable for a statutory assignment of contractual rights under the Law of Property Act 1925.

5. Know some of the other factors that apply to the assignment of contractual rights, such as rights which are not assignable.

6. Know the general principles relating to the assignment of liabilities.

Introduction

Objective 1

See Chapter 19 for the privity of contract rule.

Assignment is a method by which a party to a contract transfers the benefits they have contracted to receive from the other party to a third party, who is themselves able to enforce performance of the contract. There is no question of this situation breaking the privity of contract rule since a party is actually assigning their position to enforce the contract to the third party, the contract thus remaining essentially bilateral in character.

The right to enforce a contract is in fact a form of intangible property known generically as a 'chose in action', an expression which also encompasses property such as copyrights, patents, trade marks and actions in tort. It should be noted that the benefit assigned to the third party is not the material benefits that may result from the contract, but the right to enforce the contract. It should always be remembered that a contract is useless if it cannot be enforced and it is the fact of enforcement that produces the benefits from the contract. Thus the right to enforce the contract is a chose in action, since it is an intangible form of property that gives rights of action that may be claimed or enforced without the need for taking physical possession of the material benefits arising out of the contract.

This chapter will be concerned with the means by which this chose in action can be transferred voluntarily to another person. It is possible for involuntary assignment to take place either where a party to a contract dies or where they are declared bankrupt. In the case of death, the contract survives both against and for the benefit of the estate, thus allowing the personal representatives of the deceased to sue or be sued on any contracts entered into by the deceased prior to their death, with the exception, of course, of those requiring personal services. In bankruptcy a person who is adjudicated bankrupt has all their property vested in the trustee in bankruptcy. This property will also include any rights possessed by the bankrupt by virtue of any contract entered into by them. The effect is that if the trustee considers that the estate of the bankrupt may benefit from the contract being enforced the trustee may take steps on behalf of the estate to enforce it. The ability of the trustee to enforce the contract varies, however, where the contract involves personal services since if there is a breach of contract after the commencement of the bankruptcy, the right to enforce the contract remains with the bankrupt. The trustee nevertheless has a subsequent power to intervene and take any moneys recovered by the bankrupt which are not required for the maintenance of the bankrupt. Where the breach occurs before the bankruptcy proceedings the right to take action passes to the trustee, though this will not apply to actions in respect of the reputation or character of the bankrupt, despite the fact that such action might arise out of a breach of contract.

Voluntary assignment at common law

Objective 2

At common law the general principle was that choses in action could not be assigned, with the exception of those involving the Crown and the assignments of negotiable instruments. The assignment of negotiable instruments, sometimes referred to as **'negotiability'**, is an important exception which is virtually a subject in its own right, so discussion of it will be left for consideration elsewhere, in a more specialised mercantile law environment. The undoubted reason for the attitude of the common law courts was the desire to preserve the privity of contract rule which they feared would be undermined if the ability of the parties to assign their rights under a contract became widespread. It should be borne in mind that while the third party assignee could not enforce the contract against the promisor at common law, there was, nevertheless, a binding contract between the assignee and the assignor. The result of this was that the assignee could sue the assignor for breach of contract.

Despite the general rule of the common law not to allow assignment there were means of avoiding the rule so that the right to enforce a contract could be undertaken by a third party.

First, the promisee could always allow the third party to sue in the promisee's name. Usually the promisee would insist that the third party agree to indemnify the promisee against the legal costs of maintaining the action against the promisor.

Second, the promisee could give the third party a power of attorney, the effect of which would be to allow them to maintain the action as a representative of the promisee. This method was not particularly satisfactory for the third party since, just as in the case of the first exception above, it could be revoked by the promisee at any time and in any event it would end automatically on the death of the promisee. The rights of the third party were thus not guaranteed.

Third, it was possible for rights to be acquired by the third party by a process called 'novation'. Novation is basically a contract entered into between the promisee, the promisor and the third party whereby the benefits of the contract would henceforth be owed by the promisor to the third party. Realistically this is not an assignment since the enforcement of the contract by the third party is based on the existence of a new contract between themselves and the promisor and thus they would have to provide consideration in order that the second contract be enforceable. This exception is subject to the disadvantage that the consent of the promisor would always be required for the novation to work.

In truth, none of the methods discussed is a true assignment but merely a transaction which has the same effect as an assignment.

Voluntary assignment in equity

Objective 3

The problem of assignment at common law led to the development of a doctrine in equity which would permit the assignment of a chose in action whether or not it was in the nature of a legal or equitable chose. The means by which the assignment was accomplished and whether it could be enforced in the assignee's own name differed, however, according to whether the chose was equitable or legal and whether or not it was an absolute assignment.

The legal and equitable nature of the chose in action

Prior to the Judicature Acts 1873–75 a legal chose was one which could be enforced by action in law within the common law courts; for example, a debt due under a contract. Equity would recognise an assignment of a legal chose but was faced with a difficult predicament in that, while it would allow the assignee to succeed against the promisor, it had no jurisdiction to prevent the assignor from subsequently claiming from the promisor a second time. If the assignor undertook such an action, then the promisor would themselves have to present an action before the court of chancery in order to prevent the second recovery. Equity sidestepped this predicament by compelling the assignor, on the petition of the assignee, to sue in their own name, or at least lend their name to the assignee, the result of which was to have all the interests of the various parties decided by the same court.

If the chose in question was an equitable one, then the matter was somewhat simpler since the court of chancery enjoyed sole jurisdiction over the matter. Here the assignee could bring the action in their own name and was not required even to make the assignor a party to the action. The reason for this was that there was no claim capable of being asserted at law. This situation might arise because the parties never intended that legal rights would exist as in, for instance, rights arising under a trust. Alternatively, the equitable chose might arise out of informality, where the parties have failed to comply with a formality required by the common law; for instance, they might have failed to use a deed or been parties to an ineffective deed. Lastly, the equitable chose might have arisen because the parties themselves possessed only equitable rights, in which case it would be impossible to carve a legal assignment out of an equitable interest.

With the passing of the Judicature Acts, the above anachronism cried out for abolition. The main point of the legislation was to fuse the operation of equity and common law into a single system of courts and it was clearly incompatible to have the common law and equitable rules relating to equitable and legal choses being administered within the same courts. Section 25(6) of the Judicature Act 1873 provided for a new statutory form of assignment that would take effect in law. This statutory form of assignment will be considered later but it should be noted that it did not abolish assignment of choses in action in equity, which could and can still be fallen back on if the conditions required for a statutory assignment are not complied with.

Whether or not the assignment is absolute

Absolute assignment

An absolute assignment occurs where the assignor has assigned their entire interest in the chose in action to the assignee. This is not to say that the assignor must have completely relinquished all further interest in the subject matter of the chose. Thus it was held in **Hughes v Pump House Hotel Co**. [1902] 2 KB 190 that an assignment of moneys due under various contracts as security for an overdraft was nevertheless unconditional and absolute, despite the fact that the assignor's rights to the debts owing to them were capable of being reassigned to them when the overdraft facility was no longer required. The fact that the right to reassignment is express or implied has no effect on the absolute nature of the assignment.

Non-absolute assignment

If the assignor reserves certain rights in the chose in action in spite of the assignment then the assignment is said to be non-absolute. This may occur in three circumstances:

1   where the assignee decides not to transfer the entire chose in action;
2   where the assignment is by way of a charge;
3   where the commencement or the cessation of the assignment is conditional upon an uncertain future event.

The assignee may decide *not to transfer the entire chose in action*, if, for instance, the assignor decides to transfer only part of their rights in a debt owing to them under a contract.

An assignment may be by way of a charge. Unlike a mortgage, which transfers an entire fund to the assignee, a charge only entitles the assignee to a payment out of the fund.

Jones v *Humphreys* [1902] 1 Kb 10

In this case a schoolmaster, in consideration for a loan of £15, assigned such part of his income and salary as was necessary to discharge the loan, together with interest, or any further sums for which he might in the future become indebted to the plaintiff. It was held that this was not an absolute assignment of the schoolmaster's salary since it was only mere security that enabled the lender to have recourse to the salary should the state of indebtedness render this desirable. The assignment merely amounted to a charge on the salary and was thus not absolute.

The assignment will not be absolute where *its commencement or cessation is conditional upon an uncertain future event.*

Durham Brothers v Robertson [1898] 1 Qb 765

A firm of building contractors executed an assignment which read:

Re Building Contract, South Lambert Road. In consideration of money advanced from time to time we hereby charge the sum of £1,080, being the price . . . due to us from John Robertson in completion of the above buildings as security for the advances, and we hereby assign our interest in the above-mentioned sum until the money with added interest be repaid to you.

It was held that this assignment was not absolute but conditional. There was no question of the whole of the debt being assigned to the plaintiffs unconditionally but only such a sum as was necessary to discharge the advances made, together with interest.

Beatson, *Anson's Law of Contract*, seems to suggest that one method of testing whether or not the assignment is conditional is by having reference to the state of knowledge of the promisor. If they cannot be sure whether they are paying their debt to the right person or not without knowing of the state of the accounts between the assignor and the assignee, then the assignment will be conditional and not absolute. If, however, as in **Hughes v Pump House Hotel Co.**, the assignment passes the entire interest as security and there is a proviso for reassignment when the loan is repaid, the promisor knows to whom they are to pay their debt. The reason for this is that they will be given notice of the assignment and later, when the loan is repaid, they will be given notice of the reassignment, and the assignment will thus be absolute.

The requirements of an equitable assignment

1. Joinder of the assignor in an action by the assignee

Before discussing this requirement in detail we should note that an equitable assignment merely assigns the equitable title to the assignee. The result of this is that generally the assignee must join the assignor as a party to the action to enforce the chose in action against the promisor. The requirement of joinder, however, differs according to whether the chose in action is legal or equitable and whether it is absolute or non-absolute, as the following classification indicates:

1 the absolute equitable assignment of an equitable chose in action;

2 the non-absolute equitable assignment of an equitable chose in action;

3 the equitable assignment of a legal chose in action.

When there is an *absolute equitable assignment of an equitable chose in action*, the action is one which formerly could be dealt with exclusively within the court of chancery, so there is no need for the assignee to join the assignor in the action. The assignee can sue in their own name.

In a non-absolute equitable assignment of an equitable chose in action, as we have already seen, the assignor retains some interest in the chose in action. The consequence of this is that a court, in deciding the action between the assignee and the promisor, would not be able to make any adjudication of the rights and liabilities of the parties without having reference to the state of the accounts between the assignee and the assignor. The result is that the assignee must join the assignor into their action so that the court can come to a decision that will bind all the parties that are interested in the chose in action.

In an equitable assignment of a legal chose in action, whether the assignment is absolute or non-absolute, the assignee must in all cases join the assignor into their action. If the assignor refuses to allow this, then the assignee can sue the assignor as a joint co-defendant. It should be noted that these rules also apply if the assignor is attempting to recover the balance of the moneys owing to them by the promisor – the assignor must join the assignee into their action or treat the assignee as a co-defendant. The existence of these rules arose out of the procedural difficulties that occurred prior to the passing of the Judicature Act 1873, as already described above. Some authorities suggest other reasons but these are not particularly convincing.

2. The form of the assignment

Since equity looks to the intent and not to the form, then generally no particular form is required to give effect to an equitable assignment. This statement is, however, somewhat simplistic since statutory regulation has overlaid this basic premise. The requirements as to form differ:

1 where there is an equitable assignment of a legal chose in action of personalty;

2 where there is an equitable assignment of an equitable interest;

3 according to the terms laid down in the Law of Property (Miscellaneous Provisions) Act 1989, s 2(1).

Where there is an *equitable assignment of a legal chose in action of personalty*, the basic premise still presides, in that no particular form is required, and it is thus possible for such an assignment to take place orally. In **Thomas v Harris** [1947] 1 All ER 444 certain life assurance policies were handed by a father to his son, and at the same time it was requested that the proceeds that arose on his death be used to buy a tombstone for his grave. This was held to be effective as a valid assignment despite the fact that no notice of the assignment was given to the insurance company.

It should be noted that it is always possible for the contract itself to provide that any assignment must comply with a certain formality such as writing.

An equitable assignment of an equitable interest is void unless it complies with s 53(1)(c) of the Law of Property Act 1925. This provides:

> [A] disposition of an equitable interest or trust subsisting at the time of the disposition must be in writing signed by the person disposing of the same, or by his agent thereunto lawfully authorised by writing or by will.

It should be noted that this provision covers equitable choses in action comprising both personalty and land.

The Law of Property (Miscellaneous Provisions) Act 1989, s 2(1) provides:

> A contract for the sale or other disposition of an interest in land can only be made in writing and only by incorporating all the terms which the parties have expressly agreed in the document or, where contracts are exchanged, in each.

The full extent of the effect of this provision has yet to be decided; suffice it to say that failure to comply with the provision will render the assignment void. It can be seen that the provision is almost analogous to s 53(1)(c) of the Law of Property Act 1925 above and there should be no difference between the two provisions as they affect an equitable assignment of an equitable chose in action of land. It is suggested, however, that s 2(1) will now require an equitable assignment of a legal chose in action of land to be in writing.

Despite the fact that certain types of equitable assignment are required to be in writing there is no requirement as to the form of that writing. The writing itself need not be expressed to be an assignment. In **William Brandt's Sons & Co. v Dunlop Rubber Co.** [1905] AC 454, Lord MacNaghten stated:

> An equitable assignment does not always take that form. It may be addressed to the debtor. It may be couched in the language of a command. It may be a courteous request. It may assume the form of mere permission. The language is immaterial if the meaning is plain. All that is necessary is that the debtor should be given to understand that the debt has been made over by the creditor to some third person.

It can be seen from the above that the writing encompassing the assignment can be directed to either the debtor (promisor) or the assignee.

3. Notice

Notice may be either to the assignee or to the promisor (debtor).

An assignment is ineffective unless the assignor or someone acting on their authority has communicated it to the assignee. It is not certain why this requirement is particularly necessary since it was stated in **Standing v Bowring** (1885) 31 ChD 282 that a person can have property assigned to them without their knowledge, although this is subject to an implied right to repudiate the assignment when they gain knowledge of it.

The basic rule in notice to the promisor (debtor) is that notice of an equitable assignment to the debtor is not required to perfect the title. There are, however, sound reasons why such notice should nevertheless be given to the debtor.

First, should the debtor make any payments to the assignor in ignorance of the assignment, the assignee will nevertheless be bound with respect to those payments. The assignee will not, for instance, be able to recoup from the debtor any moneys lost by reason of the assignor absconding with moneys paid to the assignor by the debtor in ignorance of the assignment.

Second, by virtue of the rule in **Dearle v Hall** (1828) 3 Russ 1, an assignee should give notice to the debtor in order to preserve their rights of priority over any competing assignees that might exist. Failure to give notice will mean that an assignee will lose priority to another later assignee who has given notice to the debtor.

The form of the notice, as already stated, is largely irrelevant, except that in **The Balder London** [1980] 2 Lloyd's Rep 489 it was stated that the notice must clearly and unconditionally direct the debtor to pay or transfer the benefits under the contract to the third party as an assignee, rather than in some other capacity such as, for example, an agent for the promisee/creditor. If the notice does direct the debtor to pay the moneys to a third party as an agent of the promisee/creditor, then the debtor will not be liable to the assignee should they pay the money to the promisee/creditor.

4. Consideration

The question of whether consideration is needed for an effective equitable assignment is universally accepted as one of great difficulty. It should be noted that this is not an issue that may be raised by the debtor/promisee since they are bound to pay the debt or transfer the benefits under the contract whether or not the assignment is gratuitous. All the debtor/promisee is concerned with is to whom they must pay the debt, and so on, in order to avoid becoming liable a second time for the same obligation.

The problem we are then faced with is whether, as between the assignor and the assignee, there is a need for the equitable assignment to be supported by consideration. The basic premise of equity is summed up in the maxim 'equity will not assist a volunteer', but this is too wide since consideration is not an essential requirement in all situations. Before we consider voluntary assignments, it should be stated that no problems arise where the assignment is supported by consideration, since on basic contractual rules the assignment is enforceable by and against the assignor and the assignee. Where the equitable assignment is voluntary, the solution largely depends on whether the transfer is 'complete and perfect' or not, as the case may be.

To render a transfer 'complete and perfect', everything that needs to be done to effect the transfer or assignment must have been done. Thus, just as to render a gift of a chose in possession (that is, tangible property) complete, the actual property must be handed over to the donee, so that nothing remains to be done to give effect to the donor's intention, so the same is also true in the case of a voluntary equitable assignment of a chose in action. In the latter case all the formalities to give effect to the assignment of the chose in action from the assignor to the assignee must have been carried out. Failure to make the voluntary assignment complete and perfect will render the assignment invalid since 'equity will not perfect an imperfect gift'. In **Milroy v Lord** (1862) 4 De GF & J 264 Lord Turner expounded the principle in the analogous situation of voluntary settlements as follows:

> In order to make a voluntary settlement valid and effectual, the settlor must have done everything, which according to the nature of the property comprised in the settlement, was necessary to be done in order to transfer the property and render the settlement binding upon him.

The effect of the above on the various types of voluntary equitable assignments differs according to whether they are:

1 an agreement to assign a chose in action;
2 assignments of an equitable chose in action;
3 assignments of a legal chose in action.

An *agreement to assign a chose in action* relates to a future arrangement and clearly this is not capable of being 'completed and perfected' until the time of execution of the assignment arises. Such agreements then must be supported by consideration. The same is also true of an assignment of a future chose in action, since it was held in **Glegg v Bromley** [1912] 3 KB 474 by Parker J that 'nothing passes even in equity until the property comes into existence'. Consideration is thus required in respect of an assignment of such an interest.

In assignments of an equitable chose in action, if the assignor has done everything in their power to effect the transfer of the equitable chose in action to the assignee then the voluntary assignment will be valid. At that point the assignee is in a position to enforce their right to the chose in action since, as was stated in **Voyle v Hughes** (1854) 2 SM & G 18, 'an assignment without any valuable consideration is not a mere agreement but is an actual transfer of the equitable right'.

Assignments of a legal chose in action pose the particular problem of whether a voluntary equitable assignment of a legal chose in action can ever be 'complete and perfect'. The position here formerly was not clear since such choses in action had to be enforced within the common law courts by the assignee seeking the help of equity to compel the assignor to allow the assignee to sue in the assignor's name. Since collaboration of the assignor was needed to enforce the chose in action, the equitable assignment could not be said to be 'completed and perfected' and therefore consideration was required. Since the procedure now is that the assignee can simply add the assignor as a co-defendant if they refuse to collaborate with the assignee in allowing them to sue in the assignor's name, it would seem that the absolute assignment of a legal chose in action is valid despite the lack of consideration.

Statutory assignment of contractual rights

Generally

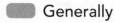

It was stated earlier that s 25(6) of the Judicature Act 1873 introduced a general form of statutory assignment. This form of assignment is now contained in s 136(1) of the Law of Property Act 1925. This provides:

> Any absolute assignment by writing under the hand of the assignor (not purporting to be by way of charge only) of any debt or other legal thing in action, of which express notice in

writing has been given to the debtor, trustee or other person from whom the assignor would have been entitled to claim such debt or thing in action, is effectual in law (subject to equities having priority over the right of the assignee) to pass and transfer from the date of such notice:

1 the legal right to such debt or thing in action;

2 all legal and other remedies for the same; and

3 the power to give a good discharge for the same without the concurrence of the assignor.

It should be noted that s 136 has not abolished equitable assignments and these will continue to exist where an assignment does not comply with the requirements of s 136. In truth all the provision has done is to allow the rights of the assignee to be exercised in a more direct manner so that they can sue in their own name without the need for joinder of the assignor arising, as stated in *Tolhurst v Associated Portland Cement Manufacturers (1900) Ltd* [1903] AC 414.

Care must be taken in construing the words 'any debt or other legal thing in action' in s 136(1). At first sight this appears to confine the statutory form of assignment to legal choses in action, that is, those choses in action which were formerly only enforceable within the common law courts. This provision has, however, been interpreted by the courts as including equitable, as well as legal, choses in action.

The provision does not require consideration to have been provided by the assignee in order to allow them to sue in their own name.

The essentials of a valid statutory assignment

The assignment must be absolute

The difference between absolute and non-absolute assignments has already been considered. If the assignment is conditional and non-absolute, then the parties will have to fall back on the use of an equitable assignment for the assignment to be valid.

The assignment must be in writing

While the assignment must be in writing and signed by the assignor, there are no provisions as to the contents, though clearly the writing must inform the debtor to pay or hand the benefit of the contract to the assignee, as an assignee and not merely as an agent of the assignor. Apparently if the date or the amount of a debt which is the subject of an assignment is incorrectly stated, then the assignment will be invalid. It would seem that the main point is that the terms of the assignment must be stated with a sufficient degree of certainty.

Notice of the assignment must be given to the debtor/promisor

It was held in *Holt v Heatherfield Trust Ltd* [1942] 2 KB 1 that notice takes effect when it is received by the debtor/promisor. The postal rules, for instance, have no application here.

Other factors affecting all types of assignment

Priority of assignments

Objective
5

The problem that arises here occurs where an assignor decides to make two or more assignments of the same chose in action to two or more assignees. This in itself presents no difficulty, but if it transpires that moneys owed under the chose in action by the debtor are insufficient to meet the respective claims of the various assignees, then the question of priority will arise.

The ranking of priority is determined by the rule in *Dearle* v *Hall* which provides that assignees will rank in accordance with the dates on which notice of their respective assignments was given to the debtor. Thus an assignee who fails to give notice to the debtor will lose their priority to a subsequent assignee who, having no knowledge of the first assignee's interest, gives notice to the debtor prior to the first assignee.

The notice may be made orally unless the interest that is being assigned is an equitable interest in either land or personalty when s 137(3) of the Law of Property Act 1925 requires the notice to be in writing.

Where the interest to be assigned is an equitable interest under a trust fund, then the assignee should give notice to all the trustees of the trust, though this is not a mandatory requirement.

Assignees take 'subject to equities'

When an assignee takes the assignment of the benefits of the contract from the assignor, they also take the risk of any defences that may be available to the debtor/promisor against the assignor should the assignee have to take action against the debtor/assignor. The assignee is thus said to take the assignment 'subject to the equities' of the debtor/promisor.

The expression 'subject to equities' needs careful consideration since it is not confined solely to equitable remedies that may be available to the debtor. It will include common law remedies, so that any damages accruing to the debtor by virtue of a counter-claim may be set off against the assignee, provided they arise out of the contract which is the subject of the assignment, as stated in *Newfoundland Government* v *Newfoundland Railway Co.* (1888) 13 App Cas 199. Further, the debtor is entitled to make use of any rights arising out of mistake, misrepresentation or breach of contract perpetrated by the assignor.

With regard to the latter point also, some care needs to be exercised since the debtor cannot raise against the assignee any personal claims they may have against the assignor. This problem is particularly prevalent in claims of fraud that may have accrued against the assignor by the debtor. The problem is well illustrated by the following case.

Stoddart v *Union Trust* [1912] 1 Kb 181

The Union Trust was induced into a contract to buy a newspaper by the fraudulent misrepresentation of a person named Price. The purchase price was £1,000, of which £200 was payable immediately and the rest by instalments. Price assigned the £800 debt to Stoddart who took it without knowledge of the fraudulent actions of Price. The Union Trust were subsequently sued by Stoddart for the moneys owing, but they counter-claimed for damages exceeding the £800 on the basis of the fraud that had been perpetrated on them by Price. They therefore claimed that they owed Stoddart nothing. It was held by the Court of Appeal that they could not owe Stoddart nothing since the claim represented a personal claim against Price and did not arise out of the contract being enforced by Stoddart. An anomaly occurs here since Stoddart was then in a better position than Price would have been under the same contract and this is clearly to the detriment of the debtor, the Union Trust. It may be that the Union Trust should have sought the rescission of the contract rather than merely damages, since this action would tend to strike at the existence of the contract itself rather than at the more personal liability of the assignor to pay damages.

Where the equities accruing to the debtor arise out of a separate contract or transaction from the contract that is the subject of the assignment, the debtor cannot set off those equities against the assignee. The only exception to this is if the independent claim accrued before the debtor had notice of the assignment to the assignee. It can therefore be seen that the serving of notice of the assignment by the assignee to the debtor is particularly important in this context and certainly, in order to prevent the debtor setting up fresh equities against the rights of the assignee, as indicated in *Roxburghe v Cox* (1881) 17 ChD 520, should not be delayed.

It can be seen from the above rules that great care needs to be exercised by the assignee when they decide to accept an assignment from the assignor, since the assignee could be acquiring an interest in a chose which is far less valuable than it appears on the face of things. Thorough investigation of the circumstances in which the chose in action arose is highly desirable.

Rights which are non-assignable

Express exclusion of assignability

The contract entered into by the original parties may expressly provide that the contract is not capable of being assigned. Any subsequent assignment is invalid as it affects the debtor, though it is effective between the assignor and the assignee. In *Linden Gardens Trust Ltd v Lenesta Sludge Disposals Ltd; St Martin's Property Corporation Ltd v Sir Robert McAlpine* [1994] 1 AC 85, it was argued that an express provision prohibiting an assignment of property rights was contrary to public policy, since it rendered those rights inalienable, a principle that lies at the heart of English property law. It was then argued that contractual rights are themselves a form of property. Putting the two arguments together then produces the result that contractual exclusion of this right to assign one's contractual rights is per se unlawful. This was rejected by the House of Lords since there may be several reasons why this right to assign may need to be excluded, as one can see below.

Rights of action

A right to sue for damages, sometimes described as a 'bare right of action', cannot be assigned since this is contrary to the rules relating to champerty and maintenance. While this principle has been affirmed in the case of *Trendtex Trading Corporation v Crédit Suisse* [1982] AC 679, the House of Lords declared that such a right may be assignable where the assignee has a genuine legitimate interest of a financial or commercial nature in taking the assignment and subsequently enforcing the right in question. An example would be where the purchaser of land is able to sue the vendor's tenants for any breach of covenant that had arisen prior to the sale. These rights of the purchaser of the reversion of the lease are now contained in s 141 of the Law of Property Act 1925, though here the right to sue the tenants only extends to the situation where there has been a breach of a covenant that 'has reference to the subject matter of the lease', that is, the covenants affect the landlord qua landlord and the tenant qua tenant rather than merely being personal in nature.

Personal contracts

If the contract involves the use of a personal skill or confidence then the parties can insist on the contract being performed personally by the other party. The reason for this is that the personal performance forms the essence of the contract and to allow assignment would be to alter the very nature of the contract itself without the consent of the other party. In **Griffith v Tower Publishing Co. Ltd** [1897] 1 Ch 21 it was held that a contract by an author to write a book for a publisher amounted to a personal contract so that the author could restrain the publisher from assigning the contract to another. The logic here is that the author entered into the contract with the publisher on the basis of the latter's skill and judgement in that capacity.

Public policy

See Chapter 12 for 'Contracts tending to corrupt the public service' and 'Contracts prejudicial to the administration of justice.'

As explained under 'Contracts tending to corrupt the public service', the law does not allow a public servant to assign their salary (**Wells v Foster** (1841) 8 M & W 149) and similarly ('Contracts prejudicial to the administration of justice') it does not allow a wife to assign her rights to maintenance on grounds of public policy (**Re Robinson** (1884) 27 ChD 160).

Assignment of liabilities

Objective 6

The general rule is that it is only the benefits of a contract that are assignable, not the burdens, unless the consent of the promisee is first obtained. The reasoning here is that it should not be possible to compel the promisee to accept performance of the contract from someone other than the promisor. It is nevertheless possible to achieve this position by novation since this results in the original contract being rescinded with the mutual agreement of the promisor and promisee, and a new one being substituted between the original promisor and the new promisee.

Summary

- Assignment is a method by which a party to a contract transfers the benefits they have contracted to receive from the other party to a third party, who are themselves able to enforce performance of the contract.
- The right to enforce a contract is in fact a form of intangible property known generically as a 'chose in action'.

Voluntary assignment at common law

- A chose in action could not be assigned.
- The assignment of negotiable instruments, sometimes referred to as 'negotiability'.
- Ways to avoid the rule and allow the right to enforce a contract by having a transaction that has the same effect as an assignment:

  1 the promisee could always allow the third party to sue in their name;
  2 the promisee could give the third party a power of attorney;
  3 third party acquires rights by a novation.

Voluntary assignment in equity

1 Equity permits the assignment of a chose in action whether or not it was in the nature of a legal or equitable chose.

The requirements of an equitable assignment

Joinder of the assignor in an action by the assignee

- An equitable assignment merely assigns the equitable title to the assignee.
- Joinder requirements differ according to whether the chose in action is legal or equitable and whether it is absolute or non-absolute.

The form of the assignment

- Originally – no particular form is required to give effect to an equitable assignment.
- Statutory requirements as to form have now overlaid this position in certain cases – Law of Property Act 1925, s 53(1)(c).

Consideration

- No problems arise where the assignment is supported by consideration since on basic contractual rules the assignment is enforceable by and against the assignor and the assignee.
- Where the equitable assignment is voluntary, the solution largely depends on whether the transfer is 'complete and perfect' or not, as the case may be.

Statutory assignment

Generally

- Law of Property Act 1925, s 136(1) now stipulates the statutory form of assignment.
- Section 136 has not abolished equitable assignments and these will continue to exist where an assignment does not comply with the requirements of s 136.

The essentials of a valid statutory assignment

Other factors affecting all types of assignment

Rights which are non-assignable

Further reading

Beatson, Burrows and Cartwright, *Anson's Law of Contract*, 30th edn (Oxford University Press, 2016)

Furmston, *Cheshire, Fifoot and Furmston's Law of Contract*, 16th edn (Oxford University Press, 2012)

Peel, Treitel *Law of Contract*, 14th edn (Sweet and Maxwell, 2015)

Glossary

ab initio From the beginning. See **void *ab initio***.

acceptance Acceptance of an offer to create a contract (i.e. an assent to all the terms of the offer) must be unqualified, and may be by words or conduct. It must generally be communicated to the offeror and must conform with the prescribed or indicated terms of the offer.

accord and satisfaction Occurs where, following the conclusion of a contract, one party obtains his release from his obligation under the contract by promising or giving consideration other than that which the other party has to accept under the contract. The new agreement is the 'accord'; the consideration is the satisfaction.

account, action for An action whereby a court can investigate sums due from one party to another resulting from transactions between parties, e.g. as between principal and agent.

adhesion contracts See **standard-form contracts**.

affirmation To declare expressly or impliedly with full knowledge of the facts an intention to proceed with a contract. Lapse of time may be evidence of affirmation.

anticipatory breach Term referring to the repudiation of a contract before the time for performance. The other party may immediately treat the contract as though it were discharged and sue for damages.

apparent authority See **ostensible authority**.

auction sales A public sale of property by an auctioneer to the highest bidder. An *auctioneer* is one who is licensed to conduct sales by auction. A contract comes into existence as the result of an auctioneer's acts, when a bid is accepted and their hammer falls (or in other customary manner) and a bidder may retract their bid until that event.

bilateral discharge Applies to executory contracts. Discharge may take the form of: extinction of the contract; extinction and substitution of a new agreement; partial dissolution of the contract, e.g. by modification of terms.

capacity The legal competence, power or fitness to enter and be bound by a contract. Thus, an infant generally lacks contractual capacity, save where they bind themselves by contract for necessaries or for other matters relating to their benefit.

cartel An association of independent enterprises, possibly companies or other business organisations, that is created to monopolise the production or distribution of goods or services.

causation The relationship of cause and effect. Thus an injured party cannot recover for all loss since a causal link must be shown to exist between the loss suffered and the breach of contract.

caveat emptor Let the buyer beware. In general, the buyer is expected to look to their own interests.

champerty A criminal offence and a tort, abolished under Criminal Law Act 1967, whereby a person pays for another's legal action on condition that the damages or subject matter of the action are to be shared by them. While champerty (and maintenance) have been abolished as a crime and a tort, champerty survives as a public policy rule capable of rendering a contract unenforceable.

chose in action All personal rights of property which can only be claimed or enforced by legal action rather than by taking physical possession.

collateral contracts Collateral contracts exist where there is one contract, the consideration for which is the making of some other contract, e.g. 'If you enter into this contract, then I will give you £1,000.'

common mistake See **mistake, common.**

compositions with creditors Sum of money accepted by creditors in satisfaction, or adjustment, of a debt or debts.

condition A condition in a contract for the sale of goods is a vital stipulation, the breach of which may give rise to a right to treat the contract as ended or repudiated.

condition precedent This is a condition which delays the vesting of a right until the occurrence of a particular event, e.g. 'to X if he graduates in law'.

consensus ad idem Literally 'total agreement'. A binding contract requires *consensus ad idem* (agreement as to the same thing) by both parties.

consensus mistake This type of mistake arises where there is a mistake as to the terms of a contract which therefore precludes an agreement from arising. In other words this type of mistake prevents a consensus from arising between the parties. There are two basic types: mutual mistake and unilateral mistake – see below.

consideration That which is actually given or accepted in return for a promise. 'Some right, interest, profit or benefit accruing to one party, or some forbearance, detriment, loss, or responsibility given, suffered or undertaken by the other': ***Currie v Misa*** (1875) LR 10 Ex 153. Example: *X* receives £50 for which he promises to deliver goods to *Y;* the £50 is the consideration for the promise to deliver the goods. Consideration is required for the formation of all simple contracts. It must be legal; it must not be past; it must move from the promisee; it must be real, i.e. something of value in the eye of the law.

contra proferentem **rule** The words or deeds should be interpreted most strongly against the person who uses them.

contributory negligence 'A man's carelessness in looking after his own safety.' A defence established where it is proved that an injured party failed to take reasonable care of themselves, thus contributing materially to their own injury.

de minimis **rule** Known more fully as '*de minimis non curat lex*'; or the law does not concern itself with trivialities.

del credere **agent** An agent who receives a higher rate of commission than that which is usual, in return for a guarantee that their principal will receive due payment for goods sold.

delegatus non potest delegare A delegate cannot delegate. See now Trustee Act 2000, Part IV. 'The law is not that trustees cannot delegate: it is that trustees cannot delegate unless they have authority to do so': ***Pilkington v IRC*** [1962] 3 All ER 622.

deposits These are essentially the opposite of a penalty in that they are payable before a breach occurs, rather than after as in the case of a penalty. Deposits are normally regarded as part satisfaction of the contract price which may be retained should the purchaser fail to perform their side of the bargain.

discharge by agreement Generally, a release from an obligation; however, in the law of contract it refers to the freeing of parties from their mutual obligations by performance, express agreement, breach, or under the doctrine of frustration.

discharge by breach Where a party fails to perform their side of the contract they will be in breach of contract, subject to mitigating factors.

discharge by performance Where the parties fully perform their part of the contract the contract will become discharged by virtue of the contract having been fully performed.

divisible contracts A contract in which the parties intend that their promises are to be independent of each other: ***Taylor v Webb*** [1937] 2 KB 283. An *entire* (or *indivisible*) contract is one in which there is agreement, implicit or explicit, that neither party may demand performance until they are ready to fulfil, or have fulfilled, their promise.

duress Actual violence or threats of imminent, although not necessarily immediate, violence to the person. Known also as *duress per minas* (by threats). A contract obtained by duress is voidable. 'Duress, whatever form it takes, is a coercion of will so as to vitiate consent': *per* Lord Scarman in ***Pao On v Lau Yiu Long*** [1980] AC 614.

economic duress Recovery of money paid under duress (i.e. illegitimate pressure resulting in compulsion), other than to the person, is not limited to duress to goods; it can include economic duress where it is constituted by a threat to break a contract, even though there is good consideration for that further contract: *North Ocean Shipping Co. v Hyundai Construction Co.* [1978] 3 All ER 1170; *The Universe Sentinel* [1983] 1 AC 366. ('The victim's silence will not assist the bully, if the lack of any practicable choice but to submit is proved': *per* Lord Scarman.)

equitable estoppel A rule of evidence (and not a cause of action) preventing a person from denying the truth of a statement they have made previously, or the existence of facts in which they have led another to believe. Under the doctrine of *promissory estoppel,* where X, by words or conduct, makes to Y an unambiguous representation by promise or assurance concerning his (X's) future actions, intended to affect the legal relationship between X and Y, and Y alters his position in reliance on it, X will not be allowed to act inconsistently with that representation.

exclusion clause This is a clause 'which excludes or modifies an obligation, whether primary. . . or . . . secondary, that would otherwise arise under the contract by implication of law': *per* Lord Diplock in *Photo Production Ltd v Securicor Transport Ltd* [1980] AC 827.

executed consideration Consideration is *executed* when the act constituting the consideration is performed.

executory consideration Consideration is said to be *executory* when it is in the form of promises to be performed at a future date.

exemption clauses Clauses in an agreement seeking to exempt the parties from general liability or excluding or modifying their liability in certain circumstances.

expectation loss Damages that arise where a party is claiming damages for the gains that they could reasonably be expected to obtain from the completion of the contract, for example, loss of profits.

ex turpi causa non oritur actio No action arises from an unworthy cause.

fitness for purpose Where goods are sold in the course of a business, and the buyer expressly or impliedly makes known to the seller any particular purpose for which the goods are being bought, there is an implied condition that they are fit for that purpose: Sale of Goods Act 1979, s 14(3).

force majeure **clauses** A superior force. An event that can generally be neither anticipated nor controlled, e.g. an industrial strike which leads to loss of profits. The circumstances must be abnormal and unforeseeable, so that the consequences could not have been avoided through the exercise of all due care.

forfeiture clauses These clauses normally arise in contract where there is a purchase of goods by instalments and the contract provides that should the purchaser default on any instalment then they must surrender the goods, at the same time forfeiting any instalments already paid. They are designed to ensure that the contract will be performed.

fraudulent misrepresentation A false representation made knowingly or without belief in its truth or recklessly, careless whether it be true or false: *Derry* v *Peek* (1889) 14 App Cas 337.

free on board contract Also known as an 'f.o.b. contract'. Goods are to be delivered on board by the seller, free of expense to the purchaser; they are not at the purchaser's risk until actually delivered on board, when property in them generally passes.

freehold land An estate of an uncertain length of duration.

frustration Where there is an extraneous event or change of circumstances so fundamental as to strike at the root of a contract as a whole and beyond what was contemplated by the parties, that contract is considered to be automatically frustrated.

hire purchase An agreement under which goods are delivered to the hirer in return for periodical payments by the hirer and the property in the goods passes to the hirer if the terms of the agreement are complied with and the hirer exercises their option to purchase or some other specified event occurs.

illegal contracts Contracts which are forbidden by statute or are contrary to common law or public policy and are, therefore, generally void.

injunction An order of the court directing a person to refrain from doing or continuing to do an act complained of, or restraining them from continuing an omission. Non-compliance is a contempt of court.

innominate terms Terms neither named nor classified. Innominate terms in a contract are also known as 'intermediate terms'.

in pari delicto, potior est conditio defendentis Where the guilt is shared, the defendant's position is stronger.

intermediate term See **innominate terms**.

intra vires Within its powers.

laches, doctrine of Negligence and unreasonable delay in the assertion of a right will defeat equities.

leasehold land A term of years or leasehold or the document used to bring into existence a term of years, i.e. an interest in land for a fixed period of a certain maximum duration.

letter of comfort This is a letter or memorandum usually written by a holding company to a lender about to lend money to a subsidiary of the holding company so as to reassure the lender of the financial viability of the subsidiary. Such letters are not guarantees in that the holding company is not willing to enter into a legally binding financial commitment.

lien A right to hold and retain another's property until a claim is satisfied.

limitation clause A clause that seeks to limit liability, usually up to a specific amount, as opposed to an exclusion clause that seeks to exclude liability entirely.

limitations of actions Provision whereby, after a certain period of time stated by statute, claims cannot be brought. Generally: in the case of land, 12 years from the date of accrual of action; in the case of tort and simple contract, 6 years from the date of accrual of action (for contract under seal, 12 years from the date of accrual).

maintenance A contract of maintenance arises where a person encourages and supports a course of litigation in which they have no interest.

merchantable quality 'Goods of any kind are of merchantable quality within the meaning of [this Act] if they are as fit for the purpose or purposes for which goods of that kind are commonly bought as it is reasonable to expect, having regard to any description applied to them, the price (if relevant) and all the other relevant circumstances': Sale of Goods Act 1979, s 14(6). Replaced by 'satisfactory quality': Sale and Supply of Goods Act 1994, s 1.

misfeasance Improper performance of some essentially lawful act.

misrepresentation A false statement which misrepresents an existing material fact: which is made before the conclusion of a contract with a view to inducing another to enter that contract; which is made with the intention that the person to whom it is addressed shall act on it; which is acted on, having induced the contract; which is not merely extravagant advertising.

mistake, common Common mistake occurs where both parties to a contract make the same mistake.

mistake, mutual Mutual mistake occurs where the parties are at cross-purposes.

mistake, unilateral Unilateral mistake occurs where one party has made a mistake of which the other party is aware, but the latter keeps quiet and does nothing to correct it.

mitigation of loss It is the duty of the claimant to take all reasonable steps to mitigate the loss caused by a breach of contract.

mutuality The general principle is that specific performance will not be awarded unless the order is available to both parties, that is, availability of the award is mutual.

necessaries Goods suitable to the condition in life of an infant or minor or other person and to their actual requirements at the time of the sale and delivery.

negotiability In relation to a negotiable instrument, the quality of it being transferable free from equities.

nemo dat quod non habet No one can give that which he has not. See Sale of Goods Act 1979, s 21(1). Thus, a person cannot give better title than they have.

non est factum Literally 'it is not [his] deed'. This is a plea which denies that an instrument (deed) is that of the defendant, e.g. where there has been a mistake as to the nature of the transaction.

nonfeasance Failure to perform an act which one is bound by law to do.

non-pecuniary losses Loss of pleasure or where physical inconvenience flows from the breach of contract as opposed to losses that can be measured in financial terms.

novation Essentially a substituted agreement. Contract whereby a creditor at the request of a debtor agrees to take another person as debtor in place of the original debtor. The original debtor is thereby released from their obligations which fall on the new debtor. The new agreement requires consideration.

ostensible authority This type of authority, sometimes referred to as 'apparent' authority, really forms an application of the doctrine of estoppel. It arises where a principal, whether by words or conduct, creates an implication that the agent is entitled to act on the principal's behalf when in fact no such authority actually exists. An agent acting within this apparent authority will bind the principal to a third party despite the fact that the agent has no actual authority to do so.

parol evidence rule Where the record of a transaction is embodied in a document, extrinsic evidence is not generally admissible to vary, qualify or interpret the document or as a substitute for it.

penalties A threat, held over a party to a contract *in terrorem*. The plaintiff who brings an action to enforce a penalty can generally recover only the damage suffered.

power of attorney An instrument authorising one person to act for another during the absence of that other.

principal One on whose behalf an agent works.

privity of contract Principle based upon the relationship between the parties to a contract.

promissory estoppel See **equitable estoppel.**

quantum meruit As much as he has deserved (i.e. earned). On breach of contract the party injured may be entitled to claim for work done and services performed to the extent that they have actually been completed.

quasi-contract Cases in which the law imposes on a person an obligation to make repayment on grounds of unjust benefit, e.g. when they have been enriched at the expense of another.

ratification Confirmation; approval. In the case of ratification of a contract made by an agent, the contract must be made on behalf of the principal; the principal must be competent at the time of the contract; there should have been an act capable of ratification.

rectification Where a written document does not accurately express an agreement between parties, as the result of some common mistake, equity has the power to rectify that mistake.

remoteness of damages In contract the general rule is that damages for breach will be too remote to be recovered unless such that the defendant, as a reasonable person, would have foreseen as likely to result: *Hadley v Baxendale* (1854) 9 Exch 341.

res judicata A final decision pronounced by a competent judicial tribunal. There must be an end to litigation at some point and therefore parties are not allowed, having had a decision from a court, to start the litigation again on precisely the same question. Known also as 'action estoppel', it is one of the fundamental doctrines of all courts.

res sua 'One's own goods'. The phrase used where a person makes a contract to purchase that which, in fact, belongs to them. The contract is void for mistake as to title.

rescission Remedy for inducing a contract by innocent or fraudulent misrepresentation whereby the contract is abrogated. A party intending to rescind must notify the other party. A rescission *ab initio* results in the contract being treated as though it had never been. Right of rescission is lost: if *restitutio in integrum* (see below) is impossible.

restitutio in integrum Restoration to the original position. Right to rescind a contract for misrepresentation is lost if *restitutio in integrum* is not possible.

restitution The equitable doctrine of restitution refers to the case where, for example, an infant, having fraudulently obtained goods, is ordered to return their ill-gotten gains.

restitution, law of The body of law concerned with claims for the reversal of unjust enrichment, the prevention of one who has committed a wrong from profiting from it, the restoration of a claimant's property rights adversely affected by defendant's actions, and the provision of appropriate restitutionary remedies. Remedies, intended to effect 'a fair and just balance between rights and interests of the parties concerned', include rescission, award of interest, subrogation, equitable damages, restitutionary damages, account of profits.

restraint of trade Any contract which interferes with the free exercise of a person's trade or business, by restricting them in the work they may do for others, or the arrangements which they may make with others, is a contract in restraint of trade. It is invalid unless it is reasonable as between the parties and not injurious to the public interest.

restrictive covenants A covenant by which use of the covenantor's land is restricted for the benefit of the covenantee's adjoining land. Known also as a 'negative covenant'.

Romalpa clause Otherwise known as retention of title clause, whereby there is a term in the contract of sale that the right of ownership shall not pass to the buyer until the buyer has paid the seller in full or otherwise discharged their liabilities to the seller under the contract. Such clauses have to be drafted very carefully for them to be valid. (Derived from *Aluminium Industrie Vaassen BV* v *Romalpa Aluminium Ltd* [1976] 1 WLR 676.)

satisfactory quality Where the seller sells goods in the course of a business, there is an implied term that the goods supplied under the contract are of satisfactory quality. Goods are of satisfactory quality if they meet the standard that a reasonable person would regard as satisfactory, taking account of any description of the goods, the price (if relevant) and all the other relevant circumstances.

***Scott* v *Avery* clause** A clause inserted into a contract that requires a party to have the case heard in arbitration proceedings before being able to pursue the cause of action in the courts. Derived from *Scott* v *Avery* (1856) 5 HL Cas 811.

severance This is the removal of the illegal elements of a contract, leaving behind a valid enforceable agreement.

solus agreements An agreement whereby a retailer binds themselves to buy a product from one source only. Example: garage proprietor agreeing to buy all their petrol from one oil company.

speciality contract A contract under seal or by deed.

specific performance An equitable, discretionary remedy whereby a party to an agreement is ordered by the court to perform their obligations according to the terms of that agreement. It is granted where the common law remedy of damages is inadequate.

standard-form contract Contracts, the terms of which were not the subject of negotiations between the parties to them.

stoppage *in transitu* Right of stoppage *in transitu* is the right, under Sale of Goods Act 1979, ss 44–46, to stop goods in transit, to resume and to retain possession until the price is paid.

tender of performance Expressed readiness to perform an act in accordance with an obligation. May be equivalent to performance: *Startup* v *Macdonald* (1843) 6 Man & G 593.

trespass The unjustifiable interference with possession of goods or land. A tort involving 'direct and forcible injury'. In trespass to the person, it involves assault or battery.

trust In essence, an equitable obligation which imposes on a person described as a trustee certain duties of dealing with property held and controlled by them for the benefit of the persons described as the beneficiaries, or, if there are not such persons, for some purpose recognised and enforceable at law.

trustee One who holds property on trust for another, known as *cestui que trust* or beneficiary.

uberrimae fidei Of the utmost good faith. Applies to a contract in which the promisee must inform the promisor of all those facts and surrounding circumstances which could influence the promisor in deciding whether or not to enter the contract.

ultra vires Beyond the powers. Term relating generally to the excess of legal powers or authority; specifically, the exercise by a corporation of powers beyond those conferred on it explicitly or implicitly.

undue influence Improper pressure on a person resulting in their being at a manifest disadvantage in relation to some transaction. Such a transaction may be set aside by the court.

unilateral contract A contract arising where an offer is made in the form of a promise to pay in return for the performance of an act, so that the performance of the act is taken to imply assent. See, e.g., *Carlill v Carbolic Smoke Ball Co.* [1893] 1 QB 256; *NZ Shipping Co.* v *Satterthwaite & Co.* [1975] AC 154.

unilateral discharge In a contract, the terms of which are carried out by *X,* but not by *Y* (the other party), the release of *Y* from his obligations by *X.*

void *ab initio* Void from the beginning; having no legal effect.

voidable contracts Capable of being voided, i.e. set aside. A voidable contract has legal effect until avoided at the option of one of the parties (e.g. where the contract has been induced by misrepresentation).

waivers These normally arise where one party requests an alteration of the terms of the contract and the other party agrees not to insist on strict compliance with the terms of the contract, so, for example, allowing late delivery at the request of the other party.

warranties A term that is collateral to the main purpose of a contract, the breach of which gives rise to a claim for damages, but not to a right to reject the goods and treat the contract as repudiated.

Index

Note: page references in bold refer to entries in the Glossary